W9-CRA-703

THE HOLLAND HOUSE DIARIES

THE HOLLAND HOUSE DIARIES 1831 - 1840

The diary of Henry Richard Vassall Fox,
third Lord Holland,
with extracts from the diary
of Dr John Allen

Edited with introductory essay and notes by

ABRAHAM D. KRIEGEL

Routledge & Kegan Paul
London, Henley and Boston

First published in 1977
by Routledge & Kegan Paul Ltd,
39 Store Street,
London WC1E 7DD,
Broadway House,
Newtown Road,
Henley-on-Thames,
Oxon RG9 1EN, and
9 Park Street,
Boston, Mass. 02108, USA
Filmset in Janson by
Weatherby Woolnough, Wellingborough
Northants
and printed in Great Britain by
Lowe & Brydone Printers Ltd
Thetford, Norfolk

ISBN 0 7100 8406 4

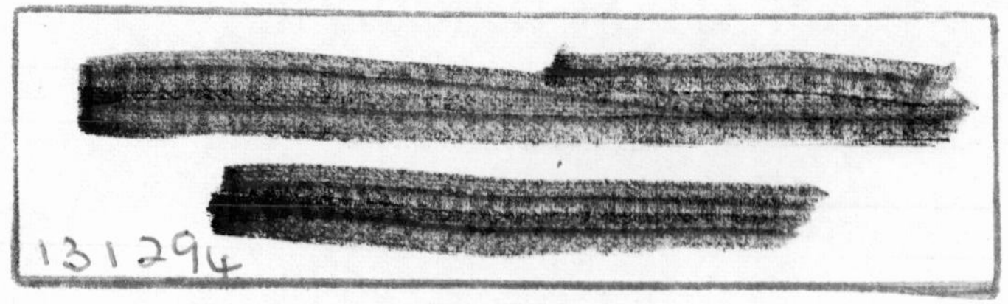

For Reva

CONTENTS

PREFACE ix

ABBREVIATIONS xii

INTRODUCTION: LORD HOLLAND, THE WHIGS, AND THE DECADE OF REFORM xiii

EDITORIAL PROCEDURE lxi

THE HOLLAND HOUSE DIARIES 1

NOTES 423

APPENDIX: THE WHIG CABINETS 1830-40 491

INDEX 495

PREFACE

Lord Holland kept his diary (BM Add. Mss. 51867-72) from 1831 until his death in 1840. During that decade he was a member of the Grey and Melbourne cabinets. Already an elder statesman of his party when the Whigs returned to power in 1830, he declined the Foreign Office because of poor health and became Chancellor of the Duchy of Lancaster, primarily a sinecure, but traditionally one with cabinet rank. At a time when the cabinet was approximating but had not yet fully realized its modern role, Holland participated in its deliberations on such crucial matters as parliamentary reform, Irish problems, and foreign affairs. To be sure, some of the material contained in the diary is available in other published sources—letters, parliamentary debates, and memoirs; but there is nothing comparable to it by an individual of Holland's stature. And even for subjects treated extensively by historians, Holland's diary provides information not generally known. For example, the cabinet's consideration of extending representation to the colonies is not included in standard accounts of the Reform Bill.

But the value of Holland's diary is not to be gauged solely by the amount of information it adds to our knowledge of events. Rather, it is so rich a document primarily because its detail enables one to perceive a society in a decade of reform from the viewpoint of a worldly and intelligent aristocrat who was intimately involved in its leadership. More than any other source, it is invaluable for studying the decision-making processes of cabinet government at a time when the effects of industrialization placed immense pressures upon established institutions and transformed political and social attitudes. Moreover, at Holland House, Lord and Lady Holland presided over one of Europe's last international salons. The diary accordingly reflects a style of life that valued urbanity and wit, a conception of international affairs that elevated the role of reigning personalities, and a lingering attitude of *noblesse oblige,* as well as an emphasis on the obligations of honor, so characteristic of the European aristocracy.

It is more valuable than Holland's reminiscences about his earlier career, *Memoirs of the Whig Party* (London, 1854, 2 vols) and *Further Memoirs of the Whig Party 1807-1821* (London, 1905), parts of the latter also having been written in the 1830s. Though printed posthumously, those memoirs were intended by Holland for publication. He had no such intention for his diary. Had he lived longer, he might have used it to write an additional memoir. But the unexpurgated diary is more substantive than any memoir could have been. It was kept irregularly and is most detailed and comprehensive for the years of Lord Grey's ministry. There are substantial gaps for the later years, and I have attempted to provide some continuity in those cases by including extracts from the diary of Holland's companion, John Allen, a permanent resident of Holland House.

Lady Galway kindly gave permission for the publication of the diaries. I have to acknowledge the gracious permission of Her Majesty the Queen to make use of material in the Royal Archives, Windsor. I am indebted to the Trustees of the Broadlands Manuscripts for allowing me to read the papers of Lord Palmerston, and to the staff of the Historical Manuscripts Commission, particularly Miss Felicity Ranger. Some material in my introductory essay is adapted from an earlier article in the *English Historical Review,* with the permission of Longman Group Ltd.

Like most American students of English history, I am grateful for having access to the facilities of the British Museum and the Institute of Historical Research at the University of London, and for the helpfulness of their respective staffs. Some of the editorial work and annotation, however, had to be done in the United States, and I was fortunate in being able to make use of the Perkins Library of Duke University. For taking the time to reply to various queries, I would like thank Professors Frederick Hollyday, Harold T. Parker, and John TePaske of Duke University, and Mr William Erwin of the Duke University Library.

The assistance of colleagues at Memphis State University facilitated the completion of this work. My friends George Leon and Cleopatra Leon spent considerable time in deciphering Holland's Greek and Latin and, on occasion, were able to provide the source for his remarks. Walter R. Brown generously assisted me with Holland's Latin as well. I profited from conversations about historical editing with my colleague, Gerald S. Pierce, who was also good enough to track down some of Holland's references to Portuguese and Spanish figures. Robert Frankle and Marcus W. Orr helped me at various times. Mrs Sandra Franklin, then a graduate student at Memphis State University, provided some clerical assistance in the early stages of this project. The Faculty Research Committee of Memphis State University provided some financial assistance when I began this work. I am indebted to Malcolm Richardson for assisting me in preparing the index and in reading proofs.

I am grateful to Memphis State University and its Board of the Press for providing a generous subvention which defrayed some of the costs of publication. I particularly want to thank Aaron M. Boom, Chairman of the History Department, for his representations on my behalf, and to acknowledge the support of President Billy M. Jones, Vice-President Jerry N. Boone, and James Simmons, Editor of the Memphis State University Press.

Although I appreciate the help given so generously by so many, the customary claim of exclusive responsibility applies. Any errors in transcription, interpretation or annotation are mine.

PREFACE

I was introduced to the study of English history by the late Professor William B. Hamilton of Duke University. His suggestions during the early stages of this work were very helpful.

My wife, Reva, read the introductory essay, and served as both demanding critic and constant source of encouragement from the commencement of this work to its completion.

ADK

ABBREVIATIONS

AP	Anglesey Papers
BFSP	*British and Foreign State Papers*
BM Add. MS	British Museum, Additional Manuscript
BP	Broadlands Papers
cr.	created
d.	died
DNB	*Dictionary of National Biography*
EP	Ellice Papers
(GB)	in the peerage of Great Britain
GEC	G. E. C[okayne], *The Complete Peerage* (London, 1910-59), 12 vols
GP	Grey Papers
HHP	Holland House Papers
3 Hansard	*Hansard's Parliamentary Debates,* third series
HP	Hatherton Papers
(I)	in the peerage of Ireland
m.	married
N.L.I.	National Library of Ireland
N.L.S.	National Library of Scotland
PP	*Parliamentary Papers*
P.P.	Peel Papers
P.R.O.	Public Record Office, London
P.R.O.N.I.	Public Record Office Northern Ireland
(S)	in the peerage of Scotland
S.R.O.	Staffordshire Record Office
(UK)	in the peerage of the United Kingdom
WND	Duke of Wellington, *Despatches, Correspondence, and Memoranda of Field Marshall Arthur Duke of Wellington,* 3rd series (London, 1913), 8 vols
WP	Wellesley Papers

INTRODUCTION: LORD HOLLAND, THE WHIGS, AND THE DECADE OF REFORM

In 1763 the barony of Holland was conferred upon Henry Fox, whose secure reputation for self-aggrandizement and cupidity attests his dexterity in the craft of mid-eighteenth-century English politics. Having leased the Kensington property of Holland House since 1749, he acquired the title as a somewhat grudging reward to an astute politician who had served both his king and himself by management of the House of Commons and venal dispensation of patronage. Nor was he left naked to his enemies, for if he could not acquire the earldom he craved, he had achieved the security and status which eluded so many of his contemporaries in the intricate politics of 'connection' and 'interest.'

Henry Fox, first Lord Holland, died in 1774, his eldest son, Stephen, barely six months thereafter. Stephen's son, Henry Richard Fox, born in November 1773, became the third Lord Holland at the age of one year. His mother died when he was five years old, and he and his sister Caroline were entrusted to their maternal uncle, the Earl of Upper Ossory. Man of letters and dilettante, Lord Ossory preferred the life of a leisured country peer to the factional strife of Westminster, though he was MP for Bedfordshire from 1767 to 1794. Holland dutifully lauded his uncle Ossory's generosity and solicitude, but he reserved his devotion for his paternal uncle, Charles James Fox, to whom the 'dear young one' of their correspondence became more than an avuncular charge. Fox enjoyed directing his nephew's political and academic education, particularly in instilling in him a reverence for the classics, poetry, and the cultivation of those refinements that became a man of parts in the late eighteenth century.

Holland's formal education was no more intensive than that of many young English noblemen—Eton for ten years, Christ Church, Oxford for two. His subsequent affection for Eton hardly impaired his recognition of its intellectual deficiency. Nevertheless, there and at Oxford he mastered Greek and Latin, beyond the mere aggregation of those classical embellishments that adorn the rhetoric of nineteenth-century English politicians. The Grand Tour, in his case a bit more extensive than for others of his generation, was probably one of the last of its kind before the accelerating Revolution arrested the continental travels of young English nobility. In the summer of 1791 he embarked for France and toured Denmark and Prussia as well before a brief return to England. In the following year, France again, then to Spain, Italy, and Austria, a tour that lasted some three years. He returned to England in the spring of 1796, in the company of Elizabeth Vassall, Lady Webster.

Then the young, alluring wife of Sir Godfrey Webster, twenty-three years her senior, she was the daughter of Richard Vassall, a wealthy Jamaican planter, who brought his family to England before the beginning of the American Revolution. Two years older than Lord Holland, she had become his companion on the continent after their chance encounter in Naples in 1795. Her divorce from Sir Godfrey, by whom she had three children, and marriage to Lord Holland in 1797 became a minor *cause célèbre,* involving as it did parliamentary inquiries, considerable expenditure, and the birth out of wedlock of their eldest son, Charles Richard Fox. The financial burden was borne by Lady Holland's substantial inheritance, conveniently made available by her father's death in 1795. The Hollands assumed the additional surname Vassall by royal license in 1800. Some years thereafter, Lord Holland's familiar correspondence came invariably to be signed 'Vassall Holland.'

The lure of the continent, even stronger for Lady than for Lord Holland, led them abroad once again in the summer of 1800, and for an extended tour after the Peace of Amiens, when they were accompanied briefly by Charles James Fox and his bride, Mrs Armistead, his erstwhile mistress. Lord and Lady Holland were presented to Napoleon, then first Consul, and were entertained by Talleyrand and Lafayette, both of whom Holland had met during his previous journey. They travelled again to Spain, where Holland renewed and extended his circle of acquaintances and engaged in his first biographical essays in and translations of Spanish literature.[1] The party returned to England in the summer of 1805, having missed the resignation of Addington and the formation of Pitt's second administration. The Napoleonic wars notwithstanding, they returned to Spain in 1808, barely a year after Lord Holland's brief service in the aborted 'Ministry of All the Talents.' With the young Lord John Russell in their charge, they remained abroad for almost a year. The end of hostilities in 1814 witnessed another year-long sojourn to Paris, Geneva, Florence, Rome, and Naples.

The Hollands' cosmopolitanism was not confined to foreign travel. When settled at Holland House, their home became an English approximation of the continental salon.[2] Purchased by the first Lord Holland in 1767, it was let during much of Holland's minority, but subsequently renovated and occupied by its owners. John Allen (1771-1843) soon became one of its permanent occupants as well. A Scottish physician, he had been introduced to Lord and Lady Holland in 1801, and became their friend, fellow-traveller, Lord Holland's occasional amanuensis and, at Holland House, dilettante, clerk and librarian-in-residence. He was absent from Holland House only for his weekly visits to Dulwich College where he was warden from 1811 and master from 1820 until his death. Allen, Macaulay wrote, was treated by Lady Holland like 'a negro slave';[3] he issued dinner invitations at her direction, allocated rooms to those staying the night, and carved at table.

Holland's dinner books[4] list the company—regular visitors such as Sydney

Smith, Francis Horner, and Francis Jeffrey, the nucleus of the *Edinburgh Review*; floating continental exiles; members of the diplomatic corps in London; and literati of such varying talents as Byron and Samuel Rogers. As its reputation grew, anecdotes about Holland House abounded.[5] The company was usually crowded round the table. 'Make room,' Lady Holland once directed Henry Luttrell. 'It must certainly be *made,*' he rsponded, 'for it does not exist.' Imperious toward intimates, her commands were occasionally mocked. Upon instructing Sydney Smith, 'ring the bell Sydney,' the Whig clergyman countered, 'Oh yes, and shall I sweep the floor.' Opinionated, she rarely abstained from judgment. To Samuel Rogers, with perhaps more justification than she realized: 'Your poetry is bad enough so please be sparing of your prose.' The accolade conferred by parody confirmed the fame of Lady Holland and Holland House in Caroline Lamb's *Glenarvon,* wherein the mistress was represented as the Princess of Madagascar, the salon as Barbary House.

Holland House opened its doors most readily to politicians in varying degrees of alienation from the existing government. Indeed, alienation was a ticket of admission. It pervaded the atmosphere of Holland House as it did the politics of the Whigs during their long years out of office. And Lord Holland's political career personified the vicissitudes of Whiggery since the French Revolution, which had refined its creed by diminishing its adherents, placing it in the seemingly permanent role of established opposition.

By the 1790s the coterie of Foxites in opposition had arrogated or inherited the appellation of Whig. The eighteenth-century descent of the 'Revolution' or 'Big Whigs' from Newcastle to Rockingham to Fox is generally acknowledged. The transition from faction to party once associated with that descent, however, has long been a matter of historiographical controversy. Holland attributed the transition to the effects of the American Revolution, when the politics of 'struggles for favour and power' by the 'cabals' of George III's early reign were succeeded by 'great questions of policy and principle.'[6] His uncle's career may belie Holland's precise demarcation. Charles James Fox's coalition with Lord North in 1782 after a decade of relentless opposition, his apparent tergiversation in advocating an unrestricted regency in 1788 after his passionate opposition to arbitrary executive power may justify the scepticism which has postponed the creation of party and tarnished Fox's once unassailed reputation as a champion of liberty. But the uneasy coexistence of faction and party invalidates neither; and Holland's consciousness of his role as a repository of Fox's political principles need not be verified by exculpating Fox from the charge of political expediency.[7]

Political principle is usually cultivated in opposition. Its attempted implementation invariably leads to compromise and the charge of opportunism. Charles James Fox remained in opposition from his dismissal in 1783 until his coalition with Lord Grenville in 1806. When Fox died later that year, Holland joined the Ministry of All the Talents as Lord Privy Seal, though he would much have preferred the Foreign Office. He aspired 'towards keeping my uncle's political friends together upon the same principles as they and he uniformly acted on.'[8] When the government was dismissed eight months later, Lord Holland commenced his career in opposition, not to conclude until the formation of Lord Grey's government in 1830—a lapse of twenty-three years, the same amount of time Fox had remained in opposition from his dismissal until his juncture with Grenville.

Holland was thirty-three years old when his uncle died. His subsequent evaluations of measures and men were strongly conditioned by his personal and intellectual inheritance which, in turn, owed so much to Fox's tutelage. He was neither uncritical nor insensitive in his judgments of contemporaries. Born to a title, a peer from infancy, perhaps his own privileged status led him to belittle others who sought honors, ribbands, knighthoods, and titles. And perhaps the example of his uncle who shunned these 'gew gaws,' as Holland called them, provided him with an appreciation for unadorned talent. As in so many of his attitudes, Holland evinced a persistent humanist tradition when he conceived of politics as an arena for the display of virtue:[9]

> The habit of ascribing great designs and elevated motives to all the actions of public characters, so prevalent in courtly writers, is not only false and foolish but mischievous. On the other hand, the passion in which vulgar minds indulge of levelling all public characters to their own standard, and branding indiscriminately the leaders and followers of all parties with the meanest selfishness, is equally false, nearly as foolish, and much more mischievous. Far from showing sagacity, it betrays an ignorance of mankind as well as malignity of disposition. Instead of deterring men from corruption by the exposure of vice, it extinguishes one of the strongest incentives to virtue, posthumous fame.

Like the classical hero, Fox would be enshrined in posterity and Holland became the agency of his uncle's fame, a role which Fox bestowed. In 1793 Fox wrote to Holland, then in France:[10]

> The truth is, that all men when they are no longer young must look forwards to something they expect to last beyond themselves. My friends whom I love most are all about my own age, and consequently one supposes they will go off the stage about the same time as oneself. So when I have a mind to build castles, and to look forward to distant times with pride and pleasure, I must think of you and only you, and I feel myself quite sure that you will not disappoint me.

In the luxury of opposition, with principle unfettered by the exigencies of government, Holland could espouse those sentiments, elusive but meaningful, that he associated with his uncle and which have been subsumed under the rubric, 'the old cause'.

The cause was liberty. In the midst of British revulsion from the radical phase of the French Revolution, Fox embraced liberty as an absolute good in itself, beyond empirical demonstration. If Locke had occasionally used property as a generic term to encompass his trinity of natural rights, Fox, like a political Socinian, subsumed all rights under liberty. Life and property, though concomitant with it, were precarious without it. Indeed, the Glorious Revolution, whose intellectual spoils Whiggery had somehow managed to monopolize, had predicated the defense of property upon liberty and the elimination of the crown's arbitrary power. By the

1780s, the Rockingham and Foxite Whigs had justified economical reform within the context of that tradition. Moreover, Fox wrote, the love of liberty exalted humanity: 'If it be an illusion, it is one that has brought forth more of the best qualities and exertions of the human mind than all other causes put together; and it serves to give an interest in the affairs of the world which, without it, would be insipid.'[11]

If true Whigs remained liberty's most eloquent exponents during Holland's youth, the equation of liberty with limited government was no longer confined to them alone. In the early utilitarian vocabulary it was reflected in Bentham's inclination toward the rules of 'probity' rather than those of 'beneficence,'[12] the removal of abuses of authority that hindered natural growth rather than promoting such growth by governmental intervention in established institutions. It received its continental imprimatur in the Declaration of the Rights of Man and of the Citizen, wherein liberty was associated with the abolition of govermental infringements. If the final cause of liberty was the elevation of humanity, its efficiency required the removal of restraints. One may reconstruct an eighteenth-century conception of liberty as essentially negative in character, its definition and immediacy dependent upon evidence of its opposite—arbitrary power.

Holland perpetuated that conception of liberty. From youth to old age, his correspondence, speeches, and diaries are incessantly punctuated by such phrases as 'friends of liberty', 'civil and religious liberties', 'the general cause of liberty', 'principles of political liberty'. His politics in opposition acquired consistency in his vigorous dissent from governmental measures which he deemed detrimental to liberty. Early in his career he revived the written protest in the House of Lords as a device to record one's principled opposition to specific legislative decisions.[13] In 1799 he opposed the bill to continue suspension of habeas corpus, 'because the alarms of Ministers are always to be received with distrust by the Legislature, when the remedy proposed is an extension of their power, andu diminution of the liberty of the subject.'[14] Union with Ireland similarly would increase the influence of the crown, impair the independence of parliament, and enhance arbitrary power.[15] The act endowing the Irish lord lieutenant with powers to proclaim martial law was not only unconstitutional but dangerous: 'Such power in its nature tends to corrupt the minds of those who hold it.'[16] The Seditious Libels Bill of 1819, along with others of the Six Acts, was intended to repress free expression.[17] Even if liberty of expression disrupted domestic tranquillity, it was paramount and unimpeachable. To resort to coercion for the sake of political expediency presaged 'the surrender of all constitutional liberty . . . .'[18] The Alien Bill of 1822 he opposed on grounds that it was cruel, unjust, unnecessary, impolitic, and unconstitutional, its unconstitutionality consisting in the creation of arbitrary power; 'and arbitrary power has always been thought to degrade those who are the objects of it and to corrupt those who possess it, and thereby to lead to tyrannical maxims and practices incompatible with the safety of a free people.'[19] In a second protest to the same bill, Holland branded it as 'hostile to the liberties and welfare of mankind.'[20]

Holland owed much of his parliamentary reputation to his consistent defense of religious liberty. But 'civil and religious liberty,' a phrase he often invoked, was a redundancy. Holland's 'religious liberty' could hardly be distinguished from constitutional or political liberty. It amounted to the abolition of governmental restrictions on the general liberty of the subject. One could in fact contend that religious liberty, in the strict sense of the term, had already been achieved in Regency England; such restrictions as the Test and Corporation Acts as well as the oaths required of public men did not circumscribe freedom of worship.[21] Rather the Whigs' defense of 'religious liberty' was another, if more passionate, expression of their opposition to any proscription of the liberties of the subject by arbitrary power, however technically justified those proscriptions might be. Holland implicitly acknowledged the tautological association of religious and political liberty in many of his protests and speeches. In 1811 he opposed Sidmouth's attempt to restrict the licensing of Methodist ministers. Hardly enamored of evangelical religion, Holland insisted that the right to preach was not contingent upon governmental sufferance.[22] Two decades later, he would plead for the Jews by contending that the constitution admitted all 'to the full enjoyment of political rights.' The equation of liberty with the absence of regulation was evident in his argument that common law, 'if unrestrained by statute,' permitted all free-born subjects to seek any political or temporal office under the crown.[23] That Catholic Emancipation should have unified the Whigs in opposition was not attributable to mere expediency. It provided an issue which varieties of Whig adherents could unequivocally support, and which Holland recognized in his injunction to Grey in 1812 to 'stick to the Pope' and pledge the party to Emancipation.[24] Indeed, Holland and the Whigs were most comfortable when the issues they appropriated could be advocated in the elevated cause of liberty, civil or religious.

Fox had converted his nephew to faith in party, comprised of educated and propertied aristocracy, as the proper guardian of such liberty and watchdog against encroachments of arbitrary power by crown or ministers.[25] But if an aristocratic Whig party was to stand for the defense of liberty, Whig aristocrats had to resolve the problem of their proper relationships to those radical groups which also aspired to limit excessive power but did not share the Whig emphasis on the primacy of the aristocracy. The problem was first evident to Holland in his observation of Charles Grey's circle, the Friends of the People, established in April 1792. Decades later, in the calm reflection of old age, Grey was to confess to a sense of embarrassment about his youthful ardor.[26] But in 1792 the Friends of the People succeeded in cleaving the split in the Whig opposition, enlisting the acquiescence if not enthusiasm of Fox, and driving the party's more conservative members to William Pitt and the support of king and country. If the Friends of the People dissipated its youthful energy amidst the reaction to the French Revolution, it helped to impose upon the Whig party a group consciousness which it had not hitherto attained. As important as its political implications, the association exemplified an indigenous attribute of Whiggery. The very name, Friends of the People, revealed that stance of benevolent condescension which sustained the Whig party in the nineteenth century. The benign ascendancy of the aristocracy and the relative rigidity of class distinctions constituted its unassailable social premises. Even in the exuberance of youth, Grey and the Friends invoked their rank and station to preclude identification with radical groups of the lower orders, whose program for parliamentary reform was presumably similar to their own. In response to solicitations by the Society for Constitutional Information, one of Grey's colleagues advised John Cartwright there could be no liaison between the two groups, for there was an underlying conflict in their attitudes, notwithstanding the transient identity of their political goals.[27] Fox had himself warned his nephew of the party's possible isolation, sandwiched between 'the Court and the Democrats.' The latter, 'unmixed with any aristocratic leaven,' might conceivably become as dangerous as the despotism of monarchy.[28]

There were probably few Whigs who experienced the same sense of urgency expressed in 1809 by Francis Jeffrey, who was convinced that an eventual conciliation between Whigs and more radical groups was essential for the survival of the former.[29] No doubt that conclusion was revolting to those of the party who considered political connection with the radicals as a prelude to the aristocracy's disintegration. It was revolting to Grey, who by that time was leader of the party and who simply refused to consider affiliation with the followers of Sir Francis Burdett; nor could he condone the behaviour of such Whigs as Samuel Whitbread, who had apparently been inveigled into contemplating a coalition on the basis of parliamentary reform.[30] Curiously, Holland, who had been aloof from the Friends of the People, was to become less hostile to such coalitions than most of his Whig colleagues. After Peterloo, Holland reluctantly recognized the necessity for some sort of association with the radicals.[31] Nevertheless, he never doubted the desirability of the aristocracy's continued ascendancy in guiding social and political change.

Whether inherited or acquired, aristocrats presumed to possess attributes which distinguished them from others. Indeed, the underlying and unspoken justification of the Whig antipathy toward radicals concerned neither power, wealth nor status so much as honor, a quality required of governors and of which radicals, given their social and economic situation, were lamentably devoid. Montesquieu had predicated aristocratic ascendancy on the social principle of honor. Burke had articulated the sentiment when he derided the National Assembly:[32]

> In asserting that any thing is honourable, we imply some distinction in its favour. The occupation of an hairdresser, or of a working tallow-chandler, cannot be a matter of honour to any person—to say nothing of a number of other more servile employments. Such description of men ought not to suffer oppression from the state; but the state suffers oppression, if such as they, either individually or collectively, are permitted to rule. In this you think you are combating prejudice, but you are at war with nature.

Honor, after all, was an aristocratic quality. From the Whig point of view, men of rank and breeding, aware of their social responsibility, sensitive about personal reputation, economically secure and exposed to the accumulated wisdom which their generation had inherited, were best endowed with the capacity to defend liberty and resist despotic temptation. Yet honor, however essential in the enlightened defense of liberty, was apolitical. Even some like Wellington, infatuated with power and therefore hostile to the cause of liberty, insisted, at the very least, upon honor in their personal relationships. It was a quality that bound aristocracy together in a consciousness of kind that transcended political and even national boundaries, almost in a perverse vindication of Marxian class struggle. When Holland recorded that Queen Adelaide must have been surprised to discover that not every radical was 'destitute of gallantry, honour or humanity,' he was referring to Sir Francis Burdett, an aristocratic radical, soon to turn Tory.[33] Lord John Russell, ruminating in later years about that fleeting association of Whigs, Radicals, and Irish Repealers called the Lichfield House Compact, insisted that it was an 'honourable' enterprise.[34] In the Grey and Melbourne cabinets, Goderich and Glenelg agonized about loss of honor when shifted from offices of function to those of dignity. Ministerial deliberations about omission or modifications of specific clauses in bills before parliament provoked animated discussion about the cabinet's collective honor, just as foreign policy invariably involved the national honor. For the preservation of Melbourne's government Holland remained prepared to 'sacrifice everything, short of honour . . . .'[35]

If honor remained an aristocratic preserve and, among Whigs at least, a defense against the temptations of power and subversion of liberty, a reverence for property distinguished Whigs from radicals as well. Holland eschewed particularly the 'impracticable' schemes of visionaries who would ultimately destroy the liberties they professed to secure by neglecting the institutions and the property which had nurtured and sustained them. In the exuberant springtime of Revolution, men like Wordsworth and Coleridge were 'smitten with notions of impracticable liberty,' Godwin with 'visionary notions of the perfectibility of the human species.'[36] The contagion of revolutionary fervor and youthful idealism affected Holland as well, though not so severely. His enthusiasm for the Revolution was tempered by his libertarianism. He qualified liberty by its 'rationality.' Rational friends of liberty or lovers of rational liberty became Holland's singular encomium for those, regardless of factional affiliation, whose political vision encompassed his own libertarianism. Burke, for all his mystical inflation of the constitution and opposition to Fox, was acknowledged to be a rational friend of liberty.[37] Impracticable liberty was distinguished by its indifference to the principle of the inviolability of property and the institutional distribution of political power.[38] Rational liberty was contingent upon both. The distribution of political power signified its separation in accord with the increasingly anachronistic conception of a mechanical constitution, wherein the abuse of power was thwarted by the delicate balance between King, Lords, and Commons. It was a theory refurbished by Lord John Russell,[39] believed by King William IV, and deferred to by most others. Holland had it in mind when he occasionally referred to the 'branches of the constitution.' Indeed, it became more frequent a part of his vocabulary in office than out. He invoked it to support extensive ministerial power presumably justified by the exercise of the royal prerogative against the encroachments of the House of Lords.[40] When in opposition, the separation of powers meant, more importantly, division between the executive and legislature, the elevation of the legislature checking the executive's invariable propensities toward arbitrary excess. If parliament was to restrict executive power, property had to be paramount within it, and to that extent a nobility in the House of Lords and an aristocracy in the form of a corporate enlightened leadership of the nation, instilled with a sense of honor, was required in both houses. Indeed, the preservation of liberty required property's continued and legitimate influence, and Holland thought he could best defend liberty in his capacity 'as a man of education and property.'[41] Insofar as Holland and the Whigs were to acknowledge the changing forms of property in a period of industrialization, they could adapt institutions to new conditions. But the inviolability of property circumscribed Holland's perception of social problems and led him, like most Whigs, to a conception of government as active in the defense of liberty but passive in matters involving the correction of social and economic grievances.

The abolition of the slave trade and, decades later, of slavery constituted an ostensible exception to limiting government's interference in property relationships. In those cases liberty and property were antithetical. In 1791 Fox had eloquently condemned slavery as a limitation on personal freedom, much less the political freedom to which any people would legitimately aspire.[42] Despite his landholdings in the West Indies, Holland characterized the slave trade as inhumane and 'repugnant to the principles of natural justice.'[43] Slavery aside, the compassion which Holland often displayed was rarely projected to government. It remained an individual obligation in a society that retained a pre-industrial dependency structure. For all his complaints about the inconveniences of dispensing patronage when in government, it was essential to the dependency relationship which Holland accepted without question. His hierarchical and corporate assumptions about society as well as his devotion to liberty informed his opposition to measures of governmental coercion. Coercive legislation constituted not only infringement of liberty; it subverted the people's acceptance of that necessary 'subordination' which endowed a society with its cohesion.[44] Perhaps consistency was not so well served when hierarchical assumptions about society conflicted with principles of liberty, as in 1831 when Holland argued against immediate emancipation of the slaves, because the measure would not provide for the subordination of the emancipated.[45] Ultimately, then, in the scale of Whig values, liberty was conditioned by and subordinated to the maintenance of a traditional hierarchical order in society.

The preservation of subordination could also be invoked as a justification for legislative concessions like the Reform Bill, which would propitiate the people and maintain order. Like the principle of utility, hierarchical assumptions could be used to sanction or oppose specific legislation. But legislation involving governmental regulation of social and economic relationships hardly attracted Holland's concern. His relative indifference to such legislation may be attributed to the circumscriptions imposed by fundamental Whig premises. Like the proposal for immediate emancipation of the slaves, social reform legislation might very well upset the hierarchical order of society and the continued and legitimate influence of the aristocracy. Moreover, and far more obvious, such legislation hardly involved the preservation or extension of liberty as Holland conceived of it. Consequently, when he returned to government during a decade that witnessed considerable expansion of regulatory activity, Holland continued to restrict his attention primarily to constitutional questions and foreign affairs. He once wrote to Lady Holland that he would regrettably return late to Holland House, for he had to endure a debate on a factory bill, 'which I could and would shirk' but for the important foreign enlistment bill to come on thereafter.[46]

Why were foreign enlistment bills more important than factory bills? One could fashion a barometer of Holland's legislative sensibilities based upon his conception of liberty and his cosmopolitanism. Factory legislation had little to do with liberty. It involved social justice, a concept which subsequent generations of liberals would heartily endorse. Whether British volunteers should be allowed to fight in foreign wars, however, was a matter of considerable import, particularly if those wars were fought on behalf of liberty. In that respect Holland remains a text-book writer's dream. The association of continental nationalism with liberalism had no more fervent proponent in the early nineteenth century. War or revolution, Holland advised John Russell, was justified if the conflict involved a quest for liberty; and liberty, on the continent at least, signified constitutional government and aspirations for national independence.[47] 'To connect the cause of liberty with that of independence' became an obvious and salutary formula in 1808 when Holland was moved by the Spanish quest for freedom.[48] In 1814 he opposed the subjugation of Norway by Sweden as 'a manifest violation of the sacred rights of national independence.'[49] He condemned the treaties concluding the Napoleonic wars because the principle of legitimacy was tantamount to 'general and perpetual guaranty of all European Governments against the governed.'[50] Similarly, if national aspirations were equated with English liberty, restrictions of the latter corresponded to suppression of the former. In their denial of liberty, the Six Acts were comparable to the nefarious subjugation of the Neapolitan revolution by the Holy Alliance.[51]

Holland's sentiments in foreign policy had him moving between the Grey and Grenville factions until the latter lost any credibility for Whigs by sanctioning the suspension of habeas corpus and supporting the Six Acts. Sympathetic toward the Spaniards, Holland had favored the peninsular war when Grey and Whitbread favored peace. He supported overtures for peace in 1813 when Grey opposed them. He would generally have aligned with the Grenville faction in foreign policy, but was at odds with them as well when he opposed the principle of legitimacy in the peace settlement and advocated non-intervention in foreign affairs. Throughout his opposition, the underlying association of liberty with constitutional movements for national independence attracted his sympathetic attention.

Holland's sympathy for Napoleon, then, appears incongruous with his libertarianism. Lady Holland, to be sure, was an unqualified 'Napoleonist,' infatuated with the heroic emperor.[52] Lord Holland, despite his protests on behalf of Napoleon in captivity,[53] was ambivalent. In his *Foreign Reminiscences,* Holland disdained Napoleon the absolutist, the opponent of liberty. But he also lauded

Napoleon for establishing 'equality before the law, impartiality in the administration of justice, and certainty of redress in case of any injury either from individuals or from civil and military authorities.'[54] Moreover, in attempting to heal the wounds of the Revolution, Napoleon must have represented the consummation of the *ancien régime*'s destruction which the Revolution had initiated. He had, incidentally, also assured for himself the 'posthumous fame' which was so eminently an aspect of the Enlightenment's secular tradition.

Holland was a more faithful child of the Enlightenment than was Napoleon of the Revolution. Cosmopolitan, urbane, ardent defender of liberty and opponent of arbitrary power, reverent of the classics and fashionably anticlerical, he exemplified the Enlightenment's secular-humanist ethos. His ethical principles were derived from classical rather than Christian tradition. Discussing an eighteenth-century commentary on the Old Testament, Holland encountered a reference to eunuchs: 'I do not recollect any mention of it in Homer,' he noted. 'It was an Eastern refinement.' Similarly the Biblical tales of the patriarchs defied the ethical principles of a generation dedicated to the advancement of virtue and talent. The story of Jacob and Esau, for example, was at best devoid of moral content. Jacob, deceitful and calculating, profits, while Esau, 'generous, affectionate and forgetful of injuries' was 'hated by God.' God, then, was *'capricious and his favours no proof of merit*—and where is the sense or morality of such a lesson?'[55] If the sarcasm of Voltaire is lacking, the similarity of sentiment is apparent. A more passionate Holland in different circumstances might well have declaimed, *'Écrasez l'infâme!'* If he delighted in expatiating about the 'clerical vermin that infest the country,'[56] such hyperbole was merely a gratifying indulgence. In early nineteenth-century England one could still entertain a worldly and comfortable 'rational Christianity,' stripped of its embarrassing supernatural elements and endowed with an ethical system derived from the classics. Indeed, classical precepts of morality underlay Whig Christianity, which has been aptly characterized as 'substituting for the dreamy ambition of establishing Christ's kingdom on earth, the nearer but no less desirable objective of the Reign of Liberty.'[57]

Was it any wonder, then, that the Tory evangelical and social reformer, Lord Ashley, sponsor of factory legislation and guardian of the underprivileged, should have found Holland the virtual incarnation of sin? The worldliness of the latter was irreconcilable with the worldly asceticism of the former. When Holland died in 1840, Ashley assessed his 'profligate life and atheistical soul':[58]

> A man of much talents in conversation, good humoured and Sufficiently accomplished; but there all ends; he had a fair portion for this world but nothing for the next. Infidel, ignorant and addicted to French opinions, he both practised and encouraged a cold and Saucy scepticism, tho he was far better than either his wife or his friend Allen. As an individual I mourn for his death for it was awfully unprepared; as a politician he is well absent; and the decoys and illusions of Holland House will now cease to tempt and pervert the unwary in public or private life.[59]

Ashley's zealous righteousness may appear more redolent of the turbulent generation that preceded the mid Victorian 'equipoise' than were the 'illusions of Holland House.' In a society undergoing seemingly unremitting change, the detached urbanity of Holland House almost suggests anachronism, not only when juxtaposed to the style of evangelical reformers. One summons images of the Bristol and Nottingham riots, the Tolpuddle martyrs, the histrionics of 'Orator' Hunt and Daniel O'Connell, and G. M. Young's memorably evocative 'age of flashing eyes and curling lips.'[60] Holland lacked the romantic striving and apocalyptic vision that were becoming fashionable even among some of the governors. If he admired the talent and agreed with the opinions of the mercurial Lord Durham, he deplored Durham's tactlessness and boorish behavior. Nor can one imagine Holland in the role of a quixotic Lord Brougham, on his knees to implore a recalcitrant House of Lords to save itself from its own folly. Yet Holland shared the supreme apprehension of the governors. He remained neither aloof from nor indifferent to the social discontent which threatened to destroy the institutions of English society. Rather, he and his colleagues in the governments of the 1830s sought to contain it, to assuage the aggrieved while maintaining the social order and its established institutions.

Those governments were popularly and properly called Whig. In the 1820s the Whig party had almost dissolved. It no longer monopolized the advocacy of Catholic Emancipation or sympathy for movements of national independence. Reform of parliament did not unify its motley adherents, although most supported motions for it in 1822 and 1826. Its solidarity in opposition was attenuated by the presence of liberal Tories in the Liverpool government from 1822, several younger Whigs lured into association with them. Moreover, the chronic lack of leadership which characterized the Whigs in opposition impaired their parliamentary efficacy. Grey, the acknowledged leader of the party in the Lords, was often an absentee. The zeal of his early years apparently spent, he roused himself from the pastoral torpor of Northumberland only when his titular leadership seemed threatened. As for the Commons, as early as 1812 Holland had lamented the absence of an effective leader who could enlist the enthusiastic allegiance of Whig members.[61] After Tierney's retirement in 1822, even less direction was evident in the lower house. Canning's succession as Prime Minister after Liverpool's paralysis in 1827 portended the permanent assimilation of moderate Whigs with liberal Tories, by default, to be sure, many ultra and moderate Tories having refused to serve in the ministry. Three of Canning's cabinet of fifteen were Whigs, led by Lord Lansdowne—junior partners assuredly, but partners nonetheless. Though not in the government, Holland acted as Whig broker for his friends and those 'attached to my uncle's memory.'[62] He obtained a peerage for Lambton, always eager for one, though he failed to persuade Lord Derby's son, Edward Stanley, to accept one. He declined an offer to join Canning's government, mainly from loyalty to Grey, who detested the Prime Minister and was precluded from office in any event by the animosity of George IV. But Holland, like many of his circle, joined the government benches in 1827. After Canning's death his role as mediator continued during Goderich's brief, abortive ministry. Considering the continuation of some Whigs in office as a barrier to the return of the ultra Tories, he became an object of controversy himself, several Whigs urging his appointment to the cabinet. Wellington's succession, his alienation of the ultra Tories in accommodating his government to repeal of the Test and Corporation Acts and Catholic Emancipation, his refusal to invite Grey into office even after the death of George IV, the departure of Huskisson and his colleagues, public agitation for economy and reform even among the ultras, and finally the organization of an active opposition in the Commons marked the unexpected resurgence of Whiggery in 1830. Grey was the only alternative as prime minister when Wellington chose to resign in November 1830 upon the defeat of the Civil List.[63]

Holland had lamented the absence of clear-cut constitutional issues in the 1820s which would define principled parties. Currency and corn were matters which hardly excited him, nor did he understand them.[64] In 1826 he wrote to his son, Henry,

> We have indeed got rid of party government and we shall now see if an Empire divided between Interests and Countries and religions, Growers and Consumers, Irishmen and Englishmen, Protestants and Catholicks constitutes a happier wiser or stronger community than one where the only distinctions were attachment to different systems of policy or adherence to opposite leaders in the State.[65]

The emergence of the Whig government of Lord Grey, pledged to peace, retrenchment and reform, hearkened back to those more desirable days when constitutional issues of great magnitude were allegedly supported or opposed by distinct parties.

That Grey's government was a coalition hardly meant that it was not Whig. The Canningites were courted and won, Melbourne becoming Home Secretary. He first had had administrative experience in the short-lived Canning ministry as Chief Secretary for Ireland. His appointment had then assuaged Lansdowne sufficiently for the Whig peer to throw in his lot with Canning. Melbourne retained his post in Wellington's government, remaining an advocate of Catholic Emancipation. That problem, however, was not originally intended to be a government issue, once again being relegated to oblivion as it had been since the formation of Liverpool's first ministry in 1812. Melbourne, along with Palmerston and Charles Grant, had thrown his support behind William Huskisson. His resignation was indirectly related to the government's refusal to continue consideration of enfranchising Manchester. Late in 1830, Wellington had renewed negotiations with Melbourne, Palmerston, and other Canningites, but the death of Huskisson and the Duke's refusal to consider a moderate reform of parliament ensured Melbourne's association with the emerging Whig opposition. Melbourne was a rather lethargic figure, content to restrict governmental activity to the enforcement of law and order and the administration of public business. Among the most conservative members of the government, he acknowledged 'that change is of itself a great danger and a great evil.'[66] Only when it seemed unavoidable could he consent to it. He was, as Holland recognized, not 'a reformer by choice.'[67] But he regarded parliamentary reform as unavoidable in 1830, and expressed the government's sense of urgency about it when he exhorted the peers, 'Do not make that measure which is safe, if adopted immediately, dangerous by delay.'[68]

His colleague, and later his brother-in-law, Lord Palmerston, became Foreign Secretary when Holland declined the office because of the nagging gout and after Lansdowne refused it as well.[69] Palmerston nearly broke up the government in his reluctance to insist upon the Reform Bill without modifications, but otherwise was immersed almost totally in foreign policy, gradually extricating himself from Grey's domination and Holland's often meddlesome intervention. Other Canningites to join Grey's government were Charles Grant as President of the Board of control and Viscount Goderich as Secretary for War and Colonies, the latter to continue as an inept administrator, the former to become one.

Viscount Althorp became leader of the government in the House of Commons and Chancellor of the Exchequer. He had been a Whig for almost all of his forty-eight years, and like most members of the new government, had never held high office. He was neither a persuasive orator nor a financial expert, but had earned the respect of the Commons. The eldest son of Earl Spencer, Althorp combined aristocratic breeding with relatively advanced political views. He was selected leader of the party in the Commons in March 1830 and his chambers became the meeting place for Whigs who were prepared to oppose the Wellington government. Althorp was able to attract the support of radicals as well as moderates. Although Melbourne and Palmerston were not enthusiastic about him, they accepted him as leader in the Commons given the alternative.

The alternative was Henry Brougham. Elected MP for Yorkshire in 1830, his fame had been established a decade earlier as advisor to Queen Caroline during the divorce controversy. Brougham was an energetic and eloquent advocate of legal and administrative reform. His motion for parliamentary reform had been averted when Wellington resigned on the Civil List. A powerful orator, Brougham could simultaneously wheedle and implore the trimmers while vilifying his opponents. He was thought by some to be on the periphery of Whiggery, a little too radical. But his reputation was established as much in the country as in the House, and to ignore him would hardly have ingratiated the government to that body of public opinion which it was disposed to mollify. Brougham's reputation was surpassed only by his insatiable ambition, and he accepted the office of lord chancellor when Grey had almost despaired of finding a place for him. He was, thereby, removed from the House of Commons, to the relief of some, and possibly of Grey, although that was not the prime minister's original intention.[70] Brougham did, however, throw a scare into some of the party's potential friends. Holland, prior to the formation of the new government, hoped that the plan for parliamentary reform would be entrusted to Lord John Russell, because Brougham would alienate some of its prospective supporters.[71] Aside from his occasional outbursts, however, Henry, now Lord, Brougham, was not a dangerous radical. He shared Grey's apprehension that the recent July Revolution might result in a weak executive, and counselled the retention of a hereditary peerage and of the influence of the crown in the Orléans monarchy across the channel.[72] Moreover, having lost the Commons, Brougham developed a love of office which overcame any hitherto outlandishly unacceptable views.

Among the moderate Whigs, Sir James Graham was perhaps the most competent. One of the few Whigs who considered economical reform to be more than a party shibboleth, his appointment as First Lord of the Admiralty was to result in an impressive departmental reorganization. Earlier in his career, he had opposed parliamentary reform. As he considered that episode in later years, he saw himself among those Whigs 'who delight in the assertion of democratic principle only when wearing the garb of aristocracy.'[73] In 1830 he approached the matter in a typically Whig fashion, 'the object being to reform to the extent necessary for preserving our Institutions, not to change for the purpose of subverting.'[74]

Lansdowne, Carlisle, and Holland, with Grey the core of the old Whig party in the Lords, assumed cabinet posts as well, Lansdowne having yielded his pretensions to leadership of the party once Grey had resolved for active opposition to Wellington's government in 1830. He became Lord President of the Council and Carlisle entered the cabinet without portfolio. Holland accepted the sinecure of Chancellor of the Duchy of Lancaster with its abundant patronage, undemanding requirements, and the luxury it afforded of intimately participating in the deliberations of the cabinet without pressure of business.[75] Lord Durham, Grey's son-in-law, was appointed Lord Privy Seal, a post which enhanced one's status if it did not demand much energy. The Duke of Richmond, an ultra Tory and recent proselyte to reform, was appointed Postmaster General.

Of the thirteen men who formed the original Grey cabinet, then, nine were in the Lords and one, Palmerston, was an Irish peer in the Commons. Three others were in the Commons, of whom one, the leader of the House, was the heir to an earldom. On the periphery of the cabinet were Lord John Russell, son of the Duke of Bedford and an enthusiastic reformer, Viscount Duncannon, an Irish peer and another relative of Grey and Melbourne, and Edward Stanley, heir to one of the oldest earldoms in the kingdom. If the cabinet accommodated Canningites and even an ultra Tory, its moving spirits were unqualified Whigs. Holland referred to the Grey and Melbourne ministries as Whig[76] and contemporaries agreed. Moreover, the most important legislation to which the government was pledged, the preparation of parliamentary reform, was entrusted to a committee of four—Russell, Durham, Graham, and Duncannon—all with impeccable Whig credentials.

The cabinet modified the committee's final draft by eliminating the ballot and, in exchange, reducing the suffrage qualification for boroughs. Russell explained the legislation to the Commons on 1 March 1831. The bill for England and Wales provided for the disfranchisement of sixty boroughs wherein population, according to the 1821 census, was under 2000 (Schedule A of the bill); forty-seven boroughs, with population between 2000 and 4000, were to have representation reduced from two members to one each (Schedule B). Representation was granted to seven large towns—including Manchester, Birmingham, and Sheffield—and four metropolitan districts which would return two members each; twenty other towns were to return one member each. Twenty-six counties were to be divided as constituencies and, in effect, return four rather than two members each. Yorkshire was to have six rather than four members. The forty-shilling freehold franchise was to be retained in the counties and the county franchise extended as well to £10 leaseholders who held leases for life and £50 leaseholders if the minimum period of the lease was fourteen years. The borough franchise was uniformly established for householders who paid rates for or occupied a house of the yearly value of at least £10. The composition of the Commons, considering intended Irish and Scottish alterations as well, was to be reduced from 658 to 596. On 22 March the second reading of the Reform Bill for England and Wales passed by one vote, 302–301. With some minor amendments in county franchise, the transfer of a few boroughs from Schedule A to Schedule B, and the elimination of seven boroughs from Schedule B, the government prepared for the committee stage of the bill in April. But they were defeated on 19 April by General Gascoyne's motion that the representation for England and Wales not be decreased. The king agreed to dissolve parliament, and the subsequent general election was among those, rare in English history, dominated by a single national issue. The government reintroduced the bill, basically the same, on 24 June, with fifty-seven boroughs in Schedule A and forty-four in Schedule B, and the £10 householder qualification more strictly defined. The second reading was carried by a comfortable majority on 8 July, but the Lords defeated the bill on its second reading in October.

Beginning his diary in July 1831, Holland presents the cabinet as preoccupied with reform. On its passage depended not only the future of the ministry, but that of the country and, indirectly, of Europe. Whether a revolution would in fact have transpired had reform failed is unanswerable and not, after all, so important. What remains incontestable is that the ministers were convinced it would, and that the king's acquiescence in reform was predicated on the alternative of revolution, a contingency which Grey assiduously fostered. The fear of revolution intensified after the elections of 1831 and the subsequent rejection of the second reading in the Lords. Nor was it mere cant for the unconverted. It is evident not only in correspondence and parliamentary rhetoric, but in Holland's diary, intended for no one but himself, and in the secret councils of the cabinet. Grey confided to his colleagues that a second rejection by the Lords would mean civil war and revolution.[77] James Abercromby warned ministers that even a slight change in the principles of the bill would subvert the constitution. And Holland repeated Grey's admonition: 'The loss of the bill is civil war and revolution.'[78]

When politics and the constitution still monopolized the historian's attention, the Reform Act achieved the status of an historical landmark at which surveys or lectures could abruptly end or conveniently commence. The traditional interpretation is that parliamentary reform, embracing the middling orders within the political nation, was a concession which averted revolution and thereby preserved the institutions and aristocratic ascendancy that sustained political stability in the nineteenth century.[79] D. C. Moore has recently challenged and, in the process, distorted the concession theory.[80] 'The act is usually conceived,' he contends, 'as the political corollary of industrialization, as a means of transferring power from the hands of a rural aristocracy and gentry into the hands of an urban middle class.'[81] Defining the social structure of each constituency and geographically segregating landed from urban interests, Grey's government allegedly sought to reestablish the traditional bases of authority in the localites, thereby 'restoring the cohesion of those local hierarchical communities through which traditional social discipline had been exerted.'[82] Moore's close and subtle textual analysis of the bill isolates the borough freeholder clause and the constituency boundaries as attesting ministerial intent to redress the landed interest's loss of power and restore the legitimate influence of the nation's traditional leaders, thereby providing a permanent cure of the problem rather than a concession of power to others.[83]

To some extent Moore undermines his own argument, for proponents of the concession theory have not considered the bill as a transfer of power.[84] Nevertheless, despite his distortion of the traditional interpretation, Moore's sociological orientation has had the salutary effect of producing a reevaluation of the Reform Bill. As recorded by Holland, the cabinet's deliberations do lend some credence to a revisionist interpretation, not so much in vitiating the concession theory as in emphasizing the ministers' assumptions about the corporate structure of society and their ambiguous conception of parliamentary representation. Holland had recurrently alluded to the desirability of maintaining proper 'subordination' in society. No doubt his hierarchical assumptions conditioned his perception of reform as well. He thought the justification for the government's continuation in office was 'that by retaining the confidence we may secure the tranquillity and subordination of the people.'[85] His few discussions about the bill's provisions reflect the cabinet's attempt to reconcile hierarchical assumptions with the compelling need to propitiate the admittedly vague but meaningful entity called public opinion.

Sensitivity to public opinion was hardly a novelty. The populace in the constituencies had often been the objects of Whig cultivation; in 1819 Holland was active, if not enthusiastic, in organizing county meetings to protest the repressive actions of Liverpool's government, and during the queen's trial the Whigs again appealed to public opinion.[86] Nor was it neglected once the Whigs achieved power. Holland wrote that one object of government 'is to inspire the people with something like affection and respect for authority.'[87] During and after the reform debates, Grey contended that government must direct and regulate 'the current of improvement and reform' and endeavour 'to adapt its institutions and policy to publick opinion and gain the affection and confidence of the governed.'[88] Melbourne went even further in 1834 when he told the king 'all that was consistent with justice must be done to adapt institutions to the real (be it conscientious or fanatical) opinion of the country.'[89] Such attitudes presupposed the necessity for concession to popular opinion for the sake of maintaining stability. Otherwise, as Holland indicated, one was confronted by alternatives of an oligarchy ruling 'at variance with the obvious tendency of the times and Society' or of 'organic Changes' which might well prove hazardous.[90] To be sure, the Whigs identified public opinion and the people with a particular if ill-defined socioeconomic group, demonstrated by Brougham's famous panegyric 'of those middle classes, who are also the genuine depositaries of sober, rational intelligence and honest English feeling.'[91] Their ominous association with extra-parliamentary unions in the 1830s alarmed ministers and made passage of the Reform Bill all the more pressing. Indeed, by the 1830s 'the people' had assumed a role in the eyes of their governors which virtually elevated them to a branch of the constitution, along with King, Lords, and Commons. Insofar as the Commons were the people's representatives, the proper effect of reform was to elevate the lower house to a position which overshadowed the Lords or the crown. Its ostensible supremacy was ratified by Melbourne's pledge in 1836 that his government would resign only if it lost the Commons' confidence.[92] Since it represented the Community, the Commons' apparent supremacy hardly surprised Holland. He noted that the Reform had, after all, extended 'to the Community a real and positive and not a mere nominal representation.'[93] The problem was to define the community. Was it now an aggregation of individuals or did it remain an association of corporate interests?

Holland's diary suggests that he and his colleagues retained their allegiance to what has been called 'the Old Whig theory of representation,' wherein the 'functional representation of interests in the House of Commons' was associated with parliament's role as the repository of sovereignty, while simultaneously approximating the subsequent 'Liberal theory,' wherein individuals replaced corporate orders as units of representation, property remaining a prerequisite for the suffrage.[94] Holland's discussions of the cabinet's deliberations in late November 1831 are particularly revealing in demonstrating the cabinet's corporate societal assumptions. When the Duke of Richmond suggested that representation be extended to the colonies, his proposal was not considered inconsonant with any accepted theory of representation. Rather Holland objected to it because it was impracticable, particularly at that advanced stage of the proceedings. For what of the legitimate claims of other 'corporate bodies—trades, guilds, professions, and classes'?[95] Similarly, some ministers urged that two to four members be given the Inns of Court.[96] Such suggestions were not rejected out of hand. Rather, their presentation attests the prevailing conception of parliament as embodying a representation of interests.

Though hardly as rigid as D. C. Moore suggests, the cabinet did proceed on the premise of balancing those interests within the broad and sometimes overlapping classifications of landed or urban constituencies. Holland unfortunately did not define the formula precisely, but he did refer 'to the proportion we had proposed to establish between land and town representation.'[97] So, for example, when they considered which of three constituencies—Stroud, Cheltenham, or Dudley—ought to return two members rather than one, ministers selected Stroud 'as an insulated district of thriving Manufactures.'[98] But Moore's contention that the cabinet deliberately structured the bill to ensure the permanent ascendancy of separate landed over urban interests presupposes a ministerial unity which is simply not justified. Although common corporate premises among ministers are evident, the provisions of the bill or of the subsequent legislation defining constituency boundaries cannot be considered as a statement of collective ministerial intention. The bill underwent considerable modification during its parliamentary sojourn, with accompanying squabbles and disagreements of varying intensity within the cabinet. To be sure, Russell's controversial 'finality' statement to the Commons in 1837 seems to suggest that the bill was designed as a cure rather than a concession.[99] But given the context of Russell's remarks, the Whig government of Lord Melbourne confronting not only a hostile House of Lords but an irascible Commons to the left as well as right, the stability of the ministry may well have required a gesture to dampen the ardor of radicals. Moreover, the recurrent ministerial emphasis on the finality of the Reform Bill may also be interpreted to signify their insistence upon full implementation of all the principles of the bill, rather than their opposition to any further alterations.[100] Assuredly, some of the cabinet's disagreements confirm a tendency among a few of Holland's colleagues to maintain the landed ascendancy over the towns. Lansdowne, for example, would have preferred the enlargement of some smaller boroughs 'with the real object probably of infusing landed interest in town elections'[101]—though such a proposal would have combined rather than segregated the two interests. The cabinet agreed that 'a general rule should be adopted,'[102] and the subsequent regulations for arranging borough boundaries did indeed result in the alteration of the electoral complexion of some English boroughs. But Holland provides no evidence to suggest that the cabinet actually adopted any such rule at this stage of its parliamentary struggle. To contend that the subsequent arrangements by the boundary commissioners were the direct results of a preconceived design by the cabinet implies collective ministerial connivance of a magnitude which the structure of nineteenth-century English politics was hardly capable of sustaining.

Other cabinet dissension suggests as well that the alleged finality of the bill was not to be construed as an immutable establishment of landed ascendancy. When the cabinet decided to retain a complement of 658 members in the Commons after the passage of the Gascoyne amendment, they did so to circumvent the claims of the Irish, however legitimate, to a greater increase in representation than the five additional members allotted them by the Irish Reform Bill. Holland thought the decision dangerous, for the very reason that it might be construed as freezing the representation. It provided 'no margin for the admission of other interests which may on experiment be found unrepresented, or for towns which, like Manchester, Bolton or Brighton, may in the course of a Century swell into places of vast importance and not be easily reconciled to a perpetual exclusion from the representation.'[103] Moreover, if others envisioned further enfranchisement while maintaining a House of 658 members, it follows that further disfranchisement would have had to be undertaken, thereby invalidating the 'finality' of the measure in terms of the permanent ascendancy of the landed interest.

Conversely, Holland's account of the now celebrated borough freeholder clause attests the cabinet's occasional predilection for urban over landed interests, rather than the other way around. Moore interprets the government's modification of that clause in August 1831 as signifying their intention to retain the separation of landed from urban interests. In its original version, the extension of the county franchise to borough freeholders was more restrictive than the amended provision in the second and third versions of the bill. The more liberal provision, Moore contends, resulted from the cabinet's response to the Chandos clause, which enfranchised tenants at will in the counties, whose lack of economic security made them totally dependent upon their landlords. Hence the more liberal provision was ostensibly to balance the anticipated 'illegitimate influence' of landlords in the counties.[104] But Holland's diary reveals that the cabinet's revision of the clause preceded the Chandos amendment, that it was not conceived in terms of balancing landed as opposed to urban representation. Rather, he notes, ministers concluded that the continued exclusion of many borough freeholders from the county franchise had to be abandoned because 'we should hardly be able to carry a provision so injurious to the rights of persons connected with town population.'[105]

To acknowledge the cabinet's corporate assumptions and their distinction, however ill-defined, between landed and urban interests hardly impairs the validity of the traditional interpretation. The Whigs' sensitivity to public opinion and fear of revolution are more telling than their vague distinctions between landed and urban interests. Moreover, when they referred to the principles of the bill, Grey and his colleagues invariably meant the abolition of rotten boroughs, the addition of representation to the hitherto neglected populous towns, and the extension of the franchise to the £10 householder, never the enfranchisement of the borough freeholder.[106] Nor is the concession theory impaired by noting that the ministers were not motivated by democratic principle. No one contends they were, and to belittle the Whigs by suggesting that the Reform Act was not the first step toward democratic representation is to turn the 'Whig interpretation of history' on its head. If the Whigs were not motivated by a conception of the newly enfranchised in terms of 'Benthamite individualism,'[107] they nevertheless did extend the vote to considerable numbers. Of course, population alone was never the sole criterion for the vote nor, after the first version of the bill, for enfranchisement or disfranchisement of constituencies. The latter was to have as its 'just criterion' not population alone but 'the combination of wealth and numbers.'[108] Given the vague distinction between interests, the recognition of numbers, however qualified by property or wealth, implies an incipient if reluctant acknowledgement of the representation of individuals.

Relatively little attention has been directed to the relationships between parliamentary reform and other significant legislation of the 1830s. Factory reform, the Poor Law Amendment Act, abolition of slavery in the empire, reform of municipal corporations, and concession to Dissenters in the form of the marriage and registration bills have generally been considered as corollaries of the Whigs' parliamentary reform. But the Whig governments' responsibility for them has not been adequately evaluated. Reform of municipal corporations was the most immediate and logical corollary. Holland certainly thought so,[109] and if those who drafted the Municipal Corporations Bill were on the fringe of traditional Whiggery, one can still legitimately consider it a Whig measure. It was the kind of institutional and constitutional reform with which traditional Whigs like Holland were genuinely concerned. On the other hand, although Holland claimed 'the country is indebted to the Whig administration of Lord Grey' for the Poor Law Amendment Act,[110] that was not a Whig measure and could hardly have been promulgated without the initiatives of radicals. Factory reform, similarly, derived its main support from paternalistic Tories and some radicals before Althorp assumed management of a more moderate bill in the Commons. True, some Whigs like John Cam Hobhouse and later Lord Morpeth were ardent advocates for factory reform. But such party stalwarts as Holland were hardly moved by the issue. In general, legislation to improve the condition of the 'lower orders' was not Whig legislation, though some individual ministers may at times have sympathized with and even promoted specific bills. Holland congratulated his colleague, the erstwhile ultra Duke of Richmond, for his concern about the Beer Bill, 'for inattention and ignorance often lead to pernicious and cruel legislation where the lower orders are concerned.'[111] But he and probably most Whigs of his ilk were bored by such matters. Abolition of slavery in the empire and the continued relief of Dissenters, reforms involving liberty and the institutions of Church and State, were more conducive to the Whig tradition, though not measures monopolized by Whigs in the 1830s.

If some reforms have been extravagantly credited to the Whig governments, others have unfairly been denied them. Legal reform has often been attributed exclusively to the influence of Benthamite theory, Lord Brougham somehow associated in this regard only with the Philosophical Radicals.[112] But reform of the legal system was hardly the monopoly of Benthamites. Holland was obviously attracted to it, naturally enough, since it had its intellectual source in the Enlightenment tradition of which Whigs as well as Utilitarians were common heirs. One had to rationalize those 'artificial laws of society' which resulted in 'disproportionate severity.'[113] Hence Holland's interest in the continued curtailment of capital punishment. The rationalization of the legal system appealed to him as well, and Brougham's Local Judicature Bill, though introduced by the Lord Chancellor as an individual, 'assumed the aspect of a Government measure.'[114]

Nevertheless, after 1832 it would be more accurate to note that the Whigs presided over rather than initiated much of the legislation of the 'decade of reform,' more active in the sponsorship of some bills, mere bystanders attending the proceedings of others. Holland's remark about the alteration of the stamp duties and the penny postage is rather revealing in this regard. Lauding Spring Rice, he lamented the latter's poor standing with the 'popular party' which had agitated for those measures. Despite Rice's management, they 'gained no credit for the Minister who acquiesced in them.'[115] Acquiescence, the adaptation of reform to mollify the discontented, remained an expedient of Whiggery throughout the decade. His colleagues agreed with Lord Palmerston when he remonstrated with the king that 'timely reforms and the adaptation of measures to opinions were the real means of preserving all institutions, even Monarchy itself . . . .'[116] And the preservation of institutions remained the Whigs' prime consideration. 'Reform on a truly conservative principle,' as expressed by Grey,[117] could be applied to every established institution and became a virtual Whig maxim. Their recognition that the preservation of institutions necessitated concession hardly diminishes the Whigs' collective importance. One may contend that Peel's projected reforms in his first brief ministry were in some cases more extensive than those achieved by his Whig successors in 1835. Whether Peel could have carried them, however, remains highly questionable.

The stratagem of concession for the sake of stability, so evident in the Whigs' implementation of parliamentary reform, recurred so often as to assume the dimension of government policy. When applied to Ireland it was compromised so that it became ineffective and embarrassing.[118] Holland's numerous entries about Ireland reflect the Whigs' chronic predicament with the seemingly intractable and ubiquitous concatenation of problems subsumed under the rubric of the 'Irish question.' The fusion of traditional grievances about land tenure and religion in the agitation for abolition of tithe was the most immediate Irish problem to confront Grey's government. Its implications were perhaps more profound than the earlier agitation for Emancipation, since they involved fundamental questions about security of property and land tenure as well as religion.

If the Whigs observed the English middle classes to be contributing to the progress of civilization by their acquisition of new wealth and property, the absence of a substantial middle class in Ireland instilled into Lord Anglesey, the Irish Lord Lieutenant, fears about the cleavage between property and poverty.[119] Indeed, insecurity of property in Ireland attested the backward state of Irish society and impelled enlightened Englishmen to conclude that Ireland had not yet attained a state of civilization.[120] It compelled even such scrupulous Whig politicians as Lord Althorp to question whether representative institutions were appropriate across the water, whether Ireland was really 'fit for a free Government.'[121] The protection of established institutions presupposed the protection of property against violent agitation. So if Whig benevolence was to encourage concession in the form of removing flagrant abuses in Ireland, the recurring agitation within that country could be interpreted in such a way as to sanction coercive legislation in the guise of protection of private property, without which no country could claim to be civilized. But security of property was not the only criterion of civilization, progress, and freedom. Some Whigs, if not Lord Holland, perhaps anticipating Macaulay's *History,* unabashedly continued to associate Protestantism with them as well, despite the abysmal failure of the 'New Reformation' of the 1820s. Melbourne suspected the Irish to be 'the most conspiring people on the face of the earth.'[122] No doubt their rejection of Protestantism and irreverence for property confirmed his suspicion. Unfortunately for the Whig government, a backward civilization was producing startlingly new methods of political agitation which would test the efficacy of the Whig ambitendency of benevolent condescension and maintenance of aristocratic ascendancy. Daniel O'Connell thought the Whig government would fail within a year: 'They will fail by attempting to conciliate things that are irreconcilable—the popular sentiments with the interests of the ruling party.'[123] The passage of the Reform Bill temporarily vitiated O'Connell's prognosis so far as England was concerned. But he was correct in assuming that Ireland would defy similar ministrations of Whig government; and after the passage of Reform, Ireland's 'English masters' appeared to O'Connell to be synonymous with the Whig party.[124]

How, indeed, were the Whigs to reconcile 'popular' with aristocratic interests? They were confronted with this essential problem, and it was appallingly more complicated in Ireland than in the rest of the United Kingdom. Admittedly, the commitment to reform with which the Whigs embarked upon government could not, without embarrassment, be restricted to one side of St George's Channel; their modest Irish Reform Bill was presented as a reluctant, if ineluctable, corollary to the English one. Holland thought Irish demands unreasonable. And even at this early stage of the Whig government, he resented the necessity of submitting to pressure. 'It is one thing,' wrote Holland, 'to grant a boon to a friend, another to have it extorted from you after you have refused it.'[125]

Whether the Whigs would have plunged into the 'Irish question' had their assumption of power not been accompanied by the 'tithe war' is doubtful. Resistance to tithe was generally considered as a prelude to resistance to the payment of rent, a far more ominous infringement upon the rights of property and an even greater threat to institutional stability. Coinciding with the debates on Reform, however, tithe agitation propitiously facilitated the extension to Ireland of the Whigs' English policy. The protection of established institutions could once again be associated with the necessity for timely concessions to public opinion for the maintenance of public order. Whigs were fond of referring to such concessions as 'remedial measures,' but some were distressed to discover that legislation that incorporated the remedies did not 'cure the disease.'[126] That was hardly surprising if one considered that the nature of such remedial measures was as historically conditioned as was the Whig reverence for property. It reflected the old Whig association of liberty with limited government and the abolition of restrictions. In the early months of his government, Grey informed the Lords that Irish prosperity depended on 'the adoption of a good system of government rather than on anything else.'[127] Similarly, Althorp told the Commons that ministers would maintain order in Ireland at all costs, and while so doing would attempt to promote Irish prosperity, which was to be achieved by undoing or repealing laws that were 'obnoxious' to the Irish people, who would thereby be conciliated.[128] Those arguments of political economists which stressed the need to create capital by massive public works programs or to reduce population by subsidies for emigration, required more active governmental intervention than ministers were prepared to sponsor. Occasional and uncoordinated proposals for public works and emigration were sanctioned by the Whig government, more so Melbourne's than Grey's. But in terms of property relationships, the extensive Irish estates of Whig families were conveniently inviolable according to the common notion of the sanctity of property.[129] And the sanctity of private property, in turn, conveniently inhibited the Whigs' consideration of any extensive reform in property relationships adumbrating the Land Acts of 1870 and 1881, organic reforms as susceptible as the Reform Bill to the charge of being a revolutionary measure. The Whigs could then persist in their traditional emphases on civil, constitutional, and religious liberties. Their essentially restrictive attitude toward governmental intervention was reflected in the limited Irish legislative program announced by the Home Secretary before the dissolution of 1831. That legislation was to be confined to rectifying the more egregious civil and religious inequities in Ireland. Melbourne's list of priorities included reform of grand jury presentments, education, and corporation monopolies; repeal or alteration of the Subletting Act; some reform of the Vestry Act; and some provision for the poor.[130] None was intended to grapple with the problems of land tenure. Melbourne considered reform of grand juries the most urgent Irish problem, 'as affecting the most deeply and extensively the property of the country.'[131] He did not even mention tithe reform as a matter for legislation.

Nevertheless by the autumn of 1831, Anglesey and Stanley, the Irish Secretary, agreed that reform of the tithe system was essential and could no longer safely be delayed. The impost simply was not being paid, and resistance to it suggested the emergence of a subversive, national organization. The parochial clergy, dependent upon the tithe, were generally unsuccessful in recovering arrears by the tedious prescribed methods. Holland alludes to the conflict that ensued between Anglesey and Stanley, each bidding for mastery of Irish policy. The Lord Lieutenant's extensive program of Irish legislation, including provisions for the appropriation of surplus Irish Church revenues for secular purposes in Ireland, was not adopted by the cabinet and Melbourne virtually abdicated responsibility for formulating an Irish program. But Stanley's control over the formulation of tithe legislation was to provide the government with an inchoate Irish policy. He suggested the appointment of select committees of both houses of parliament to investigate the tithe question, and, to Holland's chagrin, persuaded the cabinet that only Protestants should conduct the inquiries and make recommendations.[132] He presided over the Commons' committee, selected many witnesses, and arranged that the committee's report express substantially his own opinions. Stanley's tithe reform involved an Arrears Bill whereby the government advance arrears of tithe to the Irish clergy, subtracting the expenses of collection, and three bills for permanent and compulsory composition of tithe, the establishment of ecclesiastical corporations in each diocese to manage Church finances, and an intricate procedure for the commutation of Irish tithe. Only the Arrears Bill and the bill for compulsory composition were enacted by the summer of 1832.

Ministers considered the Arrears Bill to be coercive, having the government in effect assume the role of tithe proctor. Holland feared what did, in fact, occur—passing the restrictive Arrears Bill and delaying the boon, which was conceived to be Stanley's composition and commutation bills.[133] As reflected in Stanley's tithe legislation then, the policy that developed entailed an association of concession with coercion. Such an association became a premise implicit in almost all ministerial considerations of Irish legislation. Aside from the parliamentary circumstances which were peculiarly conducive to that policy, the Whig attitude of benevolent condescension along with the commitment to maintain established institutions must have facilitated its adoption. Members of the cabinet consciously thought in such terms. Holland referred to 'our intention to conciliate as well as to coerce.' The conservatives, Graham, Lansdowne, and Melbourne commended such an association; the more liberal Althorp, Durham, and Brougham accepted it as well, after their abortive resistance to any coercive measure.[134]

Many Whigs as well as Irish Repealers and Radicals considered appropriation of surplus Church revenues as the essential concession in the anticipated church reform legislation for the parliamentary session of 1833. But that concession conflicted with some interpretations about the inviolability of property, albeit that of a state church, and placed Whig ministers in the unenviable position of choosing between two hitherto complementary principles. If security of property demanded concession, surely the concession ought not to subvert that security. The ministerial dissension about Stanley's prospective Church Reform Bill in autumn of 1832 was ultimately grounded in this paradox. Holland sympathized with his House of Commons colleagues in the cabinet who, for the most part, emphasized concession. Althorp maintained that government must become popular, and along with such measures as the regulation of church rates in England and the abolition of slavery in the empire, he emphasized the need for Irish Church reform. The Commons had to be controlled, which signified to Althorp that it had to be appeased. Unless government took the lead in 'Popular Measures, the Reform will lead to Revolution.'[135] Lord Duncannon, former party whip and liberal gadfly on Irish problems, foresaw the importance of Irish Church reform for the Whig government's survival in a reformed parliament, and detected that it would succeed parliamentary reform as the most distinctive party issue.[136] Holland thought Stanley's opposition to appropriation unfortunate and unfounded, particularly when applied to 'so anomalous an establishment as the Irish Church.'[137] Personally he favored appropriation. Indeed, Holland would not have lamented the total abolition of the establishment.[138] But Stanley's bill, despite the lack of provision for appropriation, was still an extensive reform. It provided for the abolition of the church cess, reduction of Irish bishoprics, the dissolution of parochial unions and the establishment of a commission to investigate Church revenues and patronage. Surely, Holland thought, 'shades of difference' ought not to obstruct the government's progress.[139] The government was on the eve of a general election, and its disruption by any minister could prove disastrous. He then assumed a role for which he was peculiarly gifted, that of dissuading potential defectors from leaving and thereby destroying Grey's government. He convinced Russell that the bill was not inconsistent with Russell's principles and sought to appease Anglesey as well.

If Holland did not share Grey's increasingly conservative predilections concerning the Church, his loyalty to the Prime Minister was complemented by their mutual assessment of what constituted a 'practicable' reform. Was it not far wiser to encourage moderate reforms that could be achieved than to stand for all or nothing? For Grey the rights of property and the maintenance of order defined the boundaries of reform. The compelling vindication of the Reform Bill, after all, had been that concession was necessary for the sake of stability. But it was dubious whether Grey's firm defense of Stanley's Irish Church plan was based exclusively on practical considerations. His reluctance to sanction 'encroachment on the established institutions of the country', his precept of reform on 'a truly conservative principle' and his repeated emphasis on upholding the 'rights of Property and the authority of the Law' reflected a fundamentally cautious attitude toward changes which could affect institutional stability and property relationships. Disinclined to go further, he excused himself on the ground that tampering with church property was always 'a question of great difficulty and nicety.'[140] If he advised Stanley that the government could still resort to appropriation at a later time, he was obviously relieved that the matter was ostensibly avoided by the cabinet's reluctant agreement not to consider it in the 1833 session.

It was not mere coincidence that ministerial deliberations on Irish Church reform should have been accompanied by the preparation of a coercive measure. To Holland coercive legislation was always distasteful. He had excoriated the Tories for their coercion of the Irish over a decade earlier. Brougham and particularly Althorp strongly opposed proposals for suspending habeas corpus in Ireland or constituting courts martial. Melbourne and Stanley, however, were impressed with the need for additional powers if the Irish government were to maintain order. And by mid-December 1832, Grey, receiving reports of unabated and increased crime in the countryside, was inclined to agree. Anglesey forwarded a harsh bill prepared by the Irish legal officers in January 1833, having equivocated about coercive legislation earlier. Whether intended or not, coercion was once again associated with conciliation, now in the first reformed parliament of 1833. Since Holland was in the Lords, he did not have to apologize to a body which swiftly passed the Coercion Bill while preparing to limit if not defeat the Church Bill. His colleagues in the Commons, however, were confronted with the reverse. The Church Bill was well received but the Coercion vigorously opposed. Although Russell and some Commons colleagues denied that either bill depended on the other, Stanley virtually confirmed the cabinet's association of coercion with conciliation by pledging the government to the passage of both bills.[141] Compelled to reconcile so tainted a measure with Whig deference to liberty, the more liberal Whigs resorted to casuistry. Virtually admitting its unconstitutionality, they then defended the Coercion Bill as a prerequisite of liberty rather than an infringement of it. Althorp, Russell, and Macaulay suggested in turn that liberty was meaningless without the protection of property for which the Coercion Bill would provide.[142] Holland was spared the embarrassment of such public tergiversation.

The Whigs could not deal effectively with Ireland. Although the Coercion Bill and an attenuated Irish Church Temporalities Bill were passed in 1833, dissension about appropriation of surplus Church revenues dogged the ministry. Russell 'upset the Coach' in May 1834, revealing to parliament and public the division within the cabinet on appropriation. Stanley, Graham, Richmond and Goderich (since promoted to the earldom of Ripon) resigned, and Grey's government fell through the indiscretions of Brougham, Althorp and Littleton in their unauthorized dealing with O'Connell on a renewal of the Coercion Bill. Melbourne succeeded Grey after the king's abortive attempt to establish a coalition government. The Whigs had stumbled and then fallen on the 'Irish question.' In so doing, they fulfilled O'Connell's prophecy of 1830. As far as England was concerned, 'popular sentiments' and 'the interests of the ruling party' had to some extent been reconciled during, if not by, the Whig government in the reform legislation of the early 1830s. Whiggery could apparently accommodate itself to the demands of a society in which property had assumed new forms but remained inviolable. But Ireland defied both Whiggery's grace and admonition, its conciliation and its coercion. Given the premises of Whiggery and the political situation in which Grey's government was placed, Irish legislation was neither extensive enough to please the reformers nor restrictive enough to satisfy the guardians of the Church. When Grey's government tried to apply its reforming principles to a society in which property had remained essentially landed and exclusive, Whiggery revealed its contradictions and limitations. Nor was Melbourne's government more successful. Despite its association with O'Connell and his followers resulting from the Lichfield House Compact of 1835, Whig ministers were unable to implement the 'appropriation' to which they had in honor pledged themselves. Moreover, the reform of Irish corporations, like the Irish Reform Bill, lagged behind its counterpart for England, and the English Poor Law was indiscriminately imposed upon agrarian Ireland.

In July 1833, after a favorable division in the House of Lords on the Irish Church Bill, Holland observed that the proceedings would 'certainly impress foreign powers with a conviction of our Stability.'[143] He consistently predicated an effective foreign policy on domestic tranquillity and particularly on the continuity of Whig government. Holland singularly distinguished the Whigs from their Tory opponents in terms of foreign policy as well as domestic issues. Since his liberalism had long been associated with sympathy for constitutional causes elsewhere, the possibilities of a Tory reaction were commensurately more distressing for him, portending international as well as domestic disaster. Lord Aberdeen, Wellington's foreign secretary, became his *bête-noire,* personifying the unenlightened Tory predilection for legitimacy which would sacrifice the national interest for the appearance of international order. Others of Aberdeen's persuasion proliferated in the British diplomatic corps which, with the exception of a few able ambassadors, Holland found uniformly inferior. Their counterparts in London, the ambassadors and ministers of great and small European courts, invariably frequented Holland House. There Lord and Lady Holland presided among the giants and dwarfs of European diplomacy, the members of the international aristocracy who controlled Europe's destiny.

Holland, then, was more intimately aware than most of his colleagues of the ominous state of things on the continent. All, of course, recognized the immediate events which had coincided with the Whig resumption of power. The July Revolution had provoked rebellions in Belgium and Poland, as well as constitutional movements in the Germanies and the Italian peninsula. Unrest in the Ottoman Empire had already secured an independent Greece, of which England was a joint guarantor. Greek control of the Peloponnesus had diverted the ambitious Mehemet Ali, Pasha of Egypt, to seek the acquisition of Syria as his reward for having assisted the Sultan during the Greek insurrection. London was the diplomatic center for resolving some of these knotty international problems.

When Holland commenced his diary, plenipotentiaries to the London Conference on Greece were establishing the borders as well as trying to select an acceptable monarch for the new state. Some of those same ministers were involved in the protracted London Conference on Belgium. It had originated during Wellington's ministry and its labors almost spanned the decade of Whig government.

If formal conferences of the great powers were rapidly becoming the mechanism for resolving international disputes, the informal chatter of diplomats at the dinner table reinforced a lingering conception of international affairs wherein national interests were often confused or identified with reigning personalities. Holland remained on intimate terms with many of them. He was delighted by the company of Talleyrand, fascinated by the old diplomat's recitation from yet unpublished memoirs of a neglected and abused childhood.[144] He observed the despair of the poet, Niemcewicz, after the Polish revolution was effectively crushed.[145] He listened curiously to Lucien Bonaparte, who inquired about the possibilities of returning to the France of the Orléanists.[146] And he had many conversations with the Marquis of Palmella and Dom Pedro, who schemed and succeeded in overthrowing Dom Miguel in Portugal.

His presentation of international problems couched in gossip or anecdote may lead one mistakenly to assume that Holland's preoccupation with foreign affairs was casual, superficial and uninformed. That was hardly the case. Aside from Palmerston and Grey, of the cabinet only Holland and occasionally Lansdowne grasped the intricacies of diplomacy. Though dispatches to and from the Foreign Office were generally available to all cabinet members, they were specially circulated to Holland for his perusal.[147] That was a courtesy from the Foreign Secretary, who more often suffered than solicited Holland's opinions. Palmerston gradually became increasingly independent. Eventually he so monopolized the formulation of foreign policy that cabinet discussions, particularly during Melbourne's ministry, frequently signified formal ratification of decisions already made rather than collective deliberations about alternative actions. Occasionally he withheld information from Holland. No doubt Palmerston was justifiably cautious, for the notorious gossip at Holland House was not likely to preserve secrecy. Sometimes Holland had to rely upon drawing-room conversation with foreign diplomats for information about British activity. Palmella once showed him a dispatch from Palmerston which, Holland wrote, 'I had not seen and which is more favourable to Donna Maria than I expected.'[148] During the Near East crisis of 1840, an important dispatch from the Porte to the Foreign Office was not circulated for six weeks. Holland learned of it from foreign ambassadors.[149] The famous Collective Note of July 1839, requesting the Sultan to take no action, was endorsed by Britain as well as France, Austria and Russia, but never presented to the cabinet for consideration.[150]

Occasionally Holland did divulge information to foreign ministers about which he should have been more guarded. Particularly forthcoming with Talleyrand, he indiscreetly revealed to him provisions of the still secret four-power agreement about the disposition of fortresses on the Belgian frontier. Apologizing for the unauthorized disclosure, Holland protested that Talleyrand, after all, 'had told me all I knew of the Conferences about these fortresses.'[151] Palmerston on that occasion agreed that he should have been more explicit in impressing upon the cabinet the necessity for secrecy. Holland also received information from foreign courts. Carefully selective no doubt, Talleyrand occasionally showed him advance copies of his own dispatches to the Quai D'Orsay as well as replies from the French foreign minster or Louis Philippe. Moreover, Holland carried on an extensive correspondence with British diplomats of standing, especially Lord Granville at Paris and Sir Robert Adair at Brussels.

It was fortuitous for a man of his opinions that the Whig resumption of power should precede a diplomatic realignment, so that the national interest in the 1830s could be identified with a palpably ideological dichotomy in Europe. The moderate July Revolution auspiciously facilitated Holland's reconciliation of his Francophilia with his libertarianism. Almost from the inception of Grey's government, he envisioned the happy combination of Britain with France in fortifying constitutionalism against the despotism of the Holy Alliance. Holland was as much a Foxite in foreign as in domestic affairs. He insisted that any war in which England became involved be 'for liberty and against *power and in confederacy with,* not against, *Constitutional France.*'[152] He identified himself as leader of 'the old adherents of Mr Fox' in foreign affairs as late as 1840, when he opposed the sacrifice of the constitutional alliance even if it meant the erosion of the Ottoman Empire.[153] Holland sedulously fostered the association with France to which, at the end of the decade, he attributed the peace of Europe, the extension of constitutionalism, and the containment of hitherto expanding continental despotisms.

Numerous obstacles had impeded that combination. Fear of French expansionism, though diminished by the early moderation of the July monarchy, still lingered. It educed baleful recollections of the violent international upheaval associated with the Revolution. Suspicions engendered by traditional Franco-British enmity were not easily abandoned. Within the cabinet Holland confronted 'AntiGallicans,' particularly Goderich and Richmond, the latter dubious about Holland's 'predilection for foreigners.'[154] As late as December 1831, Holland lamented that even Palmerston was 'not so averse to AntiGallican and antirevolutionary systems as I at one time had hoped.'[155] The Belgian revolution of 1830 had aggravated those suspicions. French intentions remained ambiguous, so long as the 'Mouvement' and moderate parties vied with one another for ascendancy. That circumscribed Franco-British cooperation in maintaining an independent Belgium against the obvious legitimist sympathies of Russia, Prussia, and Austria. But Russian preoccupation with the Polish Revolution also precluded the Eastern powers from acting in concert on behalf of the Dutch. They were also assuaged by British steadfastness in opposing a French candidate for the Belgian throne, ensuring the withdrawal of French forces from Belgium, and the four-power agreement to dismantle fortresses on the Belgian frontier.

Holland lamented that the protracted struggle in the Low Countries prevented Anglo-French cooperation elsewhere. He suspected that the Eastern powers, wistfully anticipating the fall of Grey's government on parliamentary reform, wanted to prolong it.[156] Once it was effectively if not formally settled late in 1832, he anticipated and incessantly agitated for closer ties with France, toward which Palmerston was himself inclining. Even before the resolution of the Belgian problem, Holland supported conciliation of France. Only Carlisle and Grant joined him in inclining to accept a French offer for joint mediation on Poland.[157] Holland alone in the cabinet favored recognition of Poland.[158] On the question whether the king should consent to see delegates from the Polish provisional government, he was again in a minority.[159] He may have been outspoken in the confidence that he would be outvoted. Perhaps on such matters he conceived of his role as a catalyst, moving the cabinet toward an acceptance of the prospect of French cooperation and mutual assistance in constitutional causes. On the Polish question Holland's passion for constitutionalism was inhibited by a grudging recognition of international exigencies, having acknowledged that in Poland 'our interests are remote and our power small.'[160]

Iberian affairs offered the most promising arena for Anglo-French cooperation. In 1831 Holland favored declaring war on Dom Miguel, or, failing that, joint mediation of the Portuguese problem with France and formal acknowledgment of Dona Maria's regency. He regretted that opportunities for supporting Pedro and the constitutionalists were passed by, and often argued that if Britain were to forego them, the benefits to be derived from supporting Dom Pedro would accrue exclusively to France. Was it not far better to act in concert? Even in 1833, when the invasion of the peninsula by Pedro's forces was successful, Holland, by then in association with Palmerston and Grey, had to convince reluctant members of the cabinet that British support for Pedro and Dona Maria should be forthcoming. Ironically, the principle of noninterference which Holland had himself supported after the Congress of Vienna was now appropriated by those colleagues who questioned the government's direction in foreign policy.[161] Nevertheless, the association of eastern powers ratified by the Convention of Münchengrätz in 1833, followed by the Quadruple Alliance between Britain, France, Portugal and Spain in 1834, divided the constitutional west from the autocratic east. The association with France was strained by Louis Philippe's flirtation with the Carlists in 1835 and 1836. But it became so accepted a tendency in international relations that Holland could refer in 1836 to 'our general policy of uniting in one great Western League all the Constitutional States of Europe.'[162] To be sure, Palmerston, not Holland, was the architect of British policy. But Holland had long agitated for the association of constitutional powers and was eminently pleased at its realization.

All the more frustrating then his inefficacy and relative isolation in 1839-40, when the alliance of constitutional powers foundered in the maelstrom of the Near East crisis. The ambitions of Mehemet Ali, technically the Sultan's vassal, threatened the Ottoman Empire, whose unity Palmerston belatedly recognized as vital to the national interest. Palmerston conceived of British interests as transcending ideological ties. When France supported Mehemet Ali's ambitions in Syria, he gravitated toward association with Russia. But Holland continued to perceive foreign policy almost exclusively through distorting spectacles of ideology. The need to maintain Anglo-French amity obscured the importance of the Ottoman Empire. Rather sketchy on the details of the Near East imbroglio,

Holland's diary nevertheless conveys his desperate longing to maintain the association of constitutional powers and his simplistic rationalizations on that account. He lamented a separation of England from France, particularly on such 'remote' affairs as 'the territorial distribution of Western Asia.'[163] A letter to Palmerston of 17 October 1839, with the latter's sardonic interlineations, verifies Holland's shortsightedness on the Eastern question. He failed to comprehend why Palmerston should protest if Mehemet Ali continued to occupy Syria: 'I do not care one rush who has Egypt or who has Syria—and perhaps I do not care quite so much as I ought, certainly not so much as many others, about the Dardanelles and the Bosphorus. Were either Nicholas or Mehemet Ali to swallow them up quick tomorrow, I should not think the end of the World was actually at hand.' 'As to projects against India from the Red Sea and Persian Gulph,' he added, 'I hold them all at nought.'[164] In a tortuous postscript, Holland grudgingly recognized the strategic importance of the straits, while remaining blissfully indifferent about who controlled them:[165]

> I have alluded to my somewhat *peculiar opinions about the Dardanelles,* but I hope you understand that I am not so enamoured of my paradoxes nor are my paradoxes themselves so strong as to preclude my concurrence in measures tending to secure the free engress and egress of commerce thro' those narrow seas, and my acquiescence (to all practical purposes) in the reasoning which supposes the preservation of Constantinople in the hands of the Turks to be essential to that object. I had much rather keep things as they are though I have *not such a horror of the dismemberment of Turkey in Europe as many have* and can conceive though I do not wish to promote a state of things which by *giving one European power the Bosphorus and another the Dardanelles,* would be to the full as beneficial to countries in and out of the Black Sea as the precarious existence of the Sublime Porte which we are bound and therefore we strive to maintain is now.

Having long delayed communication to colleagues about his negotiations, Palmerston imposed his views upon a reluctant cabinet during the Near East crisis. His independence in formulating foreign policy was facilitated by Melbourne's supineness. Grey had superintended Palmerston's activity, Melbourne merely acquiesced in it. Palmerston's latitude was particularly noteworthy since, in the Talents Ministry, Holland considered the activities of the Foreign Office 'more emphatically designated . . . by usage and reason, as the objects of cabinet deliberation' than the business of other departments.[166] If Holland's assessment was accurate, it would seem that the departmental independence of the Foreign Office had increased while that of other departments diminished during the two decades of Whig opposition.

If the principle of collective cabinet responsibility were to be examined from the vantage point of foreign affairs exclusively, one might well conclude that even in the 1830s it was honored as much in the breach as in the observance. Technically, collective responsibility was not inconsistent with ministerial independence. A minister's independence did not necessarily imply his departure from the collective will of the cabinet. It might signify merely that the collective will of the cabinet was not invoked or exercised. Increasingly, however, collective responsibility implied the deliberation of all cabinet members on matters of importance, as opposed to their acquiescence in the determinations of an individual minister. It was, therefore, opposed to what was called government by departments, excessive ministerial independence considered inconsonant with the exercise of joint responsibility. The realization of collective responsibility was imperceptibly gradual. Nor was it fully achieved by the 1830s. Indeed, Holland's remarks about the Fox-Grenville cabinet could well be applied to the Whig cabinets of Grey and Melbourne:[167]

> Though the necessity of a well-concerted or party Government in a limited Monarchy and popular Constitution has generally established the wholesome doctrine that each and every Member of the Cabinet is in some degree responsible for the measures adopted by the Government while he is a member of it, yet there are no precise laws nor rules, nor even any well-established or understood usages which mark what measures in each Department are or are not to be communicated to the Cabinet.

There is no gauge to determine precisely the relative independence of a particular department at a given time. No doubt a prestigious minister in a government that commanded substantial parliamentary support would have an advantage in acting independently of his colleagues. On the other hand, the interests of the crown were not uniformly distributed among departments of state, and the extent of royal interest would affect both ministerial independence and collective responsibility. William IV's claims to the royal prerogative were at least as frequent and apparently more persuasive in matters pertaining to international than domestic affairs, particularly since he remained King of Hanover. Hence Palmerston and Grey had often to pay more attention to the inclinations of the king than to the cabinet, and the foreign minister's greater independence would be accompanied by more rigorous royal scrutiny. To be sure, there were occasions in the 1830s when the cabinet vigorously debated matters of foreign policy, and even a few rare situations when the advice of both the prime minister and foreign secretary was rejected, or at least their proposed action deferred. But Holland's accounts of cabinet deliberations generally confirm Palmerston's increasing independence.

Although Palmerston occasionally concealed his decisions from the cabinet, he vigorously objected when colleagues made policy pronouncements in parliament on domestic matters without previous cabinet discussion.[168] One encounters several such instances of ministerial independence in the Whig cabinets, when decisions were declared in parliament without prior consultation or government pledged to legislation not yet collectively endorsed. Stanley was particularly prone to such practice. His Arms Bill of 1831 would have subjected to transportation any individual found guilty of possessing unregistered arms in a proclaimed district. The bill had been drawn by counsel to the Irish Office and Melbourne was the only cabinet minister to have seen it. He neglected to bring the matter before the cabinet, so Graham was astonished and Grey, Althorp, and Holland 'appalled and disgusted' to discover it upon its introduction to the Commons.[169] Bitterly attacked by O'Connell and other Irish members, the bill was modified once the cabinet became aware of its provisions. In 1833, although Russell denied that the Irish Church Temporalities Bill was contingent upon passage of the Coercion Bill, Stanley pledged the government to the passage of both bills.[170] The most famous example of ministerial independence occurred on another Irish matter, the appropriation of surplus Church revenues. The government's abandonment of the appropriations clause in the Irish Church Bill in June 1833 was announced by Stanley to the utter surprise of cabinet members, who had not been consulted.[171] Nor were Stanley or Palmerston singular in their exercise of independence. Occasionally the pledge of one minister conflicted with that of another. Holland noted the government's predicament in 1837, when Russell pledged them to the Irish Corporations Bill while, in the preceding session, Melbourne had informed the Lords that he would resign only if defeated in the Commons.[172]

Although Lord Howick was particularly critical of Palmerston's independence, he extended his criticism to Melbourne's administration generally. Of course, he had his own axe to grind after his resignation in 1839, when he condemned Melbourne's for having been 'a government of departments some very ill some moderately administered but of which the various measures have never been animated by one spirit or directed with energy to one common object.'[173] Perhaps Howick exaggerated, but it is significant that as late as 1839 he should have considered meetings of Melbourne's cabinet to have been merely ceremonial: 'Everything of real importance is settled not in the cabinet but out of it, and . . . Cabinet meetings are merely an idle waste of time in desultory or inconclusive conversation or a mere form to adopt a decision already formally come to.'[174] That was a lamentable departure, he implied, from the ministry of his father, Lord Grey, when the cabinet presumably practiced collective responsibility.

Grey's cabinet originally consisted of thirteen members. It was expanded to fifteen in June 1831 to accommodate Stanley and Russell, because of their importance as individuals rather than the offices they held. Durham's resignation in 1833 reduced the cabinet to fourteen, at which size it remained until the end of Grey's administration. Melbourne's first cabinet numbered fifteen, his second originally twelve. Grey thought the cabinet too large and consequently unwieldy. Although no 'inner cabinet' is evident in either the Melbourne or Grey governments, smaller groups of ministers often discussed strategy before an important cabinet meeting. Relieved of departmental duties, Holland had more time than others for such pursuits. So, for example, on the question of creating peers early in 1832, he advised Grey to settle on a course with Althorp and Brougham before a formal meeting of the cabinet.[175] A friend as well as colleague of the prime minister, he sometimes functioned as Grey's confidant. Grey sought out Holland on various occasions to speculate about shifting personnel in the cabinet. When cabinet dissension threatened the government's stability, Holland functioned as a conciliator of the more liberal ministers. But there is no evidence of a permanent clique of ministers who could impose decisions upon the larger body.

Indeed, the emergence of the cabinet subcommittee in the Whig governments attests the collective need for cooperation when confronted with a multitude of complex business. The Reform Bill was itself prepared by a subcommittee of the cabinet. During the course of the debate on the bill, Grey suggested a subcommittee be formed under Althorp to prepare a defense, clause by clause, for the committee stage of the bill in the Lords.[176] Holland functioned on a subcommittee of Melbourne's cabinet to draft the Municipal Corporations Bill.[177]

These cooperative ventures, however, failed to conceal the inevitable factional alignments in a cabinet like Grey's that was, after all, a coalition. By the end of the 1833 session, the uneasy division between liberal and conservative wings was more apparent than ever. Some liberal ministers suspected Stanley and Graham of Tory proclivities. Similarly, when Edward Ellice, Secretary at War but not yet in the cabinet, changed his plans in September and decided to visit Howick rather than go to Ireland, Palmerston conjured up notions of Ellice's alignment with Lord Durham, who had resigned months earlier and would be in alarming proximity at Lambton Park.[178] The conservative members became better organized at such cabals. Graham wrote to Stanley in December 1833:[179]

> Lord Grey says we must meet in Cabinet the first week in January. The Duke of Richmond asks how this will agree with our arrangement for shooting at Goodwood on the 7th. I answer, perfectly, for if we meet in London on the 3rd or 4th, a *little* Cabinet at Goodwood on the 7th will be both useful and agreeable.

One may assume that such 'little' cabinets had their counterparts on the liberal side. But decisions were presumably to be concluded at meetings of the complete cabinet.

It met frequently, usually at the Foreign Office, but it was exceptional for all ministers to be present. Similarly, the weekly Wednesday cabinet dinners, though well-attended, were rarely full. Some ministers arrived late, others departed early. Melbourne joked that the government's Near Eastern policy would have been considerably different had Holland not been tardy to a cabinet in October 1839.[180] Their frequency may account in part for the relative informality of cabinet meetings. In his *Memoirs of the Whig Party* Holland had noted 'the slovenly and irregular method of transacting business' in the Fox-Grenville ministry.[181] He might well have come to a similar conclusion about the Whig cabinets of the 1830s, had he not become inured to the practice. When Macaulay joined the cabinet in 1839, Holland casually observed that his 'surprize at the loose construction and proceedings of what is Called a Cabinet Council and practical Government of the Country is natural enough. It struck me equally in 1806.'[182] On occasion it is difficult to determine whether or not a specific meeting of the cabinet was transpiring when ministers assembled. The presence of the prime minister was not required, and any member of the cabinet could summon a meeting of his colleagues on any subject he considered important. Grey wrote to Palmerston in September 1831, 'I see there is a Cabinet announced for today, but with a view to what subject I am not informed.'[183] One month earlier, Charles Grant, President of the India Board, summoned a cabinet to denounce as inadequate the Irish government's plan to reduce the Yeomanry corps.[184] If there was no need for advance notice, nor was there any established procedure for recording cabinet decisions. Grey did revive the abeyant practice of forwarding minutes of the cabinet to the king, but not for all meetings. He wrote these himself but they were sometimes carefully perused by his colleagues. Although Grey apparently kept copies of his minutes, no record or file was retained by the cabinet.[185] The need to maintain the king's support occasionally resulted in an entire session being devoted to the composition of a minute. Although the extant minutes remain exceedingly valuable and were generally candid, they often concealed or deemphasized cabinet dissension. After a session on 19 November 1831, Holland persuaded Grey to exclude from his minute specific detail on cabinet disagreements about when parliament should be convened.[186] The prime minister, on the other hand, sometimes took the liberty of distorting the cabinet's conclusions to accord with his own and perhaps the king's inclinations.[187]

Procedural informality and the lack of records for future reference led to confusion among cabinet members about the disposition of particular problems. Intense and protracted deliberation on important subjects often produced general ambiguity rather than collective understanding about the government's determination. As Holland noted, 'The want of all formal resolution, paper or motion . . . is, according to the usual mode of conducting business in every Ministry of which I have been a Member, no proof whatever either of the matter being postponed to further consideration or positively settled.'[188] To delay a decision may occasionally have been tactically desirable. But Holland often discussed cabinet deliberations in detail, only to lament that ministers had resolved nothing. In a discussion on Portugal in November 1831, 'We came to the worst of all decisions, namely none at all.'[189] On the creation of peers a few months thereafter, 'We settled to settle nothing.'[190] Confronted with the alternatives of resignation or creation, ministers left 'the choice quite undecided . . . . '[191] In one of Melbourne's cabinets, 'little really transacted or settled.'[192] The absence of important ministers frequently precluded decision. On one of the clauses of the Reform Bill, 'We could settle nothing in the absence of so many of our Colleagues.'[193] There was no decision on the £10 qualification in July 1831 because Grey had to leave the cabinet early.[194] In September the ministers could make 'no resolution on so delicate a question' as the removal of members of the queen's household because of the absence of Grey and Lansdowne.[195] Decision about alteration of clauses in the Reform Bill was delayed in November 1831 'chiefly on account of Lord Lansdown's Stanley's and Sir J Graham's absence.'[196]

Similarly holidays and parliamentary recesses produced the customary flight from London and abandonment of ministerial functions. The cabinet dispersed in 1833 'with a full understanding that the various important measures [were] to be considered during the recess, but returned to London, as usual, only a short time before the meeting of Parliament, without any of their projected designs, if I except the revision of the poor laws, being in a state of forwardness of preparation.'[197] The cabinet was to convene on or before 1 November 1834 to consider important legislation, 'but on Lord Duncannon's return from Ireland which was not till the first week in November, Lord Lansdown was still in Paris and John Russell in the Country, so that the Consideration of the Irish measures was unavoidably postponed, though well prepared and drawn out by Lord Duncannon.'[198] In 1837 Melbourne and Russell both left London during the Easter recess 'and nothing was done in the Cabinet.'[199] When a course of action was ostensibly adopted, the decision was often left vague or ambiguous. Holland's parenthetical qualifications about cabinet decisions may be attributed in part to the imprecision and tortured syntax that resulted from hasty transcription. But they recur so frequently as to suggest that neither Holland nor his colleagues were always certain about precisely what the cabinet had decided. Holland's diary is punctuated with such qualifications: 'It was implied and I think understood that we should not even on defeat resign our offices';[200] or 'the general opinion was I think . . . . ';[201] on the question of making peers in June 1833, 'We canvassed this subject over, but I think we on the whole acquiesced, if we did not absolutely concur in the opinion, that a few, *4 or 5*, well chosen, would be enough for the present.'[202]

This chronic uncertainty may be partially attributed to the infrequency of formal votes. Holland records only three occasions when a formal vote of the cabinet was taken. After the prorogation of October 1831, Grey preferred that parliament not convene before the new year. Holland and Melbourne opposed a postponement and the cabinet voted, eight to three, to advise the king to summon parliament early in December.[203] In March 1832 the intractable problem about creation of peers impelled Durham to propose three resolutions, the effect of which would have bound government to press for an immediate creation. He alone voted for them.[204] In May 1835 the cabinet voted 7 or 8 to 3 in favor of three year ratepayers rather than ten pound householders for the qualification of voters in the Municipal Corporations Bill.[205] The last vote aside, two of these formal divisions occurred on procedural rather than substantive issues. To be sure, procedure might itself assume substantive dimensions when the tactic being considered directly or immediately involved the government's future. Substantive issues, however, were more often concluded by informal agreement. During a crucial deliberation about Palmerston's Eastern policy, for example, ministers expressed their opinions, 'though we did not come to any vote in the Cabinet.'[206] Perhaps the paucity of formal divisions attests the fragility of both the Grey and Melbourne cabinets, which included several strong personalities. A formal vote on a substantive issue might ordinarily have obliged the minority to yield or resign. So Sir James Graham favored but voted against Durham's resolutions, because if he were in a minority he would have felt obliged to resign.[207] But Holland's discussion of the cabinet decision in November 1831 to convene parliament before Christmas suggests that the minority on a formal vote was not necessarily confronted with the alternative of yielding or resigning. Nor was it assumed that the majority decision would automatically be implemented. Holland observed that if Grey's minute to the king strongly recorded the opinion of the three dissenting ministers, 'the King might agree with the minority and we should all feel much embarrassment. It was unlucky we had not agreed beforehand to be concluded by the resolution of the

Majority . . . . ' Grey thereupon modified the minute at Holland's request, and noted 'his disposition to defer to the advice given.'[208]

If the king could have sided with a minority of his cabinet, albeit on a matter of procedure, then the king's ministers in the 1830s still remained to some extent his ministers in fact as well as in theory. As Arthur Aspinall commented, joint cabinet responsibility could not become fully translated into practice until the king ceased to govern and merely reigned.[209] William IV continued to govern, or at least to try, and Grey's cabinet was conscious of their continued dependence upon him, particularly during the struggle for parliamentary reform. The ministers' allegiance to the king thereafter, as Holland intimated, was as much the result of gratitude as of dependency. They could not bring themselves to desert him after he had done so much for them. William IV's retention of his ministers, of course, was secured by the lack of any alternative. But his confidence was neither to be taken for granted, nor was it transferable. When Grey contemplated resignation in 1833, Holland noted that he could not necessarily transfer the king's confidence to Althorp, then Grey's intended successor.[210] Clinging to office in 1834, Brougham suggested that Grey's resignation did not mean the ministry was at an end. But the king insisted it was and so did Brougham's colleagues. William IV's subsequent dismissal of the Whig cabinet was the last such ambitious exercise of the royal prerogative, and the lack of constitutional clamor signified that it was an acceptable if foolhardy venture. The sentiment to give the king's new ministers a 'fair trial' accorded with established constitutional practice. Peel's failure and the success of the combined Whig-Radical Repealer alliance in opposition dramatically demonstrated the king had indeed ceased to govern. William IV's pathetic threat in 1835 that the cabinet was not his and he would have them impeached verified its responsibility to parliament rather than the crown. Melbourne's government might delude itself into inflating its situation from the reciprocal infatuation that subsisted between the young Victoria and the older members of the cabinet, Holland among them. They even extended their tenure in office by self-serving behaviour during the Bedchamber controversy of 1839. But by the end of the decade, the vestiges of the royal prerogative had to be propped up by the ministers rather than freely exercised by the monarch.

To whom then was the cabinet responsible? When defeated in the Lords on the motion for Portuguese neutrality in June 1833, Holland wrote, 'The obvious and natural course would have formerly been, and would be in common times hereafter, to resign, for it was very questionable whether we were constitutionally justified in undertaking to conduct the affairs of the Country with the indirect hostility of one house of Parliament.'[211] That they chose not to resign signified an incipient recognition that the constitutional division between King, Lords and Commons was no longer so meaningful. The Lords' defeat of the Irish Tithe Bill in 1834 similarly did not result in resignation. Lord Roden's successful motion in 1839 to censure Normanby's government in Ireland, by implication a censure of the cabinet, moved the cabinet to appeal to the Commons. The Lords could and did obstruct legislation after 1832, but could not bring down the government unless the cabinet itself chose to resign, in order to convince the public that the peers alone were responsible for their plight. But the cabinet did not depend upon the House of Lords for their survival.

They did depend on the Commons. Calculations about government support in the Commons would seem to have ensured its stability. But modern party was still in its inchoate stages and the cabinet could not rely upon a disciplined whip. Moreover, as Holland noted, government was not attuned to the increasingly liberal disposition of the Commons and rarely sought a preconcerted understanding with MPs upon whose support they had to rely.[212] The increasing independence of Commons members, furthermore, limited government's control in the lower house. 'My Grandfather . . . was nearly impeached for saying he was to *manage* the House of Commons,' Holland wrote, 'and We are assailed . . . because we do not *command* them.'[213] The Commons could and did go further than the cabinet wished. The repeal of the malt tax in 1833 would have led to their resignation had ministers not managed, with Peel's cooperation and the belated recognition by radicals of their error, to reverse the decision. The Commons' ascendancy was implied in other actions by king and cabinet as well. William IV's ostensible justification for dismissing Melbourne's government was that Althorp's succession to the Lords prevented them from managing the Commons. Government, though they retained a majority of five on the suspension of the Jamaica constitution in 1839, thought that margin an indication of insufficient confidence and decided to resign.

It is accurate to note that the Commons could defeat a government but could not impose a policy upon it.[214] But the accepted observation that the cabinet collectively determined policy is questionable. Aside from specific bills to which government pledged itself or which otherwise came to be considered as government measures, domestic policy was ill-defined. Indeed, in the 1830s policy often signified a tactic or stratagem like the Whig emphasis on concession for the sake of stability. If one conceives of policy as a continuing process of implementing previously established programs, then only reform of parliament and perhaps of the Irish tithe system comprised legislation which fulfilled policy. Most legislation was drafted in particular departments with the assistance of legal officers. On such complex problems as Irish tithes, legislation was exceedingly technical and often beyond the grasp of ministers themselves.[215] In such cases a minister of a department might have considerable latitude in deciding whether or at what step the legislation ought to be submitted to his colleagues for deliberation in the cabinet. In the absence of policy, it also became particularly difficult to determine on what issue a government might decide that it must resign.

The cabinet's most important function, then, was to reconcile ministerial dissension, or at the very least to prevent public exposure of serious differences. It often succeeded in this task. It was particularly important to do so during the parliamentary reform struggle, when all acknowledged that the resignation of any cabinet minister would destroy the government. The prolonged controversy about creation of peers gradually resulted in the reluctant concurrence of all ministers in its necessity. Had a decision been forced beforehand, no doubt the government would have fallen. Joint responsibility was approximated once it was understood that the minority had to accept the decision of the majority or resign. One cannot detect a specific event which marked the formal adoption of such a practice. As cited above, there is evidence that in some instances the minority need not have resigned. But increasingly the assumption that dissenting ministers accept the decision of the majority or resign became the more common practice. The cabinet divided seven to two against resignation after the Portuguese neutrality resolution passed the House of Lords. Melbourne and Graham, the dissenting ministers, 'somewhat reluctantly assured us that they would acquiesce in and defer to the opinion of their colleagues.'[216] Althorp and Brougham acceded to the majority's determination in 1833 to await the second reading of the Irish Church Bill in the Lords rather than resign on another question.[217]

So long as dissension remained concealed from public view, the cabinet could continue even with severe differences of opinion. Palmerston's protests about modification of the Reform Bill, though communicated to the king, were not made public. Moreover, even if the majority decision were binding, techniques remained for dissenters to evade resignation in the higher cause of cabinet continuity. As late as May 1832, after the government's defeat in the House of Lords, Richmond refused to agree with his colleagues when they suggested to the king the creation of enough peers to overcome the Lords as an alternative to their resignation. He was dissenting from a major decision that came at the end of nearly a year of cabinet debate. Until this date, there were several ministers who had been almost as strongly opposed to a creation. Richmond concluded that he would retire if the king followed the recommendation of the cabinet, and was relieved of the necessity only when William IV accepted the cabinet's resignation and turned to Wellington. Technically, Richmond was never placed in the position of either having to defend the cabinet's decision or resign. But in 1840, when Holland strongly disagreed with Palmerston's Eastern policy, he informed Melbourne 'that the most obvious, regular, and constitutional method was to accept my resignation ....' Since he assumed that his resignation would break up the government, he concluded that a declaration of some sort to indicate his disagreement and dissociate himself from the cabinet's determination would suffice. 'I could either demand an audience of the Queen and deposit my protest with her, or, if he (Melbourne) would require the advice of the cabinet to be reduced to regular form, I could annex a separate Minute.'[218] Holland and Clarendon followed the latter course.

Generally, however, if cabinet dissension could not be contained, ministers in a minority did indeed resign. The dissension within the cabinet about appropriation was concealed from parliament, though many may have had inklings about such disagreements. When Russell 'upset the coach,' however, Stanley, Graham, Richmond, and Ripon resigned. Later that year the Grey government fell because of the indiscretions of Brougham, Althorp and Littleton, who acted without authority in negotiating a compromise with O'Connell on the Irish Coercion Bill, which Grey found intolerable. When the matter became public, Althorp resigned and Grey determined he could not carry on the government without him.

When the cabinet was approximating but had not yet achieved modern collective responsibility, the personalities of individual ministers were enormously important. Those who headed departments of state usually exercised greater leverage than colleagues, like Holland, in offices of dignity. Moreover, ministers in the Commons were increasingly deferred to. Above all, the personal stature of the prime minister was crucial. He had few specific duties. In the early nineteenth century he was particularly associated with the development of foreign policy in conjunction with the foreign secretary and he was the principal spokesman of government to the crown. He generally retained considerable latitude in recommending appointments and particularly in choosing his colleagues. Beyond that one can hardly generalize. Both Grey and Melbourne have been considered weak as prime ministers. The characterization is apt for Melbourne. His lethargy is almost legendary. Although Holland defended him from the charge of indolence, he also lamented Melbourne's apparent attraction to mediocrity, and was distressed that the prime minister should consider 'a want of genius no great defect in the government of a great nation.'[219] In his second administration Melbourne had the advantages of inheriting a political alliance which had been imposed upon him.[220] He was also dealing with a monarch who had already gambled and lost in his quarrel with the Whigs, and then with a young queen who found security rather than challenge in her prime minister's avuncular attention. Howick's criticism of Melbourne's government as one of departments may well be valid. Although Holland noted that in some areas, particularly the dispensation of patronage, Melbourne's cabinet functioned with more cohesion than Grey's,[221] Melbourne hardly emerges from Holland's pages as a commanding presence. If Holland's account of the Near Eastern crisis is accurate, Melbourne may have maintained his government by neglecting rather than directing or conciliating his colleagues.

Grey's situation was somewhat different. William IV had not yet squandered the vestiges of royal power, and Grey constantly had to solicit his support. On the other hand, the king reposed his confidence specifically in Grey. Within the cabinet Grey's stature was reminiscent of leaders of eighteenth-century 'connections'. The personal loyalty he commanded, perhaps more than any other factor, sustained a government divided on crucial matters. So on the prolonged discussion about creation of peers, Grey's reluctance for some time prevented the majority of the cabinet from insisting on anything beyond a pledge from the king that, should the occasion arise, sufficient peers to carry the bill would be created. Aware of Grey's reluctance, Holland was prepared to reconcile himself to it, though he strongly favoured creation. Althorp found himself in the same situation. As Holland indicated in March 1832, aside from Richmond, none in the cabinet would have resisted creation of peers if Grey was not himself so strongly opposed to it; non-creation might be a gamble, but 'defection from the leaders of the cause of reform would . . . be the certain and instant ruin of that cause.'[222] Holland contended that he had never considered office except under Grey. After Grey's retirement, he informed Melbourne that he would be in a rather awkward situation if the new Whig government should cease to appear to have Grey's sanction.[223]

Similarly, when approached during the king's abortive negotiations to establish a coalition government in July 1834, Stanley professed his continued attachment to the 'principles' of Lord Grey, notwithstanding his recent resignation from Grey's government.[224]

Grey's personal stature enabled him to reconcile differences, often through third parties. He smoothed over the intensifying animosity between Durham and Stanley, which threatened to destroy the government in the fall of 1832, and used Holland as a mediator to moderate the distraught Lord John Russell as well as Lord Anglesey in Ireland. Within the cabinet he could occasionally impose his own views upon reluctant colleagues. The delay in urging creation of peers is the best example of this; another, less fortunate in its consequences, was Grey's insistence that the Irish Coercion Bill be renewed in 1834. He carried the cabinet then by threatening to resign if the bill were not introduced in its entirety.[225] Grey used the threat of resignation more effectively than did any of his colleagues, in part, perhaps, because he genuinely welcomed retirement after the passage of Reform. His indispensability was evident in August 1833 when his colleagues, convinced that the government could not survive without him, had to dissuade him from resigning.[226]

Grey effectively guided the cabinet, particularly during the first two years of his government, but he did not dominate it. He was careful to submit tactical decisions to his colleagues. That was particularly evident in his reports to the cabinet about his negotiations with the 'waverers' on the Reform Bill, the topics to be considered in the King's Speech, and cabinet minutes to be submitted to the king. He would on occasion frame the alternatives which the cabinet might adopt in the form of prospective letters or minutes to the king, his colleagues then debating which course to adopt. He did this when government was defeated in the Lords on the question of Portuguese neutrality. Grey submitted to his colleagues two versions of prospective papers to the king, one recommending resignation, the other recommending a response by the king to the Lords' address. He then left the decision to the cabinet.[227]

Grey submitted to the opinion of the majority in the cabinet on a number of occasions. One has already been noted—the decision to recall parliament before the Christmas recess in 1831. He may have been persuaded to change his mind as well on the division of counties in the government's third version of the Reform Bill.[228] He was induced by his colleagues to take a stronger stand than he had hitherto in communicating to the king about creation of peers in March 1832.[229] And, though there is no evidence to suggest he felt very strongly about the matter, he would have preferred withholding the vote from £10 resident leaseholders in the Irish Reform Bill.[230] On none of these issues, however, did Grey insist that his opinion be adopted. The most interesting conflict between the prime minister and his colleagues on a substantive issue occurred on foreign policy early in 1834. By then Grey had concluded, much to Holland's satisfaction, that England intervene to assist the recently victorious but beleaguered constitutionalists in Portugal. The majority of the cabinet agreed, but Althorp, Stanley, and Richmond had misgivings. Holland noted that Grey, 'even with the full concurrence both of the King and the Majority of his Cabinet, did not feel himself equal to engaging in a War with the loss of Althorp, Stanley, Richmond and perhaps others in his Cabinet.'[231] He decided to resign. The rest of the cabinet then met and all agreed that Grey's departure and the subsequent dissolution of the government would leave the country in a 'perilous situation.' Appealing to Grey to remain, they simply did not refer to the Portuguese problem. Holland attributed Grey's retention of office to that appeal and the king's entreaties. At the time, wrote Holland, the episode reflected 'the personal attachment of the whole Cabinet to Lord Grey and . . . their concurrence of opinion in all matters excepting Portugal, or at least in all such as regarded the domestick affairs of the country.'[232] But the intervention was delayed and the immediate result was that the prime minister had conceded to a strong minority in his cabinet without whom he would have felt unable to govern. Grey acknowledged that he had 'given way.'[233]

One cannot find adumbrations in the 1830s of what is now called prime ministerial government. Melbourne was even less authoritative a figure than Grey. But concrete evidence for the approximation of collective responsibility is abundant in the sources, not the least of which is Holland's diary. Holland and his colleagues recognized its desirability, even if they did not always implement it in practice. The process was gradual, halting, and tortuous, but it was real. If Howick could indict Melbourne's cabinet on grounds that it constituted a government of departments, then its opposite, collective responsibility, must already have become the standard of value and judgment.

NOTES

1 *Some Account of the Life and Writings of L. F. de Vega Carpio* (London, 1806); *Three Comedies* (London, 1807).

2 For works on Holland House see Lord Ilchester, *The Home of the Hollands 1605-1920* (New York, 1937) and *Chronicles of Holland House 1820-1920* (London, 1937); Marie Princess Liechtenstein, *Holland House* (London, 1872), 2 vols; Lloyd C. Sanders, *The Holland House Circle* (London, 1908); Caroline Roche, 'Holland House,' *Pall Mall Magazine,* XVI (1898), 191-204; Walter Derham, 'Holland House and Earl's Court: Their History and Topography,' *Jour. of the Brit. Archaeological Association,* n.s., XXIII (1917), 57-78.

3 Macaulay to Hannah M. Macaulay, 25 July 1831, in George Otto Trevelyan, *The Life and Letters of Lord Macaulay* (London, 1959), p. 170.

4 BM Add. MSS. 51950-7.

5 Those that follow are recorded in the entry on Lady Holland in the *DNB,* VII, pp. 555-7.

6 Quoted in John Brooke, *The House of Commons 1745-1790: Introductory Survey* [*The History of Parliament*] (Oxford, 1968), p. 281.

7 For recent conflicting interpretations of Fox see L. G. Mitchell, *Charles James Fox and the Disintegration of the Whig Party 1782-1794* (Oxford, 1971) and John W. Derry, *Charles James Fox* (London, 1972).

8 Holland to Howick, 14 Sept. 1806, in *Memoirs of the Whig Party,* II, p. 59.

9 *Further Memoirs,* pp. 149-50.

10 In Lord John Russell (ed.), *Memorials and Correspondence of Charles James Fox* (New York, 1970 reprint of the 1854 London edition), III, pp. 54-5.

11 Fox to Holland, 14 June 1793, *ibid.*, p. 40.
12 Jeremy Bentham, *An Introduction to the Principles of Morals and Legislation* (New York, 1965), pp. 312-13.
13 Holland's protests were collected and published as *The Opinions of Lord Holland, as Recorded in the Journals of the House of Lords, from 1797 to 1841,* ed. D. C. Moylan (London, 1841). Hereafter cited as 'Holland, *Opinions.*'
14 *Ibid.*, p. 19 (also, Lords' *Journals,* XLII, 41).
15 (11 Apr. 1799), *ibid.*, pp. 30-1 (also Lords' *Journals,* XLII, 119).
16 (23 Mar. 1801), *ibid.*, p. 43 (also Lords' *Journals,* XLIII, 61).
17 (1819), *ibid.*, p. 99.
18 (3 Mar. 1825, Protesting rejection of an Irish Catholic petition against the second reading of a coercion bill), *ibid.*, pp. 117-18 (also Lords' *Journals,* LVII, 72).
19 (29 July 1822), *ibid.*, p. 102 (also Lords' *Journals,* LV, 464).
20 *Ibid.*, p. 104.
21 G. F. A. Best, 'The Protestant Constitution and Its Supporters,' *Trans. Royal Hist. Soc.*, 5th. ser., VIII, 111-13, 121-2. One should note, however, that the oaths prohibited Jews and atheists from holding office.
22 *2 Hansard,* XIX (9 May 1811), 1128-34.
23 (1 Aug. 1833), Holland, *Opinions*, p. 164 (also Lords' *Journals*, LXV, 544; *3 Hansard,* XX, 352-5); see below, p. 236.
24 Holland to Grey, 17 Nov. 1812, BM, HHP. (Some of the Holland House Papers were read before they were catalogued and may be cited without BM additional manuscript numbers. Some had been catalogued but not yet foliated.)
25 See his letters to Holland in 1794, *Memorials and Correspondence,* III.
26 C. Grey, *Some Account of the Life and Opinions of Charles, 2nd Earl Grey* (London, n.d.), p. 11.
27 Lord Russell to Cartwright, quoted in H. W. Carless Davis, *The Age of Grey and Peel* (Oxford, 1929), p. 101.
28 Fox to Holland, 1796, in *Memorials and Correspondence,* III, pp. 135-6.
29 Donald Southgate, *The Passing of the Whigs 1832-1886* (London, 1962), pp. 20-1.
30 Michael Roberts, *The Whig Party 1807-1812* (London, 2nd ed., 1965), pp. 208, 271-2.
31 Holland to Charles Richard Fox, 29 Sept. 1819, HHP, BM Add. MS 51872.
32 Edmund Burke, *Reflections on the Revolution in France* (New York, 1965), p. 58.
33 June 1831, below, p. 195.
34 John, Earl Russell, *Recollections and Suggestions 1813-1873* (London, 1875), p. 135.
35 Below, p. 418.
36 *Further Memoirs,* pp. 381, 383.
37 *Memoirs of the Whig Party,* I, p. 6.
38 *Further Memoirs,* p. 384.
39 John Earl Russell, *An Essay on the History of the English Government and Constitution: From Henry VII to the Present Time* (London, 1865).
40 In 1831, for example, Holland justified the anticipated creation of peers because it was an exercise within the prerogative. (Below, p. 46.) In 1839 he and his colleagues opposed the Lords' censure of the Irish government as interference with the royal prerogative. (Holland, *Opinions,* p. 194; below, p. 393.)
41 'Lord Holland's Commonplace Book,' HHP, BM Add. MS 51911.
42 *Cobbett's Parliamentary History,* XXIX (19 Apr. 1791), 344.
43 (27 June 1814, Protest against rejection of a motion to censure government for failure to secure abolition of the slave trade in the treaty with France), Holland, *Opinions,* p. 82 (also Lords' *Journals,* XLIX, 1012).
44 (10 June 1824, Protest against third reading of Irish Insurrection Act), *ibid.*, p. 113 (also Lords' *Journals,* LVI, 375).
45 17 Sept. 1831, below, p. 56.
46 n.d., HHP, BM Add. MS 51730, f. 149.

47 13 Aug. 1810, in Rollo Russell (ed.), *The Early Correspondence of Lord John Russell* (London, 1913), I, pp. 132-3.
48 Holland to Caroline Fox, 17 June 1809, HHP, BM Add. MS 51739.
49 Holland, *Opinions,* p. 79 (also Lords' *Journals,* XLIX, 860).
50 (19 Feb. 1816, Protest against passage of Liverpool's motion for an address to the Prince Regent in approbation of the recent treaties), *ibid*., p. 84 (also, Lords' *Journals,* L, 450).
51 *2 Hansard,* IV (19 Feb. 1821), 771-85.
52 E. Tangye Lean, *The Napoleonists: A Study in Political Disaffection 1760-1960* (London), esp. pp. 126-200.
53 Holland, *Opinions,* pp. 86-7.
54 *Foreign Reminiscences* (London, 1850), p. 269.
55 HHP, BM Add. MS 51896 (unfoliated).
56 26 Mar. 1837, below, p. 358.
57 G. F. A. Best, 'The Whigs and the Church Establishment in the Age of Grey and Holland,' *History,* XLV (1960), 107.
58 Lord Shaftesbury's Diary, 6 Feb. 1841, BP, SHA/PD/2.
59 *Ibid*., 24 Oct. 1840. (I am grateful to Geoffrey Finlayson of Glasgow University for this reference. A.D.K.)
60 G. M. Young, *Victorian England: Portrait of an Age* (London, 2nd ed., 1963), p. 14.
61 Holland to Grey, 17 Nov. 1812, HHP, BM.
62 Holland to Henry Edward Fox, 22 June 1827, HHP, BM Add. MS 51750.
63 See Carlos Flick, 'The Fall of Wellington's Government,' *Jour. Mod. Hist*., XXXVII (Mar. 1965), 62-71.
64 E.g., 17 June 1832, below, p. 192; Austin Mitchell, *The Whigs in Opposition 1815-1830* (Oxford, 1967), pp. 191-2.
65 Quoted in James Newell McCord, Jr, 'Lord Holland and the Politics of the Whig Aristocracy (1807-27): A Study in Aristocratic Liberalism' (unpublished Ph.D. dissertation, Johns Hopkins University, 1968), p. 399. A good study, particularly on politics in the early twenties.
66 Melbourne to Anglesey, 8 Apr. 1833, AP, P.R.O.N.I., T1068/31, f. 159.
67 22 June 1834, below, p. 259.
68 *3 Hansard,* VII (4 Oct. 1831), 1185-6.
69 John Allen's Diary, 7 May 1831, HHP, BM Add. MS 52204 (Book 2E).
70 Arthur Aspinall, *Lord Brougham and the Whig Party* (Manchester, 1927), pp. 185-6.
71 Holland to Grey (priv.), 10 Oct. 1830, HHP, BM.
72 Brougham to Duc de Broglie, 16 Aug. 1830 in Henry, Lord Brougham, *Life and Times* (London, 1871), III, pp. 46-7.
73 Graham to Roebuck, 4 Jan. 1851, in Charles Stuart Parker, *Life and Letters of Sir James Graham* (London, 1907), I, p. 118.
74 Graham to Brougham, 2 Nov. 1830, Graham Papers (microfilm, Cambridge University Library).
75 The king had suggested to Grey that Holland become Chancellor of the Duchy (Allen's Diary, 7 May 1831, HHP, BM Add. MS 52204 (Book E)); Grey to Holland, 18 Nov. 1831, in G. M. Trevelyan, *Lord Grey of the Reform Bill* (London, 2nd ed., 1929), p. 379. Holland had forty-four clerical livings at his disposal as Chancellor. HHP, BM Add. MS 51540.
76 22 June and 17 Nov. 1834, and Feb. 1839, below, pp. 261, 276, 391.
77 18 Dec. 1831, below, p. 97.
78 Dec. 1831, below, p. 102.
79 E.g., J. R. M. Butler, *The Passing of the Great Reform Bill* (London, 1914, reprinted, 1964); G. M. Trevelyan, *Lord Grey of the Reform Bill;* Elie Halévy, *The Triumph of Reform 1830-1841* [*A History of the English People in the Nineteenth Century,* III] (London, 1961); Davis, *The Age of Grey and Peel.* The most recent expression

of this interpretation is given by Michael Brock, *The Great Reform Act* (London, 1973).

80 'The Other Face of Reform,' *Vict. Studies,* V: 2 (1961), 7-34; 'Concession or Cure: The Sociological Premises of the First Reform Act,' *Hist. Journ.,* IX:1 (1966), 39-59; 'Political Morality in Mid-Nineteenth Century England: Concepts, Norms, Violations,' *Vict. Studies,* XIII:1 (1969), 5-36.

81 Moore, 'Concession or Cure,' p. 39.

82 *Ibid.*, p. 46.

83 *Ibid.*, pp. 52-6; 'Political Morality in Mid-Nineteenth Century England,' pp. 16-20.

84 Except perhaps in the nineteenth century when that interpretation was popularized by Dicey's 1898 lectures subsequently published. See A. V. Dicey, *Lectures on the Relation between Law and Public Opinion in England During the Nineteenth Century* (London, 2nd ed., 1930), p. 185.

85 16 Oct. 1831, below, p. 70.

86 Mitchell, *Whigs in Opposition,* pp. 127-30.

87 30 Jan. 1832, below, p. 122.

88 17-19 July 1833, below, p. 232.

89 Below, p. 259.

90 Sept. 1836, below, p. 348.

91 *3 Hansard,* VIII (7 Oct. 1831), 251.

92 Sept. 1836, below, p. 343.

93 *Ibid.*, p. 348.

94 These models are presented in Samuel Beer, 'The Representation of Interests in British Government: Historical Background,' *Amer. Poli. Sci. Rev.*, LI (Sept. 1957), 613-50.

95 29 [28] Nov. 1831, below, p. 86.

96 *Ibid.*

97 22 July 1831, below, p. 11.

98 11 Dec. 1831, below, p. 92.

99 Below, p. 377.

100 The point is made by John Milton-Smith, 'Earl Grey's Cabinet and the Objects of Parliamentary Reform,' *Hist. Jour.*, XV: 1 (1972) 73.

101 20 Dec. 1831, below, p. 99; See Norman Gash, *Politics in the Age of Peel: A Study in the Techniques of Parliamentary Representation 1830-1850* (London, 1953), p. 67.

102 Below, pp. 99-100.

103 29 [28] Nov. 1831, below, p. 85.

104 Moore, 'Concession or Cure,' pp. 52-6.

105 14 Aug. 1831, below, p. 30.

106 E.g., 15 Feb. 1832, below p. 130; see also John Cannon, *Parliamentary Reform 1640-1832* (Cambridge, 1973), pp. 246-7, 250.

107 Moore, 'Concession or Cure,' p. 56; 'Political Morality in Mid-Victorian England,' p. 18.

108 29 [28] Nov. 1831, below, p. 85.

109 28 Mar. 1832, below, p. 163.

110 22 June 1834, below, p. 261.

111 3 Aug. 1831, below, p. 23.

112 Cf. Elie Halévy, *The Growth of Philosophic Radicalism* (Boston, 1955), p. 264.

113 June 1832, below, p. 195.

114 July 1833, below, p. 227.

115 May 1839, below, p. 409.

116 Aug. 1832, below p. 201.

117 To Anglesey, 25 Oct. 1832, AP, P.R.O.N.I., T1068/30, f. 239.

118 For a fuller treatment of the Irish question, see A. D. Kriegel, 'The Irish Policy of Lord Grey's Government,' *Eng. Hist. Rev.,* LXXXVI (Jan. 1971), 22-45, from which some of the following remarks are taken.

119 Anglesey to Stanley, 6 Apr. 1831, *ibid*., T1068/16.

120 Radicals such as Francis Place, concerned with the improvement of England, would have found little if any opposition among Whigs to their conclusion that 'the Irish must be left to fight it out among themselves before they can be put in condition ever to commence regeneration, or rather before progress can be made toward actual civilization. I do not consider that a state of civilization in which property is not secure.' Place to Beauclerck, 26 May 1832, Place Papers, BM Add. MS 35149, ff. 156-7.

121 Althorp to Grey (priv.), 26 Aug. 1832, Spencer Papers, Althorp Park.

122 Melbourne to Anglesey (priv.), 30 June 1832, AP, P.R.O.N.I., T1068/31, f. 85.

123 O'Connell to wife, Saturday [Nov. 1830], O'Connell-FitzSimon Papers, National Library of Ireland.

124 O'Connell to P. V. FitzPatrick, 29 Aug. 1832, in W. J. FitzPatrick (ed.), *Correspondence of Daniel O'Connell* (London, 1888), I, p. 301.

125 14 Dec. 1831, below, p. 94.

126 Melbourne to Stanley (priv.), 2 Jan. 1831, P.R.O., H.O. 122/15, f. 118; Russell to Grey, 20 Oct. 1832, Russell Papers, P.R.O., 30/22/1C, f. 35; *3 Hansard,* (3 Feb. 1831) I, 119; Stanley to Melbourne, 4 Jan. 1831, Melbourne Papers, Box 32, Royal Archives, Windsor Castle.

127 *3 Hansard* (22 Dec. 1830), I, 55.

128 *Ibid.* (8 Feb. 1831), II, 325; see also the report in *The Times,* 9 Feb. 1831.

129 For the Irish interest among Whig peers, see David Large, 'The House of Lords and Ireland in the Age of Peel, 1832-1850,' *Irish Hist. Studies,* IX (1955), 367-70. Prominent Whig Ministers or advisors in the Commons who had extensive Irish estates included Duncannon, Palmerston, Spring Rice, and Stanley.

130 Melbourne to Stanley (priv.), 2 Jan. 1831, P.R.O., H.O. 122/15, f. 118; *3 Hansard* (3 Feb. 1831), I, 119-21. Some of that legislation had been recommended in the report of the select committee on the Irish poor. H.C. 1830 (667), VII (*Reports from Committees,* iv), 56-7.

131 Melbourne to Stanley, 7 Jan. 1831, P.R.O., H.O. 122/15, f. 121.

132 7 and 14 Dec. 1831, below, pp. 91, 95; Littleton's Diary, Sunday, 12 Dec. 1831, HP, S.R.O., D/260/M/F/5/26/7, ff. 256-7. For Stanley's control over the Commons' committee, see James Grattan's Journal, 12 and 16 Feb. 1832, Grattan Papers, N.L.I., MS 14147 (Grattan was a member of the committee); Stanley to Peel (priv. and confid.), 22 Apr. 1832, P.P., BM Add. MS 40403, ff. 25-6.

133 15 Feb. 1832 below p. 130; Holland to Anglesey, 10 Feb. 1832, AP, P.R.O.N.I., T1068/34, f. 280.

134 5 and 8 Feb. 1832, below pp. 125, 127; Melbourne to Anglesey, 12 Sept. 1832, AP, P.R.O.N.I., T1068/31, f. 118.

135 Althorp to Grey (priv.), 1 Jan. 1833, Spencer Papers, Althorp Park; 9 July 1832, below, pp. 197-8; Thompson to Ellice, 30 Oct. 1832, EP, National Library of Scotland, E/55, f. 17; Ellice to Grey, 5 Nov. 1832, *ibid*., E/18, ff. 94-5.

136 Duncannon to Holland, 1 Jan. 1833, HHP, BM.

137 2 Dec. 1831, below, p. 90.

138 Holland to Anglesey (priv.), 25 Oct. 1832, AP, P.R.O.N.I., T1068/34, f. 340.

139 Holland to Anglesey, 24 Oct. [1832], *ibid*., T1068/34, ff. 334-5.

140 Grey to Anglesey (priv.), 25 Oct. 1832, *ibid*., T1068/30, f. 239; 11 June and 12 Sept. 1832, *ibid*., ff. 207, 228-9.

141 *3 Hansard*, XV (22 Feb. 1833), 1104.

142 *Ibid*., 27 and 28 Feb. 1833, and 1 Mar. and 5 Mar. 1833, XV, 1226, 1333, 1362; XVI, 51-2, 273.

143 9 July–3 Aug. 1833, below, p. 236.

144 20 Jan. 1832, below, p. 117.

145 27 Dec. 1831, below, p. 104.

146 31 Aug.–6 Sept. 1833, below, pp. 254-6.

147 Sir Charles Webster, *The Foreign Policy of Palmerston 1830-1841: Britain, the Liberal Movement and the Eastern Question* (London, reissued 1969), I, p. 37. Webster's two-volume study remains the standard work on English foreign policy for the decade.
148 19 Dec. 1831, below, p. 99.
149 Below, p. 417.
150 Below, p. 412.
151 Dec. 1831, below, p. 101.
152 27 Dec. 1831, below, p. 105.
153 Below, p. 418.
154 22 June 1834, below, p. 248.
155 Below, p. 100.
156 Below, p. 204.
157 21 July 1831, below, p. 10.
158 26 Aug. 1831, below, p. 40.
159 Below, p. 437 n. 221.
160 27 June–5 July 1832, below, p. 196.
161 22 June 1834, below, p. 248.
162 Below, p. 339.
163 Below, p. 413.
164 BP GC/HO/120/1-3, Historical Manuscripts Commission.
165 *Ibid.*; italics indicate passages underlined by Palmerston.
166 *Memoirs of the Whig Party*, II, p. 85.
167 *Ibid.*
168 15 Oct. 1831, below, p. 69.
169 Sir Denis Le Marchant, *Memoir of Viscount Althorp* (London, 1876), p. 326; Holland to Anglesey, 11 July 1831, AP, P.R.O.N.I., T1068/34, f. 208.
170 Above, p. xxxviii.
171 Below, pp. 223, 464n.64.
172 Below, p. 361.
173 Howick to Ellice, 6 Sept. 1839, EP, National Library of Scotland, E/22, f. 44.
174 *Ibid.*, ff. 46-7.
175 6 Mar., below, p. 147.
176 28 Mar. 1832, below, p. 163.
177 24 Apr. 1835, below, p. 293.
178 Palmerston to Graham, 28 Sept. 1833, Graham Papers.
179 Graham to Stanley, 3 Dec. 1833, *ibid.*
180 Below, p. 411.
181 II, 89.
182 Oct. 1839, below, p. 412.
183 Grey to Palmerston, 29 Sept. 1831, in Webster, *Foreign Policy of Palmerston*, II, p. 824.
184 15 Aug. 1831, below, p. 30.
185 A. Aspinall, 'The Cabinet Council, 1783-1835,' *Proceedings of the British Academy 1952* (London, n.d.).
186 Below, p. 82.
187 E.g. 2 Jan. 1832, below, p. 110.
188 Oct. 1839, below, p. 412.
189 Below, p. 80.
190 19 Feb. 1832, below, p. 135.
191 26 Mar. 1832, below, p. 162.
192 15 July 1835, below, p. 321.
193 20 July 1831, below, p. 8.
194 31 July 1831, below, p. 20.

195 29 Sept. 1831, below, p. 62.
196 19 Nov. 1831, below, p. 81.
197 Below, p. 247.
198 Below, p. 266.
199 Below, p. 359.
200 25 Mar. 1832, below, p. 160.
201 3 Apr. 1832, below, p. 167.
202 Below, p. 218. Perhaps the most serious division occurred on the conflicting interpretations of the appropriations clause in Stanley's Irish Church bill. See Kriegel, 'The Irish Policy of Grey's Government,' pp. 35-40.
203 19 Nov. 1831, below, p. 82.
204 Below, p. 152.
205 Below, p. 303.
206 [8 July 1840], below, p. 419.
207 Below, p. 152. Although Durham had frequently threatened to resign and now had ample reason for doing so, he allowed himself to be persuaded that his resignation would break up the government and thereby endanger the Reform Bill.
208 Below, p. 82.
209 Aspinall, 'Cabinet Council,' p. 214.
210 2 July 1833, below, p. 226.
211 4 June 1833, below, p. 214.
212 Below, pp. 209, 230.
213 May-Sept. 1836, below, p. 348.
214 John P. Mackintosh, *The British Cabinet* (London, 2nd ed., 1968), p. 98.
215 Littleton wrote that those ministers involved in formulating the Irish tithe bill of 1833 considered it 'the most difficult question they have ever treated in their lives.' Littleton to Anglesey, 28 Aug. 1833, HP, D/260/M/01/2, f. 144, S.R.O.
216 June 1833, below, p. 215.
217 Below, p. 228.
218 Below, p. 419.
219 Below, p. 410.
220 See A. D. Kriegel, 'Politics of Whigs in Opposition,' *Jour. Brit. Studies,* VII: 2 (May 1968), 65-91.
221 20 Apr. 1835, below, p. 292.
222 9 Mar. 1832, below, p. 150.
223 12 Nov. 1834, below, p. 272.
224 Thomas Creevey to Miss Ord, 12 Aug. [July] 1834, in Sir Herbert Maxwell (ed.), *The Creevey Papers: A Selection from the Correspondence and Diaries of the Late Thomas Creevey* (London, 1903), II, p. 284.
225 Below, pp. 255-6.
226 Below, p. 241.
227 4 June 1833, below, p. 215.
228 Below, pp. 444-5n.361.
229 Below, p. 162.
230 24 June 1832, below, p. 194.
231 Below, p. 248.
232 Below, p. 249.
233 Grey to Holland, 16 June 1833, HHP, BM Add. MS 51548.

EDITORIAL PROCEDURE

The immediate problem that confronted the editor was to decipher Holland's penmanship. He obviously wrote many entries in haste, and his handwriting was affected by his gout. 'I scrawl lying down and in some pain,' he apologized to Palmerston (27 Feb. [1831], BP, GC/HO/66). Moreover, Holland apparently read sections of his diary long after he had written the original entries, and there is a good deal of deleted material as well as considerable interlineation. Fortunately, Holland reserved the left-hand side of his pages for marginalia, and that material can be identified as having been added after the original entry, sometimes years later. Some entries include material beyond the time of the dateline entry. Holland subsequently inserted dates as a heading at the top of pages in some of these lengthy summaries. The transcription of the diary, therefore, required considerable care and patience.

The essential task in transcribing a handwritten document, assuming it is worth publishing at all, is to make it intelligible. To be sure, its form and spirit ought, as much as possible, to be retained. But aside from holy writ or documents like *Magna Carta* or the *Declaration of Independence,* sacred to the collective heritage if not the faith, one commits no transgression by exercising a certain latitude to achieve the desired end. Precious facsimile reproductions are not only financially prohibitive. They are usually unnecessary and, indeed, undesirable. Most contemporary editors would accept the 'middle course' between exact reproduction and complete modernization advocated by the editor of *The Papers of Thomas Jefferson* (Princeton, 1950-; I:xxxix). That 'middle course,' however, is inevitably a broad and flexible one, and the editor should provide a guide for his procedures.

Capitalization and spelling have been retained as Holland had them. Given his scrawl, both occasionally require educated guesses. In doubtful cases the editor has generally refrained from capitalizing. But inconsistencies in both capitalization and spelling are retained. 'Cabinet' is sometimes capitalized, sometimes not. Holland alternated 'ambassador' with 'embassador'. He gave varied endings or inconsistent spelling for proper names: Russell or Russel, Althorp or Althorpe, Lansdown or Lansdowne, Mastutevitch or Matuscewitz. The editor has not imposed consistency upon the author; in all cases, he has retained the author's version as it appears in the manuscript.

Most *abbreviations and contractions* have been expanded silently. 'Plenipo:ies' is given as plenipotentiaries, 'bp' as bishop, 'bk' as bishoprick; 'K' or 'K^{g}' is King, 'D' is Duke. 'H^{se} of L^{ds}' and 'H^{se} of C^{ms}' are printed as House of Lords and House of Commons; 'H^{d} H^{se}' or 'H^{lld} H^{se}' are transcribed as Holland House. Holland almost always wrote 'L^{d}' and 'S^{r}', transcribed here as Lord and Sir. Similarly, he wrote 'D^{n}' and 'D^{na}' for Portuguese as well as Spanish honorifics, and these are transcribed as Don and Donna. (The last was wrong, but Holland spelled it that way when not abbreviating.) 'George the 4th' or 'William 4' are printed George IV and William IV; '25ls' is given as £25. Holland invariably used the ampersand; it is always given as 'and', except in the case of '&c'. To have retained all of these abbreviations would have resulted in a typographical patchwork both unsightly and unnecessary.

Some abbreviations, however, have been retained. Datelines are kept as Holland wrote them but are uniformly italicized, superior letters lowered to the first line of the entry and followed by a period. Abbreviations of proper names are retained, superior letters lowered to the line of the text and followed by a period—e.g., Robt. Adair, Wm. Russell. If abbreviations of proper names would, in the editor's judgment, not be identifiable to the reader, they have been expanded within brackets—e.g., R[usse]ll.

Quotation marks and diacritical marks: The editor has transcribed Holland's French, Greek, Latin, and Italian as they appear in the text. Holland often omitted diacritical marks, and these are not supplied unless his entry is otherwise unintelligible. Holland often began a quotation with appropriate marks, but failed to end it. The editor has supplied the missing quotation marks at the proper place in the text if it is obvious. If not, the ending quotation mark is omitted.

Paragraphing: Where Holland begins a paragraph, his paragraphing is retained. Occasionally, however, the editor has had to provide paragraphing for Holland's lengthy, run-on commentary. This has been done without giving notice to the reader.

Grammar and syntax have not been tampered with, except to delete such obvious slips of the pen as consecutive conjunctions or prepositions (and and, of of). If Holland obviously omitted an article or preposition, the editor has supplied it within square brackets. If the omission is probable but not certain, the bracketed word is followed by a question mark within the brackets, e.g., [to?]. If Holland seemed in his haste to have used the wrong word, the proper one is suggested within brackets and preceded by a question mark—e.g., 'in conjunction in [?with] France'.

Punctuation: Although Holland was capable of precision and literary grace, most of his diary entries were written hastily and for his own subsequent perusal. The prose style is often highly convoluted, occasionally approximating German construction. Holland often had apposite phrases within non-restrictive clauses which, in turn, were incorporated within an enumerated series, with no punctuation at all. He used the dash as a universal punctuation mark, to signify comma, period, semicolon, colon—and even dash. He used commas as well, but often in the contemporary practice of separating the subject from the predicate of a sentence. It is not difficult to determine sentence stops, and terminal punctuation is supplied by a period unless Holland used a question or exclamation mark. The problem, rather, is to punctuate the lengthy, ungrammatical constructions for intelligibility, without altering (or improving) Holland's prose style. Generally the editor has provided punctuation in accord with modern usage. But some flexibility has been necessary; for if modern usage were followed in setting off all apposite phrases, parenthetical statements, non-restrictive clauses, and series by commas, that punctuation would serve to confuse as much as to assist the reader. With a few inevitable exceptions, the following procedures have been adopted:

1 For lengthy passages, commas to set off a series are given priority. In some very lengthy passages which incorporate many parenthetical phrases, semicolons are used to set off a series.

2 In short sentences, parenthetical statements have not generally been set off. Thus: 'He was I thought bound to communicate it to the French.' 'I thought' is not set off by commas.

3 If Holland used a comma to set off the beginning of a parenthetical phrase, but did not insert one at the conclusion of the phrase, the editor has inserted the missing comma.

4 If Holland's lack of punctuation results in ambiguity not readily explicable by the context or otherwise subject to doubt, the editor has refrained from adding punctuation. In these instances a possible construction may be given in a footnote.

Interlineations and deleted matter: Crossed-out passages were generally rewritten by Holland. In those cases the crossed-out matter is ignored, unless substantially different from Holland's revised version. Interlineations are brought down to the line of the text. Holland's marginalia, written on adjacent pages, is incorporated within brackets and indicated by the words 'in the margin' italicized and in brackets.

Textual devices: All parentheses in the text are Lord Holland's. Square brackets [roman] are used for editorial expansion. Square brackets [*italicized*] are used for editorial direction and correction; for example, [*blotted*], [*sentence unfinished*], 'in October [*November*]'; [*In the margin:* roman] indicates Holland's marginalia. [*Heading:* 13 July 1837] indicates the date written at the top of a page, not the date of a diary entry. Words, letters, phrases, or ellipses within angular brackets < > indicate uncertain readings or illegibilities. The correction [*sic*] is used sparingly.

Annotation: Biographical citations are provided for all but the most prominent figures. For Peel, Wellington, Grey, William IV and others, birth and death dates are provided in the index. Except for the French, titles of continental nobility are anglicized, unless there is no English equivalent. Non-English names are given in the appropriate language, unless their anglicized forms have become familiar: for example, Dom Pedro and Dom Miguel, but King Ferdinand and King John, rather than Fernando and João. The reader is referred to *Hansard* for most parliamentary divisions, and for some important debates where Holland's entry covers more than one day. Parliamentary bills and statutes are given explanatory citations, unless the material has been discussed in the introductory essay.

Reference works have generally not been cited in biographical entries. The editor consulted the standard biographical dictionaries, peerages and genealogies, school and university registers, army and navy lists, parliamentary registers, and obituaries in the *Gentleman's Magazine*. Haydn's *Book of Dignities* (London, 1894) remains indispensable. A few more specialized reference works are worth noting. For the clergy, Joseph Foster (ed.), *Index Ecclesiasticus* (Oxford and Cambridge, 1890) lists the incumbents of every living for the period 1800-40; *The Clergy List* (London, 1859) should also be consulted. For identification of lawyers, the annual *Clarke's New Law List* was of considerable value. Among the numerous contemporary almanacs, the annual *Royal Kalendar* and the *Almanach de Gotha* were the most useful. The Institute of Historical Research has a valuable and rare hand-annotated copy of W. A. Shaw, *The Knights of England* (London, 1906). *Boyle's Fashionable Court and Country Guide and Town Visiting Directory*, published annually, proved to be a surprisingly rich source of information.

THE HOLLAND HOUSE DIARIES

This book, originally bought for alphabetical notes, is filled with a diary, beginning July 1831 and ending 24th. Octr. of the same year, very irregularly, imperfectly, and carelessly kept, and of no use but to remind the writer of the succession of events if he should ever compose Memoirs of that time, or possibly to clear up or illustrate any event of that time to any other person engaged in a similar employment.

I have prefixed a short proem which in any memoirs of these times would perhaps facilitate as it would certainly require a great enlargement.

[*no date*] V[assall] H[olland]

PROEM[1]

To understand the following diary it may be necessary to remind those who read it, or use it hereafter as historical matter, of the events that had occurred between the death of G[eorge] IV on 26 June 1830 and the resignation of the Duke of Wellington in October [*November*] of that year. Fortunately for his own fame, the interests of the country, and the peace of the World, the Duke of Wellington was disembarrassed by the hand of death of G[eorge] IV before 'the three memorable days' of July 1830 had placed L[oui]s Philippe on a Constitutional throne.[2] He had the good sense to perceive the advantage of a prompt and unconditional recognition of the new and Constitutional Government in France, and he had an early opportunity of ascertaining that at home the reigning Monarch, unlike his Predecessors, had no prejudices or vanities which the strong recommendation of a Minister he had appointed might not instantly subdue. The prompt recognition of L[ouis] Philippe perhaps rivetted him in the Constitutional throne and certainly prevented the renewal of war throughout Europe. The Example of England ultimately prevailed with the despotick Courts throughout [Europe] to acquiesce in a revolution of which they abhorred the principles and dreaded the consequences. The Court of Berlin on the very first intelligence had dispatched instructions to Mr Werter[3] at Paris, authorizing if not directing him to ask for his passports and quit his post. And a copy of those instructions was forwarded, together with the news of the events at Paris, to St Petersburgh. Fortunately they arrived before any Russian instructions had been dispatched to Pozzo di Borgo.[4] Werter however on the receipt of his communicated them to that intelligent and able Embassador and at the <same> [time?] Count Molé,[5] very much his personal friend, expressed to him his dismay at learning the contents of them. At his instigation or of his own accord, he [Pozzo] strove to dissuade Werter from acting on them, and represented in strong colours the advantage of an apparent as well as real concert between the three Great Military powers, which the departure of one of their Ministers from Paris while the other two remained would completely counteract. He urged him to wait till the decisions of Austria and Russia should arrive. If England had separately and hastily acknowledged the new order of things, that circumstance <furnished> an additional motive for proceeding with caution, and in either case, whether they should quit Paris or recognize the new dynasty in France, of acting together and on grounds manifestly the same. Werter was prevailed upon to wait, till news should arrive from Vienna and Petersburgh. When those from Vienna arrived or what they brought I know not, but those received from [Czar] Nicholas by Pozzo were peremptory enough and in fact directed him to withdraw from Paris without delay with the other Ministers of the Holy Alliance. He contrived however to evade an irreparable obedience of them; for in the preamble to his instructions, it was said, 'as Mr Werter will have left Paris before this reaches you' or words to that effect. Pozzo, in quest of some pretext for staying where he was, seized this phrase most adroitly as the basis on which the whole reasoning of the dispatch practically rested, and answered by observing, that 'as Mr Werter had *not* quitted Paris['] he deemed it more prudent to wait further instructions. That interval was no doubt employed in insinuating to his own Court, and to the others too, the manifold prudential reasons for deferring any step that had a tendency to render war inevitable. And there is as little doubt that the news of England's prompt and honourable recognition of the new Government reconciled the three Courts to the prudence and policy of Pozzo's procrastination or disobedience of his orders. Whether he acted in all this from private or publick motives, from a desire to remain in France or a conviction of the good policy of avoiding war, I do not pretend to determine, but so it was—and the friends of liberty and peace were in this instance obliged to the decision of the Duke of Wellington and the caution of Pozzo for the preservation of both those blessings, that is, to two men who from principle and temper had as little love of freedom and as much predilection for forcible means of government as any two throughout Europe. But it was of a piece with the whole event—and when L[ouis] Philippe owed his Crown to Lafayette the republican, it was natural that France should owe its liberty and Europe its peace to Pozzo and to Wellington![6]

The revolution of Belgium was mimickry rather than imitation of that of France. Nothing but the obstinacy and jealousy even of his Son deprived the Dutch King of all chance of recovering his provinces. He claimed the interference of his Allies, and England in particular, but Wellington answered correctly that England was by treaty entitled but not compelled to interfere; that it was optional and that She declined. He soon afterwards acquiesced in a mediation to prevent the effusion of blood and contrived to impose some articles of an armistice, which, when they ultimately became inconvenient to one party or the other, each was desirous but neither ventured to transgress.[7]

At home the dissolution was thought to prove and in truth did prove the little disposition entertained by the Duke of Wellington to introduce Lord Grey or any portion of the Whigs into Government. Rosslyn,[8] Jersey,[9] Scarlet[10] long cajoled either themselves or went themselves to cajole their friends that such was the design of the Duke of Wellington and that he had been labouring to subdue the repugnance of G[eorge] IV. The absence of all overtures on his decease was a pretty strong indication of the falseness of all such speculation and the dissolution was decisive. It happened <contradicting> for the Duke that the dissolution was announced before the three memorable days, and the memorable days known before the Elections were completed. The people were in a great state of excitement, and the new members chosen with a view to reforms approaching to revolution.[11] Wellington, little aware of the extent of this feeling, began the Session by a voluntary declaration against all reform, and thereby accelerated the event and lost himself and his party in publick estimation perhaps forever.

I BEGIN A DIARY—1831

15 July. At breakfast Rogers[12] and Mr Ellis[13] of Museum. The latter come to examine coins found in river Dove near Tutbury and a treasure trove to the King in right of his Duchy.[14] The number according to some amounted to no less than 200,000, but allowing for exaggeration was certainly most extraordinary, though only *1500* were rescued by the Commission of the Duchy. None later than Edward I, many Scotch. Mr Danvers[15] called in morning on the subject of the Eaubrink drainage bill[16] and other small matters relating to Duchy affairs. Went to Committee of Council sitting on Coronation between three and four, found they had finished their report and attended them with it to Court. I saw the King about Duchy affairs in Closet. He told me he thought the solemnity of a Coronation might have been useful in its time but was ill adapted to ours, and the expence it involved, in the present circumstances of the Country and those of Europe, most idle and unnecessary. However he had been told that part of it was deemed essential by some of his subjects. If so, it was better to comply. Yet if the Coronation Oath was of consequence, why was it not provided that it should be taken at the Accession? In the interval between that and the Coronation was not the King, King? And if so, where were the securities? He told me the Expence of George IV's coronation was not less than 250,000. He could not conceive how it could have cost so much. Sir Something Stephenson[17] (I think that is his name) was a very correct man and had overlooked many of the accounts. But in the furnishing out the Speakers House and all the details there had been by express orders a wasteful display amounting to extravagance and ridicule. The King was chearful and well and talked much good sense on Coronation. [*In the margin:* He is reported on one occasion to have said that he would be damned if he would be smeared. His

Majesty thus objects to the smearing—and the people to the *schmeurgeldt.* Why cannot the state vehicle proceed without stopping to grease at all?] He spoke as openly but not so well on foreign matters, described Russia (I believe truly) as in a very critical state, Nicholas (I fear prematurely) as more reasonable with his Lithuanian insurgents than he had hitherto been, and the King of Holland as a very wrongheaded man, I am afraid his Majesty said somewhat irreverently 'an obstinate Hound' and brought some traits in proof of it which he had observed in 1814. He then joined the Council, assured them that his approbation of report was not a mere matter of course; he had read and sincerely approved of it. He was the last man to spare himself trouble or hesitate in complying with any solemnity which his subjects might deem necessary, but he thought perhaps at all times and, he was sure, in these, it was prudent, nay, incumbent upon persons in his situation as well as their advisers to devize every means of curtailing useless expence and unnecessary parade. He hoped this scheme would preserve whatever could by possibility be supposed to be important in the ceremony and avoid all that led to mere shew att<ended> with expence. I rejoiced that Lord Cholmondely[18] and Mr Greville,[19] the Clerk of Council, heard this declaration. They will repeat it and cavillers will know that in this judicious step at least Ministers follow as much as guide the good sense of the King.

Undressed at Lord Grey's and went down to House of Lords to hear Lord Londonderry's[20] foolish and malevolent questions about Belgium and Prince Leopold's 50,000.[21] I understand Lord Grey parried or answered them extremely well. I did not hear his answer, for I was closeted in an adjoining room with Don Pedro, who was in the first instance anxious to have a speedy answer to the requests he had made on the manner of receiving his daughter on her arrival here and, secondly, disposed to communicate to me more of his views and schemes against Don Miguel's government than I deemed it prudent to hear, especially as he was about to consult me on the propriety of asking the Government how far they would assist, sanction, prompte, or connive at them.[22] I returned to House, told Lord Grey what had passed and then accompanied him to Lord Palmerston at foreign office. Lord P[almerston] communicated to me the letters of our King on the project of the answer to be given to Don Pedro's 5 requests,[23] which were in the main favorable and civil. We then agreed that we could not sanction or even overlook any thing like hostile aggression from our coasts, that Pedro by consulting with us upon such matters might bring before us facts which it was better for him that we should not know. The knowledge of them might be embarrassing and impose upon us the necessity of interference in a direction very different from our natural interests and wishes. On my return home I wrote a French letter to Don Pedro apprizing him of the answers he was to expect and dissuading him from the consultation he had projected. Palmerston read me a dispatch from Hoppner[24] describing discontent, fear, and cabals at Lisbon, and a report of a conspiracy and a plan for inducing Miguel to resign, which, though founded on rumour only, seemed to tally pretty exactly with some expectations which Don Pedro had avowed to me as inducements to make him sail to Terceira and from thence undertake a descent upon Portugal.[25] Throughout the conversation, Grey as well as Palmerston spoke handsomely of Don Pedro and more favorably of his character and conduct than from previous representation they had apprehended he deserved. They confirmed the accounts of the distress of Russia.[26] Lord and Lady Carlisle[27] dined here this day.

16th. July. Private accounts with Mr Currey.[28] Eau Brink bill with Mr Adam.[29] Received a letter from Lady Breadalbane urging a step in the peerage for her husband and acquiescing in a writ to call up her son.[30] Dined at Lord Dover's.[31] Heard report of House of Commons debate from Lord J Russell, who is in good heart, and of Prince Leopold's departure for Flanders this morning.[32]

July 17. Went to Cabinet at two. Cabinet full.

Decided on course to be taken in Lords with respect to two bills, one (ArchBishop's) for composition, the other (Lord Dacre's) for commutation of tythes.[33] It was agreed that with respect to both we should follow the line of Lord Grey's speech.[34] We should not deny that a commutation of tythes would be desirable if it could be adjusted on practicable, just, and equitable principles, but acknowledge that we were not prepared either to approve unequivocally of the bill before us or to frame a measure for that purpose ourselves, and therefore were willing, in the meanwhile, to assist the Archbishop in an object which he and the church so handsomely promoted. We then agreed that the vote of £16,000 for Colonial Churches might be reduced and hopes held out to the house of speedily dispensing with it altogether, reserving all opinion upon the ulterior question which might be raised, how far any or all ecclesiastical establishments in the Colonies might be abandoned and nothing but sums of money voted for general education of all religions by the respective assemblies of each.[35]

[*In the margin:* Lord Grey stated to us that he was in possession of a letter from Prince Leopold, written before his election, which announced his intention, if chosen, of leaving his annuity of *£50,000* in England to pay what remained due for the purchase of Clermont,[36] to defray expences of keeping up that place, and to pay some pensions of old servants of himself and Princess [Charlotte], carrying the residue, as long as he lived out of England, to the consolidated fund. This intention he adhered to and has recently confirmed. It was resolved to silence the questions and reports, which Lord Grey justly denominated 'malevolent', by communicating the substance of this letter on Monday to both Houses of Parliament. On the subject of his Regiment nothing explicit had been said, but Lord Durham[37] assured us that Leopold certainly did not mean to retain the pay. Some were inclined to question the propriety on point of constitutional principle of his retaining the patronage and nominal command, tho' after all the King had clearly the power of removing him.]

The necessity to prevent delay in passing the reform bill, of the house meeting at ten in the morning was discussed. And though such a step was postponed from consideration of the inconvenience to private bills and the interruption it would give to Election Committees, the notion of resorting to it as the <resource> against the pertinacious opposition of our adversaries was generally approved. We then fixed on names for the Commissioners in the bill.[38] Althorp, Lord J Russell and the House of Commons [ministers] urged the necessity of naming a considerable portion of persons inimical or indifferent to the measure. Lord Durham protested vehemently against such a principle, objected to every name, maintaining that all, aye, even Abercrombie[39] himself! were antireformers; and he very sullenly submitted to the decision of the Cabinet, muttering that 'he was often alone in divisions in that room but had the satisfaction of knowing that in the Country the great majority sided with him'.

The Duke of Sussex[40] dined with me. Maule,[41] Lord Duncan,[42] and Lord Oxford[43] were of the party. The first is I think entitled to, tho' he would not ask, a peerage; the latter [*i.e.* Duncan] wishes for a step in the peerage; and the third very modestly and fairly told me that if eldest sons were called up, he should exceedingly like Lord Harley[44] to be one, because on his entrance into life it would give him occupation, introduce him to good company, and open his mind. But he added that whether he obtained such a mark of favor or not, it would make no difference in his conduct and very, very little in his feelings about measures or Men. He was an eager reformer and the present Ministry included nearly all his political friends. He asked nothing but should vote steadily for them all.

The Chancellor, Lord Brougham, came in the evening and talked over men and things confidentially. He fancies Durham would go to Brussells and approves of the notion, more no doubt for what it would remove than for what it would confer. I learnt with great grief and some surprize that Lord Spencer's[45] health is very precarious indeed. Althorp who (as well as Stanley) dined here was much overcome with the news he had received, though no immediate danger was apprehended. [*In the margin:* There seemed something ominous. The last time he dined at Holland House he received the account of his Mother's death at table.] The Chancellor has been compelled by the conduct of Mr Long Wellesley Pool[46] to attach him for a contempt of court. He is in durance, an untoward event inasmuch as it may raise a question of privilege and enable the antireformers to postpone the bill while they are talking on a question that never fails to engage the attention and inflame the passions of Parliament. [*In the margin:* The Chancellor could not otherwise, for though I believe the whole practice to be usurpation and see no reason why the Chancellor should have powers respecting his wards which fathers have not respecting their children, the usage has been sanctioned and the jurisdiction so generally allowed that, had he permitted himself to be defied, his forebearance would have lowered him and his Court and have been ascribed to worse motives than a sudden scruple about a power so often exerted and so little disputed.]

18 July. Heard that Lord Munster,[47] to whom Duke of Wellington had given Lieutenancy of Tower, is harrassing the King for more money and distresses him exceedingly. Attended in House of Lords the Archbishop's composition and Lord Dacre['s] commutation of tythes bill[s]; the Archbishop fair, moderate, and dull, and not altogether adverse to the principle of commutation, though strongly disapproving of Lord Dacre's bill. The Chancellor made a perspicuous, artful, and good speech, highly conciliatory to the Clergy and yet far from pledging himself against the principle of commutation. Difficulties rather than insurmountable objections prevented him from voting Lord Dacre's bill; but in the meanwhile he thought the Archbishops both expedient and just and, should the experiment succeed, no obstacle to a further extension of it. Eldon[48] held high the property of the Church, deprecated laws changing the nature of property by anything like compulsion, seemed to prefer even commutation bill, because it included lay tythes, to the composition which affected the tythes of Clergy only; and then in his usual strain said he would not resist 2d. reading, but emphatically pronounced it *impossible* to pass the bill if it should come out of the Committee as it went into it. Bishop of London[49] made a better but less judicious speech than the Archbishop, seemed yet less averse to some mitigated commutation, but was somewhatsore on the nature of tythes which had, he said, been calumniated by the press and were more odious from the complicated, incoherent, and expensive state of the laws than from any inherent defect in the system itself. The property of the Church in them *was as sacred, perhaps more sacred, than that of their Lordships' patrimonial estates.* He called Brougham his learned friend, paid him more than one compliment, and neither he nor Archbishops were at all hostile or even distant to the Ministry, which augured well for the future conduct of the Bench. Dacre was persuaded by Archbishop, Lord Carnarvon,[50] and Lord Grey to withdraw his bill, reserving to himself the right to bring it in again if the Composition bill did not become an act this Session.[51]

Lord Grey announced Prince Leopold's determination to take no part of his annuity out of this Country, asserted the Prince's unequivocal right to the whole, but explained his destination of the annual sum to payment of debts and annuitants to keeping up Clermont and then to the publick Exchequer. Tis was received well in the house, and yet better at the bar. The Duke of Wellington handsomely congratulated the house and Country upon it, not, he said,forthe paltry object of the money and from any of that feeling so unjustly promulgated in the publick, but from the indication it afforded to Europe and to Belgiu of the just <view> the Sovereign lately <elected> by the latter took of the necessity of being independent of all other foreign countries—a remark just and reasonable, useful to the country, and advantageous to the Ministers. We liked it better, I suspect, than some around him, who seemed chagrined at our escape from a clamour which, however unjust, might have exposed us to some censure in the newspapers.

The accounts of Lord Spencer are bad. Lord Grey seems well aware of the embarrassments the loss of Lord Althorp in Commons would occasion. He will therefore by prepared with the arrangements to which he must in that case resort. Mr Stanley would not I thought undertake the lead. I remarked that he, Lord J Russel, or both together must; that our other friends in the Commons, however excellent in many respects, were, either from want of popularity or of eloquence or of both, unequal to the task.[52]

19 Ju. Called on Lauderdale.[53] He had taken his seat but does not mean to attend. His health he says prevents him, but I hope that his real reason is his dislike to oppose all his own friends. It was strange to pass an hour with him and avoid all unreserved conversation on politicks. I shirked the house of Lords. Lords Plunkett[54] and Sefton[55] and others dined at Holland House. Lord Brougham and Prince Talleyrand[56] in the evening.

20 July. Don Pedro called in the morning—good humoured and easy, but his countenance was clouded and he spoke with some bitterness when Lady Holland inadvertently asked what had become of the Marquis Barbacena,[57] who formerly conducted the little Queen here. Il est a Rio et c'est pour cela que je suis ici. He was tolerably well satisfied with the answers to his requests, and understood or affected to understand the difficulty, arising from the strict administration of our finances and the controul of the House of Commons, of our advancing him so small a sum as *£15,000* on his jewels. He was more than nettled, he told me, at our styling his daughter La Reine Donna Maria, instead of La Reine de Portugal, which title he observed had been allowed her by our predecessors in office. 'I say nothing about it,' said he, 'but I am not pleased at it.' The object of his visit here was very gracious—to inform me that he postponed his departure 24 hours for the purpose of dining with me on Sunday next, an honour which I was soon after obliged to decline, being invited or rather commanded with all my *Etonian* colleagues to Windsor on that day.[58]

The Cabinet dined here but the House of Commons members could not come, and Lord Durham, from alleged indisposition but I suspect from childish ill humour with most of his Colleagues and with Grey in particular (to whom he owes his office and seat and such importance and consideration as he enjoys), sent his excuse. When any individual in our councils differs with him in opinion or criticises the minutest article of the [Reform] bill which he assisted in preparing, he answers him shortly and petulantly by imputing his opposition to some mean and interested motive or by resenting the observation as a personal reflection upon himself. This, in spite of some very good qualities and yet greater talents, is intolerable and renders him both useless and offensive in council. I am afraid his forward temper will ere long furnish more matter for my diary of Ministerial transactions than will be pleasant to witness or record.

At dinner we could settle nothing in the absence of so many of our Colleagues. But Grey read us the draft of an answer to Talleyrand, drawn out by Lord Palmerston, which we all thought, as well as the Author, required curtailment and revision. The object and circumstances attaching it equally required dispatch. Prince Talleyrand had applied several days ago to Lord Palmerston for the consent of Great Britain to a proffer of mediation between Russia and Poland. We had talked that matter over at a Cabinet dinner at Lord Goderich's,[59] agreed that the matter demanded much deliberation and a full Cabinet, and in the meanwhile that Prince Talleyrand (who had shewn me, Grey, and Palmerston the dispatch from Sebastiani[60] but not communicated any formal paper) should be requested to put the request of the French Government on paper, that no misunderstanding might occur as to the nature or extent of the proposal. To this he could not accede till he received instructions from Paris, but he had within a day or two presented a note containing the official communication of the dispatch and soliciting an early and explicit answer,[61] with the avowed hope of being able to furnish the King of the French with a popular topick for his approaching speech to his chambers. Lord Goderich, the Duke of Richmond[62] and, above all, the Chancellor were vehement in urging objections to our concurrence in any such offer. The little right we had to interfere at all, the remoteness of any interest we could have in Poland, the inevitable consequence of a rejection of such overture by Russia being war, and the certainty of Russia so rejecting it were either taken for granted or argued by them. It was passing strange that Lord Brougham should take this line, and not the less so that the Poles (especially Count Walewsky)[63] who have had any intercourse with us are loud in their complaints of the coldness of our Cabinet, with the exception of Lord Brougham, from whom alone they pretend to have received warm and cordial assurances of zeal and good offices in their cause. Grey, Palmerston, Melbourne, and Lansdowne[64] acknowledged more interest in the Poles but with less passion urged the same objections to the policy and especially to the time of offering any joint mediation. Carlisle and myself were the only Members present who inclined to acquiesce in the French proposal limiting the proferred mediation to such as would not impose upon us, if rejected [by Russia], the necessity of enforcing it by ulterior measures. It was agreed to discuss it next day in a full cabinet, and before I went to bed I wrote a short note to Grey, who slept in the house, to say that if contrary to my judgement, the offer must be declined, a more conciliatory tone to France and less fulsome compliments to Russia ought at least to be adopted, and the wish to cooperate in promoting some lasting arrangement between the Poles and Russians, whenever we had a prospect of doing it without breaking our relations with the latter Power, more unequivocally avowed.

21 July 1831. Went early to the Cabinet with Lord Melbourne. All present but the Chancellor, Lansdowne, and Durham. Grey had in the interval greatly shortened and improved the draft of answer to Talleyrand and had inserted and worded some suggestions contained in my note with his usual felicity. The dispatches from Lord Granville[65] were read. They certainly furnished some arguments and provoked yet more some feelings against the proposed mediation. Even Casimir Perrier[66] in his conversation with our embassador seemed to reproach himself with too much complaisance towards England in the Belgian business, lamented that he did not meet in us any reciprocal accommodation about Poland, hinted I think at something more than mere mediation in favor of that gallant people, and professed greater apprehension of the warlike party in the Chambers, than he had hitherto admitted. Sebastiani had, as is usual with him, handled these topicks more offensively, talked of the necessity of assuming a high tone, reproached England with her cold and selfish policy in attending exclusively to her separate interests, and hinted at a determination not to recognize Leopold till all pretensions of the Germanick Confederacy to the sovereignty of Luxemburgh were formally abandoned.[67] Throughout this and former conversations, He, as indeed Talleyrand had done before him, almost acknowledged that their views were to enforce any mediation they could persuade us to offer conjointly, by armaments, recognition of Poles <or> war. These circumstances operated as dissuasives, if there was indeed any disposition in the Cabinet to concur in the proposed offer of mediation. Lord Goderich urged, and most present concurred in thinking, that mediation meant war and was *so intended by* the French, that there was great appearance of their not having either the will or the power of controulling their own actions on this matter, but that they were at the mercy of chambers and the publick, and that it became us to pause before we involved ourselves with a

Government so situated in a proposal to Russia which that power would inevitably reject. I avowed that the leaning of my mind had been and was perhaps still to join in the proposed mediation from a persuasion that, if we did so, we should strengthen Casimir Perrier's government and have it in our power to regulate and moderate the views of the French, and possibly to confine the efforts of the Poles themselves [to] such practicable objects as could be attained without general war. That I apprehended, if we declined, the French neither would nor could refrain from offering their mediation; that if rejected as unsupported by us, [as] it would infallibly be, a general war would ensue; and, if accepted and conducted to a fortunate conclusion, France would have acquired a great ascendancy in Europe and be not a little estranged from us by the very transaction which enlarged her authority and extended her influence. I acknowledged, however, the weighty considerations urged by others against this course of proceeding, and felt that it would be difficult to acquiesce with an ally and cooperator, who did not wish us to do so, in [case of?] any peremptory rejection of our proposal, without enforcing our proposal by some ulterior measures. Although I was far from being convinced that Russia, exhausted and mortified as I suspected her to be, would not be induced to accept, yet I was bound on such a point to defer to the opinion of those who had read the dispatches more diligently and had better means, from their intercourse with the foreign Ministers, to judge of the disposition and character of the Russian Government than myself. I therefore did not press, though I could not retract, my opinion that we should do better to concur conditionally with France in her offer of mediation; but I sincerely hoped that if we did decline we should in the manner of declining take great pains to conciliate France, to express some sympathy for the Poles and approbation of the object proposed by the mediation, and hint our readiness to concur in any steps that without embroiling Europe in war might at no great distance of time be likely to promote so desirable an end.

In all my views of this subject Mr Grant[68] and Lord Carlisle seemed to me entirely, and Lord Althorp and Lord John R[usse]ll nearly, to concur. Though Lord Althorp was more impressed with the difficulty or, as they considered it, the impossibility of offering a mediation without being prepared to follow it up by war than either Mr Grant, Lord Carlisle, or myself, he however was equally impressed with the policy of strengthening Casimir Perrier's Ministry and cultivating a closer alliance with France—a sentiment in which I think all except Lord Goderich and the Duke of Richmond would concur, but from occasional apprehensions of the instability and weakness of any Government in France in the present state of that Country.

We went through the paper paragraph by paragraph, Grey and Palmerston with great temper and good humour listening and generally acceding to the criticisms affecting either the sense or composition; and it was again very materially amended, generally in the sense that Mr Grant and I had suggested, of regretting that the moment had not arrived where we saw any prospect of promoting with effect a pacification in Poland, but implying that we should gladly seize it in conjunction in [?with] France whenever it did, and in the interval approved the object, though we questioned the choice of time, if the French endeavour to accomplish a lasting settlement of the Polish affairs. Grey, Palmerston, and myself remained in the office to complete what the Cabinet had decided, and in this last revision of the paper it was again shortened and every peremptory expression either softened or omitted.[69]

Mr Stanley asked me significantly if Lord Durham had dined with me the day before. He was curious on this point, because, he said, they had a report among them that he was likely to resign, after a difference with Lord Grey in which high words had passed on the subject of Lord Cochrane's (now Lord Dundonald's)[70] restoration to his rank. I know nothing of this, but Grey had complained to me and was evidently so harrassed at the unreasonable ill humour of Durham that he did not contemplate a separation as impossible. Durham murmurs at the insignificance of the place he holds, which he calls a mere sinecure; charges to the Cabinet, which has shewn wonderful forebearance and restraint towards him, with manifest personal estrangement; and attributes (Grey says with some little more reason) marked aversion to him in the King and Court. Grey is fully aware of (and indeed learns from sources that I could wish were less resorted to, except in cases of urgent necessity, viz intercepted correspondence) [*In the margin:* This practice is, I hope, confined to foreign correspondence, and I could wish were sparingly used even there.] the unpopularity of Durham and the vulgar notion that he (Grey) is entirely led by the intemperate judgement and wayward disposition of his son in law. I think however if the King is prejudiced against Durham it must be by the ill offices of others. His Majesty is of himself inobservant of manners and not liable to strong personal objections unless instilled into him. When that has been done, it may be true that it is not easy to remove them. He seldom allows even these (however inveterate they may be) to influence his reception of the obnoxious person; and if it be true that he barely takes notice of Durham in the Council chamber or at Court, it must be allowed to be a mark of displeasure more galling because it is with W[illia]m IV so rare.

In the House of Lords the tythe composition was in a Committee. Wynford[71] and Eldon made some objections. The latter flattered and harrassed the poor Archbishop of Canterbury who in anything like a debate is a most helpless man, canted usque ad nauseam about his devotion to the Church and his respect for the Archbishop, which with great emphasis he hypocritically protested to be greater than he felt for the individual who was addressing their Lordships; and he then proceeded to pull to pieces the Clauses, most of which had been adopted in the Irish act that Eldon had himself supported[72] and all of which had been privately communicated to him. The Bench was embarrassed but a little nettled too at such treatment. The result was the Archbishop is to move various amendments and, when reprinted with them, the bill itself is once more to go into Committee.

22 July 1831. Attended the Cabinet. Lord Durham was there, was very explicit, able and convincing, and for him tolerably dispassionate, in combatting the pretensions of Ashton on Line for representation.[73] It was resolved, however, that that and even stronger cases should not induce us willingly to alter the bill or vary the proportion we had proposed to establish between land and town representation. For the same reason it was agreed that Milton's[74] motion to grant double representation to 26 boroughs allowed by bill only one member was inadmissible. Mr Portman's[75] motion to admit tenants at will to vote for counties is also to be resisted. But all these amendments if carried in Committee to be submitted to by our House of Commons Colleagues, the Duke of Richmond shrewdly remarking that the original provisions would be replaced in the Lords and that it was no bad policy to gratify our house by leaving them something to do.

The answer to Talleyrand on proposal to offer mediation to Russia we give down to Windsor for the King's approbation and consequently not yet delivered. The intelligence from the Hague is discouraging. The King of Holland threatens hostilities and in the meanwhile maintains a vigorous paper war against our 18 articles.[76] Palmerston has a notion of inviting Plenipotentiaries from Brussels and the Hague to negotiate in London, but in present disposition of the French Government it is rather an embarrassing affair. Adair[77] is not unlikely to go to Brussels in preference to a choice suggested by Leopold of Lord Dover. The latter, if deficient neither in abilities nor zeal, has hardly experience, discretion, or reserve enough to be entrusted with a mission where so much of all those qualities may be required.

Grey would like to name his brother in law, Ponsonby,[78] to the Bishoprick of Derry and Lord Anglesey[79] recommends it, and nobody that I can find suggests a better *Irishman* for the See. But Grey hesitates to incur the odium of another family promotion[80] and Lansdowne protests to me that the appointment would be to the full as unpopular from the indifferent character of the Man as from the imputation of family partiality or *linajudia* as I think the Spaniards term it. I know nothing of the individuals but I hope that every where, and especially in the Church and in Ireland, political friends will be preferred to enemies. I was I own surprized to hear from Stanley that Lord Anglesey had had thoughts of promoting Mr Harcourt Lees!![81] to a Deanery. I have however remarked that my informant does not hide the Lord Lieutenant's mistakes under a bushel. Plunket, with admirable raillery, asked our new Irish bishop,[82] who attends this Session and means they say to vote against his Patron and Maker, what he terms a legal question, viz whether 'if his Lordship was made Bishop of Derry he could continue to vote during the Session as Bishop of Cork'.

I dined with Prince Talleyrand, Don Pedro, the Ministers of Austria, Prussia, and Bavaria, several Ladies, the Chancellor, and Lord Grey. Don Pedro highly satisfied with his reception at Windsor, not a little gratified at his daughter being treated as a Queen in France. He told Talleyrand that the captured Portugueze corvettes[83] should be restored to his daughter either now or at least whenever she was restored to her lawful crown. Talleyrand promised to carry the representation to his Court. He, Pedro, sails in an English ship of war for his daughter, Donna Maria da Gloria, from Portsmouth tomorrow and expects to return by Wednesday next. Harry Webster[84] accompanies him. He has, I am told, sent for all the Ex Portuguese Embassadors ever employed in London—Funchall,[85] Palmela,[86] Villa Real[87]—to repair to his daughter here and to form her council, and he is attempting to raise a loan from Portuguese Capitalists in England.

Talleyrand, when told that the new King Leopold's choice of a Prime Minister lay between two of the deputies lately in England and Mr Le Hon,[88] said he hoped it might be Mr Le Hon. And why? said some one with surprize. Car je ne le connais pas, replied Talleyrand. He seems tolerably well satisfied with the answer [of the cabinet to the proposal for mediation of the Russo-Polish dispute] which he interprets, nous le voulons bien mais ce n'est pas encore <temps>. He is in truth more than usually earnest in the cause of the Poles for three reasons: old resentment of 15 or 16 years standing to the Russians; connection thro' Mme de Dino[89] with Poles; and, let us hope if last not least, a sense of the justice of their cause.

23 July 1831. Lord Glenorchy called. He is pleased at the prospect of being called up to House of Lords, indifferent about a step in peerage for his father, and sincerely eager to promote reform. Went to London with Lauderdale, who affects confidence in throwing out the bill on 2d. reading but votes by proxy and returns to Scotland. Called on Lord Egremont,[90] whom I found much pallid and looking old, but, he assures me, recovering. Recoveries after 75 are I fear generally precarious and always painful.

Cabinet heard an indistinct but rather alarming account from a Dr Marshall[91] of Port Glasgow of a disease he pronounces Indian Cholera among the workers of flax, especially the females, in the neighbourhood. Lansdowne sent two men conversant with Indian Cholera down to Scotland without delay.

Grey consulted me on the propriety of communicating to Talleyrand some intelligence respecting France, namely an order to <H . . .>[92] to procure 150,000 stand [of arms] by a certain day at Paris, which he had collected from a source to which it seems to me that he resorts rather too frequently and too readily. Having however heard it, he was I thought bound to communicate it to the French, and he did so through Palmerston and Talleyrand without delay.

The King of Holland in a long paper combats as a departure from the Protocols the eighteen articles proposed by [the] five powers and accepted, though as the minimum, by the Belgians. He terms any Prince who can accept the crown on such conditions his Enemy and speaks in one passage of having recourse to arms. His object, if he means war, is obviously to bring the French into Belgium and then to negotiate with them and Prussia a partition of the country which shall leave him Antwerp and a large share of Flanders. But Weissenburgh,[93] who has just returned from the Hague and knows him well, thinks he may yet be brought by a little management to negotiate and by as much in the negotiation to terms of permanent peace.[94] In this view of the subject the Conference was disposed to invite him and the Belgians to appoint Plenipotentiaries to negotiate in London. Palmerston submitted to Cabinet the draft of a Protocol recording the principles of such a step and also of the two letters by which he prepared respectively to invite Belgium and Holland so to negotiate.

Here arose a very embarrassing difficulty. The Belgians, however reluctantly, had yet accepted the 18 articles proposed by the five powers. They could not therefore be invited to treat with Holland on any other basis but that of the said eighteen articles. But the King of Holland had as vehemently protested against them as a departure from the Protocols, and in the recent paper had represented them as constituting the new King his enemy and justifying the resumption of hostilities. The way suggested to bring them to a negotiation was by inviting one party, the Belgians, to treat on the basis of the articles, and the other, the King of Holland, with a view to an arrangement that might satisfy his interests and honor. This appeared to me an attempt to lure them into a negotiation on different grounds and on false pretences. Speaking for myself I declared I could be satisfied by a simple request to each to enter into negotiation to adjust their remaining differences [*In the margin:* or by a statement of the same basis for negotiation to both], but I could not reconcile it to my conscience to invite one upon one ground and to procure the acquiescence of the other from a persuasion in his mind that such was not the ground on which we pressed him [to] negotiate. In this view of the subject or something like it the Cabinet concurred, and I understood from Count Wessenburgh in the evening that the Conference, struck with the remark and the reproach of deception and duplicity to which they might be exposed, agreed to apply to both the parties to negotiate on the basis of the articles which the 5 powers had proposed and one party had accepted. Durham, though earnest and acute in protecting the Belgians from any departure from what had been proposed to and accepted by them, was conciliatory and reasonable. Palmerston was called out during this conversation by Bulow,[95] and great apprehension was expressed by that Minister and Talleyrand at the continuance of the [Belgian National] Congress, which they pressed us to recommend Leopold instantly to dissolve. This we refused to do. It would ill become a Government who plumed itself upon non interference with its neighbors. Moreover that assembly is prorogued, sine die, and Leopold has it in his power to call it or to act without it at his discretion and responsability. He presses for a Minister and wishes that Minister to be Lord Dover. Palmerston prefers Adair and with good reason. The latter will be offered the Mission and urged to go immediately.

While Palmerston was with Baron Bulow (who, dit on, is likely to succeed Bernstorff[96] at Berlin), Mr Stanley read to us a plan for new modelling the Yeomanry in Ireland and, while he acknowledged their bad behaviour at Newtown Barry and the general unpopularity of such Corps in the South, dwelt with much complacency on the cheapness and vaunted even the utility of them to the amount of 19,000 in Ulster.[97] Mr Grant and Sir James Graham,[98] Lord Lansdowne, and Lord Grey seemed equally impressed with the danger and impropriety of continuing such a force, and acquiesced in an observation of the Duke of Richmond that Yeomanry might be good against a foreign invasion, but in civil disturbances or war they often acted like bad soldiers and always aggravated the evil by exasperating the feelings that led to it, and that the regular army was our best dependency both for safety and for humanity whenever we came to blows. Such has always been my fixed opinion. One shrinks from all operations of the sort, but if one must undergo them one is safer and better in the hands of the regular practitioner than in those of men who use the knife from wantonness or experiment. Melbourne was not present, and though the new model of the Yeomanry was thought better than the old, no resolution was taken upon it or upon the yet more important preliminary question whether we should not discontinue and disband that force altogether.

Mr Shiel[99] dined and Mr Macaulay[100] dined and slept here. Lord Chancellor Brougham came late and slept. He ran on in his wildest strain. He accuses the Princesses (called by him and others Begums), the Queen and her family of intriguing to thwart Leopold to stimulate the King of Holland to resistance, and to subvert our Ministry. [He] suspects Wellington, Peel, and others of being in the plot and maintains that *they*, the Cabal of Women and Princes, plague the King out of his life and render him sometimes unhappy and sometimes discontented. There may be some truth, but there is great exaggeration in all this. Brougham was vehement about it and very foul mouthed against Her Majesty. I suspect he has learnt from some quarter, not improbably from Lady Sophia Sydney,[101] that he is not a favorite in that quarter. He is not less vehement about Scarlet, who has taken up the Privilege question and decries or at least implies doubts about the right of Chancery to commit for contempt. Wilde[102] seems upon a hint to have backed out of it and is gone into the country.

24 July, Sunday. Called according to request at Lord Egremont's. Found him better. He descanted on the value of the King's life, its importance towards keeping things quiet, and confusion which might ensue from the loss of it. Such solemnity is not usual with him and I wondered in what it would end. He then in substance told me, 'They are killing him, they will worry him to death in less than two years. The Queen, the Princesses, and those who surround [him] are adverse to the Ministers and their measures at home and abroad. The Queen sometimes goes to bed and cries her heart out and works upon him that way. They have found his secret and will use it; and they will succeed for I know him to have lost his energy. He surrendered it for some years to his brother. I never knew anybody of equal sense and shrewdness so subdued, and a Man so long inured to voluntary slavery cannot resist those who are determined to master him. His sons[103] once acted on this principle. But others now know it as well as they and will turn it to political as well as personal objects. The Queen's manner to his children had altered already. A difference was now made between them and Miss D'Este,[104] the daughter of a left hand and the children of none at all. The sons may have provoked this, but the daughters[105] who were and should be the chief comfort of his life cannot. Yet except when invited they cannot now as formerly approach their father or the Queen.'

To all this, which tallied rather strangely with Lord Brougham's wild invectives of the night before, I answered. The[re] might be and probably was some foundation for what had reached him, but I was confident that if there was truth it had been discoloured by exaggeration. Those I guessed to be his informants were likely to magnify such occurrences in their imaginations. I know my daughter in law[106] to be on the same footing as heretofore and quite well with the Queen. I told him however that his hint might be useful and was very seasonable at least, for I was then going to Windsor and might observe and ascertain the extent of the evil he apprehended. Yet, added I, to what practical conclusion can it lead? 'To getting rid,' said he, 'of bad entourage of Lord Howe,[107] of Lady Brownlowe,[108] and others.' He then observed, on the other hand, that Lord Munster (whose peerage had greatly exasperated the Queen) had contrary to usage three titles with his Earldom and one, Tewkesbury, which belonged to George I before his accession.

He could not help thinking that some analogy between Munster and a presumptive heir had glanced across the brain of the person, whoever it was, with whom that strange title of Tewkesbury had originated.

I saw Adair. He goes to Brussels, pleased but anxious about his Ambassadorial character. He wishes to draw Grey's attention to the precedent of Lord Pembroke[109] in 1807, but I am afraid it hardly applies; seems disposed to accept the Red Ribband he some time ago declined.

I went with Carlisle to Windsor Castle. He pointed out to me two curiously carved wooden capitals of pillars in a stable wall at Hounslow, which George Selwyn[110] or his father had assured him formed part of James II's chapel in his camp at Hounslow. I had often observed them but never knew what they were.

I am lodged on ground floor by an attention of Her Majesty's who thought the staircase might fatigue me. The Castle and the view from it is really magnificent. The busts, portraits, and pictures in Corridor extremely interesting. The Selection of Characters is rather strange. The scroll on Pitt's picture of 'Redemption of National debt' looks like a satire, and yet I am told it is a posthumous portrait and certainly it must from its appearance have been painted long after he had ceased to redeem in the year to the amount that he created debt. A strange bust of Sheridan. The door leading to King's apartment is between those of Wm. Pitt and Charles Fox. In one of the Cabinets are miniatures by Mrs Mea[111] of the beauties of George IV—Lady Galloway, Duchess of Argyle, Lady Conyngham, Duchess of St. Albans, Lady Heathcote, Mrs Duff, &c, &c, &c. It is to be hoped the originals deserved no such epithet, but the style of painting is meretricious in the extreme. All dark blue eyes and all much alike. The Plate [and][112] furniture most splendid, though the price of the latter, still un<paid>, was scandalously extravagant.

The King shewed civility, the Queen marked attention, to Durham. Had they been asked to do so? Their treatment of the other Etonian Ministers who had come on invitation was kind, hospitable, and cordial without constraint. The Queen spoke at length and more than once to Grey of the hard usage of the House of Orange and asked why we had not sustained the King of Holland better? To this Grey had a good answer and no doubt he gave it. But surely the Queen's frank avowal of her opinion forms a presumption, if not a proof, that there is no underhand cabal on that point, and no plot to mix up with it a resistance to reform and a dismissal of Ministry. If Lady Mary Fox can judge [*crossed out and torn*] it is not in her character. However I told Grey what Lord Egremont apprehended, because there may be truth enough in it to require circumspection.

It was Sunday, consequently no cards. The Princesses had much conversation but nothing escaped in my hearing to shew that strong political bias which, it is often reported, they cannot conceal. Yet Lady Mary confirmed to me the aversion or rather terror which pervades the female Royalties of reform. She denies however the exaggerated statement of the manner and consequences of their opposition to it, acquits the Queen distinctly of harrassing the King on that or indeed any other subject.

The Duke of Weimar[113] is indeed a warm partizan of the House of Orange and a wrong headed violent Man. He reproaches England and its government and perhaps the Queen herself, through his wife now resident in the Castle, whom he torments exceedingly, for their lukewarmness and, as he calls it, perfidy and injustice to King of Holland. This may incline the Queen to any policy which, by conciliating the Dutch King, would pacify her brother in law and make her Sister's life more easy. She has manifestly great affection for her. Even though the policy she would prefer should injure Leopold and chagrin the Duchess of Kent,[114] that circumstance would not I think make it less palatable to any in this Court, not perhaps excepting the King himself.

It is true that Lord Munster and his brothers and his sisters too, with the exception of Lady Mary, have imagined that the Queen's kindness to them has abated. But Mary maintains that it is pure imagination or grounded upon some trifling incident about lodging the children on the night of the ball, too slight to admit, much less to require, an explanation. She acknowledges that Munster's peerage displeased the Queen and she believes it was concealed from her. But she acquits her of tormenting and yet more strongly of the least design to torment the King on any of these domestick concerns or on any other. The torment, if any, for she doubts there being much, comes from another quarter—Lord Munster and his insatiable love of money, about which she had meant to speak to Lord Egremont herself. She is persuaded that Lord Munster is invariably putting forward unreasonable pretensions and instanced that of wishing to carry the Crown at Coronation, and then commuting his demands to money, and representing the annoyance he gives as the consequence of others' manoeuvres.

25 July 1831. The King, Queen, Lady Westmeath,[115] the Princess Augusta of Cambridge,[116] Lord Grey, Lord Wellesley,[117] Lord Carlisle, Lord Melbourne, Lord Durham, and myself with many others went to the Election speeches at Eton and were received in the Upper school room by the Provosts, fellows, and Masters. The English address in rhyme was spoken and written by the same boy, Daniel. It was well composed but very moderately delivered. Some poetry and good flow of verse with many commonplaces. The most remarkable feature was the dexterity and impartiallity with which praise was distributed to Etonians, Whig or Tory, statesmen or warriors, and the ingenious choice of avoiding all appearance of party by clapping the names of Wellington and Grey as the two living Premiers in one line. The boy, it was whispered to me, was a Tory, and such Whigs as had found their way into the verses were probably forced in against his inclination by the Masters. But a boy of Tory principles should learn, no doubt, to submit to authority.

The weather was fine, the scene was gay, and to us all the recollections a mixed emotion of pleasure and melancholy. The excessive and foolish delight of the Provost[118] at the Royal and noble visitors was diverting, and the innumerable portraits of faces known to us in our youth, some no more and some so altered, raised many reflections of a mixed nature in all of us. In Lord Wellesley the melancholy seemed to predominate, but in addition to his constitutional nervousness he has destined in his will Eton Chapel for his burial and written a latin epitaph in verse to be inscribed on his gravestone. And moreover he has within the year lost his eldest son, Richard Wellesley,[119] who was a pupil of the Provosts and gave promises at school of a more brilliant career than Accident or health ever permitted him to run.

On our return, Grey rode out with the Queen. After dinner I played at Cribbage with the King, and though we heard of the King of the French's injudicious and offensive speech,[120] I had little or no political conversation in the course of the day.

July 26, 1831. Grey and Durham returned in consequence of a notice given to Lansdowne of questions from Aberdeen[121] in the Lords. Lord Carlisle, Lord Melbourne, and myself remained. Witnessed the experiment of removing carriages and artillery by horses with no harness or traces but one rope to each, conducted and applied to such purposes by Mr Head,[122] who had seen the care with which horses so lightly accoutred could be made to draw in South America. The rapidity with which they are fixed and loosened and the simplicity of the whole manoeuvre is wonderful, and I can easily believe that the Duke of Wellington had expressed regret that such an invention for saving time in military operations had not reached him in Spain. We did not see the experiment made on rough ground, and it appears to me that the trail of the cannon when in rapid motion is so low that the point might strike a ridge and, if so, would come with a momentum to penetrate the earth and impede its progress. What was very satisfactory in the experiment was the readiness with which Horses from the Dragoons who had never been in harness nor employed in this manner performed the duty required them without fear, restiveness, or surprize.

We drove through a beautiful part of the Park. The day was magnificent. At dinner and the evening nothing remarkable. The King was, I understand, much pleased at learning that we all of us had expressed our satisfaction at the excursion.

July 27. Returned with Lord Carlisle. Saw Adair who has kindly offered to take Henry[123] to Brussels, an offer which Henry seems inclined to accept. Henry dined here. Lord Chancellor called in evening. Loud in his complaints of want of concert and management the night before in the House of Commons,[124] and with reason. Abercrombie is arrived.

July 28, 1831. Talleyrand called, drove round the grounds and took me to the House of Lords. Has accounts from Lisbon which he has communicated to Lord Grey. They shew that the French Admiral[125] did not rise in his demands on success, that he had landed no troops nor intended to do so, and that consequently the phrase *pronounced* by the King of the French, 'Le pavillon Tricolor flotte *sur* les murs de Lisbonne', was incorrect and could not have been written. Talleyrand said slyly that Louis Philippe had substituted *sur* for *sous dans son enthousiasme.* Certain it is that if he had constructed a speech for the purpose he could not have furnished better topicks for the opposition here nor exposed himself more, when they should be repelled by a statement of fact in our Parliament, to the attacks of those opposed to His Government in France. Talleyrand laments his propensity to court false popularity and whispers to me that in the ensuing contest for a President, which Casimir Perrier (imprudently according to Talleyrand and Lord Granville) is determined to make a trial of strength, the King's wishes and perhaps intrigues are for *Lafitte.*[126] Talleyrand recommends them to yield with a good grace and cites Sutton's[127] election here as an example or, one should say, a *precedent* in point.

Prussia's or, as far as I know, Bernstorff's phrase to Flahault[128] on Polish war, viz that they professed *inactivity not neutrality* and were avowed interested for the Russians, produces great sensation in the Publick. In the meanwhile the Poles are undismayed, speak with hopes of attacking a part of Russian force when divided by Vistula, and with confidence even if defeated in the field of holding out Warsaw till Christmas.

The Russian government has betrayed, in its conduct about the Cholera, ignorance, insensibility, cruelty, and weakness which, if it were a *democratick* Monarchy, would be ascribed to its institutions, but which none of our fashionable brawlers think of connecting with autocracy. The Russian people ignorantly suppose that the Physicians and foreigners are the cause of the complaint and intentionally infect the natives therewith. They break into hospitals, they murder the physicians, they throw the sick and dying in the Neva, they assail and massacre strangers for having precautionary medicines about them; and the Emperor Nicholas, who comes to the Capital to appease them, and who cannot listen and negotiate with the Poles or Lithuanians on their just rights or great political grievances, truckles to the ignorance and fury of a rabble, surrenders the necessary securities for health to their prejudices and leaves outrage and murder unpunished.

In House of Lords tiresome discussions in Committee on Clauses of Bishop of London's Church bill[129] and Lord Wharncliffe's truck bill.[130] On the former there had been a division before I arrived in which Kenyon,[131] Beresford,[132] Falmouth,[133] and other Ultra tories constituted a small minority of 4 or 5, the Bishops and their supporters a majority, and Grey with Ministerials, Wellington with *reasonable* opposition men (for I do not suppose that is quite a contradiction in terms), were neutral. Londonderry, who neither in opposition nor in office ever deserves that epithet, addressed a string of questions mixed with much loose and violent declamation to Grey, respecting the demolition of the fortresses, the French King's speech, the want of communication with and the general ill treatment of the King of Holland. Grey said that there was only one question which he could answer, viz whether he meant to bring down more papers than the Protocol on the subject,[134] to which he begged leave to say he had no further commands from H M. Londonderry with great violence inveighed against the assumed dignity and real inefficiency of so laconick an answer and gave notice of moving for papers next week. Lord Melbourne dined and slept at Holland House.

July 29, 1831. Lord Hastings[135] on marriage gives up the *Bedchamber,* an odd occasion some wags might say for such a surrender. I hope it is no change of opinion about Reform. The King's letter implies it is not and implies also, Grey thinks, that he has no particular person to recommend. In which case he consults me on the propriety of attempting to recover Lord Hereford.[136]

Lord Melbourne and his brother,[137] Genl. Alaba,[138] Arguellas,[139] and Don Felipe Bauza,[140] Adair, and others at dinner.

I missed the House of Lords, where Bishop Blomfield spoke so earnestly in favor of thorough enquiry and fearless reform in ecclesiastical matters, that the

Archbishop, after writhing some time, exclaimed loud enough for his brother of London to hear, 'These things should not be said without consultation'.

My son, Henry, goes with Adair. Labouchere[141] has declined on the ground of being too much connected with Dutchmen. Adair has proposed to Lord Wm. Russell,[142] now at Paris, to join him.

July 30 1831. Passed the morning with my Spanish visitors and in conversation on old Spanish stories. The state of Royal family in that country likely, even exclusive of political opinions, to lead to a Civil war on death of the King. The Salick law not constitutionally established by Philip V. Doubts upon it and a project to declare against it by the Committee of Cortes [were] entertained in 1791 and only defeated or rather postponed by the apprehensions awakened in the minds of Florida Blanca[143] and Campomanes[144] on breaking out of French revolution and a memorial of grievances presented by one of the Cortes deputies. The King has now abolished the Salick law with a view of securing the succession to his daughter and with the effect of casting a suspicion on his brothers designs? But would Charles [Don Carlos] and his Ultra party submit if the King were to die? There are many nice points on which the actual state of law may be argued, and there are strong interests within the palace as well as passions without for interpreting it both ways. Consequently much prospect of civil war.[145]

I was assured Duke of Wellington not only disapproved of Lord Londonderry's language, but however nettled at Lewis Philip's speech, acknowledged that our Protocol and the proceedings upon the fortresses were almost unavoidable, censuring nothing but the communication of it before a general recognition of the Belgian Government. If this be true, it is handsome and even magnanimous in him to sanction a sacrifice of a system of his own contriving at the shrine of reason, policy, and convenience.

31 July. Cabinet chiefly on questions of £10 qualification as arising from rates, taxes, or rents in bill.[146] Much tiresome discussion and no decision. Lord Grey was obliged to leave us and to attend the King and then sent us word that he could not return. A dispatch from Lord Granville read in which he relates a conversation with Sebastiani, who offers either to concur with England in restoring Don Pedro or Donna Maria, to effect that object alone without the cooperation but with the consent of England, or to withdraw their fleet and troops and leave matters as they were before the Expedition—in short, to regulate their conduct by English advice and in concert with us. Moreover, Pedro, to whom some communication was made, frankly and handsomely avowed that he wished to connect himself and his daughter's interests as much as he could with England and to take no step but in concert with that court. Some loose conversation not amounting to discussion ensued. I was sorry to perceive that one or two of my Colleagues were more disposed to start nice questions on the legality of French prizes &c, &c, than to seize the fair offer of concert made by them and turn it to the general advantage of Europe and of France, England, and Portugal in particular.

The Queen has chosen all her attendants, Male and female, at Coronation, excepting Lord Cawdor,[147] among our Enemies. This is bad as an indication and worse still in its effect. I wrote to Lord Hereford to offer him, as authorized by Grey, the Bedchamber. Heard many reasons for appointing an Englishman to

Derry from Plunket, who acknowledges Ponsonby to be the only political friend on the bench, but who on various private and publick grounds hopes Lord Grey will not promote him to Derry.

There are many apprehensions that Casimir Perrier's Ministry will fall and Lafitte be chosen President and afterwards, with Soult,[148] form a less pacifick administration; and there are moreover several complaints of the King Philip, who from levity, love of false popularity, weakness, or what not, indirectly weakens his ostensible Ministry and thereby lowers his own character and impairs his authority both at home and abroad.

1 August 1831. The opening of London bridge, which I declined attending from fear of fatigue, and the anniversary of the victory of Aboukir.

A Cabinet at 1/2 past ten p.m. All loud in praise of the exhibition of the day, the management both of the procession by water and of the feast, the concourse and joy of the people, and the warm and gratifying reception of the King. Some, and they unaffected, persons had been quite overcome with the genuine and enthusiastick expression of delight in such multitudes. The Duke of Wellington had perhaps prudently declined the invitation, but somewhat uncourteously gave as his reason that he was unwilling to risk exciting feelings in the people which it was desirable should not be expressed before His Majesty. Peel was in his barge with his name in large letters. He was much hissed but not otherwise ill treated. It is said that some of the Princesses dreaded or affected to dread disturbance, and I have since heard that the Duchess of Gloucester[149] has been converted to Reform by the touching proofs she witnessed of the affection of the people to her brother.

After much conversation on these subjects, we went to business and discussed many nice and uninteresting points relating to the qualifications of voters in the bill at great detail. Letters from Granville report Sebastiani's strange language about recognition of Leopold, which France will not concur in till the fortresses to be demolished are settled. Granville urged the inconsistency and unreasonableness of such conduct and the distressing situation in which it placed the new King. It is vexatious and unjustifiable, but it is as well to take the chance of Sebastiani cooling a little before we express as warmly as we feel our sense of such shuffling conduct. I was not sorry therefore that the subject was dropped. It seems Perrier did not know any thing of the offensive farce got up between Semonville and the Duke of Orleans about the Austrian standards,[150] and he has disavowed and in some senses reprimanded them. The Austrian Minister wisely takes no notice of it.

Greece is resumed and a conference was held yesterday or today on 3 propositions—1 an application for advance of money; 2d. a Sovereign from some reigning family in Europe; and 3dly. a change of the limits.[151] To the first no answer was given or proposed but the consideration postponed; on the 2d. Lord Palmerston suggested Fredk. Prince of Orange, but it is still apprehended that France may object; and on the 3d. it was agreed to instruct the Ambassadors at Constantinople to negotiate for a recurrence to the line of [the gulfs of] Arta and Volo on the ground of the impracticability and incorrectness of that last designated and of some other special arguments and proposals which may render it palatable to the Turks. Paul of Wurtemburg[152] is canvassing for the Sovereignty, acknowledges (as Talleyrand tells me) his own bad character, but urges as a strong recommendation his having children to whom, he with naiveté assures us, no such objection can apply *as he has had nothing to do with their education!* Talleyrand, whom together with Falck[153] I found on my return from Cabinet at Holland House, had not received any dispatches or instructions from Sebastiani and was or affected to be surprized and even angry at his threatened delay in recognizing Leopold. He seemed dissatisfied with his King's speech but he apologized and accounted for rather than justified it. And he is still less satisfied with the language of the King, who had intended to name *Bresson*[154] to Brussels in preference to Genl. *Belliard.*[155] A strange selection certainly since the former had been the instrument thro' which the election of Nemours[156] had been managed.

2d. August Tuesday. The Queen as well as King went down in state to the House of Lords to thank Parliament on passing an act to make provision for Her Majesty on the decease of the King.[157] There had been no occasion of the sort for 70 years. It is an indelicate if not distressing ceremony for a Lady publickly and in the presence of her husband to express her sense of the advantage of a provision which she cannot enjoy but by his death. Her Armed Chair was placed obliquely towards the House between the throne and the Bishops bench, part of which, being railed off for the accommodation of the Diplomatick Corps, was occupied by my old friend Talleyrand, *L'Eveque d'Autun!* The front seats were filled with Peers in the robes, and Ladies in full dress and feathers sat behind. It was remarked that Lords Londonderry and Salisbury[158] came unrobed and are said to plume themselves upon doing so as a practical satire on what they were pleased to imagine to be a neglect or an offence, the omission of a summons. The Queen sat near a quarter of an hour before the King arrived, and he and his attendants passing sideways by her to the throne had an awkward effect. She went through the ceremony and the curtseys with great dignity and propriety, without affectation. The Streets, though it rained, were full, and the shouts with which their Majesties were greeted as cordial as the day before. His popularity when he appears in publick has a sensible effect even on the enemies of Grey's Government and on that part of his family most adverse to reform. Though he professes, and I believe feels, much contempt for mere popular applause, which by a strange phrase of his fathers he often denominates *a mere pack of cards,* it is impossible he should not be gratified with such a heartfelt acception as the people always give him, and the refutation it affords of the rumours of a republican and revolutionary spirit which silly old women and mischievous anonymous letters are always conveying to Royalty is reasonably and justly satisfactory. Little George of Cambridge[159] had been so prepossessed by stories of the hostility of the people to his family that the moment he saw such multitudes of people he clung to Lord Albemarle[160] for protection and could hardly be persuaded that the shouts were proofs of affection, not yells of excoriation against the King and his family. The Duke of Devonshire,[161] embarking by mistake in the barge of the Duke of Cumberland,[162] was told by H R H that he had better not come there, for all *in the boat* (where by the bye was Lord Howe) *were against him.* He replied, 'I do not much mind that Sir, for if all in the boat are against, all out of it' (pointing to the immense multitude around them) 'are for me'.

Tired with the ceremony in Lords I returned home.

3 August Wednesday. Attended Levee. Transacted some Duchy business with King, who was more tired with the ceremony in Lords, owing to the weight of the Crown and heat of the weather, than with the fête of the day before. Don Pedro was at Court, having, in compliance with his promise and in spite of the earnest entreaties of the French, returned with his Empress and daughter from Cherburg to Portsmouth. The French offered him the ships they had taken. He expressed his determination to be guided in his transactions with other powers by the advice and wishes of England and throughout marked his predilection for English rather than any other foreign connection. Harry Webster remarks with truth, but perhaps with more asperity than is prudent or justified, that our indifference to Pedro forms a strong contrast to the cordiality of the French Govt. Even the Royal carriages, he says, are now withdrawn, and he and his Empress are left to lodge in a tavern and fumble about in a Glass Coach.

Dined with Cabinet at Lansdown House. No House of Commons members present. Went through the draft of bill respecting Licenses to sell beer: A dull business but many, especially the Duke of Richmond, take great interest in such matters, and it is lucky they do, for inattention and ignorance often lead to pernicious and cruel legislation where the lower orders are concerned.[163] We had retired to tea when a box from Palmerston arrived containing intelligence from Sir Ch Bagot[164] that alarmed and astonished us—namely that orders had been issued, six hours after Zuylen[165] had left the Hague with full powers to negotiate according to our invitation a definitive treaty of peace, to the Dutch army to advance. This was more strange, as Zuylen had at the Levee conversed with Palmerston for half an hour and delivered to him the sealed answer to the Conference without mentioning the circumstance. We decided on sending for Codrington's[166] fleet (now supposed to be cruizing off the Scilly islands) to the downs and, at the very judicious suggestion of Brougham, to annex to a note to Zuylen apprizing him of the intelligence of the Hague, the intimation of our orders, in consequence thereof, to our Admiral to bring his fleet to the Downs. The King of the Netherlands speaks very cooly of this outrageous breach of the armistice as une affaire domestique et nullement Europeenne. The most singular circumstance is that although the King of Netherlands answer to our invitation to treat, which was brought over by Zuylen and is not yet opened, was communicated in form or substance to the Ministers of the 5 powers at the Hague, none *but the French Chargé d'Affaires, La Rochefoucault,* understood it as a notice of immediate war. Did he so interpret it from comments made to him by the Dutch and withheld from the others? or had he any previous intimation or understanding with the King of the Netherlands respecting his views? It is clear Bagot suspects something of the sort, and some among us, always prone to suspect the French, connect it plausibly enough with the sudden objection to recognize Leopold expressed by Sebastiani and with a strange project, which Talleyrand threw out as *une horreur et impossible,* of driving the King of the Netherlands to war; making that war a pretext for marching foreign troops and introducing foreign armaments into the territories and ports of Belgium; and then dividing the Country among the powers in the way most convenient for the permanent tranquillity of Europe. Time only can solve the enigma.

4th. August. Cabinet at one. Zuylen's note apologizes in a shuffling way for his imperfect communication to Lord Palmerston, carefully avoids saying whether he knew of the approaching hostilities or not when he left the Hague, idly represents Leopold's oath, conduct, and speeches to Luxemburgh and Limburgh deputies as a declaration of war, and pretends to be at a loss to discover how the order to the English Admiral can have any relation (connexité) with the Military movements of his Govt. against Leopold. We agreed that that order should be explained to the Conference as merely resorted to for the purpose of placing the fleet in readiness to carry into effect any thing that the Conference might wish them to execute, not as implying any determination of the English Government to interfere or act separately.

Letters from Lord Granville read informing us of Casimir Perrier's resignation.[167] Sebastiani, Barthe,[168] Louis,[169] and one other had followed his example, but nothing was known of their Succcessors, the King still urging Casimir Perrier to remain and openly declaring that his endeavour was to preserve or form a moderate and pacifick Ministry. His embarrassment must be great for no Party can command a majority in the assemblies.

Lord Hereford refuses the Bedchamber but is manifestly pleased at the offer. In the Lords, Eldon confirms Lord Chancellor's law on the affidavits and the latter withdraws his declaratory bill as unnecessary.[170] Some conversation on the bill prohibiting the growth of tobacco in Ireland.[171] Lord Londonderry asks an ignorant question about reception of Donna Maria, which is answered by the fact that Royal personages are received as such without any acknowledgement or denial of their political character; and Lord Londonderry uses some hard words and takes great merit to himself, as is his fashion, for eliciting discoveries, which Lord Grey justly termed Maresnests, from Ministers.

5 August Friday. Lord Grey wished me to answer Lord Aberdeen, who moved for papers relating to supposed outrages on British flag in the Azores, and prefaced his motion by an offensive and factious speech accusing us of truckling to France, secretly conniving at warfare against Don Miguel in violation of Law of nations equity and honour, and touching, with great bitterness and sarcasm but with more than his usual talent (which is not great), on every point likely to exasparate the French and raise prejudice and jealousies of their designs in the Country. I was so little Master of the details of the cases to which the Motion referred, and was moreover so very, so childishly, nervous and uncomfortable at the dread of not being able to speak, that I very shabbily shrunk from my duty and, notwithstanding Grey's earnest request and his apparent longueur, begged him to let me off, which he did most good humouredly. I should not have forgiven myself for giving way to this infirmity if it had not been retrieved by Grey's delivering an admirable speech which destroyed all the effect of Aberdeen's insinuations and declamation and explained with perfect satisfaction to the house the nature of the cases, in themselves unimportant, few and exaggerated, which were the groundwork of the motion. The Duke of Wellington <hand>somely but very inefficiently supported his friend, his brother Wellesley leaving the house 'ashamed,' as he said, 'to hear Arthur talk such nonsense'. Grey still wishes me to speak and I hurried through a confused, indistinct, and unmethodical speech in which, however, I hit a point or two, and was gratified at the warm cheers I received on resuming, tho' with such disadvantage, my habits of speaking, now disused for more than a year. I had the still greater gratification to learn indirectly that Plunkett spoke highly of parts of my speech, and bad as it was it will enable me ere long to speak a better and possibly a good one. Slept at the pay Office. Talleyrand called in the evening. He had been ten days without news from Paris and *seemed somewhat sore at the neglect.*

6th. August 1831, Saturday. News arrived of French orders to march 50,000 men into Belgium at the request of King Leopold in an autograph letter to King of the French and a note delivered by Le Hon to Sebastiani. Ralph Abercrombie,[172] just returned from Brussels, dined with me and, having heard on Wednesday morning assurances from Leopold that he dreaded more than any thing too prompt assistance from France, was confident that neither the autograph letter, nor any communication authorized by him could contain so explicit a demand of succour as the French pretended. [*In the margin:* In this Ralph Ab[ercromb]ie turned out to be quite wrong—and his confidence convinced me that he had imbibed some of his principal's, Lord Ponsonby's,[173] hasty prejudices.] Alarmed at this suspicion, I proceeded to the Cabinet at which neither Grey, Melbourne, nor John Russell were present, at 11 p m.

We proceeded to read the dispatches from Lord Granville and several private letters from Leopold and persons about him, and after much comparison of dates and discussion on phrases, it appeared clear that an Autograph letter and also an official note from his Minister, Le Hon, had been received in Paris, which the French interpreted or chose to interpret into a distinct and earnest demand of immediate succour; that they had sent it without loss of time; and they had communicated not the letter, but the substance of it, together with their prompt acceptance of the invitation to the four foreign Embassadors at Paris, together with assurances that there was no intention to garrison or to retain the fortresses or to occupy any part of Belgium, whenever the King of Holland had been driven or retired within the ancient limits of that Country. An assurance to that effect was *promised* the next day and, in the publick declaration or announcement as well as in the form and language of the whole proceeding, nothing was omitted which, consistently with the measure adopted, could be devized to mark that the separate step was taken in furtherance of the views of the conference. On the other hand it did not appear that Leopold in any publick or private application to us had communicated the substance, much less the terms, of his application to France. Goderich, who two days before suspected an understanding between Holland and France, now seemed to suspect one between Leopold and that country or to harbour the notion that the march of the French troops was the indication of a premeditated design to dupe the conference and commit a flagrant aggression on the Low Countries. Duke of Richmond seemed to partake in these suspicions but drew rather a different and strange conclusion therefrom both on this and other occasions, namely, that we should remonstrate and protest against the conduct of France, break up the conferences and interfere neither for Leopold nor the Dutchman, but leave them to fight out their battles themselves. [*Half a page and approximately one quarter of the next page are torn out.*]

Lord Palmerston then produced the draft of a Protocol which had been agreed upon at the Conference and on which he requested our opinion. The sketch had been his own and after sundry alterations had been put into French by Mastutevitch,[174] who is considered as the readiest *redacteur.* Palmerston told us, to the great delight and relief of the Chancellor, Lord Lansdown, and myself, that when he was going into the conference the Austrians and Prussians took him aside and said, 'Now England let us know if you mean war or peace, for if you mean the latter you must not remonstrate or insist on anything like retractation or retracing their steps from France'. To this question Palmerston answered Peace, and they replied, 'we rejoice because we think by timely acquiescence and friendly explanation we may still keep the movements of the French army under the controul of the conference and on the faith of positive engagements secure from permanent occupation the dominions of King Leopold'. We made several verbal and some substantial amendments in the paper, which was very pacifick and conciliatory to France, but at the same time distinctly recorded her assurances and engagements to march back her troops to the department du Nord when the Dutch should have been driven back to their frontiers. This paper was to be shewn to Lord Grey and, with his approbation or amendments, adopted the next day at the Conference.[175] Lord Chancellor returned with me to Holland House.

August 7th. Sunday. Went to Cabinet with Lord Chancellor. The Protocol, somewhat altered by Grey, had been signed by the Conference. The promised note from Sebastiani is arrived. It is observable that the assurance of withdrawing the troops is less distinct and dogged with an additional condition, viz the settlement of the affairs or the signature of a definitive treaty for Belgium. Talleyrand tells *me* that his instructions were yet more vague but that he took upon himself to give the assurance in the same terms they had been given at Paris, for he did not approve of so shuffling a way of conducting business which, if a trick, was useless and, if not a trick, had sufficient appearance of it to create jealousy and suspicion. We went thro' several points connected with Reform bill, had tiresome discussions upon them, and came to determinations which our Colleagues in the House of Commons were upon reconsideration induced to vary and abandon. There is nothing material in this but it is a sad loss of time.

On Irish affairs we had a more important deliberation which has perhaps been too long postponed. The Irish members shew strong symptoms of discontent and hint, if they do not actually threaten, opposition on every point except the reform bill to which they are pledged. Their grievances are not very distinct, but the measures for Ireland, with the exception of the pecuniary relief, have been perhaps somewhat neglected. Mr Stanley submitted the plan of discontinuing the grant to Kildare Street Society and annexing new conditions to all the grants for education, namely such as imposing no particular religious instructions, but would leave one day in the week set apart for that object to be regulated entirely by the will of the parents. A bill for the alteration of the Subletting Act was agreed to and is to be presented forthwith. The Vestry bill and Church sess, as it is called, is not I fear in readiness.[176] On the Yeomanry we came to no positive resolution. The numbers in the north are very considerable. They cannot it is said be disbanded without breeding great discontent among the Protestants, and materially weakening the strength of government; nor can they with safety be replaced by any other local corps. In the south their numbers are very insignificant but their existence always odious and recently peculiarly offensive to the people.

I eat my 4 o'clock dinner at Brookes's and Lord Duncannon[177] and Baron Abercrombie were with me and conversed much on these Irish matters, assuring me that there was a general disappointment among our Irish friends at the cold and dilatory proceedings of our Govt. in many Irish affairs, at the delay of these measures, at the employment of the Yeomanry, impunity of Newtown Barry Magistrates and Yeomanry, and general tone, temper, and spirit evinced in many recent appointments to the Irish Government. It was in vain I recapitulated the many things that had been done, the yet greater number in contemplation, the multiplicity of important businesses pressing on Government, and the unreasonableness and injustice of witholding confidence from persons who for so many years had proved themselves the friends of liberal policy and impartial Govt. in Ireland. I was told we were on the brink of a precipice, that Irish Members were preparing for concert and opposition, that they would then infallibly fall into O'Connell's[178] wake, and that under his banner dissolution of Union and separation would shortly be their object.

Monday 8th. Lord Grey was sent for to Windsor to converse with the King on foreign, especially Dutch, affairs, and in his absence there was no business in Lords.

Tuesday 9 August. Lord Londonderry made as bitter a speech in moving for information for Belgium as he could devize, and was supported by Lord Aberdeen, Duke of Wellington, and Lord Carnarvon. Grey, who had answered fully and prudently, was anxious that the debate should not close and, even after the Chancellor had answered Wellington and severely chastized Lord Londonderry, pressed Lord Goderich to speak; but he, somewhat depressed at the events in Belgium, after hesitation declined; and I, perceiving Lord Grey chagrined at the want of support, tho' I had not intended to speak till Aberdeen's speech was nearly concluded, answered him and Lord Carnarvon by a sharp attack on the motives and tendency of the proceedings rather than by any argument on the merits of the case, which they knew and acknowledged we could, consistently with duty or usage, fully explain to the House. I recovered some fluency and self possession in this speech and was gratified by the warm and cordial manner in which it was received by my friends in the house, though I was tempted and I think justified to comment with some personality and asperity on one old friend, for whom I feel much regard, Lord Carnarvon, and had the mortification to find that he was more hurt than angry at my insinuation that his opposition to us was chiefly occasioned by the omission of his name in the appointment of offices—an omission, I must acknowledge, that was wrong in itself and which I much lamented at the time, but which he has allowed himself to resent in a manner little creditable to his judgement or character, by engaging in systematick opposition to our Ministers, even on subjects such as Portugal in which he must agree with us, and by indulging in virulent invective against the principles as well as measures of the administration. He is too formidable in sarcasm and invective to be allowed an undisputed monopoly of those articles and, some around me having furnished me with a tart epigram against him, I pointed the weapon with as much or more success than he or perhaps I expected. Our eager partizans enjoyed his smarting under it and cheared me in a way that irritated and hurt him exceedingly. I shall be sincerely sorry if the wound cannot be healed and could wish it had not occurred, though I cannot reproach myself with being the aggressor and still less with being unjust.

I saw Talleyrand in the evening but was too much tired to execute my intentions of filling up this book, and during

the 9th., 10th., 11th., and 12th., days of August the diary was not exactly kept, and the variety of events both domestick and foreign are probably not recorded in these pages in the succession in which they were conveyed to my mind.

Leopold privately informs Durham that he had not kept a copy of his Autograph letter to the King of the French. But Talleyrand, who has a copy of it, assures me that it is distinct, earnest, and even abject. From Brussels we are told by his Minister that he wrote it without consultation from Liege, and that he (the Minister) dispatched a messenger to stop the French on their march, though subsequent information made it clear that, in the treachery and defeat of General Daine,[179] further pressing instances were dispatched to the French General urging him to advance. In the mean while we were apprized from Holland, *first* that orders had been sent to the Prince [of Orange] to retire whenever he heard that the French had passed the Belgian frontiers, and secondly that, on learning the determination of the Conference, more positive orders for an immediate retreat had been issued. On this Grey was disposed to order our fleet back to Spithead, but on the suggestion of Lord Palmerston it was thought more prudent to wait till the retreat was actually commenced as well as commanded.

The Irish Members, in an interview with Lord Grey and yet more by their conduct in Commons, have shewn their discontent. It arises I think mainly from the employment of the Yeomanry and partly from the alledged reason that many projected measures of relief have been delayed.[180] But there are as usual many personal disappointments also and some heart burnings at the reported appointment of the Sons of the Knight of Kerry[181] (which after all has not occurred) to a place on the commission for distributing relief. Miserable motives for action, and enough to disgust publick men with affairs, if such paltry errors and suspicions as these are to alter the decisions of Parliament, endanger the existence of a Ministry, and even threaten the disturbance of an Empire. For these men, who affect to resent the neglect of their country and are swayed by a dread of seeing a Gentleman whose politick they disapprove employed in a subordinate place, threaten opposition in Parliament and must, if they pursue the cause they menace, either reestablish Orange authority in Ireland, or join Mr OConnel in an endeavour to separate the two countries. It is lamentable to think that even Sir John Newport and Lord Duncannon divided against Government[182] and in some sort sanctioned the proceedings of this Junto. There are no doubt faults on both sides. Some evil influence there must be at the Castle which defeats or at least retards too frequently the good intentions of Lord Anglesey, and something there may be in the complaints of Mr Stanley's manner and his want of concert and consultation with leading members of that part of the country. Lord Grey returned with me from House of Lords where Lord Londonderry postponed, sine die, a motion for the report of the Dublin Election Committee, in which he hoped to found a charge against Lord Anglesey and Lord Plunkett, and the latter urged the postponement of a bill of Lord Wynford. Lord Grey and Mr Poinset[183] of A[meri]ca, Lord Lansdowne, Lord and Lady Lyndhurst[184] at dinner.

13 August, Saturday. Fox Club at Greenwich. Lord Althorp somewhat annoyed at the attacks of the Times newspaper,[185] but better pleased at the attendance of our friends and progress of bill than I expected. Lord Tavistock,[186] with whom I went and returned, disposed to lament tho' not to oppose the changes in County Elections,[187] and to approve though not to support Lord Milton's crotchets of either giving *all* leaseholders or *none* votes for the Counties. The meeting at the Club satisfactory and I believe in good humour. Melancholy to find that among 25 or 30, there were only 7 members of the old original Whig Club.[188]

14th. August. Cabinet at 4. News from Belgium of Dutch advance and successes and of the ultimate determination of Prince of Orange, at the suggestion, instances, and threats of English Minister and Frenchmen, to withdraw his army and resist the temptation of taking Leopold in Louvain. This under the circumstances must have been an act of self denial. General Belliard informed him that if he fired a cannon, it would be war with the 5 powers, and *guerre a toute outrance.* He, Prince of Orange, either knew or affected to know nothing on the 12th. of the conditional orders to retreat, sent from the Hague on the 9th. He assured Lord W Russel the first he heard of it was the letter communicated to him, by Lord William, of Sir Charles Bagot to Sir R Adair, where he distinctly announces the orders of the Dutch Government to retire. However the Prince of Orange conducted himself in manners like a Gentleman and in substance like a good subject and son and a man of humanity. When once satisfied that the orders of his Government were to retire before a French, though not a Belgian, force, and that the French as well as the English Minister in the name of the 5 powers exacted it, he desisted from firing and promised to retreat. Not so the Duke of Weimar who was brutal and rude in manner, and was with difficulty prevailed upon to obey the orders of his Commander and not to wreak his vengeance on the unoffending inhabitants of Louvain by bombarding and assaulting that town. He said, *J'ai honte de mon beau frere Le Roi d'Angleterre,* under whose roof his wife and children have been living for this month.

We then discussed in Cabinet the knotty point of giving proprietors in towns (who had no votes for the borough) votes for the County in the character of freeholders, copyholders, and leaseholders on the same qualification as would, if their property did not lay within the borough, entitle them by the bill to vote for the county. To this Lansdown, Palmerston, and Richmond, who was absent, had strong objections founded on the apprehension of town votes overwhelming the land. After much tedious discussion, a middle course recommended by Althorp was adopted, viz to give or rather *leave freeholders* so situated a right to vote, but not to extend that right of voting for the County to Copyholders or leaseholders for land or possessions in a town. And it was further agreed that he should communicate this alteration to a meeting of friends, inasmuch as the reason for so altering our former determination was a persuasion that we should hardly be able to carry a provision so injurious to the rights of persons connected with town population.

Talleyrand called in the evening and I learnt with pleasure that the French Government adhered to the Protocol [of 6 August]. Saw Henry Webster and heard Pedro, having negotiated a loan, was going away better satisfied.

Monday 15th. August. Went with Lord John to Cabinet at one. Learnt on the way from Mr Denison[189] that the Meeting had gone off well. The Cabinet was summoned by Mr Grant, who deprecated in an elaborate paper all countenance given to the Irish Yeomanry, argued that Lord Anglesey's plan of partially disarming and regimenting them implied governing permanently by their means and would be equally repudiated by Orangemen and Catholicks, and ended, after eloquently urging the discontent that course had and would continue to create, by rather a strange conclusion *to do nothing at all,* but to allow the Yeomanry silently to expire. I read a very distressing letter from Anglesey full of alarms at the state of Ireland and not without complaint at the long postponement of this and other measures recommended by him.[190] It was acknowledged that nearly all our Irish friends would oppose any bill which sanctioned or confirmed the Yeomanry system, but some doubt was expressed whether, if properly explained, the proposed measure would or could be so considered. It was at length resolved that Mr Stanley should consult the most rational and leading Irishmen and, if asked in the house, should avow that he had in readiness a measure which he trusted would remove the crying evils produced by this corps, and yet preserve some of the advantages which were supposed to be derived from its existence.

The matter is serious, both as it affects the stability of our Government and the welfare of the Empire. Lord Goderich, both on this and the French occupation of Belgium, talked high language and recommended firmness, and betrayed I think more soreness and irritation at the necessity of managing various interests and consulting our real friends and supporters at home or abroad, than is usual for so good humoured a man to feel or to avow. When the word 'free agent' was accidently used, he exclaimed, 'Free agent! there is no such thing now any where, for ought I see there is no such person in England or elsewhere, free agent indeed'. He shook and rattled the fetters which the opinions and connections, on whom both our Ministry and the safety of the country depend, <impose>, but surely to no purpose.

I had some conversation with Palmerston on foreign affairs. He suspects French of a deep laid design of acquiring territory in Brabant and Flanders and imagines that design is the real clue to their very devious course in some part of the negotiations.[191] That they would like it, none can doubt; that Prussia would assist in a dismemberment of Belgium, if England would consent, is very probable; and that even Holland would prefer it to the present arrangement is far from impossible. But the French would not (if bent on such a project now) have entangled themselves with so solemn a declaration as is contained in the Protocol [of 6 August], to retire to the Department of the North after the Dutch had been driven back to their frontiers; because before that Protocol was ratified, their army was in Belgium and at Brussels, and the promise, if intended to be broken, was *en pure perte*, of no use to the attainment of their purpose, and not unlikely to expose them to reproaches in the Chambers and in the newspapers. Neither of those powers they are disposed, without efficient reason, to provoke. That they should deceive for the purpose of attaining an end is not perhaps improbable; but that when they had in a manner secured their end, they should gratuitously make a promise with an intention of violating it, I cannot so easily believe, and the fanfaronnades either of Sebastiani or the King can be easily explained without resorting to treachery as the solution.

[*In the margin:* Lord Grey left the Cabinet to meet the Archbishop, the Bishop of London, and the Primate[192] on a suggestion he had made of curtailing the revenue of Bishoprick of Derry and appropriating part of it to Queen's Anne [*sic*] bounty or to some ecclesiastical object. The Bishop of London, who had, he thought, encouraged him in such a project, and distinctly said that the best and safest method of reforming the Church was in particular instances and on the occurrence of vacancies, now retracted and declared he had been quite misunderstood. All three Prelates maintained the danger of such a step and would not acquiesce in Grey's view that a more reasonable distribution of the revenues of the Church would contribute to its safety. London, he remarked, was a 'slippery chap', a rash one. I believe he is.]

Pedro and the Queen Donna Maria of Portugal went down to Windsor, were received with due honors and much cordiality, and have returned to night to set off for France tomorrow, apparently in better humour with the King, Court, and Country than they were a few days ago. At the same time the contrast of their reception here and in France must strike them in a way far from advantageous to this Country. It is perhaps unavoidable but, should his projects in Portugal ultimately succeed as they ought, it may be unlucky. He leaves most flattering personal compliments to Grey, Palmerston, and myself. I missed the House of Lords this day.

16 August, Tuesday. Wrote to Anglesey and Granville. Went to house of Lords, read on the woolsacks the dispatches contained in two Cabinet boxes from Paris. Great disposition in Sebastiani to bluster and shuffle about Belgium. Casimir Perrier more reasonable and seemingly disposed to adhere to his solemn promises, though anxious to hurry the conclusion of a definitive treaty, with a view, no doubt, of representing it as the price of their retreat from Belgium. Granville combated what argument there was in the conversation of either, in palliation of the postponement of their retreat, very successfully. While I was reading this Lord Londonderry and Lord Orford[193] were harrassing Lord Grey with questions on the certainty and time of the French retreat, declaiming on the danger of their advance in Belgium, and <founding> their demands of explanation on the speeches and newspapers of France. The Duke of Wellington very handsomely and judiciously stated that it must be by documents, by notes, protocols, and treaties, and by actions that Ministers must regulate their conduct, and that they could not be responsible for, or indeed take notice of, mere speeches or writings in a foreign country. Lord Grey had I believed urged the same topicks. But Lord Londonderry persisted in assurances, which nobody ever doubted, that he should continue to ask questions and comment on publick events whether he was answered or not or whatever the Government might suppose to be the motive or effect of his conduct.

On our return from Lord Gowers[194] where we dined, found Lord Chancellor and a letter from Henry full of interesting intelligence; praise of Lord William Russell, Sir R Adair, and Prince of Orange; and full of censure on the brutality of Prince of Weimar, who continued firing as Sir R Adair passed between the armies, and treated Lord William in a way that may induce the latter to call him out whenever they are both divested of a publick character.

Wednesday 17 August. Avoided Levee and dined at home with Rogers, Lilfords,[195] and a snug family party.

Thursday 18 August. I was summoned to Cabinet at 11 a.m. Dispatches of Granville from Paris, and private letters from him, King Leopold, and others read aloud. The language of Sebastiani and his dispatches to Talleyrand, though accompanied with some general professions of leaving the movements of French army at the disposal of Conference and of having no view but that of preserving peace, and containing a communication *and a declaration* that orders had been issued to withdraw 20,000 troops immediately from Belgium, imply in some vague and indistinct sentences a notion that two conditions may be annexed to the retreat—the dismantling the Belgian fortresses immediately and the completion of a definitive treaty of peace between Holland and Belgium. The draft of a dispatch to Lord Granville on this subject was deliberately considered. Great endeavours were made to render it firm and yet conciliating. The recall of the *20,000,* with whom I understand the Princes[196] return, was stated to be satisfactory as indicating the intention of recalling the whole; the motives and nature of their march were stated correctly and civilly; their promises to evacuate Belgium whenever the Dutch were driven back within their frontiers was earnestly but not offensively insisted upon; and the solemn assurance contained in the Protocol [was] adverted to; after which the paper went on to combat most successfully the unreasonable and hazardous notion that the destruction of the fortresses was at all connected with the retreat of the French army or such as the French were entitled to urge or to execute. It was in truth a resolution of the other powers which, <being> determined, was agreable to France and which we had subsequently permitted her to make publick. With respect to a definitive treaty of peace between Belgium and Holland, though we all owed it to be desirable and urgent, we denied that a French force in Belgium would be conducive to such an end and maintained on the contrary that it might impede it. The paper, though not peremptory or offensive, was a firm, earnest, and unqualified demand of the withdrawal of French troops according to the letter and spirit of their engagement, and especially of the Protocol they had signed and ratified so recently. Talleyrand himself had wished some such earnest representation to go to Paris, and though he was still manifestly desirous at his heart to recover Marienburg and Philippeville,[197] he was obviously and sincerely anxious for Peace and as obviously aware that it could not be well concluded or secured untill the French had evacuated Belgium. In the course of our deliberations it turned out that Wessenburgh and Bulow had originally suggested the demolition of the fortresses as a necessary consequence of the separation and neutrality of Belgium, and that Bulow had written a dispatch to urge the object very early in these transactions. That dispatch recently he had shewn to Duke of Wellington to convince him of the unreasonableness of arraigning the measure as a suggestion and triumph of France, when in substance as well as form it had originated with the military powers most likely to be jealous of her. These facts seemed to strike Lord Goderich and relieve his mind from an impression somewhat burthensome upon it, that we should appear to have been outwitted or intimidated by France.

Lord Granville, when he went to urge many of these considerations on the King of the French, unluckily found Sebastiani there, who fresh from altercations in the Chamber was both irritable and insolent, bounced and boasted a great deal, 'his eyes flashing fire and his tongue shedding gall'. The King apologized for his heat, was manifestly struck with Granville's representation of opinion here in Parliament and in the publick, and Casimir Perrier, who joined the party before they separated, acknowledged that the French army must be directed by the Congress [*i.e., the London Conference*]. We agreed to the draft of the dispatch and expressed a hope that the Conference, which was to meet soon afterwards, would hold similar language on the communication from Prince Talleyrand of the retreat of the *20,000*.

While we were deliberating on these matters, Althorpe and Mr Stanley went out to meet 50 Irish Members professedly friendly to our government. They laid before these Gentlemen their plan for storing the arms and, as Lord Anglesey terms it, regimenting the Yeomanry. They all to a Man objected to the scheme. It was, they said, a permanent establishment of the obnoxious force. But they honestly admitted that immediate and entire disbanding would be impracticable and that the situation of Ministers between the two parties was embarrassing. As Orangemen would oppose the measure for disarming and our friends for organizing the force, it was deemed best not to disturb or alter what is, but gradually to let the necessity of Yeomanry abate and substitute some other force or at least with some other name for the protection of the state.

Lord Grey found the Bishops equally averse to any reduction of the Bishoprick of Derry's revenue. The surplus we thought might be well applied to the relief of the poor or to Queen Anne's bounty. The English, and still more the Irish, consider tythes as highly questionable and yet more injurious, and I suspect this obstinacy about Derry will prove the East Retford[198] of the Church, i.e., the proximate cause and forerunner of a more extensive reform.

Talleyrand dined with me. A small party and we talked of past transactions and literature (on which he converses naturally and well) rather than on politicks. He shewed me however two letters from Sebastiani, which he did not seem to approve and, to say the truth, they contained many ambiguous and indistinct expressions, which, Talleyrand assures me, he has written to his court to get softened or expunged.

19 August. A note from Talleyrand to apprize me of the majority in the French Chamber in favor of the address and of the phrase in the King's speech in which he announces his intention of recalling his troops from Belgium, *d'accord et de concert* with the Powers who, like himself, have guarantyed the independence and neutrality of Belgium, as soon as necessary measures are taken to secure her. This Talleyrand justly called *convenable;* [*In the margin:* The Young Princes are returned to France, which is a favourable circumstance, especially as Talleyrand tells me they have written some very foolish letters, qu'il n'aurat pas contre signé] and I understand the protocol settled at the conference yesterday, after our Cabinet, was less peremptory than the dispatch to Lord Granville and left a larger loophole for insisting on some security, either of armistice or treaty, before the French armies completely evacuate the territory.[199] This is lucky. Too peremptory tone would come with a bad grace when the King had voluntarily renewed his assurance. After all, it is clear that King Leopold wishes them to tarry a little longer, and it may be necessary to prevent a second expedition of the King of Holland. I learnt from Lord Jn. Russel, who went to town with me, that Lord Grey had originally drawn up the dispatch in a yet more peremptory strain, had wished it to be sent on Wednesday night, and had only at the instance of Lord Althorpe called the Cabinet of yesterday and consented to delay or alteration. He is so reasonable in council and so unaffectedly desirous of peace when left to himself, that I am half inclined to suspect, when he assumes so high a tone as he does occasionally with France, that his vicinity to Richmond gives his first impressions a tincture of the Princess Lieven's[200] politicks. I learnt from Sir J Graham at House of Commons that a dispatch had arrived from Captn. Napier[201] of the Galatea from the Azores, with an account of all those islands having been reduced, after a truly brilliant action in San [São] Miguel, by the Constitutionalists of Terceira. A glorious piece of news for Don Pedro and his daughter, whom it is unlucky that we should have neglected and the French so warmly and generously received and cultivated. I urged these considerations when he was here, but oeconomy, multiplicity of business, silly and overscrupulous fear of interference, and I am afraid some little prejudice in our King's mind prevailed, and he was allowed to depart with his Empress and his Daughter to Paris. Falck dined here. He shewed me the map of Limburg, seemed quite reasonable about Luxemburgh, but urged with great earnestness the just pretensions of his Country to Maestricht and to entire contiguity and safe road along the left bank of the Maes [Meuse] between that fortress and Holland. He seemed impressed with a notion that Palmerston was hostile to Dutch interests and disposed to chastize the King for the embarrassment he had occasioned. Something of the same sort dropped from Bulow who with Talleyrand and Baron Wessenburg called in the evening.

20 August Saturday. Went with Lord John Russell to Windsor where a great dinner of 98 covers was given on the investiture of the Duke of Saxe Meinungen[202] with the garter. The dinner was in St. George's Hall and the service of Vermeil and decorations truly magnificent. The King on the toasts after dinner made speeches of some length, which proved his desire to please both his foreign and domestick guests more than his taste or judgement in oratory. He with more judicious good nature had invited the neighbourhood, and especially those resident near his old palace of Bushy, to the Evening party; and Sir Jeffry Wyatville,[203] who was there, must have been gratified at the warm and artless admiration of the apartments expressed by foreigner or native, Prince Duke and apothecary, of all ranks. His Majesty selected me for his party at Cribbage with the Princess Augusta and Lady Mary, and seemed to me not a little relieved that the ceremony (which however he had made rather unnecessarily long) was concluded. The Archbishop of Dublin[204] is dead, and the greatness and number of such windfalls rather embarrassing. Grey seemed to me in better spirits, as he ought to be, about foreign affairs. I sat near Albermarle at dinner, learnt from him that my inscription on obelisk to Duke William of Cumberland on the victory of Culloden in Windsor Park was approved and would be placed on the pedestal. He also confirmed me in the opinion that the Queen, though averse to reform and surrounded by persons hostile to our government, was incapable of intrigue or underhand manoeuvres to thwart the King's government and equally unlikely and unable to sway his opinion. Returned to Lady Holland at Richmond with Lord John Russell and Lord Lansdowne, the last unaccountably averse to new peerages and more easily reconciled to the possibility of defeat in the Lords than I could have wished. On foreign affairs his opinions, as usual, right but rather faint, and on Irish, where he thinks more patronage is wanting for a government, practically conciliatory, more sound and better considered.

21 August Sunday. At Richmond. Drove out with Princess Lieven, Mr Mastuzewitz, and Lord John Russell. Mme Lieven very anxious that Falck should remain and that for that purpose, as well as others, we should keep a Minister with the title of Embassador at the Hague. Though She and Mastuzewitch indulged in some sneers at Leopold and his Belgians and expressed approbation of the Prince of Orange (which he deserves), they did not venture to espouse the cause of the King of Holland and seemed yet less disposed to enter upon any part of the Polish question. She remarked with some truth that it was bad taste to send the Duke of Nemours with the army, and was or pretended to be agreably surprized when I told her the French Princes had returned unto France. We dined with Lord Lansdown. He spoke with more censure than I have hitherto heard him of the opponents of bill, but speculated on many of them acquiesing in 2d. reading and making great alterations in the Committee when it comes to the Lords.

22d. August. Letters from Paris confirm the pacifick disposition of French Government, and Granville earnestly exhorts me in private letters not to allow petty points of form and punctilio to involve us in war, or even to estrange our councils when in substance we have no quarrel and when, as far as he can judge, there is no design or even wish in the French Ministry, unless perhaps in Soult, to injure us or our continental interests by war or negotiation. I was glad to find in House of Lords that Grey saw matters now nearly in the same light, and was highly satisfied with a conversation he had had with Talleyrand—explicit, cordial, and reasonable as he described. Talleyrand came to Holland House in the Evening and most justly observed that we were all most bungling negotiators if, meaning the same thing in substance and anxious to preserve peace, we should contrive to quarrel or separate upon points of honour and punctilio, instead of eventually soothing each others pride or amour propre.

[*In the margin:* Lord Wicklow[205] in House of Lords made a malignant but not mischievous speech on the meeting of Irish members and the intentions of Government to disband the Yeomanry, on both which subjects he was either imperfectly informed or grossly misrepresented them. Grey stated the facts distinctly, as well as his determination of pursuing the course he thought fit and of not being dictated to by any combination. He acknowledged he was not *prepared* to disband the Yeomanry but, with proper acknowledgements of their zeal and military merit, he dwelt enough on the unconstitutional and hazardous nature of such a force to indicate, I thought, no great disposition to continue them, whenever they could be suppressed with safety. Lord Wicklow's approbation of this statement as satisfactory to the Yeomanry was a little alarming and more mischievous in my opinion than his speech. It is better to pass for the persecuted than the supporter of so odious and dangerous a corps. Lord Londonderry as usual indulged in irregular conversation, but when called to order by Duke of Richmond and myself, desisted, with more personal civility to myself than I deserved at his hands or could account for.]

23 August. Cabinet. Palmerston related his conversation with Talleyrand, the professions he [Talleyrand] made of the willingness of the French to withdraw their troops, the readiness to give up and forget any other objects they may have once entertained such as Phillipeville, Marienburgh, and so forth, and their earnestness to concur in any or all arrangements we thought conducive to permanent peace; but added that King Leopold and Le Hon at Paris pressed the French to stay till his own army was better organized, that it was reasonable not to evacuate the country till some further assurance was taken that it would not again be invaded, and that it would be much more satisfactory to all parties if all matters (including the demolition of fortresses) were settled at the same time, and that such final settlement should accompany or precede the withdrawal of the French Forces. It was also acknowledged that Latour Maubourg[206] was employed at Brussels to accelerate King Leopold's agreement to the demolition of the fortresses. *Palmerston* very justly observed that as a condition of the French retreat the demolition could *not* be admitted; he further apprehended that any demolition of them, either settled in detail or executed while the French were in Belgium, would be in effect if not in form a humiliating proof of the ascendancy of France, would be so described by them, and so felt both here and on the Continent. As a conference was about to take place, he was anxious to have instructions what language to hold and what course to pursue on this subject. The official communication of the Dutch being within their own frontiers had not arrived, the return of the French Princes and 20,000 men into France had—and Leopold's wish that the French force might remain while he was organizing his own had been transmitted to us, not only through the French Government, but with a certain disposition to soften and explain it, through the official channels between Leopold and this government. Palmerston brought under our notice also that the three other powers had not formally recognized Leopold nor were bound to do so till the King of Holland had agreed to the 18 articles; and the demolition of the fortresses was by the Protocol made contingent on the recognition of the Belgian King by all the powers.[207] Lord Grey, after expressing his conviction of the sincerity in substance of the French Government, deprecated any thing approaching to coldness, suspicion, altercation, or war on mere points of form and on the time and manner of executing *that* which on all hands it was agreed should be done; and in illustration of the views of the powers on the fortresses, read papers from Baron Bulow and Baron Weissenburgh on the subject, in which they urged the demolition of part of the fortresses as a necessary consequence of the altered state of circumstances and pointed out those it would be expedient to preserve and those to dismantle. Weissenburgh's was a very able and well reasoned paper.

The result of our deliberations was that Palmerston should recommend the Conference to offer or impose upon the two parties an immediate armistice, either for six weeks or indefinitely during the negotiation of a definitive treaty; should signify to Talleyrand the impossibility of making the demolition of the fortresses a preliminary or accompanying condition to the performance of the French government's promise of evacuating Flanders, and the impropriety of any thing like formal negotiation on the subject of these fortresses with France, but the willingness of England to expedite with the other powers the completion of their intentions; and in furtherance and proof of that willingness that he should give him to understand that the arrangement in the details was in forwardness, and that he had no objection to apprize him, as it proceeded, of the particular fortresses they meant to dismantle, and to hear from him any remarks he had to make on the places selected for demolition and those retained. We then agreed on a dispatch to the Hague requiring, as a satisfaction for the affront offered to the King by the unmannerly reception of Lord William Russell by the Duke of Saxe Weimar, a reprimand of that officer in the service of the King of the Netherlands. Some such atonement was no doubt due for conduct amounting to a violation of the most sacred usages among Civilized nations, respect to flags of truce and persons charged with Missions and embassies; and it was whispered that the King himself was personally desirous it should be made, notwithstanding his family connection with the Duke who had himself, in spite of that tie, indulged very freely in his remarks on him and, it is said, on the Queen, his Sister in Law, also. All Kings and Princes, even the best, seem to hate one another. The Irish, said Johnson, are an honest nation; they harbour and avow a distrust of one another.

In House of Lords, Lord Wynford's bill extending the bankrupt laws to persons travelling and not in trade was thrown out on the motion of Lord Plunkett. [*In the margin:* Lord Fife,[208] possibly from a recollection of his own insolvent state, had offered the bill in its first stages in a long, tiresome, and foolish speech. This drew some notice to it. He was pleased at Plunkett's support and success, and this circumstance secured, if not his vote, his zeal and attendance for the reform bill.] Wynford called for a division and Lord Kenyon was named teller for the contents; but on Lord Eldon walking out of the house, Lord Wynford, who had begun his expedition towards the bar, exclaimed agreed, with the unappropriate remark that he would not give their Lordships the trouble of dividing, though it was pretty manifest that the trouble of all excepting himself would have been confined to sitting in their places and expressing thereby 'Non Content' to the bill. Some other bills passed their respective stages, and in a conversation on the Chancellor's bankruptcy bill,[209] he made an apology to the house for his late absence and Lord Eldon gave him a rub for neglecting what, according to the Standing order, he very ignorantly maintain<ed> to be the first and most important duty of a Chancellor—his attendance as Speaker in that house. Lord Eldon forgot that his own famous resolutions about appeals[210] had in effect and in intention destroyed the authority of that standing order and the supposed but erroneous principle of the paramount importance of the duty of attending the Lords.

Talleyrand called at Holland House late at night, and I learnt from him that the Dutch Plenipotentiaries had given official assurance of the retreat of the army within their frontiers, and agreed to transmit the armistice, proposed in the protocol of this day[211] by the Conference, *for six weeks,* to the Hague where they have little doubt it will be admitted. Talleyrand complained to me that the Protocol was *un peu trop moux,* that he wished the Conference had used the word *resolved upon,* and so intimated more directly an intention to *impose* as well as *propose* the armistice to the parties. Palmerston he said wished it otherwise, and as he supposed he [Palmerston] had parliamentary reasons, he [Talleyrand] did not like to combat his wishes. He has written to Latour Maubourgh to impress upon him the necessity of secresy and discretion, and the impropriety of any thing like ostensible negotiation on the subject of fortress[es]. He has written in the same spirit to Paris and told them that no parties in England, from Grey and Wellington to Hunt,[212] would bear the interference of French in any such negotiation.

24th. Wednesday. Lord Mulgrave[213] assures me that of Lords who have taken their seats there is a majority of 20 against the reform bill and the report of many who canvass such lists corroborates this statement. It must be for Grey or as he says the Cabinet to determine what and when efforts are to be made to counteract this frightful superiority of our Enemy. Lord Lansdowne overtook me on my way to Shene where I dined with Lord Grey and told me that Don Pedro was to be accommodated with carriages at the Coronation and every attention shewn that may induce him to attend it. It is rather late now, but the impolicy of neglecting him begins to be felt as the prospect of Miguel's overthrow becomes more certain. The Duchess of Kent, with great want of judgement if not with some sinister motive, declines on the pretence of oeconomy attending the Coronation. I had little conversation with Grey on political matters because Lord Lyndhurst and his wife dined with us, who if not actual enemies are hitherto very doubtful friends of the Ministry or the reform bill. They are not, however, judging by the Lady's language, the least attached to our opponents. I was sorry to learn from Lady Grey that Grey is despondent about the success of the bill and the duration of his Ministry. However the next good speech he makes, and that cannot be long, his spirits will revive. He tells me Gerard[214] has received orders to withdraw all the French troops from Belgium, but Leopold presses earnestly, and more earnestly than he acknowledges to us, that they may remain.

Thursday 25 Augt. Lord John Russell urges the necessity of decision about new peerages—or at least new peers. Lord Carlisle anxious about the same subject and impressed with the necessity of encreasing our strength and settling our course of proceedings in the Lords. In that house Lord Londonderry asked again if the French had retreated and, when answered by Lord Grey that Marshal Gerard had received orders to retreat with his whole force, affected to congratulate Grey, the house, and the Country on intelligence which no doubt disappointed him exceedingly. I observed that it was a great satisfaction to find that we had for once sent him contented and happy away. Lord Grey had an interview with Duke of Wellington on the fortresses to day. His Grace observed that he of course could only be consulted on the Military question and that he had nothing to do with the political state of the country, the effect of revolution, or the disposition of the people. He gave it therefore as his opinion, founded on former examination and confirmed by recent reflection, that all the fortresses were necessary to the defence of Belgium, that, if any, *all* must be preserved to render the frontier serviceable, and that an army not greater than such a kingdom as Belgium might maintain, 12,000 men, would be sufficient to man them during peace and to protect them (provided the men were to be depended upon) against any coup de main. In short it is clear he will take his stand against us on the demolition of the fortresses. Grey said he had made up his mind, subject to the consent of the King and approbation of his Colleagues, to create as many peers at the coronation as, together with those recently created, would equal the number of the last Coronation,[215] and to consider as extra such Eldest sons as he could call up. But he seemed to apprehend the majority against us to be more than twenty and to shrink from the measure of exceeding that number, remarking that one must take care not to provoke to opposition some that might vote with us by too large a creation of peers. In this view Lansdown confirms him. He asked me to add a Baronet or two to his list. He was not in spirits, and on returning home where Melbourne dined with me I learnt that Brougham, who was not in the house, had taken in great dudgeon Grey's answer in defence of C Poulett Thompson[216] and his [Grey's] Son, Lord Howick,[217] for voting against a motion of the Attorney,[218] and had probably harrassed him on the subject. It is clear the Chancellor is almost frantic on the subject and in his rage phrases escape his lips and his pen which indicate not only some dislike of Grey but regret at having accepted the seals and even an inclination to throw them up. Yet if he does so he cannot, by the signature of *HB* to which when in those paroxysms he resorts, replace himself in the Commons as Member for Yorkshire and realize the dreams of carrying all things with the people at his back. Is it his own unaccountable temper and imagination or the bad advice of his brother James[219] which occasions these frantick moods on subjects comparatively trifling?

Harry Webster shewed me Palmerston's letter which notified to him that Pedro's expences and carriages would be defrayed for him at Coronation and a Government Steam boat at his disposal at Calais whenever he should appoint. Better late than never.

26 August. The House of Lords was up before I arrived but I found Grey, Lansdown, and others in the house. Czartorinski[220] had written a letter and sent some Polish deputies to deliver it to the King. We all agree that by receiving *them and this message* the King would recognize the provisional government of Poland, and all, except myself, incline to the opinion that the time for that recognition is not yet arrived. It seems however that a distinction may reasonably be made between receiving a letter and receiving a Deputy or Embassador. Grey and Lansdown are willing to avail themselves of that distinction and to transmit the letter to the King, but Palmerston I understand has some scruples in establishing any thing like an intercourse between the King and the revolted subjects of the Emperor of Russia.[221] Idle squeamishness this, if not sheer pusillanimity and imprudence; for if the Poles are successful we must acknowledge them, though success can hardly make them more legitimate than they are. They constitute a government *de facto* at Warsaw, as much as if they were in possession of Dantzick and Riga. Yet who doubts if those towns were subdued by them that we should immediately send and receive Consuls and probably Ministers too?

The Chancellor was again absent from the House of Lords. I heard Oconnell for the first time in the Commons, a ready and powerful speaker but though pleasing, not so pleasing as I had expected. [*In the margin:* In the Commons Lord Carnarvon who passed by me gave me a friendly shake of the hand and I am in hopes he feels that any blow I may have given was all in the way of fair fighting.] Mr <Boune> engages through the Globe to counteract the evil effect of warlike articles in the Times. These as well as other symptoms of hostility in that formidable paper, the Times, are attributed to jealousy of the Courier and to the mismanagement in our publick offices, especially the foreign, by which the conductors have been in some degree offended.[222] Sir George Shee[223] (whom I do not know) is said not to be much more adroit than his father who, in 1806, as UnderSecretary of Mr Windham,[224] offended many of our best friends and let his principal<s> into innumerable awkward scrapes. Though I shut my eyes and ears as becomes a Minister in a neutral Cabinet, I suspect Don Pedro has got money, ships, and English officers, especially Captn. Sartorius,[225] and that the expedition meditated from Terceira will derive no little assistance from individual exertions in France and England. Why not repeal the foreign enlistment bill[226] at once? Lord Melbourne dined with me.

27 August Saturday. Talleyrand called after dinner and he told me Leopold had pressed for 12,000 men to remain and that the French wished to comply with the request and pressed England &c to sanction it. He was aware Wellington had given his opinion, as a Military Man, that all the fortresses were necessary to the defence of Belgium. Lord Chancellor came and slept. Very anxious and sensible about the peerages, a little irritable at the delay of bill, and sundry incidents in Commons, and vaunting about his Court of Chancery,[227] but on the whole more reasonable and I hope tractable than he had been represented to me.

Sunday 28 August. Lord Chancellor talked of necessity of obtaining 30 votes in House of Lords and after canvassing names finished by projecting a list of 17 eldest sons fit to be called up and 14 (of which some were Scotch some Irish peers and many childless and professional men) fit to be created peers. He spoke severely of the little patronage bestowed on keen reformers and party men and of favors lavished on false and lukewarm friends or even positive opponents and enemies, but he ended by acknowledging an intention of giving a living to Dr Croley,[228] a bitter adversary and one who has written and writes in Magazines and other periodical works against us. Plunkett and Sir Henry Parnell[229] dined and slept at Holland House. The latter earnest to procure offices of trust for some Catholicks such as Shiel, Wyse,[230] and others, and the former equally earnest for a provision for Catholick Clergy.

Monday 29 August. Leinster[231] from a heartfelt contempt for such gewgaws declines St. Patricks ribbon. And who can blame him? He as well as Anglesey presses for a peerage for Lord Cloncurry[232] who has certainly claims on the latter and on us for being the person about him who best counteracts the influence which Attorney General Blackburne,[233] Lord Forbes,[234] and others with antiministerial propensities have on his councils, an influence which I am told is too discernible in the disposal of small patronage. In house of Lords Lord Londonderry asked questions respecting the stay of French army in Belgium and the intended demolition of the fortresses, and as usual indulged in much extraneous matter in which he betrayed great ignorance of past transactions as well as of the state of things at home and abroad [*In the margin:* and, quoting what has passed between us in private, endeavoured without success to say something smart on my situation in the Cabinet and the interest I took in foreign affairs.[235]] Lord Grey exposed his ignorance in one particular the impropriety of dismantling Courtray which he had urged very vehemently by the simple remark that Courtray was not fortified and did not form one of the line of fortresses in question, he repeated verbatim the answer he had given, namely that Gerard had received orders to evacuate, that we had a right to expect from engagements and assurances that the French would do so, and that we had no reason to doubt their good faith and honest adherence to their promises. Londonderry had, by a practice common with him but not very correct or considerate, quoted what he termed my interpretation in private of Lord Grey's former answer and if it were to be quoted it was at least satisfactory to find it correct. Duke of Wellington threw Lord Londonderry over board on Courtray and the title of King Leopold, whom Londonderry denied to be a King till Russia had recognized him; but he approved of his vigilance in exacting explanations of the French occupation of Belgium, said he could only consider the 12,000 men as an advanced part of the French army, denied the right of Leopold to ask them to remain, and maintained that, if they remained to controul his mutinous troops and rebellious subjects, it was a direct interference by the power which had least right to interfere and for the party we had least reason to allow of any. I was on the point of retorting and ridiculing Londonderry's idle sarcasms on myself, but thought it prudent not to speak lest I should be tempted to remark on the Duke of

Wellington's view of the subject and let drop some phrase which might be misconstrued into an admission on the other side of the water and be reckoned too pacifick on this. Melbourne and Plunkett passed the Evening at Holland House and both agree in the necessity of strong measures to secure Majority in Lords and in the folly of not adopting them.

Tuesday 30th August. Cabinet at eleven. The object of meeting was to settle the Commissioners in the Reform bill and sundry clauses relating to their appointment and functions, in none of which I took any interest. The news through Berlin of disasters and what is still worse outrages in Poland is very distressing. The King of Holland agrees to armistice but Leopold and, what is passing strange, the French demur to it. The King of Holland has most wantonly and cruelly cut the dykes and inundated a large district near Antwerp. Leopold, thro' Stockmar,[236] who is arrived here, acknowledges that the stay of 12,000 French troops would be convenient and that he hopes the Conference will sanction their staying there some time longer, but at the same [time?] denies have [?having] pressed for them as earnestly as the French pretend or for the reasons which they alledge, or at least exaggerate, of the anarchy prevalent in his new kingdom. The French blame Talleyrand for acquiescing in the Protocol and Armistice [of 23 August] and Lord Granville from Paris, Lord Wm. Russell and Henry from Brussels, write pressing private letters to us not to allow the opposition either in France or England to drive two friendly governments to war, who have in truth no real object of dispute between them. True it is that If England quarrel with France about the demoliton of the fortresses or the preservation of the independence of Belgium, she quarrels for objects which we all know to be quite unattainable, and if attainable scarcely worth having. It was agreed that Palmerston should grant the Portugueze paper moved for by Mr Courtenay[237] and a letter from Mr Hoppner giving a lamentable and ludicrous account of the Squabbles in King Michael's [Miguel's] Council room was read, as well as of the negotiation between his government and the French Admiral since the capitulation, which related to the release of persons imprisoned for political offences and not to a Commercial treaty and which was rejected by Miguel. In the house of Lords I urged Grey to make peers sufficient to pass the bill and he seemed to listen to my arguments and Lord Sefton who cordially joined with me. The Archbishop made a very heavy and unimpressive speech on his Pluralities bill[238] which passed one stage and there was some tiresome conversation between Lords Wicklow, Plunkett, and Melbourne on the subletting bill.[239] The Duke of Richmond and the two last mentioned Peers dined with me, and Talleyrand called in the evening. He shewed me private letters from his King and Sebastiani which most unreasonably complained both of armistice and protocol and somewhat sharply animadverted on his conduct in signing it. He was nettled at this, made some <just> remarks on their want of steadiness and good faith, and did not seem to be pleased with Baudrand's[240] mission though he greatly extolled the Man.

Wednesday 31 August. Wrote a letter to Lord Grey advising him to create 18 new peers and call up 17 eldest sons.[241] Baron Wessemburg called. Seemed to approve of temporizing measures and was far from eager to force the retreat of French troops from Belgium. I went to the Levee and waited more than two hours before the King came out of his closet. Lord Grey is still very unwell with lumbago and unable to come to Court. This is unlucky as it is high time he should canvass the state of Lords with the King and sound him on the measures he is disposed to acquiesce in to improve it. Grey means to promote his brother in Law Ponsonby to Derry, and the Bishop of Norwich[242] having declined the Primacy, it is thought prudent and right to name none but an Irishman to the vacant See. I had some conversation with my Colleagues and others on the approaching creation of Peers. All even our enemies expect it to be large, but I was much disappointed to find both Lansdowne and Palmerston disinclined to any measure vigorous enough to be effectual. They manifestly reconcile themselves too easily to any amendment or alteration of the bill in the Lords and are not aware of the effect any violation of its principle would occasion in the Country. A Council with routine business. The new Great Seal produced and the old one brought before the King to be broken. The Chancellor stated very incorrectly that it was doubtful whether the old seals belonged to the Chancellor who holds the seal when the new one is brought into use or to his predecessor when the late King expired. The King took the seal and, humorously saying he would act the Solomon, divided it, and added that his jeweller should mount each in a Salver, one with Lord Brougham's and the other for Lord Lyndhurst's arms and then, spinning the two together on the table, bade Brougham chuse the Uppermost or Undermost as it fell, observing it was the first time a Great Seal had been disposed of by 'Heads or Tails'. After this Royal Joke the Council broke up and I hastened home to meet General Baudrand who had announced a letter to me from the King of the French which turned out to be a mere letter of enquiry and compliment and not, as I had supposed, relating to the present ticklish state of publick affairs. The Chancellor called in the Evening. He is justly elated at having heard and decided all his causes in Chancery, will now renew his attendance in House of Lords and prove to the conviction of the world the truth of what was considered to be a paradox of Romilly's[243]—that an able, honest, laborious, and decisive Man can discharge the duties of Chancellor without having an arrear and without the assistance of a Vice Chancellor. Brougham told me that on the day of the dissolution Grey was almost deterred and disheartened by the technical difficulties in drawing out the commission, hesitated in proposing to the King to go down, and was in truth only decided by his (Brougham's) and the Duke of Richmond's vigor and determination. He described the scene very dramatically and well. He was indeed the Hero of his own tale but I believe the thing passed nearly as he recounted it.[244] He does not flinch from the further consequences without which that step was fruitless, namely the creation of 30 new peers to secure the bill in the Lords as the dissolution secured it in Commons.

1 September 1831. The incessant rain prevented my going to House of Lords or visiting Lord Grey. General Baudrand, who had brought a letter to me from the King of French, breakfasted here. The letter was merely one of compliment and Baudrand, though open and communicative, had nothing specifick to say to me. He had seen Lord Grey and Lord Palmerston and seemed pleased with both, thoroughly satisfied that there [was] no hostile feeling or adverse design here, and full of earnest protestations that there was as little in France. But of the danger to Europe and to the peace, as well as to France and tranquillity <i>f any change of Ministry there, he talked much and earnestly, and then assured me that it was very necessary to the preservation of the Ministry that they should not be compelled or bullied, either in appearance or reality, into a premature recall of all their troops, when King Leopold presses them to stay and when the King of Holland kept up and augmented his army and betrayed so much disposition to renew his unwarrantable accessions. He acknowledged however that there [is] nothing in the terms of the 34[th.] Protocol the least offensive and that in Paris it had been misconceived, a circumstance which Talleyrand had hinted to me and seemed willing I should impress on his countryman. Baudrand was anxious that it should be understood that he came here with no mission or publick character, simply to give information of Brussels and Paris, both which places he had seen within the week. He spoke kindly of Talleyrand and seems himself to be a good, sensible, and pacifick man, deeply impressed with the critical state of affairs in France.

2 September. Drove over to Lord Grey's at Shene. He was writing to Palmerston and consulted me whether in tomorrow's conference he should be instructed to insist on the immediate retreat of French, now both Belgians and Dutch had agreed to the suspension of arms. I thought it was better to defer it, as it would be much better they should retreat at our earnest request and suggestion than at a peremptory demand of the Conference, and Grey was of my opinion. Werther the Prussian at Paris, though lately offered the Premiership at Berlin and high in his King's confidence, presses for the immediate demolition of fortresses and wishes that measure to be more complete as well as more speedy than Bulow here approves, who maintains that this discrepancy between them arises from Werther not having the instructions of his Court on that head. The Conference has agreed to urge on the King of the Netherlands the necessity of repairing the dykes he has cut near Antwerp and indemnifying the inhabitants and, at the same time, <insisted> on the Belgians rendering unavaileable the works which, in contravention of the suspension of arms, they have raised on the Scheldt.[245]

Grey is hurt with an unreasonable and unseasonable request of Durham and still more at his manner of asking for an Earldom. The innumerable applications for honours seem to provoke and disgust him not a little. The King not unnaturally objects to Coke[246] on account of his strange invective last Autumn against George III whom he termed that 'bloody King, the worst man that ever lived', and very unreasonably to Sir James Saumarez.[247] I was authorized by Grey to inform Breadalbane, Duncan, and Maule that it was his intention to recommend the two first to a step in the Peerage and the latter to a Peerage. He read me a list of projected creations at the Coronations—all with one or two exceptions staunch and proper men. The number however is not sufficient to secure a Majority in Lords unless followed up by writs to several Eldest sons. While I was with Lord Grey, a letter from Stanley arrived pressing for a full Cabinet to consider the measures necessary to pass the bill in House of Lords and the course we should pursue in case the house were to postpone it. I was sorry to perceive by a parenthesis in his letter that he leans to the more timid counsels and, unless we are prepared to overwhelm the majority by creations, I do not understand how we can remain in office an hour after we are beaten. The present leaning of Grey's mind is to create 12 or 15 at Coronation and to keep in reserve and for consideration the measure of calling up.

3d. September. Heard a bad report of our force in Lords. A Majority they say of 22 against us without Bishops. Lord Howe continues to hold very hostile language. The Duchess of Kent very improperly declines attending Coronation, on the pretence of oeconomy. Neglected to write this diary at night.

4 Septr. Sunday. Cabinet at Foreign Office. The three Plenipotentiaries of Austria, Prussia, and Russia had drawn out a project of Protocol, reciting the assurances of the French government that they would evacuate the Belgian territory when the Dutch were driven back and the armistice reestablished, and, after alledging the accomplishment of those objects, demanding in a peremptory tone the immediate recall and retreat of the whole French Force. The question Palmerston submitted to us was whether he should in the Conference of tomorrow propose and agree to such a proposal, or postpone the demand a little longer with a hope that France may of her own accord or on our less formal remonstrances withdraw her troops. After a long conversation in which the conduct of Leopold, in throwing himself too obviously on France, and soliciting from her separately that support which if necessary should have been continued by the Conference, was much censured, and the views of France, Belgium, Holland, and Prussia much canvassed, it was determined chiefly at Lord Grey's suggestion that the powers should separately and we, most amicably but most earnestly, press the French to execute their promise by retiring before we were compelled in form to demand them to do so; and that Palmerston should hint to Talleyrand the difficulty there would be not only to restrain the others, especially if flushed with the frightful success of Russia in Poland, much longer from strong official representation, and the impossiblility of reconciling our Parliament and our people, or indeed ourselves, to any protracted stay of the French army even at the most earnest solicitation of Leopold. Grey was obliged to attend the King. He was very pacifick in his view of foreign politicks, sadly hurt at Durham's unreasonableness, disposed to create 14 [*blotted*] 16 peers at Coronation and to listen to the necessity of resorting to Eldest Son's [*sic*] afterwards. He bade me acquaint Lord Plunkett that his son[248] should have the first dignity vacated by filling up the Bishopricks in Ireland.

General Baudrand dined with me and Talleyrand came late in the Evening. The first is a reasonable man and I believe sincerely desirous to preserve peace, but apprehensive that French Ministry could not recall the troops immediately without raising a flame in the Chambers and in the publick that must end in their dismissal. Talleyrand was impressed with a notion that, though perilous, it might be done speedily and with <vigor>. He assured me he had written to that effect. To both I stated explicitly that it must not be delayed, that we could not stave off much longer something like a peremptory demand, and that it would be better both in appearance and reality to <perform> their promise from a sense of their own honour and obligations, than to have the execution of them exacted in a less amicable way and be brought to the Alternative of defying the other powers, or incurring the reproach of submitting to them. I hope I made some way.

Monday 5th. Septr. Cabinet at twelve. The question—viz, what shall we do to prevent the Lords postponing or rejecting the bill, and if they do shall we resign?—resolved itself after much conversation into another more simple—shall we make peers enough to give us a majority in Lords? The Chancellor, who had adjourned a cause in Lords to attend this important Cabinet, spoke ably and earnestly in favor of a large creation and described, I believe in just but certainly in very strong terms, the consequences of a rejection or even postponement of the bill, unless the latter could be corrected by an immediate augmentation of the Peerage, sufficient to ensure the success of the measure at the period to which, by the hypothesis, the discussion was deferred. Duke of Richmond took fire, though with good humour, at one or two of his strong expressions as implying that we should not act under intimidation, and declared that he could not agree to making peers with the avowed view of overruling the will of the house of Lords. He could not, he said, vote it *useless.* In his view of the subject though more faintly it seemed to me that Lansdowne, Goderich, Stanley, and Palmerston concurred. Carlisle, on the other hand, very pertinently observed that the current of creations had run in the opposite direction for 70 years, and that the House of Lords was not a fair representation of the Aristocracy of the country untill a large portion of persons of a different Leaven should be introduced to it. I said little but enough to express my decided conviction, that we were in a situation to justify us in advising a large exercise of the prerogative, and that if we shrunk from doing so, we sacrificed the interests of the Country, deserted the King most unhandsomely, and exposed the institutions of the Country and the House of Lords most especially to the greatest danger. Queen Anne's twelve peers bore, I observed, the same proportion to the whole number which then constituted the House of Lords as 30 would do to the 405; and though I disapproved of the occasion because I questioned the policy and popularity of the peace of Utrecht, I could not deny that, if they had a conscientious conviction that the peace was right, The Tories acted both constitutionally and meritoriously in advising that augmentation of the peerage. Lord Grey, who had stated the question very fairly and somewhat favorably to the policy of a large creation, dwelling on the evils of a rejection of the bill, on the virulence and strength of our opponents, on the embarrassing consequences of a difference between the two Houses—especially to the King to whom in honour we were so pledged and indebted—and on the numerous peerages that had been made at the last coronation, listened with great complacency to every argument and remark that tended to corroborate the view the Chancellor and I had taken of the necessity of the measure, but prudently and adroitly admitted some of the general principles urged by Goderich, Palmerston, and Lansdowne; and none of us did more than glance at the extreme absurdity and danger of the doctrine that the will of an hereditary Assembly should be allowed unmolested to stem that of the Court, the Commons, and the Country. Lord *Althorp* questioned the propriety or rather condemned the expedient of making peers for the special purpose of supporting any measure, admitted the constitutional objections to a great encrease of the

House of Lords, and did not feel himself prepared on the present emergency to consent to a creation so large as to imply our determination to overrule the majority of the Lords and to cram down their throats by means of the prerogative a measure to which they are averse; but he thought that the constitution, which rendered the concurrence of the three branches legally necessary to the passing of a law and virtually necessary to conducting the business of the country, had provided and must provide some means of correcting the consequences of a disagreement, whenever such disagreement should amount to an obstacle to the conduct of publick affairs. I concurred in all Lord Althorp said, but differed with him solely on a point of fact. He seemed to think the crisis, which by preventing the conduct of publick affairs would justify a large creation of peers to expedite, had not yet arrived. It seemed to me that virtually and practically it *had*. The result was that we determined that a number equal to that of last Coronation should, as *Coronation* Peers and without reference to the bill, be made forthwith, but without prejudice to the question of calling up Eldest Sons or creating more, if previous to the second reading we should be brought to the alternative of resigning or of continuing in office with one House of Parliament against us. I acquiesced in this decision on that understanding and with the acknowledgement that I should infinitely have preferred the immediate creation of 30.

On the whole our discussion did good. Though there was much difference of opinion, there was not the slightest ill-humour or discontent; and I think the scrupulous went out of the room more familiarized, if not reconciled, and the timid, less averse to the prospect of a large creation than they came in. The list, which Grey half communicated and half submitted to the Cabinet, pleased the majority and was canvassed with much impartiality and great good humour. The principle I had recommended to Grey, of advancing in the peerage such as would vote for the bill more chearfully in consequence, without any strict investigation of their general political bias, but of raising to the peerage none but such as would abide by us in opposition and were staunch Whigs, was with two or three exceptions adhered to. We objected to Sir Charles Bagot as a very lukewarm friend, if any, and as a Diplomat, of which species we have already too many in the Lords. 'I am all against him' said Melbourne, who had been silent for an hour. And he told me afterwards that, 'Damme he should have been plagued to Death about his brother Frederick if Bagot had got a peerage'. He was dropped. That of Dundas of Berkshire[249] postponed, for the County would not be safe. And a peerage for Archbishop of York,[250] though promised, is not completed, that we may not exceed the number of last Coronation, nor throw away above one (Belhaven's[251]) on persons who have votes already. Grey did not mention the Dukedoms for Stafford[252] and Cleveland[253] and I much fear they are dropped. Durham was not at this Cabinet and Grey, who had written the kindest letter imaginable stating his sorrow at being compelled to refuse him an Earldom, shewed me, with tears in his eyes, his short, pettish, and unfeeling answer, in which he says he should 'not degrade himself by expressing his feelings on the occasion'. Grey expects him to resign, and asked me if Melbourne could be persuaded to change his office for Privy Seal and let Richmond into the Home office. His motive for wishing it was alledged indolence in Melbourne. I combated the grounds and told him a dislike to meddling legislation and his [Melbourne's] careless nonchalant Manner might give him the character of an indolent man with the inobservant, but those who had business with the office did not find him so. He did uncommonly well there and I strongly deprecated his removal even if he wished it. If he did not, I could not see how any of us could reconcile ourselves to asking him. Well then, said Grey, Carlisle I suppose must have the Privy Seal, and it is rather a convenience as diminishing the Number in the Cabinet. Certainly, I replied, I think it would be strange as things now stand if a vacant Privy Seal were offered to any other.

This passed in the Garden at St. James's where I had come after Cabinet and found Grey waiting for King. During his audience, I had one with Sir Herbert Taylor.[254] He told me the King, though well, was harrassed; that he contemplated the difference of the two houses with great and reasonable dismay; that he had foreseen it; and that disposed to assist his Ministers, with whom he was more than contented, cordially, He had more repugnance to making peers, especially if not rich men, than I might suppose. When at dissolution He (Sir Herbert) had at my suggestion and the King's commands felt the pulse of some opponents of bill, it had, he thought, done harm rather than good, provoked rather than softened. As to Lord Howe he had heard as I had that he had boasted that he would vote against bill and keep his place longer than Lord Grey. I suggested something might be done with Bishops through the Archbishop and he seemed to think that the King was not averse to speaking to him or others. Sir Herbert was as usual distinct and I think friendly. I tried to impress upon him the extreme embarrassment to the King as well as danger to the Country which would ensue if the Lords rejected the bill. I dwelt on the same topick in my audience with the King, who acknowledged it but felt, as people are sometimes apt to do, a little consolation in their annoyance, from the triumph of having foreseen the difficulties in which he was involved. I spoke of the Bishops but he shrugged his shoulders and said nothing. He permitted and almost commanded me to absent myself from Coronation,[255] said the Duke of Cumberland and Eldon had devized it to plague him, and then in talking of foreign affairs observed that 'nothing could justify King Leopold who entirely mistook his position'. It is manifest he dislikes him.

I arrived late at House of Lords. Aberdeen was ending an elaborate, violent, and unfair speech of some effect, which was an invective against the French Nation and government and breathed war in every syllable. Grey answered him satisfactorily but rather feebly. He had not expected so detailed a statement and was not prepared with the papers (which Palmerston had neglected to furnish me with at all), and he was in truth imperfectly recovered of his lumbago and terribly fretted and low about Lambton [Durham]. *Wellington* shewed more hostility to Government and above all more factious disposition to drive us to war than he has hitherto betrayed. He acknowledged, *totisdem verbis,* that he should have recognized Miguel in spite of his injustice to us, because such a connection would act as a counterpoise to Revolutionary spirit, and Aberdeen had spoken of strict and cordial union between Spain and Portugal as a British and European object. Nobody was disposed to answer Wellington, and Grey was mortified and displeased thereat. Fortunately Londonderry relieved us from that difficulty by one of his senseless and malignant speeches, in which he more than once taunted me with my opinions on foreign politicks and my late panegyrick on Mr Hoppner, and produced a private letter from Sir J Campbell[256] calumniating and reviling that Gentleman in the true spirit of a Miguelite. I was both from reason and inclination averse to take up the gauntlet, and Lansdowne and Richmond both more than supplied my place and terminated well a debate that had not begun very auspiciously.

Tuesday 6 Septr. Lord Wm. Russell, returned from Brussels, gives good account of my son Henry's attention to business. They seem to join with Leopold's government in censuring us or the Conference for not sending the English fleet to Antwerp and in strong suspicions of the designs of the Dutch and Prussians, founded on the augmentation of his force and on the enlistment of Prussians in his service. But they admit that there is more appearance of secret understanding and concert between France and King Leopold than the mere gratitude of the latter for his rescue can well justify, and the negotiation with Latour Maubourgh on the fortresses, separately from the Conference, is no doubt offensive and objectionable. There is a mischievous Belgian of the name of Celles[257] at Paris, who is so unpopular in his own Country from his conduct when Prefet under Napoleon, that whenever a Belgian is inclined to divert himself, he (says Talleyrand) 'hangs Mr de Celles in effigy'. This man is consequently obliged to live at Paris and anxious to annex his country to France. He is very well versed in affairs and clever in intrigue and he is married to a daughter of General Valence,[258] which not only brings him in relation with Marshal Gerard, who has married another, but with the Palais Royal where there were so many connections of Mme de Genlis.[259] He exercises also much influence over the Belgian Minister Le Hon. And Baudrand himself admitted to me that his object was supposed to be the embroiling matters for the purpose of annexing Brabant.

I learnt in House of Lords that Sir Francis Burdett[260] had declined the peerage and that Byng[261] was hurt it had not been offered to him. Why should it not be now? [*In the margin:* It was the next day, but Byng declined it unless with remainder to his brother, which could not be granted. Tho' he refused it, he was satisfied and pleased at the offer.] Lord Foley,[262] say Sefton and Brougham, must be hurt at not being an Earl. Why did he not ask for it? says Grey. And why should he not have it now? I replied. The Duke of Sussex presented a remarkable petition of Merchants and others of the City of London, in number 1100, all either Grand Jurors, Jurors, or liable to serve as such, declaring that they could not according to their notions of duty either prosecute or on evidence pronounce men guilty of offences which, unaccompanied with violence, were by law visited *by capital* punishment, and praying therefore for the abrogation of that punishment in all cases but those of murder or crimes attached with violence. The Duke of Sussex stated the nature of the petition and the prayer of it, and described the persons who signed it and the reasons why no Quakers (though all of that opinion) had been permitted to subjoin their names, with the great force and perspicacity and with a delicacy and propriety very unusual in His Royal Highnesses speeches. Nothing could be better. Brougham with great <clear>ness and force but with some little hypocrisy and at much too great length, asserted the *right* of a state to punish offences with death, and answered the petitioners who acknowledged that they had forsworn themselves by giving verdicts against the evidence they had heard. The Tories applauded and Lord Tenterden[263] complimented his speech, but surely he does not mean to change his course on this most interesting subject. Duke of Wellington talked some nonsense about what he called the *preventative Police* on the Continent. What preventive police but bad pens can hinder forgery? The Chancellor came out and slept at Holland House.

7 September. Heard from Grey that the promotions were final. Neither Byng, Foley, nor Newburgh[264] could have their wishes. He was vexed with the discontents of some and manifestly out of spirits. I went to St. James but did not see the King, for Sir Herbert Taylor told me he had sounded him, in the sense of his conversation with Grey and myself, on speaking to the Archbishop against postponement, and found him singularly and decidedly averse to it. Still however earnest for bill and anxious not to part with us, which he would be disposed to imagine and wish that neither postponement nor rejection would necessitate. I told Sir Herbert that considering that he had dissolved Parliament for us, I thought that as long as we deemed we could either be of comfort or use to him we were bound to stand by him and sacrifice even some character for him; but that as at present advised, if we submitted to the postponement or rejection, I held that we were lost with the publick and should do him more harm than good, for these were not times in which the confidence in parties or individuals was so strong as to survive appearances or stand the suspicions they created. Sir Herbert told me the King was much excited and harrassed. We dined at Lord Chancellor's with several Judges and Lawyers. Byng had the offer of the peerage and was pleased, but unless it could be settled on his brother and nephew (which it cannot), declined it. Lord Charlemont,[265] unreasonably dissatisfied at *his brother*[266] not being included in peerage though he has himself been offered one, declined it, a Lordship of the bedchamber which he declined also, and a St. Patrick's ribband which he accepted but now seems inclined to refuse. Grey always feels these reproaches too much.

8 September. Up early and at Pay office by 8 o'clock. Saw Lady William Russell[267] in her dress and witnessed from the Window the procession to and from the Coronation. The Weather was tolerable, the cavalcade well managed, the <leanings> and trappings &c of the horses magnificent, and the sides of the Street, windows and tops of houses crouded with people who received the King and Queen with acclamations, applauded the Duke of Sussex and Lord Chancellor Brougham, and occasionally but not loudly hissed and groaned at Duke of Cumberland. I met Lord Grey in St. James's park with his Coronet and Robe. We dined with Lord Essex.[268] Accounts of the Coronation may be better given by persons who were in the Abbey. Many say that at one fifth of the Expence, it was (owing to the attendance of Peeresses and House of Commons) a finer piece of pageantry than the last.[269] The King at his dinner at St. James's justly observed that as pageantry and shew it might be gratifying, but that the oath, if of consequence, should be taken at accession and that, in truth, upon that occasion every necessary oath and precaution was taken in conformity with the law to ensure the observance of the great compact between the King and the people. Any Prince who after his accession and before his Coronation imagined that he was less bound to govern by law was not fit to be a King at all and had hardly sense enough to deserve the appellation of a Man.

Septr. 9 Friday. Mr Crampton,[270] Irish Solicitor General, and Plunkett to breakfast in old Burlington Street.[271] The first full of Attorney General Blackburne's vindication against the Charge of Orange propensities in the distribution of his patronage. The latter earnest about the preferment of his son who, if Knox[272] is made a Bishop, is offered the Deanery of Derry;[273] if Lefanu[274] (Sheridan's nephew), a smaller deanery held by that Gentleman; and in certain other arrangements might be at once Bishop of Raphoe.

At Cabinet at 1/2 past one. News from Lisbon. English property and English subjects in so much jeopardy that we determined to send a Ship of the line without loss of time to the Tagus. Lord Grey stated very fairly the reasons for and against restoring Lord Dundonald to his rank in the Navy, viz the severity of his original sentence, the length of time elapsed, his extraordinary gallantry and professional abilities, and the consideration his name bore in the world and even among the younger portion of the British Navy; on the other hand, the dishonourable nature of the offence of which he had been convicted, the equivocal character of his subsequent conduct, his impracticability when serving under superior officers, and the objection felt to the measure in Most of the higher ranks in the profession. The Chancellor who had been his council [*sic*] mentioned many circumstances in mitigation of his offence and urged as well as Carlisle, Lord Lansdown, and myself the value of his services in the Navy and the possible inconvenience of leaving so great and enterprizing an Admiral in a situation to seek employment elsewhere. But Duke of Richmond and Palmerston and others were earnest against restoring him to his rank or his red ribband; and a letter from Sir Thomas Hardy[275] to Mr Croker,[276] which though private had been maliciously converted into a publick communication by the latter Gentleman and which designated Cochrane's conduct in the pacifick as *piratical,* had great weight in indisposing our Colleagues to that measure. Sir James Graham certainly related on the authority of Hardy some disgusting instances of his extortion when Admiral of Chile or Peru, and these circumstances, combined with acknowledged averseness of the King to the measure, determined the Cabinet to abandon the restoration to his rank. And Lord Melbourne put an end to the proposal of confining our measure to a simple pardon by observing justly enough that if we did not restore him to his rank we did not gain him, and yet if we pardoned him we passed some indirect censure on the law, and offended those who would sternly enforce on an officer a strict observance of the most delicate principles of honour. I called at St. James's where I found Grey waiting in Sir Herbert Taylor's room. They talked of the silly conduct of Duchess of Kent, who on the pretence of her daughter's health and her own oeconomy or from an absurd pique at the place assigned her in the Coronation had declined attending that solemnity. The King had in the first instance goodhumouredly acquiesced, but was nettled at the proceeding in reflection and still more at the comments in the publick prints to which it had given rise. Sir Herbert told me that the loss of two ships in the Baltick was among the causes assigned by the King for his unmerited prejudice against Sir James Saumarez. Grey told me he had given the Bishoprick of Worcester to Carr of Chichester,[277] the King having suggested or in a way asked it for him, and he projected making Dr Maltby[278] the new Bishop. The Greys were staying at Holland House and Plunkett and the Chancellor dined with us.

10 Septr. Saturday. Attended the Council of the Duchy of Cornwall for the first time. I heard enough to convince me of the superior importance in point of profit of that Duchy over that of Lancaster. From thence I met Charlemont by appointment at Brookes's and succeeded in persuading him to accept of St. Patrick's ribband, and in removing from his mind (if there were any) all discontent or resentment towards Grey, though he could not renounce the hope of some measure being resorted to, if we remained in office, to secure a British peerage to the descendants of the late Lord Charlemont. Cabinet at four. Spring Guns bill and special Constables bill discussed.[279] The fresh news from Oporto prove the condition of the English there to [be] worse than even at Lisbon. Palmerston and Graham acquiesce in the impolicy of our neglect of Pedro and ascribe it to the King. They think more decided measures must shortly be resorted to. The Conference has this day established an exchange of Prisoners between Dutch and Belgian governments,[280] and the instances of the latter to the French Marshal to keep his troops in Belgium are excused in a way to us that somewhat allays the suspicion of our most antiGallican Colleagues. Grey had been much touched this morning at Sir James Saumarez's complaints and had stated his vindication of the loss of St. George to the King, who agreed to see Graham and Hardy upon it and sent to Sir G Seymour[281] to ask him if the promotion of Sir James Saumarez would not displease the whole Navy. On the contrary, replied that gallant officer; I know nothing that would be more generally applauded by all that love the Service. The King in the evening wrote to Grey that *his Barony should go on,* and Grey had the satisfaction of conquering a prejudice infused by some evil spirit in the King's mind and of promoting a Professional man of great character in the Navy. He also obtained promisses to make Mr Sydney Smith[282] prebendiary of St. Pauls, vacant by Carr's translation to Worcester.

Lord Chancellor Brougham opened to Cabinet the embarrassment likely to occur from a proceeding in Chancery of Coll. D'Este, son of the Duke of Sussex, to perpetuate the evidence of an old Clergyman of the name of <G . . . >, respecting the validity of his father's marriage at Rome; and he made a suggestion not much relished I think by the Cabinet, and to me highly questionable both in principle and policy, of a reference from King to Privy Council for advice on the subject, His Attorney General having demurred to being made party in the suit for perpetuation of evidence.

Talleyrand called at night and pressed me to urge on Baudrand, if I saw him, my persuasion of the prudence in a New Government not to attempt too many things at home, or any at all at home, unless absolutely necessary.

11 Sunday. Grey shewed me a letter from Duchess of Kent in answer to one from him on subject of her absence from Coronation. The spirit of it was very bad: much indefinite complaint of past ill usage; extreme soreness at late attacks in newspapers; exhortation to Lord Grey to ascertain and chastize the quarter from whence it came, with insinuations that it was the King's family; explanation of King and Queen's coldness and estrangement by her uniform reluctance to admit the FitzClarences, as the Queen does, as the King's children; offensive and rather unintelligible reference to Lewis XIV and Charles II; vindication of charge of omitting to invite Lady Errol to dinner at Isle of Wight; retort on Lord Adolphus for intrusive visit and conduct; justification of Sir John Conroy[283] and one or two broad hints that those who now offend her may feel the weight of her displeasure if ever she becomes Regent or her daughter Queen [*In the margin:* together with phrases shewing that she does not deem that event so remote as we all hope it is]. Intercepted letters from Portugal confirm Mr Hoppner's accounts. Some remarks or rather interlineations of H M in a Belgian [dispatch?] prove that he is very quick in discovering the errors and faults of King Leopold, a faculty which the conduct of Duchess of Kent is likely to question. Miss D'Este said to Lord Grey, the King is a good man but 'the worst is, any body can bully him'. True or false, it is bad that those about him should have such a notion of his want of resolution. Chancellor and Plunkett slept at Holland House. Alvanley[284] gave in his adhesion and some good advice.

12 Monday. Saw my daughter and grand daughter. I am not entitled to a Coronation Medal, not having been present. In my way to the King's dinner, learnt with no little concern from Charles, the sad Catastrophe of poor Calcraft,[285] who put an end to his life. With all his faults, publick and private, he was an amiable, useful, and clever man. He has not left a more ready debater behind him. And if he had much of the appearance and some of the faults, he had all of the merits, of that race of unprincipled politicians who formed the majority of our leading publick men during the greater part of last century. He was frank, bold, friendly, and honourable to his party, as long as he professed to belong to it, though incapable perhaps of chusing or adhering to it from any publick virtue.

At Court I learnt that the French had signified their intention of withdrawing their troops and fixed their time. Austria and Talleyrand seemed to me unfeignedly pleased. Bulow somewhat ungraciously ascribed it to our firmness and their fear, but shrewdly remarked that it would surprize and vex our opposition here. The King, after a great banquet to the Diplomacy, Ministers &c, to the amount of <5>0 or 80, made one or two long speeches in French which proved his wish to oblige Talleyrand and his own good spirits and anxiety to please more than his knowledge of French and his taste and propriety. [*In the margin:* This propensity to make foolish speeches after dinner is the only fault the King has. It is not a very great one, a venial offence against taste and judgement and nothing more. The speeches are so unintelligible that they fortunately offend taste more than judgement, gratify the <mirth> of an enemy but in nowise commit or expose his political friends.] It was well meant but somewhat distressing. He was particularly civil to me both at the dinner and in the drawing room.

13 Tuesday. Missed seeing the King from forgetting that it was a levee day. Called on Lords Bessborough[286] and Ilchester[287] and understood from them that Mr W Ponsonby[288] was gone down to stand for Dorsetshire. At the Cabinet. It was called from a notion that part of Sir J Graham['s] representation of the Conduct of Lord Dundonald (Cochrane) in South seas since his dismissal from the British service had transpired, but before we met, Sir James had ascertained that Lord Dundonald's ground for seeking an opportunity of vindicating himself proceeded upon other matters. It was unnecessary to (prosecute) the enquiry further. But one thing was clear from our conversation—that all the evidence we had of his subsequent misbehaviour rested on the moral conviction of an honourable man, but not on any thing like judicial evidence, much less on any allegations he had had any opportunity to refute.

The assurance of the French that they will evacuate Belgium by the 30th. seems quite satisfactory in form and substance, and the alarms of the most suspicious among us are allayed. It appears from Sebastiani's assurances that there is no foundation whatever for the story of demands and refusal of commercial advantages by the French Admiral at Lisbon on which Lord Aberdeen grounded so much of his argument and invective against ministry. The King has a fancy to augment the navy and had directed Sir J Graham to submit it to the Cabinet. The report of its strength given by Sir James was highly satisfactory, and the Cabinet approved a letter he had drawn up to satisfy His Majesty that it was sufficient for any service likely to be required, in better condition than it had been for some years, and that both the expence and the alarm it would occasion would be insuperable objections to any augmentation not obviously and undeniably necessary. I arrived too late in House of Lords to hear rather a warm altercation between Lord King and the opposition, in which the latter endeavoured to have Lord King's words taken down as reflecting on the house.[289] Dull business ensued and especially the Archbishop's plurality bill, on which Lord Harrowby[290] made a sensible speech and Lord Wynford many dull ones.

14th. Septr. The Chancellor to expedite his appeals had, as I suspect, contrived to keep away the Garter King of Arms or officers necessary to the introduction of Peers. He for the same reason absented himself from Cabinet, where it was decided not to augment the number of Scotch representatives in the Reform bill, but to make in one or two instances a distribution more popular in the Counties and more agreable to the professed principle of the Union provisions. It would have been hazardous to have enlarged the numbers, for Ireland, which has already more than a share, would also have insisted on some further encrease and, if refused, have had a fresh grievance which OConnel and the repealers of Union would easily have turned to advantage.[291] <I and> Lord Plunkett introduced Lord Meath[292] by his English title of Chaworth. I saw the King who was well and gracious, somewhat vehement against both Leopold and King of Holland, extremely pacifick in his professions but somewhat jealous of any strong declaration of others against war, as if it might be intended to reflect on a contrary propensity in him. He acquiesced in the decision of the Cabinet against any augmentation of our maritime force and in the reasons assigned in the Admiralty paper, but he maintained, and I believe with truth, that our ships, though superior in that as in all other respects to those of *other nations* (I am afraid he said of *the Enemy,* which was a slip, not I trust indicating any serious design of war), were yet imperfectly manned. If his attention is directed to improving and completing the force we have and not to augmenting it, the Country will derive some advantage from his great sensibility on the subject of his fleets. In the Lords, Grey stretched a point and gave, contrary to general usage, the King's advocate's opinion and [? on] the case relating to Portugueze ships in the Tagus. Lord Londonderry made one of his most foolish and offensive harangues, breathing hatred, malice, and all uncharitableness towards France, and affording Grey an opportunity of bearing testimony to her good faith and the cordial understanding subsisting between us, and Lord Chancellor Brougham the still greater advantage of pronouncing one of the liveliest, severest, most eloquent, and most useful speeches I ever heard delivered. Neither Wellington nor Aberdeen were there, nor did any of the party shew much stomach to defend that officious supporter, who does us more good by estranging the publick from our enemies than the zeal of ten friends could accomplish.

Dined with Grey, Richmond at Lord Melbourne's. They are all in better heart about the Lords, and I think most are reconciled and all familiarized to the scheme of administering *quantum sufficit* to the composition of the House of Lords, if they should dare to reject it. A notion occurred to me, and I communicated it to Grey, that Sir Herbert Taylor's elevation to the peerage might please both him and the King and have no unwholesome effect on the Courtiers in the House. Moreover he deserves it—a laborious, distinct, discreet, and honorable Man.

September 15. Returned to Holland House. Read dispatches, but neither went to House of Lords nor saw any of my Colleagues.

September 16. Hry. Webster told me that Portugueze loan was likely to be raised and Pedro not unlikely to come over, that his expences when in London would be paid, and that Funchal was at Paris. Palmerston daily expected in London. Chancellor is disposed to dispute Lord Grey's claim to patronage vacated by Bishoprick when that patronage is in the Chancellor's gift. Esterhazy[293] and Talleyrand dined here. The latter pleased with pacifick tone of French papers and urgent on the Conference to finish the definitive treaty. It is better, he says, to finish, though imperfectly, than with hopes of improvement to delay its conclusion beyond the 10th. of October.

September 17. Visit from Lord and Lady Breadalbane. Somewhat disproportionate expressions of gratitude for their Marquisate. Cabinet. The West Indians press for a Committee of Lords to enquire into state of Slavery and means of mitigating or abolishing it. And Chandos,[294] the Chairman of the Committee of West Indians, is reported to have said to Buxton[295] and others that he would agree to a Parliamentary measure for emancipation if a loan or an indemnity to the amount of 5 millions were given to the Planters. To such a compromise however I doubt the West Indian body being a party, and I know neither Lord Seaford,[296] Lord St. Vincents,[297] nor I have been consulted thereupon. The Chancellor with great plausibility deprecated the policy of announcing enquiry when it could not be prosecuted, especially as he assured us that the Emancipators and Saints would consider it as absolute defiance and defeat (a strange admission this), and we should have meetings and petitions almost equal in number and vehemence to those of reform, reviling our Government as Slave drivers and arraigning some Members of it as apostates from the cause of freedom. He then launched out on the uncertainty and perjury of all West India evidence, and very unfairly accused them all of a design of perpetuating slavery and instituting an enquiry with a view of disproving the evils of Slavery altogether, not of ascertaining the method of mitigating and gradually abrogating it. He did not, nor could he, point out what measure short of immediate emancipation, by a law of the Mother Country and a supersession of all local authorities, would satisfy the Saints. It was at last agreed to ascertain the extent and nature of the agreement proposed or settled between Mr Buxton on one side and Lord Chandos on the other, with a view of regulating our course on a great measure thereby. Lord Goderich had difficulties in acting, even in the Crown Colonies and yet more with Jamaica and those who had legislatures of their own, on a resolution proposed but not adopted last Session of Parliament, viz of lowering the duties on Sugar grown in the Colonies who admitted our regulations and laws respecting Slaves, and keeping up or augmenting them on the produce of those who rejected all such improvements.[298] The truth is, the difficulty of the subject and the unreasonableness of both the parties with whom we have to deal led us, weakly enough, to postpone our decision on the pretence of ascertaining the extent of Lord Chandos's negotiations. Lord Grey, Lord Goderich, and Mr Stanley seemed fully aware of the distressed state of West Indian concerns, and not less so of the extravagant and impracticable plans of the party who call for immediate emancipation, but have neither views nor plan of providing for the subsistence or subordination of the Emancipated.

Lord Dundonald had applied officially to Sir James Graham and privately to Sir Ths. Hardy for information on the representations made to the Admiralty of his conduct when in Command of the Chilian or Brasilian fleet, and a proper letter declining it on the score of usage and propriety, and with a hint that his very command of a foreign fleet was a breach of the Law, was drawn up by Lord Grey. Sir Ths. Hardy had imprudently acquainted Lady Cochrane[299] that such correspondence existed and had lately been referred to, and that admission gives Lord Dundonald some, though a very faint, colour for supposing a proceeding to be instituted on his conduct and applying for the means and opportunity of defending himself. I understand he disputes the legality of his deprivation of the red ribband. How much better would it have been, by a pardon and restoration at the Coronation, to have avoided these embarrassing questions (sure to be taken up by many of our best friends) and to have recovered the first Naval Officer of the age to His Majesty's service?

Lord Grey took me to Shene in my way to Richmond. Lord Durham has ceased writing to him. The breach between Duchess of Kent and King seems irreparable. She had wished General Wetherall[300] to have a Grand Cross, and Sir John Conroy to be made a Baronet. The King would not hear of the latter and expressed more determination and even passion than is usual with him, which Grey was at great pains to conceal from Duchess of Kent, but which no doubt may have reached her thro' other channels. The whole family takes little pains to conceal their dislike to her, and the Princess Sophia is suspected of an inclination, for some reason or another, to blow the coals and keep up the estrangement.

The sad news of the capture of Warsaw arrived this day. Palmerston seems properly impressed with the urgency of making some representations, in the spirit of the treaty of Vienna, to prevent the entire subjugation of the Kingdom of Poland into a province of Russia.[301] I slept at Richmond.

18 Septr. 1831, Sunday. At Richmond. Though in the course of the Morning I saw Lord Lyndhurst and Lord Grey and heard from Henry Webster of Palmela's arrival, nothing political occurred. Lyndhurst thinks the bill entirely depends on the Bishops. Palmela reports that the little army of Terceira[302] still at St. Michael's is in high condition and spirits and amounts to 4000 men.

19 Septr., Monday. On my return to Holland House saw Palmela, who has thriven on his hard fare and poverty and subsequent success in the Azores. He was very anxious to ascertain the views of our Government with regard to Don Pedro. If we wished him to return here, if we should prefer a Government in his daughter's or in his own name, and how far we should acquiesce in any assistance given him from France; in short, whether there existed any jealousy between the two Countries on that subject. I advised him to see Lords Grey and Palmerston without loss of time, to speak openly and consult with them unreservedly as he would with me, and though there was no jealousy between England and France, to labour to render any countenance given to his cause common from both, a joint and not separate act. In the house of Lords, Lord Aberdeen restated his information that Admiral Roussin had demanded from the Portuguese Government of Don Miguel an admission to privileges for the French equal to those of the English in Portugal and brought an article of a Convention signed on the 22d. July in corroboration of that belief, because, as he contended, that article, though it contained no stipulation of the sort, related to commercial negotiations and raised an inference that some such demand had been made and eluded by the introduction of a vague and unmeaning article. Lord Grey read General Sebastiani's distinct denial of any such negotiation having occurred, acknowledged he had not seen or known of the second convention of the 22d. of July. After the Duke of Wellington, I spoke, with little or no effect, but questioned the authority on which Lord Aberdeen relied, expressed some doubts even of the existence of the convention, and yet more of the supposed negotiation of the French to be admitted on the footing of the most favored nation. Lord Aberdeen afterwards shewed me the Portugueze gazette, containing a paragraph from which he inferred the existence of the convention of 22d. July, and a written copy in French of that convention. Even if it be authentick, no article in it substantiates Lord Aberdeen's surmize or charge against the French Admiral, though it certainly is irreconciliable with *the letter,* not perhaps the spirit, of Sebastiani's denial of any negotiation on matters relating to Commerce. Aberdeen betted me a Sovereign; that is, he is to receive one if I acknowledge that I believe in the Convention and the article he shewed me or in the Admiral's demand of such commercial advantages. If at the end of two months I am still incredulous, he is to pay me one.

20 Septr. Duchy business with Mr Danvers; and sent by King's command four medals to those who had assisted the Commission for the treasure trove at Tutbury.

House of Lords. Lyndhurst attacked, in a long speech, the Bankruptcy bill of Lord Brougham, who defended it and himself in a yet longer but very able speech. Lord Eldon spoke at some length, but feebly. Little but the garrulity of age remains, but there is a good humour and mildness in his manner that is agreable. We had a division on an amendment moved by Lord Tenterden in the Archbishop's plurality bills, and 11 or 12 Ultra tory Lords and Bishops laid in with Lord Tenterden; Duke of Wellington, Bathurst,[303] Bishop of London, and others voting to the amount of 53 or 54 (with the Archbishop).[304] I found Palmela (who had seen Palmerston) at Holland House. He presses us to espouse Pedro or his daughter's cause at once, and is curious to know if we should take umbrage were the little Queen affianced to a Son of King Philip *Lewis* [*sic*]. I say we should dislike it.

21 September. At the Levee. Bulow implies some in the conference are disposed to protract the conclusion or to vary the terms of definitive treaty of peace in consequence of the reduction of Warsaw, but protests that it ought not and will not vary the views of his Government nor produce the slightest disposition to stickle for more in favor of Holland than before. Talleyrand, as usual, earnest for dictating terms and concluding the affair. The accounts from Paris manifestly distress and alarm him,[305] tho' there is much praise of Cas[imir] Perrier's courage and the army's fidelity. Lord Lyndhurst and Lord Grey at dinner. Lady Lyndhurst's conversation would lead one to hope he will not vote against 2d. reading of bill, and betrays much estrangement from the party in opposition, which, if his information is correct, is greatly divided. Lord Chancellor in Evening gave an account of a meeting of 90 Members of the House of Commons, all independent of Ministers and including Hume[306] and OConnel, where it was agreed that even in case of the rejection of bill in the Lords, it would in the judgement of all present be a desertion of the King and the Country in the present Ministers to resign.

22d. Septr. Lord John Russell and house of Commons brought up the bill to a full house of Lords. There seemed a preconcerted silence and moderation on the opposition benches and they received the distant day of Monday, the 3d. Octr., named for the second reading, and even the hint that little time would be suffered to elapse between that stage and the committal, with great composure and even approbation. I slept in Old Burlington Street.

23 Septr. Friday. Cabinet at twelve. It was agreed somewhat against our wishes to add three Members to Scotland and to the inevitable but much less reasonable consequence as many to Ireland. Althorp told us that such a concession would greatly accelerate and facilitate the progress of both bills, and he and the other Members of the Commons seemed very apprehensive that we should be beat if we resisted it by the combination of Irish and Scotch reformers and the antireforemers who, for the sake of embarrassing us and furnishing their cooperators with an irresistible argument for delay in the Lords, would vote for them. The embarrassing questions relating to Don Pedro and Don Miguel were talked over.

The substance of dispatches from Lisbon containing fresh instances of outrages and invasions was stated, and a letter of Don Pedro from Paris, detailing his conversation with Sebastiani and disclaiming in strong terms any disposition to sanction propagandism or connect himself with liberal party in Spain, was described and afterwards put into circulation. He and Palmela naturally and earnestly press for a decision. Lord Goderich seems to question our right, and Duke of Richmond the policy, of going to open war with Don Miguel, and they as well as others deprecate the unfairness and folly of inviting Pedro here, winking at his preparations and half encouraging his expedition from our coasts and against our laws, yet not openly espousing his cause. I think we have cause of war against Miguel and should declare it. And in support of that policy I urged the danger of leaving to the French exclusively the credit and advantage of restoring a good government in Portugal, and not taking the lead in so righteous a cause while France very handsomely and fairly was disposed to allow us. Palmerston and Grey and I think Stanley, Lord J Russel, Sir James Graham, and even Althorp leant to my opinion, but many were gone before the topick was introduced and nothing consequently was settled. Palmela's interview with Grey and Palmerston had inspired the first with confidence in him and revived in the latter some of his old and just indignation against Miguel. The Spaniards are so apprehensive of civil war in Portugal, that they would acquiesce in any arrangement England and France were to recommend about Portugal, provided it was likely and possible to be accomplished without a war, which would embody Spanish patriots with Don Pedro's partizans. Neither Shee nor Backhouse[307] can find any traces of the second convention of 22 July. It is not in the gazette, nor does the passage in the [Portuguese] gazette shewn me by Aberdeen prove its existence. Yet Aberdeen persists in believing it and still suspects it must be in the office, sneeringly observing that Palmerston must have put it in his pocket like the letter from Holland. In the Lords the game bill[308] by courtesy was referred to a select Committee. Wynford and Brougham spoke in the Committee on Bankruptcy bill. I dined at Talleyrands who was far from well. He, Palmela, and Lima[309] confirmed me in disbelief of the Convention. And Palmela presses more earnestly than ever for some explicit answer to Don Pedro.

24th. Septr. Saturday. Saw the King. Though in health and physical spirits he did not seem sanguine about the success of our bill in the Lords, spoke of the hostility of the Aristocracy; and when I remarked that whether that word related to the Antiquity of family or vast landed possessions—I thought they were at least pretty equally divided—he only observed that antiquity of family was nothing to the purpose; when a Man was a peer he was as much so as if his ancestors had been there for centuries. All which is true, but makes H M's remark amount only to this, that there are great numbers against us in House of Lords. He expressed surprize at Lord de Saumarez and Bishop of Bath and Wells[310] (whose preaching he admires not I suspect with much reason) voting for the bill and made another remark on the latter, in which he is probably mistaken, that he expected nothing better than his present Bishoprick. I learnt from Sir Herbert Taylor that he was more averse to any further encrease of the House of Lords than I supposed, that he plumed himself upon his sagacity and foresight in predicting so much resistance there, and dwelt much on modification and compromise and not overwhelming creations being the only safe method of overcoming it. The Chancellor came in the Evening. The King, hearing he was going to Westmoreland for air, told him Windsor was as good and nearer, invited him thither for a day and he goes tomorrow. He tells me that H M has taken great umbrage at a speech of Coll. Torrens[311] in the city, suggesting the propriety of putting the House of Lords themselves, if refractory, in Schedule A, and has written to consult the Admiralty on the propriety of striking him out of the Marines in virtue of his prerogative. In the same letter he complains of the same Gentleman's speech in Parliament,[312] any proceeding on which would be a breach of privilege. Brougham told me also that an embarrassing question was likely to arise from the too open and positively illegal preparations of the Portugueze in the river. He goes down to Windsor with strong prepossessions against the Queen. I cautioned him against hasty conclusions about her hostility and preached observation and courtesy. Lord Waldegrave,[313] whom I saw in the morning and also who reluctantly and from fear of his place will vote for the bill, let drop a word that shews he considers a place in the Queen's household more enviable than his own, because the holder of it may with impunity vote against Government. I said that might be so but I did not know how it appeared, and he said nothing.

Lord Durham's son,[314] once the picture of health, beauty and promise, is dead, and Grey though prepared for the event is much overwhelmed. I hope the grief will soften other matters in the family, and Durham be soothed by the unaffected sympathy of his father in Law in his misfortunes. But who can speculate on so forward a temper?

25th. Septr. Lord Seaford had a conversation with me on West Indian topicks—the condition of the Slaves, the disposition of the Assemblies and white inhabitants, and the means of relieving the distresses. On the first is earnest not for a Parliamentary but a Government enquiry who, he says, should exact from the two parties of West Indians and emancipators a plain statement of the points in which each thinks the other has made misrepresentations, and then direct impartial and intelligent publick officers *silently* to ascertain and report the fact. He shewed me some violent and alarming resolutions of parishes in Jamaica, demanding an absolution from allegiance and praying their assemblies to petition for it. He agreed that the only permanent relief would be a lowering of the duty on Sugar and the final abolition of foreign Slave trade, and contended that the refinery bill[315] was an encouragement of it.

Cabinet. Thinly attended. Lord Chancellor, Lord Lansdowne, and Lord Grey absent, the latter from affliction at the death of his Grandson. Sir James Graham lay before us an angry speech of Colonel Torrens of the Marines[316] and referring to the board of Admiralty the propriety of taking away his commission. The answer of the Admiralty was firm and decisive in the negative, and we concurred in their reasons of law and equity and added others of expediency of our own. The intelligence received of Don Pedro's preparation in the river and the interference of his recruiting with our press for Sailors was then brought before consideration. The frigates were not, as Lord Chancellor supposed, armed, nor did the Portuguese flag float on their masts. But the inconvenient and unjust act called the enlistment act uses the word *equip* or arm, and the report of our naval men is that the preparations are open, scandalous, and cannot be overlooked. We agreed with some reluctance to enquire, agreeing that a breach of the laws cannot come within our cognizance without endeavouring to prevent or to punish it. But I was happy to perceive that with the exception of Lord Goderich and perhaps Grant we were none disposed to be unnecessarily hasty or vigilant, and I again touched the string of a more open espousal of Don Pedro's cause in a way to familia[rize] the overscrupulous to the idea and to awaken the alarms of those who dread French preponderance to the consequences of an opposite course. We are not to meet till Wednesday and Lord Londonderry is written to to put off his motion in consequence of Grey's affiliction. San Payo,[317] the Portugueze Consul, has sent Palmerston the Convention, which I suppose was signed but contains nothing in proof of commercial proposals from the French Admiral.

Palmela who called at Holland House in the evening, had seen Grey and was satisfied with his interview. By the advice of Sir James Mackintosh,[318] who takes great interest in that affair, he is to write a letter to me to be shewn the Cabinet, and he is to do his best to get the unarmed Ships to Dieppe as fast as he can. He will no doubt reprimand the imprudence of those who on shore and without authority have crimped Seamen or enlisted Soldiers with a Portugueze flag.

Talleyrand says all depends on the next fortnight. Reform in England and definitive treaty between Holland and Belgium. On the plea or pretence of humanity, he seems inclined to foist in some provisions to prevent future inundation, to which Holland and Prussia will clearly not agree and which we should be backward to sanction. He tells me that King Philip has written him volumes and sent him a map of his own constructing with his notions on the frontiers of Holland. Tous les Rois sont geographes et pour lui il est vraiment un grand geographe. I told him our King without being a great geographer happened to plume himself too upon very particular information on the Dutch line of defence and that there was no pretence for not leaving Holland and Prussia as good frontiers as they had before the union of Belgium and Holland.

26 Septr. Monday. Unwell and did not attend house of Lords or the board of trade where I was engaged to meet Auckland and Goderich &c about wine duties.

27th. Tuesday. Anglesey came to take his seat in good health and spirits. Grey, from grief and too great apprehension of hurting Lord Durham, averse to attending Cabinet, Parliament, or Court, in all of which, especially the latter, his exertions just now are so necessary. Though ill, I attended the house of Lords where Lord Chancellor repelled the attack of Lord Londonderry for his absence from Woolsack on Monday with admirable temper, judgement, and effect, and I ridiculed both his and Lord Eldon's ignorance of the Constitution of the house and its orders with some success. On the remaining business of the day I paired off with Lord Wicklow. Lord Chancellor was with me till late at night, recounting his observations at Windsor. The King, he said, was beset with female antireformers and they, from ignorance or design, full of lies about the state of the Country and the opinion of individuals. Lord Brougham seemed to have counteracted such impressions as this perpetual supply of false reasoning and inaccurate facts might make on the King's mind with great dexterity. But H M is more irritable at the licentious intimidation of the Lords; more impressed with the aversion of the great aristocracy to the measure of reform; and more inclined to listen to the idle stories of relaxation in the desire of reform in the publick than on dispassionate enquiry would be found to be true, or than we, who are convinced of the necessity of the bill, can wish him to give credit to.

28th. Septr. 1831. Draft of <. . .> for quarterly payment of Duchy payable tomorrow. At Court communicated Palmela's wishes and letter to Palmerston and my other Colleagues; learnt that King was yet sore about Colonel Torrens's speeches, but diverted on a point of law in the Admiralty answer, which he thought incorrect, from the original cause of his chagrin. Talleyrand told me and Palmerston confirmed the news that the King of Netherlands was making active preparations and manifestly meditated immediate hostilities on expiration of armistice. I had some conversation with Goderich on West Indian matters and sugar. The Sugar refinery comes in to day in Commons and it does not appear to me that it will break Goderich's heart if we lose it. He is friendly to the West Indian interest, but agrees with me that a reduction of duty and a total abolition of foreign slave trade are the only measures that can permanently benefit the West Indian planters.

Anglesey gave a candid and interesting account of Ireland. He is for vigorous measures in England and will tell the King, whom he will see tomorrow, that we must leave no stone unturned to pass the bill. Plunkett and Chancellor in evening. Various reports of the intentions of individual peers and Bishops about voting. Persons conversant in lists pretend that the bill will be beat by nine without Bishops, and some say (preposterously I think) by 17 when they are added to th<is> number.

29th. September. At Cabinet. A Question between Lord Plunkett and the Irish Master of Rolls, MacMahon,[319] relating to the appointment of a Secretary in the latter court, which has for 25 years been constantly given by the Chancellors and the patronage of which Plunkett is desirous of retaining during his Chancellorship; but Master of the Rolls, Irish Members of Parliament, and English Lawyers (save and except the Chancellor, the Attorney and Solicitor[320]) are disposed to take from him. His present appointment is to be sustained but a bill to regulate the office will probably be the result.[321] Duke of Richmond urged the propriety of removing those of Queen's household who vote against us, but as neither Lord Grey nor Lord Lansdowne was present no resolution on so delicate a question could be taken, and we soon left positive business to converse on various matters and the approaching question of Londonderry on Belgium in Lords. Palmerston told me no answer could be given to Pedro or Palmela for some time and that the enquiries in the river were not likely to lead to any discoveries that would be injurious to the former. In the meanwhile the Miguelite officers had been landed from the Portugueze Ships in the Tagus, and the crews had declared for Donna Maria. Palmela will probably set off to Paris, and both Palmerston and myself wrote him notes that are likely to induce him to do so and at the same time to explain his having staid so long to Don Pedro.

In the Lords a brisk conversation on reform petitions in which I took a prominent part and marked with some effect the hypocritical declarations of our opponents that they are not Antireformers. Londonderry made a long, malignant speech without talent, in the course of it inveighed against the civilities shewn Prince Talleyrand, threw out suspicions and dealt in violent though ill expressed invectives against France and our policy in Belgium. Goderich answered, or rather put aside his motion well, but indulged him too much by combating his other answers and statements, and gave a colour thereby to Duke of Wellington to prolong the debate who, in one of the best speeches he has ever made, did ample and handsome justice to Talleyrand and, with the help of false reports and some exaggeration, stigmatized the conduct of Leopold in accepting French officers as unwarrantable, suspicious, and at variance with the spirit of that neutrality which is guaranteed by the great powers for his territories. I answered flatly and lamely; but such is the nature of newspaper reports, the few words which I delivered on the reform petitions, with which I and I believe the House were well satisfied, were, in the reading, flat though violent, and my answer to the Duke appeared reasonable, judicious, and befitting a Minister. In the course of this debate some angry or rather coarse words passed between the Chancellor and Londonderry, and the latter for the first time in his life disarmed his antagonist by some appearance of humility, which Brougham then treated with good humour, feeling, and propriety, and all ended amicably.

30 September. At Duchy Council, and after dining at Holland House, to Lords, where we presented many petitions, and Aberdeen opposed the 3d. reading of the bill for equalizing the duty on wines, first on the beaten and exploded ground of being a violation of the treaty of 1810 or of the Methuen treaty combined with the second one;[322] secondly on the score of the vast commercial advantages resulting from our trade with Portugal; and lastly as a proof and link in that scheme of revolutionizing Portugal and propitiating Constitutional France for which he is so forward to arraign our Government. On the two first Goderich, in a most perspicuous well reasoned and agreable speech of some length, exposed this unfairness and ignorance of Aberdeen's views, and on the third declined to enter till the materials for forming a judgement, in the shape of the Portugueze papers, were before the house; and though he disclaimed the imputations cast upon us, maintained that the measure before us, being purely fiscal and commercial, could raise no question upon our political conduct in that Country. Duke of Wellington, more hostilely to us and with much less effect to the house, persisted in believing the bill, however we might denominate it financial and commercial, a link in the series of measures by which we hoped to revolutionize Portugal in favor of Don Pedro. Clanrickarde[323] very clearly separated the political from the commercial, maintained the first was not before us, but confidently appealed to the papers which would be soon produced. The House sat late.

1 October 1831 Saturday. Saw Grey at Sheen and found him still in deep affliction, and not a little harrassed at the prospect of the debate and division on bill; the state, if not of the court, of the household upon it; and at the variety of embarrassing and painful questions a rejection of the second reading would inevitably raise. He hesitates about making more peers, is determined to call up none till he knows the division on 2d. reading, manifestly doubts the king's firmness if it should be rejected, and foresees difficulties and reproaches in any course we can steer.

For the ensuing days, namely *2 3 4 5 6 7 8th. of October,* I neglected to keep this diary. I attended in the course of them one or two Cabinets in which the limits of Belgium and Holland were discussed, and the principle of restoring and even improving the antient line of defence of Holland, but removing all impediments to the fair commerce of Belgium, was approved; but the greatest part of my time was spent in the House of Lords where we met for 3 or 4 days as early as 4 [o'clock] and, after employing two or three hours or more in presenting petitions for the Reform bill, proceeded to the debate each night and only terminated it on Friday the 7th., or rather on the morning of the 8th., when we were beat by a majority greater than our calculation.[324] Lord Grey was much overcome and very nervous when he rose to open the business, but he soon recovered his usual fluency and eloquence, and enforced the justice at all times and the necessity at this of restoring the people to their just rights and representation in the House of Commons, in a speech of great earnestness and perspicuity. In the debate which ensued and lasted five days, Lord Mansfield,[325] Lord Wharncliffe, Lord Harrowby, Lord Carnarvon, and Lord Lyndhurst were the most prominent opponents of the bill; and Lord Grey, Lord Lansdown, Lord Goderich, Lord Radnor,[326] Lord Plunkett, and Lord Chancellor [Brougham] the most successful supporters, each and above all Lord Brougham in his own style of eloquence and argument surpassing himself. Lord Brougham's display was almost preternatural and miraculous. His voice, delivery, and action, perfect; the variety and versatility of his genius, his general knowledge and particular information, his readiness of retort and reply, and the soundness of his philosophical views delighted and astonished the house, though interest or prejudice were too strong to allow any marks of conviction to appear in their votes. The majority against the bill was greater than we had apprehended. It was remarked the twenty Bishops and twenty one Peers who are proprietors of boroughs and voted against the bill made up the number of 41 by which we were beat. The Chancellor in the course of his speech drank at least a bottle and half of mulled port and, taking some more after he had returned to the Woolsack, was so intoxicated that he could hardly put the question. And yet he wished to proceed three hours after the division to the trial of causes, and was only prevailed upon by the exhausted state of the Clerks to defer them till 1 or 2 o'clock in the day of the 8th. We of the Cabinet who were not such men of iron, deferred our meeting till three, where the Chancellor joined us from the house of Lords and was as marvellously lively, vigorous, and vehement in our councils of

Saturday the 8th. as he had been in the debate not twelve hours before. The King had answered Lord Grey's short and usual report of debate and division in a letter which expressed some little regret but no surprise at the event; reminded us of his having foreseen such a catastrophe to our bill; glanced with regret at no modifications having been devized to disarm or convert opponents; hinted at the propriety of such policy in future; deprecated the encrease of the peerage; but avowed a hope that the loss of the bill would not lead to the retirement of the Ministry.[327] It was, after much discussion but little if any difference of opinion, agreed to defer any minute or answer from the Cabinet till our strength in the Commons was known, and the course they meant to pursue ascertained. The Chancellor seemed confident that our continuance in office, even without any ostensible demonstration of power, would ensure the confidence of the country, and was somewhat alarmed at the peril of asking the King any thing which he was indisposed to grant at the close of a Session, because, he argued, it was always easy to form a Ministry at the close, and always difficult to do so at the opening of a Session. He inferred that all unpalatable steps that were necessary to our end should be deferred to the meeting of Parliament. We all concurred that no creation equal to constitute a Majority could, for the present at least, be resorted to; but with the exception of some faint distinctions of Palmerston, Lansdowne, and Richmond, the opinion of all was that the principles of the bill must to their full extent be adhered to, and that it was fair to the King to apprize him of our persuasion on that point as early as possible, and was no less prudent for our own character to give some pledge of our unaltered determination, as well as some signs of our power to the people. As we drove away, the Chancellor's horses were taken out of his carriage at Charing Cross and drawn by the people, through the acclamations of an encreasing multitude of well dressed followers, to his house.

A meeting of House of Commons of nearly 200 met this day and agreed to support, on the Monday following, two temperate resolutions to be moved by Lord Ebrington[328] adhering to the principles of the bill and expressive of their entire confidence in our administration.

Talleyrand called on me this day, was earnest that Granville should return to Paris, vehement in his apprehensions of the consequences of any change here, and loud in his complaints of the encrease of arrogance in the Russians within the last week when our defeat was foreseen.

Lord Palmerston and Lord Granville dined here. The latter hints that Bagot at the Hague adopts surmizes of French designs and artifices upon very slight evidence and sometimes without any ground whatsoever.

9th. Octr. Sunday. Called on Lord Grey who was prevented by illness and medicine from going this morning to Windsor. I represented to him the necessity of some indication of power in us and of will in the Court to carry the bill or one not less efficient in order to enable us, with any honour or advantage, to remain in office; and I suggested that if any thing necessary to attain our object was unpalatable to the King, it was now, when he pressed us to remain, that we should in prudence and indeed in fairness insist on it. Grey entirely concurred in these views and determined to speak openly to the King about Lord Howe and to offer, if it was disagreable to H M, to explain to the Queen in an audience the effects which in this country an opposition from persons in her household to the King's ostensible Ministry must infallibly produce. In the course of conversation other demonstrations of power, as substitutes for these, were canvassed, such as two Dukedoms for Cleveland and Stafford, some other advances in peerages, and one or two creations. Grey was in good heart and spirits. Lansdowne, Lord John, and others dined with me at Holland House.

10th. Monday. Grey went to Windsor. He had received in the morning a letter from the King very indignant at an intemperate speech delivered at Devizes by Coll. Napier and earnestly desirous of dismissing that officer from the service.[329] He was apprehensive that the King in this temper of mind might be more disposed to compromise and modifications, at which his first letter seemed to glance, less inclined to sacrifice Lord Howe and the refractory voters in place, and more unwilling than before to prorogue Parliament in person, with the necessary phrases adhering to the Reform bill. He was however agreably disappointed. The King was reasonable and friendly. He acquiesced in the imprudence of dismissing Napier and readily approved of removing Lord Howe. He declined Grey's offer of breaking that resolution to the Queen and said he and Sir Herbert Taylor could undertake it with more propriety and less offence to Her Majesty, who was an excellent woman but did not understand this country and who might take fire if a change in her family was notified to her by a Minister. He gave Lord Grey full power to dismiss all inferior placemen for refractory votes, and after a little reflection agreed to prorogue in person, because his Ministers thought it useful and because George III, before his blindness, usually did so, altho', he added, he had some repugnance to the appearance of being made a puppet of popularity.

The debate and division in the Commons[330] were most gratifying to Ministers and beneficial to the Country. The tone taken by opposition was very low. They feel how much they have lost themselves in the Country, and the dismissal of Lord Howe and other symptoms prove they have made no way with the Court. OConnel and the Irish were cordial. Palmerston had written a strange letter to Grey deprecating the creation of peers (of which there is at present no project); hinting at extensive modifications as the only method of propitiating the Lords, in whose sentiments he supposes many of our Gentry concur; and expressing some scruples about the declaration to be made by Lord Althorp in the Commons, viz that this Government will never be a party to proposing a bill less efficient than that which the Lords have rejected, nor remain in office but with the prospect of passing that bill, or one equivalent to it, into Law. However Lord Lansdown's, Grey's, or Althorp's remonstrances reconciled him to the proceeding, for he was silent in the Commons when Althorp most distinctly and to the great satisfaction of Ministry, house, and country made that declaration[331] and he also on

Tuesday 11 Octr. in the Cabinet acquiesced in the answer drawn up to the King's letter which expressed our readiness to continue to conduct the King's affairs, but avowed that we expected the full support of His Majesty in promoting the same bill or one not less efficient as essentially necessary to the peace and well being of the Country.[332] An answer to the address of the City of London was also drawn up by Lord Grey, the topicks which should form the King's speech on Prorogation discussed, and the necessity of an early recourse to that measure acknowledged. Lord Anglesey was at this Cabinet and urged the necessity of taking into consideration the state of Irish affairs and the conduct he should pursue with respect to OConnel, before he returns to Ireland. Lord Granville returns tomorrow after Levee to France. He is very earnest that we should discard from our minds all jealousy about little matters and unreasonable suspicions about great ones; is confident of the sincerity of the present French Ministry about peace, but persuaded that they require every reality as well as appearance of mutual confidence to strengthen them, and thinks we might now and then afford a sacrifice of minor objects of mere form and etiquette, and not substantial national interest, for so great an object of confi<rm>ing their power in the Chambers and the publick. He manifestly thinks Bagot, and even to a degree Adair, negotiates in a more Antigallican spirit than is favorable to peace, or warranted by any designs of the French Govt. He confirms the change of tone which others had observed in the Princess Lieven and the Russians, since the rejection of the Reform bill. The Opposition Peers are manifestly alarmed at their own handy works. Many of them anxious to propose and pass some general resolution of reform, but finding that, if very vague and unsatisfactory, we should oppose or move to amend it, and that, if distinct and satisfactory to real reformers, their late allies would abandon them and oppose it, they have hitherto abstained from any motion whatever. The dismissal of Lord Howe (which his Lordship deplores and resents in a most undignified manner) discomfits the whole phalanx, and Lord Wharncliffe, who is as honest and frank as he is whimsical and inconsistent, acknowledges in private and publick that he would now support a bill founded on nearly all the principles contained in that which he helped to reject, and is as vehement as the keenest reformer in urging the folly and impossibility of resisting speedy and effectual reform.

Wednesday 12 Octr. Prevented by violent cold from attending Levee, where the King received the addresses. The concourse of people was immense but the incessant and violent rain dispersed them soon. The shops were shut up either from marks of sorrow at the loss of the bill or fear of the populace, who on the whole conducted themselves peaceably, though they broke some antireformers windows, shewed something like a savage thirst of revenge in pursuing Sir Robert Peel and the Duke of Cumberland, and struck Lord Londonderry, one day on his arm with a stick and another on his head with a brick bat, in consequence of his imprudent defiance and threat of carrying pistols about him. The Queen cried abundantly on Lord Howe's dismissal; at first said she would not come to dinner but thought better of it and made her appearance. Lady Lyndhurst announces the intention of going to Paris with her Lord, who, though he has disappointed and exasperated us, does not seem to have engratiated himself with our enemies.

Thursday 13th. October. Early Cabinet which Lord Anglesey and Lord Plunkett attended. We were all anxious for an early prorogation and the King signified his willingness to stay over Saturday that it might be prorogued over that day. Lord Brougham however urged the necessity of passing his Law reform or Bankruptcy bill, and Lord Althorp stated the little prospect of getting it through before Tuesday, or the earliest Monday, and the possibility or even probability, if opposition with a view of delay were offered, of it requiring a week. The Chancellor was inflexible and even nettled at our hesitation. It was at length agreed that the attempt should be made, that if on Friday night there was a prospect of getting it through on Saturday or Monday, the prorogation should be deferred till tuesday; but that if that were hopeless, the King should prorogue on Saturday or Monday. It is no doubt vexatious to Brougham and the publick that his bill should be lost, but it will be renewed next Session; and a revival every night of angry discussion and recrimination between the two parties for and against reform is highly injurious to the cause and hazardous to the tranquillity of the Country.

Grey told us that there was reason to think that Mr OConnel would accept from this Government either the Attorney Generalship or Mastership of the Rolls, that there were means (somewhat objectionable) of vacating the latter office immediately, and that there were but too well grounded apprehensions that OConnell, returning to Ireland without any positive connection with the Government, would revert ere long to his system of agitation and, both on the reform bill and repeal of Union, embarrass exceedingly the government of that Country. Both Lord Anglesey and Lord Plunkett bore testimony to the extent of his power, his disposition to exert it mischievously, and the certainty that he would so exert it if furnished with no motive of interest to abstain. It was a choice of evils most perplexing. Duke of Richmond and Mr Stanley seemed to spurn the notion of employing or ingratiating a Man whom we could not trust and who was so recently an object of prosecution himself. They argued that advancement would not diminish his means or his desire of mischief, would lower the character of our Government, and estrange all those on whom we might in extremities be compelled solely to rely. To all such arguments I thought Lord Grey leant too willing an ear, and Plunkett acknowledged his apprehensions that many even of our best and oldest friends would be estranged and our Orange enemies to a Man exasperated by any such promotion. Anglesey, in the handsomest and clearest way imaginable, stated the danger both ways, acknowledged the impossibility of his making the offer after D[a]n[iel] OConnel's conduct to him, but added that, if he was named he should act openly and cordially with him. Brougham, Althorp, Lansdowne, Carlisle, Palmerston, and myself were for a more explicit communication with him without delay but, after long canvassing, a half measure (possessing in my judgement the advantages of neither) was offered. He was to be thanked for his support of Govt. in the latter part of the Session; and hopes that if persevered in it he might enable us to connect him more closely with us were to be conveyed to him. Lord Anglesey undertook to do so much and told us the plain and frank manner in which he should perform his task, which was inimitable. Many thought OConnel too greedy to be brought by distant prospects only and many too vain and too open to impressions to be able, even if now willing, to abstain from his usual course for two months unless actually fettered by office. I heard soon afterwards that he acquiesced in the impossibility of any high office immediately and was only desirous of a patent of precedency at present, to which his professional station well entitles him. Anglesey had left London before this last intelligence reached him, but Plunkett and Brougham approve and I trust Grey will when he hears it.

To resume what passed in Cabinet: Anglesey enumerated the measures which he deemed necessary for Ireland and said if they were not all granted except OConnell was gained we must give him 10,000 more men. The King, whom I did not see, is by all reports in great health and spirits. I suspect the act of vigor in turning out Lord Howe, though appalling before hand, gratifies and exhilarates him, when executed. In the Lords, Lords Harrowby and Haddington[333] took an opportunity of declaring themselves friendly to reform and sanction the principles, though not the extent to which they were applied, of the late bill. Wellesley shrewdly observed in a whisper that this was the first time he had known Lords protest against their own votes.

14 October. I was kept at home by a severe cold. Dined at Prince Talleyrand's who is overjoyed at the prospect of bringing the definitive treaty to a conclusion, though he says the extreme equity and impartiality of it will render it odious to both parties. The Chancellor is vehement in his exhortations to get the Bankruptcy bill through before the prorogation and somewhat loose in his assertions respecting the means taken and the motives felt for retarding or defeating it. He tells me OConnell will have his patent of precedency forthwith. He refused it on our coming into office. The Queen scarcely spoke to Lord Grey at dinner, and Her Ladies affect sorrow, indignation and surprize at the dismissal of Lord Howe.

15th. October. The five powers settled the definitive treaty this morning at four.[334] A great work if the two contending parties of Belgium and Holland submit as no doubt they will. A negotiation on a difficult and complicated matter between five great powers and of a year's duration brought to an amicable conclusion without a moment's hostility or even estrangement does the negotiators great credit and is almost unprecedented in History; and if the result of their labours be to disband four immense armies prepared for war, without firing a shot, they will deserve the thanks of Europe and mankind. I was sorry to find that Palmerston, who has so large a share of merit in his department, has still some strange scruples and yet stranger methods of expressing them about our reform. He writes to Grey on the 11th. of this month to protest against individual members pledging a Government to the reform bill or a bill not less efficient without modification; says such a practice leads to dictation instead of discussion and cannot reconcile it to his conscience to be concluded by such prospective declarations of the intentions of Government. If he alludes either to Lord Grey's or Lord Althorp's declaration that they would not depart from the principles of their measure nor be parties to any less efficient (though willing to consider modifications consistent with those principles), he surely is wrong in censuring such declarations as the act of individuals, inasmuch as Althorp more than once consulted the Cabinet on what was to be the nature of his language, and Lord Grey suggested nearly verbatim what he afterwards said, in Palmerston's presence, and as we all understood with his full acquiescence and approbation. We are in truth pledged to so much by our actions and by the course we have pursued at the dissolution and since, to the full as strongly as any declaration of an individual member or as the Cabinet itself collectively can pledge us. I spoke a word to Goderich at St. James's on this matter and hope he will pacify Palmerston. I saw the King, who was well but not disposed to talk politicks and somewhat tired with his foreign Visitors.

16 Sunday. Cabinet at one. The King has handsomely consented to the removal of

Sir Byam Martin,[335] though a sailor and a favorite. But he would not vote with Ministers and boasted, though a placeman, that we could get no vote out of him. We had much conversation about the time and duration of the ensuing prorogation. It was agreed that there must be but one prorogation between the ending of this and commencement of the next Session, and that in the first instance the usual period of forty days was the most prudent. In this discussion Lord Lansdowne and perhaps Lord Grey were too susceptible of the indignity of admitting publick opinion or dictation, as they call it, into consideration, forgetful that our only motive, reason, or justification for remaining in office is that by retaining the confidence we may secure the tranquillity and subordination of the people, and that consequently we must do all in our power consistently with honesty and principle to retain that confidence. The topicks of the King's speech were discussed. It was hoped the settlement of Belgium and Holland might form part of them, Poland, being a delicate and difficult subject, to be avoided. Portugal to be mentioned in a way not to expose us to censure or reproach, if hostilities or open espousal of Pedro's party should occur in the recess. The King's repetition of the words of his opening speech respecting reform and his hope that the object there described will upon the reassembling of Parliament be speedily accomplished was agreed to be the most material part of the speech, and all, including Palmerston, appeared to acquiesce in the necessity of some such paragraph. It is said Leopold will protest against the distribution of the debt and some other articles of the treaty, but in protesting agree to it, a course which, Talleyrand justly observes, invites attacks on his government and betrays a want of firmness of purpose that cannot but be injurious.

17th. Monday. I was confined to the house and indeed to bed with a heavy cold.

18th. Tuesday. Still confined at home with a cold. Lord Grey sent me a correspondence with King, in which His Majesty somewhat vaguely and indefinitely pointed at the necessity of modifications in the reform bill to disarm opposition and reconcile house of Lords; deprecated party violence, hurry, and warmth; and complained of a letter by Lord John Russell to the people of Manchester, which termed the opposition to the bill, including therein, remarks His Majesty, the Majority of the Lords, the 'Whisper of a Faction'.[336] Lord Grey, in a letter to Sir J C Hobhouse[337] and in a speech in House of Lords[338] has explained his own views so clearly that none can mistake them but those who are determined to be dissatisfied. The King's speech, which was drawn up by Grey and sanctioned at a Cabinet which I did not attend, pledges the government distinctly to the bill or an equivalent measure. H M, by approving that speech and by telling Anglesey and others that the bill or an equally efficient one is virtually carried, concurs in our views; and his occasional displeasure or apprehension at intemperate expressions, infused into his mind by the swarm of antireformers who surround, lead to no practical consequence whatever, much less to any breach with Ministers for whom he professes more attachment than ever.

19 Wednesday. Talleyrand, Grey, and Melbourne dined with me. Lord Howe's correspondence with Sir Herbert Taylor last May gave his Lordship some colour to suppose that, if he abstained from factious opposition out of doors, he might vote against the bill, but his offensive manner of urging his case to the publick puts him in the wrong and is more likely ultimately to provoke than to convince His Majesty.

20 Thursday. Parliament prorogued. King well received, read his speech distinctly and forcibly. Many ladies present and among them the Grand Duchess Helen[339] (a Wertemburg Princess) on the woolsacks in virtue of being a descendant of the Electress Sophia and consequently in the succession. Dined at St. James. The Queen was civil to most of the Ministers, particularly so to me, but absolutely cut Lord Grey and hardly spoke to the Chancellor. This is extremely silly but will, if taken no notice of, pass off. It would be almost as silly to resent it by not attending her parties, which Grey tonight said he thought he should do. Talleyrand assures me that at Paris they are doing all in their power to persuade and to drive Leopold to prompt acquiescence.

21 Friday. Saw the King. In good health and spirits, satisfied that King Leopold must accept the treaty, pleased thereat, but not much disposed to talk of home politicks. Palmerston who called in the evening was as well as Talleyrand in good hopes about Belgium, but cold about reform, dismissal of <refractory> placemen and promotion of friends in the diplomacy [*four lines torn*].

22 Saturday. Dined at Lord Staffords. Talleyrand gave me letters from Brussells and notes from Palmerston full of good news and prospects: Leopold and Council resolved to recommend acceptance of treaty to Assemblies; Assemblies well disposed and treaty, when read well received, and Leopold resolved, if it were rejected, to dissolve the assembly, secure that Priests and the pacifick would ensure him a majority. Letter of same date but contrary tendency from Henry.

23d. Sunday. At Holland House. Palmerston dined with me, sanguine about Leopold's signature of treaty and effect of Gerard's mission from Paris to Brussels who is to inform Leopold's government that, if they provoke hostilities by declining the treaty, they must expect no assistance from France, whose honour and interests are engaged in enforcing the terms of pacification which the five powers have devized. Palmerston has conducted all this business admirably and has reason to be satisfied with his success. On home politicks and reform he is studiously silent and reserved.

October 24th. Monday. Saw Grey at Shene in the morning. A dispatch from Bagot informed him that the King of Holland, when asked what he would do on the expiration of the armistice tomorrow, and solicited to give an assurance of waiting till the answer of Leopold to the treaty was known, assumed a mysterious, haughty, and even suspicious air, maintained that neither England nor the Conference had a right to demand a communication of his intentions, and, with general words of a resolution to act in the way most conducive to the interests of his people, eluded the question. Bagot added that he (Bagot) did not believe he meant to resort to actual hostilities. But Lord Grey, within ten minutes of reading the dispatch, answered Palmerston—who had asked him whether he should not recommend the Conference to send a demonstration of English force to the Scheldt and the Dutch coast to intercept their commerce if they should again invade Belgium—that with or without the consent of the Conference, some ships should immediately be sent for that purpose. The Duchess de Dino who dined with me told me from Talleyrand that a similar resolution had been taken by the Conference, and no doubt the orders are given and received and acted upon while I am writing.

Grey is much irritated at the distrust expressed in the Sunday papers of our designs; in considerable anxiety about the means of retaining the confidence of the Country, and yet acquiring votes in the Lords; and not without some apprehension of the weakness of the King, surrounded as he is by enemies of the bills, and exasperated as he [Grey] supposes the Queen to be with him. I urged him to come to some understanding with the Bishops, and the Bishop of London in particular, and I told Lady Grey[340] that this and a little courting and consultation of the Queen were parts of the dutys or talent of a Prime Minister which he neglected.

He sees great difficulties in espousing Pedro or his daughter's cause and thinks that if such a line of policy were adopted all mention of Constitution or even Cortes should be suppressed, for he is convinced that any thing of the name even is unpopular in Portugal. [*In the margin:* In this he turned out quite wrong. I never agreed with him or others in their disparagement of Portugueze enthusiasm for liberty, but I had no notion that their attachment to the Constitution was so intense as it was and far exceeded that they felt for Miguel, Pedro, or any of their Princes.] Lord Durham seems to urge and even provoke him by intelligence of the impatience of the people in the North and the impracticability of proroguing Parliament beyond the 1st. of December or altering an iota in the bill. He, Lord Durham, thinks of going to Brussels. [*End of BM Add. MS 51867.*]

[*Beginning of BM Add. MS 51868.*]

Tuesday 25th. October 1831.

Wednesday 26th. Octr. On the road from London to Brighton.

27th. Thursday. Letter from Lord Chancellor urging the propriety of some better place for Sir James Mackintosh and the advancement in the Ministry of Mr Stanley. I wrote to Lord Grey.

28th. Friday. Brighton. The Grand Duchess Helen obliged to put back to Margate roads on 26th.

29 Saturday.

30 Sunday. The King at Brighton. Well received but no illuminations.

31 Monday. Saw the King, who was well in health, pleased with definitive treaty; confident that the King of Holland will be compelled to consent on the appearance of our fleet; not indisposed to propitiate OConnel for the sake of quiet in Ireland, and justly reprobates the bill which at the period of Catholick Emancipation estranged him from the English Government;[341] did not shew any inclination to speak of reform bill; and though I spoke of Lord Grey as likely to be better for sea air, said nothing of a wish to see him here. We received news this evening of the Grand Duchess Helen's and Charles's arrival at Rotterdam.

1 November. Letter from Mackintosh about Palmela and Portugal, and I wrote my opinion to Lord Grey, that as the French had proposed to us to espouse the cause of Donna Maria and there were so many reasons to justify and so many motives to induce us to do it, we should without delay acknowledge Donna Maria's

Regency, accredit Ministers to it, and offer jointly with France a mediation for the pacification of Portugal.

2 November Wednesday. The King at half an hours notice set off to London to hold a Council and issue a proclamation in consequence of the riots at Bristol, where the Jails, the Bishop's palace, and a large part of a Square have been burnt by the populace.[342] Saw Palmela, who came down to apprize and to consult me on the practicability of prevailing on our government to act in concert with France in countenancing the party of Donna Maria in Portugal. After conversing with him, I wrote again to Lord Grey to recapitulate the grounds on which such interference might be justified, and to recommend at least the immediate recognition of Donna Maria and her father as Regent and other steps tending to the pacification of Portugal and the settlement of that country without giving just umbrage to Spain. The French still pay us the compliment of deferring to our opinion on Portugueze matters and waiting for our decision. But they are earnest we should decide soon and very desirous that it should be in the affirmative and in favor of Donna Maria. It is clear, therefore, that even if we decline, their inclination towards the Anti-Miguelite party will be the same; it is unlikely that with such inclination they should long continue to forbear gratifying it out of mere deference to us. And if they should act separately it is quite obvious that jealousies, disputes, and finally war must ensue. Surely then it is better to concur in their views and to concert measure together.

3 November Thursday. Brighton.

4 November Friday. ditto.

5 Novr. Saturday. Saw King on Duchy business. Found him well but somewhat sleepy. He is much annoyed at Unions and meetings, scared at the sound of national guards and tricolor cockades, and has written this day a letter to Lord Melbourne suggesting the propriety of establishing some constabulary police in lieu of such dangerous associations in the towns and places where, on the pretext of preserving property, some such projects are promulgated. He does not say any thing or even listen with much pleasure to any thing said on the subject of pressing the reform on House of Lords, but he agrees that the rejection of the bill before it had been in Committee was an injudicious and violent proceeding. In talking over the subject with him, that is the only nail that drives, at least from one like myself who have no immediate duty to urge a measure upon him. The Queen passed thro' the antechamber while I was there, was to the full as gracious as ever, but I thought more than usually ugly.

The King, reasonably enough, thinks riots and publick meetings less permanently dangerous to legitimate authority than the self constituted Unions and national guards, but is not sufficiently impressed with the undeniable truth that the delay, postponement, or uncertainty in passing the measure of reform is the real cause of those Unions, and that they can only be prevented or put down by removing the inclination in the middling classes of society to join them.

6 November Sunday. It seems by letters from Lord Lansdown, who has come up to London on the occasion, that there were seven cases of Cholera at Sunderland but that 48 hours have elapsed without it spreading further, that what precautions are possible have been taken, and that there is good reason to hope that even if it does appear in England its ravages will be less fatal and extensive than they have been represented to be elsewhere. Saw old General Dalrymple,[343] 96 years of age; remembers Lord Lovats trial and execution.[344] Is sprightly, sees, hears, and walks well. An early riser.

Monday 7. The meeting of the working classes, which was much apprehended, postponed if not abandoned, chiefly by the good sense and management of Melbourne, who in a frank, careless, and coarse but easy and plain manner frightened their leaders without offending them.

Tuesday 8 Novr. Wrote a long letter to Grey on the question what must be done with the Lords? News of cholera and dispersion of intended meetings highly satisfactory. That of Pedro's ships in the river being seized by Custom house, not equally so.[345] Palmerston's paper, which I have not seen, is circulated, but nothing I fear yet done to assist Don Pedro morally or physically. Dined at Pavilion on Princess Augusta's[346] birthday. Queen very civil. King as usual. Nothing remarkable.

Wednesday 9.

Thursday 10. Brighton. Packet from Dieppe announced that Quarantine is established in that port. In the meanwhile the official reports from Sunderland, sent to me from Lansdowne and communicated to me by Sir Herbt. Taylor, are far from satisfactory. The disease, be it contagious or epidemical, seems inevitable, but it may be less extensive and less fatal than has been represented in other places, and the skill of our Physicians, with the experience of foreign and Indian practitioners to boot, may render it manageable. Palmerston's exposé of the Portugueze question is admirable, and not less agreable to me from leaning strongly to immediate treaty with Pedro and to the opinion that Miguel must abdicate or be deposed.[347] I am told the King has sent word to Lady Jane Peel[348] that he cannot invite her to the Pavilion while the Duchess of Richmond[349] is with her, for her Grace is so vehement against his Government that it would have the appearance of insincerity to shew attention to so bitter an opponent. This is well for effect, but why exclude this old Lady and admit other younger and full as violent.

Friday 11 Novr. Very bad accounts of the Cholera from Sunderland of 8th. Novr. Saw the King who does not despair of its being kept out London, and approves highly of the advice of the Physicians to refrain from resorting to any vexatious precautions which may induce the lower orders to conceal the disease, the most dangerous of all <practices> if it be contagious.

Saturday 12. Accounts of Cholera discouraging. Belgian Minister Vandeweyer[350] arrived. Treaty with Leopold in forwardness. The King of Holland still refractory, but a decisive though somewhat verbose answer of the Conference will shew him that he cannot prevail on them to alter the terms or to withold their assistance to Leopold if He should attack him.

Sunday 12 [*13th.*]. Long conversation with Lord Chancellor Brougham who came last night to Brighton. He is in high health, spirits, and good humour, vehement for an early meeting of Parliament and the immediate introduction of an unaltered bill. He tells me that on the 5th. instant Duke of Wellington wrote a somewhat unusual not to say improper letter, to the King, explaining, not very correctly, the state of the country and the formation of armed unions and associations, throughout describing what is intended or announced as actually done, exposing the evil tendency and predicating the illegality of such unions, and obliquely insinuating that the Ministers had not chosen to exert the powers they possessed to put down practices, which, under the pretence of supporting them and the government, were constituting and organizing a force that must ere long overawe King, Lords, and Commons, and place us under Mob government. To this the King sent an answer in Sir H Taylor's hand but signed with his own, and did not communicate the receipt of the letter or the substance of his answer to Lord Grey till after it was sent.[351] It truly and somewhat archly reminded the Duke of Wellington that the Unions, though illegal, had subsisted for some time and remained unmolested under his own administration; but it acknowledged and stated, as strongly as Duke of Wellington and perhaps stronger than the truth, the illegality of voluntary armed associations except at the suggestion and under the controul of Government, adding, in vague but earnest and almost intemperate language, his fixed determination while he wore the crown not to permit any general arming of the people except under the authorities of the State. Brougham in conversation with me descanted on the constitutional and hazardous nature of such correspondence, contended that, altho' as a Peer the Duke of Wellington might give his opinion in an audience (but even in the closet the etiquette and late usage had been that H M should give no answer, assertion, nor deliver in writing any explanation of his intention), he was not therefore warranted in writing, and much less in eliciting an answer from the King on subjects which the Crown can only decide after consultation with his Confidential Servants and act upon at their responsibility. He, the Chancellor, saw the King twice today, and in two conversations impressed on his Majesty forcibly the alarming state of the Country, the probable necessity of calling parliament soon, and the extension of unions and of intense feeling in the country on the subject of reform. He denied that such feelings were confined to the lower orders. He drew a clear distinction between the middling classes and the mere rabble, and between the determined reformers which composed the last and the lovers of plunder which had no doubt too much preponderance in the latter. He stated yet more forcibly the utter impossibility of keeping down the plunderers in a community like ours, if the middle classes were adverse to Government and disposed to be the allies of the mob or even neutral and indifferent in the hour of tumult and confusion. The Unions even at Birmingham and elsewhere were composed and composing of those who must stand between us and the plundering mobs of Hunt and Bristol. No army could keep them down without the assistance and cooperation of those who now formed or were forming Unions. After earnestly assuring H M that tradesmen and small proprietors, not mere rabble, were already either in Unions or on the eve of joining them, I glanced at the propriety and prudence of some measure by bill or otherwise to give to the Government or Civil power the appointment of officers and the controul of any voluntary association formed with a professed view of keeping the peace. In these views the King seemed disposed to acquiesce, but he was not aware of the extent to which Men of some property had engaged and were engaging in these Unions, nor perhaps alive sufficiently to the distinction of Unions on account of wages, Unions for political objects, and armed associations. These topicks led Lord Chancellor to advert in his conversation both with him and Sir Herbert Taylor on the letters from and the answer to Duke of Wellington. He explained respectfully but distinctly the irregularity and possible inconvenience of such a proceeding. The King observed, and Lord Chancellor said it was true, that before he received Duke of Wellington's letter, he had received others from Lord Grey and Lord Brougham himself denouncing the illegality of these associations and that He thought (as there was no doubt upon that point) there could be no objection and might be some advantage in his expressing it immediately. And Sir Herbert Taylor hinted that it was thought more delicate to Ministers for the King to express what he deemed to be their opinion as his own, when the promptitude of the reply shewed that he could not have consulted them. He implied however that such a correspondence should not occur again. I suppose (said he, asking the question) the best way would be in case of any further letter merely to acknowledge the receipt and then see My Ministers? The Chancellor answered 'Certainly Sir'. The Chancellor on the whole was satisfied with his audiences, convinced that he had impressed the King with a just (too true) notion of the dangerous state of the country, prepared his mind for any measures Ministers may deem it their duty to recommend in order to avert it and to secure the reform bill, and persuaded him of the inconvenience of conferring much more or corresponding with the Duke of Wellington or any body but his ostensible advisers on such difficult and momentous topicks. Charles and Henry returned together by Calais and Dover and along the Coast through Hastings from Brussels.

Monday 14 Novr. The Chancellor set off at 5 in the morning. Sir Herbert Taylor, whom I saw at his house adjoining pavilion, read to me the draft of the King's letter to Lord Chancellor and Lord Melbourne commenting somewhat angrily on Unions, relating (as I afterwards found somewhat hastily and inaccurately) what had passed at Crown and Anchor with Sir Francis Burdett,[352] but containing many judicious remarks on the opportunity, afforded by riots and cholera, and by the proposal of people to arm for the protection of property, of establishing some force of the nature of constabulary police and, in truth, separating the great class of respectable reformers from those who had other and ulterior revolutionary objects and those among the rabble who had none but plunder and impunity. He told me the King was more uneasy than could be described on this subject. He not only acknowledges but earnestly maintains that the Reform bill is *not* the cause of the danger which, in truth, existed and was growing rapidly when the bill was proposed; but he does not perhaps perceive that the bill, and the prompt passing thereof, presents the only and the best chance of dispelling the danger and applying a remedy to the disorders of the community. Sir Herbert gave me the Duke of Wellington's letter, the King's answer to it, and Lord Grey's observations on the correspondence to read. The Duke's is more, the King's far less, objectionable than the Chancellor's representation had led me to suppose. Inclosed in the Duke's letter is a paper, ill written and ill reasoned, containing some obvious legal and constitutional truths, loosely applied to unions and meetings very vaguely described; some very inaccurate illustrations from recent English, Irish, and French history; one allegation of an unknown fact (the order of arms at Birmingham for the use of the Unions); and an unwarranted insinuation that these matters are overlooked by His Majesty's government, and that they have the means and power of checking these practices if they chuse to exert them. The King, in his answer (written the day after he had received the letter and before he had shewn it to his Ministers), assures the Duke that he has watched the unions and contemplated their possible perversion to the worst ends with as much apprehension as himself, that he and his Ministers are fully aware of the means and power they possess to protect the property of his subjects, and fully determined to exercise them with vigor, whenever any illegal project and particularly any plan of arraying a military force independent of his authority has taken a *tangible* shape. He declares in warm terms that while he wears the Crown no such unlawful Military combination shall be allowed to subsist, but he observes that the Unions existed both for the purposes of raising wages and, in some instances, for political purposes too, before the Duke of Wellington left office; that the Duke's notice was drawn to them, that the too natural transition from trade to politicks and from petitioning to overawing the government had been contemplated and dreaded, was apparently in progress before the Ministry was changed or the bill for reform proposed, and that it was idle to suppose that they had been created by the bill. Nor had the Duke any right to infer from the absence of all publick notice of such transactions that His Majesty or his Government were blind to the danger or remiss in the precautions necessary to avert it. Sir Herbert Taylor subjoined a note in which he apprized the Duke that the King, after seeing his answer, had communicated the correspondence to Lord Grey. Lord Grey in his comments slightly adverted to the inaccuracy of the historical allusions in Duke of Wellington's paper; admitted the undeniable and undisputed law quoted against armed associations; observed that none such had as yet assumed any *tangible* shape; [*In the margin:* said that he would institute enquiries about the order for arms (and has, I understand from Sir H Taylor, sent to the Duke of Wellington himself to furnish him with the sources of his information upon that point)]; and repelled the insinuation of any remissness or irresolution on the part of Government, thanking the King for the justice he did his servants in vindicating them against any such charge, and reiterating his assurances that every measure necessary for the protection of property and for the maintenance of the Civil Authority, of which the King is the head, should be recommended whenever it became necessary, but adding that premature or undue or disproportionate severity would, he knew, be equally repugnant to the King's disposition and to the dictates of prudence in the present circumstances of England and the World. The King wrote an acknowledgement of this letter to Lord Grey[353] in which he speaks in warm terms of approbation of his sentiments and, in allusion to former correspondence, accounts for the readiness with which he expressed such sentiments to the Duke of Wellington from the knowledge that he shared them with his Confidential advisers and indeed from a persuasion that he had a right to expect and exact from those entrusted with his government a recognition and, in case of necessity, a vigorous assertion of those principles upon which its safety might depend. Sir Herbert Taylor in his conversation was very earnest to vindicate and even apologize for the King's answering such a letter without previous concert with his Ministers; he urged (and I believe most truly) the King's chief and sole motive to be desire to prove the entire and cordial union of sentiment between him and his Ministers, and, he observed more than once, that he was the better enabled to do so from letters he had received from Lords Grey and Melbourne, in both of which there were the same opinions and, in some instances, the identical expressions which His Majesty had used respecting the law and respecting the tendency of these Unions &c. Sir Herbert added however that such a correspondence should not occur again, that the best method would be, if such letters were written, to answer dryly but civilly that they were received and should be communicated and considered by the Government and leave it there. Sir Herbert however remarked and perhaps truly that the Duke of Wellington must have liked this answer still less, and that it was written not with a view of pleasing him but of shewing the cordiality subsisting between Lord Grey and the King. Throughout Sir Herbert seemed impressed with the firm adherence of the King to his Ministers, of the danger to the country of any change of men, and of the necessity, *now the* bill was proposed and the country was excited, of passing it without delay and without any material alteration or modification, to which, however, the King has invariably clung as one of the means of reconciling the Lords. From these premises I hinted that there might be a necessity of an early meeting of Parliament and, without naming it directly, a further creation of peers. To the first he evidently thought the King himself inclined; to the latter he said nothing, though in London he had told me that the King was much more averse to it than I supposed. I dined at Pavilion and had, in five minutes conversation *sotto voce* with the King, an opportunity of enforcing the Lord Chancellor's statement of the dangerous situation of the Country; the necessity of appeasing the publick soon; and the policy of combining with concessions and precautions against Cholera some establishments which might serve the purposes of police, remain in truth under the controul of the Civil powers and the government, and yet satisfy the spirit in which these projects of Unions originated. He seemed struck with an observation I made, from Allen, that in granting the right of representation to great towns it was right, natural, and expedient that some new regulation of their municipal government, either by Charter or bill or otherwise, should be adopted. He told me to mention it to Lord Grey.

OConnel has again run out of the course, scurrilously abusing Mr Stanley and disparaging Lord Anglesey in a letter to the Newspapers,[354] without provocation. The King is reported to have said, 'the gloss was not off his Silk gown before he began flinging dirt and kicking up a dust to defile it'.

15 Novr. Slept at Ryegate.

16 Novr. On my arrival at Holland House found Marquis of Palmela waiting for me. He is in great anxiety about our decision on Portugueze affairs, confident that if we decide to acknowledge and espouse the cause of Donna Maria, in conjunction with France, Spain will follow and, should she be invited to a conference and treaty, acquiesce in and facilitate the retirement of Don Miguel. Palmela shewed me a letter of instructions from Don Pedro, authorizing him to promise every sort of security for Spain, an entire amnesty (save and except the resumption of confiscated property and the expulsion of some very few persons) for his own subjects, and disclaiming with reasons of great delicacy and honour all notions of resuming his own pretensions, which, he contends, he could not in consistency or honour resort to without reestablishing the constitution he had offered; whereas as Regent and Guardian of his daughter, he might be guided by her council, her allies, or the force of circumstances, without incurring the reproach of inconsistency and duplicity or sacrifice of the nations's rights to his own vanity and ambition.

Lord Carlisle told me the treaty with Leopold was signed.[355] Portugal undecided and to be discussed tomorrow, and the question of prorogation in truth a choice between an immediate Session or such a creation of peers as by affording a prospect of ultimate success would preclude the necessity.

Lord Melbourne is deeply impressed not to say alarmed at the state of the Country, thinks some convulsion must happen, but adds with some pleasantry that neither Bristol nor White Conduit Street nor the innumerable information he has received make him half so gloomy as an hours conversation with Abercrombie, who had just left him and is going to Scotland, fully convinced that a weeks delay in passing the bill or the change of an *iota* will subvert the whole frame of our constitution and throw the whole island into confusion. It seems by Lord Brougham's report who came in after dinner that in the Cabinet yesterday the question of meeting Parliament was discussed and great reluctance expressed by Lord Grey to accede to it. With the exception of Lord Carlisle's earnest testimony to the impatient feeling in Yorkshire, none, according to the Chancellor, combated Lord Grey's wishes, though nearly all, according to the same reporter, are in judgement against him save Goderich. Althorp is somewhat apprehensive of the bill not being in readiness, and it certainly seems strange that Gregson[356] who either from hostility or carelessness played them such a trick about the qualifications early in last Session, should be admitted to the councils of those who are drawing up the bill and employed in framing it. Talleyrand, who goes to Brighton tomorrow, says the treaty with Belgium was signed at three o'clock in the morning, praises Palmerston as a *Grand homme d'affaires.* He is anxious we should lose no time in recognizing Donna Maria and securing Spain from a Civil war in Portugal; acknowledge her, sign a treaty, in which she engages to promulgate a satisfactory amnesty, to exclude all Spanish refugees from Portugeze territory; and then invite Spain and Austria to a Conference for the final arrangement of the terms between Miguel, Donna Maria, and Spain herself, and all, he says, is done. You prevent war in the South as you have in the North.

I had a letter from Sir Herbert Taylor expressing the King's wish that I should communicate my notion of a grant of Municipal police, or Government by Charters, to the great towns.

17 November 1831. Met Lord Althorp and Lord John Russell at Lord Greys. The latter averse to meeting Parliament till after Christmas and somewhat sore at the alledged impatience of the country and our friends, saying that if he cannot be trusted for 3 weeks it is high time to go out &c &c. But it is not suspicion of his intentions, but doubt of his power and success that renders men so impatient of delay. John Russell whispered to me that he had been struck with Allen's suggestion of creating 8 or 10 peers at the time a prorogation was announced, as an indication of his power at court and an earnest of his continued exertions for reform. In the Cabinet, all present but Graham and Durham; much of foreign and domestick matters was discussed, little business done. A draft of dispatch to Heytesbury, instructing him how to represent to the Russian court our persuasion that the substitution of provincial assemblies and other institutions in the Polish provinces instead [of] a general constitution for the whole was a departure from his [Russia's] engagements in the treaty of Vienna, was approved of; but the notion of converting it into the shape of actual and official remonstrance and still more of any thing like menace of war was deprecated, not from any doubt of the justice of such a course, or approbation of the Russians, but from a strong averseness to war, from considerations that Russia had already rejected some such insinuations from France with unbecoming haughtiness, and above all from a knowledge that Austria (changing her original views and overbalancing her fears of Russia by her dread of free institutions) and Prussia would acquiesce and support Russia in her intended change of system to her Polish Provinces and give another construction from us to the treaty of Vienna. The draft furnishing Lord Heytesbury[357] with the arguments and authorizing him to maintain them in conversations and conferences, but not directing him to make any formal and official remonstrance on paper, was approved, and the propriety of consulting or communicating these views to Austria and Prussia referred to further consideration or to Palmerston's discretion.[358]

The justice, necessity, expediency, and urgency of a treaty with Don Pedro as regent of his daughter, the Queen of Portugal, with the avowed object of settling the disputes of the family of Braganza and with the practical effect of preventing a civil war in Portugal, dethroning Miguel, and placing his niece on the throne were discussed at some length. The present state of things seemed by all admitted to be such as could not last. But scruples as to the grounds of such an act of hostility against a King de facto from whom we have exacted and obtained an observance of treaties, and a prevalent opinion (unfounded or at least exaggerated) that the Mass of the Portuguese are really attached to that tyrant, weighed even with those who are not prepared to acknowledge Don Miguel and who admit that, while he remains unacknowledged and king de facto, we shall have a continual succession of wrongs and outrages to remonstrate against and redress by menace or by force. We came to the worst of all decisions, namely none at all, when the golden opportunity of reclaiming Spain from her ultra Miguelite policy in Portugal, of cementing our union with France, and restoring English ascendancy in Portugal had offered itself. I fear the consequences of neglecting it will be long and perhaps speedily felt. Poor Palmela dined with me. He is disappointed at our want of decision and broken hearted at the dismal consequences to himself and his countrymen. He is overwhelmed with the responsability of having engaged so many Portugueze in an enterprize now nearly hopeless, and confesses that the reproaches which will follow, however unmerited, will overwhelm him.

Friday 18th. Came to town. Lord John Russel at dinner. Chancellor and Lord Wharncliffe after dinner. Persons of wealth in the City, and among them the Archbishop's brother in Law Palmer,[359] who were averse to our bill, shewed Althorp some resolutions approving all the main principles thereof, asserting the absolute necessity of giving them effect speedily, and objecting only to some minor details, as those likely to be agreed to at a meeting of the Merchants in London. Althorp prudently declined committing Government to any opinion about them, but individually acknowledged that, in his judgement, such sentiments adopted by those who had formerly hesitated about the bill could not but be useful.

19 November Saturday. A long Cabinet of more than 5 hours. We went through and considered many proposed alterations in the Reform bill, approved of some few and dissented to others, but abstained from any final decision upon them, chiefly on account of Lord Lansdown's, Stanley's and Sir J Graham's absence. Wharncliffe has had a long conversation with Grey,[360] in which he acknowledged his wish to agree with Government and the impossibility and even impropriety and danger of their yielding any material point, much less any principle, to which they were pledged; and he proceeded to state what he thought consistent with their pledges might be altered, and would in a great measure reconcile him and, he believed, *though without being authorized to say so,* others in the Lords also to the bill. There was a remarkable coincidence between the amendments he dwelt upon and those to which the Merchants, coming round on the subject in the City, pointed in their resolutions and conversations with Althorp. Many of the amendments this day discussed in the Cabinet were framed with a design to propitiate these half reforming enemies of the late bill, and were even their own suggestions.

[*In the margin:*

They were nine

1	To send down Commissioners before meeting of Parliament to invite enquiry as to each boundary proposal?	Rejected
2	The King to issue a Commission to report on said boundaries and that Report to be accepted in the gross and alluded to in bill?	Rejected and bill adhered to.
3	Division of Counties?	Not to be proposed, but not pertinaciously resisted.[361]
4	Freeholds in boroughs to vote for County	Let it remain as it is.[362]
5	The rights of Freemen by birth or servitude, *if resident,* to continue[363]	Agreed.
6	To take houses and assessed taxes not population as criterion for disfranchising, and I think enfranchising, Boroughs[364]	Referred to future consideration, but favorably received.]

It is rather singular that almost all of them had a tendency to extend rather than narrow the elective Franchise, though some would destroy (which is no great objection in my eyes) the uniformity of the right of voting. These considerations, rumours founded perhaps on gossip—such as a marked declaration of the Duchess of Gloucester to a female friend that as the bill must pass it ought not to be delayed; more than one expression of repentance from the Bishops; Bloomfield's explanation of his absence, and the strong report of Bishop of Winchester's[365] dangerous illness—made many [of] us more sanguine than we have hitherto been of passing the bill in the House of Lords, without any, or at least any great, addition to that house. We proceeded to the question of the meeting of Parliament. Grey, from personal inclination and from a just sense of the manifold inconvenience of a session before Xmas, was decidedly and earnestly bent on a prorogation to the first week in January. The arguments of convenience were all on his side, but the state of the country, the pressing representation of all our friends, the dread of the unions made us all shrink from the responsability of leaving the Country in its present state for another month without a Parliament. We felt, whether with reference to measures for suppressing, or diverting or legalizing the Unions, or to the rapid progress of reform as the sole cure of the propensity to form them, that an immediate session of Parliament was, in spite of inconveniences, by far the safest course. This view of the subject was much confirmed by Lord Melbourne's report of the state of the publick mind and his somewhat reluctant but decided opinion that it would be aggravated very materially by a postponement of the meeting. Palmerston however faintly and Duke of Richmond earnestly supported Grey's view of the subject, and Lansdown and Stanley, who were absent, were quoted as concurring with it. When we came to voting, Goderich, who had been converted to the disagreable necessity of calling Parliament immediately, gave that opinion, with his face covered with his hands; we all felt it a painful duty and Carlisle very feelingly expressed his unwillingness to differ from Lord Grey, but by a division of 8 to 3 we decided to advise his Majesty to fix the day for the dispatch of business early in December. Grey drew up the minute. In it he stated strongly that He, Palmerston, and Richmond could not concur in the advice. A pause ensued. I observed the King might agree with the minority and we should all feel much embarrassment. It was unlucky we had not agreed beforehand to be concluded by the resolution of the Majority, which I own I should have been, had it been the other way. Grey, with great good nature but evidently not without pain, altered the phraseology of the minute and, tho' he recorded the difference of opinion, implied his disposition to defer to the advice given.[366] It was really painful, and not the less so for the extreme good temper and considerate conduct of Lord Grey. Althorpe, who had taken little part in the discussion and seemed to be undecided, told me that he was quite convinced the immediate meeting was necessary and wise, and had only refrained from urging his opinion more strongly from the pain he knew it gave Lord Grey. He now thought the bill might be got thro' the Lords without making new Peers. Why I do not know.

A strong opinion of Attorney and Solicitor General on the illegality of Unions was read, a proclamation founded thereon suggested. In this I silently acquiesced, though in truth neither opinion nor proclamation nor even indictments for conspiracy, even if followed by convictions (which is a result at least problematical), amount to more than scolding and railing—Brutum fulmen—utterly unequal to prevent the formation of unions or disperse them when formed, if there be a determination in the people to persist. Let us hope Parliament, the bill, and wise popular measures for the preservation of the peace under the guidance of government, but <closing> with the plan of the Unions, may divert the resolution of the people and convert their zeal to the strengthening instead of impairing the authority of the State.

Palmerston shewed me the projet of a convention admitting reciprocal search for slaves offered by France. The Admiralty pro formâ must be consulted on some particulars, but I trust no time will be lost in concluding it.

20 November 1831. Sunday.

21 Novr. My 58th. birthday. The King had, with his usual good humour and readiness, come up to go through the usual formalities of signing the Commission and proclamation for prorogation, and took that opportunity of signing two others in Council and receiving the Recorder's report. The first proclamation, respecting the Unions, was shewn me by Lord Melbourne and Grey. It was merely to warn persons of the illegality of armed associations and assumed authority; but I am assured that nearly simultaneously the Union of Birmingham will be dissolved, and the framers of it acknowledge that there were some technical illegalities in their scheme. I rely more on the meeting and the reform bill than on this promulgation of laws which, tho' indisputable, may yet be found impracticable and, even if practicable, yet inadequate to its real object. I observed Grey was more sure about the early meeting to day than he had been on Friday; not perhaps so much hurt with us, but low and oppressed at the prospect of business pressing upon him, and strangely suspicious of some design in the Chancellor in urging the meeting so vehemently. He asked me, significantly, if I had remarked his manner was satisfied that he meant to resign had the postponement of Parliament been determined upon, and added that he believed he was disappointed that it had not been; for he must have, in the project of resignation on such a point, some desperate game in view. I tried to soften Grey; told him that if Brougham meant to be beat in the Cabinet, he would not have been at so much pains to convert us all, as he had done me, to his opinion; and that far from widening the difference or triumphing in his victory, he had spoken with earnest commendation and feeling of Grey's behaviour throughout, and lamented the painful necessity of differing from him.

Tuesday 22 Novr. Sat Commissioner with Duke of Richmond and Lord Chancellor to prorogue the Parliament to 6th of December. Saw the new Gallery and other alterations in House of Lords—improved ventilation, additional space &c &c; and succeeded in prevailing on Richmond not to attempt the exclusion of Commons from under the throne, but leave them an option between that and the bar, rendering the latter more convenient and comfortable.

Wednesday 23 November. Cabinet at one. Much time spent or rather lost in discussing some projected alterations of great moment in Reform bill, in the absence of the Chancellor, without whom on such points nothing can well be decided. Lord Lansdown, who had been brought up from Bowood, seemed dissatisfied with every alteration proposed and far from pleased with any part of the business. Lord Grey was unwell, still complaining of our decision, and the trouble and risk it will occasion. He is manifestly chagrined at the Chancellor. He bade me write to Lord Northampton[367] to ask him to move the address, told us confidently Bishop Bloomfield would support second reading. In the meanwhile the City Meeting of pretended converts to bill has failed and there is little assurance of any real proselytes. The Treaty of Mutual search[368] is returned from Admiralty and to be sent off I trust to Lord Granville tonight.

King of Holland witholds all answer, seems to prepare war, and meditates it, says Bagot, next Spring. Ouvrard[369] urges him to raise a loan of 48 millions of Florins and, if the chambers consent, it is thought he will. Yet <Pr>ussia dissuades him from this frantic course.

Thursday. Monterond[370] told me Lord Brougham had been vehement for early meeting on account of some mistake in his bankrupt bill which must be rectified before Xmas.

Friday 25 Novr. Cabinet at three. Lord Chancellor present. The general leaning of his mind, in which most of us concurred, was to leave the bill as little altered as possible, to listen indeed to the suggestions of Wharncliffe and others, and where their amendments were reasonable or even indifferent, to adopt them if there was a reasonable prospect of gaining votes thereby, but on no account to sacrifice a tittle of our principle or a grain of the Confidence we had gained in House of Commons and Country by any thing like negotiation. Many details relating to the qualification for voting—the rates, the taxes and rent—were discussed at length over again, and the nature of such objections or differences as subsist in the minds of our Colleagues respectively on the various proposals even better ascertained and understood, with a good prospect of coming to a full agreement, though from Lord Grey's and others absence we postponed any decision upon them.

Saturday 26 Novr. 1831. Cabinet at 1 O'clock. Further communications from Lord Wharncliffe[371] and many vague speculations on other's opinions talked over. The Bishop of London has distinctly told Lord Grey he should vote for 2d. reading of the bill. It is manifest that most of his Cloth and many Lay Lords too would be glad to recall their vote against 2d. reading, but not equally clear that they will correct that vote and, still less so, that the alterations they affect to call for would secure them or that the rejection of them would prevent them from voting with us, if they have from fear an inclination to do so. Wharncliffe, frank, manly, and open though he be, is not excempt from some little vanity in acting as a self constituted mediator, without any positive authority and perhaps with very little concurrence of opinion with any body; he has communicated to Peel and Wellington his late conversations with Lord Grey, and the former returned a dry answer which he does not relish. From the latter he received one more civil in form with which he is satisfied, but which to my understanding when construed, breathes hostility to Ministry and management of the middle party with a view to future union or rather employment of them, but carefully avoids pledging himself either to the support of any bill, however modified by the present Government, or on the other hand to any thing like perpetual hostility to the cause of reform. It may insinuate that, in the hands of more moderate reformers, he might acquiesce in a general measure and rejoice that it has fallen into such prudent hands; but it much more broadly hints to those who recollect his former conduct that he means to keep himself open, after resisting the reform of others, to carry one of his own, provided he is at the same time entrusted with the full powers of the state which it is necessary to exert with the vigour and decision that, perhaps he flatters himself, none but himself can supply. He expresses satisfaction that any agreement should be probable between the reformers and the opponents, because *it must,* he deems, *be the result of mutual concession;* observes that, desirable as a settlement of this great subject may be, the final suppression of the armed associations and political unions and the vindication and assertion of the authority of the state are yet more so; expresses his fervent hope that some method may be devized of preserving the system of Government under which this happy country has so long flourished; and insinuates tho' on the information of others, that the disfranchisement, in addition to its unwarrantable extent and questionable principle, has been partially and therefore corruptly applied by the framers of the late bill. In short, he throughout the letter cultivates the good will of his correspondent without encouraging him in his approaches to the present Government, and affects, on other points as well as reform, great alarm and consternation at the state of the Country, with a hint that such efficient measures as he might devize have not been adopted, and confirms in my judgement the opinion expressed of his Character by two who know him well, namely Fredk. Lamb and his brother, the Marquis [Wellesley], the former of whom said, 'He is so d——d cunning. People don't know him, he's the cunningest fellow in the world'; and the latter told me, 'there never was a more crafty Villain than my brother Arthur'.

Sunday 27th. No Cabinet. Talleyrand much annoyed at insurrection at Lyons and strongly deplores the sending of Duke of Orleans. Soult, he observes, is suited to the object, though ten years ago he might have been a dangerous man to employ on such a commission,

Monday 29th. [*28th.*] Confirmed in Cabinet many of the points we had formerly discussed, viz: that the criterion of places to be disfranchised, and I think enfranchised too, should not be taken from any census of population, but from the number of houses together with the amount of the assessed taxes which it pays—a more just criterion of the combination of wealth and numbers in itself, and one much less liable to fraud and to mistake than the census; 2dly., that we should fill up the number to 658, a determination arising from the apprehension of an *immediate* embarrassment, namely the pretensions of the Irish, but fraught in my judgement with future and growing inconvenience by leaving no margin for the admission of other interests which may on experiment be found unrepresented, or for towns which, like Manchester Bolton or Brighton, may in the course of a Century swell into places of vast importance and not be easily reconciled to a perpetual exclusion from the representation; 3dly., we decided on filling-up the complement in pursuance of the above resolution with 8 or 11 restored to Boroughs in Schedule B [*boroughs to lose one representative*], and with as many added to towns in Schedule

D [*new boroughs to return one member each*], thus diminishing the number of boroughs to be represented by one member only and encreasing those to be represented by two.[372] In the course of the discussion on this proposition, it was earnestly urged by some to give at least half of the additional votes to Counties and to give two or four members to the Inns of Court. The Duke of Richmond suggested and argued very ingeniously in favor of extending the right of representation to Colonies, where members, without appearing so, would be, he said, a sure counteraction to the force of popular clamour and temporary excitement in the House of Commons. But so large and new a principle was most reasonably objected to at this stage of the proceeding; and without delivering any judgment on the measure or the wisdom of it, I urged on the Duke of Richmond and the Cabinet the many fair pretensions and claims the admission of constituents so totally new in our constitution would open to various corporate bodies—trades, guilds, professions, and classes—and how impossible it would be either to satisfy them or ourselves, or indeed to methodize the machinery of such a bill before the Parliament met tomorrow Sennight. It was generally thought that a substitution of two additional Members for Middlesex instead of one for Marylebone and one for Tower Hamlets would remove some objections sincerely felt by our opponents, or at least reconcile more than one to the measure.[373] This however was vague, as indeed most of the reported conversions seem to be. Not so that of Dr Copplestone,[374] Bishop of Llandaff, whose twaddling letter to Lord Goderich contains some foolish and unsatisfactory remarks but one sensible and satisfactory proposition, that he will vote for the 2d. reading of bill. The resolution comes late in the day. Better late than never, and while I am glad he at length comes to the right course, I am not altogether sorry that he did not by any provident speed in his decision outstrip some better and wiser Men of his Cloth.

It is intended to combine some plan of Municipal government or Corporation, either by Charter or act of Parliament, with the Elective Franchise to the new boroughs, and Lord Althorp means to announce such an intention on first presenting the bill. I wr<i>te with Greys and Althorp's approbation to Sir Herbert Taylor to apprize him of this determination, which will gratify the King, and with reason, for it is a seasonable and provident measure.[375]

Tuesday 29 November. Palmela pleased at release of Pedro's ships. Expects Pedro to sail shortly for Terceira and when on board to address a demand at least of Neutrality from us; states that reports from Madeira say the Cape of Verd Islands have declaired for Donna Maria, and urges us most anxiously to introduce two words in the Speech, saying that no sooner had we recalled the Ships sent to redress some injuries to our Country men in Portugal, than fresh ones occurred, and all hope of recognizing Miguel had disappeared.

Palmela thinks Russia still harbours projects hostile to free institutions in Germany and the West of Europe. Duncannon ridicules the notion of having put OConnel in a state of probation, says he might have been fixed and saved. He, Duncannon, for vigorous measures and ten Eldest Sons being called up on tuesday next.

30 November. Duke of Richmond told me that he had been down into the country yesterday to demand an explanation from Henry Drummond to Lord Grey for a letter signed with his name and reflecting on Lord Grey's conduct and motives in the Times.[376] Richmond called him out from a parish vestry he was attending. Mr H Drummond behaved in a very gentleman like manner, and gave without reserve and without any apparent constraint or shabbiness a satisfactory explanation both in words and writing.

Cabinet dinner at Lord Althorp's; the whole Cabinet, including Durham, except Lansdowne were present. It is determined to send a special Commission to Bristol. It is usual to include the local Magistracy in the Commission, and Bristol being a town and County, the Mayor, and the Recorder, Wetherall, [377] as well as other Aldermen would in the common course of things be named in the Commission. But could we trust Wetherall's delicacy not to act as Judge in a cause which in some senses is his own? And could we justify either the appearance or the consequences if he did? The King has the undoubted prerogative of naming and omitting whom he pleases, and we decided that, in the peculiar circumstances of the case, it was safer and even more desirous to omit all the Magistrates of the place, and we negatived the notion started by somebody of writing an explanation to Wetherall, or consulting him on his feelings about it.

Lord Grey then opened the topicks of the Speech and consulted us upon them. It was agreed that Reform should be mentioned and recommended as strongly as it was possible without using words that would invite and provoke an amendment; that our proclamation against the Unions should be adverted to or the words of it nearly repeated in lamenting the propensity of some of the King's subjects to form them illegally; and that the intention of a special commission for the trial of Bristol rioters should be announced. The treaty with Belgium and the expectation of an early ratification thereof should be mentioned, and I suggested that the entire concurrence of the five powers in all their views should be emphatically expressed and a hint conveyed that ulterior measures would be resorted to if, on the ratification of the treaty, the King of Holland did not shortly agree and proceed to execute the articles of it. The treaty for mutual search is expected on Saturday. A paragraph in Speech will no doubt allude to the conclusion of so useful and popular a convention. With respect to Portugal, the continuance of the interruption of our diplomatick relations with Don Miguel together with his unwillingness to agree to the conditions of an amnesty (offered by Duke of Wellington's government) will be adverted to; and Grey having added that he thought something yet stronger should be introduced, I thought it prudent to take the chance of his language being as strong as I could wish it, without inviting too much discussion on a topick where the Chancellor, Lord Goderich, Richmond, and most of the Cabinet are less disposed to agree with me than Lord Palmerston and Lord Grey, with whom the construction of the periods naturally rests. Poland it was agreed with some regret to omit altogether. It would do no good, would sour Russia and encourage the King of Holland with hopes of an estrangement of that Court from England. The Cholera, and the Commercial and financial state of the Country, on which the said Cholera unfortunately has a pernicious effect and is likely to have more, must also be mentioned and are not very agreable topicks. Even of reductions to any great extent we have nothing positive to boast and the general notion was that we should promise little and do as much as we can. The East India Charter, which does not expire till 1834, is to be omitted, and the Bank Charter, which expires in 33, is to be referred to a Committee, but it is questionable whether its renewal has ever been alluded to in a King's Speech. Mr Stanley observed most justly that some commutation of tythes pressed exceedingly in Ireland and, though no bill was drawn out, he was prepared with the principles of one sufficiently perhaps to justify some mention of it in the King's speech. His plan was to give the Clergyman relief against the Landlord as well, or even in preference to, the tenant, and to grant the former, as a compensating boon, the right of purchasing it [*the tithe*] at 17 years purchase and of mortgaging his estate, whether entailed or not, for the amount of the purchase money. The plan seemed to me to be conceived in a spirit less favorable to high Church notions than the tone and temper in which Stanley explained the grounds of it. And after some cursory remarks upon it, Lord Grey acquiesced in the propriety of glancing at it at least in the Speech, and undertook to make a draft of the whole speech by nine o'clock on Friday when we meet at his house to settle it. Throughout these discussions Lord Durham, who had appeared for the first time at the Cabinet since the death of his beautiful and remarkable son, and who had lately returned from an excursion to Brussells and Paris, expressed his surprize and disapprobation at many things that had been done or left undone in his absence in no very measured terms and in a way to undeceive us in the sanguine delusion that his misfortune (which he felt most deeply) might have softened his temper. But after all the 9 topicks for the speech had been agreed upon, he observed that 'we have acted our play but the Character of Hamlet had been left out for we had scarce touched on the subject of reform'. The form of the observation led one to suppose that he made the remark in good humour. Lord Grey said he had begun the discussion with it. Althorp, the Chancellor, Richmond, and all confirmed the observation, and I said so little foundation was there for the criticism that the Prince of Denmark was on the Stage when the Curtain drew up. He said pettishly that he did not know what reform or what bill was to be named in the speech. Was it the old one? or was it a new one? had it been altered? Richmond told him he was under a misapprehension if he supposed much altered, but the best way of judging of it would be that Althorp should inform him of what had been resolved. And on Grey telling him that he could not blame us for omitting the discussion of the details on that day because he could not judge of the time and deliberation we had spent upon the subject during his absence, he lost all command of himself; said he was a Member of a publick government; he could not and by God he would not agree to things he did not know; that he had a right to see all that had past and he would; that he had heard and he believed there had been alterations, and great ones, and he now as a Cabinet Minister demanded to know what they were and why they had been adopted; that his absence was not his fault, that it was a blow of Providence, that he should least of all men have expected that Lord Grey would twit him with it; that his objections were received with a laugh; that he did not wish and was not likely, nay, was determined not to remain long in the Government, but that while there he would discharge his duty and insist on his rights. During all this unprovoked and ungovernable tirade, Lord Grey behaved with the greatest temper, feeling, and dignity, and thereby rendered the whole more disgraceful to Durham and more distressing to the bystanders. Some of them construed the latter part into a premeditated notice of his intended resignation. I am not sure that a wish was not father to the thought, but there certainly were some strong symptoms of a predetermination to differ with Lord Grey and more asperity towards him when differences occurred than to all others at table, though less connected with him. Is it possible that the refusal of the Earldom still rankles in his breast? How strange that a man with so keen a sense of ridicule in others, of so clear and just an understanding where his own selfish vanity is not concerned, and capable too of so much generous and elevated feeling, should be swayed by such silly and paltry objects to language and conduct at once disgraceful, ludicrous, and mischievous.

1 December 1831 Thursday. Some of Durham's strictures on our conduct as a Ministry, if more temperately and less hostilely and contemptuously expressed, might well deserve our consideration. The want of decision in some foreign affairs, especially Portugal, the overscrupulous forbearance in removing enemies in the diplomatick corps, in the horse guards, and in other departments unquestionably beget an opinion in the publick that we are not strong in court or that we are not united in opinion. On such matters Palmerston is either constitutionally or systematically cold and dilatory, and Grey, whose talents in council and debate are as fresh and efficient as ever, has lost some of that energy which, though often termed rashness and violence by his enemies, gave a force to his opinions and stability to his influence over other men, which perhaps a less resolute course may lose.

2 Decr. 1831. Cabinet at foreign office at 9 p.m. Heard from Lord Chancellors the result of enquiries about precedents for the official Commission to Bristol. It is clear that in the ordinary course the Recorder must attend the Sessions or assizes and that the Rioters consequently would be tried by Sir Charles Wetherall. It is equally clear that the King has the prerogative of inserting or omitting what names he chuses in a Special Commission, and that of Dunning himself, then recorder of Bristol, was omitted, though manifestly with his consent and probably at his desire, in a special commission to try one case of forgery (in which Dunning's[378] own name had been forged) in 1769. Grey then read us his sketch of the King's speech. He seemed himself dissatisfied with it, but I thought it prudent and good, and that it handled the two difficult topicks of Reform and Union[s] with great dexterity, urging the speedy termination in terms which the warmest reformer must approve and yet without any such direct allusions to the provisions of the bill as should invite or provoke the opposition of those who disapprove it. On the Unions, the King is made to assert the full right of the people to discuss and represent their grievances and to disclaim all wish as well as intention of interfering, but at the same time to trust to the loyalty of his faithful subjects in assisting him to put down any illegal combinations and to protect the peace and property of the Country. [*In the margin:* The King stickled for the word 'Unions' but it was deemed, and justly deemed, more safe and more dignified to avoid it.] The words on Portugal alledged the impossibility of recognizing Miguel, and alluding to the distracted state of that country said that it arose from the differences subsisting between the Princes of the House of Braganza. To the latter proposition some subtle and ingenious but not convincing objections were urged by Duke of Richmond, and the consideration of the sentence was postponed; but I have no doubt that even in its most mitigated form it will be sufficient to imply a wish for the final settlement of Portugal and a persuasion that under Miguel it can never occur. A Commutation of tythes in Ireland was pointed at as one important remedy of the grievances at present most felt in that Country. Mr Stanley, from a hope of propitiating the Churchmen and perhaps from too great a liking to that body himself, had introduced a phrase, pledging the Government to the *more effectual* support of the Protestant established Church, in terms which, the Chancellor justly observed, would sound menacing to the ears of the Irish people. Some conversation ensued on the nature and character of that species of Ecclesiastical property in which it was manifest that Mr Stanley and the Duke of Richmond deemed them more inviolable than law and reason would <shew> them to be, and the latter even questioned their injurious pressure on the industrious part of the agricultural classes in Ireland. However the phrase was altered, softened, and much amended. The measure that Stanley pointed to was such as should satisfy Catholick as well as protestant and really just and considerate to the Community, but I can easily understand that the statements and arguments by which he justifies and, in some sort, palliates its necessity are by no means conciliatory to those Irishmen who do not share with him in the respect he professes for so anomalous an establishment as the Irish Church.

3 Saturday [*December 1831*]. During the whole of this week I neglected my diary.

4 Sunday. Our Cabinets were chiefly occupied with discussing the intended
5 Monday. alterations in the Reform. The result of them will be seen in the
6 Tuesday. bill to be presented next week. Durham in the course of them
7 Wedy. (which he attended pretty regularly) abstained from any repeti-
8 Thy. tion of the painful scene witnessed at Lord Althorp's and seemed
9 Friday. to acquiesce with tolerable chearfulness in many of the alterations.

10 Saturday. The King's speech had great success on the publick, and though the Duke of Richmond had been somewhat earnest to prevent any allusion to Don Pedro in the Speech, the sentence attracted animadversion from Lord Aberdeen, who unintentionally injured Miguel's and assisted Donna Maria's cause very materially by provoking Lord Grey to comment on the text in a way far more severe on Don Miguel and his government than the original Speech. Lord Grey answered Lord Aberdeen triumphantly but not sufficiently so to deter him from giving notice of a motion on the settlement of the Belgian question.[379] Lord Camperdown spoke manfully and sensibly on Reform without offence to the House. Lord Lyttelton[380] shewed more zeal than taste, and more sympathy with publick feeling than respect for his audience. Nothing proved the subdued tone and spirits of the Antireformers more than the faint manner in which they repelled the attack of Lord Lyttelton on their late 'contumelious rejection' of the bill, his description of the consequences to them and the Church and the religion of the Country if they did not shortly retrace their steps, and his direct exhortation to

Ministers to create Peers enough to carry the measure. Harrowby spoke temperately and behaved courteously and even handsomely about an amendment rather of form than substance in the address, but none manfully avowed conversion to Reform and still less to our Bill. Yet the address, pledging the House as it did to 'a *speedy* and satisfactory settlement of the question of Reform which the King's Government was avowedly to introduce' and approving by implication the whole policy of the Ministry at home and abroad, was voted nemine dissentiente. [*In the margin:* Yet Lord Stormont,[381] Lord Wynford, and others of the high flying party who describe Reform as revolution and Robbery were there. It is no business of mine to reconcile their principles with their actions; but what does such forbearance indicate? real change in the elements of their opposition or greater depth in their design? Time will shew.] Such a result, especially after rumours of amendments and motions innumerable, was some relief to Ministers and must create a great opinion of their strength and stability abroad. Nothing occurred in the Commons to impair this feeling.

On Wednesday we dined at Lord Grey's, the whole 15 of the Cabinet present. The alterations in bill were the chief topicks of discussion, and all I think amicably and I hope finally arranged. In general the improvements were either necessary or reasonable. They were granted to none as the price of their votes, but should they furnish decent opponents with an excuse to come over, so much the better. The names of those who should be appointed to *tythe* Committees in both houses were mentioned and the propriety of admitting any Catholicks canvassed, on which Stanley and Palmerston and some others were decidedly against the admission, Goderich, Grant, and myself as decidely for it. They will I fear be omitted.[382] A strong proof, this, of the propriety of altering the oaths, if any opportunity should occur, and of devizing one and one only for all his Majesty's subjects. If even in a liberal Cabinet like ours the distinction of Catholick and Protestant is still so much considered, how obviously must the separation of oaths perpetuate it among feeble and vulgar politicians!

It was after some conversation agreed that Althorp should *postpone* his resolutions on the Condition of Slavery in the Colonies. The Order in Council is gone out.[383] It is full of regulations little adapted to the state of society or even to the accomplishment of its object and of course strongly repugnant to the feelings of those on whose observance of it the success must depend. I fear the Jamaica assembly will reject it; and I see no benefit arising from a collision between the legislatures of the Mother Country and the Islands.

I was too late for the House of Lords on the 9th., Friday, when Aberdeen announced an intention (unless the Duke of Wellington were well enough to do it himself) to bring on some motion on Belgian affairs. This notice justly provoked Grey as factious in the extreme. The King of Holland is said to be instigated in his obstinacy by Ouvrard, who offers to advance him a loan and suggests, that if the King can persuade the Chambers in their present loyal and warlike mood to sanction it, he may, when he has got it, yield in time to prevent hostilities and so pocket both the money and the supposed affront it was voted to resist. These manoevres are not only dishonourable and from the loss of lives they will occasion inhuman, but they are dangerous in the extreme and may lead to war.

Sunday 11th. December 1831. The Chancellor has been much censured for the distribution of the Church patronage to 'Undeservers' and political enemies. He had heard the charge, and vindicated himself, at some length but great good temper, on the ground of the Chancellor's patronage not being devoted to party and political purposes and on the merits of each particular case, in which, *if his facts* are *correct*, his justification may safely rest.

A Cabinet at foreign office at 2. The Chancellor came late, some conversation on the renewal of East India company's charter, which, till the House of Commons Committee be closed, Mr Grant thinks should not be determined upon, negotiated, or announced. It was determined to send a special commission to try the offenders at Nottingham. The opinion of Attorney General leant the other way but Denman on such a point might find it difficult to divest his mind of all prepossession. There was a difficulty about the Judges. Why not Lyndhurst? I asked; and it was agreed he should go.

We then once more went through the bill and the schedules. A Question arose which of the three places—Stroud with its environs, Cheltenham, or Dudley—should have two instead of one Member. Their numbers according to our criterion were nearly equal. We decided on Stroud, which as an insulated district of thriving Manufactures <seems> to me well entitled to a good representation. Lords Wharncliffe, Harrowby, and Lord Chandos had a meeting with Grey, the Chancellor, and Lord Althorp; and a paper containing their very unsatisfactory, incoherent, and inadmissible suggestions remained in the hands of our Colleagues. Grey told them without reserve the nature and extent of such alterations as we intended, and Harrowby observed it was impossible for him to agree to the provisions of such a bill, though in the principles of disfranchisement, enfranchisement, and extension of qualification he was prepared to acquiesce. The interview went off as all these half negotiations, half intrigues, and half concerts ever have and ever will do, unsatisfactorily to both parties. Lord Chandos had an audience of King in his character of Chairman of West Indian Committee, and took occasion to talk of the Reform bill both to H M and to Sir Herbert Taylor, one of whom told him he had better state his suggestions to the Ministers. They have somewhat expeditiously and industriously, Lord Brougham thinks scandalously and almost treacherously, bruited this about as a negotiation sanctioned by the Court; and he [Brougham] shrewdly suspects [*crossed out:* the Enemy] them of a design of affixing upon us the imputation of some concession, with a view of undermining our popularity and lulling [us] into a false security by one and the same manoeuver. The[n] after beating us on the bill, they may come in on our defeat and move the same or a stronger measure to pacify the people. There is perhaps something in this.

The Clemency and amnesty of the Emperor Nicholas are of a piece. The latter consists in the banishment of all who have opposed him and the illegal confiscation of their lands; the former, in various devices, under hypocritical pretences, for extirpating the Polish race in Podolia and Lithuania. The King of Holland still obstinately persists in witholding his assent to the treaty, though the reduction of the Prussian army, the earnest remonstrances of the Prussian Minister at the Hague, the somewhat angry representation of the Germanick confederacy who have signified their intention of acting with respect to the Duchy of Luxemburgh as if he had agreed, should he continue to maintain his disdainful silence 15 days longer, and a variety of other appearances have given him a fair warning of the consequences of his obstinacy. He sends a special mission here with the idle hope of again opening the negotiation. He is encouraged, no doubt, in these dangerous practices by the secret instigations of Duke of Wellington and Aberdeen, and by that silly delusion which always perverts the brain of Princes—that a Crown once worn can never be finally or irretrievably rent from their brows. Talleyrand wishes King Philip to withold his ratification of the treaty till those of the three other Powers arrive, in order to give to that act still more character and appearance of entire concert and cooperation. The delay in terminating this affair, in addition to the danger of exciting jealousies between the arbiters, and war between the parties, impedes the progress of all other affairs, renders England and France cautious in their language and remonstrances about Poland, and tends perhaps to deter us from adopting a distinct line of politicks in the Affairs of Portugal.

In the Cabinet of this day Lord Durham was calm, judicious, and conciliatory, and Lord Grey's manner to him quite touching as well as considerate. Durham, whom I set down at his house, spoke to me on the state of affairs, on the necessity of making peers, and on the obvious designs of our enemies and danger of their success, with infinite temper, discernment, and sense. No two men are more unlike than Durham when in good humour, and Durham in his angry, tetchy and, I am afraid one must add, usual mood. Durham is to meet Stanley and others to prepare the tythe measure.[384] He likes this.

Monday 12 December. I did not go to House of Lords. In Commons there was great appearance of moderation in our opponents, though Sir Robt. Peel attempted a high tone and failed, being half disavowed by Lord Clive[385] and others. The only untoward appearance was the general complaint of the Irish at the small additional number (5) granted to their representation and the sympathy expressed by Hume and Labouchere and felt by many of our friends with this most unreasonable as well as inconvenient cause of complaint.

13 Decr. Tuesday. Idle report of a revolution in Spain, confuted by a comparison of dates. Strange that one should dread and deprecate the dethronement of such a wretch as Ferdinand, but his death or a civil war would just now aggravate the calamities of Spain and probably lead to a War in Europe.

Ellenborough[386] moved for papers relating to the dispute between China and the East Indian Companies factory at Canton, in which he laid the blame (perhaps justly) on the latter, and inveighed in gentle voice but strong language against the assumed license of an English press in that place, in a strain better suited to the Chinese than the English Senate. Our Mandarins however nodded from sleep if not from approbation and he cautiously withdrew his motion at the request of Lord Grey.

Wednesday, 14 Decr. Cabinet dined at Admiralty. Ebrington had written a letter to Althorp, which Althorp read to us, urging the policy and justice of granting more representatives to Ireland and suggesting one or two methods of doing it, and ending by acknowledging that he felt it his duty to move it, partly from his conviction of its necessity and justice and partly with a hope that such a motion or measure in his hands would be less injurious to the Ministry than if taken up by any Member less disposed to consult their interests. A very incorrect report of a communication between some Irish Members and Lord Althorp and Mr Stanley had been lithographed last September, and among other inaccuracies it was stated therein that it was probable some further addition to the Irish representatives might be adopted by the Government. This both Stanley and Althorp said was—as well as various matters in the paper which Sir J Newport and OConnel had approved, but which neither Stanley nor Althorp had ever seen till now—quite incorrect; and they both (acknowledging however that at one time they had not been adverse to some further addition) declared that they could not recommend and scarcely assent to any concession of the sort *now*. Lord Grey was still more decided. He would rather resign at once than acquiesce. Some others spoke with resentment of their Irish friends. Carlisle and Grant and the Chancellor (the latter very faintly) were the only persons who doubted of the propriety of adhering to our solution, i.e., of granting the 5 additional and *no more.*[387] We must do so, and I have less reluctance in doing so because the pretensions of the Irish are nearly as unreasonable as their method of enforcing them is of bad example and unfriendly. At the same time the object contended for *(three additional Members)*, though not just, was not of importance enough to incur so serious a danger as the estrangement of our Irish friends, could we have foreseen it. But it is one thing to grant a boon to a friend, another to have it extorted from you after you have refused it. It is the more vexatious, because with a view of preventing this very inconvenience we have saddled ourselves with another and filled up on the House of Commons to its original number (though inconveniently large) with the hope that it would shut the door to all disturbance about the additional representatives of Scotland and Ireland. Lord Althorp said there was another point on which an early decision was advisable, as affecting the disposition of the Irish Members. They had asked him if the new provision in English bill which continued votes to freemen by birth and servitude was to be extended to Irish Boroughs. If so, the effect would be to perpetuate the *Protestant* Monopoly in each of the Incorporated boroughs; if *not,* the discrepancy maintained in the Irish bill would be somewhat of a boon and might act as a set off with those among them who were disposed, where they dared, to support our Ministry even against OConnel. Althorp, who was firm against extension of numbers, was decidedly for this step and the substantial justice was clearly that way. We could not, however, avow the objection to Protestant ascendancy as our justification. The vehemence of the Duke of Richmond against it was a pretty clear indication how such an argument would be received. But Goderich justly remarked that the Irish and English bills were already dissimilar in many principles, provisions, and details, and ought to be so from the dissimilarity of the circumstances; that it by no means followed that a provision that might be harmless or even useful in Corporation towns here, where many were to be added and many taken away, might not be very injurious in Ireland, where all the old ones were to be preserved and scarcely any new ones to be created; and that in truth they had been partially and injustly administered and all in a direction and with a view unknown in England. Some conversation arose on the nature of that practice. The Chancellor agreed to see Mr Spring Rice to ascertain the state of the law and the way that it worked, and it was agreed that unless he saw reason to question the propriety of doing so, Lord Althorp should inform the Irish that *as at present advised he had no intention of extending the obnoxious provision to Ireland.*[388]

Burdett had signified to Althorp an intention of moving the repeal of 'Foreign Enlistment bill' with a view (among others of a more publick nature) of stating Lord Dundonald's case and vindicating his character. This would be embarrasssing to Government and injurious to Lord Dundonald, for reasons not easy to assign even to Burdett. Lord Grey in truth informed us that Dundonald had memorialized and subsequently seen the King and not without effect; that His Majesty was struck with his abilities and less prejudiced against his case than hitherto; that he thought he should be furnished with such charges or insinuations as existed against him in the Admiralty and other offices in order that he might have an opportunity of vindicating himself; and that He, the King, should rejoice if so great an officer could be restored to the Service without scandal or offence. Though Richmond repeated his somewhat violent prejudices against this remarkable man, it seemed to me that our Colleagues received the intimation of a change in the King's sentiments very favorably and that, when we come to reconsider the subject, a more lenient decision than the last may be taken, now that it is known that such Unity will not be altogether displeasing at Court. In the meanwhile Archbishop will endeavour to prevail on Burdett to postpone his motion.

A conversation ensued on the form of motion for a Committee on tythes and the extent to which Mr Stanley should open his plan for a Commutation. It was clear that Hume would move an amendment to enquire into the whole state of the Irish Church.[389] We agreed that the grievances should be urged at length, that the general object of a Commutation should be pointed at, but that any particular means of effecting it should be stated hypothetically and not as if finally resolved upon and prepared by Government. We then canvassed the projected names in both houses. More than one of us thought the omission of Catholicks injudicious and unfair, and if Bishops in Lords, Goulburn,[390] and Orangemen in Commons are admitted, why should Lord King and Mr Hume be passed over?

The Convention concerning the fortresses is signed and Mons, Ath, Menin, Marienburgh, and Philippeville are to be dismantled.[391] On my return I found Talleyrand. He was earnest to know if *Tournay* was on the list. I told him I could not recollect and I sent to Palmerston to ask. His answer made me conscious of my indiscretion in telling Talleyrand any thing about it, but it was too late to recall. France was particularly anxious that Tournay, of which they had boasted, should be one of the dismantled fortresses. It seems to me a pity that their amour propre (in a matter substantially of no moment at all) should not be indulged. We are very earnest upon such points ourselves; we ought to do as we would be done by, when it is our wish and policy to keep well.

It was settled at the Cabinet dinner of this day that a sum not exceeding

£100,000 should be given in relief of the sufferers by the hurricane in Barbadoes and St. Vincents, and more lent on security if security can be found. The whole amount of the loss is estimated at more than *£1,700,000.*

Thursday 15 Decr. Melbourne moved in rather a slovenly manner a committee on tythes in pursuance of the King's speech. Though he put hypothetically the measure he had in view of rendering the Composition compulsory, making the Landlord answerable but giving him a good bargain and a release from entails to redeem the tythe—enabling him to raise money for the purchase by mortgage and then commuting it to land—he too broadly acknowledged that we were not in a situation to prepare a bill, and laid himself somewhat open to the observations of Wicklow, Ellenborough, and Carnarvon, the first of whom, disclaiming hostility, made a bitter invective against our policy in Ireland, threatened us with Orange and Protestant associations which he said he might be compelled to join, and inveighed against OConnel and Doyle[392] in sundry, extravagant, and prepared sentences. The second objected to a Committee which he preposterously called an unconstitutional innovation to screen Ministers from responsability; and Carnarvon, though not averse from the motion or measure to which it would lead, hung upon this peg a string of antithetical epigrams on the folly and irresolution of our Ministry, with the shew and perhaps the intention of impartiality, instead of the fear and respect we had incurred the contempt and aversion of both parties and had no authority but with our troops and agents. They were all well answered by Clanrickarde, Lansdown, and Lord Grey: the first exposing Wicklow's departure from the question, unhandsome abuse of Doyle, and factious attempt to widen the breaches he affected to deplore; Lord Lansdown ridiculing Lord Ellenborough's ignorance and presumption most happily, and vindicating the proceeding by committee and supplying the omission of Melbourne by a clear exposition of the measure to which it pointed; Lord Grey, with his usual correctness of memory and justness of reason, recapitulated the arguments in favor both of the proceeding and the measure, expressed in strong and pathetick terms his disappointment at the introduction of party topicks on an occasion where he had hoped all might agree, and vindicated the conduct of Ministry by a simple and full recital of all that had passed or rather not passed between them and Mr OConnel and their disposition towards him.

Lord Aberdeen put off his Belgian motion and, in alluding to Duke of Wellington, was studiously earnest to impress on the house the Duke's entire concurrence with his opinion on these matters.

In the Commons the tactics of Dawson,[393] Peel, and the rest of the opposition was different. They more artfully complimented us for our attention to tythes, and endeavoured to sow dissensions between the Government and the Catholicks by hailing it as a commencement of a series of measures to maintain the full power of the Church and exhorting us to persist in that laudable design.

Friday 16 Decr. Saw Lord Grey, who was somewhat despondent in his view of Ireland and the internal concerns of the Country. Able and vigorous as he is in Parliament, and amiable and sensible in Council, he has I fear lost some of his energy and ardor. I missed the Lords, where Aberdeen asked some questions and attempted to affix some blame on Ministers for neglecting to enforce the provisions of Foreign Enlistment bill against Don Pedro's partizans. Macaulay's speech in Commons made a great sensation and proves how valuable an acquisition he will be to Administration. Some appointment for him should be found without loss of time. The Lords adjourned to *17 Jany. 1832.* In this Session Reporters, Ladies, foreign Ministers, and people were for the first time admitted to a gallery allotted exclusively for that purpose in the House of Lords, and English Bishops appeared to great advantage without wigs, in conformity with the antient Canon, Cleris deperuetur.

17 Decr. Saturday. Commons at 12, and sat till 1/2 past one into Sunday. The debate and division triumphant for Ministers and reform.[394]

For Second Reading	324	
Against	162	two to one
Majority	162	

Lord John made a very judicious and Stanley a brilliant, lively and argumentative Speech in which he exposed Mr Croker's inaccurate quotations and precedent and, difficult as it should seem, abashed him entirely. Sir Robert Peel declared that he never could support or share the responsibility of supporting reform, he might be compelled to submit to it. His speech was a good one and by mismanagement the last (Hunt's excepted) in debate. It was remarkable that he said nothing to cover Croker. I dined at Talleyrand's.

18 Decr. Sunday. Cabinet at two. The whole 15 present. Grey called our attention to the state of the two houses and the prospects of passing the bill, observing that although he had strong reason and confidence, without however positive assurances, of the accession of 7 or perhaps 8 or 9 Bishops, he could not reckon upon any further additional force in the House of Lords as at present composed. Many who had expressed alarm at any second reading of the bill, and as Harrowby worded it, professed an anxiety to find a loophole through which to creep thro' to it, appeared nevertheless discontented with it as it now stood and at the best irresolute unless such alterations were made as in prudence and honour we are equally bound to resist. The conduct of their representatives in Commons (John Wortly,[395] Chandos, and others) warn us that we can not reckon on the votes of such as, professing to be half converts at least to the necessity, dwelt earnestly on many of the most indispensable provisions of the bill as formidable and insuperable objections to it. It followed that we had little prospect of a majority of the House of Lords where, according to our most favorable calculations, the opponents outnumbered us by 20 or 25. He then stated in language sufficiently earnest his conviction that a 2d. rejection of the bill was equivalent to a subversion of the state, civil war and revolution, and that our duty to the King and the country called upon us to provide against such a calamity; but he suggested, I thought rather faintly and with much hesitation and many admissions both as to its efficacy and its propriety, the only effectual and obvious expedient for the prevention of such a catastrophe, namely the Creation of peers. Some difficulties, he more than hinted, he might find with the King. Great repugnance he should feel if he did, in throwing on the King after his noble and handsome behaviour all the odium of defeating the measure and dismissing the ministry, and some doubts he expressed that, by introducing new friends into the House of Lords, he might lose the support of some old ones who would be disgusted at that measure. There were two, Lord Francis Osborne[396] and Mr Dundas of Berkshire, who were in a manner promised and to whose elevation there could, he apprehended, be no objection. The Chancellor, after recapitulating the difficulties of the situation, acknowledged that of the two evils—the loss of the bill or a very large encrease of the Lords—he thought the former the greater, but he at the same time *admitted and even exaggerated* the objections to the latter. He exercised a little more ingenuity than was necessary or in the circumstances prudent to prove that we were not in a condition to judge what number would really secure our bill. He suggested however that a moderate number as an indication of our strength might be made immediately, and he dwelt on some length on the difference between the calling up eldest Sons, the creation of presumptive heirs and childless old men, and the creation of such as were likely by succession to add permanently to the numbers of the house. A long conversation ensued, several admitting, hastily I think, that the creation of peers would estrange some that are friendly and therefore doubting the efficacy of such a measure if in a large scale and the good effects of the threat and indication of strength if on a small one; Lansdowne and Richmond deprecating most earnestly what they called preposterously the destruction of the House of Lords; and Palmerston, less covertly than hitherto, recommending an indirect concession of material parts of the bill by an understanding that we would acquiesce in having many which are obnoxious to us forced upon us in the Committee, provided they would vote for the second reading. Lord Carlisle, Lord Goderich, and myself, and I think Sir James Graham and Lord Althorp combated slightly the notion of a large creation destroying the Lords, which I contended the rejection of the bill would practically effect, and [I] urged more earnestly the creation of a few, as a demonstration of our power with the King and as likely to deter those who were really averse to any large creation on strong constitutional views of the subject from driving us to an expedient that they might think yet worse than the bill itself. An admission of the Duke of Richmond that, in his belief, the Archbishop of Canterbury, if convinced we would make peers, would vote himself and make half the Bishop's bench vote for the bill in order to reduce the number of new peers seems to me to answer at once the idle doubts whether any creation now would as a demonstration of power do us good or harm. Grey would not press the Cabinet to an immediate decision. He referred the question to our further consideration, on which Durham, with somewhat too much solemnity and a little tho' suppressed asperity to Palmerston, summed up with great perspicuity and readiness the three points submitted to us: whether to make peers sufficient to carry the bill; whether, with the hope of avoiding the necessity of making a large batch, we should *now* proceed to call up some (which he adroitly termed my proposition); or whether we should trust to modifications, arrangements, and understandings about amendments in bill for obtaining us a majority out of our opponents in Lords. The first plan, he said, he was ready to adopt and disposed to recommend; the next he would assent to as a means of postponing the consideration of the first; but to the latter [*i.e. the last*] he must solemnly protest as one neither reconcileable to honour or prudence, an evasion of Lord Grey's pledge, and an uncertain expedient for securing votes, inasmuch as many of our friends would probably, as he himself certainly would do, vote decidedly against a bill so mutilated and the offspring of such compromise and contrivances. His manner was far less offensive than usual and his reasons and firmness made much impression on us all.

Stanley and Lord Grey then called our attention to Ireland, the encreasing violence and numbers of political associations for repeal of union and other popular measures suggested by OConnel and the agitators, and the no less violent and factious combination of Orangemen and Brunswickers on the pretence of protecting the Protestant Church. Some of the latter were Lord Lieutenants, officers in Militia and army and held honors or offices under the Crown. Were they to be allowed to pass resolutions directly tending to charge Government with a dereliction of duty and avowing an intention of over<com>ing and superseding it? and could they be deprived of their commissions unless by some even handed justice we equally endeavoured to put down OConnel's associations, and how was the latter to be done but by coercive laws? Althorp pertinently remarked that in dismissing Lord Lieutenants or Officers we advised the King to exercise his undoubted authority, and in allowing the other Associations to subsist, we shrank from no responsability in exerting the law, because we were enabled by no law to put them down.[397] He seemed disposed to remove Lords Lorton[398] and Farnham[399] from their situations, but not to apply for any further powers against the other associations. Stanley (whose eyes sparkled with delight at the success of his last night's speech) said little on this subject, but quoted Duncannon's admission that Kilkenny was in a state to justify coercive measures, an admission, Althorp remarked, which would have been conclusive had it been made with respect to any county but Kilkenny.[400]

19 Decr. Monday. Palmela shewed me Palmerston's answer which I had not seen and which is more favorable to Donna Maria than I expected, though it does not expressly say we will not allow of Spanish interference in Portugal. Palmela is in spirits and hopes Pedro will take Madeira before he reaches the Azores.

Talleyrand shewed me letters from his King and Sebastiani quite vexed and irritated at the choice of Philippeville and Marienburg and the omission of Tournay in the list of fortresses to be dismantled. He affects apprehensions that it may subvert Perier's government, says they will withold the ratification of Belgian treaty, and but for the King would have witheld that of the reciprocal search with a view of prevailing on us to amend it. Dined at Master of Rolls.[401]

20 December. Went late to the Cabinet, where I found them discussing the boundaries of smaller boroughs. Lord Lansdowne very earnest to include some adjacent parts which he calls 'arrondisements' with the real object probably of infusing landed interest in town elections, with the ostensible one of preventing these boroughs becoming close by enabling more than one proprietor in case of need adding votes by building £10 houses. Agreed that a general rule should be adopted.[402] Sir James Graham consulted in the Cabinet on a reduction of several 1000 Seamen which after discussion was approved. It appears the Americans go upon the plan of building [*crossed out:* the body] but not completing Ships, and Graham says it is a wise and oeconomical plan and fit to be adopted here. Goderich asked what were the French designs and what our relations with Algiers?[403] did the French succeed to the treaties of the Dey and had we a right to such privileges from the Conqueror as we enjoyed under the conquered and exiled Dey? He justly observed that if questioned on these matters in Parliament we should have a distinct answer to give, but he betrayed, as is usual with him, more suspicion and jealousy of France than the occasion required. Codrington means to press for head money for the seamen at Navarrino, an unpleasant and embarrassing question. Lord Grey seems to me to regret that our selection of fortresses to be dismantled should be such as to disappoint the French, but Palmerston with some asperity to Talleyrand maintains that the inclusion of Philippeville and Marienbourg, not the omission of Tounay [*sic*], is the real source of his displeasure and that he and the Government of France harbour a hope of recovering that nook of territory by force or by craft and wish to keep the fortresses upon it. There is some justice in Palmerston's argument that unless they had such views the destruction of those two places would be the next agreable thing to France to the possession of them, but I am inclined to believe their real motive of displeasure at this arrangement is that it confirms the prediction of Mauguin[404] and gives a handle to him and the opposition in the Chambers. A similar dread of Wellington is in truth our motive for making the selection we have made; for the point in dispute is three blue beans in one blue bladder, of no intrinsick value but suited to make a clatter and call attention. Palmerston thinks Don Pedro will take Madeira. He tells me Grey thinks his paper in answer to Palmela too strong, as I do too weak, against Miguel. On that topick Palmerston is generally right, but I think he is not on domestick or even on foreign matters generally so averse to AntiGallican and antirevolutionary systems as I at one time hoped. His continuance of our political enemies in office both at home and abroad is very unpopular with our friends. It may proceed, and I believe it does, from forbearance, good nature, indolence, or principle, but coupled with some estrangement from our reform measures, gives rise to suspicions of his lukewarmness in the cause of the party and Ministry to which he belongs.

21 Wednesday [*December 1831*] During this whole week I neglected my Diary. From Wednesday to Sunday I was at Lord Grey's at East Sheen.

22

23

24

25 Sunday

26

27 Tuesday

I found him on the whole well in health and chearful in spirits, though he had a small but a new physical annoyance to disturb the first, and much uncertainty about the House of Lords, Ireland, and France to discompose the latter, without adding that of Durham's temper which is often more irritating to him than any publick or private grievances whatever. Nothing can be more natural and amiable than Grey in his family, and his anxiety to soothe Durham with a view of gratifying his daughter is most touching. Grey shewed me a letter of Palmerston and Palmerston called to enforce the topicks of it on Lord Grey while I was at Shean, but by accident or design he did not seek to see me. Grey also shewed me the fortress treaty and the secret article. The latter is unobjectionable in any sense but that of being secret. When however there is a patent Quintuple treaty renouncing all exclusive interest or separate advantage, Vide 11th Protocol, the right of four of the contracting parties to make *separate and secret* engagements as security against the fifth may be questionable and is at least a suspicious exercise of a right. I learnt from Lord Palmerston's letter that the French had shifted their ground of objection from that of the particular fortresses selected to the concealment with which the negotiation was conducted and the anomalous principle of subjecting the state of the defence of a guaranteed neutral power to the perpetual superintendence of four of the guaranteeing powers and to the exclusion of the fifth. He ascribed the whole difficulty to Talleyrand's activity and intrigue and his secret desire of getting back Marienburgh and Philippeville, and he ascribed the opportunity he had seized of doing this mischief, a little more than appeared just or friendly, to my indiscretion in informing him [Talleyrand] the night of the signature that Tournay was not to be dismantled and Philippeville and Marienburgh were.

I was not apprized of its being a secret, Talleyrand had told me all I knew of the Conferences about these fortresses, and in April last and during the whole summer he had been not officially but confidentially apprized and in some senses consulted on the subject. Palmerston candidly acknowledged that he was to blame for not admonishing me and the full Cabinet, to whom he communicated the signature of the treaty, the necessity and advantage of concealing it from Talleyrand. Of the policy and wisdom of that concealment I certainly have strong doubts, of the justice of the prospective stipulations I have some, and to the base notion or possibility of a war upon such a point I have the most unconquerable repugnance. All these views I should have urged in the Cabinet if the treaty had in any shape come under our consideration before it was concluded. But when it was so concluded and on the point of being ratified and after the French had urged many disingenuous, unintelligible, and inconsistent arguments against it and resorted to some equivocal manoeuvres both at Brussels and in London to prevent the ratification, it was too late to retract. The appearance of being detected and defeated in a hostile measure would have sown more discord between us than the persisting in one liable to such an imputation but certainly not conceived in any such spirit. When therefore it came on Monday the 26th. before a very thin Cabinet, I contented myself with stating my scruples and apprehensions, lamenting that I had not had an earlier opportunity of canvassing the question, and I acquiesced in the decision to proceed to the ratification of the treaty. In the course of this discussion Lord Durham read a letter full of ill humour and suppressed menace from Louis Philippe to King Leopold and other communications he had received from Brussells which indicated the fears of King of Belgium and his reluctance to give umbrage to the French. This was manifestly interpreted into mere intimidation and bluster by Palmerston, but he acknowledged that in a letter from Leopold to Louis Philippe 5 other places with the omission of Philippeville and Marienburgh had been named as those he should wish to see dismantled, a communication which explained if it did not justify the French King's reproach of Leopold for deceiving him. In Sebastiani's discussion with Lord Granville, the latter adroitly retorted on him the unjustifiable endeavour to cajole or intimidate Leopold into a separate engagement to demolish the fortresses, and in exposing the incorrectness and inconsistency of the French language and conduct, was very successful, though I think in vindicating our own he had a harder theme to sustain. For my part I recorded my view of this subject in a letter to Palmerston, which if I have time I will transcribe on the opposite page.[405] Palmerston in his letter to Grey had hinted somewhat tartly, I thought, the determination of himself and other of his Colleagues to resist any thing that could be construed into truckling to France and warned Grey of the consequences to his government of exposing it to any such reproach. To Grey I did not remark this, for he is perhaps too apt to take fire at any thing of the sort and I should have been sorry to have made ill blood. But when I reflected on all the circumstances of Palmerston['s] language and conduct, his renewed intimacy with Lady Cowper[406] and her incredible and unaccountable subserviency to Mme de Lieven, I was not sorry altogether to learn from him that the Emperor Nicholas had written to lament, with some censure, the signature of the treaty and to withold at least if not to refuse his ratification till the King of Holland shall have consented. This may estrange Palmerston from Russian councils, especially if it be true that the Princess Lieven had intelligence of the refusal to ratify before her husband and was more rejoiced than chagrined at it. Lieven is himself a plain Man and of course anxious that what he has signed should be ratified. But the Princess is unquestionably more Antigallican than he and seems of late to have imbibed much of that Ultra spirit which, according to rumour, Mme Nesselrode has taken from the Carlist Ladies at Dieppe into Russia, where She inculcates in her husband and the Emperor the wickedness and instability of the Revolutionary Government of France. If the Russian refusal to ratify [the treaty of 15 November] impresses on the English and French Government the necessity of drawing their connection closer for the preservation of peace, it may dispel the transitory ill humour produced by the fortress treaty and counteract the objectionable tendency of that engagement to unite us with the three great Military powers of the Continent in a sort of defensive confederacy against France. I was glad to hear Durham express a wish that all the fortresses were destroyed.

Lord Grey somewhat reluctantly acquiesces in the necessity of making peers or at least of obtaining from the Crown full powers to do so. He feels some apprehension lest the King should object, but we are to have a Cabinet before he goes down to Brighton to consider of this most important matter. The conversions to our bill in House of Lords, except some few on the Bishops bench, are all problematical, and the majority against us is at least 25. The loss of the bill is civil war and revolution and, above all, the loss of the Lords to which our Aristocracy is so str<onge>ly attached. It seems an odd effect of love for that institution to risk its existence merely to prevent its encrease, and thus to prefer to a large House of Lords the having none at all. Lady Grey, who in a quiet way has great influence with her husband, is manifestly for vigorous measure and a large encrease of the peerage rather than the risk of a 2d. defeat in Lords. The King will no doubt be averse to it. It is right he should be, but if convinced that it is a choice of evils, that the only alternative is a large creation or the confusion consequent upon rejection of the bill, he will I think acquiesce in the same spirited and manly way he did in the dissolution.

Arguelles and other Spaniards applyed to me to intercede for that unfortunate and misguided Man, General Torrijos,[407] and his followers. I suggested and did all that occurred to me as likely to plead for mercy, but as I foresaw it was too late. He and his fifty six companions, among whom there were two Ex Deputies of Cortes, were shot without mercy in the Square at Malaga. Their lives were doubtless forfeited to the Law, but the Spanish Consul at Gibraltar, the officers at Malaga, and other Agents of Ferdinand, under the direction of Government, stooped to the base and cruel artifice of enticing them on to their destruction and took pains to conceal from the Governor of Gibraltar[408] the preparations of Torrijos, knowing that he would prevent them, and send away the conspirators, but at the same time give them a safe conduct to some distant and neutral port. Ferdinand was not content to be safe from the project. He was determined to be revenged of the authors of it.

The King, at the suggestion no doubt of some Miguelite, has taken offence at a British officer of the Navy, Sartorius, commanding the expedition of Don Pedro, and confounding the provisions of the Foreign enlistment [act] with the exercise of the prerogative, urges Sir Js. Graham, in conformity with that statute, to admonish Captn. Sartorius that he will lose his rank and commission if he persists. He has not drawn for his half pay, which requires an oath that he has no foreign employment. We agreed that no admonition could be given but by a proclamation, and that must be a general measure affecting officers in all foreign services and in Miguel's as well as Pedro's. The time for such a measure would be most cruelly unfavorable to Pedro and hardly in unison with our views or consistent with our honour. It was thought better that Graham should in the first instance expound to his majesty the distinction between the law and the Prerogative, observe to him that the former was open to Miguels' agents, and that the exertion of the latter would be at least premature, and perhaps somewhat partial and severe, if not extended to many Officers now serving in foreign armies and fleets. At least some time would be gained in these explanations. The truth is the provisions of the Enlistment bill are utterly illusory; the very act which constitutes the crime puts the criminal out of the reach of the law.

Mr Grant suggested the propriety of sending an embassy to China and hoped Mr Elphinstone,[409] now in Italy, might be induced to undertake it. Some questioned the use of an Embassy which had notoriously failed in the only two instances they had been tried, and others seemed to grudge the expence, though all agreed in the excellence of the selection of Mr Elphinstone for that or any other employment of importance. Durham said jokingly, 'If the Embassador is to go to Pekin, pray send me'. I smiled at the recollection that both Macartney[410] and Amherst[411] had discovered the necessity of an Earldom to reconcile their approach to the Emperor of China, because He can only receive the relations of a Sovereign Prince, and an Earl is, according to form, styled by the King a *cousin* as well as a councillor. Were Durham taken at his word he would not neglect this circumstance, for he is childishly bent on an Earldom. Pauvre humanité!

27 December tuesday. I met Prince Adam Czartoriski and a Pole who had followed the fortunes of Kosciusko,[412] Niemkewitzh,[413] at Prince Talleyrands. Czartorizki, though not much altered in looks, is interesting and melancholy, and the old Patriot and Poet, broken hearted. The former ascribes the original insurrection in Warsaw of 1830 to accident, the extravagances of Constantine,[414] and the despair of the young men at College; its conversion to revolution and civil war, to the pusillanimity and incapacity of Constantine; and the ultimate failure chiefly to the unreasonableness of the Clubs, the factious and base conduct of a rival of Shrynecki,[415] whose name I forget, and the want of some maritime court through which they might have communicated without traversing Austrian or Prussian provinces. The Court of Berlin was most hostile to them, and he suspects that the Empress animates rather than allays the resentment and severity of Nicholas, whose nature, in itself stern and relentless, requires no such stimulus. The Austrians received Czartorizki on his escape not only with humanity but with favor. Their Ministry, with the fearful exception of Metternich, had compassion for them in their misfortunes and some disposition to succour them in their struggles. The Hungarians particularly betrayed much common feeling in their cause. But great as the Austrian dread reasonably is of Russian encroachment, they fear liberty and revolution more, and their hostility to Russia was silenced by the sound of insurrection in Italy. Czartorizki spoke of the late Emperor Alexander as suspicious and distrustful in the extreme, seemed to acknowledge that he had some illusions approaching to mental derangements, and observed that all the Emperors and Princes of the House had the apprehension of a violent death deeply imprinted on their imagination. He as well as Constantine had harboured notions of abdicating and retiring in a private character to *Warsaw!* The same reminiscences that alarm Russian Princes with the image of a violent Death possibly suggest to the Princesses and Arch-Duchesses of that Country ambitious notions of seizing the supreme power.

Talleyrand had seen Palmerston, and he shewed me the dispatch he had written a few minutes before he delivered it to Young Perier[416] who set off this evening to Paris. The whole object of it is to pacify his Government, to account and apologize for our ratification of the fortress treaty, ascribing it to causes which, though not flattering to us, are not offensive to France, viz our timidity, our disposition to court opposition and to shun the appearance of affronting the Duke of Wellington and rendering the sum expended on the fortresses (5 millions!) utterly and obviously useless, and above all to recommend forbearance and good humour in minor points, with a view of drawing England and France closer together, when it is obvious Holland and Russia would like to separate them with the hope of a general war.

The refusal of Nicholas to ratify the Belgian treaty furnishes a fresh argument in favor of this excellent policy. Talleyrand protests that he neither suggested nor enflamed the discontent of his Court at the treaty, though he does not deny that he was nettled at the concealment of the negotiation and dissatisfied at the provisions of the treaty. I believe there is more truth in his protestations on this subject than in the suspicions of Palmerston and our Cabinet. Yet neither may be entirely unfounded and both be greatly exaggerated. As I told the Cabinet yesterday, when I came into office I determined that all my endeavours should be directed to maintain peace, but that if that was impossible, I was yet more determined that any war into which I could be forced should be one for liberty and against *power and in confederacy with,* not against, *Constitutional France.*

28 December 1831 Wednesday. At home. Talleyrand in the evening, much out of spirits at the illness both of Perier and Sebastiani and the general aspect of affairs at Paris, which have been much affected by the ugly lawsuit about Duke of Bourbon's[417] will. There is nothing really injurious to the King's moral character or honour in that business, but with a sensitive publick like that of Paris, it would have been wise to make some sacrifice to keep such a transaction from the notice, sneers, and censures of his various enemies. C'est un procès bourgeois et c'est bien vilain pour un Prince. Improve and legislate as you will, how much the good government of Mankind depends on accident and individual Character!

29 Decr. 1831 Thursday. Dined at Prince Esterhazy's. Though the intelligence from Berlin was discouraging, and conveyed the opinion of that Court that the refusal of Russia to ratify was final and the yet more extravagant opinion that the non ratification of a treaty between five allies and another power by one of the five annulled the agreement altogether and released the remaining four from their engagements, the Plenipotentiaries, who, with the exception of the Russians, were all present, seemed to me in great spirits. They had discovered that Palmerston meant to take up the disavowal of the Plenipotentiaries at St. Petersburgh and at Berlin in a high and severe tone, and were manifestly satisfied that Prussia would be reclaimed from her heresy and Austria deterred from committing it by the fear of war and by the apprehension of close alliance between England and France. Through his noise, his laugh, and his chatter, it is difficult to penetrate the real feelings of Esterhazy and, moreover, his private affairs, the effect of his father's extravagance and want of principle are likely to affect his spirits just now. He professes however great cordiality with England, he has suppressed the instructions we know he has received to press the recognition of Don Miguel, and he is confident that his Court will ratify the treaty with Belgium. A word dropped from him that shewed a latent apprehension of England and France ratifying alone was among his motives for wishing his own Court to comply without delay. Palmerston, though fatigued with business, was in good heart, and to my great satisfaction did not seem to me to dislike much less to shrink from the notion of proceeding with France and without Russia.

30 Decr. 1831. Cabinet at one. Palmerston read us the draft of his intended instructions to Berlin, which were firm, spirited, well reasoned, convincing, and severe—so much so that the few remarks I made went to soften rather than heighten the tone, though not the substance, of the indignation, astonishment, and resentment we conveyed. Mr Ancillon[418] in this able paper was convicted of inconsistency, exposed for his fallacy and ignorance, reproached with bad faith, and threatened with the consequences of witholding his ratification of the treaty—a dissolution of the Conference, a separation of England from Prussia, and not improbably an active alliance between England and France. To Austria we were less peremptory, implied no doubt of her ratifying, but gave her by some expressions and, still more by the confidential communication of the dispatch to Chad,[419] a glimpse of what might ensue if she did. This hint will not be thrown away upon her. She as usually is under the operation of fear—fearful of the Russians and yet more fearful of Constitutions. She would not feel less dread of an entire, exclusively, and cordial union between France and England.

The King's letter to Sir J Graham on the question of Captain Sartorius and the Foreign Enlistment bill was read. His Majesty, as I foresaw, on hearing the distinction between that bill and his prerogative, lost some of his predilection for it—a good preparative for the repeal. The Cabinet was a very thin one. Lord Grey told me he was ready with an arrangement for bringing Mr Macaulay into office, had written to Lord Lansdowne but found that Calne could not be safely vacated. I urged him to speak to Macaulay himself, and I at the same time bid him sound Lord Ponsonby on his inclinations to go to Jamaica as Governor.

The illness of Sebastiani, an apoplectick attack, will disable him for a month. Lord Granville writes that Perrier will be in no hurry to fill up his place and will do the business himself in the interim, an arrangement that will not be disagreable to us for two reasons: he is a more direct and manly Man than Sebastiani; and he will be chiefly swayed by Talleyrand, whose dispatches and opinions are all in favor of connection and good fellowship with England as a Nation and Grey's Cabinet as a Ministry. Talleyrand however says that Granville must warn him to beware of Pozzo, who is insinuating and on the spot, and of whom Perrier has a high opinion.

31 December 1831. Dined at Carlisles. Much correspondence, some conversation, and a good deal of reflection this day on the propriety and necessity of creating Peers and on the general policy and Stability of Lord Grey's administration. How much depends on the lives and health of three or 4 Men—William IV, Lord Grey, Lord Brougham, Casimir Perrier. It is strange and will somewhat pique the Russians to find that English funds keep up and French actually rise after their hesitation to ratify the treaty is known. So little is their power of mischief apprehended.

At home Grey meditates placing Macaulay in board of Controul or Ordnance. An offer to employ him does not come too soon. Sir James Macdonald[420] says evil Counsellors have been at him, but without success hitherto, to preach discontent and advise ambitious projects. Macdonald most handsomely would resign to make way for him, but the purpose may I believe be managed otherwise. In meanwhile Calne cannot be vacated, but I hope Grey will apprize him that that circumstance alone postpones the arrangement.

1st January 1832. Sunday. The only complete year from 1st. of January to 31st. of December which the Whigs have seen Office for near seventy years is elapsed.

And their prospects both at home and abroad are brighter on this than on the last New Years day.

Monday 2 Jany. 1832. Cabinet at one o'clock. Lord Chancellor, Lord Goderich, Sir James Graham absent, and Lord Lansdowne from Bowood did not arrive [till?] late.

A Dispatch from Berlin or the Hague informed us that the letters of 16 December from Petersburgh to the King of the Netherlands were not decisive as we had imagined. They deferred, indeed, according to some promise, the ratification of the Emperor till he should learn the consent of the King of the Netherlands to the treaty; but they exhorted that Prince to consent and urged very cogent arguments, viz: that if he went to war it was impossible for Russia to afford him any Military (materiel) assistance, and counselled him accordingly to signify his concurrence in treaty to the Conference without delay, with a representation or hope that some particulars which he might specify would, by the intervention of the five powers, be altered.

The extreme factions in Ireland seem to vye with each other in intemperate language and equivocal actions. The Orangemen talk sedition and treason and threaten force, and persons with offices and commissions attend these meetings. <Query>: shall they be removed? The followers of OConnel avow their hostility to Government and the Reform bill, encourage the people in resisting the law (and the tythe especially), and threaten to call the Irish representatives together to instruct them how to act in Parliament. Shall laws be framed to render these Associations illegal and shall force be used to suppress them?[1] The Irish Attorney General seems to lean, and Plunkett rather listens, to insurrection acts and other coercive laws, but Anglesey hesitates. They speak of referring the question of prosecutions for libellous resolutions and speeches to the English Lawyers, who will no doubt report that the words are libellous, but that of the certainty of conviction, the Irish Law advisers, not they, must be the judges, and of the expediency and consequences of a prosecution, the Government a more adequate Judge than either.

Lord Grey then opened the great question of the day by reading two long letters from the Chancellor.[2] He painted in strong language the dangers of the country and the absolute necessity of passing the bill, and he inferred, from a variety of facts and reasoning, that some creation of peers would sooner or later be necessary for that purpose. He then gave his opinion (together with abundant and cogent reasons for it) that prudence, honour, and fair dealing called upon us to apprize the King of this state of things, and he suggested the propriety and wisdom of proposing a certain number, such as 10–12 or more, as a demonstration of our power and of the King's determination to support us, in the hope that such an indication might render all further creations superfluous or at least less numerous than they must be if deferred to the last Moment. A letter from Mr Coke strongly urging the measure on the same grounds and stating the earnest expectation and wishes of the people of Norfolk was also read, and ample testimony was given of the exceeding desire for the measure in those best able to form a judgement and most disposed to further the cause of reform and support Lord Grey's administration. Lord Grey then repeated with great sincerity and earnestness his original aversion to such a measure and his reluctance even now to comply with so strong and so unusual and, as he perhaps too severely stigmatized it, so unconstitutional an expedient. But he said we were compelled, he feared, to adopt it or to incur yet greater calamities, and he then, with great earnestness and feeling but without affectation or exaggeration, painted the state of things in which a second rejection of the bill by the Lords would leave that house, the Ministers, the King, and the Country – especially Scotland which, satisfied at the prospect of passing the bill, was nevertheless concentrating and composing its means of resistance in case of disappointment, with a foresight, intelligence, and determination peculiar to that people, and inaccessible to the Law till the blow should be struck. Palmerston strongly objected on constitutional principle to creating peers for an immediate purpose, still hankered after possible conversions, and manifestly would not personally grudge very great and even unjustifiable concessions to obtain them. He could not consent to a batch of peers, though two or three or four he might, because he thought any number amounting to a batch, which I think he meant to be *ten* at least, implied his readiness to go beyond it if necessary, and he was not *(as at present advised)* prepared to do so. Duke of Richmond argued, or rather conjectured, that we should carry the 2d. reading without creations, deemed amendments in Committee no objection, and with some vehemence but great good temper, opposed the whole measure, maintaining somewhat preposterously that any but a very small creation of two or three would irritate without overwhelming our opponents, would involve an unconstitutional principle, and would be shewing our teeth without biting. Mr Stanley faintly opposed the measure or rather the time of proposing it and suggested the postponement of it till the exact number wanted, the *quantum sufficit,* should be known after 2d. reading. Lord Melbourne urged the danger of the precedent, contended it was a much more violent and permanent measure in its effects than a dissolution, and exaggerated the magnitude, importance, and danger of so extraordinary an expedient. In this *Lansdowne,* who entered the room while he was speaking, cordially and emphatically agreed, but in the course of discussion acknowledged that the question was a choice of evils and, somewhat inconsistently, that it was entirely one of degree. As a demonstration he could acquiesce in creations to a certain extent, but must deprecate, till the last necessity should arise, all overwhelming of the Lords which would render that branch of the legislature a dead letter in the Constitution and at the moment we were strengthening the democracy to a fearful degree annihilate for all practical or efficient purposes the only barrier we had against them. He made great admissions, though his aversion to the expedient was very apparent, and he mingled with his argument some reflections on those who not only liked the Reform but liked these means of carrying it as subversive of aristocracy, favorable to democracy, and partaking of a revolutionary character. In the course of his conversation (for I have put the substance of various remarks into one speech) he set aside the opinions or authority of many good friends we quoted, as partizans who always preferred expedients to principle, and violence and impatience to caution and circumspection, and in mentioning some names, betrayed that weakness in his disposition which leads him to prefer the councils of feeble men and to suppose that any opinion which is espoused and enforced with determination and vehemence must be ill founded, hazardous, or unjust. The Duke of Richmond, whose character is composed of the very opposite foibles, though agreeing with him in opinion, whispered to John Russell when Lansdowne was making his admissions and qualifications that it was strange how, even in his strongest opinions, when he came to the decision he seemed to melt them down to little or nothing.

These objections, which with the exception of a little impatience expressed by Palmerston at an article in the Times, were urged during two hours conversation, with great calmness and good humour, were combated as temperately by us all, including Lord Durham, who without any asperity questioned many of the speculations on conversions and conduct of the Lords, and read a very able paper in which he urged our obligations to the King and the Country to exercise every legal means in our power to carry the bill and the impracticability of doing so without a large and immediate creation of numbers sufficient to secure it in the Lords. He proceeded to examine and confute the objections, maintained with great clearness of reasoning that it was constitutional and would be beneficial. Althorp and Lord John acknowledged that they felt some but no insuperable objections to such a measure. They both stated the question as a choice between two evils, and both, with reference to immediate effect and ultimate operation on the Constitution, thought the creation of peers or at any rate a demonstration of the power of creating them the least evil of the two. Mr Grant was yet more decisive. We were not justified in having gone so far if we did not go through with our measure. We had now no choice. Lord *Carlisle* denied that such a measure was as unconstitutional as it was represented, far from injuring would both improve and save the house of Lords; and when the question degenerated to the silly one of whether Grey should recommend six or ten to the King tomorrow, he very opportunely urged the ten. In the course of the conversation, I recapitulated all I had at various times stated to Grey: avowed that I was prepared for the whole number; deprecated as unfair to the King, injurious to the measure, and a yet greater indignity to the Lords any concealment of delay; but acquiesced in a present *demonstration,* as it was called, of *ten,* though I should have preferred *fifteen* (for I was an old tennis player and loved that way of counting – fifteen, thirty, forty, game – and had no objection to a bisk to boot);[3] and I suggested that the King might possibly wish to promote some friend of his own (I had Sir Herbt. Taylor in my <eye>) and, if so, he should be allowed one for every ten at least. The notion that a Courtier might be added seemed to please and was acknowledged to be an additional *demonstration* and as such desirable.

That phrase of *demonstration* was very serviceable. I know not how, but in the gravest discussions and sometimes with men of great sense and command of words, a handy *term* for an action under consideration seems first to familiarize and then reconcile them to it. I know not with whom the word *demonstration* for such a creation of peers as would indicate the King's continued confidence in us and imply our power to create more if needful originated; but it greatly facilitated the discussion, enlarged Lord Lansdowne's admission, and somewhat stifled Lord

Palmerston's chief objection, viz an unwillingness to pledge himself to any further step. So *Demonstration* it was, and under that name a half consent to a number not less than ten was obtained from three or four of the Members who came to the Cabinet this day firmly resolved, I suspect, to resist all new peerages but those of Mr Dundas of Berkshire and Lord Francis Osborne, to both of whom they had been previously promised. Nothing could exceed Lord Grey's judgement, candour, and ability. He acknowledged most distinctly and gracefully that the late meeting of Parliament, contrary to his apprehensions, had been productive of the most beneficial effects to the country; spoke of the conduct of the people as deserving as well as requiring a prompt compliance with their reasonable wishes; and displayed much good and sincere feeling, without affectation, for the King, who was, he said, averse to these large creations and whom he should, if he were to decline them, be most earnestly desirous to screen from the odium in any way he could with honour and consistency, but that he felt it his duty to lay before him the appalling state of the country and to apprize him that there was too much prospect of an approaching necessity of a measure to which he, Lord Grey, had a repugnance almost as strong as His Majesty. This he is to lay before him tomorrow. In a few words conversation with Grey after the Cabinet was over, he told me that he did not think himself quite authorized by the Cabinet (I think he was) to propose the ten, but he should tomorrow confine himself to a more general statement of the condition of the country, the possible necessity of a large creation of peers to avert yet greater and more instant calamities, and the expediency of an immediate *demonstration* of the King's confidence by calling up or creating a few.

Talleyrand called in the evening, much vexed and dispirited by the answer to his dispatch from Perrier and the King, both of whom are as sore as ever about the fortresses. Talleyrand says he now apprehends the very quality he admires in Perrier, namely his inflexibility (voideur), being turned to foreign as well as domestick politicks, will thwart all his (*Talleyrand's*) hopes and prevent the cordial union and good understanding he hoped to bring about. He had no very great confidence in Sebastiani nor predilection for him, mais du moins il etait plus souple.

3 January 1832. Mr Le Tellier, Talleyrand's Secretary, called and read me the answers of the King of the French and of Perrier to his dispatch of the 27th., and they are far from satisfactory, somewhat peremptorily instructing him to withold ratification of Independence treaty till that relating to fortresses is revised, postponed, or altered. This, after his urgent instances to accede with good humour and after the communication of our dispatches so well calculated to restore it, is vexatious. Talleyrand's reply to both the King and the Minister is earnest, eloquent, and judicious, insists on the insignificance of the object of the fortresses, the importance of cementing the concert and cordiality between the two countries, the willingness and disposition of England to meet them half way, and the golden opportunity which the estrangement produced by Russian hesitation affords them. Talleyrand and the Plenipotentiaries were seven hours in conference this day!

4 Jany. 1832. Letters from Brighton not encouraging. The King's averseness to a large creation is (according to Taylor) unabated.

Talleyrand sadly discomposed at the sensation produced by the fortress treaty, though satisfied that the King of Holland will be brought to his senses, especially if our Ministry (which the Dutch King wishes at the bottom of the Thames) gains strength and solidity. Talleyrand manifestly thinks that the report of 30 Peerages is true and that that expedient will secure us. He remarked again that Perrier's ,rmness and decision, which qualified him so admirably for the place of first Minister in France, was not just now equally fortunate when acting as Minister for foreign affairs, of which he understood little or nothing. When much might be attained by time, decision, unless accompanied with experience and understanding, became a dangerous quality. He was afraid Perrier would be rash, whereas time would heal and appease the ill humour which existed. King Louis Philippe was he said a *faiseur,* loved writing and talking too much, and had written hastily, angrily, and imprudently to King Leopold. I do not believe, as Palmerston, Adair, and perhaps Granville do, that he wrote at the instigation of Talleyrand, but I am sure the style and substance and length of his letter was not such as Talleyrand did or would have advised.

Goodwin[4] called to tell me somewhat mysteriously from a Medical Man that the Duke of Wellington's mind was going or gone, but I do not believe it and sincerely hope that it is not true. One does not wish to see from a

> second Marlborough['s] eyes
> the tears of dotage flow.

I should not have remarked the rumour, but in the course of the evening I heard from more than one quarter that great depression of spirits was part of his malady, that his deafness encreased, and that his attendance in Parliament was over.

5th. News from Brighton more encouraging. The King's confidence in Lord Grey unabated. He acknowledges the urgency of the case and it is manifest that his averseness to creating peers may yield to a sense of necessity.

6th. The King acquiesces, with much reluctance and some agitation, in the measure of creating peers to ensure carrying the bill in The House of Lords, but he deeply laments the necessity of it exists, and wishes on so important a matter to have the written opinion of the Cabinet. Lord Grey has taken a minute of the conversation and the nature of the points His Majesty wishes to refer to us.[5] He shewed the minute to the King and tomorrow it is to be submitted to us.

7th. [*9th.*] *Monday.* It was so submitted. It contained many kind expressions of regard and even gratitude and unabated confidence in the Ministers, lamented but acknowledged the alternative to which the state of affairs seemed likely to drive him of losing the Bill and his Ministry or creating Several peers with a view of securing it in Lords, declared not only confidence in the intentions and approbation of the labour of his Ministry, but expressed a strong opinion that in the present state of affairs, abroad and at home, which he described as critical and even alarming, that no body of men would be found capable and willing to replace them. He said that before so very important a step, which he had in some measure foreseen and dreaded, and to which, unless urged by extreme necessity, he was still very averse, could be taken, he should like to have the opinion of the Cabinet in writing. He added that if it was resolved to encrease the House of Lords, he preferred doing it at once to any demonstration of the intention and to providing the competent number by degrees, so that he was ready, if Lord Grey confided in the calculation he had made of a majority at present of 20 against the bill, to create or rather call up *21* immediately (an avowal which when read seemed somewhat to surprize those among us who had been for advancing with an irresolute and trembling step in this matter),[6] but he urged the propriety of confining the new votes to be created (with two or three exceptions which stood on other grounds) to Eldest sons, collateral heirs and, if necessary, Scotch and Irish peers. He strongly deprecated the advancement of any who had been forward in agitating the people, but neither Grey nor Sir Herbert Taylor imagined that he had any particular person in view by this remark, and he exhorted us most earnestly to take our stand against the disorganizing principles which were so actively enforced in meetings, Clubs, Union, and thro' the medium of the press, and which he said were peculiarly levelled at hereditary authority, with an allusion, I think, to the late vote of the Chambers in France.[7] Grey told us that he was much agitated, even to tears, protested that the state of the Country was no fault of his nor of his Ministers, but that the mischievous activity of the press and the demagogues was such that the foundations of our institutions or hereditary rights and of property itself might be subverted. He urged, both in the paper which was read to us and the conversation of which Grey had taken a minute, the necessity of taking a stand and other phrases of the kind, which glanced, I thought, at some coercive laws. Grey said he had taken some little fright at Althorp's conceding too much, and observed he should recollect that he was heir to Lord Spencer's titles and possessions. In general his letter and conversation pleased us all and somewhat softened, and if it did not overrule, the opposition to the measure of encreasing the peerage. It was agreed to come to no final resolution till the Chancellor was present, and to assign his absence as a reason in our apology to the King for not sending an immediate answer.

Some other matters of inferior importance were talked over. I was sorry to find Lord Palmerston quite stiff and inflexible about the fortresses, and Lord Grey more disposed to dwell on the undeniable inconsistencies of the French in their language, and the occasional shuffling in their conduct in this business, than to listen to the grave objections in principle and yet graver errors in policy of maintaining a system of hostile confederacy against one of the powers with whom we have covenanted to maintain the neutrality of Belgium, and of estranging the French Government and perhaps <ruining> the Ministry of Perrier for a point which, in truth, affords no additional security to Belgium or Europe, and for which neither Parliament nor people would willingly sacrifice a shilling.

9th., 10th., January. I again neglected this diary for several days. Recollect nothing particularly worth recording.

11th. January. Wednesday. Cabinet. While we were waiting for the Chancellor, the practicability of proposing, without loss of time, a vote of *120* or 130,000 per annum in payment of the Roman Catholick Bishops and Clergy in Ireland was discussed. We learnt from a letter from Mr Blaike[8] to Lord Lansdowne that the R C Clergy would not be unwilling to apply for such a grant, and it was agreed that the proposal had better come from them. Mr Stanley was authorized to convey to them an assurance that any such application from them would be favorably entertained and, should it lead to a final arrangement, be considered by His Majesty's Government as highly advantageous to the publick service and the welfare of Ireland. This determination will please Lord Lansdown (who was gone down to Bowood), for he had earnestly urged the consideration of the subject, tho' he had never put it into so practical a shape as it now seemed to assume.

On the Chancellor's arrival much of the former discussion on the creation of peers was revived, but the Duke of Richmond was in some degree less confident of conversions and of carrying the bill without creations. Lord Palmerston still averse to the principle and evidently so little disinclined to purchase votes by large concessions, that it raised a shrewed suspicion that he liked the payment of the price almost as much as the article to be obtained by it. However the propriety and even necessity of obtaining from the King the power of creating an indefinite number was generally agreed to, but some faint hopes that that power might not be extensively exerted expressed by some, and a preference of our original scheme of an immediate demonstration by the creation of 10 or 12, over that suggested in the King's letter of 21 at once, seemed to prevail—Lord Durham and myself being the only two present who acknowledged that we should have advised taking the offer of 21 immediately, with an explanation to the King that, though we hoped, yet we were not sure that more might not be required, and that unless all requisite were to be ultimately made, it was better to make none. We however chearfully deferred to our Colleagues, and Grey was to embody such opinion as he could collect from them and bring it under consideration on the ensuing Friday 13th. He took me from thence to Sheen where I spent the

12th. Thursday.

13th. Friday. He was somewhat more despondent about the state of affairs both abroad or at home than the aspect of things seemed to me to warrant. The impressions he had received from Palmerston on the subject of the fortresses made him less disposed than his own prudence, sense, and love of peace would lead him to be, to some postponement or evasion of a treaty which secures no solid advantage, and weakens and estranges the present Government of France. His repugnance to the Creation of Peers is certainly strong and the reluctance with which he yields to the necessity by no means words of course. The notion or illusion of the dependence of that branch of our constitution on his vigor and talents for support, with which for some years back he has been frequently tickled, hangs occasionally about him and sounds a faint note of self reproach in his ear. This, reason and reflection should silence. He drew out a paper which he shewed me on Friday. It was ably argued and eloquently written. It explained and lamented the hopelessness of passing the bill without some fresh creations, assured H M of our reluctance in resorting to such a measure and our willingness to postpone it to the last moment and to limit its extent most scrupulously to its necessity, but forcibly urged that it was incumbent upon us to ascertain whether we had the power to surmount our difficulties, and to submit to him that, with that view, we might be compelled to recommend the creation of peers to an extent which could only be defined by the number necessary to constitute a majority in the Lords. It ended by requesting an assurance that such power should not be witheld if actually necessary, and that in the meanwhile 10 or 12 as a demonstration should be created; for we could not conceal from His Majesty that if the larger number of 21 were adopted, we were not prepared to say it was sufficient, as we could not ascertain at present what force in the House of Lords the Enemies of our measure might be able to muster. The paper, in a Cabinet which sat long *and which on account of Gout I did not attend,* was altered rather than improved. The immediate creation of any was postponed, but the permission to reckon upon the exercise of the prerogative to an extent commensurate with the necessity, whatever that might be, was yet more earnestly enforced.[9]

Saturday 14th. 1832. I returned to London. The Times of this morning contained a very virulent and personal attack on Prince Talleyrand, insinuating that he divulged the secrets of the Conference and misrepresented the motives and conduct of his Colleagues and the states they represented. There was in it some indication of jealousy at another paper (the Courier) obtaining early intelligence, but few read the paragraph who did not, like Talleyrand, suspect that the impulse came or was at least encouraged from some higher quarter. The coincidence of Palmerston's anger at a supposed communication of Talleyrand to the Courier, which led him to withold the usual intelligence furnished from the Foreign Office to that Evening paper, and with appearance of this unhandsome and scurrilous article, is certainly singular, and I am not quite satisfied that Palmerston may not have expressed his indignation at Talleyrand's connection with the Courier (which is erroneously surmized on very imperfect evidence) in the presence of some Underling. This petty warfare, if it subsists, is as pernicious as it is undignified. Talleyrand affects not to enquire about it, has refused to furnish the Courier with facts or hints for a reply, and has the affectation at least of wishing no publick answer to be given. But I think he is nettled, and am afraid he suspects it is connived at and encouraged, if not written, by persons connected with our Government.

The news from Berlin arrived by Couriers from Mr Chad and Mr Bresson before the Telegraph which had been arranged for the purpose of conveying the dispatch more expeditiously. The King of Prussia sends his ratifications but insists on what his pedantick Minister, Ancillon, terms the solidarité of the treaty, maintaining that till all have ratified it is no treaty, and declining, for that as well as other reasons, to exchange the ratifications till *all* the contracting powers are ready to sign. In the dispatches conveying this intelligence, many conversations between Chad and Ancillon and Chad and Bernstorff are recounted, in which it is remarkable that the indifference of Prussia to the question of fortresses, asserted by Talleyrand and denied by Palmerston, is distinctly confirmed by the avowal of both Ancillon and Bernstorff. The manner in which the apprehension of a closer alliance between France and England is received by Ancillon and the obvious and instantaneous effect it has, not only in damping all appetite for war but of rendering him more courteous and accommodating in peace, speaks volumes in favor of that policy, which I sadly forebode the foolish pique about the fortresses may impede or at least retard.

Sunday. Talleyrand showed me Bresson's dispatches, full of satisfaction at the cooperation of Chad, somewhat confident of the ultimate compliance of Prussia of the French and English should determine to ratify, and confirming the remark I have above made of the salutary effect which the prospect of English and French cooperation every where produces.

Monday 16. Remarkable only for a dinner singularly agreable. Scarce any politicks were talked and Melbourne, Jeffray,[10] and Sydney Smith in their different ways were very particularly agreable. The origin of the Edinburgh review, at the instigation of Sydney Smith, in the company of Horner,[11] Lord Webb Seymour,[12] and Jeffray and at the flatt of the latter in Buccleugh Square, Edinburgh (now 30 years ago), was described with great humour by Sydney. He told us that he had further proposed to adopt for a motto

We cultivate literature on oats
Musam meditamur avenâ

but that the two Scotchmen vehemently protested.[13] I scarcely ever heard more wit, learning, and good sense in any society, and the remaining part of the Evening did not fall off when Talleyrand came and closed it with some anecdotes, both political and literary, in which his conversation abounds.

Tuesday 17 January 1832. Mr Danvers on Duchy business. Mr Palgrave[14] on his project of a bill for incorporating the towns to which the right of representation in Parliament is to be extended.

Cabinet at 2. Lord Grey read us the King's letter,[15] which distinctly but reluctantly consented to give us the full power of recommending such an addition to the House of Lords as we should deem on further enquiry and knowledge necessary to the attainment of a majority in favor of the reform bill in that house. It affixed no limitation to the amount of the numbers but peremptorily confined the augmentation to such as were Eldest Sons, Collateral heirs of peers who had no children, and, in default of them, Scotch and Irish peers of large property. To these rules it admitted but of three exceptions. The objection to vacating Counties by the elevation of Eldest Sons was somewhat controversially answered by a sneer that, if the opinion in favor of reform was so general and intense, no risk could be incurred thereby. And there was in more than one passage a recurrence to his original apprehension of the collision between the two houses which had taken place, his deep sense of the value of that house in the Constitution, and his hopes that for a temporary object his Ministers would never lend themselves to measures that might lower and degrade it. The consent however was explicit and handsome. There were indeed here and there symptoms of more ill humour at the measure than is common in the King when he has once made up his mind to a course, however disagreable it be to him. Grey then read his reply as an individual to it, in which he thanked His Majesty for his gracious compliance, acquiesced in the limitations but hinted some doubts of the solidity of the reasons on which the Commoners of large landed possession were excluded, and combated, with great respect but with great success, the notion of any change in the publick mind, or the justice of any inference of such an apprehension being drawn from an averseness to vacate Counties just now. Grey expected the Cabinet to write a separate reply to this Royal answer. None were disposed to take up the pen. The Chancellor declined doing so, and Goderich observed that all we had to say was that Lord Grey had also communicated his written answer, and that in all the feelings and reasonings contained in it we entirely concurred. This was unanimously approved.[16]

Grey read us first the proof of Lord Blayney's[17] application for a peerage *last May* to support Government, and then his virulent attack and unfounded assertions concerning the Household Troops. He has been written to, at the suggestion of the King as well as Grey, by Lord Hill,[18] and will be either cashiered the Army or reprimanded, unless he publickly retracts his unfounded and unwarrantable Charge against Lord Grey of having in furtherance of radical objects proposed to the King to disband his Household Guards &c &c &c.[19] Duke of Richmond maintained paradoxically that he should not be given an opportunity of contradicting the charge or called upon to criminate himself, but should be prosecuted at once by a Court Martial.

In house of Lords neither motion nor notice occurred. The opposition benches were full. The Duke of Wellington much emaciated and deaf, but better in health than rumour had taught me to expect. His adherents about him seemed to me in brisk spirits and quite ready and panting for action.

Grey gave me a better reason for the despondency he occasionally expresses than I have hitherto heard. The defalcation of the revenue is very great.

Talleyrand thinks the Ministers of Vienna and Berlin, and perhaps Paris, too, if Sebastiani resumes the portefeuille, not unlikely to thwart the objects of the Conference from jealousy of the Plenipotentiaries who compose it. On the whole however he is in better spirits than he was.

18 January Wednesday. Cabinet dinner at Lord Melbourne's. Grant related the embarrassing circumstances of Canton, where the Supercargoes have quarreled with Chinese and at one time threatened to suspend their commercial operations. The Supercargoes or Merchants seem to be quite in the wrong, and have introduced European Women and Sedan Chairs, printed newspaper, reviled the Chinese Government, and what not, contrary to the Stipulations on which they were admitted. This is strange as they were sent thither to supersede <other> Supercargoes who had committed the same indiscretions and were strongly disapproved of, both [by] Lord Wm. Bentinck[20] in India and the Board of Controul here. But what is *stranger* Lord Wm. Bentinck, who so disapproved of the old lot, has sent Sir John Owen,[21] one of the Most headlong of our Seamen, with such force as he commands, to support this new Set. Sir John G <. . . . .>[22] is about to sail to supersede him. There seemed some doubt whether he should proceed directly to China or stop for further orders and communication at Singapore. It was at last resolved to send him in the first instance to Calcutta (which, when I first suggested, was said to lose too much time) to avoid the possibility of all conflicting authority, and dispatches both by Sea and Land have been already sent to Lord Wm. Bentinck to apprize him of the view taken, both by the Company and the Government, and strongly to admonish Him not to sanction any war or resistance of the Chinese.

A complicated question of the Secretaryship of the Master of Rolls in Ireland, which is disputed between Plunket and Macmahon, was discussed, and agreed that Stanley should allow the bill for McMahon to be brought in, but keep himself open to oppose it afterward. Plunket is right but the English and Irish bar are against him. We then spoke on the financial prospects of the Country, which are very gloomy. The deficiency of Revenues below expenditure not less than £700,000! ! ! This to nearly a half may be compensated by diminished Naval estimates, for Sir Byam Martin, expecting us out soon, made us apply for more stores than were necessary in hopes we should have <had> the odium of the Charge, and his friends, our successors, the benefit of the articles. In the meanwhile trade seems creeping up and the prospects not discouraging if there was a chance of fair play and time being allowed us. But in the present ferment of Men's mind and the active and virulent opposition in Parliament that is not likely. Force may be required in Ireland. We have only the Yeomanry in reserve without a fresh act of Parliament. If we apply for any fresh act or force, the Orangemen will say why not call out the Yeomanry? The Catholicks will say why call out any? And both extremes concurring will prevent our having other resources than the Yeomanry, which is Orange Government. We have neither authority to keep peace, nor resources to make war. Lord Grey is manifestly depressed and nettled at this state of things. The Chancellor, though well in health, is not yet in his usual vigor and spirits. The necessity of preparing measures for a general police, a constabulary force, and corporation governments in towns was talked of, but nothing settled. It is curious that the Irish revenue improves as the tythe diminishes and the rent becomes precarious. The Consumption of <Luqur> too, is said to be encreasing rapidly. The Emigration, without assistance from Government, was last year prodigious—50,000 to Canada only, and all provided for by employment at good wages immediately on their arrival.

Sir James Graham brought me home where I found Prince Talleyrand and was kept by the charms of his conversation to a late hour.

19 January, Thursday. Grey was prevented from attending House of Lords by a slight bowel complaint. Lord Aberdeen gave notice of a motion on Belgium and Strangford[23] on some other topick connected with trade. Both betrayed some asperity to Government and the first was cheered by Lord Wharncliffe.

I forgot to mention that Palmerston intends to move Harry Fox[24] to Rio, which he, Harry, prefers to Buenos Ayres, and to name Goodwin's son[25] to the reduced Consulship at Naples.

20 January. Remained at home. Talleyrand in the evening read the early part of his memoirs, beautifully written, full of wit and *feeling*. He was *shy and nervous* in reading them! They spoke with great taste and delicacy but with deep and natural feeling of the conduct of his parents, and Mother in particular, who neglected and slighted him in his childhood and forced him into the Church when grown up, from an indulgence of their own passions of family pride and wounded vanity on his becoming lame from an accident during his infancy. We sat up till three. I could have sat up till sunrise and from thence to sunset to hear these memoirs.

Saturday, 21 January. Saw Lord Grey who shewed me the Duke of Buckingam's[26] letter to the King inveighing against press and Union, deprecating a creation of Peers as subversive of that hereditary assembly, and stigmatizing the bill as a revolutionary measure, all which was an exordium for an oblique offer of forming a new administration, which without the aid of such a bill could, he assured His Majesty, conduct the affairs of the Country in a way satisfactory to the people, advantageous to the crown, and conducive to the stability and improvement of our happy Constitution. The King dryly answered by a note in Sir Hebt. Taylors hand that he acknowledged the letter and transmitted it to Earl Grey!

Melbourne in the evening, disposed at all events to Peace and sanguine about preserving it.

Sunday, 22 January. With some gout attended the Cabinet, where I learnt that a paper had been drawn up on the subject of the fortress treaty from the Four Powers to King Leopold, explaining that there was no intention or right preserved of employing money to raise or keep up the fortifications, and that the expences merely related to the destruction of them. It contained also some other assurances indirectly disclaiming hostility or even jealousy of France. It is to be officially communicated to Talleyrand, who has not seen the words but did, in truth, suggest in some degree the substance, and it is hoped by him and us that it will soften the objections to the treaty and, above all, stifle the expression of them in Paris.

Various matters foreign and domestick discussed but none, as far as I recollect, determined upon.

23d. Monday. I was confined with the gout and for the ensuing

24 Tuesday (There was a Cabinet this day on reform which I did not attend.)

25th. Wednesday was detained at home by that disorder and the Colchicum administered by Sir Henry Halford.[27]

26 January Thursday. In spite of gout, attended the House of Lords where Aberdeen, in a better but not less bitter speech than usual, introduced a motion for an address against the treaty signed by the Plenipotentiaries of the 5 Powers and King Leopold but not yet ratified. Such a violent interference with the prerogative has never been resorted to since 1711, when the Whigs, under a Tory leader Lord Nottingham (whose nick name would not be inapplicable to Aberdeen—Don Dismallo), moved and carried by a majority of eight an amendment to the address, on the announcement of the approaching treaty of Utrecht, that no treaty which left Spain or the West Indies in the hands of any branch of the House of Bourbon would be satisfactory to the House. These words, which were carried on the 7th. Decr. 1711, convinced the Harley Administration that they could not get their treaty sanctioned without an addition of friendly votes to the House, and consequently before the ratifications were exchanged, i.e. on the 30th. of that very month, 12 peers were introduced by writ or patent to the house. The Coincidence would have been striking, had the whole body of Antireformers supported Lord A's intemperate address. But we beat him by a Majority of 37,[28] and are still left in the dark as to the precise muster roll of our enemies army and, consequently, as to the amount of reinforcement we may stand in need of to resist them. The Bishops and the Modification Men, at least Wharncliffe, Binning,[29] and Harrowby, staid away. Aberdeen's motion, tone, and temper breathed utter abhorrence of France and Belgium and the newly established Governments thereof, and both in spirit and tendency the motion was a motion for Change of Ministry and War. Aberdeen, when charged by Grey with encouraging the King of Holland in his perverse and infatuated resistance, seem[ed] to plead guilty, or rather to plume himself on the avowal of the object and, in other parts of his conduct, appeared to me to offend the diplomacy of all other courts by his taunts, sneers, and invectives, almost as much as he purposely and advisedly did those of France as well as the feelings of the English publick. Grey made an admirable full and statesmanlike answer. His circumspection, accuracy, and discrimination in stating his view of the probability of the ultimate ratification of all the Powers, without exposing himself to the taunts or triumphs of his adversaries should he be disappointed, were quite inimitable, and that part of his speech was executed with a nicety of judgement and prudence that I do not think Mr Fox or Mr Pitt, even with all the latters exquisite command of language, were ever known to display. So true is Mr Fox's remark that Grey, who is artless, hasty, and imprudent in a private room, is discretion personified in debate, a circumstance the more reasonable inasmuch as spirit and vigor are the characteristicks of his eloquence. Grey had let me offfrom speaking, and perhaps judiciously, certainly with the greatest success, spoke second in debate. The opposition seemed very hot and factious but mustered only 95 votes present or proxies.

In the House of Commons the awkward question of the Russian loan was brought on against us by Herries.[30] It was faintly resisted by Althorp and very inefficiently and ill argued by our Law Officers. Our friends trembled for the result and division and we were barely rescued from defeat by a spirited speech from Lord John Russell and a very able one from Lord Palmerston.[31] Lord Althorp very unaffectedly dislikes office, but he very imprudently says so to all our House of Commons supporters and very unfairly wishes to be beaten on these collateral occasions and does not assume the tone which is necessary to induce partizans to acquiesce in a reluctant vote.

27th. Friday. Dined at home and had little political conversation or intelligence. Our Crown Lawyers in Commons are said not to have distinguished themselves last night, and our adversaries, though they knew we were in the right in paying the Dutch Russian loan, were not averse to joining in a vote with our deserters, who for the sake of economy urged the house to violate the faith of the Country. Baring,[32] who but a few days before told LaBouchere that we could as well as withhold the 3 per cents as these payments under our engagements, voted against them and exhorted the Members to do so because they would not, as in the case of a vote against reform, have any unpopularity to encounter; they might truly say that they had voted for saving millions to the Country.

28th. Janry. Lord Grey tells me the King is much displeased with Aberdeen's speech and motion and those who supported it. The French are satisfied with our declaration with fortress treaty. Talleyrand delighted and at eleven o'clock on the 31st. summons, he says, Palmerston and the other Members of the Conference to exchange ratifications. Grey spoke rather less confidently on this subject and much less so of the new creation of peers than I could wish. He still harbours a hope, a vain one I think, of carrying the bill without them. Parnell, our Secretary at War, would not vote on Thursday![33] Is this to be borne. Grey laments that if a vacancy occurs, Calne should prevent Macaulay from filling any office that vacates a seat.

29th. January Sunday. A full cabinet. Palmerston apprized us that dispatches had arrived from Holland to Zuylen and Falck containing a counter project of the treaty and an angry answer to the last note from the Conference. He did not know the exact stipulations of the first, but he had reason to suppose that it did not recognize the separation of the Crowns of Belgium and Holland, and the Members of the Conference had some notion of asking him that question as a preliminary, in the expectation that the answer would be in the negative or that the Plenipotentiaries, Falck and Zuylen, had no instructions. In this we concurred with a proviso of mine that if they answered in the affirmative it was to lead to no postponement of ratification. We then discussed the propriety of that measure, and I was sorry to find Lord Grey dwell too much on the embarrassment we should be exposed to if left alone to the French and the Belgians and forced to cooperate with them in forcing the Dutch to accede to our terms. He acknowledged however that good faith left us no option, and it was agreed that the ratifications should be exchanged next tuesday but an assurance given to the three hesitating parties that the Protocol will be kept open, by which phrase is meant in diplomacy that they may at any subsequent period accede to the agreement and date their accession from the day it was ratified by England and France, in a way to give them all the benefit of the stipulations from that day. It was also suggested and settled, unnecessarily I think, that we should state to the French and Belgians that they must not press us to *act* hostilely against the Dutch for some time and till the other Courts have had full time to come in, unless the Dutch themselves are the Aggressors. It is difficult to reconcile some of our Council such as Goderich to the notion and consequences of a cordial union and concert with France, and others, not excepting Lansdowne, have from constitutional caution a very *rash* predilection for 'half faced fellowships'.

The Russian Loan and the treaty we have made to continue it as well as the way of meeting Lord Wynford's motion were considered. It was agreed that an act of Parliament was necessary and the announcement of it and of the probability of the treaty (which later Althorp seemed inclined to keep back) the best method of disarming or at least postponing opposition. The treaty had I believe been read before it was signed in Cabinet, but we had not attended to its nature or consequences as accurately as we should have done, and there are objections and blemishes which will not escape so vigilant and factious an opposition as we have to encounter.

Lord Grey read us some letters of the King to him on the late divisions in the Lords and Commons, on the admission of Mr Tennison[34] to the Privy Council and Kennedy's[35] accession to his office. There was nothing specifick in these letters to call for our decision, but the tone and temper of them were far from agreable, very unlike most we have received from the King, and evidently manifesting that some impression has been made on the Royal Mind by the importunity and number of the booby Lords, who came to protest against an encrease of the peerage, inveigh against the Democratick current of the times, insinuate the weakness and connivance of Government, and suggest the means of defeating, evading, or rendering inefficient the reform bill. Great disgust at popular leaders, great apprehension of the encroaching spirit of the Commons and its Committees, and strong preference of the Lords and even a disposition to identify the feelings of that house with his own pervaded these compositions. In acceding to Mr Kennedy's appointment, the character of that Gentleman's political sentiments was mistaken and exaggerated for the purpose of introducing a strong admonition against the promotion of popular leaders, agitators, and Demagogues and in truth, under such opprobrious terms, persons who have distinguished themselves by zeal for our political service and for reform. Sir Henry Parnell would not vote last Thursday. It is pretty clear that he is looking out for popular grounds to resign. His conduct in office has been far from friendly to the Government or even meritorious in his department. Not Grey only, but Althorpe, who has great personal regard for him and estimates his talents and principles of political oeconomy very highly, agrees he should be dismissed. We all think Sir John Hobhouse should succeed him, but the Kings exhortation to abstain from popular names seems to threaten some obstacle. However Grey writes to recommend him tonight. And the necessity of a popular name to resist the retrenchments which no doubt Sir Henry will urge when out of office was suggested by Palmerston as a topick likely to prevail with His Majesty. Truth is that Hobhouse is as unlikely a man to be intractable in office as any I know and more likely to run the career, though with superior talents and taste, of his father[36] from demagogue to Ministerialist, from Ministerialist to placeman, and from placeman to Courtier, than to embarrass a government he is connected with [by] any austere notions of retrenchment or any visionary plans of reform. Anglesey writes word that he can do without coercive laws. In the course of conversation Grey shewed more averseness to the creation of peers, more doubt of the means of ascertaining the number necessary, and more apprehension when that is ascertained of not being enabled to complete them, than I thought prudent. He seems, too, more confident of carrying the 2d. reading than any facts he has communicated to me justify. In general this Cabinet exhibited gloomy faces and broke up under a vague persuasion that in one of the houses of Parliament or at Court our fate would speedily be decided and a change of Government take place. I do not see why, and I shall be unfeignedly sorry though most of my colleagues say they shall be glad. But loss of place and such powers as I ever had or ever aspire to have, is not likely to break my heart.

January 30, Monday. Went with Lord John Russell to Brighton. We talked over and agreed upon the general state of things, on no part of which were we so gloomy as most of our Colleagues. He has a notion that the Commons might force the Lords to agree to the Reform bill by voting the Mutiny act for a short time, from Month to Month or fortnight to fortnight only, and His Uncle, Lord Wm. Russell,[37] and other old Whigs have suggested that such a mode of proceeding is more *constitutional* than a large Creation of peers. What their definite meaning of *constitutional* is, it may be hard to guess. A less violent proceeding it can hardly be said to be, a more democratical, Whig, and Parliamentary one it may be; but if one object is to inspire the people with something like affection and respect for authority, the gratification of them by an exercise of prerogative which we hope to keep, rather than by the zeal of a house of Commons which we mean to reform, is surely preferable.

I saw the King for an hour and half. He was very well and very chearful, and none of the tone or temper of distrust which we thought had pervaded his letters of date was discernible in his conversation. He expressed concern and surprize at Aberdeen's motion, and Wellington's support of it he termed I think factious and unusual, and he condemned the absence of the Bishops. He highly approved the intended promotion of Sir J C Hobhouse to be Secretary at War and said he *was a Gentleman* and had behaved with great judgement and moderation on the late occasions. His opinions might be strong but he was not capable of resorting to base or wicked means of enforcing them. He praised Grey and blamed the Saints and Orangemen in Ireland for the course pursued in Ireland about the Protestant Church, which they were running the course to expose and destroy, and Grey, he said, labouring to save. The Queen was gracious but looked thin. With the exception of some little asperity about the Radical oeconomists, there was no appearance in the King of ill humour and very little of alarm. I was told that Londonderry, arriving late to dinner, had his audience of the King afterward; that for near an hour he was extremely dull and prosy, and then grew so violent and frantick with reform Ministry and politicks foreign and domestick that the King, who had borne all in patient silence, said at length, 'And now My Lord you had better go and see your Mother', old Lady Londonderry[38] being at Brighton.

Janry. 31. Returned to London. The Plenipotentiaries met at the Foreign office at 11 and France and England exchanged ratifications with Belgium.[39] Each power read and put in a declaration explanatory of their reasons for not exchanging their ratifications then, and England, in proposing to keep the Protocol, made also a declaration highly conciliatory, urging the advantages of union and speaking confidently of the prospects of accession. Talleyrand, when asked what he would declare, said with adroit nonchalance that he thought that he could not do better than adopt in substance and indeed verbatim the Declaration of England, a symptom of agreement if not of concert which discomposed Mastuzewitch, who looked as blue as the Cholera and gave an intimation highly useful to the three Courts that England and France could act with cordiality. They had themselves prepared and rehearsed their dialogue and the protocol which was to embody it with Palmerston; but this entire concurrence of Talleyrand in England's views (which they no doubt supposed was equally preconcerted) somewhat surprized them.

Wednesday. 1 Feby. [*In the margin:* I this day sat for the first time to hear an appeal in the County Palatine court Westminster with two puisne Judges, Vaughan[40] and Park,[41] as assessors. They or in forma I reversed the decree of my Vice Chancellor Holt.[42]] Cabinet dinner at Mr Stanleys which John Russell and Althorp, occupied in Commons, could not attend. Talked over the line of argument by which the payment of the Russian loan, the nonapplication to

Parliament for an extension of the act, and the renewal of the treaty if <glanced> at was to be defended. Goderich suggested that we should previously settle the course of the debate, wished Brougham to lie by for Lyndhurst, and me to answer Wynford on Precedents, formality, and the tendency of his motion and, as he not very complimentarily styled it, to throw a wet blanket on debate.

A letter from the King which proved that he was neither so much alarmed nor so disposed to find fault with us as imagined was read. The state of the House of Commons, the unmanageable temper and crotchets of our friends were the subject of some fruitless invectives, and the state of the Lords was cursorily discussed, the only positive convert being Lord Northwick,[43] who has given his proxy to Duke of Sussex and acknowledges that he repented of his vote the moment he had given it.

Thursday 2 Febry. Prepared my precedents and arguments against Lord Wynford's motion and went down to House of Lords with all the nervousness of a maiden speaker (I cannot conceive why) to take my allotted part in debate. I was relieved by the Chancellor telling me very early that he could not from indisposition wait to the end and that he preferred speaking after Lord Wynfords speech. He did, and not only demolished that very imperfect and incoherent composition as well as the irregular motion with which it concluded, but pronounced one of the most ingenious, powerful, and convincing legal arguments as well as most finished harangue and statesmanlike speech that ever was delivered in that house since Lord Mansfield and Lord Hardwicke. He seemed to match them both respectively in the talent in which they excelled. Eldon acknowledged Wynford's motion, which he had at first encouraged, to be untenable; no other Lord supported him and, after all of them had come down determined to vote and to shew great strength, he was compelled by their desertion to abandon and withdraw his motion and retired, abashed and beaten by his Enemy but yet more mortified and chagrined at his friends. He would have been to be pitied, were he not a presumptuous, ignorant, and interested Man. Wellington and Ellenborough both agreed that Brougham's speech was the best they ever heard, and this debate (if debate it can be called which Sefton more appropriately styled a *Monodrame*) completely retrieved our half discomfiture in the Commons. I am told Mr Holmes,[44] the opposition whipper in of the Commons, curses Lord Wynford for not letting well alone.

Talleyrand with Weissenburgh and Bulow has urged Vanderweyer to ascertain what points, if any, can be ceded or modified by King Leopold and to advise him if possible to open a negotiation with King of Holland before the advices come from Russia, which are too likely to bring a contreprojet. He (Talleyrand) tells me there are symptoms of some little hesitation in the King of Holland, and flatters himself that the proof the Protocols will afford of that Prince's real wish to recover the Crown of Belgium will greatly damp the ardor with which he at present is supported in Holland.

3d. February Friday. The dispatches from Germany prove that both at Berlin and Vienna the Ministers of these courts contemplated with great delight the possibility of France declining to ratify on account of the fortresses, and look forward to a coolness and separation between England and France; their consternation and dismay at their joint ratification and the opposite prospect of close union and concert will be proportionate. It will no doubt render them more submissive and compliant, tho' not a jot better pleased.

4th. Saturday. Talleyrand dined with us. He is sanguine and in good spirits in spite of the detected conspiracy at Paris. Our opposition say 'No wonder, he has duped us'; and the French opposition say that 'we have duped him'. Strange that in human affairs it should be deemed impossible that two States should cordially agree without one <overreaching> the other. We have no conflicting interests and we have the common one of preserving peace and shewing the rest of the world that we are willing as well as able to enforce what we deem essential to it.

Lord Sefton and Duncannon urged vehemently the manifold and forcible reasons for creating peers and the dangers of neglecting or even postponing that measure.

[*February*] *5 Sunday—1832.* Lord Cloncurry urged the necessity of an immediate commutation of tythes; represented, with strong acknowledgements of his useful and powerful talents, the unpopularity of Stanley; and enumerated 5 Irish peers—Lismore,[45] Milltown,[46] Llandaff,[47] Kenmare[48] and Gormanstown[49]—who might be made Peers of the United Kingdom. A Cabinet was held at Foreign Office at two. Some loose conversation about the state of the House of Lords and creation of peers. Lambton [Durham] read a calculation of the Lords from whence he inferred that we could not *command that assembly* without the addition of 50 or even 60, and that under the most favorable hypothesis, that is with the accession of all the doubtful, we could hardly carry the bill in the present house. Many however and among them Grey leant to that opinion it would be carried. Many reports, letters, and expressions were quoted which gave fair prospects of conversion, but nothing containing positive proof of above one or two accessions was produced. I ventured to urge the infatuation and indeed the dishonour of allowing the bill to go to a second reading in the Lords without ascertaining that we should carry it in the house as now composed or encreasing that house in the way to secure it. If we were sincere in our opinions of the dreadful calamities which would ensue on the rejection, we were <bond[ed]> with the power of averting, not to encounter them; and as to the notion of waiting for a vote of the house against us and then proroguing and making peers, it seemed to me exposing the country to all the perils we apprehended and reserving, as a desperate preventive or remedy, an expedient tenfold more degrading to the house of Lords than an immediate augmentation of its numbers. Before they had voted on the present bill the practical result of making peers to carry it would be the same, but quite safe as well as expedient; but the creation of peers immediately upon a vote with a view to rescind or correct it would be an open declaration that the House should not be permitted to render its opinion valid. I was supported by Durham and in some measure by the Chancellor. But it was said that we were bound to the King not to urge peers till the last moment, and the Duke of Richmond and Grey seemed to think that expression pointed directly to the day the bill should pass the Commons. This was combated. The confinement of peerages to eldest sons was lamented as inconvenient and it was said many in that predicament would decline the honour and some votes be lost by our resorting to it. The Bishops, though not above two or three have promised their support, are said to be likely to vote to the number of 12 for us and 8 against us—and there is I suppose more reasons than I know of to reckon upon Harrowby and such as will follow him. Some clearer understanding should be come to, but tho' Grey and others agreed in that remark I am not satisfied that he or they have any practical method in view of executing that intention. Durham told me that he could not and would not remain on the Ministerial bench if he had not before the 2d. reading some better security than we yet had for passing it. It is unlucky that we did not accept the King's offer of 21 some weeks ago.

We had a long discussion on the means of enforcing the laws for collecting the tythes in Ireland and on the best method of effecting a commutation of them and the extinction of their very name in a short time. The notion of transferring them to Government and giving a power to levy them as any other debt of the Crown seemed generally approved of, but it is a very unusual, anomalous, and violent remedy. Sir James Graham and Lord Lansdown very justly observed that the measure or at least the announcement of a measure to commute and abolish tythes should accompany any proclamation or enactment of stern proceedings, and it was settled that the Irish Solicitor General and Mr Greene[50] (both of whom had been present during part of our discussion) should throw the project of a proclamation and another of an act of Parliament on paper before Wednesday, when at a Cabinet dinner we may consult about it.

Talleyrand and Bulow in the evening, the latter very angry with Aberdeen, very indignant with the King of Holland and Zuylen, and somewhat chagrined and nettled at being told by his Court that his dispatches are more English in their spirit than even the representations of Mr Chad. However all conspires to persuade us that the three powers will shortly ratify, and though Mr Bernstorff by an affected refinement calls two of the five powers in conference merely 2 fifths of a moral being, he may find that the moral force they possess will largely outbalance the other three.

Adair writes privately that he fears Leopold and his Belgians may be impatient to attack the Citadel of Antwerp. But as the Protocol is left open he cannot do so with honour, and as his army is improving and the Dutch resources wasting away in the meanwhile, and all the ratifications likely to arrive, he ought in policy to remain quiet. Vanderweyer will go to Brussells to urge this view of the subject, and Talleyrand writes earnestly in the same sense to his Court. Poor Lord Hardwicke[51] died yesterday—a vacant ribbon [*The preceding sentence is crossed out and there follows in the margin:* The fact untrue and the remark incorrect. Lord Hardwicke is alive and were he dead, a supernumerary ribbon having been given to Grey, none would be vacant.]

6 Febry. Monday. Lord Ebrington at breakfast expressed his conviction that our friends in commons lamented their squeamishness about Russian loan, were anxious to retrieve the false step they had made and disposed to uphold our Belgian negotiation and treaty and our union with France in a high tone. He further told me that on a petition from Hertford Tom Duncombe[52] would in all probability open on the necessity of making peers and ridicule and expose those who wearied with the King with audiences of dissuasion. I told him of the abrupt dismissal of Lord Londonderry from the presence and suggested that the booby Lords who pestered His Majesty with these audiences, though they might not have the wit to point any argument in favor of their views, furnished a practical one against an augmentation of peers who would all be invested with the right of obtruding their advice on their Sovereign. This Ebrington thought Tom Duncombe might make use of. I went to Court. Grey promises to ask Harrowby distinctly what he means to do and what numbers will follow him, with an intimation that on the greater or less certainty of conversions must depend the measure of a creation of peers to pass the bill. Soult has contradicted Grey's statement and the truth by denying that France ever espoused the House of Orange in Belgium, and Casimir Perrier engages to set the matter right. Sir R Vivyan[53] has given up his motion on Belgian affairs. A council to swear in Sir J Cam Hobhouse, who seems mightily tickled with his appointment and honours, and a Recorder's report from which I escaped before the painful cases came under consideration. Two I understand are to be executed.

Tuesday 7 February. Duchy business with Mr Danvers and offered the solicitorship, vacant by death of Mr Minchin,[54] to Stephen Moore.[55] In house of Lords a conversation on Irish tythes arose on a petition in which Lord Grey, Lord Lansdown, and Lord Plunkett took occasion to expose the factious misrepresentations of the orangemen to persuade the publick that the Government connived at the lawless resistance to tythes. Aberdeen censured Grey for not explaining the treaty, threw out something like doubt of the validity of a treaty signed by five but ratified by two only on one side and signed and ratified by the only party on the other. Lord Strangford, Lord Auckland, and Lord Wynford spoke on the glove duty. I went to the commons to hear Stanley who, in a short debate on the fees payable on Irish commissions and warrants by the Magistrates, shewed his acuteness, self possession, judgement, and authority in the house, and proved to me that he was or will soon be the leading man in that assembly.

Wednesday 8th. Febry. Lord Chancellor after dinner took me to a Cabinet at Lord Greys at which Plunket as well as the members—excepting Lord Carlisle, Lord Althorp, and Lord John Russell—were present, and all annoyed. Grey exceedingly nettled at the manner in which his speech about tythes last night had been treated by the press and spoken of even by friends in the House of Commons this evening. He had said that he would enforce the law in putting down outrage and resistance to tythe by exerting all the powers with which the Executive government was entrusted and, if they were insufficient, come to Parliament for more, but that he was at the same time anxious and determined to frame and carry as speedily as possible such an entire alteration of the present odious and dangerous system as should ensure the tranquillity of the country, protect the people from oppression, and afford the Clergy additional security. The former part of this declaration was hailed by the Orangemen as the announcement of coercive laws and railed at by the Catholicks and radicals as proof of such an intention, and the second part was dropped and unnoticed by both parties. Lord Grey was nettled and reportedly declared that he should stand by his words, and if his friends in the house of Commons would not stand by him, he would not stay in. Sir James Graham, Durham, and myself urged the hazard of proposing any coercive Law unless accompanied with some substantial pledge of a practical commutation of tythes and extinction of the very name. In the principle of such a measure and the expediency of a prompt and distinct announcement of it, all concurred. But much embarrassment was felt in announcing a measure which was not in readiness and in making the Committees of the two houses adopt a report pledging them to a bill of which they had not the outline. Stanley seemed to undertake that the committee of the Commons would go the full length of recommending a transference of the Charge from the tythe to land tax, from the tenant to the Landlord, and an Abolition of the very name of tythe, provided they were at liberty to urge at the same time the immediate enforcement of the law by some new legislative act.[56] That act in the shape of bill is drawn out and it was agreed to put it in circulation and decide on it next Sunday, Lord Durham declaring he should oppose it and somewhat petulantly remarking that it was worse than the six acts and that Grey's language in Lords had done infinite mischief. Our intention to conciliate as well as coerce must be distinct and prompt, and embodied at least in resolutions if not in a bill without loss of time.

Some discussion on the ensuing motion of Mr Courtenay on Don Pedro's enlistment of Sailors and purchase of Ships, and some discussion on an intended drawback of duty on sugar, introduced in his, Althorp's, absence and at his request by Goderich. Durham grumbled at the possible loss of £100,000 to revenue and very coolly declared the case of West Indians to be hopeless and better left to be ruined. After the Cabinet The Chancellor, Grey, Duke of Richmond and myself had some conversation on peers. Harrowby has written to Wellington and is much affronted at his answer, which disdains all compromise about Reform, says that Ministry have introduced a bill to subvert the constitution and government and he will never lend himself to <mend> it in a Committe or elsewhere.[57] The High tone and impracticable spirit of his reply has nettled Harrowby and affronted his followers, and they are not pleased with the cold and cautious answer of Sir Robert Peel.[58] They intend, says the Duke of Richmond—and Lord Grey asserts belief if he does not confirm the report—to state their determination to support the second reading in a day or two and can engage positively, it is reported, for 22. They wait however till they have consulted the Archbishop. This may diminish the number of peers necessary to our object, but does it dispense with the necessity of the measure. They are bitter enemies to our government; they may not lull us into security, separate us from commons and people, desert and overthrow us? I tremble—and must have certainty before 2[d.] reading.

9 February. Saw Grey in the Lords where there was no business. The King thro' Sir Herbert Taylor has written both to the Chancellor and Grey, expressing his satisfaction at the prospect of Wharncliffe, Harrowby, and several peers voting for 2d. reading and the consequent escape from the 'dreaded and obnoxious' measure of creating Peers.[59] According to Sir Herbert he has never had an hour's ease since he acquiesced in resorting to that expedient and is much relieved by what he considered a disproof of its necessity. That chiefly consists in a paper of

Wharncliffe, written as the substance of his conversation before him by Sir Herbert, submitted to the King and then transmitted to Grey. It contains an adherence to his former opinions, but a readiness to vote for the second reading and to engage to do so, *provided no peers are made*; but if that prerogative is exerted to facilitate the passing of the bill, the King's Government is menaced in no very measured terms with the active hostility and inveterate opposition of a considerable number of peers who will, without reference to any consequences, do their utmost to reject the measure, embarrass and remove its authors.

There seems a better prospect of some strong measure for commutation of tythes being prepared and accompanying the coercive Law and menacing declaration than there was yesterday. Anglesey is all right on this subject.

10th. February Friday. Bad news that Tipperary is proclaimed. Took Duncannon to the Commission for conducting the affairs of the Duchy of Cornwall at Somerset house, where we spent more than an hour, and I took Sir Wm. Knighton[60] from thence to the Duchy of Lancaster, where we dispatched some business. Dined at Falck with many of the Diplomatick corps. Lieven is confident his court will ratify, and builds his confidence on the conviction that the late papers and conduct of the King of Holland will open the Emperor's eyes to his real design—that of embroiling Europe in war with the hope of recovering Belgium. I called at Lord Greys where the Lievens had driven before us. When they were announced Grey and his family were sitting with Czartorinski, and Grey met the Lievens on the stairs and apprized them of the company they would find in the Drawing room. Lieven had made a formal complaint to Lord Palmerston that Czartorizki was received, and of course he and the Princess turned back and drove away when they learnt he was there.

There has been some conversation in Commons about the creation of Peers, but few members of any weight in the country took part in it, and OConnell unluckily enough said something for it, which will not much reconcile the King to the measure. What is more I do not find Lord Grey more decided than he was about it, tho I have reason to believe all his private friends and all his family have been persuading and even goading him to it.

11 Febry. Saturday. At Richmond. Rogers of our party. Slept at Star and Garter.

12 Febry. Sunday. Drove from Richmond to Lord Grey's Downing Street, urged him as did Lady Grey and Durham not to trust too implicitly to the prospect of converts to reform in the House of Lords. Harrowby as he assured me had told Lord Lansdowne that he could answer for 25 (including Bishops), provided no peers were made in the interim, and Grey seemed to think his language was fair and explicit and his view of the subject more reasonable than, supposing him sincere, it seems to me to be; for if the dread of the calamity resulting from a rejection of the bill forces him to concur in a measure that he disapproves, how can the creation of a few peers deter him from doing so? or why does he suppose the rejection to be less fatal after than before the creation?

At the Cabinet at foreign office the opinion of Attorney and Solicitor General n the conduct of the Magistrates at Bristol was read, and it was agreed unanimously that they should be prosecuted for neglect of duty. Grey leant to a proceeding by Ex Officio but that point was left to the judgement of the Crown Lawyers.

There were alarming accounts of cases of Cholera at Rotherhithe and on the river.

Lord Plunkett was requested to attend, and some recent letters from Lord Anglesey, containing enclosures from Sir Hussey Vivian, on the amount of the force and state of the Country in Ireland were read. They differed materially from reports given us by Stanley, by Mr Greene, and others. The opinion of Anglesey was distinctly, that if the law was to be enforced and no preceding or accompanying measure of conciliation adopted, that not only his amount of force was insufficient, but that not less than 40,000, and Sir Hussey said not less than 100,000, men would prevent a general rebellion or enable Government to collect the tythes. Althorp stated as distinctly his opinion that the House of Commons would vote for no great augmentation of force for such a purpose and scarcely any unless an immediate commutation were announced and the possibility of a considerable reduction of Ecclesiastical revenues at least left open for discussion. He said that he might possibly pass something of the sort, but it would be by the help of his enemies, the Tory and Orangemen, and in the teeth of his friends; and he did not like to offend those on whom he depended, and to depend on those with whom he was on all points at variance. The respective Committees were then talked over. Stanley read us a report, on which he thought that of the Commons would agree, declaring that while the incomes of the Clergy should be secured, the tythes should be abolished and the very name extinguished; and Lord Lansdown shewed us a resolution nearly to the same purpose, though in more measured terms, to which the Lords Committees, with the exception of the Archbishop, was, he said, ready to comply. The said Archbishop is unwilling to commit himself to a *commutation*. In which case, with the help of the Bishop of London, he must be overruled.

This indeed seemed to be the general opinion. And till such a resolution is agreed upon in both Committees and in the houses, and till further evidence is gone into, I hope the coercive measure, so impracticable and so hazardous, is, I hope [*sic*], virtually postponed.[61] Durham is decidedly against any such measure—and hot. The leaning of all our House of Commons Colleagues, Stanley excepted, is the same way, and I think the entire contradiction between his and Lord Anglesey's opinion a proof that they have not communicated in so unreserved a manner as they ought. Anglesey has sent over a plan, somewhat complicated and much objected to by Stanley, on the success of which he relies perhaps too confidently.[62] Part of it cannot it is true be immediate, but the Commutation of tythe to Land tax might be so and I hope will. With his whole plan he hopes to do without reinforcement, but we think of furnishing him with 10,000 and, I trust, a conciliatory measure (worth 30,000 to boot). Grant was on this topick as on most quite right. Agreeing as he and Durham do in their opinions on these matters, how singularly different is their manner of enforcing them!

13 Febry. Monday. Returned from Richmond. In House of Lords a conversation on fees of Irish Magistrates tiresome, but strongly indicative of personal spirit of

Irishmen. Grey is to see Harrowby on Thursday. Harrowby defers the conversation till then from a persuasion that by that time he can tell what numbers will vote with him on 2d. reading. Grey sent me some letters from Sir Herbert Taylor and King, urging some understanding with Harrowbites, insinuating the policy of modifications in Committee and, while he admits and adheres to his promise of making peers if unavoidable, earnestly imploring him to avert that 'dreadful measure' and arguing that it will not secure success. The tone of the correspondence is not agreable, but I suspect it indicates less hostility or soreness than Grey supposes. I drove down after dinner to see him and found him low, though Lady Grey and her brother, who were with him, preach the necessity of creating peers and distrust of Harrowby's power and of the sincerity of his friends. Lord Ponsonby maintains that the King is far from being so averse to the measure of creating Peers as he pretends, and reports, on better authority I suspect, that the Duke of Wellington is in spirits from a conviction that we shall not venture to make peers and persuaded that, if we do, our triumph will [not] be permanent.

14 Febry. I was too late for the Lords, and saw few of my Colleagues. The Cholera is undeniably in Rotherhithe, Souhwark, and some of the adjoining parishes. The Board of Health, the Privy Council, and the constituted authorities active and vigilant, and the Parochial authorities at length alarmed. This day Althorp explained and vindicated Lord Grey's declaration about Irish tythes with great success. Our intention of endeavouring to extinguish the whole system is avowed, the Committees are to report tomorrow, and many of our best Irish friends—Lord Ebrington, Carew,[63] Sir John Newport, &c—are satisfied. Tythe is safe. Peers and reform only remain.

15 Febry. Wednesday. Cabinet dinner at Lansdowne House. Carlisle from gout and four others, from business in the Commons, absent. Lord Grey apprehended some difficulty in Lords in passing a resolution pledging Parliament in this stage of business to the extinction of tythes by commutation, but when assured by Stanley and Palmerston and confirmed by most of us in the opinion that without it the bill for relieving the Clergy and transferring the means of enforcing the payment of tythes to Government would never pass the Commons, consented, with some remonstrance from Richmond, to try it. He then consulted us on his tomorrow's appointment with Harrowby: should he, on his assurance of enabling us to pass the second reading, renounce the thought of making peers? or should he exact some further understanding for the Committee? or should he insist on every part of the bill and immediately make peers to the number of 50 or 60, with the uncertainty even if that or any number would secure his object. He spoke feelingly of his responsibility, but read us a very handsome and satisfactory letter from the King, which, though it still recommended modifications (provided they do not touch what Grey had called the three cardinal principles of the bill, namely, disfranchisement in Schedule A, enfranchisement in Schedule C, and the ten pound qualification) and exhorted him to avert if possible the 'dreaded' measure of a large creation, distinctly repeated his promise of acquiescing if the necessity existed and his assurances not to shrink from his promise when claimed; and this was accompanied with many personal expressions of kindness to Lord Grey and hopes that the dissensions in the opposition, or, as he termed it, 'The Enemy's camp', might be turned to account and facilitate the carrying of the bill.[64] Melbourne and Duke of Richmond were vehement against any creation, and the latter, with Lansdowne, confident of passing the second reading without resorting to that measure. Durham was manifestly averse to any negotiation and considered the Government pledged to take all measures to pass the bill as it is and avowed that the one certain way was the creation of 60 peers immediately. He and Brougham maintained that if we went into the Committee without a Majority at our command we probably should lose the bill and certainly lose all the confidence of our friends and the country. They did not lay much stress on what, I confess, weighs much with me—that the second reading passed and the power of creating peers in our hands, no manoeuvre in Committee can deprive us of the power and the time to retrieve any defeat we may experience there. I stated that I should have preferred the direct creation of the number requisite but, having promised the King to do all in our power to ascertain the state of the House and to avert if possible the necessity, we could not honourably go to him with a lie in our mouth and state that the necessity had occurred, if we should receive from Lord Harrowby and others a moral certainty of carrying the first stage and principle of the bill. I remarked that *speculation, hopes, conjecture, intimations* would not do. We must not risk the bill—but if we had real assurance of the second reading, we should accept it with the tacit and implicit contract of making no peers for the purpose of carrying the bill thro' that stage; but I questioned the prudence of negotiating with them now upon the subsequent stages and Committee, because I thought it better to reserve the power of making peers, which would be quite effectual to retrieve any defeat in the Committee. I disclaimed all belief in the defection of friends on account of the creation of peers, and I quoted the opinion of Duke of Bedford[65] and other Grandees in disproof of the assertion of Duke of Richmond that none but radicals encouraged us in adding to the Peerage. Grey went away with a heavy heart to manage his conference with Harrowby tomorrow, and Durham, who set me down, observed with asperity that it was not the poor King who prevented the necessary measure, but that our difficulties were in the Cabinet itself, that Grey and others shrunk from the measure and from the redemption of a pledge he had openly and explicitly given to the Country. Durham distinctly added that he would not remain in office if the Peers were not made before the second reading, though he would do his best to assist our bill and sincerely hoped we might succeed.

16 February, Thursday. In House of Lords the first reading of Cholera prevention bill[66] and the report on tithes from the Committee passed with little or no observation.

Grey in the Chancellor's room shewed me a letter from the King and his own minute of the substance, or rather result, of what passed between Lords Harrowby and Wharncliffe and himself.[67] The King's letter began by expressing his satisfaction at the interview being postponed, inasmuch as what he heard from Lord Grey of a conversation between Mr Wood[68] and Lord Sandon,[69] and what Lord Wharncliffe had recently told him, led him to hope that some conciliatory method of passing he bill might be devized, in which case both Lord Grey and himself should congratulate themselves on having deferred and averted a step so objectionable and unconstitutional as a large creation of Peers. He repeated, however, yet more distinctly and firmly than ever, not only his adherence to his promise of making peers if that measure was deemed necessary, but expressly said that he left the consideration of that necessity *entirely in Grey's hands* and, from the constitutional principles which had guided him thro' life, was confident that he would not abuse that power; he went on to say that to avert an evil of *greater magnitude,* which for the first time he described the loss of the bill to be, it might become the duty of his station to adopt even the inconvenient and dangerous expedient, and he was ready to do so at Lord Grey's suggestion, if he should find it impossible to carry the bill without such a measure, or a surrender of such parts of the bill as were essential to its object and necessary to the satisfaction of the publick. He did not wish, on the contrary he should deprecate, Lord Grey's uselessly sacrificing any part of his measure, unless by that sacrifice he secured not only the second reading but the final passing of the bill and the Committee; and he authorized Grey to shew these, his strong expressions of unrestrained and unqualified confidence, to Lords Harrowby and Wharncliffe. Grey did so, and Wharncliffe seemed much startled at the unreserved *carte blanche* with which Ministers were furnished by this fair, direct and manly Prince. He and Harrowby were open and fair enough, but their promises far from satisfactory. They thought, they hoped, they were confident, but they were not and could not be *positive,* that 26 proselytes amounting to 52 votes would support the bill on second reading, and they supposed many others would stay away provided no peers were made. And Wharncliffe distinctly, Harrowby more cautiously, implied that to the disfranchisement, enfranchisement, and qualification of the bill, which Grey calls the three cardinal points (Schedule A, Schedule C, and the £10 voters) they would agree. But on the other hand they acknowledged as distinctly that they could not be answerable for this amount of support; that many of the 26 were likely to take umbrage at slight matters in the Committee, and that a large portion of them would abandon the bill and oppose us in every possible way, if a single peer were made, which they should consider as a signal of a determination to lower and almost extinguish the House of Lords; that if the bill came out of committee as it went in, they could not engage to vote for the 3d. reading, and a word was dropped that, should another bill be proposed by any other peer, they should reserve an option of supporting which they liked best. This seems very unsatisfactory and vague. However we are to have a cabinet to consider of it on Sunday. Grey was tickled at King's letter, disposed to believe that the two Lords, especially Wharncliffe, were fair and honest, though obliged to acknowledge, I think too reluctantly, that it was intimation, conjecture, and hope, and not certainty, and that it was therefore unsafe to trust to. The two Lords undertook to inform Lord Grey in time if on enquiry they found many of their expectations too sanguine. The Archbishop of York votes for bill and affects to believe that 14 Bishops will vote the same way and none the other![70]

17th. Febry. Friday. Attended the Duchy of Cornwall committee wih Lord

Duncannon. The lease of the property in the Scilly Islands has fallen in by the refusal of the Duke of Leeds[71] to pay any fine for the renewal. The tenants petition the Treasury instead of petitioning the Commission, and this both in form and substance creates some embarrassment.

In house of Lords a conversation on the tythe report, very irregularly introduced by Lord Wicklow without any question or proceeding, degenerated in hands of those who followed him into a vague but virulent attack on the whole system of Government in Ireland, and even into a defence of the Orangemen and attack on the Catholicks by Wicklow, Buckingham and, horresco referens, Carnarvon. They were answered most satisfactorily by Grey, and somewhat less forcibly or judiciously by the Chancellor, Lord Plunkett, and Lord Clanrickarde. I reproach myself for not speaking, but I am nervous, I hate speaking when there is no point to argue and no question before the house, and I had just swallowed my dinner, when it is unpleasant to listen and yet more so to utter.

18 Febry. 1833 [*1832*]. Saturday—at home.

19 Febry. Sunday. In a Cabinet at foreign office, in which all the Members but Lord Carlisle (ill with the gout) attended, we were detained near 5 hours. The King had been applied to by Lady Dundonald without the knowledge of her husband to pardon him, and His Majesty was much inclined to do so but thought it right to act by the advice of his Ministers. We all agreed that the pardon should be granted, but the Duke of Richmond begged to be understood that he was not thereby pledged to concur in the restoration of his rank, and many of us observed that neither we were pledged not to propose it, and there the matter ended. Captain Sartorius had applied for leave of absence and somewhat incorrectly affirmed that he wished to pass the winter at Palermo, when it was notorious he was about to take command of Don Pedro's fleet. And the same day that a question was asked about him in the Commons, the Admiralty had summoned him to attend, in consequence of the papers announcing his oath of allegiance to Donna Maria.

Lord Grey then read the letter from the King of the 15th., and the result of his conversation with Harrowby and Wharncliffe—of both which I have given an account under Thursday—and he related to the Cabinet at greater length and more distinctness all that had passed. He read also one or two letters received from the King[72] in which expressed his disappointment at the vague and unsatisfactory engagement offered by the two Lords, acknowledged that there was not sufficient security, but still hoped that they might be able to give it when they knew that full power of creating peers was given to Lord Grey, and he ended by repeating his adherence to his promise and his exhortations not to exact it till all endeavours to render it unnecessary had failed. Lord Grey then exposed with great clearness, feeling, and force the difficulties of our situation, acknowledged the imperfect hopes held out by the two Lords, though he said that Harrowby assured him that if the second reading was tomorrow he was morally certain we should carry it, and only refrained from undertaking that we should from a knowledge that it was possible events might occur to make those he reckoned upon waver. It appears however that he has written a sort of circular to those disposed to confide in him, in which he urges two reasons for voting for the bill and preventing the creation of peers: the first, the obvious danger to which the Country and state would be exposed by a second rejection; and the other, the strength which *a new creation of peers* would give to a Ministry which they wished to remove, and the difficulties it would expose them to, if they or their friends should succeed them. Lord Grey said that it certainly was not hitherto sufficient security even for the second reading, much less for the Committee, for us to proceed upon, but that it afforded some hopes of obtaining that security and he repeated above once his conviction (to my mind a very strange one) that neither fifty nor sixty peers would necessarily ensure the carrying [the] bill, because we could not calculate what numbers, both of the new accessions and of our own old friends, might fall off from disgust or resentment of that measure.

We then conversed at some length on the state of the <thing> or our prospects, and even Palmerston agreed that we were called upon to 'confide in Lord Harrowby's confidence' but not in his knowledge or assurance. Several names in the course of the discussion were mentioned and about 5 Bishops and 7 Lay Lords who voted against us in Autumn were deemed certain proselytes now, making 12 additional supporters subtracted from the enemy's force which is equal to 24, to which five others were with confidence added as unquestionable accessions—in all 29, but all as it was contended to be considered subject to the condition of no peers being created. Lord Althorp stated very shortly and distinctly that, though his repugnance to making peers was not so great as that which some of us possessed, he felt bound to the King, after the handsome and direct manner in which he had conducted himself (of which we had declared ourselves sensible in the warmest times), not to recommend such a step till he was satisfied that the second reading could not be carried without it. On the other hand he could not but say that with such vague hopes as the late conversation of Lord Harrowby and Lord Wharncliffe held out, it would be impossible for us to go to the second reading in the Lords. Unless therefore something more distinct and certain were offered, he foresaw that he must recommend a large creation, and in some part of the conversation I think he expressed his persuasion that few if any votes of our friends would or could be lost by a creation. If however he was satisfied that the 2d. reading was sure, he was ready so far to take his chance in the Committee and third reading that he would postpone any recommendation to make peers till he had been able to ascertain the necessity and the amount in that Committee.

In all this I agreed so exactly and entirely that I did little more than signify my full concurrence in what Lord Althorpe had delivered as his opinion, though I somewhat more earnestly insisted on the staff being in our <hand> if we should once get into the Committee, and I scouted as utterly incredible the defection of any of our friends or indeed of any man of common honesty and sense merely on account of the creation of peers. I should have preferred making them now and at once, but my anxiety to avoid pressing the King to a measure he abhorred, unless upon the most incontrovertible necessity, made me as anxious to do every thing to avert that necessity as those who had much stronger repugnance to it than myself. I would therefore give Lord Harrowby and the rest ample time to collect any security they could give us, but unless both in nature and amount it was much more satisfactory than any they had yet offered, I saw no safety in any course but that of creating Peers. The reluctance to the measure seemed to me much abated in all but the Duke of Richmond, who declaimed against it warmly and <eagerly> but with great good temper and some talent. Lord Lansdowne acknowledged that Harrowby had spoken of the possibility of another bill being offered and seemed to wish to reserve a right of preferring it, but he assured Lord L that it was not likely, and both he (Lord L) and Lord Palmerston argued that it was not practicable, though somebody said he had heard the bill was drawn and even printed. That such a course was inadmissible all present allowed and Grey said he must have an explanation on it with Lord Harrowby, but none seemed to me to consider it, as I did myself, as an indication of a spirit even in Harrowby, not only of hostility to us as the authors of the bill, but irreconcilable with any cordial concert with us for the purpose of carrying it. The Chancellor was more earnest than he has hitherto been for an immediate and large creation. He dreads the Committee and seems to think that a defeat even there would lose us all publick opinion, raise the suspicion of treachery, and expose us to half if not all the consequences of rejection and defeat. He as well as others remarked that they were making us instrumental to concentrating a third party to overawe us, and that they would then coalesce with the Duke of Wellington and Peel and turn us out without remorse. Richmond, Palmerston, and Lansdowne combated this opinion.

There was much more conversation and not a little canvass of names. Grey seemed, if not confident, disposed to expect sufficient accession to pass the 2d. bill and unaccountably apprehensive of numbers falling off if any creation is resorted to. At the end Lord Durham very offensively asked, after looking as black as the night and preserving a sullen silence, if he might now be permitted to speak. He said we were pledged to the principle and efficiency of the bill and to his understanding we were about to violate that pledge by compromising both, by accepting from the enemies of the measure the 2d. reading if they condescended to grant it, and then entering the Committee at their mercy and with our eyes open to their intention of mutilating the most essential parts; that to such an abandonment of our professions he could not and would not assent; and that he could not agree with me that once in the Committee we had the staff in our hands, for we could not and dare not use it, that not only the King but many in that room, some of whom as we knew would have liked the modifications they proposed, would clamour against peers being created for a clause. A few sharp words passed between him and Richmond, which I interposed with success to allay and divert, and we settled to settle nothing on this most important point but to postpone the consideration of it till Wednesday. In the meantime Grey would try to procure from the two Lords and the Bishops something more distinct, and each would exert himself with his personal friends among the doubtful and wavering to obtain some positive assurance and ascertain the degree of reliance that may be placed on their vote or their absence.

[*The following verse appears on an adjacent page:*

A tale addressed to Grey to persuade him to make peers
Febry. 1832 or April 1832

Wearied with trudging many a mile
Hodge stopped before an awkward stile [*margin:* 2d. reading in House of Lords]
And seemed in need of aid

The Lane was long—and at the end
Stood many a stout and gallant friend, [*margin:* more than 120 Candidates for peerages]
But Hodge no signal made.

Two tramping fellows, lurking bye [*margin:* Wharncliffe and Harrowby]
With sourish looks and evil eye
'We'll help you over,' cried

Hodge heard or thought he heard them add
'To do him here would be too mad
'Get him on 't' other side

'We then indeed in snug Committee
'Beyond the reach of aid or pity
'Safely may do the job

'Force him to give us half a crown [*margin:* to coalesce or to yield the essence of the bill and all the popularity of it]
'Or fairly knock the blockhead down
'And murder maim and rob' [*margin:* turn him out]

And will not Hodge call for the true
To crush that false and smaller crew
Who are such mischief brewing?

If he does not—in faith and troth
I can't but own with shame, he both
Meets and deserves his ruin]

The news of a black insurrection in Jamaica, great loss of life, severe executions, and the destruction of 52 estates arrived while we were in Cabinet. A long and tiresome discussion arose on the question of appointing a Committee in Lords to enquire into the condition of Slavery in the West Indies. Lord Chancellor is greatly against it. He said the West Indians would have it all their own way and it would be all 'deception'. I said, though no great friend to the scheme of Committee, I did not see why 'the deception should be all on one side; and though I could not deny the propensity of the Slavedrivers to lie, I was quite sure they could not outdo the saints in that accomplishment'.

20 Febry. Heard from Mr Byng[73] a more accurate report of Lord Harrowby's circular letter, which is somewhat less unfriendly to Ministers than was represented and well adapted to its purpose of prevailing on those who are hostile to vote for the second reading and acquiesce in the bill, rather than drive us to make peers.

I this day swore in Mr Stephn. Moore solicitor to the Duchy.

Prince Talleyrand read me his interesting memoir on the Duke de Choisuls[74] administration and character.

21 Febry. Tuesday. Met Lord Seaford at Colonial Office. In addition to the calamity in Jamaica, where there is too much reason to believe he is a great sufferer, he had this morning heard of the death of his brother.[75] He bears these cruel misfortunes with unaffected calmness and philosophy, and discussed with Goderich and myself the policy of publishing a proclamation to undeceive the Negroes and enforce the laws (which we all three agreed should be done without loss of time) and of moving a Committee in the House of Lords to enquire into the condition of the Slaves, which is a measure Mr Burge[76] and several West Indians insist upon as a matter of justice. The policy of resorting to it struck both Lord Seaford and me as very questionable: 1st., it implies on the part of those who requested it a recognition of a right in the British Parliament to legislate, and in some senses invites them to do so; and 2dly., it would be impossible to avoid a corresponding committee in the Commons, and a difference in the evidence and report of the two Committees, which it might be helpless to prevent, would be infinitely worse than no Committee or enquiry at all. Goderich added that many and strong cases of cruelty had been reported to the office, that they could not be witheld if an enquiry was instituted and, tho' every thing had been done to redress any wrong inflicted on the Negroes, one knew by experience the certain effect that the production of particular cases, commented upon by orators and preachers, would have in exciting a general disgust against the whole government and frame of West Indian society. All these matters Lord Seaford undertook to state to Mr Burge for his consideration. The bias of Lord Goderich's mind as well as my own was that, if the West Indians are still persuaded that such enquiry is due to them and likely to assist them in their vindication, it would be wrong and hazardous to withold it, and if necessity or policy required Committees in either or both houses, I strongly preferred Government moving and keeping the business in their own hands to acquiescing in the motion of others and leaving the conduct of so nice and important a subject in the hands of persons over whom we had little or no controul.

I saw Lord Grey. I find Lord Bradford[77] will follow Lord Harrowby. Aylesbury[78] is also certain. The Bishop of London is directly and openly for 2d. reading, but reports that Bishop of Gloucester (Monck[79] I think) is less to be reckoned upon than he formerly expected.

22 Wednesday. After the Levee had a long conversation with Sir Herbert Taylor. He told me that Lord Wharncliffe had originally mistaken the King's reluctance to make peers for a determination not to make any if the second reading were passed and a disposition to acquiesce in and even promote considerable modifications in the Committee. The passage in the King's letter to Lord Grey, distinctly giving him his option of the time of making peers if necessary, whether in the Committee or before the 2d. reading, and the permission to shew that passage to Lords Harrowby and Wharncliffe, were introduced with the express purpose of correcting all such misapprehension. It is probable that Lord Harrowby's letter to his friends with reasons for voting the second reading was written under the same false impression as Lord Wharncliffe's, for it holds out the hope of great alterations in the Committee and urges that, if once the bill is read a 2d. time, Lord Grey dare not and cannot make peers and the house is rescued from such degradation. At least the substance of the letter is so reported to us, altho' Lord Grey collected from Lord Harrowby that he would expect and almost approve of peers being created if in the Committee the bill should be much mutilated. It is possible that the knowledge of the *Carte blanche* given to Lord Grey and communicated to Lord Harrowby in the King's letter may have altered his view of the case and occasioned this discrepancy, which otherwise would imply some duplicity.

Sir Herbert Taylor told me much of Lord Munster's undutiful and ungentlemanlike behavior to his father and the uneasiness all his Sons except Adolphus occasion him. We had some conversation on the leases of the Duchy of Cornwall and he agreed with me that a sale of the estate in the Scilly islands to the Crown would be advantageous to the King and the State. But the treasury does not lend itself to that scheme.

A cabinet dinner at Lord John Russell's. The necessity of a boon to such of the West Indian Colonies as accept the order of Council was after some discussion allowed, but whether a loan of 5 millions Sterling taking security for the payment, a reduction of duty or an encrease of bounty on exportation should be adopted was after much deliberation left still unsettled. Lord Althorp objected strongly to the bounty, and most were startled at the notion of the advance and doubtful of its being attainable.

There was a proposal of a friend in the Commons to bring in an amendment of the enlistment bill, but we agreed that it would be prudent to prevail on him to postpone it, though many of us prefer an entire repeal of the act to any amendment.

We reverted to the perplexing question of the state of the House of Lords and the propriety of making peers. But we had not the materials for forming a correct judgement of the necessity. Durham petulantly and offensively urged an immediate decision, and said he saw the Cabinet were determined not to create peers, the enemy knew it, and so did the publick, but he would not submit to the disgrace. Althorp somewhat earnestly, the Chancellor more faintly, urged the necessity of creating several, but both acknowledged that the number required could not yet be distinctly calculated and all agreed that there were some hopes of a declaration which would throw light on the state of our numbers, either publickly upon the petition to be presented to morrow against reform by Duke of Rutland,[80] or in private from Harrowby and Wharncliffe, from whom Grey is to exact more explicit declarations.

23d. Febry. Thursday. Lord Roden[81] at Lord Grey's request postponed his petition and speech on the discontinuance of Kildare Street Society Grant till Monday, on account of Lord Plunkett's absence who has lost his Sister, and whose conduct upon an affair of patronage formed a subject of unpleasant discussion this very night in the Commons.[82] The Duke of Rutland presented a petition from Cambridgeshire, which he represented much more adverse to reform than the words of it imputed and argued as a proof of reaction in good or rather in better set terms than has been usual with his Grace. We all expected Lord Harrowby or some of the halfconverted Reformers to seize this excellent opportunity of disclaiming all intention of resisting the Reform generally or the 2d. reading of our bill in particular. Wharncliffe, Harrowby, and Haddington were in close consultation, and I am assured that Harrowby intended to speak but was deterred by Kenyon's getting possession of the house and moving some other matter.

24 Febry. Friday. I did not go to the Drawing room and escaped the fatigue and the fog. Both Lord Wharncliffe and Charles Greville successively were anxious to vindicate to me a passage in Lord Harrowby's letter. The date, which was the 27th. of January, certainly exonerated him of the suspicion of holding disingenuous or inconsistent language in it after he had seen Lord Grey. The topicks were in truth, though not complimentary or friendly to Lord Grey's government, very fair and well selected for the purpose of prevailing upon Lord Talbot[83] (to whom it was written) or others of his colour in politicks to vote for the 2d. reading. On the other and the main question, the strength they could bring in the Lords, they were far less satisfactory, though Lord Wharncliffe was very confident. On going over a list which had been made out by the Clerks at the table and comparing it with my own, I was inclined to take a more gloomy view of our prospects, *without new peers,* than ever, and wrote to Grey to warn him of it.

Saturday 25th. February. Saw Sir Herbert Taylor and had a long audience of the King. The former spoke to me in a most open and friendly manner of our prospects in the house, told me confidentially that his brother in law[84] would vote for the 2d. reading, but admitted that delay in declaring themselves and other parts of the conduct of those who professed some inclination to vote were, if not suspicious, at least ominous and unsatisfactory. He concerted with me an answer to the treasury about the lease of the estate of the Duchy of Cornwall in the Scilly Islands and promised me to forward Mr Palgrave's and Captain Marshal's application for the Guelph.[85] The King very gracious and communicative, seemed to me not to shrink the least from the notion of creating peers if necessary and listened to the prognostics I dwelt upon of such a step becoming necessary. He told me Glasgow[86] would not vote, nor the Bishop of Hereford,[87] but seemed to think Lord Mayo[88] would. 'He is' said he 'a d——d blockhead. He comes to solicit things from me and I always say "how can you My Dear Lord be such a damned fool as to suppose that I can *have the face* to ask Lord Grey for any thing for you or your friends when you vote against his Government." I have said so above once but I can do no more'. He spoke well of foreign affairs, held up his hands and eyes at the King of Holland's obstinacy and observed the Dutch would find him out soon and the ratifications must come. He praised most of the Ministers in the Conference, Bulow and Talleyrand in particular, and seemed more aware than usual of the extreme importance and value of good understanding as well as peace with *France.* On the Scilly island Lease he was reasonable and proper.

He inveighed against the Saints especially in Ireland and said that the enormous revenues of the Church could not be preserved but by sacrificing some of it to other purposes, and especially to the payment of the Roman Catholic Clergy. He told me that young Sinclair[89] corresponded with him on this subject, but though otherwise sensible, he was both a Saint and a fool on the question of paying the Priests and, advantageous as it was to hear what all parties said on such matters, he could not approve of his notions. Ireland however and the Irish was a strange chapter and a strange people, but he had not expected Preaching and fanaticism to break out there.

He talked but little of Jamaica.

26 February Sunday. There was no Cabinet and I missed seeing Lord Grey. Lord Carlisle in the gout authorized me to give his opinion in favor of making peers and, in expressing his regret, to disclaim any surprize at the necessity of doing so, which he had long foreseen. Lord Mulgrave, who has been offered the Government of Jamaica, is a little scared at state of that Island and the instructions which have been sent out. Lord Belmore[90] has been instructed to call an extraordinary meeting of the assembly to propose *without modification or delay* the obnoxious orders in Council for their adoption. [*In the margin:* This was incorrect.] These dispatches he must have received soon after the insurrection, and to complicate the whole matter yet more, the recall of Lord Belmore was sent out a few days or a few hours before the account of the insurrection arrived in London. Lord Mulgrave wishes for time to look about him on his first arrival and leans to an opinion held by Lord Seaford and myself that operations of all sort—orders in council, vindictive or rewarding duties, and what not—should be suspended till the new Governor should try to negociate some arrangement with the Planters, to which their present distress may induce them to listen, and the alarm created by the insurrection *herein* render the Saints less averse than hitherto. [*In the margin:* I hear Foxwell Buxton is so already.] Lord Chancellor objects or at least demurs to this proposal and for some reason or other seems to discourage Mulgrave from accepting the situation.

27 February. Spent my morning in making out lists of House of Lords—very perplexing they are. If no peers are created, the division of 2d. reading will be fearfully close, and if the defection on our resorting to that measure be not (as I suspect it is) grossly exaggerated, it is difficult to ascertain and not very easy to make the number necessary for that purpose.

A very long, virulent, and most irregular debate in the Lords on Non Intervention, tythes prosecutions, silk gown to OConnel and what not, in which Wellington assumed a high tone, and Eldon attacked Bishop Maltby for an imprudent letter published in newspapers which styled the majority of the Lords an ignorant faction and glanced at a large creation of peers as the only constitutional method of repressing it. Lord Melbourne and Lord Grey answered Wellington, and Lord Plunkett, Eldon, very successfully, and the Bishop of Chichester vindicated himself with temper, modesty, judgement, and address, considering the original and almost indefensible imprudence of his letter. The Converts, if Converts they be, the Harrowbites as they are called, held aloof and said nothing, and the Irish Orangemen, especially Roden and Lorton who are fanaticks, were virulent in the extreme. Lord Gosford[91] in a spirited vindication of himself did us much service and in general the tone of the opposition, tho' cheering and animating to their partizans, was more likely to exasperate and estrange the publick out of doors both in England and Ireland than to strengthen them within the House. Such undisguised appetite for coercive Laws at home and war abroad must surely displease.

28 Febry. Tuesday. Lord Roden in a long, violent, yet canting speech on presenting a petition arraigned Ministers for witholding the grant of *£25,000* from the Kildare society and substituting a plan of National Education, in which the Bible should not be read in the schoolhours, destined to the joint instruction of Catholick and Protestant Children.[92] Lord Plunket stated the real case and vindicated the conduct of Ministers admirably. And though the Archbishop of Armagh, who stammered through a speech ill gotten by heart endeavoured to maintain the exaggerated objections of Lord Roden—as if the permission to educate Roman Catholicks and Protestants together without reading the Bible amounted to a prohibition of its being read by either and a general surrender of the Protestant principle—all who followed in debate, and the Duke of Wellington especially, felt themselves compelled to admit that the new plan was nothing but a fresh endeavour to accomplish a purpose long deemed desirable by Parliament and persons of acknowledged piety and patriotism, and to confine their objection to the practicability of the measure and not to question even the principle, much less the motive and intention with which the new institution was proposed. The Bishop of London did in fact take this ground. He acquitted the projectors of the scheme of any love of innovation, acknowledged that they were striving to execute what had been often recommended, but doubted of the practicability of uniting Catholicks in any plan of education in which Protestants could concur, without a *practical* surrender of some principles essential to all Protestant education. His view of the subject was not irrational, and his language was courteous and even complimentary to the government, but yet the manner, the reason, and the effect of it were far from inspiring much confidence or cordiality or efficacy of his promised support of the reform bill. The political feeling which pervaded it was that of courting and propitiating both the Tories and the Saints, rather than the Whig and Ministerial reformers. None of the other Orangemen or Saints supported Roden—even Lord Lorton slid out of the house and the discussion was advantageous to the Government.

Wednesday 29. Gout prevented my attending the Levee. Lord Londonderry, imitating and outdoing the Duke of Wellington, read aloud to the King a petition against the Reform bill and the reforming administration. The King, receiving and throwing aside with manifest contempt the petition, said 'very *young* counsellors! My Lord' and turned on his heel.

After dinner I went to a Cabinet at Mr C Grant's with the Chancellor. I had a notion that the great question whether we should create peers or run the hazard of the division on the 2d. reading in the Lords would be determined. Nothing was said upon it, but in truth every subject we started ended in a remark that proved the expediency if not necessity of that measure, namely that we had no hold upon the majority of the House of Lords and that they were able and likely to impede all publick business from hostility to the Government, who had brought in a reform too popular in the country to be directly and successfully resisted. The West Indians press for a Committee, to enquire into the state and condition of the Slaves in the West Indies, in the House of Lords, with a view to repel the many imputations of cruelty cast on their body. To this course of proceeding there are many and weighty objections, and various and even opposite feelings on the subject concur in taking exceptions to it. I question for one the prudence of submitting matters which can be much more soundly considered and more effectually acted upon by an enlightened Executive Government so decidedly and avowedly to the cognizance of the British parliament, whose jurisdiction over them, to say the least, is likely to be disputed and is technically disputable. And tho' some exaggerations of the evils of Slavery and the cruelty of the masters and drivers have no doubt been industriously circulated, I am far from believing that the truth of the case will so entirely refute those allegations as many West Indians fondly imagine. Sure I am that a few insulated instances of barbarous severity and injustice (of which there must needs be many) will be quite sufficient to stamp on the whole system the character of cruelty, in a publick predisposed to receive such impressions, at this moment. Many think that after Parliament has adopted resolutions, and orders in council grounded on those resolutions have been sent out to the West Indies, it would be an indecorous relinquishment of its own acts and an unnecessary investigation of the facts on which one has already proceeded to admit of or establish any enquiry. And Brougham vehemently protests against the measure because he sees in it a triumph of the West Indians, who solicit, over the Saints, who deprecate, it. He is afraid the latter will suspect him of abandoning the cause he has for years instigated and prevailed upon them so warmly to espouse. It is clear that all thse considerations would naturally overrule the only consideration that had weight in the opposite scale with the Cabinet, viz some compassion for the losses and for the unjust unpopularity of the West Indians. But there comes the objection. Does the determination depend entirely on our discretion? Are we sure of rejecting a motion for enquiry if it should be made by a peer unconnected with or hostile to Ministry? And we were compelled to acknowledge the painful truth that we have not strength enough in that house to command a majority on such a question!

Again, on the tythe question we are similarly circumstanced or indeed yet more perplexed. The Commons will not pass the Clergy relief bill unless thay have a pledge that the bill for Commutation and extinction of Tythe be also passed,[93] and nothing short of a resolution to that effect in the Lords will they consider as security. But the Lords it is obvious *like* the relief bill but do *not much relish* the Commutation; and it is doubtful, whether from sincere dislike of the measure or from a desire of embarrassing Ministers whom they dislike still more, they will not decline all concurrence in such a resolution or alter it so as to render it unpalatable to the Commons, and involve us in inextricable difficulties in accomplishing our twofold measure. Is it possible to conduct the Government with a house of Lords so ill disposed to assist us? And are we not called upon, both by the publick voice and by the legitimate object of reconciling the two houses, to mould it to our purposes by an infusion of friendly members?

Lord Goderich stated at length and with perspicuity the dates and purport of the different instructions to Lord Belmore, and the possible situation in which the island might be placed by his execution or by his postponement of the orders he must have received soon after the insurrection, namely to convoke the assembly and to propose in a peremptory manner the orders in council, and afterwards the dispatch to recall him. It was determined to send a proclamation, which Goderich read and which, with some amendations rendering it less offensive to the local legislature, was approved of, and to authorize him to postpone yet further the submission of the orders in council to the Assembly if he had, as is probable, already taken upon himself to defer that part of his instructions.[94] In general Goderich seemed earnest and agitated on this perplexing affair, but more anxious I thought to frame instructions and dispatches, which if produced in publick would vindicate retrospectively his conduct in office, than to devize a clear line of policy and engage in it promptly and decisively, which is surely that which the occasion requires. Such however is too often the effect on orders for foreign, distant, or contingent events in a representative government. So true is the observation of Machiavel that even the <d>earest and greatest advantages are in human and political affairs never to be attained or in truth unaccompanied with correspondent evils. Non si puo <. . .>are lo conveniente senza il inconviente.

Thursday 1 March. In bed wih the gout. Saw Mulgrave, who is very irresolute about Jamaica because others, he thinks, are irresolute about the instructions and powers to be given to him. Lord Dover went over the list of the Lords with me. There are some additions to those who vote for, and some diminutions from absence and unwillingness of those who vote against. There is in short quite [a] shew of probable success sufficient to furnish the adversaries of the measure of creating peers with strong arguments against its necessity, but not sufficient to render the relinquishment of it either safe or prudent.

Friday 2 March. Still confined with the gout and thereby prevented from attending the Lords, where Lord Londonderry, by his outrageous and almost ungentlemanlike breach of courtesy and order and propriety, drew down upon himself the displeasure of the house and one of the severest chastizements ever inflicted on presumption, ignorance, and <illmanners> from Lord Plunkett. Lord Londonderry made an awkward half apology for his breach of order and the House, who would have been embarrassed in following up censure by imprisonment, goodhumouredly and prudently agreed to be satisfied with it.[95]

Saturday 3d. March. Dined with the Duchess of Kent at Kensington. The Princess Victoria dined at table. She is a healthy, well behaved, and observant little girl, has much natural modesty and propriety in her manner, and without beauty bears great resemblance to her fathers family, without the defects of white eyelashes or unsteady eyes. My daughter in law assures me that the King does *not* like the notion of a large creation of Peers.

Sunday 4 March. At a Cabinet at foreign office where, after settling the words of the intended resolutions on tythes and dispatching one or two other matters of minor importance, Lord Grey opened to us the question of creating peers, persisting, more than I could have wished and more in truth than I expected, in his strong repugnance to the measure, and stating the prospects of succeeding without any fresh creation, in the second reading, more positively perhaps than the vague assurances of support through third persons can warrant. He read us a letter from Goderich, who was confined by illness, in which he leans to the opinion that the necessity for creating peers is not actually proved and that there is sufficient prospect of success on the 2d. reading to justify the postponement of that measure. Lord Carlisle has authorized me to say that, though he should have wished to avert the necessity of making peers, he had long foreseen it could arise and had made up his mind to it, and from the best consideration he could give the subject and the report of the lists, he thought that time had arrived. We then went thro' the lists, canvassed names, discussed rumours, and heard calculations on the numbers. The certainty of a majority of at least 5 and probably 12 was strongly insisted upon and the measure of making peers argued to be unnecessary as well as objectionable by Duke of Richmond and Lord Palmerston. Many exceptions to the list and still more to the certainty annexed to it as proving a Majority on the second reading were taken by Althorp, myself, Lord John and Sir James Graham, and Brougham urged with much force the little reliance to be placed either in the intentions or power of these new accessions. Althorp pressed the indispensible necessity of either making peers or exacting from the new converts on second reading a pledge of the extent of alterations they would propose in the Committee, and the propriety of a clear understanding on what points we should, if beaten, be disposed to recommend a Creation of Peers. In this Lansdowne and Palmerston seemed to me to acquiesce. All contemplated the possibility and some the probability of our being ultimately compelled to resort to the measure and, though some more and some less fervently deprecated the necessity, none, not even the Duke of Richmond, denied that in certain cases we might and ought to resort to it. Sir J Graham with great earnestness and perspicuity shewed that if it was to be done or if here was even a chance of our being compelled ultimately to resort to it, it would be much less offensive to the Lords, more gratifying to the publick, and advantageous to Ministry to do it now, when the King permitted and the Country called for it, when it was done to secure the principle of the bill and to rescue the Lords themselves from the consequences of a second rejection. Though no dishonourable motives or conduct were attributed to Lord Harrowby, the language of his letter was argued by myself and others to be an indication of the temper and design with which the support of such hollow and hazardous auxiliaries was offered us. They offered to help us over the stile because, as they acknowledged, we could be more easily dispatched on the other side of the hedge—a motive which might justify such avowed enemies of the bill and the Ministry to lend their help but would render it very silly indeed in us to accept it. Althorp told me that Lord Spencer was earnest for the creation of peers and, when it was said that it would be a violent measure, replied, 'If no violent measure was required by the times, you should not have dissolved Parliament, nay, you should not have proposed such a bill'. The discussion alas! ended in no resolution except that Lord Grey should rather dissuade Lord Harrowby (who had consulted him) from making any declaration tomorrow, inasmuch as an avowal and explanation of his letter, which could scarcely be avoided would lead to much animadversion in the commons, the declaration would give us no certainty as to Numbers and, if made at our suggestion, it might imply an engagement on our part, which we were far from being secure enough to contract.

After these discussions I urged Palmerston in private to send some one to Paris during Lord Granville's absence, and half in joke half in earnest attacked him for opposing an immediate creation of peers which would be ultimately necessary, when he knew that nothing would so effectively strengthen our authority and influence in all the Continental Courts, where they were speculating on our defeat and dismissal and consequent adoption of other and opposite principles of foreign policy in the British Cabinet. To Melbourne and Lord Lansdowne I urged the manifest necessity, sooner or later, gradually or at once, of assimilating the temper of the Lords to that of the Commons and the Community by a fresh infusion of persons of liberal and popular opinions, and I combated, with all the ingenuity I could muster, the notion of the violence and unconstitutional character of such a proceeding. These two original enemies of the measure listened, and I was pleased by observing that the minds of both had been somewhat familiarized and softened by time to a scheme from which at first they revolted. Lord Lansdown, as I brought him home, very sensibly shewed that we had delayed our measure too long, that an indication of power, 'a demonstration', some weeks ago might have rendered any further creation unnecessary, but that now we should have the air of restoring to it precisely at the moment when we had apparent reasons at least to convince us it was unnecessary. I agreed it would have been better some time ago, but I said it would be better now than hereafter, and better hereafter than not at all—and so I think. Durham spoke litle but temperately and to the purpose and so did Mr Grant.

5 March 1832. Heard from Grey at House of Lords with great concern that the French had entered Ancona by force, taken the governor and the Papal troops prisoner and garrisoned the place. The report adds what is still worse, that that part of the expedition came from Algiers [*In the margin:* This I hope and believe is not true.] which would imply premeditation and combined movement and would be inconsistent at least with the spirit of all the assurances we have received about the armament at Toulon. However we have received assurances from Perier since the arrival of the intelligence, that the officer had not only exceeded, but acted in direct violation of, his instructions; and Talleyrand, on first hearing of it, hurried to Lord Palmerston and boldly and judiciously urged him to remonstrate, to urge the disavowal of the officer and the evacuation of the town without delay, but at the same time to dispatch a courier to Vienna to express the conviction of the English Government that the orders had been exceeded and that the French would evacuate Ancona, and to engage that they should do so by a settled day, provided the Austrians would continue to cooperate with them and the French in insisting yet more peremptorily than ever on the improvements in the civil administration which the Pope had already promised and which the three powers had agreed to recommend.[96]

Lord Londonderry, in a subdued tone but with his usual malignity and without other information than a newspaper, rose to ask Lord Ponsonby and Lord Grey if sundry libels he had seen in print against the former were true. The former Lord, who spoke for the first time, repelled the assertion of the foreign journal, gave it and through it Lord Londonderry a direct and unqualified contradiction, and appealed to his employers for his character and conduct to his justification, and spoke with proper indifference and scorn about the opinion of Lord Londonderry himself. His speech was a parliamentary method of giving a Man the lie and shewing him that you defied and despised his malice, though you deemed it to be great. Lord L rose immediately after it to express his satisfaction, satisfaction at the lie having been given to charges which he had thought sufficient to bring forward and even to sanction, and expressed much regard and even confidence as well as private friendship for Lord Ponsonby.

I met Talleyrand at Lansdown House at dinner and learnt from him that Palmerston had taken his advice and that he (Palmerston) would send or had sent, this very night, dispatches to France and Vienna, exactly in the spirit he had proposed, engaging France to disavow and evacuate Ancona as soon as possible, and promising Vienna that she should do so, but not abandoning on that account the amicable instances we are making conjointly to the Pope to improve the administration of his provinces and of Bologna and the legations in particular. This is however a troublesome and *untoward* incident; and the spirit of Metternicks conversation on Belgium and the ratification is far from satisfactory. It is not such as promises much forbearance or reasonable moderation on the receipt of this awkward news from Ancona, nor is it in itself judicious or agreable to England or France.

6 March 1832. I called on Lord Palmerston and was glad to find he harboured no suspicion and felt little discontent at the Conduct of the French Government about Ancona and was more sanguine about bringing the matter to an amicable issue without collision between Austria and France than from Grey's statement I had feared. He had written to Lord Granville to urge Casimir Perrier to make a prompt disavowal of the officer and to give us assurances that he did not mean to keep forcible possession of Ancona but would evacuate it immediately in certain contingencies which Austria as well as we should approve. At the same time He had forwarded under flying <sail> to Lord Granville dispatches to Lamb at Vienna, instructing him to communicate and in some sense to answer for the sincerity of the French assurances and promises, and to express the conviction of our Government that the expedition had not been undertaken with any design of taking forcible much less permanent possession of that port. I suggested to Lord Palmerston, who had consulted me upon that point, that Sir Arthur Paget[97] was the *Ex Diplomat* of rank best qualified by talents and character to supply Granville's place during his absence on the Committee, and perhaps the one most likely to accept it without ulterior views.

This suggestion was approved of by Lord Grey, whom I visited in the evening and found engaged in deep and somewhat warm dispute with Lord Durham, before the Ladies of his family, on the merits of Lord Harrowby's letter, the prospects of passing the 2d. reading and the subsequent stages of the bill without any creation of peers, and the policy or necessity of resorting to that step. Lord Grey with Lord Lansdown present had had an interview in the morning with

Lords Harrowby and Wharncliffe, and the latter had been more explicit than hitherto as to the force they could bring in support of the 2d. reading, the main parts of the bill which they should be disposed to submit to in the Committee, and the latitude of creating peers, without breach of honour exprest or implied, which would be left us after their support. They seemed to have satisfied Lord Grey of the Majority. He repeated again and again his confidence that it would not be less than 20. It was obviously the inclination amounting almost to the determination of Lord Grey's mind not to create peers before the second reading. The two Lords (Grey added) would leave the Schedules A and B untouched, had no disposition to meddle with any principle involved in the Enfranchisement of Boroughs and towns, and would only suggest an alteration from the value of the rate as the criterion of a qualification to vote. To the clause of the Metropolitan districts they expressed great hostility, and I was sorry to hear Grey, without denying the reasonableness of extending the right of voting to these districts, allow that for such an object only, he would not and could not propose that Peers should be made. Indeed his rooted aversion to that necessary and useful expedient broke out more forcibly when he was goaded by Durham, than I had ever hitherto known. He bitterly lamented that he had undertaken a task in the government of this Country for which he was too old and quite unfit; acknowledged that had he forseen that such a measure as making 60 Peers, which he termed *an act of violence unparalleled in our history and equivalent to a Destruction of the House of Lords,* could have been contemplated, he would never had proposed the Reform bill; and with great earnestness declared that he wished any one of his Colleagues would take his place and free him from a responsibility which overwhelmed him—that he would gladly support him. All was left to *him.* He was almost unassisted in the House. He knew not how to go thro' it. He told us he had stickled for the right of making peers if the bill should be carried by a bare and narrow majority on the 2d. reading, and though he acquitted Harrowby of the duplicity and rooted enmity of which Lord Durham accused him, he acknowledged that he was adverse to our whole system of policy and very disagreable to deal with in negotiation or council. He still dwelt on 7 or 8 friendly peers who would desert us if peers were made, but he named but two. Suffolk and Segrave (neither of whom would, I suspect, execute their threat),[98] and he harped upon the old string that even 60 would not necessarily and certainly secure our bill. I told him partly in discussion and partly in a more private way that if he decided to make no peers, *I should bow to his decision and should strive* (no doubt with success) to reconcile myself to it, for I thought any thing like separation or division of the Ministry was the last of evils to the country till the bill was passed. Though till that decision was made, I should continue to press my earnest conviction that it ought in prudence and sense to be in the affirmative. I added to him privately that I thought the Cabinet should as a preliminary agree not to separate and how to come to some determination to which all should submit, that I should argue against him but vote for him whichever way he decided, but that he should on all policy settle with the Chancellor and Althorp what should be their course, and that on that they 3 should agree, before the opinion of the Cabinet was formally asked. On my mentioning that Althorp's being called up for the

Committee was frequently suggested as a convenient step, he said it would give great umbrage in the Lords, for I could not conceive what a notion there was that Althorp was a republican, and how much some people especially in the House of Lords dreaded him. Durham both in his sarcasms and arguments was I thought very powerful, and his feelings at the opportunity afforded, and as he contended likely to be neglected, of 'sweeping the tories from the face of the earth' (an expression used in Harrowby's letter to Lord Talbot) were those of a zealous, consistent, and wise party Man; but his way of expressing them was as usual harsh, scornful, and repulsive to Grey and the latter, though depressed and nettled at the perplexities surrounding him, bore all he said with admirable temper and treated him with a tenderness and delicacy that ought to soften him and bend him to something like compliance or accommodation. I agree with Durham and I differ with Grey in their respective views of this embarrassing question, but as to their manner and character: Malo cum hoc errare quam cum isto bene sapere.

7 March 1832 Wednesday. A Cabinet dinner at Duke of Richmond's. None of the House of Commons (except Lord John Russell for half an hour) present. Some conversation on the ensuing motion upon tythes and Lord Lansdowne read the resolutions he intended to move. The Chancellor suggested the propriety of Government bringing in a bill for the abolition of capital punishment in cases of forgery, which would otherwise be forced upon them. It was observed that the majority against it in Lords was very great two years ago,[99] but we were all favorable to the measure and some as well as myself earnest it should be brought in, but nothing was determined. Grey than asked Lansdown to state what passed between them and Lords Harrowby and Wharncliffe, and on Lansdowne declining, began himself by saying that he thought they had proved the certainty of passing the second reading, afforded good hopes of making no alteration in the Committee that would affect the principle of the bill, and in short convinced him that there did not exist that necessity which could alone have reconciled him to such a creation of peers as would alone have secured the measure. Brougham and myself and Lord Goderich questioned him a little about names and particulars, and he was proceeding to answer our questions and to state the additional reserve he had made, in which Wharncliffe distinctly and Harrowby more reluctantly had aquiesced—viz that in the case of a bare majority on 2d. reading, he might, without forfeiting their support in subsequent stages, make some peers to be useful in Committee—when Durham, who knew the statement before, began to throw in some observations. 'Pray listen My Dear Lambton one moment' said Grey interrupting him. 'I thought' rejoined Lambton, disdainfully, 'I might remark on what Harrowby said, but very well I will not say another word', and sat looking black and sullen for three minutes, than [*sic*] rose and rang the bell and asked if his carriage was there; on hearing it was not, bade the servant apprize him when it came, and sat in sulky and dignified silence while we all attempted to start subjects on the details of the bill likely to engage his attention, till the carriage was announced and he, declining Richmond's offer of Coffee and tea, marched out of the room and drove off. Grey was manifestly hurt and distressed, and it added much to the depression of spirits under which he was labouring. I am afraid Lord

Durham's reproaches hurt much more than convince, and act like the taunting, insolent, and menacing paragraphs in the times [*Times*] to confirm rather than shake his aversion to the measure of creating Peers.

We talked the matter over. The Chancellor argued sensibly but not vehemently on the peril to which we were exposed and it was clear that, with the exception of the Duke of Richmond, none in the Cabinet would resist or even struggle against the Creation if Grey did not himself revolt from it. It is clear he will *not* create peers and I hope it is nearly as much so that we shall carry the 2d. reading without them. I lament the decision, but if taken by Grey, shall do my best to reconcile myself and others to it, not only from affection and devotion to him, which would and ought to make me and I think all connected with him in politicks do much, but from a conviction that any change in the Ministry, much more one that would endanger the Ministry itself, would be as fatal or yet more certainly fatal to the publick tranquility of the country than the rejection of the bill. The resignation of a single Member of the Cabinet may lead to the result and for that reason the abrupt departure of Durham alarmed as well as disgusted me. Yet his views are just, his remarks keen and penetrating, and his arguments convincing.

8 March Thursday. Went to Court. Had some conversation with Althorp, who thinks that he risks his publick character if he remains in without peers being made and makes the sacrifice of running the chance of the 2d. reading from deep devotion to Lord Grey and a persuasion, like my own, that resignation now is fatal to Lord Grey's Ministry, and the downfall of his Ministry, fatal to the Country. Althorp spoke with great emotion and great good sense. He distrusts the majority more than I do. And he says clear reserves must be made with them and the King about the right of making peers in the Committee, and he considers any amendment in the qualification clause nearly equal in danger to a rejection of some principle in the bill. Lord John Russell said he was struck with my having said that the majority was literally certain and wished I would go over the list with Duncannon.

In the House of Lords Lord Lansdown in a judicious and luminous speech moved the resolutions on tythes. They were nearly verbatim the report. Borne down by the weight of authority, namely a Committee of which Bishops, and that lay Prelate, Lord Harrowby, as well as Rosslyn and others formed a part, the Tories were compelled to acquiesce in the vote and to confine their opposition to captious criticisms on the words of the resolution, to invectives against our delay in resorting to measures to repress violence, and to taunts on our pledging the house to measures of which we could state neither the details nor the outline with any precision or certainty. The most remarkable incidents in the debate were the sneers of the Duke of Wellington and the invective of Eldon against the Bishops for abandoning and betraying the interests of the Church—an indignation probably quickened by the well founded rumour that many of them would support the Reform bill. The imputation was repelled with some spirit by the Archbishop of Canterbury, and the Bishop of London delivered a very sensible, judicious, and manly speech in which, tho' he disclaimed all servility or indeed connexion with Ministers, he manfully defended the expediency and justice of such commutation of tythes as the report and resolutions printed and as he believed the Government intended to recommend. Talleyrand tells me that Appony,[100] Granville, and Casimir Perrier are likely to come to an amicable understanding on the Ancona affair, and augurs a good result from Count Orloffs[101] language at the Hague, so much so that he even says he shall not be surprized if Russia after all entraine les autres dan [*sic*] les ratifications.

9 March 1832 Friday. Convinced much to my regret that Lord Grey's aversion to creating peers before the 2d. reading is insuperable, I endeavoured as well as I could, and not I think without success, to prevail on some of our eager and earnest friends not to condemn too hastily his resolution, or as they would term it, his irresolution, and to reflect that the Non Creation of Peers may be hazardous, but a separation of the Ministry or defection from the leaders of the cause of reform would at this moment be the certain and instant ruin of that cause—would lead either to the total discomfiture of the whole system and [?or] to the success of it by the means which we were labouring to prevent, convulsion and revolution.

Lord Strangford in House of Lords made a speech for an enquiry into the state of glove trade, <founded> on the distress of some classes engaged in that manufacture, which, if not very factious and malignant in its intention, was very foolish and ignorant and which, in either hypothesis, was very inefficient and replete with bad taste as well as bad logick. He was very satisfactorily refuted by a plain statement from Lord Auckland, and Lord Ellenborough and the Duke of Wellington, who somewhat factiously and very feebly supported a motion they manifestly disapproved, were well answered by Lord Clanrickarde and Lord Grey. Many Bishops, and among them two or three on whom we are called upon to depend for the Reform bill, voted against us, and we rejected the unreasonable request by a narrow majority of 41 to 33.[102] This was in some measure owing to negligence in summoning an attendance, and not much to be lamented if, as Auckland imagines, the fear of any resumption of our prohibitive system may contribute to induce the French, already half inclined, to abandon theirs which, though much more injurious to themselves than to us, nevertheless impede the good effects of our more liberal system.

10 March Saturday. Lord Mulgrave, who has accepted Jamaica, is not much pleased with the spirit and still less with the manner in which Lord Howick exercises his ascendancy over Lord Goderich. Lord Lansdown is disposed to regret that no Peers were made at Christmas and that any negotiat<ion> was resorted to with the Harrowbites, and to think that we must be prepared to create what may be necessary in the Committee, and to prorogue and create if the bill be rejected on 2d. reading. He justly observes that he has less repugnance and Grey more to the measure of carrying the bill by a large creation than they respectively had when the question was first started.

11 March Sunday. A Cabinet at foreign office. Lord Goderich has been applied to by Mr Burge in the name of the West Indians to reinforce Jamaica and, though neither Sir Wby. Cotton,[103] Lord Belmore, nor Lord Hill ask for greater force there, it was agreed that a Regiment should be sent from Bermudas, but the Assembly in Jamaica called upon to fulfill their engagements and provide better quarters for our troops than they have hitherto done. The orders of Council are better received in Trinidad than elsewhere, and in Demarara with good management and some modifications it is thought our projected improvements may be accepted. Lord Goderich means to recall the Governor of the Mauritius[104] and consulted the Cabinet whether it should be offered to Sir Henry Hardinge.[105] Lord Fitzroy Somerset,[106] if he would go, was preferred, as it is impossible that the Duke of Wellington's influence should not be exerted or at the least suspected as long as he remains at the Horse Guards.

Bad news from Ireland. The Grand Jury found the bills presented against three Catholicks who were wounded in a fray, and ignored those against the Protestants who shot them, while on the other hand the petty Jury acquit on the suspicious grounds of an alibi the murderer of a tythe collector, fully proved to be a premeditated crime.

Lord Grey then resumed the endless question of making peers. He seemed confident of a majority on second reading, went over some of the names, expressed his conviction that if amendments were made in the Committee which appeared to him materially injurious to the bill, he should find the King willing to make peers to replace the original clauses, but at the same time had distinct authority to do so only in the case of changes affecting the three great principles of the bill—disfranchisement of nomination boroughs, enfranchisement of populous towns, and the qualification of voters for £10 houses. He avowed that he could not bring himself to propose a larger creation of peers for two plain reasons: *first,* he was not persuaded that such a step was indispensably necessary but, on the contrary, harboured confident hopes that the bill might be passed without it; 2ndly., he was far from satisfied that the measure of creating peers to the number of 40–50 or even 60 peers might not endanger the bill rather than ensure it, for he was apprehensive that all the new converts and possibly some of our old supporters would fall off or change sides. A conversation ensued on the degree of certainty which the assurances we have received conveyed of reading the bill a second time, in which Lord Chancellor and Lord John Russell expressed great distrust and Lord Althorp and myself stated that we thought it far from satisfactory. Lord John suggested the propriety of an actual written declaration from the new converts or at least a direct personal assurance from each to Lord Grey, and not through those whose general hostility to the principle of this reform bill was known; and Lord Althorp urged somewhat earnestly a previous understanding on those points in Committee which we should deem of sufficient importance to be protected, and reestablished, if disturbed, by a creation of Peers; and the Lord Chancellor recommended full preparation, by correspondence with the individuals, for the immediate accession of 50 or 60 to House of Lords. The difficulties, impracticability, hazard, and insufficiency of declarations from the Harrowbites other than Harrowby and Wharncliffe themselves was adverted to, and the no less difficulty of anticipating the value, nature, or affair of each particular case <even of detail> was very justly urged by Palmerston. With respect to Lord Brougham's suggestion it was thought by some not without reason that it would excite hopes, provoke animosities, and give scandal, and might subject us to some of the defections and half the odium the measure itself would expose us to, without securing the prize to be obtained by it. Lord Lansdowne was disposed and even earnest to secure from the King distinctly the power of making peers in the Committee, was inclined to *fear* that such a measure would sooner or later be necessary, thought however that we stood in need of greater bitterness and hostility to us and to reform to justify us for resorting to it *now*, but seemed, even in the event of a small majority in our favor on second reading, to acquiesce in and almost to press the creation of a few peers. Richmond looked rather disconcerted at these more than admissions from one with whom he had expected to agree, and the conversation like so many others seemed to lead to no practical conclusion, when Durham, somewhat <solemn>ly but less offensively than he had <implied> his intention before moved 3 resolutions: the first declaring that the certainty of success on the second reading was far from satisfactory; the second that the persons on whom we depended for that stage openly avowed their intention to oppose us in the Committee; and thirdly that it was necessary and expedient *now* to create peers sufficient to assure the Government the passing of the bill. We all declared we could not vote for these resolutions because, if Lord Grey was convinced that we should succeed on a 2d. reading, we were unwilling to harrass or endanger his Government by any obnoxious proposal; but many of us and among them myself gave to our vote the character of a previous question and openly acknowledged that we should prefer the measure of an immediate creation, were far from satisfied with the effect going into a Committee without a majority of tried friends might produce, and were yet further from apprehending that the Creation would lose us so many votes as some of our Colleagues supposed. None but Durham voted for the resolutions. Lord Brougham said that in justice to Lord Grey those who concurred in his reluctance to make peers should say so, and Lord Melbourne avowed that he should have some scruple in annexing the signet to the warrant of creating any large number of peers before the 2d. reading—a sentiment in which Palmerston and the Duke of Richmond, but nobody else, concurred. Graham gave his vote and opinion in this Cabinet with great distinctness and some solemnity. He agreed nearly with the resolutions of Lord Durham, but if he voted with them should feel, were they not acted upon, called upon perhaps to tender his resignation. The resignation even of one of the Cabinet would be the dissolution of the Ministry, and that dissolution being fully equivalent to the rejection of the bill in disastrous consequences, he was unwilling to be responsible for them. He acquiesced therefore in Lord Grey's decision and so did I, hoping that we should come to an understanding to leave the discretion of making peers in the Committee entirely to him and that he might be at liberty to secure the progress of the bill after the second reading whenever he thought fit by recommending the creation of peers to any number he deemed <meet>, without further deliberation or reference to the Cabinet. This was not so well received as I hoped. Duke of Richmond deprecated pledges and the others were too much fatigued with the discussion to say much. Goderich ended the day with an exhortation, somewhat tardy and useless, to keep our councils and determination of this perplexing question very secret. He agreed however that we should speak confidently of passing the bill, *without* any creation if possible, *with* a creation if necessary.

12th. March Monday. In Lords Lord Eldon vindicated himself from what he called an aspersion cast upon him by Mr Spring Rice[107] in the House of Commons, that he had given a prodigious number of lucrative places to his son[108] in his first elevation to the seals; he told the House that he had been prevailed upon against his inclination to take the seals, that he had for many years resisted G[eorge] III's earnest directing to him to grant these reversions to his son, that his son had not to this hour come into possession of the two largest, and that all his predecessors in office had considered these offices as provisions for their family. He interspersed among these statements and arguments, which tho' uncalled for were no doubt true and reasonable, many protestations of his disinterestedness and many specimens of querulous egotism in which his speeches abound. Lord Clanrickarde vindicated Lord Plunkett from the charges of Lord Londonderry and Mr Dawson, from whence this degrading crimination and recrimination, defences and rejoinders, had originated, in a clear and spirited speech. The Duke of Wellington acquitted both Chancellors of any improper avidity for their family, Grey bore witness that Lord Plunkett's son was made a Dean without the solicitation of his father and upon an enquiry into his merits, and Plunkett refuted with much modesty, taste, and eloquence the catalogue of offences with which he had been charged.

13 March Tuesday. In House of Lords Lord Aberdeen, on the pretence of asking a question about the occupation of Ancona, inveighed in bitter terms against the perfidy, ambition, and injustice of the French, stigmatizing their conduct as worse than any of the Republick or of Napoleon, and maintaining that a proper resentment of such an outrage was the way to prevent, not to provoke, war. He arraigned Mr Casimir Perrier's speech[109] as unintelligible and unwarrantable, and implied that we ought to insist at the risk of war on an immediate evacuation of the town. *Lord Grey* with great temper but with great earnestness animadverted on the unfairness, the irregularity, and the pernicious tendency of <hanging> such invectives on a mere question regarding a transaction on which it was manifest the <s>eason of explanation and disclosure could not be arrived and, in declining to give any positive answer with respect to what passed, stated luminously and dexterously that the French Govt. had been almost as much surprized at their officer having exceeded its instructions as England, the Pope, or Austria could have been at the event; that the officer was recalled; that a prompt communication had been made by the French Minister to England, Austria, and Rome of the intelligence; that explanations had been required and there was every reason to believe they would prove satisfactory; and that the steps by our Government to demand explanation from the French were such as would satisfy Austria; and that there was every prospect of the whole terminating amicably, for there was no reason to suspect the French Government of any sinister design. Even Lord Aberdeen acknowledged himself satisfied. Duke of Wellington gave notice of a motion for papers founded on the necessity of reporting some part of Casimir Perrier's speech, and after some irregular conversation about an Irish Magistrate the House went into a Committee on Lord Kenyon's labouring poor bill.[110]

Wednesday 14 March. At Court. Learnt from Durham that he had written a letter to Grey, lamenting his decision not to make peers, pointing the consequences to him and his Ministry, and assuring him that, tho' from personal regard and affection and a sense of the consequences which ensue from breaking up the Government he would not be accessory to such a result, he thought from the insignificant office that he held no such consequences would ensue from his individual retirement, and should accordingly have withdrawn, but as a Member of the Cabinet whom he would not name to Lord Grey (it was Lord John Russell) had signified his intention to resign if he (Lord Durham) took that step, and as the Member he alluded to was much too prominent a person in the great business of reform to render his resignation a matter of indifference, he had with much pain determined to submit. He was manifestly much tickled with the notion of leading one of his Colleagues and in a better humour than he has lately been. I mentioned to Lord Palmerston and Lord Grey, Lord Granville's wish to be an Earl (why one of the most sensible men I know should wish for so very foolish a thing, I cannot guess) and the latter told me that had he known of it at the Coronation he should have had it, and that he would gladly seize any special opportunity for conferring it, but that as I well knew any step of the kind would open many new claims and there were more, in themselves reasonable, than he could well satisfy already.

Dinner at Palmerston, few of House of Commons Members present. It was agreed that the two Ratifying powers should decline answering any note presented by the King of Holland in conjunction with the 3 powers who had witheld their ratifications as they stood in a different condition. To enable the 3 courts to take part in any deliberation or act of France and England with respect to the relations of Belgium and Holland, they must by ratifying the treaty place themselves under the same engagements to the King of Belgium to enforce those articles. Much was said but nothing determined about any foreign politicks. The notion that Ancona will not lead to war seems to prevail, and I think our most reluctant colleagues reconcile themslves more and more to the true policy of cultivating a close union with France and preserving the peace of Europe by proving that no power in making war with France can expect England as an ally and that she will have some danger of having her for an enemy. Lord Grey at the suggestion of the King consulted us on following the pardon of Lord Dundonald by a reference of his memorial for restoration to rank to the Board of Admiralty, and after some conversation in which Durham was hot and pettish with the Duke of Richmond, it was agreed that his petition should be granted, and the consideration of any restoration to the order of the Bath postponed till the other was finally reported upon and disposed of.

Thursday 15th. March. Saw Sir Herbert Taylor and the King at St. James's. The former told me the King was more earnest than ever to get the bill passed, and the whole of his conversation convinced me that the opposition and the Duke of Wellington especially had nettled and exasperated the Court by their conduct in Parliament and their language in private, in which the King is not spared. Lord Londonderry read to H M a letter written by Duke of Wellington to Lord Strangford, in which the sacrifice of the constitution and happiness of the kingdom to the maintenance of Lord Grey's *honour* and consistency is spoken of with indignation and irony, the notion of the King not being aware of the state of the case scouted and exploded, and his degeneracy from his progenitors, if he wants firmness and spirit to rescue himself from the measures of the present Ministry, urged in very unmeasured terms and with offensive expressions. The King, thinking the reflections on Lord Grey were so personal that any publicity given to the letter might lead to unpleasant consequences, abstained from speaking of it [to] Lord Grey or any body; but allusions have been made to it, and to its communication to the King by Lord Londonderry, in the Papers, and Sir Herbert was rather anxious, he said, to apprize a friend of Lord Grey's of the circumstance and the reason why the King had never mentioned it to him. I recommended no notice of it in publick and suggested the probability of its passing unnoticed and unpublished.

The King has just seen the Archbishop of York who, he said, was an agreable man to talk to and a 'Statesman'—a conclusion he had drawn from his willingness to vote for the 2d. reading and his yet greater readiness to concur in temperate and conciliatory measures in Ireland about the Church. His Majesty is manifestly anxious and nervous about the bill and, if it be not a contradiction, I should say less averse to the creation of peers to secure it, than he says or imagines himself to be. I impressed upon his mind the dreadful consequences which would ensue on a second rejection or even a considerable mutilation of the bill,and hinted at the necessity even if the bill were passed of imposing a spirit more congenial wih the times and the House of Commons into the House of Lords, and I remarked that the accessions to that house for these last 30 years had not been from the great landed proprietors. I ventured too to suggest the inconvenience to a Govt. of too many Irish Lords in the House, for they seldom voted in a pinch for any Ministry without exacting some favor or honour as the price. These remarks I made with a view of persuading the King, if ever a batch of peers is to be made, to relax some part of the condition he has annexed of limiting them to eldest Sons and peers of Scotland and Ireland. I found both from his conversation and a subsequent examination of the lists, which he bade me revise, that some peers on whom we had reckoned had not pledged themselves as distinctly as in Cabinet they had been represented to have done.

16 March Friday. Once more perplexed myself with the lists of the Lords and sent the result of my calculations, which make the division much too near to Lord Grey. Lord Aylesbury, I was assured by King and Sir Herbert, did not pledge himself distinctly.[111]

In House of Lords Duke of Wellington read part of Casimir Perrier's speech, in which, as Wellington pretended, he declared that the French Government had promoted and supported the Belgian revolution and had protected them from the interference of other powers by threatening war. Both these propositions were, he said, incorrect. The first, if true, would attach to Louis Philip's Goverment a breach of faith, of which he believed it incapable and knew it to be innocent, for Louis Philip was as he termed it *admitted* to all the benefits of the European treaties by our recognition and was bound in duty to observe them, and any disturbance of the Kingdom of Netherlands would have been a violation of the engagement. He disclaimed with great earnestness and at some length all intention of interfering with Belgium; took credit to himself for the openness, sincerity, and cordiality with which he had constantly communicated the applications from the Dutch Government, the answers to them, and the general view of His Majesty's government on all matters connected with Belgium to France; denied that the French had ever intimated a wish or intention much less a menace of interfering. He spoke however with much more forbearance of the government and greater respect and even admiration of the people of France than Aberdeen, professed an anxiety to preserve peace with France—an acknowledgement that, next to honour, it was the one thing most necessary to the Country's welfare—but he contrived to insinuate that if France and England were to separate themselves from the other great powers, the latter would inevitably become the dupe of the former and slide as she [France] heretofore so often done into a career of aggression, interference, and aggrandizement, and he quoted the affair of Ancona as a warning to Government. He concluded a speech with some good sense, some plausible argument, a little misrepresentation, and no little cunning by moving for a long list of dispatches of August, September, and October to refute a passage on which I think he put a wrong construction in the French Ministers. Lord Grey, with great sobriety of judgement and delicacy as well as propriety of language, urged the objections to institute a proceeding in Parliament for the purpose of refuting the speech of a Minister in a foreign assembly. He contended it was unusual, proved that if it became a practice it would be hazardous in the extreme, and assured the Duke and the House that in this instance it would be, to say the least of it, inconvenient to the publick service. He hoped however that Duke's purpose might be answered by his full and entire confirmation of his statement of the conduct of Government at the period alluded, which he described in much more luminous language than his Grace eulogized, and explained in a way that perhaps tickled the vanity and certainly disarmed the opposition of the moment. He expressed some tho' not perhaps sufficient doubt of the construction put on Perier's words, professed his desire of preserving peace and close union with all the powers, disclaimed any intention of separating ourselves or France from the rest, and repelled with yet more earnestness any, the slightest, inclination to sacrifice a particle of our honour or our interest to French connection, though as the Duke seemed to acknowledge, it was most desirable and almost indispensable to maintain it at any other cost. Nothing could be more perfect than his discretion and dexterity in neither appeasing the Champion of the Frenchman's speech, nor yet omitting a topick which the French Government might think necessary for his defence or to be expected from the cordial understanding between us. In these statements Lord Grey's judgement and execution exceed those of the greatest orators or Statesmen I have known. He is more perspicuous, clear, and methodical than Mr Fox, more conciliatory and just than Mr Pitt, and more circumspect and cautious than Mr Canning, yet as full of spirit, life, and energy as any of them. The Duke of Wellington withdrew his motion. He should have done so, he said, on the bare assurance that the production of the papers would be inconvenient to the service, but he did not wish to deny that he was equally satisfied with the ample and handsome testimony Lord Grey had borne to the accuracy of his statement and the policy of his conduct.

A conversation ensued on plurality bill, remarkable only for the attack of Lord Kenyon on the Bishops and on the Bishop of London in particular, whom he twitted with having held too large livings before he was on the Bench and now depriving the inferior Clergy of the privileges he had enjoyed, quoting some droll <Ra>kish verses from drunken Barnaby, or some such author: A quod juvenis gaudebat habere modo Pontifex cupit idem abdere. The Bishop answered him with spirit.

17 March Saturday. Came to Holland House. Lord Wellesley called and was much disconcerted at an account he had heard, from what he deemed good authority, of the designs of his brother and the party. They were determined to drive Lord Grey to a resignation and prepared to form a Ministry and to substitute <some> plan of reform for the bill, and to compass these ends they meditated defeating or postponing the bill before the 2d. reading. He would not mention his informant, but his information tallying so much with reports I had heard from Scotland, I thought it worth my while to apprize Lord Grey and urge him to see Lord Wellesley.

18th. March Sunday. No Cabinet but tho' I staid all day at Holland House I saw in the course of it Lord John Russell, Lord Melbourne, Lord Chancellor, and Lord Grey. The two latter are somewhat startled at <hearing> that Sir Frederick Adam's[112] appointment to Madras is deemed a Company's nomination and yet more so at the rumour, I trust a false one, that the Adams[113] in canvassing for their brother have promised their own and their connections support for the Chair to *Mr Astell,*[114] who is one of the bitterest enemies of the Ministry in the House of Commons. Lord Grey seems more confident of a majority in the house on second reading and of success even in the Committee than ever, and of course is more averse than ever to creating peers, though I hope resolved upon it if any trick like that apprehended by Lord Wellesley is played off against us.

19 Monday. Came to town. News favorable to the prospects of Don Pedro both from the Azores and Lisbon. Nothing material in the Lords. I dined at Prince Talleyrands.

Tuesday 20 March. Duchy business and a Committee on Scotch peerages in the Morning. I dined at the Club.

Wednesday 21 March. Deference to publick hypocrisy prevented a Cabinet dinner on the fast day,[115] and compelled the Government to disperse, with some broken heads, the radical unions who had a plan of converting it to a feast and met in great numbers at Finsbury Square. Nine tenths or 99 hundredths of the reasonable class of society contemn in their hearts the observance of such superstitions and are equally conscious of the utter uselessness of them with the rabble; but each in looking grave, abstaining from his usual avocations and going to Church tickles is own vanity by flattering himself that he is of the humbugging and not humbugged portion of Mankind and so encourages the hypocrisy he despises.

We met at nine p.m. Our Cabinet was dull. We talked much and did little. Althorp is to give West Indians hopes of a loan to relieve the sufferers by hurricane and insurrection, and those islands who accept the orders in council are to be rewarded by some drawback or reduction of duty on their sugars. Other methods of relief, more efficacious and perhaps less objectionable in principle, were stated, but they were all abandoned as impracticable from a fear either of the Saints or the Country Gentlemen. A guarantee of a loan to the Greeks on the acceptance of the Crown by King Otho[116] was, from a similar fear of the House of Commons, negatived or at least postponed, though it is quite evident that without some such assistance from the three powers, the new King and his State cannot be maintained and it is a question whether, after all that has occurred, we are not bound in honour to assist him and in policy and prudence not to leave him exclusively to the protection of Russia and France. The latter power handsomely and frankly offers to be guided entirely in this affair by our example. Goderich and the AntiGallicans hear of these instances of French cordiality and forebearance with the greatest composure, and never seem to be the least shaken in their preconceived notions of French perfidy and ambition by any proof of conciliation and confidence.

Grey then propounded for Sunday's consideration the great question. If the 2d. reading in the Lords is rejected shall we immediately resign or shall we prorogue and make peers? Most seemed to admit and Richmond vehemently asserted that the bill would *not* be rejected, but it was justly contended that we ought to be prepared for the worst. Grey evidently leant to immediate resignation, and those who contemplated prorogation and creation of peers as the course in that case to be pursued, in which Class Lansdown and Richmond too were included, agreed that it might be necessary to be prepared, and that the knowledge and suspicion that we were so might have salutary effects on the votes of their Lordships. The Chancellor urged the necessity of having our course clearly understood by ourselves and I think explained to the King beforehand; but it was remarked that if it was resignation it should *not* be divulged—if prorogation and creation, it should be implied. And Althorp expressed a wish that the debate in the Commons should not be allowed to close without some Cabinet Minister protesting against Sir Chs. Wetherell's position that any large creation of peers (whatever be the circumstances) must be *unconstitutional.* Lord Lansdowne thinks if the majority is very small, it will be right to make peers. Durham was not present.

Thursday 22. Lord Wicklow moved in Lords a resolution that the new plan for joint education of Irish Children of whatever persuasion was a practical exclusion of the Bible from the education of that people and that the House disapproved it. In short he moved what in plain words might be termed a notorious lie, with a view of deluding the zealous fanaticks in both countries by an apprehension that he knew to be groundless, and for the purpose of raising or continuing a clamour in the distracted country of Ireland, thereby embarrassing the Government. The chief features of the debate was the shabby and hostile conduct of the Bishops who, with the exception of Maltby and Knox, all voted with Lord Wicklow. The Bishop of Exeter[117] made a long, elaborate, virulent, and eloquent speech, but the extreme laboured and subtle unfairness of his argument, and the malevolence and hypocrisy of the whole were so disgusting that they almost eclipsed and obliterated the talent and certainly injured the effect of his speech, which was well answered by Lord Radnor and Lord Plunkett, and part of which, relating to Archbishop Whately, he was obliged to retract. We had good service done us by several Irish Lords and Lord Gosford in particular. The Duke of Wellington studiously raised the standard of Protestantism or rather Orangism in Ireland, laboured hard to reinstate himself at the head of a political party he had once deserted and then discomfited, and he indulged in his usual strain of dogmatism on figures and reports of number, though he was more abashed than I ever remember him at the exposure of his misrepresentations and flimsy sophistry by Lord Grey. For he in an animated and feeling speech, which was delivered with all the fire of his youth, upbraided the Duke with his factious proceeding and contrasted it with great felicity and effect, but without the least descending from the dignity of his character, with the handsome assistance lent by him and his friends to the Duke of Wellington and his government on the Catholick emancipation. We were beaten by a majority of one by the presents but recovered a majority of 38 by the proxies.[118] This is in itself a warning of our weakness and there were other symptoms in spite of our triumphant debate.

Friday 23d. A committee with Lord Roseberry[119] in the Chair on the regulations necessary to be adopted in the election of the Scotch peers. Great irregularity prevails. No discussion or decision is permitted at the Election, and it may happen and often has happened that persons claiming a title on the Roll, without the slightest right to it, have been admitted to vote. The subject is one of no little perplexity. If the roll made at the Union is tampered with, there is great danger of our passing judgement on peerages without any opportunity for the parties being heard, of our recording a presumption that some are extinct to which fair and just claims may exist or of our admitting that some are in existence to which there may be no legitimate claimant. On the other hand while the roll is considered as primâ facie evidence of the existence of the peerage, and the Clerk Registrar is a simple Ministerial officer not entitled to institute enquiry or to exercise any discretion, it must be difficult to prevent false notes unless some preliminary proof of qualification is exacted, and none such can be easily devized which will not expose the Scotch peers to the trouble, vexation, and expence which it was manifestly the intention of the legislature at the time of the Union to spare them.

In the house there was a long debate on the Archbishop's plurality bill. It is liable to all the objections which half measures of reform are sure to meet with. It does too much or too little. It admits the existence of abuse and it does not remedy it. It must be allowed the Bishops are placed in this particular in rather a hard situation. They have been badgered for years for not doing something, and when they bring forward their plan they are attacked by one party for abandoning the interests of the Church and by the other for deluding the publick by the semblance of reform while they in fact perpetuate and even aggravate the abuses of it. They do not deserve much compassion just now, for their political conduct is at once irresolute and factious.

I dined at Lord Grey's.

24 Saturday. The Austrians are very placable and reasonable about Ancona and they give us assurances of speedily ratifying the treaty. I am afraid Pedro's affairs are in some jeopardy for want of money. But there are strong symptoms of Miguel's downfall.

Sunday 25 March 1832. Went over the list of House of Lords with Lord Grey's son in law and Secretary, Mr Wood, and found it, tho' far from unfavorable, not quite so certain as to warrant us in suspending all precautions in case of defeat.

In the Cabinet, they discussed the propriety of giving Don Miguel the Royal Salute as we had given it to Donna Maria. Lord Grey thought that as a king de facto he was entitled to it but, when we ascertained that it had been refused repeatedly to Don Miguel since his usurpation and once by Captain Gordon,[120] Lord Aberdeen's brother, it was thought better not to vary the order at this critical conjuncture, when it would be equivalent to an army in favor of Miguel, but to have the Commanders in the Navy to follow the example of their predecessors.

Lord Grey then brought before our consideration the state of the Reform bill, that of the Commons and the Lords and the necessity of coming to some early decision how in certain cases we should decide to act. If the bill were lost should we resign? and if not, were we prepared with a large creation and a sudden prorogation? and would it be more prudent to prorogue for a period and make peers afterwards or to make peers first and take the chance of resolutions against us retrospectively and against new Peers prospectively. On all these points we agreed to meet after the conversation which would probably occur the day after on the first reading of the bill. It was settled that on that occasion the less was said on our side the better and the choice of topick and phrases was left to Lord Grey, who is so admirable a steersman in a narrow channel where deviation to the north or south is likely to prove so fatal. It was implied and I think understood that we should not even on defeat resign our offices, but that before that event, we should apprize the King that the necessity of making peers, which he had imagined was averted by the accessions, might become more urgent. The notion of resignation was thus silently abandoned, but the King was to be apprized beforehand that the rejection of the bill would constitute the necessity of making peers and that in preparation of so unlikely but yet possible event we should be authorized by him to take every precaution to secure our adopting that step, promptly and efficaciously, when the necessity should occur. Whether it would be advisable that a sudden prorogation should precede any large creation of peers, or a creation of peers precede the prorogation, was discussed at some length. The question necessarily involved an enquiry into the state in which a prorogation would leave the publick service, and it was agreed that the second reading should be deferred till the 5th. of April, with a view of giving Althorp time silently to pass a new Mutiny bill and other votes which would enable the King to prorogue without publick inconvenience. Lansdowne and Richmond were among the most decided for prorogation and creation of peers in case of the rejection. Strange that these Lovers of the House of Lords should think it a greater indignity to that body to introduce a few quiet Gentlemen into their company as associates who might prevent them from committing an act of Madness, than to wait till the outrage was perpetrated and then to call in their keepers to knock them down and put the strait waiscoat on. Lord Lansdown very sensibly and forcibly urged that even if our majority were small, some peers should be created.

26 March 1832. A day of great interest. Lord John Russell brought up the reform bill to House of Lords where there was a considerable assemblage of peers and strangers in some degree of anxiety from a rumour that the opponents meant to make a sudden assault on the measure in hopes of taking its supporters by surprize, and from a more reasonable expectation that much would transpire from the new and reluctant converts to the bill which might render the speculations on its final success somewhat more certain. The best informed were well aware from the state of the proxy book and indeed from reason and probability that the decided antireformers would not make so desperate attempt as that of throwing out the bill on the first reading. Nor did they. Lord Harrowby avowed that he should alter his course. He appealed to the recollection of the House that he had originally doubted that he had even last year had a strong inclination not to refuse the consideration of the bill, and he grounded his charge on the difference between this and the former bill, which were all, he contended, in favor of this, on the additional conviction which time and observation had impressed on his mind that the people were intensely bent on some great reform, on the great inconvenience and even hazard of postponing it, and on the hopes of improving it in the Committee. He guarded these remarks by some distinct and strong declarations of his repugnance to many parts of the bill. He stigmatized its democratick tendency as mischievous and hazardous, and he implied that unless that spirit was much softened in the Committee he should vote against the third reading. Lord Wharncliffe, who followed him, was yet more decisive in his determination not to 'consent to the bill as it stood passing into law'; he somewhat earnestly exhorted the peers to attend the Committee with a view of removing the obnoxious parts of the bill, but disclaimed all intention of mutilating it in that stage. The most satisfactory of our new supporters was the Bishop of London, who in a short, clear, and manly speech avowed that he should have voted for the last bill had he been able to attend, that he should support the second reading of this, and attend the Committee with a view of supporting many improvements of which it was susceptible, and of enforcing not impairing the principle, certainly not of mutilating or rendering it inefficient for its great purpose of satisfying the publick. He strongly implied if he did not positively declare that even if it came out of the Committee unamended, he could not vote against it on the 3d. reading. Lord Carnarvon with some little asperity contrasted his own direct and straightforward and consistent opposition of the bill with Harrowby's changeableness, and observed smartly enough that the alterations which in the 2d. bill had won over Harrowby were such as he might well have expected last year to introduce in the Committee, and therefore left his opposition to the second reading of the first bill inconsistent with his sudden support of the second. He as usual indulged in some hard words about the authors of the measure, and Lord Grey, in a very discreet and well worded speech, said every thing that could conciliate the new converts, propitiate and invite more, without yielding a tittle of his principle and consistency; he vindicated, in the way of answer to

Carnarvon, Lord Harrowby's line of argument, and repeated his adherence to the principle and efficiency of the bill, urging the necessity of speedy settlement of the question to put an end to the excitement and suspence who were harassing every part of the Community. The Duke of Wellington in a subdued tone questioned the propriety of premature discussion, disclaimed all warmth, but avowed his unabated hostility to the bill, though he cunningly announced his intention of attending the Committee and trying to improve it. He vindicated himself from the charge of *party* spirit and denied the principle of the bill being that of *reform* in a manner that only proved that he did not understand the meaning of the words *Party* and *reform*. Most of our House of Commons friends though with some exceptions were better satisfied with the result of this very critical and arduous conversation in the Lords and with the prospect it held out of ultimate success, than they had expected to be. The Chancellor however is very nervous about it, and if the Press should preach suspicion and distrust we are lost.

[*End of BM Add. MS 51868; beginning of BM Add. MS 51869*]

[*Cover page:* This book contains a Diary irregularly and carelessly kept from 26th. March 1832 to 26th. July 1833.]

At 10 p m and after the conversation in House of Lords we met in Cabinet at Foreign Office. After discussing the impression, generally favorable, which the conversation in Lords had made on our friends in the Commons, and canvassing some names in Lords (once reckoned certain of supporting us on 2d. reading but now doubtful), we proceeded to business. Grey, jaded and unwell, read a draft of a minute less judiciously drawn and less perspicuously worded than is usual with his compositions. It stated to the King the three different results which we had to contemplate in Lords: 1) the passing the 2d. reading by a satisfactory majority; 2) passing it by a bare majority; 3) the losing it. In the first case our course was clear. In the second the propriety of adding some peers to the house to facilitate the passage thro' the Committee would probably suggest itself but did not now press. In the 3d. which *we denominated very improbable!* the consequences were so serious that we were bound to be prepared as to the line we should recommend H M to adopt. The paper then went on to state the alternative of resignation or a creation of peers with or without prorogation, seemed to leave the choice quite undecided, and even left upon my mind the impression that it must be intended to convey to the King, if not a positive wish and determination, a strong inclination and hope that he would accept our resignation in the event of a rejection of the bill. After much conversation on the necessity of our *deciding* now what in the event of a rejection we should do, the Lord Chancellor Brougham at Grey's request revised the latter part of the minute, omitted the passage about resignation, and somewhat strongly urged the expediency and necessity both of a creation of peers and a prorogation of Parliament in the case supposed. We once more deferred the final settlement of the paper till

Tuesday 27th at three p m when we again met. Grey had introduced Lord Brougham's phrases and earnest recommendation in that part of his minute which related to the prorogation and creation of peers, and by the addition of the word *Therefore* rendered that alternative the one which the Cabinet advised, but he retained the form of his original draft and thereby in my opinion brought the alternative of resignation on the rejection of the bill too obviously and forcibly before the King's mind—it being a step that nothing but the King's refusing to prorogue Parliament and create Peers could justify us in thinking of. I expressed tho' faintly my objections. Some few passages were altered and the sentence which drew a deduction from the premises that the course of prorogation and Creation of peers would become necessary was made more direct and pointed. It was then agreed that Grey should deliver the minute so amended tomorrow.[121]

Wednesday 28 March. Went to court. Was introduced to Count Orloff the Russian just arrived from the Hague, and Mr Vandeweyer, the Belgian Minister, whose respective statures are no bad Emblems of the size of the two states they represent. The athletick figure of Orloff brings to one's recollection the nature of the services which more than one of that name have been destined to perform and qualifies him for the acts of love and violence for which his family have been so celebrated. He seems a frank and sensible man. He reports his conversations with the King of the Netherlands very distinctly and the avowal of that Prince that he will *never* sign the 24 articles as they now stand. He does not seem to think the King of Holland can adhere to so obstinate a resolution, he firmly announced to him that he must expect no assistance from Russia if he did, and he is said to have written to his Court in terms of strong disgust his sense of the perfidy and obstinacy which has characterized the King of Holland's proceedings. He at the same time is persuaded that the Dutch people are deluded by his pretences into as violent and insurmountable a repugnance to the treaty as their King.

The rumours of defections from our very scanty Majority are to me appalling, but Lord Grey is impatient at any mistrust of it. We dined, a small cabinet, at Lord Melbournes. I urged that we were pledged to the country to bring forward some general law or regulations for a police in the large towns about to be represented, and nearly as much so to the King, to the institution of Corporations by charter or act of Parliament. That if we were not soon prepared with one or both of these measures we should be exposed to ridicule and disgrace, but that a knowledge that any such measures were in forwardness would facilitate the progress of the Reform bill, as might be collected from Harrowby's profession of the expectation of such an expedient being one of the circumstances that had reconciled him to this second bill of Reform. Grey declared that he was unable to fight the great bill in the Committee, complained with some little soreness of the little assistance he derived from his Colleagues, and exhorted us to prepare for the Committee by meeting in a Sub Committee with Lord Althorp to go thro' the bill clause by clause and collect the voluminous matter and local peculiarities of each place, a full knowledge of which was necessary to a defence of the Clauses. Of the labour and difficulty of such a task the Chancellor drew a picture sufficient to appall the most diligent and, though we agreed to undertake it, I think none of us had much stomach for the enterprize. The King received the intimation of the possible necessity of creating peers and proroguing Parliament, with good humour and approbation, and was yet more delighted at the prospect of carrying the 2d. reading of bill, which he calculated we should do by 18 or 20, thereby preventing the necessity of any such measure as the creation of peers.

29 March. At 12 o clock this day Talleyrand received the contents of a Telegraphick dispatch from Paris of 4 p m the preceding day. It related the communication of the Austrian ambassador to the French Government that an Austrian Courier had arrived on his way to London bearing the Emperor's ratification of the treaty of the 15th. Novr. Count Appony <added> that he had reason to suppose that Prussia had by this time sent her ratification also.

In the House of Lords Lord Winchelsea[122] in a ranting speech railed at what he chose, I will not say without, but in the teeth of, proof, to stigmatize as an exclusion of the Bible from national education in Ireland and, though he was temperately but triumphantly answered both on fact and argument by Grey, his monstrous and preposterous statements were still maintained by the Arch Bishop of Armagh, Lord Roden, and Lord Wicklow. In the course of his speech Lord Winchelsea unhandsomely inveighed against the political letter and arraigned the Heterodoxy of some of the writings of the Bishop of Chichester, Dr Maltby, who vindicated himself especially from the last Charge with as much dignity and temper and with more spirit and talent than before. Orloff, I hear, foretells the speedy arrival of the Russian ratifications and implies that it is by agreement between the two Emperors that Austria and perhaps Prussia ratify first, that he may have to urge to the King of Holland the impossibility of standing out alone.

30 March. Called on Grey. He hesitates about calling up Althorp to the Lords. He had written to Durham, and enclosed him the last minute of Cabinet, which Durham, who has absented himself from Cabinet and Lords for near a week, answered pettishly, called mere twaddling and ended his letter with the exclamation, Que Diable avois je [*sic*] a faire dans cette Galere là![123] Leopold has also written a wrongheaded letter to Palmerston, expressing great impatience and determination not to be bamboozled (mystifié) much longer. He avows an inclination to attack the Dutch.

Soon after I left him Grey received a long letter from the King commenting on Minute of Cabinet and suggesting I fear compromise and modifications of the bill.[124] It is lucky Grey goes to Windsor tomorrow and we meet in Cabinet early to strengthen him with our support, which will I trust be for vigorous measures. Lord Minto's[125] account of the state of Scotland is tremendous. The loss of the bill there is indeed Civil War and revolution. Austrian ratifications arrived but not with orders for an immediate exchange. They are to be exchanged when those of Russia shall arrive, and both the Austrian and Prussian Ministers expect them immediately and speak as if the speedy arrival of them had been announced from their courts.

The King's answer to the Minute of Cabinet was read. It is certainly far from favorable. If experience did not prove that on paper His Majesty is more difficult and controversial than he is either in conversation or action, it would be the forerunner of a dissolution or dismissal of Ministry. It does however commend our general policy and conduct, deprecate resignation, and assure us that the promise of making peers if *necessary* shall be sacred. But on the other hand it hesitates as to the expediency and number of peers to be created in the supposition of carrying the 2d. reading by a very small majority; somewhat uncourteously hints at *some* of his confidential advisers being reluctant to recommend creating many; launches forth at length on the difficulties which have attended the Progress of the Reform bill; refers to former opinions that without modifications it could never pass to the Lords; and openly recommends in the case of rejection some understanding, not only with the followers of Harrowby but with the moderate opponents of the measure, as the most eligible not to say only method of carrying it. We all agreed that some further explanation on the main point should be attained. Both Grey and the Chancellor deemed a minute necessary, which to say the truth I much doubted. The Cabinet which was thinly attended concurred in postponing the answer till Lord Grey had seen him at Windsor, and Somewhat earnestly recommended the Chancellor not to press any of the contingencies in the Committee too distinctly, because a prospective view of an unpalatable remedy is more likely to meet with a refusal, than the submission to the most disagreable, when enforced by urgent and obvious necessity. I remarked that the Chancellor was inclined to suspect the King, very unjustly, of being indifferent to our fate and even disposed to abandon us, if the 2d. reading were once over. Palmerston avowed a strong difference of opinion on the state of the country and Government, thought the people would gladly accept the Reform bill though materially altered, and was far from acknowledging that we were precluded from the course suggested by the King—of accommodating matters with the more reasonable of our adversaries, if the second reading be rejected. Grey cut this short by observing that even if compromise or understanding could be safely or conveniently resorted to with any of the Ultra Party, He and his ministry were not the men that could conduct such a system conveniently and that we should by discrediting our own character deprive ourselves of all power of doing good to the Country and conducting the King's affairs with advantage. The Chancellor was requested to draw up a paper, but the propriety of sending any was, together with the paper, left open for discussion after Lord Grey shall have reported the substance of his audience.

1 April 1832. Dined at Lord Dudley's.[126] The reports of the state of his health and mind, in addition to the many years of estrangement between Lady Holl[an]d and him, made it an awkward dinner;[127] but he did not appear at table and by the good management of Sir Hry. Halford and his confidential servant was spared the excitement. The party was somewhat strangely composed but went off decently well. [*In the margin:* He never appeared in public afterwards. He became quite insane, and after a few months his bodily health and strength declined and he died early in 1833. A man of a highly cultivated mind and of exquisite and refined though somewhat elaborate wit. He was accused of wanting affections but I think that, although confined to a few and certainly not in proportion to his bitter hatreds and unwarrantable resentments, that he was not entirely devoid of benevolence and even generosity.]

Lord Brougham sent his draft of a minute to three or four of his Colleagues. The topicks are well selected, but perhaps it is not necessary to press the King in this preliminary stage to any premature decision on points obviously unpalatable to him. Lord John Russell suspects that the Chancellor presses it from a wish to break up the Government, but how is he interested in doing so? And if he is, how much more advantageously he might have taken his stand on the question of Peer making many weeks, nay months, ago? Durham's resignation is much bruited abroad. It is believed and rejoiced at. That he is out of town and temper I know, that he is out of health I fear, but that he is out of office I have not heard. I have really great regard for him. I know him to have many good capabilities as well as extraordinary talents, but I do not very much deprecate his retirement *even now,* so generally unpopular has he made himself by his haughty and disdainful demeanour as well as petulant and ungovernable temper. Even if he retires on the most popular grounds, it is not clear that the reformers and democratical party will not hail the event as joyfully as the most virulent Tories. The King has probably heard this report, and It is not impossible that some passages in his letter to the Cabinet were composed with a view to accelerate that event and provoke Durham to a resignation, which will gladden His Majesty. If on the present irritable state of the publick mind the avowed cause does not excite some distrust of Ministers, his retirement in itself would add to our comfort in the Cabinet and strengthen not weaken us with society and the publick. Some pretend that it would encrease our Majority in the Lords. The report of it raised, if the newspapers speak truth, the funds 1/2 per cent.

2 April Monday 1832. In the Lords Lord Suffield[128] made a tiresome and Lord King somewhat unfair attack upon the Archbishop's bill against pluralities. It is a weak and unsatisfactory measure but, as Lord Grey observed, a bill which endeavours to correct an obnoxious abuse with which the Church has been often reproached, originating with the Bishops, deserves to be treated with some little indulgence and may, even by those who are not satisfied with it, be hailed as the harbinger of further and effectual reforms. The Bishops seemed pleased with Lord Grey's temperate and gallant defence of them, but will one of them give him a vote for the reform bill more readily?

The Chancellor brought me after the debate to Holland House. He had sketched an answer to the King's last letter, but after Lord Grey's detailed report of his audience on the subject it will require some revision. The King was anxious in his conversation with Lord Grey to impress upon him that his notion in case of defeat on 2d. reading of proroguing and bringing in a modified bill, with a view of gaining over adversaries instead of augmenting friends by a large creation, was only thrown out *as a suggestion* and did not imply a refusal to prorogue and create as he may be advized. He was as cordial and as warm in his commendations of the Ministry and manifestly as attached to Lord Grey as ever. But he reserved all positive answer till the Cabinet should again advise upon it; tho' he argued as usual against the measure of making peers, tho' he doubted the possibility of ascertaining the number requisite and seemed to shudder at the number (50 or 60) which Grey stated might be necessary, and though he manifestly leant as he had uniformly done to the expedient of compromise and modifications, it is nevertheless quite obvious to me that should the case arise he will handsomely and even readily acquiesce in the advice given to its full extent. [*In the margin:* In this I was wrong, be it a proof of my simplicity or of the court's duplicity. Stet.]

3 April tuesday. In Cabinet at 1/2 past one, considered Lord Grey's minute of conversation at Windsor[129] and Lord Brougham['s] draft of an answer to the Royal letter. In the conversation on the latter, the Chancellor pressed and Lord Palmerston deprecated too earnest an instance to the King to decide on proroguing and creating peers in a case which we in the same paper acknowledged to be very improbable, and still more any hint that even in case of a refusal we should resign before the 2d. reading. The general opinion was I think that we should now urge him to decide on the contingency but that, even if he decided in the negative, we should be called upon both by duty to him and the country not to abandon our posts till we had stood the hazard of the div[ision] on the second reading. Lord L[ansdowne] bore testimony to the earnestness of the publick, and of grave soberminded Men among them, for an immediate creation of peers, and to their dismay at the very apprehension of a possibility of the bill being rejected a second time. Some doubts were murmured by Palmerston respecting both these points, and Duke of Richmond paradoxically maintained that we should lose the confidence of our friends by a creation and that excepting Schedule A the country took little interest in the provisions of the Bill. Palmerston was as usual civil, courteous, and fair, but he marked his disagreement with our statements, respecting the indispensability of the bill nearly as it stands, both to the satisfaction of the publick and the maintenance of our own character, in a way that made others remark that he could without any breach of honour to his Colleagues remain in with a Government which propitiated the <......> of reform by any sacrifice, however small and insignificant at her shrine. Grey repeated that neither in honour nor expediency could he follow such a course and in that opinion most expressed their concurrence and none but Palmerston any dissent.

It was however thought by more than one that Lord Chancellor's paper too peremptorily implied immediate resignation even before the 2d. reading, unless the King previously determined in the course to be pursued on the loss of the bill *now*, and that point was reserved for further consideration in the evening. We parted for a few hours.

In the evening I was stopped for an hour at the literary or Johnson's Club to ballot for Lord Dover who was chosen, and drove down with Lord Lansdown to Lord Greys [*In the margin:* where we revised the paper, omitted the passages which pointed to any resignation before Monday next, softened some others, but firmly urged the absolute necessity both of prorogation and a large creation of Peers in the event of the bill being rejected on second reading.[130]] Lord John Russell questioned the policy of the whole proceeding and would have preferred meeting the second reading this week and advising the King according to the result but not pressing him on hypothetical or contingent cases. Perhaps His view is not incorrect but it was now too late to enforce it. Palmerston, though he assisted in correcting the phraseology (and he is a great dab at such a task) and acquiesced in the paper as a whole, expressed sufficient doubts of our view of the necessity of immediate and extensive Reform and of our dismay at any thing like compromise or modification to justify him in taking another course, if that on which we shall decide should turn out unsuccessful. Others of my colleagues observed this. It seems strange, for to use the vulgar phrase of a Servant, I think he is of all the Ministers the one least likely to better himself by a change of Men. He has always been on bad terms with Wellington, he does not like Peel, he has the office of most fame and credit in the Ministry, he conducts it to the satisfaction both of the Court and the Country, has been uniformly supported by his present Colleagues, and seems at least pleased and satisfied both in his department and with his Colleagues. The Duke of Richmond manifestly disliked the paper, implied that nothing but his intimate conviction that a good majority on 2d. reading would render it unnecessary to act upon it would induce him to agree to it, and he avowed to me that he had rather lose the bill than make a single peer at any stage of it for the obvious purpose of carrying it. However, by way of preparing ourselves for the event, we went through a list of the Candidates for a seat in the House of Lords. The King had fairly enough remarked that before he could sanction such a measure he must know whom we prepared to make. The list, including nearly all who had applied or had been suggested to Grey, was hastily made. Melbourne read it nearly thro' with some lovely and blunt remarks on the character and pretensions of each, and we saw enough of it to draw two rather unpleasant conclusions: viz 1, that our means of decision were not much advanced by any knowledge of the inclinations of individuals, and the certainty of their attendance and support; and 2dly., that the King's restrictions of our choice to Eldest Sons, and Scotch and Irish peers would, if adhered to, drive us to many improper and some very uncertain men.

For the ensuing ten days
4 Wednesday [*April 1832*]. I neglected this journal. During the first five days
5 Thursday. much correspondence passed between the King and the Ca-
6 Friday. binet related to the conduct to be pursued in the event of the loss
7 April. of the bill or of a very scanty Majority. The substance of the
8 Sunday. King's letter, while he adhered to his promise of making peers if
9 Monday. necessary, was yet more stedfast in his adherence, not unmixed
10 Tuesday. with pertinacity and a little soreness, to the inconvenient con-
11 Wednesday. ditions he had before annexed, of confining the new seats in
12 Thursday. Lords to Eldest Sons, Scotch and Irish peers. There was one
13 Friday. very long letter,[131] recapitulating and quoting the words of all
that had passed on this subject since December or January last and assuming an air of controversy and self justification, which, combined with a sort of valedictory encomium, very unlike his former warm commendations of our Ministry, persuaded some of us that the moment of separation was approaching. It seemed to incline the Chancellor to a breach on the refusal, or at least witholding of acquiescence, to our proposal, in the contingency. It convinced us *all* that in that event we must instantly resign, unless He consents to prorogue Parliament and create peers *instanter*. He was however persuaded to come to town during the debate which commenced on the 9th., and I learnt from Sir Herbert Taylor that the long recapitulating letter was a device of that Gentleman to remind the

King of the strength and nature of his promises to make peers, which had, he told me, escaped the Royal Memory and was succeeded in his mind by an aversion to the measure stronger than ever and a *notion that he had been consistent in resisting it!*

On his arrival in town he became more softened and cordial, spoke with great earnestness of the second reading of the bill and, though full of attentions to the Queen as far as presents and great civility and deference go, marked more than ever the little influence she had or could acquire over his councils. When she praised the eloquent but factious speech of Bishop of Exeter against the Reform, he said at breakfast 'It may be clever or eloquent, Madam, of that I am no judge; but though the *peers* may occasionally be factious, By God, the *Bishops* are in that house to defend my crown and not to follow vagaries of their own'.

That speech was the leading feature of the three first days of our prolonged debate, and never did an oration more artfully and malignantly convey the bitterest Charges against his adversaries or excite more mischievously the angry passions of his own party. It was itself and rendered a great part of the debate a strong contrast to the judicious and temperate manner in which Lord Grey had introduced the subject. My strange and culpable nervousness, which for the first days had not only the pretext but the reality of a severe cold and hoarseness to excuse it, prevented my speaking, but I had the satisfaction of hearing many of my thoughts far better expressed and many of my expressions and points better delivered by Lord Grey, than I could have done, in his admirable reply, which in spirit, judgement, recollection, and reasoning would have been an extraordinary display at any time and from any man, and was surely, after a fatiguing debate of four nights and at six o clock in the Morning of the fifth from a man of near seventy years, almost miraculous. Lansdowne distinguished himself by an excellent speech. Brougham spoke with less brilliancy and with less energy than usual but with great judgement. Lord Durham rather exceeded the bounds of parliamentary language in his indignation against the Bishop of Exeter. I availed myself of my very undeserved but high character for knowledge of order to embarrass those who interrupted him as to this mode of proceeding against him, and he not only extricated himself from his scrape with dexterity, credit, and honour, but had the satisfaction of drawing from the Bishop a vindication and explanation of his insinuations and conduct, which materially damaged him in the estimation of the house. Lord Goderich's rebuke of the Bishop, flowing as it manifestly did from strong and sincere as well as deeply religious feelings, was affecting and eloquent. On the whole the debate, especially that of the last day, was triumphant, for tho' Mansfield, Ellenborough, and Lyndhurst spoke well against the bill, they and the Duke of Wellington maintained extravagant parodoxes on the state of publick opinion *now* and, above all, exhibited such practical ignorance of the nature and effect of popular elections, as deprived their judgement of all authority in such matters with men of reflection.

The debate in truth turned during a great part of the time as much on the changes in men's votes as on the changes in the Electoral body which we were called upon to consider. Wharncliffe and the Harrowbites on the whole did well and vindicated their change of course with spirit and ingenuity, and the Bishop of

London, who had however no variation in conduct to justify, took the plain, decided, and manly course of acknowledging that the bill, with all its imperfections or sins, of which he thought it had many, was not such an evil as its rejection would be, that he would attend to the Committee to improve it as much as he could, but that he was not prepared to vote against it even in its present form, nor would act the insidious or unmanly part of attempting indirectly to defeat by mutilating it in Committee. This, considering his character and abilities, was sufficient to cower such timid prelates as were at all disposed to reconcile themselves to the Court and the Ministry, and we had the support of twelve of that Reverend Bench. Though the Archbishops—the most timid, irresolute, and helpless of them all—gave a silent vote against the bill and a foolish unmeaning countenance to the opposition against it. The majority of nine, however scanty, will I hope be sufficient to enable us to feel our way in Committee and to persuade the foreign courts of the stability of our Ministry.[132]

Talleyrand says it must hasten the ratifications; if it does not, he suggests some decided or as he calls it dignified step, and thinks England and France should recall their Embassies and Missions from the three non-ratifying Courts and have mere Charges d'affaires to transact ordinary business—a measure which, he observes, and I believe justly, pledges us to no war, but would have the effect of bringing them to their senses and alarming them with the consequences of a total estrangement, in a way that would render them ere long much more tractable. He told me in confidence that the loss of Perier would have led, in addition to the obvious and dreadful consequences we all apprehended, to a resumption of power and presidency in the Council by King Louis Philippe himself, which, he added, would be fatal to the tranquillity of France. During Perrier's illness, he, the King, shewed dispositions to resume that ministerial ascendancy. His and his Sisters[133] strong predilections both for democracy and the party of the 'Mouvement' was, he said, most singular, and much greater than could be accounted for by mere love of popularity or weakness. The only personage in the Tuilleries who had the slightest repugnance to such popular and democratick courses, or the least preference to a government with any aristocratical leaven in it, was the Queen[134]—and strange to say she was the only one for whom the people in general and the democratical party in particular felt any respect or consideration whatever.

It is gratifying to see Lord Grey restored so entirely to the confidence of the whole party, by success, though one cannot but reflect on the injustice of that eagerness which will not between the notion and first acting of a serious thing give the leading actor credit for some judgement as well as sincerity.

14 to 21 April. I still continued to neglect my diary. We had some debates and I think two Cabinets between the 14 and 19th., on which day I went to Lord Seftons at Stoke. The King wrote a very strange, unexpected, and somewhat embarrassing letter to Lord Grey, in consequence of a word which dropped from the latter of the necessity there would be of remonstrating with the Russians on their manifest breach of the spirit of the treaty of Vienna in their avowed and violent determination of annihilating the independence and nationality of the Poles.[135] The King's letter expressed much apprehension at the prospect of too close a connection with France, allowed that the present Govt. and Casimir Perrier's Ministry were disposed to maintain peace but not he feared from 'honest' motives, but from a sense of their own interest and that of France—expressed some suspicions of their designs of aggrandizement and ambition especially in the Mediterranean, quoted the silly reports (circulated by the Russians and somewhat officiously repeated by Lord Heytesbury) of a project against Minorca, and exhorted Lord Grey and his Government not to estrange himself from the other Courts whose cooperation might be so necessary for our protection, observing somewhat invidiously that with a view of acting in the spirit of the times and maintaining a policy falsely denominated 'liberal' we might imperceptibly slide into a system of a revolutionary and insurrectionary character, which he earnestly deprecated, and to guard against which he insisted on examining and approving all instructions sent to our foreign Ministers. By this latter distinct injunction he seemed to imply either that matters of that nature had been witheld, or a suspicion that, unless further precautions were taken on his part, this Ministry would be disposed and capable of deceiving him. Grey wrote a spirited answer.[136] He adverted to the repeated approbation, nay, cordial commendations, of our foreign policy to be found in the King's letters, expressed grief and surprise at one in so different and even opposite a strain, and firmly observed that if his Majesty's advisers, after a general concurrence with H M in his views of foreign affairs, were not to be trusted with such instructions as they might deem proper to their Ministers and Ambassadors, he could only say that they were not fit to enjoy their offices, as none could after losing the Confidence of the King. Both in writing and in conversation the King distinctly and earnestly disclaimed all intention of hurting Lord Grey or of seeking either to dismiss or disturb his Ministers, but he did not specifically retract the strange injunction his first letter had imposed nor in substance deny the apprehensions of our predilection for France, which were the grounds of his uneasiness. On the contrary, he said to Lord Palmerston, I have some notions on foreign politicks which are entirely my own and by God I am too old to change them. In short, though he softened his tone and conceded many principles which his late letter seemed to combat and though he shewed no wish to quarrel with his Ministers, he was, nevertheless, more sore and discontented that [?than] we had hitherto known him to be on any matter except perhaps on the reform bill. It was more remarkable that the topick he selected to express discontent upon was precisely that which he had hitherto singled out for eulogy and which, he more than once declared, had reconciled him to matters of domestick policy that he did not entirely like, from a persuasion that none could conduct his foreign policy so well, or perhaps at all, excepting Lord Grey and his present Colleagues. There was, we thought, some indication of extraneous influence of assiduity, and our suspicions fell on the Duke of Cumberland. In the mean while the Austrian and Prussian Plenipotentiaries were prevailed upon by Palmerston and Talleyrand to exchange, as they were in truth authorized to do, the ratification of their respective courts of the treaty of November. The Russian Mastuzevitch was much vexed at this determination, and Russia will not doubt be nettled at a practical avowal that the four powers can come to a final agreement on a matter of importance without her concurrence and in defiance, if not of her resistance, at least of her irresolution and delay. The truth is that few in England and France and perhaps not many who think independently in Germany will regret this result. They are not sorry that her pride should be somewhat humbled by discovering that she is not all powerful at a distance, and her conduct to the Poles is not only repugnant to the common feelings of mankind but manifestly at variance with the spirit of the real interests of all the states contiguous to her Empire.

21st. to 30 April. [*In the margin:* On the 28th. April Lord Wharncliffe had an interview with Lord Grey and I have seen Lord Wharncliffe's own minute of what passed. Lord Brougham and Palmerston were I think present. Wharncliffe disclaimed having any following. He spoke only for himself, acknowledged that, though in principle he was not averse to postponing disfranchisement to Enfranchisement, he deemed such an attempt in the Committee highly inexpedient and liable to misconstruction in the publick and, although none could say that he declared an intention of *voting* against it, Palmerston and the others understood him to say that he (and he should think Harrowby) would resist it. By his own note of the Conversation, it is substantially proved that Lord Grey distinctly declared that whatever arrangements at the commencement of the bill might have been practicable or admissible, the postponement of the disfranchisement at this stage and in the present circumstances would in his mind be *fatal to* the satisfactory termination of the business and that he never could consent to it. If this was not to imply or rather to avow, totisdem verbis, that if the Majority decided to postpone the Clause he should either resign or insist on making peers, there is no meaning in words; and yet Lord Wharncliffe as well as Lord Harrowby had subsequently the face to impute trick, manoeuvre, and <management> to Lord Grey! ! ! Quis tulerit?]

I spent Easter week at Ampthill Park, heard little of Politicks and collected nothing for this diary. On my return to Holland House I learnt from Talleyrand on

1 May that the Russian ratifications and order to exchange them were arrived, though with a desire of modifications in 3 articles of the treaty of 15 November,[137] which rendered Palmerston's absence from town exceedingly vexatious, inasmuch as the manner of compromizing, evading, or postponing such modifications as well as the determination on what to do immediately after the exchange was completed, required some preparation, and all delay was inconvenient and even hazardous. I clearly perceived that his knowledge of Louis Philippe's activity, who is *de sa nature un peu faiseur pour ne pas dire intrigant,* and his dread of it during Cas[imi]r Perrier's illness added to his uneasiness at any prospect of delay; and he told me in confidence that Monterond was employed to correspond with the King of the French, who had paid his gaming debts for him in London. Cas[imi]r Perrier is by no means well and is far from likely to resume his functions as Minister for some time. I much suspect that the King considers the interval as a holyday or rather as a promotion to business for himself and will meddle more than is advantageous or wise.

With respect to our King, he is in good humour with his Ministers personally, but still harps on the necessity of distrusting France and preserving a cordial understanding with the other powers, with a view of repressing her ambitious designs and counteracting her revolutionary principles. Absurd and hazardous as these apprehensions appear to me, it is not surprizing that the perusal of our official diplomatick correspondence should excite such suspicions in the mind of the King. With the exception of those from Lord Granville, Mr Seymour,[138] and perhaps Mr Addington,[139] all our official dispatches breathe the spirit of a jealous and controlling system of policy against France and contain, with little and very feeble efforts at refutation, the fallacies and sophistries of Ancillon, Nesselrode,[140] and Metternich, reported at great length and with considerable ability and manifestly not very repugnant to the feelings of the Reporter. On

Wednesday 2 May I urged these remarks to Lord Grey at Court, and learnt from him and others that the Antireformers in House of Lords meant to give up their motions of instructions to the Committee and were at much variance with one to another on the method of proceeding.

3d. May. Transacted some Duchy business with Mr Danvers. The Bishop of Hereford is dead. The Dean of Exeter[141] is dying. The King declines giving the peerage of Berners, pronounced to be in abeyance, to the claimant who made it out and who is a friend to reform. This we think is no good sign.

The declaration with which Russia proposes to accompany her ratification seems to contain conditions utterly inadmissible: 1, there shall be modifications; 2, Those modifications shall be in favor of Holland; and 3dly. no means of coercion must be employed against either party in any case. Palmerston, in explaining by letter to Lord Grey these pretensions, combated and exposed their unreasonableness and seemed persuaded that the difficulty was insurmountable. Talleyrand had been more sanguine about the means of softening or explaining away the reserve accompanying the Russian ratification and in his conversation with me did not seem aware of the yet more unjustifiable protest by which Russia declares that *in no case* will they admit of any coercive means being adopted against Holland or either party.

4 May Friday. A note from Talleyrand implying that after a conversation with Bulow and Wessenburgh he had satisfied them and himself that it was better to accept the Russian ratification with the explanation that the modifications were understood to be made grè a gre than to postpone the matter once more for two months. I answered the note somewhat ambiguously with the remark that the *defectuosités,* as he called them, of the Russian ratification were more serious and more difficult to be got over than I had imagined. Before I went to the Cabinet the Duchess de Dino called and I learnt from her that the place of President or Prime Minister *sans portefeuille* had been destined by the King to Talleyrand and she had received letters to sound him. He from personal reasons and I think with great judgement at once declined any such offer. The wish to place him there is however an indication of the pacifick and reasonable disposition of the Court. It is so far good. I attended a Cabinet at 1/2 past four. Lieven had communicated his instructions *confidentially* to Palmerston, and Grey read them to the Cabinet.

Nothing could be more peremptory than the directions in them: 1, to preserve the modification of the three articles and to develop the meaning of that reserve by insisting on the very stipulations which the Dutch plenipotentiaries had prepared, and 2dly., to protest against the employment in any case of coercive measures (that as as Palmerston justly remarks 'a declaration in ratifying a treaty that they never will consent to its execution'); however Palmerston assured us that in talking the matter over with the three Russians—Lieven, Mastuzevitch, and Orloff—he found them disposed to give in a declaration (which might be recorded in a Protocol) that the modifications were to be introduced by the mutual consent of the parties (de grè a grè) and to consider themselves as authorized to proceed to the exchange without any further protestation against the employment of coercive measures, which they confined to force of arms, than the communication of their instructions and their verbal explanations might imply. How they can reconcile the evasion of one injunction and the total omission of the other to their instructions I cannot divine, but that is their affair and it is by no means impossible that they have authority from their court to relax the peremptory orders they were empowered and enjoined, with a view of bullying and bragging, in the first instance to communicate. Vanderweyer, notwithstanding Sir Robt. Adair's predictions to the contrary, seems to be more accommodating than ever, and he would be satisfied to accept the Russian ratification as he has done the Prussian with a simple, vague, and general declaration that he does so with reference to the guarantee contained in the 24 articles and thereby implying that any deviation from them must be the result of further negotiation and effected by mutual consent only. This consideration in addition to many obvious motives of convenience induced us to prefer an exchange of the ratifications, accompanied even with these reserves and declarations, to an immediate postponement. The appearance of a settlement, even if the reality could not be immediately had, was something, and might accelerate rather than retard that reality. I suggested however that some means should be devized of putting on record that we did not concur in the reserve if the sense contained in Lieven's instructions was put upon it, and that we yet more peremptorily rejected the notion that coercive measures were not in any case to be resorted to.

The King insisted on making Grey's brother Bishop of Hereford.[142] would take no refusal, likened this act of favor to one bestowed on Lord North's brother [143] by his father, and accompanied what he called this testimony of regard and gratitude with some equivocal phrases that had a sound of somewhat a valedictory nature, especially when combined with some incidents and expressions that have lately come to our knowledge. Whatever might happen, he said, he was anxious that a tribute of his affection and a record of the sense he entertained of the handsome manner in which Grey had come forward on the dissolution of his last Ministry should be preserved. He told Grey he had no intention whatever of conferring the peerage of Berners on Mr Wilson,[144] who had made out that it was in abeyance and who was the representative of the Elder Sister. When Grey had cautioned him not to commit himself to the East India Company at the dinner (which he very unnecessarily gives them to day) about the renewal of the Charter,[145] he took the admonition (conveyed thro' a private letter to Sir H Taylor) very goodhumouredly but wrote word that he had a great objection to opening the trade with China and that Grey would find that objection in his mind unalterable. [*In the margin:* He afterwards in April or March, 1833, was convinced by Mr Grant's letter and conversation, and said both were 'inimitable'. He was wonderfully struck with Grant and quite reconciled to the inroads on the Charter—so much force have truth and simplicity on a mind which means well as the King's always does.] He gave a wipe at the Order in Council for the West Indies and above all, in his conversation, marginal notes, and correspondence, he is more than ever earnest in deprecating any estrangement from the three Northern Courts and in admonishing us of the dangers and consequences of too close a connection with France. It is clear an unfavorable impression of our policy has been recently produced in his mind; part no doubt may be ascribed to the Antigallican and silly tone of many of our diplomatick agents, so improvidently continued in their appointments, but some we have too much ground to suspect has been instilled into his mind through channels which intriguers either foreign or domestick have discovered for conveying imperceptibly their own views to the Royal ear.

5th. May Saturday. Morning at Duchy Office; 1/2 past 2 in Cabinet, Foreign Office, where I learnt that the King had decided in favor of Mr Wilson for the Barony of Berners, lately proved to be in abeyance, and thereby given us another vote for Reform in the Committee. He spoke likewise more cordially of his Ministry and more in unison with their system of policy than he had done lately. The Conference had sat up till 3 o'clock in the Morning, when the Ratifications between Russia and Belgium were exchanged with a note explanatory of the reserve contained in the Russian ratification, and another from Vandeweyer, temperately and adroitly penned, in which he annexes a sense to the reserve contained in Russian ratification which leaves all the stipulations of the treaty of 5th. [*15th.*] November peremptorily binding on the Contracting parties and supposes the modifications to be subject to the consent of both the Belgians and Dutch and only applicable to a subsequent definitive treaty to be agreed upon between them, and not to be alterations in the original treaty itself. In a declaration reciting the very words of the Belgian's note and consequently implying some acknowledgement of the construction put thereby on the Russian reservation, Palmerston and Talleyrand, after much cajoling and wrangling prevailed on the Russians as well as the others to concur.[146] Orloff was himself anxious to be the bearer of the instrument completed, and Bulow and perhaps Lieven were desirous that he should first announce the completion of their work, inasmuch as he would give a favorable impression both at Berlin and St. Petersburgh of the transaction. The ratifications and accompanying papers were not finally completed till three o'clock in the Morning and Count Orlof, who had been waiting with impatience with his horses to the carriage, left London at 5, after complimenting Mr Vanderweyer on his handsome and conciliatory manner of admitting and explaining the reservation and whispering him that he would now find Nicholas equally and perhaps more earnest and friendly in supporting King Leopold than any of the others. We talked over two drafts of circular letters to the Crown and legislative Colonies in the West Indies. The latter, though it agreed to defer the enactment of order in Council while the Lord's Committee was sitting, was menacing, angry, and scolding, and better calculated to justify Government in House of Commons against the Saints, than to persuade or to induce the West Indian assemblies to cooperate in our views. It was far from a good paper.[147] We mitigated the harsh expressions and somewhat softened it, and it was agreed that it should be submitted to the King and if approved sent next tuesday or thursday. Dined at the Academy. Talleyrand in the evening, much pleased at the ratification and accompaning documents and somewhat tickled at a note from Lieven which tells him he was 'inexorable'.

6 May Sunday. The Cabinet dined at Holland House, and we agreed to move to omit the words 'fifty six' and introduce the names, amounting to 56 of the Schedule, into the first Clause of the bill, and we further agreed that any postponement of the first clause, as subversive of the principle of disfranchisement, should be resisted to the utmost. It was thought that, in that resistance, many of the Waverers and certainly Wharncliffe, who acknowledged he disapproved of such postponement, would join.

7th. of May. I went to town and staid till the twelfth and consequently during that time neglected this diary. I may at my leisure fill it up from recollection. On going into the Committee on the 7th., Grey rose when the Title was moved to be postponed to announce that in the first clause he should move to leave out the words fifty six and to insert after "following places" the word namely and the enumeration of the fifty six boroughs in the Schedule A, so that a question might at the will of any member of the Committee be raised on each. When the Preamble and Title had been postponed, Lord Lyndhurst rose to say that his amendment was in point of order before that announced by Lord Grey, for he should move to postpone the first Clause, and the second, with a view of considering those relating to Enfranchisement first, because he could not consider Disfranchisement as a principle in itself to be adopted, but such as could only be admitted to the extent which Enfranchisement and a due regard to the Members of the House of Commons enjoined. He was manifestly as much agitated and as nervous as his nature destitute of shame well could be, but he travelled thro' an elaborate speech to prove that the disfranchisement principle if acted upon was a revolution and led to the subversion of the Monarchy and property itself, and that it must not be resorted to till the necessity arising from the enactment of Enfranchisement was clearly proved. Lord Chancellor Brougham answered him in a calm and well reasoned speech without much effect and without that peremptory and fearless repudiation of the motion, as utterly inimical to the principle of reform and fatal to the bill, which seemed necessary to expose the plot. That plot was obviously to get the Management of the bill entirely in their own hands, to shake the confidence of the people in the Government, and then to mutilate and impair our measure in a way that would force us in honour to resign on some point upon which neither King nor Country would support us in making peers. When Harrowby, who followed Brougham, spoke and declared for Lord Lyndhurst's amendment, it was clear that the Waverers were willing to postpone those points on which they differed with the Ultras with the view and effect of combining with them in wresting all power of proceeding from us, and mangling our measure in a way either to disgust us, and to discredit us, if we submitted to it, with the Country. One or two, such as Lord Bexley[148] and Duke of Newcastle,[149] honestly avowed that they voted for the postponement of the Clause with the hope and intention of materially diminishing or utterly suppressing the disfranchisement. I attempted in a hurried and ill delivered speech to expose the tendency of the amendment. I maintained that disfranchisement was one leading principle of the bill, the first in point of order and not the last in importance, and above all that which, if disturbed or impaired *in the slightest degree,* would alarm and estrange the House of Commons and exasperate the people. I inveighed against the Nomination boroughs, maintained in reason and precedent the right of altering the Elective Franchise, and exhorted the House on every principle of prudence to reject the Amendment. My speech had little or no merit as a speech, but it put the question on the right ground. It pleased our friends, especially those of the House of Commons who were most apprehensive of any acquiescence in modifications or compromise with the Enemy. We divided and were beaten by a majority of 41![150] All the waverers, Wharncliffe included, and most of the Bishops, save London and Chester[151] and our own,[152] voting against us! We had scarce resumed our seats and heard the divisions when Ellenborough, with unembarrassed countenance, gravely announced his intention of substituting a plan of reform in the shape of amendments nearly commensurate to our own and in one respect, the preservation and extension of the Scot and Lot qualification, more popular or democratick, as he had the face to contend, than the bill. This artifice, if any thing so shallow or so gross can be so termed, was disclaimed by the Duke of Buckingham and shortly but admirably exposed by Lord Grey.[153] The latter after such a defeat said time must be taken for deliberation, and adjourned the Committee, and I think the house, for two or three days, having consented as a consequential amendment to the postponement of the 2d. Clause relating to Schedule B.

8th. Tuesday. We met at Foreign office at 11 AM, and agreed on a minute to the King relating the defeat of last night and tendering our resignations as a natural consequence, but adding that, in the peculiar circumstances of the Country and after what had passed, we felt it our duty to state the alternative of creating peers presented itself to us as one that might enable His Majesty to carry the bill without any change of Government, and that we were willing with that additional means of securing our measure to undertake it. It was deemed prudent that Lord Grey and Lord Chancellor should deliver the minute and convey the determination of the Cabinet to His Majesty—namely, to resign, unless they were allowed to create a sufficient number of peers which, we did not disguize, would be 50 or 60. This minute, the exact terms of which I have forgotten, was agreed to unanimously with the exception of the Duke of Richmond, who acknowledged that he could not recommend a creation of peers or remain in if that measure were resorted to. Grey and Brougham saw the King, presented the Minute, talked the matter over with him, and returned in the expectation, tho' not from persuasion, that H M would reluctantly and somewhat sulkily comply with our suggestion.[154] But on

Wednesday 9 May in the morning we received a letter accepting our resignations,[155] and attended the Levee where many of my Colleagues and some of the Household and other offices had audiences of leave to announce their resignation. The King was gracious and civil to all, but felt or expressed something like annoyance and agitation. He attempted to prevail on Richmond and I believe Palmerston to remain in. The former had openly recorded his difference with his Colleagues on the advice contained in the last Minute of the Cabinet, and the King probably knew or shrewdly surmised that the latter, though he acquiesced in it, had very earnestly deprecated the advice. In both of these attempts he failed, but engaged in even a more arduous undertaking, viz to persuade Brougham that the Chancellorship was not a political office and to retain the seals whatever Minister he might appoint, a view of the subject which some shrewdly suspected to have been suggested by Lord Lyndhurst. That unblushing lawyer was certainly on the next day, namely

on *Thursday 10 May,* with the King. He saw him frequently in the course of the 24 hours and in some sort clandestinely. Of what passed between the Duke of Wellington and his friends either before or after he kissed hands I of course can know nothing but such points as they in their speeches, newspapers, and private conversation subsequently divulged. Carnarvon on Thursday in the House of Lords and Baring, I think, in the Commons implied or expressed that a new Ministry was on the eve of being formed and both of them were supposed to be willing to accept high offices. It was shrewdly suspected from the beginning that Sir Robt. Peel's timidity or principle would prevent him from joining. He saw the impossibility of crushing reform and shrunk from the shameless inconsistency and profligacy of carrying it. In the mean while the accounts from the Country were appalling, the encrease of the political unions rapid, and the notions and preparations for resisting taxes, barricading towns, establishing communications and organizing simultaneous movements, more or less questionable in point of legality, manifest and undeniable. Yet it was thought, and I still believe, that the Duke of Wellington would have persisted, had he found a sufficient number of leading Men in the commons willing to assist him. Talleyrand told me that he thought he would succeed car il avait une volanté si fort, et je crois, added he, a la puissance d'une volante forte. [*In the margin:* Talleyrand was abused by our eager partizans for this language—but why? should he not have done his best when he thought a change of Government inevitable to propitiate our successors and preserve the pacifick system?] It is said that he gave further proof of the sincerity of his belief, by paying great court to him and Lady Jersey[156] and writing to Paris that Wellington when in office would be as pacifick as his predecessors. He laboured however to keep Aberdeen out of the foreign seals. So intense was the interest taken in our domestick affairs during these six or seven days, that neither the Cholera, nor the death of Casimir Perrier (a signal misfortune to Europe and the World), were deemed worthy of much notice, and even at Paris, I have been assured that the publick were more occupied with the dismissal of our Premier than with the illness and death of their own.

Monday 14th. May. I went with Lady Mary Fox to St. James's. We had scarce arrived when the Speaker entered the room where we were waiting, and Sir

Herbert Taylor took him into his Cabinet to speak on business. The King sent nearly at the same moment to me, and I had hardly time to apologize for having postponed my audience of leave, to express in the usual and respectful terms my sense of the kindness with which I had been treated and my regret at the circumstances which rendered my resignation a duty, and to observe his Majesty's earnest desire to divert the conversation from any of the late political events, before Sir Herbert Taylor came in to apprize the King that he wished him to step into an adjoining room for a moment. I of course made a motion and an endeavour to retire, but was forbidden to do so. The King went out, staid for two minutes, returned to talk entirely and exclusively of pictures, old Stories, and indifferent matters. It is clear that the conversation, so pressing and necessary, was one with the Speaker, and it seems to imply that at least attempts are making to shake his determination of declining Office. As to the King, I believe our tête a tête was nearly the only one in London which lasted this day for two hours without a single allusion to the cause or effect of the Change in which His Majesty was deeply engaged. He told me that his father had assured him that he did *not* know who wrote Junius, that he (George III) was satisfied as a critick in language and style (a character which I never before heard he had aspired to) that more than one hand had been employed upon it and that he doubted the Duke of Grafton having ever discovered the secret, for, had he done so, it would have been his duty to communicate it to him. He confirmed a story which I have related elsewhere of the concise funeral oration pronounced over Lord Rosslyn[157] by George III on hearing of his death. He said, 'There is one great rascal less in my dominions' though all persons and particularly the Queen thought Rosslyn had been a favorite. Throughout his conversation the King shewed neither emotion nor sorrow, but he manifestly studied to talk much and gaily. I heard with some chagrin that the King had given yesterday as a toast 'the virtuous men who are forming my new administration'. Nothing can exceed the warmth of Lady Mary Fox's feelings on this occasion. She was so impatient, that she prevailed on her husband to resign yesterday. In the Lords Lord Carnarvon, saying that no New Ministry was yet completed but there was a prospect of its speedily being so, postponed the Committee on Reform till Thursday and nothing more was said. Far different was the event in Commons. The debate on a petition was protracted to nearly 11 o'clock, and Henry Webster, who brought over the account to me late at night, described it as a total discomfiture of the Great Captain's forces and surrender at discretion of most of his leaders and partizans. I heard too, from Grey, that Baring allowed that the King was pledged to the bill and even admitted when pressed that the propriety of withdrawing all opposition to the bill and leaving Lord Grey in Ministry without making peers was a mode of proceeding well worthy consideration. In this Lord Ingestrie,[158] Charles Wynn,[159] and Davies Giddy[160] joined, and added that if Reform was to be carried it was much better to be carried by a Whig than a Tory administration, and Hunt added the people *would take it from no hands but ours*. Can even the Duke of Wellington, Hero as he is of an unembarrassed countenance, stand this? The motion of Lord Ebrington to address the King to keep his Ministers was carried by a Majority of 80.[161]

May 15. The debate of last night has produced such a sensation in the publick that Tories, waverers, and Court must yield. The Duke of Wellington at 1/2 past 11 slunk ignominiously away from the enterprize he had so imprudently undertaken, and told the King he was unable to form any Ministry. He could scarcely draw any other conclusion from the general reprobation of all respectable men, Reformers and antireformers, and the loud, universal, and dangerous indignation of the Country. In aid of these tremendous monitors I have reason to believe Rothschild[162] informed him that, if he persisted, a demand for Gold in England would encrease to a frightful amount, and the Movement Party in France would precipitate a war. [*Holland gives no indication where the following marginalia should appear, but it most likely refers to Rothschild:* He moreover learnt for the first time by the communication of the King's correspondence with His Ministers, that His Majesty had yielded the principle of making peers at an earlier period of the transaction and even consented to create 41—a fact which I am afraid the King had so much forgotten in his interviews with Lyndhurst and Wellington that he had led them to a contrary conclusion and to a supposition that they should come in to protect him from a measure which he had uniformly deprecated, resisted, and rejected.]

The King sent a letter to Grey,[163] and grounding his motive exclusively on what passed in Commons and the prospect of passing the bill in consequence thereof with modifications not affecting the principle and without any addition to the peerage for the purpose, offered and solicited Lord Grey to continue. He made no allusion to what Mr Holmes terms, aptly enough, the Interlude of the Duke of Wellington, and manifestly pointed to modifications, arrangements, and compromises with the Antireformers as furnishing the means of passing the bill without peers. To this, after deliberation at Lord Grey's, we dispatched a Minute of Cabinet[164] in which we adverted to the failure of the attempt to form a new Ministry, repeated the necessity of having a full security that we should pass the Reform bill unimpaired in its principles and essential provisions, and requested an assurance that H M would enable us to strengthen his Government in the House of Lords. In the house Grey announced the communication but, as nothing was settled, avoided all further explanation and adjourned the House till Thursday. The intelligence of this renewal of communication with Grey checked the active and encreasing violence of the people and suspended the frightful demand of gold and converted many hundreds of meetings throughout the country in the ensuing days into meetings of joy instead of consternation and despair. The tone however of the letter and the language repeated to us by Court Gossips were far from encouraging, and indicated soreness if not hostility in the King and yet more bitter hatred in the Queen to Lord Grey and his Colleagues. At the levee, where I arrived late, Grey told me that he thought 'the thing would do', and that the King in his audience, though neither cordial nor satisfactory, was better than his letter. I afterwards found that Grey alluded to a letter[165] (the reply to our answer in Cabinet) which he had received this morning, and which was full of irritation, soreness, and reluctance, and indicated as much repugnance to our measure and ourselves as was consistent with any possibility of admitting us to his councils, and more design of getting us in the wrong if a rupture ensued than of desire to prevent one [*In the margin:* recapitulating, with great earnestness and not much accuracy, his various *and uniform* objections to the creation of peers, and yet vindicating himself from what he considered as a complaint made against him—that he had shewn any unnwillingness to strengthen his Ministry or any want of sincerity or honesty in his dealings with them]. Even in his conversation the King avowed to Grey that he had always been hostile tho' he had yielded to Reform and that his hatred of it was not abated, and he still persisted in his incredulity of any very general and intense desire for it in the community. To this second letter we framed, after long and earnest deliberation in the Cabinet at Foreign Office and at Mr Stanleys, A Minute,[166] the substance of which was that to secure the bill through the Lords where, as at present composed, there was a Majority against it, there were but two methods of proceeding: the one, to prevail on the existing Majority to desist in their opposition, or the second, to produce a Majority in its favor by the introduction of friends to the measure. The first alternative was not in our power, and the last was the only one which suggested it to our minds unless some other security could be devised. We therefore must either advise the creation of peers or, on any probability being shewn us of passing the bill unaltered, resume the Government and proceed with an understanding that if any obstacle should arise we should be at liberty to surmount it by a creation of peers. We urged in this and all our minutes that security to pass the bill was indispensible as a condition to our remaining in office, but we did not insist on a creation of peers being the only security, although we glanced at it as the only one which we had a prospect of obtaining.

Thursday 16 [*17*] *May.* A Cabinet at Lord Grey's to consider of the answer received to our Minute of yesterday. The King in his letter distinctly acknowledged our right to exact some security for passing the bill unmutilated in its principles and essential provisions and as nearly as possible in its present form. He suggested the hopes that such security might be obtained and spoke of the creation of Peers as a measure to which he believed his Ministers were as averse as himself. In the meanwhile, though not in his letter, but through Sir Herbert Taylor and to Mr Stanley, he informed us that not less than twelve peers, who had given him their autograph signatures, had the intention this night of declaring that they would wave their opposition to the bill. The substance of what they meant to say was communicated in a written paper to Mr Stanley and, on his objecting to some phrase in it as equivocal and improper, he was assured that he King would suggest an alteration and that there was little doubt it would be adopted. In the twelve were included names which surprised us, such as *Duke of Newcastle* [*In the margin:* This must be a mistake of mine or was a mistake of Taylor's or Stanley. Absurd as Duke of Newcastle has been, is, and ever will be, he was consistent and invariable in his absurdity and, as a man of independence and honour, appeard to advantage throughout this transaction when contrasted with the Wellington, i.e. the profligate, or the Wavering, i.e. the conceited party.] Lord Mansfield, and many of the most uncompromising enemies of reform. This surrender of their opinions and pledges, solemnly recorded and passionately proclaimed within these three weeks, seemed unquestionably a strange device for vindicating the honour and independence of the House of Lords, rescuing it from degradation and contempt. However that was not our affair but theirs. We could not be any parties in such a transaction, but after due deliberation we thought we might await the result, as no doubt the knowledge of opposition being withdrawn might induce us to substitute for the advice of creating peers a request of an assurance that, if we should deem it necessary for passing the bill, the prerogative should be exercised and that on the existence of such necessity our judgement should be trusted.

With these views we framed an answer in substance, deferring a final and categorical one till Friday morning, stating in the body of it that the withdrawal of opposition to bill could not depend on us and that we could take no steps either with propriety or honour to diminish it, and that,if it were not diminished, we remained in the same state as we were on tuesday the 8th. May when we humbly tendered, through Lord Grey and the Chancellor, our resignation, unless a creation of peers was resorted to. However, glancing at, but not mentioning, the expected declaration in Lords, we were willing to wait till the next morning; from Lords Grey's we went to the House of Lords, in full expectation and with no little curiosity, to hear The Duke of Wellington and other of the protesters against the bill, as revolutionary, injurious to property, contrary to justice and nearly impracticable, state their reasons for supporting an attempt to form a Ministry to carry this heinous measure and, on the failure of their attempt, absenting themselves from Parliament in order that it might be carried by others. On moving a petition, Duke of Wellington related the transaction in which he had been engaged; vindicated his devotion to the King who, he said, had bade him assist in forming a Government founded on an extensive plan of reform; inveighed against the bill loudly, and yet more loudly against any creation of peers to carry it; said that he should have considered himself as the basest of men if he had refused to succour his Monarch when 'left alone'; and described the Man who should threaten, as criminal as the one who should create, peers, and the Peer who was swayed by the dread of such a measure, as degraded and contemptible as the one who had lost his relative importance in that house and the Country by the admission of them. Hitherto there was neither declaration nor any thing approaching to it. On the contrary, every sentence breathed enmity to the principles details and authors of the bill. Richmond, who had been most confident that all opposition would be waved, whispered to me that he began to believe no declaration whatever would be made. Lyndhurst, who followed the Duke of Wellington in the same strain and extolled him to the skies for his devoted conduct, said indeed that Reform had triumphed, that the waters were out, and much more of the same sort of metaphor which implied that it was now hopeless to stem the current, but made nothing like an explicit avowal of a determination to secede or to withdraw his opposition. Lord Grey in a calm, dignified, but well reasoned speech stated the motives and course of his conduct, repelled the insinuation of having left the King 'alone'—a character which Wellington had preposterously endeavoured to affix on his resignation—and at the same time acknowledged that the communication from the court had not hitherto led to any final settlement of the

Government. This speech, which Grey himself deemed too tame and guarded, but which every dispassionate or impartial observer admired for its calmness, judgement, discretion, and temper, was assailed successively by Mansfield, Haddington, Londonderry, Salisbury, and above all, Carnarvon, with a virulence of language, extravagance of gesture, and fury of sentiment such as I have never witnessed in the House of Lords. We let it pass; all Grey's colleagues sat silent, which at the time disappointed and hurt him—so much so that on Carnarvon's sitting down, I was, with some reluctance and against my judgement, rising to answer him, but gave way to Mulgrave who made a spirited speech, though on Lord Carnarvon's conclusion of 'having us to our duty work', The Duke of Wellington and about 50 or 60 peers rose in a marked way and quitted the house in a body—a proceeding they wished us perhaps to consider as an indication of an intended Secession, though it bound them neither in faith nor honour to any subsequent forbearance in their opposition to a bill which they had stigmatized as injustice and revolution.

We certainly acted judiciously in avoiding all angry debate and allowing the undisciplined rattle of words let loose against us to rave and riot at their will, without furnishing them with a pretext for charging us with rash or offensive language, or any thing unlike conciliation and forbearance. To such it was one of their objects to provoke us, and in that they failed. In another object—to exhibit themselves as a combined body ready to act in or out of office in any emergency—they succeeded. In a third, to afford us some little ground of hope of their absenting themselves from the Committee and the house during the Reform bill and, thereby, to deprive us of any plea for making peers, and yet at the same to keep us in a state of uncertainty and entirely dependent for the success of the bill on their perseverance in a course which they were in no way pledged to adopt, they were not altogether unsuccessful, and we felt our embarrassment. Grey wrote an account of the debate to the King and a more detailed report of his excessive disappointment to Sir H Taylor.[167] From others, especially Lord Errol,[168] the King received other accounts and had he grace to acknowledge next morning his deep mortification and disappointment at the absence of all publick declaration of secession or of support.

May 17 [*18*] *Friday*. The King's answer to Lord Grey's letter on the result of the debate was submitted to the Cabinet.[169] He spoke in terms of disappointment and almost of chagrin of the turn which the debate had taken, and ordered the copy of an answer he had sent to a letter of Lord Mansfield, received on the night of the debate; but he again deprecated the creation of peers as a measure to which he believed Lord Grey himself very adverse, and so as one which, forgetting his distinct consent to creat 41 three months ago in certain contingencies, he considered as against his *honour* and his *conscience* and fatal to his future *peace of mind*. The answer to this required both firmness and caution. We met at foreign office at 12, and we were full 4 hours in deliberation. Lord Althorp as well as myself came into the room in a full persuasion that nothing but actual and immediate creation of a large number would do, and both Lansdowne and Palmerston were prepared and even desirous to press for 10 or 15 as a demonstration. It was however agreed by all, after canvassing that question, that the full number requisite, if any, should be prepared, or that the power of making them, when we judged it expedient and necessary toward passing the bill, should be distinctly granted. Some letters and more reports which we received from many staunch friends in the course of our deliberation inclined us to avoid if possible any rupture on the question of immediate creation.

[*Heading:* 17 to 24 May.] Here again to the *24th. of May,* my diary, owing to my removal to London and attendance in Lords, was neglected, and I must fill it up at my leisure and according to my recollection, which however, on the succession of small events and details, unless refreshed and rectified by notes, is always imperfect and scarce to be relied upon. Nothing could exceed the violence and acrimony of the invectives of the Lords still attending the house in all the debates before going into the Committee, and occasionally in the Committee itself. The Duke of Newcastle announced a motion denying the King's right to create peers, questioned Lord Grey on what had passed between him and the King, and arraigned Ellenborough and the waverers and seceders as almost as bad as the Reformers themselves and less honest and consistent. The Archbishop of York, with more talent than I ever knew him display, lamented the indecent asperity with which the debates had been conducted, declared that the disgust and alarm he had felt thereat had prevented his speaking, and took a late opportunity of bearing his testimony, founded upon observation in his extensive, populous and industrious diocese, that to avoid an efficient Reform was impossible, and to delay it much longer would be hazardous. The Bishop of London redeemed his pledge in the Course of the Committee and, though he suggested or supported some amendments, both by his manner and votes proved that he was earnest and sincere in his profession of forwarding the bill and preferring a great measure of reform, even with blemishes, to the hazard of delaying and defeating it under colour of perfecting or improving it. The other hostile Bishops for the most part staid away, or voted with the antireformers when there was any division in the Committee.[170]

Thursday 24th. May. Still at Lady Afflecks.[171] Went to St. James's but the King was on the point of driving out and could not see me. I spent more than an hour with Sir Herbert Taylor, who praised Coll. Fox for his conduct, acknowledged that neither he in his private or I in my ministerial capacity had ever pressed the King to make Charles an Aide de camp, that it was the fulfillment of a *spontaneous* promise and that he ought not to have declared it so premptorily to Charles, if he was not prepared to insist on it with Lord Hill. He fully entered into the feelings of Charles about the money, assured me that if ever [he] had an opportunity he would explain it to the King as a necessary consequence of delicate and honourable feelings, and not a haughty and ill tempered rejection of any kindness or favor for him, which, even of a pecuniary sort, his son in law would always receive as a mark of his affection, but which an officer could hardly accept as a compensation for a professional disappointment. He added, what is strange, that the King never spoke to him on the subject, nor on that of Charles's resignation of the Equerryship. Lord Grey came on the subject of the estrangement with the Duke of Sussex and begged me to stay while he and Taylor discussed it. The King, according to Taylor's account, was and still is greatly incensed with the Duke of Sussex for thinking even of presenting an address which he, the King, construes into a menace of rebellion and civil war.[172] He says he is at least impartial, for in the same week he reprimanded the Duke of Cumberland, drove the Duchess into Hystericks, and forbade the Duke of Sussex to come to Court. He persists in the impossibility of receiving the Duke of Sussex without some written explanations from him, which he terms an apology. *Not Under* that name certainly, and under no other, I fear, will the Duke take such a step, unless invited to do so with some degree of brotherly kindness. It is a bad business, for if it gets into the publick prints and House of Commons debates, the breach will be widened and the Cumberland faction at Court greatly strengthened. They will not fail even to represent the poor Duke of Sussex as the *Egalité* of the family, and I am afraid by Taylor's report of the King's soreness at the libels at the Attorney General's admissions and other things, his mind is still in a state susceptible of being perverted and enflamed.

Attended the Lords, and was tempted or provoked by the ignorance and offensive tediousness of Lord Wynford to speak with more earnestness and violence than the occasion required and thereby possibly against good policy, lengthened the debate on granting a vote to freeholders within the precincts of a borough, for the adjoining County. On my return found My Son Harry just arrived from Flanders. My daughter in law, Lady Mary Fox, seems to think her father will insist on Charles being appointed his Aide de Camp. He distinctly allows that in his judgement Lord Hill is wrong in objecting to it, and Sir James Kempt[173] calls Lord Hill's resistance to it most extraordinary and unjustifiable.

25th. May Friday. My Son Charles, while on Guard at St. James's, was sent for by the King, whom he found at luncheon with his family and Sisters and who, rising, bade him kneel down immediately. He then told him to kiss his hand and exclaimed, 'Now rise *Colonel* Fox and My Aide de Camp'. All this was done de proprio Motu. Neither Ministers, I, Charles, nor Sir Herbert were further aware of his intentions than from his having promissd Charles himself, in 1830, that in March 1832, he would make him his Aide Camp. There was an angry article full of false statements in the Morning Post on the subject, the facts of which my son set right with great calmness and temper in a paragraph in the Morning papers of Saturday.

In the Lords, Lord Londonderry made an irregular, virulent, and ungentleman-like attack on Ministers in an invective against a seditious and extravagant speech of a man of the name of Larkin[174] at Newcastle. That man, I discovered, was the son of a gardener who lived with me. He was born at Holland House, and christened Charles Fox, has recently been employed and dismissed from the Police, and by a libellous, scurrilous, and indecent speech against the King and Queen at Newcastle, gave occasion to one against Lord Grey in the House of Lords from Lord Londonderry equally deserving those epithets. Lord Goderich, justly exasperated at the irregularity of such attacks and foaming with rage at them, deprecated any thing like an answer from Lord Grey, and Lord Wynford, who attempted to palliate if not to justify Londonderry and censure the Government for not prosecuting the outrageous attacks on King and Queen, with zeal, was admirably exposed and rebuked by Radnor for his extrajudicial violence and prejudgement of the law and fact in arraigning Men, untried and unheard, as traitors and Criminals. The Duke of Cumberland again stepped forward as a peacemaker. In the Committee on reform we made considerable progress, and the debate though dull was all to our advantage. It is rather comical to observe Brougham, who inculcates the necessity of calmness and moderation in the Committee, act that part to the life, so happily as to become humdrum and prosing upon the details, even to tediousness. Durham and Radnor are the two who are of most service to the cause in this stage of the bill, and even Lord Bathurst and Lord Gage[175] acknowledge that on two points upon which they had the strongest antipathy to the bill, namely the Metropolitan boroughs and Gateshead,[176] they have been satisfied by Durham that there is nothing either partial or extravagant or that is not fairly a consequence and of a piece with the measure, if a measure of reform of such extent and principle is once to be admitted.

On *Saturday the 26th. and Sunday 27th.* we had Cabinets chiefly to decide on the question of amendments which had been proposed in the Committee and which, on the statement of our adversaries, seemed reasonable, but many of which, on further enquiry and discussion, turned out quite inadmissible.

The King is certainly much agitated and his manner as well as conduct are, by the account given me by Charles, so inconsistent and even incoherent as to raise some apprehensions in the minds of persons immediately about him. This is unpleasant. In Charles's affair he is at least friendly, just, and candid, insists on his right of conferring and adhering to the appointment, and acquits Ministers, me, and Charles of any importunity, advice or application about it. I understand his reception in the streets on his way to the exhibition at Somerset house, though unattended with violence, was far from flattering and, in spite of his affected disdain of popularity, he feels the loss of it. Does he draw the right inference? That to secure it he must steer a steady consistent and popular course?

Monday the 28 May 1832. We were unexpectedly summoned to Cabinet after the [King's] birthday (which I missed), chiefly to consider of a letter from the King to Lord Grey of an unpleasant and discontented nature.[177] He described himself though long silent as deeply and sensibly alive to the question of reform, as *surprized* at so few modifications having been admitted in English bill and yet more at the tone assumed and prospects held out about the Irish bill, which, unless there was a *remedy* in *store* he described as fraught with evil consequences. He quoted supposed admissions of Lord Grey entirely at variance with the fact, affected to consider him as inclined to let the Irish bill be defeated and willing to admit modifications in the English bill, hinted at an unfair disappointment if not a violation of engagements to the seceders and opposition who had disarmed themselves, and throughout urged the necessity of conciliation. He betrayed great soreness at the licentiousness of language both in meetings and in writings, termed the state of the bill *unimproved,* and argued that he had a right to use that term because, as he erroneously supposed, Lord Grey had admitted that many of the points now introduced into the bill ought to be altered. There were even other topicks introduced indicative of ill humour and whim—strong lamentations at the mention of further reforms in Church or state and especially on Hume's speeches views. To this remonstrating and in some degree reproachful letter, Grey, before he went to court, dispatched a spirited and respectful reply,[178] vindicated himself from the aspersion of inconsistency about modifications, to some of which he had before the late unlucky occurrences stated that he might submit without a creation of peers, but none of which he had ever approved, much less recommended, and most of which, from the encreased excitement of the publick, he believed to be now incompatible with some of the main and immediate objects of the bill and not the least likely to reconcile or soften any of the opponents of his Majesty's Government, the more reasonable portion of which acknowledged themselves much shaken if not convinced both on the Metropolitan boroughs and the £10 qualification. The substitution of a second member for Kilkenny in lieu of the additional one for Dublin University, on which the King felt apprehensions, had not been acquiesced in, and whatever might be our opinion of the original addition of a member of the University, we were disposed to adhere to it.

While we were discussing or rather commending this answer of Lord Grey's, Melbourne, who had been commanded to wait after the drawing room, came fresh from his audience and told us that on the *perusal* of the reply the King had vehemently disclaimed all intention of urging modifications, recommending any negotiation with our opponents, or threatening their return to the house, and had authorized him to assure Lord Grey and the Cabinet that Grey had *entirely* mistaken the purpose and intention of his letter. In short it was clear from Melbourne's report that he had expressed his uneasiness, perhaps vented some ill humour and dissatisfaction in his epistle, but that he was so far aware of his situation as to shrink most earnestly from bringing any dispute with us to a practical crisis. He has recently appointed a Lord of the Bedchamber not in Parliament and suspected to be an Enemy, Lord Ashbrook,[179] without consulting Lord Grey, and he has filled up the places of Attorney and Solicitor to the Queen with two names which, though not hostile, are not those of the gentlemen who resigned on our retirement. He continues as much inflamed as ever against the Duke of Sussex. He alledged in proof of his impartiality that, almost on the same day that he had forbidden the Duke of Sussex the Court, he had <rated> the Duke of Cumberland and his Duchess[180] so sharply that the latter <fronted> away. He had told her that the conduct of her husband was *une infamie.* She complained bitterly of this to the Queen, who reminded her, with some readiness and dignity, that if the King had given her so much pain by censuring in strong terms her husband, She, the Queen, could not receive much pleasure in hearing such intemperate language about her own.

My son Charles, who thought that without solicitation he had, at the expense of some calumny and misrepresentation and consequent jealousy and odium, acquired, through the favor or remorse of the King, the rank of Colonel, was not a little hurt and exasperated at finding that he was gazetted as Aide de Camp, without the usual rank accompanying that office. [*Heading:* 29 May Tuesday] He had not been apprized of this intention by Lord Hill or the King, and his first impulse was to decline the whole promotion, nay, it required some persuasion to prevent him from actually quitting the army. After reflection however and consultation with Sir James Kempt, who was singularly friendly to him throughout, he determined to consider the gazette as a professional command which he could not disobey, and satisfied himself with reminding the King that the favor had been offered, and as he thought conferred, without any solicitation much less importunity on his part, that divested of the rank it was in truth no favor but the omission of the advantage usually accompanying it, a sort of ridicule, and that the appointment which he had been authorized to announce, and now compelled, after the King had publickly made him kiss hands and called him a Colonel, to forego, exposed him to all the odium and none of the advantages of the intended promotion. To Lord Hill he said that he could not complain, for he could not disapprove of his remonstrances against the favor which would have put him over the head of so many older officers; he had certainly thought that after the King had spontaneously and publickly not only announced but persisted in his intention and, as far as lay in him, <completed> it, it was at least a strong and ungracious measure to force him to retract it, and that he could not deny that after he had himself in the most open and, as he thought, handsome and considerate way apprized Lord Hill before his friends or even his own father of every step taken or word spoken by the King, he was hurt, and indeed never could forget that he was shorn of the usual honour attached to his appointment, without being allowed the opportunity of declining it and without being apprized, though others were, of the unusual step his Lordship determined to advise the King to adopt. It seems Lord Hill, after repeating his remonstrances and citing some precedent in peculiar circumstances of naming an Aide de camp without advancing him to the rank of Colonel, sent two drafts of the article to be inserted, one omitting and one, as usual, conferring the rank, and the King signed and returned the former!

30 May Wednesday. Lord Munster made a speech which he termed an explanation of his conduct, but which left his opinions more unintelligible and his proceedings or intrigues more liable to suspicion than before. We proceeded through the Committee smoothly enough.

May 31 Thursday. No House of Lords.

1 June Friday. With the exception of a few deliberate and angry epithets from Lord Carnarvon, little more was said on the Report than was necessary to afford the opposition Lords an opportunity of protesting; and the Duke of Newcastle, at the request of the Duke of Cumberland, who lectured or frightened by his Majesty, acts the part of a peacemaker and does not act it ill, put off his Motion on Creation of Peers sine die.[181]

On *Saturday* the *2d. June,* I returned to Holland House, and staid all *Sunday*.

On *Monday 4th. June* Lord Winchelsea in a ranting speech, which, as Lord King truly said, he delivered so loudly that one could hardly hear him, arraigned Grey for subverting the Constitution, degrading the Lords, and threatened him with revolution and bloodshed, remorse on his death and damnation afterwards, and once more declared that he never would set his foot in the house again if a single peer were to be made. [*Heading:* Monday 4 June—George III's birthday and 3d. reading of Reform!] Lord Harrowby followed with equal malignity, turned some laboured periods on the degradation of the house, consigned Lord Grey to the judgement of the people when grown sober and posterity, maintained with more sophistry than ingenuity that the amendment which postponed schedule A was a matter of *no principle* to the supporters but of some to the opponents of the bill, and drew from these premises the monstrous and revolting conclusion that the resignation of Lord Grey was a trick to trample on the Crown and degrade the Lords and to rivet the power of the Whigs. Lord Grey with wonderful animation and effect retorted the Charge of political manoeuvring, and without descending too much to details vindicated himself from the malignant and unfounded charge. I thought Harrowby quailed under the merited chastizement he received. Wharncliffe, manifestly hampered, did not relieve him by disclosing more frankly the course of policy he had pursued, and acknowledging that he had voted for Lyndhurst's motion, not because he deemed it important or even right, but because it was the only way of enlisting thoroughstitch AntiReformers in their scheme of altering the bill against the will of its supporters. They had planned a *Coup de Theatre* and were to rise in a body and walk out of the house when the question was put; but this was disconcerted by Roden, who would divide, and who consequently perplexed them to a degree that was ludicrous, some running away, and some, to the number of 22, staying to divide.[182] Never were men more bitter or more discomfited. <In triumph>.

Tuesday 5. Nothing but congratulation on 3d. reading and hopes ill founded that King will go down to pass bill.

·*Wednesday 6 June.* Went to Levee, where I heard from Talleyrand that the Duchess of Berry[183] was certainly in the Vendee and that she had passed through Bourdeaux on the outside of a Diligence disguised as a serving maid, and through other places in male attire. Talleyrand is not alarmed but laments the bloodshed and sacrifice of foolish people which it must occasion. Palmerston was invested with his red ribband, the Duke of Wellington and Duke of Gloucester[184] attended the ceremony. The King made a short speech to Palmerston expressing his satisfaction at his foreign policy, which is rather at variance with sundry passages in his conversation and correspondence and not much of a piece with the irritability and soreness which he shews about everything connected with our liberal politicks. He has written a very improper letter through Sir Herbert Taylor to Sir John Dalrymple,[185] accusing him of disloyal language and conduct (upon light and false testimony as well as incorrect newspaper reports) at the meeting and clearly hinting at a removal from the army. All this, too, without consulting the Horse Guards or his Ministers! He remonstrates with Althorp for acquiescing in a bill extending the power of granting reprieves,[186] and very strangely sends for Tenterden to the closet to authorize him to oppose it as an encroachment on the prerogative, and he writes to the Chancellor that he will not go down to pass the Reform, for that after the Manner he and his Queen have been treated by the people he should feel himself disgusted and degraded by their applauses. Wellesley, hearing of his inflexibility on this point, will abstain from pressing him to go down as he intended. There is evidently a fear of *exciting* him (that is the term) too much, and I hear it whispered that his <dinners> and his wine tend to aggravate the said excitement.

Business at the Duchy. Dined at a Cabinet at Lansdown House but as Grey and others were absent no business was done. Palmerston wishes to see Henry and offers to make him Precis writer or paid attaché to Washington.

7 *June Thursday*. Henry has seen Palmerston, and his leaning is to prefer the transatlantick employment. I sat as one of the Commissioners to pass The Reform Bill. We were six in our Robes and on the bench, and I reflected with some satisfaction that five of us were members of the old opposition who uniformly maintained the principles of peace and reform,[187] and that the three bills which I had hitherto sat as Commissioner to pass were the Abolition of Slave trade, the alteration of the Game Laws, and the Reform Bill. We were all astounded with the news of insurrection in Paris,[188] of which the origin and object seem unintelligible, and the issue, though scarcely doubtful, not decided when the Telegraphic dispatch at 12 o'clock yesterday came away.

Friday 8 June. The letters from Paris which <reach> to yesterday morning prove that the insurrection is put down, that the force employed against it both of troops of the line and National guard has been considerable, and so much so as to give rise to some natural surmises that there had been great preparation for such an event, and that the measures of vigour, such as the suppression of several publick prints, the declaring of Paris in a state of siege, and the dissolution of the Polytecknick school, all suppose great division of parties and a very uneasy and unsafe state of society.

In the Lords: the Duke of Buccleugh,[189] Lord Haddington, and Duke of Wellington pretended difficulties and scruples about the bill regulating the Court of Exchequer in Scotland[190] and prayed for time and information, which the Chancellor deemed it prudent to grant them, against my judgement, at the hazard of not passing the bill in time to admit Abercrombie into Parliament for Knaresborough on the vacancy occasioned by the death of poor Sir James Mackintosh. Mackintosh is some loss in politicks and much greater in society, and the greatest of all in literature, where his knowledge, good nature, and talents rendered him most useful and delightful. The last fortnight has been painfully remarkable for the loss of men, distinguished for attainments in law, politicks, philosophy, and strength of intellect. Sir James Mackintosh, Sir William Grant,[191], John Clerk,[192] and Jeremy Bentham.[193]

Talleyrand, Wessenburg, and Lord Granville, who remains to hear the result of the Paris event, dined with me at Holland House whither I returned this day. The Mob government at Paris is put down, but is not the military power, in the person of Soult who put it down, set up? and is that for the interests of Europe and peace? Time will shew.

Saturday 9th. June. Holland House. In the evening went to the Duke of Sussex, who receives the Royal Society, and I was really much pleased at the assemblage of men remarkable for science learning and various attainments and at the propriety with which R H Highness [*sic*] does the honours of his house. His disgrace at Court is not repaired and the King is injudicious and I think unjust in excluding him from favour. H M vindicates himself from the charge of partiality by observing, as is true, that in the same week he reprimanded Duke of Sussex for Radical and the

Duke of Cumberland for Tory faction. He remarks, as is also true, that the Duke of Cumberland altered his course and adopted a mild, mitigated, and conciliatory tone, though he (the King) had thrown the Duchess of Cumberland into Hystericks by the severity of his reproof. Of this the Duchess complained to the Queen with some asperity and with tears bewailing the indignity put upon her husband. When she launched out into reflection on the King's conduct the Queen very properly interrupted her by observing that if it was painful to the Duchess of Cumberland to hear her husband abused by the King, it was not less so to the Queen to hear abuse of her own from the Duchess of Cumberland.

There was among our House of Commons friends a great outcry at the report of Sir Charles Bagot going on a temporary Mission to St. Petersburgh. He declines going and there is an end of that, but as the feeling which led to the outcry is produced more by the prevalence of Tory politicks in many of the offices and missions and not by the particular case, we shall probably hear more of the same sort of remonstrance. There has been one of a yet more formal kind from many of our friends in Parliament. I suggested some new men to Grey, such as Gower, Minto, Auckland,[194] &c &c.

10 June Sunday. Little business and no company but Duncannon, who confirms Sir James Kempt's opinion in the case of Charles and approves of his not actually resigning the Aide de campship, though forced upon him and shorn of its usual and legitimate <beams>, because the gazetting is technically a professional order that he should discharge the duty and a soldier ought not to disobey, and secondly, though the gazetting him without his consent or knowledge is either inconsiderate and [un?]<friendly>, yet the possession of that post will insure the acquisition of rank when other Officers are promoted with rank to the same office, and that event cannot be very remote. He is considered as a sort of Martyr and no less than 4 Boroughs–Kidderminster, Dudley, Brighton, and Christchurch–have been in some degree offered to him. The dissenters are the chief promoters of such a measure.

Monday 11th. June.

Tuesday 12th. June. Much conversation in the course of these two days respecting Scotch elections, where there is some difficulty in procuring Candidates who unite the manner and character of Gentlemen with strong popular feeling, but none in finding places and electors who will chuse such in preference to visionaries and radicals, if they can be found.

13 June Wednesday. Went to Court and saw King on Duchy business. He did not touch on politicks. Sir John Dalrymple who was on the eve of an audience told me he looked quite savage at him at the Levee, but he must be more unjust than I believe him to be, if he does not relax when he hears of Sir John's statements and the documents by which he substantiate them. The Calumnies and exaggerations propagated about the Edinburgh Meeting and against this meritorious officer have already occasioned one fatal duel and were near producing another. Mr Dundas[195] however acknowledged to Sir J Dalrymple that he had been <misinformed>, but a hot young man, Markham,[196] nephew of Lady Mansfield,[197] chose the Mess of the 98th. for the theatre of his invectives, founded on false reports, against the Colonel Sir John Dalrymple. He was consequently challenged thereupon and shot on the spot by the Lt. Colonel of the name of McDonald.[198] I am told that Clanrickarde, Anson,[199] and Foley, all in the Household but all persons who recently resigned and were restored, are omitted in the invitations to Queen's ball. It may be accidental but it is an odd accident. Lady Foley[200] and Lord Kinnaird's Sister[201] are asked but not Kinnaird.[202] Folly about such trifles is not confined to the Court itself. Lord Dundonald has embarrassed Grey by applying to have Lady Dundonald presented.

14 June Thursday. Attended the House where, after some trifling matters, the Scotch Exchequer Court bill was postponed, and it was also agreed to put off Lord Roden's motion[203] till Friday sennight which I hope will enable Lord Plunkett to attend. Dined at a splendid dinner at Devonshire House. Grey much chagrined at Lord Duncannon and other friends in and out of office voting against Government on the additional Member for Irish University.[204] The King much less cordial even in manner to Lord Grey than he was, and his correspondence both to him and to Lord Althorp, very sore and irritable. I strongly advised Grey to avoid so much intercourse by letter and to seek more in conversation and society. The Queen at Drawing room was gracious to him and Whig Ladies. I suspect she is much less political than her advocates and calumniators suppose, but more occupied with matters for which her appearance does not particularly qualify her, than has hitherto been apparent.

15 June Friday. Saw Sir Herbert Taylor. Sir John Dalrymple has completely vindicated himself in the King's judgement. At least H M admitted he was satisfied and listened to the testimony of Sir John, who moreover referred him to Lord Mansfield, in favor of John Murray's loyalty, on whom the King was disposed to shift the charge brought against Dalrymple. I left a letter from Murray with Sir H Taylor to shew His Majesty. Attended the West India Committee and the House. In the latter the Dukes of Buccleugh and Wellington and Lord Haddington, from party spite to Chief Baron Abercromby, virulently and pertinaciously opposed the bill for reducing that Court and trsferring the business of it to a Judge of the Court of Session, and styled it a violation of the Union, an injury to Scotland, and what not, tho' only a year ago they had let it pass thro' the House without notice or objection.

Saturday 16 June. Returned to Holland House. Falck, Talleyrand, and Weissenburgh, the two former on the point of quitting England, dined with us. The Chancellor, Melbourne, and Palmerston as well as Falck staid at Holland House.

Sunday 17 June. Palmerston offered Henry a step in Diplomacy to Turin if he would first be gazetted as paid attaché to Washington, which Henry gladly accepted. Attended the Cabinet at two. Althorp is anxious for some decision on the business of the Bank as he is likely to be pressed to explain his views either in the Committee or the house.[205] I know little of these matters, but unless the notion of entire free competition and the suppression of all exclusive privileges for a Government bank are determined upon (as I think they ought to be), I prefer keeping things as nearly as possible as they are, to tampering and tinkering an artificial system and introducing regulations and contrivances of which one cannot from experience judge the consequences. The plan, to which Althorp leans, and which I suspect is the suggestion of the Chairman and of Poulett Thompson, would extinguish all small Country bankers at once and produce a very extensive change in the currency and mercantile transactions in the country. The Chancellor, Lord Melbourne, and Falck slept at Holland House.

Monday 18 June. In House of Lords Duke of Buccleugh persisted in captious objections and amendments to the Scotch Exchequer court bill, but it was read a 3d. time and passed without a division. Some trifling Duchy business in Morning with Mr Danvers and Mr Harper.[206]

Tuesday 19 June. Yesterday some of the rabble followed by boys insulted the Duke of Wellington, who had been on the anniversary of the victory of Waterloo to deposit the flag either at Lincoln's inn or the city, and to day, at Ascot, a mad or drunken old Sailor with one leg, who had been deprived of his pension for bad behaviour at Greenwich, threw a stone at the King on the race ground and struck him a blow which the King at first mistook for a bullet and which might have been more serious but for the padding of his hat. The Man was immediately taken up, and his motives were clearly private and personal, arising from resentment at the right of a petition he had transmitted to be laid before the King against his dismissal from Greenwich. These outrages are disgusting and not a little provoking too as they furnish the wicked and the weak with popular topicks for arguing that the Government is entirely at the mercy of the people.

[*In the margin*: Prince Talleyrand took leave of us this night. He was manifestly affected at leaving England, and though earnest in his assurance of returning, seemed to me to have misgivings that he should not. He has however placed here Mr Durand (Baron Mareuil[207]) and has, I suspect, thereby disappointed and hurt, *possibly dejoue,* Flahault, whose desire to fill his place was no doubt mingled with some design of *permanently* replacing him. Our King, who was strongly prejudiced against Talleyrand on his arrival in England, complimented him in his audience of leave extremely on his conduct, attributed to his talents and good disposition the understanding subsisting between the two countries, vehemently expressed a hope he might return, and directed Palmerston in his presence to write to Paris to assure Louis Philippe that nothing would be more pleasing to the Govt. here, or more calculated to prove his earnest desire to preserve cordiality af peace between the two countries, than his return.]

June 20 Wednesday. Lady Afflecks 84th. Birthday. I staid at home all day.

June 21 Thursday. The address moved yesterday in both houses on the Ascot outrage was right in itself both in reason and precedent and has had the happiest effect on house, country and, I hope, court. Among the good consequences an injudicious speech from our opponent Sir Robert Peel and a castigation which he felt from Stanley are not to be overlooked. The people, though no doubt in some degree estranged from the King by his late conduct, were justly indignant both from moral and loyal feeling at the Ruffian, and Richmond, who was on the spot, seemed inclined to censure both them and the Magistrates and witnesses for displaying more passion than was decent and more conviction of unproved facts than was just. In the Lords, Lord Roden was prevailed upon to postpone his threatened motion on Ireland till 1st. of July.

Cabinet dined at Lord Melbourne's. Stanley anxious for instructions how to proceed with the tythe bill, said he must announce some measure as in readiness tomorrow and fix a day for presenting his bill or bills for next week. He wishes us to decide on Sunday what measure we will recommend. Great difficulties beset his plan, and his speculation that on the arrest and imprisonment of some rich and leading recusants of tythe the others will come in seems very precarious. Should it fail, our embarrassment is increased and the reproach of weakness and impotence on Government greatly aggravated. Prompt relief and an immediate and compulsory commutation would be the simplest and safest remedy, but is it practicable? The Committees are far from being up to the Mark, and in the Lords, though the report was softened and rendered somewhat ambiguous and irresolute, Harrowby protested against it and denounced opposition in the house because strong measures of coercion should, he said, be recommended, and the law at all hazards and by all means enforced. He knows as well as we do that such means are not at our command, but baffled in his plot against our reform, he labours and chuckles at any other perplexity, however dangerous to the Country, in which we may be involved. The Irish Members press for some further extension of the franchise in Irish Counties to repair in some degree the injustice of the forty shilling freeholders disfranchisement bill. Their arguments on some of the details are plausible, but their motives may be suspected; the consequences of any alteration cannot be thoroughly understood without further enquiry and those who recommend it may have some private interest in view. It is safer to abide by the bill as it is; the only solid reason for any change was the exhortation of OConnell to some Irish Member not to press it, 'for', said he, 'Ministers may yield that point and then the bill is better and less of a grievance for us'. This however did not outweigh the other objections. Both Althorp and Stanley think some concession, reasonable in itself, would smooth the passage of the bill thro' the commons, and are willing to give way. The King is still rather cross and troublesome about the Unions.

Friday 22d. June. In town and at Lord Grey's in the Evening.

Saturday 23rd. Saw the Museum, dined with Fox Club at Greenwich.

Sunday 24th. Cabinet at two. Reconsidered an alteration solicited by Irish Members by which votes are to be given to £10 tenants with a 21 years lease who reside, and the concession, after much discussion and explanation, granted, somewhat against Grey's and much against Richmond's will.[208] We then entered upon the more arduous question of bills relating to Irish tythe. Grey preferred and I think most justly the prompt and simple method of an immediate commutation to land tax, but met with little encouragement from any present except myself, who was prepared to go yet further and convert the Irish Church revenue at once into an annuity on the publick funds. It was agreed on all hands that if a more specifick commutation were to be made, the first step on which all the rest must depend was a bill of compulsory composition, and the principle and provisions of that prepared by Stanley were approved.

In two other bills, involving many difficult and important details, he means to establish an Ecclesiastical Commission in each diocese, composed of beneficed Clergymen, to superintend the Composition value and exchange of tythes, to facilitate the sale of tythes at 16 years purchase, and to convert hereafter the money raised by the sale into land or glebe.[209] By one of these bills the subject is to be relieved from the Church cess and a new valuation of benefices to be made with a view of enlarging the first fruits and tenths and applying their proceeds to the building and repairing of the Churches.

The case of Collins, the prisoner who assaulted the King at Ascot, is to be referred to the Law Officers. It is difficult to avoid trying him for high treason and will be equally difficult to convict him thereof. The King was much tickled with the joint address which took him by surprize and not a little pleased at Sir Francis Burdett's speech, in which he reprobated the base and unmanly attacks on the Queen, who was herself struck and perhaps surprized at the propriety of his feelings and expressions, being taught to believe by the narrowminded gossips who surround her that every Reformer or at least every Radical is destitute of gallantry, honour, or humanity.

25 June Monday. Lord Middleton[210] accepted the Stewardship of Tickhill from the Duchy of Lancaster. Sir John Newport called on leaving England, not without some chagrin, natural enough, that his nephew's claim to some promotion has been hitherto neglected. Few deserve more from the Whigs than Newport. None can have got less, and the old Man feels it.

In the Lords a bill for abolishing the punishment of death for Horse and for Sheep stealing and for stealing above five pounds in a dwelling house[211] was as usual combated by the three Law Lords—Tenterden, Eldon, and Wynford—who, begging the question that the terror of death, notwithstanding the continual evasion of the law by the unwillingness of prosecutors, of juries, of judges and of the Executive government to execute such revolting rigour, did nevertheless deter persons from the commission of the crime, inveighed against the possibly heinous nature and cruel consequences of the offence, and turned periods and produced illustrations of the sacredness of property. They were well but not vehemently answered by Lord Chancellor Brougham, who however made greater admissions respecting the lawfulness and humanity of such punishments than sound reason or possibly his own real opinion would approve. He knew the King to be jealous of the general principle which leads to the abrogation of capital punishment, and thought, perhaps justly, that the narrow ground, founded on the specifick inefficacy of the Statutes proposed to be repealed, was more likely to prevail than a bold avowal of that broad principle which enjoins the relinquishment of all capital punishments for offences unattended with violence, inasmuch as the feelings of the pious, the tender, and the just portion of Mankind have always and will always revolt at all disproportionate severity and above all at capital punishments for offences created entirely by the artificial laws of society.

The Chancellor came home with me to Holland House. He blamed and lamented the intended appointment of Durham to St. Petersburgh and sneered at what he is pleased to call Lord Grey's nepotism; but the appointment is in many respects good. A Man of authority, vigour, and decision is much required in Russia, and even the defects of Durham's character and his unpopularity with the Ultras and Tories both at home and abroad may inspire salutary terror in the Autocrat. I am told too, that He, Durham, was much pleased with Palmerston, which removes the only solid objection, a fear of jealousy or difference between them. After all, who that knows Durham's great qualifications, as well as his defects, and reflects on his misfortunes, but must rejoice at his being employed in a way likely to divert his grief and in a line where his abilities may be of real service to his country and his employers?

26th. Tuesday. The King's accession. He reviews some Regiments in the morning, gives a dinner of 100 covers at St. James's, and goes to a ball at the Duke of Wellingtons in the Evening, where I am the only Minister uninvited, though I believe by mere accidental omission and I know to my great comfort and satisfaction.

A new qualification for Scotch Members has been introduced in the Scotch bill by a strange acquiescence of Althorp in the suggestion of Sir G Clark.[212] This has spread dismay in Scotland and it must be altered again.

27 Wednesday. At Court and dined with an ill attended Cabinet at Lord Goderich's. Pmerston has drawn out a dispatch to Fredk. Lamb explaining to him the various objects of Lord Durham's mission to Petersburgh, and apprizing Metternich distinctly that he must not expect any assistance either by negotiation or otherwise from us in the prosecution of his Italian policy, inasmuch as it is clear that the Austrians in Rome have not acted in concert with Mr Seymour or the French, but rather endeavoured to thwart them, and that in consequence thereof Mr Seymour's presence in the Roman territories is no longer necessary or useful, the English having taken no other interest in the concerns of the Papal Government than such as might be instrumental in preserving harmony between the respective parties and the general peace of Europe.

At dinner Grey and others seemed more disposed to prosecution for libel and intemperate language than is ever useful or prudent, and the Chancellor, meaning to divert the object with address, did, with that cajolery usual with Lawyers and with none more than himself, make greater admissions about the atrocity, the bad effects, dangerous tendency, and necessary suppression of publick libels than, with a view to future discussions on similar questions, it was right or prudent for him to make. To defeat the immediate object of a particular prosecution, he unnecessarily and earnestly inculcates a principle that may lead to many he would yet more earnestly deprecate. The Scotch qualification is given up.

From *27th. June to 5th. July* this diary was neglected. There was no cabinet. Durham, who dined with me on Sunday the 1 July, spoke much of his instructions, which I have not seen, and lamented as Grey had done that the intemperate language in the House of Commons would disgust the Emperor Nicholas and render him averse to listening to our remonstrances about Poland.[213] Such language may no doubt estrange and even exasperate foreign Courts, and in matters like Poland, where our interests are remote and our power small, we may defeat our objects by offending those who have the means of disappointing us. Yet it is not unwholesome that Russia and that all the despotick courts should know that neither this nor any Government in England could procure men or money against French or Continental liberty, and that, in the event of a general war of opinion,

England would be more likely to side with the liberal than with the Ultra party in Europe. Lord Carlisle had some thoughts of retiring on occasion of his health from the Cabinet and wrote to Lord Grey to that purpose. Grey's answer and my representation of the bad effect it might have, persuaded him to relinquish this resolution and I hope a hint I gave Palmerston will prevent the renewal of any little disappointment he may have felt at not being regularly informed of the foreign dispatches and instructions, which have not been regularly sent to him during his absence from the Cabinet.

I keep this diary so irregularly, that I must curtail or abandon it.

Sunday 9th. July. Two letters from Anglesey of 5 and 6 July announce much alarm at state of things in Ireland, some apprehension of immediate insurrection and rebellion. They speak of extraordinary measures such as Suspension of Habeas Corpus Act and Martial Law as expedients to which he may find *himself compelled* to resort. It is a little ambiguous whether he consults or apprizes Lord Grey of his having such resources in contemplation. Some curious letters of Pelham[214] in 1797 and Peel in 1829 were read, and it was agreed that Grey should write to explain to him the nature of his legal powers and the extreme cases in which only he could be justified in exceeding them.

The embarrassing measure of tythes and Irish Church was discussed and it was after much deliberation determined that we must get the Compulsory composition through, but that the Ulterior measures should be left over till the next Session, and the Government to reserve to itself the nature as well as the extent of that ulterior measure, entirely open. It is clear that all the Cabinet are not agreed on the policy to be pursued with respect to the Irish Church, some wishing to preserve its character of an established and endowed Church, others thinking it must be reduced to a Stipendiary one. Both may and do agree in the composition bill, but it is the groundwork of a different and even of an opposite policy in the contemplation of the two parties, and there their agreement must terminate.

The Irish Members in the Commons, bullied themselves by O Connel, their constituents, and the apprehension of a speedy election, factiously urged us on to measures which they must know are unpracticable in the state of Parlient and Court, and they were nevertheless, as usual, unwilling to give their friends any credit or confidence, though they would submit at least for a time to positive rejection and contumely from their enemies. Unless we adopt resolutions tantamount not only to the extinction but to the reduction of the revenue of Church and clearly avow the principle of subverting the character of an establishment, they threatened to oppose our Government in a body on other matters, and specially on the *Russian loan*! On this it was impossible to do any thing but defy them, and even their advocates such as Ebrington and Duncannon are disgusted with their unreasonableness and feel that if our measures do not go the full length of their wishes, they are as much as can be safely and speedily attained, they are a step in that direction if it shall please Parliament, and above all they are and must be, if rejected by Parliament, the ruin of the present Government and the renewal of the experiment of an Orange Ministry and a coercive system. Lord Anglesey despairs of the effect of conciliatory measures. He is as he must be disgusted with the violence and ingratitude of the agitators and with the outrageous and undeniable conspiracy by which it is proposed to withdraw all labour and renounce all intercourse with those who pay or exact any tythe and take any step to advize any other person to do so. Grey says the Law must be enforced and he dropped some words in his speech at the Mansion House recommending vigorous <councils> both at home and abroad which perplexed many of his supporters with the fear of war abroad and disturbance at home. He is in truth nettled as he well may be with the Irish. He and Anglesey think that the large Antitythe meetings, which are unquestionable conspiracies and consequently illegal, may be suppressed by law and force. But tho' the Law and yet more the reason of such law is <obvious> and reasonable enough, the means of enforcing it is more perplexing. Minto is to go Envoy to Berlin, an excellent appointment. Our discussions in Lords on Scotch reform bill were temperate even to dulness, but the Duke of Buccleugh, who displayed no talent or acuteness, shewed that he was disposed to be troublesome.

I shall discontinue this diary. It is impossible to keep it regularly, and the utmost that I can expect from myself in assisting any future work of memoirs or recollection is to record here and there a fact not known to the publick, with a date and such remarks as may serve to indicate its nature and the sensation provoked thereby on the publick.

The Princess of Weimar[215] died on the 11th. It was a hopeless and distressing case and both her Mother and the Queen were deeply affected by it. The Duke of Sussex was no doubt much censured at Court and by Duke of Cumberland for attending the Civic feast given to Ministers on that very day. Pains will be taken to widen his breach with Windsor; and there is less disposition than can well be accounted for, in so goodnatured and just a mind as the King, to forgive him in a matter where he was scarcely to blame and in which the King was both hasty and unjust. Lord Chancellor, from waywardness or from a weak wish of courting Enemies whom he cannot gain, allowed the Anatomy bill[216] to be further postponed and thereby endangered.

End of regular Diary [*July 1832*]. It may possibly be occasionally resumed but it must always be irregular and imperfect.

[*Heading*: July 1832] There was about this time among our House of Commons supporters some jealousy and even dislike of Stanley who, notwithstanding his great parliamentary abilities, his high station in the Country, and his uniformly honourable upright conduct, has not the good fortune to ingratiate himself with those he deals with, and who is unaccountably unpopular with all Classes of Irishmen. Fortunately however for him and perhaps for us, the Irish Members were so very headstrong and unreasonable that those of their English supporters most likely to concur with them on matters affecting the Church and the tythes were compelled by principle and honour to dis<dain> cooperation with them and to give us a temporary and qualified support to the tythe bills.

We had sundry reports about the 15th. and 20th. of this Month of an attempt to defeat us in both houses, and after many of our partizans and several of our adversaries too had left London for the season, the latter were sent for back from the country and a great appearance of a *rally* took place with a view of bonifying the prediction that as soon as the Reform bills had passed Lord Grey's administration would fall and the Duke of Wellington, with the aid of Sir Rt. Peel and of such as had been squeamish about assisting to complete reform, construct a Tory administration—all which would, they said, be accomplished before the 1 of August. The endeavours in House of Commons were directed against the payment or the manner of treating to pay the Russian Dutch loan. At first the divisions were very near and the impression rather unfavourable to Ministry, but the improving Majority, the eloquence of Mr Stanley, and the blunt declaration of Joseph Hume that a vote against the measure, tho' that measure was wrong, would turn out a good Whig Reforming administration and let in a vile corrupt Tory one, and *would not save the Money* and that on that account he should vote with the Ministers, turned the tide both in and out of the house and converted their battle to a triumph for Lord Grey's government. The last divisions in the House of Commons encreased the Majority for Ministers,[217] and the hungry of the beaten party were manifestly discouraged and chopfallen. Their muster in the house of Lords on Irish bill turned out a false alarm, and it passed with some few near divisions on the details in the Committee and one concession regarding Freeman's votes, of little consequence in itself but rather annoying to those who in commons had at the request of Ministers resisted OConnel upon it, quietly and easily enough. The Russian Dutch loan passed in the Lords without a division and with little debate, for tho' Wellington as well as Aberdeen made it a peg on which they chose to hang their philippicks and epigrams against the foreign policy of Lord Grey's government, the first distinctly acknowledged that the payment could not have been witheld, and both confined their objection to the measure itself within the limits of the Constitutional question. Aberdeen seemed to plume himself on his accurate knowledge of the state and details of our negotiations in Holland and laboured to confirm the King of Holland in his obstinacy. The Duke maintained that the best method of preserving peace and friendship with France was to avoid all connection and alliance with her, and he as well as Aberdeen was much cheered in such sentiments by Duke of Cumberland and Lord Stuart of Rothsay.

During the latter days of July the intelligence of Don Pedro's landing and taking Oporto arrived, but there was no intelligence of any thing that indicated signal or certain success reached England during that month, and if there is not while I am writing on the 31 of that month any positive marks of discomfiture or despondency, there are some unfavorable symptoms, among which a growing propensity to murmur at our neutrality and to reproach our indifference and impartiality as amounting to an intended support of Don Miguel may be reckoned. In truth we have been guilty of a great error in policy in not espousing Don Pedro's cause or at least shewing more openly and ostentatiously our countenance and good wishes.

August 1832

On Wednesday 1st I went to Court, and the Cabinet short of its House of Commons Members dined at Holland House. Richmond, Goderich and myself considered a sketch for the report of West Indian Committee. Grey read us a draft of Palmerston['s] dispatch to Lord Erskine[218] on German affairs in which we disclaim all intention of remonstrating or interfering at present but communicate without reserve our apprehension of the consequences and dislike of the spirit of the late proceedings of Austria and Prussia in the Diet.[219] It is like all from Palmerston's pen, clear, judicious, and forcible, and we all agreed that something to the same purport should be communicated to the Courts of Berlin and Vienna. Palmerston has also written a private letter to Leopold which, from the report I have heard of it, is admirable and persuasive. The object is to prevail on him to wave all points of form, etiquette, and all pretensions about words, in order to bring matters to conclusion with the King of Holland, who has now with great reluctance and some very unreasonable and untenable, but in themselves really unimportant, conditions complied with the substance of the treaty. If Leopold holds out and keeps us to the strict letter of our engagement, hostilities may ensue on points, the value of [?or] importance of which it will be difficult to impress on Parliament and the publick. On the other hand Leopold has, no doubt, his difficulties in reconciling his Chambers, full of noisy and ignorant people, to any relaxation of pretensions which the 5 powers in the Conference, or at least France and England, have consented to sanction and support. I saw and was introduced to the Elder Fagel[220] at the Levee. He is just arrived from the Hague and the bearer, I presume, of some secret instructions to Zuylen. The absence of Talleyrand is indifferently supplied on these delicate and important matters by Mr de Mareuil who is scarcely par negotiis and does not aspire to be supra.

Durham has been received in a very marked way by Emperor Nicholas, who has no doubt had a hint from Princess Lieven that personal attentions and distinctions are not thrown away upon him.

The state of Ireland and especially Kilkenny is most perplexing. Juries acquit Murderers, provided the Murder is in prosecution of a plan to prevent the payment of tythes, in the teeth of evidence, and there is such abundant proof of a systematick intimidation of witnesses and Jurors with a view of defeating the execution of any law for the levying of tythes, that it is scarcely justifiable to prorogue Parliament without some additional powers to defeat such a conspiracy. The two or three verdicts at Kilkenny furnish however but narrow and disputable ground for any extraordinary law, and we agreed that if we copied and renewed one which in the early period of George III's reign enabled the Government to remove the trials for murder from the neighbourhood and lawful men of the neighbourhood to Dublin and the juries of that county, we must find in the notorious practices of the people, not in these few and disputable verdicts, the rationem justificatoriam of our measure. Lansdowne, Melbourne, and Grey are for the measure. The Chancellor doubts but suggests the substitution of others, perhaps more objectionable in principle and certainly more difficult of attainment.

In truth Stanley with all his virtues and talents is an obstacle to our Government in Ireland, inasmuch as he hates and is hated by all parties in that country and no proposal coming from him is considered on its own merits either by the High Protestant faction on one side or the body of the Catholick people on the other. Some arrangement must ere long be devized to remove him to an office which will gratify as well as suit him better than that he holds.

On Sunday 5th. attended a Cabinet at Foreign Office where two letters from the King to Lord Palmerston were read, upon the revolutionary spirit prevalent in Germany, the necessity of avoiding every thing that would countenance or promote it, and objecting to the topicks and opinions contained in the draft of a dispatch to Lord Erskine at Munich which had been submitted to the King's approbation.[221] Both these letters, especially the last, were not only of a controversial but of an angry and almost hostile character, abounding with general phrases of keeping things as they are, preserving institutions, &c, &c, and with bitter invectives and sarcasms against the revolutionary spirit of the times, the scurrility of the press, and the growing prevalence of a party bent upon subverting order, morality, and religion. His Majesty was throughout these letters at great pains to vindicate himself, as King of Hanover, King of England, and individual, from the supposed censure of not conforming to the spirit of the times, but at the same time to display the firmness, the consistency and, above all, conservative character of his Monarchical principles, and in the course of his argument [*In the margin*: in which he termed the most offensive of the articles of the Diet, purely *inquisitorial* and at the worst <inquisitional>] it was pretty plain that he purposely employed phrases and maintained principles which, though brought forward in a speculation on German events, were easily convertible to English policy, and either betrayed or ostentatiously exhibited a dread of all reform and popular improvement and an aversion amounting to abhorrence of the Press, which he termed dominant and supreme in England and France and the fruits of which in neither country, he tartly remarked, were such as reasonably to reconcile the Princes of Germany to its free growth and diffusion in any part of that Confederation. To this Palmerston had drawn up a long, spirited, judicious, and able reply, in which the Cabinet present unanimously concurred. It was very respectful in form but stout in substance. It maintained free principles of Government and such liberal opinions as, since the revolution of 1688 and the accession of the House of Brunswick, had prevailed in England and secured the honour of the Crown, the stability of our institutions, and the welfare of the Country. It proceeded to vindicate the advice we had given from the aspersion of interfering with independent nations, and argued from recent circumstances and general principles that timely reforms and the adaptation of measures to opinions were the real means of preserving all institutions, even Monarchy itself, that we had a right to give friendly advice to an ally or friendly power when, as in this case, they seemed to be adopting a course of policy hazardous to themselves and injurious to Europe—and more likely to provoke and occasion revolution, war, and invasion than prevent it—and it proceeded in support of the latter proposition, to cite passages in Mr Cartwright's[222] dispatches (from which the King had quoted many things with high approbation) which predicted resistance both from the states and the people of the smaller governments to the six articles of the Diet, arraigned the policy and exposed the designs of Austria, and foreboded, from such illtimed, illconsidered, and unjustifiable attempts, internal confusion, external war, and not impossibly a result the very opposite of that which Austria professed to promote. The whole was well reasoned and spirited and, without soreness or offence, resolutely maintained that both at home and abroad liberal policy was as truly '*conservative*' and almost necessary to the preservation of Kingly authority. A sentence was added at the suggestion of Grey to justify our admonition to the two Courts not to persist in their intentions by observing that, after previous notice of our views of their proceeding, we were less likely to be called upon and should be more warranted in refusing any call to support them, should confusion, war, and invasion be the consequences of their proceedings. The letter was stout as well as well reasoned and written.[223] I shall be curious to observe whether the invitations to Palmerston to Windsor and St. James's, which have been somewhat more frequent than those to most of his Colleagues, since his and the Duke of Richmond's unwillingness to make peers, become more rare after the receipt of this letter. There is I think in this transaction as in some others grounds for suspecting that the Antiliberal spirit which occasionally breaks out in the King's language is infused into him by foreign rather than English intrigue, or at least that persons connected with Germany, such as the Queen, Duke of Cumberland, are the Channels of Communication. Lord Grey, who set me down at Holland House, though he acknowledged that his health was good, spoke feelingly and earnestly on his situation and, comparing his prospects of declining years and energies with that of continual and encreasing labour and excitement, avowed a disposition if not a determination to retire shortly and consulted me on the arrangement I thought might ensue. I avoided much conversation upon it and only urged postponement of all such plans, especially as there was the prospect of a recess of three months to recruit his health and spirits and it was essential to his glory to launch and steer out of port the great vessel of Reform he had constructed.

The arrangement for Ireland was, as I urged, more pressing, and he gave me some letters from Stanley and others, which confirmed me in the opinion that He (Stanley) and Lord Anglesey differed too widely in principle to conduct the tythe measure to a satisfactory issue. One or both must be removed to some other situation. If Anglesey could be placed at Horse Guards our government would be greatly strengthened thereby, and Melbourne, Lansdowne, or Goderich might go to Ireland. Grey agreed that the first would be the preferable appointment, as he has already been employed there and is liked, but he has told me he would not go; yet he may not be inexorable. [*In the margin*: The Irish bill for removing the venue was dropped by Stanley, from a want of attendance and fear of losing time. It is in my mind lucky. These peevish and angry laws of coercion are generally Evaded and baffled. They exasperate and they seldom intimidate.]

On the next day, the 6th., Palmela arrived from Oporto with accounts not quite so desperate as his arrival seemed at first to imply, but yet far from encouraging.

On the 6th Monday. The King answered Lord Palmerston at great length and <subjoined> a note in his own handwriting. The letter, which I have not seen, contains compliments to Palmerston and civil but reluctant acquiescence in his policy, and the note enjoins him to warn Lord Erskine not to travel out of his record or convey any opinions on the proceedings in Diet in any language but such as he finds in the dispatch.

On the following Wednesday, viz. 8th, the King at Levee was in high health, spirits and good humour. The attendance in Lords during the rest of the Week shewed that the Tories despaired of any success, and on the tythe bill Duke of Wellington recommended a unanimous support of the Ministerial measure as the groundwork for the final settlement of the question. Q[ue]ry: what final settlement but the entire abolition or at least ultimate and complete commutation of Tythe? In this debate, Lord Westmeath[224] having described Ireland in actual rebellion or on the verge of it and declaimed on the necessity of meeting the emergency by some extraordinary measures of legislation, which the separation of Parliament would render impossible, the Chancellor, at my suggestion, stated the extraordinary powers with which by a law exclusively Irish the Lord Lieutenant was actually armed in cases of invasion and *rebellion*, and he gave a definition of rebellion to which he pledged himself as a Lawyer and which if correct would certainly enable the Lord Lieutenant to suspend the Habeas Corpus without any fresh act of Parliament, should matters assume an aspect but a little more turbulent than hitherto they have done. He thus hinted to Oconnel, that if the mischief he did exceeded all bounds, he might be taken up, and he confuted the supposed necessity of any sudden, angry, and occasional law by holding up the full efficacy of those in existence *in terrorem*. This declaration produced a very sensible effect on the house, extorted praise as well as wonder from Wellington, and entirely dispelled that sort of clamour which had been raised of the weakness and irresolution of the Irish Govt. It exposed the ignorance and defeated the malice of one faction and it may not improbably somewhat appall the nerves of the other.

On the 10th. Lord Grey dined with me and announced his kind intention of proposing My Son Charles to the King for a place in the Ordnance.

On the 13th. The bill for abolishing Capital punishment in cases of Forgery was in Committee, and both Lord Lansdowne and Lord Grey acquiesced in an exception of forgeries of wills and of powers of Attorney, to which in my judgement there is the same objection in principle as to the Law we intend to abrogate.

13th. to 15th. August 1832. The Chancellor and I both objected to the amendment but did not deem it prudent to insist in a way that would have been misconstrued into any substantial difference with our Colleagues. It is something to get so near the general principle of abolishing Capital punishment in all cases exempt from violence, and that once recognized and acted upon, the exceptions must inevitably be done away and the principle followed out ere long to all its consequences.

On Wednesday the 15th. the King dined at Holland House. Grey, Lansdowne, Leinsters, Sir J Kempt, Lord Ad[olphus] FitzClarence, and my family—22 covers. His Majesty gracious to all and cordial to some. *Parliament prorogued.*

[*In the margin*: I wrote the following short recapitulation of events from August 1832 to May 1833 on my return to Holland House in May 1833.]

Summer and Autumn 1732 [*1832*]

I renounced all notion of keeping this diary regularly. It was well I did so as soon afterwards I was confined to my bed and my couch for weeks and months,[225] and should have fretted at leaving a task I had undertaken unaccomplished whenever I heard any thing of importance passing among my Colleagues. They dispersed during the summer and autumn and Grey was in Northumberland. There were more symptoms than ever of bad faith to the Conference and cool designs to France in the three despotick powers. We ascertained from secret sources of intelligence that Mastuzevitch absented himself on pretext of health and amusement, with the view of keeping the negotiation open till we were out of office and the Tories and Duke of Wellington once more in possession. They speculated with some plausibility, for they knew that we could not, without publick inconvenience and suspending the operation of one great provision of the Reform bill, viz the registration, dissolve before the 2d. December, and they calculated that before that day, want of money, something like war with Holland, or other embarrassments would force us to recall the old Parliament, which they well knew would now be unmanageable by us. In truth our situation was somewhat embarrassing, but we had the good sense and spirit to surmount it, and confiding in an obvious principle much urged by Lord Lansdown—that a new parliament would be a favorable tribunal to try us on the charge of not having called the old one—we determined neither to slacken our efforts against Holland, nor to call the old Parliament, but have recourse to the dissolution the first moment we could with convenience. Yet till Lord Grey was returned from the North none would believe that such would be our Course, and Mme Lieven was active in promoting the notion that *Palmerston only* was bent on acting in concert with France against Antwerp and that Lord Grey was too averse to any such violent proceeding and too well aware of the King's averseness to it also ever to sanction it. [*In the margin*: She canvassed me by presuming from a saying which somebody did me the honour of repeating that I was averse to vigorous measures against Holland. When our policy was questioned as too dilatory and irresolute by some eager friend at table and the numbers of our Protocols ridiculed, I had answered, 'better have 100 Protocols than one Bulletin'.] The Tories were astonished at the length of our prorogation, and the King somewhat reluctantly acquiesced, though he foreboded misfortune from any joint operations with France! Insinuations first against the success and then against the good faith of France were greatly listened to at Court, especially among the Ladies, but fortunately such calumnies were refuted by the honourable Conduct of the French Government, and the long prepared sneers on French perfidy and ambition were laid aside for a season, and Lord Aberdeen compelled to acquiesce in that part of the address which acknowledged the concert and cooperation of Gt. Britain and France. [*In the margin*: Though he could not refrain from sneers at Lewis Philip and Marshal Soult, to the latter of whom he imputed misconduct, founded on a vulgar story of his giving battle after peace was signed, which the Duke of Wellington very handsomely and very explicitly contradicted.]

[*In the margin:* Beginning of 1833[1]] In Ireland likewise great difficulties were likely to occur. Lord Anglesey's notions of Church Reform and of other measures of conciliation and popularity went far beyond those of Mr Stanley, and our House of Commons Colleagues were not satisfied that the plans of Stanley went far enough. Still less could they agree on one of the principles to which Stanley limited his bill, viz that it was unlawful to divert any property applicable by Law to ecclesiastical purposes to any other not strictly within that description, such as relief of poor, general education, &c &c.[2] Both Stanley and Richmond were at first inclined to insist on a distinct recognition of this most questionable principle. Few of the Cabinet could agree and such a course would have led to an actual breach or separation. After some discussion however and more reflection, it was felt that Stanley's plan, if neither perfect nor complete, was yet a great improvement and might satisfy the Reformers. Above all it was attainable, because Stanley had engaged to bring large Masses of Churchmen and dignitaries to acquiesce in it.[3] On the other hand a larger and better plan, however preferable in reason and policy, could not be obtained, and possibly would be revolting not only to Bishops and Aristocracy but to a considerable portion of the English publick. It was thought therefore that we should do better to be satisfied with what we could get, than to risk losing all by trying to get more. But it was as distinctly understood that while we acquiesced in not enforcing any diversion of Church property from ecclesiastical purposes, we by no means disclaimed all such diversion of it as irreconcileable with principle. We simply consented to wave it on the present occasion, and to try the experiment of a plan which fell short of it. Stanley's difficulties however were not confined to the principle or details of the measure or to the diversity of opinion about them in the Castle or among his Colleagues. He was nettled at the openness and indiscretion with which, he contended, Lord Anglesey commented on his projected measures, and he more than once in letter and conversation strongly urged th impossibility of his remaining in the Irish Office with Lord A[nglesey] as Lord Lieutenant.

I was employed to sound Lord Anglesey on these subjects, to ascertain how far he might be brought to acquiesce in a measure less extensive than he himself recommended, how far India the Horse Guards or any other seat in the Cabinet would reconcile him to quitting Ireland and whether, if a change took place, he would be nettled at the notion of Stanley's policy being preferred. I, in a great measure, succeeded in this delicate correspondence, but it was entirely owing to the noble, disinterested, and friendly nature of My Correspondent, whose devotion in politicks and in private left us at liberty to dispose of him as most convenient to our Ministry which, he very unfeignedly assured us, was in his judgement synonymous with the publick service. Though he recommended a wider measure of Church Reform, he was ready if we wished to urge the adoption of a more narrow one, to wave the objections he felt, or if we preferred it to make way immediately for any other Government in Ireland, or keep it for an interval to prepare any line of policy his Successor might wish to adopt. Nothing could be so handsome. Never was there a more manifest disregard of all considerations of Self. In the mean time he more reluctantly than our other friends but yet more earnestly urged the absolute and cruel necessity of a strong coercive Law, but coupled with all such representations he never failed to press the necessity of proceeding rapidly and firmly and simultaneously with many measures of improvement. Stanley agreed to return to Ireland and Anglesey was contented to confine the Church Reform to Stanley's project with some small additions and improvements, and the

Irish Government were employed in preparing the tremendous Martial Law bill,[4] and the other Measures of a more conciliatory aspect relating to tythes, Grand and petty Juries,[5] Church reform and Church Cess. A few days or weeks before the meeting of Parliament, Stanley wrote again and more formally to Grey to urge the impossibility of his remaining Secretary in the present Government of Ireland and alledging some grounds, founded on Lord Anglesey's conduct, for believing that *he* [Stanley] did not enjoy his [Anglesey's] Confidence and that other *irresponsible* persons, glancing no doubt at Lord Cloncurry and Mr Blake, did.

[*In the margin:* February 1733 [*sic*].] On the eve of Parliament opening and while Anglesey was in London, the expediency of changing the Irish Government was discussed in Cabinet and Melbourne reluctantly consented to go Lord Lieutenant of Ireland, and Goderich, by accepting the Home department or Privy Seal, to make way for Stanley in the Colonial. The inconvenience and danger of making such a change—the difficulty of the reelections, the triumph of OConnel, and above all the strange prelude it would make to the introduction of our Coercive bill—flashed on every man's mind. A somewhat ungracious consent was extorted from Stanley to remain where he was, till Easter, provided he had a direct promise that his resignation would then be accepted. It was at the same time implied that a higher office should be offered to him, and that not only He but Anglesey should be removed from the Irish Government; for he did not imitate that noble minded Minister's generosity in deprecating all notion of sacrificing the interests of the Ministry or of the publick to any private consideration of his feelings. Anglesey had told me in the morning that he begged the Cabinet to do what they thought best with him—that he should prefer leaving Ireland altogether or remaining there, to any destination here or in India—but he hoped that it would be decided with reference to what we thought best and most convenient to *ourselves* and not to *him*. He was when he gave me this commission in the anguish of an attack of his agonizing complaint, the tic douloureux. Knowing his sincerity, I ventured to answer for him, which I hardly would have done for any other living man, that he would return to Ireland even with the disagreable prospect of being recalled in two months and the condition annexed that he must keep his intended return at that period an impenetrable secret from the publick and from his family. That last condition was no doubt irksome to him and many of his detractors implied that he could not and did not observe it, but I believe he *did most scrupulously*.

In the mean while the protraction of the debates on the Coercive or protective bill, the turn those debates took, and the authority acquired and assumed in the House of Commons by Stanley, before whom Oconnel manifestly quailed, altered the state of matters, when Easter Came. The fulfillment of our intention of recalling Anglesey was actually impossible as well as disagreable to us all. Many, and Ebrington in particular (one of the most important of our popular members in the House) had supported the bill because *Anglesey* was to administer it, and there was moreover no man either capable or willing to engage, in the Infancy of his appointment to the Lord Lieutenancy, in the execution of so tremendous a measure. [*In the margin:* Spring and Easter of 1833.] Stanley, satisfied in all probability with the great and well deserved fame and political authority he had acquired, had the good sense not to stickle for a triumph over Lord Anglesey, and the latter, to his credit and the advantage of the Government, remained where he was. Sir John Hobhouse succeeded Stanley, but the anomaly and inconvenience of having the Irish Secretary in the Cabinet were relinquished. Hobhouse was rechosen for Westminster without any difficulty, and Mr Ellice,[6] who succeeded him in the War office, with some at Coventry; but there was a fatality attaching that Irish Secretaryship. Hobhouse not long after his election, from over scrupulous deference to the wishes of his Constituents to repeal the House and Window tax and from unwillingness by voting for such repeal to endanger his Colleagues, thought proper to resign both his place and seat, and was on the election beaten by Coll. Evans.[7] Abercromby, hardly recovered from his disappointment about the Speakership, declined the office on the score of not being combined with a seat in the Cabinet, and Spring Rice, on the more reasonable plea of being an Irishman declined it also. The difficulty of reelections on acceptance of offices circumscribed our choice. It is to be hoped that inconvenience may be remedied by a bill proposed by somebody independent of Government.[8] It was not the only vexatious consequence of the internal Changes in our Government. Lord Goderich was mortified at being removed from an office of business to one of dignity though, if he had made a just estimate of himself and considered his superiority of talents in debate, and his irresolution and difficulty of coming to a point on transactions of importance, he would have rejoiced at the leisure which the *Privy Seal* left him for displaying his useful, agreable, and ready eloquence in the Lords and at his escape from the many and painful duties of the Colonial Office. He was however prevailed upon to acquiesce in the arrangement, and in proof of his good humour to accept the Earldom of Ripon. Every one who knew him wished him to be satisfied, for in addition to his great abilities and clear knowledge of details in debate he is a most amiable and agreable man. [*In the margin:* Lord Durham from some ill humour with our measures and our Colleagues, from family afflictions and bad health, had resigned the Privy Seal some weeks before and been gratified with an Earldom for which, in spite of his understanding and his half republican principles, he had long panted with childish vanity. Many were glad and more sorry at his secession. His manner to all was insufferable, and when he differed as he often did with Grey, to him most inexcusable and disgusting.]

Other ill humour occasioned by the change was no so easily allayed. Lord Howick, who had been convinced by enquiry or swayed by Mr Stephens[9] to espouse the cause of immediate and almost unqualified emancipation and had devoted his time and talents, which are very great and greater than generally admitted, to the formation of a project by which Slavery was to cease on the 1 Janry. 1835, and the vagrancy and idleness of the Slaves to be prevented by a heavy tax on their provision grounds and severe penalties on the occupation of waste land, took great dudgeon at the relinquishment of his plan (which all West Indians had vehemently repudiated), and betrayed no little soreness and ill temper at the elevation of Stanley to the head of the department.[10] His injudicious language and conduct hurt Lord Grey deeply, disgusted many indifferent spectators and injured his reputation with the publick. The Chancellor, who denied him the credit he deserved for sincerity and earnestness and talent, attributed all to vanity and pique. 'It was hard' he said, 'upon Grey to be visited with another Lambton in his family only with an ugly instead of a handsome face'. [*In the margin:* May 1833] True it is that Howick is one to whom the disadvantages of person are extremely injurious, for I think they induce people to attribute the impetuosity of youth to violence of temper, and the ardor of his mind to presumption and ambition. Whatever be the cause, he is very unpopular and his defection and opposition, however painful to Grey's friends, did no damage to his administration. None cheared Lord Howick (tho' his speech was an able one[1]**X**) but OConnel and a few of the Repealers, and they manifestly chuckled at it as a vexation to Lord Grey, but lent him openly no assistance, and bestowed on him, I suspect, in secret, as little commendation.

Stanley, in opening his plan which prepared the Negroes by the means of apprenticeship and sundry regulations for entire freedom in 12 years and in the meanwhile withdrew them from all arbitrary and capricious punishment, made a most able exposition and, with great dexterity, eloquence, and effect, brought back the great body of Emancipators to an acquiescence if not an approbation of the plan. The apprehensions we had felt for our Ministry were dispelled and the project on which we dreaded a defeat became in appearance, in [?at] least, a portion of our strength and defence. The King was in some measure by Stanley and in some by Mr Ellice (the Secretary of War) reconciled to the Emancipation and persuaded that part of the plan originated with himself; and the Chancellor, who had been dreadfully appalled at the prospect of reproaches from those whom he had formerly hallooed on to sudden and unqualified emancipation, was agreably disappointed at finding that, without forfeiting their confidence, he could sanction and support the mitigated scheme of his Colleagues. [*In the margin:* It must be confessed that the Chancellors conduct on this great question of Slavery had from his acceptance of office been somewhat strange and equivocal. After working up the people to a state of madness on the topick of immediate and unqualified emancipation, he, like other abolitionists, had no plan for carrying their object into practical execution, and he even uniformly abstained from the discussion of it in Cabinet, either quitting the room or confining his remarks to some personal reflection on those publick men who took part in the debates. It was not till Stanley's accession to the Colonial Office that he took any, nor till his successful speech in House of Commons of 14th. May 1833 that he seemed to take lively, interest as Minister in the measure which out of office had been his chief engine of popularity.] It is to be hoped that the West Indians will (I write 17 May 1833) have the good sense to acquiesce, for fear of worse; and if their foolish opinion of this day, viz that they would have preferred Lord Howick's plan (against which they so vehemently protested) to this be true, It should at least admonish them that it is not the interest of the weaker party to reject altogether such terms as are offered by the stronger, but to mitigate or modify; but by utterly repudiating them, they incense those who make them to devize yet worse.

Although we have a prospect of steering thro' this very formidable and difficult pass, it is too manifest that our hold on the country is less firm than when the Reform Parliament met. Some affect to attribute our decline of popularity to the unmanageable character of the new House of Commons, others to the harsh provisions of our Irish coercive bill; but the Parliament, tho' a little more talkative and in want of experience as to the consequence rather than grounds of its votes, is on all material questions as tractable as most of its Predecessors and to the full as well disposed to confide in the leaders of a Government as a really representative body can or ought to be.[12] The Irish bill, not disliked even by Irishmen, is I believe approved of and applauded by the great majority of Englishmen, but there is, however, some disappointment at the comparative <longuer> of all measures of redress and improvement. The budget was far from satisfactory and the *impossibility* of large diminutions of taxes is not duly considered by the publick.[13] The tone and language of our Ministry is not quite in unison with that of those parties of men to whom we owed our Elevation and continuance in office. Lord Grey naturally and laudably looks to closing his career and leaving the country in tranquillity and prosperity. He is consequently averse to the agitation of any great questions that are not actually forced upon him. When they are, he expresses perhaps a little too much chagrin and impatience and he certainly is more irritable at the manoeuvres and scurrility of the Demagogues and Radicals than might be expected from one of his experience and real superiority of mind. [*In the margin:* There is another peculiarity in Grey's manner and character which, with foolish, inobservant, vain, and proud persons not well acquainted with him, leads to conclusions the very reverse of the truth. He is thought by such persons to be impatient of contradiction, averse to hear any thing which does not accord with his own views, deaf to remonstrances and provoked rather than grateful for any advice against his inclinations; Whereas there is no Man with whom I have ever been acquainted more truly candid in deliberation, more open to reason, more certain to reflect and exercise a calm judgement on all that is said to combat his first impressions, and less disposed to confound the advizer with the advice and to be nettled or estranged by such difference. At the moment however that any thing disagreable is suggested, he is so artless that he cannot disguise his chagrin and seems disposed either to question the facts or scout the reason on which it is founded; and this is deemed most falsely repulsive by the timid and offensive by the vain and proud. The appearance however is the very reverse of the reality. He is perhaps *too open* to conviction, and he is certainly both candid and generous to all who in sincerity take upon themselves to advise him.] These little blemishes, if indeed they amount to any such, are confined to words and fleeting projects of strong proceedings, which on calmer reflection and the representation of his Colleagues are abandoned, but they get out in the publick, give a tincture to the language of such among our party as are by nature more Tory than Whig and more conservative than reforming, and, combined with the untoward but necessary support of many odious taxes, produce an appearance of unpopularity and encourage Hume, Cobbett,[14] OConnell, Attwood,[15] and Whittel Harvey[16] to foment discontent and turbulence. The latter, nettled by an over righteous rejection of an application for office on the score of his more than suspicious character, is full of malignity and activity—and an able, cunning, and formidable man. Throughout the contests which have led to this temporary clamour against us, the gallantry with which Sir Francis Burdett has risked and indeed for a season forfeited his darling popularity should be mentioned with praise as a proof of the sincerity of his professions and affections. His feelings are always generous and his language frank. His conduct upon them simple, bold, and direct, but these very merits prevent him from using any art or hypocrisy in disguising the motives on which he acts, and it must be acknowledged that they not unfrequently expose him to the reproach of inconsistency and even incoherence of publick principle. [*In the margin:* The truth is his conduct, especially towards individuals, is always honourable and benevolent, but his political creed is a strange medly of monarchical and republican notions, of Tory and democratical prejudices and maxims.]

Sunday the 19 May 1833. At a Cabinet at Lord Althorps, lamented the unpleasant sensation produced by the inquest on the murdered policeman in Cold bath fields,[17] and discussed inter alia the necessity of forwarding some general police bill and some measure for new Corporations which will be presented in the shape of a bill this year but not passed. We instructed Palmerston to <close> with the <most> favorable proposal we have hitherto received from Holland by signing a preliminary convention in his own words, which gives up to him Maestrict, question of transit, and adding an article, explanatory of the extent of the armistice he agrees to, and of the freedom of the Scheldt which he also consents to. The first is to abstain from all hostilities with the *Belgian troops,* and the latter to place the navigation of the Scheldt on the footing on which it subsisted prior to 1832, that is, subject to no duty, till the conclusion of a definitive treaty Between Belgium and Holland. Some such explanation by note or in an article, or some alteration of the Dutch Monarch's phraseology is prudent and necessary as by styling himself Majesté < . . . . > landoise without the usual addition of Duke of Luxemburgh and disclaiming all hostilities against *La Belgique* instead of Belgian troops, he might have some pretence of having reserved to himself the right of attacking Luxemburgh or Limburg, and by the vague expression of *liberté entiere de navigation* he might, as once before, have contended that he meant free passage, but not exemption from duty. His Embassador, Dedel,[18] will be pressed and is certainly well disposed to sign, and the French and Belgians (the latter somewhat reluctantly) will accede. If Dedel has powers, sign he will. If not, what Dutchman can maintain that his King does not prefer war to peace and that his object is not to recover Belgium? He may be relieved from blockade and embargo[19] and he is complimented with an advantage at Maestricht which the five powers deemed he was not entitled to and, in rejecting terms of his own proposing, he will shew that he worded them ambiguously and unusually for the purpose of deluding and evading the obvious intentions of the other contracting party and the interests and wishes of his people, including his Embassador Mr Dedel. Lyttleton[20] is Irish Secretary—and thought a good appointment. I hardly know him.

20. Holland House. Palmela called. He has seen Grey and Palmerston and is on the point of sailing with reinforcements to Oporto, but goes with a heavy heart at finding that the English Government will not define the contingency which would induce them to espouse more openly the cause of Donna Maria, nor even suggest the advice which they would be best pleased Don Pedro should follow, whom Palmela thinks he could persuade to abandon the Regency, or take any other step we might deem proper, provided he could hold out to him with any certainty the prospect of England's countenance or interference in behalf of his daughter. It seems to me, we lose an opportunity, and throw the Liberal party if successful into the arms of France, without the slightest prospect of attaching the opposite faction to us in case of the total discomfiture of Donna Maria. Palmela assures me that the money he has unexpectedly raised does not come from France. General Baudrand called and seems much pleased with the Duke of Orlean's reception here and with the improved condition of France. Chateaubriand,[21] when told by some brother Carlists that the Duchess of Berri, now she was pregnant, could no more serve the good cause answered, 'Yes but she can, if she has sense and spirit to die at Blaye'. She has however committed the folly of living and the game is up. [*In the margin:* When it was observed that the Carlists were furious with the Duchess of Berri, Talleyrand said, 'Pardy, Je le crois, elle les a fait "tous Cocus." ']

I am sadly afraid that the Police, who have generally conducted themselves so discreetly, acted with precipitation and violence in the late affray at Cold Bath fields and were in the wrong. We should have done much better not to proclaim the meeting, but to have stationed Police and perhaps Military in the neighbourhood and, if breach of the peace occurred, to have read the riot act and dispersed them. This proceeding on the authority of Common Law, which if not questionable is unknown and unusual, is after all very odious, and the denouncing meetings by proclamations and menaces is a species of <thunder> in the index to a contest in which the Constitution gives a vast advantage to the people over the government.

21st. May Monday. Preliminary treaty with Holland[22] signed by Palmerston, Talleyrand, and Dedel, after some little difficulty suggested by Dedel about the name to be given to the Article Palmerston had drawn up—'additional' 'explanatory' or 'separate'. Such a question appears trifling but I hope they have chosen one of the two first, for 'separate' would be illogical, inasmuch as it is declaratory of the meaning of the others and, what is more material, would give the King of Holland some pretence for demurring. N.B. They chose the best, 'Explicatif'.

22. The King has written an earnest letter to Palmerston on Turkish affairs, on which he is always particularly anxious. In the result he is not perhaps very wrong, for he wishes to avoid entangling ourselves either with Austria or France. The first of which powers seems cajoled by Russia, and the latter is, he thinks, full of perfidious designs secretly connected with Mehemet Ali[23] and tenaciously attached to certain projects connected with the possession of Algiers. All this is I believe more unfounded suspicion but the conclusion he draws of keeping reconciliation and management open with Mehemet Ali, 'though a rebel', is I think sound policy and in his mouth an unexpected admission. That the French will ultimately have him, if we do not, is a I think more probable; but they have constantly, uniformly, and openly offered to share with us, share and share alike, all influence at Constantinople or Alexandria, and even pressed us to take the lead, and we have as constantly held back. If we refuse to act jointly we cannot in reason or justice complain of their acting separately. Portugal is something of a similar case and in policy yet more inexcusable.

23 May. Account arrived of my son's marriage at Florence on 9th. instant.[24] A letter from Mulgrave shewing that he is nettled at want of support in the Colonial Office, dissatisfied with the plan of the land tax (which we call Lord Howick's and which is now abandoned), and much inclined to quit his situation. I sent his letter to Stanley and urged him to prevail on Mulgrave to stay.

24th. May. Palmela left London for Falmouth last night. Prince Canino[25] and his brother, Joseph Bonaparte,[26] dined with us. It is curious to see a Man, eight years a King and six years Monarch of one of the largest kingdoms in Europe, in private society. His manners are very plain and simple, he shews less talent than Lucian, and in appearance is perhaps homely and heavy but unaffected, unassuming, and easy. Their manner to each other seems to bespeak confidence and affection, and is creditable to both.

25th. May At Cabinet (Lord Althorp and Mr Grant absent) Lord Ripon exculpated himself most satisfactorily of any want of confidence in or refusal of support to Mulgrave, and traced his discontent to its true cause—the misrepresentations or rather falsehoods of the Jamaica Agent, Mr Burge, who to animate the opposition in Jamaica, had written out to his friends that the Colonial Office disapproved of and were about to recall the Governor. Steps are to be taken to expose him. I am sorry to find that the Master of the Rolls has taken effectual steps to expose himself by soliciting a Committee of House of Lords on Chancery bills, volunteering unfounded charges against the Chancellor, and acknowledging, in his vehemence to prove offices and patronage freehold, practices of his own, directly violating an act of Parliament. He is a warmhearted, highminded man, but injudicious, rash, and wrongheaded.

Saturday. Sunday. Monday. At Burlington Street. On Monday saw the King, who on politicks was more communicative and cordial than I have seen him since the fracas of last year. He talked sensibly and temperately of Belgium, Turkey, and even the West Indies, and I collected from Taylor that he was just now particularly anxious that Lord Grey's administration should not, even if beat in Commons, resign their power. The Ratifications from Holland are confidently expected, for French, English, and Russian agents at the Hague describe the Dutch Cabinet as decidedly favorable and Dedel looks delighted. There is some little apprehension that the propensities of German Prince and the wish to retrieve his military fame may indispose King Leopold to disarm, even after the Dutchman has ratified. Talleyrand says pleasantly enough that he must be pressed to encourage arts, Manufactures, letters, and science, that he must leave off his Uniform the day the peace is signed and make himself 'an old Arch Duchess'. Under the article of Neutrality Brussells must become a Northern Florence, and Flanders a flat Switzerland.

27 Monday. There was a Meeting of West Indians, tremendously numerous and attended by respectable classes and individuals, which shewed a very hostile and formidable spirit against our plan and our Ministry. Some parts of it must be remodelled. They are unpracticable. I heard Mr Sharpe's[27] reports and comments, and recommended Stanley to do so too. The Duke of Orleans returned highly delighted with the railway and wonders of Manchester; he came to Lord Grey's, where I was, in the evening. His appearance, conversation, and conduct while in England have gained him the good word of all parties. His presents and charities have been well judged and distributed with taste and delicacy.

28th. Tuesday. Returned to Holland House. News from Constantinople arrived that the Sultan[28] had agreed to give up Adana to the Egyptian, and peace would be concluded. The Russians however had urged the Divan to retract such an offer. Mme Lieven told Talleyrand that the Emperor Nicholas never would consent to the cession of Adana. 'I thought' said Talleyrand, 'that Adana belonged to the Turk not to Nicholas'.

The Duke of Orleans went to the drawing room and left London at seven. The Duke of Brunswick[29] having absurdly put forward a pretension of taking rank of the Heir Apparent of France, the King, who had invited the Duke of Brunswick as head of his family to dine with him on his birthday, thought he could not invite the Duke of Orleans, and the latter very justly observed that there would be an impropriety in dining with the diplomacy at Lord Palmerston's. He therefore determined to pay his respects and take leave at the drawing room and quit London before dinner, which was in good breeding and good taste.

29 Wednesday. Dutch ratification is arrived, and the peace between the Turk and Egyptian is signed manque the Muscovite.[30] The Cabinet (Carlisle excepted who is unwell) dined at Holland House. We had some discussion on the bank and a great deal on the resolutions abolishing Slavery. We settled that Althorp or Stanley should announce the change of 15 Million loan to a grant, convert the fund for paying the interest to a duty on sugar from a tax on the Negro's labour and, at his discretion, consent to augment the sum from 15 to 20 millions. [*In the margin:* After discussion was over, Melbourne on one couch and Ch[arles] Grant on another went fast asleep. Grey said jokingly we should blow out the candles and leave them; and about a week or ten days a caricature by HB[31] was in all the shops representing our two colleagues asleep at Holland House and the rest of us escaping with the Candles!]

30th. On debate upon the Slavery resolutions, the alterations we announced in our plan answered well: the 'Saints' says Stanley, 'are satisfied and the West Indians divided'. There must however be yet further alterations to render the plan practicable or safe.

31 May 1-2-3-June 1833

Sunday 2 June A Cabinet was held at Althorpe's on Sunday. A letter from Ireland as a reference to the act of last year apprized us, to our great annoyance and surprize, that the remaining moiety of the unpaid tythes of Ireland of 1830 and 1831 was vested in Government as assignees for the Clergy. Yet Althorp with full authority from the Cabinet had promised in the House of Commons that no more arrears should be levied,[32] and Mr Lambert[33] and 5 other Irish Members, who had been induced as they say to vote for the coercive bill on that assurance, were bent on bringing on a motion on the subject on Wednesday next. We decided that the money (I think about £114,000) must be advanced to the parsons, who are clamorous and factiously pertinacious in keeping us to our bargain, and repaid to the state by a temporary land tax, and that Althorpe shall give notice of it without delay.

We decided also to reject a proposal of the 'Chairs' of the East India Company, reserving to them a right of protesting against the decision of the Board of Controul, with reasons to the House of Commons. Grant, when asked what he would do if the Proprietors as well as Directors rejected his whole plan on this account, answered, with his usual nonchalance and courage, that it was unlikely, but in that case he would propose an Indian Secretary to take the whole Management of India into the hands of government.[34] Stanley has the gout again.

3 June Monday 1833. Duke of Wellington moved in the Lords and carried by 80 to 68 presents (proxies not called for) an address to the King, prefaced by a speech both from him and Aberdeen, full of censure and bitter animadversion on Ministers, to enforce the neutrality which His Majesty had declared in the contest now carrying on in Portugal.[35] The Chancellor made a speech full of close reasoning and good law, and exposed the tendency, intention, and effect of the motion with great force and vivacity. This step of the opposition had, I understood, been suddenly resolved upon at Lady Hertford's[36] three nights ago, and it is clear that a great muster had been made to combine the forces of those Ultra tories who openly and honestly avow a wish and design of subverting the Ministry and those who have hitherto thought or pretended that the time was not ripe for such hostile proceedings as they were not prepared to form a new administration. All depends on Commons, press, and publick—if they support us our situation is improved, if not, the coalition between Tories and Radicals must take place, and the latter, in all probability, ultimately triumph. Nous verrons.

4 June 1833 Tuesday. A Cabinet at twelve oclock at Lord Althorps. All present.

Grey opened the delicate question on which we had to deliberate by observing that he had directed Courtenay,[37] the Clerk of the House of Lords, to search for precedents respecting such addresses implying or expressing censure, as had been either answered angrily or not at all by the crown, and he then briefly but pointedly alledged the grounds upon which he must consider the address as a censure, and the awkward predicament in which any Ministry censured by a branch of the legislature and manifestly not enjoying its confidence must be placed. This was in our case much aggravated by reflecting that a much larger majority than that on this motion were hostile, both to our measures and our persons, and that their vote of the preceding night was an indication that they were disposed to exert the power they possessed. It was clear that they must think themselves prepared to form a new Government, and were determined with that view to force us to resign or the King to dismiss us. The obvious and natural course would have formerly been, and would be in common times hereafter, to resign, for it was very questionable whether we were constitutionally justified in undertaking to conduct the affairs of the Country with the indirect hostility of one house of Parliament. The point upon which that hostility was shewn was obviously not such as would warrant a large immediate batch of New Peers. On the other hand the state of the

House of Commons and of the Country was such, and the multifarious measures pending so important, that it was a fearful thing to forfeit the favor of the King, and the Confidence of our friends, and risk confusion and revolution by throwing up the Government at such a moment. He had accordingly drawn up two papers: one, tendering our resignation; and the other, shortly explanatory of the difficulties of our situation, but recommending an answer to the address, civilly but firmly denying the inference it conveyed of having acted in violation of his neutral professions and assuring them of his intentions to continue, as he had hitherto done, to adhere to them.

Lord Melbourne and Sir James Graham were strongly in favour of immediate resignation—the former saying that it was the plain, obvious, constitutional course, and the other feeling more strongly than justly that though we might rebuke the Lords, we should be degraded by their censure and avowed hostility. Though Althorp's desire for retirement strongly inclined him to resignation, he candidly acknowledged that his judgement disapproved of it and that the consequences were sufficient to appall us—indeed such as we could never satisfy our friends and perhaps scarcely justify to the Country or our consciences, occasioning. The Chancellor, Lansdowne, Palmerston, Ripon, Richmond, and myself were very decided and earnest in deprecating resignation, and I think Lord Grey, who left the determination entirely to the Cabinet, was in his heart of our opinion.

After canvassing the question at some length and after Melbourne and Graham had somewhat reluctantly assured us that they would acquiesce in and defer to the opinion of their colleagues, we unanimously decided to advise the King to give the answer which Grey's second paper suggested, but to explain to him that it might be followed up with yet more hostile votes from the Lords, that they had it in their power and seemed not averse to use it to drive matters to extremities, in which case we must in honor or duty tender our resignation or engage in that sort of contest with the Lords which it was the wish of His Majesty if possible to avoid. At my suggestion it was agreed that Grey should simply write to the King that the Cabinet had met to consider what course they should advise HM to adopt on the late vote of the House of Lords, and that he would bring down the result [of] their deliberations early on the ensuing Morning to Windsor. This course seemed to me to present the double advantage of urging our views on the subject face to face rather than by letter, and giving Grey some further opportunity of judging of the temper of the publick and the House of Commons, which might in some degree guide his own opinion and, if as favorable as we expect, give force to the advice we offered to the King. Accordingly Lord Ebrington in putting a publick question to Lord Palmerston on the subject of our policy to Portugal, took occasion to express a strong dissent to the views taken by the Lords, and the manner in which his remarks were received sufficiently indicated the adverse feelings of House and Country to the vote of their Lordships.[38] The conversation of the town and the language of the newspapers confirmed this speculation, and the day did not pass without many instances reaching our ears of the doubt, regrets, and fears of many of the Tory Lords themselves at the imprudent step they had taken. These reports confirmed me in the strong persuasion which I had expressed in the Cabinet and which had been received almost as a paradox, that if the King acted *without* hesitation or delay on our advice, the Lords would not be at all disposed to follow up their blow by another, but silently submit to the gentle rebuke they would receive from the Crown and the menace of a much more serious one from the Commons and the People. The King's answer to the intelligence was very favorable. He had heard of the vote with regret, he deferred to Lord Grey's judgement on the impossibility of agreeing to the motion, which he had at first suggested, and indeed acknowledged that from what he had heard and read of the debate it seemed much too broadly to imply a censure to render it practicable for Ministers or Government to acquiesce. There were many, some very sensible and all very friendly, remarks on the state of the Country and of parties, a little more inclination to coalition or at least approximation between Whigs and Tories if practicable than one could have wished, but a decided preference of keeping the party now in power in their places, and a strong sense of the inconvenience and danger of immediate or frequent changes.

5 June 1833 Wednesday. The Chancellor accompanied Lord Grey early to Windsor and found the King, as a private letter from Sir Herbert announced to me that they would, 'steady and quiet tho' anxious', surprized and annoyed at the opposition, satisfied with Grey and the Ministers, exasperated with the Bishops. He of his own accord remarked that the Lords would be mad to drive things to extremities for, after all, the supreme power, and above all the purse, resided in the Commons. A Government did not depend so much on the House of Lords as on the Commons. A Collision between them would be a Calamity and might be ruin, but nothing so likely to produce and to aggravate it as a struggle for power and a want of stability in the Government. His first notion was to give no answer at all, but he was soon reconciled to that which Lord Grey had suggested to him, and seemed fully convinced that a change of Ministry would lead immediately to dissolution and through dissolution to confusion and revolution. He, I think of his own accord, declared that he should write to the Archbishop of Canterbury to lament and reprehend the Bench for voting against the government and, on receiving next morning a hint from the Chancellor that such letter if written at all should for effect be dated and delivered before any vote of the House of Commons was known, he and Sir Herbert between them penned an epistle full of good sense and, if not very constitutional in its language, well calculated to make a deep impression on those to whom it was addressed.[39] It exacted in pretty direct terms unqualified support on all party questions from the Bench of Bishops and hinted in terms almost as plain at the possible consequences which a connection of the Church with an imprudent and obnoxious faction or party in the state might produce. The Cabinet dined at Lord Melbournes, and after talking over many matters in very good spirits, we empowered Stanley to acquiesce in an additional grant of five millions to the West Indians, provided he thought that by such concession he could secure the cooperation of a large portion of that body and possibly of the local legislatures themselves, as the delegates from Jamaica as well as the representatives of Glasgow, Liverpool, and Bristol gave him hopes that he might.

Thursday 6 June. Returned to Holland House. The Archbishop of Canterbury must have received his reprimand at three, and probably some of the Bishops who looked very low in the House of Lords had heard of its purport by the time Lord Wellesley read, with becoming solemnity, the King's answer to the address at the table of the House of Lords, soon after 5 oclock. The little Marquis laid the proper emphasis on the words *'had already'*, which gave the lie indirect to their Lordship's foolish address; and though the Bishop of Exeter said something about the Church bill, not one Lord Temporal or Spiritual wagged his tongue about the answer and shewed any stomach for renewing the contest.

On this or the preceding day died my excellent friend Lord King. We came into the House of Lords and voted together thirty seven years ago, and I believe we never voted and very seldom thought differently on any publick subject afterwards. He was an amiable, honourable, unaffected, and very acute, perspicuous, and inflexible man. His speeches were full of matter, well expressed and not deficient in language or in wit, though the latter was delivered with so little delicacy or taste and in so harsh and crude a form that it made him pass with Strangers for the very reverse of what he was, an illnatured man.

In truth He had rather a childish love of mischief and enjoyed plaguing the Bishops and the Clergy. In his hatred of every species of exclusion, Monopoly, tyranny, and corruption, he was very sincere, disinterested, consistent, and persevering, and on all questions of currency, finance, and political oeconomy, had greater knowledge and sounder opinions than any peer in the house, but he delighted to present his thoughts, which were in themselves not very palatable, in the shape most revolting to the taste of the audience before whom he produced them. Numquam libentius locutus quam <quam> quod locutus est auditoribus displicebat.

Colonel Davies's[4P] motion to express 'grateful acknowledgements for the policy pursued towards Portugal' was carried by 361 to 98 in the House of Commons, OConnel and the Irish repealers, as well as most of the English Radicals, voting with him! Such has been the result of the Duke of Wellington's manoeuvre.

7th. June Friday. A good answer prepared for the King to Commons by Lord Grey. The progress on West Indian resolutions in Commons but slow. There are however symptoms of both sides becoming more reasonable, though Buxton, chiefly I am told at the instigation of Lord Howick, who made a clever speech, announced his intention of moving to shorten the apprenticeship of the Emancipated Negroes, and the House shewed some distaste to any *encrease* of the money, grant or loan, proposed for West Indians.

Saturday 8th. of June. The Dutch Minister Dedel invited to go back to Hague for further instructions, and the King of Holland reported by our Minister there to be discontented at having ratified so soon, and probably <bro>ught to regret his compliance, tardy and forced as it was, by <learning> of Duke of Wellington's triumph in House of Lords on Monday. The subsequent events may reconcile him to the course he has pursued.

The King has written an admirable Comment on Austrian policy and Russian designs in the East to Lord Palmerston. It is in composition, feeling, and reasoning, an excellent paper, animadverting severely on the false policy of Austria, describing the evil consequences of Russian preponderance in a crumbling Empire, arguing that Mehemet Ali is more likely to revive the Mussulman power than the Sultan, and deprecating any European confederacy in effect or intention similar to the Holy Alliance to which, he shrewdly observes, England was never a party. He also blames the half concealed hostility of Austria to the French Government, though he reverts to his favorite topick of Algiers, and suggests that France, by a timely relinquishment of it, would acquire greater weight in insisting on the evacuation of the Turkish territory by the Russian. These letters of the King, though often too long, are always well composed and well written and often shew much reflection and knowledge and more enlarged views than are ever to be collected from his conversation in publick speeches. That Sir Herbert Taylor, so long practiced in holding the pen, should furnish the language and style, I can easily understand; but exclusive of his repeated assurances that he furnishes little or nothing of the substance and, when he ventures to do so, generally advises omissions rather than suggests new topicks, the turn of thought and nature of policy contained in them are not such as one should suppose even Sir Herbert to entertain, much less to obtrude upon the King. Combined with the King's good humoured manners and his uniformly constitutional conduct, they do His Majesty great credit indeed, and I own they rather surprize me.

Sunday 9th. June. Cabinet at Althorps; empowered him and Stanley to offer the reduction of the period of Negro apprenticeship from 12 to 7 years and the encrease of the grant to West Indians from 15 to 20 millions, with an expectation held out in debate that, should a loan become necessary, such a proposal founded on any thing like a good case should be favorably entertained by the Government. We also directed Stanley to give full powers to Mulgrave to hire <Mansions> or take any other steps he deems necessary for the distribution of his forces in the way most conducive to the safety of the Colony and the preservation of order and property. We went through many of the heads of the intended bill and considered many suggestions originating with Mr Stephens, who is said to be nettled at not being made under Secretary, and whose remarks, ably written, seemed better calculated to impede and embarrass than to smooth the way for our bill. I urged strongly Lord Mulgrave's and Lord Seaford's arguments for additional force and power &c &c.

We then spoke of the state of Parliament and the Country, the necessity of pressing on Irish tythe bill, and the numberless important affairs in Parliament. Some and especially Althorp were for a considerable batch of peers. We canvassed this subject over, but I think we on the whole acquiesced, if we did not absolutely concur in the opinion, that a few, *4 or 5,* well chosen would be enough for the present. The Archbishop has acknowledged the King's letter and, in assuring him that 'he will communicate it to the parties concerned in the way most agreable to H M', adroitly conveys the fact that he did not give the obnoxious vote himself.[41]

Grey dined at Holland House.

Monday 10th.

Tuesday 11th. At Holland House. On one of these days the West Indian resolution, including or at least implying the grant of 20 millions to the planters, the entire abolition of Slavery, and the principle of apprenticeship for the Negroes, was carried by a large majority,[42] Lord Chandos voting against so large a sum of money, and Alexr. Baring, by the good management of Mr Bernal,[43] the Chairman, actually telling the division!

Wednesday 12th. A Cabinet dinner at Lansdown House, all the House of Commons (Sir J Graham excepted) absent. We talked over the state of the Lords, the disposition of the King, and the great probability as well as obvious and fearful consequences of a defeat of the Irish Church bill on 2d. reading in the Lords. Lord Fortescue[44] has given his proxy to Lord Harrowby, and it is thought that the conceited and wavering party are inclined a second time to play the game of last year. The King, however, albeit disposed if practicable to temporizing and compromising, is more aware than he was that it is the unreasonable conduct of our enemies, full as much as as any apprehensions of our own, that renders such approximation difficult and impossible. He very justly remarked to Sir J Graham that they never would forgive Lord Grey and Schedule A, and censures them bitterly for driving matters to extremity, to Collision, and perhaps to revolution from a feeling of revenge if not of personal ambition. He authorizes the Chancellor and Grey to shew the letter he had written of his own accord to the ArchBishop of Canterbury, either to the Archbishop of York or the Bishop of Hereford, as there is some reason to suspect that Canterbury, at the suggestion of Aberdeen, enjoins the strictest secresy to each of the voting Bishops to whom he communicates it, and thereby hopes to deprive the Ministry of the benefit of the admonition to the remaining part of the Bench. The knowledge of his earnestness to support us, to avert a collision of the 2 houses and to be spared the anxiety and hazard of a change would perhaps appall some of the Members of the House of Lords, and we agreed that, if that earnestness was conveyed by some little preference of our supporters and some marks of address to our opponents, it might be of great service to the cause. Accordingly

on *Thursday 13th* Lord Grey conversed with him at length on the subject, was well and patiently listened to and seemed to make much impression. I wrote also to Sir Ht. Taylor a letter in the same spirit and quoted the example of his [the King's] father, who on important occasions insisted on having accurate lists of the divisions sent to him for the purpose of regulating thereby the proportion of favor or discountenance he should so [?show] to persons attending his Levees. The Queen went this day to St. Pauls and somewhat ostentatiously to the Mansion House where she received an address. Her political attachments or rather antipathies have long been no secret, and from rumours which reach me she seems likely to divulge other secrets to the publick which will be nearly as unpalatable to them. The text and Sermon of the Bishop of Hereford, who preached before her, was much animadverted upon as coming from Lord Grey's brother. The text was falsely represented to be the same as Sacheverell's and, though the innovations deprecated in the sermon probably were in the intention of the preacher merely of a doctrinal kind, they were misconstrued by inattentive or malicious hearers to allude generally to reforms in Church and State. I dined with Talleyrand.

14 Friday. Dined with Lord Grey. Lord Ponsonby's letters impute very openly ambitious and perfidious designs to Russia. He perhaps refines too much and may exaggerate the utter helplessness and dependence of the Porte, but I am not sorry his suspicions take that direction. I believe there is more reason and am sure there is less mischief in inculcating distrust of the Muscovite than of the French.

The Infant Don Carlos, for whom his brother's Government had sent a frigate to the Tagus to convey him to Civita Vecchia, decamped with all his family the eve of the day he was expected to sail and proceeded to Don Miguel at Coimbra, with whom he had manifestly concerted this flight. The Spanish Embassador, Cordova[45] (originally the Lover of the Infant's Wife), is or affects to be furious at this event and, if the dispatches which are shewn by him to Lord Wm. [Russell] are really sent by him to the Court, will bring matters shortly to a crisis. These documents and other notes and conversation have convinced Lord Wm. of his sincerity, but some there are at Lisbon who suspect him to be in the plot and that Zea[46] and perhaps Ferdinand himself entered to reestablish the Salick law[47] on the meeting of Cortes and are in deep cabal with Carlos, Miguel, and the Portuguese Princesses to subvert the ascendancy of the Queen of Spain and what they invidiously term the Neapolitan influence at Madrid.

15 Saturday. Returned to Holland House.

16 Sunday. Lady Coventry[48] dined at Holland House. Grey, Chancellor, and Richmond at dinner. I received a long and well written answer from Windsor,[49] in which the King professed to take my hints in good part, fixed an early day for dining here, entered into a detailed vindication of his conduct, good humouredly acknowledged the hostility of all branches of his family, except the Duke of Sussex, to the Ministry, justified his own equal reception of Whigs and Tories on the ground of never being a party man and, acknowledging his father's and brother's conduct in that respect to have been different, justly remarked that they were censured for being too exclusive. He repeated his former aversion to making peers and with some little asperity remarked that the embarrassment we foresaw was drawn on ourselves by an unnecessary declaration that we should stand or fall by the Irish Church Reform bill.[50] The case was well argued and there is truth in his view of the subject. But there is good and bad in the letter, and the prospect is very discouraging. Some of our friends, and among them John Russell and Duncannon, are for striking out the most obnoxious parts of the bill. At this I am surprized, tho' if the Majority of the Lords had not exasperated our House of Commons friends and the publick, it might have been the most judicious course. But now will any modification disarm the Tory hostility in Lords? and will not even reasonable concessions displease the Commons and rouse the suspicions of the People? On the answer to these questions our determination must turn. In the meantime we hear the Tories are softening or taking fright. [*In the margin:* Mr Rogers consulted me upon an inscription upon Crabbe[51] the poet, and in the framework furnished by his family we patched up one together which is I think simple, short, and yet full. The Monument is to be erected at Trowbridge by his friends and parishioners.]

17 Monday. We were threatened with a great attendance in Lords and formidable division on the Lord Chancellor's local Jurisdiction bill.[52] The House was a full one and the Chancellor, after a very artful exordium alluding to the state of the house and the reports of the day, made an able exposition of the bill. Lord

Lyndhurst opposed it bitterly and with many malignant insinuations and inflammatory topicks addressed to the house and the [*word missing*] but in manner and delivery temperate and solemn and in execution as is usual with him clear, copious, and forcible. He however indulged in the fallacy of treating the proposed law as extensive and general, though he knew it was confined to debts under £20, and treated it as an entire substitution of local for central or circuit Courts. He was answered in one of Broughams most powerful speeches, replete with argument, eloquence, invective, and irony. I observed Duke of Wellington earnestly dissuading Lyndhurst from a division, and several Tory peers went away unable and unwilling to give a vote in the teeth of so convincing a speech as Lord Broughams. They did not divide, and one of the various merits of the Chancellor's speech consisted in the artful manner in which he identified both his bill and the Government with popular feelings at this critical period when it is so essential to reconcile the press and the publick to our administration.

Tuesday 18. Cabinet at one. Brougham read a letter from Windsor in the same spirit but more detailed and perhaps in rather a more irritable tone than that I received on Sunday.[53] [*In the margin:* There was one passage in the letter extremely unjust and ill founded which indicated considerable soreness and, in my judgment, afforded much ground for suspecting that pains had been taken to infuse jealousy and discontent in his mind. He complained of the manner in which our advice to answer the House of Lords had been conveyed, namely in a visit of Grey and the Chancellor to Windsor, as implying an apprehension and raising in others a suspicion that he was likely to hesitate. He implied by this complaint that we had been anxious to secure all the merit and popularity of the answer to ourselves and to leave with him the odium of hesitating about it. This is surely a perverted way of considering a measure which the nature and importance of the question and indeed personal respect to the King seemed to us all and certainly to me, who earnestly recommended it, to enjoin.] The King lamented, as in the other, our declaration of standing or falling by the Irish Reform bill, urged yet more openly a coalition with some of our Tory opponents which would, he said, be the happiest day of his life, and, in some ambiguous and mysterious sentences with compliments to the transcendent talents of the Chancellor and deprecating his engaging in a factious opposition, hinted at the possibility of his remaining in office even if the Ministry were changed. He took merit to himself for the strong measure of writing to the Bishops and for his earnestness in supporting us, though he repeated his vehement aversion to encrease of the peerage, which would, he say[s], degrade both the house and himself. Our impression was that he had a deep sense of the embarrassment he was likely to have to encounter, that he ascribed it to the passions and prejudices of both parties but more to the Tories than to us on this occasion, that he would rejoice and assist to a limited <degree> in procuring us acquiescence in the Lords, but that he had made up his mind, in the case of our defeat, to accept of our resignation and take the chance of either negotiating some coalition and compromise or conducting the government with Wellington and the Tories. [*In the margin:* N.B. his letter of 6th. June to the Archbishop not only distinctly answers the voting Bishops for lending themselves to a party but as distinctly charges that party with the design of embarrassing and harrassing the King's Government at the risk of producing an instability in His Majesty's councils dangerous to the welfare of the Country.] We then discussed the propriety of dividing the Irish Church Reform bill. John Russell, Lord Melbourne, and myself were earnest for doing so, and the Chancellor was so inclined; but Grey, and above all Althorp, was averse to it and, after a good deal of conversation, we deferred to the opinion of the leader in the Commons and agreed to substitute an amendment in the obnoxious clause for a division of the separate parts of the bill. The produce of the alienated lands is not to be left generally to be disposed of as Parliament deems fit, but to such *religious and charitable* purposes as Parliament deems <meet>. Grant of Rothemareas[54] is made puisne Judge at Calcutta, and the Cabinet recommend the King to recall Sir Coln. Halkett,[55] who has treated Lord Clare[56] most <insolently> from Bombay. The King dined at Duke of W[ellingto]n.

Wednesday 19th. The King seems pleased at my second letter in which I acknowledged his notions of impartiality to his subjects to be right and honourable generally but confine the departure or apparent departure from it which I had ventured to suggest as justifiable only for very peculiar circumstances and with a view of removing unjust but not quite unaccountable impressions of partiality the other way. There was no Cabinet dinner.

Thursday 20 June. The King dined at Holland House and was remarkably chearful and good humoured. Many of the company, which consisted 21 including His Majesty, were exceedingly pleased, especially the Clanrickardes, Lord Roseberry, Lord St. Vincent, and Lord Poltimore.[57] His Majesty seems to me to be somewhat comfortable in a society where he has neither the Queen nor his brothers to observe him, to take him to task, or to reprove him for what he says. In truth I collect from those who know his habits well that the Queen's ascendancy, such as it is, is as much founded on his fear and his indolence as on his love, and that her hostility to the Whigs, arising from personal mortification in the matter of Lord Howe, is inveterate and insurmountable. The King has a more sincere anxiety to do right than is usual in persons of his exalted rank, and is more exempt from bad passions, especially rancour, vanity, or pride, than is common in any.

Lord St. Vincent told me that the Duke of Wellington checked Mr Burge in his violence, moderated Mr Barrett[58] and the other West Indians, and persuaded them to entrust their petition in the hands of a West Indian proprietor rather than his, because it was a national and not a party concern, and in his hands would be misconstrued into hostility to the Ministry, which it was in their interest and the publick advantage should be avoided. This does his judgement and his publick spirit credit, and as I often blame him in these notes, it is fair to record his good deeds and to give him praise where, as on this and on other not unfrequent occasions, he deserves it.

21 June Friday. In Lords some questions and rambling conversation on foreign politicks, Algiers, and Turkey from Lords Aberdeen and Londonderry, strongly indicative of hostility and wish to do mischief but not otherwise remarkable. A Motion of Lord Wicklow's for certain returns respecting Irish tythes gave that

Lord and the Duke of Wellington an opportunity of venting their spleen against the whole system of Government in Ireland and censuring by anticipation the bill for paying the Clergy the arrears and repaying the country by a land tax. Lord Grey made a very excellent and I thought satisfactory reply; he expressed more resentment and indignation towards OConnel, I will not say, than he deserves, but than it is in present circumstances prudent or perhaps in any, dignified, for a first Minister to display towards an individual not in the house. The Chancellor attempted to do away that impression by strong and possibly exaggerated commendations of his professional eminence, describing it as sufficient not only to justify but to commend the patent of precedency we g<a>ve him. Brougham told me afterwards that OConnel had some thoughts of coming to the English bar and would be much pleased at so opportune a testimony to his professional talent. In the mean while, or rather while Brougham was speaking, he was bitterly inveighing in the Commons against Stanley and an amendment on Church Reform which he knows to be useful in promoting the measures he affects to approve.[59] After a slight attempt to delay the Local legislature bill,[60] we went into the Committee pro formâ and by agreement of Lyndhurst and Brougham are to consider the Clauses on Monday. The transactions in the Commons as reported in papers to me unpleasant and unintelligible.

22 June. The papers represent Stanley as withdrawing not amending the Clause relating to Bishop's lands in Ireland, and Lord Carlisle, who dined with me, assures me that Abercromby and other important personages voted in the minority.[61]

OConnell made an angry but powerful speech, and Mr Grote[62] and Mr Gisborne[63] more calmly arraigned us for giving up the principle of applying Ecclesiastical funds as surplus to publick purposes and for tacitly compromising with the Bishops and the Lords.

Sunday 23d. June. Cabinet at Althorp's. The debate and division of Friday have much estranged our friends there. The great fault however seems to have been the want of early decision and more general communication. The absence of Althorp *from gout* was unlucky, and Stanley somewhat injudiciously urged a fear of collision with the Lords as a motive for omitting the Clause, whereas many are so heated against the Bishop[s] that in their hearts they think that would be sufficient reason for retaining it. I urged on the Cabinet the necessity of settling beforehand, communicating to friends, and adhering afterwards to the course we intended to pursue with respect to any further amendments, such as reduction of the Bishop of Derry's or Primate's income. We seemed to agree on what should be done; but will Althorpe communicate and will Stanley adhere to it? Though at Windsor the division of Friday is very erroneously deemed a triumph, the state of the Commons is far from comfortable.[64]

We went thro', clause by clause, the West India Slavery bill. The accounts from the Admiral at Jamaica (of 23d. April) are encouraging. It is clear that if they take time to hear our plan, the Planters will be satisfied with the Apprenticeship plus 20 millions, and the Negroes, submissive to the restrictions on their liberty, when they find themselves exempt from all arbitrary punishment.

24th. to 30th. June. Passed this week in Old Burl[ingto]n Street. Monday and several days of the week were employed in the House of Lords in discussing the principle and details of the Lord Chancellor's local Judicature bill, which is a bold and benevolent attempt to administer cheap law to all the poor of the Country. The debate was chiefly between Lord Lyndhurst and Lord Chancellor. The former spoke with great perspicuity and eloquence, but seemed to me to beg the question throughout, to argue a bill which confined the jurisdiction it established to causes under 20 or £50 as if it extended to all, and to conceal, under a calm and suppressed manner, much real bitterness and personal malignity to Brougham, who repelled it in a speech of great and various powers. There was some appearance of a design to throw out the bill on a motion of Lord Eldon's, which was rejected however by a majority of ten.[65] The Tories, who attended in numbers at the beginning of every day, deserted Lyndhurst, Wynford, and Duke of Cumberland in the discussion of the details.

On the tuesday Lord Ripon opened the West Indian resolutions. He had taken too large a canvass for his speech and was more than once unable to proceed, but his known talent and yet more his amiable and natural manner of acknowledging his sudden and temporary inefficiency bespoke the favor of the House; he recovered and delivered a very good and sensible speech. Lord Harewood,[66] Duke of Wellington, and Lord Ellenborough spoke on the other side: Lord Harewood mischievously, unhandsomely, and incorrectly complaining of want of communication to the West Indians and commenting of the bill, which had been communicated to him in part and confidentially; The Duke of Wellington dwelling at length on the commonplace topicks against Emancipation and dealing after his fashion in strong assertions and bold non sequiturs, but agreeing to vote for the resolutions; and Lord Ellenborough, who alone opposed them, applauding himself for superior sagacity, thinking to cajole the people by <some> hopes of great oeconomy and much liberality from the <tories>, reviling the house of Commons, and lauding the condition of Slavery. Grey answered Wellington admirably and the Chancellor exposed Lord Ellenborough unmercifully. The Resolutions were passed,[67] but not till the Duke of Wellington, with that contempt or ignorance of publick opinion which distinguishes him, had proposed to omit the words 'liberal and comprehensive' before the Education destined by the resolutions to the Negroes; and to the vote retaining them, he and several other peers afterwards protested—a trait of judgement nearly equal to that which induced all the Bishops, save one, to be absent when a unanimous vote abolishing Slavery was passed! We dined on the *Wednesday* at Lord Ripon's and heard with some chagrin that the French Ministers had allowed their law for empowering the King to relax the commercial restrictions during the recess to be rejected without debate or division! Many disposed to distrust the French, crowed over what they determined to consider their bad faith and duplicity and what was, even to make the best of it, at least weakness and mismanagement or want of foresight and sagacity. *Thursday* I assisted at the Christening of my Grandson, T Powys,[68] and Friday I dined with Sir J Kempt. Saturday at Lord Carlisles.

On the Wednesday at Ripon's, Lord Grey read a letter to him from the Duchess of Kent, complaining of the fortresses having received unusual orders restricting their salutes to her, and also some comments from Windsor on the complaint, which amply vindicated the order but betrayed no little soreness at the complaint and at some other proceedings of the Duchess of Kent, who, instigated probably by Sir J Conroy, seems more disposed than hitherto to court publick notice and to represent herself as an aggrieved personage. Melbourne was somewhat maliciously diverted at her expostulation about the declining number of 'salutes' and Sir J Graham devized an order from the board of Admiralty which, in regulating a variety of other matters relating to Salutes both at Sea and on ports, places all the Royal family except the King and Queen upon a new and separate footing—an alteration which the trouble, expence, and inconvenience of the present arrangement renders in itself very advisable, but which will no doubt be very unpalatable to them all, not expecting even the Duke of Sussex, unless he is previously apprized and apparently consulted upon it. The value of that little artifice, if such attentions are to be so called, is not sufficiently understood either with great or little personages by our Ministers.

Sunday 30th. June. At Holland House—no political event.

Monday 1st. July. Holland House.

Tuesday 2 July. Cabinet at Althorp's. Division of legal tender resolution discouraging and Althorp disposed to give up one half of his project.[69] The postponement of the West Indian bill recommended by St. Vincents and other West Indians, though it would unquestionably propitiate the Jamaica assembly and facilitate their cooperation, was on discussion deemed impracticable, as the House of Commons and publick would never vote or adhere to the 20 million unless the article of emancipation, enforced in the shape of an act, were secured. Burge, by not only pressing the postponement but protesting against the principle and canvassing some of the details of the bill with a strong and premature assurance that the Jamaica legislature would not agree to it, indisposed the Cabinet yet more to any thing like postponement.

Intelligence has reached Government that Genl. Bourmont[70] is in London with several officers on his way to Lisbon, where he is to take the Command of Don Miguels army. It is said he has hired a steam boat, and already equipped, with the assistance and knowledge of Marshal Beresford, several vessels with ammunition, troops, and warlike stores for the Tagus, and private intelligence from the city (corroborated by information from yet more secret and authentick sources) apprizes us that he has interviews and consultations with Vial, the Spanish minister here, much secret correspondence and concert with the Carlists in Spain, with Zea himself, and with some agents of the three Northern courts, as well as a very large command of money. Palmerston taxed the Spanish Chargé d'Affaires[71] with meddling in a way inconsistent with neutrality, but he of course denied the facts and, as we cannot produce our secret evidence to substantiate them, it is not easy to confute him.

The King has approved Sir James Graham's plan about the salutes, and Grey wrote last thursday to the Duchess of Kent withdrawing the order, assuring her that it was not intended as any diminution of respect to her or disparagement of her or her daughter, and apprizing her that some new and *general* regulation respecting signals is in contemplation. That intention has been communicated to Duke of Sussex and he takes it well and reasonably. The Duchess of Kent has not answered but is gone, they say, to Cowes. I had written to Sir Herbert Taylor once more venturing to hint that, if the King would permit Lord Grey to recommend Mr Coke to a peerage, it would be tantamount in effect to the creation of twenty, but I received a civil and well written but firm and determined letter, written at the King's request, saying that he could not, after Mr Coke's unmeasured language about George III grant him any such mark of favor without lowering himself in the opinion of his brothers and Sisters (Sussex perhaps excepted) and indeed in his own. It is a matter of *feeling* and he cannot subdue them. I am sorry but it is neither blameworthy nor unnatural and we must acquiesce in it.

Grey expressed this day to me even in stronger language his sense of his inability to attend to the various business and to decide the weighty matters on which a man in his situation was called upon to deliberate. When I told him, as in conscience and truth I could, that there was neither in Council nor Parliament any symptom of decaying powers or impaired energy, he earnestly assured me that he could not apply his mind as formerly, that he hoped to tide over the Session and that in the recess some arrangement might be adopted. He thought Althorp, called up to the House of Lords and appointed to his office, would be the best. I observed to him that it was not clear that he could transfer to another the King's confidence and deference to his authority, and my apprehension that if the King had not the protection of him (Lord Grey) he would resort to the Duke of Wellington as, in his view of the matter, the only alternative. Grey, the Archbishop of Dublin and Talleyrand and Sydney Smith dined at Holland House this day.

Wednesday 3d. Went to town and staid till the 13th. The Cabinet dined at Lord Carlisles on the 3d. On Friday the 5th. Lord Lansdowne in a very luminous speech moved the East Indian Resolutions, was opposed by Ellenborough in a very eloquent and ingenious and less injudicious speech. Ripon answered him and was answered by Duke of Wellington more wretchedly than usual. [*Heading:* Friday 5th.] Lord Lansdowne's reply was full of spirit, vigour, and argument.

In the course of the ensuing week there were one or two Cabinets, but few matters of any great interest discussed. Speculations on the intentions of our enemies on the Church Temporalities bill, on the time it would arrive in the Lords, and on the attendance we could procure chiefly occupied our attention. We heard of few votes in the Lords purchased by the relinquishment of the Alienation Clause in the Commons, and had good reason to suspect that such concessions as weakened our popularity either in Parliament or in the Country, however congenial to the principles of our adversaries, animated their hopes and did not soften the virulence in opposition. The local Judicature bill lingered in the Committee and in the Report. Lord Lyndhurst and Lord Wynford pertinaciously urged amendments and cavilled at details, but whether from the intrinsick tediousness of the discussion or for some other reason, they were generally abandoned by their friends at the dinner hour, and Lyndhurst, both on his legs and in private, seemed to be sore at the thinness of the audience he addressed. Some appearance there was and more rumours there were of dissentions in our enemies councils, but yet the canvass for attendance and activity of Rosslyn and others seemed to announce a battle and accordingly on the 9th. tuesday, on the 3d. reading of the local Judicature bill (which Brougham had originally introduced as an *individual* and had in truth never opened or communicated to the Cabinet, but which had assumed the aspect of a Government measure) the forces of the two parties both in presents and proxies were very numerously arrayed. Lyndhurst made a very elaborate, eloquent, ingenious speech which Plunket, in a good but not brilliant answer, termed masterly, and after a long and tedious discourse from Wynford, the Chancellor delivered one of his most successful displays of reasoning, knowledge, eloquence, and sarcasm. He absolutely annihilated Wynford, and with great temper and matchless judgement exposed Lyndhurst's ingenuity and faction, and conveyed to the house the frightful consequences which might ensue from their rejection of a bill which he adroitly described as more popular than it perhaps was and well deserving the name of the Poor Man's bill. Our numbers of present were equal, 81 and 81, Lord Cawdor from Welsh propensities and private pique voting against the Chancellor, and Harrowby, at the head of the Waverers, giving to our dismay and surprize the proxy of Lord Fortescue against the bill. The proxies gave the opponents of the bill a bitter majority, and the matter was not I think mended by a vexatious call for a second division from some of our friends after several peers had left the house, and an endeavour of objecting to their votes after they returned.[72] Even before the debate, the Bishop of Exeter and Duke of Cumberland had sounded the Alarm of the Coronation Oath upon the Church Temporalities bill, and The Duke of Buckingham was so impatient to brand it with the names of Spoliation that he could not wait till it was offered for a first reading, but thundered at the index of its being brought up from the bar.

We met on one of the ensuing days to consider of the consequences of our recent and approaching defeats and of the unpleasant condition in which, with a Majority of hostile peers, we are placed. It is impossible for a Ministry to conduct the affairs of the King with advantage to the Country and with honour to itself, if the hostility of one branch of the legislature is manifestly, permanently, and decidedly against them; and it seems, as far as our experience has gone, to be as impossible to convert or to intimidate the present Majority in the house of Lords, who may have occasionally been restrained by fear or prudence from driving us from the helm, but who have clearly the will and the power and are only waiting to seize the most advantageous opportunity for subverting our administration. In this statement of our condition and in the unpleasantness of it we were all agreed, nor did we differ on three other important points: first, that the creation of a large batch of peers would *now* be impracticable, and if practicable, not perhaps either justifiable or efficacious; and 2dly., that the loss of the local Judicature bill was not an advantageous occasion to resign upon; and 3dly., that the loss of the 2d. reading of the Church temporalities bill, pledged as we are in words and yet more strongly in feeling and reason to carry it, will render the immediate tender of our resignations an absolute and indispensible duty. On all these points we were unanimous. But there was in several an inclination, and in some a strong and earnest desire, not to wait till the rejection of the bill, but to urge in the interim either the general aspect of the Lords, or some measure which the King would hesitate to adopt as a motive for immediate retirement. Lord Hill had absented himself from the house on Brougham's Judicature bill, and Althorpe, Brougham, and Lord J Russell, especially the last, urged us with some warmth to request his immediate dismissal and to tender our resignations if it was not as immediately granted by the King. To this however Lord Lansdowne, Palmerston, Stanley, and myself and, indeed, most of the others vehemently objected. It was desirable that, if we did leave our posts, our motives for so doing should be intelligible, important, and popular. It should be distinctly understood that it was a majority of the House of Lords turned us out, not a want of favor at Court or loss of confidence in the Country. If we went out because the King would not remove Lord Hill, We went out on a personal question and we quarreled with the Court, not the House of Lords. We had three courses to pursue: 1, to insist on the dismissal of Hill and resign if it was refused; 2d., to resign in anticipation of a defeat on the Church bill and the notorious hostility of a Majority in Lords; and 3dly., to wait the event of the second reading, and resign on the rejection of the bill or any essential mutilation of it in the Committee.

The first course appeared to me unfair to the King and, considering many little circumstances both of the office and the individual, unjust to Lord Hill, as well as a disadvantageous ground of resignation for us; and it was agreed that he should not be dismissed, but his disposition to support put to he test on the eve of next division, by a letter from Grey, urging his presence and support upon so vital a question.

The 2d. course was certainly justifiable, but with some prospect of passing a great and useful measure, and of forwarding many others, it was not expedient to relinquish our post, till it was made manifest to the World as well as ourselves that we could no longer retain it. We accordingly decided on the 3d. course. Althorpe and the Chancellor acceded, but J Russell somewhat pettishly declared that he could not act or attend the house of Commons as a Minister till Hill had either pledged himself to support us or was dismissed. He was, he said, discontented that something had not been sooner done to secure the Lords, some peers been made and the Horse guards cleansed of enemies, open or disguised, and he appeared to me strongly to suspect the Court and the King himself (I am satisfied *unjustly*) of hostility.

Here we are then, in July 1833, much as we were in June 1832. The same helplessness in the Lords! the same dependence on the Waverers! the same embarrassment, though on a bill of somewhat less importance, between the 2d. reading and the Committee—but with much less hope and less reason for resorting to the expedient of making peers and with diminished popularity in the Country and perhaps impaired support in the Commons. It is clear however that the dread of the Tories revives in the same degree the favor we had lost in the publick, and enhances in the eyes of the people the merit of the measures on which we apprehend a defeat. The Duke of Wellington took an early opportunity, after the rejection of Lord Chancellor's Law bill, to sound high the alarm of the Coronation

Oath and, tho' all such designs were disclaimed by his immediate adherents, his whole deportment announced a disposition for battle and a persuasion of immediate victory. Pains were taken to imply that he will not be first Minister [*In the margin:* that Sutton the Speaker may be Premier with a Peerage], and that a dissolution may not be necessary. It is utterly impossible that a Ministry should be formed without Peel and Wellington being virtually the leaders of it and, yet more so, that they should conduct the affairs of the Country without a new Parliament. It will be marvellous even then if the Government should last 3 months or the institutions of the Country 12. The King is aware of the perilous course the Tories are steering and I think displeased at it. He is acting fairly by us, but he appears occasionally indifferent, preferring us perhaps, and certainly not betraying us, but he occasionally lulls his anxiety with the delusion that when things are come to the worst Wellington and Peel can *form* a Ministry more easily than they could last year, and in that case he would be prepared to submit the rest to the chapter of accidents. We are assured that the House of Commons is determined to stand by us, and even OConnel is under such an alarm at the approach of a Tory Ministry that he has given notice of a motion in favor of 'local judicatures' by which he hopes to indicate the determination of the house not to submit to the controul of the house of Lords and the Bishops. Sir John Wrottesley[73] on Friday 12th. gave notice of moving for a call of the house, implying that the object of it was to prepare for a collision of the Lords.

In the early part of this week arrived intelligence of Palmella's and Terceira's (Villa Flor) expedition having taken possession of the whole coast and many towns in the Algarvis—but per contra Bourmont has sailed for Lisbon, and Beresford, if not Wellington himself, is active in directing the employment of the money sent from the Continent by Don Miguel's supporters in equipments, recruiting, &c.

Saturday 13th. Duke of Sussex dined at Holland house. Chancellor Brougham and Plunkett came over and slept. We talked over the question of Coronation Oath and on.

Sunday 14th The Chancellor shewed me Grey's letter and the King's answer on the state of the Ministry and the Lords. Grey had sent a shorter letter on the subject, not actually declaring that he should resign if defeated nor pointing directly at the creation of peers, but complaining of Hill's vote, painting in strong colours the hostile spirit which animated the house of Lords, and the painful predicament in which his Ministry is placed with the weight of one branch of the legislature opposed to it. The King's answer was friendly and satisfactory, directly acknowledging the embarrassment arising from a Collision of the 2 houses, the probability of such a Collision and the part which Wellington and Peel had had in producing it, deprecating in warm and friendly terms the dangers of a change, expressing a hope that even if beat and forced to resign we would give him a fair opportunity for accommodating matters and avoiding the evils of instability or shortlived administrations. He earnestly disclaimed all knowledge or intercourse with the Tories, agreed distinctly to remove Hill if he should again either absent himself or vote against us on any important occasion, and avowed in direct terms his unwillingness to part with us, and the yet greater danger he should apprehend from a House of Commons hostile to his Ministry than from a House of Lords so indisposed to them.

Mr Barrett and Mr Sharpe called and seemed to have in contemplation an address from the City to the King, representing that a Change in his government would be 'hazardous to the publick interests abroad and at home'. Soon afterwards arrived the news of Napier's victory over Miguel's fleet off Lagos on the 5th. instant. One line of battle ship struck without firing the shot, the others were taken after a vigorous resistance but by a force wonderfully inferior. Lord John Russell called but was still firm, not to say obstinate, in his purpose of resigning, for I can call it by no other name since he does not seem to me to propose an alternative and is not satisfied with the King's letter, the substance of which had been communicated to him by Althorp. Lord Grey called and Sir James Graham dined and Lord Lansdown came in the evening. All pleased with Napier's victory and struck with the exploit.

Monday 15 July. Went to London and staid till Saturday the 20th. The report of a determination on the part of the Tories to throw out the Irish Church Temporalities subsided, and consequently the notion of meetings and resolutions on the subject in the City and elsewhere were abandoned, though in the House of Commons Sir John Wrottesley brought in his motion for a call of the House and resisted Lord Althorpe's earnest entreaties to withdraw it. There should in truth have been some previous concert on the subject, for the motion was intended and supported chiefly with a view of preserving the Ministry and terrifying the Lords into an acquiescence, and there was something ungracious and offensive in repressing publickly the zeal of our friends and exposing the impropriety of their proceedings. Stanley allowed his personal enmity to mislead his judgement so far, as to reproach O'Connel in his very endeavour to save us and our bill, with his inconsistency after reviling the one and voting against the other. This and the suddenness of Lord Althorpe's resolution to oppose the motion was resented by some and lamented by more of our friends. However Sir John Wrottesley was satisfied with the respectable names and considerable number of his Minority,[74] and in the course of 48 hours Duncannon, Mr Ellice, and others acknowledged that neither motion nor rejection of it had done material mischief, though the conversations and murmurs about it sufficiently betrayed some habitual faults in our Management of the House of Commons, and particularly the little Concert which subsists between the Ministers and their leading friends out of Cabinet and office, and the frequency of abrupt and unexpected deviations from the Course of proceeding once announced and maintained by our friends in conversation. The Intelligence of the great action of Napier had arrived on Sunday. It gladdenned every enemy of tyranny and oppression, depressed the abettors of all Ultra opinions, and should have induced our Government to send a Mission to the Regency *forthwith* and to recall by proclamation all our subjects from the service of Don Miguel. I urged but in vain the policy of taking such steps before Lisbon was in possession of Queen Maria's party, that we might have the grace of serving her cause in its adversity and have some right to assume authority in advising the settlement of the Government and the marriage of the Young Queen. The French were alarmed and are chagrined at the appointment of Bourmont but I am assured by Lord Granville (just returned from Paris for the Church bill) that they are still ready to acquiesce in the policy and cooperate in the measures we are inclined to adopt. As the day for the 2d. reading of the Church bill,

Wednesday 17th. July, approached, the existence of a schism in the Councils of the Tories acquired more credit, and it is confidently rumoured, that Peel adhered to the resolution of taking no office, that Wellington and a portion who are branded by the High Flyers as worshippers of Expediency would vote for the 2d. reading, and that the meetings of the latter had been transferred from Apsley House, to the Duke of Cumberlands, Duke of Newcastle. Of this or something like this symptoms had occurred in publick. Wellington, in some of the preliminary skirmishes on petition, wheeled manifestly to the flank of the position he first intended to occupy and pretended that the Coronation Oath in his view of the subject was not a positive bar to legislation, but yet served as an indication of the antient and uniform policy of this Country. Indeed some of his adherents did not scruple to insinuate a falsehood, viz that he had communicated his waver of all opposition to the bill on 2d. reading and that he had for political purposes of our own suppressed that intelligence. The Duke of Newcastle and Lord Winchelsea on the other hand were forward and earnest to disclaim and inveigh against *Expediency* as the ground of action, and in their zeal to disprove their own prudence (which nobody ever suspected), asked questions about the King's letter to Archbishop, which the Bishop of London answered discreetly and smartly enough. The Debate then began and last[ed] 3 days.

Wednesday 17, Thursday 18, and Friday 19. Grey's speech was luminous, temperate, argumentative, and persuasive. On the side of the Opposition the speeches of Bishop of Exeter and Lord Mansfield (both elaborate and malignant and the former intolerably and unnecessarily long and irrelevant) were remarkable for eloquence, talent, and research, but were answered effectually and in many points triumphantly by Lansdowne, Plunket, the Chancellor, and Grey. The Duke of Wellington, though he waved opposition to the 2d. reading for fear of provoking the Commons to withold the indemnity to Irish Clergy, reprobated both principles and details of the bill, arraigned bitterly the whole conduct of Government, ascribed to their weakness, folly, or wickedness all the evils of Ireland, all the dangers and difficulties that beset us, and particularly to the appointment of Lord Anglesey, who was the most unfit Man in England for that situation and had disqualified himself by that dangerous letter in which he counselled the Irish to 'agitate agitate agitate'. [*In the margin:* He thought no doubt that he might soften the resentment of his Ultra friends at his not voting against the 2nd reading, by railing at their Common enemy, the Ministry. He is manifestly anxious to recover and retain the command of the Ultra party and especially of the Orangemen and Protestants in Ireland! They say *Roden* has <attended> a political meeting at Lady Jersey's!!!] He ridiculed however the Duke of Newcastle's horror of expediency, and by some sophistry or another endeavoured to prove that his view of the Coronation Oath was not inconsistent with the principle of expediency or the vote he was about to give. *Lord Melbourne,* in the best speech I ever heard him deliver, indignantly and ably repelled and retorted the attacks of the Duke of Wellington and exposed his want of fairness of justice and *generosity* in arraigning the conduct and character of Anglesey, reminding him of his own letter not less imprudent than that of Anglesey. Wellington, who has a sort of notion that all prudent Combatants are bound to keep their hands off Hector however he may assail them, was evidently surprized and annoyed at the success of this personal retort. The Bishops of London, Bath and Wells, and Hereford as well as Archbishop of Dublin all spoke for the bill, but all, except in some degree the Archbishop, rested their votes more on the fatal consequences of rejecting, rather than the consequences of passing, the bill. The Bishop of London managed that topick with great address, and drew the distinction between expediency and principle, or rather reconciled the former, in cases like the present, to the latter with great talent and success; the other two English Bishops gave very reluctant votes—similesque coactis—and cut a poor figure. Bishop Grey regretted not being cordial with his brother on the bill, and Lord De Grey[75] was anxious to disclaim, in voting with a Ministry of which his brother was a part, confidence in them. These strange brotherly exhibitions were soon followed up by a short debate between the Dukes of Cumberland and Sussex, and the spirit of Miguel and Pedro—Acies fraterna et ineluctabile bellum—not to mention Lord Wellesley and the Duke of Wellington, seemed to pervade the House of Lords.

The Chancellor satisfied me that the argument on the Coronation Oath with which I had furnished him and Plunket was sound, by putting it forcibly and well. He proved that if political oaths were to be considered as indissoluble vows to God and not engagements between Man and Man, the necessity of some dispensing power on Earth, some infallible Church such as Roman Catholicks are supposed to acknowledge in Popes, Conclaves, or Councils, would be undeniable. Lord Grey closed the debate in a reply of some length, full of mental and bodily vigour, and wonderful for both in a Man near seventy years old, after anxious attention for three successive nights in a heated and unwholsome atmosphere. He handled both Wellington and the Bishop of Exeter severely and exposed the inaccuracy of the latter in a way that mortified him and surprized the house; but the manly d earnest manner in which he avowed the necessity and determination of acting in the spirit of reform, in which he vindicated the conduct and character of the Reformed House of Commons, and in which he exposed the hopelessness of conciliating the Tories, who were on the watch to avail themselves of any unpopularity to which a desire of removing their objections might lead him, for the purpose of subverting his administration, was eloquent, impressive and, above all, judicious and statesmanlike. He repeated that a Government in these times had to chuse between a repressive; coercive, and forcible system or one which, by directing and regulating the current of improvement and reform, endeavoured to adapt its institutions and policy to publick opinion and gain the affection and confidence of the governed. The first system he and his Colleagues could not, ought not, and would not adopt; and if they were not allowed to prosecute the latter in the way they deemed most beneficial to their country, they were bound in duty to quit a station in which they could no longer be useful. The Duke of

Wellington went away and many including Haddington followed his example. Ellenborough and Duke of Buckingham voted with the Highflying Tories against the 2d. reading. Harrowby, Wharncliffe, and most of the Waverers with us. The Division including proxies was 157 for and 98 against the bill, and of these latter, 68, a number exceeding by 10 or 15 what the Duke of Wellington or we had calculated, were present—a circumstance of portentous omen for the ensuing Committee.[76]

Saturday 20th. The Chancellor and Lord Melbourne slept at Holland House and the former assured me that the Tories were determined to put forth their strength in the Committee and beat us upon some one point. It is manifestly his opinion and Althorpe's determination that we should resign if beat on the minutest particle of the bill. I doubt the policy of this, and above all of not attempting to recover any ground we lose in the Committee on the report or on 3d. reading. Burdett, if any criterion of the opinion of House of Commons friends, would clearly condemn resignation even for the material objects of the bill.

Sunday 21. Attended Cabinet at Lord Althorpes; by our hasty promise to advance the arrears due to Irish Clergy for [18]30, 31, and 32 and not to raise the tythes from the people, we have involved ourselves in a dilemma from which it is impossible to extricate ourselves with honour or perfect justice to all parties. The only honest method is impracticable, and we determined on as fair a compromise as we could devize.[77]

I went to London and staid till *Saturday 27.* The week was chiefly occupied in the Committee on Church Temporalities in Lords. It would be very difficult to remember and tedious to report all the points canvassed in the Committee. It was clearly the object of our opponents to beat us in some trifling object which we could not in honour, and with the good will of our House of Commons friends, concede, and which nevertheless would not furnish us with a good case with the publick for resignation and desertion of the King in a critical period. They played the game (tho' with occasional interruptions by the Ultra Tories and Lord Rosse[78] on the coronation oath and an imprudent expression or two of deep distrust in the Ministers by Lord Wicklow) with much hypocrisy and some skill, but they were nevertheless entirely baffled for the first 4 days by the temper, judgement, readiness, and ability of Lord Grey and the Chancellor, assisted constantly by Lord Plunkett and relieved by useful and good speeches from Lansdowne, Ripon and Melbourne. We beat them on one division by a Majority of 14,[79] though only four Bishops including the Bishop of London voted with us. Many other amendments we anticipated, some we admitted and others we compromised, and some, want of agreement between themselves or between the Bishops and them enabled us to resist. It was manifest all through that two distinct and even opposite views of policy prevailed [in] the ranks of adversaries; that the Duke of Cumberland and the Ultras were for exerting all their strength and throwing out both the bill and the Ministers; while the Duke of Wellington protested that he only attended the Committee for the purpose of improving the bill and disclaimed vehemently all intentions of harrassing the Government or defeating the measures by a mutilation of its details, though he had prefaced his attendance with the committee, and sometimes diversified his speeches in it, with denunciations of breach of the Coronation oath, spoliation of property, and subversion of the Protestant religion, a view of the subject not very compatible with improving the bill and propitiating those who conducted it.

On Wednesday 24th. there was a close division in the House of Commons against the grant of Money to the West Indians, at the motion of Mr Buxton, who was supported by the Anti Slavery party and by Lord Howik, who did not scruple to stigmatize the Ministry of whom his father was the head as guilty of the grossest duplicity and little better than Slavedrivers, pirates, freebooters and what not.[80] These circumstances were hailed, say some, by the Tory faction as symptoms Grey's declining authority in the Commons and popularity in the Country, and they plucked up spirit accordingly. It certainly was not unlikely that the prospect of uneasiness which Howick's conduct held out might have had the effect of inclining Grey's mind more easily to the relinquishment of his post. Be that as it will, Certain it is the Tories mustered strong in the Lords on

Thursday 25th. and moved sundry amendments in the Clause<s> enabling Commissioners to suspend the appointment of Parsons in parishes without duty.[81] They were all calculated to gratify the Bishops and to catch uncertain votes, but Grey and the Chancellor discussed them all with so much candour and fairness as well as ability and receded on minor points or suggested equivalents with so much address, that the Committee was on the point of passing the Clause without the opportunity of a division on an amendment in it, when Archbishop of Canterbury declared that there was one part of his amendment (which amendment in other respects had been improved and adopted by Lord Grey) from which he was not *authorized* to recede. The word *authorized* was strange and seemed to imply some engagement or promise, if his Grace was not a Man whose words very often involuntarily imply the very opposite of that he means to express. The clause in amendment which he thus stickled for at the 11th. hour was, it must be admitted, of little or no importance;[82] but there had been such a succession of compromises and apparent concessions, and the tone of Lord Grey had been throughout so conciliatory, that it appeared to us that yielding another point, which was in itself unreasonable tho' unimportant, would leave to our friends both within and without so much the appearance of pusillanimity or secret agreement that, with very rational hopes of beating them, we divided and were beaten by two, Lord Grey's brother, the Bishop, voting unexpectantly against, and two of our friends, including Belhaven, not returning from their dinner after the hour, at which those paring had expired, was past.[83] *Grey* after a minute's consideration moved that the house should be resumed. *Kenyon* wished to have it understood whether the bill was to proceed or not, but Wellington checked him and the Committee broke up. We met in the Chancellor's room to deliberate on what was to be done. Brougham was at some pains to mark how insignificant the amendment was, said that it was chiefly in his own handwriting, and manifestly lent at least to immediate if not ultimate acquiescence. I maintained that we were hardly authorized to consider it as an indication of hostility in the house till we had appealed to the Report or 3d. reading, and that even after those two stages, if the Commons acquiesced, we had no great reason to be discontented at so trifling an alteration; if they rejected the amendment then the Lords must either submit and give us a triumph, or they must adhere to their amendment, in which case we retire on a quarrel between the houses, because we side with the Commons a ground of separation which the publick will understand, and not on the narrow question of more or less discretion in the Board which they would neither approve nor comprehend. Lansdowne and Melbourne seemed to agree with me, but Grey [and?] in some measure the latter dwelt on the frequency of defeat, the hostility of the Lords, and the inextricable difficulties we were involved in. At My Suggestion Althorp was sent for and acknowledged that the ground was so narrow that a dissolution of Government upon the point and in this particular stage would be dreadfully inconvenient. I wrote to Granville before I went to bed to suggest his deferring a journey till our course was decided, and his answer was clear, well written, and earnest on our not quitting our posts. We had on

Friday 26th. A Cabinet at Althorp [*In the margin:* a very friendly and earnest letter from the King deprecating any hasty step on this amendment and pointing out its insignificance was read] in which it was decided after some difficulty that we should proceed, but Grey should state his regret at the decision, should reserve to himself the liberty of attempting to rectify the error on the report or 3d. reading, should declare that all further concessions were impossible, and should discharge himself of all responsibility for the outward consequences which might follow from an adherence to this amendmentm All this he executed as usual with admirable delicacy and judgement. The Enemy said nothing, allowed the Clauses against which they had railed so loudly to pass *sub silentio,* and offered no further opposition during the Committee, which terminated its labours at 11 o'clock. It is confidently asserted that there is great schism between the Duke of Wellington and the more violent tories, and there is a strange rumour that Lord Lyndhurst, who somewhat indecorously came up from the circuit to vote, is invited to take the lead of the Conservative party and destined by them to become in case of a change, not Chancellor, but Premier!—a notion so absurd that I should not record it here, if some ambiguous phrases that dropped from Lady Lyndhurst did not so far corroborate the suspicion as to shew that preference of a political to a judicial station had trotted through her head very recently. [*End of BM Add. MS 51869.*]

[*Beginning of BM Add. MS 51870.*]

CONTENTS[84]

1. The first 38 leaves of this book contain a Diary, imperfectly kept and carelessly written, from the 28th. July to the 5th. Septr. 1833.
2. The ensuing 63 leaves contain various incomplete and unmethodical reminiscences of events and transactions between 28 July 1833 to the 10th. November 1834—all written on or subsequent to the 10th. June 1834.
3. then follow 65 blank leaves which may hereafter be filled up with reminiscences or notes relating to 1833 and 1834.

4. 23 or 24 leaves containing a desultory but regularly kept diary from the 10th. to 20th, November 1834, during which the dismissal of Lord Melbourne and the delivery of the government to Duke of Wellington occurred.
5. There follow eight leaves containing recollections of the early part of the Session and a diary of the first week or 10 days of April 1835, written on the 15th. of that month, and after some 8 or 10 blank leaves,
6. A Diary from 15 April to the end of the Month, imperfectly but regularly kept, occupies the remainder of the book.

Note of April 1835 V[assall] H[olland]

July 27th, and 28th, 1833. I remained at Holland House.

29th. July Monday. till 3 August Saturday, when I was in London. The report and 3d. reading of Church bill, though, with exception of a strong and powerful and not long speech of Lord Ellenborough's against it, a dull and long debate, terminated prosperously.[85] The majority was such as it is presumed will sicken and silence our enemies during the remainder of the Session and will certainly impress foreign powers with a conviction of our Stability. The Commons, after some good humoured and well merited pleasantry on our amendments, acquiesced in them.

Grey has been much fatigued with the debates and spent Wednesday and Thursday at Sheen. He was in truth lukewarm if not adverse about the Jews, whose bill was discussed in the Lords on Thursday the 1st. in his absence.[86] I had prepared matters for a speech and thrown it into the form of a protest, and though still from nervousness and lameness unable to deliver one, was in hopes that Lord Clanrickarde, who is improving as a debater, would have used them. The Archbishop of Dublin, very ably and with great propriety as well as force of argument, supported the bill, as did Maltby, Bishop of Chichester. Canterbury and London opposed it, on grounds silly enough but very narrow, and in a tone and temper very different and much milder than the lay Lords, including Winchelsea and Duke of Wellington. The latter of whom delivered one of the worst and perhaps the most injudicious speeches we have yet heard from him; every word of it implied or avowed that no relaxation of exclusive laws should ever be made but under the pressure of necessity, i.e. intimidation, and that the repeal of test act as well as of Catholick disabilities had been granted to the formidable number of the petitioners had their determined manner of demanding relief, not to the reason or justice of their cause. The burthen of proof lay, according to his Grace's notable philosophy, on those who claimed, not on those who refused, constitutional rights. A more inveterate worshipper of power and a more bigotted enemy of the fundamental principles of political liberty certainly never existed. His theory of human society is truly that of an army. All right and authority in the Chiefs, obedience the sole duty of the mass, and every enjoyment or, as he termed it in his speech, *'indulgence'*, to be measured by the convenience of the Commanders, not by the wants or wishes of the army, who are the means not the object, formed to obey not to think, act, or enjoy. I resolved to enter my protest as containing principles so opposite to those avowed by Wellington in debate.[87] Lord Segrave avowed himself anxious to uphold Christianity, and therefore charitably voted to exclude the Jews. One of the Newspapers remarked that they often observed his Lordship's proceedings, which were busy enough in propagation, but they had never been aware till then that it was Xtianity He was propagating. On

Friday 2d. August in the evening arrived dispatches from Admiral Parker[88] and Lord Wm. Russell announcing the proclamation of Donna Maria in Lisbon and the subsequent arrival, after a skilful march and manoeuvre and a brilliant affair on the south of the Tagus, of Villa Flor. Nothing could be more satisfactory, though the intelligence of Pedro departing immediately on hearing the event, from Oporto to Lisbon, does not encrease confidence in the speedy establishment of a good Government there.[89] On the ensuing Cabinet of

Saturday 3d. I found many of my colleagues, and among them Grey himself, more apprehensive of the baneful influence of Pedro's uncertain and ill regulated character than I think either his previous conduct or the circumstances in Portugal warrant, and much slower in availing themselves of the event than either Palmerston or myself wished and recommended. However though we did not instantly accredit Lord Wm. Russell, receive Funchal, offer a frigate to convey Donna Maria to her dominions, and restore Napier to his rank, all which steps I would have had taken before Sun set that day, we did frame a Minute, recommending:[90] 1st., contingent instructions to Lord William to produce credentials to Donna Maria's Government, instructing him at the same time to advise the formation of such a Regency as would inspire confidence in us and dispel the alarms of Spain; 2dly., instructions to Addington to hold firm language at Madrid and menace actual interference by force if a Spanish Soldier crossed the frontier. 3dly., the placing vessels and troops at the disposal of Lord Willm. and Admiral Parker at Gibraltar and Cork; and 4thly., a communication and concert with France. If Grey and my Colleagues were more slow and phlegmatick than Palmerston and myself, H M was to the full as much slower than they. He was indeed in words much pleased at the success of the cause of the *legitimate* Queen Donna Maria, and anxious for the final settlement of Portugal and a revival of our connection and influence at Lisbon; but he still apprehended that Miguel's force was entire, deprecated entangling ourselves too deeply in a quarrel of which the issue was not certain, dreaded giving umbrage to Spain, distrusted Lord Wm. Russell's judgement, and very earnestly insisted on Parker's being consulted and deferred to, pointedly expressing his distrust and dislike of Pedro [*In the margin:* There is much in Don Pedro's character, disposition, ill breeding, and levity to dislike, but it happened, as usual in personal interviews between Princes, that the dislike felt towards him was aggravated into hatred by his visit to England last year. It is greatly to the credit of the Duke of Orleans that his visit had an opposite effect and rather disarmed and softened previous distaste and prejudice.] and both in his publick answer and private letters, vehemently deprecating concert and even communication with France—as if the most effectual and easy as well as most honourable method of baffling any sinister designs which France either does or hereafter may entertain about Portugal (of which however there are no symptoms) was not to take the lead in countenancing, assisting, forming, and advising the Government, and the Marriage of Donna Maria, while the French are at least in profession willing to give us the grace and precedence and while the novitas regni of the Queen and the Regency will make such counsel and assistance something of a favor and give us hereafter a claim to our former predominance as well as better means of securing it. If *we* were not sufficiently elated, the *Tories,* and *Duke of Wellington* particularly, seemed properly depressed by the Lisbon news.

3d. August to 8. I spent these 5 days between London and Burlington Street and had little time to keep a diary. Anglesey wrote earnestly to be released in Autumn on the score of health and from the necessity of a milder climate. Althorp is, I understand, determined not to remain leader in Commons in another Session. Grey too spoke very seriously and earnestly and, I believe unaffectedly, to me, to Althorpe, and to the Chancellor on the necessity of his retirement from the premiership and the lead in the House of Lords, to which he maintains, contrary to appearance, that his physical strength is unequal. With these prospects of changes, some of which are inevitable, it is I am afraid impossible to shut one's eyes to the necessity of a new arrangement or to disguise from oneself the many embarrassments which will beset it. Brougham, however, and I agreed that for the present we should direct our efforts to two points: 1st., the postponement of the evil day, and 2dly., the persuading Grey, even if he must quit the treasury (which Althorp reluctantly would consent to accept), to remain in Cabinet and the Channel of Communication on many points, especially patronage, with the King. No doubt health, age, press of business, and a natural desire to close his career with credit and glory, combine with the unavoidable retirement of Anglesey from Ireland and Althorp from Commons to induce Grey to relinquish the post he occupies, but it is not impossible that the unreasonable conduct of his family, and of Howick in particular, confirm and accelerate the adoption of that step, by the unpleasant prospect which it holds out of his continuance in office, with Stanley leader in the House of Commons. Though his superiority over Howick is conferred by the publick voice of Parliament and the Country, or rather by Nature herself, Yet Howick would deem his acting in that capacity under Lord Grey a proof of his father's injustice and preference, and the prospect of dissention in his family is yet more intolerable in Grey's affectionate mind than the fatigue and pressure of business. The King is not I presume aware of these approaching difficulties, but he has obviously a strong inclination to coalition with the more moderate tories, and tho' he has recently shewn some personal attentions to other of our Colleagues, such as Lansdowne and Richmond, there is none among us of whom he stands in that awe in whose strength and energy he has that confidence with which Grey, and perhaps Wellington and Peel, inspire him.

The Russians have signed what they call a defensive treaty with the Porte,[91] and Metternich pretends they have deceived him, but very manifestly means to pocket the affront if it is one, or go snacks in the profit if it is (as it not improbably will turn out) a plot. Palmerston attributes this event to our unwise decision of not interfering between the Porte and Egypt at an earlier period, and Talleyrand presses for a joint representation to the Porte and to St. Petersburgh to prevent the ratification, tho' without pledging ourselves to any act of resistance or hostility.

The Netherland Conference meanwhile goes on slowly. For two or three hours, the Dutch contended against the introduction of the usual and indispensible article of 'there shall be peace &c' ! ! ! and the Prince of Orange snapped his fingers at the Hague when the Conference was mentioned, and said, 'it was a farce which all who knew his father knew must end in nothing'. Nous verrons.

Friday 9 August 1833. The King, though he naturally feels and warmly professes indignation at the Duke of Cumberland's protest on the Church bill,[92] which in truth amounts to a personal insult on him and nearly to treasonable language in denying the supremacy of Parliament, yet occasionally shews him unnecessary marks of attention, and recently Commanded Lord Ailsa[93] to ask him to a dinner where Grey also had been invited to meet His Majesty. After hearing that the party annoyed Grey, he advises him (Lord Grey) to send Lord Ailsa an excuse! This is the more strange and reprehensible in His Majesty because, while he overlooks such offences in his Brother of Cumberland, he continues to visit the minor offences of Duke of Sussex in an opposite direction, with disfavour, sternness, and even injustice, and he is not only nettled at the Duchess of Kent for laying out for vulgar popularity by parading her daughter as Heiress apparent of the Crown, but actually urges Lord Melbourne and his Ministers to animadvert on her language and conduct which, if it offend against delicacy, taste, and judgement, is not certainly, like that of the Duke of Cumberland, open to the censure of defying or calumniating any constituted authority in the state. The truth is that the Duke of Cumberland knows how to bully H M and, partly through other branches of his family and partly by direct and intrepid remonstrance or menace, persuades him occasionally to act in contradiction both to his judgement and his inclination. Grey, who spoke to me on this subject in House of Lords, is much annoyed at it.

10 August. Dined at Holland House. Melbourne and others. Bank business said to be smoother in House of Commons.

11th. August. News and reports from Portugal. I hear with much concern that Lord Uxbridge has apprized his father, who was altogether unprepared for it, that he has a debt of *£110,000,* which must be provided for on his ensuing marriage with Miss Bagot.[94] This will combine with his health, spirits, and inclination to confirm him in his intention of leaving Ireland before November and spending the Winter in the South.

From 12th. to 16th. August inclusively. I spent my time in town and might almost say in House of Lords. The Committees on the East India, the Slavery Abolition, and the Scotch boroughs[95] bills detained us generally to 11 or 12 o'clock. It was really singular to see the Duke of Wellington apply his mind with all the assiduity, though not with much of the astuteness, of a laborious young Attorney to the minutiae of the phraseology of the Clauses and to all the financial and technical details of these various subjects. He was occasionally assisted by Lord Ellenborough, who spoke well, and by Lord Wynford, who was captious and tiresome in the extreme. Our friends in the Lords attended these tedious debates very regularly, and on the frequent divisions which occurred, our majorities encreased rather than diminished.

From 16th. to 24th. August I equally neglected this diary, and spent part of the time in London and two days of it at Windsor, where I was invited to the splendid banquet on the King's birthday in St. Georges Hall, really a magnificent sight. I remained the next day and saw the additions to the Castle and the remains of the late King's cottage &c &c.

The project of Don Pedro and his Empress[96] to marry Donna Maria the Queen of Portugal to the Duke of Leuchtenberg[97] gives great umbrage to Louis Philippe, and the clandestine manner in which the Duke of Leuchtenberg was invited to accompany the young Queen and her Stepmother to Portugal was not calculated to dispel any suspicion or allay any anger such a project might give occasion to. The King of England, somewhat to the surprize of his other Ministers but not at all to mine, far from deprecating such a match (like the King of the French) acquiesces in it readily and is in truth disposed to approve and to promote it. This does not surprize me, first because I think that for the interests of England such a marriage is infinitely preferable to any with a Neapolitan, Spanish, or French prince of the Bourbon branches, and secondly because I know and regret the strong antipathy borne by our Court to the reigning dynasty in France, and am well aware that our Gracious Sovereign would be easily reconciled to far more disagreable events, if he fancied that, without actually provoking war, they would estrange and mortify the Court of the Tuilleries. He is as anxious to keep it at arm's length as the more considerate of his subjects and servants are of conciliating and drawing towards them.

The Conduct of Pedro on his arrival at Lisbon is reported to have been very injudicious and offensive. He has (dit on) estranged as much as with common decency or indeed safety he could, The Duke of Palmela and the Moderate party, he has named inefficient and violent Men, and he has had recourse to arbitrary illegal and precipitate measures of a revolutionary and vindictive character. [*In the margin*: Such were the first impressions given us by the official reports from Lisbon, and Hoppner, our Consul, was in truth recalled (I suspect against Palmerston's wishes) because his accounts were at variance with these reports and chiefly because he expressed his conviction of the necessity of revolutionary measures to secure the success of a revolution in somewhat uncourtly and violent terms.] They are marked with the same cruelty and injustice as those of his brother, but they are said to be nearly as irreconciliable with the spirit, temper, or form of any regular or constitutional Government. Palmela, with the hope no doubt of identifying the English with the Cause of Donna Maria and with the artful and pardonable design perhaps of strengthening his own party by shewing his influence with the English, applied to Parker to land the Marines. Hoppner seems to have previously approved, if he did not instigate, the application, and Parker, who declined immediate compliance with the request, promised something equivalent in the contingency of an approach of the Miguelites and a danger of the recapture of the City, annexing however a condition that English colours *alone* should be hoisted on any <forts> which English Marines should occupy. By this offer our Admiral, cautious and excellent Man as he is, was deemed, too precisely and captiously I think, to have exceeded his instructions. Fresh instructions, earnestly admonishing him not to land troops unless in the positive case of English Subjects or English property requiring protection, were sent out, and a Recall of Hoppner, to my great regret, accompanied those instructions. Palmerston softened the tone of the recall as much as possible and spared Hoppner's feelings, but I am afraid the fact of his departure will make an unfavorable impression on the Portugueze.

24th. to 29th. August. Saturday and Sunday, the 24th. and 25th. of August, Grey dined and slept at Holland House. He was visited by most of his Colleagues. We were all (chiefly at the instigation of the Chancellor and Lord Lansdown) anxious to prevail on him not to think of retiring from office and urged with great earnestness the manifold and forcible arguments which would render such a retreat extremely unreasonable and dangerous, and the announcing of such an intention, before it was irrevocable and before the <time> of executing it arrived, unpolitick and unnecessary. On Sunday morning we prevailed upon him distinctly not to propose, much less announce, any such design, either in the approaching Cabinets or to the King, before leaving London, and reserving to himself the right of recurring to such a project, if he felt it indispensible to his health and comfort before the opening of the next Session; he agreed to continue where he was and preserve both the form and substance of his Ministry, as undisturbed as was practicable, for the present. It was lucky that the notion of any premature division on this subject was abandoned. For exclusive of the uncertainty of prevailing on the King to continue a Whig and Liberal administration with any but Lord Grey at the head of it, I was assured by Lord Lansdown two days afterwards that more than one of our Colleagues would, in the case of Grey's quitting the treasury even for another Cabinet office, tender their resignation and resolutely adhered to the determination of breaking up the Government. Fortune came to assist and confirm our decision. For while we were *on tuesday 27th.* considering the draft of the King's speech at Althorpe's and speculating how far we could venture to announce in it the resumption of diplomatick relations with Portugal, the news was brought us by the Spaniard Mendizabal[98] (Don Pedro's chief money agent) that he had arrived a few hours before in the Africaine Steam boat from Oporto and Lisbon, and that the day before he left the latter, Lord William had delivered his credentials, the agreable intelligence had been printed in the Chronica, and the town illuminated on the occasion. This, together with the successful sortie at Oporto, which had entirely liberated that important town from the besiegers, and several other favorable reports of the state of parties and public mind at Lisbon were confirmed shortly afterwards by Official and private letters from Admiral Parker, Lord William Russell, Mr Hoppner, Mr Sorrell,[99] Palmela, and Admiral Napier. The difference between the violent and the moderate, between Pedro and Palmela, is not so wide, nor the misconduct of Pedro by any means so flagrant as has been somewhat studiously and malignantly reported. Palmela, in a letter remarkable for magnamity [*sic*] good sense, and ability, vindicates Pedro from many of the aspersions cast on him, strongly and earnestly inculcates the justice and policy of propitiating rather than rebuking him, *acknowledges the necessity of establishing the constitution,* and presses for the assistance of an English force. [*In the margin:* On this point [*i. e. establishing a constitution*] Pedro had always been *inexorable.* He could not, he said, establish much less form part of a Government which did not in substance restore the Cortes. His honour was pledged to it. He could not, if He resumed the title of King, postpone the promise of the constitution an hour; but he would serve his *daughter's* cause till she was triumphant at Lisbon and willingly conform his language in the interim as her Regent and Officer to the views of her Council. Palmela, satisfied in his own mind that the Constitution was unpopular, fondly imagining that Royalty and Nobility still commanded favor in Portugal, and perhaps not overfond of a free government, uniformly deprecated all declaration of a Constitution; and this was the reason that Pedro served under his daughter's colours and never raised his own, and he did so with the reservation of being at liberty to convoke Cortes and proclaim the constitution the moment the Usurper was restored. The Fidalgo party there and perhaps many Carlists and Tories elsewhere soon had an inkling of his sincerity and determination on these points—they hated him for his honesty more than for his views—and soon betook themselves to denying and calumniating the first and very grossly exaggerating the latter.] On the other hand, I am afraid the disputes between Hoppner and Lord William or more particularly Lady Willm. Russell run very high. As Hoppner is intemperate in his language and somewhat suspicious and disposed to take umbrage, he may have put himself in the wrong, but he has been zealous, and at great personal hazard sustained the cause of his country men and the Character of the British Government in a time of difficulty and danger, and if uncourtly in his form of uttering, he has proved correct in surmizing and exposing the intrigues and cajolery of the Spanish Minister Cordova and the Miguelites. The former boasts in a letter written to Santarem,[100] and now intercepted, or as Lady Wm. maintains, purloined, of fomenting the quarrel between Lord Wm. Russel and Hoppner, many of the latter [*i.e. Miguelites*] obtained not only the <countenance> but the protection and recommendation of Lady Wm. to her friends in London, where they were in fact employed in recruiting for the government of Don Miguel. Hoppner is also right in his estimate of the publick predilection for the Constitution. If he is wrong in the notion of preferring a more energetick and less scrupulous Ministry to the conciliatory policy and Cabinet which Palmela would recommend, Lord Wm. Russell himself leans to an opinion not altogether dissimilar in the letters he has written after observing Palmela's character and conduct, both which he represents as exemplary and praiseworthy but far from decisive or vigorous or adequate to the emergency.

The sketch of the King's speech had been drawn up at Grey's request by Spring Rice. The topicks and the enumeration of the great acts passed during the reformed Session of Parliament were much approved by us all, but after sundry criticisms both on the phraseology and the substance of various passages, it was left for Grey to revise, who with his usual felicity of language presented it in an amended shape the next day, when we all pronounced it to be a most able, judicious, eloquent, and spirited exposition of the publick conduct and policy of the Government and a just encomium by implication on the result of our great act of Reform and of the practical spirit and wisdom of the New House of Commons. The King on the Wednesday seemed highly pleased with it, said he felt no objection to its length, for he had a good voice and was not afraid of raising it, as Mme Lieven should perceive, if she were present, when he came to deliver the sentence about Turkey. He bantered the Chancellor about the word 'transference', saying he must have owed it to his Scotch education, for it was not English nor in Johnson's dictionary, and he changed it to 'Conveyance'. Lord Grey had been extremely nervous about the tythe arrear bill,[101] which was certainly a very intricate and a very questionable measure, only to be justified by the extreme difficulty of the situation we were in, and the impossibility of extricating ourselves without, on one hand, a departure from the strict rules of law and justice, or a renewal of all that resistance to it which we had done so much to prevent and which, if once more provoked, we might not have it in our power to repress. The Duke of Wellington however, though tiresome and pertinacious about the details, was extremely temperate in language and conciliatory in manner. He acknowledged he should be sorry to lose the bill, and with the aid of Plunkett's law and Lord Melbourne's easy admission of the difficulties and objections to his measure, we got through it without a division, without disgrace, and with less trouble than could well be expected, or perhaps than for so bungling a measure we deserved. With this bill the business of the Session Closed; for The Chancellor, unwilling to be longer detained, postponed several measures, both of his own and other people's, that had come up from the commons, and when he incurred the anger of some of our friends, and particularly of Mr Kennedy for so doing about the Small debt bill,[102] he redeemed his Character by suddenly appropriating to himself the merit of a bill of Lord Althorps on English Corporations, which he announced and in some measure described for the subsequent Session, and which was next day represented in many of the papers as a work of consummate wisdom, conceived and nurtured in his powerful and prolifick brain. On the whole the news from Portugal, the easy close of the Session, the excellence of the Speech, and the Approbation which it received reconciled Grey very cordially to his decision, and one saw in his face, manner, and conversation that a total relief from occupation and responsibility was by no means necessary, as he imagined sometimes, to his happiness. He consulted the Cabinet on the Successor of Lord Anglesey, compelled by the state of his health to quit Ireland before the Cold Weather commences, and it was agreed that it should be offered to Lord Wellesley. He is very agreable to the King, but His Majesty's suggestion that Mr Johnston,[103] who has an undue ascendancy over him, must not accompany him, is deemed well worthy of attention.

Palmela in his private letter urged the succour of English troops (a circumstance which rendered it prudent not to communicate his letter to the King, who would have peremptorily refused it). He grounded this application on the great danger of a war of guerrillas and on the carnage, misery, and turbulence which would ensue, whereas, if Lisbon were occupied by English forces, Donna Maria's army would be sufficient to suppress the guerrillas. In this reasoning we could not acquiesce. Perhaps under the treaties no internal insurrection would, certainly the bare apprehension would *not,* justify our interference in arms; but on the other hand the possibility of Spain being with or without her consent involved in the civil war, sufficiently indicates the necessity of being prepared; and we, consequently, after some discussion, resolved that as many as 5000 Men, and transports to convey them, should be collected at Cork, though, at the somewhat earnest expectation of the Chancellor, we acquiesced in the precaution of their not being allowed to proceed till the Cabinet should be again summoned and had approved of it. True is it that the Members are dispersing in all directions and till the 4th. November, when they dine at Holland House, it is not expected they will meet.

30th. August. On this day the King of the French is to be at Cherburgh and he and yet more Talleyrand was desirous of some compliment from the British Crown or Navy, such as the arrival of a British ship of war or the King's own Yatch [*sic*] to greet him, but on sounding King William's disposition, it was pretty clear that he could not be brought to consent to it without its being made a question of state, which it scarcely deserves to be. In truth, his aversion to Louis Philippe is personal as well as political and dates from some old story of the late Duke of Kent's[104] correspondence and supposed influence with the House of Orleans. Our good King's prejudices against persons are often strong, and yet oftener unreasonable, but where the matter is of importance they can by representation be surmounted, or at least he can be prevailed upon to act in opposition to them. Among his antipathies is a strange one against General Flahault. He is particularly apprehensive of his coming here as Embassador, and for that as well as other reasons praises and courts Talleyrand with the hope of retaining him where he is. When a report of Flahault's appointment was mentioned at Court before Mme de Lieven, the King incautiously said, 'No no that cannot be. I should have a right to a voice there, n'cest ce pas?' Mme. de Lieven with her usual quickness and dexterity said, 'Assurremment Sire, C'est de votre droit', thus answering by anticipation any remonstrance that <sh>ould be made to the Emperor of Russia's unwarrantable objection to Sir Stratford Canning.[105]

That Gentleman wishes for a peerage or mark of favor to shew the approbation of his own Court when a foreign one so unjusly and unusually takes upon itself to censure him, as an 'homme de manières angulaires et peu traitable' &c &c. Diplomatick peerages are among the worst. They infuse no popular feeling into an assembly which stands much in need of some. Yet if it opens the budget of creations, it will do good. Grey is however strangely averse, even to the less offensive and more plausible measure of feeding the House of Lords from time to time and during the recess with friends. He does not like urging the King, he has no small dread of exasperating the numerous candidates by any preference of a few, and he perhaps has himself a little aristocratical propensity to heighten the value by encreasing the rarity of the honour. He consulted me on the Successor to Wellesley's Stewardship if he goes to Ireland and on the blue ribband if Lord Chatham[106] shall die. To the first I should recommend Argyll[107] for three strong reasons: first, his personal and political merits, 2dly. his great want of money, and 3dly. the gratification it would give Scotch Whigs. Grey suggests Clarendon,[108] Essex, or Grafton.[109] Either of the two last, if they would take it, would be proper and popular and in some little degree strengthen the Ministry. The first, though Clarendon has behaved very handsomely *since Grey was Minister,* would gratify no

Whig, because he never voted with them out of office, and would weaken us, on account of his numerous sinecures, with the large body who are scandalized with the very existence and name of such eyesores. As to the ribband, I was sorry and a little surprized (though less than I should have been two years ago) to find that Lansdown wished for it. He is well entitled to have whatever he likes, though he is very ill advised to have so foolish a taste. The Duke of Grafton, to whom Lord Grey more naturally destines, well deserves it and I should hope that, their respective ages considered, Lansdown will wave his pretensions in his favor.

Grey seems quite reconciled to remaining where he is.

31st. Aug. to 6 September. I spent these days between Richmond and Holland House and saw few persons. Grey and Palmerston were at Windsor and afterwards at Stoke, and it seems the visit at Windsor and the King's dinner at Stanley's at Putney passed off admirably. At court on Wednesday the King invested the Speaker with the Bath and made a speech with a better selection of topicks than is usual with his Majesty, full of personal compliments to Sutton, reminding him that a predecessor of his, Sir Spencer Compton,[110] had been among the first to receive the honor of the red ribband on the revival of the order, descanted on his experience, learning, and authority, on the utility of it when so many of the Representatives had been new in Parliament, and ended by expressing his satisfaction not only at rewarding so meritorious and useful a publick man, but at the opportunity of expressing through him, to the body whose confidence he enjoyed, his sense and gratitude for their unwearied attention to business, their loyalty, and their usefulness. Nothing could be better. Wellesley goes to Ireland at the end of the Month and Anglesey, who is both glad of his own release and highly pleased at his Successor, returns to Dublin to receive him and deliver over his Office in <form>, which they both agree will please in Ireland and mark the entire accordance in principle of the outgoing and incoming Lord Lieutenants. Duke of Argyll succeeds Wellesley in the Lord Stewardship and I rejoice to think that I have been useful in reminding Grey of the justice and advantage of gratifying so good a friend and so steady a Whig; the King is highly pleased at the appointment and affects to believe, chiefly to teize his Sisters, an idle piece of Scandal of G[eorge] IV, that Argyll is their half brother— a story in which there is not, I believe, the least semblance of truth or possibility.

[*Heading:* 5 September] Prince Canino called, and told me in confidence that he was desirous of recovering his rights as a French citizen, that he lamented and disapproved some rash expressions of his family, especially his brother Joseph and his nephew Lewis, that since the death of the King of Rome, it was not only wrong but foolish in any of his family to keep up pretensions or foster recollections which, perhaps it would have been well, had never been excited in that direction;[111] and after a preface of this kind mingled with many well turned and obliging but undeserved compliments to my general views on these subjects, he asked me As an Englishman if I believed there would be any great objection to restore the remains of Napoleon to France, and then proceeded to consult me upon a delicate point, whether it would be becoming his situation, character, and general course of conduct as a publick man to accept of a Commission from Louis Philippe to solicit, and if successful to accompany, the remains of his brother to France. To the first question I answered that 'I could not know as I had not ascertained the sentiments of others, that there seemed to be no objection, that unless it was *at the request* of the French Government, there might be some political obstacle to a step which would excite so many feelings and recollections in a country with the government of which it was our policy and wish to maintain the most cordial terms, but that if it was with the consent, much more at the desire, of the reigning dynasty, I could foresee little or no difficulty. In such matters however there was of course a possibility of some formal difficulty or prejudice connected with past transactions in quarters where it was always good policy and indeed duty to avoid pressing any thing, in itself indifferent, that was disagreable. I did not however know that there was any where any such feeling. With respect to the other question or consultation, I found upon enquiry that L[ouis] Philippe had conveyed to him *thro' Mr Laborde*[112] a disposition to employ him, and had asked if he would accept it. I did not hesitate to say that it was a Commission which under the circumstances of the two Princes would do credit to him who offered and him who accepted it. He wished this part of his communication to be kept secret. It was a conversation between private friends. On the probability of such a request being made he did not lay any injunction of secresy. He should be glad if I could ever give him a hint whether it would be favorably received or rejected, for of course if there were no chance of success he should not like to undertake a fruitless negotiation. I thought but did not remark aloud that this project of L Philippe, as well as his late restitution of Napoleon's statue to the Column, was not of a piece with the feverish and silly jealousy he on many occasions shews of every branch of the Consular or Imperial family of Napoleon. Before Lucian had quitted my room Lord Grey had entered it and he soon afterwards recounted to me the injudicious and embarrassing manner in which Louis Philippe had evinced these petty feelings in the affair of the Duke of Leuchtenberg. Not only were the Queen Donna Maria and her StepMother coldly received at Havre, but the Sous Prefet took upon him to admonish Leuchtenberg that his appearance on French soil was an infraction of the Law. The Young Prince, who be he German or Beauharnais is full of high spirit and vivacity, answered him in a letter of which Grey speaks in high terms, and which even Talleyrand, to whom he has shewn it, acknowledged to be excellent. He denies the construction of the Law as regards him, questions the justice of it as affecting others; maintains that the restored Government of France more than once, and recently through Polignac,[113] disclaimed its extension to the House of Beauharnais; argues from the hospitable and even kind manner in which he and his family have been received in Courts where such a law might have been supposed to be more cherished than in that of Louis Philippe that it has never been so interpreted; and ends by remarking that it would be strange if a free and constitutional Government should, with respect to him or those connected with him, be more harsh and aribitrary than the restored dynasty, and that France, the country of his father and family, should be the only Kingdom in Europe which withheld its protection and even refused him its hospitality. There is moreover in the latter a hint which is interpreted as an announcement of an intention to appeal to the Chambers against the infraction of the law in his person. The same day he wrote and sent a long letter to Lord Palmerston containing an exposition of his conduct, by which it appears that he was solicited to visit and accompany his Sister and her [step]daugher, the Queen, that he hesitated in doing so, and when he at last acquiesced, urged with great candour and great force the objections both in principle and policy of any project of marrying him to the Infanta—arising from his want of connection with Portugal, the nature of their laws, and the peculiar circumstances in which the young Queen was placed. He annexed therefore as a condition that he should be considered as agreeing to the visit and the voyage only and not to any ulterior step. It is thought he is averse to the marriage, but whether he be or not, he left Havre on the rebuff he met from the French, and is returned to Munich, while the little Queen has announced her intention of coming here. The King and Queen of England have seen this correspondence, approve much of Leuchtenberg, and express satisfaction at the arrival of Donna Maria. [*End of first part of BM Add. MS 51870.*]

22 June 1834. The duty of Keeping a diary is so irksome that I have renounced it. It is now more than 10 Months since I have written a word in it. Many events have occurred in that interval, but I recollect too little or too much (I know not which) of the causes which led to them and the transactions which attended them to record more of their progress than can be collected from publick documents, newspapers, annual registers, and debates.

Soon after the prorogation, a pamphlet written by Mr Le Marchant,[1] with the assistance of Mr Stanley, Mr Senior,[2] and others, was published in which the labours and success of the Reformed Parliament and the Reform Ministry were duly enumerated and extolled. The Publick, who had been suspected of being disappointed with the results of reform as falling far below their expectation, were really surprized when the number and importance of the great measures atchieved in the East and West Indies, in the foreign policy of the Country, in the Bank, in the Irish Church, &c, &c, &c, were fairly before them. Much however *it was felt* remained to be done, and the Cabinet separated with a full understanding that the various important measures [were] to be considered during the recess, but returned to London, as usual, only a short time before the meeting of Parliament, without any of their projected designs, if I except the revision of the poor laws, being in a state of forwardness or preparation.

Events abroad did not indeed equally wait the pleasure of Ministers. Don Pedro's government pressed earnestly for assistance, and urged the active recruiting of Don Carlos's party in Portugal and the actual existence of Spanish troops under the Command of Don Carlos officers on Portuguese territory as furnishing a casus foederis in which they had a right to claim the assistance of British Troops. The policy of affording it was yet clearer than the obligation. The bare moral effect of British succour would secure the rapid success and permanent establishment of Donna Maria's Government, and by such a step we might recover all our pristine ascendancy in Portugal, and ingratiate ourselves with the liberal government in Spain indirectly secured and established by our ascendancy in Portugal. So thought Lord Palmerston, Lord Grey, and indeed the majority of the Cabinet, and Lord Howard of Walden,[3] recalled from Sweden and named Minister to Lisbon, was waiting in London in the expectation of carrying out the welcome assurance of immediate succour and in the meanwhile authority to Admiral Parker to land the Marines. But Lord Althorp, Mr Stanley, and Duke of Richmond had scruples founded on the principle of non interference and yet more strongly misgivings that Parliament would not sanction a war or vote the necessary supplies. Lord Grey, though earnest, positive, and able in his view of our policy, was somewhat dilatory in urging an immediate decision, and the loss of time as usual encreased the fears of the timid. We found that our House of Commons' Colleagues, with the exception of Palmerston and Sir James Graham, *who were earnest for immediate interference,* would not consent to recommend such a measure to Parliament; and Lord Grey, even with the full concurrence both of the King and the Majority of his Cabinet, did not feel himself equal to engaging in a War with the loss of Althorp, Stanley, Richmond, and perhaps others in his Cabinet. He consequently determined to resign.

We dined at Althorp's (14 January 1834) and Grey was to carry his resignation to the King next day; when he left Lord Althorps, The Chancellor called the attention of the Cabinet, who, with the exception of Mr Grant and Lord Carlisle, were all present, to the perilous situation in which the retirement of Lord Grey and the consequent dissolution of the Ministry would leave both the King and the Country. He exhorted us to press Lord Grey to remain, insisting, with his usual vehemence and exaggeration, that the question relating to Portugal was as nothing and suggesting a paper of remonstrances to Lord Grey in which, according to his first draft, the very opinion which the majority and among them the Chancellor himself had solemnly expressed on the affairs of Portugal was treated as a matter of indifference, if not distinctly abandoned and condemned. In the picture he drew of the consequences of Grey's retirement we all concurred, and in the propriety of making some sacrifices ourselves and calling upon him to make yet more we all acquiesced. Some of us indeed, and particularly Sir James Graham and myself, objected strongly and inflexibly to any words which should imply a change in our view of the necessity of succouring Portugal and still more a pledge expressed or implied of relinquishing all intention of advising such interference. The Duke of Richmond, though in his usual good humoured way, was full of taunts at my predilection for foreigners, and Portuguese in particular, and somewhat provoking in his manner of perverting and misrepresenting the question. The Chancellor, eager, vehement, and <rude>, used all his weapons of ridicule, invective, abuse, and menace to drive us and especially me from my purpose, but he at last acquiesced in the omission of the words to which Sir James Graham and I had objected. We signed a paper, deprecating Lord Grey's retirement from office and painting the consequences of it in strong colours, but not touching upon, much less underrating or depreciating, the grounds which had inclined him to contemplate such a step. With this paper in his pocket and with Mr Ellice in his post chaise, he went down to Brighton on the 16th. Janry. No doubt, the contents of the paper and the conversation on the road prepared him for what happened—his acquiescence in the King's earnest entreaties that he should remain, though the King both acknowledged and lamented, as much as he could, the impractibility of giving immediate succour to Portugal. This incident, tho' much misrepresented and never understood by the publick, had the good effect of proving the sincere desire of the King to retain Lord Grey in the Ministry and of restoring more entirely and more manifestly that confidence between him and the King which, according to the speculations of many, had been shaken materially by the events of 1832. [*In the margin:* It seemed too for the time to mark the personal attachment of the whole Cabinet to Lord Grey and to imply their concurrence of opinion in all matters excepting Portugal, or at least in all such as regarded the domestick affairs of the country. The events of the ensuing months belied all expectations of stability drawn from such circumstances.]

Lord Howard of Walden had been named to Lisbon without my knowledge, but Palmerston never meant to convey disapprobation, nor could it be construed to convey any, of Lord Wm. Russell. On sending out his credentials to him in the summer Palmerston had apprized him thro' Lord John that, even if he delivered them, he must consider his situation at Lisbon to be temporary, inasmuch as it was destined to Lord Howard the moment a permanent mission could be named to Portugal. This circumstance, combined with the complaints I heard that Lord Wm. had expressed at the inadequacy of the appointments and unpleasantness of the residence at Lisbon, induced me to urge what I sincerely thought upon both Lord Palmerston and Lord Grey, namely that the publick service required as little interval as possible between the appointment of Lord Howard in the gazette and his arrival at Lisbon. No temporary and superseded Minister can speak with that effect or authority which it is always desirable that an English Envoy should command at Lisbon. I mention this because owing to Lady Wm. Russell's foolish surmizes and mischievous tracasseries Lord William and even Lord John Russell himself imagined that I had acted an unfriendly part upon the occasion, and that it was founded on gossiping stories of the Spanish Minister's intimacy with Lord and Lady William and scraps of his intercepted letters to the latter. That those letters, albeit insignificant enough, indicated Mr Cordova's disposition to take credit for his intimacy with the English Mission and proved his Knowledge of a coolness between them and the Consul, Hoppner, is undeniable. It is equally so, that general rumour at Lisbon and in London described Lady Wm. as associating exclusively with the Miguelites, a charge which her very unmeasured and ill bred abuse of the opposite party does not disprove. But I do not believe that her Ladyship's opinions or conduct, whatever they may have been, had the slightest influence in determining Lord Palmerston to appoint Lord Howard. I *know* that they formed no part of my motive in recommending his speedy departure when named. The truth is that Lord William's language like that of all his family is never very measured or qualified, and was at various periods in Lisbon inconsistent and contradictory. At first Earnest and Eager for any and all interference against Miguel, and afterwards stigmatizing one party as bad as the other. On Pedro's arrival at Lisbon he implied in contradiction to Hoppner that the appointment of a Moderate and Palmela Ministry should be a sinequânon condition of recognition and assistance, and yet upon the receipt of credentials to be used at his discretion [*In the margin:* and in a great measure entrusted to him in the persuasion that he would *not* produce them unless the Portugueze Ministry was changed], *he immediately* [*In the margin:* and to the surprize of the anti Pedro part of our Cabinet] presented them to Freire,[4] describing for the first time his radical advisers to be as reasonable and well disposed as a Ministry named by himself could have been, or as Hoppner, who was recalled for too much partiality to that party, could himself have described them. He inveighed against the folly and supineness and the restlessness and violence of Don Pedro's party almost in the same breath, and maintaining that but for Pedro's extravagance all might have been settled long ago, he yet acknowledged that little or nothing had been done but by his personal exertions and hasty and decisive temper. In sober truth Pedro may be a Madman and perhaps is, but as Allen well and justly observes, he has done more for the recovery of a legitimate throne than any Prince since Henry IV of France. [*In the margin:* There had been throughout, in the mind of many of my Colleagues, in some from fear of war, in others from dislike of foreigners, in some one or two from a dread of democracy, and in Lord Grey from some private and very *prejudiced* sources of information, an unwarrantable repugnance and suspicion of Pedro, but Lord Palmerston was always more just to him and I was at a very early period satisfied from the admission of those who complained of him, and of Palmela in particular, that tho' ungovernable in his temper and yet more in his language, and tho' occasionally swayed by most unwarrantable affections and resentments, he was yet full of good and even great qualities and true to his word, zealous in the cause of his daughter and the people, incapable of disguise or dissimulation even to a fault, affectionate his family and his friends, and, though intemperately violent in language and sometimes hasty even to brutality in his actions, by no means implacable or unforgiving.]

The English had better luck than they deserved in the events of Spain—the death of Ferdinand, the helpless character of Zea, the downfal of that base politician and the appointment of Martinez de la Rosa.[5] Sir Stratford Canning failed to wean Zea from his Miguelite propensities. That Minister was no doubt directed in his view of Portuguese or of all foreign politicks by the Holy Alliance, if he was not swayed by the same pernicious councils in his domestick policy, and by the idle hope of maintaining tranquillity in Spain without either acknowledging Don Carlos or crushing his party by a cordial cooperation with the liberals. He had once been guilty of murdering judicially two Chiefs of the opposite factions in the course of a Month and, in his ignorance of his own country and of mankind, he inferred from the impunity that his cruelty enjoyed that an unsparing effusion of blood constituted vigor of mind and served the purposes of wisdom of design. He conciliated no party, foreign or domestick. He had indeed agreed to quarrel with Don Miguel unless Don Carlos were expelled from the territory of Portugal, yet His continuance as Minister at Madrid would have palsied all the efforts of English as well as Portugueze Councils to rid the Peninsula of such nuisances as two Pretenders in arms against the Constitutional governments. Mr Villiers[6] was perhaps too courteous to him on his fall and Don Martinez de la Rosa, partly from his example and more probably from his own humane disposition, treated him wih singular indulgence and forbearance. Martinez de la Rosa wrote me a letter on his appointment. In the course of it he shortly adverted to his occupations in preparing and reviving the liberal institutions of his country, correcting abuses and healing dissensions, and urged with much warmth and apparent sincerity his sense of the advantages of an early and open concert with England on all foreign matters, and especially on those of Portugal, where he hoped for our assistance in expelling Don Carlos, and expressed a willingness to acknowledge Donna Maria *after* such a measure had been accomplished and the Portugueze Cortes called. To this I answered in a tone of congratulation, assumed the probable convocation of the Spanish Cortes, gave some crude and general opinions on the way of convoking them, lamented the limited nature of the Amnesty and especially the marked exclusion of General Mina[7]—an omission that was in the first instance so deeply resented by Spanish patriots that many of them and among them Arguelles refused the offer of appointments and the advantages of the amnesty. In the meanwhile Don Carlos had connected himself more and more with Don Miguel, and the latter Prince not only afforded him a species of countenance but permitted him to engage Portugueze in his service and to raise his Standard and collect such Spanish forces as he could within the Portugueze territory. Don Pedro justly argued that these circumstances brought the case within the spirit and even letter of our treaty, either by the actual presence of a Spanish force under a Spanish King (Don Carlos) in Portugal, or by the just provocation and excuse it gave to the acknowledged Government to march troops against the Rebels on their frontier. Miraflores,[8] the Spanish Minister who had superseded Vial, urged these topicks with great success and—while the Spanish Government was <busiest> in correcting their errors in acknowledging Donna Maria—in marching their troops into Portugal, calling the Cortes, and recalling Mina it prevailed on the Ministers of France, England, and Portugal in London to sign the quadruple treaty.[9] I believe before it was signed and certainly before it was ratified, the Duke de Broglie[10] had retired from the French Ministry and the Duke of Richmond, Sir James Graham, Lord Ripon, and Mr Stanley had resigned their seats in the British Cabinet. The loss of the Duke of Broglie seemed to us irreparable. It was not mitigated by a suspicion very widely entertained that Louis Philippe, though he did not contribute to it, was not sorry at an event that removed from his councils one more jealous of Royal interference and more capable of resisting it with effect than any of his Colleagues or probable successors. However the assurances that the friends of peace and even the party of Broglie himself considered as a doctrinaire and a liberal would be as strong in the new as in the former cabinet, of which Guizot's[11] continuance and De Rigny's[12] appointment seemed some indication, reconciled us sooner than we expected to the change.

Perhaps we were too much occupied with vexatious and lamentable divisions at home to examine the consequences and tendency of those abroad. It would be tedious and difficult to explain all the causes that led to Stanley's and the other three Ministers retirement from Office.[13] In truth they dated as far back as Lord Anglesey's viceroyalty, and at the beginning of the Session of 1834 Lord John Russell had faintly but frequently revived the question of diverting the enormous revenues of the Irish Church, and especially such as were derived from Parishes without Protestants, to some more general and national object.[14] Two means were suggested, one by direct legislation, the other by a commission of enquiry. We had once hoped that Stanley would have acquiesced in the latter, for in one of his early panegyricks of the Irish Church he had declared that 'to be loved she needed but to be known', and that he did not deprecate but court investigation. Perhaps the reference to that rhetorical flourish (in truth it was no more) rivetted him in his determination of resisting all enquiry and confirmed his inclination to separate from his Colleagues rather than embark on a series of measures leading to the subversion of the Church. His distinctions indeed between what constituted *reform for ecclesiastical purposes,* and what *a diversion of Church revenues* to other purposes, were somewhat nice, subtle, and unintelligible; but he had too much sagacity not to perceive, and too much spirit not to avow, that enquiry into the revenue and uses of such anomalies was equivalent to a project of subverting them; and he manfully resisted it. He was willing however in 1834, as in 1832 and 1833, to wave the consideration of any abstract question and to acquiesce in such measures, as were on other grounds adviseable, or as he thought at least innoxious, although his Colleagues supported them on a principle which he was determined to resist. All he stipulated for was that the measure should not be recommended as depending upon the principle he condemned, nor be considered by its authors as sanctioning that principle and pledging their Colleagues and supporters to it. But Lord John Russell was more impatient, either to procure the sanction of Parliament to the opposite principle which he deemed just and necessary to act upon, or to lay in his claim betimes to the merit of urging a measure which he knew to be inevitable. He spoke unnecessarily warmly and prematurely on the subject in the house of Commons.[15]

It was with difficulty and chiefly on the consideration of their having so recently urged Lord Grey to continue in office, that Duke of Richmond, Sir J Graham, and Mr Stanley were prevailed upon to remain. Richmond said to me, 'You must acknowledge We are good humoured fellows to remain to the end of the Session with a knowledge that the Majority of our Colleagues will have us out soon after, by preparing and suggesting measures in which we never can concur'; but our adversaries or our over busy friends out of office would not allow us to wait so long. Notice of a motion directly approving of the appropriation of Church revenues in certain contingencies was given in the House of Commons by a Mr Ward.[16] If not with the intention it was with the effect of perplexing Government, and Oconnel himself as well as others aware of this were active in dissuading Mr Ward from withdrawing it. Though the Majority of the Cabinet agreed in the substance of the proposition, they were averse to the form and yet more to the time. With considerable reluctance Althorp at first consented to oppose it. But when the yet stronger reluctance of our friends out of office to concur with him became manifest, Stanley and *his* friends in Cabinet found it necessary to announce their full intention of resigning in case the resolution was carried. Our friends in general were as averse to the notion of breaking up a Ministry because a proposition of which the Majority of the Cabinet approved was passed in a shape and at a time not entirely consonant with their convenience and wishes. Thus the difference in the Cabinet became notorious. It added to the probability of a defeat. Lord Lansdown and others were disposed to postpone all steps till the division should have taken place, under the erroneous persuasion that we should be in a large and not an *unwilling* majority, or from a yet idler notion that a bare majority, composed of reluctant and discontented supporters who endanger their future seats by their votes, does not weaken a government more than a timely retreat or even an actual defeat.

It was clear that in either event A Cabinet notoriously divided could not, with such opponents as Oconnel on one side and Sir Rt. Peel on the other, be kept together for many days. Stanley and Sir J Graham felt therefore disposed to tender their resignations and, after much private discussion at St. James's between the King and Grey and Sir Herbert Taylor above stairs and Lansdowne, Grey, Sir Herbert, and Mr Ellice and myself below, the resignations were accepted just as Lord Althorp was about to rise in the House of Commons, and the announcement enabled him to prevail on Mr Ward to postpone his motion to a future day. A Commission for Enquiry into Irish Church was signed in the interim. And it furnished an argument and motive for abandoning the motion altogether. That Commission was instantly and somewhat hastily if not irregularly constructed, but the King did not hesitate to sign it [*In the margin:* with an observation however that it pledged him to nothing but an enquiry and a willingness to consider on the result of that enquiry, if any, or what measure was expedient and necessary]. It was rapidly filled up by the Chancellor with names of many who declined to act and of some who, on the renewal and revision of it, were <continued>.

The King again and earnestly pressed Lord Grey to remain. A body of the House of Commons signed a paper deprecating the possibility of his retirement and pledging themselves in somewhat cautious and equivocal terms to the support of his Government; to this Lord Grey gave a dignified and judicious answer, containing however a delicate admonition against precipitate innovation produced by a pressure from without, which was a more faithful interpretation of his own policy than exact resemblance of their intentions and wishes.[17] [*In the margin:* Stanley, who had always admitted not only that the majority of his Colleagues but of his party were averse to his principles, was nevertheless surprized at the indignation and disgust with which his very able but hostile and intemperate speech on the subject of the Commission was received and by the extreme smallness of the number of Whigs whom his eloquence and success had attached to his fortunes. He somewhat atoned for the virulence of his harangues by a handsome letter to Grey. Sir James Graham, in whose succession there was supposed to be more calculated and less real prejudice than in Stanley's, seemed they say disconcerted at the discouraging result of his manoeuvres and spoke not a word in the house. Such was the interpretation put on his conduct by the eager men of our party who, for some reason or another, seemed to me to be always particularly harsh and unjust to him.] The vacant places were not filled up immediately and much imprudent language as well as some ill blood appeared during the few days in which the appointments were matter of enquiry, speculation, and curiosity. Mulgrave, having been prematurely complimented on being first Lord of the Admiralty by some officious friend or sneering Enemy, as prematurely and hastily scouted the notion of accepting the Post Office without Cabinet. Lord Durham declined the Embassy to Paris, on the score of his unwillingness to serve under Palmerston, and in the course of that transaction I learnt that Lord Granville preferred remaining in his Embassy to the Admiralty or even to the Foreign Seals or to Ireland.

The Chancellor was in a state of much agitation or, as the fashionable phrase now is, 'excitement', and as usual with him on such occasions vehement, indiscreet, unscrupulous in his assertions and over bearing in his manners, but full of eloquent invective, satirical wit, extraordinary knowledge, and singular resources, sometimes hyperbolical and sometimes scurrilous, in arguing the pretensions of those he favored or the disqualifications of those he disliked, but yet more anxious to have the fame of doing all than to do it, and willing therefore even when thwarted to adopt and father the appointment which had thwarted him as the offspring of his own designs. [*In the margin:* Thus he dropped all at once his declaration of not submitting to see a seat in the Cabinet offered to Mr Ellice and half assumed the merit of recommending him.] He *deprecated* the appointment of Auckland (which Lansdowne (I believe but do not know) us earnestly urged)[18] [*In the margin:* but he acquiesced in it when done, with many comments on the advantages]. The Post Office, partly to gratify the Duke of Richmond, which it did not do, was given to Lord Conyngham.[19] This not unnaturally hurt Lord Clanrickarde, who announced in a friendly and polite manner his determination to resign. Lord Carlisle was prevailed upon somewhat reluctantly to take the Privy Seal, which Lord Ripon I believe as reluctantly, in consequence of the language he had held to Stanley and Richmond, deemed it necessary to resign. The only new appointment which all concurred in approving was Mr Spring Rice. But it was felt *out* if not *in* the Cabinet, that a larger portion of the reforming branch of our party was still required in our councils to secure the zealous support of our house of Commons friends. The question lay among Abercrombie, Duncannon, Dacre, Durham, and Radnor—the last either then or subsequently declined, not from any positive averseness from office and still less from want of cordiality to Grey or the Government, but from a consciousness that his opinions on currency, on ballot, and other matters were so singular and so strong that his appointment would be obnoxious to many and might be troublesome to some of his Colleagues. The King had certainly some dread of him and Grey, possibly for that reason and possibly from deference to others and to Lansdown in particular, did not press him to accept. Dacre was disabled by an attack which he deemed apopletick. With Durham at least three of the remaining Cabinet would not have acted even if Melbourne and *Brougham* could have brought themselves to do so. [*In the margin:* Brougham was above once in the course of the Summer and Autumn inclined to urge his admission, though full as frequently during that time loud and vehement against any such step.] To Duncannon Grey would not consent, tho Melbourne and Althorp recommended him. It was thought that recent family connection with Lord Lansdowne[20] rather indisposed than inclined the latter to accept him as a Colleague, for he has perhaps greater dread of the reality or appearance of being swayed by his connections than a more perfect knowledge of his own character and a more thorough confidence in his own judgement and understanding would lead him to entertain. Many circumstances, however, though not Lord Lansdowne, recommended Abercromby. He handsomely accepted and he had hardly been returned for Edinburgh in either sense of the word before it was manifest that a seat in the Cabinet had a tendency to remove one of the most plausible objections to offering him one, namely his propensity to take an unfavorable view of the conduct of affairs. The Chancellor, though he had recently inveighed against the notion of introducing so crotchety a Man [*In the margin:* not only accepted, as he had done both Lord Auckland and Mr Ellice (to both of whom and especially the former he had felt and avowed the strongest possible repugnance) but *actually*] *hailed* the appointment as an act of his own and he did, I believe, in truth mainly contribute to it.[21] Among his devices for that purpose, the omission of the Martial Law Clauses on the revival of the Coercion bill was one—and even the few who, with myself, thought the bill should be either dropped altogether or renewed with all its hideous and frightful features to make it formidable, acquiesced in the omission of those clauses more readily, because we felt that it paved the way for Abercrombie who had strenuously opposed them.

The Irish Government, Lord Wellesley and Mr Littleton recommended that omission, whether de proprio motu or at the instigation of others it is not easy to determine; but they certainly did not hint to Grey, or Grey to the Cabinet, the least disposition to relax the *other* parts of the bill or to consider the prohibition of agitation and publick meetings one jot less necessary than the suppression of predial disturbance. The Chancellor however, directly to Wellesley and indirectly to and through Littleton, conveyed the notion that the omission of those Clauses regarding publick meetings would facilitate the passing of the bill,[22] and Lord Wellesley distinctly retracted his former opinion and in a letter to Grey signified his readiness to conduct the government of Ireland with no other addition to the ordinary power of a Lord Lieutenant than those which related of the nightly outrages and the excesses which had obtained the name of predial disturbances. In thus writing, Lord Wellesley was chiefly actuated by a desire to accommodate the Government at home, but Mr Littleton and perhaps Lord Althorpe himself as well as others were instrumental in producing such false impression on Lord Wellesley's mind by the machinations of the Chancellor. In the mean while Lord Althorp had the imprudence to give Mr Littleton some authority to feel the pulse and obtain if he could the acquiescence of Oconnel in the mitigated bill, and Mr Littleton had the still greater indiscretion to exceed that authority by rendering such conversation in form and substance a formal communication, thus disclosing the existence of some difference of opinion in the Cabinet and assuring him that by forebearance he would ensure the concurrence of the whole in the omission of the Clauses to which he most Earnestly objected. Of this however nothing was known or at least nothing was said in the Cabinet.

We had parted on an understanding that the bill with the exception of the Courts Martial was to be soon proposed to the Lords by Lord Grey. It was at a Cabinet dinner at Holland House on 25th. June Wednesday, that Lord Wellesley's letter to Lord Grey, suggesting the possibility and safety but not urging the propriety of omitting the prohibition of meetings, was first read. The Chancellor, who had in truth suggested the letter, affected prodigious surprize and commented on the contents as creating in his mind for the first time some scruples about the Clauses. We agreed that Grey should ask an explanation of his opinion from Wellesley. Althorp and our House of Commons Colleagues with the exception of Lord John seemed somewhat averse to proposing a bill more coercive than the Irish government required, and all manifestly alarmed, lest the fact should transpire and they incur the odium of rejecting mitigation when actually recommended by Lord Wellesley. Grey was as manifestly determined on pressing the bill as it was. He was disposed, rather than yield even to the opinion of Lord Wellesley, either to resign or to persist in proposing the whole bill. The reply of Lord Wellesley (tho' the proposal originated in an erroneous view of satisfying persons on this side of the water) repeated his assurances that Government *could dispense without* danger with the obnoxious clauses. In the mean while Grey *had* proposed the first reading of the bill with those clauses in a speech which dwelt on the inseparable connection between agitation and predial outrage, and the Chancellor in answer to Lord Durham, who temperately objected to that part of the bill, forcibly described the injustice of depriving the peasantry of their natural rights and leaving Oconnel and the agitators in the full enjoyment of theirs, though directed to such mischievous purposes, thus bearing with a weight of <Gun stores>, said he, on the weak and defenceless and leaving the mighty evildoer unpunished and unquestioned. There seemed no great relish for this part of the measure, either among those who were to support or those who were to propose it in the Commons—but though an unpleasant debate and an unpopular cause were foreboded, there was little or no doubt expressed of the measure being carried, till OConnel [*In the margin:* fully justified by what had passed] revealed what Mr Littleton had in words and by implication promised him and complained of being cheated into forbearance by false expectations.[23] Though Littleton had exceeded his powers and endeavoured to atone for his fault by taking that whole blame upon himself, the reluctance of Althorp to acquiesce in the whole measure, the recommendation of Wellesley to drop part of it, and perhaps the wish of the former to purchase the forebearance of Oconnel by a relinquishment of the Clauses most obnoxious to him were obvious to the house and the publick. There was great doubt whether the question so loaded with odium could pass. There was yet more, whether Althorp could be brought to support it. He determined to resign and Grey was equally determined not to continue in office without him.

The King accepted the resignations [*In the margin:* with less appearance of chagrin or reluctance than I think Grey had expected. At least Grey has more than once observed to me since, that he neither offered him any little favor or mark of honour nor requested him to give him his bust.] In his reply, He spoke of 'the *dissolution*' of Lord Grey's government and requested the component parts of it to remain in their respective offices till he had had time to resort to some new arrangement. It was pretty obvious that his wishes pointed to a mixed or Coalition administration, but he was not blind to the obstacles which presented themselves to such a scheme or to the yet more insurmountable difficulties in the way of an entire restoration of the Tories. The frequent and somewhat imprudent declarations of Lord Grey during the last year of his intention of retiring and the shock the Ministry had received by the secession of Stanley and Richmond had already led to speculations even within the Palace on Lord Grey's successor, and had familiarized the King's mind to a comparison of the individuals on whom the first office would necessarily devolve, should he be compelled or inclined to continue the same system as Lord Grey under another nominal head. Lord Grey had laboured to prepare the way for Lord Althorp, but the King's predilection never pointed that way, and the unforeseen circumstances which attended the final retirement of Lord Grey, however unpleasant in all other respects, were perhaps less unpalatable to His Majesty from originating in a tendered resignation of Lord Althorp and more by precluding the possibility of the ostensible transfer of Lord Grey's power to him.

To the Chancellor the King was equally averse and His [Brougham's] strange declaration that Grey's and Althorp's retirement had not dissolved the Ministry, and his still stranger correspondence with the King, in which he exolled the Lords and disparaged the Commons, were not calculated to weaken his repugnance to such an arrangement, to remove any suspicions he entertained of such a design, or to raise in his Royal Mind any additional respect for his judgement, temper, principles, or prudence. There were indeed in these notable performances, as well as in many other passages of the Chancellor's speeches and conduct at that time, no very covert threat of resorting to furious popular courses if driven by despair to adopt them, but there were also many assurances and declarations which, if divulged, would have shaken all reliance in the sincerity of such a course, and the King moreover was well aware that his position in the House of Lords was of itself an insurmountable bar to such a career and that the Commons were by no means so favorable as to give him in his situation of exclusion from its debates so unusual an advantage as an ascendancy over its decisions. Of this latter misfortune and the signal loss of his popularity in that house, some gleams must have flashed on his mind, however his vanity strove to fortify him against them. His idle practice of signing *H[en]ry Brougham* and his ill concealed jealousy of Lord Althorp afforded some proofs that he was not blind to the fact, and that circumstance among others leads me to acquit him of all those designs, of Undermining Grey and placing himself in his post, which so many both in the palace and in the publick attribute to him and of which they considered his unjustifiable and restless conduct throughout these transactions a strong indication. That he was the original if not chief cause of Lord Wellesley's and Mr Littleton's disposition to wave the Clauses, and that he in a clandestine manner organized an intrigue to cajole or compel Lord Grey into a relinquishment of them there can be no doubt. Indeed, when in his indignation at the probable dissolution of the Ministry he reproached Althorp with being the chief cause of the catastrophe by his imprudent communications with Littleton and his subsequent precipitation in resigning, Althorp very quietly but significantly observed, 'I am I grant the immediate cause but you my Dear Brougham are the ultimate cause'. All however must acquit him of any actual design of bringing in Tories or Radicals, and *I* believe it was as little his intention to worm out Lord Grey. Restlessness and a desire to curry favor with the Commons and the publick by appearing to force or cajole his Colleagues and especially Lord Grey into popular courses were, I believe, his chief motives in this most unnecessary, unlucky, and discreditable intrigue. He hardly expected to be looked to by the Court as Lord Grey's successor, but he did perhaps hope that the Commons would be chiefly guided by him in transferring their confidence to any Member of Lord Grey's Cabinet. In this he was grievously disappointed. There was much consternation at the retirement of Lord Grey and Lord Althorp, great desire and many efforts to retain both and much earnest expectation and hope that the latter would either be called to the helm or continue the leading Minister in the House of Commons. To these objects private conversations, court communications, club discussions, and parliamentary debates, management, manoeuvres, persuasion, and contrivance were all exclusively directed. [*In the margin:* no mention or thought of Brougham but such as marked curiosity, wonder, and even distrust—certainly not a word implying confidence or hope.]

The King in the meanwhile asked for time and sent for Lord Melbourne, *his home Secretary*—a designation studiously repeated, to mark that it did not imply his selection of him as the framer of a new administration—to be the channel of communication to such persons as he thought necessary to have intercourse with before he determined to whom to entrust the formation of a new Cabinet.[24] He did not directly consult Lord Grey as to his Successor; but though his inclinations manifestly leant to the construction of one [ministry] formed by a Coalition of parties, he never took any step to establish that principle as a basis of negotiation, nor even consulted any one distinctly on the propriety of adopting it. He drew out a paper which he commanded Lord Melbourne to communicate to Duke of Wellington and Sir Robert Peel.[25] Lord Melbourne was distinctly to consider himself as merely the official channel of communication and he took an early opportunity of avowing his own opinion that, whatever on general principles or on peculiar occasions might be the advantage of a coalition of parties, the present emergency was not such as he would admit of it with any Safety and honour to the parties. The paper itself contained neither demand of advice nor basis for negotiation and seems to have embarrassed both the Duke and Sir Robert, who, if not disappointed at the extreme formality and insignificance of it, were at a loss to know if it required any or what answer. One I think merely asked if he was expected to do more than acknowledge the receipt, and the other confined himself to the acknowledgement of it, observing that he did not seem to be authorized by it to enter into any communication with Lord M[elbourne]. I forget how the correspondence, if such it could be called, terminated, but the impression was that both were disposed to agree in the impracticability and danger of any mixed administration, but Sir Robert Peel, this time, less averse than Duke of W[ellingto]n to the notion of forming one exclusively Tory, and some of his party, especially the Speaker (who was ready to run the glorious career of Wilmington and Addington),[26] grievously mortified at no such offer being made.

Lord Grey, much affected at the beginning of his speech, had made in the Lords a plain, luminous, and explicit statement of the untoward circumstances which had immediately led to his retirement and of those which had long induced him to contemplate it in the ensuing recess, and he had followed it up with an eloquent, feeling, temperate, judicious, and unpretending exposition of his policy and conduct in Office.[27] His friends and indeed the whole house were deeply affected with this pathetick close of so glorious and consistent a career, though the Duke of Wellington had the bad taste to comment on it in a dull speech which would have been mischievous [if] it had possessed a spark of genius or talent or a grain of ingenuity or argument. It had neither, and some one observed that 'he would not have made so bad and so heartless a speech even to gain a battle of Waterloo'. Lord Grey shewed a great desire, and Lord Althorp almost as much reluctance, to see the Members of the late Cabinet construct a new administration.[28] Though pressed by many of his friends Lord Althorp would not and indeed could not have consented to accept Grey's place, if the King had actually offered it to him, which he did not; and at length His Majesty brought himself to resort to the other branch of the alternative which Lord Grey had frequently submitted to him in the contemplation of his probable retirement, namely the placing his Ministry in the hands of Lord Melbourne. He had studiously, from the first appointment of Lord Grey's Ministry and particularly on the recent retirement of Mr Stanley, limited his pledge of confidence and support to Lord Grey and those Lord Grey recommended and employed, and he manifestly marked in his first intercourse with Lord Melbourne on the retirement of Grey that he employed him as His existing Home Secretary and not as the publick Man selected by him to be his Premier. He was, however, determined in a short time to place the helm in his hand from a variety of considerations—recollection of Lord Grey's recommendation of him, decided personal preference of him over Lord Althorp, despair of forming what he miscalled a strong, i.e., a mixed administration, and satisfaction at the plain and manly avowal of his views which Lord Melbourne made to him in the course of their communications.[*In the margin:* Many thought that his decision would not have been so absolutely or so promptly taken if the Queen had not been in England,[29] for she misunderstands Lord Melbourne's paradoxes and humour and, affecting or feeling many religious scruples, thinks his principles too loose.] He perceived what indeed was the truth, that Melbourne was neither in Church nor state a reformer by choice, that on the contrary it was in his nature to lament the necessity of it, but it was in his understanding to perceive it and not to impair the grace of unavoidable boons by too slow, niggardly, or ungracious a compliance with them. Melbourne told him that on Church Matters particularly he should have wished things to remain as they had been, for he had no religious and scarce any political objections to the establishment, but that the times and the people of the Country would not leave it alone and that all that was consistent with justice must be done to adapt the institutions to the real (be it conscientious or fanatical) opinion of the country. On Corporations he declared himself by inclination as well as conviction a very keen reformer. The King in general acquiesced in these views and, after cautioning him against the admission of persons with visionary fanatical or republican principles, gave him full assurances of support in continuing, replenishing, or supplying his Cabinet. He or Sir Herbert communicated to him all the strange letters which Lord Chancellor had written, and Melbourne clearly perceived that he should have more reason to dread the disgust than the cooperation of his Royal Master in such designs as his restless Colleague might set afloat.

Lord Grey's family, both in speculations on his retirement beforehand and on the event occurring, expressed and I believe felt a strong conviction that a continuation of a Ministry founded on his principles and chiefly composed of his friends, supporters, and Colleagues was necessary to complete his glory and consolidate his domestick policy. He had for some time designated in private conversation with me and others, and I am confident with the King and Sir Herbert Taylor, Lord Melbourne as well as Althorp as one who might fill his office with less danger of divisions than most publick men. I think that in the circumstances he naturally preferred him to Lord Althorp, and I am not sure that that preference had not been imperceptibly gaining strength in his mind before those circumstances occurred, and ever since Lord Howick had been his Under Secretary, certain I am from phrases which escaped Lord Grey, that he was a little nettled at finding that Melbourne limited his offers to Howick to earnest and repeated exhortations to him to keep his place which Howick as peremptorily declined. Grey manifestly thought, though too proud to express or to imply it, that being qualified for the seals which Lord Melbourne had quitted, He [Howick] was entitled to have the offer. In truth he was so, if his discretion were at all in proportion to his honour and talents and if his manners, appearance, impetuosity, and impatience of contradiction did not counterbalance his natural and acquired abilities both in debate and business. On the [*blank*] of [*blank*], when many of the Ministers and among them the Chancellor and Lord Duncannon as well as Lord and Lady Grey met his Majesty at dinner at Holland House, I observed that the reception of Lord Brougham by the Ladies of the family was colder than ever and that the appointment of Duncannon was *not* one of the ingredients which rendered the new mixture less unpalatable than might be apprehended. The choice of Mr Benjn. Stanley,[30] a follower of Lord Durham and suspected on no light grounds of reviling Lord Grey and his Ministry in the times [*Times*], for an Under Secretary was not a lucky one. It did not reconcile the cavillers at Duncannon's appointment. Lord Carlisle, who had announced his intention of retiring, delivered up his Privy Seal. It was given to Lord Mulgrave. The Woods and forests after some deliberation were offered to and accepted together with a Cabinet place by Sir John Hobhouse.

Two embarrassments presented themselves on our first meeting after Grey's audience of leave—the first whether to accept or decline Mr Littleton's offer of resignation, and the 2d. how to proceed with the Coercion bill. The first question was got over rather than settled by agreeing that Mr Littleton should remain to the end of the Session according to the manifest wish of Lord Althorp, but in the full expectation that some successor should be appointed soon afterwards;[31] the 2d. was determined in a way suggested to me by Mr Allen which in a choice of difficulties seemed the least objectionable and least troublesome course. It was to leave the Coercion bill, already brought to the stage of the 2d. reading or Committee in Lords by Lord Grey, untouched, and to let Lord Althorp move another without the obnoxious Clauses in the Commons. <Thus> the original supporters of them were furnished with the solitary pretext for abandoning them, namely that the Commons had agreed to a bill without them, which might probably be lost altogether at that period of the Session if the Lords should stickle for their reinsertion. Grey acknowledged on his legs that such a course was the best that could now be adopted and, in answer to Lord Wharncliffe's motion for the production of the letter in which Lord Wellesley recommended the omission of the clauses, he delivered a speech equal to any of his best in spirit and perspicuity and excelling them all in generosity of feeling and magnanimity.[32] He vindicated himself, he accused nobody. He praised Melbourne and Althorpe too for undertaking the government and he rejoiced that it was established.

This conduct and indeed His consistency, high sense of honour and elevation of mind were all deeply felt and generally acknowledged throughout society, and it was gratifying to those who had acted with and followed him in politicks and party for years to see the wisdom and justice of the principles he had maintained so generally acknowledged and honoured in his person. A Subscription for a Statue of him to be presented to Lady Grey, visits, dinners of individuals and Clubs, addresses and resolutions from private societies and publick corporations almost immediately, and subsequently yet larger meetings and celebrations to his honour throughout the Country, marked the gratitude of the Community for the benefits conferred and the admiration of that force of eloquence talent, Character, and consistency which had atchieved them. As far as he was personally concerned, he could never have retired more honourably or creditably. But the untoward circumstances which accelerated, if they did not occasion, his retreat certainly afforded a sort of triumph to a very different personage, namely Daniel OConnel. His complaint that faith was not kept with him by the Irish Secretary led to the embarrassment and resignation of Lord Althorp and he had at last the satisfaction of beholding the Government of the country compelled to adhere to the unauthorized promises made to him by a subordinate agent and comply with the terms he thus exacted even at the expence of their head, and that head Lord Grey! Before the end of the Session, he had another scarcely less important, but far less pernicious, triumph.[33]

In the meanwhile, however, Parliament and especially the House of Lords were chiefly occupied with the amendment of the poor Laws, a measure as difficult in its details as important and I trust beneficial in its consequences, and perhaps as arduous in its undertaking as any, not excepting the Reform bill, to which the country is indebted to the Whig administration of Lord Grey.[34] There was however one facility which could not be foreseen and which is creditable to the Community, the House of Lords, and even a large portion of the Tory Party. The Duke of Wellington, Lord Ellenborough, and others of that party disdained to sacrifice their conscientious opinion to their manifest party and political interests, or to recover in any degree their lost popularity with the multitude by joining in the vulgar, but not unnatural, clamour of denial of rights to the indigent, and cold, unfeeling barbarity to the lower orders of the people and especially the weaker sex. Lord Ellenborough in particular gave Ministers distinctly great credit for wisdom and courage in perfecting a measure which many enlightened governments had wished to establish but none had had the hardihood to accomplish or even attempt. No doubt the authority of these Men contributed to enable the sense and firmness of the reformed Parliament to disregard and repel the invectives and menaces with which the Press from the basest motives continued to assail the supporters of the bill. It was the first signal proof of the truth of my prediction, the reform would strengthen Parliament against the Press and shake the dominion which the latter, in the hands of a Monopoly, was disposed to exercise and abuse. The conductors of the Times, very soon after arraigning the new Poor bill, were said to have some inkling of the insignificance of their efforts to over awe the House of Commons. The first divisions, where, in spite of many virulent and some elaborate paragraphs denouncing the bill, the majorities were overwhelming and the minorities contemptible both in names and in numbers, appalled them. [*Crossed out:* It was currently reported that] a meeting of its proprietors was held and that the chief proprietor, Mr Walther,[35] who plumed himself in the Magistracy of Berkshire on the title of the poor man's friend, earned by improvident adherence to all the worst abuses of the administration of the poor laws, had considerable difficulty in animating the exertions of his associates and dependents, and of Mr Barnes[36] in particular, to write down the new bill and its authors. However, they redoubled their exertions with small effect on the divisions in Parliament and with less on the publick mind than might have been expected, but they irritated Lord Chancellor Brougham, who animadverted in bitter and contemptuous terms on their ignorance and malevolence and was perhaps goaded by their diatribes to a somewhat unnecessary and extravagant invective against illdirected and injudicious charity in various branches not immediately touched by the bill. This provoked a warfare from which many consequences ensued, but the bill passed. Lord Grey somewhat injudiciously did not attend it. The Chancellor made several able and eloquent speeches, but more on the principle than the details of the measure, and the debate was chiefly remarkable for the contest on the bastardy Clause between the Bishops of Exeter and London, and for Lord Alvanley's opposition. He shewed, without any high oratorical talents, considerable acuteness, many just general principles, and extraordinary diligence and memory in studying the details of the subject. The whole from so idle a man excited surprize. It was falsely considered as the starting post of an *opposition career* in a course of decided opposition, and apprehension he dispelled by placing his proxy soon after the bill was disposed of in the hands of a Ministerialist.

In the meanwhile a measure for the commutation and extinction of tythe, and composition in Ireland in 5 years and the payment of the established Clergy—from the Bishop's [*sic*] lands, the Landlord's [*sic*] rents, and other funds in lieu of the produce—was brought forward by Lord Althorp. It was somewhat intricate in its provisions and contemplated five years treaty and arrangements before its ultimate object was obtained. Oconnel very adroitly seized the opportunity of suggesting an amendment, which rendered it more simple, speedy, and efficacious, and gave in truth better security tho' less nominal income to the Clergy but which, if originally proposed by Government, would hardly have been accepted by the Irish Landlords.[37] On a division where Many of our friends in office with Althorp at their head voted against their conviction[*In the margin:* and in which the bulk of Irish Landlords supported OConnel] the Ministers were beaten and they readily perhaps gladly acquiesced in their defeat, a second but a well earned triumph to Oconnel.[38] The Church and the tories were exasperated and, sacrificing their interests to their passions, chiefly at the private instigation of the Primate, Lord John Beresford,[39] a weak though gentlemanlike man, they rejected the bill by a considerable majority in the Lords.[40] [*In the margin:* He [*the Primate*] had no seat this year in the House, but The Conservatives and Bishops consulted him.] They probably knew that a defeat on that measure would not break up the Ministry. They perhaps would have been yet more scared at the consequences of their temerity and passion had it done so. Even as it was they felt some compunction when they began to reflect on the ruin to which their vote exposed the Clergy of Ireland and the fatal consequences to the importance of that order of which they were so proud, when their recorded want of confidence in Government should be known to fall imbelle sine ictu and effect no change whatever in His Majesty's councils.

This was one of the first practical and ostensible proofs of the comparative insignificance to which Reform and their fruitless and obstinate resistance to it had reduced the House of Lords. Whether it will be the last, time will shew. Grey did not attend the bill, but his brother in Law, the Bishop of Derry, manfully supported it, while Bishop Grey of Hereford, released from his allegiance to his brother, voted with those who are the natural associates of priestly prejudice and narrow principles in Church and State. His views and opinions were not likely to have now or at any time much weight with Lord Grey, but the language of the younger branches of his family, naturally and amiably indignant at the treatment he had received and not over scrupulous in repeating and exaggerating stories in disparagement of his late Colleagues and remaining friends, might not have been so innoxious had the Session and Grey's residence in town been much further prolonged. His childish aversion to OConnel could hardly be encreased by a change in his situation, but his dread of the machinations, influence, and success of that agitator since his own retirement and Duncannon's acceptance of the seals was somewhat more loudly expressed. Any compliances with him, however inevitable, were arraigned with less delicacy or disguise than was agreable to Lord Melbourne or indeed compatible with a full, efficient, and cordial support of his measures.

It was well I think for the interests of the Ministry and even for the credit and comfort of Lord Grey himself that a dispersion of the principal actors soon took place. The splendor of his reception in Scotland,[41] the unaffected and cordial admiration of all his friends, and not impossibly a consciousness of the contrast between the sentiments which he and the Chancellor respectively inspired in their followers soon extinguished or eclipsed any false or glimmering lights that seemed at one time capable of diverting him from his course and misleading him from the solid path of glory he had chalked out for himself. The Chancellor, who in the course of the late transactions could not have overlooked the unpleasant truth, and indeed was distinctly and plainly told it by Duncannon, namely that the House of *Commons* had little regard and no confidence in him, attempted at one time to cajole the Lords by tardy panegyricks on their usefulness as a branch of the legislature, at another to curry favor with the King by long and imprudent diatribes, communicated in writing to Sir Herbert Taylor against the licentiousness of the press and the dangers of Democracy, and then by an indecorous exhibition of itinerant oratory at various publick meetings from Johnny Groat's house to Salisbury. In all these manoeuvres he did not do enough to cajole either the Court or the aristocracy, but full and more than sufficient to forfeit the confidence, at least for a time, of the reformers and the people. In truth his hasty promises to those he wishes at the time to gain, his unmeasured abuse of all who displease him, both forgotten by himself with as much readiness as they are uttered, are too often recollected by the objects of them. They had embodied a host of personal enemies, on the watch to embitter any hostility his political errors provoked in the publick. In the case of any other man, his popularity and consideration would have been irretrievably lost and he so little formidable to friend or foe as that he might have been discarded by the first or defied by the second without disgrace or danger; but after committing faults and offences without number, he has so often displayed his many miraculous qualities so opportunely and atoned for his occasional violence and ungovernable sallies by so long a course of controul over his temper, that it is not impossible for him, if he discover his error, to regain his lost ground with the publick almost as rapidly as he lost it. His brother James was carried off at the beginning of the year. Lord Brougham felt his loss deeply, and though he was far from an agreable or judicious man, it is said that he spoke openly and firmly to his brother, had great weight with him, and more power in checking his extravagancies than any of his family and friends. There certainly seemed some want of such a counsellor for eight or nine months after his death. He, Lord Brougham, was guided by a series of bitter paragraphs in the times [*Times*], sometimes disgusting and scurrilous, often unjust, but occasionally difficult to be answered and always ingeniously malignant and galling. He at one time had serious thoughts of prosecuting them for libels and in the meanwhile either wrote or caused to be written an article in the Edinburgh review which Lord Durham and even Lord John Russell very naturally considered as a libel upon them. The former retaliated in a speech at his Glasgow dinner, where his vanity and presumption led him to assume the Character of the great popular leader of Reform, and his imprudence, to pledge himself to many various visionary measures, fatal to his real wishes and ambition for office, honours, and distinctions from Government. The Chancellor somewhat reluctantly abandoned his wild project of prosecutions, and Lord John, on consulting Lord Althorpe and myself, prudently and reasonably relinquished all thoughts of a controversial correspondence with him or Durham on their respective shares in the great work of reform. [*Heading:* Autumn 1834] I sent Brougham quotations from Cicero, Tacitus, Aulus Gellius, Dio Cassius, Suetonius, and the Theodosian code (some of which are curious enough) deprecating the persecution of lampoons and libels, in which he was not displeased to be likened to Julius Caesar, or told that there was a greater disparity between him and Durham (as there surely is) than between Caesar and Cicero. Yet Caesar when Consul thought that by any notice of Cicero's invectives against him, he should lower himself and place his inferior on a level with him and therefore abstained.

There was another incident that must have feelingly apprized Brougham of the enmity which his intemperance of tongue had provoked in quarters where it was most for the interest and comfort of a Lord Chancellor to purchase golden opinions. Sir John Leach, after surviving and surmounting by his fortitude and spirit so many dreadful operations, died suddenly of erisipelas and obstinacy in travelling with it upon him at Edinburgh. The Chancellor appointed the Solicitor Pepys,[42] though it gave him pain to sacrifice his feeling to the publick interest and again overlook Horne, whom he had originally with great levity made Solicitor and Attorney and afterwards and reluctantly been compelled somewhat ungraciously to remove. The only Eminent Equity Lawyer of congenial politics with the Govt., whose accession to the office of Solicitor would reflect credit on the Government, was Bickersteth,[43] and the Chancellor was willing and earnest that he should be appointed, though he had so frequently and so bitterly reviled, slighted, and calumniated that Gentleman. He perhaps felt little enmity to him when he did so, and certainly none after the subjects in contest were over; but though he forgot the injuries [and] who had inflicted them, Bickersteth, who had sustained them, did *not*, and from the first mention of the entailed offer (which was, thro' the Chancellor's impatience and wish both to do and to appear to do every thing himself, conveyed from him and not as it should have been from Lord Melbourne) determined to decline it. Lord Melbourne in a private interview and afterwards at a dinner here with Allen and myself in vain endeavoured to persuade him. He was inflexible. He would not place himself in a situation where he was bound to defend Lord Brougham and his measures, and tho' he unequivocally avowed his support of our General policy and disclaimed, with the exception of the Chancellor, all distrust of the Men now in Office, he declared his feeling about him so rooted in his mind as to render his acceptance of any such office impossible. The Chancellor felt mortified. He would they say have liked had he dared to appoint Serjeant Wylde, though a Common Lawyer and somewhat decried for his origin and manners in the profession, but he more prudently acquiesced in the propriety of an equity Lawyer and named a good Whig and honest man, though of moderate standing and eminence, Mr Rolfe.[44]

The new Bishoprick was filled up by a Clergyman of respectable character, Dr Allen,[45] chiefly remarkable as tutor of Lord Althorp and consequently liable to the negative censure of not encouraging active friends in the Church, but exempt from that at first very liberally bestowed upon it, of promoting a treacherous friend or hidden enemy. Dr Allen if not a warm is a good Whig, and an honourable man. The blue ribband vacant by the death of Lord Bathurst, the most amiable and nearly the most sensible of our tory opponents, was bestowed on the Duke of Norfolk,[46] who felt a natural pride in being the first of his family or religion who have received such a favor from the House of Brunswick or any constitutional King of England. It had however been offered to Duke of Grafton, who in deep affliction for the loss of a favorite son,[47] declined it in a letter full of good feeling and sound sense, remarking that such decorations were of little value but when associated with some signal service or peculiar occasion. The letter was seen by the King. The philosophy of it was not particularly palatable to Royalty, and the refusal contained in it was deemed unintelligible and offensive. The knowledge of this impression has I am told reached the Duke of Grafton and he has attempted to redeem his supposed error by attributing it exclusively to domestick affliction and soliciting an early repetition of the offer. This may lead to some embarrassment. For to my surprize (shall I say concern?) Lord Lansdown (who I should have imagined set no value on such gew gaws and assurances) has both to Lord Grey and Lord Melbourne applied for the second blue ribband that should fall.

The Cabinet had agreed to meet on or before the 1st. November to consider of the various questions of Irish Church Reform, Corporation Reform, Dissenters claims &c &c, but on Lord Duncannon's return from Ireland, which was not till the first week in November, Lord Lansdown was still in Paris and John Russell in the Country, so that the Consideration of the Irish measures was unavoidably postponed, though well prepared and drawn out by Lord Duncannon. The time of those Members who were in town was chiefly occupied with the enquiry into the causes of the fire which consumed the two Houses of Parliament and on measures and speculations on the means of replacing [them] first by a temporary building and afterwards by a more permanent national edifice. The King, who in truth dislikes the new Palace of Pimlico,[48] lost no time in offering it for the immediate and, if the Country approved, the permanent accommodation of Parliament, but he had not the King Craft to conceal that part of his motive was the indulgence of his own inclination and therefore got little credit for the generosity of the offer. Perhaps the fear of its entailing additional expence at St. James's and of the obloquy that would follow induced and will induce the Ministry and the country to decline it. The nature and result of the enquiry into the causes of the fire are generally known and it was somewhat fortunate that the accident which led to it was so unequivocally proved that neither folly nor malice could well withold its assent to the report, tho' one of the reporters, the Speaker Sutton, displayed in the course of the examination an abundance of the first quality quite sufficient to lead to any preposterous or ridiculous opinion, and to extort from Melbourne as he went down stairs an involuntary exclamation of 'What a damnation fool that Speaker is!'

In Ireland, Lord Downshire[49] announced to Lord Wellesley his intention of calling and attending a *Protestant* Meeting in the County of Down, with the hypocritical assurance that he deemed it a measure likely to strengthen the King's Government. Lord Wellesley in his answer expressed his disapprobation of Lord Lieutenant of a County binding himself to a proceeding which might lead to a disturbance of the publick tranquillity and in a word, somewhat unusual from a superior to an inferior Officer, *protested* against it. He thus warned him of the responsability he incurred, but he neither resorted to nor threatened dismissal for calling so partial a meeting but put his <future> determination in fact on the issue of the meeting itself. The meeting substantially was alarming enough from the numbers, order, and organization, as well as determination of the people who attended, but the language was guarded, tho' decisive, and the whole demeanour of leaders and followers such as gave no handle to a charge of sedition, much less actual breach of the peace. Yet Littleton, Wellesley, and even Plunkett were eager for the immediate dismissal of Lord Downshire and some proceedings if practicable against his son, Lord Hillsborough,[50] who attended it. They contrived by leading questions to extort from the Attorney General and Solicitor General an opinion that the Meeting was actually illegal, founded upon doctrines utterly subversive of all publick discussion or meetings, and they earnestly and almost passionately urged the Government to resort to dismissals. There were among some of us strong suspicions that Littleton might again have been tampering with OConnel and promised him that Downshire, if he attended such a meeting, should be recalled. What a Man once does he will in some situation always do again, was a maxim of the late Lord Lansdowne,[51] and the few instances of folly being corrected by an experience of its consequences too frequently tend to confirm that severe remark on human nature. Duncannon however was decidely adverse on the grounds of policy and the Chancellor on that of law and dangerous tendency to any such proceeding, and the Cabinet was unanimous in rejecting the advice to dismiss him. We received a Royal answer to the Minute containing this prudent determination, so highly laudatory thereof, that we did or might have inferred from it a resolution in the King's mind not to accede to the proposal had it been in the affirmative, and even, si mens non<lava> fuisset, an apprehension that the menaces or the cajolery of the Orange and Tory party had not been altogether devoid of effect on his Majesty's mind.

When Portugal and Europe were about to derive the full advantages of the gallant resistance to Tyranny, the ultimate expulsion of Don Miguel, the establishment of representative governments in the Peninsula, and the signature of the Quadruple Alliance, the ardent and spirited Prince, Don Pedro, to whom they were mainly indebted for these blessings, was languishing under a Mortal disease and snatched from the scene of his glory and triumph before it was entirely crowned and completed by the marriage of his daughter. A fall from his horse and his fatigues at Oporto and in Lisbon had brought on a confirmed consumption. He could hardly go thro' the necessary ceremonies on the first convocation of the Cortes, and he lay on his death bed, in the very room he had been born, while the Cortes were deliberating on the rank and confidence they should confer on him and on the choice of a Regent after his death. At the same time the Fidalgo party headed by Palmela and Terceira, and too much supported by England and France, were urging, if not a change, an extension of the Ministry in a manner harsh, indelicate, and offensive to the dying Prince. He was fully aware of his approaching death. His whole thoughts were employed in the preservation of his honour, in affectionate advice and provisions for his daughter and the Empress and, above all and to a degree almost unequalled by any dying Sovereign, on the means of securing to his people not only the independence he had conquered, but the practical and permanent benefits of the popular government and wise laws he had introduced or recommended. Count Villa Real, who had originally rebelled with Chaves[52] against the Constitutional government, who in quarrelling with the Usurper resented the personal indignities he received rather than the national oppression, who during the struggle had ignominiously declined All civil and military service in the cause of his country and had returned from Paris after the recapture of Lisbon and the frequent repulses of Don Miguel's army, now marked by his votes in the Cortes his exceeding distrust of Pedro and his dislike of the Empress, and was supposed to be gratifying the foolish wishes of Louis Philippe's court, 1st. by urging restrictions on the Regent Don Pedro, 2dly. by endeavouring the [?to] exclude the Empress on her death from that station, and thirdly by limiting the choice of A King Consort for the young Queen to the son of some reigning Prince. Yet the Duke of Terceira insisted on the introduction of Villa Real to the Cabinet as the condition of his acceptance of office. He was too much sanctioned in that pretension by Lord Howard's not unnatural construction of his dispatches. Pedro, enfeebled as he was, readily consented to a Coalition between his Chosen Ministers, Carvalho,[53] Frerre &c and the Palmela or Terceira party. He would admit, he said, any friend of the latter into his councils, save Villa Real. He considered his recent votes as actual personal affronts to him and not less than an impeachment of his honour. Yet he would give him an Embassy, a Command, a title, or whatever they liked, but dying as he was, he would rather resign his situation at once and end his few remaining days at sea or in exile, than submit, after all he had done for Portugal, to the imputation of treachery to the cause and country he had restored. In spite of Villa Real's revolting opposition, the vote passed and the Choice of a husband was left to Donna Maria and her father, and no time was lost. Pedro's recommendation of the Duke of Leuchtenberg (to whom the foolish women of the Fidalgo party on the score of mesalliance, and the designing politicians with a view of courting the Tuilleries, objected) and the little Queen's consent to that arrangement were obtained and executed without delay.

She as well as the Empress spent many hours at the side of the dying Emperor's bed and received from his lips many earnest injunctions to preserve the privileges granted to the people, as well as assurances of affection and devotion. His touching interview with the Officers and his farewell message to his troops are faithfully recorded in publications of the day, and I have been assured by persons present at that interesting scene that there was not a rugged face of all the veterans but was bedewed with tears at the interview. As the fatal moment approached he made signs for the Uniform of that Regiment which had first declared for his daughter in Terceira and which he had adopted and served with as peculiarly His own. It was put on with some difficulty, and himself once more in a Soldier's dress, he surveyed with complacency [and] He seemed soothed with the scenes of glory it recalled and then, sinking on his bed as on a field of victory, closed his singular and adventurous life in the very room in which he was born.[54] The station he was born in necessarily and the education he received purposely were formed to corrupt a nature, by constitution susceptible and irascible to a high degree; is it then a slight panegyrick to say that he personally did more, he grew both wiser and better every year he lived, that he displayed more personal vigor and spirit on recovering a crown and more political honesty and zeal in extending the freedom of his people, than any legitimate Prince for a century?

His eyes were scarcely closed before the endeavours to remodel the Ministry were renewed with success and Terceira and Villa Real actually installed in their places. The New Ministers, not unwilling in their hearts to defeat the project of a Marriage with Leuchtenberg, either suspected or affected to suspect that the

Young Queen's consent to it had been improperly or imperfectly obtained. A council was held to decide whether they should not again submit the point to her consideration and, before they took any ulterior step, put the somewhat indelicate question to a young Lady, whether she really and personally approved of her person being offered to the Duke of Leuchtenberg. While they were deliberating, the object of their deliberation was clandestinely conveyed to Donna Maria by the Spaniard Mendizabal, and she had time to prepare for the reception. She answered, with some spirit but with great propriety, that she was firmly determined in all things to regulate herself by her late father's wishes, that he had consented and indeed <enjoined> her alliance with the Duke of Leuchtenberg and she was surprized that any should have deemed her capable of departing from her engagement. After this the Council could not openly combat the intention, but some Members were suspected of a design to elude it. They hinted that the Gentleman named by Pedro and the Queen was not of sufficient rank to undertake the mission to Munich, but the Queen's better judgement or advisers suspected an intrigue and, on the same ground of adhering religiously to Pedro's injunction, dispatched Mr Bayard,[55] who is to bring back the procuration and then to be followed by the Duke. [*End of second part of BM Add. MS 51870.*]

Sunday 10th. [*9th.*] *November 1834.* The Chancellor called early and found John Russell and me in the library. After speaking of the dissenters and the Universities and other matters with great good sense and moderation, he said that in contemplation of Lord Spencer's death, which he hoped was not yet certain, he came to impress upon us the necessity of being prepared with some arrangement whenever that event should happen, and then, with little further preface, urged as the most advantageous and practicable the appointment of Howick to the Exchequer and of John, still Paymaster, to the lead in the Commons. He spoke of the former with some flattering expressions to John as a matter almost of course, and he alledged many judicious reasons both of feeling and policy for the latter, illustrating his arguments with much of the ingenuity and vehemence and some little of the exaggeration and satire which are usual with him. I thought I perceived symptoms of a consciousness that the period when it was prudent to draw up and check the career of scorn, defiance, and pugnacity was arrived. He told me carelessly and with some detail of fresh offences of Durham's, that he had dropped all thoughts of prosecution, and seemed unusually accommodating and reasonable about questions of patronage.

In the evening I mentioned what had passed to Melbourne. He approved of the cautious answers I had given, namely that our House of Commons friends could alone judge who could lead them and that till Melbourne had seen both Althorpe and them it was impossible to give a sound opinion, tho' it certainly seemed obvious that John, if willing to undertake it, was the most eligible person, and that with regard to Howick, he was unquestionably an able man both in business and Parliament, and that I believed in policy and I was sure in feeling, at least with me, the advantage of gratifying Grey and indeed the deference due to his wishes would largely counterbalance any inconvenience his temper or his unpopularity might occasion. Melbourne received *both* suggestions very favorably. He questioned indeed the policy or practicability of giving the Paymaster the lead, but he agreed unequivocally in the advantages John would have over any other competitor and he expressly said that Palmerston would not only acquiesce but approve and urge his (John's) taking the lead—a circumstance which pleased John, when I told him, exceedingly and will I trust tend to soften the opprobrious and unjust epithets which he is too much disposed to lavish on Palmerston's measures and manners. In general John is tickled with the notion of the lead, and ready to undertake it with or without the Exchequer, though his reelection for Devonshire is somewhat precarious.

Tuesday 11th. Novr. 1834. News of Lord Spencer's death arrived—an amiable and respectable Man.

I met several of My Colleagues at Lord Melbourne's. They all agreed in the indelicacy and impracticability of settling any thing till Althorpe was in a frame of mind to be consulted, and Melbourne was satisfied with conjuring him by letter to come to no hasty determination about himself and at the same time apprizing the King of the event and signifying his hope that some high and efficient office might be found to offer Lord Althorpe, now Lord Spencer, to mark the sense entertained of his great and useful services. It seems Lord Wellesley has written another urgent letter for the dismissal of the Lord Lieutenant and Sheriff of Downe, grounded on a forced construction of Law by Plunket, the Attorney and Solicitor-General in Ireland, by which the calling of any Meeting hazardous from its numbers is <tortured> into an indictable Offence, and the dismissal of those who called it, though the meeting has passed without any breach of the peace, is with great subtlety and ingenuity but without success urged to be an act of enforcing a due respect for the law. The notion of dismissal was however exploded by the English Law Officers, the Chancellor, and the Cabinet. Brougham was inclined to send a circular to the Lord Lieutenants, strongly censuring Lord Downshire's conduct and warning them at the peril of their office not to follow his example. But upon duly weighing the charge of pusillanimity to which such a course would be liable, and other consequences such as resignations meetings and motions of remonstrance to which it would give rise, he very good humouredly withdrew his opinion, and acquiesced in one expressed in Wellesley's dispatch that unless Lord Downshire were dismissed, it would be better his conduct should not be noticed at all. Melbourne and Duncannon half suspect that Mr Littleton has again promised <some> repealers more than he was authorized or can perform. If it be so, it will be a strong confirmation of Old Lord Lansdown's maxim that what a Man does once he will always do again. It will also be a sad embarrassment, Melbourne apprehends, the absolute ruin of his Ministry, but will be no more than he and all of us deserve for keeping Littleton after his conduct last Summer in the post he still occupies.

1834 Wednesday 12 Novr. Ellice, in Melbourne's anteroom, agreed with most others that John alone could be leader of the Commons and He may be so without removing to Exchequer. He acknowledged that a Cabinet Office for Lord Howick would propitiate Lord Grey and soften the irritation of his family, and from affection and reason professed to think *that one* reason sufficient for offering it to him, though he added there were at least 99 strong reasons against it, and He deprecated earnestly the notion of making him Chancellor of the Exchequer.

I found Melbourne, who reported very favorably of his conversations with Palmerston, Abercrombie, and Rice, none of whom were looking to and most would be unwilling to undertake the lead or the exchequer, and all agreed that the first devolved upon John Russell as of necessity, an opinion in which I think Tavistock and, not less than Tavistock, John Russell himself cordially concurs. Melbourne says he finds less aversion or jealousy to the lead being annexed to the Paymastership, and not to the Exchequer or signets, than he had apprehended. Although from other reasons he very rationally admits the inconvenience of the separation of those active offices and the lead, he is satisfied that the objection on the score of etiquette, usage, or authority is little or nothing. A letter from Althorp, saying his decision would require little deliberation for his mind has long been made up in contemplation of the event which has happened, seems to indicate an intention of retiring from publick life altogether—a determination foolish and even wrong in him and certainly inconvenient if not fatal to Melbourne's government. The King approves of Althorpe (now Lord Spencer) being appointed to some office and justly observes, in his letter to M[elbourne], that the management of the House of Commons is that which on his removal to the Lords presses most urgently for consideration.[56] [*In the margin: N.B.* It must be confessed that this answer of the King to the first intelligence of Spencer's death was very incompatible with his subsequent conduct and might be construed into duplicity; but on the other hand, Melbourne's admission that the Confidence of the Commons in Lord Althorpe was 'so main an ingredient in the resolution adopted by the King in placing him at the head of the Govt. that he was bound to ask H M if he would go on' (recorded on the opposite page[57] at the time and before our dismissal) goes far to prove that the King was not altogether *unjustifiable* though very foolish in reconsidering his determination when Lord Spencer's death was announced.] Melbourne, reflecting that the declared confidence of House of Commons in Lord Althorpe was a main if not the chief ingredient in the resolution adopted by the King of placing the Government in his hands, justly conceives that he is bound to ask the King in some formal and solemn manner if it is his pleasure to employ him in repairing the breach made by Lord A[lthor]p's removal from the House, and in reconstructing the Ministry on the same principles. This is right, and at my suggestion he goes to Brighton to speak to the King in preference to a communication by letter. Though not averse to the admission of Howick to the Cabinet, M[elbourne] is less cordial and more doubtful both of its propriety and practicability than yesterday or Sunday. The Greys, he laughingly observed, in or out were always dissatisfied. When *in* they wanted to be *out*, when *out* they wanted to be *in*, and while he was ready to acquiesce in any thing devized to gratify or honour them, he doubted any device answering that purpose. Howick could not be Secretary of State or Chancellor of Exchequer. Many and especially Grant would never bear his being put over their head, and he hardly knew how, after he and his father had both distinctly said that he could not remain in office consistently with his opinions, he (M)[elbourne] could offer him an office. He could not at least till he was sounded. He agreed, however, in what I said of the impolicy and danger of driving all connected with or personally attached to Grey into positive opposition and closer alliance with Durham, and he assured me, when he spoke seriously on the subject, that he partook of those feelings which I represented to him very strongly would render the position of many and mine especially most irksome, if the Ministry should cease either in substance or appearance to enjoy the sanction of Lord Grey and the character of a continuance of his *Government.* He well knew that I had never contemplated office but with or under Lord Grey, and I could not bear in declining life to belong to a Ministry which he opposed, even tho' I did not approve and would not out of office support his opposition. Melbourne had seen Lansdowne but thought him cold and reserved. He acquiesced in the necessity of chusing a leader of Commons from among the Ministry but lamented the exclusion of Stanley. (But how we can look towards Stanley, till the Irish Steeple which he has raised between us is shortened or removed, I cannot for the life of me comprehend.) He justly said that the choice of leader lay between three—Abercrombie, Rice, and John Russell—but added that great objections and, in his judgement, nearly equal, lay to all three. The objection which he afterwards urged to me also, namely that it would shut the door on Stanley, seems to me, if valid, conclusive against any thing like permanent arrangement; and yet is not an arrangement which acknowledges on the face of it that it cannot be permanent, more objectionable than any one, however bad it may be, and even than actual surrender? Melbourne assured me with great confidence but not unmixed with surprize that L[ansdowne], in canvassing the comparative advantages of the three, seemed to have no strong preference of Rice.

I saw Lord Lansdown at Foreign office. According to his report Lewis Philip has an unpardonable repugnance to Broglie; Talleyrand, if he does not actually encourage, shrinks from all endeavours to combat it. Palmerston is right in his suspicions that Talleyrand does not mean to return to this country and that he leans to a close connection between Lewis Philip and the Northern Courts. Weak, foolish, and inconsistent—a proof of declining faculties or of female influence. It gives to his personal anthipathy to Palmerston, which seemed accidental, the character of political design.

Melbourne, having prepared the King by a letter in which he observed that the Ministry had been formed *mainly* on the ground of the confidence reposed by Commons in Althorp and that it consequently appeared his duty to receive fresh instructions and to lay a fresh statement of the condition of his Government before His Majesty ere he submitted his plan of arrangement,[58] *received permission* [*Heading:* transcribed and corrected from opposite page] to repair to Brighton in an answer which somewhat emphatically concurred in Lord Melbourne's statement of the principle on which his (Lord M's) Ministry had been formed. This gave Lord Melbourne some inkling of the Royal disposition.[59] Soon after his arrival at Brighton on *Thursday the 13th. November* that disposition was more distinctly developed. The King received the intimation of embarrassments arising in the Commons, on Lord Althorp's removal from it, with much more readiness to acquiesce in their existence than he listened to the methods by which in

Melbourne's judgement the loss could be supplied. He at length remarked that as the confidence of the House of Commons had become more doubtful, or at least the means of managing that house more problematical and uncertain, *He did not see how Melbourne's Cabinet could conduct the affairs of the Country*. He mingled other matters, all betraying a dislike or at least an apprehension of Lord Melbourne's offer of continuing. He spoke of measures in contemplation regarding Irish Church, to which, if they contained provisions reported to him by Duncannon, he could never be brought to consent, and he occasionally dropped some expressions of displeasure and discontent at the Lord Chancellor's itinerant harangues, general demeanour, and very troublesome correspondence with him with respect to the Irish measure. Though he had in fact both before and after Lord Duncannon's accession to the Cabinet agreed more distinctly and even cordially, in conversation, with that Lord's general views than he now acknowledged or recollected, he *reminded* Lord Melbourne that he signed the Commission of enquiry on an express understanding that it pledged him to enquiry only, and he then asked if any and what measure was intended? He thus intimated that *a Declaration that no measure of the Character he apprehended should be submitted to him* might materially alter his views of difficulties.

Lord Melbourne honestly replied that no bill on the subject had been submitted, much less considered or sanctioned by the Cabinet; he acknowledged that there might be some strong shades of difference as to the extent to which such measure should be carried and consequently many alterations in the details of any likely to be brought before the Cabinet; he further acknowledged that the Commission of enquiry pledged neither His Majesty nor his Cabinet to any specifick measure or indeed to any Measure at all. But at the same [time] he could not disguise from his Majesty that that Commission raised and indeed was found on an *expectation* that some such step would be necessary; And Unquestionably the outlines of such measure was in great forwardness for Lord Duncannon and the Irish Government to lay before the Cabinet for its immediate Consideration, *And that as far* as he, Lord Melbourne, knew of it, the general principles and features of it had his full concurrence.[60] [*In the margin:* He might have added that of all his Colleagues, but he did not know at the time that Lansdowne, Spring Rice, and others so entirely approved of the scheme as they in fact did.[61]] *Indeed the general bias and leaning* of His Majesty's advisers, both when they counselled the Commission and now, was that a reform or reduction in the Irish Church would on investigation be found reasonable, expedient, and necessary. Melbourne thought that the dread of this measure, which the King deemed a step to the subversion of the English as well as Irish establishment and also an attack on the principle of property, was his main and leading motive, though no doubt some dis<taste> to our Colleagues in the Commons, and unconcealed disgust at the conduct and language of one in the Lords together with a <returning> predilection for the Majority of the latter Assembly were ingredients in making up his determination to part with him. If Melbourne however could have guaranteed him against any such Church measure, He would according to his conjecture have obtained his concurrence in the other arrangements. The truth is that ever since Stanley's resignation he has been alarmed at the prospect [*corrected and expanded copy in the margin:* of being reproached with a subversion of the Irish Church and of those institutions to which his father professed such attachment, but for which W[illia]m IV himself feels little or no reverence. Sir Herbert Taylor warned me and others at the time of the Commission being signed that persons about him (the Princesses and others I presume) had created in his mind some feverish sensibility on the subject of the Church particularly, and of the reproach to which he would expose himself by practically repudiating the conscientious maxims of his fathers life.] His Correspondents from Ireland were many. If common report be not a liar, the Queen was active in cherishing all such morbid scruples in his Mind. Yet he did not talk to her about Melbourne's visit, for when on his asking Sir Herbert Taylor if he had told his Wife that Melbourne was coming and Sir Herbert answered yes, he exclaimed, I did not tell the Queen; to which Sir Herbert replied, 'No Sir but you told the House keeper'. In addition to this trifling incident in disproof of much immediate influence of the Queen, there was no appearance in the Pavilion either on Thursday night or Friday Morning of the result having transpired.

On the *Friday 14 Novr.,* Melbourne had another long audience with the King in which he offered him an Earldom, which Melbourne declined, and he authorized him to offer the vacant blue ribband to Duke of Grafton and was in all respects personally very gracious cordial and communicative; [*corrected and expanded copy in the margin:* gave him a paper in his own hand writing in which he <sh>ortly alluded to the inducement which Lord Althorp's possession of the confidence of Commons had afforded for the formation of the Ministry, and his conviction of the embarrassments his removal offered to the continuance of it, and added that this consideration *and other contingencies,* or some such expression, led him to part wih his present Confidential Servants.[62] There were in this paper, as in his conversation since, expressions of approbation and praise of Lord Melbourne's conduct throughout. He returned with it to London and apprized the Chancellor and two of his Colleagues that night. The [*others*] were not aware of it. But the news of the dismissal was in the Times and Morning Chronicle of

Saturday 15 Novr. from which, and the report of the Mad Whig John Goodwin, I first learnt the fact. [*In the margin:* N.B. It is now quite certain that these two unpardonable and indecent disclosures were made to the respective Newspapers by Lord Brougham.] We met in Cabinet to hear the particulars of our dismissal at twelve, and Melbourne gave a plain, manly, goodhumoured, report of the whole transaction. It was agreed that, being a dismissal, not a resignation, we were to keep our insignia of office and not tender any resignation till the appointment of our Successors. Taylor wrote me and others a very handsome letter and, though there can be little doubt that Many and the King himself had long contemplated the probability of the event on the death of Lord Spencer, I doubt his having actually determined it before hand and still more discredit the suspicion of his having in any underhand way communicated such an intention to our enemies. The Chancellor had on Friday night written him a harmless but foolish and hypocritical letter, half menace and half flummery, in which he took credit for going about the country allaying the impatience for unreasonable innovation. In this he said he had in some degree succeeded and he exhorted the King in strong language not to dissolve Parliament. 'Lord Cowper', observed Melbourne drolly, 'gave the same advice to Queen Anne and she dissolved it next day'.

Sunday 16th. November. A Note from Melbourne in the morning apprized me that the King had ordered him to summon the three Secretaries of State to council tomorrow for the purpose of delivering up their signets. One is necessary to a new commission of the Treasury and it is probably to expedite the Duke of Wellington's, *who has been sent to,* kissing hands as first Lord of the Treasury. The movement is somewhat rapid and gives a strong colour, it must be owned, to the suspicion of premeditation and concert with the Tories, which the report I subsequently heard of the Queen's Secretary Hudson,[63] humorously called the master of the Maids, being sent to Italy to bring back Sir Robt. Peel, will by no means *efface.*

The Chancellor called. He has filled up some vacant stalls and livings with excellent and liberal and distinguished Cantabs such as Thirlwal,[64] Sedgewick[65] and others, and as he has actually promoted Mr Eden[66] to Battersea, Hertingfordbury is actually vacant and I must lose no time in signing the presentation of Mr Archibald Home[67] (my son Henry's friend and vouched by him to be liberal) to that living, for I found to my regret that it would not suit that true philosopher, Malthus,[68] to whom I thought it my first duty to offer it. The King has answered the Chancellor's letter courteously and sensibly, telling him that the patriotick sentiments in it gives him pleasure, as he knows the vigor and talent with which he pursues any line he adopts, encouraging him to adhere to them and assuring them that his remarks on the danger of dissolution will be duly weighed by him if the subject is ever brought under his consideration. It seems that in this or in some other letter His Majesty hints at the surrender of the Great Seal next Thursday—a step which Brougham in his answer has somewhat roughly stated to be wantonly injurious to the suitors—adding to me that, if the King persists, he will read him such a lesson in the Court of Chancery as King never received. In truth he seems well prepared for action and the seat of his adversary on the Woolsack will not be a bed of roses, when he, undiverted by any other occupation, has the House of Lords exclusively for the arena of his oratorical contentions.

We are thus fairly dismissed. The loss of my place is to me personally disagreable enough, for it impairs my fortune and curtails much of my occupation and amusement. In its publick consequences I unaffectedly believe it to be a very great misfortune; and yet so far from being stunned at the blow, I see much to console me and even to gratify me in the manner. It is in a great degree a release from embarrassments which in prospect were many and appalling. Our dismissal can require neither vindication nor explanation from us. There is no variety of conduct or shade of opinion among our Colleagues to trace or to canvass. No possibility of misrepresenting or misunderstanding our motives, no impropriety with which enemies and no indiscretion with which friends can even with plausibility or ingenuity reproach us. It is an act of the King and the King only, and I fear, for him, poor man, a very fatal one. It is I feel no small honour to have belonged to a Government that has done so much for the Country and the World and both the heads of which, Grey and Melbourne, have left their posts in higher estimation and with a greater character in their country than they possessed when they assumed it. Melbourne's acquisition of character for sense, firmness, temper, discretion, sagacity, and simplicity during his Premiership is not only pleasant to his friends and creditable to him but beneficial to the country. The times require men to whom the publick can look in an emergency, and there are few.

In the evening Sarmento,[69] the Portuguese Minister, called with Bayard who is returning with 'procuration' of the Duke of Leuchtenberg to enable the Duke of Terceira to marry the Young Queen of Portugal by proxy. Bayard shewed us with some little mystery the well painted yet more beautifully mounted miniature of the Duke set in diamonds, and Allen took the opportunity of urging them both to hasten over Leuchtenberg for a real marriage, an advice which the dread of Wellington's politicks and yet more of Beresford's pestiferous interference inclines them eagerly to adopt.

Monday 17th. November 34. Went to council whither the 3d. [*three*] Secretaries of State and other Ministers were summoned to surrender their insignia. Wellington, Lyndhurst, [the] Speaker, Maryborough,[70] Cowley,[71] Goldburn, Rosslyn, and Jersey in the Anteroom through which we passed, but the offices to which they were respectively destined, to us unknown. The King was very gracious and even personally kind to some of us, more calm than we expected. The Chancellor's Brougham audience was short, and I think his countenance shewed that he thought it so as he came out; I am told that as he passed thro' the Anteroom it betrayed yet stronger marks of mortification. He had that morning betrayed soreness at the newspapers *attacks* by injudiciously railing at slander in the Court of Chancery. After my interview with the King [*In the margin:* in which he approved of the County Palatine seal remaining in Lancashire till my Successor is appointed] I saw Sir Herbert Taylor, who is I sincerely believe sorry on personal grounds at the dismissal of the Whigs, but who in justification of the King reminded me that Grey had always spoken of Lord Spencer's death and Althorpe's removal from Commons as the termination of his Ministerial career; 2, that the King had throughout that epoch confined his engagement of support to *Lord Grey's* Ministry; and 3dly., that when he acquiesced in the experiment of Lord Melbourne, it was expressly on the assurance that the confidence of the Commons in Lord Althorpe made things comparatively easy and that without him there the Whigs were not able to continue the Government. From these premises, on the most material points undeniable, he concluded that the King in honour was not engaged to continue the present Ministers after Lord Spencer's death and had some plausible grounds and indeed some prudential reasons for well weighing the practicability, the wisdom, and the consequences of such a step. Sir Herbert did not in this conversation directly advert to the other motives which swayed him in determining on a Ministry, for he had before told me enough of the King's positive disgust at Lord Brougham's proceedings,[72] and his misgivings about the projected innovations in the Irish Church, to make me understand that he had long contemplated the possibility, if not actually meditated the plan, of the step he was now taking. With respect to the manner of accomplishing his purpose, Sir Herbert vindicated him from all trick and all underhand proceeding, but allowed much secresy and some possible premeditation in his proceedings. The Queen certainly knew nothing of the immediate nor, though she may have contributed to it by the general tenor of her opinions, of the original design, if any such there has been. The mission of Hudson, her Secretary, to Peel was purely accidental and entirely Sir Herbert Taylor's, settled not only without her suggestion but almost without her knowledge.

I am inclined to believe all this, of both the King and Queen. Yet odd phrases of His Majesty's censuring the liberal opinions of Bishop Maltby and speaking of the instability of things a fortnight ago are mentioned. The observations with which the Queen received the news of the Change from the King, viz '*to* the great joy of the whole nation', does not exculpate her from all suspicion of labouring to produce it, especially as the King's reply, viz '*that* is as it may be Ma am', implies that he knew her hostility to the Ministry which he had dismissed.

The Times of this morning was favorable to the Duke of Wellington, retracted its obloquy on the Queen, and attempted, lamely enough, to reconcile the Reformers to a Tory Government by hinting that the Duke would make them act on pure Whig principles. That active Minister had in truth secured the Times by furnishing them intelligence and promising them more, even on Sunday. He paid his court to 'King Press' before he kissed hands of King William.

18 Novr. Tuesday. It appears that the Duke (they call him his Highness) holds pro tempore nearly all the offices and they are in his hands no sinecures, for early in the morning he was at almost all of them, reading his dispatches, directing the details, sorting the boxes and what not; and he did not even neglect to answer, the same day, the official letters of his Militia Officers on regimental details, as Lord Lieutenant of Hampshire. But he will fill up no offices except such as are absolutely necessary till an answer from Peel is obtained, and it is confidently reported that the whole arrangement is considered by him as purely provisional and temporary—indeed the language of the Standard and times [*Times*] (now a Ministerial) newspaper on

Wednesday the 19th. seemed to indicate a change. Instead of the praise hitherto lavished on the Duke for decision and promptitude, great pains are taken to disclaim all exclusive spirit or indeed any final determination in the measures which he has taken.

The chief motive for the dismissal is alledged to be the King's displeasure, dread, and disgust at Lord Chancellor, against whom almost exclusively the invectives and scurrility of the Times are directed. [*Corrected and expanded copy in the margin:* A paragraph appeared in the Times, on Saturday Morning, containing the Intelligence with an Emphatick Sentence at the End—*The Queen has done it all*—and another longer and more inflammatory one in the M[ornin]g Chronicle of the same Morning. The Lord Chancellor Brougham was pretty distinctly charged with having sent both these paragraphs. The times [*Times*] of this very day, Wednesday the 19th., challenges the globe [*Globe*] to drive them to a disclosure in a way broadly insinuating that Brougham was their informant. Melbourne, who arrived from Brighton between 7 and 8 P M on the Friday night, communicated the result of his visit to no soul but Palmerston, Duncannon, and Brougham, and the latter did not leave him till past Midnight. On the other [hand], it was not mentioned in the Pavilion till Saturday Morning.

N.B. I had related these suspicious circumstances on the 19th., but since that period the suspicion has been more than confirmed. Lord Brougham no doubt peremptorily denies it. But the fact and the Channel through which at least one of these paragraphs was conveyed are well ascertained.

This transaction both in conversation and in debate has been alledged, and not improbably with truth, as the chief reason as well as solitary excuse for the precipitate, unusual, and offensive manner in which Duke of Wellington took possession of the publick offices and demanded the instant resignation of the insignia.]

Thursday 20th. Little known and little conjectured but from the publick papers. Strange that it should be on them The Duke with all his lofty pretensions should lean for support, and from them we are compelled to guess at his policy and system. Yet so it is. With the Press he probably imagines he can now beat the Commons, and the question seems, as John Russell well observes, is whether the representatives of the people or the anonymous monopolists of the periodical press shall lead publick opinion. If the former, The Duke of Wellington's project must prove abortive; but if the latter, the reform bill has failed to accomplish one of the great purposes intended.

Grey seems less surprized than most of us and less indignant or annoyed at this sudden event than his friends should wish him to be. He palliates, excuses, and almost vindicates the King for his conduct. He attributes His determination to the discussion among Reformers created by Durham and Brougham, to the disgust which the speeches and behaviour of the latter have excited in the Court and the Country, and to the misconduct of the Irish Government, in which he very erroneously supposes that Duncannon has his share. This is I think wrong and I lament it; but it tends to shew that He, his family, and immediate followers would have held language if not pursued a course of conduct on the meeting of Parliament which would have been very distressing and thus reconciles one to an exit in which there is nothing mysterious to clear up, no reproaches to repel, and no differences or jealousies to apprehend. Lord Melbourne goes out with a reputation not only untarnished, but greatly heightened by his conduct in power; with one exception, the whole administration and party have gained rather than lost character by the whole piece including the Catastrophe.

That Catastrophe over, I am no longer behind the scenes and can neither listen nor prompt more than other spectators. I therefore may close my book. Before I do so I may mention a small epilogue. Brougham, the day after he was out, wrote to Lyndhurst to offer himself for Chief Baron of the Exchequer, which he would hold without any addition to his pension and thus save the publick 5 to 7000 per annum. Lyndhurst answered that till Peel arrived, to whom the King entrusted the forming of the new Ministry, He and the Duke of Wellington abstained from giving any appointment or making any pledges about places or measures, and Brougham went off to Paris on the 25th. of November 1834. [*End of fourth part of BM Add. MS 51870.*]

[*From the diary of Dr John Allen*[1]]

6 February 1835. The Elections are now over; and if we credit the Whig Newspapers, there is a majority of 150 in favour of Reform, but many of these will not join in expressing a want of confidence in Ministers. Some will keep out of the way and others will declare for giving them a trial. The first question will probably be decided in their favour, many reformers objecting to vote against Manners Sutton, on the ground that he has done nothing since 1833 to justify those who voted for him before for voting against him now.[2] The first defeat will, in my opinion, be decisive as to any want of confidence or address to that effect. The great danger of Ministers will arise from divisions among their own friends. To keep their places they must reform the Church; but if they propose extensive reforms in the Church, the real Tories will separate from them as they did before on the Catholic question. I see no reason to think there will be a complete victory on either side. Questions will be alternately won and lost till some compromise or arrangement is effected by which a mixed Government will be formed under the guidance of either Peel or Stanley, the extremes on both sides being laid aside. How long it will take to bring about this result depends on the measures of Reform brought forward by the Ministers. If they be such as to alarm the real Tories Peel will be abandoned by those who constitute the real strength of his party and a Government more liberal, most probably under Stanley, will replace the present one. If they are such as not to alarm the real Tories, there is danger that the Moderate Reformers will be afraid to support him. His safest course will be to gain time by issuing Commissions of Enquiry and making this a pretext for delay in the final measures he recommends. The application of any surplus that may come out of the Irish Church is the bar between Stanley and the rest of the Opposition. It is not the business of Peel to remove that bar and therefore the final settlement of the Irish Church is the last question he will be inclined to bring forward. Nor can opposition force the question upon him without they hazard the widening of the breach between them and Stanley.

12 February 1835. According to present appearances Abercromby will have a majority.[3] What will follow if he succeeds? Nothing immediate. Ministers will not resign, and if they do, I see no possibility of any efficient Minister to replace them.

Feb. 17 1835. Parliament is to meet on the 19th. The Session is likely to be of importance; I shall therefore keep a short journal of the more remarkable events that come to my knowledge.

18 [*February 1835*]. The meeting today was attended by about 130 persons.[4] Lord Euston[5] came but went away when he found it was about the Speakership, saying he was to vote for Sutton. Lord John said a few words recommending that no personal reflections should be made on the late Speaker.[6] O'Connell in private expressed to Lord John his approbation of that advice. Graham, they say, has declared to some of his friends that he must separate, though with regret, from his old Colleagues.

19 [*February 1835*]. Abercromby has been elected Speaker by a majority of 316 to 306.[7] Stanley and his friends voted against him. Several persons calling themselves Reformers voted in the same way. How many I cannot say. Of the members who were absent and did not vote, the Morning Chronicle reckons 25 Reformers and 7 Tories, which with the two Tellers and one pair during the debates makes up the whole of the House. Burdett had determined till this morning to attend and vote for Sutton, but was persuaded by Otway Cave[8] to stay away. Of the Scotch reformers Sinclair and Agnew[9] voted for Sutton, McTaggart[10] staid away.

22 [February 1835]. The following account of the speech to be delivered on Tuesday has been given to Lord Holland by one who had it from a person who had seen a rough draft of the speech. It is to announce:

1. A reform in the English Church—an equalisation of Bishopricks, enforcement of residence and a prohibition of pluralities, but it was [not] recollected whether any mention was made of Chapters or arrangement proposed with respect to advowsons.
2. the adoption of those reforms in the Scotch Kirk which have been favourably received by the last General Assembly.
3. the communication of a report from the Corporation Commissioners and a willingness to follow it up by an efficient reform of Corporations.
4. redress of the grievances of Dissenters, as to marriage, church cess, and it was believed registry and burials, but not with regard to the Universities.
5. Extinction of tithes in Ireland, but has no recollection of any reduction of revenues or suppression of benefices, and is sure there is no appropriation to any but ecclesiastical uses.

The length and character of the Speech [is] confirmed from other sources. The Duke of Wellington told Rothschild that it would be more liberal than Lord Grey or Lord Melbourne could have ventured to recommend.

In addition to the above I have to add some particulars communicated to me by Mr Hodgson[11] (Secretary to the Bishops) whom I met accidentally on Saturday: Benefices in commendam to be altogether abolished, Canterbury to be reduced to £16,000 a year, York to £12,000, London, Durham and Winchester to be fixed at £10,000 each, and the other Bishopricks to be £4,000 each or about that sum. Chapters to be greatly reduced, and the reductions applied to the smaller Benefices on the principle of Queens Anne's bounty. He seemed to think there would be no difficulty in Crown and Episcopal Livings, in taking from the greater and adding to the smaller Livings, but saw no way of introducing such a reform in Livings in the gift of private patrons; Residence to be enforced, pluralities prohibited, And Unions effected, wherever it was found to be expedient.

23 [February 1835]. Stanley had a meeting of his friends this morning—31 is said to have been the number present—but I have neither heard their names nor anything of the line they mean to take.[12] While he was speaking against Abercromby, O'Connell, I am told, could not conceal his joy.

The speech was neither so long nor so explicit as was expected.

Lord Grey very much out of humour with the conduct of his friends, cannot bear the communications they have with O'Connell, is afraid they are widening the breach with Stanley and drawing towards the Radicals.

24 [February 1835]. Brougham's speech last night one of the best debating speeches he ever delivered—but during Lyndhursts reply he became impatient and disorderly. Peel's speech in the Commons also said to have been very efficient. Howick declares he would have been ready to vote with him, but for his opinion on Church Temporalities.

27 [February 1835]. Lord John's speech on Wednesday night, as well as his speech on the election of a Speaker, considered excellent and justifying the selection made of him to be the leader of the party. Fox Maules[13] speech last night seems also to have made a general impression in his favour—Majority 307 to 302.[14] 6 pairs and 5 on one side absent. In the Lords Brougham and Plunkett had a great advantage over Lyndhurst on his assertion that the Corporation Commission was illegal. He confessed that he had not read it when he made the assertion, but took his opinion from Lord Abinger.

Howick, in speaking for the amendment, said that he would not vote for it, if he thought it would make the Ministers resign. That family are full of rage at what they conceive to have been the forced resignation of their Father. Howick went further and expressed his hope that carrying the amendment would lead to a reconstruction of the Cabinet. This suggestion joined with a word that dropped from the Duke of Richmond this morning 'that all would end well', convinces me that some scheme is in agitation to bring in Stanley and his friends and get rid of some or all of the ultra Tories.

Gisborne's speech was decidedly the best of last night.

March 1. Rumour of changes, but nothing announced. Hobhouse, Thomson, and others of the late Cabinet are manifestly desirous of widening the breach with Stanley, and Graham for a different purpose is supposed to be working to the same end. The more moderate men of the party wish on the contrary to heal the breach, thinking it impossible to form a stable Ministry without the cooperation of him and of those disposed to act with him, and if it were possible, fearing the consequences of a Ministry entirely Radical. Holmes has offered to bet 50 guineas that Lord Grey will be sent for within three months. No immediate fear of dissolution.

7 [*March*]. Nothing of importance has occurred during the last week. There are still rumours of changes, but nothing has taken place. Graham supposed to be more anxious for a junction with Peel than any other of Stanley's friends. Opposition divided into at least two parties, Lord Grey dissatisfied that O'Connell was invited to the first and only meeting of the party. Howick violent against O'Connell and many persons, like him, look forward with apprehensions to the resignation of Ministers. Others contend that nothing effectual can be done without a closer connection with him. Lord John finds it difficult to avoid breaking with one side or other. The more eager and violent complain of the mildness of the amendment and call for a direct vote of want of confidence in Peel, without considering that they would be unable to carry it. Violent altercations about the Orange Lodges and on the other hand great dissatisfaction among the Tories at the determination of Ministers to maintain and even extend the new system of education in Ireland. Both sides are composed of discordant materials, and it will depend on events which party is first broken up. Brougham active and discreet in public.

March 9. Much difference of opinion on Humes notice of a motion to grant the supplies for three months. Some call it a vote of confidence for three months to the

Ministers. Some propose to grant the supplies for the army and navy in the usual manner, but to declare that no supply shall be voted for the Ordnance or Extraordinaries till the Corporation reform becomes law. Peel had a meeting of 189 of his friends on Saturday to urge the necessity of opposing Lord Chandos' motion for the repeal of the Malt Tax. Three or four declared that they must vote against the tax, but the remainder acquiesced in the Minister's request. Application has been made to Lord Chandos not to persist in his motion, but he is said to be obdurate. I trust he will persist and be beat. The opposition of Ministers to such a motion will lessen the chances of a second dissolution.

15 [*March 1835*]. The motion of Lord Chandos for the repeal of the Malt tax was rejected by a much larger majority than had been anticipated, the Tory country gentlemen having (with some few exceptions) voted against it in opposition to pledges given to their Constituents to which they owed their Elections. There is no longer any fear of a second dissolution.

At a meeting on Friday morning of the Opposition it was discussed whether a motion should be made to grant the supplies for three months.[15] Hume is said to have [been] angry and to have reproached Warburton[16] bitterly for changing his mind, but at length he was induced to acquiesce in the general sense of the Meeting. O'Connell was present, not so Lord Howick. Can it be the intention of the Grey family to break with the Opposition unless the Opposition break with O'Connell? If so, Peel has nothing to fear, and may reform or not reform as he pleases. The report on the Irish Church has been delayed by the Duke of Wellington leaving the Commissioners without money during the interrugnum.

March 17. The affair of Lord Londonderry must have damaged Ministers very much.[17] Stanley's speech shews no disposition to conciliate them, and neither Peel nor the Duke of Wellington have said or done any thing to lessen the odium they had incurred by so improper and unpopular an appointment. Lord Londonderry himself is the only person concerned who has gained credit by his conduct. His resignation of the Embassy was judicious and placed on proper grounds. Lord Grey came to town last night.

19. Language held by Lord Grey unsatisfactory, doubts whether he is to consider himself in opposition to the present Government, cannot find that he differs on any point from Stanley, averse to the discussion of any abstract question on the appropriation of any surplus from the Irish Church, should vote for the previous question.

22 [*March 1835*]. Notwithstanding their defeat on Friday night[18] the Opposition are in good spirits and confident of a majority of 40 or 60 on the Appropriation question. Howick made a stout speech in favour of it, and Stanley declared the question must be brought to a decision. Peel lost his temper on Friday and is said to be harassed and much annoyed with his present position. Ministers are now committed on the Malt Tax, the new Education in Ireland, the Dissenters Marriages by a civil contract, and on the Irish appropriation. Palgrave is said to have presented, without proper notice, a protest against the report of the other Commissioners.[19]

23. Stanley seems to consider that in the present state of things the abstract point of appropriation must be decided by the House, and thinks it cannot be deferred. Thinks Ministers will be beat upon it, that Peel will next morning resign, and that the Opposition will find it impossible to form a Government that can last ten days, and shews no disposition in such an event to join his former Colleagues. Graham still more determined, in all appearance, against any such junction. Talks of Church appropriation as if it were a question of religious principle, and expressed great abhorrence and apprehension of the doctrines on National property inculcated in Senior's pamphlet.[20] There is to be a meeting of the Opposition today to dissuade the more violent members from any division on the Irish Church before the 30th.[21]

26. Nothing of importance occurred except violent language in the House of Commons and the defeat of Ministers on an insignificant question on which they were induced unnecessarily to provoke a division in consequence of an assurance from Mr Charles Ross[22] that they had a majority in the House.

27. The signal defeat sustained by the Ministers last night on the motion to address the Crown for a Charter to the London University without waiting for any report from the Privy Council has the appearance of a disinclination in the friends of Government to support them any longer[23]—whether from despair of success, or disinclination to Peel on account of the liberal measures he has lately proposed—and in that view it may be considered as a hint for him to resign before Monday. Nine or ten additional members have this morning put down their names for the dinner to be given tomorrow to Lord John Russell. Peel is said to be unwell and last night he made, I am told, a very bad speech.

29. The dinner given yesterday to Lord John Russell appears to have gone off well. It was attended by more than 250 persons. Names put down were 272. At Bridgewater House there was in the morning a meeting of the Tories and an address, it is said, agreed upon to Peel, urging him not to resign, though he should be defeated on the Irish Church question. Wetherell says that Peel's Government is founded on the *not going out principle.* Nothing can be more scurrilous than John Bull, the Guardian, and other Tory newspapers. Rabble, Canaille, &c are the terms they apply to the majority of the House. Factious, nay traitorous, are the motives attributed to their conduct. The chief object, it is said, of the meeting at Bridgewater House was to secure a better attendance of the Tory members, and for that purpose the town was divided into districts with a superintendant over each, who is to summon the absent from Balls, dinner parties, Clubhouses &c wherever they are to be found. All this bustle and activity have been excited by the defalcation of members on the London University question.

April 3. The majority last night of 33 was greater than had been expected in the course of yesterday, but much the same as had been reckoned on ten days ago.[24] Peel will not resign upon it, and if he does, it will be no easy matter for any other person to form a Government out of the discordant materials that compose the present House of Commons. According to the analysis made of it by Mr Ellice it consists of 281 Tories and followers of Peel, of whom he reckons 100 to be decided Tories and the rest willing to follow Peel under any circumstances in all the measures of reform he has brought forward. He reckons the followers of Stanley at

18;[25] the Radicals at 112; the Waverers and uncertain people, on whom no one can reckon, at 7 or 9; and the remainder to be Whigs. According to this calculation the Whigs are not more than 238 or 240, a number insufficient to form an Administration without constant dependance on the Radicals. What opinions he considers such as to afford grounds of a fundamental difference between Whigs and Radicals I cannot say, but to justify his conclusion, it must be definite and strong. The numbers who voted last night, including pairs and tellers was 643: 338 in the majority and 305 in the minority, being the whole House with the exception of 15, or 14, besides the Speaker, who did [not] vote.[26] This was the calculation I heard from Lord Grey, who added that so great a proportion of the whole House had never voted on any former occasion.

6. I have been so much taken up with quarrels and dissensions at Dulwich that I have neglected to notice many things for the last eight days. There was a meeting of the Opposition this morning which agreed to the proposition of Lord John that, instead of an address to the Crown, they should proceed by moving a resolution of the House that the appropriation to other than Church purposes of any surplus that may arise from the reform of the Irish Church should form part of the tithe Bill. Some think that after the declaration made by Peel he must resign if this motion be carried. Others, and among them Lord Grey and Lord Holland, think he will remain in office, and put off till after the Holydays the further progress of the Tithe Bill.

[*Lord Holland's diary resumed.*]

15 April 1835. I returned to Holland House, Melbourne being once more employed in forming an administration. The Duke of Wellington's proceedings, the return, declaration and conduct of Peel, the dissolution of Parliament and the votes of the New Parliament are as well known to the publick as to me, and even the composition of the Majorities and the manner in which they were brought together are to be found in the speeches, pamphlets, and our newspapers of the day. The general effect of the Change in England and Scotland had been to dispel among Dissenters and Whigs their suspicions of Grey's and Melbourne's administrations and to convince them that there existed greater obstacles to the rapid progress, even of rational reform, than their ardent minds had hitherto imagined. But in Ireland the Catholicks and even Reformers were alarmed at the possibility and virulence of an Orange Ascendancy. The effect of the dissolution in England was to encrease, especially in agricultural districts, the number of Tory Members, but not to vary so much as was apprehended the relative force of Whigs and Radicals and to convince the latter, especially in the South of England, that they were not so strong in proportion either to Whigs or Tories as the language of the press had led them to suppose.

This rendered them for a time humble and accommodating. The English Radicals with Mr Warburton and Mr Grote, two sensible and honourable men at their lead, were very amenable to reason and willing to cooperate in every endeavour to replace the power in the hands of avowed and consistent, though, as they thought, somewhat lukewarm and dilatory reformers, and to leave to chance or future consideration the pace at which they would travel in the direction towards which all professed to turn their heads. Oconnel was still more profuse but not perhaps for that reason more depended upon his professions. Yet fear and hope combined to give him that impulse, and there is some truth in his acknowledgement that he is a Man of impulse. Persons of variety and levity can yet be 'constant while possessed' and Oconnel courted more concert and union than the Whigs were willing to grant him. He disclaimed however any claim, personal or political, after the Tories were driven from power, and only asked to be allowed to cooperate in that first necessary and preliminary work. Some squeamish Members of the party hesitated about meeting him even on these terms. Grey from a distance deprecated all approximation and even all communication with him, and his Sons, Howick and Chs. Grey,[27] exaggerated his feelings. <They> repeated and imitated them, and exasperated them by their reports of all that was passing. However Meetings did take place at which OConnel was present. The questions on Speakership, on amendment, on London University, and on appropriation of surplus revenue in Ireland were carried. Howick speaking on more than one and very ably on the last.

DIARY RESUMED APRIL 1835.

On Tuesday the 7th., Lord John Russell's Resolutions (to appropriate the surplus of the Irish Church revenues to purposes of education and charity without distinction of religion, and to express an opinion that no tithe measure in which such a provision was not embodied would be satisfactory) were carried in a very full house by a majority of 25.[28]

On Wednesday Peel and his Cabinet resigned and announced their resignation to both Houses of Parliament. It was not I think till *Thursday 9th.* that the King sent to Grey and it was on the afternoon of that day that he saw him. The King began by reminding him that when he had sent to him [in] 1830 he had done so at the recommendation of all those who had resigned their office, but that on this occasion sent to him without *any such recommendation,* solely on account of the satisfaction with which he reflected on his conduct throughout the four years he was Prime Minister and because he thought his weight and authority and his having been aloof from the recent contentions of parties which had followed his retirement from office might render more easy for him to unite persons of different shades of opinion without giving a triumph to any. He dwelt on the little difference of opinion subsisting between all the former Ministers, and especially Lord Grey's particular friends and Lord Stanley, or indeed Mr Peel, and he manifestly leant to a hope that a Coalition might be effected and even hinted that Peel might remain 1st. Lord of the Treasury. [29] He spoke at the same time handsomely of Melbourne, but I should suspect by Grey's report of the conversation that he dwelt, with some degree of complacency if not with design, on all the past transactions which he thought most likely to weaken his predilection for the liberal part of the Cabinet that succeeded him, and above all he inveighed against the notion of junction with dangerous men, meaning OConnel and others,[30] described the object in constructing any Ministry as mainly that of stemming the tide of revolution and resisting the designs of incendiaries, a topick which I fear Grey must have <chimed> in with more than was prudent or wise. Grey professed his readiness to do any thing in his power to extricate the King from a position which he allowed to be most embarrassing. He admitted that little difference seemed to exist between them and Lord Stanley but on the subject of the Irish Church; but then, that difference was unfortunately so entangled with the circumstances which had made a second Change unavoidable and the necessity of acting on the principles of the House of Commons was so urgent that he saw no prospect of bringing the respective parties to an agreement and as little of being able to postpone, avoid, or modify the measure to which the Majority of the Commons and those who enjoyed their confidence were pledged. He distinctly stated that he thought the sort of Union of publick men to which the King pointed, however ultimately desirable, was for the present at least impracticable. He was ready to convey any views or to ascertain any opinions of Lord Stanley and even of Sir Robt. Peel, but he should deceive the King if he did not tell him that he thought his best and indeed only practicable course was to consult Lord Melbourne or some of his late Ministers, and the conversation ended by Grey receiving directions to bring Melbourne and Lord Lansdowne to St. James's at 12 o'clock.

From Friday the 10th April 1835 to tuesday the 14th. inclusive: Several audiences granted to Lord Grey, Lord Lansdown, and Lord Melbourne, separately and jointly. The King's hopes of some coalition or compromise with the Tories and Sir Robt. Peel, or with Stanley and his small squad, were manifest, and his soreness and apprehension of what he termed the visionaries and the incendiaries in the House of Commons yet more so. More than two days elapsed in these preliminary conversations. Melbourne and Lansdown foresaw or imagined many difficulties, and the former was half inclined to answer the King's enquiry whether he could undertake to form a Ministry (for he had not hitherto been formally authorized to do so much less had he kissed hands as first Lord) with an acknowledgement that *he could not.* This would have been an ignominious surrender indeed! And Lord Lansdowne, though less sanguine than any of us as to the success of a Whig Government and averse to the whole thing, yet felt forcibly that in honour Melbourne was bound to proceed or endeavour to proceed, unless there should occur some ostensible publick ground on which to break with the King or with those with whom we had acted for the purpose of turning [out] Peel's Ministry and on whom we depended, no doubt more than he could wish or approve, for the success of establishing another. In this and indeed in a yet stronger view of our duty, our interest, and our honour being engaged, not to shrink from the attempt, nearly all our friends warmly concurred. Lord John, Lord Granville, Lord Palmerston, and above All, Mr Ellice, whose activity, good sense, and good humour have acquired very great influence in the party, were vehement and earnest; and even Sir Fredk. Lamb, though an antiliberal in grain and far from cordial with any of us, told his brother that he had gone too far in opposition to recede, that he (Fred) deemed the endeavours to harrass and overthrow Sir R Peel were wrong, but that if after success he shrunk from replacing him, he gave those efforts the character of faction, resentment, and even folly. Spring Rice was the only one among the leading advisers of the party who seemed seriously to hesitate in the Course to be pursued. Whether his motives were enmity to Oconnel, some secret understanding with Stanley, or genuine fear of the consequences it is difficult to determine.[31] Irishmen are usually swayed by personal passion or personal interests and he, notwithstanding his many good qualities, may not be an exception. He was however somewhat deterred from his pusillanimous course by Ellice's hint that he would take his place both in office and debate if he persisted, and yet more by the milder persuasions of Lord Lansdown, who suggested an expedient that reconciled him and indeed greatly strengthened Lord Melbourne's means. Lord Lansdowne prevailed on Rice, Palmerston, Melbourne, and myself, with the approbation of John Russell who was gone with his bride into the Country, to draw up a letter to Lord[32] [*unfinished; end of fifth part of B M Add. MS 51870*].

Wednesday April 15th. Diary resumed for a time. At Melbourne's in the evening. Ellice, John Russell, Duncannon there. Melbourne had on Sunday night Monday Morning written to the King a reasoned letter, claiming in distinct terms those powers respecting Peerages, Household, and other matters which can alone mark the Confidence of the Crown in its advisers.[33] To this he had no answer till tuesday, and the answer, which I read for the first time to night, was far from satisfactory and more suspicious and even hostile in spirit than directly objectionable in matter or distinct propositions. Nothing but the household was distinctly accorded; a jealousy of individuals, though with a disclaimer of the principle of exclusion, was earnestly, frequently, and somewhat offensively expressed; and what was yet more alarming, the subject of the bill regarding the Irish Church was retrospectively introduced with phrases indicative of an unwillingness to support the principle of it. As these objections would a fortiori be fatal to any bill founded on the House of Commons resolutions, it was necessary to clear this matter up, and Melbourne, after shewing the paper to Grey, waited on His Majesty and urged upon him the necessity of considering an appropriation of the surplus revenue of the Church of Ireland to general and charitable purposes as the principle on which the new Government must be formed, and of his Majesty sanctioning not only the introduction and carrying of such a legislat<ion>, but specially signifying his consent to those parts of it which affected the possessions or interests of the Crown. The King seemed embarrassed, perplexed, and uneasy in the extreme, said he had never understood the matter in that light and (what was true tho passing strange) that the subject had not been mentioned either in Melbourne's letter or in the audiences which he had given to Lord Grey, Lord Lansdowne, and Lord Melbourne.

He at last desired Melbourne to write to him, and Melbourne, after consulting Grey, Lansdowne, and others, returned home this morning to draw up an answer. Before However he had sent it and about the time (1/2 past 9 p m) I arrived at his [house], another letter came from H M in which, after some explanation of a point or two in his former epistle, he distinctly admitted that by accepting Peel's resignation and sending for those who had prepared, voted, and carried the resolutions, he had sanctioned the proceeding to carry the House of Commons resolution into effect on the part of the New Ministry; but he contended that he had not been aware of the necessity of what he was pleased to denominate his *special* sanction of the appropriation, by signifying in an early stage his formal assent. He then proceeded to start a doubt that his Coronation oath might be violated by such a proceeding and somewhat strangely requested Melbourne to ask the opinion of the 15 Judges, which he said might easily be done during the holydays and, with an assurance that he did not wish the arrangements to be hurried, manifestly implied that they should be postponed till the Judges answer was obtained and the Easter Holydays over. Melbourne read an admirable answer to the first and longest letter, and it was agreed that together with one to the last letter it should be sent; the last should advert to the distinct admission that Melbourne, if Minister, must act forthwith on the principle of the resolutions, should decline all discussion of the Coronation Oath, observe that it was not for him to refer questions of the sort to the Judges, and end by declaring that till such scruples were removed and a Government be formed which had His Majesty's sanction to introduce a bill on the principles of the resolution and to signify His Majesty's sanction thereto, he could not undertake to conduct H M's affairs in Parliament.[34] Melbourne said that Grey, since Howick's admission to the Cabinet had been fully announced, was he thought more disposed to surmount difficulties than before, and Ellice, who communicated the King's 2d. letter to Grey, returned from him saying that he thought the notion of a reference to the Judges on the Coronation oath would be nonsense, but the whole by a little Management might yet be settled amicably. Ellice somewhat satirically observed, 'if you write to the King, Grey thinks you should have spoken, if you speak he thinks you should have written'. Johnny was so recently on his nuptial couch that he slept soundly on Melbourne's. He seemed however disposed to declare the whole negotiation for a ministry off to morrow, and said he hoped the King and the Tories would try another dissolution.

Thursday April 16th. 1835. I called again at Melbournes about three oclock and found there Lord Duncannon, Lord John Russell, Mr Spring Rice, and Mr Ellice, waiting with some anxiety for an answer from the King, which might enable Lord John and Lord Melbourne to announce something definitive to the respective houses or induce them to adjourn to the unusual day of Saturday with the hopes of moving some writs on that day; for since last night much had occurred. Melbourne had seen the King; he had explained to him the nature of his scruples, which appear to me somewhat too subtle and discriminating to be of his own invention. He would it seems have no scruple in his legislative capacity to consent to a bill as strong or stronger, in contradiction to his Coronation Oath, if recommended by the two Houses of Parliament, but he hesitates in his individual capacity signifying beforehand his willingness to allow such a subject to be discussed and waving, for the purpose of enabling the Commons to proceed on it, that share which he may have on the rights, privileges, and possessions of the Church so to be dealt with. He disclaimed however all pertinacious adherence to his suggestion of consulting the 15 Judges as well as all wish to defeat the object by the pretext of scruples he did not feel, and he would be satisfied with Lord Lyndhurst['s] opinion and wished Lord Melbourne to agree to meet him and be present at the questions put and answers received. He ended by putting a paper into Melbourne's hands. That paper recapitulated shortly his proposal of consulting Lyndhurst and his reasons for it and repeated, in terms much stronger than Melbourne's disclaimer would warrant, the personal objections which he felt to OConnel and other Members of the House of Commons. On the latter topick Melbourne justly thought he had said sufficient for the present, and he confined himself entirely in his answer to the proceedings necessarily arising from the resolutions, to the scruple the King felt regarding, them, and to the plan he had suggested for relieving his mind from them by an interview with Lyndhurst. Melbourne told him either in this paper or in conversation that he had not but three courses open to him: 1 to sanction the immediate proceeding in the spirit of the resolutions, and to give his consent; 2d. to withold his consent and endeavour to rescind the resolutions; and 3dly. to dissolve the Parliament. He added that the first course was the only one in which he, Lord Melbourne, could hope that his services could be of any advantage to his Majesty and indeed the only one which, with regard to his own honour, consistency, or opinion, he could advise or assist him in adopting. He could not for a variety of obvious reasons advise the consultation upon the scruple. The scruple seemed to him far from valid or sound. He was not yet constituted his Majesty's official adviser. He was politically unconnected with Lord Lyndhurst and could not recommend any consultation with him; it would be submitting the conduct and fate of the New Ministry he was forming to the judgement of a political adversary and it would be apprizing that adversary, and through him many others, of a difference in views and feelings between his Majesty and his Government which could not but prove injurious to the latter. He ended by conjuring His Majesty to come to an early decision and the King promised to let him know soon after three. It was near four, however, that he learnt from him that his opinion was unchanged, that he had sent for, but had not seen, Lyndhurst, that the houses had better be adjourned to Saturday, and that He was setting off to Windsor. Lord Melbourne wrote a hurried reply, deprecating delay and stating the inconvenience of it and entreating him not to leave London till *he had seen Lyndhurst* and could definitively inform him whether he adhered to or was relieved from his scruple. I remarked to Melbourne who told me this in House of Lords that the words *underlined* had better have been omitted and he agreed with me, tho', having distinctly stated that he could *not* advise sending for Lyndhurst, no material reference could be drawn from them. It was observable that in his conversation, when he mentioned *dissolution*, the King eagerly interrupted, 'That My Lord is quite out of the case, impossible, in the present state of the Country it must not be thought of'.

Wellington moved the adjournment of Lords. Nothing was said, and their Lordships were again disappointed, 'Much Ado about Nothing', said Lord Chancellor Lyndhurst as he left the house. He might with more truth have said, 'Nothing Ado about something of great importance'.

The King's papers, conversation, and proceedings throughout this business have been so very ill conducted, that I acquit him of all concert or cabal, but he has been probably predisposed to raise such difficulties by sundry previous apprehensions and remarks expressed by those who surround him. The sensibility of G[eorge] III to all matters relating to the Church, and the Irish Church particularly, has no doubt been brought frequently before his view and even Sir Ht. Taylor's testimony, perhaps his own individual feelings, might corroborate it. Lord Stanley emphatically expressed a doubt last year if he had yet seen a King who could consent to divert the revenues of the Irish Church from its object, and the argument of Peel and others, as was supposed to catch and gratify Stanley; but not impossibly to alarm the King, was directed to the necessity of a previous consent from the Crown and the impossibility, in his view of the matter, of advising it. As a proof of the silly tales reported to St. James's, John Russell, when asked by Lord Londonderry 'What next?' answered in a banter, 'Oh we mean now to establish the American Constitution'. Londonderry reported it to Buckingham, Buckingham put it down in his tablets, and the King very gravely mentioned it to Lord Grey in his audience as an indication of the violence of Lord John Russell's opinions and the dangerous tendency of his designs.

17 April 1835. Good Friday. Grey came over from London and told me that Lyndhurst had very properly declined giving any opinion to the King, that the King had waved his scruples, and that the outline of the Ministry was formed and the number of the Cabinet reduced to 12. Howick is to be one, and Secretary of [?at] War. But Grey did not seem to me to be pleased with one or two of the names, Hobhouse and Poulett Thompson especially. I cannot but think that it would have been better to overrule many objections felt by others and to have made Howick, who with all his blemishes is an able, laborious, and honourable man and a good speaker, Colonial Secretary. I had afterwards letters from Melbourne [and] Lansdowne confirming the news and informing me that the King comes for his new Ministers to Kiss hands tomorrow at twelve.

18 April Saturday. At ½ past 2, not twelve, we all attended the council, somewhat of a solemn not to say painful proceeding, for the King, poor Man, was constrained and nervous in declaring, with an 'I think fit' or an 'I think proper', the appointment to each in their turn to their respective offices. There were some there and more I suspect out of Cabinet very disagreable and in my judgement more really objectionable than those whom, to avoid shocking him, were more carefully than prudently avoided. In general the New Cabinet did not seem to me pleased and I suspect Melbourne himself is not satisfied and Grey far from being so much gratified as he expected. For myself I am only annoyed at having so good a place when I can do nothing for it, and I told Melbourne, Lansdown, and Johnny, with great sincerity, that I was ashamed of accepting the office, though I must own it was so agreable and so convenient to me that I could not refuse. It is in truth kind to have room for me at all, and certainly, helpless as I am, it is the seat I can fill with least discredit as well as most profit to myself. Some little difficulty occurred about Privy Seal. Wharncliffe, who held it, is in Yorkshire. He writes word he has left it [in] London, which he should not have done, and somewhat cavalierly says they may send to his house for it.

19 April Sunday. The appointments seem to please exceedingly. In truth the Subordinate Offices are admirably filled, and the Scotchmen and Young men—of both of which there was a dearth in 1830—have their due share in this arrangement. Lord Wellesley is I fear much hurt but will be pacified by the

Chamberlain's office, though a long visit from Brougham to him this day sufficiently indicates that the latter will take the line *in private* of fomenting the discontent of those who, like himself, are omitted. *In publick* he seems yesterday (for I was not in the house) to have been zealous and was disproportionately vehement in protecting Melbourne from the questions of Alvanley. Melbourne however judged right in answering them and answered them well; he disclaimed the obnoxious opinions and all positive treaty with OConnel, but avowed those opinions on Church Appropriation introduced in the resolutions, and expressed with emphasis his determination to enforce them. I wish he had added a phrase of accepting, where he had the fortune to agree, the votes and assistance of any man enjoying a portion of his Countrymen's confidence, with gladness and satisfaction.[35] But many are more squeamish than him on such points and Oconnel moreover is quite satisfied with Melbourne's answer.

The dispatches of Wellington, and especially those to Morier[36] in Switzerland, adhere not only to the treaties and engagements, but concur entirely in the instructions of Lord Palmerston and even congratulate themselves on their satisfaction with persevering in a course of Policy already adopted. They adhere to the policy and language of their predecessors and rejoice that they can and ought to be uniformly supported and pursued. These are strong admissions after the emotions and speeches of himself and Aberdeen. Lord Elliot's[37] mission is confined to exhortations of establishing a Cartel to avoid the cruel effusion of blood, to assurances of no intention of assisting the cause of Carlos, to representations of the hopelessness of that course, of the little assistance which the Northern Powers if so disposed could give him, inasmuch as they must conquer France and Spain and perhaps England and Portugal before it could be efficient, and to hints that if the endeavours to prevent an European war were to prove useless, France and England would commence operations by crushing him and his party. All these topicks except the first are merely unofficially treated; the exchange of prisoners is the only ostensible object of the Mission and directed of course to both parties. I understand that Genl. Alaba checked the Duke's disposition of offering mediation, compromise, or marriage between A Son of Carlos and the Queen of Spain, and even went so far as to assure him that any mention of such a project would make him return to Spain without loss [of] time. In short he justified the remark I have often made—that had the Spaniards in 1820 or 1821 sent him instead of Frias[38] to England, the Conduct of the latter power would have been very different.

20 April 1835. First Cabinet. All present. Should Lord Heytesbury's appointment to India be cancelled? Both Grant and Hobhouse disposed to cancel it, but two strong arguments urged by Lansdowne and others against it. First, although there is a clear right in the Government to cancel the appointment, there is not an equally clear power of substituting a Governor whose principles are more in consonance with those of Govt. or of the late Bill than Lord Heytesbury, and secondly, the exertion of the power of cancelling, in the very first instance after the bill, is likely to make such a proceeding the rule rather than the exception on the change of Government at home, an effect that would be injurious in two different ways to the publick service—by rendering the government of India less stable, permanent, and uniform, and by encreasing the difficulty of appointing proper Governors inasmuch as, if entirely dependant on changes at home, the Governorship General would cease to be such a prize for Statesmen, and indeed would be hardly worth the acceptance of those best qualified to fill it. It was agreed that Hobhouse, without any actual promise or even hint of his final intentions, should, on the score of his convenience, occupations, and election, request Lord Heytesbury to defer his departure and promise him an interview soon after his election and a consideration of his instructions. It was thought that Lord Amherst's appointment[39] should be confirmed and his Lordship dispatched as soon as Mr Grant had looked at the outline of his instructions. Mr Grant seemed rather reluctantly to acquiesce in this decision and, I have since understood, intends submitting it to our reconsideration. He was at the same time advised to accept and indeed to require the resignation of Mr Hay,[40] who has got his retiring pension and who is an inefficient officer from his state of health as well as a bitter political opponent, extremely inconvenient to our three successive Colonial Ministers—Ripon, Stanley, and Spring Rice. Howick was decided and vehement for his dismissal, but for Barrow[41] of the Admiralty, tho' equally averse to our politicks, there was more indulgence on the score of his long services and the good report Graham and Auckland concurred in giving of them. In general I thought there was more disposition in this Cabinet than in others of which I have been a Member to consider such personal questions as general rather than departmental. Melbourne and John must hold a firm hand on such discussions. John is clear, firm, and short and not all indisposed to assume, without offence, the authority his station as leader of Commons should invest him with in Council. He brought in the Attorney General to report on the little progress made on a bill for the regulation and reform of Corporation[s], to urge the necessity of proceeding immediately therein, and to press for a statement without delay of the general principles or outline on which it is to be drawn. It is impossible to settle such an affair in a Cabinet of 12 without some canvass to work upon. A Subcommittee, of which I am a Member, is named, and with the assistance of the Attorney and of one or two of the Commissioners we shall no doubt soon [have] digested some plan.[42]

22d. April 1835. Cabinet dinner at Lord Melbournes. Much conversation on appointments, dismissals, elections on the vacancies; and some on Canada, Speakership of Lords, and practicability of putting that, as well as Great Seal, in Commission (which Lord Denman very handsomely facilitates); on a letter from Don Carlos to the King, styling himself his Brother and asking for facilities, i.e. a King's Ship to convey his family, now in England, to Italy, also a letter from King or rather Sir Herbert to Palmerston, marking Duke of Wellington's entire approbation of his policy and indicating as usual the King's aversion and suspicion of Russia and her agents and especially of Pozzi di Borgo. Melbourne very chearful and pleasant but yet as he tells me almost confident that the discontented at arrangements will pare down our scanty majority and expose us to defeat and discomfiture. Tom Duncomb is among the most vehement of such Malcontents.

23. April. At Court and received the Duchy Seals. Lyndhurst gave up the great seal and shook hands gaily and good humouredly enough with his Successors, the three Commissioners—Pepys, Shadwell,[43] and Bosanquet[44]—as well as with myself and others of my Colleagues his acquaintance. Three impressions of the seal were taken and one of each delivered by the King to each of the Commissioners. The Senior of whom took the bag and seal and all three were sworn in together. It seems that the Speakership of the House of Lords can also be put in a sort of separate Commission which (as Denman is very handsomely willing to preside at political debates, and Lyndhurst, Brougham, and Abinger not indisposed to take the Appeals in rotation or by understanding) will be an arrangement useful to the publick and convenient to the Government. Wellesley was in attendance and appointed Lord Chamberlain. He is deeply hurt and spoke to me with great resentment, tho' he assured me he had discarded all such thoughts at the treatment he had received. I know not against whom that resentment is directed, for he seemed to make an exception of Melbourne. He had on the first suspicion of not returning to Ireland somewhat ludicrously assured me that he was ready to start for his post at a moment's notice and never felt so vigorous in mind and body, and he yet more ludicrously went about to all our friends in the House of Lords to impart to them severally the miraculous effects of a dose of physick which he had taken for an influenza, but which had swept away together with that disorder every ailment under which he had suffered for months or even years and left him more equal to action than ever! Yet in spite of these little foibles and ridicules and in spite of the deep chagrin and disappointment under which he was then labouring, the little Great Man, in the course of his ten minutes whisper with me this day, displayed an enlargement of views and developed a system of policy in Ireland which it will be well if those who succeeded him are half as capable of conceiving or even executing as he is. With all his foibles or vices he is more of a Statesman than those who laugh at the first or inveigh against the other immoderately.

24th. Introduced Mr Howard,[45] Lord Suffolk's son, a fine young man full of political zeal, to Lord Palmerston, who has named him Precis writer. Attended the Subcommittee of Cabinet on Corporation Reform at Home Office, and settled the outline (with some knotty points reserved for consideration) on which a draft of a bill is to be procured by Sir J Campbell,[46] Attorney General, who has no opposition at Edinburgh. Palmerston is very wisely desirous to consult his Colleagues on the Choice of his Embassador to Petersburgh.

25 April. I saw Melbourne and Lord Grey. The latter just returned from Stoke. He does not take a very chearful prospect of things. Indeed, unless by reversing Tubal's dexterity with Shylock. one speaks of his Child and praises (as one conscientiously may) the talent and application of Lord Howick to business, one is not likely to extract much of a favorable aspect to Melbourne's Ministry either in the way of remark or prediction. The King just before the Change, but when he no doubt foresaw it, asked him for his bust. The determination to place none but Members of Parliament <is> certain, adopted I believe at the suggestion of Ellice and Duncannon, is a wholesome and necessary one but not without objections. It compels the Ministry in some instances to appoint less efficient Men in the Offices, and hurts and disappoints many who have the claims of former service with the addition of having fought, tho' unsuccessfully, for a seat in Parliament and incurred expence for the cause.

26th. April 1835. Rogers gave me an account of the manner in which the literary pensions, for which Peel derives so much well earned credit, were granted. Aberdeen applied to Taylor,[47] the author of Philip de Arteville and a Clerk in the Colonial Office, for a list of those whose genius best entitled them to, and whose circumstances most required, pecuniary reward. Taylor drew up a paper containing the principles on which such relief should be administered by a government and describing the claims and circumstances of those who were the proper objects. Peel acquiesced and, according to Rogers, applied to that benevolent and judicious purpose the money which was left at the disposal of government by the extinction of Mr Arbuthnot's[48] pension and which he pointedly observed the Whigs had neglected and would have continued to neglect appropriating to any such beneficial object. It seems that in the papers which they had shewn Rogers was a correspondence between Brougham and Southey[49] on the former's accession to office. Brougham made great professions on the subject of rewarding literature and gave himself the air of consulting Southey on the means of doing so, ending by an offer of the Guelph (which he had not the power to bestow or Southey the inclination to receive), and Southey in a sarcastick answer exposed the hollowness and insincerity of B[rougha]m's profession, declined the favor, &c &c. There is something mortifying in the contrast which can plausibly at least be stated between this proceeding of Peel and the neglect in which men of genius such as Moore,[50] Wordsworth,[51] Farraday,[52] and others have been left to languish during these last few years.

The neglected or omitted among our own or former friends with the exception of Brougham and Durham (both and especially the former very painful but quite unavoidable omissions) are not numerous, nor likely to swell to any formidable amount the bulk of our enemies. Durham's dissatisfaction is not likely to be allayed by Lady Grey's intimation to him that the whole arrangement was settled by his friend, Mr Ellice. Mulgrave attempted to reconcile him some little time ago to Brougham, but Durham required a disavowal of the obnoxious article in the Ed[inbur]gh Review, which Brougham said he would willingly make, if the disavowal of one did not imply the avowal of such, as when required, he could not or would not disavow—a specious and adroit answer.

It is said that Alvanley has seriously requested Mr OConnel to wave his resolution of not fighting a duel, and to give him satisfaction for the insulting expression of *bloated buffoon.* The latter word it is added he does not care about, but *bloated* exasperates him beyond measure. Such scrurrility is disgusting and a bad sign of the times, but Alvanley brought this on himself by an uncalled for and unusual attack on an individual.[53] It is clear by Alava's account that Duke of Wellington adopted the spirit as well as letter of our Quadruple treaty, estranged himself from Beresford who is mortified and hurt thereat, reprimanded both Londonderry and Strangford for being officious in Miguel's or Don Carlos's and Duchesse de Beira's[54] affairs, observing that members or expectants in Diplomacy had nothing to do with unacknowledged Princes, and told some agent of Miguel, who was hinting at facilities to be granted for fitting out an expedition against the

Azores, that he would give as orders as peremptory and as instant to sink it as he did that of Saldanha. [*End of B M Add. MS 51870.*]

[*Beginning of BM Add. MS 51871.*]

[*On cover page:* These notes are generally written when I am half asleep, with a view of assisting my own memory (which is much fainter than it used to be) hereafter if I should have the leisure and perseverence to record the events of Lord Grey's and Lord Melbourne's administration. I should not be able, without some such assistance, to recollect the leading occurrences much less the succession, connection, and hidden causes of them.

By all whom it may concern

Be it remembered that this and other volumes of a similar diary imperfectly and irregularly kept in my hand writing are not intended for any thing like publication or general inspection. They may occasionally furnish materials for myself or any others if engaged in writing memoirs or any historical or biographical work, and yet more probably rectify or elucidate the dates and circumstances of other documents used for that purpose; but they are much too rambling, careless, and incorrect to be in themselves either a composition or part of a composition intended to convey my observations to posterity, or to augment or continue such memoirs of my own time as I have written or may however imperfectly compose hereafter.]

V[assall] H[olland] 23 July 1837

1835. May. The King somewhat reluctantly acquiesced in cancelling Lord Heytesbury's appointment and leaving Metcalfe[55] in the Government of India till Lord Wm. Bentinck's return. He significantly reminded Lord Melbourne that, before November last, the latter step had been represented to him as improper and even hazardous.

6th. May. The news of John Russell's defeat in Devonshire was confirmed and many plans suggested for bringing him into Parliament, among which My Son Charles very handsomely had one of vacating Stroud. He wrote both to John and his own friends in Stroud to prepare for it without apprizing me. I attended the Levee but not the Privy Council, where Labouchere was sworn in, and I also attended the Lancaster Duchy Council and transacted much of that business which forms the chief occupation of that grave body. A Cabinet dinner at Lansdown House. Long, important, but dull discussions on Irish Church bills and English Corporation bill in Cabinet. The delays of the Commissioners on Irish Church or at least of their Central Committee in England (arising from some little jealousy of authority about their brother Commissioners in Ireland[56]) threaten to embarrass us much and must be corrected by strong admonitions from Melbourne and Duncannon. Peel told OHanlon,[57] a blundering busy Irish Attorney who contrived to stay in with both Governments, that he might communicate his intended bill on Irish tithe to Duncannon on condition that the concessions proposed in it should not be brought up against him in debate. The subject is very perplexing and complicated. Our general notion seems to be to adhere as much as possible to the provisions of our last years bill with the addition of a clause for appropriating the surplus and of some provisions for the reduction of livings where no Protestant service is required or performed, which will give the publick a chance of obtaining such surplus. The Franchise in Corporate towns was much canvassed, that of the £10 householders, tho' adopted in Reform and found to work well in the Scotch Burghs, would be impracticable and inconvenient in England.[58] It is better to alter the qualification altogether and Coll. Drinkwater,[59] Mr Blackburne,[60] and the Commissioners as well as most of our House of Commons Friends strongly recommend the payment of rates for three years as the safest and best qualifications. Spring Rice vehemently opposed it. The decision deferred till Lord John's return who is expected tomorrow. All decisive measures to ensure his return are likewise suspended till he is consulted. Melbourne has written to Lord FitzWilliam, and My Son Charles very handsomely taken steps to secure his return <here> for Stroud on a vacancy, and offered on finding it sure to make that vacancy and retire. This at least does him credit.

The King was very averse to recall Lord Aylmer,[61] holds in horror the idea of substituting an elective for an appointed Council in Canada, and is in general very suspicious and very difficult about the instructions relating to that Colony.

9th. May Saturday. Attended a Cabinet which was long and tiresome owing to the details of the Corporation bill and the very complicated and perplexing questions of the arrears of tythes and debts to and from the Clergy of Ireland. Grant, now Lord Glenelg, left us to see Lord Amherst and returned with the intelligence that he had declined, but in a manner and with expressions highly satisfactory and indeed creditable both to himself and to us. He acknowledges not only with frankness but with gratitude that Lord Glenelg and the Cabinet's conduct to him has been honourable and considerate, begs him to convey his sense of obligation to us, assures us that so far from being dissatisfied at the proposed addition of other Commissioners[62] he thinks it a wise and prudent measure and one which would render his appointment, if he accepted it, more satisfactory to himself, and he has no scruple in acknowledging that such alterations as we had suggested in the instructions seemed to him an improvement of them.

By the evening mail Charles and John Russell went down to Stroud. It was cold and John Russell, who was unwell, sleepy, and faint, was much wrapped up and extremely silent and languid. Charles very attentive to him. A Gentleman in the Mail, who by his conversation shewed himself to be a very violent tory, is said to have persuaded himself that our spirited little patriot, Leader and bridegroom as he is, was a damsel in disguise and in the act of eloping with Charles. However on the arrival of the Mail at Maidenhead, he ascertained the names of his Companions and imagined his discovery of such importance that he abandoned his projected journey and returned in a post Chaise to communicate the important intelligence to the Conservative Club. They no doubt took immediate plans to ascertain the possibility of meeting Lord John with an opposition at Stroud, and there is as little that they can find hardly any to harrass and none certainly to endanger his return.

From 10th. to Wednesday 13th. May. Lady Holland was, I think unreasonably, disposed to lament Charles's generosity in giving up Stroud for Lord John and to censure the latter for accepting it. But surely it is natural that he should prefer being obliged to a friend rather than a stranger, and it is prudent and right that he should be rechosen to Parliament by a Constituency really independent and yet not connected with radicals and Oconnellites. He thus exempts himself and his party from the reproach, either of having preserved snug family boroughs for their own convenience or truckling to OConnel or the Radicals for the seat of our leader. Lady Holland fears that this incident may separate Charles from Stroud (to him the most convenient, creditable, and fortunate connection that he could have formed) for ever. That there is some danger of this result cannot be denied, and that that danger enhances the merit of the sacrifice I think Lord John and the party must, for they ought, to feel.

13 May Wednesday. At a very crouded Levee. Alava very naturally anxious about Spain, seems desirous that our Govt. should take into early consideration some means of assisting the Queen in subduing the insurrection of Don Carlos without any introduction of French troops into Spain. There is in his head as well as in others some vague notion of the possibility of employing Portugueze troops and English and French cruizers in that enterprize, but would Portugueze be efficient? [*In the margin:* At the same Levee Palmerston told me that Lewis Philip indicated some little design of proposing one of his sons for Donna Maria's hand (a project that must be resisted), but was in his heart as averse to armed interference in Spain as we could be and willing and even anxious to regulate his course and his language on that subject by our advice—a reason for determining our own course.]

The Chief Commissioner Adam was sworn in Privy Councillor and the King was really gracious and cordial in his reception of him as an old friend. These Royal virtues of graciousness and cordiality do not seem to me to be in daily wear with His Majesty just now. He is manifestly constrained and unhappy not to say discontented and sulky. He observed more than once with <*humour*> to Argyll that *Wellesley* was totally unable to execute his office of Chamberlain, sneered at his way of crossing the room, and grumbled at his absenting himself another court day on the plea of health. Whether these remarks were repeated to Lord Wellesley, or whether his mortification at not being reappointed to Ireland recurred so strongly that he could not endure it, or whether he discovered that by keeping up the state of Lord Chamberlain he would more than exhaust the salary which was in a prudential view his chief motive for accepting it, Certain it is that he resigned and alledged in his letter tendering his resignation that the *Constitution* of the Irish Government was such as he could not but consider as 'derogatory to his honor'. But as there has been no change in that constitution since his acceptance of the Chamberlainship, the reason will hardly justify or even explain the step he has taken.

We dined this day at Palmerston's. Nearly all the time was occupied in the renewal of those topicks relating to Corporation bill, Church of Ireland bill, and Canada which have occupied us so incessantly of late. On the outlines of Corporation bill we are however pretty well agreed. In the relinquishment of the £10 Qualification and the substitution of payment of rate, Spring Rice at last seems reluctantly, and not without some occasional recurrence to his opinion, to have acquiesced. Mr Poulett Thompson's earnestness for a Magistracy elected for ten years in preference to an election for life was overruled by rendering the number of Magistrates indefinite and thus providing against the inconvenience of a large majority of incapable and superannuated Men.[63] The Surplus appropriation and still more the adjustment of the various claims of Govt. upon Clergy, of Clergy upon the Land and of land owners on the Government, all which must be comprehended in our Irish bill, appear more and more perplexing the nearer we approach it. This necessity of some simple, distinct, and intelligible plan may drive us to the adoption of one which, if successful, will effect a great good, and if rejected, will at least do us credit with the country and posterity for having manfully endeavoured to atchieve what common sense and reason require and what must be sooner or later accomplished, viz the suppression of an endowed Church for the minority of the people and the substitution of a stipendiary Clergy, well provided in proportion to the duty they are called upon to perform for that minority—the residue of the same provision to be applied to the education of all without reference to their religion [*In the margin:* and then but longo intervallo some provision derived from other funds for the Catholick Clergy].

May 14 to May 19 inclusive. On my return to Holland House I was confined with some gout in my left hand. Many of the various persons suggested for Canada—Minto, Seaford, and others—have declined. It came to my knowledge that Durham, if it were proposed, would go, but when I mentioned this fact to Melbourne, without venturing opinion for or against the offer, I ascertained that the other Northern appointment, Russia, is in contemplation for him! a much safer one for the country than the other and I suppose less disagreable to him than it was. Palmerston is said to have corrected the habits which rendered him unpopular and Durham may possibly find some pretext for overcoming his *invincible* repugnance to serving under him. I wish those little blemishes in Palmerston's Ministerial character may be as much obliterated as it is said they are, but I learnt from Granville that he had kept Lord Cowley an hour and half and Lord Eliott nearly three waiting at F[oreign] O[ffice], and had not seen either after all. Pozzo di Borgo dined with me on the Friday. He is out of spirits and disconcerted at his removal from France. They say that he often insinuated to the Emperor Nicholas that Russian affairs in England were ill managed and that his agents here did not understand the Country, and that Nicholas, either from conviction or from malice, said, 'Since he understands England so well, Let him go there and manage matters himself'. Minto justly observes that our King is wrong in disliking his being here, for Pozzo will be less Russian in his views than any other Embassador employed by that Court. He will of course do what he is bid, but in nothing but European politicks and certainly not in Turkish, Persian, or Asiatick designs will he ever originate any thing or even act with any relish or zeal whatever. Right however or wrong, the King cannot surmount his repugnance to the two Corsicans now Embassadors at his Court—Pozzo and Sebastiani. Melbourne and Palmerston are distressed at his incivility to them. His repugnance is so strong that he avoids inviting the Austrian—who has come to acknowledge the compliment on the accession of the Emperor[64]—to Windsor and the giving any balls, dinners, or parties at St. James's, mainly because he thinks he can do neither without including Pozzo and Sebastiani.

Conyngham is Chamberlain. Lichfield,[65] whom Melbourne reckons the pleasantest and even one of the ablest men in England, the Postmaster. He is fighting Staffordshire to great disadvantage. Lord Hatherton's (Littleton's) peerage, in addition to its many other objections, was very unseasonable for securing a Whig Member for the County. The peerage, owing to the implied promise of Althorp, could not well have been avoided, but it has hurt Grey and provoked many exceedingly. Duncannon has thought of substituting a general quit Rent (in other words a new and practical acreable land tax in Ireland) for the rent charge and composition intended for equivalents of tithes, and contends that by loans whose interest shall be charged on it and by its annual proceeds all the payments (save that of the million from Clergy) may be amply provided for and a larger surplus left for education, according to [the] resolutions [of the House of Commons]. To this I understand Spring Rice vehemently objects, and he has persuaded Lord Lansdown that it is unjust to vary the proportion of burden hitherto borne by the respective Landholders in Ireland for the maintenance of Anglican Clergy. The two schemes however are to be circulated and the comparative merits and objections of each to be clearly [*unfinished. In the margin:* Note June 5: This was not done this Session and the better scheme abandoned, partly from difficulties in reconciling some of the Cabinet to it, but chiefly from the facilities which the concurrence of Irish Members in a further sacrifice afforded the other less satisfactory and more complicated plan. I am sorry; to this complexion if not *we* some *successors* of ours must come at last.]

19th. May. Lord Melbourne and Mr Ellice dined here and we had much agreable and confidential talk over men and things. Melbourne seemed to me in great spirits, and not averse to the notion of proceeding rapidly and decidedly with Corporation bill first and then framing a plain and intelligible measure for rendering the Protestant Clergy in Ireland stipendiary in future, for providing for the general education of that people, and for entirely abrogating tythes, compositions, arrears, lands &c, &c, and meeting the expences by a new and equitable valuation and tax on Irish Land. He is aware of the difficulty of passing such a bill, but he seems to me aware of the interminable difficulties and small advantages of any other course and, above all, of the advantage and comfort, if we are beat, of falling back on creditable, tenable, and important ground. He bade me see Anglesey the moment he arrived to explain to him what happened about Ordnance, and ascertain if he has any, and if any, what, wishes. His brother, Sir Arthur, has declined Canada. I hope he would do the same, for I have a stronger affection for him than for that Colony.

20th. May. Cabinet dinner at Lord Glenelg's: in going thither called on Lord Anglesey who had arrived in 11 hours from Calais through Dover. [*In the margin:* He was generally friendly to Melbourne's Government but had his misgivings about OConnel.] [*The remainder of this page is crossed out, with the marginal comment,* 'repeated afterwards'. *Some of the material, however, is not repeated, and is therefore transcribed as follows:* He (Anglesey) assured me that he should not have liked the ordnance as far as his own pleasure went, should have disliked it with Cabinet worse than without, but but should yet have felt it awkward to accept it without when he had once held it with the Cabinet. He seemed to me not absolutely disinclined to high Military office, criticized our disposal of Ordnance as lowering the Station and Rank of the Master, and our acquiescence in the continuance of Hill as a virtual surrender of the Army to Wellington, and spoke with approbation of a scheme of consolidating the two offices as a measure of oeconomy and one, he contended, not unpleasant to the army. He was generally friendly to Melbourne's Government but had his misgivings about OConnel.]

We had still the eternal discussions at Glenelg's on the details of Corporation bills, Magistracies for lives or for ten years &c; but John, who is returned in both senses from Stroud, gives notice and asks leave to bring in the bill tomorrow. It was also agreed that he should announce to his friends and to the house the inclination of the Govt. to confine themselves this year to the Corporation and Irish Church bill and to leave Church rates[66] and other matters on which he should be questioned to future consideration, and that he should hold a meeting for that purpose on Saturday. Some conversation on Spain, on the impossibility of permitting French armed intervention, on the expediency and difficulty of devizing any thing short of intervention which would extricate the Queen and Cortes of Spain from their present precarious condition.

On the 21 or 22 or 23 Ellice and Melbourne and others dined with me,[67] and Melbourne, on being pressed though without indelicacy or importunity to employ none where opinions were known to be adverse to our politicks, broke out into an abrupt, violent, and extravagant fury, in which however there was little enmity and no bitterness or personality against any one. He clenched his first, stamped his foot, gnashed his teeth, crying, 'Let's hear no more of the subject'. 'Now have done with it forever.' 'I will not hear of it, So by God say no more on the subject', and similar ejaculations with similar gesticulations ensued; but as there was nothing to provoke the passion, so there was nothing in the passion itself to hurt anybody. It was ludicrous rather than injurious, and there was in truth nothing to lament but that such an exhibition of anger had occurred in the presence of persons unconnected with office, who had no motives to suppress their comments on so strange an outbreak [*In the margin:* but a delicate sense of propriety which, however, to their great credit, was found quite sufficient to seal their lips]. Melbourne ended all by a laugh. He did not wait for the arrival of Mrs Norton[68] and Lady Seymour,[69] full of the atchieved elopement of their brother with Miss Grant,[70] to put him in good humour. He learnt from me with some disappointment but with great candour and acknowledgement of Whishaw's[71] honourable conduct that he could not resign his Auditorship for Gossett.[72] He told me and Charles that he would place him as Secretary of Ordnance without loss of time, and he adopted my suggestion of offering Lord Clements[73] to be Vice Chamberlain [*In the margin:* who afterwards refused it].

I had on the 21st. called on Anglesey. He assured me that he would not have taken ordnance without Cabinet, tho' in fact he should have liked it better than with that honour. He also assured me he *wanted* nothing, which I believe; he added however that a junction of Mastership of Ordnance and Horse Guards would be a very judicious measure, and dwelt on it in a way that persuaded me he would not dislike or at least might easily be prevailed on to accept it. Wellesley was with him when I went to Uxbridge House. He wished not to see me, from which I gathered that he very erroneously suspected me of concerting and concealing the design of excluding him from Ireland, whereas I knew nothing of it till it was done and wrote to him the moment I suspected (contrary to my first expectations and yet more so to my wishes) that such was to be the case. I wrote and called to explain, and he acquitted me but protested against the usage he had received as unequalled 'in antient or modern record'. Melbourne shewed me subsequently his letter upon a paragraph in the Times respecting his resignation, in which he distinctly denies that either the procession[74] or Oconnel furnished the grounds of his resignation, and says that with respect to the latter he agreed with Melbourne and 'deprecates persecution or exclusion of Mr OConnel, and as much the being governed by him'. When questioned in the house he denied the procession being the cause as *stoutly*, but somewhat shabbily left the topick of OConnel untouched. [*In the margin:* In truth he had in his passion held a different language and assigned different reasons to the Duke of Cumberland, who together with Londonderry was disposed illnaturedly to Wellesley and Melbourne to make his weakness and inconsistency subservient to factious purposes.]

Saturday 23d. A Cabinet at Treasury. Much Parliamentary business discussed. The Gaol bill[75] contains excellent regulations, but are made on some subjects so peremptory and absolute (such as on separation and silence of all before or after conviction) that I cannot support it unless altered. Spring Rice has suggested an admirable method of relieving the County rates from various expences to the amount of 80,000 per annum or more, and yet making it the interest of Magistrates and Country Gentlemen to keep down the expences of prosecutions both at Assizes and Quarter Sessions. It was agreed to make the Privy Council report forthwith on the London University.[76] And I am to apprize Radnor to defer his bill for abrogating subscriptions.[77]

24th. May 1834 [*1835*]. Saw Mr Coke; delighted at his association and full of health and vigor; and Anglesey pleased with his conversation with Melbourne and not wrought upon by the Malcontents who besiege him. Palmerston who dined here went away without speaking to me about Spain, but Mendizabal who called afterwards urged me to enforce his request of repealing the Foreign Enlistment bill without loss of time and allowing and encouraging English subjects to join corps and enter into the Service of the Queen of Spain. General Alaba is to present a note to press us to do so.

25th. May. Renewal of questions about the procession in honour of Lord Mulgrave. One would really suppose that 'a flag with a cap of liberty', 'a harp without a crown', and what not were sins against the Holy Ghost, in such set terms do the Godly rail against these harmless symbols of liberty and national feeling. However the testimony of Lord Leitrim,[78] the only peer who witnessed the procession and was present in Lords , and the manifest folly of the whole charge, have mitigated the language and feeling of the house. Granville took leave of me. Writ for Tiverton was moved and Palmerston thinks himself sure of being returned.[79]

26th. May. The news from Spain contained in French dispatches from Madrid and communicated by Sebastiani is very bad, announcing discouragement and division in the Queen's army, almost equal discomfiture in her councils, approaching application for French assistance and little prospect of salvation with out it. These lamentable reports are to be corrected in some little degree but not wholly by the reflection that the writer, Rayneval,[80] is more disposed to intervention than his court, that Cordova, on whose report from the army he chiefly relies, is an intrigant, and that even in his account of the anxiety for French protection there are admissions which prove that that desire is far from being universal. It proves however the urging of some such plan as that which Mendizabal suggested, and accordingly at the Cabinet it was resolved that Alaba should make some application for permission under the Foreign Enlistment bill to engage British Subjects in the service of Spain and that the repeal of that bill altogether should be facilitated by Government. At the same Cabinet held at Chancellor of Exchequer's a perplexing question from Lord Mulgrave was laid before us by Lord John and Lord Duncannon respecting the employment of Military force to maintain peace and the difficulty of distinguishing between keeping the peace and levying the tithes. It was agreed to follow as nearly as we can the instructions and system of the late Secretary and the Attorney General, and to circulate some letter or general orders to the officers to make them understand and communicate to all concern[ed] that they c<a>me to prevent or put down a breach of the peace and not to levy tithes, and that if their presence be thought to facilitate the levy of it, it cannot and ought not be thought to protect those who, *contrary* to law, attempt to raise it at night and by force. Palmerston not gone to Tiverton but confident. Spring Rice much and justly pleased with his successful reply to Peel.[81]

In House of Lords, Bishop of Exeter [was] exposed in a good humoured but powerful speech of Lord Brougham for his disingenuous and uncharitable attack on two Commissioners for Irish Church, He felt abashed, and Orangemen themselves, especially Lord Farnham, seemed ashamed of him. These instances of intolerance and intemperate language of Churchman in Ireland, together with the inordinate disposition between Catholicks and Protestants in number, and between the endowments of the latter and their duties, performed or required, divulged in reports, insensibly have their effect on the soberminded in England and I think in spite of party spirit the publick and even the Lords themselves are better reconciled to the notion of a reduction of Church revenue in Ireland, in a Ministry disposed to accomplish it here, than they were three Months ago. They will vote however for neither. If Brougham could conduct himself as he did this day, he would soon recover his lost ground. His speech cheered our side, disarmed the other, and delighted all but the Bishop himself, who smarted under it.

27 May 1835. Cabinet dined at Lord Duncannon's. London dissenters friendly, but apprehensive that their brethren in the Country will be less so at the postponement of general Registration, Marriage bill, and abolition of Church rates. They urge a declaration from Lord John, if not some resolution of the house, pledging government to a favorable consideration of all these matters.[82] They are entitled to it and, in spite of foreseen difficulties in the detail, we consented to gratify them. Renewed discussion on the qualification of voters in municipal elections. Decided after an appel nominal by 7 or 8 to 3 in favor of resident three year ratepayers instead of ten pounders. I think this right. It is necessary to confine the vote for Members of Parliament to men of some independence and intelligence, but there is no reason to confine votes for the management of their own funds to the same class, and it is wholsome that the voters for Parliament should be taught that they have not a monopoly of all rights—that others, incapable of voting on these occasions, yet Enjoy privileges, and that it was not the intention of Parliament in extending the franchise to create any species of oligarchy in the country.

The compliance with vote of House of Commons about London University is unavoidable but perplexing, and the more so as Lord Brougham, who will attend Privy Council, deludes himself with the notion that he can prevail with them to come to a resolution and report far beyond that for which they are prepared. It was agreed to reject the application for charter as there prayed for in Privy Council on Friday, and then to settle on Saturday how to comply with the House of Commons address.[83] Gosford will go to Canada and the King highly approved the suggestion, saying he was a sensible, firm man and had shewn himself to be so in discharging the duties of Captain of the Yeomen, which should be known.

28th. May. King's birthday kept. Lameness prevented me from going to crouded drawroom, but not from receiving the Officers of Duchy at dinner. Mendizabal and Count [*blank*], the companion and Mentor of the poor Duke of Leuchtenberg, called in evening. The first told me the King had consented to our order in Council permitting British Subjects to enlist in Army of Queen of Spain,[84] but that intelligence had arrived from Madrid this day of an intended application to France and England for joint and armed cooperation, and information that the Councils were weak divided and torn by intrigue and faction and all in consternation and confusion. Mendizabal was anxious to find Palmerston. The French Count seemed really deeply affected at the death of Leuchtenberg and spoke with much feeling and emotion of the event.

29th. May to 5th. June. I was in South Street and this book at Holland House. In the course of those six or seven days I attended Duchy Council once, Court and Council, Parliament and Cabinet. At the first, ordinary business; at a Council held after the Levee, The Recorder's report of the Central Criminal court contained a case of rape on a child not ten years, in which, after much deliberation and a discussion highly creditable to the humanity and discrimination of King, Chief Justice, and Recorder, we came to the painful but I think necessary and just conclusion of leaving the convicted criminal to execution. The King, with tears in his eyes and with more propriety of diction than is usual with him, owned that in so painful a discharge of duty as that he was performing, he could not but confess that he had one consolation, that the case, in which a Man so humane and so just as Lord Denman abstained from recommending the Culprit to Mercy, must be one of an atrocious nature, and he could not but take this melancholy opportunity, and he had hitherto sought one in vain, of expressing his satisfaction at the manner in which his Lordship discharged this part of his duty and secured him from the possibility of reproach from himself or others from being betrayed into any unnecessary severity.

Our Cabinets, including a dinner at the Admiralty, were chiefly occupied with the difficult and tiresome subject of the Irish tithe commutation and surplus appropriation. Its somewhat unintelligible provisions were well expounded by Duncannon, Spring Rice, Mr Thompson, Lord Howick, and Lord Lansdowne, but it must be owned that the dulness of the subject was not relieved by the practical rather than oratorical way in which Lord Duncannon submitted each clause to our consideration. We altered the criterion for regulating the payment of the Curates and Incumbents from a scale founded on the number of Protestants to a less definite but less hazardous phrase of the amount of duty to be performed. This alteration will, it is hoped, obviate or at least soften the Archbishop of Dublin's objections, who considers the mention of numbers as an instigation to the Catholicks to murder Protestants and to Protestants to eject Catholicks.[85] Howick throughout these discussions and those on Corporations and other matters shews great knowledge, perspicuity, and good sense, and if his impetuosity now and then betrays too much confidence in his own opinion, it is not such as to my taste renders the discussion painful or unpleasant.

The Spaniards, including Martinez de la Rosa and Alaba, hitherto the most averse to French intervention, urged the prompt entrance of a French army into Spain, and the reports not only of Rayneval but of Villiers, Lord Eliot, Gurwood,[86] and Wylde[87] confirmed the apprehension that without such intervention the Queen's Government must fall a victim to Carlist insurrection or to some revolutionary movements at Madrid. There was however great reluctance in both our Kings, for different reasons, to listen to any such proposal, though both manifestly might be brought to concur in it, more readily as the means of crushing revolutionary designs than as a necessary precaution for keeping out the Pretender. Alava, tho' empowered to ask this assistance formally, was instructed however to feel the pulse of the Government first, and Broglie wrote a private letter to Sebastiani, which he shewed to Palmerston &c, and which distinctly bid him ascertain, first whether we considered ourselves and the French bound by treaty to furnish assistance to the Queen; secondly, if there was in our judgement no such obligation, whether we thought in policy we should offer a joint cooperation; and thirdly, whether, if it did not suit us to take any steps of the sort in conjuction in [?with] France, we should nevertheless approve and sanction the march of her army into Spain and consider ourselves *solidaire* in such an undertaking, that is, prepared to make common cause with her, if a general war should ensue. These questions, especially the last, were precisely the same as those which Talleyrand had put to Palmerston at the time of the [Quadruple] treaty, and Palmerston had met by postponing the answer till the case of necessity should arise. That case seemed fast approaching and, embarrassing as it was in itself, it perplexed us yet more from the various opinions and inclinations both in the French and English Courts and Councils on the propriety and practicability of any armed interference that would be efficacious. However we at last learnt from Lord

Granville that Louis Philippe was positively determined, *come what will,* not to consent that a French army should enter Spain, and that He, Louis Philippe, had assured Lord G[ranville] that there were only 12,000 disposable men now in France and that it would require at least three Months to procure or march a force (which should be 80 and could not be less than 50 thousand men) at all adequate to the undertaking. This was conclusive as to marching an army across the Pyrenees, but Alava was earnest in his entreaties to us not to send a flat refusal of all succours or assistance and Palmerston was equally anxious to devize some method, short of an army entering Spain, that in the spirit of the treaty would tend to rescue the Queen from her difficulties, to crush the Carlists and pacify the anarchists in Spain. The reinforcement of the French Cordon to intercept supplies might be officially insisted upon and ostentatiously made. British subjects by an order in Council might be encouraged to enlist in the armies of the Queen and relieved from the penalties of the Foreign Enlistment bill, and that step might be accompanied with restoration to British rank of Sartorious, Napier, and other Volunteers in Portugal. A Frigate or two might visit Passages or St. Andero [*Santander*] and the French and English Embassadors at Madrid be instructed to enforce all advice, however unpalatable, which would tend to pacify the parties and remodel the armies in Spain, such as the removal of disaffected, suspected or intriguing persons from all places of trust, attempts to reconcile the existence of provincial privileges in the Cantabrian provinces with general representation and, above all, the establishment of any army of reserve under the command of some Foreign General to be organized by foreign and for the most part British officers. To the latter expedient, All Spaniards will feel a repugnance, for their pride is so constructed that they conceive it less degrading to be ruined, oppressed, overun, and conquered in consequence of notorious cowardice, dishonesty, and incapacity, than to receive improvement and security at the hands of strangers at their own invitation and of their own appointment. Alava is aware of this wrongheaded propensity of his Countrymen, but does not partake of it. His presence here is agreable to us and may be highly beneficial to his Country, and he has moreover greater influence in softening his friend the Duke of W[ellingto]n's distrust of our policy than in furnishing him or his followers with materials for attacking it.

Wellington both in private and publick not only speaks well of our past negotiations but deprecates all harrassing questions on what is going on and very handsomely rebuked Lord Londonderry in the Lords for his inconsiderate motions for papers &c. He (the Duke) says our first duty is to protect Portugal and all that is necessary to that end must be done. Grey, less aware out than in office of the difficulties too fatally attending deliberations of this sort, was decidedly for interference and will no doubt think our councils pusillanimous. Perhaps if in office he would find, as he often did in the case of Portugal, that a bolder and better policy was impracticable and a fruitless attempt at it more subversive of the end proposed than the relinquishment or modification of the undertaking in contemplation.

6 June Saturday. A Cabinet where we decided on a Commission to enquire into the Accomodation of Churches in Scotland and talked over many matters pending in Parliament and other things, among the rest the necessity of granting forthwith

Charters to the London University and King's College and of consulting Lord Brougham thereupon.[88] The plan most approved, to constitute both of them by Charter, Colleges, but to establish a separate board to grant degrees to those educated thereat. The qualifications of examiners and the appointment of them postponed for consideration. Saw several House of Commons friends all pleased with Corporation bill, some surprized at Peel's admission of principle to its full extent.[89] His Tory friends said to be yet more so. Stanley's friends annoyed and his enemies in our party much delighted at his silence, which Peel's more popular course renders yet more offensive.

Sunday 7th. John Russell had given up his visit to Woburn in consequence of some circumstances that have transpired respecting the Man left for execution next Tuesday, or rather respecting the child he was convicted of violating, which may lead to a respite and commutation of punishment. There are stories which would prove her, young as she is, not only to be artful and possibly false and malignant, but more depraved and debauched in body and mind than her tender years would imply. John Russell has seen Melbourne and Denman. The truth will be further sifted to morrow and in all probability the punishment commuted to transportation for life.

Monday 8th., tuesday 9th. At Holland House. The Man Williams was pardoned, at least his punishment commuted. The whole matter should have been sifted before, but in the result the decision is right. Such seems the depravity of the Child that Denman doubts even of the Man's guilt.

10th. Dined with Cabinet at Mr Spring Rice and remained in South Street

till 14th. during which time and till 16th. I neglected this diary.

10th. to 16th. June. Little of an interesting nature in Commons, less of course in Lords—a foolish attempt to prevent travelling on a Northern railroad on a Sunday made by Bishop of Hereford, supported vaguely by Roden and the Saints and, for the sake of appearances I suppose, by all the Bishops present (of whom Maltby was not one) led to a curious division shewing the force of the Saints, who were left however in a Minority.[90] Lord Harrowby voted with, Wharncliffe spoke and voted against them. Aberdeen in moving for a copy of Canada commission took occasion to lament and somewhat to misrepresent the change from Amherst to Gosford, to infer from it great change in the instructions, and to withdraw his responsibility from instructions on which, if they had remained unaltered, he would willingly have borne his share. Grant, now Glenelg, answered him clearly and courteously, with a good and unassuming manner, but Aberdeen contrived in his explanations to imply that any change which had been made must have impaired the liberality of the measure, and Melbourne and Glenelg allowed the artful insinuation to pass without exposing it.

Strangford asked a foolish question about the Volunteers in Spanish service, which was no further remarkable than it led to a notice from the Duke of Wellington for Monday 15th. which he afterwards abandoned—a circumstance which confirms the conjecture of a great difference between him and the Ultra Tories on the propriety of stirring foreign questions and proves the justness of a remark I have long since made, that the presence of General Alava as Spanish

Embassador is, with reference to the confidence he inspires and to the hostility he disarms, worth an army to the Spanish cause. We issued at his request on Wednesday 10th. an order in Council permitting British subjects to engage in the service of the Queen of Spain, but we admonished him that the Men so enlisting could not consistently with our Laws be formed and trained in this Country. He has advertized for Volunteers and Recruits and has, I understand, engaged Coll. Evans and several other Officers. He has acted on his own responsibility and prevailed on us to substitute these and similar measures in France, England, and Portugal in lieu of the invasion of Spanish territory, which, chiefly owing to the repugnance of L[ouis] Philippe to the step (enforced with some disingenuous and suspicious arguments), was impossible. At Palmerston's suggestion I wrote to Martinez de la Rosa in praise of Alava's zeal and intelligence and extolling the importance and value of this suspension of the Foreign Enlistment bill. It is evident that Mendizabal prefers it to actual Military intervention and, if his way of seeing it is any indication of the feelings of the Ultra liberal party in Spain, it may possibly do as much for the cause of the Queen and excite less discontent in the publick than the entrance of a French army.

The Changes in Portugal have an ugly appearance—the effect or cause of them, I know not—which has been an estrangement between the Empress and the young Queen. The latter has been prevailed upon through Females of the Palmela party to dismiss suddenly and unexpectedly part of the Ministry who had secured her majorities in Cortes, and she has done so at the moment when those Cortes are prorogued. The Queen, Saldanha,[91] and Palmela write most earnest and even fulsome letters to Mendizabal, entreating him to continue their agent in finance matters, but he with great truth and disinterestedness, though he complies with the request, remarks both to Palmerston *and to them* that such solicitations to an individual are proofs of weakness and want of real system and plan rather than of confidence. 'If,' he said to me, 'it was a bad thing for a King of near 70 years of age and after a reign of four prosperous years suddenly to dismiss Lord Melbourne who had a majority of the House of Commons in his favor, what is it for a raw girl of 16 to do the same at the instigation of a Court intrigue?' I strongly urged Palmerston to read Palmela a lecture thro' Howard [de Walden] on the folly and wickedness of sowing divisions in the Royal family as well as on the danger in appearance as well as reality of departing from the policy of Don Pedro.

At our Cabinets we decided sundry home matters—the suppression of Militia staff a skeleton, a measure of oeconomy which will be very disagreable to King but which is right; resistance to Buxton's motion on West Indies, which would open the whole question of apprenticeships, alarm the West Indians about the compensation, and thereby discourage those who are bona fide exerting themselves at much trouble and expence to make the new system work well.[92] They reckon on the indemnity money as part of their means. It seems, by a very sensible letter from Sir Wm. Gage,[93] our Admiral in the Tagus, that the young Queen in the late transactions has shewn great levity and caprice, some duplicity and much intrepidity, not to say violence of character. When Freire was admitted to her presence one day, she greeted him by expressing a hope that he was come to 'tender his resignation'; he hesitated, and said he was not prepared to do so. She replied, you had better, for 'if not I will dismiss you directly'. She affected the greater tenderness for her Stepmother the Empress, protested with tears that she never could be happy but with another brother of hers,[94] insisted on sleeping in her room &c, and was all the while employed in defeating the negotiation for the marriage with the Leuchtenbergh prince and conveying messages, perhaps with the knowledge of Palmela and the Ladies of his faction, to the Duke of Nemours. When that intrigue was defeated and she learnt that even L[oui]s Philippe hesitated about it, she stamped with her feet, clenched her teeth, and exclaimed she should like to tear him to pieces &c.

[*In the margin:* Duke of Leinster dined here the 13th. and 18th. He declined, as I foresaw he would, the St Patricks. I told him that as A Minister I should have pressed him to take it, but as a friend I was glad he persisted in his uniform contempt for such baubles. 'To be sure,' said he, 'but you know they say it's because I am so ambitious and would be content with nothing but a blue Ribband. The truth is I had just as <leave> have one as the other.' He laughed heartily and I believe he is quite sincere and therefore much more philosophical and sensible than many who pass for wiser men.]

On the 16th [*In the margin:* Duke of] Lavradio,[95] formerly Almeyda, called with Sarmento, now raised to the title of Torrecorvo [*Torre de Moncorvo*] and he assured me that the quarrel between the Queen and Empress at Lisbon was not so serious as reported. It is said however that the Empress is to come away.

17th. Went for an hour and 1/2 to Cabinet dinner at Lord John's. The King took the opportunity of the scheme for reducing the remains of Militia (which Melbourne always foretold he would dislike) to read the Cabinet a long lecture on the dangerous projects and prodigious armaments of Russia and on the necessity of being prepared for war, when a Power, *not shackled as the Kings of England and France are by assemblies niggardly in their supplies, indifferent to the foreign relations of their country* till the *hour of jeopardy* was come, and *shortsighted* and *speculative* (rather different qualities these!) in their views, was pursuing a systematick plan of military encroachment and aggression and had formed an Armament on the Baltick of 26 or 38 sail of the line, with which he might suddenly transport an invading army to the British shores or at least sweep the Channel and the seas of our Commerce before we could put out a fleet at all ready to cope with him.

There was much exaggeration and some nonsense in these Royal apprehensions, but yet the statements of the Russian Naval force and the small means of actually meeting it on the seas was deserving the attention of an English Government, and some of us, especially Melbourne, seemed to think the admonition against entire Confidence in the impracticability of war from the North not altogether unseasonable. I remarked and all agreed that such a state of things if there was any truth in it, furnished grounds for encreasing our naval establishment, but none whatever for preserving the simulacrum of a Militia allowed to be inefficient and expensive. The unsettled state of Holland, the vindictive and mischievous spirit of the King of that Country, and perhaps the excellent condition of the small but formidable fleet of the Danes (8 sail of the line) might be plausibly urged by H M as additional motives for vigilance and precaution. In the mean while Spain and Portugal too press for Naval demonstration. I understand there are many young Officers eager to engage with Coll. Evans, but his comparatively low rank in our Army disinclines older Officers from serving under him, and perhaps the character of his politicks somewhat checks the ardor of young men of name and distinction from engaging. He will take none but English subjects and has refused the Poles who have applied to him. They are somewhat burthensome to us, but under the auspices of Lord Dudley Stuart[96] and Calder Ferguson[97] have obtained some relief and certainly have not forfeited their title to it by any misconduct or indiscretion since their residence in England. Lord Palmerston was not at our dinner.

[*In the margin:* Cobbett, a Man of genius, died on the 18th. He had been a common soldier and was entirely self educated; he made himself perhaps the ablest and certainly the least scrupulous political writer of his time. His style was plain and masculine. His perspicuity in statement unrivalled and matchless, his acuteness in reasoning equal and his wit, humour, and vehemence very superior to most of his rivals and contemporaries. The pride or the virtue of the Whig Aristocracy disdained in 1806 or in 1807 to admit a person of so low an origin, of such instability in principle, and of such scurrility in controversy to their councils or their Society. Had they prudently acted otherwise, Cobbett would have probably felt the value of a decently honest Character and laboured to preserve it. As it was he despaired of obtaining countenance or equality; he became desperate. He cast away all shame and was restrained by no scruple. Unable flectere Divos, he determined morere <........> and refrained from no devilish arts that language can supply for that purpose. The impudence and effrontery with which he assailed all who opposed him were unequalled and revolting. Like most vain men he was very sensible to small obligations and very impatient of great ones. His ingratitude to Burdett was intolerable. His humour did not desert him to the last, if it be true that on his deathbed, on its being observed that the Whigs had 'put Brougham on the shelf', he exclaimed 'put *him* on a shelf? they might as well put a live Rat there'. Lord Essex says Brougham's book is so full of Ologies that he cannot read or understand it and Allen yet more maliciously proposes as a Motto to it the words of Scripture, 'Is Saul also one of the prophets?']

18th. June. Waterloo Anniversary. King at Duke of Wellington's. He has seen the outline of our Irish Church bill and, though he does not approve, acquiesces and promises his support, candidly owning that Melbourne's Ministry was formed on the principle of carrying such a bill and that he could expect no less when he accepted office. This is more manly and satisfactory than if the expressions had been so cordial as to prove gross inconsistency or raise the suspicion of insincerity. He has been beaten and submits, if not with a good grace at least in good earnest. The *truth* is there was neither intrigue nor treachery in his abrupt and hazardous experiment of last autumn, but natural disgust at Brougham's restless and irregular conduct, unfeigned dislike of Lord John, real dread and repugnance to much further reform in Ireland, and a persuasion, artfully produced perhaps by those who surround him, that Wellington and the Tories would find sufficient support in the Country to enable them to conduct his affairs with ease to himself—a persuasion in which the newspaper virulence against Brougham and the great Orange or Protestant Meeting in the County Down had strongly confirmed. He now feels he was wrong, is sorry thereat, but not, like his father, busy in contriving means of subverting those to whom he has capitulated.

Friday 19th. June. Wrote to Palmerston and Granville urging them to exert themselves to keep Alava in England, and to dissuade the new Government in Spain from placing him there instead of keeping him here; touched also on the necessity of encreasing our Naval force on the coast, especially the North Coast of Spain, as nearer at hand should Russians come round to the Dutch Ports.

Saturday 20 June 1835. Heard an appeal in Duchy Court. Baron Park and Baron Alderson[98] the assessors. This made me late for the Cabinet where we discussed the course to be pursued on the proposed amendments on Corporation bill,[99] and the steps to be taken on a proposal conveyed in a letter from Broglie to Sebastiani to send joint Squadrons of English and French to the Mediterranean and Northern Coasts of Spain. Auckland, Melbourne, and Palmerston seem to think that without going to Parliament, we may from our present force afford three line of battle Ships and some frigates for such a purpose, and they and others agreed with me that some augmentation of our Naval force would be preferable, for our present establishment was scanty low for the circumstances of Europe, but our House of Commons Colleagues doubted if any additional vote could be procured unless by statements which would spread much alarm and justify, if true, a very large one. Palmerston dined at Holland House.

The King was at first rather pleased at the encouragement to British Officers to enlist in the Service of the Queen of Spain, suggested recruiting parties for her in Ireland, assurance of half pay &c, and observed that it would be a vent for many turbulent spirits in Ireland and that a Catholick country was a good receptacle for the superabundant population of that Country. He has since that time betrayed a great disrelish to Evans Commanding it, and he revolted immediately when the restoration of Napier's English rank and the extension of local rank to officers engaging with Napier were suggested. When he asked Wellington what he thought of Spain, W[ellingto]n answered, 'I think every body is wrong about it, and as to Carlos I would not give a pinch of snuff for his chance of success'. Palmerston assures me that he will leave no stone unturned to keep Alava here.

Much sensation in London at Sir G Grey's[100] useful and excellent speech of Friday, which persuaded Mr Fowell Buxton to withdraw his mischievous motion for enquiry into West Indians' title to compensation, and induced Lord Stanley to give up speaking in answer to Buxton. Sir G Grey's manner reminded the house of his Uncle. The warmth of praise on this occasion proves among other things the great demand there is for a first rate young Orator. Will, as in other matters, the demand secure the supply?

Monday 22d. June 1835. House of Lords nothing remarkable. Slept in South Street.

Tuesday 23d. South Street. At Committee for Western Railway.[101] King, tho' engaged to Lord Hertford's fête and tho' he commanded some of His Ministers to be invited, did not go himself. The Courtiers whisper that he avoids going out to escape meeting the Duchess of Kent and to lay in an excuse for not making his annual visit to her. There is unquestionably much ill humour between the two courts, more tracasseries in the Palace than is consistent with the King's ease or comfort. Madamoiselle D'Este is accused of having a design to complete Prince George of Cambridge's (A Lad of 15 or 16) education too rapidly, and whatever foundations there be for the scandal, it is certain that her long visits to the Castle are discontinued. [*The following verse appears in the margin in Greek characters:*

Fair d'Este's hands were in a situation
With Princely George that did not seem to suit
'Tis to complete would she his Education
And teach the young idea how to shoot]

A Conversation is repeated between the Duke of Cumberland and Alava. The Duke attacked him on the Character of the Corps he was raising. Vous n'aurez, he said, que la canaille. Dans ce cas on devrait, ce me semble me scavoir bon gré d'en avoir debarrassé le pays. Mais la malheur est, Monseigneur, qu'il en restera toujours.

In the Commons Graham and Stanley in support of him adopted a hostile line to Ministers, and were well answered by John Russell. Peel, tho' he voted, was silent and is supposed to mark his comparative liberality to the great disadvantage of Stanley. The Divisions have been good, and that against the Freemen, considering how formidable that body is to many Members, shews no little virtue in the House of Commons.[102] Melbourne's government is allowed by his enemies to acquire strength imperceptibly, but it is probable that they, and possibly that some who do not avow themselves to be such, may lie in wait for the Irish tithe bill.

Wednesday 24th. June 1835. At Court. Sir Harford Jones Brydges[103] sworn in Privy Councillor, and Duke of Richmond, Lord Lieutenant of Sussex. To the latter the King said that he never had bestowed a Lord Lieutenancy with so much satisfaction to himself, and that he liked to mark his approbation of one whose residence in his County was so useful and whose talents and executions of them on all publick occasions were so creditable to his Station. Many of our party friends do not respond to this Royal panegyrick and the Duke's family[104] has not reconciled them to the promotion by voting against Melbourne's government in the two last divisions in the Corporation bill Committee. Yet the appointment was surely right, and what passed of Sussex and of the poor laws, considered, the appointment of Duke of Norfolk the first Roman Catholick Lord Lieutenant in England and merely residing in the County would have been very objectionable.

Alava, with whom I had much conversation at Court, was in better spirits about his country and very sanguine about his *10,000* Englishman, loud in his praises of Coll. Evans and satisfied with the manner in which Duke of Wellington and Lord Aberdeen check the factious language and proceedings of the Ultra Tories, who would support the Carlist and revive the Miguelite faction in the Peninsula. Alava wisely declines the office offered him in Spain, is aware and gratified at the acknowledgement of his usefulness here, and has been manifestly persuaded by Mendizabal that the countenance and assistance we shall afford to the Queen's cause will be as efficacious and much less objectionable than that of a French Army in Navarre or Catalonia. The appointment of Mendizabal[105] is very popular in Spain, and Wellington admitted to Alava that it was the wisest step the Queen had yet taken. He, Mendizabal, will go to Madrid by Lisbon and strive to repair the mischief which the intrigues of the Court and the caprice of the young Queen have occasioned by sowing dissensions between her and the Empress and by dismissing, in the person of Carvalho, a popular and virtuous Minister who enjoyed the Confidence of the Chamber but was contumeliously dismissed immediately after the prorogation of that Assembly. It was bad, said Mendizabal shewdly, for a King of 70 years and of some success in his station to turn off Lord Melbourne in similar circumstances so unceremoniously, but what is it for an inexperienced, wayward girl of 16 to have such a power and to exert it so peremptorily, suddenly, and unexpectedly!

Malthus, the philosophers son,[106] having declined the living of St. Andrews, Hertford, I gave it to Mr Bayley,[107] the Curate of Ampthill,[108] who has been liberal and useful about the schools there and who has moreover as Proctor in Oxford resisted the intolerant petitions meditated against Lord Radnor's bill by that University. Yet I am not quite sure that he may not, like most of his cloth, turn out a Tory and that I may not consequently incur, and in some measure deserve, censure, for omitting to ascertain his politicks. So unpleasant a thing is Church patronage! viz Even if there be not this alloy, there are others—in the disappointment of my old friend Lloyd[109] and I fear of the Cowpers too—though that was unavoidable. The miserable feather of the honour of Tickhill, vacant by the death of Lord Middleton is I find acceptable to a staunch Whig, Lord Scarborough,[110] and he of course shall have it. Thanks were voted to Lord Devon[111] in the House of Lords for his conduct when Clerk. I thought I could trace the wishes of all the Lords, and particularly the Ex Chancellors, who spoke in his commendation, as to his Successor. Brougham in particular, who would place his brother William,[112] dwelt on the advantages of having a barrister, and seemed to think that it had been an additional recommendation of Courtenay that he was a Master in Chancery before he was appointed, as Wm. Brougham is now. Lord Abingdon,[113] who on some occasion had been chosen Speaker to swear in a Lord, with good grave buffoonery said he was bound to add his testimony to the other Lords that he, too, while on the Woolsacks had derived the greatest assistance and advantage from Mr Courtenay. Melbourne is beset with applications, and the friends of the Candidates dwell on the advantages of placing a barrister at the table and they quote a dictum of Lord Liverpool to that purpose—but many think there are other and weightier reasons, besides the oeconomy of suppressing a superfluous office, for promoting the Assistant Clerks and not introducing a Stranger, who either by servility or presumption might warp the judgement of the Chancellor on judicial questions, and who, if exempt from such failings, might tempt and almost justify a Minister in conferring The Great Seal on inferior persons.

Thursday 25th. A Cabinet at twelve. Lord Morpeth[114] was present and we went thro' the Clauses of the tythe bill. No very material alterations was determined upon, but many unnecessary Clauses were omitted. Morpeth was less nervous than

I should have expected him to be. It is a very complicated and in many senses very imperfect and objectionable and unsatisfactory bill, and yet on its fate may depend that of the Ministry.

Broglie holds cheap the notion of Russian armaments.

26th. Friday. Alava expects the first detachment of his expedition to sail for St. Sebastians the day after tomorrow. I wish the Port they landed at were further from the theatre of war, for the Spaniards, if they can, will hurry them into action and disperse them about in small and indefensible positions before they are formed, disciplined, or completed.

I saw the Duke of Bedford. His head is clear, his mind occupied, and his fortitude most exemplary, but his appearance has not improved and he is frequently blooded, tho' his strength is somewhat recovered, and he walks and rides. Lord Morpeth opened the tithe and surplus appropriation bill very perspicuously, firmly, and eloquently, and placed himself on the first form of publick men and Parliamentary Speakers.

27 June Saturday. A Cabinet. J Russell reported King's reception of the Militia scheme. He would prefer a better preparation for war, for 'he trembles' he says 'in his shoes' when he thinks of the armaments of Russia; however after disclaiming all responsibility for the result of such a disbandment of forces, he acquiesces in the recommendation of his Ministers and acknowledges that this 'penny wise and pound foolish' country would not easily be brought to engage in the expence necessary to prevent aggression, tho' he does it the justice to acknowledge that it would spare no exertion to repel it when made. Morpeth, whom success last night had greatly animated and improved, attended our revision of Clauses of the tithe bill, and Palmerston and Auckland agreed to keep in some measure out of deference to the King's whims or prejudices, our Squadron distinct from the French. They take care of Alicant and the East coast of Spain, and we of Lisbon, Ferrol &c on the North. The news from Spain is on the whole good. They accept the French Legions but they again instruct Frias at Paris to press for a French army, which will be again refused.

28th. Sunday. Went to South Street. Lord Melbourne and Lord Palmerston had suggested Lord Durham for the Embassy to Petersburgh and the King urged, among many strong objections, the probable averseness of the Russians to receive him. In order to remove that objection Melbourne wrote the King word that a letter had been received from Count Nesselrode which assured Pozzo di Borgo that Durham would be agreable to the Emperor. Melbourne added that the letter had every appearance of sincerity and he pressed upon the King the many advantages likely to result from the appointment. To this he received on the same day an answer from Windsor stating that the King had not seen Count Nesselrode's letter, believed Lord Mel[bour]nes report of it to be correct, and 'therefore withdrew his objection'. He thought Durham's language at publick meetings had disqualified him from representing his Sovereign at any great court, but if 'the Great Autocrat had made up his mind to receive him' he would not withold his acquiescence, as he fully admitted that 'this Country would be benefited by the absence of Lord Durham'. But this letter was followed by another of the same day, after the King had seen Count Nesselrode's dispatch to Pozzo which had raised his fury to a high pitch. This second but short epistle directed to Lord Melbourne was written in the King's own hand. The King expresses 'his surprize and highest displeasure at Lord Palmerston for *daring* to write to a Foreign Minister on any subject without the previous obtained consent of his own Sovereign'. He then avows an inclination to dismiss Lord Palmerston and hints that if the cause were known it might lead to and would justify impeachment! He does not withdraw his consent to Durham's appointment, but he repeats his 'high displeasure and extreme disapprobation of Lord Palmerston'.

The next day *Monday 29th. June.* Lord Melbourne in a very plain, firm, and handsome letter acknowledged not only his participation but advice in the proceedings of Lord Palmerston, takes the full share of blame if any to himself, but contends that nothing improper had been done and takes upon himself so far to act on that conviction, as 'to withold from Lord P. the strong expressions of HM's displeasure which he had the mortification to receive'.[115] To this the King answered by an acknowledgement of Lord Melbourne's handsome conduct to his Colleague and an expression of regret at not being satisfied by Lord M[elbourne]'s vindication. He repeats his former reasons, and represents the transaction as mainly obnoxious to him because it made him appear 'a Mere Cypher and his consent to an Appointment a mere matter of Course'. He wrote also on the same day another letter to Lord Melbourne detailing more at length the causes of his displeasure with Lord P[almerston], and speaking bitterly and ironically of the *humble proceeding* of his Minister and *condescending answer* of the Emperor Nicholas; and Lord Melbourne in reply maintains that HM was not made to appear a mere cypher, that it was more considerate to prevent beforehand, and without making the King a party, the recurrence of a refusal from the Emperor to receive the destined Embassador of this Country; and in declaring himself unconscious of guilt or error, says that in conveying the King's displeasure to Palmerston he must disclaim all concurrence in such a censure upon a measure by which he confidently hopes and thinks that he had rendered no inconsiderable service to the King by proper and justifiable means.

Tuesday 30th. June. Lord Melbourne sent the King Palmerston['s] justificatory letter in which he clearly relates the whole transaction, disproves the charge of undignified or disloyal submission to the Emperor Nicholas, and civilly proves by dates, though he does not allege it, that the King was aware of the contents of Nesselrode's letter and consequently of the application to Russia, when he signified his reluctant acquiescence in Durham's appointment. To this communication the King wrote a civil answer to Melbourne, but does not retract his opinion. He wishes however to 'drop the discussion'. In doing so he animadverts with some bitterness both on the Emperor and Lord Durham, says that the being represented by the latter in a foreign Court is *naturally* and particularly painful to him, and hints that even his introduction into the Cabinet would be less so. In another letter of same date, commenting on Lord Palmerston's vindication of himself, he, tho' ungraciously, acquits Palmerston of intentional misconduct, but attempts, unsuccessfully enough, to combat his arguments, and in his endeavours to draw a distinction between Lord Londonderry's appointment and Lord Durham's, betrays considerable soreness at the conduct of those who were in opposition on the former occasion.

Wednesday 1st. July. The King wished to avoid seeing Lord Durham in the Closet, and when he was urged and in some senses compelled to do so, he stipulated that there should [be] *no discussion,* and adhered so strictly to his stipulation, that he did not utter a syllable. The Door opened, Durham came in, kissed the King's hand, and retired and the door Closed. What a farce is a Court! and how Childish the performances Great personages go through!

The irritation or excitement produced in the Royal Mind by this appointment broke out in other subjects and in the Privy Council on an occasion and in a manner that might have led to very serious consequences indeed. Sir Charles Grey,[116] one of the Canada Commissioners, was at the King's own <intimation> sworn in at the Privy Council; he had no sooner kissed the book, than the King in a prepared, solemn, and peremptory and emphatick though agitated speech addressed him to the following purpose. He magnified the importance of his mission, descanted on the obligation of obedience to which he had bound himself, and described the peculiar Character of the Colony to which he was going, which, not being Chartered or proprietary nor originally peopled by Englishmen, had been gained by the sword and was therefore, according to His Majesty's Royal logick, peculiarly subject to the prerogative and had no pretensions to set up any rights of Its own. He forbade Sir Charles Grey on pain of his high displeasure to allow the prerogative to be altered or violated. He disclaimed all apprehension of Sir Ch. Grey entertaining any such projects or opinions, but he warned him, because he knew there were individuals, and those too who ought to know better, who fostered and expressed, nay, had ventured *even in his presence* to express, opinions inconsistent with the maintenance of those prerogatives which were essential to the preservation of the Colony and the Connection with the Crown of this Country'.

We all guessed that what he by a misnomer called the prerogatives was the appointment by the Crown of the Members of the legislative council, which was however established by an act of the British Parliament; but who he meant by the persons *who ought to know better but who nevertheless had ventured* to express dangerous opinions in his presence, we were at some loss to conjecture. Lord Glenelg, who some weeks ago had discussed with him the question of Canada and in some few topicks seemed amicably to differ with the King, had an inclination to ask an audience and seek an explanation, but after some reflection and consultation he contented himself with a conversation with Sir Herbert, from whom he received an assurance that the King in all probability did not allude to him, but that he, Sir Herbert, would ascertain for whom the censure was intended. The King, whom I saw on Duchy business, was gracious and talkative, but evidently much agitated and very nervous. He was among other things very peremptory in his dislike of railways, and evidently nettled when I said that called the Western would go thro' My Wilts property and benefit it.[117]

2d. to 6th. In the course of the 4 or 5 days that I staid in town, I attended several

Cabinets in which we consulted on the means of obviating some objections to the tithe bill of the Archbishop of Dublin, fostered if not suggested by Mr Blake and enforced by a formidable threat of both those Commissioners resigning their seats at the Education board, unless their objection to its dependence on the death of Protestant Incumbents were removed. Melbourne stated truly enough that the Archbishops resignation would at this period of the discussion be fatal to the bill and the Ministry, and added with humour and emphasis that Blake's would at all times be an unmixed benefit. Lord Glenelg, subsequently to his interview with Sir H Taylor, had received from that Gentleman a letter, regretting that the person alluded to in the Censure pronounced by the King in Council was his Lordship. Glenelg consequently summoned a Cabinet to consult what was to be done on the Occasion. All concurred in the absolute necessity of some remonstrance. The sketch of a written one which had received the assistance of Lord Grey was read and commented upon, but it was finally agreed that though it should be prepared and finished, it should not be delivered till Lord Melbourne had seen the King and failed to obtain from him an assurance that he would abstain in future from so unusual and inconvenient a method of conveying instructions to those who were to receive others from his responsible Ministers and Secretaries of State.[118]

On *the 7th. Tuesday* Lord Melbourne went to Windsor and on

The *8th. Wednesday* there was a Levee and a Cabinet dinner. I attended both. The King at first was in better spirits, humour, and health, but far from that state of composure which secures him from imprudent speeches. He spoke somewhat strangely, both to Sir Robt. Adair about the Court he had quitted and to the Dutch Minister Dedel on that which he represented. If there was any indication of impartiality or fairness in his remarks, it consisted in equal tokens of hatred, not of love, to both the Kings of the New Countries. He was also strangely adverse to the Western railway and disposed to withold his consent to the second reading in Lords tho' he had granted it in Commons. [*In the margin:* He did not speak *one word* to Mendizabal, tho' Minister of finance in Spain, and presented to him as such by Alava. The only reason as I conjecture was that he had seen in some letter that he was in the soul of the Movement party in that country! Indeed, according to Alava's account, when told by him that there were two Generals in Don Carlos's army equal or superior to Zumalacarreguy,[119] he said, 'J'en suis bien aise'! but Palmerston who stood by did not think his observation was so decidedly improper, tho' it certainly implied no disappointment.]

At our dinner at Sir John Hobhouse's, Lord Melbourne gave us a very diverting but satisfactory, judicious, and conciliatory report of his audience on Lord Glenelg's business. He began he said with an expression of confidence in the King's patience and goodness, which he had always experienced, and lamented that it was his duty to state to H M the inconvenience that might result to the publick service, in the unanimous judgement of himself and his Colleagues, from a recent step of H M, and he was sure H M must perceive that he alluded to what passed in Council on Wednesday, for he supposed H M had foreseen that, when by Sir Ht.'s Taylor [*sic*] letter to Glenelg it was known to his Servants that the words of severe censure which dropped from him were in truth intended for one of them, some explanation of the circumstance would necessarily ensue. 'Indeed' replied the King, 'I neither expected nor foresaw any such thing. I was very angry with Lord Glenelg and thought, and I still think, he deserved a reprimand for the dangerous opinions he held'. Melbourne said there was some misapprehension about those opinions and that much time had elapsed since they were expressed and that His Majesty in many private audiences and opportunities had never said one thing about them to Lord Glenelg. 'All that may be true' rejoined the King, 'but they were never out of my mind and I always intended to reprimand him for them, and as to misapprehension of his words, I know what they were and am confident about them'. When however Melbourne urged the injustice of arraigning one of his Servants publickly in council for language which he had no opportunity of explaining, and the yet more serious consequences of lowering the authority of the Secretary of State with those employed under him and even of injuring His Majesty's own authority and the publick service too by creating a discrepancy between the verbal instructions delivered by the Sovereign and those written at his direction and with his consent by his Secretary of State, he acknowledged that he had been hasty, allowed that there might be a danger of mischievous consequences from such a practice, and said he would take care in future to avoid such sudden and publick ebullitions of displeasure, but he persisted in maintaining that Glenelg had held strange and dangerous doctrines which had naturally put him in a d_____d passion and added that, though he would say nothing in publick, he would give it him well in private. Melbourne said he would of course see Lord Glenelg after the Levee, and the King significantly assented with a gesture implying that he would manage the interview so as to heal matters or at least not make them worse. But When Glenelg did see him, he talked much about Canada and the instructions, was communicative and gracious, but altered not one syllable either on his own unusual sally in Council or on Glenelg's alledged opinions which had occasioned them.

Gossett had retired from his place in Ireland and Seymour[120] announced his resignation of the black rod. When Conyngham mentioned Gossett as the person to succeed, the King expressed very properly his acquiescence in the appointment and his general approbation of Gossett, but when Melbourne spoke of these places, The King said with some shrewdnesss: It is well enough to call Gossett's retirement from Ireland a resignation, but gloss it over as you will, it is a removal and one I cannot approve, for I think him a useful and loyal man; however as you chuse to remove him, I am glad you give him so good a retreat and I have given my sanction to Lord Conygnham. The Vice Chancellor, Shadwell, is to sit as Speaker of Lords while Denman is on the Circuit. Alava and Mendizabal speak in high commendation of the talents, zeal, and disinterestedness of Evans.

Thursday and Friday, 9 and 10 July. The King in a conversation with Lord Gosford spoke peremptorily against the surrender of his territorial revenues and any alteration in the appointment of the legislative Council in Canada. He would never consent to either. Yet he had already sanctioned the first in Lord Aberdeen's Instructions and the earnestness of his objections is only an additional indication of his irritability and excitement.

Saturday 11 July. Long Cabinet, important but unanimous. Lord Melbourne said he would read to us what had passed between the King and Gosford, as it was right, he added with a laugh, that we should know how We all stood in His Majesty's estimation. He then read the substance of Gosford's recollection. His Majesty told him that it was not likely the instructions would be ready or he be able to go as soon as he expected. But he was glad he was to go because he thought he was a *Gentleman.* The instructions drawn by the Ministers were not likely to be such as he could at once agree to. At any rate they would not be his instructions, for 'this Cabinet', he said, 'is none of mine'. However that might be, Canada must not be lost and by God it should not be by surrendering the territorial revenues and rendering the legislative Council elective. Either of those measures would ruin and lose the Colony and he would turn out ten Ministries [*In the margin:* and have them all impeached] rather than sanction such a dismemberment of the Empire.[121] He said this to Lord Gosford because he believed him to be a Man of principle and a Gentleman, and he was sure that if he encouraged any such notions as he had just adverted to and as he never would agree to, he might get into a scrape and difficulty and therefore he warned him beforehand. [*In the margin:* He implied that he suspected some of harbouring such notions and that the instructions might be tainted with such dangerous opinions, but I have forgotten the words.] Gosford was not quite sure of the very words, especially of the 'scrape and difficulty', but he was positive of the substance and especially of his speaking of 'the Cabinet not being his', 'of dismissing several rather than yield points which would in his judgement, lose the Colony', and 'of getting such as advise him to do so impeached'. We all agreed that this strange language, held privately in the Closet, should not become the subject of any animadversion or remonstrance, though it furnished additional motives for framing with special care the instructions we were about to consider and in a manner which if possible would reconcile him to the course of policy we meant to pursue, and if not would put us quite in the right in our difference both in this Country and in the Colony.

Before proceeding to that very delicate deliberation, Palmerston submitted a question about the gum trade on the Coast of Africa near Senegal and Permandick [*Portendic*] which had arisen between our Merchants and the French Government. The latter had by various stratagems and practices endeavoured to elude the article in our favor of the treaty of 1783, and had made a war with an inland tribe who occasionally trafficked on the coast belonging to France a pretext for blockading the coast and thus debarring us from the access and barter, to which (though not to settlement) we were by treaty entitled. We resolved to send a ship and a Steamer to protect our commerce, to apprize the French that, deeming the blockade illegal and our right to trade in gum and other articles, *not contraband of war,* indisputable, we had done so, but that we were ready to acknowledge and had signified to our merchants that during the war the French had a right to seize all arms and contraband of war and, therefore, in declaring to them that their innocent commerce should be protected, had also cautioned them not to expose themselves to seizure by dealing in arms, ammunition, and contraband of war.

We then proceeded to the long, able, and artful paper which Lord Glenelg, aided I should judge by Howick and Stephen of his office, had drawn up for the instructions of the Canada Commission. The nature of the Commission was defined to be that of enquiry and, though a general willingness to hear and a disposition to conciliate were generally strongly and repeatedly inculcated, nothing was actually conceded on most of the points that the King had not actually agreed to give up by sanctioning Lord Aberdeen's instructions, and the admissions and reasons of that paper were carefully repeated and eloquently enforced. On the delicate question of the evils alledged by the Canadians to result from the constitution and appointment of the legislative Council the King's *reluctance* to enter in any discussion was distinctly declared, nor was his persuasion that neither any new facts nor any further representations would be sufficient to induce him to depart from so vital a principle of the act of 1792[122] in any degree softened or concealed, but the right of petitioning and canvassing every part of our institutions and every supposed grievance arising from them being allowed, it followed of necessity that it was the duty of the Executive Government to weigh the representations that it was bound to receive; and the Commissioners were therefore permitted to receive and to discuss such representations against the present mode of nominating the legislative council, though enjoyed as it had been by the King's ancestors for more than 40 years, universally approved for the greater part of that period, and sanctioned by use and experience, nothing short of indispensible necessity, of which there was no appearance, would justify the King in relinquishing it. In short the purport of this part of the instructions was not peremptorily to close or forbid the discussion of this point, but at the same time to imply the greatest possible disinclination and aversion to consent to the proposed alteration. On the subject of the primary assemblies, the refusal to comply with the request was yet more peremptory and emphatick, and the whole was so admirably penned that it appeared difficult for the King to take any exceptions to the conciliation recommended, and yet the tone and temper in which the Commissioners were instructed to proceed, and the large scope given to their enquiries and discussions, afforded a reasonable hope that the Canadians might be propitiated. The paper with some slight verbal alterations and omissions (enough to elicit some little solicitude of a parental appearance from Howick) were adopted and then the question was when, where, and how it should be submitted to the King. It was determined that Glenelg should solicit an audience and read it as his sketch to the King, before he was formally requested to sign it, in order that he might endeavour to recast any part which contained expressions or involved opinions at all questionable in H M's judgement.

The whole business, considered as an indication of the King's real disposition to us, is full of bad omens and bad appearances, and there is, moreover, in the manner and abruptness of his expressions on this and several other, less important, matters, some symptoms calculated to awake apprehensions yet more alarming, while *no heir apparent or presumptive* is of an age to assume the government of the Country as Regent.

The King told Lord Hill to discourage officers on full pay from taking half pay with a view to serve in Evan's corps—a fresh proof of his hostility to that course of the Queen of Spain which his government openly and by treaty countenances and encourages and ought to assist.

Sunday 12 July. The King does not confine his extravagances to the topicks of Canada, Durham's embassy, &c, &c or to his Ministers and persons concerned in publick affairs. He speaks imprudently, not to use harsher terms, to many, and I was requested by a common friend today to caution a great Officer of the Household against the indiscreet report of his language and proceedings, for the said Officer openly represented him as *quite Crazy*. A Rumour of that calamity, well or ill founded, cannot be long prevented.

Lord Glenelg shewed the King the Canada instructions this morning and writes me word 'he succeeded very well'. The King suggested some alterations which Glenelg thinks he can make, and it is clear, he adds, 'that the King expected much worse'. There were however (he says in his P S) some 'fervida dicta'. Some say the perpetual movement, reviews, dinners, &c of the King increase his excitement, others that they give an innocent vent to restlessness which would otherwise break out in more serious extravagancies. I understand that a foolish altercation took place at the late review about the position taken by the Duchess of Kent's carriage, who, though warned that the etiquette required that she should retire behind or beyond the Queen, would not budge from the post she had chosen, till positive[ly] apprized that the King would stop the review till she had resumed her proper station. I am told another misunderstanding has arisen about the Princess's confirmation, and the Duchess of Kent insists, somewhat injudiciously as it appears to me, that no communication about it from the King could or ought to be conveyed to her or her daughter thro' the Duchess of Northumberland[123] or indeed thro' any body but the Archbishop of Canterbury.

Monday 13th. Staid at Holland House.

Friday 14th. Lord Radnor made an excellent yet temperate speech on 2d. reading of bill for abrogating subscription. The Bishops and Tories mustered in strength and, tho' Wellington had in truth counselled the University of Oxford to comply with some modifications, he spoke and no less than 163 peers in person or by proxy voted to reject a bill for abrogating this immoral and revolting practice of requiring subscription to propositions which the subscribers are not expected to understand. Melbourne spoke with great spirit and effect.

Wednesday 15 July. Met Bishop of Lincoln[124] and ArchDeacon Goddard[125] at Duchy about building Churches in the Fens. Failed to attend Levee and council, the latter of which, on a Recorders report, was kept late by the detention of the Chief Justice in Court, which gave the King an opportunity of again complimenting Lord Denman; he assured him that he had done right not to quit his post and the important duties that he was there discharging so well, that He the King would readily have waited hours rather that [?than] take him from those duties, or proceed on the important consideration of the Recorder's report in the absence of one who was such a comfort and an assistance to him. All this was mighty handsome, and in his audiences, even with Glenelg, he was calm and civil if not gracious, said the Canada instructions were now quite satisfactory. He boasted to Melbourne that he had received Lord Glenelg as Melbourne had wished him to do and had shewn his wishes to regulate his instructions by the advice of his Ministers and his own sense of right to both which propositions Lord Melbourne coldly assented with a bow. But the King did not like his somewhat emphatically remarking that the instructions as he had now approved of them were in substance the same as the Cabinet and Lord Glenelg had all along projected and recommended, and still less did he relish being reminded that Lord Aberdeen's instruction, *which he had signed and approved,* authorized a more complete cession of the territorial revenue than that now submitted to his approbation. He attempted to deny that he had ever sanctioned more than was contained in Glenelg's instruction and, when he found his argument on this point untenable, coloured up and was manifestly disconcerted in being detected in assuming high language to us on the very point he had conceded to our more favored predecessors.[126]

The Cabinet dined at Lord Melbourne's. General conversation on pending businesses but little really transacted or settled. [*Corrected copy in margin:* Senior, far from persuading the Archbishop, is almost persuaded by him to adopt his objections, and the Archbishop will resign if the surplus as such is to be paid to the Education fund, or the supplies for the Education board made to depend upon and fluctuate with the surplus.[127] Nay, he is bent on making his objections known, *to save his character* he says, even if the clauses are proposed or pressed in that shape, though they are not carried.] He is sincere and friendly, but he defends his view of the case most strenuously and ably and is not to be pacified but by great alterations. This is embarrassing and vexatious.

Thursday and Friday, 16-17 July. In the Lords much idle, unprofitable, and mischievous conversation generally originating with Bishop Philpotts on the errors and abominations of Popery and on the comparative merit of the Roman Catholick and Protestant Priests in Ireland. In point of scurrility and intolerance there seems not a pin to chuse. The old trick of selecting revolting passages from books of general authority which the party will not disclaim even if they disapprove was in the case of Dens Theology and other works resorted to by Phillpotts.[128] The retort on an English Churchman who had signed the articles and through them acknowledged the Athanasian Creed and the Homily of obedience was obvious enough, if it had been prudent. Melbourne, without using it, spoke with derision and indignation of the unnecessary revival of polemical divinity and of the years of persecution the Roman Catholicks had undergone in Ireland. The tone and temper of his speech was excellent, in a high strain of confidence. It will do him great good in Ireland, as his exposure of the sophistry and hypocrisy of the Churchmen about the 39 [articles] will with the dissenters in England. He is manifestly somewhat nettled at the aversion of the Court and the hostility of the Aristocracy, and his manly defiance of them ingratiates him with the popular party and has obviously strengthened his Govt. in the Country. Yet the rumours of the dissolution of the Ministry and the revival of the King's November experiment were much credited, and the elation of the Tories joined with the activity and attendance of all Wellington's party in the Lords seemed to Countenance such a speculation. He has assumed a much more decided tone of High Church politicks in the course of the last week, throws his shield of protection over Oxford and the Bishop of Exeter and encourages in his late Colleagues, especially Lord Ashburton, the adoption of high Orange and Protestant language. Some however who know him well imagine that such compliance with the prejudices of the more wrongheaded of his party is one of his *straight forward* manoeuvres for acquiring authority and thereby checking the impatience of his unruly types whom he is anxious to restrain from any direct assault on the second reading of either the Municipality or the Irish bill.

He'd work more mischievously slow
Disfigure first and then destroy.

A great meeting of the Conservative Tories at his house ended, we are told, in exhortations to discipline and attendance, a promise neither to pair off or vote by proxy or to leave London before the two bills were disposed of. The Slackness of our attendance and the general absence of many leading Men and especially Grey no doubt encourages them.

Saturday 18. A Cabinet. The Archbishop has almost persuaded us all that it would have been both in principle and expediency better to have obviated his objections at first. And Even now if we can reconcile him to the whole measure, by fixing a definite sum for the revenue of the education Board, in lieu of an annual vote depending on the decease of Protestant Clergymen and fluctuating with the encrease or decrease of Protestant Parishioners, we are determined to encounter the inconvenience and untoward appearance of so late an alteration in our measure. We sent thro' the Clauses of Irish Corporation bill.[129] Many think we cannot actually carry it this year, but we owe it to our Irish friends who have attended and supported us so steadily to try, and the more so as a bill in lieu of the expiring Coercion bill, but of a severe nature, will be necessary and is in contemplation.

Sunday 19th.

Monday 20. At the Duchy Council for 3 hours and House of Lords afterwards.

Tuesday 21. A Charge against the Duke of Cumberland, arising from evidence given before A Committee in the House of Commons, of having, contrary to positive and reiterated orders of the Commander in Chief, corresponded with Soldiers and Officers in the Army in the Character of Grand Master of Orange Lodges much talked of and canvassed. Hume, tho' not of the committee, denounced the fact and called for the evidence in the Commons on Friday, and it is understood that on Monday the Committee determined to report what evidence they had collected to the house. The Duke of Cumberland in no very measured or delicate terms is said to have defied his accusers, but unless they overrun their scent, which with such a headling huntsman as Hume to direct them is not impossible, the chase may drive him from the Coverts which he now haunts, and materially impair his powers of mischief. [*In the margin:* It ended however with the death of the Orange Society the next year. As the whole transaction may be seen in printed papers, Parliamentary or publick, I say no more about it.[130]] The attendance of Tory peers in Lords is very marked and very formidable. Read and suggested many omissions in Irish Protection bill of which a confidential draft was sent me by Duncannon. It must be greatly mitigated.

Wednesday 22d. I was sorry to perceive by a conversation with Lord Strafford, who breakfasted at Holland House, that many of our friends in Lords had not even taken their seat, and in contemplation of the Municipal bill, to be read a 2d. time next tuesday, and the Irish Church bill, soon to come up to us, we took some means to call in the Stragglers. I went to the Levee but was too late. The King was aghast at finding that he could not fill up a vacant stall at Windsor with Lord Aug[ustu]s FitzClarence and was not aware that he had precluded himself from doing so by promising a suspension of such patronage till the Ecclesiastical Commission shall have executed their task. He would be in all probability more loud in his compliants, tho' not more vexed in his heart, if it had been his present and not his late Ministers who had surprized him into such a virtual surrender of his patronage—a surrender which only yesterday the Archbishop recorded in the bill he moved,[131] and commended and explained in the speech with which he introduced it. The Tories may steal the stalk as well as the stud, and less noise be made than at the Whigs looking over the Hedge with which the Church is fenced in.

The King approves of Lord Howard of Effingham[132] for the Yeomanry [*In the margin:* but Effingham would not take it and Ilchester has it]. He is angry at Mulgrave appointing an Usher of the order of St. Patrick (tho' given to the Lord Lieutenant in the King's absence by act of Parliament) without apprizing him; a place he says of such *importance* ought not to be conferred without his knowledge. Is your son, said he to Berkeley Paget,[133] still aide de Camp to the Lord Lieutenant of Ireland. 'No Sir he has left it', answered Paget. 'I am *very* glad of it' replied the King with emphasis. He is in a very vituperative mood, but perhaps it is rather a proof that he regards all change as hopeless than an indication of a decision to make one. Howick made an excellent speech this night in answer to Graham on Irish Church bill. Not less than three Members attached to Tories or to Stanley have been reclaimed by the force of argument or rather by a statement of the facts of the Case—Evelyn Denison, Mr Young,[134] and Mr Pewsey.[135]

Fazakerly[136] has been offered Canada by Glenelg and Brussells by Palmerston, declined both but pleased by offer. Harry writes me a strange project of Jerome and Louis Bonaparte[137] of marrying one of their sons to the Queen of Portugal and wishes me to sound Palmerston, who agrees with me in thinking that we should certainly not meddle in it and yet more certainly not promote or encourage such a scheme.

Thursday 23. The debate on Irish bill or rather on Peel's motion for dividing it,[138] protracted to the third night, was closed with a triumph for Ministers—319 to 282; a Majority of 37 is a trifle better than we expected and enough, I presume, to shew that our Enemies cannot conduct the Government with this house of Commons. If half we hear of the registration be true, they cannot easily procure a more manageable one. It is manifest, in spite of fanaticism and dread of Popery, [that] the state of the Irish Church, the disproportion between the revenues enjoyed and the duty required, and many other circumstances hitherto unknown to the publick gradually reconcile the English, both in and out of Parliament, to the sensible and necessary measure of applying the surplus to some beneficial object.

24th. July. Staid at home all day. Mr Sheil's speech seems beautiful and unanswerable.

Saturday the 25. A long Cabinet. I had the satisfaction of finding that my objections to two provisions in the intended Irish Protection bill—namely, 1, to all the Clauses against secret societies and associations, which I believe to be utterly inefficacious and, like Women's anger, impotent and loud; and 2dly., to the power, under the word, visiting, of entering a house by night to ascertain that the inmates are at home—had been duly considered. The Assembly clauses were abandoned, and the power of visiting confined to summoning the persons from without and constituting their not answering to be primâ facie evidence of being out at undue hours, an offence in cases of proclamation under this bill. The Irish Corporation bill was once more gone thro', and the proposed alteration of voting a specifick sum for the education board and charging it on the consolidation fund on one hand, and paying the surplus not to the Education board but to the Exchequer on the other, was read and approved as propitiating the Archbishop of Dublin, and is to be announced, with as few reasons as possible on going into the Committee, by Lord Morpeth, who was present in our Cabinet this day when these Irish bills were considered. He understands them well and is stout and conciliatory in his management and defence of them.

The question of reducing or repealing the duty on Newspaper is forced upon us by the large and yet more largely threatened encrease of unstamped papers and by the manifest and mischievous disposition of several, and especially Brougham, to encourage the practice, as a means of annoying the leading journals, of courting popularity for themselves, and of injuring the revenue. There is in my judgement no doubt that the tax is unwise as well as odious, but it cannot be entirely repealed without greater injury to the revenue than the publick interest allows us to incur, and the violation of the law to the extent now existing and still encreasing cannot be submitted to without disgrace to the Govt. so permitting or conniving at it, or without flagrant injustice to the lawful printers, who pay for their stamps. The Govt. is in a perplexing dilemma. Howick from high notions of a slim execution of law, and Spring Rice from fear of a defalcation of revenue and of a combination of the established legal presses with the illegal to defraud the Exchequer, are strongly disposed even at this season of the year to lower the duties to a penny and to raise the powers of proceeding and the penalties against the offence to the level of the severest revenue laws we have.[139] [*Heading:* 25th. July to 2nd. August] The Clamour which such powers will excite with some Radical writers and talkers and the yet greater topicks of invective with which a relaxation of revenue, refused to the landholders and granted to newspaper writers, will furnish our Tory enemies, appall others and, combined with the natural repugnance to start afresh, have at the close of the Session incline[d] John Russell, Lansdowne, Hobhouse, and others to leave matters as they are for a time and to postpone the consideration to next year. In the meanwhile the extraordinary and unusual powers of the act requiring registry of printing presses, passed in 1799[140] and having no reference to the revenue, have been by Sir Fredk. Roe[141] and the police called into activity, 40,000 unstampt papers have been seized and the types and utensils of two Unregistered

Presses are actually seized. This matter was discussed in one or 2 Cabinets between the 25 of July and 2 of August, but left after all to Lord Melbourne's decision. The business in the two houses, dinners at Court and elsewhere, and communications with the King prevented a Cabinet dinner and much interfered with our meetings during the whole week. The King's licence of language, especially on Mulgrave's government, continues and encreases, and he has recently taken to scolding and rating people especially his Ministers in a manner indicative either of what is called 'excitement' and means something like 'derangement' or of more settled enmity and deeper designs or revenge than I am willing to suspect him of. He reverts often and violently to his objections to the proposed reduction of Militia Staff, but he nevertheless admits the necessity and propriety of some reduction and, with the exception of Lord Howick, the Members of the Cabinet acquiesce in some arrangement and compromise on the subject. The King is not more tractable on this subject from the circumstance of John Russell being the Channel of Communication. But John is firm, determined, and imperturbable and has secured his acquiescence in sufficient reductions for the present.

Tho' I was at Holland House from the *2d. to the 7th. August,* I neglected this diary. There were no great political events but such as Newspapers recount as well as private notes, such as the infernal Machine at Paris,[142] the murder of some English Marines at St. Sebastians by the Carlists, the Parliamentary debates, and the departure of Alava and Evans for Spain.

There were few if any Cabinets and no Cabinet dinner. This was chiefly owing to Parliamentary business and the necessity of Melbourne's attending the examination of witnesses on Corporation bill. That evidence was entirely directed to the disparagement, exposure, and crimination of the Commissioners, not to any proof of injury to property inflicted by the bill. The high tone taken by Melbourne against hearing any evidence greatly nettled the Tory Lords and surprized them yet more. He manifestly despairs of gaining any proselytes in that house and wisely directs his efforts to animating, gratifying, and recruiting his support in the Commons and the Country. In this I believe he succeeds. In the mean while the King has betrayed much irritability to his household and Lords of the Bedchamber on occasions of little or no importance and in a way very unlike himself as well as unbecoming his dignity, for if he is not remarkable for his taste in preserving the latter, he is generally good tempered, good humoured, and good natured to those about him. His brother of Cumberland [*unfinished*].

26th. August 1835. For three weeks I have neglected this diary and shall very probably not have time to recapitulate what passed at Court, in Parliament, or in Cabinet during that time; but I open my book to record my having at length said a few words in the Lords last night and overcome that nervousness which made me once think I should be dumb evermore. I really feel this morning like a boy who has first discovered that the water will support his body and swam across a river which he deemed impassable. Yet the few words I said were hurried, confused, and insignificant; they will however enable me to speak better another time. In addition to this self congratulation I was touched, and should be an insensible brute if I was not so, by the good nature and feeling of the house, both friend and foe, who seemed pleased to encourage an old and shattered debater and treated the somewhat fumbling efforts of an old performer of 62 with all the tenderness which a Maiden speech generally secures.

7th. Septr. 1835. During the few remaining days of the Session I continued occasionally to say a few words for the sake of keeping up the habit and familiarizing my ears with the sounds of my own voice in publick. I did not recover even the full possession which I formerly had and which was never great, but still enough to enable me to be of some use in a house, *where we rather want debaters,* and to rescue myself from the mortifying feeling of being [a] useless Member and an encumbrance upon my friends and party rather than an assistance. The Lords led by Lyndhurst and bound by some unknown compromise between the Duke of Wellington and the more bigotted Ultras contrived to let the popular election remain in the Corporation, but to amend in the Committee almost all the provisions which rendered that popular election palatable or useful.[143] The alterations which preserved the old Aldermen and the Town Clerks, which substituted monopoly of power for equality of rights, and substituted an irresponsible for a responsible Government in every town were indignantly rejected by the Commons, but others, scarce less objectionable in principle, were treated at the instance of Lord John with great forbearance and conciliation. [*In the margin:* Lord John, contrary to the advice of most of his house of Lords Colleagues and of myself in particular, very doggedly and obstinately to appearance but in truth most sagaciously, judiciously, and successfully adjourned the house over Saturday and gained 48 hours, in which he prevailed on his hot partizans in the Commons to check their impetuosity and acquiesce in his more temperate course.[144]] And Sir Robt. Peel in a very marked but very judicious manner signified his entire adherence to the leading principles of the bill and practically inferred his strong censure of the intemperate and unreasonable conduct of his party in the Lords. They felt no doubt deeply mortified but they had no alternative but submission. They acquiesced in all the main disagreements and adhered only to two important amendments of their own, that which gives the power of nominating the Borough Magistrates absolutely to the Crown and that which insists on introducing the division of Wards into <zones> and extends the number of divisions into wards of several of the enumerated towns. The spirit or the animus of all these alterations were bad, but the practical effect, particularly if Lord Melbourne remains in office 6 months, will be little or nothing. The recommendation of Town Councils will become as necessary to the appointment of a Town Magistrate as that of the Lord Lieutenant to a County Magistrate, and few Ministers will be found bold or wicked enough to resist the appointment of any body of respectability recommended by the principal inhabitants, and still fewer who will be profligate enough to place obnoxious and unpopular names in defiance of the publick opinion of the place. As to the wards, the bill restricts the King with respect to the places enumerated, but it leaves unrestricted as to the number he may appoint in any new corporation, and there is no reason why he should in incorporating Manschester itself, divide it into any wards whatsoever.[145]

But tho' the points in dispute were in truth of little practical importance, there was a latent jealousy of authority in the two houses which it will require great temper and dexterity and, with both, no inconsiderable share of luck, to divert from consequences infinitely more important than the difference between the two set of Clauses proposed by the Commons originally and those endeavoured to be substituted for them in Lords.

The Impossibility of averting much longer what is called a Collision between the two houses is now generally acknowledged on both sides, and the probable consequences of that collision, such as the remodelling, the reforming, or the controlling the House of Lords, are calmly discussed with various comments and feelings of pleasure or regret, in a way that six months ago would have exerted merriment as too chimerical, or disgust as too monstrous and mischievous for speculation. Unless some new hare should start to divert the pursuit of the publick pack, these symptoms are somewhat ominous for the Lords Spiritual and Temporal. If the two houses meet in the same frame of mind in which they part, the consequences of the rash and infatuated conduct of the Lords will not be confined to the mutilation or rejection of a bill or two, but expose their legal and constitutional power, if not existence, to the greatest possible peril. The manifest determination of Peel not to be dragged into an unpopular and unavailing struggle against the inevitable progress of publick opinion has mortified and disgusted those who are honestly as well as foolishly violent, but it may reclaim some of the less unreasonable. Its immediate effect is a conviction, both in the Court and in the Country, that he is not prepared to renew the experiment of last year, and the consequent continuance of Lord Melbourne in office, till accident or time deprive him of the support of the country and enable the King to get rid of him without risque of another Parliamentary defeat.

His Majesty, for the first time since the change of Ministry, has expressed himself civilly and even cordially to his Minister in the House of Commons, and though the largest proportion of his praise is bestowed on Sir Robt. for the handsome manner in which he has redeemed his pledge of not harrassing any Government of his Majesty, a share and no inconsiderable is reserved for and graciously administered to Lord John for the very judicious, considerate, and conciliatory manner in which that forbearance has been met. It is manifest that the notion of Coalition again crossed His Majesty's mind, but whatever may be the motives of such language, the effect is to produce either indignation or despondency in the ranks of the soi disant Conservatives. Brougham nobly defended the Muncipal bill and the Ministers. But towards the end there was or there appeared so much of private understanding or even mysterious compact between him and Lyndhurst, and there certainly was so much fulsome flattery of the latter in a highly wrought and laboured encomium on him by Brougham, that he failed to inspire the party he served with any confidence, or to enable or even perhaps incline the Ministry, who owed him so much, to repay their obligations by the admission of so irregular and uncertain [an] inmate into their councils.

Minto is to have the Admiralty. He has scruples of accepting his brother's[146] resignation and it is deemed invidious to have so many near relations at one board.

Wednesday 10 Septr. Attended the Levee and Council. The King's speech read. It is a safe, prudent, and moderate one and much approved of by the King, tho' it expresses satisfaction at the establishment of responsible governments in the towns and at the Coercion having been allowed to expire in Ireland. To the word *crime*, or the *epithet* inhuman, applied to the African Slave trade, His Majesty, with more regard to consistency in his personal than political capacity, strongly objected, and it was omitted. Before the speech was read, some orders in Council were read and approved and among them one reducing still further the Militia establishment.[147] The King, before he reluctantly pronounced the word *approved* to this reasonable and necessary measure, thought proper to deliver a strange speech on the Militia, of which, he said, being older than any Man he addressed, he of course must know more than any of their Lordships. He told us a *Whig* Ministry had forced the Militia on George II against his inclination, that it was a constitutional force; that as our Army was smaller in time of peace than that of other Armies and of Russia in particular, the Militia was our only security; that his consent to this reduction was only temporary and extorted from him chiefly by an unwillingness to expose the misconduct and neglect of the Colonels, which must have transpired had it been reorganized; and that he delivered this opinion purposely in the presence of the great officers of State, because they were either Colonels of Militia themselves or connected with those that are, and he wished his sentiments on the nature of the duty of those Servants of the Soverign should be known. He ended by repeating that, while the Militia remained in the reduced state in which this order left it, it was his conscientious opinion that the United Kingdom was in danger of Russia!—and he then said, Approved!

10th. to 26th. Septr. The Cabinet parted without a dinner but with plenty to digest before they meet again in the gloomy and ominous Month of November—such as Registry bill,[148] Irish Church Measure,[149] and last but most difficult of all, arrangement about Great Seal. Brougham naturally enough waxes impatient. He wrote me a letter full of bitter complaint and reproach but meant in truth for a pump rather than a ducking. I kept my secret, however, as well as Lady Percy and for the the same reason. I could not tell what I did not know, nor could Melbourne say what was not decided in his own mind, much less in the Council of his Cabinet. Though B[rougham] sarcastically observes that Adelphi should be substituted for Admiralty on the Board of Minto's office, the appointment is generally approved and more satisfactory to the King than any not really objectionable which could have been suggested. For these or other reasons the King is either in better humour or more resigned to his fate than he was while Parliament was sitting. He was cautious to Sebastiani and the Duc de Nemours. He has had more of his Ministers at Windsor than is usual and, tho' he occasionally inveighs against the disorganizing doctrines of the Radicals and has allowed the politicks of Evans to counteract his good will to the Queen's cause, he acquiesces chearfully in the promotions which Palmerston and Melbourne recommend. Harry Fox to Washington, Seymour to Brussels, Anglesey I believe to Gilbraltar [*In the margin:* which Anglesey declined with a little ill humour unlike himself], and Lansdowne to Garter. The latter are vacant by the death of Lord Chatham, a strange man whose friends promulgated and whose demeanour indicate[d] much of the talent and genius of his brother and father, but whose conduct shewed wondrous insensibility to their glory or to his own fame. His indolence was never roused to exertion unless it was for the objects of emolument, rank, and decoration, which they despised, and even for those very rarely and very imperfectly. I have long known that Lord Lansdowne wished for the garter though when the knowledge reached me it surprized me. [*In the margin:* He waved it this time, foolishly I think, for Duke of Hamilton.[150]] He is every way entitled to it, and it is much better for the state, or at least for those who administer it, that such as are entitled to it should like it than they should, as it is natural to expect they would, despise it; but it seems that even elevated Minds are but Children of a longer growth.

The King gave his daughter and my daughter in Law the profitable place of Housekeeper at Windsor, but this was as it ought to be a mark of fatherly affection not of political preference. On the arrival of Mendizabal at Madrid the whole weight of business fell upon him and it seems as heavy a one as ever one man's shoulders were doomed to bear. Had he arrived sooner he might have made it lighter. He is fully aware and indeed early foretold his difficulties, but judging by his first acts he is not appalled. OConnel's Tavern speeches,[151] the natural fruit of his situation, are sad, offensive trash. They provoke many good men but they are more offensive than injurious to Govt., and he manifestly avoids the topicks most likely to *embarrass* he Govt. he professes to support, though he dwells on many they must condemn and <despize>.

1835 November. The Members of the Cabinet, with exception of Lord Duncannon, detained by the illness of Lady Fanny Ponsonby in Ireland, had several meetings and dinners in the course of this Month. The Principal measures of the ensuing Session were again talked over and the materials and in some instances the projects prepared. They were Chiefly the Irish Church bill [*In the margin:* The comparison of the land tax scheme and one founded on the less simple basis of last year was circulated early November. The tax however is proposed to be on the value or rent of *titheable lands only*. The objection to the principle seems abandoned or overruled, but the time and difficulty of making an accurate valuation is by some thought an insuperable objection. Till it is done in the avowed shape of a tax and the Clergy become to all intents and purposes a stipendiary Church, the question will never be at rest and ought not to be.] the English tithe bill, the Registration and Marriage bills, the Irish Corporations, and the English Church rates. In the details of all some and great difficulties are likely to occur, and the narrowness of our Majority in Commons, the peril of losing our Radical and OConnel friends on one side and the policy of not exasperating moderate Tories or shocking lukewarm and squeamish Whigs on the other, required and require great caution, temper, and circumspection, but we have hitherto the advantage of undivided councils, there are few shades of difference on the principles of our intended measure[s?] or on the objects of our policy among the members of the Cabinet, and none whatever the least connected with designs or intrigues of personal ambition, resentment, or vanity. The King seems softened if not reconciled to those even among us who were most obnoxious, and the adverse faction at Court has every appearance of feeling itself beat. [*In the margin:* He was very much pleased with Lord John's speeches in Devonshire and at Bristol and expressed himself satisfied of the prudence of postponing rather than inviting discussions on what is called the reform of the House of Lords.] The chief and only clamour against Lord Melbourne's Government is what his enemies are pleased to denominate the mysterious connection with Mr OConnel and, ridiculously enough, the chief proof of the mystery hitherto detected is the fact of that Gentleman dining at the Castle and the Phoenix with Lord Mulgrave and Lord Morpeth. The former did not take this very innocent and natural step without asking Lord Melbourne, who told him that he highly approved of his inviting all Members of Parliament without reference to their political opinions or to the method they adopted, within the law, of enforcing them. [*In the margin:* Lord Melbourne with his usual frankness and generosity avowed this advice to those who were most scandalized at the invitation, and on my acquainting Lord Grey of the fact, I observed that his censures were much softened and that he did not dwell on what he thought the errors of Lord Melbourne with the same emphasis as he denounced them when he imagined they were exclusively Lord Mulgrave's. There remains alta menti repostum much odium provinciale between the Greys and the Liddels[152]—and odium provinciale as I have often observed is more bitter even than theologicum.] Surely after the various attempts and failures of excluding Men for their publick conduct from the common courtesies of private life and the experience in the cases of Wilkes and others, Lord Mulgrave and the Ministry who support him are right both in feeling and policy. It is not possible to indict Mr OConnel for enjoying the Confidence of his Countrymen and exerting it to keep them loyal and contented under the present Government, and it is not true that any measure has been adopted, or any promotion made, with a view to propitiate him, which Lord Melbourne would not, from other considerations of publick duty and convenience, have advised. Lord Morpeth, whose success both in and out of Parliament delights all his friends and exceeds their most sanguine expectations, says that all he knows of OConnel is that of all our Irish supporters, he is the only one who asks for nothing for himself or his friends. It would indeed be better for the Ministry and ultimately more creditable and advantageous for himself, but not perhaps quite so conducive to an encrease of *rent*,[153] if he would abstain from the disgusting personalities and revolting intemperance of langauge which furnishes our common enemies with a plausible pretext for representing all intercourse with him as contamination, and which neither the peculiar hardships, amounting to persecution, to which he has been exposed, the provocations which he has received, nor the general bad taste which pervades the oratory of his country can excuse, though they in some little degree palliate and account for it.

Sir Francis Burdett felt or affected great squeamishness on this subject, and forgetting that many with whom he had been more closely connected in publick and private than by mere association in a St. James Street Club, and perhaps he himself, had at periods been exposed to similar reproaches and threatened with parallel exclusions, called upon the Club,[154] thro' an hostile newspaper, to expel him. He came to explain his motives to me, but he was manifestly disconcerted at the general disapprobation his letter had met with, acknowledged that it would have been more judicious to apply to the Committee of the Club privately, regretted that the Members of it were out of town and yet more that he had not, as he once intended, alledged that reason for writing in the Newspaper, and talked generally of his preference of a Country life to politicks, and that it was odd that he had been immersed in the latter, for that his natural destination was to be a Foxhunter and *that sort of thing*. He feels he has lost Westminster, and some shrewdly suspect that the Otium cum dignitate to which this quondam Agitator but well mannered and kind hearted Man looks, is to be The Tory Knight of the Shire for Derbyshire! He has always been swayed by those he lives with and the gossip of London says that Mr Sinclair and Mr Croker! are now his chief advisers. Peace to all such! but OConnel is the cause or pretext of much animadversion from other and yet more painful quarters. I wish I could think an apprehension of him the real and only cause, and not in some degree the indication, of a temper of mind in Lord Grey somewhat incompatible with his conduct and disparaging to the motives which led him to retire. Every thing is done and has been done to remove all jealousy of neglect or estrangement, and if attention, favours to his family, and deference to any publick opinion of his can remove a disposition to find fault or to complain, I am satisfied Lord Melbourne and nearly all his Colleagues will strive hard to find and to avail themselves of such opportunities.

True however it is, that there are many persons of weight and importance for whom we feel and ought to feel more or less consideration and even affection, who are more excluded from power and confidence than they very naturally suppose is either kind or reasonable—Wellesley, Anglesey and, above all, Brougham. Anglesey was hurt at being offered the Government of Gilbraltar's on Chatham's death and perhaps more so at being offered India on Lord Wm. Bentinck's return. With his usual manliness and frankness he told me that he thought the first, after the professions made him at the formation of the Ministry, was an insult and only to be accounted for by the influence of OConnel! I told him with truth that if it was a mistake to think it would gratify him, it was one for which I was responsible, for Melbourne had consulted me, and certain I was that neither in what was offered or what was not offered was OConnel either consulted or thought of.

Brougham is a more difficult chapter. Something must be done about the Seal—a Chancellor appointed or a new arrangement for the performance of duties attached to that office devized. Campbell, our Attorney General, is a good Common Lawyer and stout politician and of a spirit not to brook being overlooked. But on the other hand he has little or no Equity, has little judgement in debate and, though not deficient in courage, hardly equal to sustain any thing like a contest in debates judicial or political with Lyndhurst and Brougham, who could combine with more virulent zeal against him than any body we could raise to the Woolsack. Bickersteth is untried as a debater and his elevation would exasperate Brougham almost as much as Campbell's and not improbably provoke Campbell himself to resign. Such difficulties are not unfrequently the rounds of the ladder by which *supposed* Mediocrity arrives at heights to which it could not in the ordinary course of things pretend to aspire. [*In the margin:* I put in supposed because till it was tried such was supposed to be the Character of Pepys; but it has turned out (I write in 1837) that far from being the description of our Chancellor, he is in his judicial capacity the very best since Lord Hardwicke, and his Senatorial and political, useful, straight-forward, conciliatory, *acute,* and intrepid.] Brougham has broadly hinted that Pepys, a good equity lawyer and good sort of man, tho' neither a Statesman nor an orator, would somewhat soften his *dis*appointment at the disposal of the Great Seal. If the Rolls were in consequence to devolve on Campbell, it would smooth all difficulties with respect to Our Attorney General, but Brougham is in a very accepting humour and may possibly, in deference to an office long his favourite, stomach the indignity of a descent from the Seals and <look> the Rolls, with a Deputy Speakership of House of Lords and the Scotch Appeals, as his share of the spoil in such a distribution of legal offices. It will not do to have a Chancellor inefficient in debate for the purpose of propitiating Brougham and find him defied and exasperated at the arrangement after all. He has taken the first place in the Charity Commission[155] at the Offer of Lord John, and then, probably to throw on Lord John the odium of rejection, proposed Whittle Harvey, whom he had laboured so hard and so successfully to exclude, as one of the Members. He studiously eschews the society of Ministers and haunts that of Statesmen on the Shelf, discontented individuals and occasionally actual enemies, especially if professional. Melbourne, who he does occasionally see, assures me that he diverts the conversation if you remark on his Metaphysical work. [*Heading:* 29th. November 1835] He, like Grey and Burdett, is loud in his condemnation of OConnel, whose *vituperative and itinerant oratory!,* He gravely asserts, is not to be borne. It is lamentable that with such powers and with so many good qualities, his restlessness of mind, inscrupulous employment of means to accomplish his immediate object, and little respect for truth should disqualify him from filling any station with comfort to his Colleagues, with safety to the publick interest, or with real advantage or comfort to himself.

The King, as well as most of his subjects, has recently made this remark to Lord John, and Lord John by his speeches in Devonshire and at Bristol, deprecating all agitation of a reform of the House, has ingratiated himself with his Majesty without injuring himself with any reasonable reformer. Certainly those who for very solid reasons prefer our form of constitution as established to any experiment not absolutely necessary must feel that little is to be gained for the House by canvassing in the abstract the reasonableness of an Hereditary legislature. At the same time the prospects of an accession of a majority of the Lords to any liberal system do not improve, and the occasional favors which a Minister has to bestow on that order of Men, far from gaining over enemies, has the effect of cooling and even exasperating disappointed friends. Lord Chatham's garter, waved by Lord Lansdown, to whom it had been promised with the knowledge of the King both by Grey and Melbourne, was given to Duke of Hamilton. It will please him prodigiously for a week, hurt the feelings of one or two good men who should have sense enough to despise such baubles, and exasperate others who perhaps overrate their own pretensions and certainly greatly undervalue those of their competitors. The death of Duke of Beaufort[156] followed soon afterwards and Lansdowne has accepted his garter. Some and especially Duke of Cleveland will be unreasonably disappointed, but any other disposal of it would have exasperated more and Melbourne would feel obliged to L[ansdowne] for not declining it, if he did not know (to his and my surprize) that he does no violence to his own notions of distinction or dignity in accepting it. He certainly deserves whatever he likes, though in this instance he likes what is hardly deserving of him.

During the whole of the Autumn there have been strong proofs of an endeavour on the part of Russia to detach France from her intimate alliance with England and there have been more symptoms, and in more than one quarter, of Louis Philippe listening to such suggestions and even misconstruing, neglecting, and thwarting the objects of the Quadruple Alliance than are agreable. These intrigues, however, tho' fomented it is said by Mme de Lieven, Duchess de Dino, Talleyrand, &c, were to appearance dissipated by the sensible and earnest representations of Sebastiani and King Leopold, and disconcerted by the unproductive and unsatisf[act]ory meetings of Kalisch and Toeplitz,[157] where there was little Cordiality and no real concert between the Sovereigns, and by the publick indignation so suddenly and so naturally excited in France and Europe by the Czar's insolent speech and barbarous manners at Warsaw [158] The professions of cordial connection with England have been renewed by Louis Philippe and are as strong as ever. It is difficult to believe that so honest a Man as Broglie could know of, much less approve of, any deviation from that line of policy to which the faith of the French Crown and the honour of the Govt. of which he is the head are so distinctly pledged. Yet the supply of stores and horses to the Carlists in the North of Spain is ascribed by English Consuls and Naval officers, as well as by Spanish patriots, to French connivance; additional and unforeseen difficulties in the way of augmenting and reforming the Spanish army is gravely and confidently, and without any passion or prejudice, attributed by Mendizabal to Rayneval, Miraflores, and the hostile language of French Agents at Madrid and at Paris; and the sudden, rapid, and unjustifiable changes of Ministry in Portugal are pretended to be traced by Lord Howard, Admiral Gage, and several leading Portugueze Statesmen to French influence and advice. Palmela, in confidence and in some little confusion, admitted that L[ouis] Philippe had admonished him not to let Portuguese troops enter Spain, and there are many other slight symptoms, as well as positive reports, that would lead a suspicious mind to conclude that the acquiescence of England in the marriage of Leuchtenberg with Donna Maria, and still more her unwillingness subsequently to replace him by the Duke of Nemours, have been deeply resented by L[ouis] Philippe. It is I fear clear and lamentable that, if he be not actually perfidious as well as false, Louis Philippe has derived from the education of Mme Genlis such a love of intrigue and manoeuvre, that it is impossible to judge of his design by his language or ostensible actions. In the mean while he has paid England the compliment, and no slight one it is, to place his subjects in the United States under the protection of the British Minister at Washington upon the recall of the French Chargé d'Affaires, and he is on the point of soliciting our Mediation for the termination of the quarrel and the renewal of diplomatick relations.[159]

Lord Durham's mission has hitherto been productive of one long dispatch containing an able exposition of the designs of Russia and means of Turkey to defeat them, some reasonings more Specious and injurious, I think, than valid and some reports of his own conversation with Turkish and Russian Ministers at Constantinople, mingled with a due portion of self commendation for the judgement and ability with which he conducted it and exaggerated expectation of the happy results it is likely to produce. He does not seem to neglect in the hour of his greatness his more humble fellow labourers in the vineyard of vulgar popularity, and his convivial speeches and Noble appearance on every occasion of compliment are duly reported in our newspapers. His earnest good wishes for the prosperity of the Russian Navy, however well turned in point of eloquence, came a little unseasonably, as it made its appearance on the same day and on the same sheet in which Nicholas's less courtly harangue at Warsaw was printed to the indignation of every zealous friend of freedom in the Country. That speech and the activity of some pamphleteers are stimulating not without success the publick, the opposition, and the government to hostile measures against Russia. Lord Ponsonby, early imbued with hatred to Russian influence by Sir Ths. Maitland[160] <in Casse> and not much restrained by any generous enthusiasm for Greece or any Christian horror of infidel oppression at Constantinople, listens with much complacency to the ingenious suggestions of his own mind, and of paradoxical and conceited travellers in the East, in favor of the Mahometan system and the practicability of directing it to the improvement of those countries it has desolated and oppressed for more than 300 years. [*Heading:* 30th. November 1835] We must not allow our disgust, natural as it may be, at Russian insolence and oppression in Poland to involve us in a war for interests which are either not really English, or are quite unattainable. It should be recollected that many of the views imputed to Russia in the East are not only natural and tempting but justifiable in themselves, not injurious to the real and <permanent> interests of Mankind, and not to be prevented, if steadily and judiciously pursued, but by complicated combinations and extensive wars more calamitous to the rest of Europe than the actual accomplishment of the suspected designs. Palmerston seems a little, and Ponsonby a great deal too much, inclined to *Warlike and angry language* on these topicks. I should prefer less complaint, less apparent ill humour, but great reserve, amounting almost to mystery, and some such augmentation of force and employment of individuals as should impress on Russians, Turks, and Austrians a well founded notion of our power and a wholesome dread of not provoking us to exert it. Till Austria thinks herself threatened and is determined to resist, we should hold aloof. When invited to accede to an Anti Russian policy, we may be equal to projects which instigated by us and forced upon unwilling allies would inevitably fail.

The King is not unlikely to renew his proposal of encreasing our Mediterranean force, issuing a Brevet in the Army, and promoting to flags some distinguished Naval Officers, and if the appointment of Lord Dundonald to a Command and the restoration of Sartorius and *Da Ponza*[161] to the service could be combined with such measures, they might I think be conducive to the peace of Europe and the credit and glory of Great Britain, to whose strength and power, operating upon the fears of foreign Courts, that peace would perhaps with justice be chiefly ascribed. The Carlists of Spain receive more stores and money than the Ex Princes of Bourbon or Braganza, even with the aid of such Potentates as the Pope[162] and the Duke of Modena[163] or of such adherents as the Fauxbourg St. German can supply, could furnish.

Sligo[164] in Jamaica, though zealous and honest in his views and full of attention to business, wants judgement and has somewhat hastily dissolved an assembly which he had unnecessarily called at an inconvenient period of the year, without putting himself in the right in his quarrel with the dismissed legislature or securing for himself a less hostile majority in the next. Glenelg exposed in a very able dispatch the futility of his reasons for calling and for dissolving his assembly, and shewed that the grounds alledged for his conduct were either inaccurate in fact or deficient in reason. Unless the refutation of Lord Sligo's reasons soften the impression he must receive from the publick dispatch, it should seem likely that on the receipt of it Lord Sligo will tender his resignation. Such a triumph for the faction of the Old Slavedrivers would be very unfortunate and it will be well, if a due attention to his private affairs and a love of business prevail on Lord Sligo, to overcome any little chagrin or disappointment which the view taken of his measures at home must, upon his first reading the dispatches, occasion. In addition to the evils of a triumph of the Slave party, the selection of a new Government would be attended with considerable embarrassment, if one can judge by our difficulties in procuring fit men for Lower and Upper Canada. Neither Lord Gosford nor Sir Francis Head were nominated till after much discussion and after we had learnt, from many rejections of the offer, that persons best suited for such situations are not easily prevailed upon to accept them. The truth is that the Salaries and emoluments, so long lavish and improvident and the sources of unjustifiable jobs in the appointment of greedy and incapable men, are now pared down in an opposite extreme and are quite insufficient to tempt Men of Character, ability, and Station, which afford any prospect of advancement or distinction at home, to undertake them. If this goes on, Men of inferior rank, and less tried, must be selected and on every occasion and <their> appointments to foreign stations will become tickets in the lottery, to the great peril of the publick service.

Soon after Parliament was up I cast the materials I had collected for a speech which I never delivered on the Irish Church into the form of a letter to Lord Granville, and I determined on printing it in the form of a pamphlet. But John Russell suggested to me that it would be known to be mine and be misconstrued into a Manifesto of the Cabinet. The remark struck me as just and I suppressed it, at least for the time. It was afterwards published without my name under the title of Parliamentary Talk.[165]

30th. November. November our predicted Ides of March are over, to the grievous disappointment of many of our enemies and perhaps mainly owing to the premeditated plan of some.

December 1 1835. Saw Palmerston and learnt from him and the dispatches of this day fresh proofs of the hostility and activity of Nicholas in counteracting the spirit of the Quadruple treaty, in inculcating in other powers the propriety of recognizing Don Carlos, in urging King Otto to govern on the principles of Russia, and in various other Manoeuvres. Fresh accounts from Lord Howard at Lisbon, more apprehensive than ever of the consequences of the late changes, more decided in his censure of the inexcusable methods by which it was effected, and to the full as suspicious of the motives and of the quarters from which it originated; yet he allows some of those appointed to the Ministry to be able and respectable men, and seems to dread the Constitution of 1820 and the fall of the funds as the most immediate evils resulting from the change, with a conviction that the Cortes and publick opinion will compel the Queen to recall the Ministry of Palmela, Saldanha, and Carvalho. Moncorvo (Sarmiento), though he equally laments the interference of the Army and the hasty and precipitate conduct of the Queen, so indicative of a hasty and despotick disposition, criticises the policy and propriety of the late Ministry, and especially Carvalho, in forcing the Queen to retract her conduct in a letter to be published. It was, he says, crying *peccari* in a way derogatory to her dignity; and the moment she was apprized of the nature of the step she had been advised and, in a way compelled to take, her objections to the policy of her advisers, which had hitherto been ignorance, levity, and childishness, became resentment. She wished before to govern or rather misgovern them and have her way, she is now bent on dismissing, mortifying, and punishing them. He is far from thinking that they will be reinstated by the Cortes, where, he contends, they will find themselves in a small Minority. Their successors, excepting Loulé[166] and perhaps Campos,[167] are he contends not ill selected, and he attributes any obstacle Loulé may devize to the marriage with Ferdinand of Coburgh[168] to no predilection for Nemours or French intrigue, but to a secret and absurd hope that his Wife may ultimately be elevated to the throne, he become King Consort, and his children succeed to the throne. He says the treaty for the Marriage with Ferd[inand] of Coburgh is advancing and that Lavradio hopes to complete it before the 2d. of Janry. when Cortes meet.

The King thro' Taylor takes up a hint dropped by Palmerston of augmenting the Navy. On such subject he is apt enough, and not only jumps at the prospect of augmentation of force in the Mediterranean, but urges what he calls a Straight forward course, which is little more or less than an avowal of hostility to Russia and her policy, directly reproaching her with a variety of ambitious designs and taking upon ourselves, not without some jealousy and suspicion of others, the task of resisting her and keeping the rest of the world in order. The whole tone is warlike and imprudent even to extravagance, but there are circumstances, justly touched upon in his paper, which seem to call for some augmentation of force and some precautionary policy, either to prevent a war or to enter upon it, if inevitable, with a competent fleet. Lord Howick who dined here has a different opinion and is somewhat overearnest and positive in maintaining it. Nothing can according to him justify the addition of a Soldier or Sailor, and A Brevet or promotion in Army or Navy he would resist at the risk of his office <or> of any thing else in the Commons, and knows he could prevent it. He made some remarks on Palmerston having even hinted such a measure without taking the sense of the Cabinet—and though sincere and communicative, seems somewhat headstrong on this subject.

December 1835 to May 1836. For near five months I wrote nothing in this book. The King's strong aversion to Russia, the unpardonable conduct of that power at Cracow[169] and still more the little pains taken beforehand to palliate or account for it, the prejudices and resentment of Lord Palmerston, the yet more unreasonable and silly suspicions and injustice of Lord Ponsonby, and the indefatigable activity, intrigue, and Anti Muscovite Mania of Mr Urquhart[170] seemed at one time likely to embroil us in a foolish and unnecessary war. The latter Gentleman, who had some mysterious protection at Court and was falsely said to be A natural son of Sir Herbert Taylor, was hastily appointed Secretary of the Embassy to Constantinople by Lord Palmerston, tho' the Duke of Wellington had refused to do so, as it is supposed, when pressed by no less than Royal Solicitation. As he not only continued to print with or without his name a variety of intemperate pamphlets extravagantly magnifying the importance of Turkey and as extravagantly inveighing against the ambition, perfidy, and hostility of Russia and Mehemed Ali, but was notoriously the instigator if not publisher and translator of a Collection of intercepted or purloined dispatches which, under the name of the Portfolio,[171] made a great sensation in Europe and exposed in the secret correspondence of Russian agents (and especially of Count Lieven, Mastuzewitz, and Pozzo di Borgo) the <views> of that court in 1829, 1830, and 1831, his appointment was not unreasonably considered as a symptom of hostility, if not an open affront and avowal of enmity to Russia. Many pamphlets of this same Gentleman were published under the encouragement of the Foreign Office and some MSS were circulated in Cabinet boxes. They all breathed the most unmeasured hatred of Russia, alternately urged this Government to war with her by describing her as exposed to conquest and dismemberment, or alarmed us to resistance by magnifying her means and assuming her determination of aggression and arguing that, unless instantly resisted, it would infallibly become irresistible and overwhelming. It was strange that, with a slight variation of name, A Gentleman of the name of Urquhart should in 1835 be acting over again the part performed by Mr Ewart[172] in 1791, who succeeded in prevailing on Mr Pitt, Lord Carmarthen,[173] and Lord Grenville[174] in England, and on the Prussian Cabinet in Berlin, to adopt a warlike policy against Russia from a sense of the mischiefs which would ensue from her aggrandizement and the Black Sea, and was only defeated in his project of a vast, gigantick, and unnecessary war, by the large divisions in the House of Commons.

I left off here in *May 1836* and did not resume my task till *September 1836*.

The Russian question on which I was writing died away in that interval, partly from the intrinsick absurdity of the alarms entertained by Mr Urquhart, the King, and Lord Ponsonby; partly from the success of the latter in removing the Reis Effendi[175] and the publick indication that circumstance afforded of the falsehood of Russian Preponderance at the Porte; partly, I must in candour acknowledge, from the talent and good conduct of Lord Durham; and mainly, no doubt, from the intimate conviction in the Councils of Russia, that war with England, and yet more with England and France conjointly, would be the annihilation of her Navy, the loss of her commerce, and not improbably the dismemberment of Poland from her Empire and some violent convulsions and revolutions at Petersburgh itself. [*Heading:* 1836 from January to September] These considerations were no doubt strengthened by observing the Anti Russian spirit of our press and publick meetings and the ease with which an augmentation of the Navy was obtained from a reformed House of Commons, when the most distant notion of a war with Russia was afloat. It was remarkable in the course of the 9 months of which I am speaking that, in spite of the hostility felt in England to Russia and in spite of the known repugnance to Louis Philippe in the breast of Nicholas, that [*In the margin:* he not only rendered the review of his ships and the cruize on the Baltick less ostentatious or formidable than was expected, with a view of propitiating us, but] the language and conduct of his Ministers and Embassadors bore less marks of ill humour and seemed less directed to the object of separating England and France than either Prussia or Austria and certainly than Holland. The unwarrantable but not quite unaccountable interference with Cracow, though originating no doubt in the policy of Russia, was maintained on less high and insolent grounds and discussed with more temper and reason by that power than by Metternich and Ancillon, and they, especially the latter, seemed nettled at the calm and conciliatory tone with which the Court of Petersburgh let down the somewhat lofty pretensions of her Allies in her vindication.

At the same time it was thought, how truly I know not, that Mme Lieven and Talleyrand, still actuated by personal resentment to Palmerston, were active and stirring in their intrigues to wean Louis Philippe from his English connection, to involve him in practices injurious to the Constitutional cause in Spain, and to incline him to projects of Marriages and treaties which would reconcile him to the three despotick Governments of the North, in contravention of that very treaty of the Quadruple Alliance on which Talleyrand so recently had plumed himself. How far or with what success Talleyrand laboured in this vineyard, I do not pretend to ascertain, but it was generally believed that one branch of the scheme was ripened by his fostering cultivation, and that he had the gratification of worming out Broglie, tho' not that of excluding Palmerston, from Foreign Affairs. If Thiers was his pupil, he soon emancipated himself from his tutor. But in the mean while Lewis Philip himself, terrified and disgusted naturally enough by the Assassination plots, singularly sensitive at all times to all republican movements in Spain, and wrought upon by the artful insinuations of advantage and security resulting from a closer connection with the great continental powers [*In the margin*: he met however very little encouragement either at St. Petersburgh or Vienna to prosecute with either of those courts a Matrimonial alliance for his Sons. They returned from their tour in Germany little pleased with their reception.] did by various acts of omission and commission weaken the government of Mendizabel, encourage the Queen Regent of Spain to offend and dissolve her Cortes, and to retain Generals and admit Ministers odious to the people, by which she ultimately provoked the very catastrophe Lewis Philip strove to avoid—the declaration of the constitution of 1812 and the triumph of that party whom it pleased the weak or corrupt to stigmatize with the name of Anarchists.[1] These events may have been more or less occasioned by the intrigues and practices of Lewis Philip. He certainly steered a tortuous and suspicious course through all these affairs. His influence, and perhaps his intentions, have however been much exaggerated. The Queen Regents secret deference to her favorites, her love of authority, and her marked dislike to Mendizabal were the more immediate causes. Mendizabal is said to have been guilty of the folly and vanity of making love to her and of the yet more unpardonable offence of failing to take advantage of the moments in which his imprudent and unbecoming suit might have met with success. This seems incredible, but Villiers, himself suspected of flirtation, believes it. It is clear she hated him and it is also clear that, like most Princes and Princesses in her situation, she imagined that the power of naming Ministers and Generals, confided to her by the constitution, was in good earnest to be regulated by her own judgement and caprice and not by the wants or wishes of those whose affairs were to be administered. In these false and fatal notions she was countenanced and assisted by many who pretended and thought themselves patriots and should have known better; and perhaps Villiers himself, who did not like Mendizabal, never enforced the principle of his admonitions with all the vigor that was necessary to give them effect. Certain it is that at the Close of the Session of Parliament [*August 1836*], and still more manifestly some weeks after it, our prospects in the Peninsula were more gloomy and our alliance with France less firm and satisfactory than at the Commencement. Thiers,[2] who had succeeded Broglie, all along assured Lord Granville and Mr Aston[3] that he was more disposed to act in the spirit of the treaty in favor of Spain than his Colleagues and that his Master was far less so. He followed up his assurances by sundry underhand manoeuvres to elude the vigilance of both and to Strengthen the Foreign Legion, acting in Spain with Men and Officers beyond and even contrary to Lewis Philip's intentions. This (and no wonder) had nearly led to a dissolution of his Ministry before the declaration of the Constitution of 1812, but on that event—which the French King and his Minister allowed had or *might* change the whole question—they agreed to suspend their differences and their measures, and the Ministry seemed once more patched up; but Lewis Philippe began withdrawing the forces he had near the frontiers of Spain, and Thiers, conceiving that such a step was a departure from the state of suspense agreed upon [*In the margin*: precluding the possibility of his policy being resumed], remonstrated and resigned, and this terminated in a Change of Councils yet less favorable, it was surmized, to our views on Spain or our general policy of uniting in one great Western league all the Constitutional States of Europe.

Upon all these foreign transactions, or at least on all that preceded them, the Duke of Wellington took and deserved great credit for forbearing to harrass Melbourne's government with embarrassing questions or hostile motions. He was, I believe, even where he disapproved, unwilling to say or do any thing which could by possibility embroil the Country in war. He might in contemplation of succeeding to power be cautious of pledging himself either for or against the policy we pursued, for he had felt on assuming office in 1834 that much which he condemned in opposition, he must applaud in Government, and he was perhaps disinclined to accelerate a change at home for which he did not feel that his party was ripe by a premature triumph on Matters on which he knew the Country felt little or no interest. Certain it is that he not only abstained himself, but repressed and rebuked Lord Londonderry and very faintly seconded even Aberdeen and others in any observations on the most vulnerable parts of our position, viz the instability of a French Alliance and the unfavorable prospect of the Spanish contest.

Though on domestick affairs his opposition was far more active and kept up by large and constant meetings out of the house of Lords and by great attendance and frequent divisions and triumphs in it, yet there were many symptoms discernible to an observant eye that he and Mr Peel were less prepared than their followers and perhaps the Court wished them to be, to repeat the experiment of November 1834. He determined, and I suspect with some difficulty prevailed on his followers to adhere to that determination, to wait for our measures and oppose them and to take the chance of our loss of bills driving us to resign, but not by any direct motion of censure in the Lords or any indirect representation to Court to procure our dismissal or take our places. If indeed we lost either the majority in the Commons or the Confidence of the publick by any rash act of our own, the Tory Conservative and Expedient party were sufficiently compact to enable them to act together in any emergency; to keep them in that condition their concert both in the Commons and Lords was uniform throughout the Session and, though some differences and even warm words among them at their meetings at Apsley House transpired, they compromised matters even with the most intractable Ultras so far as to prevent any thing like disunion in publick, and they threw out in the house of Lords bills important and numerous enough to give them rational hopes that we might be exasperated into resignation. The most important of these were the Law Reforms,[4] the Irish Corporation, and the Irish tithe bill. The English tithe, a great and a useful measure though too favorable to the Church, was allowed, and probably for that bad reason, to pass the house of Lords.[5] Some part of the Church Reform scheme also became law, but on other parts of it the house of Commons took very reasonable alarm and they were, to the injury of the whole scheme and with a little discredit to Government, rather awkwardly dropped for the Session by Lord John Russell, tho' introduced at the instance of the Ecclesiastical Commission of which he, Melbourne, Lansdowne, and, I think, Spring Rice were Members.[6] It seemed to our warm reforming friends, and it is not impossible that there was some ground for the opinion, that the art and assiduity of the Bishops, Lord Harrowby, and of Mr Hobhouse[7] (The Tory), who were joined in that Commission, prevailed over the better judgement of our Colleagues and made them adopt and further schemes very inconsistent with the principles on which they meant to act. At any rate the quarter from whence these proposals were supposed to spring bespoke little favor for them in the Commons and the Country, and the omission of any repeal or regulation of Church rates was with suspicious Dissenters the source of much uneasiness and somewhat diminished the satisfaction with which the General Registery and the Dissenters Marriage Act[8] (two very difficult and much Solicited, if not important measures) were greeted by that body.

On the very opening of the Session, Duke of Well[ingto]n and Mr Peel objected to certain words in the address pledging the houses to legislate for Irish Corporation on the same principles as that which had been adopted in England. The words were retained in the Commons upon a very good division, but they were altered by the Tories in the Lords, the Ministers somewhat hastily and weakly acquiescing in the amendment without a division. Clanrickarde and Cloncurry protested, and si mens non lava fuisset, we should have foreboded from this incident what the subsequent treatment of our Irish Corporation bill would be. In the spirit of the House of Lords amendment the Course adopted by the Conservatives in both houses was not to retain the Old Orange Corporations or even to assimilate them to such institutions as they had acquiesced in last year for England, but to suppress corporations altogether in Ireland. They speculated, no doubt with some plausibility, that the great impatience felt by the Catholicks to extinguish the Orange Municipalities, which had so long insulted and oppressed them, would induce them to submit to the indignity of being deemed incapable of Municipal institutions rather than risk the loss of the bill in the Lords and the consequent countenance of the hateful tyranny of the Corporators. They were not entirely wrong in their speculations. Oconnel and others were at first not indisposed to the Compromise, but a little reflection and, above all, the eager and offensive arguments urged in favor of it by their bitterest foes, combined with the knowledge that the loss of that question would compel us to resign, reclaimed them, and they secured us a Majority sufficient to surprize as well as discourage the eager partizans of our enemies, who were speculating with more confidence than their leaders on our speedy discomfiture and resignation.

When the bill came into the Lords, Lord Lyndhurst and the more violent portion of the Tory faction, either purposely or improvidently, clouded the matter by grounding the proposal on an entire distrust and defiance of all the Catholick body in Ireland. Lord Melbourne had, I know not why, a sort of theoretical and abstract but strong aversion to Corporations in general, and while he felt the propriety and even necessity of resisting the entire suppression of them in Ireland, he felt also that the line of argument which was required to give that resistance force went against the grain, and that he could not urge it with that earnestness and vigor which a full and entire conviction in principle as well as expediency alone confers. He told me that he trusted to my reading the House of Commons debates and defending the bill and, when the Chancellor had delivered a sensible but somewhat inefficient speech, he bade me answer Scarlet and FitzGerald.[9] I wanted at least as much encouragement as this and to be put upon my mettle to induce me to rise, and my nervousness was so great that for the first two minutes I had no notion that I could have strung two sentences together. However I spoke in a way to resume such station as I formerly held in the house and, if not to come up to my conception of what I meant to say (which Cicero observed no man with a grain of oratory in him ever does), at least to exceed my expectation of my powers of saying it. I was as usual rapid, confused, and unmethodical, but on the whole I pleased my friends and served the cause, and I gratified myself by reflecting that I might contrive to give some further assistance to my Colleagues in debate, who in truth were from the state of the House of Lords in some want of it. During the rest of the

Session, though I made no really good speech and some very bad ones, I took a part not discreditable to myself nor unuseful to the government, and I think our bitterest adversaries felt that I did so, for both the Bishop of Exeter and Lord Lyndhurst went out of their way on two separate occasions to make a personal and unprovoked attack on me, which in both instances I repelled without fear and without acrimony, and, my friends were good enough to say (and I believe to think), not without success.[10] But enough of self.

Grey himself in one of the last stages of the bill came down and supported us in a calm, moderate, but able, impressive speech. By so doing he did us great service, and relieved his friends from much apprehension and himself from very unjust but very widely circulated reproaches. He had I believe on sundry little and perhaps some great matters affecting men and measures indulged in censures more freely than was quite reconcileable with the part he took in the formation of Melbourne's Ministry, and his invariable but surely childish resentment at OConnel's scurrilities and other men's imprudence or intemperance of language had betrayed him occasionally into expressions of warmth liable to much misinterpretation. Secret enemies and injudicious friends had as usual exaggerated these outbreaks, which are in him little venial infirmities, and his studious and ill judged absence from the house had confirmed the tories in the hope, and some even of his best friends in the fear, that when he did come there, he might let his disgust at OConnel and his disapprobation of the more politic and temperate conduct of other Whigs, and particularly his indignation at the subscription of the Duke of Bedford, Fergusson, and others, transpire.[11] He was however as usual on his legs, all that his friends could require and wish. The tory press vented their spite in a way to which he was not quite insensible, viz by disparaging his eloquence most absurdly, and that circumstance, together with the somewhat cavalier rejection by Wellington of a suggestion he had made to reconcile the differences on one clause of the bill, did great good. They served to confirm him in the more friendly tone he had assumed, and Melbourne's good humour, John Russell's marked and respectful attention, gradually effaced the neglect which he imputed occasionally to Palmerston; and the latter's offer to place his youngest son[12] in the office or in a mission, as well as the promotion in the Church of his newly married Son, John Grey,[13] checked perhaps in some degree the querulous tone in which he is too often reminded by some near him of the contrast between the attentions a Minister and a Statesman out of Office can command. For some private and some publick reasons the seat Lord Howick, whom he both loves and admires, holds in the Cabinet does not tend to soften these little asperities. In the first place Grey does not think the Office suits his talents, in the 2d. his opinions are widely different from his fathers, and 3dly., the opinions neither on public or private matters of the two Ladies[14] seem, to common observers at least, entirely to coincide. Grey was invited to Windsor to the Knights of the Garter day, graciously treated, stayed over a night and was pleased; but this civility might have been suggested by those about the Court who entertained some hopes that he might help to destroy what he had helped to form. They were grievously disappointed. He was more reconciled to the Ministry when he left than when he arrived in London, but it was full as well that he left it before the Irish Church bill was discussed in the Lords and before a reform in that house was rendered, by the mischievous activity of Lord Lyndhurst and the majority in throwing out bills, so familiar a subject of conversation and discussion.

Melbourne manfully declared in the house, and his supporters, especially the Irish and Radicals, warmly Applauded his declaration that as long as he had the confidence of the House of Commons he should not resign,[15] and he somewhat rudely or at least roughly defied his enemies in the Lords by telling them that they dare not attempt to remove him and knew they could not form a Ministry or acquire the Confidence of the Commons and Country if they did. Though the imprudence and scurrility of OConnel occasionally shocked the prudish English publick, and though the shape which the question on Irish Church had assumed was neither very defensible in argument nor attractive or plausible to indifferent persons, yet the endeavour to raise the Cry of the 'Church in danger' and even of 'Popery being about to be established' failed to produce any general effect. The latter [*i.e., former*] at the most extorted an inconvenient or disingenuous pledge from two or three popular representatives to dissenters or Scotchmen, and the latter, limited in its effects to Clergymen and the Universities, had no pernicious influence on any thing but on harrassing Lord Melbourne's mind in the distribution of Church patronage and terrifying him perhaps from selecting for a Mitre the men best able to serve his Ministry in that capacity.

In aid of that odious cry a very intolerant set at Oxford who dubbed themselves *κατ'ἐξοχην* [16] Orthodox attempted to obstruct Dr Hampden's[17] appointment to the Divinity Professorship in that University. They accused him of Heterodoxy and even insinuated absolute Socinianism in his works, tho' since those works and almost in consequence of them he had obtained Academical honours and been advanced to the government of a College and was sustained by Dr Copplestone and the Master of Oriel[18] and acquitted, as far as words and conversation go, of all heresy or impropriety by the Archbishop of Canterbury himself, who acted however a very cowardly or a very disingenuous part on the occasion. The Clamour had its effect on the King, and Melbourne's manly way of meeting it still more. He was frightened by the intolerant Parsons and foolish Old women, at the threatened schism in the Church, and he was mortified at the indignity of Lord Melbourne's going down to Brighton (which he did at my instigation) to insist on the appointment or to resign on his Government not being supported by H M. Hampden, <through> his

Nomina sunt ipso pane timenda sono

will conquer his adversaries by his unrivalled learning and reasonable conduct; but a fresh endeavour was made to crush him and [was] arrested by the unusual and spirited exertion of the Proctors, who put a Veto on the proceedings in full Convocation. It was a satisfaction to me to find Mr Bayley, the first proctor whom I had appointed to a living in Hertford, so liberal in his opinions and so firm in enforcing them. He had indeed originally engaged my interest in his favor by his private and very lively reports of the manoeuvres of the Orthodox faction at Oxford, and the propriety and ability with which he conducted his opposition to this flagrant attempt at Persecution fully justified my choice of him for the living and will, I hope, procure, as it entitles him to, much further preferment. I had soon after another living vacant in the Duchy, which I offered to Mr Reynolds,[19] the other Proctor, a Welshman, but he declined it and I gave it to Mr Pickthall,[20] a supporter of Mr Blamires[21] in Cumberland. Melbourne was more harrassed in selecting his Bishops. There was a great push on the part of the Prelates to get Lincoln advanced to Durham[22] and some Tories and Churchmen talked of the claims of Bishop Grey of Hereford in the hopes that, so doing, they should either get an intolerant narrowminded Man in an elevated situation, or breed some discontent in Lord Grey's mind at the pretensions of a brother being overlooked. Grey was however quite satisfied at the preference given to Maltby, and every Man who loves liberality of sentiment on civil and religious matters, respects great learning, and esteems modest worth was rejoiced at his advancement. The new Bishopricks were not filled with such entire satisfaction to the Reformers. Melbourne hesitated too long. I had once hoped, and indeed Melbourne told me, that one of the vacant Mitres might fall on Dr Shuttleworth's[23] head, but when the choice was talked of either in the Cabinet or in Whig Societies, it was soon clear that his offence in signing in 35 the address to Peel to remain in office could not be overlooked and, in truth, that circumstance and his conduct, though he voted right, on Hampden's business thoroughly persuaded me that, with all his integrity and disinterestedness, and he has both, he lacks the nerve, the spirit, and the energy which would render him a useful friend in the hour of need. His conscientiousness, tho' sincere, has the gait of indecision and his conciliation and ingenuity assume the appearance, and perhaps in some degree the reality, of timidity and compromise. The earnestness with which his name was caught at by the Archbishop of Canterbury, and with which Melbourne was exhorted to prefer him, did not sharpen my pangs at his disappointment. I hardly know how to account for Longley,[24] who has never voted with us and declared at the outset that he could not support the appropriation. Butler[25] had claims of long standing; it was an appointment gratifying to many old and steady adherents, though his health and age have hitherto prevented him from giving any active support. The merits of Otter[26] are said to be firmness and liberality. But the Clamour raised about Hampden deterred Melbourne, I think, from taking the marked men on the side of Liberalism such as Thirlwall, Sedgewick, Arnold,[27] and Sydney Smith or even those approved and suggested by the Archbishop of Dublin,[28] who wrote several sensible, candid, manly and confidential letters on the subject and, though perhaps the whole correspondence was tinctured with a little Oriel predilection, was as just and impartial as he was acute and discriminating in his estimation of Men.

The Ecclesiastical Patronage was, I think, next to the personal transactions connected with Mr Norton's[29] action against him, the matter most harrassing to Lord Melbourne during the Session. That action originated no doubt in private spite and sordid motives, but it was soon espoused if not actually contrived by some few base political opponents. Lord Wynford spontaneously and solemnly disclaimed any knowledge of it; he prevailed on the Duke of Cumberland to bring

Lord Melbourne across the house to hear his asseverations of knowing nothing about it, and yet it is the firm persuasion of those who resisted the cause, and I believe the suspicion of those who conducted it, that it was prompted and got up by him, and it is remarkable that Lords Abinger and Langdale, Sir John Campbell and I believe Lord Lyndhurst do not consider his peremptory and solemn denial of it any proof whatever that it is not true. So much for the high Character of the bar and the bench which has been so loudly extolled in my time! The disavowal on the part of Melbourne thro' his Counsel of all sexual intercourse with Mrs Norton, though of a more equivocal character, was much more credited and, tho' one might say

Forse era ver ma non peró credible,

many even of a light Character and some of a censorious turn implicitly believed it. The great wit and greater beauty, the fashion and somewhat indelicate and unguarded language and manners of Mrs Norton had made her female enemies who would not have lamented her exposure or her degradation. But yet, in a sort of race for unpopularity, the disgust felt at the meanness, the spite, and the cruelty of the Whole Norton family so far outstripped the indignation kindled at the Lady's beauty and success, that the whole Publick as well as the political adherents of Lord Melbourne sincerely rejoiced at the favorable verdict, and the more respectable of the Tories, especially the Duke of Wellington himself, discountenanced every attempt to affix any imputation on the private character either of Lord Melbourne or the Lady. It was much manifest and it was certainly true that the husband sought to establish rather than prevent an intimacy between the Minister and his Wife, that he endeavoured but in vain to make it subservient to his own promotion, that far from feeling any jealousy of Lord Melbourne, his anger and his separation arose from causes entirely different, and that he had been instigated by some from political motives and by others of his family from personal enmity to Mrs Norton to produce letters and describe scenes, unnecessary and inadequate to the proof of any criminal act, with the mere view of harrassing their feelings and lowering them in the estimation of the World. But the Jury were disgusted at such lowlived malignity and the publick yet more so. Even the austerity of the dissenters relaxed and they overlooked for once the more venial offences of levity and indiscretion in their detestation of the coldblooded malice and sordid contrivances of the Plaintiff and his connections. I must do the King the justice to observe that he did not allow his political antipathies or convenience to sway him on this occasion, and he either scorned to take advantage of a proceeding he disapproved or perhaps felt some sympathy for a Lady whose beauty and descent might remind him that he had not himself been insensible to the attractions of her sex and her family. The incident from which the vulgar of the tories hoped, and the liberals both at home and abroad had apprehended much, turned out so well, that it rather endeared Lord Melbourne to the popular party than estranged them from him. While it was pending I think I could perceive occasional languor and corresponding irritation in his publick speaking, and it formed an additional motive with me for endeavouring to furbish up my own. On the Whole however Lord Melbourne rose as a Speaker as well as a Minister in the Session of this Year. Though his language is good, his manner and voice fine, and his knowledge and learning extensive, yet there is a want of Parliamentary aptitude and ready apprehension and logick that always leaves one something to desiderate in his speeches. But on the other hand his admissions, though apparently imprudent, give an air of frankness and candour, and his sudden and sometimes unprovoked bursts of passion imply such fearlessness of character and such singleness of purpose, that they in a great degree disarm his enemies, endear him to his friends and, above all, ingratiate him with the publick, with whom he is become not only politically but personally too a real favorite.

The absence of Brougham and the assistance of Lord Cottenham as Chancellor were the greatest Changes in the house, for the accession of Lord Langdale made little sensible difference; he had stipulated some What affectedly to be a mere judicial and in no wise a political character in the house, and though he often seemed to take a warm interest on our side in debate and voted pretty constantly, he never spoke throughout the Session but on questions connected with Law, and on those more frequently against than in favor of the project entertained by Ministers. On the Great Law Reform bill, on which he had been much consulted, he urged his objections with as much force and earnestness and with more effect in the house than he had in the Cabinet, and though he voted with us and the opponents took different and even opposite views of the Measure, his speech and authority greatly damaged the measure and was among the main causes of its ultimate discomfiture. Our Chancellor had an uphill to fight and had no Learned friend to support him. Perhaps the want of Brougham, in spite of his power, his brilliancy, and his activity, was in his favor as well as in ours. If we missed the sevenfold shield and tremendous Shafts of Brougham, we were relieved not only from the apprehension of their being turned against his friends, but from the distress to which his perpetual and indiscriminate use and abuse of them often exposed us. The Political Sacharissa who excites admiration and applause and to madness doth incline inflicts many pangs on her soberminded worshippers, and though there may be less of rapture with Amoret and though even the food may not be quite so delicious as the poet feigns, there is comfort and repose in a quiet and wholesome diet—and such, though sparingly and modestly, our new Chancellor never fails to administer to us. The very contrast, and it was a strong one, between his merits and Broughams gave a relish to it. I will not say as Talleyrand did of his loves with Mme de Stahl[30] and Mme Grant,[31] Il faut avoir aimé Mme de Stahl pour connoitre le bonheur d'aimer une bête—for Pepys is in no sense of the word a Bête. He is a quick, sensible, and learned and ready Man and, though he neither dazzles nor delights, he always pleases his audience and often refutes without actually confounding nor provoking his audience. He gained on the house by his courtesy and good sense and though at the [*blank*] they were disposed to accuse him of mediocrity, they felt especially on the last debate with Lord Lyndhurst that in a quiet way he could blunt the edge of keen and bitter sarcasm, and dim the brilliancy of showy rhetorick and invective. Brougham was seriously ill in the winter and Spring, and that was the cause or pretext of his absence. If it was design, it was well judged; for With much publick spirit and great private Affection he had so entirely lost the Confidence of Parliament and People and made such numberless individuals his enemies by heedless promises and subsequent breaches of them, accompanied with bitter and unmerited abuse, that a full year was required to soften the prejudices and the resentments he had inspired. It is not quite clear that, had he been present, Lord Lyndhurst would have ventured to play such gambols and it is not unlikely that, having once attained to the extent he has the ear and admiration—for I will not say the confidence—of the Lords, the reappearance of Brougham on the field will be too late to force him to abandon it. In all other respects, his retreat has been an advantage to Government, to the Country, and I am most willing to hope to himself. I suspect however that he courts the outlying and discontented of our party. He strove hard but in vain to divert Lord Anglesey from his generous course, and he had I suspect more success with Lord Wellesley. He is I believe as much estranged from Grey as ever, and Durham will be confirmed in his unjust suspicions of his having decided against him on a suit in Equity from personal or political enmity when he learns that his decree has been reversed.

In the Commons Lord John shewed more discretion, judgement, and talent than ever. He inspires respect even in his enemies and gratifies and even warms his friends more than could well be expected. Lord Stanley betrayed a mixture of levity and violence which alienated his old friends more than ever and seems to acquire him no new; and though Sir James Graham continues the main object of Whig and Radical resentment, he seemed to adopt a more rational ground for his line of policy than his angry and inconsiderate friend. Howick did well on many occasions and particularly at the Conference, but among the Statesmen of that age, it seems to me that Lord Morpeth, steady, firm, diligent, and conciliatory, has risen most rapidly and most surely in publick estimation. [*In the margin*: tho' Lord Howick has not only maintained but advanced his post in Parliament, and gains with great reason, notwithstanding a little occasional but amiable impetuosity, the affection approbation and even admiration of his Colleagues in Cabinet—He is a little too apt to magnify the importance of those objects to which, like Canada, the post office, and the details of the Colonial department, he has paid particular attention and to undervalue those of which he knows nothing or has been comparatively negligent. At the free Conference[32] which was altogether a strange scene he shone extremely and his earnestness of manner, his closeness of logick, his propriety of language and manifest spirit and determination reminded one much of his father. He has none of his personal advantages, nor has he so much candour, good taste, judgement, and generosity, but he is not grossly deficient in any of those qualities and his principles are more fixed and his love and perhaps powers of application yet greater. He has, too, more originality of mind.] The Commons shewed throughout, in my judgement, great temper and forbearance. Lyndhurst and Wharncliffe were most indiscreet, unconstitutional, and almost unparliamentary in their insinuations and invectives against that branch of the legislature and individuals composing it. The burthen of their song, especially Wharncliffe's, was that a democratick faction governed the Commons and that the Ministers had no authority over them. Times have changed, and words with them. My Grandfather in 1755 or 1756 was nearly impeached for saying he was to *manage* the House of Commons and We are assailed with invective and menace because we do not *command* them. This sounds like an epigram more showy than sound, but there is truth and philosophy in it, for the objection, felt as well as stated, to Lord Melbourne's government is that the House of Commons do really represent the people and, so representing them, have, necessarily the virtual supreme government in their hands. They forget that such is the intention of a popular and representative Monarchy and they shut their eyes to the obvious truth that such must be the effect of a reform which gave to the Community a real and positive and not a mere nominal representation. It is to be hoped the House of Lords will ere long discover and act upon this undeniable truth, for as is observed with as much sagacity as drollery by Mr Creevey,[33] the people of England like the rich and Noble, they doat on the House of Lords, but yet by dint of working to disgust them they may succeed and some little progress had been made in the course of this Session of 1836. A Change of conduct or the Chapter of Accidents may arrest that progress, but if not the Country will be driven to the Alternative of being governed by an Oligarchy at variance with the obvious tendency of the times and Society, <or> of producing organic Changes and embarking on a series of somewhat hazardous experiments. Peerage Reform is already the topick of conversation, and persons not yet reconciled to the project are nevertheless more familiarized with the notion than they were, and behind that measure may be discerned, by the observing, the yet more unmanageable question of a change in the Law of Primogeniture. Some who have assumed the attitude of provocation and defiance, and Lyndhurst especially, must be aware that the natural consequence of the line they have adopted is to bring matters to an issue between extremes. They have been actuated by impatience, resentment, or a reckless desire of distinguishing themselves in confusion. The wiser portion of their party, and Peel and Wellington in particular, are supposed by us to disapprove and check them, but the Court in all probability was during this whole session on the Watch for some opportunity to effect a Change and the Duke of Cumberland did not scruple veris addere falsa with the view of impressing them with the policy of accelerating the Crisis.

Not only the King's discontent with the Ministry (which he had all along denominated the Ministry of the House of Commons, not his) broke out in occasional tirades to them and to Lord Glenelg, whom he dislikes more particularly, but actual avowals of a hope of getting rid of us were whispered about the Palace as having been made to his family and to foreigners, and in his publick speeches at dinner, passages not unfrequently occurred that the audience could not fail remarking were improper in themselves and indicative either of an aversion to the general policy of his government, or of an irregularity of mind that might lead to serious consequences and embarrassments. He told one of the Coburgh family (whom he was by no means predisposed to treat confidentially) that he ought to stay in England till the 10th. of September, because a Change of Government was always a curious event for a foreigner to witness, and he marked especially after the rejection of the Irish Church bill, by sundry acts of restlessness and irritation and by a general ungracious demeanour, his disappointment and chagrin that It had not led to a resignation. It is just, however, to add that he never on this nor on any other occasion has been known to *consult* others than his Constitutional advisers. His fears that the Tories would not undertake the government, or that undertaking it they would be beaten, alone restrained him no doubt from repeating the experiment of 1834; but tho' he might infer their intentions from their publick conduct and from his own observation on speeches, publications, and gossip of one kind or another, he never sought by any intrigue for advice or assistance to undermine his Ministers, nor even encouraged (though it was perhaps sometimes officiously conveyed to him) any communication likely to sway his determination. He was no doubt like all Princes, especially Germans, lofty and arbitrary in his notions of Government and panting for the moment of breaking thro' restraints, but from weakness or principle, from diffidence or from fear, he was strictly constitutional in his conduct, and where in language he exceeded the bounds of propriety, it was the effect of impulse or folly and no premeditated design of counteracting his publick advisers. On one subject he was certainly more irritable, more unjust, and more determined than any other. This was his jealousy and enmity to the Duchess of Kent. He hardly preserved decorum in speaking of or before her and his first impulse was to refuse and thwart every request she preferred to him, and She, being a wrongheaded woman, not unfrequently put him in the right by preferring very foolish and imprudent ones. The real cause of this estrangement was the unconscionable dislike of the King, and perhaps some equally strong and more secret partiality of the Duchess, to Sir John Conroy. The King hardly ever admitted him to Windsor or the Palace and resisted all applications both from Lord Grey and Lord Melbourne for his advancement.

The latter did indeed, as a matter of courtesy as much as policy, give some subordinate office to his son, though it is not impossible that had the King known of it at the time, it might have encreased his jealousy and estrangement from the Ministry, for there is little doubt that his unconquerable aversion both to Durham and the Speaker Abercromby is founded on a notion that they are the advisers of the Duchess of Kent, and in the latter case His Majesty is not quite wrong in his conjecture, though certainly Abercromby never gives her any advice that would, or at least should, tend to widen the breach between the two courts. That is kept up *αυτηοιν αταυϑαλιηοιν*[34] The Duchess takes umbrage at trifles, remonstrates upon small points of etiquette in which She is often wrong, and would fain regulate her motions in a way to attract notice and applause and invidiously to contrast herself with the King and Queen. She had a project of visiting Ireland and she had thoughts of asking permission to take the little Princess to Belgium. On the other hand the King sneers and even inveighs in conversation against her and Sir J Conroy, and at the Accession or birthday dinner this year, repeated *in her presence* his ungracious oration on minorities and female Regencies, describing them as the greatest of calamities, inasmuch as they, many female Regents, were necessarily surrounded by the worst, the very worst, of men, and he ended by congratulating himself and the Country on the robust state of his own health and the prospect of its averting such a calamity. The Duchess cried all the evening and the speech was so bad that the Queen felt it necessary to comfort her by assuring her that the King, when once he began speaking after dinner, hardly knew what he said and distressed his family and audience by similar outbreaks continually. She might in confirmation of that excuse have cited many recent examples, for he avowed in one his hope that in the next war he might crush the French, being, as he said, so good an Englishman as to hate a Frenchman wherever he met him!

The same hatred of [the?] foreign made him discourage if not actually refuse Lord Glenelg permission to make an excursion to some Genevan Spa for his health, observing that the same illness which would require a Secretary of State to quit his Country should require him to quit his office also, and he was displeased at Plunket and other Lawyers in high office taking Continental trips during the vacation without asking leave at Court. He secretly expressed a wish that Leopold might visit England, with the hope of persuading or frightening the Duchess of Kent into parting with Sir Jn. Conroy; but surely, if the surmizes about her amour with him are false, she will not, unless actually forced, consent to remove him. If the object be either to destroy his influence or to prevent scandal, the means taken are calculated to defeat rather than promote the object.

It is now whispered in Portugal that the Young Queen has been a second time unfortunate in her Consort, and either from her own person not being attractive or from the coldness or debility of both her bridegrooms, neither Marriage has been consummated.[35] This will not satisfy a Portuguese constitution and this observation brings me to the news of the day.

Saturday 17th. September 1836, when I resumed this book to enter in the form of diary that Lord Palmerston dined here and gave a woful account of the revolution of Portugal.[36] The Queen had been compelled to concede the Constitution to the military and *Carvalho,* the best Minister they have, to fly to English vessels for Protection. The Queen I fear considers herself in duress and with less judgement or sense than the Queen Governess of Spain, is disposed to represent herself so and to defeat the system she has consented to establish.

18 Sunday and Monday 19. Lord Plunkett who atoned for his omission of asking leave by writing to the King. I was involved, a little by Lord John Russell's fault, in a dispute or rather negotiation between Lord Nugent[37] and Mr James Stuart[38] of the Courier, the latter being promoted to a place in a Scotch Commission, to the exclusion of Mr Lauder Dick[39] [*sic*] and the disappointment of our best friends north of Tweed, pending a prosecution by Lord Nugent against that paper for a false and atrocious libel upon his administration of the Ionian Islands. Nugent has been hardly treated as well as neglected, for after all few men have sacrificed more to their principles, friends, and party and few men have been more consistently [loyal?] to those now in Office and denominated Whigs. With Lord Ebrington's assistance, who luckily dined and slept here, it may I hope be amicably arranged.

20th. Septr. Read the dispatches from Lisbon. Lord Howard seems to me to have given the Queen bad advice and She to have followed it in making and communicating to the diplomacy a declaration that in accepting the Constitution she was *not* a free agent. If she could have resisted doing so, or could have escaped, it might possibly have been wiser and more justifiable to have done so; but if she yielded, though it were in fear of life, she had much better have assumed the appearance of being a free agent and striven to make the best of a bad bargain. She has acted as persons of her Class almost always in a way to satisfy no one of any thing but her weakness and insincerity—Charles I and Lewis XVI, over again to the end of the Chapter. The Queen of Spain did rather better for, tho' reluctant, She had dignity and honesty enough to espouse to all appearance at least the measure she executed. Mr Spg. Rice saw the Governor and Director General of Bank this morning and is satisfied with his arrangement about the Exchequer bills.

21st. Council on Recorder's or Central Court's report. The King manifestly excited. He is in somewhat angry controversy with Minto upon the reduction of the fleet during winter, in which question his expectations or rather hopes of war make him somewhat peremptory and irritable. He is I understand more irritable about Lord Durham than ever, indeed the somewhat queer phrases by which Durham designates those whose jealousy dictates disproportionate precautions against Russia, even in his publick dispatches, namely *Russophobites,* is not likely to bespeak the favor of the King. It is not the way for the latter to get his Red ribband and star non sic itur ad astra.

24th. to 27th. September. At Brookes. Palmerston and Glenelg and Mr Bulwer[40] there.

Bad news from Lisbon and Madrid. At the former the Queen seems to have provoked the revolution by misgovernment, favouritism, and intrigue, to have met it without courage or dignity, and finally to have submitted to it with duplicity and insincerity. She lodged with the Diplomats a paper protesting against the act she communicated to them as invalid and extorted from her by force!—and they had the folly not to say more, to accept and conceal it! It is by such practices Ch[arle]s I and Lewis XVI arrived at the Scaffold, and surely a Stern Moralist might say *ως απολοιτο και αλλος ὁ'οτις μεν ταυτα γε ρεζει*[41] Forced or not, the moment a Sovereign yields, the thing yielded becomes his own and, if he has common sense or common honesty, he will abide by it. The Queen of Spain, equally forced and more insulted, has acted with more dignity and more honour. She adheres to her capitulation. Both Villiers and Howard and our Correspondents from St. Sebastian, Bayonne, &c report many symptoms and more suspicions of plots and underhand practices of the French Government; but in the mean while the protestations of adherence to British Alliance by Lewis Philip and Molé are so earnest and frequent to Lord Granville, that he deprecates any thing like irritating language to them and seems to think that, tho' all hopes of active cooperation by sending troops to Spain is out of the question, France may yet be shamed and cajoled into witholding her connivance at all assistance to the Carlists. Palmerston wrote at Brocket an exposition of our respective policies to Spain in the form of a dispatch to Granville and consulted Melbourne and myself upon it. It argued forcibly but courteously that the principles of the Quadruple Alliance were at issue, that practically the object of that treaty was to secure the prevalence of a representative and liberal government and the expulsion of a Carlist and legitimate one from Spain, that the same reasons existed now that subsisting [*subsisted*] then for wishing it, that we were both deeply interested in maintaining this sort of Western Constitutional Confederacy, and it hinted delicately that France was yet more interested in system than England. Philip Lewis [*sic*] is annoyed at our publick papers and especially the Globe. Palmerston has taken some steps to mitigate and check his hostility, but the difficulty of doing so is great and perhaps the existence of such difficulty not altogether unwholsome. Apropos of Papers, I was dragged into a foolish correspondence with the Editor of one, the Courier, who had libelled Lord Nugent falsly and scandalously, and was afterwards and while a prosecution was hanging over him inadvertently promoted by Lord John to a lucrative Office. Lord Nugent naturally felt offended and I suggested to Lord John that he should in justice to Nugent prevail on Mr Stuart to retract. The proprietors of the Newspaper ultimately did so and paid the Costs but Stuart, a wrongheaded and obstinate man, who had equally libelled his greatest benefactor, Lord Brougham, persisted in disavowing the disavowal. Lord Nugent throughout behaved with great good temper and honour, and not without much good nature to me, who by my own negligence furnished Mr Stuart with the only plausible pretence or excuse for publishing an imperfect retractation and asserting that Lord Nugent was satisfied with it.

28th. to 30th. Nothing fresh. The news from Spain rather better. The Bishop of Salisbury[42] dying.

October 1836. Moncorvo the Portuguese Minister gives a dreadful account of the state of Lisbon, is disgusted with the late revolution and appalled at the consequences. He wishes to resign, seems to think all true Pedroites will do the same, attributes the discontent and revolution more to secret societies and disorganizing principles propagated throughout France, Spain, and Portugal, and less to the mismanagement and corruption of the Queen's government than I believe the real truth would exhibit it. At the same time it is clear that the Country does not approve of the late transactions and there is reason to apprehend that they will pave the way for a Miguelite insurrection in the Algarves, which the Anarchists or lovers of confusion are said to <preserve> to the Constitutional system established by Pedro. With this true, bands of troops and companies of Ruffians have as in Miguel's time been introduced into the city with a view of over-awing the inhabitants. Such is the frightful picture he draws; it may be and probably is darkened and distorted by passion, but there is some ground for his apprehension. All depends on the success of Mendizabal in Spain.

From 1st. to 20th. October 1836. The state of Lisbon grew more and more unsatisfactory. Whatever might be the defects or offences of the Queen's government, and I suspect there were both in it, the Method of redressing it was as bad as possible, and the persons who conducted the Revolution, to all appearance men of no honesty, no honour, no sense, and little popularity. All who were connected with the late Ministry, and Many opposed to it, are terrified and disgusted with this and most of them have engaged in counterplots which, though detected and in law certainly indefensible, the new Government dare not denounce or punish. It is the obvious wish of the Government to drive the Queen to take refuge in our Ships, but they are alarmed lest we should resort to more active interference, for they are aware that the least appearance of regular force would produce a reaction and that nearly all that is wealthey or respectable in the Pedroite party would rally round the Queen and Prince [Ferdinand], the latter of whom has refused to take the last oath and is panting for more spirited measures. King Leopold is equally earnest and, forgetting the neutral basis on which his throne stands, urges us and longs himself to send troops in aid of his Nephew. We have determined to order Our cruizing Ships and those ordered out to the Mediterranean to appear off the Rock of Lisbon and to deposit a considerable reinforcement of Marines, for tho' we can only interfere in case of foreign or Miguelite Invasion or, according to instructions more sanctioned by precedent than principle, of actual personal danger to the Royal Sovereign, yet the moral effect of an appearance of force, activity, and some concealed design may do good and restore the late or at least some better men to power than those who now hold it; and for that reason Admiral Gage's ambiguous language when questioned about his instructions by Portugueze and the unauthorized threats of some of our Merchants may not be amiss, especially as the French have been induced by our representations to recall Mr St. Priest,[43] who seems to have been mischievously busy in intriguing against the late Ministry and has certainly given both our Admiral and Minister a notion, I trust and believe erroneous, that he was instructed to counteract British Influence in the councils of Portugal—a policy which, from previous prejudice, he would be too much disposed to foster, but which also, Lord Howard and Sir Wm. Gage would be too hasty and ready to impute to any Frenchman. Their representations, the persuasion at Madrid, and the frequent and uniform assertions of our Agents and Naval officers on the North Coast of Spain respecting the connivance of French authorities (General Harispe[44] always excepted) at supplies to the Carlist Army from France, have induced Lord Palmerston, somewhat against the judgement of Lord Granville, to require further explanations of the French Government respecting their adherence and interpretation of the Quadruple Alliance. Granville read Molé a dispatch on the subject which dwelt much on these supplies lamented that the treaty as far as France was concerned had been a 'dead letter', and required a frank exposition of the views of the new Ministry, together with a little argument on the imprudence and danger of embracing a policy opposite to that of the treaty and either fomenting federal governments or establishing Arbitrary Authority in Spain. Molé took fire at the strength of some of the expressions, vehemently disclaimed any change of policy, and urged the difficulty of hermetically sealing a long frontier. It was shrewdly remarked by Lord Melbourne that the last topick came with an ill grace from a Government who were threatening to bring Switzerland on her knees by shutting out all trade on the frontier—Unless they could prove that against Ultraliberalism they had the power but against UltraRoyalists and Carlists not.

During these days Sir Wm. Knighton died—a Man of business and sense and of a strange career. He was mindful of kindnesses and not less resentful of injuries. His timidity and his love of mystery made him pass, I suspect, for a much worse man than he really was. We shall soon know if he was so rich as he was supposed to be. He held two places and large ones in the Duchies of Cornwall and Lancaster. That in the latter, which had been augmented from 8 to £1200 for him by G[eorge] IV, was in my gift. I suggested the reduction of £400 and proposed to give it to Allen, but the King before he heard my proposal, and yet more earnestly afterwards, though without any objection to Allen, pressed and insisted on my giving it to Charles, observing truly that Charles was a good man of business, and familiarly and truly too, that he had done all he could for his daughter, it was now my turn to seize the golden opportunity of doing something permanent for my Son. He somewhat *ominously* add[ed] that he spoke to me as he had done to Grey about making his brother a Bishop. (He did so just at the time he refused making peers and nearly forced Grey out.) It would I felt be affected if not wrong to combat his wishes and resist his Commands yet so kindly meant and in truth so advantageous. So Charles is receiver[45] with 8 or £900 Per annum, but I think it would have been better for the fate of the Duchy whenever it comes again to be considered in Parliament, and I do not know that it would not have been as pleasant to me, to pay a long debt of gratitude to Allen as to provide somewhat more permanently and largely than I have hitherto been able for my son, who, however, deserves from me and I think from the publick, too, any good of the kind that can befall him. This he owes to the King.

On 20th October 1836, I with Lord Chancellor and Lord Langdale sat Commissioners to prorogue Parliament to 8th. Decr. Lord Melbourne arrived just too late from Brocket. The Queen at Lord Howe's earnest instances has consulted Dr Chambers[46] on her state of health. He thinks her lungs delicate if not positively diseased. Her German and Homopathick Quacks have injured, perhaps demolished, a constitution not naturally strong.

March 26th. 1837. For five months this book entirely neglected.

We agreed to postpone the meeting of Parliament for a variety of good reasons and among them to take the chance of some more favorable turn of events in North of Spain, where we had but too much reason to dread at the end of the year and commencement of 1837 that Bilbao would be taken by the Carlists and Evans and his Legion compelled to embark for England. The little resistance which the Carlist General Gomez[1] encountered in his predatory incursions over the whole surface of Spain, and the numberless instances of want of concert, subordination, and vigor in the Queen's General conjured ill for the cause of the Constitutionalists, tho' on the other hand the few converts or recruits who joined Gomez and the comparatively temperate conduct of the New Cortes indicated in the minds of the best informed the impossibility of any permanent success for Don Carlos. On Christmas day Bilbao was relieved and the Carlists obliged to raise the siege and retire. Though Old Espartero[2] raised himself from his bed of sickness to which he was confined by the stone and from his habitual sloth and procrastination and shewed great courage in the attack, the merit of his exertion as well as the brilliancy and glory of the action was chiefly ascribed to the British Officers, Lord John Hay,[3] Coll. Colquhoun,[4] Coll. Wylde, Lapidge,[5] and others, who urged, directed, and in some parts of the field executed the attacks.

The admiration and gratitude of the Spaniards for the English seemed to be unbounded, both in Cantabria and at Madrid, the contrast between their success in a generous cause and the failure of the French in an unjustifiable aggression on Constantina in Africa was galling enough to French vanity at Paris,[6] and the improved prospects of the Legion and the Constitutional cause damped the ardor and almost silenced the oratory of the Tories at the meeting of Parliament, for which it seemed by the tone of their papers during the autumn and winter that they were preparing philippicks and invectives against piracy, buccaneering, meddling policy, mercenaries, meanness, and what not. Nor were they elated with the prospect of foreign misfortunes only. They had a notion that some reaction had occurred in the Country, and one or two untoward Elections, especially Renfrewshire, seemed to confirm their speculations. The election of Peel to the Rectorship of Glasgow gave him an opportunity of a display, of which however he did not avail himself so largely or so ably as his partizans expected.

Some Conservative and more Radical dinners, especially one at Bath, made the enemies of Lord Melbourne's government flatter themselves that a great schism between the Whigs and Radicals was approaching and that the division of the two formidable branches of their enemies would enable them to regain that post, which in spite of six or seven years exclusion they still conceive to be their natural and lawful inheritance and possession. But the vanity or malignity of a few hot or designing demagogues served to call forth an expression in favor of union from the large mass of Whigs and Reformers. OConnel and the Irish, if not from higher and more generous motives, clearly perceived that any disunion with the Whigs would expose Ireland to the fearful experiment of a Tory Government and the effect of these <factious> dinners of the two extremes in various parts of the Country was in no little degree counteracted by a great meeting in Drury Lane Theatre of the Electors of Middlesex, at which Lord [John] Russell very handsomely consented to preside and acquitted himself with great credit to the delight of his family and friends. The King, chiefly I believe from the bad health of the Duchess of Gloucester (who was in a state of delirious excitement) and of the Queen, and partly possibly from disinclination, determined not to come up to open Parliament himself, but tho' that circumstance fortified some in their suspicions or hopes of a speedy change of Ministers, it had no effect on the debates on the address or on any of the early Proceedings of Parliament. Peel and the Duke of Wellington yet more remarkably were temperate and considerate in their tone, especially on foreign matters. Some shrewdly inferred from that moderation their expectation of an early accession to office and great unwillingness to pledge themselves to a line of policy it might in office be impracticable to pursue.

Our Speech[7] and addresses were studiously framed to invite unanimity. They did little but announce the topicks that would be afterwards brought forward, and avoided in speaking of Spanish affairs all mention of our Ally Lewis Philip, who in his speech had indulged in a French flourish which might be construed into a sneer at the policy of allowing British subjects to serve under Spanish banners. This silence, while it mortified and perhaps corrected the French Government for its coldness and want of faith in the Spanish cause, withdrew another topick from the quiver of our opponents and the meeting from which such contests were expected went off with little but reservation of opinions for future discussion and engagements. It was soon clear that the Radicals (and especially Mr Roebuck[8] whose improvement in speaking and earnest application to business shewed that he was destined to rise to some importance), however disposed to inculcate distrust of the Whigs and the Ministry, felt the necessity of supporting their Measures and the impracticability of involving their own partizans out of doors, in visionary or violent causes. There was in truth more symptoms of irreconcileable and inconvenient dissensions between the Ultra Tory, and the more reasonable or Expedient branches of the Conservative party than between the Radicals and the Whigs, and a knowledge of this inward rottenness was supposed to disincline Duke of Wellington and Peel to all active operations which might drive them to the alternative of acknowledging their incapacity of conducting the government or of undertaking it with materials which could not hold together during a Session. Others inferred from their forbearance and inactivity in the Lords, which lasted in truth till Easter, that they were apprized and appalled at the prospects of the Money Market and of Commerce, expected an approaching crash, and preferred leaving the odium and the remedy of it to their opponents to the charge of accelerating it and the difficulty of encountering it with which, if they occasioned any sudden change, they would have to contend. Meetings however at Apsley House at the beginning of the Session were frequent, and tho the absence of Duke of Cumberland and some expressions or occurrences among them which transpired served to confirm the speculation on their differences, few actual defections took place in the House of Commons divisions, and those, such as Sir George Crewe's,[9] fairly attributable to the conscientious opinions of individuals and not to any cabals indicative of a real change in the state of parties.

The division on the Irish Corporation exceeded our expectations and the debate was said to be yet more triumphant on our side. One incident in it was remarkable. On Mr Shiel's eloquent and witty exposure of Lord Lyndhurst's <impudent> and offensive phrase at the end of the former Session, representing Irishmen as Aliens in blood in language and religion, Lord Howick remarked Lord Lyndhurst sitting at the other end of the house and, having directed the attention of his neighbours to him, the whole house caught the hint, and rising like one Man, the whole Ministerial side of the house continued to greet him with an insulting cheer for full two minutes and half without the Speaker, Sir Robt. Peel, or any of his Conservative friends shewing the slightest demonstration or wish to protect him from so overpowering an ebullition of scorn and indignation. It is not to be supposed that Lyndhurst came into the Commons as Hortensius into the theatre, ut suum gaudium gaudirent, but the remaining part of the passage applied most remarkably—Hic ille strepitus fremitus clamor tonitrum <&> audientum sibilus &c ut in totam vilam cuivis satis esset et pauiteret cum <. . . .> vicisse. He felt it, as I was told by a foreigner who sat by him, most acutely. I can believe it, for tho' a shameless, he is not a callous nor I believe a really bold man. However he carried it off well, and said, 'I think Shiel must feel obliged to me for coming down here'. Sheil improved in brilliancy and effect and OConnel fell short of his former force on this occasion. In general Lord John Russell rose wonderfully in publick estimation both as a speaker and a leader of the House. His temper and decision were admirable and his knowledge, judgement, and eloquence as much beyond the expectation of his best friends as his resistance of fatigue and physical exertions were beyond his appearance of bodily strength. He announced, some think incautiously, the determination to stand or fall by the Irish Corporation bill and he postponed, according to agreement in Cabinet, with some little ambiguity as to his final determination, the question of Irish tithe and Appropriation. This line of policy disconcerted the Tories, who had no doubt settled among themselves to compromise or acquiesce in some Corporation measure, feeling the opposition to be unpopular ground, but to provoke or at least risk an entire rupture between the two houses, and two parties in the Country, where they reasonably calculated that the publick feeling in England would not be bonâ fide against them. The origin of our Ministry certainly made it difficult for us to recede with honour from the appropriation, which we had been brought in to accomplish, but those most anxious to bring and keep us in, who were the very same persons who devised that measure for the purpose, were now not only averse to our sacrificing ourselves for it, but in truth somewhat averse to the measure itself, or at least satisfied of its insufficiency and insignificance, and earnest in their hearts that we should deal with it in the manner most likely to retain our power.

We determined if not to abandon at least not to gratify our enemies and disappoint our friends by hazarding our existence for it early in the Session. In this all the Cabinet more or less reluctantly acquiesced. Hobhouse indeed seemed alarmed at giving it up and at the reproaches we might occur, but as Duncannon observed to me, he was yet more alarmed when we seemed to be inclined to bring it forward. He is frightened all ways—qui <tuitu molesta> est—and the responsibility of office not only clouds his judgement but has spoilt his speaking. He ruined one night's debate by making a lamentable display of weakness after Sir James Graham, whom Lord Howick would have answered and exposed with spirit and effect. There are few except his old Colleague, Sir Francis Burdett, now a relapsed and childish Tory, who have lost more by late events than Hobhouse, whose powers of language and extensive knowledge serve him in no stead in debate or in council. Younger Men have however got on. Lord Morpeth improves as a speaker and wins every body by his unaffected good nature and accurate knowledge of all he undertakes. Howick has improved in temper and manners, and experience in business has either softened his presumption, or the real originality and justness of his views, combined with the intrepidity and talent with which he enforces them, have greatly reconciled the world to it. In truth his impetuosity and pertinacity, though sometimes inconvenient, are of an open, generous, and amiable character and not really offensive. Two among the radicals, Mr Roebuck and Mr Ch. Buller,[10] have given indications of becoming considerable men in debate. On the other, some Irish as well as English seem to acquire the ear of the house, but tho' Stanley's powers are unimpaired, his relative importance to Peel and even to Sir James Graham seems to grow less from his total want of temper, cunning, or even judgement.

Two great questions of some difficulty, announced at opening of Parliament and prepared during the recess, were opened before Easter by Spring Rice and Lord John with very different effect both on the house and the Country—The Irish Poor Law[11] and the Abolition of Church Rates.[12] The first was received with great moderation by all parties. Its difficulties were by all sides acknowledged, and those who in their hearts wished it might not pass, of whom OConnel was no doubt one, were afraid of forfeiting all popularity in Ireland by openly opposing it. The Church Rate bill met with a different bill [*sic*]. It had been from a punctilious feeling of propriety incautiously communicated to the Bishops composing the Commission for Church Reform, and those timid but artful Priests had expressed their doubts, apprehensions, and disapprobation, prevailed on most of their Colleagues on the Commission to postpone if not abandon it, and at the same time prepared the body of the High Church Clergy and party to take measures <further> for resisting it with effect. The moment it was signified to the Archbishop that such a measure would be resorted to, cabals, consultations, and correspondences were instituted to counteract it, and little doubt can be entertained that the conservative party were apprized by their Clerical adherents or guides that the ensuing question of the Church rates would serve their turn almost as well as the appropriation Clause, and that they would lay the train and blow the flames in a way that would rouse the Country and perhaps the House of Commons itself against us. With this view innumerable petitions from the most remote rural parishes were procured by Archdeacons, Rural Deans, and other clerical vermin that infest the country, and it was evident from the language they contained and the comments with which they were delivered that the grossest arts of delusion had been practised to misrepresent the measure as one adopted and intended for the demolition of parish Churches and the elevation of dissenters at the expence of all Churchmen, lay and ecclesiastical.

On the eve of the first stage of the business in the Commons, the Archbishop of Canterbury and the Bishop of London came down and denounced the approach of Sacrilege and Spoliation, and loudly proclaimed that 15 Spiritual Lords had in a separate chamber and among themselves vowed to strangle the infant or rather embryo bill.[13] With all these manoeuvres, it is perhaps strange that they did not reduce our majority lower than 23,[14] tho' that was sufficient to animate our enemies and to discourage many of our friends and in truth to render the success of the measure and the Ministerial existence of its authors entirely dependent on the manner in which the dissenters and the liberal part of the Community would support us. For some days the Country seemed flat, but owing to the meeting of the dissenters and to two excellent pamphlets addressed as much to Churchmen as to dissenters by Messrs. Kemble[15] and Rich[16] and more than all owing to the active cooperation of Fonblanque[17] and other writers in the Newspapers, the current seems to me on this day *2d. of April* to be turning very fast in our favor.

On the death of that voluminous but obscure pamphleteer and polemick, Dr Burgess, Dennison,[18] a young Oxonian and brother of Mr Evelyn [Denison] was appointed to the See of Salisbury. Denison had so little preferment that the appointment was at least a disinterested one, and there was no ground for doubting the wisdom of it but the readiness of our Tory opponents in joining our friends to applaud it. Some too thought the reason alledged against Wm. Herbert,[19] that he had been a civilian, was not only an insincere and insufficient one, but that the one really felt and perhaps suggested by his Archbishop, that *he* was somewhat unclerical in his habits and that his wife, a Woman near fifty, had been yet gayer in her time, was no good ground for excluding a Man of learning, family, and character, who had proved his disinterested and unshaken attachment to his party and his principles on every trying occasion for the last 40 years.

Lord Abercrombie[20] had the Lord Lieutenantcy vacant by the death of Duke of Montrose,[21] and Lord Carlisle, to the delight of many, the disappointment or at least the reasonable disappointment of none, had his blue Ribband. The King by letter and at the levee and at the institution of him expressed his approbation of Carlisle in the warmest terms, though he would not even speak to his Son Lord Morpeth, very foolishly determining to shew that mark of displeasure to all connected with the Irish Government—Plunkett, Whately Archbishop of Dublin, &c. To the last mentioned Prelate, when he approached him at the Levee, he merely said 'pass on My Lord', by which he certainly did not mean to Lambeth. This was the Archbishops year for attending Parliament and he shewed occasionally both in debate and yet more rarely in Committees in conflicts with Bishop Phillpotts, the superiority of genius over art, and simplicity over cunning. [*In the margin*: His health taste and habits made him culpably averse to attendance. He was at least idle and some said a little lukewarm on any matter affecting our Ministry from disgust he had taken at our disregard of his impracticable advice about Irish poor Laws[22]—but he was honest, original, and full of genius.] He checked and exposed tho' he could not abash or silence Phillpotts.

Lord Melbourne and Lord John Russell both left town during the Easter Holydays and nothing was done in the Cabinet, though it is to be hoped that on the many important measures of Irish Poor Laws, Canada, Currency,[23] Registration,[24] Law Reform, Army, &c, &c, the Ministers in their respective Departments were not idle and our partizans connected with particular boroughs or with the press, unusually active. The unexpected return of Mr Collins[25] a Whig for Warwick gave some practical answer to the widely and industriously circulated report of a Tory Reaction. Melbourne was much harrassed with rumors of more Bishops dropping, but I fear that he will still neglect to prepare himself for that event by making up his mind in the interim what stout Clergyman to prefer, and shutting his ears after the vacancy to all the objections which should be considered and overruled before he absolutely designates a Man for the Bench. Lord Lieutenantcies and Ribbands are not so difficult. The death of Lord Bath[26] has vacated one of each. The Lord Lieutenantcy is to go to Lord Cork,[27] the garter to the Duke of Somerset,[28] who has in no unequivocal terms signified his adhesion, though I am afraid for my old College friend that his frequent absences from the house were to be accounted for by his ill humour at not having the garter or at his connection and enemy, the Duke of Hamilton, getting it before him.

The new Bishop, on the death of the Bishop of Norwich who left little property, a pure and unblemished name for disinterested benevolence and liberality, and two or three mad and unreasonable sons, was Stanley,[29] the brother of Sir John[30] and the author of some very liberal letters on Ireland, as well as of the only candid, correct, and full account of the Massacre at Manchester, which about 15 years ago made so deep an impression on the neighbourhood and country and was, in truth, a most unjustifiable proceeding.[31]

June 3d. These last two months have been productive of various speculations but few events, if we except the Spanish campaign, The French King's marriage,[32] and the Westminster Election. On the 16th. of April Evans was repulsed with considerable loss from Hernani, part of his legion took panick and disgraced themselves and, according to the version of many, though not of Lord John Hay or Col. Wylde [*In the margin*: eye witnesses and good judges], he himself betrayed negligence, indecision, and rashness. Sir Henry Hardinge availed himself with bad taste of this disaster to attack the Whole Spanish policy of government, though he in words disclaimed all direct censure of Evans's military conduct, with whom he had had some personal altercation in the house. He retailed many calumnious stories picked up from discontented officers, inveighed against hostilities without declaration of war, mercenaries, &c, &c, and endeavoured to fix the sanguinary nature of the war in some measure on the British legion and to argue that by the aid afforded on shore by British Marines we had exceeded if not departed from the stipulations of the treaty; he ended by a Motion deprecating the renewal of order in Council allowing our Officers to engage. The Spanish war was not popular with our best friends and still less with our Radical supporters, and it was nothing but the persuasion that the effect of the motion, if carried, would be to provoke our resignation, which prevented many from staying away and some from voting against us. However they behaved handsomely by us, and a Majority of 23 rejected the Motion,[33] re<formed> if not actually created by the excellent speeches of Dr Lushington,[34] who established incontrovertibly the conformity of our proceedings with the law of nations and their necessary connection with the general cause of liberty all over the world, and of Palmerston, who in a Masterly, statesmanlike, and forcible speech vindicated our general policy and exposed the fallacies and insidious designs of those who affected to recommend neutrality. I sat out the debate, which lasted three nights. I was much struck with Follet[35] and much disappointed with Peel, who spoke I suspect less well and less adroitly than usual and was certainly refuted as well as nettled by a short, sharp, and effective reply of John Russell's. Alvanley brought on something of a similar discussion but upon a mere motion of course in the Lords. Duke of Wellington adopted a more prudent tone than his friends in Commons and was thought by many to be reserving to himself the power of acting up to the spirit as well as letter of the treaty in case of a Change of government. I thundered through in a hurried and confused manner the matter of a well reasoned defence of our policy, owing to nervousness and pain and to the want of support and repose which I last year derived from my Crutches. Melbourne, by a warm declaration in answer to Alvanley of his determination to support any Officers he employed, pleased the country and the two Military professions and did himself credit as a Minister, though not as a reasoner, for the observation was in truth inapplicable to the question before the house. The division, though the majority was scanty, strengthened us abroad and at home, and Evans in May retrieved the Character of his legion by the reduction of Yrun and Fentarabia and by a display of humanity as well as gallantry highly honourable to the British name.

The conceit of the Radical party in Westminster and the restlessness of some busy bodies such as Coll. Jones[36] and I am afraid Fred:k. Byng[37] drove Burdett to the necessity of resignation and tempted a very bad candidate, Mr Leader,[38] to stand against his reelection for Westminster. He was however reelected by a large majority, and in spite of letters and speeches in which he declared himself a Tory, encouraged the No Popery cry, inveighed against Irish agitation and patriotick Cant and belied every profession and every friendship of his early life. This notable manoeuvre lost us Bridgewater also, and the Tories hailed it with some plausibility as a symptom if not a proof of rapid reaction. The events in Spain, a triumph at Glasgow, and Great failures in the City which alarmed reasonable men at the prospect of any political change or convulsion, gradually retrieved these losses and improved our prospects of stability. John Russell had declared that the Irish Corporation bill was considered by Govt. as a Vital measure,[39] tho' Melbourne at the Close of last Session had at my suggestion also declared in the House of Lords that while he was supported by the Commons, and the Commons were supported by the people, he would not abandon his post. These conflicting declarations embarrassed and annoyed our friends and the eager among the Tories were satisfied that on the rejection of the bill in the Lords we should resign, *in which case,* Peel had directly announced, and Wellington was supposed to think, that they could accept office, though they would not concur with their warm partizans in any direct measure to obtain it by driving us from our posts. But for some reason or another, probably from feeling the justice and necessity of some such measure as the Irish Corporation bill, the Duke of Wellington, Lord FitzGerald, and Lord Ellenborough, and the most sensible of that party in the Lords were averse to meeting the bill with a direct negative, and on the pretext of considering it in combination with the other Irish measures, postponed it, without announcing the course which they meant to take, to a distant day the 9th. of June—a step so offensive to the Commons and so injurious to their own party that it could in our judgement only be accounted for by a disunion in their councils. It relieved us from many embarrassments and we are now enabled to accept any reasonable compromise about the measures if they have any to offer, sure of the support of the country if they have none. The Irish and the dissenters, though eager for their respective objects of Corporation Reform and abolition of Church Rates, are firmly persuaded both of our sincerity and our difficulties in urging <either> and will not permit us to retreat even if baffled in either or in both. Resolutions to that effect are passed in both those bodies and serve to damp the ardor of the Tories, and to undeceive the few radicals who were mischievously disposed to sow dissensions as to their comparative strength. Indeed the defeat in Westminster, injurious as it was to the interests of the liberal cause, had yet the good effect of shewing Mr Hume and others that when they decline all concert and cooperation with the Whigs they expose themselves to discomfiture and disgrace.

Of the King of France's marriage I know little or nothing but what appears in publick papers. The event and the amnesty that preceded it seemed to soften the aversion of the people to L[oui]s Philippe, which, well or ill founded, was at a fearful height at the beginning of the year. My Son Henry (on a visit to me for three weeks in May) heard last summer or autumn at Vienna from St Aulaire[40] during the negotiations for a marriage between Duke of Orleans and an Austrian Archduchess, that he, St Aulaire, was extremely perplexed by the contradictory instructions he received—that his publick instructions pressed him urgently to procure the assent of the Court of Vienna and that he received from King Louis Philippe himself very earnest private letters telling him that he had set his heart upon the match and that his private happiness as well as publick honour was at stake; while the same post brought him secret exhortations from the Queen, Princess Adelaide, and the *Duke of Orleans*! himself most pathetically soliciting him to break it off. He said that so beset by conflicting wishes he should think it prudent to execute his positive commands and be lukewarm and slack about every thing not actually enjoined in his publick dispatches.

But to return to our concerns we were at the end of May and beginning of June involved in Court tracasseries of our own. [*In the margin*: The joke was that Ministers had silenced the Circassian 'Vixen' successfully enough but that they would find the Kensington 'Vixen' more troublesome, and the most efficient agent in such an operation, Lord Durham, less willing to assist them. The tracasseries had been preceded by many recent offences on both sides in which both had been equally reprehensible. Poor Lady de Lisle, tho' on no terms with the Duchess of Kent, was the King's favorite daughter and housekeeper of the palace in which the Duchess of Kent was living, and yet on the very day of her death and while her body was yet lying in the palace, The Duchess persisted in entertaining a large party to dinner under the very same roof, tho' more than one of her invited guests gave her a hint of the impropriety by sending in the morning to ask if the party was not put off. The King was hurt and angry at this pitiful spite or unfeeling pride, but he was as undignified in his way of shewing his resentment, if his refusal to admit her Son, the Duke of Linangen,[41] to the Closet, or to invite her daughter in law the Duchess[42] to the ball, ostensibly founded on the marriage being a Mesalliance, was intended as retaliation.] The King, on the Princess Victoria's approach to the age of 18, when tho' not of age as a subject she is on the contingency of her succession to the Crown declared to be so, expressed to Lord Melbourne his wish to mark his affection to his Niece and his respect for his presumptive heir by an augmentation of her establishment and pecuniary means. He asked Lord Melbourne if he did not think Parliament would agree to an additional 10,000 and approve of the appointment of a Lady Privy Purse, on which the Princess should herself be consulted to administer it—The Princess still living under her Mother's roof, but the Lady Privy Purse (not the Duchess of Kent) under the same roof, having the controul and superintendence of the expenditure. Melbourne, after examining the precedents in point, strongly dissuaded a Lady treasurer; the sum was large for any Lady's management, the residence under the same roof with the Duchess would lead to many female jealousies and intrigues, and the solitary precedent of the Duchess of Marlborough and Princess Anne was not particularly encouraging. Melbourne preferred the appointment of a treasurer or auditor, as had been meditated and approved in the case of Princess Charlotte. The King acquiesced, he sent the offer without loss of time, but he added a Postscript and adopted a mode of conveyance and delivery which Lord M[elbourne] had not suggested. In the Postscript he named as from his own authority Sir Andrew Stephenson,[43] a Gentleman peculiarly obnoxious to the duchess of Kent and one with whom she had had a publick quarrel, and he directed the Lord Chamberlain to put the letter in the Princess's own hand and to request her to read it, as if implying that it would never reach her if entrusted to her Mother or Sir John Conroy. The Princess said she would take, read, and answer it after communicating with her Mother and she sent an answer avowedly concerted with her Mother, full of warm gratitude for the mark of affection and the offer of appointing such Ladies as she named, but added that she had no wish for more Ladies than at present and declined the money, as her youth and inexperience disqualified [her] from administering such matters herself and she was accustomed and disposed to be entirely guided by her Mother in them and to leave all expenditure regarding herself entirely to her better judgement and kind discretion. The Duchess of Kent was earnest in her letter to Melbourne to fix on him the responsibility of the advice, and in reply to a temperate, civil, and judicious representation of the propriety of proposing to Parliament some arrangement agreable to both the Courts, she answered in a querulous and angry tone that she perceived the design of separating her from her dear Child, that she had long been left helpless and alone, that she had struggled thro' many difficulties, practised forbearance under many mortifications, and made many sacrifices to the preservation of peace in the Royal family, but that she knew what was due to her own character and dignity and that of the Mother of the Princess, and that she would never accept herself nor counsel her daughter to accept any thing derogatory to either, as this proposal, implying distrust of her and separating the interests of herself and her daughter to whose education and welfare she had devoted herself, manifestly was. This letter, perhaps unguardedly, Lord M[elbourne] communicated to the King, instead of softening the substance and submitting it so softened to the Duchess, as his communication of her feelings to the King. The King, apt enough to take umbrage at any thing from that quarter, was furious and in very unmeasured language in which he alluded to Sir John Conroy (King John I think) declared that he could not lower himself to any thing like compliance with her wishes which was manifestly to obtain the money to defray her own and other extravagancies. In the mean while he was ill and the drawing rooms and balls to celebrate the birthday of the Princess, which he would not allow to be postponed but which neither he nor the Queen could attend, took place under the auspices of the Old Princess Augusta.

There were many remarks, perhaps the offspring of mere imagination, on the conduct and appearance of the Duchess of Kent, the Princess, and Sir John Conroy. Some accused the latter of an air of triumph and others, the whole party of rudeness and ill humour, which was confirmed by their staying only an hour and retiring before Supper. Conroy did not diguise from some of our Colleagues to whom he spoke that the Duchess would reject any arrangement which placed the new grant under any controul but her own, and he still less concealed his conviction and *delight thereat* that the whole correspondence and <negotiation> must ere long transpire. It was they say evident that he at least reckoned upon the Duchess acquiring and the King losing much popularity, and there was enough in his manner and demeanour to account for, if not justify, the imputation of triumphing at an approaching demise of the Crown and the unwillingness of the King to allow of any indications from which a dangerous state of his health might be inferred. The Speaker from scruples or from timidity declined all consultation with the Duchess on a matter which might come before Parliament, and Stockmar, whom King Leopold sent to inculcate temper, conciliation, and accommodation, arrived too late. The King wished that the whole 10,000 should be given to the Princess with full power to dispose of it herself without the superintendence of her Mother, or of Privy Purse or treasurer Male or Female; but after some deliberation at the suggestion of Lord John Russell and Lord Palmerston, the sum was thought large for a girl of 18 and of no experience to manage and the positive rejection of the proposal by the influence of the Duchess of Kent as implying strong distrust of her was apprehended, and it was proposed to place 6000 of it at the disposal of the Duchess and 4000 as pocket money, given as a mark of affection by her Uncle, in the private purse of the Princess Victoria herself. Lord Melbourne solicited an audience with the Duchess as he had a Message to deliver from the King. She drily answered that as commanded by the King she would see him, but must desire him to make his communication in writing as she had resolved to have no intercourse by mere word of mouth on the subject or to listen to any conversation on the topick. She drily received the letter and as drily and peremptorily refused the offer in her own name and that of her daughter.

It is an ill wind that blows nobody good and this breeze with Kensington seems to have brought H M to a sense of the merits of his Ministers, for he complimented Melbourne on his honour and high mindedness, apologized for having brought him and his Colleagues into contact with 'low and vulgar' upstarts, spoke kindly to and of Lord John Russell, and sent even a civil message to the Speaker for his late arrangements for expediting publick business. His spontaneous offer of a red ribband to Durham was yet more gracious and far more politick and useful. Durham, such is the vanity even of Clever Men, may be disarmed by it for a time, and if he is fool enough to prize such a bauble he is entitled to his plaything, for his good sense, diligence, abilities, and judgement have helped to bring the awkward affair of the Vixen to an amicable conclusion. A fortunate quarrel between Urquhart and Ponsonby, which led to a disclosure of the unwarrantable intrigues of the former and possibly to a suspicion of some incautious connivance in the latter, facilitated this happy arrangement by disgusting us with those who had designedly, and with a view to embroil us in war, exposed the Vixen to capture. It is now known by Urquhart's own confession to Mr Strangways[44] that Bell[45] was *urged* by Mr Urquhart (then (most unadvisedly) in a publick and ostensible employment) to undertake the voyage. Such unpardonable intrigues make one almost rejoice at what I hear this day (*4 June*) that Bell is a bankrupt. His bankruptcy and Urquhart's recall from Constantinople may check such wicked speculations in future, but Lord Ponsonby is still at Constantinople and, though he pressed for leave of absence with some little soreness at its delay, is now, it seems, unwilling to quit his post, though Sir Charles Vaughan[46] has been several weeks at Malta <or> Naples with orders to replace him when he comes home.

The Duchess of Northumberland has resigned her place about the Princess Victoria and is this day 4th. June gone to Windsor to assign her reasons.

12th. June. She assigned two: the answer to the City was such as had rendered Duke of Northumberland[47] averse to her continuance with the Duchess of Kent; and she had herself taken umbrage lately at a change in the manner of conveying orders to her, which used to be by letters from the Duchess of Kent herself, but had lately been written and even signed by Sir John Conroy. A less offensive and plausible reason might have been assigned from the title of her office, as it should seem that a person entitled to succeed to the Crown and discharge all the duties of a Queen could hardly require a *'Governess'*. Many either implied or asserted that she had other reasons, and her resignation was often quoted in confirmation of a report that the Princess was kept in too great subjection by her Mother and Sir John Conroy, that she (the Princess herself) began to think so, that she had a will distinct from her Mother, and a very decided dislike of Sir John, and that she had on occasions manifested an inclination very shortly and peremptorily to act on her own impressions.

The speech in answer to the City of London's congratulations was very artfully drawn. It implied much more than it expressed of hardship and neglect which both Mother and daughter had experienced and of attachment to and even zeal for strong liberal and democratical policy. It is not known and hardly surmized Who was the author of the paper, which had deeply offended the Conservative party in the Country. Durham is away, Abercromby from squeamishness or timidity has studiously and affectedly abstained from all intercourse and council, and Conroy is hardly supposed to be equal to penning so judicious, so artful, and yet unobjectionable an answer.

In the mean while the King somewhat reluctantly consented to the publication of *bulletins* and the turn of his complaint enabled them in the first instance (10th. or 11th. of June) to announce some improvement in pulse and appetite and some prospects of returning strength. Melbourne however was manifestly not only apprehensive of an unfavorable termination (which I think he is pretty confident and I suspect from some more positive knowledge than he divulges, would not lead to any change of Ministry), but of protracted illness which would incapacitate the King from transacting business or at least render any agitation or excitement upon it extremely hazardous to his health. Such a state of things would be perplexing, it is thought, in the extreme to a Government which may be thwarted in its views by a hostile Majority in the Lords or even by a failure of its measures in the Commons.

[*In the margin:* Death of W[illia]m IV.]

These speculations were put an end to by the poor King's death who grew feebler though he never lost his recollection and expired between 2 and 3 in the Morning of

the 20th. of June 1837. All his children visited and attended upon him as well as the Queen assiduously in his illness, and I collected from various reports and from those of my Son Charles in particular that nothing could exceed his patience tenderness and composure during the whole of his illness. In a short interview with Charles 12 hours before his death, he spoke most affectionately of my Sister[48] and called her 'an excellent creature' (a term God knows she well deserves). Charles in writing the account of this last scene to her very naturally and truly adds that 'none high or low can leave this world with less to be sorry for, inasmuch as whatever may have been his prejudices or indiscreet words, absence of guile [*In the margin:* and he might have added of hypocrisy, vanity, conceit, affectation and presumption], kindness of intention and acting from what he thought his duty have invariable been the leading points of his Character since he has known him'. Certainly they have been so since his accession to the Crown and he was on the whole the best King of his race and perhaps of any race we have ever had, and the one who has left the greatest name as a Constitutional Sovereign and the first Magistrate of a free and improving People.

[*In the margin:* Nearly all his Children were in the room when he expired and Charles, who was also there, assured me that he was manifestly sensible of their presence, pleased at it to the last. He grew somewhat inarticulate the last day but often uttered words of tenderness and kindness. One incident occurred which, in the hands of what is called a picturesque or graphick Historian, might be made striking and dramatick. Early in the morning of Sunday 18th. June he was thought by Lady Mary, Sir Herbert Taylor, and the Queen, who were present, to have said, 'I hope I may live to see the sunset of this *horrible* day'; the last word but one was very indistinct nor could they divine his reason for terming the day *horrible,* as he expressed no other impatience and his sufferings did not appear aggravated, tho' his strength was fainter and fainter. In relating the circumstance to Lord Munster, *he* quickly and . . . ly remarked that the word he intended to use was 'Memorable', for the day was the Anniversay of the Victory of Waterloo. Accordingly, before the Sun set or the poor King expired, which was not till 2 A.M. of the 20th., the usual flag presented by the Duke of Wellington arrived and Lord Munster, with attentive and affectionate presence of mind, hastened with it into the room and laid it at the feet or across the knees of the almost expiring King, who had still strength enough left to raise his hand and touch it and to murmur, tho inarticulately, 'Glorious, Glorious'.

How often are similar speeches attributed to persons of high station in their last moments and how seldom is it that they have the least foundation in truth! But it is strange that in this instance, which I have been assured by Charles, who was in the Castle, literally passed as I have related it, tho' some hours before his death [*margin:* about <36>, it has been repeated in no public papers and little observation has been made on it even in conversation.]

Melbourne had been previously authorized by the young Queen to draw up her Speech at the Privy Council. He saw her early this morning and the Council was called to Kensington and very numerously attended at 12 o'clock. She appeared and to some advantage quite alone in that awful assembly. Her two Royal Uncles, Cumberland and Sussex, by her side and Melbourne and Lansdowne at her shoulder. The Speech was thought to be beautifully written and all agreed that it was yet more beautifully read in a distinct, firm, and harmonious voice with enough of tremulousness to denote some feeling and modesty, but not to obscure the sense or disfigure the delivery. In general her deportment was much approved and her countenance and demeanour impressed the audience with the idea of good sense, good taste, and considerable firmness and self possession. She whispered and smiled with Melbourne once and she spoke occasionally to her Uncles. To all others without distinction she was gracious, courteous, and well bred. In short, on the first drawing up of the Curtain the performance has been very successful, all the audience acknowledging the talents of the performers, and all those friendly to us, highly satisfied with the prospect of its continuance. The speech contrived adroitly enough to eulogize the late King for the extension of liberty during his reign and, though it pledged her to the support of the reformed Religion *as by law established* (which last words Tories and Churchmen always strive to pervert as inconsistent with the legislative and ecclesiastical reforms), they are qualified by some phrases in the same clause in favor of religious liberty and of justice to all classes of her subjects. There had been some doubt about the propriety of the King of Hanover—Duke of Cumberland's appearance at the Council or in Parliament in the Character of subject or peer of another Kingdom from that of which he is Independent Sovereign. There can however be no doubt of his right, and Though he might hestitate to take the oath of a Privy Councillor, that was a point for the King of Hanover to consider, not for the Queen of England to object to. I examined this subject with some care and was diverted and pleased to find that at my age I could be as earnest, as eager, and as diligent about a trifle, which in no wise affected me, as I could have been about the quantity of a word or the ending of a Pentameter when I was at Eton. The instances of William King of Scots in Richard I's time, of Richard Duke of Cornwall and King of the Romans in Henry III's and of John of Gaunt Duke of Lancaster King of Castile and L(e)on, in Edward III's and Richard II's time were curious and interesting, the last very directly to the purpose and the last but one very diverting in Matthew Paris's sarcastick narrative.

3d. July. I somewhat perversely neglected this diary during the whole fortnight, tho' I was on my couch in illness, had nothing else to do, and heard a variety of anecdotes and incidents in the new reign that were curious and interesting at the time and might, if recorded, be yet more curious when compared with subsequent events. Will they be natural forerunners of them or will they form a contrast to them? Not only the general voice of all who approach our new Sovereign are loud in commendation of her manner and demeanour, but the traits which Melbourne naturally and without [*word missing*] recounts of her seem to me to indicate much sense and much determination too, and yet no absence of feeling and delicacy. 'I am sure you will approve,' said she, 'of the answer I have given to the FitzClarences to remain in the Castle as long as they like. Poor people they must be very unhappy'. She then told him she had written to Queen Adelaide to offer to go down to Windsor to see her, or to defer the interview till after the funeral as most soothing to her feelings, and she then consulted Lord Melbourne as to mode of directing the letter. Lord Melbourne said that it was so very soon after the event (it was the very next day), he thought 'the Queen Windsor', tho' not the most formal or correct, would be the most delicate direction. I thought so too, said she, and have so directed it and will now send it. She acquiesced, most readily and perhaps most advisedly, in suppressing the office of private Secretary as unconstitutional and improper, and when asked if she could go thro' all the fatigue of the signatures and arrangements of the papers, answered sprightily, 'I don't know but I will try'. This was lucky at least, for it saved her Majesty the painful necessity of either pressing Sir J Conroy or passing him over to the annoyance of the Duchess of Kent, and Melbourne the embarrassment of demurring about him if he had been named. The Queen either proposed or acquiesced in giving him a Baronetcy, and she accepted Lord M[elbourne]'s recommendation of Sir Henry Wheatley[49] to be continued as Privy Purse, which perhaps was as a great mortification to Conroy as the suppression of the Secretaryship. In general I think I can collect that the Young Queen is far from indifferent in these appointments and, tho' willing to consult and to defer to Melbourne's judgement, is not likely to be governed entirely by any body and hitherto certainly by none but her ostensible advisers.

22d. July. I have been at South Street and attended House and Court and dined at Court and talked much with Melbourne and others about the New Queen and her Court.

It seems that not only she conveyed to Melbourne before the King's death her commands to prepare her speech to the privy council, and her determination to remove quickly from Kensington to Buckingham palace, but the King on his deathbed found means to convey a message to her, unknown to her Mother, advising her, unless she had a very strong repugnance to the Ministry in Existence, to continue Lord Melbourne and his Colleagues and to signify that intention to them without loss of time, or, if she must change, to discard all thoughts of a middle or an Ultra Radical Government and to send at once to Peel and Wellington. The conveyance of such messages, to and fro', must have required some management, if there be any foundation in the reports of the extreme watchfulness of the Duchess of Kent and the excessive and injudicious restraint under which she kept her daughter. That such was likely to be the error of her management, Leopold had early foreseen and conveyed to Lord Grey when he assumed the Crown of Belgium, thro' Baron Stockmar, which was the same channel through which the communications were made by the Princess to Lord Melbourne during the King's life. The constraint under which she lived was to the full as Great as W[illia]m IV and Sir Herbert Taylor supposed, for though it seems almost incredible, I have been confidently assured by those well informed persons, Stockmar, Melbourne, and others, that the King's letter and offer of an establishment, which she was made to answer and decline, was never communicated to her and she certainly since her accession has occasionally acknowledged in words, and still more implied by actions, her regret at the little deference shewn to her Uncle's court and her wish to mark her sense of the affectionate duty paid to him in his last moments by the Queen Dowager, his family and attendants. Whatever the constraint was, she does not disguise from Lord M[elbourne] and those more immediately about her and in her confidence her full determination to emancipate herself from it entirely and, when she declines any advice or interference from that quarter, observes that really she can do no otherwise, for if the law has given her the <choice> and authority, it is her duty to exercise it according to her own judgement. In outward appearance however she is respectful, attentive, and even affectionate to her Mother, and the Duchess of Kent has the sense to disguise at least to common observers the deep mortification she no doubt feels at perceiving the entire loss of all influence as well as authority.

It is clear that the Queen positively dislikes Sir John Conroy and as clear that the dominion of that Gentleman over the Duchess of Kent stimulates her to attempts that the least reflection would shew her must be fruitless, and which when thwarted add to her vexation. She asked for an English peerage and red ribband for him. This was of course refused, but a Baronetcy, the promise of an Irish peerage when one should become vacant, and the payment of an annuity of 3000 per annum out of Privy Purse, the largest, I believe, ever settled on that fund with the exception of Mrs Fitzherberts,[50] have been assured to him; and the Queen was not only willing but earnest that the money should be allowed to him. When however her Mother said He must ride with her if she rode, she somewhat pettishly answered, 'Then I am determined not to ride', which she had before expressed her great desire to do. The day I dined at Court, she bestowed so much of her attention on myself and Lord Melbourne that Lord Templemore,[51] the Lord in waiting, came and whispered Lord M[elbourne] that Lord Hertford,[52] who was in the room, was manifestly nettled at being neglected, and Melbourne bade me ask her Majesty to wheel my chair from her side to look over the Whist table and to whisper to her my reason for so doing. 'Do you think so', said she to me. 'I do', and I wheeled off and she called Hertford. She told Melbourne next day I was right. Hertford was very sulky and had been so to her sister in law. In all these matters she is observant, goodhumoured, and has evidently a sense of ridicule, which a stronger sense of propriety checks and chastizes. She had urged Lady Forbes[53] from a knowledge of her poverty and a recollection of her intimacy to be a Lady of the Bedchamber, but after acquiescing but inquiring about it, Lord Melbourne, who had <found> that She, Lady F[orbes], was an active political enemy, remonstrated and the appointment was suspended. She recounted this to Stockmar. Do you know, she asked him, what Lord Melbourne says? he says—*and as she repeated it she blushed*—he says it would *play the Devil!* It is quite clear to me that he is more afraid that the estrangement between Mother and daughter, if it comes to be known, will have that effect to a much greater degree. He thinks resentment at past and extravagant subjection, mixed with some degree of suspicion of some strange cause <for> Sir J Conroy's dominion over the Duchess, has sunk deep in her mind, and it is his wise and good natured wish to allay it as well as the acute disappointment it creates in the other party. Such are the blessings of a court—and if Monarchy be a good, such is the price which all who have to do it pay for enjoying it.

On the 23d. July. Mme de Lieven, Lord and Lady Durham,[54] and Lord and Lady Clanrickarde[55] as well as Duke and Duchess of Sutherland[56] dined here. Durham in good and Clanrickarde in bad humour. The Duke of Sussex, on whom I called in the morning, is very anxious for some mark of favor from a New Sovereign and friendly Ministry. A Captain Generalship of Artillery and the Civil Mastership of the order of the Bath will I hope be given him and I urged Melbourne to let it be soon. Coke's Earldom of Leicester pleases every Whig.

24th. July. Minto shewed me a letter from Melbourne ordering a frigate to be prepared with accommodations for a Governor to sail to Canada and without loss of time. So I infer that Durham goes there! and he was in high good humour yesterday when he dined here with Mme de Lieven and Duchess of Sutherland.

I extracted for the Queen, with some additional notices and comments, Sheffield, Duke of Buckingham's account of Buckingham House.[57] It cost me some pains to ascertain the facts.

Elections as usual represented to be going well for the side which speaks of them. There is a lack of money, compared with former elections, among the Tories—and perhaps a zeal in both parties—but the apathy, which proceeds from content or love of quiet, tells after all in favor of those in possession, though their adversaries brand them with the character of Revolutionists and dub themselves *Conservatives.* That feeling, The illusion naturally produced by growth and power in the person of an interesting Girl, her own extraordinary propriety of behaviour indicative of great sense and some strength of Character, and the disgust which the King of Hanover's mad and wicked proceedings have produced, all tell and strongly in favor of our Ministerial Candidates.

26th. July 1837. A Duchy Council held in the library, and I afterwards attended Privy Council at Buckingham House where I heard that Durham had declined Canada but professed to be pleased with the offer, and that it *was* the intention of the Queen to *keep* the key of round tower at Windsor, when upon Munster's delivering it into her hands, she did not return it. She imagines he might be an unpleasant inmate of Castle and Castle Yard. Bishop of Hereford dead. Melbourne said nothing of his Successor. Duke of Sussex very properly made Captain General of Artillery, but Melbourne says he is avarus honorum. King of Hanover has made a demand of Queen Charlotte's diamonds, given her in 1662 [*1762*] and bequeathed by her (by what authority?) to Crown of Hanover, now a foreign Sovereign. They were bought of Willm. Duke of Cumberland for £54,000 in 1662 [*1762*] or about that time [*In the margin:* See my Grandfather's memoirs[58]], they are now owing to the depreciation of jewels valued at 25 or 30,000. The question about them may be awkward, but our little Queen vows she won't wear any of them till the question is settled.

30th. July. The Round tower, resigned by Munster, is given to Duke of Sussex. It is right Sussex should be gratified and he is vastly by this favor, but there is an appearance of a want of magnanimity in accepting Munster's resignation. The place has generally been treated like one for life, and was given on the death, not on the removal, of Lord Conyngham to Munster. It is therefore natural that the FitzClarences should all feel sore and unless something is done for the only warm friend we have among them, Lord Frederick, who has been somewhat harshly and, I believe, chiefly at Duncannon's suggested [*suggestion*], deprived of his

Equerryship, they will have some reason to complain and will find I believe much sympathy in the feeling part of the community. I know not if Munster's removal be Melbourne's or the Queen's own; if the latters, it is not a very good omen.

31st. July to 2d. August. Duke of Sussex, who dined with me Sunday, is not yet installed as constable of Windsor Round tower and Melbourne thinks it requires some consideration. Fredk. FitzClarence is anxious about his privy Purse annuity of £700 per annum which stands on a different footing from those of his brothers. He is also desirous of a Mission or a Government. The first he will not get but to the second, if equal to it, he is in some sort entitled. Musgrave[59] not Wm. Herbert will be new Bishop. Lady Durham is a Lady of the Bedchamber but, I suspect, Durham is far from pleased, tho' hitherto he directs his shafts chiefly against small game, appointments or continuances of Tories, favor to wavering politicians.

Rats and mice and such small deer. Brougham, writing to John Russell a complaint of the hard usage he receives from Newspapers, says that from principle he has abstained from injuring a Govt so weak. but had been almost tempted and provoked to do so by Mulgrave's unwarrantable abuse of the prerogative of Mercy, tempted I suppose by Wellesley, who wittily remarked that the theatrical Lord Lieutenant knew not how to get up his miserable pantomimes and Melodramas and, having heard that Justice was blind, the blockhead thought it would be a trait of Genius to make Mercy so too. Among these malcontents I am afraid Clanrickarde must be classed. He must naturally have been mortified at having been so long neglected, but he bore it well till his Lady resented the omission of her name among the Queen's Ladies. There are perhaps plausible and reasonable grounds and possibly some felt by the Queen herself to this omission, but a little surprize and indignation at it on the part of Clanrickarde were to be expected and are pardonable. Not so his way of expressing them, which is undignified and injudicous. He has reproached Lord Melbourne 'with neglect amounting to disrespect' and Melbourne, tho' diverted, is nettled at the expression and angry at his refusing his support to the Ministerial Candidate in Galway. The Borough Elections have not been brilliant and those of the Counties have begun ill and threaten to be worse. In Scotland we maintain our ground. I wait till we know how far our hopes are realized in Ireland to speculate upon the ultimate result. Reports are confidently asserted of Peel being seriously ill. His death would be a publick loss and his Enemies as well as friends would feel it to be so, but it would possibly alter the relations of parties in the new Parliament and certainly the *speculations* on the respective strength of them at the meeting.[60] I do not believe that the interior of the Palace is a whit more harmonious (except in the sense of musick) than it was a week ago. The Queen will not, I am told, though asked by Duchess of Kent, invite Conroy or his family to dinner. Surely this is rather too ungracious of a manifestation of a spirit which it may not be possible or even right entirely to subdue or suppress, but which should not be ostentatiously displayed or even avowed without necessity.

from 3d. to 20th. August. The Elections, especially those of the English Counties, have somewhat disappointed our eager partizans and, I am told, surprized and a little mortified our Queen, who takes as warm and even warmer interest in our liberal politicks both at home and abroad, and especially in the Peninsular affairs and the concerns of her two Sister Queens of Spain and Portugal, than I had imagined. She has a common feeling with them and a strong predilection for her Uncle Leopold, whose recent elevation to a throne has, she seems to think, identified her family interests with those of representative governments and constitutional or parliamentary Monarchy. This is lucky for the interests of freedom, though perhaps it is rather mortifying to philosophy to perceive how much the destinies of Europe, and the institutions and happiness of Mankind, still depend, in spite of the pretended march of intellect, the schoolmaster, the representative system, the press, or what not, on the accidental and personal character and will of a girl of 18! Melbourne is I think struck with her sagacity and yet more with her calm and deliberate determination, pleased *on the whole* with her feelings, but not without misgivings that her aversion to Conroy, and her estrangement from her mother mixed with something like contempt of her understanding, may break out in some way harsh and unamiable and injurious to her character. He is too very naturally apprehensive, that she and those about her must in the ordinary course of things have stronger passions ere long to deal with than, under her late restraint and in her present girlish enjoyment of novelty and curiosity, have yet crossed her mind. Her family complexion and blood, her period of life and her inordinate love of *musick*, all in his judgement indicate the germ of a warm constitution, and she has too much sagacity and intrepidity in her character not to ascertain that she is under no restraint but such as her own sense of prudence and propriety may impose.

Melbourne told me that he had ascertained lately what would have been the steps which the late King would have taken had he and Lord John resigned on the postponement or rejection of the Irish corporation bill. He had drawn up a paper explaining and vindicating his own conduct in the appointment of the four administrations formed during his reign, and appealing to the testimony of the four respective Premiers—Wellington, Grey, Melbourne, and Peel—that he had given them during their respective Ministries his fair Constitutional support and never, indirectly or by any communication with other than his ostensible advisers, sought to thwart their measures or divide their counsels; that from no fault of his, the Country was without a Government and a very frightful crisis approaching, and that he called upon those four persons to consult and give their joint advice on what principles and composed of what materials to form a government, in the hope that they would be able themselves to assist in forming it and act in concert sufficiently to give the Crown and the people the benefit of a strong and stable Government.[61] This paper was to be sent to Duke of Wellington, to Lord Grey, then to Mr Peel and to Lord Melbourne in succession, and to mark that in soliciting their advice and assistance it was not His Majesty's wish to mark any preference of individual or party. The King before his death contrived to convey his advice to his Niece to continue Lord Melbourne and his Ministry in office but, if she could not place any confidence in them, to send to the Duke of Wellington and Mr Peel, dissuading her from making any unnecessary Change or new experiment. Whether this was cautioning against Duchess of Kent or Durham or simply the result of his judgement of what was best, I know not, but I think it was good advice and does the adviser credit. He thought either one or the other party would act fairly by the Crown and the Country, and he had a confidence in both and especially in Melbourne's not leaving her entirely in the hands of Conroy and Duchess of Kent, which was his ruling terror for some months before his death.[62]

[*From the diary of John Allen*[63]]

Augt. 21 [*1837*]. The Elections are now so nearly over that the relative strength of the two parties may be compared with some approach to accuracy and the result seems to be that the ministers have a majority of not less than 38. Lord Melbourne reckons 29 on ordinary questions. The losses of the Reformers have [been] chiefly in the English counties and their gain in Ireland. In Scotland the loss and gain has been nearly equal. The causes of the reaction in England have been chiefly:

1, the violence and activity of the Clergy, who with very few exceptions have been indefatigable in their exertions to influence the farmers and landed gentry against the ministerial Candidates;

2, the Poor Law Amendment Bill, which has indisposed the labourers, small farmers and all the jobbing shopkeepers and vestrymen. The Tories, though they supported and approved of this measure have, with very few exceptions, most unscrupulously availed themselves of the discontent it has created;

3, dislike of O'Connell and of a government deriving its support from the Irish members. Many merchants and country gentlemen feel indignant that England should be governed, as they say, by Ireland.

To these general causes may be added bribery and intimidation—though it is probable that these instruments have been used on both sides—better organisation of committees on the Tory than on the Liberal side, apathy from the non-fulfilment of the expectations entertained from the Reform Bill without considering to what causes this disappointment is to be attributed, and with some, perhaps, the fear of a prolonged collision with the House of Lords. Many persons in the employment of government are also said to have taken part against them. Besides the services rendered by the Clergy at the actual elections, they act as a vigilant police in rural districts to ensure the registration of voters in the Tory interest or under the control of Tories. It would require a Committee of Reformers in every parish to counteract them.

Aug. 25 [*1837*]. Among other causes that have operated against Ministers in the West of England the fear of Popery has had an effect. I have heard of Dissenters and even Quakers declaring that they look to the established Church as the only security against the Papists!

[*Lord Holland's diary resumed*]

4 Septr. I have neglected this diary, but I have had little to record—gossip and tittle tattle from Court of traits of the Queen. She is now at Windsor, riding constantly and improving in health, looks, and horsemanship. Palmerston tells me as a trait of her determined temper that, though she likes riding excessively, she would not mount a horse for two years! because before she was Queen, the Duchess of Kent insisted on Conroy's accompanying her. She is now taking out her two years without the fear of Conroy.

Her reception of King Leopold and his Queen was cordial, natural, and affectionate. She ran down stairs and jumped into his arms, and afterwards did the honors with her wonted grace and composure. She takes great interest in the Queens of Spain and Portugal, especially the latter, but the intelligence from both countries has been lately so bad that it deadens and disgusts all who felt about them.[64]

I was at Windsor Castle from

14th. to 16th. Septembr., slept in the room (now much altered) in which the poor late King died, and which had been destined by the Comptroller or Chamberlain in the first instance for the breakfast and luncheon room of Maids of Honour, but was discontinued by the Queen's orders from an apprehension that it might be deemed indelicate to convert it so recently after a melancholy event to any thing like a scene of festivity. I saw the Queen to advantage as the King and Queen of the Belgians were at the Castle, and her affection for her Uncle seemed to improve her spirits and excite her natural and kind emotions, and her successful exertions to please his Queen and cultivate the acquaintance and friendship of one, in station and age so near to herself, shewed her powers of pleasing to much advantage. The entire absence of any haughty assumption, any unbecoming levity or triviality, or any thing like awkwardness, ill humour, inattention, or rudeness would alone be remarkable in a girl of 18 who had seen so little of the world, but attended as it is with every indication of quick perception, good taste, and kind disposition, It really makes her a pattern of propriety without impairing the least the charm of youthful and light hearted manners. [*In the margin:* The restraint under which she was kept was perhaps useful and necessary but certainly unusual. She has said since her accession that she was never alone in a room with any person whatever, her Mother excepted, till within three days of her accession. I think she should also have excepted Mme Letzen to whom I suspect She and the Country are chiefly indebted for the admirable education she has received and the happy fruits that it is likely to produce. Mme de Letzen[65] is a Woman of sense and information, great judgement and yet greater strength of mind. She had been employed in superintending the education of another daughter of the Duchess of Kent, half sister of Victoria, and she contrived, without eclat and without too much subserviency, with the Countenance of Leopold, to maintain her post at Kensington against the wishes, as it is supposed, of both the Duchess of Kent and Sir John Conroy and without furnishing either with any just cause of complaint. I was much struck with the frankness and sagacity of her conversation.] She sat at dinner between King Leopold and Melbourne, and though there was greater familiarity and a stronger approach to filial attention in a manner to Leopold, both seemed to inspire her with the confidence and ease of a girl with two of her favorite Uncles or Elder relations. There is melancholy as well as interest in the reflections which the change of scene or the Change of possessor of a palace naturally inspires, and I think the contrast of what is with what had been and what might have been must have struck Leopold, now a Royal Guest with a Princess of France for his Queen in the Castle of which his first wife would have made him master, more forcibly than any of us. His language was as usual very deliberate and cautious, but friendly and judicious. He certainly would inculcate a cordial understanding and close alliance with the constitutional Governments in Europe and France in particular abroad, and would lean to a preference of Whigs over Tories at home with a view to maintaining that system, though he may have and probably has more notion of the practicability of union between the moderates of Conservative and liberal politicks in England, and a stronger leaning to commercial jealousy and to artificial contrivances for rivalling or ruining our great superiority, than is reconcileable to reason or prudence. On the latter point he is too cautious and too sensible to fancy that he could sway his niece, and on the former he would I believe from timidity dissuade rather than advise making any early experiment. In the interior of the Palace his visit had manifestly done good. The Duchess of Kent looked more comfortable and the Queen, if possible, was more at ease. She seemed to enjoy her ride and company, and reigning appears by its effects to be wholesome for the body as well as agreable to the Mind. She is fresher in complexion, firmer in gait, and I think even larger in person than she was on her accession. When she first learnt, at 8 years old according to her version, at 10 according to Mme Letzen, that she was the successor to W[illia]m IV, she is said to have looked frightened and said, 'then I must be a very good girl', and she said that for some days she disliked the thought, but afterwards grew reconciled and even pleased at it. She does not now conceal her satisfaction at it from herself or from others. 'Far from being fatigued with signatures and business' (said she in answer to Duchess of Sutherland) 'I like the whole thing exceedingly.' I did my best to find fault but really could discover none but the inconsiderate habit of keeping her Ladies standing too long. When the Ladies retire from dinner, she seldom sits down till the Gentlemen follow them, and I hear the Duchess of Kent first remonstrated and has since retired from the Drawing room for half an hour every evening to repose herself in her own room, till she can return and *sit* by her daughter or at the Whist table in the Evening. It was droll enough to see the Ladies, young and old, married or unmarried, with all their *rumps to the wall* when we came from the dining to the drawing room and eagerly availing themselves of their release when the Queen took her seat on the Sofa. [*End of B M Add. MS 51871.*]

[*From the diary of John Allen*[66]]

Nov. 26 [*1837*]. There was a meeting yesterday at the Reform Club at which 50 members of Parliament were present. Molesworth[67] made a speech against Ministers, O'Connell answered him and said that if they wished to bring in a Tory Government they must not count on the support of the Irish members, and that he in particular would do his utmost to expose them to the indignation of all true Reformers. I know not who else spoke but there were only five—Molesworth, Leader, Wakley,[68] Grote, and Whittle Harvey—who were for withdrawing their support from the Ministry. Brougham is supposed to have had some share in setting them on these proceedings. Roebuck has been for a considerable time his chief political Ally. He has accepted an invitation to dine at Lady Tankerville's,[69] but made it a condition that no Cabinet Minister should be there to meet him. Lord Johns unnecessary and ill-judged declaration in favour of the landed interest against the towns[70] has given offence to many and on the other hand the appointment of a committee to examine into the Pension List has given much satisfaction. The general opinion seems to be that the Ministry will go on till February, and that it will then depend on the measures they bring forward whether they have the support of the Radicals or not. Many who are anxious they should not go out are nevertheless dissatified with them. Warburton I am told is one of the number. Lord Melbourne thinks this is a beginning of the dissolution of the Govt.

Decr. 13. The House of Commons continues in a very feverish state and the Government in a very precarious state. Bullers motion for changing the mode of trying Election Petitions and the reference of the Pension list to a Committee were carried by triumphant majorities, but in the debate on the Spottiswood subscription[71] the Ministry had the worst of it and all agreed that nothing was to be done. The question at present is whether Whittle Harvey shall be member of the Pension list Committee which he originally proposed. Lord John is against it. The Radicals and even many of the Whigs are for it and Sir G Sinclair (a Tory) had proposed it. No one thinks him an honest man, but many say he can do no harm in the Committee and that his exclusion will do great mischief.

Brougham has been very active of late, making speeches, not directly hostile to the Ministers, but full of insinuations against them. After one of these speeches last night Lord Melbourne burst out with great violence against him, to which Brougham rejoined with equal or greater violence. The Tories in the House thought he had hardly given provocation sufficient to justify Lord Melbourne's sally. Lord Holland was not present. Some days ago Brougham dined with Molesworth <and Leader> who had a small party of Radicals to meet him; Grote, who was one of them, had declared, I am told, for a Tory Ministry in preference to the present.

[*Lord Holland's diary resumed*; *beginning of BM Add. MS 51872.*]

Christmas 1837 December. For more than 3 Months I have entirely neglected this journal, from business, indolence, infirmity, or necessary exertions in other ways. I have no chance or prospect of preserving any thing like a regular narrative of events. [*In the margin:* The opening however of Parliament was auspiciously preceded by the Queen's dinner in the City, for which fortunately the fog of the preceding day in a great measure dispersed. The whole of the pageantry went off well and the concourse of people, their orderly conduct and their unaffected curiosity, enthusiasm, and delight were almost unexampled. The contrast of the whole scene to the disappointment which had occurred under Duke of Wellington's government in 1830, when even *he* deemed it unsafe for the Sovereign on his accession to accept the Lord Mayors festivities and traverse a *disaffected* city, occurred to every mind. The tories were twitted with it in every journal and almost in every conversation. It furnished a ready and a striking topick whenever it was necessary to expose the false report of a great reaction throughout the country in favour of soi disant Conservatism, but our debaters with equal taste and magnanimity generally abstained from it.]

There was hope among the Tories, and expectation in the publick, without apprehension among our friends, that on the meeting of Parliament we should be beaten in the Choice of a Speaker, that on foreign affairs and even on Irish enquiries we should be hard run by the Tories, and that a division between Radicals and Whigs, ensuing immediately, would render us too weak to continue in office even till Xmas. It was however soon surmized that neither Wellington nor Peel (who had been abroad and was very cautious in his language while there) approved of the policy of any very early attack or deemed their own party either strong or compact enough to form a government, if they should drive us from the helm. [*Heading:* 28 December] Indeed Peel, to whom John Russell had somewhat strangely written to ask if he had any intention of opposing Abercromby for Speaker, answered him that he would give him notice in time if he had any such design, but remarked smartly enough that he did not recollect that John, in 1834, previous to the rejection of Mr Sutton, had shewn that he deemed such announcement of his intentions any necessary part of the courtesy to be preserved between political adversaries. Abercromby was rechosen without opposition. On the address little was said on foreign policy in Commons. All passed most amicably in the Lords where the Duke of Sussex at his own request moved the address in a speech of much good feeling and, of what was far less usual with him, some felicity of language and some judgement in the selection of topicks.

The opposition in the Commons was from an Ultra Radical party. The small numbers they divided and the little dexterity, concert, or management they displayed rather lowered than raised their importance as a party. Lord John answered them with great spirit, firmness, and effect, but perhaps too tartly and personally. He was misunderstood to say that the reform bill was 'final', a stand should be made, which is a form of defence against proposed improvements vicious in itself and particularly odious to all class of reformers [*In the margin: NB.* The word 'finality', which he *never used,* was repeatedly quoted against him and he was occasionally taunted with it for full two years.[72] The spirit of the speech was however more repulsive than was prudent in a Minister so dependent as he was on the occasional forbearance of the party he repelled. The mischief of it was more lasting than that occasioned by mere ἔπεα πτεροεντα[73] generally is.] and on the 2d. day's speech on the report, [*sic*] (which was generally better in judgement and temper) he unluckily stated with some complacency and triumph that the reform had left the land a considerable ascendancy over the boroughs or monied interest, that it was intended so to do by its framers, and that it was right that it should be so. An imprudent and ungracious declaration! Imprudent as shaking the confidence of all town reformers in his designs, ungracious as exulting over the weakness of his Chief supporters, the town representatives and their constituents, and approving of a political superiority in the class where he and his friends were least likely to meet any favour, viz the land. Yet the firmness and manifest determination to give up office, rather than be hallooed into measures he disliked and disapproved, did good, and the large inequities with which Ministers set off in the new Parliament impressed distant parts, at that very time expectant of their defeat, with an exaggerated and false notion of their strength—a persuasion which the obvious favor enjoyed by Lord Melbourne at Court and the judicious predominance of Ministerial company, though without exclusion of leading Opposition Characters, at the Palace tended greatly to confirm. This persuasion contributed to create the strength it supposed.

Such impressions were yet further confirmed by the divisions and results of the Civil list bill, two Duchies and the pension list, for tho' on the two latter heads the principle of mystery and concealment was completely abandoned, and the former bar to all revision of the past pensions somewhat ignominiously though necessarily relinquished, yet the analysis of the divisions manifestly shew that there were more skulkers, lukewarm friends, or deserters among the tories than among the Whigs, and that even when the larger portion of tories factiously supported the Radicals against the Whigs and a smaller number of their friends, they found themselves left in a minority. On Irish topicks Ministry was yet more successful. In the Lords not only Lord Mulgrave vindicated himself triumphantly from the charges of Lord Roden; but Lord Roden's charges were themselves much mitigated in comparison with those which had been thundered throughout tavern meetings and blazened forth in papers, and the Lords (Donoughmore[74] and the Duke of Wellington particularly) who supported Roden made admissions almost as advantageous to Mulgrave's government as his own defence.[75] In the Commons every accusation recoiled on the Orangemen, and the whole terrifick apparatus which No Popery declaimers had vowed they would exhibit on the <grandest> edge

Fell flat at once and shamed its worshippers.

We had some difficulty about the Duchess of Kent's debts. She owed 60 or £70,000, and she said the Queen on the morning of her accession had promised to pay her debts; but when it was offered to do so by an application to Parliament, She declined peremptorily being a party to any such proceeding and implied and even insisted that the Queen had engaged to supply the Money from the Privy Purse. We could not honestly establish that fund for the Queen's private comfort without the knowledge that it was so exonerated from so exorbitant a charge. On the other hand, we could not apply to Parliament for the payment of her debts without the sanction and in the teeth of a protest of her who had incurred them. We thought however that the change in her situation fairly entitled the Duchess of Kent to an augmentation of income, and that the strong and in many respects just persuasion of her merit in educating our youthful Sovereign would dispose Parliament and people to acquiesce and perhaps even to go beyond the *£30,000* which we proposed. That sum was only half what had been allotted more than seventy years ago to the Princess Dowager of Wales, whose situation and character and rank was most analogous though not exactly parallel to her own. It was not a third of what had recently been fixed on the Queen Dowager. Leopold her brother, as the Widower of an heir presumptive, had had £50,000 per annum assigned him. Her £30,000 was obtained without much difficulty, but it was not voted with the alacrity and much less censured as unsufficient as we once apprehended and she, I believe, confidently hoped it would be. No actual provision was made *co nomine* for any debts, and we were compelled by the Duchess's unreasonable tenacity to have matters so far in an unsatisfactory state, namely, that the Duchess had not released the Queen from the alleged promise of providing for them from her privy purse or pocket money. The Duchess when at Brighton saw Conroy privately in the Pavilion. This it is whispered exasperated the Queen, and though there was to all outward appearance nothing but reciprocal affection and deference and attention, the real estrangement between Mother and daughter did not escape some keen observers and probably has reached or will soon reach the lovers of gossip. Lord Melbourne was anxious, friendly, and successful in averting all separation. He considers the Duchess foolish and even stupid—entirely devoted to and governed by Conroy, who is a vulgar Man and on the same point quite unmanageable. On the other hand, though he has great confidence both in the feelings and good sense of the Queen, he obviously thinks that it is safer to trust to the arguments which reason and prudence suggest, than to the remains of affection or filial devotion, to induce her to avoid the reality or appearance of rupture or separation between the two Courts.

The Queen is natural cheerful and even merry, so much so that Melbourne rather checked a little harmless and playful disposition to mimickry. She is very considerate of other person's feelings, but her kindnesses seem more the result of consideration than of strong impulse and affection, and with all her gaity and apparent happiness and just observation, She is certainly not unnecessarily communicative of her real feelings about persons and things. She must have reflected very deeply for one of her age on the duties of her station, is very observant of them, Self possession, discretion, and reserve have not been omitted in the Catalogue and they accompany, though they do not subdue, her natural and youthful relish for society, business, splendor, and occupation with which she is surrounded. Melbourne seems much struck by the report of a Scotchman who was near her when she walked into the house and wrote to his friends that she had a thoughtful brow, an all watching eye, a resolute nostril, and (I think) a considerate mouth.

Brougham when he dined at the Palace slipped rudely enough away, and he took or rather made an opportunity of twitting the Ministers with an unconstitutional use of the Queen's name and Melbourne in particular with 'bowing, bending the knee and glazing' at Court—a Charge which Melbourne retorted by observing that he knew no man more disposed to do so when he had opportunities than Brougham. This, which was an outbreak, grieved a few, especially Brougham's friends, if he had any, gratified more Tory enemies, and diverted many of all parties as well as neutral and indifferent men. It did not I suspect captivate the Radicals, and though the accession of such a man to ballot and extension of suffrage cannot fail to be hailed as an advantage by the professed advocates of those measures, the declaration has not I believe inspired any confidence nor abated one jot of the distrust in the professions of Brougham which pervades the Radicals in the State and the dissenters in the Church. He will persuade no one to accelerate the period of entire Negro emancipation, which is already within near two years of its completion. His only formidable theme is Canada, and even on that the plain, direct, and earnest eloquence of Lord Glenelg is not unlikely, when thoroughly provoked, to display itself and may probably discomfort him. The Speaker during this short Session was over sensitive and irritable. He once from the chair, and afterwards yet more seriously in a letter to Melbourne, talked of resignation, said he was not supported by his friends and complained of his being overruled by the house. The Ministerialists say that he put himself in the wrong and was then nettled at their getting him off with honour, and the tories maintain (while lukewarm friends listen to them too courteously) that his whole speakership is a tissue of mistakes and that no person in the Chair ever made so many blunders. He agrees to go on till Easter but his very unfriendly intentions of retiring are no doubt known, and the knowledge of them breeds as much speculation among our friends and our enemies as the fact itself. Add to which, the consequential promotions will be perplexing and draw forth the pretensions and wrong headedness of others besides Abercromby.

A question arose as to the right of the late King's executors to all the rents paid *or due* to the Duchy of Lancaster. I felt a delicacy considering my relationship to Lady Mary and my friendship for some of her brothers and sisters in deciding the matter without a regular consultation of my legal advisers. It was lucky I did so, for the amount of the sums then due and hitherto unpaid is much larger than I had supposed—*7* or perhaps *£9000*. The moment the Civil list bill was passed and the Queen's privy purse settled, she in the most gracious feeling and proper manner conveyed to the FitzClarences her intention of continuing the pensions on it (amounting to a very considerable sum) which the late King had conferred on them, and she did so she said, from good will to them and unfeigned respect and regard to W[illia]m IV's memory. [*Heading:* 1838, January] In all such matters she acts gracefully as well as generously and seems guided by good feeling and good sense, in both of which she will be confirmed by Melbourne's observations and advice. The Duchess of Kent was not a little appeased when she found that her actual income would amount to 30,000 per annum, and that it would enable her to raise money to pay all the tradesmen's and other bills and to provide for the interest and very rapidly to reduce the capital so raised (amounting it should appear by Lord Duncannon's statements and Sir John Conroy to not more than £63,000) by instalments. She prudently placed the whole management in the hands of Lord Duncannon. He with great good nature undertook, and with great good sense completed, a very reasonable and, to her, comfortable arrangement with the Coutts's. The reception of Conroy at Court and even his employment abroad cannot be quite so smoothly settled. The aversion of the daughter to that favorite is to the full as strong as the attachment of the Mother. She is willing to acquiesce in any pecuniary reward of his services in compliance with her promise on the day of accession, but she does not construe that promise as implying the slightest appearance of countenance and favor. She therefore objects to his appearance at Court on publick occasions and refuses, I understand, to let him represent her either abroad or in a Government, though it would without branding him with her displeasure remove an obnoxious subject from his [?her] presence. This is determined and perhaps harsh. He seems by what I hear more reasonable than might have been expected, but having instituted a prosecution for a libel against the Times, is likely to provoke, if he does not himself start, many topicks for publick discussion that had better have been confined to themselves, and left to time and temper to soften and allay.

The appointment of Lord Durham[1] very much facilitated the quiet passage of our Canada bill[2] through Parliament, by dividing or rather reducing to the very minimum of a Parliamentary Minority the Radical opposition to it. It silenced also the speculations and perhaps prevented the reality of any political interference with those little coolnesses and dissensions in the Royal family which have been recounted above. Nothing could be more friendly than Durham's acceptance of the Office, and Nothing more manly, judicious, and satisfactory than the view he took of the policy, both in his publick speech in the Lords and in his discussions on the bill with the Cabinet. His brother in Law, Lord Howick, was far from being equally conciliatory and tractable. With the assistance of Mr Stephen (his great guide and adviser in these Colonial affairs) He half drove and half entrapped Glenelg and the Cabinet into an acquiescence in a preamble indefensible in form and in substance. This had well nigh overset and did greatly lower us in the Commons. Howick himself was obliged to abandon it and give Sir Robert the triumph of exposing the unprecedented impropriety and possible mischief of embodying the instructions of a Governor in an act of Parliament empowering the Crown to appoint him.[3] In other respects the intelligence from the Colony itself and the unpopularity of the Canadian Cause in the Metropolis seemed to strengthen the Queen's Government, and the good sense of the Tory Leaders and especially of the Duke of Wellington directly or indirectly prevented that party from putting forth their strength in a way that might have dislodged us, but could have given them no permanent or satisfactory possession of power. [*Heading:* 1838, January to May] The Duke of Wellington openly refused lending himself to any factious opposition on the Canada question and expressly exculpated us from the charge to which we were in appearance most liable and which, unquestionably, without his great authority and his spontaneous, noble, and candid testimony we should have found it most difficult to repel—that of not reinforcing the Military establishment of the two Colonies, tho' we had so many grounds for apprehending disturbances. He did more however than this; he willingly listened and, without courting, encouraged Melbourne in consulting him on all connected with the Military establishment and the officers there, and in the course of this intercourse it was quite clear that he was far from impatient for a change and, both from publick principle and private inclination, unwilling to molest the Queen's Government. He was obliged however to keep the Tories together and he was disposed some times, by the nature of his general opinions, to gratify his eager partizans by a warm speech of censure, such as he made on sundry questions relating to the Ecclesiastical establishments in England, Ireland, and Scotland, and such as he indulged in when he *con amore* inveighed against a free press in Malta.

Brougham, after speaking every day, making upon the subjects of the poor law,

Canada, the Slave trade and the Negro apprentices several long, elaborate, and in point of talent marvellous speeches, in all which as well as in his daily speeches and motions facundia prisca remansit Raraque [*Raucaque*] garrulitas studiumque immane loquendi[4] set off in the Easter Holydays to Paris. He was chosen of the Institute and he edified the beau monde with some new phrases or at least new pronunciations in the French language, which were not much admired. [*In the margin:* He talked before Ladies of having passed *une nuit* agreable mais fort agreable entre Princesse Charlotte et Mme de Flahault,[5] the latter being present at his blunder, and in extolling Mme <. . . . . .>'s excellent pronunciation of French said, Elle ne dit pas comme toute autre Dames Italienne, *Je fous!* mais je *fus.*] He then proceeded to Cannes where he is building a house, of extreme bad taste and very uncomfortable, though with a beautiful view of the sea, unless the Villa now also building by Sir Herbert Taylor, and they say most elegant and convenient, should intercept it.

It was thought expedient with a view of deadening the animosity hastening the close of the Session to fix the coronation in the Middle of it, and the 26th. of June was named, without the circumstance of George IV having died on that day being adverted to. Whether hypocritically or sincerely, very general dissatisfaction was expressed at this coincidence and Melbourne, to silence the clamour and soothe the feelings real or affected of near relations, *persuaded* the Queen, who was not so disposed, to acquiesce in the postponement to the 28th., tho' it is obvious that the day of one Sovereign's death is the accession of another and a day, consequently, of festivity as well as mourning—and that George III's jubilee was purposely celebrated on the anniversary of his Grandfather's death. But the Tories were on the look out for grievances, especially on the approach of the Coronation, which they felt might strengthen us by the exhibition of Royal favor and by the promotions which it will naturally occasion. This feeling led them in Lords to harrass us more or less successfully with trying little Questions about the Scotch Church and the Yeomanry reduction[6]—the first rather a difficult matter on which there is vast irritation on both sides in Scotland, and the latter a measure somewhat hastily adopted by Lord John which, if right, as I believe it is, should have been prepared, matured, and <effected> to a much greater extent, but which has exasperated many of our best friends and is incredibly offensive to the Nobility, Gentry, and Farmers of the Country. In several Skirmishes, especially on Irish matters, Duke of Wellington with admirable candour and real patriotism stepped forward to repress and disclaim the factious language of his supporters. Lyndhurst, the Minutius of this Fabius, kept the knights in the House, but was suspected in common with the Mass of the troops to be panting for a general engagement and somewhat shrewdly, though with little regard to the interests of the Country or to any view truly *conservative,* remarked, it is said, that 'it was madness to wait till we were reinforced by the Coronation, the great object was to drive us from our posts before that event, force the closet in time enough to leave the promotions incident to that ceremony at their own disposal'. Whether Lyndhurst's intrigues or their own natural impatience suggested such a step, Certain it is that the Tories, by a dinner early in May and a Motion of Sir Ths. Aclands[7] on the 14th., mustered all their force, displayed the entire junction of Stanley and Peel, manifested with ostentation their readiness for office, and gave the Ministers a triumph both in debate and division which materially altered the relative position of the two parties, greatly to the Advantage of the Whigs.

[*In the margin:* Memorandum of Past Times

On the 10 June 1838, I had a curious conversation with Lady Keith about Princess Charlotte. It seems she had before she was 17 a project of emancipating herself by a marriage with Duke of Gloucester—a project suggested by her own brain or possibly by Duke of Sussex or Miss Knight[8]—and communicated by the Princess herself by post to Lord Grey and Miss Mercer (afterwards Lady Keith). By Lord Grey's advice she dropped this scheme but still persisted in consulting him—an honour he was rather disposed to shun—and she afterwards made Miss Mercer introduce herself to Lord Grey, and professed to be guided by his or her advice, though she also consulted on all her affairs and projects Miss Knight and thro' Miss Knight Mr Hallam.[9] The plan of the Marriage with Prince of Orange, originally disagreable to the Princess, became gradually less so, notwithstanding the abrupt manner in which he was introduced to her on his return from the Peninsula, as her husband, and the very unprepossessing appearance of a miniature which had preceded him. She was in some measure reconciled to it by Lady Keith, The Prince's own behaviour on the question of her visits to Holland, and the great desire she felt of emancipating herself from her father's dominion as well perhaps as her Mothers designs. But her encreasing reconciliation to the plan never ripened into strong attachment to the young Prince, although sufficient to create jealousy at his flirtations with other women. It was most probably rather checked by Miss Knight's and the Duke of Sussex's representations as well as by all such as had access both to her and the Princess of Wales. In aid of their remonstrances or intrigues many little Chagrins—the prohibition of her presence at balls while she was a betrothed bride, the little resentment of the Prince of Orange at tha prohibition, his neglect of her, his attention to other women and a scene of drunkenness into which he was betrayed (perhaps artfully at the instigation of Russians) by Paul of Wurtemberg—contributed strongly to estrange her. *And above all,* a predilection amounting almost to love for Prince Augustus of Prussia,[10] who thro' Miss Knight's imprudence or intrigue was admitted to secret interviews, led her to an abrupt rupture with the Prince of Orange to whom she wrote a letter which he answered very impertinently and offensively. The Prince Augustus was alarmed and taking Miss Mercer aside at Devonshire house, lui faisoit <. . . . . .> qu'il etait deja marié de la main gauche en Allemagne. In the mean while rumours of private interviews had readied Carlton House but the person really favoured was not ascertained and by a strange mistake or fatality supposed to be Leopold.]

[*From the diary of John Allen*[11]]

Feb. 27 [*1838*]. The division on Grotes motion gave in favour of the Ballot a minority of 200, including a great majority of the friends of Government and some persons, such as Sir H Vivian,[12] in high official station. It cannot be denied that the system of intimidation resorted to by the Tories at the last General Election has added greatly to the partizans of ballot, and its advocates, after this division, consider its ultimate success as certain.

Last night, in a question affecting O'Connell, the Ministers were beat, in a House of 521 members by a majority of 9.[13] A scene of confusion followed, several members repeating in the face of the House the words for which O'Connell had incurred their indignation. More will follow tonight.

Brougham is sliding more and more into a junction with the Tories. He and Lady Jersey are reconciled.

March 2. O'Connell reprimanded, but the House took no notice of several members who rose in their places and repeated the obnoxious expressions he had used. House disgraced and Election Committees so discredited that some new system must be adopted.

Ministers beat on the question of the pay and promotion of Marines by a junction of Tories and their own friends. Goulburn and four other Tories voted with them. By this vote the House of Commons directs the Crown to increase the pay and alter the condition of part of the army.[14]

8 [*March 1838*]. Brougham has made several brilliant speeches against Glenelg, who on the last occasion was only saved by the Duke of Wellington. Brougham has expressed in private (in presence of Lady Cowper) his surprise that the Duke should interpose to save a base and worthless Ministry. He (B[rougham]) is become the pet of the Tory ladies whose flattering attentions he repays by a corresponding return of flattery. Lady Salisbury[15] is surprised she should have lived so many years in London without having before been acquainted with so delightful a man; and he in return pronounces her the most delightful of women. He is full of undisguised vanity, and though neither trusted nor believed by any one, he lives in a Fools paradise of his own creation.

The division of last night was considerably better than had been anticipated.[16] The most sanguine and best informed had not reckoned above 25 and E[dward] Stanley did not reckon on a greater majority than 20. Only 4 of the Ultra Radicals went away without voting. Peel is said to have been forced into the line he took by the importunity and impatience of his friends. The Tories are getting very much dissatisfied with the Duke of Wellington. Brougham had calculated that he could carry his motion on the East India importation of labourers into Guiana and had boasted that he would turn out the Ministers by it. Judge of his wrath when the Duke of Wellington moved the previous question.

9 [*March 1838*]. The Duke of Wellington had been for some time in communication with Lord M[elbourne] before the late Kings death, as I believe, and most certainly since the accession of the young Queen, in whose quiet and comfort he takes a deep interest. He will not separate from his friends, but thinking, I presume, that his party are not strong enough to carry on the Government, he is desirous that she should not be thwarted or disturbed, and therefore does his best to restrain them and prevent their having any temporary success which could only breed confusion and annoy her. She was in great agitation before the division on Molesworths motion[17] and was much rejoiced at the result, the probability of which Lord M[elbourne] communicated to her late in the evening.

28 March 1838. Nothing remarkable has happened except that Brougham has continued to make very excellent and effective speeches—at Exeter Hall on the immediate Emancipation of the Negro apprentices and in the House of Lords on the poor law amendment Bill.[18] The Clamour out of doors for the immediate emancipation of the Negroes has shaken Glenelg and intimidated the members for populous places, who are afraid of the effect on their future elections of any vote they give against it. Accounts from Washington are less favourable. The House of Representatives are weakening the provisions of the law passed by the Senate and creating delays in order to wait for events.[19] Lord Elliots motion is under discussion.[20]

It is impossible not to see that the Ministers are losing strength and reputation. Resting on the popular support of a variety of parties, they must yield to the pressure from without of any one of them, and the vacillating policy which is the consequence of their position must necessarily lower them in public Estimation. In the Lords they have few speakers on their side, and even in the commons they are frequently out spoken. The Queen is very eager for the continuance of Lord Melbournes government, but its chief strength, as it appears to me, lies in the opinion entertained by the Leaders of the Opposition that they are not strong enough to form an efficient government. Nor do I see how such a government can be formed without a coalition of the moderate party on both sides, to the exclusion of the Ultra Radicals and Ultra Tories.

5 April 1838. The ridiculous termination of Lord Eliots motion, occasioned it is said by a mistaken calculation of the numbers in the House,[21] has cast a slur on the Opposition, and the next by a majority on the motion of Lord Chandos,[22] while it arose from the negligence of their Enemies, has shewn <how> disunion arises among themselves, several having gone away before the division because they would not vote for any motion proposed by him after the part he took against the W[est] I[ndian] Planters. In the debate on the Negro apprentices the speeches of Sir Geo. Grey and Mr Gladstone[23] gave them as decided a victory in debate as the numbers did in the division. But the orations at Exeter Hall seem in no way daunted and Brougham, who is gone to France, has addressed to them two most vituperative letters against the Ministers. One salutary result of these dis<cuss>ions has been to terrify the West Indians and make them compliant, and Glenelgs Bill will give the Specials the means of checking the rancorous spirit that still exists among many of the Planters and their Agents.[24]

June 17. The occurrences of the last two months have not been remarkable for any great results. The loss of Sir T Aclands motion shewed the Opposition they had no chance of success during the present Session. Peels professions of a desire to settle the Irish questions are probably sincere, but he has difficulty in managing his own friends and cannot break with them entirely.

The offer of the Rolls to O'Connell has been declined on grounds that do credit to his patriotism as an Irishman. Brougham has been a troublesome customer to the Government but he has no followers who put their trust in him.

11 July 1838. The Ministers had a narrow escape last night in the House of Lords, the numbers on a division for the production of the instructions to our naval commander on the coast of Spain being even. They were saved by the Duke of Wellington, Lord Aberdeen, and four or five others quitting the House. Brougham indignant with the Duke for this conduct, Lord Mansfield, Lord Ellenboro' and Lord Harewood separating for the first time from their leader and voting for the motion. The Duke who is manifestly unwilling to drive the Ministers to resign, seems to be losing his influence over his adherents in the Lords, as Peel for the same reason is doing in the Commons. Yet, as far as I have heard, there is no approximation to a coalition between the Duke and Lord Melbourne—so far at least as relates to office.

The intention of Mehemet Ali to declare himself independent of the Porte, which with the grounds for that declaration were communicated some time ago to the English and French Consuls, has excited apprehensions of a war in the East. The Four powers have determined to remonstrate against, and if necessary, to resist an attempt that might render it necessary and most certainly would furnish an excuse for another Russian Armament to enter the Bosphorus. The plan conceived here, with the approbation of the Russian and Austrian Ambassadors, is that the English and French fleets in the Levant should be reinforced and employed, if necessary, against the Egyptians and that an Austrian land force should be embarked at Trieste and sent to the same quarter and the Russians not to stir if it can be avoided.

August 10. The Irish Poor Bill and Tithe Bill had passed—the latter with alterations by the Lords, the omission of the Appropriation clause, and instead of it the grant of a million to discharge the arrears of the Irish Clergy—with discredit to the Ministers, but possibly with future advantage to the tranquillity of Ireland;[25] and the Irish Municipal Bill, after concessions from the Government, had been loaded with such obnoxious clauses by the House of Lords that it was on the point of being rejected (as it was last night by the Commons) when a new breeze sprung up which threatens to sink the Ship, or leave her little better than a wreck on the Ocean. Lord Durham, with the best intentions and with real humanity to the leaders of the late insurrection in Canada, has made illegal ordinances, banishing those who were in custody to Bermudas, and awarding the punishment of death to them as well as to those who have escaped to the United States if they ever return to Canada.[26] Brougham, Lyndhurst, and the Duke of Wellington have taken up the matter warmly in the House of Lords and after a triumphant debate have carried the 2d. Reading of a Bill which indemnifies Durham for what he has done but stamps with illegality his proceedings. A Cabinet is met today to consider what is to be done.

11 [*August 1838*]. Ministers have submitted. They have agreed to disallow Lord Durham's ordinances on the ground that the part relating to Bermudas being confessedly illegal, they could not maintain it, and Canada being a chartered Colony, they could not disallow one part of the Ordinance and confirm another part. In vain they entreated to have some legislative explanation of Follet's clauses.[27] It was refused on pretence of the lateness of the Session. Lord Durham is left to act or rather to do nothing as he shall judge best. I have little doubt that he will return and leave Canada to be fought for between the French and English parties.

The weakness of the Government in the House of Lords is deplorable, not merely in numbers, but in speakers. Lord Melbourne, Lord Lansdowne and occasionally the Chancellor are their only regular debaters. It is clear that unless this defect be remedied they cannot go on for another Session. Langdale gives them no assistance even in questions of law and internal reform; Argyll, Albemarle, Conyngham, and Lichfield are mutes; Lord Holland from gout gives them little assistance; Radnor and Hatherton speak rarely and are not in office; Clanricard (after being half in opposition from disappointment) is going to Petersburgh; Duncannon (if he were well), though useful in concocting measures, is no speaker. On the other side are Brougham, Lyndhurst, Wellington, Aberdeen, Ellenborough and many others. In the Commons Lord John Russell has done well and Lord Morpeth has risen very high in reputation; Sir Geo. Grey, Labouchere and others are rising men. But in the Lords there is not one of the young and ministerial peers who promises to become a man of any importance.

13 [*August*]. Lord P[almerston] gave us tonight the following history of the Portfolio. It was the custom of the Russian Government in the time of Alexander to send copies of all important despatches to Constantine at Warsaw. In the insurrection of 1830 these fell into the hands of the Poles, and in 1834 a Pole who had been recommended to Lord P[almerston] by Czartoriski put a bundle of them into his hands. Lord P read two or three of them and gave them to Backhouse to put in order. When the change of government took place in Novr. they remained in Lord P's possession, and in Feb. 1835 another Pole called on him with authority to receive them back, when they were delivered to him. It was not till the Novr. following that they were shewn to Urquhart by the Poles, and so far from being consulted about the publication of them, Lord P was not aware of the existence of the Portfolio till informed of it by Van de Weyer. He admits however that one paper about to be published was shewn to Mr Strangways and by him shewn to Lord P., who recognised it as one of the papers he had had from the Pole and recommended that certain passages with respect to the Duke of Wellington and Lord Aberdeen should be omitted, which was done accordingly. Urquhart had been appointed Secretary of Embassy at Constantinople before the publication of the Portfolio, and before he sailed Lord P. had a conversation with him in which, after stating that he was the supposed Editor of the Portfolio, he (Lord P) added that he must abstain from such publications in future. Urquhart listened in silence and made no answer. He was at one time connected with Poulet Thomson, and though now so decided a Turk, he was then devoted to the Greeks. He was very much patronised by Sir Herbert Taylor.

16 [*August*]. Parliament to be prorogued today. The House of Commons in very bad temper with the House of Lords; and the friends of government very much dissatisfied with the state of the Ministry, especially in the Lords. Many changes talked of, but none so probable as to deserve being mentioned. Lord Johns speech on the Indemity Bill[28] very spirited.

[*Lord Holland's diary resumed*]

1838. From May to August I neglected this journal and the character of a diary has been long since lost.

The Coronation, which without the expence or Magnificence far exceeded in popularity, numbers, attendance of foreigners, and general festivity that of George IV, must have ingratiated the Young Queen with the publick. That pageantry and the manifestation of real preference for Lord Melbourne and his Ministry in the Young Queen were the most favorable circumstances which occurred during the summer of 1838, or at least that were matter of observation to the publick. There was however in the leaders of the soi disant Conservative party and especially in the Duke of Wellington a strong disinclination (founded perhaps on a consciousness of their inability to undertake and maintain any Government) to a change, and they or at least the Duke hardly took the pains of concealing this opinion from his political opponents. And to Melbourne, I half suspect, he communicated this view of the matter. On Military matters relating to Canada and India he communicated with him most freely, honestly, and usefully, and even in public abstained from giving his sanction to more than one device of his over ardent followers, such as Lyndhurst and others, or of Brougham, for combining discordant materials for the purpose of embarrassing Government. Towards the close however of the Sessions, but unfortunately before the Prorogation, the news of Lord Durhams irregular, ill constructed and, in form, indefensible ordinances arrived, without any explanation from him either of his views or even of the transactions which had led him to issue them. They were (except under very special circumstances) quite indefensible and, to appearance at least, unnecessarily irregular and offensive. It was hazardous to surmise the grounds on which they had been adopted, which the next packet would have belied, and the temper neither of Parliament nor of the publick was such as, in the face of a Majority of Lords and a host of great legal authorities (without one very cordial in his approbation of them, for about one part of them the Chancellor himself had scruples), would have enabled us to stand on the high ground of confidence in those whom we employed. Brougham, with all his accustomed malignity and activity and with more than his usual dexterity, brought the Duke of Wellington and Conservative side of the house to concur in calling for a disavowal of them. Resistance would have been fruitless and resignation upon being beaten would have left us with little or no support, Durham with no protection, and the Colonies almost without a government. A less irritable man than Durham might have felt chagrined and even exasperated at this disavowal of his ordinances, but a less rash man could not have issued any in a shape and with circumstances so difficult, not to say impossible, to defend or approve. Wellington is said to have observed that the disavowal placed him in an advantageous situation if he had temper and judgement to remain and avail himself of it; but he had not, and his proclamation, unauthorized return, and silly vain Speeches on landing were the consequences. They have hitherto (I write in Febry. 1839) been more injurious to himself than others, but they might have been hazardous to the security of the Colony and threatened to be extremely perplexing to the Government.

I returned from a visit to Paris in November 1838, about the time of his arrival in England, and I found a great expectation even in the Cabinet, and yet more out of it, that these events and others would compel us to adopt some arrangement for strengthening the Government in one or both houses of Parliament. Melbourne however justly observed that the common and obvious meaning of strengthening a Government by a new arrangement was by the conversion of political adversaries, or at least hitherto unconnected parties, into Colleagues and allies. From this however we were precluded, and our efforts must be confined to new casting the <points> or introducing Men of our side already in or out office into our Councils; that altho' there might be some advantages in such an expedient, there were always counterbalancing inconveniences, the removal of one stone often disturbed the harmony of, even shook the stability of, the Whole fabrick. He was much pleased at the zealous and good humoured offer of Lord Normanby to lend himself to any arrangement that was deemed advisable and to go to Canada if he was required. He sounded Lord Spencer both on that and on Ireland. He was averse to quitting his retirement but owned that he thought he could do better in Canada than Ireland, and that if he was prevailed upon to accept any thing, he should prefer the former to most employments. The introduction of Lord Morpeth to the Cabinet was agreed on all hands to be most desirable, but out of delicacy to Lord Normanby, who would have consented tho' reluctantly to it during his Viceroyalty, it was deemed as well to defer such a step till Lord Normanby himself came over to fill a Cabinet place. These matters were not spoken of, though often glanced at and hinted at meetings of the Cabinet, but Melbourne consulted Lansdowne, myself, Duncannon, and others of our Colleagues privately, acknowledging that some new arrangements were likely to become unavoidable, but avowing his apprehension of the consequences of any *dislocation.* It was rumoured and seemed likely that Sir Robert Grant's[29] death and the embarrassed state in which he had left his affairs, as well as his Brother Glenelg's affliction at his loss and own narrow circumstances, had rendered Glenelg disposed to accept some lucrative retirement, and Lord Melbourne, partly with the view of gratifying his wishes in that respect but chiefly with that of sounding his feelings about the office he held, offered him Sir John Newports auditorship, with an assurance that, if it suited him, Sir John was ready and even eager to retire at his advanced age of 80 on a pension. Glenelg had no project of the sort at present and he would not (he said) think, while his conduct in his office regarding Canada was likely to be the subject of hostile animadversion, of voluntarily quitting his post. From this period Lord Melbourne gave up all thoughts of pressing him to resign. He reverted to a determination which he had all along preferred, of keeping matters as long as he could in their present state.

But before or very soon after Parliament met, on the occasion of preparing measures for Jamaica and superseding the refractory Assembly thereof, Lord Howick with more than his usual impetuosity urged a more general measure for all the West Indies. To this Glenelg objected and I believe all, but certainly a large majority, of his Colleagues agreed, tho' for various reasons, in the adoption of the Jamaica, and the postponement of all consideration of the general, Measure. Howick wrote a letter tendering his resignation. And upon hearing of it, Lord John Russell unexpectedly informed Melbourne that, tho' he differed with Howick on the particular question at issue, he agreed and had long agreed so entirely in the necessity of a Change in the Colonial Office that, if Howick resigned, he, Lord John, must tender his resignation too. Howick, after some communications with Melbourne, agreed to remain, provided there was a fair prospect and understanding that ere long the Colonial Seals would be in other hands, and John Russell urged strongly the necessity of some immediate change in that department. On finding that such was not only the opinion but the determination of two such leading House of Commons Members of the Cabinet, there [was] no alternative but either to break up the government or set about making an arrangement which would not long leave the Colonial seals in the hands of Lord Glenelg. It was felt however that no part of that arrangement could be settled and begun without apprizing Lord Glenelg, and Lansdowne and myself and I believe others felt that it would not only be unhandsome, but actually unjust and unfair to him, in requesting him to lend himself to any Change of Offices more convenient to Government, not to offer to consider his very natural and honourable wishes of retaining the office he held till the charges laid against his exercise of it in Canada, now on the tapis, had been met and repelled. Melbourne wrote to inform him that arrangements which would bring Normanby and Morpeth into the Cabinet, and to which his exchange of the Colonial Seals for the Privy Seal would be necessary, were deemed by almost all his Colleagues so essential to the support of the Queen's Government that he felt himself compelled, with a view of keeping the Govt. together, to propose to him to accept the Privy Seal; but as he knew that from the most natural and honourable motives he was desirous of defending himself in office for the measures now denounced, as the subject of attack he did not deem it necessary that he should resign the seals till Easter or till a New Canada Bill had been actually introduced by him into the House of Lords. It was thought his honor would be saved by retaining the post while under an attack, and that he might be reconciled to quitting it for one of less business but more dignity, and the yet more certain prospect it held out of a provision for life; but unluckily he had severely animadverted on Lord Goderich's want of spirit in submitting to something like a similar arrangement in 1833, and he had resented the treatment he had received from Lord Liverpool many years before, the recollection of some particulars of which the present offer or scheme was well calculated to revive. Lord Melbourne's letter (which I never saw) was, I am assured, not only judicious but kind, but Glenelg was hurt at being written and not spoken to. The matter might perhaps have been comfortably and amicably settled, had there been time for sounding, explaining, and discussing, which the impetuosity of Howick and the peremptoriness of Lord John's determination precluded. Glenelg, a good, and in some respects, very able man, without gall and without guile and of a gentle spirit, was not separated from his Office and his Colleagues without a wound; and all one can hope is that, altho' he disdains the salve of the Privy Seal, it may be brought to heal by the first intention, and he may be ere long reconciled to the solid comforts of the auditorship for life, with the consideration, good will, and respect of all with whom he has acted, including even those who thought that the particular office which he filled was but ill adapted to his peculiar talents and character.

[*Heading:* February 1839] This incident and the hazard to which it exposed the

Ministry brought forward more manifestations of the importance attached by the Queen to the Maintenance of Lord Melbourne's administration. When it was in jeopardy she did not conceal her uneasiness, and I think I perceive, in some of the subsequent arrangements and other circumstances, little symptoms of her having more of a voice than hitherto in suggesting the means of keeping it together. As Durham had originally supposed that the avenue to Court favor might be thro' the Duchess of Kent and Conroy, he had been attentive to them and theirs, but had no doubt discovered soon after the accession that such was not the Queen's high road to the objects in his view. But the impression made by his first policy very possibly remains on the Queen's mind, and she certainly had betrayed no mortification or disappointment at the political estrangement of her mother's and of both her Uncles (Leopold and Sussex's) quondam counsellor from the Ministry she employs and supports. In proportion as her Character developes itself, in such proportion will it be difficult for her political enemies or even libellers to represent it as childish, trifling, insignificant, or weak. The late King before his death had dictated a long statement of all his transactions with the Whig Ministry and their party, whom he said she would find in possession of office at his death. Sir Herbert Taylor, who had probably drawn it up though entirely at the King's suggestion, delivered it some months after the accession to the Queen as a confidential paper intended for the sole perusal of her Majesty by her Predecessor. The Queen received it and thanked Sir Herbert, but after observing that it related to bye gone transactions, she handed it over to Lord Melbourne unread, as a proof of her entire confidence in him. The paper tho' in some sort a vindication of the dismissal in 1834, and a proof of the reluctant capitulation in 1835, as well perhaps of the half discontented and uneasy feeling with which W[illia]m IV regarded Lord Melbourne's Ministry till his death, was yet measured in its language, correct in the details, and though strongly tinctured with what is called Conservatism, or rather alarm at innovation, was neither angry nor unjust to individuals or parties.[1]

The Duke of Sussex was much chagrined during the Session of 1838 at the rejection of Mr Gillon's[2] motion for augmenting his allowance, and yet more hurt at the early declaration of Lord John in debate that Government opposed it.[3] He on that and many subsequent occasions expressed his disappointment in an undignified not to say unbecoming way, yet the undeniable fact that the only steady Whig of the Royal family was at the end of nine years in a Whig administration left worse provided for than any of his Brothers and the recollection of many untoward accidents and disappointment which, when favors to him were projected and altered, had been dashed from his lips, abruptly and unceremoniously, made an impression on many minds besides his own and set some of our best and most powerful friends on the alert to discover some method of allaying his mortification and gratifying his expectations. Many thoughtless persons had listened to and repeated his wish to be sent to Ireland. The employment of a Prince of the blood in that station would be highly objectionable, inconvenient to the publick service, and in many possible contingencies painful to the feelings of the head of the family, who might be called upon to disavow, recall, or reprimand a near relation or at least to comment or censure his acts. Lord Melbourne in conversing with the Queen found her much disposed to adhere to this maxim of her predecessors and not to employ Princes of the blood (unless necessary) in any great Civil capacity. She said if Melbourne thought it very advisable (which he was far from thinking) she would acquiesce, but she had much rather be spared not only the pain of refusing such a request but the difficulty of complying with it against her conscientious judgement by never having it laid before her.

She was equally sensible but much more earnestly affectionate about her other Uncles's (the King of the Belgian's) proceedings. She wrote to him privately and I believe quite spontaneously to urge him to acquiesce in the proposal of the 5 powers. She pointed out the manifest advantages to him and the great personal comfort to her of a final settlement which should establish him on the throne, the comparative insignificance of the minor objects and, above all, the impracticability of obtaining, and the danger of attempting, them against all the great powers in Europe. Leopold was slow and irresolute. He wished to court popularity by shewing reluctance in conceding points, tho' he well knew, he could not retain them; <invita dato> similisque coacta may do from a lover to a Mistress compelled to yield to the embraces of his rival, but a compliance with it lowers rather than ingratiates a Government. If compelled to adopt an unpopular measure, it should seem to yield to principle and conscience and not to force. A people may respect a difference of opinion in their Sovereign, but they will not so easily pardon apparent pusillanimity in maintaining wishes which coincide with their own. The matter is yet pending, but the progress already made by the signature of the 5 powers and the compliance of the King of Holland (or Netherlands)[4] as well as our treaties with Austria [and] Turkey[5] were highly advantageous to the Government on the opening of the Session, and though there appeared by various notices in the Lords some inclination for active warfare in the opposition, they were gradually postponed and abandoned and more than the first fortnight, even in spite of Corn Law Agitation. Durham's expectation of Canadian discussion was belied and the whole passed off with little discussion and no asperity. Lord Glenelg's resignation took the publick and especially the most stirring politicans by surprize. It of course provoked some sarcasms and imputations upon the treatment he received from his Colleagues, it did not produce any great impression against us, and it is felt by dispassionate men that a post requiring decision and authority will be better filled by Normanby, though far from being his superior or even equal in knowledge or talent, than by Glenelg.

April 1839. The latter has consented to accept the pension of retired Ministers, but we must trust to time and an unfeigned respect and deference for his character to wear away the effects of his personal disappointment. His successor, Normanby, is more active in his office and far more handy and successful, tho' not so eloquent, in the house. After some very irregular and intemperate strictures from Lord Lyndhurst on the choice of his Successor, which were repelled with great dignity perspicuity and effect by Lord Ebrington the day he took his seat on being called up to the House of Lords, and after a question brought on by Lord Fitzwilliam for a revision of the poor [*corn*] laws,[6] *for* which two Cabinet Ministers (Minto and myself) and against which three (Melbourne, Lansdowne, and the Chancellor) voted, had been rejected by a vast majority, the Tory opposition determined to support as a party the Motion of Lord Roden on Ireland. It was in its natural construction, and it was so intended by its immediate Mover, a Parliamentary censure on the government of Lord Normanby.[7] In its ordinary consequences it should have led either to some penal proceedings against him or to the dismissal of those who employed him. There can be little doubt that Wellington, Aberdeen, and the more circumspect of the party, not being impatient to bring about an immediate change and least of all to undertake a Government on the principle of supporting the Orange Party in Ireland, had reluctantly consented to support the motion at all. They did so for the sole purpose of keeping their friends together and they laboured to give it both in form and effect the character of a preliminary step to an amendment of the law, and not an inculpation of Lord Normanby or a practical expedient for removing the Ministers. Indeed such an endeavour might have been collected by a very attentive and critical observer of Duke of Wellington's speech. But the Duke was not the Mover, he did not convey the distinction between the grounds taken by Lord Roden and himself very explicitly and clearly to the house, and much matter liable to another interpretation was mixed up with it. From these considerations and from others independent of them Lord Melbourne described the motion as one pregnant 'with no light consequences' and broadly hinted to the House that by the adoption of it they would be quitting the cautious grounds they had hitherto occupied, would be endeavouring to impose a Government of their own on the Crown, and hazarding, if not inviting, a Collision with the Commons, and certainly with publick opinion in Ireland. The Tories from accident or design refrained from calling Proxies, and the Majority, which if they had put forth their strength might unquestionably have been 50 or perhaps 100, consisted of 5.[8] Three courses were supposed to be open to the Government: 1, to treat the vote like other defeats experienced and, notwithstanding Normanby's and Lord Melbourne's speeches, to regard the Committee as a mere measure of enquiry with a view to an improvement in the law; 2dly., to resign; and 3dly., to proclaim a determination of resisting the Lords by making six or eight peers and thereby proclaiming.

To remain and submit would, even if practicable, have been base and degrading; at least two (Normanby and Lord John Russell) would have felt it to be so and, indeed, none of us could easily have been reconciled to such a course. *To resign* seemed upon the first impression to be the natural and necessary course, and Lord Normanby from pardonable resentment and personal feeling was all for adopting it in his own case without calling on his Colleagues to follow his example. They however all concurred that if he resigned their resignation must accompany his, and it was shrewdly remarked and afterwards most earnestly urged that such a step would be a desertion both of Court and of Commons and a valid excuse for the Tories, in quest of one, for accepting office. They could in such event make a plausible case to prove that their motion for Committee in Lords was not conceived with any design of disturbing the Government. *As to swamping* the House of Lords, there was hardly a case to justify so strong a measure, and besides there was hardly publick opinion enough in its favor to render it efficacious or means enough within our reach to render it practicable. And after much deliberation and more reflection we determined, in justice to ourselves, to the House of Commons, to the Queen and the publick, to appeal from the Lords to the Commons, and in forming that determination the recollection of a declaration made by Lord Melbourne and strongly urged and enforced upon him by me three years ago, carried great weight with us all. 'As long' he had said, 'as we retained the Confidence of the Commons and the people and had the honour of being employed by the Crown, he would not abandon his post at the instigation of any set of Men not even of their Lordships'.[9] In strict conformity with such a resolution it was felt that he was bound to *ascertain* how far he continued to enjoy the Confidence of the Commons, and Lord John in a short, manly, and explicit speech gave notice of a Motion which would put the truth to the test.[10] The Tories who were averse to a change (and especially on Irish grounds) were manifestly disconcerted and perplexed by this proceeding. They would greatly have preferred a resignation which would have thrown upon us the whole responsibility of a Change or a resistance which would have lowered our character and exposed us to defeat on less popular ground than our Irish policy. Those Radicals (and they are not few) who either from cabal with Lord Durham, from personal enmity to individuals, from disappointment caprice or conceit, were anxious to get us out, hardly concealed their chagrin at being reduced to the alternative of voting for us or openly abandoning the principles which for some years had kept us together. They laboured (and they had, I fear, some coadjutors even in office) to disseminate jealousy and discontent among their constituents, to misrepresent us as cold in the Cause of Reform, and to construe perhaps an imprudent or rather an imputed expression of Lord John's (viz the 'finality' of the Reform bill) as an announcement of a Closing of the Account and an avowal of resisting henceforward to all endeavours at improvement. The press very actively seconded these mischievous designs. Those (especially the M[ornin]g Chronicle) who derived their sale from being supposed to be the organ of government were not disavowed or checked (perhaps they were even encouraged and instigated by the very persons who should have been the channels of communication between them and the Ministry) to direct column after column to their discomfiture. Durham, if afraid to strike, was certainly not unwilling to wound, and without assailing or even leading others to assail, He perhaps rewarded them by smiles and countenance and perhaps something more for doing so.

It is not impossible that another faction of court rather than Country growth cooperated underhand in these Manoevres—Sir John Conroy and the Duchess of Kent. They were exasperated equally against the Queen and Lord Melbourne, they had endeavoured to give to the tracasserie about Lady Flora Hastings[11] (the ugly offspring of prudery, tittle tattle, and folly) the character of a plot, with the hope of involving Mme Letzen, their arch enemy, in the charge of conspiracy and of affixing on the little Queen herself the odium of harshness, indelicacy, spite and injustice. [*In the margin:* In these circumstances and recriminations both parties seem to have been equally regardless of facts. Lady Flora was not with child—nor, as far as I had an opportunity of judging, did she even appear to be so—and the

Duchess of Kent and Lady Floras family and friends entirely failed in fixing on Mme Lehtzen any share in what they were pleased to denominate the 'Conspiracy'.] Whoever conveyed to the Queen suspicions (clearly unfounded) arising from the appearance of Lady Flora's person without having first communicated them to the Duchess of Kent, to the Lady herself, or to her Mother was inconsiderate and wrong. But whether it was Lady Portman's[12] prudery, or Sir James Clark's[13] extreme want of propriety and judgement, The Duchess of Kent [*two lines torn*] was very active, under colour of asking advice, in spreading the story and complaining to her friends personal or political of the cruelty practised and the plot contrived against A Lady of her household. She applied for Council to Abercromby the Speaker. Though not averse to being the depository of secret *grief* against the Queen, he was, as he is apt to be, startled at the responsibility about to be thrown upon him. He earnestly and I believe sincerely shrunk from the perilous office, speciously urged that a Speaker was the last Man in the Kingdom fit to be the adviser on such affairs, and unexpectedly but not unwisely recommended H R H to be guided by the *Duke of Wellington's* opinion! The Duke of Wellington did, as on all such occasions he is prone to do, what was right, honourable, and judicious. He exhorted the Duchess to obey the mandates of the Queen and, If she had grounds of complaint, to convey them through her Majesty's legal and ostensible advisers, male or female, avoiding all unnecessary asperity and publicity. It does not seem that she or Lady Flora's family were much inclined to confine their confidential consultations to the Duke or that the temperate course he suggested to them produced any such inclination. Lord Hastings, a man of no sense, called Lord Winchelsea, an honest but passionate and wrong headed man, to council, and the Duke declined all further interference when he found others had been consulted. In the course of these transactions he is reported to have said to the Duchess, If once these things become publick, the enquiry will cease to be which among you Ladies at the palace is with child, and It will be who among you is not? Sir Hry. Halford's observation was that of a Physician and Man of the World. When the Ladies of the Court, said he, remarked any thing of the sort on his patient's appearance to Sir James Clark, he should have scouted all such suspicions as perfectly ridiculous and pledged himself as a professional Man that they were untrue and then have conveyed to the Lady Herself or her protectress, the Duchess of Kent, what had occurred, in a way to give them full assurance if it was untrue, and a good opportunity of withdrawing herself from notice if it was true. Whether he believed it or not, he as a professional man was bound to give not the slightest countenance or probability to such a suspicion to any but the Lady herself.

I suspect and have long suspected or rather known that these Court dissensions harrass Lord Melbourne and engross his Mind too much. He strives no doubt to pacify and soften the Queen, and he has been more than once useful and successful in doing so. She too has sense and feeling enough to acknowledge her obligations to him for doing so, but I am afraid constant intercourse with her on the subject has warped his judgement and nearly obliterated all dispassionate view of any part of the Duchess of Kent's or Major Conroy's conduct. Duncannon, the only one among us (and far the best that could be selected among us) who is in friendly communication with all parties and enjoys in any degree the confidence of all, clearly partakes the apprehension that I have expressed; for myself, I have no opportunity of any personal observation and, if I had, should avoid, as I have throughout life, rather than court any interference with the private concerns of Royal personages. I am afraid however that the inconveniences, twinborn with Royalty, will haunt the palace of Queen Victoria as much as that of weaker sovereigns of her sex, and that political events in her reign as in others may on some occasions depend on female caprices, passions, and resentments.

Brougham during the Session before Easter was nearly as active and perhaps full as hostile to Melbourne's government as he had been the preceding year, but he was not so rude in his manners, nor so obviously discontented with himself and others. His vanity had been satisfied by the success of his various publications, which afforded abundant proof of the extent, tho' not perhaps the accuracy, of his attainments and of the facility and intenseness of his application, though not of the fastidiousness of his taste and judgement and still less of the steadiness of his principles or consistency of his opinions. His utter disregard of that was well exposed by Normanby in debate,[14] and he shewed more effrontery than ingenuity in his attempt to extricate himself from the Charge. It was surely remarkable, and highly creditable to the political morality of this Country, that A Man 5 years Lord Chancellor, of transcendent talents as an Orator and a Writer and indefatigable in the devotion of those talents to the object of acquiring influence over parties, should yet fail to overcome the repugnance to unprincipled and unscrupulous selfishness and levity so entirely as not to carry with him on any one occasion a single vote or adherent from among the numerous admirers of his abilities on both sides, either in the House of Lords or House of Commons. Those who agree with him enjoy his bitter sarcasms and vehement philippics against their enemies, some and among them Lord Wellesley perhaps furnished him with fresh topicks and are delighted that their own epigrams and periods are delivered by him with encreasing effect in the House, but none gave him the disposal of their vote or even their proxy!!! Not one occasion occurred on which his adoption of an opposite line would have made the difference of more than his single vote in the division! Yet his inordinate vanity persuades him that in fortune and influence he bears some resemblance to Lord Shaftesbury, Lord Bolingbroke, or Lord Chatham. In unscrupulous profligacy he may be on a level with two first. Some traits of eccentricity and effrontery in his career may remind one of the last; but where is the private honour and friendship which attached so many partizans to the two first, and where are the high demeanour, enlightened views, and noble disinterestedness which extorted admiration for the artificial but stately and dignified character of Lord Chatham? Brougham may mount the stilts of his pretended Prototype and even display yet more surprizing feats of agility, but he can at the very most excite applause for the diversion he occasions. He will never be looked up by the Multitude for elevation of mind or even for well directed Ambition.

Early in May we brought forward a bill suspending for a limited time the legislature of Jamaica and transferring, during that suspension, the legislative functions to the Governor and the council, newly constituted and subject to the authority of the Mother Country. This was rendered so necessary by the outrageous language and conduct of the Assembly, which amounted to defiance and libel of the Parliament and of abdication of its duties, and it seemed to follow as so obvious a consequence from those circumstances, combined with the acquiescence of all parties in the late proceedings of parliament legislating for the management of persons in the island, that we apprehended little opposition in either house to securing the benefits of the Emancipation, for which the Country had made such glorious sacrifices. We were mistaken. Faction triumphed over patriotism and prudence, and the Duke of Wellington (altho' the one among the tories most susceptible of those wise and honorable motives) was misled on the subject of Negro labour by his own early prejudices as well by the Shameless falsehoods of the planters. His party seized his dislike to the measure. Many of them knew it to be judicious and salutary yet they resolved to try their strength against a Ministry and by a party triumph to force them from the helm. They succeeded so far as to reduce the majority, on a question requiring all the authority of Parliament, to five.[15]

7th. May 1839. This after a short deliberation seemed to us all too insufficient a hold on the Confidence of Parliament to enable us either to proceed with the measure or to continue in office, especially as some few who set up for ultra virtuous reformers openly professed that they preferred a Tory administration to one so moderate or, as they termed it, irresolute and compromising as Lord Melbournes. They actually voted against us to the number I think of nine; yet more who were numbered among those on whom our strength mainly depended staid away or voted reluctantly and with many insinuations that their support implied neither good will nor confidence in the administration. We accordingly tendered our resignation thro' Lord Melbourne. When Lord John Russell, who saw the Queen first, acquainted her with this resolution, she burst into tears, said she greatly lamented but had expected it. She repeated as much and more to Lord Melbourne and, on her pressing him to tell her what to do, he advised her, as after much reflection he had previously determined to do, to send to the Duke of Wellington to form her administration and advize her upon it; [*In the margin:* he had consulted me a fortnight before on this question. I sent him a statement pro and con for recommending Wellington as the person, and another for recommending Spencer.[16] My reasons for both are among my papers. My first impression was strongly for Wellington, but four and twenty hours reflection made me waver exceedingly and my judgement, like my paper, was pretty equally divided between the two courses. As it turned out few liberal friends will blame the course taken; but had Wellington formed a Peel Ministry I am not sure that the friends of liberty and reform would readily have excused Lord M[elbourne] for advising the Queen to resort to it.] to express a hope that the new administration would conduct the government of Ireland on the principles professed of late years in Parliament and in the spirit of the Catholick Emancipation; to offer the entire patronage of the Crown to her Ministry, hoping that in the household the Changes might not extend beyond Members of Parliament (for neither Melbourne nor the Queen dreamt of any interference with the Women); and to reserve the question of dissolution as one on which no decision could be taken till the occasion on which it was recommended had actually arisen and had been considered by responsible advisers. She followed this advice, but I believe that even in this first interview She, together with very artless and earnest assurances of fair dealing and surrender of all the authority of the Crown necessary to support her ostensible advisers, frankly acknowledged the pain with which she parted with her late Servants, whom she personally preferred and with whose political principles she agreed. These protestations or avowals she renewed yet more earnestly to Sir Robert Peel, to whom in compliance with Wellington's advice She sent to form the Ministry. [*Heading:* 7th. and 8th. May 1839] She told him that his Ministry should have all her support and countenance, but that she had been educated in the principles of the late Ministry and that it was painful, very painful, to her to part with them. As that or some subsequent conversations went on, she stated without reserve her predilections and dislikes to individuals, but where Sir Robert did not readily substitute others she acquiesced. When he came to the Household She surrendered all the great offices and all the places held by Members of either house, but expressed or implied some inclination to stickle for such as were not Members of Parliament; but when, without having finally settled that branch of the question, Sir Robt. started the notion of removing such Ladies as he deemed convenient to the New Government, She interrupted him by observing that she was not disposed to place that part of her household at his disposal, and according to his report peremptorily said she would not give up one. [*Heading:* May 1839] He was as she described it afterwards with some humour, greatly disconcerted. 'She never saw a Man so put out.' He turned pale and looked frightened and asked for time to consult his friends, and he then came back to her with the Duke of Wellington. He asked if she would like to see them together or alone. She left it to their Choice and she gave them at their request separate audiences. A Night had passed and she had entirely recovered her composure. The Duke was extremely civil and respectful and seemed to shew interest and real regard, but he argued earnestly and at some length. He drew distinctions between a Queen Consort and a Queen regnant and pretended that the Civil list Act, by constituting Ladies of the Bedchamber under a Queen Regnant, placed them in the situation of Lords under a King, to which the Queen smartly replied that it did not place them in the House of Lords or give them votes or political influence, and that she did not see why, if *her Ladies* were *her Lords,* the Parliament should have given her eight Lords besides. The Duke of W[ellingto]n found her, as he acknowledged, fully conversant with the Law, History, and Constitution which could bear on the subject and ready to discuss the subjects with a spirit, a propriety, and a composure that surprized him. A King who had practised the craft for forty years could not [have] performed his part with more propriety, and yet there was no artifice or duplicity. Sir Rt. Peels very complaints prove that she was open, fair, and unreserved, inasmuch as I understand that part of his defence for exacting the hard and unusual terms he did, is that Her Majesty's aversion to his party and his principles was so manifest and so avowed that he was bound in prudence to require a larger demonstration of ostensible confidence—a feeling which seems to me to be of a piece with his selfish and ungenerous policy and, I believe, for I do not know him, his not less ungenerous nature. The result was certainly to rivet any dislike the Sprited little Princess felt, not only to the party but to his [?its] chief, whom she suspected of a design to enthral her and to surround her with his creatures, founded on a notion, of which he was soon undeceived, that she was a foolish, ignorant, and weak young girl, easily intimidated or cajoled. Sir Robert and the Duke had I think another consultation with their leading friends and returned <in> respectful language (whether in writing or by word of mouth I forget) for answer, that they could not without any certainty of the support of a majority in Commons undertake the arduous task of conducting Her Majesty's affairs (though deeply sensible of the honour of the offer) unless they had every possible demonstration of the countenance and support of the Crown, that they considered, in a Queens reign, the entire disposal and controul of Her Majesty's household, including the Ladies, as one of those necessary indications. [*In the margin:* Up to this period the Queen had constitutionally considered herself in communication with Wellington and Peel for the formation of a Ministry and had *scrupulously* abstained from all consultation with her former Ministers or with any body unconnected with Wellington and Peel;[17] but she considered this answer as final, and herself at Liberty to apply to any advisers; and with that impression, sent *for Lord Melbourne.*]

The Queen on this sent for Lord Melbourne, and She was evidently pleased, not to say elated, at the rupture of a negotiation. From its success she had foreboded much mortification. She asked Melbourne what he advised and pressed him for a prompt answer. He desired permission to consult his friends, and happening to dine with me in South Street that very day, arrived late in consequence of writing summons to his late Colleagues to meet him that very night at his house. He came in late. He was evidently much excited. Lady H[olland] pressing him before he actually quitted office to advise the Queen to make Lord Elphinstone[18] an English peer, he suddenly exclaimed, 'Why are you in such a d——d hurry. How the Devil do you know that I am out?' and then outburst before Allen and Ellice, who were at dinner, the whole story, related with great emotion and some humour and indicating the high spirit and quick understanding of the Queens, together with her strong predilections for Melbourne and his friends. [*In the margin:* He read us two letters from the Queen relating what had passed in a sprightly natural style, and full both of good sense and kind feeling to Melbourne. 'I behaved quite well', says she, 'and as I am sure you would have approved'. These letters quite warmed us, and had some effect in Cabinet too, but Melbourne did not read them to Grey, and seemed afterwards to be *very* and I think *over*cautious about them. The substance was known, quoted, and repeated, and people are always tickled and sometimes reasonably more touched by seeing the originals than by a report. Qua sunt oculis subjecta fidelibus affect one more. The substance of these letters is contained on the annexed extract from the Examiner of July 7th., the passage containing it is marked with lines of black ink. It may be considered as an authentick report of that curious interview between a Queen of 20 and a Great General and Stateman of near 70.] Allen, Ellice, and myself all caught fire and, be it the bias of one's own interest or the real merit of the little Lady herself, combined with that favor which spirit and sense in youth and especially in youthful woman naturally bespeak, we waxed more loyal than I believe any of us had ever before been, and did then and have since reconciled zealous and eager support of her determination with our unaltered notions of the obligations of Royalty and the subsidiary nature of regal splendour to the support of its legal and ostensible advisers. Most of the Cabinet and all the Elders of it partook of this spirit, but I observed with surprize that what hesitation was felt as to the answer to be made arose with the younger Members, and especially with Howick, who seemed to Wish that some further explanation should be required by the Queen from Sir Robt. Peel. His father, Lord Grey, was not of that opinion. Tho' not of the late Cabinet, he had been privately apprized and consulted by Melbourne *at my suggestion,* and the event proved that my advice to speak to him and to write to Lord Spencer was judicious. Howick's crotchets and some few others prolonged the deliberation of Cabinet, but at length Lord Lansdowne drew up a short, plain, and decisive paper, to which all consented to recommend to the Queen as her answer to Peel. The substance was that she had considered his proposal and, believing it to be contrary to usage and knowing [it] to be repugnant to her feelings, she must decline complying with it. We thus made ourselves constitutionally responsible for the rejection of the proposal. She sent it most readily and chearfully, and Peel having in a long, laboured, and far from well written paper endeavoured to insinuate rather than to prove that he meant to exercise the power of dismissing the Ladies of the household, very sparingly and mildly but still acknowledging that he must have that power accorded him, the Queen considered the negotiations entirely at an end and asked Lord Melbourne if he and his colleagues would resume their situation. Melbourne, in laying this question before us, observed very pertinently that after we had advised the Queen to answer as she had done, we were bound in honour to do all consistently with our publick duty to support her, but at the same time we could not hope to alter that condition in which we stood with House of Commons, and which had induced us to resign as insufficient to our purposes, without being prepared to make concessions of a popular nature to reclaim a portion of those who had been estranged from us by the moderation and caution of our policy. We unanimously agreed to go on, though we were all aware of our difficulties and one among us, Howick, to wit, had a hankering after his original crotchet of further explanation and seemed to think that Sir Robert's paper raised a presumption that the Queen had misunderstood him. The Chancellor, however, silenced this scruple by dispassionately observing that the proposition which we had advised the Queen to pronounce unusual and repugnant to her feelings was the preliminary surrender to an incoming Minister of the practical power of removing the Ladies of the Household, not the extent of the exercise of it, and that Sir Robert Peel's paper distinctly admitted that he had requested that power and still stickled for it as the condition of accepting office. The Queen had said to Lord John before the Cabinet was held: I have stood by you; You must stand by me. It seemed clear by her conversations with Lord M[elbourne] that if we had shabbily and pusillanimously declined her offer, she would not have been brought even by Melbourne's advice to send for the Duke of W[ellingto]n a second time and still less for Peel, to whom She has contracted an invincible aversion.

I was taken ill with gout and an inflamed Chalkstone the very evening of this decision and confined to my Couch for nearly a Month. I consequently was neither in Parliament or Cabinet, and heard the explanation of what passed in neither house. Lord John was very nervous and not so clear or so decisive as usual, but he made no injudicious admissions and he asserted no obnoxious or untenable doctrines. Peel's explanations were very elaborate and some say very artful, others evasive.[19] If they were intended to pacify or propitiate the Queen they were not successful, for the unnecessary introduction of Mme Lezen's name, though professedly to disclaim all design of disturbing her and even all acquaintance with her name, was deemed at Court very offensive and seemed designed to raise in the Mind of the publick some notion of secret influence or to sanction the odious insinuation of a female faction against the Duchess of Kent and a plot against Lady Flora Hastings, and to imply some intention in the new Ministry, if installed, of defeating it by enquiry and dismissal of the accomplices. Lord Melbourne's speech was manly and decisive but he [made] an admission beyond the truth and used rather an unlucky expression by allowing that the Queen had received 'an erroneous impression of Sir Robt's views and intentions'. The main impression, that he stickled for a preliminary acknowledgement of full power to dismiss the Ladies, was not erroneous, and the persuasion that if obtained he meant to use it harshly or unsparingly, if it was erroneous, was an apprehension and not an impression. The Duke of Wellington, though he maintained somewhat pertinaciously the propriety of full power over the female part of the household, and even vindicated the exercise of it in the case of wives, daughters, and connections of active politicians, yet disclaimed all opposition to the reinstated Ministry, applauded some of the principles of Melbourne's speech, and expressed surprize and concern at his having deemed it necessary to resign because his majority was small. His speech sadly disappointed the violent as well as the placehunters of his party. Brougham, who had promised the bitter tories and Lord Lyndhurst to speak, urged as an excuse to them the presence of Lord Grey and Lord Spencer, who would in case of his speaking have been provoked to say some words and whose statements, as he observed, would have done Ministers more good than his Philippicks could have done them harm. To Duncannon and others he said that, tho' pressed and ready to speak, he abstained from unwillingness to harrass the restored Ministry too much! Unprofitable duplicity! It was true that Grey went down prepared to vindicate our course, and Lord Spencer would certainly have corrected any mistatement of past facts within his own cognizance, to which it is almost certain that Brougham on such a topick would have resorted. There is some ground to suspect that B[rougham]'s overweening conceit and ignorance of the estimation in which he is held, deluded him into the notion that, in their want of strength, the Ministers might make some offer to him, and it is not impossible he would accept of almost any. To such a degrading position has the abuse of transcendent abilities reduced this extraordinary but unscrupulous man! He was panting to vent the venom of his speech and was I suspect held back by the Tory Leaders and the Duke of Wellington's speech rather than any feelings of forbearance or judgement of his own. When Lord Winchelsey (who had in private assured Lord Melbourne that he had never contemplated any question on Lady Flora Hastings, an assurance to which he steadfastly adhered) asked a question on the future policy of the administration, Lord Brougham seized the opportunity of delivering his long meditated speech, full of venom, invective, wit, eloquence, and fallacy, and well calculated to gratify the tories and vex the Whigs, but not, considering the Speaker, to assist the former or damage the latter very materially. It all through assumed that the Queen's resistance to Sir Rt. Peel's proposal was a resistance to a Government forced upon her by the House of Commons, which was the only circumstance that could make any resistance to his proposals unconstitutional and which in this instance was not only not true but the reverse of the truth. It also grossly misstated past transactions, and especially those of 1812. If correctly recounted they form a contrast rather than a parallel to Sir R Peel's and Duke of Wellington's proposal of 1839. Melbourne had spoke and was idle. Lansdown was absent from illness, as well as myself, and Normanby though he said enough to shew his spirit, corrected Brougham only on the point of Lady N[ormanby]s[20] resignation. The Speech was much puffed by the Tories and became a text book for our opponents. It did not gain the Speaker of it a single follower in either house.

The divisions on the Jamaica bill,[21] and on Peel's motion for rescinding the order in Council regarding Education,[22] in the Commons were barely sufficient to save our honour, and in the Lords a large majority reduced the Jamaica measure (though already nearly what the Tories had prised to support) to a mere nullity, and yet larger censured by implication the Order in Council for a comprehensive national education and, by a very unusual not to say irregular step, prayed her Majesty to take no step therein without consulting them as a branch of the legislature.[23] On this latter occasion Lord Brougham did, for once in the Session, adhere to his former principles and support a measure founded upon them, but the event of the division shewed that he had gained as few adherents in the ranks of his new friends as he retained on those of his Old. When he voted with the Tories he was the single Whig who did so, and when he voted with the Whigs he was the only one composing the Tory Majority who had deserted them. And yet he fancies, or affects to fancy, that *he governs the world!!* The scanty majorities in Commons and the actual defeats in the Lords, however discouraging, were not the most alarming symptoms for Melbourne's administration. He had to contend or at least to provide against much growing discontent and some fearful seditions in the country, and though firm in the good graces of his spirited little Sovereign, the court itself was beset with dissensions of a very distressing nature.

The Duchess of Kent under the guidance of Conroy was doing every thing to inflame animosities and to lead to an open separation or rupture between herself and her Daughter the Queen. An apprehension of such a catastrophe and an idle hope that all estrangement between the Mother and daughter might be kept secret made Lord Melbourne, at the instigation and with the knowledge of the Duke of

Wellington, do every thing in his power to stifle all discussion and silence all vindication in the unlucky affair of Lady Flora Hastings. These precautions, if one may judge by the event, were most injudicious, for the Queen was exposed to the opposite imputations, both utterly false, of a connivance and participation in disgusting tales of licentiousness in her court, and of a harsh, unfeeling, indelicate, and revolting exercise of authority. It was supposed that She had entertained and encouraged if not invented and propagated tales against Lady Flora's chastity, founded on the appearance of her person, that she had done so out of malignity to her Mother's household, and that she, de proprio motu, had given the coarse and indecent direction to have the virginity of the Lady personally inspected by Sir Chs. Clarke.[24] It cannot be denied that the unfortunate Lady Flora, herself, had (in all probability at the instigation of Conroy) given some handle to these atrocious calumnies by writing to a vulgar relation, FitzGerald,[25] at Brussells a somewhat gross, indelicate, narrative of all that had passed, and authorizing that ill judged Irishman to make what use he chose of the letter. He would have published it at length but the Editor, Fonblanque, to whom he fortunately shewed it, declined exposing himself to a prosecution for libel, and FitzGerald confined himself to quotations of the letter which, tho' inaccurate in fact and somewhat revolting to good taste, were said to be less offensive than the suppressed passages. [*In the margin:* The original letter, or at least a paper purporting to be so, has since been published and is not in the respect of delicacy more offensive than FitzGerald's extracts.] Yet they raised a surmize that Lady Flora's enemies, or even the Queen herself, had compelled her to submit to the disgusting examination of her person or at least suggested that strange expedient. This false version of the whole transaction was allowed (in spite of Lord Tavistock's and Lord Portmans earnest remonstrances) to circulate uncontradicted, though the Lady of the latter, who was cognizant of the whole matter, had taken notes of all that passed and very fortunately conveyed a copy of them to Lady Hastings[26] or to some branch of the Hastings family before Lady Flora's illness had assumed any alarming appearance. Besides the letters from Lady Hastings and others of the family which have been published, there were several communications and remonstrances from Lord Hastings and various branches, urging sometimes the dismissal of Sir James Clarke, at others some other proceeding, and at one time a challenge to Lord Melbourne for not attending to their remonstrances, which was suppressed by the Duke of Richmonds good sense and had been, according to his own account, prevented for a long while, according to the suspicion of some, instigated by Lord Brougham, who was ridiculously anxious that no notorious event should occur in which he could claim no share and who is reported to have said that this business must end in blood. When however Lady Flora's illness was manifestly likely to prove fatal, <and> the malignant libels in the Morning Post and other newspapers were at pains to impress on the publick that both she and her Mother were dying of a broken heart, the victims of base calumny, falsehood and conspiracy, Those who knew the truth of the whole transaction could not submit to remain entirely silent and the facts, though unfortunately not hitherto published in any authentick shape, transpired in private conversation, and in the opinion of all candid minds (though not I fear of the vulgar and of many who ought not to have ranged themselves under that denomination) rescued the Queen from the unfounded aspersions of harshness, indelicacy, and injustice. It appears that on first learning, it is supposed from Lady Portman, the suspicions to which Lady Flora's appearance had given rise, she simply and justly observed that it should be mentioned to the Duchess of Kent, and that after that communication had been made, after Sir James Clarke had incautiously acknowledged to others that he, Lady Flora's medical attendant, had his misgivings that she was with child, and after the propriety of calling in another Physician had been suggested by either the Duchess of Kent or Lady Flora herself, The Queen observed that Lady Flora had better not appear at Table till her health was reinstated or till the Consultation was over. Sir Charles Clarke, the Eminent accoucheur, was fixed upon at Lady Flora's own request [*In the margin:* This is Tavistock's story] and He, who tho' eminent in his profession is remarkably abrupt, hasty, and peremptory in his proceedings, being in a room with, I think, Duchess of Kent, Lady Portman, Sir James Clarke and Lady Flora, and having heard the object of their consultation, suddenly bade Lady Flora go to her bedchamber and Lady Portman to follow her and, on the spur of the occasion and without further deliberation, proceeded, much to the surprize and annoyance of Lady Portman, to manual and professional enquiry, and pronounced, in as decisive a tone as any enquiry or inspection of an adult woman could justify, the entire and inviolate state of her Hymen and her therefore undoubted virginity. Of any such intention The Queen could not be aware, nor is there reason to suspect she was at all apprized of the nature of the transaction till the publication of FitzGerald's letter and other indelicate and unpardonable calumnies founded in it must have forced on an intelligent, though pure and innocent mind, a knowledge of the nature of the proceeding.

The activity with which every incident, true or false, was converted to the disparagement of the Queen as well as the encreasing uneasiness between the Mother and daughter convinced those acquainted with the interior of the Palace that nothing could restore comfort or harmony within its walls but the absence of Coll. Conroy from England. He was much suspected to be the chief agitator of these matters in the papers and journals, and it was known that, if not the positive adviser of all the Duchess of Kent or the Hastings family said and did, the effect of his intercourse with both was to influence their animosity. In the policy of removing him, not only the Duke of Wellington but all the Coburgh family concurred, and this latter circumstance, full as much as any other, is said to have prevailed upon him to absent himself. On the day of the Queen's accession he extorted a promise of money, which has been paid, and of honours, which are to come, but the Queen has uniformly resisted all appointments of authority for him, remarking that she has too much experience of his arbitrary and unjust disposition to place willingly any of her subjects under his controul. Her antipathy to him certainly exceeds the bounds of prudence, but without knowing, as I certainly do not, the extent or nature of the provocation, I am not prepared to pronounce it unnatural or unreasonable. He is said to be a coarse, vulgar, and unprincipled man, and it is insinuated that where women are concerned he is particularly so. Certain it is that in his intercourse with almost all the Ladies of the Court it has been his fate to excite the passions of love or hatred to a very extraordinary degree. He left England before Lady Flora's death.

When that unhappy Lady's life was despaired of, the Queen redoubled her attentions, shewed her and her family every mark of respect, and conducted herself with so much tenderness and propriety that she extorted from them all an acknowledgement of her unfeigned graciousness. It did not escape impartial observers that the conduct of the whole Hastings family somewhat belied the expressions of indignant pride and high resentment attributed to them, for would they have left a dying daughter or Sister, whom they deemed so cruelly injured and insulted, under the roof and exposed to the malice and in some measure dependent on the good offices of those who, according to their supposed complaints, had injured and offended her. She not only acquitted the Queen on her death bed of all unkindness, but before her illness and indeed before the charge against the Ladies of the Bedchamber had been brought, she somewhat inconsistently with her subsequent language expressed her gratitude and affection to Lady Portman for accompanying her during the unpleasant ceremony of the enquiry, and for her friendship to her throughout. I have noted down at more length than is agreable to me, or likely to be to my readers, the relations I have heard of this nasty and foolish affair, because I much fear that the false impression which misrepresentation and slander had made on the publick regarding it is likely to impair even permanently that popularity to which the qualities, even more than her station, entitled Queen Victoria.

The unfavorable impression equally or more prevalent about our Education bill is likely to be more transient. Never was there a greater ado about nothing, but the Church affected to take offence at the Douay version of the Bible being admitted in schools and the Bishops, predisposed to embarrass our Government, were unusually active in agitating the publick. The event certainly betrayed the extent and available strength of the machinery possessed by the Church for fomenting any clamour and affecting any political purpose. The House of Lords, at the instigation of the Archbishop of Canterbury, resolved by an immense majority to address the Queen on her order and, having at the commencement of the Session assumed the functions of the House of Commons by establishing an inculpatory inquest into Lord Normanby's government in Ireland, seemed disposed to close by modestly requesting the Crown to admit them to a participation of its prerogative. [*Heading:* July 1839] The Queen's answer,[27] on which we very prudently consulted Lord Grey, was [a] well mannered but firm and dignified rebuke to the House of Lords, expressive of the regret at the step they had taken, indirectly vindicating her past conduct and future intentions from the censure implied in their address, and firmly but civilly intimating that the object she had in view by her order in council would be stedfastly pursued. The Queen delivered the answer with great spirit but with good taste and propriety from the throne at Buckingham house to more than a hundred peers headed by the Chancellor exofficio (who was supposed to read the address purposely in a somewhat slovenly and unimpressive manner) and the two Primates of England and Ireland. When the object of the address and the question in dispute between the Crown and the Lords is considered, viz whether the Queen's government should be at liberty to advance 10 or 12 thousand pounds for education to Presbyterians and dissenters without the consent of the Lords or not, the whole ceremony, otherwise striking enough, becomes absolutely ridiculous, and the reflection is forced upon one that human government, even among the most enlightened people and in the most civilized and refined form, is often a mere humbug— *παντα γελως και παντα κονις και παντα το μηδεν*[28]

I could have fancied that the very hypocrites who had promoted this notable farce smiled in their sleeves at it, but the subsequent conduct of the Lords in rejecting many useful and necessary bills and in encouraging and abetting if not concerting the endeavours of Lords Lyndhurst and Brougham to mortify, lower, and embarrass the Queen's Government belied my expectations. The Committee to enquire into the causes of the encrease of [crime in] Ireland seemed indeed to end in nothing; they could not agree in any report, and the evidence, amounting to many folio volumes which they did report, seemed to cut the ground under them by proving or at least sanctioning the surmize that Crime had not *encreased* but actually diminished in frequency and in intensity under Lord Normanby's ViceRoyalty. Brougham, however, after many hypocritical assurances of meaning no hostility to Government and many mysterious and unintelligible hypotheses of what his motion on the evidence might be, brought forward one, inculpating Lord Normanby by implication for neglect of the Judges, for mistaken and lavish Clemency and, above all, for not consulting the Judges on the exercise of it; and this latter charge was conveyed by an abstract and prospective resolution, that it was the duty of the Executive Government to consult them, applicable to both England and Ireland and at variance, in my humble opinion, with principle and practice in both. [*Heading:* July and August 1839] Brougham's speech was very elaborate and full of eloquence, wit, knowledge, and argument, with the usual fault of being extremely long and in many parts hyperbolical and exaggerated. It was however prodigiously admired and, though ably answered by Melbourne, Plunkett, Hatherton, and several Irish Members, was carried by a considerable Majority.[29] I entered a protest against the principle of making a consultation of the Judge who tried the criminal compulsory on the Crown in the exercise of the prerogative of Mercy, and I had the satisfaction of finding it signed by 26 Peers besides myself,[30] as well as the still greater of learning by the newspapers next day that Lord John Russell in the Commons had declared Lord Broughams recommendation contrary to the practice of himself and his predecessors and avowed his determination of adhering to usage and not being swayed by the unauthorized resolution of one house of Parliament. So ended the Committee on Irish Crime, an endeavour of the House of Lords to Usurp the functions of the Commons and of Lord Broughams resolutions, an endeavour of the same body to force themselves into a partnership of the Prerogative with the Crown. There was something ludicrous in the extravagant and fulsome compliments which the different Members of the Committee, though of opposite opinions, lavished on their Chairman and on one another and, indeed, on all the Witnesses who had been brought before them. One Expected (so laudatory was their strain) that they would have extended it to those whom they had been appointed to inculpate and that the Catholick Priesthood and Lord Normanby himself would come in for his share. A somewhat theatrical, and as some pretended, hazardous and improvident exercise of mercy *four years ago,* under *another* reign and productive of *no inconvenience whatever,* was after all the utmost offending that industry and malevolence could lay to the Charge of Lord Normanby, and surely the state of Ireland, the safety of reducing the army there to one third of its former amount, and the avowal of Lord Ebrington, whom even Lord Normanby's enemies concur in eulogizing, are practical answers to such a charge, quite sufficient to refute and to silence it for ever.

Portugal evaded and violated our rights under treaties and connived at and instigated a trade in Slaves which she had passed laws and contracted treaties to suppress, and which for an equivalent in money and other articles she had given us a right to intercept. To enable us to enforce that right against both Portuguese and Pirates of no Nation an act of Parliament was necessary. It passed the Commons almost by acclamation, but the Duke of Wellington, from a strange misunderstanding both of its object and provisions, prevailed on a Majority of the Lords to throw it out.[31] Brougham, possibly from mere levity, possibly from shame at assisting yet willingness to connive at the mischief of his Tory friends, was dining at the Fishmongers when this outrage on his favorite measure was perpetrated. Dr Lushington heard of the vote and that very night moved in the Commons to search out journals with a view of counteracting the vote, and Brougham, roused in all probability by this promptitude of Lushington and jealous of the well earned popularity he would obtain by it, dexterously moved, the very next sitting day of the Lords, an address to the Queen to pray her to take all necessary measures to put down the illicit Portugueze Slave trade and to pledge the cooperation and assistance of Parliament in all such measures. We joyfully and unreservedly accepted and supported the motion and I think he was for once tickled at our readiness to adopt his suggestion. When however a bill founded on that address and purged of all the vices which the Tories had so squeamishly imputed to the last was brought up from the Commons, who had passed it unanimously, the Duke of Wellington, to the surprize and to the mortification of some of his friends, persisted in his far fetched objections, founded as they were on an entire misapprehension of the bill, and of the nature of the obligations of a treaty and its entire independence of any Municipal Law.[32] Brougham earnestly and honestly exposed the fallacy of the objections and urged the wickedness and the danger to the Lords of rejecting the bill. Some Tories from principle or conviction and some perhaps from dread of unpopularity were unwilling to follow this perverse course of the Duke of Wellington, and by voting with us, rescued the Crown and the Ministry from the disgrace of submitting to the perfidy of the Portuguese.[33] They, even the most disposed to English connection such as the Minister here, Baron Moncorvo, affect to be highly indignant at such an insult on their independence which, according to them, consists in the notable privilege of breaking their engagements with impunity for the glorious and honourable purpose of Man Stealing on the Coast of Africa. They say our manly course would have been to go to War and whimsically enough taunt us with treating them in this unwarrantable way because they are a weak power, whereas they well know that if a strong power were to make and break such engagements, war would be the consequence, and that it is consideration for them rather than ourselves which deters us hitherto from visiting them with all the consequences of such a calamity. They have no doubt the power, if they prefer it to the pretended indignity, to drive us to general hostilities.

All these endeavours to harrass the Government in the Lords, and especially those in which the friends in the House of Commons took little or no part, afforded proof of a studied attempt on the part of the House of Lords to regain all or more than they had lost by the Reform bill and to establish in that branch of the legislature the supreme and controuling power, the ascendancy of the State—to render themselves Lords Paramount—and substantially and practically superior both to Crown and the Commons. This scheme would perhaps have succeeded had King William IV, who in his heart would have concurred with it, lived, or had his Successor been less spirited, less intelligent, less firm, and less sincerely inclined to liberal policy than our little Queen. Perhaps however chagrin at the discovery of that obstacle rather exasperated, embittered, and accelerated the attempts to surmount it, and the violence and impatience of the Ultra Tory and Orange Party often drove or tricked their leaders into abortive demonstrations of malice, which the sober minded among them could not approve. The other, less numerous and less prominent but perhaps not less dangerous class of our enemies, viz the Ultra liberals, though they rendered the existence of our Government uneasy, and exposed us occasionally to mortifications which, but from a sense of honour and gratitude to the Queen (forbidding us to abandon her for any thing short of extreme necessity) we could not and perhaps ought not to endure, began themselves to perceive that in the state of publick opinion, parties, Parliament, and Court, the downfal of Lord Melbourne's Ministry was synonymous with an immediate and possibly permanent triumph of the Antireformers; that another, and still more an ultra Reform Ministry, was impracticable, and that their only option was to be satisfied with such benefits as a slowly progressive and much impeded system of improvement offered, or to run the peril of a party hostile to all such improvement assuming the ascendency. Lord Brougham during the whole of the session did his utmost to sow dissensions between the popular party and the Whigs, to soften the publick prejudices against the Tories, and to entice the latter to adopt many disingenuous and disgraceful manoeuvres to ingratiate themselves with the publick and to ruin their opponents in publick estimation; but in spite of his assiduity and talents, which were heightened rather than dimmed by his malignity, he had little success in estranging from us lukewarm partizans and none whatever in detaching from either party any individuals by inspiring them with the slightest confidence in himself, or exciting in them hopes that exertions so extraordinary or abilities so dazzling must ultimately triumph over the enemies they had in common. All listened and admired, several were diverted and enjoyed, from their hatred of the objects of his invective and ridicule, his masterly command of those weapons, but few expected any results from his efforts and none, not one, trusted his sincerity or felt any obligation to him for his exertions.

Towards the end of the Session a financial operation of funding Exchequers which was equivalent to raising a loan of 3 or 4 millions, was effected in terms which not only proved the flourishing state of the publick credit, but shed lustre on the close of Mr Spring Rice's administration of the Exchequer.[34] It should have created regret, and perhaps did, in those who in conversation had long disparaged the services of that active, honourable, and able Minister and thereby contributed to his disgust and retirement. He had indeed foolishly for us and for himself set his heart on the Speaker's chair. He handsomely relinquished his pretensions when he discovered the strong repugnance in most of the independent supporters of Government to placing him there. But from that time he probably looked to a seat in the house of Lords, and while he relaxed neither in parliamentary attendance nor Ministerial duties, felt less confidence than he had done in the perfect concert and cordiality of the party who keep us in power and possibly some resentment to that portion of it who, under the name of Whig Radicals, are always too much disposed to ingratiate themselves with their constituents by countenancing unjust suspicions of abatement of zeal in the cause of freedom in their leaders. In the Course of Mr Sp. Rice's administration of the finances he had removed the grievances most complained of by the Ultra liberal party. Yet they retained more resentment towards him for depriving them of topicks of complaint than thanks for redressing actual grievances. The Change in the Stamp duties and the penny postage, though loudly called for by the popular party, and possibly satisfactory to them, gained no credit for the Minister who acquiesced in them. This was in some degree owing to much injudicious reluctance he betrayed in granting them. He accepted a title and chose one somewhat objectionable, Lord Monteagle, by which Lord Sligo already sits in the Lords. He was also made auditor and was succeeded in the seals rather unwillingly by Francis Baring.[35]

In services, in standing, and in qualifications as well as other considerations, Lord Howick would have filled the place more to his own satisfaction and perhaps to the expectation of a large portion of the publick. But his somewhat overweaning confidence in his own, and his yet more unwarrantable disparagement of other men's, judgements and His frequent menaces of resignation together with perpetual and triumphant references to past differences of opinions disinclined more than one of his Colleagues and, what was most material, Lord Melbourne himself, to any measure that would place him in so prominent a station as the Exchequer. Yet the labour and responsibility would not improbably have extinguished those sparks of temper and restlessness from which we had experienced so much and He is honest, honourable, diligent, and able, understands well all he engages in, and has much sounder as well as stronger views than most of his Colleagues. True policy perhaps required either that his presumption should be gratified or at least allayed by being placed in a high situation, or that he should be removed from that which he filled. In real high and responsible station he would perhaps have been more manageable than in discontent, and I am not sure that it was not an oversight not offering it to him. [*Heading:* 1839 24 to 29th. Augst.] He objected on Saturday the 24th. to augmenting the number of the Cabinet and, dwelling with much emphasis on the services of his brother in law, Mr Wood, at the Admiralty, maintained that none of the three promoted—Sir G Grey, Mr Labouchere or Mr Baring—had equal pretensions, adding with no little *humour* that *in Mr Wood's situation* he would resign. Minto and those who know Wood best were satisfied that Howick transferred his own feelings to his friend and that, though he was nettled at Colonial Office, Board of Trade, and Exchequer seals being disposed of without any of the three being offered to him, that Wood was not dissatisfied at remaining where he was or being removed to the treasury without any seat in the Cabinet. However the result was that both Lord Howick and Mr Wood, probably at Lord Howick's but more at Lord Grey's suggestion, *did* resign. It was a loss of vigour and intelligence, talent and honesty to the Government, and if it was unavoidable, it yet imposes on Melbourne the duty of repairing it by some efforts to introduce Members not open to the disparagment of Mediocrity.[36]

The interchange of Colonial and Home office between Lord Normanby and Lord John Russell, suggested I believe by the latter and equally agreable to both, is not I suspect much relished by our friends, nor does it strike me as more likely to fulfill than to excite any favorable expectations. It arose from sincere but I believe erroneous representations from the Colonial Office of Lord Normanby's utter inefficiency (a bad reason, *ce me* semble, for placing him at the head of the home office) and from a strong persuasion in John Russell's mind that Colonial questions were the most critical at this moment, and that he who determined them should have the defence thereof in the Commons. In all these dislocations and accessions and in the Consequential appointments, I own I perceive a want of energy, boldness, and decision, and a sort of jealousy and fear of any thing like ambition and intrepidity, the usual concomitants of powerful minds. That reflection makes me tremble for the fate of Lord Melbourne's government. I have stated to him my apprehension that in all branches, and especially in the Commons, it was fast assuming the fatal character of Mediocrity and narrowness of views, and I was not a little startled to find that he thought a want of genius no great defect in the government of a great nation, and quiet and ease more the aim of a wise Statesman than popularity, authority, or splendor. As if a Command of the Confidence and, in some degree at least, of the admiration and applause of Mankind is not necessary to the preservation of the peace of those governed, and the quiet and ease of those who govern too. There is however great spirit and firmness and possibly some inequality of mind in the little Queen herself, and her character may assume an ascendancy to which few promoted under her seem to [be] either able or inclined to aspire. In the meanwhile we have lost Abercromby, one of the oldest, Spring Rice, by far the most ready, Howick, perhaps the most earnest and vehement, Poulett Thomson, one of the best informed and efficient, debaters, in the House of Commons, Lord Glenelg and Lord Clanrickarde in the House of Lords, and we have no *accession* officially connected with Government in either.

1839 October. Soon after the above was written, offers of the Privy seal to Lord Clarendon and of the Secretaryship of War to Mr Macaulay were made with seats in the Cabinet to each. From Lord Clarendon, who had rejected the offer of post office without Cabinet, no answer had been received on the 3d. of October, and Macaulay was in office and had sat on two Cabinets at Windsor before that day. His accession to the Cabinet is justly deemed an experiment, but surely it is a right one, and though he could not with his other Colleagues attend the Queen's cavalcade, good humouredly excusing himself by saying he was used to Elephants in India and afraid of exposing his bad horsemanship and falling in the presence of his Sovereign, his appearance at Court seemed to me advantageous, and the three new Cabinet Ministers—Baring, Labouchere, and Macaulay—to be much approved of. Their first Cabinets, *for which I perversely arrived too late related to very important subjects*—our rupture with China[37] and our measures for enforcing the policy we have espoused in the Levant of forcing Mehemet Ali to abandon Syria and to restore the fleet and content himself with the declaration that his Pachalick in Egypt is to be hereditary. [*In the margin:* Note: July 1840. Melbourne half in joke and half in earnest has more than once reproached me and Lady Holland for my arriving half an hour too late for the Cabinet held at Windsor in October 1839, adding that if I had been there the Government would not have got itself so deeply entangled in the Turco Egyptian question. But why, if his views coincided with mine, did he not himself prevent or at least postpone any step in that direction being taken? and why on my talking to him on the subject did he and Palmerston assure me that nothing was definitively settled? and why did he emphatically repeat to me, above once, that I need not vex myself so much about it, for there would [be] no embarrassment and above all no necessity of coercion or war whatever? in short, that by temporizing and leaving things to chance, we should very possibly hear no more of it? I cannot reproach myself with indifference, for though I brought nothing officially or formally before the Cabinet, I repeatedly explained to Palmerston my doubts of his policy and my dread of the possible consequences of it; and I pressed usque ad nauseam to Melbourne my views of the question. From Palmerston I always received civil, long, elaborate, but to me inconclusive answers, great assurances of ultimate success both in prevailing on France to cooperate and in repressing Mehemet Ali, either with or without French assistance; and from Melbourne exhortations to be quiet, for in fact he (Melbourne) was much of my opinion about the whole matter, and if I left it alone it would all turn out as I wished and in probability the whole be settled amicably some way or another, by which I understood him to point to an arrangement between the Porte and the Pacha. The great obstacle to such an *euthanasia* of the whole concern was the presence and advice of such a quack as Lord Ponsonby alongside of the patient; and upon this point I found Melbourne so entirely of my opinion that I was not without hopes that he meant to recall or supersede him.] With regard to the first I am both so ignorant and so indifferent that my conscience would have been in the hands of my colleagues had I been present, and I believe a resolution has been adopted for vigorous measures for supporting the acts of our Minister, Captain (the son of the late Hugh) Elliot,[38] and for leaving to his judgement and that of Lord Auckland the conduct of the business. There was, I believe, and indeed hope, *no such final decision* taken about our measures in the Mediterranean and Levant. The subject, a very perplexing one, is, I should infer from the report of some of my Colleagues, open, though the want of all formal resolution, paper, or motion (which seemed to surprize our new Colleagues, and Macaulay particularly, not a little) is, according to the usual mode of conducting business in every Ministry of which I have been a Member, no proof whatever either of the matter being postponed to future consideration or positively settled. Macaulay's surprize at the loose construction and proceeding of what is Called a Cabinet Council and practical Government of the Country is natural enough. It struck me equally in 1806. Macaulays manner of philosophizing thereupon was indeed somewhat characteristick of the author and reviewer—'Did I not think a very entertaining dissertation might be made on the causes which had led to many gradual changes in the Machinery of our Government and on the necessity and the effect of them?'

The Government is pressed for an answer by the Russian Special Mission.[39] We have in fact been induced by exaggerated suspicions of Russia hastily to suggest a policy against Mehemet Ali; Russia, by promptly and eagerly adopting it and offering even unexpected facilities and even sacrifices to execute it, somewhat disconcerts us and alarms France. France flies off from her agreement and takes umbrage at the cordial agreement of Russia with us to relieve Turkey of Mehemet Ali in Syria, and Russia, animated by the hope of separating England and France and thus resuming the station of a first rate power (from which a strict union between England and France necessarily removes her), is disposed to bribe us, if not to a rupture, to an estrangement from France by concurring in measures which France shabbily, some say faithlessly, hesitates to adopt by sacrificing many minor advantages within her reach which have given us umbrage heretofore, and by offering cordially and without reserve to concert and cooperate with us in Persia. If the object of these concessions were really to conciliate our good will, preserve peace, and place our relations permanently on a footing advantageous to both parties and to the preservation of permanent tranquillity, they would no doubt be very tempting; but as it is very obvious that they are offered chiefly with the design of separating us from France, we must be cautious in accepting their proffered friendship not to alienate that power with whom concert and cooperation are nearly synonymous with the Universal peace of the World or at least of Europe. I cannot yet describe in detail the state of the negotiation and the respective proposals of the various powers. [*Crossed out:* but it is very obvious that the joint note pledging ourselves to the maintenance of the independence of the Turkish Empire was somewhat hastily adopted] It has *embarrassed* more than one of the powers who are parties of it. [*In the margin:* NB 1840: There may be papers I have not seen. The Collective note was presented to the Porte on the 27th. July 1839 by the five Embassadors, without being submitted, much less explained, to the Cabinet. It was drawn up I believe by Prince Metternich, and it asserted, or at least implied, that the 5 Powers had concerted and agreed among themselves on the advice they would give to the Porte and on the means of enforcing what on that advice should be resolved; but in words it merely invites 'the Porte to suspend all definitive determination without the Concurrence of the five powers and to wait the result of the Interest they feel about her'.[40] It was vague and in truth pledged them to nothing; but it was premature and, in alledging agreement and implying previous concert, told a lie which has embarrassed us ever since and at the distance of a year threatens the most disastrous consequences.] Qui vult antecedens non debet nolle quod consequitur. France ought to have foreseen that one of the consequences of that Note was that she might be pressed to *do* as well as to *say* something against Mehemet Ali, and England ought to have foreseen that Russia, by acquiescing *contrary to her expectations in the policy* proposed, would remove the real tho' not the ostensible grounds for proposing it. Yet France shews unwillingness to do any thing and some inclination, if she had vigour and courage to indulge it, to resist others doing any thing without her. England, appalled at the consequences of too close an alliance with Russia for objects so remotely affecting her own separate interests as the territorial distribution of Western Asia, is or *ought to be* anxious to confine the endeavours of the Confederacy to objects that can be attained without disunion and, if possible, without recourse to force by an apparent if not real concurrence of views in all the Members of the Confederacy. If we *go to war* even with Mehemet Ali to make him evacuate Syria, we go to war simply to alter a state of things which has subsisted for at least five years without any national injury to us whatsoever; and if successful in a forcible ejectment of that rebel, we shall find it difficult to shew what national benefit, commercial or political, has been purchased by the expence of a War; but if, in addition to the employment of force against Alexandria, the Coast of Syria, Candia [*Crete*] and the Pacha's fleets and arsenals, we risk an actual war, or even a Menacing attitude, between ourselves and France, how can we reconcile the Parliament or the Country or, what is yet more important, our own sense of duty to such sacrifices for such precarious and worthless objects? The only justification in sound policy (if that be any) for meddling with such remote affairs is jealousy of Russia and anxiety for the safety and independence of Austria, and yet more undeniably the only feeling that could induce Parliament and people to take an interest in so remote a struggle would be exclusively hatred of *Russia* and not of Mehemet Ali. He is known not to be unfavourably inclined to our Commerce. He is thought to be a fine and spirited fellow, He is puffed off as an Abolitionist by Brougham and the Saints, and by the very supposition I am handling He would appear not the ally or favorite of Russia, but the object of her implacable disgust, terror, and hatred as well as of all the Holy Alliance. Would we, could we, or ought we to go to War with France in such a Cause and with such allies? Is it not a fragment of the Holy Alliance? a chip of the Old block?

The exchange of offices between Normanby and Lord John and the appointments of Thompson to Canada and Shiel to Vice presidentship of board of Trade are not popular and some of our friends are at no pains to reconcile the publick to them. Ellice disclaimed unhandsomely, tho' not without some provocation, all participation in advising the one and Duke of Richmond is, I understand, very vehement against both. It is a sad pity that Lord Tweedale,[41] who would have taken the Military Command in Canada, was not sent, and entirely owing to the etiquette about precedence and seniority at the Horse Guards. Lord Normanby during his short stay at the Colonial Office is accused, how justly I know not, of never saying No to an application, and the joke in the office, with allusion to the languor and dilatoriness of his predecessor, Glenelg, was that they had left the land of *Nod* and were then in the land of *promise*.

Novr. 1839. The remainder of the Autumn was saddened by the Death of several of My friends—Lord Lauderdale, the Duke of Bedford (a sad loss to many and nullo flebili<er> quam mihi), Duke of Argyll. The Reported death of Lord Brougham at first shocked both friend and foe exceedingly, but afterwards enlivened the town by an eager controversy (in which Brougham took much the largest share) about the author of the hoax. It was generally suspected to be himself. He denied it distinctly and with a vehemence which implied more serious guilt in so bad a joke than it would, if of his own perpetration, have actually involved. In the course of the Correspondence about it to me and others, he professed some personal regard and much feeling for many of his old friends in office, insinuated a strong inclination to reconnect himself with them, talked of having held out flags of truce which had been fired upon, and ended by denouncing battle on the late acquisitions to the Cabinet and against Lord Clarendon and Lord Normanby in particular. He was thought by those best conversant in such matters to shew a great desire for office of *any sort*, for he chiefly reproached the Government with not offering station or promoting either him or his friends—declaring that any advancement of Lord Clanrickarde (to whom and to Lady Clanrickarde he is or affects to be quite devoted) would have mollified him—though on the other hand he wrote Lady Clanrickarde a letter intended to be shewn, scouting the bare possibility of his ever holding any office under or with any Government except the seals, and the equal impossibility of his accepting them from the Tories. He writes in all directions vindications, explanations, and boasts, and he is not unaptly compared to the inkfish who, to elude his pursuers, involves himself in obscurity by spreading around all his actions a vast mass of that opaque fluid of which gall seems, but really is not, the chief ingredient.

The two Princes of Coburgh,[42] first cousins of the Queen prolonged their visit at Windsor for some weeks. The Queen was easy and chearful with them both, but those Ladies who thought themselves experienced in affairs of the heart maintained for a considerable time that the very ease and familiarity with which she treated the most prepossessing of the two, Prince Albert, was an indication that there was no strong attachment or disposition to Love or Marriage. However she communicated her intentions to her Mother, family, and Household, and even to the Young Prince himself before he left Windsor, and a circular was issued to summon the Privy Council on the [*blank*] of [*blank*] 1839 on important business. [*In the margin:* The Queen wrote to all her family herself, but by some oversight the letters were entrusted to the Common conveyance and no special Messenger sent to each. The Duke of Sussex, who was at Howick, at not being apprized of the object of the summons (tho he of course like all others understood it) when it arrived and the letter to the Queen Dowager came enclosed in a letter directed incorrectly to Lord How[e] by a servant. However all the family including the Cambridges, and more particularly the Queen Dowager, wrote letters of warm congratulations and entire approbation and the Queen was unfeignedly pleased and gratified thereat.] Great pains were taken in the form of summons and in the speech announcing the Marriage by the Queen to adhere as nearly to precedent as difference of circumstances and propriety would admit. The latest Precedent was that of G[eorge] III. The summons to Privy Council, in announcing that the business was 'important', omitted the word 'urgent', and the Queen in her speech very decorously dropped the assurance which George III had given his council, that his thoughts had been employed on marriage ever since his Accession. Besides these omissions, there was another which drew forth some animadversions—the religion of the Prince was not mentioned. There was no popish pretender to the Crown, and the Law and notoriety were sufficient guarantees that the object of the Queen's choice was not a Roman Catholick; and it was justly thought that the unnecessary mention of the fact and superfluous allusion to the Law would, after the admission of many Millions of Roman Catholicks to their rightful share in the Management of their own concerns by the Union of Ireland and the abrogation of the Exclusive and penal laws against them, be invidious and offensive. The endeavour to insinuate that Prince Albert was, or was likely to become, a papist was laughed at and scouted, and even the censure of the Omission of all allusion to the Protestant religion as an act of meanness to court popularity from the faction of OConnel was not only disavowed but discouraged by all that division of the Tory Opposition which had supported the measures of the Duke of Wellington in 1829. The Queen read her speech admirably. Her paleness and her tremulous voice were enough to betray inward feeling and nervousness, but not to impair in the slightest degree the grace of her delivery or the clear, mellow, and pathetick tones of her voice. The Ceremony was a strange one. A Modest girl of twenty, unaccompanied by any one of her own sex, had to announce to a grave and observant assembly of 85 men her *determination* to take as a bedfellow a young man who had lately left her palace. When asked by the Duchess of Gloucester if she had not been alarmed at the Ceremony, she answered naturally, 'A little, but not much, for I had to propose it to Albert himself and had gone thro' that much more awkward ceremony before I mentioned it to the Privy Council'. Nothing I am sure could be more natural, frank, and yet modest than the way in which she received my congratulations in a private audience and assured me with an unaffected blush and smile that 'she really thought the event would contribute to her comfort in life, that she regretted I had not seen Prince Albert and that she was confident I should like him and approve of her preference'.

1839 December. Dr Butler, Bishop of Lichfield, died; the bishoprick was offered and even pressed on Lord Wriottesley Russell,[43] who modestly, unaffectedly, but stedfastly declined it, alledging that he left himself every way unqualified for a station of this importance. I believe he is sincere and I am sure he is disinterested in this determination, for neither his present circumstances nor his prospects are very prosperous and I should think those most nearly connected with him will lament and even disapprove of his determination.

The French having peremptorily, and much to Lord Palmerston's chagrin, though surely not unreasonably, declined to cooperate with the plan Russia had suggested of employing French and English force against Mehemet Ali in Syria, and of sending Russian ships to Constantinople in case he should march against the sublime Porte, we made another proposal, that England and France should, in the same contingencies as would justify the Russians coming through the Bosphorus, be at liberty to come through the Dardanelles to the rescue of the Porte. It was thought that Russia would deem such a stipulation a virtual abrogation of the treaty of Unkiar Skelesi and reject it. But she accepted it, anxious, it is thought, to sow dissensions between England and France and to represent the latter as insidiously employed to thwart all the measures of the Alliance and of England in particular.

1840. Brunow in the Spring of 1840 came upon a 2d. Mission to England and with fresh proposals, instructed no doubt to be very accommodating in all views England might take of the subject and more especially on such points and particulars as he could ascertain or foresee that France would be most averse to. Austria, sincerely desirous of an amicable accommodation of differences, but as usual timid and circumspect in her proceedings and, above all, in dread of any thing that should separate her from Russia or connect her too closely with France, held at various periods of the negotiation equivocal and even contradictory language—at one time, recommending and rejoicing at the avowal of very Conservative not to say Holy Alliance principles against a revolted subject, and insisting on the Assertion of the Supreme rights of the Sultan; at another, insinuating the advantages of a temporizing and conciliatory policy, dwelling on the necessity of gratifying French vanity and managing the Pacha's amour propre, dwelling on the little importance to Europe of the provinces in Syria and Arabia, and hinting at the danger of employing in the distribution any European and especially any Russian troops, but on all occasions abstaining from any thing like an offer of efficient assistance from herself.

In the meanwhile Lord Ponsonby was busy in his cabals and intrigues for what he called the independence of the Porte, that is, excluding from the Divan all who are averse, and introducing into it such as are disposed, to the predominance of Warlike councils in the Divan. He was occasionally very successful in these views, and A Turk or Reis Effendi was sent on a Misson to London, who early in Spring drew up a long paper, manifestly manufactured by the diplomatick Corps here, perhaps in concert with Palmerston himself, pressing the powers to concert some plan of action and requiring from them the imposition of very hard terms indeed on Mehemet. A Copy of this paper was sent to all the five, and four answered conjointly that they would take the proposal into favorable consideration, before the answer from Paris instructing the French Embassador how to answer it had arrived and without any general or previous consultation with him on the answer to be given. Lord Clarendon, who thought there was a marked disregard of France in this method of proceeding, urged very forcibly the necessity of some communication more cordial in appearance and obtained the acquiescence of Palmerston to a more immediate communication than he had originally intended. The Turk who had presented this note was a very dull and timid man. It was soon known that he had as little influence or authority at home as he had means of acquiring them abroad, and either owing to that circumstance or the Changes in the Divan a second Special Mission was dispatched, who soon after his arrival here delivered another note to Lord Palmerston, pressing indeed for an answer and for interference, but implying that a little more than the Porte had originally intended to exact, or even those proposals themselves, would satisfy them.

[*Heading:* 1840 Summer] This note, which seemed to open the door to further concessions and on which either a separate agreement between the Sultan and the Pacha, or a fresh negotiation for French concurrence in very moderated views, might have been founded, was *unaccountably* neither circulated nor read in the Cabinet for *six weeks;* and thought I heard of its substance, it was from France, from Guizot, and from the Ministers of Prussia and Austria (who both seemed to rejoice at the mildness of its tone), and not from Palmerston or my Colleagues that I learnt its contents. It was communicated to our Embassador at Paris by Mr Thiers, not from the Foreign Office, but at the end of June a fresh and third paper was received (for I will not say *obtained*) by Lord Palmerston from the Turk, in which a speedy determination is most earnestly solicited, and the advantages of delay to Mehemet Ali and its disastrous consequences to the Porte very forcibly and somewhat rhetorically urged. This was communicated to the Cabinet. Palmerston, in communicating it, alluded to the painful and difficult circumstances into which he had been placed, owing to differences of opinion subsisting in the Cabinet and the manner in which those differences had been foreseen by, or intimated to, those with whom he treated; he seemed to allude to me and to Clarendon and he openly complained of the language of some of our friends out of Cabinet, and Ellice in particular; he not very covertly attributed that Gentleman's conduct to personal enmity to him and to a design of driving him from the Office he held. He disclaimed however any intention of answering or accusing, and he mentioned the circumstance with the sole purpose of inculcating discretion and silence.

Much difference of opinion, much variety of views, but no ill humour, crimination, or recrimination ensued, altho' I and yet more Clarendon were well aware that Palmerston harboured a suspicion that Ellice was labouring to remove him from the Foreign office and to place Lord Clarendon there, and that Clarendon and I were, more or less, abetting his designs. The mischief of these suspicions, which, even as they regarded Ellice, were quite unjust, was that he disregarded all individual opinions or information which combated his ruling passion of expelling Mehemet Ali, and when told either of the folly or wickedness of the attempt or of the strong persuasion in the publick mind of its impolicy and impracticability, he laid the flattering unction to his soul that it was not the reason of the thing but Ellice's enmity to him that spoke in such remonstrances. The 8th. of July was fixed for a final decision whether Palmerston should be authorized to draw up a treaty for the Expulsion of Mehemet Ali from Syria by the Cooperation of Austria, Prussia, and England; and before that day arrived, Palmerston wrote to Lord Melbourne saying that he perceived some of his Colleagues disapproved of the line of policy he was pursuing, that his judgement of its necessity was unshaken, that his honour was engaged, and that therefore he tendered his resignation if it was likely to embarrass Lord Melbourne's Government. Melbourne communicated the letter to me and I replied thus to his note enclosing it:

7th. July

Thanks for the letters. They give me great pain but as you well know, the difficulties of this business are not altogether unexpected by me. I should like to see you after the debate to night, or before the Cabinet tomorrow. You know how essential I think your Ministry both to the Queen and the Country and how advantageous and necessary I think Palmerston's holding the Seals to Your Ministry. But, I am afraid I cannot honestly concur in any acts of Coercion to wrest Syria from the Pacha, that are either single handed or combined only with two or three of the Confederates, especially when the obvious tendency of such an attempt is to embroil Europe in War and to break up the system which for ten years has preserved Peace. However I put myself entirely in your hands as to what to do, short of making myself responsible for what I should think a Publick Misfortune.

signed Vassall Holland.

[*In the margin:* I had literally pestered him both in conversation and in correspondence with my dread of the consequences of the course we were pursuing in the Turco Egyptian question, and of the danger not to say infatuation of Lord Palmerston's views about it. To this he always answered that he was nearly or quite of my opinion, but that there was no danger of a contrary one prevailing, and that if I would be quiet there would be no warlike proceedings in the Levant and no danger of a rupture with any European power; that Palmerston's views were erroneous but that events and, as he implied, his own way of taking them over, would prevent them leading to any serious consequences.]

[*Heading:* 8 July 1840] I saw him that night and the next morning. I stated to him that the most obvious, regular, and constitutional method was to accept my resignation, as I understood from him that he and the majority were inclined, tho' reluctantly, to authorize the conclusion of the treaty. I observed that my nullity in debate, from age and infirmities, would enable me to retire if he wished it upon that plea, that such would be the proper course and the one I should in common circumstances be resolved to adopt, but I allowed that there were some circumstances (to which perhaps it was rather vanity in me to give much weight) which rendered me apprehensive that my retirement, and yet more the real causes of it, which would inevitably transpire, might break up a Government. That I would sacrifice everything, short of honour and conscience, to keep that Government in power. The near balance of parties in Parliament; the old adherents of Mr Fox who were partial to my name; the resemblance of the questions relating to peace to those upon which they had formerly adhered to Mr Fox and had been accustomed to support under him and with me; the fact of *one* of our most active and able Colleagues agreeing entirely with me, and more than one, half averse to the measure I was deprecating; These considerations combined made me apprehend that my resignation, old and worn out as I was, might in fact be a dissolution of the Government. And altho' for the satisfaction of my own conscience I must record in some tangible shape, and be prepared if war should unfortunately happen, to produce and urge my entire disapprobation of the Measure, Yet I would leave to Lord Melbourne to chuse or to suggest the method of recording my dissent least injurious to his Government and least disagreable to him. I could either demand an audience of the Queen and deposit my protest with her, or, if he would require the advice of the Cabinet to be reduced to regular form, I could annex a separate Minute.

He preferred the latter method, acknowledged that I could not with my opinions honestly do less, and that I acted considerately by the Queen and handsomely by the Ministry in not doing more. He assured me that he should so explain my conduct to the Queen, and we then crossed over to the F[oreign] O[ffice], where the Cabinet was held and after some discussion it was agreed by the Majority that Palmerston should prepare a Convention founded on the Principle of the Collective Note and of his subsequent Negotiation, and that he should embody the resolution in the shape of a Minute to the Queen, to which Lord Clarendon and myself might have an opportunity of annexing our dissent and our reasons for dissenting from it. In these discussions many were entirely silent, two or three, especially Lord Morpeth, expressed some concurrence in the general views avowed by myself and Lord Clarendon, lamented a departure from the policy which had hitherto preserved an alliance with France, and dreaded the consequences, but thought we were concluded (that was Morpeth's word) by the Collective Note and therefore acquiesced in the obligation of signing the treaty. This seemed to be the view, or rather apology, of the measure which most accorded with Melbourne's feelings about it. The Chancellor, who seldom says much but whose little is for the most part greatly to the purpose, observed that the French, by refusing to resort to any coercive measures, did in fact acknowledge that they would do nothing for the common object. If therefore that object be a wise one, or if we are pledged to attain it, it follows that we must do something without them. Lord Lansdown remarked that we should consider what we meant to do and what we could do, and what our Allies would do for us before engaging in the attempt; but having made that pertinent and just remark, he left it there and, though we did not come to any vote in the Cabinet, seemed to acquiesce in the determination of the Majority. Palmerston was throughout very calm, explanatory of past transactions, but in the sanguine assurance that no unpleasant contingency would occur, did not say much on the means of encountering such as might. He dwelt much on the Syrian insurrection, not only as rendering a decision urgent but as ensuring, if the decision were taken, immediate and entire success. A Persuasion that it was formidable and even a jealousy lest it should effect the object of driving Mehemet Ali from Syria without our intervention and deprive the Confederacy of the eclât of accomplishing us was urged as a motive for the immediate conclusion of the treaty. The only Members who seemed to me cordially and entirely to agree with Palmerston were Lord Minto and Sir John Hobhouse. Lord John Russell expressed indeed somewhat indignantly his repugnance to regulating our demands by what he called the dictates of the French or the wishes of Mehemet himself, but he was neither so confident of success nor so satisfied of the vast advantages to be obtained by it as Palmerston. Normanby suggested the propriety of offering it before it was signed or at least communicating it when signed to the French, and even Minto pressed not only an early communication of the fact, but consultation, explanation, and a request of the French to suggest such modifications in the terms as would reconcile them to the contents.

I then stated to the Cabinet nearly what I had stated to Melbourne, said I was disposed to regulate my conduct by what he and My Colleagues deemed least injurious to their administration, but that I could not in any way render myself responsible for the treaty and must in some shape record that I could not; that the most natural method and which I should prefer was resignation, but that Melbourne's partiality supposed, and I had vanity enough to believe in his partiality, that even *my* retirement would be dangerous to the existence of his Government and, as I thought its dissolution would be a publick calamity, I should be reconciled to remaining in it, provided it was fully understood and recorded that I was in no way responsible for this measure and its consequences. Those consequences both Clarendon and myself painted in pretty strong colours. Lord Morpeth said he reluctantly acquiesced in the treaty because we were concluded by the Collective note. Others said (what was true) that the subsequent negotiations were more conclusive, and all but Clarendon and myself agreed that a minute should be drawn up, dated that day, 8th. July, and recommending that Lord Palmerston should be authorized to draw up a Convention between the 4 powers and the Porte, founded upon the Principle of the Collective Note and in accordance with the spirit of the subsequent negotiations. *Ainsi fut fait,* and when the Minute was written, the following dissenting Minute of Lord Clarendon and myself was subjoined:[1]

> The Earl of Clarendon and Lord Holland in fulfillment of those duties which Your Majesty's gracious appointment imposes upon every Confidential Servant of Your Majesty's Crown feel themselves painfully compelled to acknowledge that they cannot concur in the minute submitted this day to the consideration of Your Majesty. Your Majesty is therein advised to accede to a treaty which has for its object the expulsion of Meh[eme]t Ali from the Syria and Candia and of his Son from the Pachalick of Arabia conferred upon him by the late Sultan. Such interference appears to Lord Clarendon and Lord Holland to be questionable in Policy and neither necessary to the honour of Your Majesty's Crown in satisfaction of the obligations contracted in the Collective note of July 1839 nor directly or obviously advantageous to Your Majesty's subjects.
>
> The Means by which it is proposed that these objects in the event of Resistance should be attained seem to them insufficient and yet onerous and above all hazardous in the extreme. Your Majesty in no remote or impossible contingency may be required in virtue of the stipulations of such a treaty to wage war on the Coasts and to sanction the introduction of Foreign and European Troops into the Asiatick Provinces of Turkey. Such operations in themselves humiliating to the Mussulman Powers and ominous of the dismemberment of the Sultan's dominions, even if they should be eminently successful, cannot in the actual state of those districts be expected to enlarge the resources or to consolidate the strength of the Ottoman Empire. They must in the 1st. instance interrupt the Commerce of Your Majesty's subjects with the countries now occupied by Mehemet Ali or his Son. They must also intercept

or suspend the convenient intercourse recently established through Egypt with Your Majesty's Eastern Possessions. These Sacrifices would in the apprehension of Lord Clarendon and Lord Holland be of no inconsiderable importance, but the more remote and indirect though it is feared not less undeniable tendency of the treaty and of the Measures of Coercion arising therefrom threatens consequences far more extensive and disastrous. They may lead to a disturbance of that System of Policy and Alliances in Europe which under the happy Auspices of Your Majesty and Your Predecessor has succeeded in preserving the Peace of the World and has redounded to the Glory of Your Majesty's Crown by increasing the prosperity of your People and enabling their industry and enterprize to extend the Intercourse and improve the Condition of Mankind in every Quarter of the Globe.

Apprehensive of consequences so alarming, should any Coercion be resorted to for effecting the purposes of the treaty, Lord Clarendon and Lord Holland could not but refrain from becoming the advisers of such a Step and although earnestly solicitous to prevent all appearances as well as reality of difference in Your Majesty's Counsels, they yet feel it incumbent upon them to explain without reserve, but they trust with [no] impropriety the fact and grounds of witholding their assent to the advice, this day submitted to the consideration of your Majesty.

15th. July. The Treaty was signed.[2] The Russian, Mr Brunow, felt or affected to feel some doubt whether his signature of it would be approved at Petersburgh, and Bulow and Neumann,[3] who perhaps had sincerely some reluctance to the measure, spoke warmly of the satisfaction at having terminated the affair so happily. The French Ambassador was apprized of it in a paper or Memorandum drawn up by Palmerston and skillfully worded in which France is assured that no difference of object is in view and that the separate act only implies what they, the French, had repeatedly expressed, that in the object of pacifying the Levant by a restoration of the integrity and independence of the Porte, they agreed, but that they differed as to the means. It ends by requesting them, if they cannot concur in any means of coercion, to use their moral influence with Mehemet to persuade him to acquiesce in the proposal. Though it is to be hoped that in such professions Lord Palmerston and the English are sincere, yet by speaking in the name of all the four powers he must have subjected his sincerity to some animadversion, for we were pretty sensibly reminded afterwards of the hollowness of such professions if in the mouth of one of the Allies. Nicholas, in his raptures at the news of the signature, openly avowed and boasted to our Chargé d'Affaires, Mr Bloomfield,[4] that he cared not a rush about Syria and not much even about the Dardanelles and Turkey, but that he was overjoyed beyond measure at the estrangement which the treaty occasioned between English and France, that he looked forward perhaps to another March to Paris or at least to a downfall of the dynasty of Louis Philippe! ! ! The King of Prussia, who had lately acceded to the Crown,[5] though he resisted the dissuasions of the French against ratifying, executed that act with a distinct reserve that he contributed his moral influence only to the objects of the treaty. To

Austria, or at least to Metternich, St. Aulaire was dispatched from Paris with the same *fruitless* commission of dissuading him from ratifying. The Austrians ratified it more readily, did not <further> the purposes of the treaty much more sensibly than the Prussians, being confined to two or three Sloops, fair words and congratulations and hearty wishes. The Russians had many affairs on their hands, had in their various expeditions the year before lost many more men than they acknowledged, some say not less than 100,000 by sickness and war, were unprepared for any vigorous exertion and fully aware that, if they were too forward and alert, they would excite as much jealousy and distrust as gratitude in their British Allies. [*Heading:* August 1840] Hence at the Commencement of the Struggle the whole burthen of the War seemed likely to fall upon us. The Syrian insurrection from which such wonders were expected was, according to Captain Napiers own phrase, entirely put down before the proposals were delivered to Mehemet Ali, and put down by a reinforcement seasonally and promptly sent by the Pacha, and by the Native Chiefs and tribes, especially Emir Bechir[6] himself, on whose hostility to the Egyptian rebel Lord Ponsonby had taught us confidently to rely. Napier (Da Ponza) justly perhaps saw from the beginning that signal success was only to be insured by prompt and instant measures, and though he relaxed no exertion, very soon apprized us that it was too late to turn the Syrian insurrection to much account. His appetite for fighting a little alarmed the peaceable among us, but it is but justice to such a firebrand to observe that very unlike our more bellicose Civilians, he never misled us by false or extravagant expectations. He was ready no doubt to attempt impossible, and to achieve incredible things, but he never described them as easy. [*End of BM Add. MS 51872.*]

[*From the diary of John Allen.*[7]]

Oct. 21 [*1840*].[8] Alas!

NOTES

1831

1 The 'Proem' must have been written after 1831. Holland usually wrote on the right-hand side of the notebook page, reserving the adjacent side for marginalia or corrections. The 'Proem' however (BM Add. MS 51867, ff. 2-5) occupies adjacent pages and runs over a number of lines of Holland's first diary entry. The slip about the month of Wellington's resignation also suggests a later date of composition.

2 News of the July Revolution was received 'when K[ing] W[illia]m [IV] was dining at H[ollan]d H[ou]se.' (BM Add. MS 51917, loose and unfoliated.)

3 Heinrich August Alexander Wilhelm, Baron von Werther (1772-1859), Prussian Ambassador to France, 1824-37.

4 Carlo Andrea, Count Pozzo di Borgo (1764-1842), Corsican-born Russian diplomat; Ambassador to France, 1814-35; to England, 1835-9.

5 Louis Matthieu, Comte Molé (1781-1855), French Foreign Minister, Aug.-Nov. 1830; Prime Minister, 1836-9.

6 Cf. the loose, unfoliated document in Holland's hand, labelled 'Pozzo's conduct in 1830 from his own account—[dated] 1837,' wherein Holland attributes Pozzo's actions in part to his resentment at not having been previously informed of Charles X's Ordinances and at 'the neglect of his advice.' Holland noted that Pozzo persuaded the Austrian ambassador to remain as well. (BM Add. MS 51917.)

7 Established as King of the Netherlands after the Congress of Vienna, William I (1772-1843) was confronted with a revolution of his Belgian subjects in August 1830. His eldest son, William Frederick, Prince of Orange (1792-1849), tried at first to effect a peaceful settlement and entertained prospects of becoming king of an independent Belgian state. His efforts were disavowed by his father, and after a brief sojourn in England, the Prince of Orange returned to Holland and took command of the Dutch army from his brother, Frederick William Charles, Prince des Pays Bas (1797-1891). The Prince of Orange succeeded as King of Holland on his father's abdication in 1840.

With representatives of the five powers in attendance, the London Conference on Belgium convened during the last days of Wellington's administration in November 1830 and succeeded in imposing an armistice upon the two parties.

8 Sir James St Clair Erskine (1762-1837), second Earl of Rosslyn. Lord Privy Seal, 1829-30; he had been a Whig before his succession to the title in 1805; an intimate friend of Wellington; Tory whipper-in in the Lords.

9 George Child Villiers (1773-1859), fifth Earl of Jersey. He had been associated with the Whigs until 1830. Lord Chamberlain of the Household 1830, 1834-5.

10 James Scarlett (1769-1844), afterwards (1835) first Baron Abinger. MP Peterborough 1819-30, Malton, 1830-1, Cockermouth 1831-2, Norwich 1832-4; Chief Baron of the Exchequer, 1834-44; a Whig, he turned Tory after 1830 in reaction to the Reform Bill.

11 The alleged causal relationship between the July Revolution and the British general election of 1830 has been effectively challenged by Norman Gash, 'English Reform and French Revolution in the General Election of 1830' in Richard Pares and A. J. P. Taylor (eds), *Essays Presented to Sir Lewis Namier* (London, 1956), pp. 258-88.

12 Samuel Rogers (1763-1855), the then acclaimed poet and habitué of Holland House. He refused the poet laureateship after Wordsworth's death in 1850.

13 Henry Ellis (1777-1869), Principal Librarian of the British Museum; knighted, 1833.

14 In early June 1831, a cotton-mill owner began operations to deepen the River Dove, near Tutbury, in order to provide increased water power for his factory. In the course of the operation, workers engaged in removing gravel from the river bed discovered the treasure. Many coins were kept or sold, until Holland, as Chancellor of the Duchy of Lancaster, issued a commission which claimed the treasure on behalf of the crown, the area belonging to it as part of the Duchy. See the account in *The Penny Magazine,* III (1 Nov. 1834), 430-2.

15 Frederick Dawes Danvers, Clerk of the Council and Keeper of the Records of the Duchy of Lancaster; appointed secretary to the Chancellor, April 1831.

16 Enacted as 1 & 2 Will. IV, c. lxxiii, a local act which increased tolls on the Eau Brink cut of the River Ouse, to King's Lynn, Norfolk. Holland had opposed it in the interest of the Duke of Bedford.

17 Sir Benjamin Charles Stephenson (1766-1839), Surveyor General of Works, 1814-32.

18 George Horatio Cholmondely (1792-1870), second Marquess of Cholmondely. Joint Great Chamberlain of England, he exercised the honors for his mother at the coronation of 1831 and inherited the office upon her death in 1838.

19 Charles Cavendish Fulke Greville (1794-1865), Clerk to the Privy Council, 1821-59. His journals remain a favourite source for nineteenth-century English history. The best edition is Lytton Strachey and Roger Fulford (eds), *The Greville Memoirs 1814-1860* (London, 1938), 8 vols.

20 Charles William Stewart-Vane (1778-1854), third Marquess of Londonderry; he succeeded his half-brother, Castlereagh, in 1822, after the latter's suicide.

21 Prince Leopold of Saxe-Coburg (1790-1865), m. (1816) Princess Charlotte (1796-1817), the only child of the Prince of Wales, afterwards George IV; m. (1832) Louise, daughter of Louis Philippe. He was in receipt of £50,000 per annum as a pension by Act of parliament. He also derived emoluments from his colonelcy in the Dragoon Guards. He had declined the Greek crown in 1830, and was invited by the Belgian National Congress to be King of the Belgians in June 1831, after their earlier choices of the Duke of Leuchtenberg and the Duke of Nemours had been opposed, the former by France, the latter by England and the eastern powers.

22 Dom Pedro (1798-1834), eldest son of John VI of Portugal, declared himself emperor of an independent Brazil in 1822, its independence achieved, in part, through English intervention. When John VI died in 1826, Pedro renounced his title to the Portuguese throne in favor of his seven-year-old daughter, Dona Maria (1819-53), whose succession was associated with the concession of a constitution. Pedro's younger brother, Dom Miguel (1802-66), seized power in 1827, his arbitrary rule tending to confirm the belief that Portugal was divided between absolutists and constitutionalists. Driven from Brazil by a revolution in 1831, Pedro arrived in England on 26 June to claim the Portuguese crown for his daughter.

23 Pedro's requests were that England receive Dona Maria as Queen of Portugal rather than as Duchess of Oporto; that an English ship of war carry him to France and Dona Maria to England; that she be placed under the domestic charge of the queen when in

England; and that he be advanced a sum of money on the security of his jewels. (Palmerston to the king [copy], 14 July 1831, BP, RC/AA/16/1-2; the king to Palmerston, 15 July 1831, *ibid.*, RC/A/42/1.)

24 Richard Belgrave Hoppner (1786-1872), Consul General at Lisbon, Jan. 1831-Aug. 1833. See C. S. B. Buckland, 'Richard Belgrave Hoppner,' *Eng. Hist. Rev.*, XXXIX (July 1924), 373-85.

25 Terceira, in the Azores, was held by the supporters of Pedro and Dona Maria.

26 The cholera.

27 George Howard (1773-1848), sixth Earl of Carlisle, minister without portfolio in Grey's cabinet. Lady Carlisle (1783-1858), née Lady Georgiana Dorothy Cavendish, was the eldest daughter of the fifth Duke of Devonshire.

28 Holland's family lawyer since 1816.

29 Probably William George Adam (1751-1839), MP 1774-94, 1806-12; the Duke of Bedford's auditor and, since 1816, lord chief commissioner of the Scottish jury court; a counsel to the East India Company.

30 John Campbell (1762-1834), fourth Earl of Breadalbane, raised to a marquisate, Sept. 1831, as a coronation peer; m. (1793) Mary Turner, daughter of David Gavin of Langton House, Berwick (d. 1845). Their son, John, Lord Glenorchy (1796-1862), styled Earl of Ormelie after his father's elevation, succeeded as the fifth Earl of Breadalbane; MP co. Perth, 1832-4; Lord Chamberlain, 1848-52, 1853-8.

31 George James Welborne Agar-Ellis (1797-1833), cr. (June 1831) Baron Dover; MP 1818-31; named Chief Commissioner of Woods and Forests in Grey's government, but surrendered the office because of ill health to Lord Duncannon, Feb. 1831.

32 Leopold had refused to accept the crown until the Belgian National Congress came to an understanding with the London Conference on the terms for separation from Holland. The National Congress agreed to the Eighteen Articles (see below, p. 428 n. 76) on 9 July.

33 William Howley (1766-1848), Archbishop of Canterbury since 1828. Thomas Brand (1774-1851), twentieth Lord Dacre, Whig MP Herts 1807-19. Composition referred to the procedure whereby those liable to pay tithe could conclude an agreement with the titheowner about the amount of tithe owed, that amount then being apportioned among occupiers of the titheable and in the parish. Commutation had a more restricted meaning and suggested the permanent conversion of tithe, which hitherto may have been paid in kind, to a fixed money payment. The terms were occasionally used interchangeably. Both bills referred to were based on the Irish Tithe Composition Act of 1823. Dacre's was the more extensive bill in providing for a permanent commutation of tithe on a money basis, and gave the advantage in arranging agreements to the tithepayers. His bill also included lay impropriators—laymen who received tithe—as well as clergymen. The archbishop's bill would have facilitated a temporary arrangement in parishes, the initiative remaining in the hands of the titheowner, and was restricted to tithes owned by the clergy. (*3 Hansard,* IV [18 July 1831], 1362-82.)

34 In the Lords on 24 June. *Ibid.,* IV (1831), 293-5.

35 The supply was technically to defray the expenses of the Society for the Propagation of the Gospel. Althorp stated that government intended to reduce the grant and 'do away with it entirely as soon as possible.' The £16,000 appropriation passed, 65-27. *3 Hansard,* V (25 July 1831), 295-301.

36 Usually spelled Claremont, Leopold's country house in Surrey.

37 John George Lambton (1792-1840), first Lord Durham, Grey's son-in-law; Lord Privy Seal, 1830-3; earldom, 1833; Ambassador to Russia, 1835-7; Governor General of Canada, 1838.

38 These were the commissioners, listed in the second Reform Bill, who were to report to parliament on the geographical divisions of counties and boundaries of boroughs. When the second Reform Bill was defeated in Lords, it was determined that the commissioners should not themselves settle the boundaries, but that the information they collected be

used by government to propose a separate Boundaries Bill. 'The persons employed in this task were 20 gentlemen, part of those who had been mentioned when the former bill was under discussion,' said Russell. *3 Hansard* (16 Feb. 1832), 417-18. The reports submitted to three men—E. J. Littleton, Captain Beaufort and Lieutenant Drummond—who helped to prepare the Boundaries Act for England and Wales.

39 James Abercromby (1776-1858), afterwards (1839) first Baron Dunfermline. MP 1807-30, 1832-9. Chief Baron of the Exchequer for Scotland, 1830-2; joined the cabinet as Master of the Mint, 1834; Speaker of the House of Commons, 1835-9.

40 Augustus Frederick (1773-1843), Duke of Sussex, sixth son of George III and a younger brother of King William; President of the Royal Society, 1830-8; the most liberal of the royal family, but with virtually no influence.

41 William Maule (1771-1852), cr. (1831) Baron Panmure. Whig MP 1796, 1805-31. One of William IV's coronation peers.

42 Robert Dundas Duncan Haldane (1785-1859), second Viscount Duncan, cr. Earl of Camperdown, Sept. 1831, a coronation peer.

43 Edward Harley (1773-1848), fifth Earl of Oxford.

44 Alfred Harley (1809-53), styled Lord Harley, afterwards (1848) sixth Earl of Oxford.

45 George John Spencer (1758-1834), second Earl Spencer. Althorp's father; Home Secretary, 1806-7.

46 William Pole Tylney Long-Wellesley (1788-1857), formerly Wellesley-Pole, afterwards (1845) fourth Earl of Mornington. MP Essex, 1831-2; m. (1812) Catherine Tylney Long (d. 1825), a rich heiress, and then assumed those additional surnames. His name inspired a couplet by W. T. F[itzgerald], 'Loyal Effusion' [1812]:

Bless every man possess'd of aught to give
Long may Long Tilney Wellesley Long Pole live

in Horatio and James Smith (eds), *Rejected Addresses: or the New Theatrum Poetarum* (London: 19th ed. 1839), p. 5. Even by the aristocratic standards of his day he was considered to be a dissipated character, and the children of his first marriage were placed as wards of the Court of Chancery. He abducted his daughter in July 1831 and refused to surrender her. Lord Chancellor Brougham, committing him to Fleet Prison, informed the Speaker that an MP had been held in contempt. Long-Wellesley claimed a breach of privilege, which a Committee on Privilege of the Commons refused to sustain. He then gave up his daughter and was released. See the summary of the case in the *Annual Register, 1831* (Chronicle, pp. 301-7). Long-Wellesley squandered his fortune and died in poverty, having been supported in his last years by a £10 weekly allowance from his nephew, the second Duke of Wellington.

47 George Augustus Frederick FitzClarence (1794-1842), first Earl of Munster, eldest son of William IV and Mrs Jordan; peerage, May 1831.

48 John Scott (1751-1838), first Earl of Eldon. Lord Chancellor, 1801-6, 1807-27; an ardent opponent of parliamentary reform.

49 Charles James Blomfield (1786-1857), Bishop of London since 1828.

50 Henry George Herbert (1772-1833), second Earl of Carnarvon, turned Tory on the introduction of the Reform Bill.

51 It did not.

52 Lord John Russell (1792-1878), cr. (1861) first Earl Russell, began his ministerial career as Paymaster of the Forces in Grey's government, Edward Stanley (1799-1869), afterwards (1851) fourteenth Earl of Derby, was Chief Secretary for Ireland. Both were admitted into the cabinet in June 1831. Grey already looked to Stanley as the next leader of the Whig party in the Commons. Grey to Anglesey, 5 March 1831, AP, P.R.O.N.I., T1068/30, f.79.

53 James Maitland (1759-1839), eighth Earl of Lauderdale, turned Tory in the 1820s and voted against the second reading of the Reform Bill.

54 William Conyngham Plunket (1764-1854), first Baron Plunket, Lord Chancellor of Ireland, 1830-4, 1835-41.

55 William Philip Molyneux (1772-1838), second Earl of Sefton, MP Droitwich, 1816-31; cr. Baron Sefton (UK) 16 June 1831.

56 Having accommodated himself to every French regime since the Revolution, Prince Talleyrand (1754-1838) was Ambassador to England, 1830-4.

57 Felisberto Caldieria Brant (1772-1842), Marquis of Barbacena, Brazilian marshall and senator; negotiated Brazilian separation from Portugal and was then given his title.

58 Holland's 'Etonian Colleagues' then in the cabinet were Grey, Durham, Melbourne, Carlisle, and Stanley; Althorp, Palmerston, and Goderich had attended Harrow; Lansdowne, Graham, Richmond, and Russell, Westminster; Brougham attended Edinburgh High School.

59 Frederick John Robinson (1782-1859), Viscount Goderich, afterwards (1833) first Earl of Ripon; Chancellor of the Exchequer, 1823-7; Prime Minister, 1827-8; at first Secretary of War and Colonies in Grey's cabinet (1830-3), and then Lord Privy Seal (1833-4).

60 General François Horace Bastien, Comte Sébastiani (1772-1851), French Foreign Minister, Nov. 1830-Oct. 1832; Ambassador to England, 1835-40.

61 The dispatch is printed: Talleyrand to Palmerston, 20 July 1831 (with enclosure: Sébastiani to Talleyrand, Paris, 7 July 1831), in *BFSP*, XXXVII (1848-9), 1413-14.

62 Charles Gordon-Lennox (1791-1860), fifth Duke of Richmond, associated with ultra Tories against the Duke of Wellington's concession of Catholic Emancipation; in Grey's cabinet as Postmaster General, 1830-4.

63 Alexandre Florian Joseph Colonna, Comte Walewski (1810-68), an illegitimate son of Napoleon; envoy in London for the Polish Provisional Government. He assumed French citizenship in 1833, and was later involved in French African affairs in military and diplomatic positions, as well as being a dramatist and publicist. French Foreign Minister, 1855-60.

64 Sir Henry Petty-Fitzmaurice (1780-1863), third Marquess of Lansdowne, Lord President of the Council in the Grey and Melbourne governments, and again in Russell's, 1846-52; in cabinet without office, 1852-63.

65 Lord Granville Leveson-Gower (1773-1846), cr. (1833) Earl Granville, Ambassador to France, 1824-41.

66 Casimir Périer (1777-1832), French Prime Minister, Mar. 1831-May 1832.

67 The Duchy of Luxemburg had been ceded to William of Orange at the Congress of Vienna, in compensation for his abandonment of claims to estates in the Rhineland which went to Prussia. The Duchy had since been administratively incorporated within the Kingdom of the Netherlands. But King William, as Grand Duke of Luxemburg, was in that capacity a member of the German Confederation; and Prussia garrisoned the fortress town of Luxemburg. The Belgians claimed Luxemburg as part of their new state, and representatives from Luxemburg attended the Belgian National Congress which convened in October 1830. William claimed Luxemburg as his own. Talleyrand and Louis Philippe's government had designs upon it for France.

68 Charles Grant (1778-1866), cr. (1835) Baron Glenelg, one of the Canningites in Grey's cabinet; President of the Board of Control, 1830-5; Secretary for War and Colonies, 1835-9.

69 The dispatch is printed: Palmerston to Talleyrand, Foreign Office, 22 July 1831 in *BFSP*, XXXVII (1848-9), 1414-15.

70 Thomas Cochrane (1775-1860), tenth Earl of Dundonald, admiral, and son of Admiral Cochrane, the ninth earl. Accused of a stock fraud in 1814, he was expelled from the navy, parliament, and the order of the Bath. He served in the navies of Chile, Brazil, and Greece in the 1820s, in sympathy with their quests for independence. Succeeded to earldom, July 1831; reinstated in navy, 1832.

71 William Draper Best (1767-1845), first Baron Wynford. MP 1802-6, 1812-18; Chief Justice of Common Pleas, 1824-9.

72 The Irish Tithe Composition Act of 1823. 4 Geo. IV, c.99.

73 Ashton-under-Lyne was added to Schedule C of the Bill—new boroughs to return two members to parliament. *3 Hansard,* VII (15 Sept. 1831), 66; this arrangement was altered once again in the final version of the bill, and the new borough returned only one member under the Reform Act.

74 Charles William Wentworth-Fitzwilliam (1786-1857), styled Viscount Milton, afterwards (1833) fifth Earl Fitzwilliam, Whig MP 1806-33, sitting for Northants, 1831-2.

75 Edward Berkeley Portman (1799-1888), afterwards (1837) Baron Portman; Viscount, 1873; Whig MP Dorset, 1823-32; Marylebone, 1832-3. Colonel Sibthorp, Tory MP for Lincoln, had originally given notice of such a motion in April with a minimum rental per annum of £30. (*PP,* 1830-1, II (34), 255). He subsequently raised the minimum to £50 (*ibid.*, p. 257). Lord Chandos, MP for Bucks, gave notice of a similar motion on 5 July. Sibthorp resented Chandos's appropriation of his motion, but there is no mention of Portman in the debate on 18 August, when the so-called Chandos clause was passed as an amendment to the Government's Reform Bill by a vote of 232-148. It extended the franchise in the counties to tenants-at-will who paid a minimum rental of £50 per annum. Ministers opposed the amendment on the grounds that it would enfranchise a class totally dependent upon their landlords, but Whig squires as well as Tories apparently voted for it. *3 Hansard,* VI (18 Aug. 1831), 278-87; see also the fuller debate in *Mirror of Parliament,* II (1831), 1467-78.

76 The Eighteen Articles were the terms of separation between Belgium and Holland, determined by the five powers in Protocol 26 of the London Conference, 26 June 1831. The territorial limits of Holland were to be those of the Dutch Republic in 1790, the remainder of the Netherlands to comprise Belgium. The Grand Duchy of Luxemburg was recognized as part of the German Confederation and subject to a separate negotiation. The Articles also established liberal terms for Belgium with regard to apportioning the national debt of the Netherlands, and reaffirmed the principle of freedom of navigation for the new state. Belgium was to be a perpetually neutral state, the five powers to guarantee her territorial integrity. *BFSP,* XVIII (1830-1), 802-5. The Eighteen Articles were to be modified by the Twenty-Four Articles of 14 October which became the bases for the treaty of 1839.

77 Sir Robert Adair (1763-1855), engaged in missions to the Low Countries, 1831-5. He had requested Holland's assistance to secure the ambassadorship to Vienna. Adair to Holland, 28 Nov. 1830, BP, GC/HO/63/2 (enclosed in Holland to Palmerston [most private], 29 Nov. 1830, *ibid.*). With the exception of Lord Granville, Adair was the oldest ambassador still active in the service.

78 Richard Ponsonby (1772-1853), Lady Grey's brother; Bishop of Killaloe, 1828-31; he did become Bishop of Derry, Sept. 1831-4; of Derry and Raphoe, 1834-53.

79 Henry William Paget (1768-1854), first Marquess of Anglesey, Lord Lieutenant of Ireland, 1828-9, 1830-3. He had favored Emancipation and was recalled by Wellington.

80 For a list of Grey's relatives who held office, see Lord Ellenborough's Diary, 24 Nov. 1830, in A. Aspinall (ed.), *Three Early Nineteenth Century Diaries* (London, 1952), p. 25.

81 (1776-1852), an Irish Protestant Churchman and staunch advocate of the Protestant ascendancy in Ireland. He did not get a deanery.

82 Samuel Kyle, who had been Provost of Trinity College, Dublin; Bishop of Cork, 1831-48.

83 With English acquiescence, a French fleet had been sent to the mouth of the Tagus in July 1831 to exact reparations for maltreatment of French citizens in Portugal. The French captured two Portuguese warships.

84 Henry Vassall Webster (?1793-1847), Lady Holland's youngest son by her first marriage to Sir Godfrey Webster; a lieutenant-colonel in the army; knighted, 1843; committed suicide.
85 Domingos António de Sousa Coutinho (1760-1833), Count of Funchal, Portuguese Minister in London after the Napoleonic Wars.
86 Dom Pedro de Souza-Holstein (1781-1850), Marquis of Palmella, Portuguese Ambassador to England, 1819-20, 1825-7. A supporter of Pedro and Dona Maria, he remained in exile in England, Miguel having declared him a traitor. Portuguese Minister of Foreign Affairs, 1835; Prime Minister, 1842, 1846; dukedom, 1834. He had long corresponded with Holland on Iberian affairs.
87 José Luis de Sousa Botelho Mourão e Vasconcelos (1785-1855), Count of Vila Real, Portuguese minister in London, 1820-1, 1823-5. He returned to Portugal to join the first constitutional ministry under Palmella in 1833, and then served in the ministry of the Duke of Terceira, which was deposed by the revolution of 1836.
88 Charles Aimé Joseph, afterwards Comte Lehon (1792-1868), Belgian Minister Plenipotentiary at Paris, Mar. 1831. His title was conferred upon him by Leopold and he remained at his Paris post until 1842.
89 Dorothée de Courlande, Duchesse de Dino (1792-1862), daughter of Pierre, Duc de Courlande. Her Marriage to Talleyrand's nephew was arranged by Talleyrand with the Czar in 1809. The couple separated shortly thereafter, Mme de Dino becoming Talleyrand's mistress. She accompanied him to the Congress of Vienna and was hostess of his London salon during Talleyrand's mission to England.
90 Sir George O'Brien Wyndham (1751-1837), third Earl of Egremont. A Whig in his early years, he had long turned Tory; patron of the arts.
91 Unidentified.
92 Unidentified. Allen refers to a foreign gunsmith on Oxford Street being commissioned to send several thousand stand of arms to the Political Union at Birmingham. HHP, BM Add. MS 52204E.
93 Johann Philipp, Baron von Wessenberg (1773-1858), Austria's second representative at the London Conference on Belgium, he later left his post in disagreement with Metternich's policy.
94 The dispatch of the Dutch government to the London Conference (12 July 1831) and Wessenberg's comment upon it to Palmerston (17 July 1831) are included in Protocol 28, 25 July 1831, in *BFSP*, XVIII, 808-16.
95 Heinrich, Baron von Bülow (1792-1846), Prussian Ambassador to England, 1827-41; Foreign Minister, 1842-4.
96 Christian Günther, Count von Bernstorff (1769-1835), Prussian Minister of Foreign Affairs, 1818-31.
97 An almost exclusively Protestant and Orange force, the Yeomanry was particularly strong in Ulster. On 18 July 1831, Irish peasants attempted to prevent the sale of cattle seized in default of payment of tithe at Newtownbarry, co. Wexford. The Yeomanry were accused of killing a number of the demonstrators.
98 Sir James Graham (1792-1861), First Lord of the Admiralty, 1830-4; Home Secretary in Peel's cabinet, 1841-6.
99 Richard Lalor Sheil (1791-1851), then MP for co. Louth. He had been second only to O'Connell in the agitation for Catholic Emancipation in the 1820s. The government secured him a safe seat early in 1831, before his return for Louth, in an attempt to gain support among Irish representatives and detract from O'Connell's dominance in the 'Irish Party,'
100 Thomas Babington Macaulay (1800-59), afterwards (1859) Lord Macaulay; the historian.
101 Lady Sophia FitzClarence (1796-1837), daughter of William IV and Mrs Jordan, m. (1825) Sir Philip Charles Sidney (1800-51), afterwards (1835) first Baron De Lisle and Dudley.

102 Thomas Wilde (1782-1855), afterwards Baron Truro, Whig MP for Newark-on-Trent, 1831-2, 1835-41; Lord Chancellor, 1850-2; knighted, 1840; peerage, 1850.

103 The king's sons, all illegitimate by Mrs Jordan, were: Lord Munster; Lord George Adolphus FitzClarence (1802-56); Lord Frederick FitzClarence (1799-1854); Lord Augustus FitzClarence (1805-54). Another son, Henry, died in India. When the eldest received his peerage in May 1831, his brothers were given the titles and precedence of the younger sons of a marquess.

104 The marriage of the Duke of Sussex to Lady Augusta Murray in 1793 had displeased George III, who had it annulled according to the provisions of the Royal Marriages Act of 1772. The two children of the marriage were given the name D'Este, after a common ancestor of the Duke and Lady Augusta. The daughter, Augusta Emma D'Este (1801-66), m. (1845) Sir Thomas Wilde, later Lord Truro. Her brother, Sir Augustus D'Este (1794-1848) pleaded his legitimate future succession to his father's title in 1831, and retained Wilde as counsel in 1843 in another abortive attempt to inherit his father's peerage.

105 In addition to Lady Sophia Sidney and Lady Mary Fox (see next note), the King's daughters by Mrs Jordan, all surnamed FitzClarence, were: Elizabeth (1801-56), m. (1820), the eighteenth Earl of Errol; Amelia (1803-58), m. (1830), Viscount Falkand; and Augusta, m. first, John Kennedy Erskine, and second, Lord John Frederick Gordon of Halyburton.

106 Lady Mary Fox, née Lady Mary FitzClarence, second daughter of William IV by Mrs Jordan, m. (1824) Charles Richard Fox (1796-1873), the first and illegitimate son of Lord and Lady Holland, MP for Calne, 1831-2, Tavistock, 1832-4, Stroud, 1835, Tower Hamlets, 1841-7.

107 Richard William Penn Curzon (1796-1870), first Earl Howe, Lord Chamberlain to Queen Adelaide, 1830-1, 1834-7. He was forced to resign in 1831 for voting against the Reform Bill. See GEC, VI, 601-2n.

108 Emma Sophia, Lady Brownlow (1791-1872), daughter of the second Earl of Mount-edgcumbe, became (1828), Earl Brownlow's third wife. She was a lady of the bed-chamber to Queen Adelaide, 1830-49.

109 George Augustus Herbert (1759-1827), eleventh Earl of Pembroke, Ambassador extraordinary to Austria on a special mission, July-Sept., 1807, replacing Adair who was then provisionally minister plenipotentiary. Adair wanted to retain his ambassadorial rank in Belgium, though to do so would have signified formal diplomatic recognition. Adair to Holland, 28 Nov. 1830, BP, GC/HO/63/2; Holland to Palmerston, n.d., *ibid.*, GC/HO/79/1.

110 George Selwyn (1719-91), MP 1747-80; a rake and a wit; an intimate of the fifth Lord Carlisle.

111 Anne Mee (?1773-1851), a miniaturist.

112 Blotted.

113 Bernhard, Duke of Saxe-Weimar (1792-1862), went into the military service of the King of the Netherlands after the Congress of Vienna; m. Ida of Saxe Meinüngen, sister of Queen Adelaide of England.

114 Victoria Mary Louisa, Duchess of Kent (1786-1861), Leopold's sister and Princess Victoria's mother. She would, from 1830, have become Regent in the event of Victoria's succession as a minor.

115 Emily Anne Bennett Elizabeth, Lady Westmeath (1789-1858), second daughter of the first Marquess of Salisbury, m. (1812), Lord Westmeath, whom she divorced in 1827; one of the Queen's ladies to the bedchamber.

116 The Duchess of Cambridge (1797-1889), Augusta Wilhelmina Louisa, daughter of Friedrich, Landgrave of Hesse Cassel. She had married the Duke of Cambridge in 1818.

117 Richard Colley Wellesley (1760-1842), first Marquess Wellesley, Wellington's older brother. Foreign Secretary, 1809-12; Lord Lieutenant of Ireland, 1821-8, 1833-4.

118 Joseph Goodall (1760-1840), Provost of Eton since 1809; a staunch conservative. 'He was a showy scholar and quick man, but with as little usage of the world or solidity of judgement as his colleagues.' Holland, *Further Memoirs,* p. 311.
119 Richard Wellesley (?1787-1831), one of Lord Wellesley's illegitimate children. MP 1810-17, 1820-6.
120 In his address to the Chambers on 23 July, Louis Philippe said that the fortresses on the Belgian frontier, which had been erected to menace France rather than protect Belgium, would be demolished and, in another context, that France would engage in war if driven to it. The remark that caused particular anxiety in England was an allusion to the French expedition to Portugal. Louis Philippe reportedly said that the Tricolor 'flies on the walls of Lisbon,' probably an inadvertent departure from the written text, which stated that it flew 'sous les murs de Lisbonne.' See text, p. 18, for Talleyrand's explanation to Holland; *Archives Parlementaires de 1787 à 1860,* LXVIII (23 July 1831), 764-5 gives the written version; *The Times,* 25 July 1831 gives both.
121 George Hamilton Gordon (1784-1860), fourth Earl of Aberdeen, Foreign Secretary, 1828-30, 1841-6; Secretary for War and Colonies, 1834-5; Prime Minister, 1852-5.
122 Francis Bond Head (1793-1875) served in the royal engineers 1811-25 and spent several years in South America in an abortive mining enterprise; knighted, 1835; Lieutenant-Governor of Upper Canada, 1835-7.
123 Holland's only surviving legitimate son, Henry Edward Fox (1802-59), afterwards fourth Lord Holland, at this time about to enter the diplomatic service.
124 The House was in committee on Schedule A of the government's Reform Bill—the list of boroughs to be totally disfranchised. Ministers conceded the removal of the borough of Saltash from Schedule A to Schedule B—the list of boroughs to lose only one member. *3 Hansard,* V (26 July 1831), 328-82.
125 Albin Reine Roussin (1781-1854), French admiral; Ambassador to Turkey, 1832-4.
126 Jacques Lafitte (1767-1844), French financier and statesman; one of the conspirators of the July Revolution; Prime Minister in the new government, Nov. 1830-Mar. 1831.
127 Charles Manners-Sutton (1780-1845), afterwards Viscount Canterbury, Speaker of the House of Commons, 1817-35. He was not actively challenged by a Whig candidate until 1835. Peerage, 1835.
128 Auguste Charles Joseph, Comte de Flahaut (1785-1870), Talleyrand's illegitimate son. French minister at Berlin, 1831; Ambassador to Austria, 1841-8; to England, 1860-2.
129 An amendment to the Church Building Acts, designed to facilitate the building of churches in populous areas. Enacted as 1 & 2 Will. IV, c. 38.
130 James Archibald Stuart-Wortley-Mackenzie (1776-1845), first Baron Wharncliffe. A follower of Canning and supporter of Catholic Emancipation, he became one of the leading 'waverers' in the Reform struggle, trying to reach an accommodation with government or effect a compromise which would enable him and his friends to accept the bill. His Truck Bill was actually two separate bills which provided for the abolition of payment to laborers in kind rather than in money. Enacted as 1 & 2 Will. IV, c. 36 and c. 37.
131 George Kenyon (1776-1855), second Baron Kenyon.
132 William Carr Beresford (1768-1854), first Viscount Beresford, general; he had been a marshall in the Portuguese army, which he reorganized during the peninsular war; returned to England, 1822; Master General of the Ordnance, 1828-30. See text, p. 225.
133 Edward Boscawen (1787-1841), first Earl of Falmouth.
134 In the Protocol of 17 April 1831, the English, Austrian, Prussian, and Russian representatives to the Conference on Belgium agreed that Belgian neutrality would not require the maintenance of all the frontier fortresses that had been erected since 1815, and that those to be demolished would be determined in subsequent negotiations. The Protocol of 14 July 1831 formally communicated the agreement to Talleyrand. *BFSP,* XVIII (1830-1), 921-2. Presented to Parliament, July 1831. H.C. Journals, LXXXVI, part 2 (1830-1), 1086.

135 George Augustus Francis Rawdon Hastings (1808-44), second Marquess of Hastings, supported the Reform Bill but turned Tory shortly thereafter.
136 Henry Fleming Lea Devereux (1777-1843), fourteenth Viscount Hereford, had been generally Whiggish, although he supported George IV's divorce proceedings against Queen Caroline a decade earlier. He voted against the Reform Bill.
137 Frederick James Lamb (1782-1853), afterwards third Viscount Melbourne, was Ambassador at Vienna, May 1831-Nov. 1841. Melbourne's youngest brother, George Lamb (1784-1834), was Under Secretary of State at the Home Department.
138 Don Miguel Ricardo de Alava (1771-1843), Spanish general and statesman, in exile in England and Belgium. He returned to Spain after the death of Ferdinand VII. Ambassador to England, 1834; France, 1835. Supposed to have been the only man present at both Trafalgar and Waterloo.
139 Agustin Argüelles (1775-1844), a Spanish exile in England, he returned to Spain after the amnesty of 1832; appointed guardian for Queen Isabella during her minority, 1832-43.
140 Felipe Bauza (d. 1833), Spanish geographer, exiled in England since 1823.
141 Henry Labouchere (1798-1869), afterwards (1859) first Baron Taunton, MP Taunton, 1830-59; held non-cabinet offices in the Grey and Melbourne ministries; President of the Board of Trade, 1839-41, 1847-52; Irish Secretary, 1846-7; Colonial Secretary, 1855-8.
142 Lord George William Russell (1790-1846), second son of the sixth Duke of Bedford; attached to Adair's mission in the Low Countries; special mission to Portugal, 1832-4; minister to Württemberg, 1834-5; Ambassador to Prussia, 1835-41.
143 Jose Monino y Redonda (1728-1808), Count of Floridablanca, Spanish minister under Charles III and Charles IV.
144 Don Pedro Rodriguez (1723-1802), Count of Campomanes, President of the Council of Castile, 1783-93; essayist.
145 Holland's account is not quite accurate. The traditional Spanish law preferred the female succession in the absence of a direct male heir. In 1713, Philip V introduced the Salic Law which preferred the male succession, even of a collateral heir. In the Pragmatic Sanction of 1789, Charles IV abolished the Salic Law with the approval of the Cortes, but the Pragmatic was not published and remained generally unknown. Ferdinand VII (1784-1833), who succeeded in 1808, remained without an heir after three marriages. His brother, Don Carlos (1788-1855), was then considered to be heir presumptive. But in March 1830, still in anticipation of an heir, Ferdinand reissued the Pragmatic of Charles IV, which was to exclude Don Carlos from the succession even if the heir were female. She was. Ferdinand's fourth queen, Maria Cristina of Naples, gave birth to a daughter, Isabella, in October 1830.
146 In the second Reform Bill, the £10 householder qualification was further restricted by requiring that the householder pay his own poor rates and assessed taxes in order to be eligible to vote. This amendment excluded a considerable number, particularly in the metropolis of London, who would have been qualified to vote in the borough by the less restrictive definition of £10 householder qualification in the first Reform Bill. The second Bill also stipulated that the rent of a £10 householder must be paid no more frequently than in semi-annual installments. This, too, would have reduced eligible voters where the custom of paying rent monthly or even weekly prevailed. This latter amendment was discarded when ministers realized its limitations and, to obviate the possibility of undesirable voters, there was introduced in the course of the second bill an amendment which stipulated that the £10 householder must be resident in the same tenement within the borough for one year prior to registration in order to qualify for the franchise. *3 Hansard,* V (13 Aug. 1831), 1375-80; Le Marchant, *Althorp,* p. 325. The third Reform Bill eliminated the provision for yearly payment of rent and, though it retained a twelve-month residency requirement for the £10 household suffrage, the residency qualification was no longer restricted to living in the same tenement. For the

electoral qualifications established by the bill, see Charles Seymour, *Electoral Reform in England and Wales: The Development and Operation of the Parliamentary Franchise 1832-1885* (London and New Haven, 1915), pp. 7-45; Gash, *Politics in the Age of Peel*, pp. 86-101.

147 John Frederick Campbell (1790-1860), first Earl Cawdor, bore the queen's ivory rod at the Coronation. He voted for the Reform Bill, but joined the Tories shortly thereafter.

148 Nicholas Jean de Dieu Soult (1769-1851), French Minister of War, 1830-4, 1840-5.

149 Princess Mary (1776-1857), fourth daughter of George III, m. (1816) the Duke of Gloucester.

150 Charles Louis Huget, Marquis de Semonville (1759-1839), Great Referendary in the Chamber of Peers. The Duc d'Orléans (1810-42), eldest son of King Louis Philippe. When the Chamber of Peers convened on 25 July, Semonville displayed the Austrian banners which Napoleon had seized at Ulm in 1805. The banners were reclaimed in 1815, but the Austrians were then informed that they had been destroyed. Semonville told the Chamber that they had been hidden, and he was now presenting them anew as a symbol of France's regeneration. His chauvinistic speech was followed by one from the Duc d'Orléans in the same spirit. *Archives Parlementaires*, LXVIII (25 July 1831), 766-7; *Annual Register (1831)*, pp. 354-5; *The Times*, 29 July 1831.

151 The London Conference on Greece had convened in February 1830 and recognized Greek independence, the new kingdom being placed under the joint guarantee of Great Britain, France, and Russia. The boundary adjustments and the problem of finding a monarch were not fully resolved until the spring of 1832. Convention and Protocols of 7 and 8 May 1832, in *BFSP*, XIX (1831-2), 32-43.

152 Prince Paul Karl Friedrich August of Württemberg (1785-1852), brother of the King of Württemberg.

153 Anton Reinhard, Baron Falck (1777-1843), Dutch Ambassador to England, 1824-32.

154 Charles, Comte Bresson (1798-1847), Secretary of the French embassy at London; he and an English envoy were charged with communicating the resolutions of the London Conference to the Belgian government; French Ambassador at Berlin, 1835-8; received title (1838) from Louis Philippe for negotiating the marriage of the Duc d'Orléans and Princess Helena of Mecklenberg.

155 Augustin Daniel, Comte Belliard (1769-1832), French general and diplomat; minister at Brussels, 1831-2.

156 The Duc de Nemours (1814-96), second son of Louis Philippe, was offered the Belgian crown by the National Congress in February 1832, but prevented from accepting it by his father, who was pressured by other governments. Louis Philippe had earlier prevented him from accepting the Greek throne when offered in 1830.

157 1 & 2 Will. IV, c. 11, providing for an annuity of £100,000 and residences at Marlborough House and Bushy Park.

158 James William Gascoyne-Cecil (1791-1868), second Marquess of Salisbury, father of the later Prime Minister.

159 George William Frederick Charles (1819-1904), afterwards (1850) seventh Duke of Cambridge.

160 William Charles Keppel (1772-1849), fourth Earl of Albermarle, Master of the Horse, 1830-4, 1835-41.

161 William George Spencer (1790-1858) sixth Duke of Devonshire, Lord Chamberlain of the Household, 1827-8, 1830-4.

162 Ernest Augustus (1771-1851), Duke of Cumberland and later King of Hanover, the fifth son of George III; an ultra Tory.

163 Richmond had been a leading opponent of the Wellington government's Beer Bill of 1830 and sought, unsuccessfully this session, to restrict the licensing of beer houses. Most of his colleagues in the Grey ministry had supported the Beer Bill. See Brian Harrison, *Drink and the Victorians* (London, 1971), pp. 79-80.

164 Sir Charles Bagot (1781-1843), Ambassador at the Hague, 1824-32; Governor General of Canada, 1841-3.

165 Hugo van Zuylen van Nyevelt (1781-1853), Dutch envoy at the London conference on Belgium, 1831-3.

166 Sir Edward Codrington (1770-1851), admiral; commanded the Channel Fleet, Oct. 1831; MP Devonport, 1832-9.

167 He resigned on 2 August, after his candidate for the presidency of the Chamber of Deputies received only a one-vote absolute majority, which Périer chose to construe as a virtual defeat. By the time Holland made the above entry, Périer had already withdrawn his resignation upon receiving news of the Dutch invasion of Belgium.

168 Felix Barthe (1795-1863), French Minister of Public Instruction, 1830-1; Minister of Justice and Keeper of the Seals, 1831-4.

169 Joseph Dominique, Baron Louis (1755-1837), French Minister of Finance, 1830-2.

170 Brougham had expedited the hearing of appeals in Chancery and sought to continue to hear them, though term had ended. The bill, though a mere matter of form, was designed to give the lord chancellor unquestioned authority in this arrangement. It was dropped when Eldon insisted that the lord chancellor had authority to hear appeals at his discretion, before or after seals, and hence the legislation was unnecessary. *3 Hansard,* V (3 and 4 August 1831), 645-7; 724-6.

171 Passed as 1 & 2 Will. IV, c. 13.

172 Ralph Abercromby (1803-68), afterwards (1858) second Baron Dunfermline, secretary to the English mission of the joint Anglo-French Commission from the London Conference to the Provisional Government of Belgium, 1830-1; secretary to the English legation at Berlin, 1831-5; minister at Florence, 1835-8; to the German Confederation, 1838-40; at Turin and The Hague in the 1840s and 1850s.

173 John Ponsonby (?1770-1855), second Baron Ponsonby, minister at Buenos Aires, 1826-8; at Rio de Janeiro, 1828-30; envoy at Brussels, 1830-1 and, with Comte Bresson, Joint Commissioner of the London Conference to the Provisional Government of Belgium, Dec. 1830-June 1831; envoy at Naples, 1832; Ambassador to Turkey, 1832-7; to Austria, 1846-50; cr. viscount, 1839.

174 Count André Joseph Matuszewic (d. 1842), special Russian envoy to the London Conferences on Greece and Belgium. He was considered a rival by Princess Lieven.

175 It was adopted as Protocol 31 of the Conference, 6 Aug. 1831, *BFSP,* XVIII, 824-5.

176 The Kildare Street Society, theoretically nondenominational but effectively controlled by Protestants, had received annual parliamentary grants from 1815 through 1831 to promote education in Ireland. In 1831 Stanley established the commission for national education in Ireland to supervise nondenominational primary education, with provision for separate religious instruction. The Subletting Act, 7 Geo. IV, c. 29, was designed to prevent further subdivision of land, in the interest of owners-in-fee; but the consolidation of land in Ireland had made little appreciable progress by 1830, and the act was strongly opposed by Irish representatives. The vestry cess, abolished by the Irish Church Temporalities Act of 1833, was voted by the parish vestries of the Church of Ireland for the repair and building of Protestant churches and imposed upon the occupiers of land, the preponderance of whom were Catholic.

177 John William Ponsonby (1781-1847), Viscount Duncannon, afterwards (1844) fourth Earl of Bessborough, was on the committee of four which drew up the parliamentary reform bills, and was specifically responsible for the Irish bill. Chief whip of the Whig party in the 1820s; First Commissioner of Woods and Forests, 1831-4, 1835-41; Home Secretary in Melbourne's brief ministry, 1834; instrumental in effecting the Lichfield House Compact of 1835; Lord Privy Seal, 1835-9; Lord Lieutenant of Ireland, 1846-7; raised to the Lords in his own right as Baron Duncannon, 1834.

178 Daniel O'Connell (1775-1847), 'the Liberator.' After his victory of Catholic Emancipation, O'Connell commenced his campaign for repeal of the Union. After two abortive efforts to entice him into office, the Whig government had tried to immobilize him by

arresting him for defiance of a proclamation which had prohibited meetings of his latest association. It was tacitly understood that O'Connell's support of reform and suspension of repeal agitation during the elections of May 1831 would result in the government's suspension of his prosecution. O'Connell did not resume intensive agitation for repeal of the Union until after the parliamentary reform bills were passed.

179 Nicholas Joseph Daine (1782-1843) had been a general in the French army and was in the service of the Dutch since 1815. He defected in 1830 to join the Belgian insurgents and assumed command of the Army of the Meuse, the main Belgian force. In August 1831 he was to join his army with the forces led by Prince Leopold, but his inexperienced troops fled in disarray before a Dutch attack at Hasselt, near Liège, on 8 August. Accused of treason, he was stripped of his command, but was subsequently acquitted and reinstated in the army; dismissed from the army again in 1840.

180 With the exception of Stanley's educational reform and establishment of a Board of Public Works (enacted later in the session as 1 & 2 Will. IV., c.33), Irish legislation had been delayed. Nor were the government's anticipated projects extensive. See introductory essay, above, pp. xxv-vi

181 Maurice Fitzgerald (1774-1849), Knight of Kerry, represented co. Kerry in the Irish and imperial parliaments continuously from 1794-1831. The knighthood was a fourteenth-century honor retained in the family.

182 Sir John Newport (1756-1843), MP Waterford City, 1803-32, a long-time Irish Whig. The vote referred to was on a motion for the House to print a petition from Waterford City for the disarming of the Yeomanry. Newport and Duncannon voted with the minority for the motion, which was opposed by ministers. *3 Hansard,* V (11 Aug. 1831), 1208.

183 Joel Roberts Poinsett (1779-1851) of Charleston, South Carolina, member of Congress, 1821-5; Secretary of War, 1837-41.

184 John Singleton Copley, the younger (1772-1863), first Baron Lyndhurst, Lord Chancellor, 1827-30, 1834-5, 1841-6. Lady Lyndhurst (1795-1834), née Sarah Garay, widow of Lt Col. Charles Thomas of the Coldstream Guards, married Lord Lyndhurst in 1819.

185 *The Times* objected to those provisions of the government's Reform Bill, then being discussed in committee of the whole House of Commons, which divided some twenty-six counties in two, each division to have two members. Leaders of 12 and 13 August criticized Althorp's defense of these provisions and suggested that the division of county constituencies would facilitate the extension of 'pocket' constituencies in the counties, which the bill was simultaneously abolishing in the boroughs.

186 Francis Russell (1788-1861), styled the Marquess of Tavistock, afterwards (1839) seventh Duke of Bedford. MP Bedfordshire, 1812-32; raised to the Lords in his own right as Baron Howland of Streatham, 1833. Lord John's eldest brother.

187 In addition to the forty-shilling freeholder, the first Reform Bill had extended the county franchise to leaseholders whose rent was not less than £10, if they held leases for life. Those who held shorter leases, at not less than £50 per annum, were to be enfranchised if the minimum period of their lease was fourteen years. The second Reform Bill, as explained by Russell and Althorp, reduced the period of lease in the case of the £50 leaseholder to seven years. A £10 leaseholder had to hold a lease for a minimum of sixty years to be enfranchised. *3 Hansard,* IV (24 June 1831), 339; V (13 August 1831), 1374-5. The county franchise was to be extended further by the controversial Chandos clause, amended to the bill on 18 August.

188 The Whig Club of Westminster, founded in 1784 to assist in the election of Charles James Fox.

189 Probably John Evelyn Denison (1800-73), MP 1823-37, 1841-72, then sitting for South Notts; generally Whiggish; Speaker of the House of Commons, 1857-72; cr. Viscount Ossington, 1872.

190 In addition to revision of the Yeomanry, Anglesey had advocated extensive public works programs to be administered by a board in Dublin, a labor rate upon land for general employment, introduction of poor laws, payment by the state to the Catholic clergy, and adjustment of the education grant hitherto given the Kildare Street Society. Anglesey to Grey, 14 Aug. 1831, AP, P.R.O.N.I., T1068/8, ff. 160-2.

191 Palmerston had been informed by Bülow, the Prussian Ambassador, that Talleyrand had privately suggested to the latter the desirability of partitioning Belgium. Palmerston to Grey, 12 Aug. 1831, Webster, II, pp. 817-18. Webster's remains the most comprehensive study of English foreign policy for the decade.

192 Lord John George Beresford (1773-1862), Archbishop of Armagh, 1822-62, in which capacity he was, technically, the Primate of *all* Ireland, the Archbishop of Dublin holding the title of Primate of Ireland. But the term invariably referred to the former.

193 Horatio Walpole (1783-1858), third Earl of Orford.

194 George Granville Sutherland Leveson-Gower (1786-1861), Baron Gower, afterwards (1833) second Duke of Sutherland.

195 Thomas Atherton Powys (1801-61), third Baron Lilford, m. (1830) Mary Elizabeth Fox (1806-91), daughter of Lord and Lady Holland.

196 The Duc d'Orléans and the Duc de Nemours.

197 The sites of two of the frontier fortresses.

198 In 1828, the boroughs of East Retford in Nottinghamshire and Penryn in Cornwall were found guilty of corruption. The Wellington government agreed that the representation of the former be dissolved into that of the county, that of the latter to be transferred to Manchester, still unrepresented. When the Lords vetoed Penryn's transfer to Manchester, William Huskisson, then a member of Wellington's cabinet, voted against the government on the East Retford proposal. He offered his resignation which, to his surprise, Wellington accepted. Huskisson was followed out of office by the other Canningites—Charles Grant, Lord Dudley, and Palmerston—and the East Retford case contributed, as Holland suggests, to the revived interest in extensive parliamentary reform.

199 Protocol 33, printed in *BFSP*, XVIII (18 Aug. 1831), 830.

200 Dorothea, Princess Lieven (1785-1857), the ubiquitous social gossip, wife of the Russian ambassador to London, Prince Lieven (1774-1839). They were in London from 1812 to 1834, and in the later years, especially, Princess Lieven was virtually Russian ambassador; an intimate of Metternich, Castlereagh, Canning, Wellington, Grey, Guizot, and others. Chateaubriand wrote of her: 'Ministers and those who aspired to become such were all proud to be protégés of a lady who had the honor of knowing Metternich, in those hours when the great man, in order to divert himself from the burden of affairs, amused himself undoing silk.' (My translation.) Chateaubriand, *Memoires D'Outre Tombe*, ed. Maurice Levailland (Paris, n.d.), III, p.104.

201 Charles Napier (1786-1860), sent to the Azores to oversee activity by partisans of Dona Maria; accepted command of the Portuguese navy in 1833, and was successful in the victory at Oporto; defeated Mehemet Ali, 1840; MP Marylebone, 1841-7; knighted, 1841; admiral, 1858.

202 Bernhard Erich, Duke of Saxe-Meinüngen (1800-82), abdicated, 1866.

203 Sir Jeffry Wyatville (1766-1840), architect; responsible for the renovation of Windsor Castle from 1824, especially the Royal Apartments.

204 William Magee (1766-1831), had been Archbishop of Dublin since 1822.

205 William Howard (1788-1869), fourth Earl of Wicklow, Irish Representative Peer, 1821-69.

206 Just Pons Florimond de Fay, Marquis de Latour-Maubourg (1781-1837), French minister at Brussels, 1835-6; at Madrid, 1836-7.

207 This interpretation is implied, if not explicity stated, in the Protocol of 17 April on the Belgian fortresses. *BFSP*, XVIII (1830-1), 921-2.

208 James Duff (1776-1857), fourth Earl Fife (I) and Baron Fife (UK), a Canningite who then associated with the Whigs.

209 To establish a separate court of bankruptcy; 1 & 2 Will. IV, c. 56 relieved the lord chancellor from involvement in bankruptcies.

210 During the session of 1823, a select committee on the appellate jurisdiction of the Lords resolved to expedite appeals by having that House hear them for five rather than three days each week, and to appoint a deputy speaker in the Lords to relieve the lord chancellor. Eldon, who had been criticized for his lengthy judicial deliberations, used the occasion to vindicate his conduct as Lord Chancellor, and noted that the business of the Court of Chancery demanded more of his time than did his function of presiding in the Lords. *2 Hansard,* IX (30 June 1823), 1326-7.

211 Printed as Protocol 34, 23 August 1831, *BFSP,* XVIII, 830-1.

212 Henry Hunt (1773-1835), 'Orator Hunt,' radical MP Preston, 1831-3.

213 Sir Constantine Henry Phipps (1797-1863), second Earl of Mulgrave, cr. (1838) Marquess of Normanby. MP 1818-26; Governor of Jamaica, 1832-4; Lord Privy Seal, 1834; Lord Lieutenant of Ireland, 1835-9; Secretary for War and Colonies, 1839; Home Secretary, 1839-41.

214 Étienne Maurice Gérard (1773-1852), French general and politician; Minister of War in the early months of Louis Philippe's reign; led the French army in Belgium, Oct. 1831.

215 Both George IV and William IV created twenty-two coronation peers. (GEC, II, 654.)

216 Charles Edward Poulett Thomson (1799-1841), afterwards (1840), first Baron Sydenham. MP Dover, 1826-32, Manchester, 1832-9; President of the Board of Trade, 1834, 1835-9; Governor General of Canada, 1839-41.

217 Henry George Grey (1802-94), styled Viscount Howick, afterwards (1845) third Earl Grey, eldest son of the Prime Minister. MP 1826-45; Under Secretary for Colonies, 1830-3, and an ardent supporter of total abolition of slavery; Under Secretary for Home Department, 1834; Secretary at War, 1835-9; Secretary for War and Colonies, 1846-52.

218 Sir Thomas Denman (1779-1854), afterwards (1834) first Baron Denman. MP 1818-26, 1830-2; Attorney General, 1830-2; Lord Chief Justice of King's Bench, 1832-50; along with Brougham he had been a leading advocate for Queen Caroline. The motion was to institute proceedings against those charged with bribery in the Dublin City election; carried, 224-147. Howick and Thomson voted in the minority. *3 Hansard,* VI (23 Aug. 1831), 506-8.

219 James Brougham (1780-1833), MP 1826-33, had advised his brother not to accept the office of lord chancellor.

220 Prince Adam Jerzy Czartoryski (1770-1861), adviser to Czar Alexander I, from whom he obtained the Polish constitution of 1815. He participated in the insurrection of 1830 and led the Polish provisional government, 1830-1.

221 The cabinet's advice to the king on this matter is in BP, CAB/A, ff. 2-12. Most joined Palmerston and Grey in urging the king to receive the letter but not the delegation. Holland agreed that receipt of both the letter and delegation would be tantamount to recognition, which he favored. Acknowledging that his colleagues would not agree, however, he formally advised receipt of the letter only.

222 Pro-ministerial newspapers in 1831 were *The Times, Morning Chronicle, Globe, Sun,* and *Courier,* the latter perhaps the most favored.

223 Sir George Shee (1784-1870), permanent Under Secretary for Foreign Affairs, 1830-4; Ambassador at Berlin, 1834-5; at Stuttgart, 1835-44.

224 William Windham (1750-1810), Secretary at War, 1794-1801.

225 George Rose Sartorius (1790-1885), engaged by Dom Pedro to command his fleet against Miguel, 1831-3; knighted, 1841; admiral, 1861; admiral of the fleet, 1869.

226 59 George III, c. 69 prohibited British subjects from entering the service of a foreign prince or serving in rebellions against established governments. It also forbade the fitting-out of a vessel for purposes of war.

227 Probably the three bills relating to Chancery proceedings which Brougham had introduced this session—establishing a court of bankruptcy (cited above, p. 38), removing jurisdiction in cases of lunacy from the Court of Chancery, and payment of Masters in Chancery by salary rather than fees and abolishing sinecures. The Bankruptcy Court was established this session; the other bills were later incorporated in 2 & 3 Will. IV, c. 111 and 3 & 4 Will. IV, c. 84.

228 George Croly (1780-1860), a contributor to *Blackwood's* and the *Literary Gazette,* he was a distant relative of Lady Brougham. Brougham offered him a living in 1834 near Dartmoor, which Croly declined as too isolated. Brougham recommended him to Lyndhurst who, in 1835, gave him the rectory of St Stephen's, Walbrook.

229 Sir Henry Brooke Parnell (1776-1842), afterwards (1841) first Baron Congleton. MP Dundee, 1802, 1833-41, Queens County, 1806-32; Secretary at War, Apr. 1831-Jan. 1832, he was dismissed because of his opposition to the Russian Dutch loan; generally a liberal Whig, influential in Irish matters; Paymaster General, 1835-41; committed suicide by hanging.

230 Thomas Wyse (1791-1862), MP Tipperary, 1830-2, Waterford, 1835-47. A leading agitator for Catholic Emancipation, he thereafter devoted his efforts primarily to Irish educational reforms and claimed that Stanley appropriated his educational scheme. Lord of the Treasury, 1839-41; Secretary of Board of Control, 1846-9; knighted, 1851.

231 Augustus Frederick FitzGerald (1791-1874), third Duke of Leinster (I) and Viscount Leinster (GB). A liberal Irish Whig.

232 Valentine Browne Lawless (1773-1853), Baron Cloncurry (I), raised to the peerage of UK, Sept. 1831; a liberal Irish Whig and intimate of Anglesey.

233 Francis Blackburne (1782-1867), Attorney General for Ireland, 1830-4, 1841; Chief Justice of Queen's Bench, 1846-52; Lord Chancellor of Ireland, 1852. His appointment by Grey enraged O'Connell, since Blackburne had voted against Emancipation.

234 George John Forbes (1785-1836), styled Viscount Forbes, MP co. Longford, 1806-36. Associated first with the Whigs, he turned Tory in the 1820s.

235 Londonderry referred to Holland as 'the noble Deputy Secretary of State for Foreign Affairs, or Principal Secretary, for he understood, that it was the noble Baron (Holland) who directed the proceedings of the noble Lord (Palmerston) who ostensibly held that situation.' *3 Hansard,* VI (29 Aug. 1831), 742.

236 Christian Friedrich, Baron von Stockmar (1787-1863), secretary to Prince Leopold, 1816-34; he assumed the role of unofficial advisor to Queen Victoria and was influential in promoting the marriage of Prince Albert, Leopold's nephew, with the queen, Leopold's niece.

237 Thomas Peregrine Courtenay (1782-1841), MP Totnes, 1811-32; politician and literary dilettante. His successful motion requested presentation to parliament of documents concerning the British and French expedition to the Tagus. *3 Hansard,* VI (30 Aug. 1831), 877-80.

238 Introduced in Lords in June 1831, it was exceedingly modest in scope, and would have limited pluralities by vesting discretionary power in the archbishop of Canterbury to revoke dispensations to hold pluralities. It never reached the second reading in the Commons.

239 2 & 3 Will. IV, c. 17, which repealed the Subletting Act of 1826.

240 Marie Etienne François Henri, Comte Baudrand (1774-1848). French general; peerage 1832. His mission was to persuade Grey's government to consent to French troops remaining in Belgium. (Palmerston to Holland, 31 Aug. 1831, HHP, BM Add. MS 51599, f. 91.)

241 To which Grey replied, 'I am afraid I shall not be able to screw my courage to the sticking place for so large a creation.' *Ibid.*, Grey to Holland, 31. Aug. [1831], BM Add. MS 51555, f. 149.

242 Henry Bathurst (1744-1837), Bishop of Norwich, 1805-37. Considered to be the only liberal bishop in the House of Lords, he had supported Catholic Emancipation.

243 Sir Samuel Romilly (1757-1818), the eminent Whig legal reformer.

244 Brougham's account of the dissolution is in Henry Lord Brougham, *Life and Times* (London, 1871), III, pp. 111-19.

245 Protocol 38, *BFSP*, XVIII (1 Sept. 1831), 841-3.

246 Thomas William Coke of Holkham (1754-1842), afterwards (1837) first Earl of Leicester. Whig MP Norfolk, 1776-84, 1790-1807, 1807-32. Coke's remarks were made at a public dinner at Lynn in 1830, in reply to a toast to the memory of George III. (GEC, VII, 563n.) Associated with agricultural improvement, he was a staunch protectionist.

247 Admiral Sir James Saumarez (1757-1836), cr. (1831) first Baron de Saumarez. Politically associated with the Whigs.

248 Thomas Span Plunket (1792-1866), afterwards (1854) second Baron Plunket, Dean of Down, 1831-9; Bishop of Taum, Killala, and Achoney, 1839-66.

249 Charles Dundas (1751-1832), cr. (1832) first Baron Amesbury, MP 1775-84, for Berkshire, 1794-32.

250 Edward Vernon Harcourt (1757-1847), Archbishop of York, 1807-47. He declined the offer of a peerage in 1838.

251 Robert Montgomery Hamilton (1793-1868), eighth Lord Belhaven (S), cr. Baron Hamilton (UK) at the Coronation of William IV, 1831. A Whig and Scottish Representative Peer, 1819-32.

252 George Granville Leveson-Gower (1758-1833), second Marquess of Stafford, cr. (1833) Duke of Sutherland.

253 William Harry Vane (1766-1842), Earl of Darlington, cr. (1827) Marquess of Cleveland; dukedom, 1833. Controlled six boroughs, but supported reform. It was said of him, 'he bought his boroughs to be made a Marquess, and gave them up to be made a Duke.' GEC III, 284n.

254 Sir Herbert Taylor (1775-1839) had been private secretary to the Duke of York and then to George III; lieutenant-general, 1825; private secretary to William IV, 1830-7.

255 Because of Holland's gout.

256 Sir John Campbell (1780-1863), had been lieutenant-colonel, sold his commission in 1824 and associated himself with Dom Miguel, becoming major-general in the Portuguese army. He tried unsuccessfully to raise a naval force for Miguel in England, evading the provisions of the Foreign Enlistment Act. He returned to England after Miguel's defeat.

257 Antoine Philippe Fiacre Ghislain De Visscher, Comte De Celles (1779-1841), supported the candidacy of the Duc de Nemours and subsequently, assuming French citizenship, served under Louis Philippe.

258 Cyrus Marie Alexandre de Timbruen-Timbronne, Comte de Valence (1757-1820), French general; son-in-law of Mme Genlis.

259 Stéphanie Felicité du Crest de St Aubin, Comtesse de Genlis (1746-1830), writer; she had been Louis Philippe's tutor.

260 Sir Francis Burdett (1770-1844), Radical MP Boroughbridge, 1796-1802, Middlesex, 1802-4, Westminster, 1807-37, North Wilts, 1837-44; turned conservative in the 1830s.

261 Sir John Byng (1772-1860), cr. (1835) Baron Strafford; earldom, 1847; general; Commander in Chief of the Forces in Ireland since 1828, he resigned his Irish command in 1831 and became MP for Poole, 1831-5; among the few military men who supported the Reform Bill.

262 Thomas Foley (1780-1833), fifth Baron Foley, a Whig peer.
263 Charles Abbot (1762-1832), first Baron Tenterden; Chief Justice of King's Bench, 1818-27; a Tory opponent of Catholic Emancipation and Reform.
264 Thomas Eyre (1790-1833), Roman Catholic and styled Viscount Kynnaird, 1814-27. He assumed the title or Earl of Newburgh, but no proceedings were taken on his claim in the House of Lords.
265 Francis William Caulfield (1775-1863), second Earl of Charlemont (I), cr. (1837) Baron Charlemont (UK).
266 Henry Caulfield (1779-1862), MP co. Armagh, 1802-7, 1815-18, 1820-30.
267 Lady William Russell (1793-1874), née Elizabeth Anne Rawdon, Married Lord William in 1817.
268 George Capel-Coningsby (1757-1839), fifth Earl of Essex.
269 Greville, who was in a position to know the figures as Clerk to the Privy Council, estimated the cost of the coronation at £30,000 compared to £240,000 for the coronation of George IV. *Greville,* II. p. 183.
270 Philip Cecil Crampton (1782-1862), MP 1831-2; Solicitor General for Ireland, 1830-4; Justice of King's Bench, Ireland, 1834-59.
271 The Hollands rented 30, Old Burlington Street for several years from Sir Thomas Neve. See Lady Holland to Henry Edward Fox, 16 August [1831] in Lord Ilchester (ed.), *Elizabeth, Lady Holland to her son 1821-1845* (London, 1946), p. 113.
272 Edmund Knox (d. 1849), Dean of Down, became Bishop of Killaloe, 1831; translated to Limerick, 1834.
273 Holland probably meant Down, not Derry.
274 Thomas Philip Lefanu (d. 1845), Dean of Emly, 1826-45.
275 Sir Thomas Masterman Hardy (1769-1839), first sea lord at admiralty, 1830-4; vice admiral, 1837.
276 John Wilson Croker (1780-1857), the ultra Tory; he retired from parliament after passage of the Reform Bill; associated with the *Quarterly Review.*
277 Robert James Carr (d. 1841), Bishop of Chichester, 1824-31; translated to Worcester, 1831-41.
278 Edward Maltby (1770-1859), Bishop of Chichester, 1831-6; of Durham, 1836-56. One of the few Whiggish bishops.
279 The Special Constables Bill was passed as 1 & 2 Will. IV, c. 41, and provided for the appointment of special constables in emergencies by justices of the peace. A similar act was later passed for Ireland: 2 & 3 Will. IV, c. 108. The Spring Guns Bill, which passed the Lords, prohibited the setting of spring guns in specified areas by occupiers of land without the consent of a magistrate at Quarter Sessions. It never reached the second reading in the Commons.
280 Protocol 40, *BFSP,* XVIII (10 Sept. 1831), 844-5.
281 Sir George Francis Seymour (1787-1870), naval aide-de-camp to William IV; lord of the admiralty, 1841-4; vice admiral, 1850; admiral, 1857; admiral of the fleet, 1866.
282 Sydney Smith (1771-1845), intimate of Jeffrey, Brougham, Horner, and involved in the inception of the *Edinburgh Review.* Made canon of St Paul's in 1831, he was often critical of religious orthodoxy and the religious establishment.
283 Sir John Conroy (1786-1854), Comptroller of the Household to the Duchess of Kent and her private secretary; he received a pension of £3000 and a baronetcy upon Victoria's succession.
284 William Arden (1789-1849), second Baron Alvanley. He voted for the second reading of the Reform Bills in October and in April.
285 John Calcraft (1765-1831), MP 1786-90, 1800-31; a Whig until 1828 when he joined the Wellington government; he provided one of the surprise votes for the majority in the 302-301 division in the Commons on 22 March 1831.
286 Frederick Ponsonby (1758-1844), third Earl of Bessborough, a Whig peer.
287 Henry Stephen Fox-Strangways (1787-1858), third Earl of Ilchester, a Whig peer.

288 William Francis Spencer Ponsonby (1787-1855), cr. (1838) Baron de Mauley; third son of the Earl of Bessborough. Whig MP Poole, 1826-31; he contested Dorset against Lord Ashley and was defeated; MP Dorset, 1832-7.

289 Peter King (1775-1833), seventh Baron King of Ockham, a Whig and noted anti-clerical. Holland's reference is to King's suggestion that the Lords not be intransigent, lest the public 'question its utility, and find a pretext in its conduct to ask why it should not be got rid of.' *3 Hansard,* VI (13 Sept. 1831), 1365.

290 Dudley Ryder (1762-1847), first Earl of Harrowby, was a leader of the 'waverers,' who opposed the Reform Bill in 1831 but voted for the second reading in 1832. Greville wrote of him: 'He was at the top of the second rate men, always honorable and strait-forward, generally liberal and enlightened, greatly esteemed and respected.' *Greville,* VI, p. 1.

291 The Scotch Reform Bill, like the Irish, was relegated to a corollary of the bill for England and Wales by both government and parliament. The third reform bills for Scotland and Ireland were not read a second time until May 1832. The best discussion of the provisions and background of the Scottish bill is in Gash, *Politics in the Age of Peel,* pp. 34-50; for the Irish bill, *ibid.,* pp. 50-64, and Angus Macintyre, *The Liberator: Daniel O'Connell and the Irish Party 1830-1847* (London, 1965), pp. 29-36.

292 John Chambré Brabazon (1772-1851), tenth Earl of Meath (I), cr. (1831) Baron Chaworth (UK), a coronation peer.

293 Paul Anton, Prince Esterhazy (1786-1866), Austrian Ambassador at London, 1815-42.

294 Richard Plantagenet Temple-Nugent-Brydges-Chandos-Grenville (1797-1861), afterwards (1839) second Duke of Buckingham and Chandos, styled Marquess of Chandos since 1822. M P Bucks, 1818-39; a leader of the landed interest and the West Indian interest in the Commons; author of the 'Chandos clause.' Holland must be referring to Chandos's role as Chairman of the Standing Committee of West Indian Planters and Merchants. See *3 Hansard,* VII (28 Sept. 1831), 747.

295 Sir Thomas Fowell Buxton (1786-1845), MP Weymouth, 1818-37, the evangelical; engaged in prison reform and then succeeded Wilberforce as the leading advocate of slavery-abolition.

296 Charles Rose Ellis (1771-1845), first Baron Seaford, Tory MP 1793-1826; a leader of the West Indian interest in the Lords.

297 Edward Jervis Ricketts Jervis (1767-1859), second Viscount St Vincent, a Whig until the passage of the Reform Bill.

298 These were Althorp's resolutions: *3 Hansard,* III (15 Apr. 1831), 1426. Slaves owned by the Crown had already been emancipated and slave labor was legally regulated in Crown colonies.

299 Katherine Frances Corbet Barnes (?1796-1865), m. Lord Cochrane, afterwards Lord Dundonald, secretly in 1812 and publicly in 1818.

300 Sir Frederick Augustus Wetherall (1754-1842), aide-de-camp, equerry, and executor of the Duke of Kent; knighted, 1833.

301 Russia claimed that the constitution granted the Poles in 1815 was abrogated by the Polish rebellion. The Czar's plan abolished the constitution while preserving the kingdom.

302 Antonio José de Sousa (1792-1860), Count of Villa Flôr, Duke of Terceira, Portuguese general and politician. An opponent of Dom Miguel, he commenced a campaign against him from London in 1828; seized the Azores, 1829-30, defeating the *Miguelistas* in Portugal in 1833.

303 Henry Bathurst (1762-1834), third Earl Bathurst, had served in various capacities in Tory governments since 1812 as Foreign Secretary, President of the Board of Trade, Lord President of the Council, and Secretary for War and Colonies.

304 Tenterden moved to substitute 'forty five' for 'thirty' in the clause which prohibited clergymen from holding two benefices at a greater distance than thirty miles from each other. *3 Hansard,* VII (20 Sept. 1831), 230.

305 Riots in response to news about the fall of Warsaw.

306 Joseph Hume (1777-1855), the radical politician; MP Weymouth, 1812, Aberdeen burgs, 1818-30, 1842-55, Middlesex, 1830-7, co. Kilkenny, 1837-41.

307 John Backhouse (1772-1845), permanent Under Secretary of State for Foreign Affairs, 1827-42.

308 Mostly Althorp's measure, it provided that anyone killing or selling game be licensed by the Inland Revenue Department. Enacted as 1 & 2 Will. IV, c. 32.

309 Luis Antonio D'Abreu e Lima (1785-1871), afterwards Count of Carreira, Portuguese diplomat in London since 1830 representing the constitutionalists; later minister at Madrid and Paris.

310 George Henry Law (1761-1845), Bishop of Chester, 1812-24; of Bath and Wells, 1824-45.

311 Robert Torrens (1780-1864), political economist; MP Ipswich, 1826-7, Ashburton, 1831-2, Bolton, 1832-4; his speech to the London Common Hall is printed in the *Morning Chronicle,* 20 Sept. 1831. See Frank Whitsun Fetter, 'Robert Torrens: Colonel of Marines and Political Economist,' *Economica,* N.A. XXIX (1962), 152-65.

312 *3 Hansard,* VII, 519.

313 John James Waldegrave (1785-1835), sixth Earl Waldegrave, a Tory Lord of the Bedchamber, 1830-1, he voted against the second reading in October and did not vote in 1832.

314 Charles William Lambton, Durham's eldest child by his second marriage to Lady Louisa Elizabeth Grey, Lord Grey's eldest daughter; he died at the age of 13 on 24 Dec. 1831; the subject of Sir Thomas Lawrence's famous portrait, 'Master Lambton.' Durham lost three children from December 1831 to December 1832.

315 I.e., the sliding scale of reduced duties on imported raw sugar, instituted in 1830 and annually renewable. Duties on the importation of raw sugar to be refined in England were abolished in 1833. 3 & 4 Will. IV, c. 61.

316 At the Westminster Reform meeting, reported in the *Morning Chronicle,* 22 Sept. 1831.

317 Francisco Teixeira Sampaio, Portuguese consul-general.

318 Sir James Mackintosh (1765-1832), political theorist, historian, and intimate of Holland House.

319 Sir William Macmahon (1776-1837), Irish Master of the Rolls, 1814-37.

320 Sir William Horne (1774-1860), Solicitor General, 1830-2; Attorney General 1832-4; MP Helston, 1812-18, Bletchingley, 1831, Newtown (Isle of Wight), 1831-2, Marylebone, 1833-4; Master in Chancery, 1839-53. He was promoted to the Court of Exchequer in 1834, assuming that the prospective reform of that court would eliminate capital punishment, to which he was opposed. When the reform was abandoned, Horne had to be removed from the court by Brougham.

321 The bill would have enabled the Irish Master of the Rolls to try the question of his right to appoint his own secretary before some judge other than the Irish Lord Chancellor who was his adversary in this case. Defeated in committee. *3 Hansard,* X (22 Feb. 1832), 637-63.

322 The Methuen Treaty of 1703, in effect until 1836, admitted English woolens into Portugal in return for Portuguese wines, which were imported at two-thirds the duties payable on French wines, the adverse balance paid in gold. (*BFSP,* I, 502-5.) The treaty of 1810 (*BFSP,* I, 513-45), establishing most-favored nation status in trade relations, retained the wine-woolen arrangement but stipulated that either party could make alteration upon notice at the end of a fifteen-year period. The bill to which Holland referred equalized the duties on foreign wines and redressed the balance which had existed against France. Enacted as 1 & 2 Will. IV, c. 30.

323 Ulick John de Burgh (1802-74), second Marquess of Clanricarde. Ambassador to Russia, 1838-41; Postmaster General, 1846-52.

324 The division rejected the second reading 199-158, including proxies. *3 Hansard,* VIII, 339-44.

325 David William Murray (1777-1840), third Earl of Mansfield, a Tory peer.

326 William Pleydell-Bouverie (1779-1869), third Earl Radnor, MP 1801-28, a prominent Whig.

327 Printed: 8 Oct. 1831 in Charles, Lord Grey, *The Reform Act: The Correspondence of the Late Earl Grey with His Majesty King William IV and with Sir Herbert Taylor* (London, 1867), I, pp. 362-4. Hereafter cited as 'Grey, *Correspondence.*'

328 Hugh Fortescue (1783-1861), styled Viscount Ebrington, summoned to the Lords in his own right, Mar.1839 as Lord Fortescue, afterwards (1841) second Earl Fortescue; a Whig when in Commons, 1804-9, 1812-39; Lord Lieutenant of Ireland, 1839-41.

329 Sir William Francis Patrick Napier (1785-1860), the historian of the peninsular war. His speech at Devizes, 30 Sept. 1831, condemned governmental lethargy in pressing reform and warned of the dangers of delay. Reprinted in full in the *Globe,* 7 Oct. 1831.

330 On Ebrington's motion of confidence in the government, carried 329-198. *3 Hansard,* VIII (10 Oct. 1831), 465-7.

331 During the debate on Ebrington's motion. *Ibid.,* pp. 458-62.

332 Printed: Minute of Cabinet, 11 Oct. 1831, Grey, *Correspondence,* I, pp. 372-4.

333 Thomas Hamilton (1780-1858), ninth Earl of Haddington. Lord Lieutenant of Ireland in Peel's first ministry, 1834-5; First Lord of the Admiralty, 1841-6. He was one of the 'waverers' who voted against the Reform Bill in 1831 and for it in 1832.

334 Protocol 49, 14 Oct. 1831, *BFSP,* XVIII, 893-903. The provisions comprised the Twenty-Four Articles, a compromise between the Eighteen Articles of 26 June which had favored Belgium and earlier protocols of 20 and 27 January which had been more favorable to Holland.

335 Sir Thomas Byam Martin (1773-1854), MP Plymouth, 1818-31; Comptroller of the Navy, 1816-31; admiral of the fleet, 1849.

336 King to Grey, 18 Oct. 1831, in Grey, *Correspondence,* I, pp. 385-8. Russell's letter was addressed to the people of Birmingham, not Manchester, in response to thanks by the Birmingham Political Union for his efforts on behalf of the bill. He said, 'It is impossible that the Whisper of faction should prevail against the voice of a nation.' Russell, *Early Correspondence,* II, pp. 25-6. Russell later assured the king that he intended to calm an excited populace. Spencer Walpole, *Life of Lord John Russell,* I, pp. 172-3.

337 Sir John Cam Hobhouse (1786-1869), cr. (1851) Baron Broughton; associated with Byron; MP Westminster, 1820-33, Nottingham, 1834-47, Harwich, 1848-51; Secretary at War, 1832-3; Irish Secretary, Mar.-Apr. 1833; Commissioner of Woods and Forests, 1834; President of the Board of Control, 1835-41, 1846-52.

338 On the last night of debate on the second reading. *3 Hansard,* VIII, 311-38.

339 The Grand Duchess Hélène, daughter of Prince Paul of Württemberg, married the Grand Duke Michael, Czar Nicholas' younger brother.

340 Mary Elizabeth Ponsonby, Lady Grey (1776-1861).

341 Probably the revocation of the forty-shilling freehold franchise in Ireland.

342 The Bristol riots began when Wetherall, the Recorder, and an ultra Tory opponent of Reform, arrived on 29 October to commence the assize.

343 General William Tombes Dalrymple (1746-1832).

344 Simon Fraser, eleventh Lord Lovat (?1667-1747), the Jacobite; beheaded for high treason.

345 The ships were released shortly thereafter, government maintaining that they were bound for France and that, if indeed violations of the Foreign Enlistment Act pertained, proceedings under that statute were optional, not mandatory. See the debate in Commons, *3 Hansard,* X (9 Feb. 1832), 108-86, especially Palmerston, 153-62.

346 Augusta Sophia (1768-1840), sixth child of George III, unmarried.

347 Palmerston emphasized that Pedro become Regent, not King; that England and France associate formally with Pedro on behalf of Maria; and that Spanish intervention in Portugal on behalf of Miguel be averted by modifying the Portuguese constitution, 'the fear of which is the real cause of her support of Don Miguel.' 'Memorandum on the Affairs of Portugal,' Foreign Office, 1 Nov. 1831, HHP, BM Add. MS 51599, ff. 94-113.

348 Lady Jane Peel (1798-1861), daughter of the fourth Duke of Richmond, m. (1822) Laurence Peel, one of Sir Robert's brothers.

349 The Dowager Duchess of Richmond (1768-1842).

350 Jean-Sylvain Van de Weyer (1802-74), Belgian minister at London, 1831-67.

351 Wellington's letter to the king and his memorandum on unions of 5 Nov. 1831 are printed in *WND,* VIII, 30-4; the king's reply, 9 Nov. 1831, *ibid*., pp. 43-4.

352 At the meeting on 31 Oct. 1831, Burdett had accepted the presidency of the newly constituted National Political Union, from which he resigned in February 1832.

353 13 Nov. 1831, in Grey, *Correspondence,* I, pp. 417-18.

354 To the *Dublin Register,* 7 Nov. 1831, partially reprinted in *The Times,* 11 Nov. 1831.

355 Protocol 52, 14 Nov. 1831 (*BFSP*, XVIII, 913-14), whereby the five powers made the Twenty Four Articles a treaty between themselves and Belgium, which in effect guaranteed the independence of Belgium and its neutrality.

356 William Gregson (1790-1863), had been secretary to Sir Robert Peel, who appointed him an under secretary at the Home Office. The trick to which Holland alludes was the restriction of the £10 qualification in the second Reform Bill to those who paid rent no more frequently than in semi-annual installments (see above, n. 146). Gregson was responsible for that provision. See Le Marchant, *Althorp,* p. 325.

357 William A' Court (1779-1860), first Baron Heytesbury, Ambassador to Portugal, 1824-8; to Russia, 1828-32; Lord Lieutenant of Ireland, 1844-6; Holland scoffed at 'the false logick of Heytesbury and his uniform bias towards any thing that looks like Confederacy against France or Holy Alliance.' Holland to Palmerston, 21 May 1831, BP, CG/HO/68.

358 Heytesbury, noting the ambiguity attaching to the Polish constitution as defined at Vienna, had solicited precise instructions about his representations concerning Poland. The dispatch to which Holland refers, sent on 23 November, urged Heytesbury to urge lenient treatment toward Poland, and provided him with arguments emphasizing the liberal nature of the Polish constitution. *BFSP,* XXXVII (1848-9), 1422-30.

359 John Horsley Palmer (1779-1858), Governor of the Bank of England, 1830-2. His wife was Archbishop Howley's sister-in-law.

360 See Grey's 'Minute of the Conversation between Lord Grey and Lord Wharncliffe on November 16, 1831,' East Sheen, 16 Nov. 1831, in Grey, *Correspondence,* I, pp. 464-70.

361 This is a curious item, since the division of counties was an integral part of the bill since its introduction. Excluding the division of Yorkshire into its three ridings, the division of Lincolnshire in two, and the separation of the Isle of Wight from Hampshire—all specifically listed in the text of the first Reform Bill—Schedule H attached to that bill listed twenty-five counties to return four members each. H.C. (1830-1), *PP* (247), 14 Mar. 1831, II, 197-217. In committee, three representatives rather than two were given Buckinghamshire, Cambridgeshire, Dorsetshire, Herefordshire, Hertfordshire, and Oxfordshire, and two instead of one to Glamorgan, although these counties were not divided. The third bill, introduced on 12 December 1831 (H.C. [1831-2], *PP,* III, 1-54), contained essentially the same provisions about division of counties and additional representation for eight undivided counties, including Monmouthshire, which the amended bill of 14 March had omitted. Holland may have intended to write 'opposition to the division of counties,' 'alteration of the division of counties,' or 'elimination of the division of counties.' Many Tories had opposed the county divisions and, after the incorporation of the Chandos clause in the bill, radicals as well as some liberal Whigs opposed it on the grounds that it would leave

no independent county constituencies and would facilitate the carrying of county elections by the great families, the division of counties in effect increasing their influence by augmenting their constituencies. On the other hand, Holland's comment is also questionable because the opposition to county division was indeed 'pertinaciously resisted.' But Grey, indicated that Wharncliffe had said, with the exception of Yorkshire, Lincolnshire, and Lancashire, there were great objections to division of counties. Grey then referred to the division of counties 'as one of the points I would give up, thinking it a doubtful question, though my own opinion is upon the whole in favour of the division, in which he [Wharncliffe] agreed.' (Grey, *Correspondence,* I, p. 468.) Grey may have been overruled in cabinet.

362 As it was when Holland made the entry, forty-shilling freeholders in the borough who did not otherwise qualify for the borough franchise could vote in the county. (Text, p. 30.) See Althorp's remarks, *3 Hansard,* VI 689; Gash, *Politics in the Age of Peel,* pp. 91-2. In his conversation with Wharncliffe, Grey had stated he would reconsider this matter (Grey, *Correspondence,* I, p. 467); after the cabinet meeting, when Wharncliffe raised the point again, Grey reneged: 'This would be quite inconsistent with the principle adopted in the late Bill of continuing persons now in the enjoyment of existing rights.' 23 Nov. 1831, *ibid.,* p. 474.

363 Ministers' original opposition to all the ancient rights of franchise had included the freeman franchise, except for existing holders. (*3 Hansard,* II, 1069; *ibid.,* VI, 737, 886, 903.) The second bill extended the freeman franchise to children of existing holders. Tories vehemently, if abortively, tried to salvage the freeman franchise, as well as other ancient rights. In the preparation of the third bill, ministers thought concession on this point might palliate the 'waverers.' (Le Marchant, *Althorp,* p. 373.) Accordingly, although other ancient rights were to lapse, resident freemen by birth or servitude would retain the franchise in perpetuity. Freemen status achieved since March 1831 was excluded, because many corporations had created numerous freeman since that date. See Althorp's speech, *3 Hansard,* X, 52. See also Seymour, *Electoral Reform,* pp. 29-34.

364 Unlike the previous versions, the third bill was based on the 1831 census, which revealed that Schedules A and B of the first bills were based on distorted population returns of the preceding decade. In addition, government in the interim had accepted the Gascoyne amendment which required that the representation for England and Wales not be diminished. Twenty-three members for England and Wales then had to be restored. For the intricate formula combining population and local taxes as the criteria for borough representation, see Seymour, p. 58. Grey contended that this procedure was his own suggestion to Wharncliffe, not the other way around. 'LordWharncliffe's Plan for Altering the Reform Bill (with Grey's marginalia),' Grey, *Correspondence,* I, p. 473.

365 Charles Richard Sumner (1790-1874), Bishop of Winchester, 1827-69.

366 The cabinet minute is printed, enclosed in Grey to Taylor, 19 Nov. 1831, Grey *Correspondence,* I, pp. 432-3.

367 Spencer Joshua Alwyne Compton (1790-1851), second Marquess of Northampton, a Tory when MP for Northampton, 1812-20, but Whiggish as a peer.

368 Convention between Britain and France for the more effectual suppression of the traffic in Slaves, signed at Paris, 30 Nov. 1831, *BFSP,* XVIII (1830-1), 641-4.

369 Gabriel Julien Ouvrard (1770-1846), French financier, speculator in government loans in France, Spain, and Holland.

370 Comte Casimir de Montrond (1760-1843), an intimate of Talleyrand whom he accompanied to London.

371 [Wharncliffe's] 'Plan for the Alteration of the Reform Bill,' 23 Nov. 1831 and Grey's marginalia upon it is in Grey, *Correspondence,* I, pp. 471-8. Grey informed Wharncliffe that he would present the plan to the cabinet the next day. *Ibid.,* pp. 478-9.

372 Holland's phrasing is misleading. In the third bill twelve seats were added to boroughs originally in Schedule D; that is, they were now placed in Schedule C—boroughs to return two representatives. Eleven boroughs were withdrawn from Schedule B and

retained two representatives, instead of being reduced to one each. Palmerston proposed in cabinet that the complement of twenty-three be attained by restoring eleven members to Schedule B, five to counties of Hertford, Bucks, Cambridge, Dorset and Oxford, one to Chatham, and six to the largest towns in Schedule D. The counties listed would be divided and have four members each, rather than the three each was to have without division. This plan was rejected by the cabinet, as was Palmerston's later suggestion to leave the composition of the additional twenty-three members to the determination of the House of Lords. (Palmerston to Taylor [priv. and confid.]. 5 Dec. 1831, BP, RC/CC/1/1-2.)

373 This was not done. Marylebone and Tower Hamlets retained two members each in the final version, as did Middlesex county.

374 Edward Copleston (1776-1849), Bishop of Llandaff, 1827-49, supported Catholic Emancipation but opposed the Reform Bill. For his suggestion to Goderich see *DNB,* IV, 1100.

375 Not until 1833 did Althorp move for a select committee to inquire into the state of municipal corporations. *3 Hansard,* XV (14 Feb. 1833), 647. Althorp in this same speech reported that he had prepared a measure to give corporations to the new boroughs created by the Reform Bill, but moved this general inquiry into corporations instead. See text p. 210.

376 Henry Drummond (1786-1860), MP 1810-12; 1847-60; founded the professorship of political economy at Oxford, 1825. His letter is printed in *The Times,* 29 Nov. 1831, wherein he contended the laboring poor would not benefit from the Reform Bill and were misled by Grey and Brougham.

377 Sir Charles Wetherell (1770-1846), Tory MP Boroughbridge, 1830-2, and various constituencies since 1812. He remained Recorder for Bristol until his death.

378 John Dunning (1731-83), cr. (1782) Baron Ashburton, prominent in the Rockingham faction and mover of the famous resolution about excessive influence of the crown.

379 *3 Hansard,* IX (6 Dec. 1831), 30-6.

380 William Henry Lyttelton (1782-1837), third Baron Lyttelton. MP Worcestershire, 1807-20; a Whig peer and outstanding orator.

381 William David Murray (1806-98), styled Viscount Stormont, afterwards (1840) fourth Earl of Mansfield. Tory MP Norwich, 1830-7, Perthshire, 1837-40.

382 They were.

383 An order in Council of 2 November, actually comprising two orders, repealed all previous orders since and including the Trinidad Order of 1824 and codified and amended previous orders in council for the amelioration of slavery. *PP,* XLVI (1831-2) Cmd, 89-142. Holland is probably referring to Goderich's dispatch to the governors of colonies, 10 Dec. 1832 [*1831*], *Ann. Reg.* 1832 (Chronicle, pp. 282-6), wherein the Colonial Secretary extended the concession of further reduction of sugar duties, if the chartered colonies had their legislatures give the Order the force of law, which presumably it was to have in the Crown colonies. See Althorp and Howick, *3 Hansard,* III, 1423; XI, 807, 815. The Order in Council reached Jamaica after the commencement of the slave insurrection of December 1831.

384 There is no other reference of which the editor is aware to suggest that Durham was involved in the preparation of the Irish tithe bills.

385 Edward Herbert (1785-1848), styled Viscount Clive, afterwards (1839) second Earl of Powis. Tory MP Ludlow, 1806-39.

386 Edward Law (1790-1871), second Baron Ellenborough; earldom, 1844. In Wellington's cabinet as President of the Board of Control; Governor General of India, 1841-4; served in the Peel and Derby ministries.

387 The five additional members were added to the towns of Belfast, Limerick, Waterford, Galway, and to Dublin University. A uniform £10 household franchise was to apply to all boroughs, the freehold qualification in the counties retained at £10, thereby retaining the abolition of the forty-shilling freehold suffrage which had accompanied Emancipa-

tion. For the electoral qualification of the Irish Reform Bill, see Gash, *Politics in the Age of Peel*, pp. 50-64; Macintyre, *The Liberator*, pp. 29-37. Lord Duncannon—one of the committee of four—was primarily responsible for the Irish bill. Durham to Russell, 21 Oct. 1834, Russell Papers, P.R.O. 30/22/1C, f. 141.

388 But resident freemen already in possession of the borough franchise could, in most instances, retain it in perpetuity, and non residents who had attained freeman status before 30 March 1831 retained the franchise for life.

389 He had done so in 1824.

390 Henry Goulburn (1784-1856), Tory MP 1808-56, sitting for Cambridge University, 1831-56. Chief Secretary for Ireland, 1821-7; Chancellor of the Exchequer in Wellington's government; Home Secretary in Peel's first ministry; Chancellor of the Exchequer, 1841-6.

391 Convention between Great Britain, Austria, Prussia, and Russia, and Belgium, relative to the Belgian Fortresses, signed at London, 14 Dec. 1831, *BFSP*, XVIII (1830-1), 664-9. It was intended to be secret, submitted to Leopold for his agreement, and then presented as a *fait accompli* to France. See text, p. 101, for Holland's account of his blunder, and the letters exchanged between Grey and Palmerston on the matter, in Webster, II, pp. 818-19, 826-7.

392 James Warren Doyle (1786-1834), Roman Catholic Bishop of Kildare and Leighlin, 1819-34; wrote pamphlets under the initials J. K. L.; often testified before parliamentary committees on Irish conditions.

393 George Robert Dawson (1790-1856), MP co. Londonderry, 1815-30; Harwich, 1830-1; Peel's brother-in-law, and the first Orangeman to have declared for Catholic Emancipation.

394 *3 Hansard*, IX 547-56.

395 John Stuart-Wortley-MacKenzie (1801-55), afterwards (1845) second Baron Wharncliffe. MP Bossiney, 1831-2, West Riding, Yorks, 1841-5.

396 Lord Francis Godolphus Osborne (1777-1850), cr. (1832) Baron Godolphin, second son of the fifth Duke of Leeds. MP Cambridgeshire, 1810-31.

397 See below, p. 448 n. 1

398 Robert Edward King (1773-1854), first Viscount Lorton, an Irish representative peer, 1823-54.

399 John Maxwell-Barry (1767-1838), fifth Baron Farnham, Tory MP 1806-23; Irish representative peer, 1825-38; an Orangeman.

400 Duncannon was then MP for Kilkenny county, having narrowly won the by-election of February when he joined government as first Commissioner of Woods and Forests. O'Connell had organized opposition to Duncannon's return, but cooperating with government in the general election of 1831, compelled Duncannon's opponent to withdraw from the contest. (O'Connell to Bennet, 7 Feb. 1831, O'Connell-Bennet Papers, N.L.I; O'Connell to Duncannon, 29 Apr. 1831, FitzGerald (ed.) *Correspondence of Daniel O'Connell*, I, p. 258.) In the election of 1832, Duncannon was compelled to surrender the contest for the county, being opposed by a candidate pledged to repeal. The tithe agitation begun in 1830 originated in Kilkenny, where it subsisted.

401 Sir John Leach (1760-1834), Master of the Rolls, 1827-34.

402 A reference to the plans for the boundary acts necessitated by the Reform Bill. The rules adopted were explained by Russell, *3 Hansard*, III, 1025. See Gash, *Politics in the Age of Peel*, pp. 67ff.

403 Algiers had fallen to the French on 5 July 1830.

404 François Mauguin (1785-1854), a leader of the left-wing opposition in the Chamber of Deputies; supported the liberal movements in Spain, Belgium, and Poland.

405 Not transcribed. See Holland to Palmerston (Dec. 1831), HHP, BM Add. MS 51599, ff. 5-7.

406 Emily Mary Lamb (1787-1869), Lord Melbourne's sister, m. (1805) the fifth Lord Cowper (1778-1837). She married Lord Palmerston in 1839.

407 José Mariá de Torrijos (1791-1831) Spanish general, in exile during the 1820s. He led an abortive invasion of Spain in 1831 and was executed with fifty-two other revolutionaries by firing squad, 11 December 1831.
408 Sir William Houston (1766-1842), Lieutenant Governor of Gilbraltar, 1831-5. The Earl of Chatham was Governor General.
409 John Fullerton Elphinstone (?1784-1854); in the service of the East India Company, he spent most of his life at Canton.
410 George Macartney (1737-1806), first Earl Macartney, Ambassador to Peking, 1792-4.
411 William Pitt Amherst (1773-1857), first Earl Amherst; as envoy to Peking, 1816-17, he was received discourteously; Governor General of Bengal, 1823-8. Nominated by Peel to be Governor General of Canada in 1835, his nomination was cancelled by the succeeding Melbourne ministry.
412 Tadeusz Kosciusko (1746-1817), the Polish patriot.
413 Julian Ursin Niemcewicz (1757-1841).
414 Grand Duke Constantine of Russia (1799-1831), the second son of Czar Paul and Nicholas' elder brother, had secretly renounced the succession. He had married a Polish woman and held the title Viceroy of Poland.
415 Jan Zygmunt Skrzynecki (1787-1860), Polish general, defeated the Russians at Grochow.
416 Casimir Périer, the younger (1811-76), son of the French Prime Minister, was engaged in minor diplomatic functions from 1830 to 1846; Minister of the Interior in the Third Republic, Oct. 1871-Feb. 1872.
417 Louis Henri Joseph, Duc de Bourbon (1756-1830). He died by hanging, probably murdered. His will provided for his mistress, Mme de Feuchères, but the bulk of his estate was bequeathed to his godson, the Duc d'Aumale, fourth son of Louis Philippe.
418 Johann Peter Friedrich Ancillon (1767-1837), succeeded Bernstorff as Prussian Foreign Minister.
419 George William Chad (?1784-1849), Ambassador to Prussia, 1830-2.
420 Sir James MacDonald (1784-1832), Commissioner of the Board of Control, 1830-2, Lord High Commissioner to the Ionian Islands, 1832.

1832

1 Although the Lord Lieutenant theoretically could declare martial law or suspend habeas corpus as a preventative measure, it was generally accepted that a separate act of parliament would be required for either. The use of the Protestant Yeomanry was thought to exacerbate rather than relieve difficulties. The Constabulary, reformed by Sir Robert Peel, was limited in numbers, regulated for each barony, and could only be augmented at the request of local magistrates. Under the Peace Preservation Act of 1814, the lord lieutenant did have the power to 'proclaim' baronies to be in a state of disturbance and dispatch a salaried magistrate and fifty constables to any half-barony so proclaimed. Anglesey had utilized the power during the disturbances in Clare in the spring of 1831. The regular army in Ireland numbered approximately 20,000, but was considered as 'dissipated.' The Insurrection Act, enacted in 1807, repealed in 1810, reenacted in 1814 and continually renewed until 1822, had vested in local magistrates summary power to arrest persons and confiscate arms. But Anglesey refused to call for its reenactment. The most important power remaining to the lord lieutenant, and one which Anglesey used with limited effectiveness, was the Associations or Proclamations Act of 1829, which gave to the lord lieutenant the power to 'proclaim' any association or

society whose meeting he considered dangerous to the public peace. ([Stanley's] 'Memorandum on the Existing Means of Suppressing Disturbances in Ireland', Apr. 1831, GP, Durham University.) O'Connell evaded it, Anglesey remarking, 'No sooner had the last Proclamation put a stop to the meeting of the new Association, than another *Breakfast* was announced for to-morrow—and another Proclamation is now printing to stop it.' (Anglesey to Grey, 10 Jan. 1831. AP, P.R.O.N.I., T 1068/3, f. 84.) The Proclamations Act had expired at the dissolution of 1831 and was not renewed.

2 Brougham to Grey, 29 and 31 Dec. 1831, in Brougham, *Life and Times,* III, pp. 151-8.

3 This allusion occurs in the same context and almost in precisely the same language in Holland to Brougham, 31 Dec. 1831, *ibid.,* p. 454.

4 John Thomas Goodwin, a clerk in the Excise Office and onetime Whig election agent. Holland had called him 'a hair-brained, zealous man.' *Further Memoirs,* p. 49.

5 4 Jan. 1832, in Grey, *Correspondence,* II, pp. 68-73.

6 The figure of 21 is not in the minute, but in a letter from the king to Grey, 5 Jan. 1832, *ibid.,* pp. 72-9.

7 A reference to the abolition of hereditary descent of peerages and the restrictions imposed regarding the creation of new peers.

8 Anthony Richard Blake (1786-1849), Chief Remembrancer for Ireland until 1836.

9 Minute of Cabinet, 13 Jan. 1832, in Grey, *Correspondence,* II, pp. 96-102.

10 Francis Jeffrey (1773-1850), afterwards (1834) Lord Jeffrey, the Whig lawyer, critic, and essayist; one of the founders of the *Edinburgh Review* and its editor, 1803-29; Lord Advocate, 1830-4, MP Malton, 1831-2, Edinburgh, 1832-4, helped to prepare the Scottish reform bill and Scottish burghs bill; Judge of the Court of Session, 1834-50.

11 Francis Horner (1778-1817), MP 1806-17; one of the founders of the *Edinburgh Review.*

12 Lord John Webb Seymour (1777-1819), younger son of the tenth Duke of Somerset.

13 Cf. Sydney Smith's account in *A Memoir of the Reverend Sydney Smith By his Daughter Lady Holland with a Selection of His Letters* (London, 1855), I, pp. 22-3.

14 Francis Palgrave (1788-1861), the son of Meyer Cohen, a London stockbroker, he converted to Christianity and took his mother-in-law's maiden name; lawyer and antiquarian; contributor to both *Edinburgh* and *Quarterly*; edited the 'Rotuli Curiae Regis' for the Record Commission, 1822-34; Deputy Keeper of Her Majesty's Records, 1838-61, he promoted the study of English medieval history; knighted, 1832.

15 To Grey, 15 Jan. 1832, in Grey, *Correspondence,* II, pp. 108-15.

16 Minute of Cabinet, 17 Jan. 1832, *ibid.,* pp. 127-8.

17 Andrew Thomas Blayney (1770-1834), eleventh Lord Blayney (I).

18 Rowland Hill (1772-1842), first Baron Hill, afterwards (1842), Viscount Hill; Tory MP Shrewsbury, 1812-14; general; commander in chief, 1828-42.

19 Blayney's speech had been reported in the *Dublin Evening Mail*; his retractions and apologies in *The Times,* 17 Feb. 1832.

20 Lord William Cavendish Bentinck (1774-1839), second son of the third Duke of Portland; Governor General of Bengal, 1827-33; Governor General of India, 1833-5; liberal MP Glasgow, 1836-9.

21 Probably Rear-Admiral Sir Edward Campbell Rich Owen (1771-1849), Commander in Chief in the East Indies, 1828-32; admiral, 1846.

22 Probably Vice Admiral Sir John Gore (1772-1836), Commander in Chief East India Station, 1832-4.

23 Percy Clinton Sydney Smythe (1780-1855), sixth Viscount Strangford, diplomat until 1828; intimate of Croker, Moore, and Rogers.

24 Henry Stephen Fox (1791-1846), only son of General Henry Edward Fox; Chargé d'Affaires, Sardinia 1824-5; Sicily, 1827-8; Ambassador to Argentina, 1831-2; to USA, 1836-44.

25 John Goodwin, consul at Cape Verde Islands, 1828-32; Naples, 1832-4; Palermo, 1834-70.

26 Richard Temple Nugent Brydges Chandos Grenville (1776-1839), first Duke of Buckingham and Chandos.

27 Sir Henry Halford (1766-1844), President of the College of Physicians, 1820-44; attended George IV, William IV, and Queen Victoria.

28 *3 Hansard,* IX, 891-2.

29 Probably Lord Haddington.

30 John Charles Herries (1778-1855), MP Harwich, 1823-41, Stamford, 1847-53; Chancellor of the Exchequer in Goderich's ministry, 1827-8; Master of the Mint, 1828-30; President of the Board of Trade, 1830.

After the Napoleonic Wars, the British and Dutch crowns had each assumed one-half the interest on a loan which Russia had borrowed from a Dutch banking house. The charge was to cease should the king of the Netherlands lose sovereignty over Belgium. Since Britain subsequently supported Belgian sovereignty, Russia demanded that Britain was bound to continue payment of the charge. Palmerston eventually agreed, in a convention of 16 November 1831, that Britain continue to defray her share; that agreement probably induced Russia to sign the Twenty-four Articles of 15 November. In parliament, however, ministers could only plead that they were bound in honor to continue payment. Herries' resolutions contended such payments were now illegal and unwarranted, and two subsequent debates on the Russian Dutch loan ensued in the 1832 session, until the convention of 16 November was ratified, 2 & 3 Will. IV, c. 81. The loan was not paid off in full until 1907. See Frank Whitsun Fetter, 'The Russian Loan of 1855: A Postscript,' *Economica,* XXVII (Nov. 1961), 422.

31 Government carried the division, 238-214. *3 Hansard,* IX, 968-72.

32 Alexander Baring (1774-1848), afterwards (1835) first Baron Ashburton; second son of Sir Francis Baring, the London merchant banker; MP 1806-35. Opposed to the Reform Bill, he controlled three seats, two for Callington and one for Thetford. He agreed to join Wellington's uncompleted ministry in 1832 as Chancellor of the Exchequer.

33 In divisions on resolutions to suspend the Russian Dutch loan.

34 Charles Tennyson (1784-1861), after Tennyson-D'Eyncourt, Whig MP 1818-52, then sitting for Stamford; Clerk of the Ordnance, 1830-2.

35 Thomas Francis Kennedy (1788-1879), Whig MP Ayr, 1818-34; Lord of the Treasury, 1832-4; Clerk of the Ordnance, 1832-3; Paymaster of the Irish Civil Service, 1837-50; Commissioner of Woods and Forests, 1850-4; a friend of Cockburn and Jeffrey, he helped in preparing the draft of the Scottish Reform Bill.

36 Sir Benjamin Hobhouse (1757-1831), MP 1797-1818.

37 Lord John's uncle, Lord William Russell (1767-1840), third son of the fourth Duke of Bedford; murdered by his valet.

38 Frances, Lady Londonderry (d. 1833), eldest daughter of the first Earl Camden, had married the first Marquess of Londonderry in 1775.

39 Protocol 55, 31 Jan. 1832, *BFSP,* XIX, 92-3.

40 Sir John Vaughan (1769-1839), Baron of the Exchequer, 1827-34; Justice of Common Pleas, 1834-9; brother of Sir Henry Halford and Sir Charles Vaughan.

41 Sir James Parke (1782-1868), cr. (1856) Baron Wensleydale. Justice of King's Bench, 1828-34; Baron of the Exchequer, 1834-55.

42 Francis Ludlow Holt (?1780-1844), Vice Chancellor of the County Palatine of Lancaster, 1826-44.

43 John Rushout (1770-1859), second Baron Northwick, voted against the second reading in 1831 and for the bill in 1832.

44 William Holmes (?1778-1851), MP 1808-32, then sitting for Haslemere; MP Berwick-on-Tweed 1837-41; chief Tory whip in the House of Commons for thirty years; treasurer of the Ordnance, 1820-30. By special permission of the Duke of Wellington, he was allowed to vote against Catholic Emancipation.

45 Cornelius O'Callaghan (1775-1857), first Viscount Lismore (I), cr. (1838), Baron Lismore (UK).

46 Joseph Leeson (1799-1866), fourth Earl of Milltown.

47 Francis James Mathew (1768-1833), second Earl of Llandaff, had opposed the Union and supported Catholic Emancipation.

48 Valentine Browne (1788-1853), second Earl of Kenmare (I), cr. (1841) Baron Kenmare (UK).

49 Jenico Preston (1775-1860), Viscount Gormanston, a Roman Catholic.

50 Richard Wilson Green (1791-1861), then a clerk in the Irish Office; law advisor in Dublin Castle, 1831-5; First Serjeant at Law, Ireland, 1838-42; Solicitor General, Ireland, 1842-6; Attorney General, Ireland, 1846; Baron of the Exchequer, Ireland, 1852-61.

51 Philip Yorke (1757-1834), third Earl of Hardwicke, had generally been Tory, though he supported Catholic Emancipation; Lord Lieutenant of Ireland, 1801-6.

52 Thomas Slingsby Duncombe (1796-1861), MP Hertford borough, 1826-32, Finsbury, 1834-61; at first Whiggish, he turned more radical in the 1830s.

53 Sir Richard Rawlinson Vyvyan (1800-79), ultra Tory MP 1825-37, then sitting for Okehampton; MP Helston, 1841-57. A leader of a rather amorphous group of ultra Tory country gentlemen in the House of Commons, he repeatedly attacked the Whigs' foreign policy, especially on Belgian affairs. See B. T. Bradfield, 'Sir Richard Vyvyan and the Country Gentlemen, 1830-34,' *Eng. Hist. Rev.*, LXXXIII (Oct. 1968), 729-43.

54 William Minchin (d. 1832) had been Solicitor and Clerk in Court for Plaintiffs in the Duchy Court of Lancaster.

55 Stephen Moore (d. 1841) succeeded Minchin.

56 The second report of the Committee in June 1832 had in effect already been formulated by Stanley. See A. D. Kriegel, 'The Irish Policy of Lord Grey's Government,' pp. 29-31.

57 Harrowby's letter is in *WND*, VIII, 176-8.

58 5 Feb. 1832, in Parker, *Peel*, II, pp. 199-202.

59 Taylor to Grey (priv.) with enclosures of Taylor's Minute of Conversation with Lord Wharncliffe, 8 Feb. 1832, in Grey, *Correspondence*, II, pp. 193-4.

60 Sir William Knighton (1776-1834), physician to George IV when Prince of Wales, he then served as George's IV's private secretary; employed on confidential missions abroad, 1823-6.

61 I.e., Stanley's bill to advance tithe arrears to the Irish clergy, subsequently to be collected as crown debt, endorsed by the Commons Committee on Tithes ('Committee on Tithes: Stanley's Observations,' circulated 5 Jan. 1832, P.R.O., HO 100/241, nos 38-42); Stanley to Anglesey, 20 Dec. 1831, AP, P.R.O.N.I., T1068/36, ff. 139-40.

62 Anglesey advocated an arrangement which would have incorporated tithe reform with the reduction and sale of bishops' lands, abolition of church cess, and payment by the state to the Catholic clergy. Most important, Anglesey assumed that a surplus would remain even after paying the Catholic clergy, and that it should be appropriated for secular purposes in Ireland – a question which was eventually to split the Whig party, consolidate the opposition, and provide the most cohesive issue in English party politics. [Anglesey's] 'Paper on Tithes and Church and Bishops Lands, for the Consideration of the Cabinet,' 18 Jan. 1832, *ibid.*; Anglesey to Grey, 19 Feb. 1832, *ibid.*, T1068/8, p. 228 [typescript copy].

63 Robert Shapland Carew (1787-1856), cr. (1834), Baron Carew (I), cr. (1838) Baron Carew (UK); Whig MP co. Wexford, 1812-30, 1831-4.

64 The letter was written by Taylor to Grey (priv.), 14 Feb. 1832, in Grey, *Correspondence*, II, p. 216; *ibid.*, 15 Feb. 1832, pp. 223-5.

65 John Russell (1766-1839), sixth Duke of Bedford, a Whig elder statesman; one of the originators, with Grey, of the Friends of the People.

66 Passed as 2 & 3 Will. IV, c. 10.

67 The letter was from Taylor to Grey (priv.), 15 Feb. 1832, Grey, *Correspondence*, II, pp. 223-5; Grey's minute of his conversation with Harrowby and Wharncliffe is printed, *ibid.*, pp. 230-1.

68 Charles Wood (1800-85) cr. (1866) Viscount Halifax, m. (1829) Lord Grey's fifth daughter, Mary. MP 1826-66; Whig whip in the 1830s; Joint Secretary to the Treasury, 1832-4; Secretary to the Admiralty, 1835-9; Chancellor of the Exchequer, 1846-52; President of the Board of Control, 1852; First Lord of the Admiralty, 1855; Lord Privy Seal, 1870-4.

69 Dudley Ryder (1798-1882), styled Viscount Sandon, afterwards (1847) second Earl of Harrowby. MP Tiverton, 1819-31; Liverpool, 1831-47; he had joined the opposition on the civil-list motion which defeated Wellington's government. Secretary to the Board of Control in Grey's government, Dec. 1830-May 1831, when he resigned.

70 The Archbishop of York and eleven other bishops voted for the second reading on 14 April 1832. Fifteen bishops voted against.

71 George William Frederick Osborn, (1775-1838), sixth Duke of Leeds, was Governor of the Scilly Isles, 1801-38; Master of the Horse, 1827-30; one of the few greater noblemen who followed Wellington's switch on Catholic Emancipation.

72 Taylor's letters to Grey (priv.), 17 and 18 Feb. 1832, Grey, *Correspondence*, II, pp. 233-6.

73 Probably George Byng (1764-1847), MP Middlesex, 1790-1847; elder brother of Sir John Byng.

74 Etienne François, Duc de Choiseul (1719-85), French Foreign Minister, 1758-70.

75 John Ellis (1757-1832), Seaford's older brother.

76 William Burge (?1786-1849), MP Eye, 1831-2; he had spent twenty years in Jamaica, becoming attorney general of the island for twelve years, then agent for Jamaica in London; advocated representation of the colonies in the imperial parliament.

77 George Augustus Frederick Henry Bridgeman (1789-1865), second Earl of Bradford, voted against the second reading of the Reform Bill in 1831 and for it in 1832.

78 Charles Brudenell-Bruce (1773-1856), first Marquess of Ailesbury, had voted against the second reading in 1831 and again in 1832.

79 James Henry Monk (1784-1856), Bishop of Gloucester, 1830-6, of Gloucester and Bristol, 1836-56. He voted against the second reading in April 1832.

80 John Henry Manners (1778-1857), fifth Duke of Rutland, a Tory.

81 Robert Jocelyn (1788-1870) third Earl of Roden (I), cr. (1821) Baron Clanbrassil (UK), was Grand Master of the Orange Society.

82 The matter of the secretaryship to the Irish Master of the Rolls, *3 Hansard,* X, 637-63.

83 Charles Chetwynd Chetwynd-Talbot (1777-1849), second Earl Talbot, Lord Lieutenant of Ireland, 1817-21.

84 Edward Bootle Wilbraham (formerly Wilbraham-Bootle) (1771-1853), cr. (1828) Baron Skelmersdale, m. (1796) Mary Elizabeth Taylor, Sir Herbert's sister (d. 1840). Tory MP 1795-1828. He was Stanley's father-in-law. He voted against the second reading in 1831 and did not vote in 1832.

85 Captain Sir John Marshall, admiral, 1850, KCH, 1832. The Guelphic order, founded by George IV in 1815, was designed to recognize Hanoverian troops who had distinguished themselves at Waterloo. It was usually distributed thereafter to military and naval officers ineligible for the Bath, and was liberally conferred by William IV, who nominated 569 British subjects. See Charles R. Dodd, *A Manual of Dignities, Privileges and Precedence* (London, 1842), pp. 245-7.

86 George Boyle (?1765-1843), fourth Earl of Glasgow, a Tory and Scottish representative peer, 1790-1815; cr. (1815) Baron Ross (UK). He did not vote on the second reading of the Reform Bill in April 1832.

87 George Isaac Huntingford (1748-1832), Bishop of Gloucester, 1802-15, of Hereford 1815-32; did not vote in April 1832 on the second reading of the Reform Bill.

88 John Bourke (1766-1849), fourth Earl of Mayo, a Tory and Irish representative peer, 1816-49. Voted against the bill on the second reading in April 1832.

89 George Sinclair (1790-1868), second baronet (1835). MP Caithness-shire, 1811-12, 1818-20, 1831-41; supporting the Reform Bill, he refused an invitation to dine with the king in 1832; associated with Stanley and Graham in 1835; chairman of Burdett's election committee in 1837.

90 Somerset Lowry-Corry (1774-1841), second Earl Belmore, an Irish representative peer, 1819-41; Governor in Chief of Jamaica, 1828-32.

91 Archibald Acheson (1776-1849), second Earl of Gosford, a Whig and Irish representative peer, 1811-49; cr. (1835) Baron Worlingham (UK); Governor of Canada, 1835-8.

92 The Commission for National Education in Ireland had already been established by the Irish Office, circumventing the need for statute. Stanley's Education Bill of 1831 never reached the second reading. Subsequent votes for Irish education were actually votes for sums to be granted the lord lieutenant for support of the new national education scheme. Until 1848 the Commission for National Education was funded by the lord lieutenant.

93 The Clergy Relief or Arrears Bill, was enacted as 2 Will. IV, c. 41. The remainder of Stanley's tithe plan, which included proposals for permanent and compulsory composition, the establishment of ecclesiastical corporations in each diocese, and the intricate procedure for commutation of tithe to a charge upon the land, comprised three separate bills. Since the government had to await the reports of the parliamentary committees on tithes, Stanley was unable to present his legislation until 25 July 1832. The government carried the first bill, which made composition permanent and compulsory and provided for its eventual assumption by the owner-in-fee. 2 & 3 Will. IV, c. 119.

94 Lord Belmore had declared martial law in Jamaica on 30 Dec. 1831. Goderich's dispatches of 1 Mar. 1832 incorporating the postponement of the orders in council is in H.C. 1831-2, *PP,* XLVII (285), 297-306.

95 With no question before the House, Londonderry delivered a tirade against Plunket's misuse of patronage and extensive emoluments. Called to order, he stated that he intended to present a petition and continued his harangue. When the petition was called for, he refused to submit it, apparently not having been equipped with one or having one on another subject. Londonderry apologized for a breach of order. *3 Hansard,* X, 1040-57.

96 The revolutions of 1830 in Bologna and the Papal States had been repulsed by Austrian intervention. The subsequent establishment of a conference to reform the corrupt administration of the Papal States averted the prospect of French invasion of Italy through Piedmont to counter Austrian influence. A subsequent rising in the Papal States, however, led to another Austrian intervention and this time, in early 1832, France responded by the occupation of Ancona. The French commander hoisted the tricolor and issued manifestoes which suggested the incitement of revolution in the peninsula.

97 Sir Arthur Paget (1771-1840), diplomat; Anglesey's brother.

98 Thomas Howard (1776-1851), sixteenth Earl of Suffolk; William Fitzhardinge Berkeley (1786-1857), cr. (1831) Baron Segrave, cr. (1841) Earl Fitzhardinge. Both voted for the second reading in April 1832.

99 11 Geo. IV and 1 Will. IV, c. 66, eliminated capital punishment for forgery with the exception of forging coin, the seals of office, exchequer bills, and negotiable securities. The retention of capital punishment for these offences resulted from Eldon's amendments of the bill in the Lords. Brougham's bill passed as 2 & 3 Will. IV, c. 123 and commuted the death penalties in the earlier bill to transportation, except for forgery of wills.

100 Anton Rudolph, Count Apponyi (1782-1852), Austrian diplomat; Ambassador to France, 1826-48.

101 Alexis Feodorovich, Count Orloff (1788-1861), Russian diplomat; cr. prince (1856) and president of the council of state.

102 *3 Hansard*, XI, 30-1. Bishops who voted for the motion and against government were: Rochester, Bath and Wells, Bangor, Carlisle, Exeter, Lichfield and Coventry.

103 Sir Willoughby Cotton (1783-1860), general; Lieutenant Governor of Jamaica, 1829-34.

104 Lieutenant-General Sir Charles Colville (1770-1843), Governor of Mauritius, 1828-32; succeeded by Sir William Nicolay (1771-1842), Governor of Mauritius, 1832-40.

105 Sir Henry Hardinge (1785-1856) afterwards (1846) first Viscount Hardinge. Tory MP 1820-44, sitting for Newport, 1830-2; Secretary at War, 1828-30, 1841-4; Irish Secretary, 1830 and 1834-5; Governor General of India, 1844-7.

106 Lord Fitzroy James Henry Somerset (1788-1855), afterwards (1852) first Baron Raglan, youngest son of the fifth Duke of Beaufort; military secretary to the Duke of Wellington as commander-in-chief, 1827-52; Master General of the Ordnance, 1852-5; commander of British troops in the Crimea, 1854.

107 Thomas Spring Rice (1790-1866), afterwards (1839) Baron Monteagle; Secretary to the Treasury, 1830-4; Chancellor of the Exchequer, 1835-9.

108 William Henry John Scott (1795-1832), secretary of decrees and injunctions, 1816-21 and registrar of affidavits in the Court of Chancery; MP 1818-30.

109 Before the Chamber of Deputies on 7 Mar. 1832, a summary and justification of French foreign policy since the July Revolution; printed in *The Times*, 10 Mar. 1832.

110 Kenyon's version was abandoned in the Lords, but a similar bill originating in the Commons was passed as 2 & 3 Will. IV, c. 96.

111 Ailesbury voted against the second reading on 14 April 1832, as he had the previous autumn.

112 Sir Frederick Adam (1781-1853), fourth son of William Adam; Lord High Commissioner of the Ionian Islands, 1824-31; Governor of Madras, 1832-7; general.

113 The other sons of William Adam were Sir Charles Adam (1780-1853), admiral, MP Kinross, 1831-2, Clackmannan and Kinross, 1833-41, a lord of the admiralty, 1835-41; William George Adam, who succeeded his father as auditor to the Duke of Bedford; another brother had died in 1825, having served as acting governor general of Bengal.

114 William Astell (1774-1847), Tory MP Bridgewater, 1807-32, Bedfordshire, 1841-7; a director of the East India Company since 1800.

115 An Ember day on the Church calendar.

116 Otto (1815-67), second son of Louis I of Bavaria; King of Greece, 1833-62.

117 Henry Phillpotts (1778-1869) was Bishop of Exeter (1830-69); a vigorous opponent of the Whig governments and frequent advocate for the property rights of the Church.

118 The division for government and against the motion was 125-87. *3 Hansard*, XI, 648-50.

119 Archibald John Primrose (1783-1868), fourth Earl of Rosebery, joined the Whigs in the late 1820s and supported the Reform Bill; grandfather of the prime minister.

120 Two of Aberdeen's five brothers were then captains in the navy. The reference is probably to William Gordon (1785-1858). MP Aberdeenshire, 1820-54; a lord of the admiralty, 1841-6; vice-admiral, 1854. The other Captain Gordon was the youngest of Aberdeen's surviving brothers, John Gordon (1792-1862).

121 Minute of Cabinet held at the Foreign Office, 27 Mar. 1832, in Grey, *Correspondence*, II, pp. 288-91.

122 George William Finch-Hatton (1791-1858), tenth Earl of Winchelsea, a zealous Tory and guardian of the Church. He had a duel with Wellington in 1829 because of their clash on Catholic Emancipation.

123 See Molière, *Les Fourberies de Scapin*, II, vii.

124 The king to Grey, 30 Mar. 1832, in Grey, *Correspondence*, II, pp. 292-9.

125 Gilbert Elliot (1782-1859), second Earl of Minto; ambassador to Prussia, 1832-4; First Lord of the Admiralty, 1835-41.

126 John William Ward (1781-1833), first Earl of Dudley. Tory MP 1802-23; Foreign Secretary, 1827-8. First associated with Pitt, he then joined Grenville and the Whigs and later became a Canningite; opposed the Reform Bill; went mad in 1832.

127 See Sanders, *The Holland House Circle*, pp. 315-16; Lord Ilchester, *Chronicles of Holland House*, pp. 142-4.

128 Edward Harbord (1781-1835), third Baron Suffield.

129 Grey's 'Minute of Conversation with the King,' 1 Apr. 1832, in Grey, *Correspondence*, II, pp. 299-306.

130 The paper was submitted as a Cabinet Minute, 3 Apr. 1832, *ibid.*, pp. 307-11.

131 The king to Grey, 4 Apr. 1832, *ibid.*, pp. 311-27.

132 The division on the second reading upheld the bill, 184-175. *3 Hansard*, XII (13 Apr. 1832), 454-60.

133 Adelaide, Princess of Orléans (1777-1847), younger sister of Louis Philippe.

134 Marie Amélie of Naples and the Two Sicilies (1782-1866) married Louis Philippe in 1809.

135 The king to Grey, 16 Apr. 1832, in Grey, *Correspondence*, II, pp. 351-5, enclosed in Taylor to Grey (priv. and confid.), 16 Apr. 1832, *ibid.*, pp. 355-7.

136 Grey to the king, 17 Apr. 1832, *ibid.*, pp. 358-65.

137 Articles IX, XII, and XIII concerning navigation of the Scheldt, the construction of roads, and the division of the public debt of the Netherlands. See Bulwer, *Palmerston*, II, p. 135. Austria and Prussia had ratified the treaty on 18 April with reservations about the rights of the German Confederation in Luxemburg. (Protocol 57, *BFSP*, XIX (1831-32), 97.) The Russians ratified on 4 May with their reservations. (Protocol 58, *ibid.*, 98.)

138 George Hamilton Seymour (1797-1880), diplomat; minister resident at Florence, 1831-6, to Tuscany, Modena, and Parma; special mission to Rome, 1832; envoy to Belgium, 1836-47; knighted, 1836.

139 Henry Unwin Addington (1790-1870), Ambassador to Spain, 1830-3; permanent Under Secretary for Foreign Affairs, 1842-54.

140 Karl Robert, Count Nesselrode (1780-1862), Russian Foreign Minister, 1821-56.

141 No, he was not. Whittington Landon (?1758-1838), was Dean of Exeter since 1813.

142 Edward Grey (1782-1837), Dean of Hereford, 1830-2; Bishop of Hereford, 1832-7.

143 Brownlow North (1741-1820), Lord North's brother; Bishop of Coventry, 1771-4; of Worcester, 1774-81; of Winchester, 1781-1820. His rapid advancement was attributable to his brother's situation. When North was made Bishop of Coventry at the age of thirty in 1771, Fox questioned whether he was not too young to be a bishop, to which Lord North replied 'that his brother was no doubt young to be a bishop, but when he was older he would not have a brother prime minister.' Quoted in GEC, VI, 217n.

144 The barony of Berners had been in abeyance for ninety years, when Robert Wilson (d. 1838) was summoned to parliament by writ as Lord Berners. A colonel in the army, he was liberal politically.

145 The East India Company's charter had been extended for twenty-year periods in 1773, 1793, and 1813. In 1813, however, it lost its monopoly in trade with India, but retained its administrative control and its trading monopoly with China. The India Act of 1833 compelled the company to divest itself of commercial operations in India and compensated proprietors £630,000, the sum to be charged on the Indian territorial revenues.

146 The Protocols and the Belgian declaration are in *BFSP*, XIX (1831-32), 98-9.

147 The reference is to the suspension of the Order in Council of 2 Nov. 1831 by Goderich on 12 May 1832 during the inquiries of the parliamentary committees which sat through the end of the session.

148 Nicholas Vansittart Bexley (1766-1851), first Baron Bexley. MP 1796-1823; Chancellor of the Exchequer, 1812-23; Chancellor of the Duchy of Lancaster, 1823-8.

149 Henry Pelham Fiennes Pelham Clinton (1785-1851), fourth Duke of Newcastle, an ultra Tory. He had evicted tenants at Newark for refusing to vote for his nominees in the election of 1830, remarking in Parliament, 'Is it not lawful for me to do what I please with mine own?' *3 Hansard,* I (3 Dec. 1830), 752. He became Gladstone's patron.

150 *3 Hansard,* XII, 723-8.

151 John Bird Sumner (1780-1862), Bishop of Chester, 1828-48; Archbishop of Canterbury, 1848-62; voted for Catholic Emancipation and the Reform Bill.

152 Maltby of Chichester and John Banks Jenkinson (1781-1840), Bishop of St Davids, 1825-40.

153 Cf. Ellenborough's Diary, 7 May [1832], in Aspinall, *Three Diaries,* pp. 239-40.

154 The minute is in Grey, *Correspondence,* II, pp. 394-5. It did not specify a number, but referred to 'such a number of persons as might insure the success of the Bill in all its essential principles.'

155 The king to Grey, 9 May 1832, *ibid.,* pp. 395-6.

156 Sarah Sophia, Countess of Jersey (1785-1867), daughter of the tenth Earl of Westmoreland, m. (1804) Viscount Villiers, afterwards (1805) Earl of Jersey.

157 Alexander Wedderburn (1733-1805) first Earl of Rosslyn, Lord Chancellor as Lord Loughborough, 1793-1801.

158 Henry John Chetwynd-Talbot (1803-68), son of Earl Talbot, styled Viscount Ingestre (1826-49), succeeded (1856) his distant cousin as eighteenth Earl of Shrewsbury. MP Hertford, 1830-1, Armagh, May-Aug. 1831, Dublin, 1831-2, South Staffordshire, 1837-49.

159 Charles Watkin Williams Wynn (1775-1850), MP Old Sarum, 1797-9, Montgomeryshire, 1799-1850; President of Board of Control, 1822-8; opposed the Wellington government after he failed to obtain office; Secretary at War in Grey's ministry, Nov. 1830-May 1831, he objected to the disfranchisement provisions of the Reform Bill and resigned; supported General Gascoyne's amendment, but voted for the second reading; Chancellor of the Duchy of Lancaster in Peel's first ministry, 1834-5.

160 Davies Gilbert, formerly Giddy (1767-1839), assumed his wife's maiden name of Gilbert in 1817. MP Helston 1804-6, Bodmin, 1806-32. President of the Royal Society, 1827-30.

161 On 10 May. *3 Hansard,* XII, 866-8.

162 Nathan Meyer Rothschild (1777-1836), the financier, established the family's branch in London, 1805.

163 The king to Grey, 15 May 1832, in Grey, *Correspondence,* II, p. 406.

164 *Ibid.,* pp. 410-11.

165 *Ibid.,* pp. 411-17.

166 16 May 1832, *ibid.,* pp. 418-19.

167 *Ibid.,* pp. 423-4.

168 William George Hay (1801-46), eighteenth Earl of Errol, cr. (1831) Baron Kilmarnock (UK); Master of the Horse to the Queen Consort, 1830-4; Scottish representative peer, 1823-31; Master of the Buckhounds, 1835-9.

169 In Grey, *Correspondence,* II, pp. 426-9.

170 There were three such divisions: on May 22 May the Lords divided, 91-36 in favor of giving members to metropolitan districts; on 23 May Lord Ellenborough's proposal to give six members to the county of Lancaster was defeated, 70-15; on 24 May Wharncliffe's amendment to prevent freeholders resident in towns from voting in the counties was defeated, 84-23. *3 Hansard,* XII, 1255-8, 1394-6, XIII, 31-4.

171 Lady Affleck (1748-1835), Lady Holland's mother, was the daughter of Thomas Clarke of New York and widow of Richard Vassall of Jamaica. She married Sir Gilbert Affleck (1740-1808) in 1796. They had no children. In 1835, Lady Holland inherited her mother's house in South Street, so small that she called it the 'Nutshell.' See Ilchester (ed.), *Lady Holland to her Son,* p. 159.

172 This might refer to the presentation of a petition from the Lord Mayor, Alderman and Common Council of London in favor of the Reform Bill. *3 Hansard,* XII (7 May 1832), 669-72.

173 Sir James Kempt (1764-1854), general; Governor General of Canada, 1828-30; Master General of the Ordnance, 1834-8.

174 Unidentified.

175 Henry Hall Gage (1791-1877), fourth Viscount Gage. One of the twenty-two Tory peers who refused to abstain and voted against the third reading of the Reform Bill.

176 Gateshead's inclusion in Schedule D—new boroughs to return one member—was opposed on grounds that it be included within the constituency of Newcastle. Gateshead, along with the new boroughs of Tynemouth and South Shields and the established boroughs of Newcastle and Sunderland, comprised what Tory interests conceived to be a bloc vote for the government.

177 Taylor to Grey (priv.), 28 May 1832, in Grey, *Correspondence,* II, pp. 447-9.

178 *Ibid.,* pp. 450-3.

179 Henry Jeffery Flower (1776-1847), fourth Viscount Ashbrook, a lord of the bedchamber, 1832-7.

180 Duchess of Cumberland (1778-1841). See the gossipy note about her by the Duchesse de Dino in GEC, III, 575.

181 Newcastle intended to move that the Lords express their opinion about the prerogative of creating peers, and subsequently he withdrew a motion for an address to the crown for production of the circular letter to peers which urged them to abstain from further obstructing the progress of the Reform Bill. *3 Hansard,* XII (21 and 22 May 1832); 1096, 1218-20.

182 The Not Contents on the third reading are listed in *3 Hansard,* XIII, 374.

183 Marie Caroline de Bourbon, Duchesse de Berri (1798-1870), daughter-in-law of Charles X. She led a Bourbon rising in the Midi and Vendée during the spring and summer of 1832; captured and subsequently released in June 1833. The Bourbons then disassociated themselves from her and she moved to Venice with her second husband.

184 William Frederick (1776-1834), Duke of Gloucester, m. (1816) Princess Mary, fourth daughter of George III. He postponed marriage until the age of 40, lest Princess Charlotte, who married ten weeks earlier than he, find no eligible foreign prince to wed. GEC, V, 746n.

185 Sir John Hamilton Macgill Dalrymple (1771-1853), afterwards (1840) eighth Earl of Stair, cr. (1841) Baron Oxenford (UK), then a colonel in the 92nd foot, 1831-43; Whig MP Edinburgh co., 1833-4; Baron of the Exchequer, Scotland.

186 Sponsored by William Ewart (1798-1869), then MP for Liverpool, the bill provided for the abolition of capital punishment in specified cases. See Taylor to Grey, 6 June 1832, in Grey, *Correspondence,* II, pp. 463-4.

187 The five were Grey, Wellesley, Brougham, Lansdowne and Holland. Lord Durham was the sixth commissioner.

188 It began on 5 June, on the occasion of the funeral of General Lamarque.

189 Walter Francis Montagu-Douglas-Scott (1806-84), fifth Duke of Buccleuch. Lord Privy Seal, 1842-6.

190 Passed as 2 Will. IV, c. 54, it provided that vacancies not be filled, the court to be abolished upon the death of the last Exchequer judge, whereupon its duties would be assumed by one of the lords of the session to be appointed by the crown. Administrative duties of the court were transferred to the Treasury by 3 & 4 Will. IV, c. 13. Subsequently modified by 2 and 3 Vict. c. 36 and 19 & 20 Vict. c. 56. See Haydn, *Dignities,* p. 523.

191 Sir William Grant (1752-1832), MP 1790-1812; Master of the Rolls, 1801-17.

192 John Clerk (1757-1832), assumed the title Lord Eldin, 1823; Scottish judge, 1823-32.

193 Jeremy Bentham (1748-1832).

194 George Eden (1784-1849), second Baron Auckland, earldom, 1839; President of the Board of Trade and Master of the Mint, 1830-4; Governor General of India, 1835-41.

195 Robert Adam Dundas, later Christopher, later Nisbet-Hamilton (1804-77), MP Ipswich, 1827-31, 1835, Edinburgh city, 1831-2, North Lincolnshire, 1837-57; Chancellor of the Duchy of Lancaster, 1852.

196 Frederick Markham (1805-55), a grandson of the Archbishop of York, then a captain in the 32nd foot.

197 Frederica Markham, Lady Mansfield (1774-1860), daughter of the former Archbishop of York.

198 Possibly John MacDonald (d. 1850), then in the 92nd foot; knighted, 1847.

199 Thomas William Anson (1795-1854), Viscount Anson, cr. (1831) Earl of Lichfield. Master of the Buckhounds, 1830-4.

200 Emilia Olivia Usher St George, Lady Foley (1786-1863).

201 Probably Lady Olivia Kinnaird (d. 1897) eldest daughter of the eighth Lord Kinnaird.

202 George William Fox Kinnaird (1807-78), ninth Lord Kinnaird (S), cr. (1831) Baron Rossie (UK). Master of the Buckhounds, 1839-41.

203 To address the Crown to uphold Protestantism in Ireland. Debated and defeated 120-79 on 2 July. *3 Hansard,* XIII, 1189-237.

204 On Sir Robert Heron's motion in the committee stage of the Irish Reform Bill that the University of Dublin continue to return one member only. Rejected, 147-97. *3 Hansard,* XIII (13 June 1832), 608.

205 In late May 1832, Althorp had moved the establishment of a secret committee to consider renewal of the bank charter. Having made no report by the time of prorogation, its testimony was printed and the committee dissolved. H.C. 1831-32, *PP,* VI (722).

206 Robert John Harper, since 1825 Surveyor of Woods in the North Parts of the Duchy of Lancaster.

207 Joseph Alexandre Jacques Durant, styled Durant de Maureuil (1769-1835), French diplomat; interim ambassador in London after Talleyrand's departure; Ambassador to Naples, 1834-5.

208 The leasehold qualification for voting in the Irish counties had originally been set at £50.

209 These other two bills were not introduced before the end of the session.

210 Henry Willoughby (1761-1835), sixth Baron Middleton. A Tory, he voted for the second reading of the Reform Bill in April 1832.

211 Brougham continued reforms of the criminal code which Peel had initiated a decade earlier. Felonies for which capital punishment was retained when Peel left office included murder, attempted murder, rape, forgery, coining, highway robbery, cattle-stealing, arson, burglary, and house breaking. It could also be imposed for sacrilege, letter-stealing, returning from transportation, and other specified offences. Horse and sheep stealing, housebreaking, and coining false money were removed from the list of capital crimes in 1832. (2 & 3 Will. IV, c. 34 and c. 62.) Most cases of forgery were removed by 2 & 3 Will. IV, c. 123, but the Lords insisted on retaining the death penalty for forgery of wills, powers of attorney, and transfers of stock.

212 Sir George Clerk (1787-1867), MP Edinburgh co., 1811-21, 1835-7, Stamford, 1838-47, Dover, 1847-52; Tory whip 1833-7. Clerk suggested the imposition of a landed qualification for borough members, hitherto exempt from any. The amendment was withdrawn before final passage.

213 O'Connell referred to the Czar as a 'miscreant conqueror'; his remarks were followed by similar criticism from Cutlar Fergusson, Sandon, Morpeth, Ebrington, and Ruthven. *3 Hansard,* XIII (28 June 1832), 1115-52.

214 Thomas Pelham (1756-1826), second Earl of Chichester, Home Secretary, 1801-3.

215 Princess Louise of Saxe-Weimar (1817-32), Queen Adelaide's niece.

216 To regulate the acquisition and use of corpses by medical schools or schools of 'anatomy.' (2 & 3 Will. IV, c. 75.)

217 *3 Hansard*, XIV (12 July 1832), 346-50; *ibid.*, 16 July 1832, 493-5; *ibid.*, 20 July 1832, 619-21.
218 David Montagu Erskine (1776-1855), second Baron Erskine, diplomat; Ambassador to Bavaria, 1828-43.
219 The Six Articles, pressed by Austria and Prussia upon the Diet of the North German Confederation and approved unanimously on 28 June, curtailed freedom of the press and restricted extension of the franchise in member states.
220 Hendrik, Baron Fagel (1765-1838), Dutch diplomat and minister; Ambassador to England, 1813-24.
221 The Draft specifically condemned the Six Articles, emphasized their danger to the peace of Europe, and hinted at the possibility of subsequent English intervention, though the right of interference was not yet warranted. BP, RC/AA/43/5-9.
222 Thomas Cartwright (1795-1850), diplomat; minister to the Germanic Confederation, 1830-8; to Hesse-Cassel, 1831-8; Ambassador to Sweden, 1838-50; knighted, 1834.
223 The letter is printed, almost in full, in Webster, II, pp. 799-800.
224 George Thomas John Nugent (1785-1871), Marquess of Westmeath; an Irish representative peer, 1831-71; an ultra Tory.
225 Because of the gout.

1833

1 But much of the material discussed under this heading transpired in the autumn of 1832.
2 Stanley's plan provided for the abolition of church cess (a rate for the repair and building of Protestant churches), a reduction—originally six, later ten—of the number of bishoprics and sinecure dignities, the establishment of a commission to investigate church revenues and patronage, and the dissolution of parochial unions. A graduated tax on all ecclesiastical benefices valued over £200 was to be paid to a newly established ecclesiastical board which would defray the loss of revenue of the cess. Should sinecures be discovered among certain dignities where neither residence was required nor spiritual duties performed, the revenues of those dignities would be placed at the disposal of the board and employed for the augmentation of smaller livings. Revenues were to be applied primarily to defraying the expense formerly provided for by the cess or 'to such other purposes, not particularly specified, as shall appear to the Commissioners to be connected with the support of the Established Church and shall have been sanctioned by Parliament.' A provision enabling tenants of bishops' lands to purchase their leases in perpetuity constituted an exception to the general principle of non-appropriation. The purchase money would constitute a new value created by parliament and would not curtail the present state of Church property. In this case, Stanley was amenable to applying that revenue to purposes not connected with the Church if a surplus remained after the needs of the Church had been met. 'Stanley's Plan for Church Reform,' 10 Sept. 1832, GP, Durham University. This provision was incorporated in the bill when presented to parliament and referred to thereafter as the 'appropriations clause.'

Professor Akenson's remark that the appropriations clause was apparently an afterthought, not to be found in the first version of the bill, is not true. (*The Church of Ireland: Ecclesiastical Reform and Revolution, 1800-1885* [New Haven and London, 1971], p. 175.) The appropriations clause was clause 147 of the second bill, but clause 142 of the first bill. 'A Bill to Alter and Amend the Laws Relating to the Temporalities of the Church of Ireland,' H.C. (1833), *PP*, I (59), 412.

The bill was delayed in the Commons on 14 March when Charles Wynn charged that it was a tax bill and must, therefore, proceed before a committee of the whole house prior to the second reading. The government then produced a revised version which contained some minor concessions to the Tories: the tax on benefices was delayed until the death of existing incumbents; 'benefice' was substituted for 'parish' as the office from which commissioners could suspend the appointment of incumbents if divine service had not been performed within the previous three years. For the bill and the divisions in cabinet on Stanley's plan, see Kriegel, 'The Irish Policy of Lord Grey's Government,' pp. 33-40. The second reading of the bill passed the Commons on 6 May.

3 Stanley had been in contact with three churchmen, especially the Primate, Lord John George Beresford, Archbishop of Armagh, from the inception of Grey's government. Beresford Papers, no. 37, Library of the Representative Body of the Church of Ireland. Beresford was easily persuaded and soon convinced that Stanley was among the few remaining friends in government of the Irish Church and of the British connection. Beresford to Stanley, 24 Jan. 1833, *ibid.*, no. 27.

4 The Coercion Bill of 1833, which empowered the lord lieutenant to suppress all meetings and declare disturbed districts under martial law. Offenders in these districts would be subject to trial by courts martial. See Kriegel, 'The Irish Policy of Lord Grey's Government,' pp. 41-2.

5 Stanley's unsuccessful Grand Jury Bill would have removed the county cess from the occupiers to the landlords. *3 Hansard*, XV (19 Feb. 1833), 955-63. The bill that passed this session regulated grand jury proceedings, but omitted that provision. (3 & 4 Will. IV, c. 78.) A modified version of Stanley's Grand Jury Bill was enacted in 1836 – 6 & 7 Will. IV, c. 116. For the work of Irish grand juries see R. D. Collison Black, *Economic Thought and the Irish Question 1817-1870* (Cambridge, 1960), pp. 168-70, 175-6. The Petty Jury Bill, similar to one that passed the Commons in the previous session, regulated the qualifications and return of jurors. *3 Hansard*, XVI (21 Mar. 1833), 902-5, enacted as 3 & 4 Will, IV, c. 91.

6 Edward Ellice, the elder (1781-1863), MP Coventry, 1818-26, 1830-63; Grey's brother-in-law, having married Lady Hannah Bettesworth, widow of Captain Bettesworth and Lord Grey's youngest sister (d. 1832); Whig whip; Secretary to the Treasury, 1830-2; Secretary at War, 1832-4, and in the cabinet from June 1834. Among the most liberal of the Whigs, he was constantly advising about party and electoral tactics. One of the founders of the Reform Club.

7 George De Lacy Evans (1787-1870), MP Rye, 1830, 1831-2, Westminster, 1833-41, 1846-65; commanded the British Legion aiding Maria Cristina of Spain against Don Carlos, 1835-7; knighted, 1837; general, 1861.

8 Lord Northampton initially proposed the abolition of this practice as an additional clause to the Reform Bill. Fearing it would provide a pretext for Tory opposition on the third reading, Grey persuaded him to produce a separate bill. *3 Hansard*, XIII (1 June 1832), 291-2. The separate bill, in turn, was opposed by Wellington and others who contended that, the electoral system having been altered by the Reform Bill, such a measure should be originated by government, preferably in the Commons. The bill was then abandoned. *Ibid.* (14 and 28 June 1832), pp. 611-18, 1086-7. The practice of seeking reelection when joining government was not abandoned until 1919 by the Reelection of Ministers Act, 9 Geo. V, c. 2, which abolished the requirement for reelection if a member joined government within nine months of a previous election. This time limitation was rescinded in 1926 by 16 & 17 Geo. V, c. 19.

9 James Stephen (1789-1859), the permanent counsel to the Colonial Office and Board of Trade; assistant Under Secretary for Colonies, 1834-6; Under Secretary for Colonies, 1836-47; credited with preparing the bill for the abolition of the slave trade, 1833; knighted, 1847.

10 Howick's proposal for emancipation by a land tax on their provision grounds would have compelled the Negroes to work the planters' fields at fixed hours for fixed wages, the tax also to relieve the planters of the payment of interest on a large government loan. Lord Howick's memorandum, 31 Dec. 1832, in Bell and Morrell (eds), *Select Documents of British Colonial Policy, 1830-60* (Oxford, 1928), pp. 383-9. Stanley's plan, communicated to the West Indian committees before being presented to the House of Commons, involved indentured labor and apprenticeship. It was presented in the form of five

resolutions to the Commons. *3 Hansard,* XVII (14 May 1833), 1193-231. The best comparison of the various emancipation schemes considered by Grey's government —Howick's, Stanley's and an earlier one by Henry Taylor at the Colonial Office—is in W. L. Burn, *Emancipation and Apprenticeship in the British West Indies* (London, 1937; reprinted, 1970), pp. 108-20; see also William Law Mathieson, *British Slavery and its Abolition 1823-1838* (London, 1926), pp. 228-42.

11 In opposition to the resolutions presented by Stanley as the bases of the government's plan. *3 Hansard,* XVII (14 May 1833), 1231-59. Howick had resigned from the government on 2 April.

12 The composition of the first reformed House of Commons was estimated by Tories to be 'Conservatives 150; Whigs or Ministerialists 320; thick-and-thin Radicals, Repealers from Ireland, members or friends of the political Unions, and so forth, not less than 190.' Lord Mahon to Peel, 8 Jan. 1833 in C. S. Parker (ed.), *Sir Robert Peel: From His Private Papers* (London, 1899), II, pp. 209-10. Joseph Parkes calculated '514 Liberal members and 144 Tories in the New House.' Parkes to Littleton 8 Jan. 1833, HP, S.R.O., D/260/M/F/27/8. More traditional Whigs who chose not yet to associate themselves with Radicals in a 'Liberal' party provide estimates more useful to the historian. With five or six returns still to come, Charles Wood analyzed the first reformed House of Commons as follows:

137 tories—opposition.
22 waverers—Sandon, George Bentinck . . . and the like who are not always to be depended upon, tho' 3/4 of them will always vote with us.
303 steady supporters including all those members of the Govt., Ellice &c. whose opinions are perhaps more liberal than those of the *compound* cabinet.
123 supporters of different shades from Ebrington to Warburton—men agreeing mostly with Althorp in opinion, and who voted steadily with us under the bond of the Reform Bill, but upon whom we cannot depend on so entirely to sacrifice their own opinions.
34 English and Scotch radicals. Hume & co.
38 Irish Repealers.

Wood to Grey (confid.), 31 Dec. 1832, GP, Durham University.

13 Holland's brevity conceals the seriousness of the government's problem. In late April a motion for reducing the malt tax to half its present rate passed the Commons by a majority of ten, primarily because of carelessness in whipping-in government supporters. (Littleton's Diary, 26 Apr. 1833, HP, S.R.O., D/260/M/F/26/8, f. 209.) The ministers divided upon the question of resignation. Althorp favored it, as did Grey; but the king, aware of his lack of alternatives, strongly exhorted Grey to remain. (Broughton, IV, p. 302; Le Marchant's Diary, April 1833, in Aspinall, *Three Diaries,* p. 323). Many of the Radicals who had defeated the government urged them to remain, and Hobhouse reported that Brooks's was in an uproar, the vast majority of members insisting upon the government's retention (Broughton, IV, pp. 302-3). The government was saved by Peel's support when Sir John Key announced his intention of moving the repeal of the house and window taxes, a motion considerably stronger than the reduction of the malt duty. Althorp stated that the revenue lost by the reduction of the malt tax and the repeal of the tax on houses could only be supplied by a tax on property, inexpedient and unpalatable. With Peel's support, this manoeuver saved the government. (Althorp to Peel [confid.], 28 Apr. 1833, P.P., BM Add. MS 40403, ff. 239-40.) Peel ostensibly agreed with John Wilson Croker, who considered the government's financial policy 'bungling and fraudful,' but was certain that its defeat forebode 'a most alarming crisis.' (Croker to Lord Hertford, 30 Apr. 1833, in Louis J. Jennings (ed.), *The Croker Papers* (London, 1884), II, p. 210.)

14 William Cobbett (1762-1835) the radical journalist and essayist, MP for Oldham in his last years.

15 Thomas Attwood (1783-1856), had founded the Birmingham Political Union in 1830; MP Birmingham, 1833-9; upon entering parliament, he associated himself with O'Connell and then with the Chartists.
16 Daniel Whittle Harvey (1786-1863), the radical politician. MP Colchester, 1818-20, 1826-34, Southwark, 1835-40; Commissioner of London Police, 1840-63.
17 During the meeting of political unions there on 13 May. The Home Office had attempted to prevent the meeting. The inquest found a verdict of justifiable homicide on the grounds that the Riot Act had not been read, the government had not taken proper precautions, and the police had acted brutally. See the account in the *Annual Register 1833* (Chronicle, pp. 79-82). The Solicitor General moved on 29 May for a writ of certiorari to have the verdict quashed in the Court of King's Bench. It was. The murderer's identity remained unknown.
18 Salomon Dedel (1775-1846) afterwards (1844) Baron Dedel. Dutch diplomat; Ambassador to England, 1833-46.
19 France and England had agreed on 22 October 1832 to force this treaty upon the Dutch (*BFSP*, XIX, 258), and had required that Holland withdraw troops from Belgian territory by 12 Nov. 1832. When this requirement was not complied with, an embargo was laid on Dutch shipping. Antwerp had capitulated to a French army in late December 1832.
20 Edward John Littleton (1791-1863), cr. (1835) Baron Hatherton, MP Staffordshire, 1812-32, South Staffordshire, 1832-5. Chief Secretary for Ireland, 1833-4.
21 François-René, Vicomte de Chateaubriand (1768-1848), the author; French Foreign Minister, 1823-4; retired from politics after the accession of Louis Philippe.
22 The Convention of 21 May 1833 between France, Britain, and Holland, established the temporary settlement that subsisted until the final treaty of 1839. *BFSP*, XX (1832-3), 282-6.
23 Mehemet Ali (?1769-1849), Pasha of Egypt since 1805, was virtually independent of the Ottoman Sultan. When the Sultan refused to fulfill an earlier promise to make him governor of Syria, Mehemet commenced his invasion.
24 Henry Edward Fox, later the fourth Lord Holland, married Lady Mary Augusta (1812-89), daughter of the eighth Earl of Coventry. They became Roman Catholics in 1850.
25 Lucien Bonaparte (1775-1840), Prince of Canino; Napoleon's brother.
26 Joseph Bonaparte (1768-1844), Napoleon's elder brother; King of Naples, 1805-8; King of Spain, 1808-14.
27 Henry Edward Sharpe (1794-1867), barrister, was Attorney General of Barbados since 1826; Chief Justice of St Vincent, 1846-66.
28 Mahmoud II (1784-1839), Ottoman Sultan, since 1808.
29 Karl Friedrich, Duke of Brunswick (1804-73), had been overthrown in his duchy in 1830, whereupon a regency under his brother was established. Brunswick became an exile in London and Paris, and was briefly a subject of Princess Victoria's interest.
30 The peace agreement gave Mehemet Ali effective control of Syria.
31 John Doyle (1797-1868), the political caricaturist, whose signature was HB. His identity remained generally unknown to contemporaries.
32 *3 Hansard*, XV (27 Feb. 1833), 1226-7. The Irish government had halted the collection of arrears during the elections. It was thereafter temporarily resumed with ill success under the provisions of the Arrears Bill of 1832, since the government failed to inform Lord Anglesey of its decision, stemming from Althorp's statement to abandon the collection. Melbourne to Anglesey, 2 May 1833, Melbourne Papers, Royal Archives, Windsor Castle; Melbourne to Anglesey, 9 May 1833, AP, P.R.O.N.I., T1068/31, f. 116. The abandonment of the collection resulted in the need for further governmental subsidy of the Irish clergy. See text, p. 233, and below p. 464 n. 77.
33 Henry Lambert (1786-1861), MP co. Wexford, 1831-4.

34 The reference is to the government's India Act of 1833, 3 & 4 Will. IV, c. 85, which continued the administrative functions of the East India Company on the subcontinent, but eliminated its monopoly of trade with China. The bill passed the Commons in an almost empty house. See Greville's Diary, 3 Sept. [1833], II, 413.

35 *3 Hansard,* XVIII (3 June 1833), 298-9.

36 Lady Hertford (?1771-1856); her father was probably the Duke of Queensberry, though she had been adopted by George Selwyn. See GEC, VI, 513n-14n.

37 William Courtenay, Assistant Clerk to the House of Lords.

38 *3 Hansard,* XVIII, 376-7.

39 The king to Archbishop of Canterbury, 6 June 1833, in Brougham, *Life and Times,* III, pp. 275-8.

40 Colonel Thomas Henry Hastings Davies (1789-1846), MP Worcester city, 1818-34, 1837-41. For his motion: *3 Hansard,* XVIII, 444.

41 Those bishops who did vote the motion were: Bath and Wells, Bristol, Gloucester, Rochester, St Davids, Ossory, and Exeter.

42 Two of the government's five resolutions. *3 Hansard,* XVIII (10 and 11 June 1833), 515-47, 597-9.

43 Ralph Bernal (?1785-1854), MP 1818-52, sitting for Rochester, 1820-41.

44 Hugh Fortescue (1753-1841), first Earl Fortescue, had associated with the Grenvillites and later with the Whigs.

45 Luis Fernández de Córdoba (1798-1840), Spanish soldier and diplomat; Ambassador to Portugal, 1831-3. He supported the queen after the death of King Ferdinand and commanded the army until 1836.

46 Francisco Cea Bermudez (d. 1834), Spanish minister under Ferdinand VII; he was subsequently discharged for his reactionary politics.

47 Having reissued the Pragmatic Sanction in 1830, King Ferdinand had since abandoned it once and then reissued it once again. See text, p. 20, and above, p. 432 n. 145.

48 Lady Coventry (1791-1845) née Mary Beauclerk, daughter of the sixth Duke of St Albans, had married the Earl of Coventry in 1811.

49 In reply to Holland's letter of the 13th. Taylor to Holland (priv.), 16 June 1833, HHP, BM Add. MS 51523, ff. 57-64.

50 Stanley had pledged the government to the passage of both the Coercion and Irish Church Bills. *3 Hansard,* XV (22 Feb. 1833), 1104.

51 George Crabbe (1754-1832).

52 Brougham suffered one of his few defeats in judicial reform on his Local Courts Bill, designed to alleviate congestion at central courts by having judges paid and appointed by government. It passed the Commons, but not the Lords.

53 The letter was from Sir Herbert Taylor to Brougham, 16 June 1833, in Brougham, *Life and Times,* III, pp. 281-90.

54 John Peter Grant of Rothiemurchus (1774-1848), MP 1812-26; puisne judge at Bombay and then at Calcutta, where he later became Chief Justice; knighted, 1848.

55 Sir Colin Halkett (1774-1856), lieutenant-general and commander-in-chief at Bombay, 1831-3; general, 1841.

56 John FitzGibbon (1792-1851), second Earl of Clare; Governor of Bombay, 1830-4.

57 George Warwick Bampfylde (1786-1858), cr. (1831) Baron Poltimore, a coronation peer.

58 Richard Barrett, speaker of the Jamaican Assembly. He had been commissioned by that body to go to London to lobby against the government's colonial policy.

59 Although the famous appropriations clause was withdrawn by Stanley on this date and encountered considerable opposition by O'Connell, Holland must here be referring to the debate on clause 132, which was concerned with the method whereby tenants of bishops' lands in Ireland, usually let for twenty-one years, could purchase their leases in perpetuity. The amendment by government was in turn amended by Lord Oxmantown. Oxmantown's amendment, which O'Connell supported and Stanley opposed,

prevented the evaluation of tenants' improvements in the calculation of the purchase price. It was contended that if such improvements were considered and thereby the purchase price raised, there would be no incentive for tenants to purchase their leases; rather, they would simply remain tenants of the bishops and pay a yearly 'fine' on the renewal of leases. The 'fine' by custom did not vary, regardless of tenants' improvements of property. Oxmantown's amendment passed, 85-49. *3 Hansard,* XVIII (21 June 1833), 1065-72; H.C. *Journals,* LXXXVIII (1833), 511-12. Holland probably wrote his entry before the appropriations clause was debated. The Commons sat until 2.30 a.m. on Saturday morning. H.C. *Journals, ibid.,* 513.

60 I.e., the Local Judicature Bill.

61 Here Holland refers not to the clause on bishops' lands proper, but to the application of monies from their sale, that is, the appropriations clause—clause 147. H.C. 1833, *PP* (210), I, 493-4. The division that the clause stand part of the bill was rejected and won by government, 280-149. *3 Hansard,* XVIII, 1098-102.

62 George Grote (1794-1871), the historian. MP City of London, 1833-41; retired to devote himself to history.

63 Thomas Gisborne (?1790-1852), MP Stafford, 1830-2, North Derbyshire, 1832-7, Carlow, 1839-41, Nottingham, 1843-7.

64 Precisely which members of the cabinet were aware of the intention to drop the appropriations clause remains unknown. Le Marchant, then Brougham's secretary, wrote that Grey obtained the consent of Brougham, Graham, and Holland and then went to see the king. (Le Marchant's Diary, 21 June 1833, in Aspinall, *Three Diaries,* p. 338.) Obviously he was wrong about Holland, whose surprise is recorded above and in a letter to Anglesey, in which he wrote, 'till after it was done neither I nor half the Cabinet knew of the change in our course.' 25 June [1833], AP, P.R.O.N.I., T1068/34, ff. 396-7. Perhaps the most convincing account is Littleton's summary of the episode for Anglesey: 'The project of omitting the clause altogether . . . was suggested to Govt. by Sir George Grey, a nephew or cousin of Lord Grey's, who married a daughter of the Bishop of Lichfield and who is connected with the Harrowbys and Wharncliffes. He satisfied the Government their support in the Lords wd be procured by the change. Sir J. Graham, I believe, spoke to the King about it on Friday morning and he, & Stanley, & Lord Grey decided on the change without consulting their colleagues. Indeed, there was no time for it.' 23 June 1833, *ibid.,* T1068/30, ff. 222-3.

65 The majority was fourteen, a vote of 52-38. *3 Hansard,* XVIII (24 June 1833), 1117.

66 Henry Lascelles (1767-1841), second Earl of Harewood.

67 The Lord's approval of the five resolutions passed by Commons. *3 Hansard,* XVIII (25 June 1833), 1228.

68 Thomas Lyttleton Powys (1833-96), afterwards (1861) fourth Baron Lilford.

69 Althorp's resolution to make Bank of England notes legal tender passed, 214-156. *3 Hansard,* XVIII, 1361-401. It was incorporated in the Bank Charter Act of 1833. 3 & 4 Will. IV, c. 98.

70 Louis Auguste Victor, Comte de Ghaisne de Bourmont (1773-1846), French general and supporter of right-wing causes within France and on the continent. He had opposed the July Revolution, and supported the cause of Dom Miguel in Portugal.

71 Antonio López de Córdoba, Spanish Chargé d'Affaires in London.

72 *3 Hansard,* XIX (9 July 1833), 372-5.

73 Sir John Wrottesley (1771-1841), cr. (1838) Baron Wrottesley. MP Lichfield, 1799-1806, Staffordshire, 1823-32, South Staffordshire, 1832-7.

74 His motion was rejected, 160-125. *3 Hansard,* XIX (15 July 1833), 662-3.

75 Thomas Philip Weddell, formerly Robinson, afterwards de Grey (1781-1859), Baron Grantham, cr. (1833) Earl de Grey. First Lord of the Admiralty in Peel's ministry, 1834-5; Lord Lieutenant of Ireland, 1841-4; Lord Goderich's brother.

76 The division on the second reading of the Irish Church Bill in the Lords. *3 Hansard,* XIX (19 July 1833), 1016-18. More government supporters voted in this division than in any

other in the House of Lords between 1833 and 1841. David Large, 'The House of Lords and Ireland in the Age of Peel, 1832-1850,' *Irish Hist. Stud.*, IX (Sept. 1955), 377-8.

77 The compromise was the Church Millions Act, which advanced £1,000,000 to the Irish clergy. The provision for collection of tithe arrears under Stanley's act of the previous session was rescinded. 3 & 4 Will. IV, c. 100 (royal assent, 29 Aug. 1833). The loan was to be repaid beginning November 1834 but it never was.

78 Lawrence Parsons (1758-1841), second Earl of Rosse, an Irish representative peer, 1809-41.

79 On the Duke of Wellington's amendment to the clause about the reduction of bishoprics. The amendment would have vested the intended amalgamation of bishoprics upon expiry to the king and his heirs, 'if the Crown should be so minded,' rather than having parliament instruct the Crown to do so. It therefore would not have guaranteed the abolition of the specified bishoprics upon the death of present incumbents. The amendment was rejected, 90-76. *3 Hansard,* XIX (23 July 1833), 1104. Wellington must have been relieved at the defeat of his amendment, which he made in an attempt to control the ultras. The Earl of Rosslyn was satisfied that the division 'reconciled many of our friends and happily we were beaten many of our friends not voting. I went to the division with less anxiety that I was pretty confident that we were in a minority.' Rosslyn to Mrs Arbuthnot, 24 July 1833, in A. Aspinall (ed.), *The Correspondence of Charles Arbuthnot* (London, 1941), pp. 172-3.

80 The division was not about so simple a matter as Holland indicates. On the question being put that the Speaker leave the Chair, Buxton moved that the Committee be instructed 'that they shall not, for the sake of the pecuniary interests of the master, impose any restraint or obligation on the negro which shall not be necessary for his own welfare, and for the general peace and order of society; and that they shall limit the duration of any temporary restrictions which may be imposed upon the freedom of the negroes to the shortest period which may be necessary to establish, on just principles, the system of free labour for adequate wages.' *3 Hansard,* XIX (24 July 1833), 1192. The vote of 158-151 was on the original motion that the Speaker leave the Chair. So Buxton and the anti-slavers voted in the negative, and they, not government, were defeated by the vote. *Ibid.,* 1218-20.

81 Non-cure benefices, not parishes.

82 The Archbishop of Canterbury moved that the consent of the bishop of the diocese be required whenever the Commissioners recommended the suspension of benefices, to which Grey agreed. But the archbishop further stipulated that sequestered funds from any such suspended benefice be earmarked for building churches and a glebe house in the benefice. The subsequent division was on that issue. *3 Hansard,* XIX, 1231-2.

83 The vote was 84-82. *Ibid.,* 1232-3.

84 Holland's divisions of the manuscript are noted in the text.

85 The vote was 135-81. *3 Hansard,* XX (30 July 1833), 126.

86 The Jewish Civil Disabilities Bill passed its third reading in the Commons on 22 July. It failed the second reading in Lords, 104-54. *Ibid.* (1 Aug. 1833), 249-50.

87 Holland's protest, *ibid.,* 252-5; Holland, *Opinions,* p. 164.

88 Sir William Parker (1781-1866), then in command of British naval forces on the Tagus, Sept. 1831-June 1834; knighted, 1834; a lord of the admiralty, 1835-41; Commander in Chief in China, 1841-4; command of the Channel fleet, 1846-52; admiral, 1851; admiral of the fleet, 1863.

89 Napier, who had succeeded Sartorius in command of Pedro's fleet in June 1833, had defeated Dom Miguel's fleet off Cape St Vincent on 2 July. A successful landing in the Algarves led by Terceira and Palmella then enabled Pedro's supporters to capture Lisbon.

90 The Cabinet Minute is in BP, CAB/A/19.

91 The treaty of Unkiar Skelessi was signed on 8 July 1833. Resulting from Russian military intervention on behalf of the Sultan to arrest the conquests of Mehemet Ali, it

provided for mutual assistance if either power were attacked. Russia promised naval and military assistance to preserve Turkish independence. A secret clause stipulated that ships of foreign nations be prevented from entering the Dardanelles in time of war. H.C. 1836, *PP*, I (50), 635.

92 *3 Hansard*, XX (30 July 1833), 127-8.

93 Archibald Kennedy (1770-1846), Earl of Cassellis (S), cr. (1831) Marquess of Ailsa; a coronation peer.

94 Henry Paget (1797-1869), eldest son of the Marquess of Anglesey; styled Lord Uxbridge; raised to the Lords in his own right (1833) as Lord Paget de Beaudesert; afterwards (1854) second Marquess of Anglesey. Whig MP Anglesey, 1820-32. Henrietta Maria Bagot (1815-44) became his second wife in 1833. She was the third daughter of Sir Charles Bagot.

95 3 & 4 Will. IV, c. 76, 77. Cf. the Municipal Corporations Bill for England and Wales in 1835. See below, p. 474 n. 58.

96 Amélie (1812-73) third daughter of Napoleon's step-son, Prince Eugène de Beauharnais, subsequently the first Duke of Leuchtenberg, m. Dom Pedro in 1829 as his second wife.

97 Auguste, second Duke of Leuchtenberg (1810-35), m. (Jan. 1835) Dona Maria and died two months thereafter.

98 Juan Alvarez Mendizábal (1790-1853) a Spanish Jew; politician and financier. Associated with the liberal movement in Spain, he sought refuge in England in 1823. He was commissioned by Pedro to finance the reestablishment of Maria on the Portuguese throne and had helped to organize the expedition which left England on behalf of Maria. In June 1835, while still in London, he was named Minister of Finance by the Spanish government and effective leader of the ministry. He remained in ministerial capacities in Spain through 1837; Minister of Finance again in 1842.

99 Thomas S. Sorrell was British Consul at Oporto.

100 Manuel Francisco de Barros e Sousa da Mesquita de Macedo Leitão e Carvalhosa, second Viscount of Santarem (1791-1856), Portuguese minister under Dom Miguel; dismissed, Mar. 1833. After the convention of Evora Monte he declared his attachment to the constitutional government and moved permanently to Paris.

101 The Millions Bill was all that the government introduced of a more extensive tithe reform plan. It amounted to a postponement or suspension of the tithe question rather than a solution of it.

102 To abolish imprisonment for debt, except in cases of fraud.

103 Edward Johnston, Wellesley's illegitimate son, who had served as his private secretary and confidant during his lord lieutenancy in the 1820s.

104 Edward, Duke of Kent (1767-1820), fourth son of George III.

105 Sir Stratford Canning (1786-1880), cr. (1852) Viscount Stratford de Redcliffe; diplomat; he had been gazetted Ambassador to Russia in 1832, but the Czar had refused to receive him; he nominally retained the designation of Ambassador to Russia, but was on a special mission to Spain in early 1833; his appointment as Ambassador to Russia was finally cancelled in July 1833. MP Old Sarum, 1828-30, Stockbridge, 1831-2, Lynn, 1835-42.

106 John Pitt (1756-1835), second Earl of Chatham, Governor General of Gibraltar since 1820.

107 George William Campbell (1768-1839), sixth Duke of Argyll, Lord Steward of the Household, 1833-4, 1835-9.

108 John Charles Villiers (1757-1838), third Earl of Clarendon.

109 George Henry Fitzroy (1760-1844), fourth Duke of Grafton.

110 Sir Spencer Compton (?1673-1743), first Earl of Wilmington, Speaker of the House of Commons in the reign of George I.

111 Louis-Napoleon Bonaparte (1808-73), President of the French Republic, 1848-52; Napoleon III, Emperor of the French, 1852-70; the son of Napoleon's brother, Louis, he

had in early 1832 published his *Revéries Politiques,* wherein he declared himself a candidate for the imperial succession. He assumed leadership of the Bonapartist cause after the death of his cousin, François Charles Joseph Bonaparte (1811-32), Duke of Reichstadt, Napoleon's son, upon whom Napoleon had bestowed the title of King of Rome.

112 Etienne de Laborde (1782-1865), an ardent Napoleonist; imprisoned for two years for participation in a Napoleonic rebellion in 1840.

113 Jules Auguste Armand Marie, Prince de Polignac (1780-1847), Charles X's ultra-royalist minister. Captured after the July Revolution, he was sentenced to life imprisonment, the sentence commuted to exile in 1836.

1834

1 Denis Le Marchant (1795-1874), Brougham's secretary, observed the proceedings of the House of Commons for him and the ministry during the reform debates; clerk of the crown in chancery, 1834; secretary to the Board of Trade, 1836-41; chief clerk to the House of Commons, 1850-71; baronetcy, 1841; author of the biography of Althorp. The pamphlet, *The Reform Ministry and the Reform Parliament,* ran through nine editions.

2 Nassau William Senior (1790-1864), political economist; frequent contributor to the *Edinburgh Review*; Master in Chancery, 1836-55.

3 Charles Augustus Ellis (1799-1868), sixth Baron Howard de Walden, later (1845) second Baron Segrave, Under Secretary of State for Foreign Affairs, 1824-8; minister at Stockholm, 1832; at Lisbon, 1833-46; at Brussels, 1846-68.

4 Augustinho José Freire (1780-1836), Portuguese soldier; supported Pedro; named Counsellor of State and Minister of War, 1833-4; Minister of Marine and Minister of the Kingdom, 1835; abandoned his ministerial duties after the revolution of 1836; assassinated by soldiers of the National Guard, Nov. 1836.

5 Francisco De Paula Martínez De La Rosa Berdejo Gomez y Arroyo (1787-1862), Spanish politician and writer, appointed by Maria Cristina to lead the constitutional ministry which promulgated the Constitution of 1834.

6 George William Frederick Villiers (1800-70), afterwards (1838) fourth Earl of Clarendon. Ambassador to Spain, 1833-9; Lord Privy Seal, 1839-41; Lord Lieutenant of Ireland, 1847-52; Foreign Secretary, 1853-8, 1865-6, 1868-70.

7 Francisco Espoz y Mina (1781-1836), Spanish general; constitutionalist, he invaded Spain from France in October 1830, but retreated and made another unsuccessful attempt in 1832. He returned to Spain after the amnesty of 1833.

8 Manuel Pando Fernandez de Pinedo, Marquis of Miraflores (1792-1872), Spanish politician, diplomat, and writer; a constitutionalist; Ambassador to England, 1834-8; to France, 1838-48.

9 The Quadruple Treaty was concluded on 22 April 1834. It provided for Spanish assistance, supported by the British navy and sanctioned by France, in ejecting the now combined forces of Carlos and Miguel from Portugal. It effectively settled the Portuguese problem, Miguel's forces being routed in May 1834 near Lisbon. The subsequent Convention of Evora Monte provided for the permanent departure of Carlos and Miguel from Portugal. The Quadruple Alliance is in *BFSP,* XXII (1833-34), 124-35. Palmerston wrote of the Treaty: 'I carried through the Cabinet by a *coup de main,* taking them by surprise, and not leaving them time to make objections.' Palmerston to Temple, 21 April 1834, in Bulwer, *Palmerston,* II, p. 189.

10 Achille Leon Victor, Duc de Broglie (1785-1870), Prime Minister in Louis Philippe's first government, 1830; in the Foreign Ministry, 1832-4; Foreign Minister, 1835-6. A liberal in foreign affairs.

11 François Guizot (1787-1874), French Minister of the Interior, 1830; Minister of Public Instruction, 1832-7; Ambassador to England, 1840; Prime Minister, 1847; historian.

12 Henri Gauthier, Comte de Rigny (1782-1835), French admiral; Minister of Naval Affairs, 1831-4; Minister of Foreign Affairs, 1834-5.

13 Stanley, Graham, Richmond, and Ripon resigned in May 1834, protesting against the government's half-hearted compromise on the question of appropriating surplus Irish Church revenues to secular purposes.

14 Duncannon originated the proposal for an inquiry to determine the state of parishes in Ireland and the number of Protestants in each, presumably with the intention of further reducing the Establishment and applying surplus funds to non-Church purposes. Duncannon to Wellesley (priv.), 13 Dec. 1833, WP, BM Add. MS 37306, f. 246. Littleton pressed the issue and secured the agreement of Althorp, Grey, and Melbourne, as well as Russell's enthusiastic support, before the matter was dropped. Littleton to Wellesley, 31 Jan. 1834, HP, S.R.O., D/260/M/01/2, ff. 394-5.

15 After a conciliatory speech by O'Connell on the government's tithe bill, Russell 'upset the Coach' by saying 'that if there were ever a just ground of complaint on the part of any people against any grievance, it was the complaint of the people of Ireland against the present appropriation of tithes,' and that he would adhere to his principles even at the risk of separating from his colleagues. *3 Hansard,* XXIII, 666. Donald Southgate's contention that Russell had contrived to split the cabinet and expel Stanley in order to inherit the party leadership in Commons is unsubstantiated. (*Passing of the Whigs* [London, 1962], p. 50.)

16 Henry George Ward (1797-1860), MP St Albans, 1832-7, Sheffield, 1837-49; first secretary of the Admiralty, 1846-9; knighted, 1849; Governor of the Ionian Islands, 1849-55. His motion is in *3 Hansard,* XXIII (27 May 1834), 1396.

17 Grey's reply is printed in the *Annual Register 1834,* p. 43.

18 Grey consented to remain in office only if Lansdowne could be persuaded to remain. 'Minute of Occurrences at the Levee in 27 May which produced my [Graham's] resignation that day at St James's,' Graham Papers. Lansdowne was as conservative on the Church issue as those who had resigned; even after the matter was purportedly resolved, he continued to remark in the Lords that the revenues of the Irish Church be restricted to church purposes. *3 Hansard,* XXIV (6 June 1834), 293. He was induced to remain and reportedly consented to the establishment of the commission proposed by Brougham in return for nomination of some of the replacements for the retired ministers. Littleton to Wellesley, 30 May 1834, HP, S.R.O., D/260/M/01/3, f. 214; Le Marchant, *Althorp,* pp. 488-9.

19 Francis Nathaniel Conyngham (1797-1876), second Marquess of Conyngham, a pro-Catholic Tory until 1830, he associated with the Whigs thereafter. Postmaster General, July-Dec. 1835, and May 1835; Lord Chamberlain, 1835-9.

20 Lansdowne's eldest son, the Earl of Kerry, married Lady Augusta Ponsonby, second daughter of Lord Duncannon, in March 1835.

21 Abercromby became President of the Board of Trade and Master of the Mint; Ellice retained his seat as Secretary at War but was elevated to the cabinet; Carlisle became Lord Privy Seal; Auckland, First Lord of the Admiralty.

22 That is, that the Irish tithe bill was to be secured by enlisting O'Connell's support for it in return for the deletion of the meetings clauses in the Coercion Bill. Much of the subsequent correspondence to which Holland refers about this episode is printed in Edward, Lord Hatherton, *Memoir and Correspondence Relating to Political Occurrences in June and July 1834* (London, 1872).

23 *3 Hansard,* XXIV (3 July 1834), 1099.

24 Brougham deluded himself by attributing the king's call for Melbourne to his own grand design. Brougham had suggested Melbourne. But King William selected him independently of Brougham's advice and, initially, as Holland correctly remarks, in an abortive attempt to establish a coalition government. Melbourne had been notified of the king's

summons by Grey at the cabinet meeting on the evening of 9 July. Brougham's letter to the king was delivered on the afternoon of 9 July and not immediately placed before him; for the king was already engaged in his interview with Melbourne which began at 1:30 p.m. The king to Melbourne, 8 July 1834, P.P., BM Add. MS 40303, f. 190; Melbourne to Peel (secret), 11 July 1834, in Sir Robert Peel, *Memoirs* (London, 1858), II, p. 1; Taylor to Brougham (priv.), 10 July 1834, in Brougham, III, pp. 401-2.

25 Melbourne was also directed to communicate with Stanley. Melbourne to Peel (secret), 11 July 1834, in Peel, *Memoirs,* I, pp. 1-2. Peel and Wellington this time acted in concert. *Ibid.*, p. 12.

26 Henry Addington (1757-1844), cr. (1805) Viscount Sidmouth; Speaker of the House of Commons, 1789-1801; Prime Minister, 1801-4; Lord President of the Council, 1805, 1806-7, 1812; Home Secretary, 1812-21. See the similar comment in 1832 about Sutton and Addington, *Greville,* II, p. 327.

27 *3 Hansard,* XXIV (9 July 1834), 1305-19.

28 Perhaps Holland wished to think so, but Grey, secretly at least, thought a Tory administration under Wellington or Peel to be the king's only alternative and, indeed, seemed inclined to welcome it. Grey to Wellesley (priv. and confid.), 12 July 1834, WP, BM Add. MS 37307, ff. 115-16.

29 Holland meant that she was in Germany. The queen left England in early July and returned at the beginning of September.

30 Edward John Stanley (1802-69), cr. (1848) Baron Eddisbury, afterward (1850) second Baron Stanley of Alderley. At Oxford he had been nicknamed Sir Benjamin Backbite for his incisive wit. Served as Durham's private secretary; Whig MP Hindon, 1831-2; North Cheshire 1832-41, 1847-8; Under Secretary for Colonies, 1833-4; for Home Department, July-Nov. 1834; patronage secretary to the Treasury and party whip, 1835-41; Under Secretary for Foreign Affairs, 1846-52; President of Board of Trade, 1855-8; Postmaster General, 1860-6.

31 Melbourne had refused to serve without Althorp, and Althorp, in turn, altruistically declined to serve unless Littleton were welcomed back. As Melbourne remarked, Althorp was 'the tortoise on which the world reposes.' Littleton to Wellesley, 14 July 1834, in Hatherton, *Memoir,* p. 97.

32 *3 Hansard,* XXV (18 July 1834), 118-21. The Coercion Bill was reenacted, with the courts martial and meetings clauses deleted.

33 See text, pp. 262-3.

34 4 & 5 Will. IV, c. 79, the Poor Law Amendment Act.

35 John Walter (1776-1847), chief proprietor of *The Times.* MP Berks 1832-7, Nottingham, 1841.

36 Thomas Barnes (1785-1841), editor of *The Times,* 1817-41.

37 The government's bill at this stage would have converted the tithe to a land tax payable by the parties liable to the tithe composition. After five years, 80 per cent of the tax would be converted to a rent charge on the first estate of inheritance, the charge payable to the Church Commissioners who would transfer it to the tithe owner, subtracting 2½ per cent for the expense of collection. In late June, the government added a provision which would have enabled landlords voluntarily to assume the burden of the rent charge rather than wait for it to be converted from a land tax after five years. Those landowners would be partially reimbursed by the government through the Consolidated Fund, the sum advanced to be repaid to the Treasury by the proceeds of the Perpetuities Purchase Fund established by the Church Reform Act of the previous year. O'Connell's amendment made the rent charge on the landlords compulsory at once. This procedure, he argued, would produce a uniformity in the collection of tithe in Ireland and prevent a disparity in the amount of tax to be paid by the peasants in various parts of the country. *3 Hansard,* XXV (30 July 1834), 755-8.

38 The division was 82-33 for the amendment. *Ibid.,* 771-2.

39 See above, p. 459 n. 3.

40 The vote was 189-122. *Ibid.* (11 Aug. 1834), 204-7.
41 Grey was invited to Edinburgh in September 1834 to receive the thanks of the people of Scotland for the Reform Bill.
42 Sir Charles Christopher Pepys (1781-1851), cr. (1836) Baron Cottenham; earldom, 1850. Solicitor General to the Queen, 1830-2; Whig MP Malton, 1831-6; Solicitor General, 1834; Master of the Rolls, 1834-6; Lord Chancellor, 1836-41, 1846-50.
43 Henry Bickersteth (1783-1851), cr. (1836) Baron Langdale. In February and September 1834, he declined offers to become a baron of the exchequer and Solicitor General, respectively. Master of the Rolls, 1836-51.
44 Robert Monsey Rolfe (1790-1868), cr. (1850) Baron Cranworth, MP Penryn and Falmouth, 1832-40; Solicitor General, Nov. 1834, 1835-9; knighted, 1835; baron of the exchequer, 1839-50; Lord Chancellor, 1852-8.
45 Joseph Allen (?1770-1845), Bishop of Bristol, 1834-6; of Ely, 1836-45.
46 Bernard Edward Howard (1765-1842), twelfth Duke of Norfolk. A Catholic, he was admitted to the House of Lords after Emancipation; a Whig and supporter of Reform.
47 Lord James Henry FitzRoy (1804-34), MP Thetford, 1830-4.
48 Buckingham Palace.
49 Arthur Blundell Sandys Trumbull Hill (1788-1845), third Marquess of Downshire, had been associated with the Whigs until 1834.
50 Arthur Wills Blundell Sandys Trumbull Hill (1812-1868), styled Earl of Hillsborough, afterwards (1845) fourth Marquess of Downshire. Conservative MP co. Down, 1836-45.
51 Probably William Petty, Lord Shelburne (1737-1805), who became the first Marquess of Lansdowne.
52 Manuel Silveira Pinto De Fonseca Teixira, Marquis of Chaves, Count of Amarante (1784-1830), Portuguese general; he led the anticonstitutionalist forces in the 1820s.
53 José da Silva Carvalho (1782-1856), Portuguese constitutionalist; exiled in England in the 1820s; Minister of Finance, 1832-5, April-Sept. 1836.
54 Pedro died on 22 September 1834.
55 Ildefonso Leopoldo Bayard (1785-1856), Portuguese soldier and diplomat; affiliated with the cause of Pedro and Maria since 1828; in charge of the mission to arrange the marriage of Dona Maria with the Duke of Leuchtenberg, Sept. 1835. Portuguese minister to Brazil, 1829-43.
56 Printed: The king to Melbourne, 12 Nov. 1834, in Lloyd C. Sanders, *Lord Melbourne's Papers* (London, 1889), pp. 221-2.
57 The remarks immediately preceding and following the brackets.
58 Melbourne to the king, 12 Nov. 1834, in *ibid.*, pp. 219-21.
59 It is likely that King William had already decided to dismiss the Whig government. Though written by the king months after the event for Peel's perusal, the 'Statement of His Majesty's General Proceedings,' 14 Jan. 1835 (reprinted with some errors in Baron E. von Stockmar, *Memoirs* [London, 1872], 2 vols), states 'when he [Melbourne] intimated his intention of coming to Brighton, His Majesty persuaded himself that he was coming to tender his Resignation and had made up his mind to accept it.' P.P., BM Add. MS 40302, f. 204.
60 The anticipated position of the government regarding the Irish Church was perhaps the king's fundamental grievance. William to Melbourne, 14 Nov. 1834, *ibid.*, BM Add. MS 40403, ff. 227-8; Memorandum of the king (priv.) 14 Nov. 1834, *ibid.*, ff. 229-30 (reprinted in Charles Stuart Parker (ed.), *Sir Robert Peel: From His Private Papers* [London, 1899, reprinted New York, 1970], II, pp. 254-5). Although a draft of the new Irish tithe bill was not yet completed, plans for it under Duncannon's direction included provision for suspension of non-cure parishes as well as appropriation. 'Plans for the Draft of a Bill' [Nov. 1834], WP, BM Add. MS 37307, ff. 185-6; Duncannon to Littleton (priv.), 2 Oct. 1834, *ibid.*, ff. 181-2. Unfortunately Duncannon acted prematurely in disclosing to the king his intention to suspend non-cure parishes. 'A Statement

of His Majesty's General Proceedings . . . ,' 14 Jan. 1835, P.P., BM Add. MS 40302, ff. 205-6; Duncannon to Melbourne, 18 Dec. 1834, in Sanders, *Melbourne Papers*, p. 230. As Norman Gash has noted, the king's antipathy to Russell as the new leader of government in the Commons must be associated with Russell's attitude toward the Church. *Reaction and Reconstruction in English Politics 1832-1852* (Oxford, 1965), pp. 11-12.

61 The king bolstered his case by contending that the cabinet was deeply divided on the Irish Church issue, with Rice and Lansdowne opposed to more extensive reforms. Such dissension, he rationalized, might lead to a dangerous schism within the cabinet during the next session of parliament. Memorandum of the king (priv.), 14 Nov. 1835, P.P., BM Add. MS 40403, ff. 229-30.

62 Gash suggests that Melbourne induced the king to modify the language of the paper, the original version having emphasized the king's objection to Russell, the final version the loss of Althorp. *Reaction and Reconstruction,* p. 12n.

63 Sir James Hudson (1810-1885), then assistant private secretary to the king and usher to Queen Adelaide. He later served as a diplomat; knighted, 1863.

64 Connop Thirlwall (1797-1875), historian and Bishop of St Davids, 1840-74.

65 Adam Sedgwick (1785-1873), Woodwardun Professor of Geology at Cambridge, 1818-73; canon of Norwich, 1834-73, the stall Brougham procured for him.

66 Robert John Eden (1779-1870), succeeded his brother as Lord Auckland (1849). Chaplain to William IV, 1831-7; to Victoria, 1837-9; Vicar of Battersea, Surrey, 1834, a living in the gift of the Lord Chancellor; Bishop of Sodor and Man, 1847-54, of Bath and Wells, 1854-69.

67 William Archibald Home (?1801-1848), was appointed rector of Hertingfordbury, in the gift of the Chancellor of the Duchy of Lancaster.

68 Thomas Robert Malthus (1786-1834), the political economist. He declined a living offered him by Brougham, in 1834, in favor of his son.

69 Cristovao Pedro de Morais Sarmento, Baron, later Viscount, of Torre de Moncorvo (1788-1851), Portuguese diplomat; minister at London 1831-51.

70 William Wellesley-Pole (1763-1845), cr. (1821) Baron Maryborough, succeeded his brother, Lord Wellesley (1845) as third Earl of Mornington (I); Master of the Mint, 1814-23, with a seat in cabinet; Postmaster General, 1834-5.

71 Henry Wellesley (1773-1847), first Baron Cowley; Ambassador to Spain, 1809-22; to Austria, 1823-31; to France 1835, 1841-6. Holland thought his conduct, when ambassador to Austria, encouraged 'a line of policy which they should be dissuaded from taking.' Holland to Palmerston, 8 Apr. 1831, BP, GC/HO/67/2.

72 In Scotland where Brougham engaged in a series of speeches in the autumn of 1834, boasting of his intimate council with the king and impugning the reforming zeal of some of his colleagues.

1835

1 Selected from HHP, BM Add. Mss 52204 E, and 52204 F, ff. 1-6. (These were tentative Additional Manuscript designations when the material was read – Ed.)

2 Since the dismissal, the tactics of the Whig opposition, including the ousting of Manners Sutton as Speaker, were determined primarily by Hobhouse, Duncannon, and Poulett Thomson. Melbourne, Russell, and other nominal leaders of the party were confronted with and reluctantly accepted an association with Radicals and Repealers to defeat Peel's government. See Kriegel, 'The Politics of the Whigs in Opposition,' pp. 65-91.

3 Abercromby had to be persuaded to make the contest. Holland had originally preferred Sir James Graham as an opposition candidate in an effort to reunite the Whig party. Lord Howick's Journal, 23 Jan. 1835, GP, Durham University.

4 The first of those meetings comprising the Lichfield House Compact, which associated Whigs with Radicals and Repealers in an effort to defeat Peel's government. Howick noted that 135 members attended this first meeting. Lord Howick's Journal, 18 Feb. 1835, GP, Durham University.

5 Henry FitzRoy (1790-1863), styled Earl of Euston, afterwards (1844) fifth Duke of Grafton. Whig MP Bury St Edmunds, 1818-20, 1826-31, Thetford, 1834-42.

6 Russell was to have been tacitly acknowledged at this meeting as leader of a unified opposition. Howick's vehement resistance to such action convinced Russell that the moderate Whigs would be alienated by the formal establishment of a more cohesive opposition party. Kriegel, 'The Politics of the Whigs,' pp. 84-5.

7 *3 Hansard,* XXVI, 56-61. O'Connell was credited with delivering sixty-one Irish votes, overcoming the majority which Manners-Sutton had on the basis of English and Scottish votes alone.

8 Robert Otway Cave (?1796-1844), MP Leicester borough, 1826-30, Tipperary, 1832, 1835-44.

9 Sir Andrew Agnew (1793-1849), MP Wigtownshire, 1830-7.

10 John McTaggart (1789-1867), MP Wigton, 1835-57; baronetcy, 1841.

11 Christopher Hodgson (1784-1874), secretary to the governors of Queen Anne's Bounty, 1822-71; treasurer to Queen Anne's Bounty, 1839-71.

12 After the dismissal of Melbourne's government, Stanley intended to develop his own party in parliament, comprised of moderate reformers who could no longer follow the Whig leadership but were still too far removed from the Tories. Stanley to Ripon (confid.), 27 Nov. 1834, Ripon Papers, BM Add. MS 40863, ff. 133-5; Graham to Stanley (confid.) 21 Nov. 1834, Graham Papers. O'Connell scorned this diminishing rump as the 'Derby Dilly.' Of the meeting to which Holland refers, Lady Stanley reported to her brother, Sir Herbert Taylor, that 'above forty' attended. 24 Feb. 1835, P.R.O. 30/12/28/5, ff. 199-200.

13 Fox Maule (1801-74), afterwards (1852) second Baron Panmure, and (1860) eleventh Earl of Dalhousie. Liberal MP Perthshire, 1835-7, Elgin burghs, 1838-41, Perth, 1841-52; Under Secretary for the Home Department, 1835-41; Secretary at War, 1846-52, in cabinet from Dec. 1851; Secretary for War, 1855-8.

14 The vote was 309-302, the amendment a broad affirmation of the previous Whig government.

15 In this second Lichfield House meeting, Hume agreed to abandon his motion, Russell to move a resolution for appropriation of Irish Church revenues; should that motion pass, the opposition agreed to support a motion of non-confidence in Peel's government. Edward Baines, *The Life of Edward Baines, Late M.P. of the Borough of Leeds* (London, 1851), pp. 211-12.

16 Henry Warburton (1784-1858), radical politician; MP Bridport, 1826-41, Kendal, 1843-7; instrumental in the Lichfield House Compact.

17 Londonderry's proposed appointment as ambassador to Russia encountered vigorous criticism in the Commons, after which Londonderry voluntarily withdrew his name.

18 On Spring Rice's parliamentary maneuver in amending the government's resolution on Irish tithes, defeated 213-198. *3 Hansard,* XXVII (20 Mar. 1835), 82-4.

19 Palgrave dissented from the report of his fellow commissioners on municipal corporations and refused to sign it.

20 Nassau Senior, *On National Property and on the Prospects of the Present Administration and of their Successors* (London, 1835).

21 Russell's motion had been set for 23 March. This third meeting at Lichfield House resulted in an agreement to postpone it until 30 March. *Greville,* III, p. 180.

22 Charles Ross (?1800-60), Tory MP Oxford, 1822-6, St Germans, 1826-32, Northampton borough, 1832-7; assistant Tory whip.

23 The address of 26 March, carried 246-136, is in *3 Hansard,* XXVII, 301-3; see below, p. 475 n. 76

24 On Russell's motion that the House resolve itself into a committee to consider the state of the Church establishment in Ireland. The vote was 322-289. *3 Hansard,* XXVII, 770.

25 At least twelve of the 'Derby Dilly' had defected to the opposition after a meeting called by Stanley on 28 March. See W. M. Torrens, *Memoirs of the Right Honourable William Second Viscount Melbourne* (London, 1878), II, p. 101.

26 Inflated figures. See *3 Hansard,* XXVII, 772-7.

27 Charles Grey (1804-1870), second surviving son of Lord Grey; lieutenant-colonel, 1833-42; private secretary to his father, 1830-4, to Prince Albert, 1849-61, to Queen Victoria, 1861-70; MP High Wycombe, 1831-7; general, 1865.

28 The majority of twenty-five was on Russell's motion in committee that surplus church revenues be applied to general purposes of education regardless of religious affiliation. *3 Hansard,* XXVII, 861-4. Russell's resolution that any tithe measure which did not incorporate the principle of appropriation would not be acceptable to the House of Commons was carried 285-258. *Ibid.,* 969-74.

29 Indicating that he would cooperate with Stanley and Grey, Peel had insisted that he would accept no office other than prime minister. Ellenborough's Diary, 8 Apr. 1835, P.R.O. 30/12/28/5, ff. 266-8.

30 The 'others' were Sheil and Whittle Harvey. Taylor to Queen Victoria, 8 July 1837, Royal Archives, 50491-2.

31 The king, aware of Rice's reluctance, apparently tried to entice him into negotiations with Peel for a reconstructed ministry. The king to Peel, 12 Apr. 1835, P.P., BM Add. MS 40303, f. 177; Ellenborough's Diary, 12 Apr. 1835, P.R.O. 31/12/28/5. 274-5.

32 The letter was to Grey, and requested him to return to office as prime minister or foreign secretary. It was signed by Melbourne, Lansdowne, Holland, Palmerston, and Rice. Printed in Walpole, *Russell,* I, pp. 231-2, and Sanders, *Melbourne's Papers,* p. 267.

33 Printed in Sanders, *Melbourne's Papers,* pp. 269-72.

34 The letters are in *ibid.,* pp. 273-7.

35 Duncannon advised O'Connell of the opposition to his inclusion in the government, not only by the king, but by a considerable number of moderate Whigs, the most important of whom was Spring Rice. Ellice to Durham (confid.), 11 Apr. [1835[, in Arthur Aspinall, *Lord Brougham and the Whig Party* (Manchester, 1927), p. 296; Littleton's Diary, 11 Apr. 1835, S.R.O., D/260/M/F/26/9, ff. 80-1; Torrens, *Melbourne,* II, p. 121; Lord Howick's Journal, 11 April 1835, GP, Durham University. Howick recorded that Lord Holland had favored appointing O'Connell Irish Attorney General. Lord Howick's Journal, 10 Apr. 1835, GP, Durham University. O'Connell wrote to his confidant that he was offered but declined the office of Master of the Rolls. To FitzPatrick (priv.), 14 Apr. 1835, in O'Connell, *Correspondence,* II, pp. 11-12.

36 David Richard Morier (1784-1877), diplomat; with the English delegation at Vienna, 1814; consul general at Paris, 1815-32; minister to the Swiss Confederation, 1832-47.

37 Edward Granville Eliot (1798-1877), afterwards (1845) third Earl of St Germans, diplomat; MP Liskeard, 1824-32, East Cornwall, 1837-45; special envoy to Spain, 1834, where he sponsored the Eliot Convention for the more humane treatment of prisoners; Irish Secretary, 1841-5; Lord Lieutenant of Ireland, 1853-5. The Eliot or Logrono Convention, signed 27 April 1835, is printed in *BFSP,* XXIII, 912.

38 Bernardino Fernández de Velasco, Duke of Frias (1783-1851), Spanish diplomat, politician, and poet. Spanish representative in London, 1820-3. He later became associated with liberal factions in Spain.

39 As Governor General of Canada.

40 Robert William Hay (1786-1861), Under Secretary for Colonies, 1825-35.

41 John Barrow (1764-1848), second secretary of the admiralty, 1804-6, 1807-45; baronetcy, 1835.

42 The government's draft of a bill was founded on the report of the commission on municipal corporations, which had evolved from the Commons' select committee established in 1833. The commission's final report, drafted by its secretary, Joseph

Parkes, and its chairman, John Blackburn, MP for Huddersfield, severely criticized the structure of existing corporations, but made no specific recommendations. See G.B.A.M. Finlayson, 'The Municipal Corporations Commission and Report 1833-35,' *Bull. Inst. of Hist. Research,* XXXVI (May 1963), 36-52.

43 Sir Lancelot Shadwell (1779-1850), last Vice Chancellor of England, 1827-50; one of the joint commissioners of the great seal, 1835-6.

44 Sir John Bernard Bosanquet (1773-1847), Judge of Common Pleas, 1830-42; one of the joint commissioners of the great seal, 1835-6.

45 Henry Thomas Howard (1808-51), second son of the Earl of Suffolk. MP Cricklade, 1841-7.

46 Sir John Campbell (1779-1861), cr. (1841) Baron Campbell. MP Stafford, 1830-2, Dudley, 1832-4, Edinburgh city, 1834-41; Solicitor General, 1832-4; Attorney General, 1834-41; Chancellor of the Duchy of Lancaster, 1846-50; Lord Chief Justice of Queen's Bench, 1850-9; Lord Chancellor, 1859-61.

47 Henry Taylor (1800-86), a senior clerk in the Colonial Office, 1824-72, where he favored a gradual solution of the slavery problem; his play, 'Philip van Artevelde' was produced in 1834, after which he was a guest at Holland House, but discontinued visits because 'he could not speak well of the hostess and thought it unfair to accept her hospitality.' *DNB,* XIX, 411; knighted, 1869.

48 Charles Arbuthnot (1767-1850), Tory MP 1795-6, 1809-31; Chancellor of the Duchy of Lancaster, 1828-30; an intimate of Wellington.

49 Robert Southey (1774-1843), poet laureate since 1813. Peel gave him a pension of £300 per year. The correspondence with Brougham is in Rev. Charles Cuthbert Southey (ed.), *The Life and Correspondence of Robert Southey* (London, 1850), VI, pp. 129-36.

50 Thomas Moore (1779-1852), the poet. He did receive a literary pension of £300 in 1835 through Russell's interest.

51 William Wordsworth (1770-1850) received a pension of £300 from the civil list in 1842, when he resigned his post at the stamp office.

52 Michael Faraday (1791-1867), the scientist, was given a pension of £300 in Melbourne's second administration, 1835.

53 See *3 Hansard,* XXVII (18 and 20 Apr. 1835), 997ff., 1009. On his father's behalf, Morgan O'Connell fought an inconclusive duel with Alvanley. It is recounted in *Greville,* III, pp. 199-201. Althorp wrote to Drummond, 'I never heard of such a thing as a man missing Alvanley three shots running.' 7 May 1835, Drummond Papers, N.L.I., MS 2150, ff. 891-2.

54 Maria Theresa, Princess of Beira, Dom Miguel's sister and sister of Don Carlos' first wife. She married Don Carlos in 1837.

55 Charles Theophilus Metcalfe (1785-1846), cr. (1845) Baron Metcalfe. Provisional Governor General of India, 1835-6; Lieutenant Governor of the North-West provinces, 1836-8; Governor of Jamaica, 1839-42; Governor General of Canada, 1843-5.

56 Holland must here be referring first to the board of ecclesiastical commissioners established by the Irish Church Temporalities Act of 1833 and, second, to the Ecclesiastical Commission established by Peel and retained by Melbourne's government to consider English Church reform — technically the Ecclesiastical Duties and Revenues Commission which became, in 1836, the Ecclesiastical Commissioners. See G.F.A. Best, *Temporal Pillars: Queen Anne's Bounty, the Ecclesiastical Commissioners, and the Church of England* (Cambridge, 1864), p. 298.

57 Henry M. O'Hanlon, counsel to the Irish Office. Peel's Irish tithe bill had been similar to that introduced by the Whigs in 1834, providing for the reduction of rent charges to 75 rather than 80 per cent of the composition, and omitting any provision for appropriation.

58 In terms of the extension of town councils, the reform of Scottish corporations had been more extensive than the plan for England and Wales. Thirteen of the towns provided with councils had received representation in the Scottish Reform Act of 1832, but had

not been royal burghs, a limitation in the bill for England Wales; the Scottish bill was less liberal in so far as it restricted the municipal franchise to those who qualified as £10 householders for the parliamentary borough franchise. 3 & 4 Will. IV, c. 76, c. 77.

59 Probably John Elliot Drinkwater Bethune (1801-51), son of Lieutenant-Colonel John Drinkwater; counsel to the Home Office, 1834-7. While holding this office he drafted the Municipal Reform Act, Tithes Commutation Act, and County Courts Act.

60 John Blackburne (d. 1837), MP Huddersfield, 1834-7. With Joseph Parkes he drafted the report of the commission on municipal corporations.

61 Frederick Whitworth William Aylmer (1777-1858), sixth Baron Aylmer, Governor General of Canada, 1830-5, recalled by Melbourne's government.

62 The commissioners were the new Governor General, Lord Gosford, Sir Charles Grey, and Sir George Gipps.

63 The initial version of the bill provided for appointment of magistrates by town councils. This provision was opposed by the Lords. Russell and the government agreed, but sought the consent of the Radicals in the Commons by suggesting that the recommendations for magistrates by town councils would be considered before any appointment was made by the Crown. *3 Hansard,* XXX (1 and 7 Sept. 1835), 1221, 1405-6. See Halévy, *Triumph of Reform,* p. 216. See text, p. 326.

64 Ferdinand I, Austrian Emperor, 1835-48.

65 Thomas William Anson (1795-1854), first Earl of Lichfield. Master of the Buckhounds, 1830-4; Postmaster General, 1835-41. In the by-election for South Staffordshire, occasioned by Littleton's elevation, Lichfield's younger brother, George Anson (1797-1857), was defeated by the Conservative candidate.

66 Althorp's unsuccessful bill of 1834 would have eliminated church rates, and provided for the repair and building of churches from the land tax.

67 On Friday 22 May, the party including Melbourne, Ellice, Ebrington, Rogers, and Luttrell. Lord Holland's Dinner Books, HHP, BM Add. MS 51955, f. 101.

68 Caroline Elizabeth Sarah Norton (1808-77), daughter of Thomas Sheridan, m. (1827) George Chapple Norton, brother of the third Lord Grantley; she engaged in literary pursuits and was one of the beauties of her day. Her liaison with Melbourne became a matter of considerable gossip and litigation.

69 Jane Georgina Sheridan (1809-84), Mrs Norton's sister, m. (1830) Edward Adolphus Seymour (1804-85), styled Lord Seymour, afterwards (1855) twelfth Duke of Somerset.

70 Richard Brinsley Sheridan (d. 1888), grandson of his namesake; MP Shaftesbury, 1845-52, Dorchester, 1852-68; m. (1835) Marcia Maria, only surviving child and heiress of Lieutenant General Sir Colquhoun Grant.

71 John Whishaw (?1764-1840), commissioner for auditing the Public Accounts, 1806-35, long a habitué of Holland House. See W. P. Courtenay, 'A Memoir of John Whishaw,' in *The 'Pope' of Holland House: Selections from the Correspondence of John Whishaw and his Friends, 1813-1840,* ed. Lady Seymour (London, 1906).

72 Sir William Gossett (?1782-1848), Under Secretary for Ireland at Dublin Castle, 1831-5, succeeded by Thomas Drummond; Serjeant at Arms in House of Commons, 1835-48.

73 Robert Bemingham Clements (1805-39), eldest son of the second Earl of Leitrim, styled Lord Clements since 1831; MP Leitrim, 1826-30, 1832-9.

74 To welcome Lord Mulgrave to Dublin as the new lord lieutenant.

75 This bill became the Prisons Act of 1835, 5 & 6 Will. IV, c. 38, which provided for central inspectors of prisons under the supervision of the home secretary.

76 The non-denominational University College, London, had applied for a charter as a degree-granting University of London in 1834. The question was submitted to a committee of the Privy Council, which was inclined to advise against a charter, but felt unable to do so because of the king's response of 1 April to the Commons' address of 26 March (text, p. 283). The king implied approval, but referred the matter back to the

Privy Council, which decided to make no recommendation and leave the matter to the new ministry. For the king's reply to the address, see *Annual Register 1835* (History) p. 156; see Greville's entries of Friday [5 June 1835] and 14 June, *Greville,* III, pp. 204-6.

77 Lord Radnor's bill would have abolished the requirement to subscribe to the Thirty-nine Articles upon admission to either of the universities.

78 Nathaniel Clements (1768-1854), second Earl of Leitrim (I), cr. (1831), Baron Clements (UK).

79 Palmerston had lost his seat for Hampshire in the general election of 1835. He was returned for Tiverton in a by-election in June 1835 and continued to represent it until his death in 1864.

80 François Maximilien Gerard, Comte de Rayneval (1778-1836), French diplomat, active in Spain in the 1830s.

81 In the debate on Lord Chandos' motion for an address to the king to ameliorate agricultural distress. *3 Hansard,* XXVIII (25 May 1835), 118-24; motion defeated, 211-150, *ibid.,* 127-8.

82 Russell's unsuccessful Marriage Bill of 1834 had attempted a compromise by providing for banns in church and marriage in chapels. Peel's Marriage Bill would have allowed civil marriage for dissenters, if registered with the rector or vicar of the parish church.

83 See above, p. 475 n. 76

84 *BFSP,* XXIII (1834-35), 738-9. Promulgated on 10 June, the Order facilitated the establishment of the British Legion, commanded by Colonel de Lacy Evans, to support the Queen Regent, Maria Cristina, against the Carlists.

85 A measure for the resolution of the tithe question as well as for Church reform, the bill included provisions for the elimination of benefices in which Protestants numbered less than fifty, the theoretical surplus to be used by the Educational Commissioners. Archbishop Whately, one of those commissioners, objected that the dependence of the Irish Education Commission upon a theoretical surplus resulting from the suspension of benefices would set Catholic against Protestant in Ireland, and make national education dependent upon the spoliation of the Church. He threatened to resign from the Education Board unless government established another way of funding it. Lord Morpeth introduced the bill in Commons on 26 June. Subsequently, because of Whately's attitude and Howick's arguments in cabinet, government added a provision in the committee stage in late July for allocating the National Education Board £50,000 from the Consolidated Fund, presumably to be repaid in future by the anticipated surplus of Church revenues. Whately to Melbourne 3 Mar. 1836, Melbourne Papers, Box 40, Royal Archives; Lord Howick's Journal, 25 July 1835, GP, Durham University. See text, pp. 316, 321, 324.

86 John Gurwood (1790-1845), colonel; private secretary to the Duke of Wellington, and editor of the first series of *Wellington Dispatches,* 1837-44. He had been sent on a mission to Spain by Wellington in late 1834 to establish an arrangement on prisoners.

87 William Wylde (1788-1877), military commander at Dom Pedro's headquarters in 1834; served in the Queen of Spain's army, 1834-8; general, 1866.

88 The Anglican King's College had received a charter in 1833. The charter for University College and the incorporation of King's and University College within a degree-granting University of London was effected in 1836.

89 *3 Hansard,* XXVIII (5 June 1835), 558-71.

90 On the third reading of the Newcastle-upon-Tyne Railway Bill, the Bishop of Hereford moved an amendment which would have prohibited operation of the railway on Sundays. Rejected, 40-19. *Ibid.* (11 June 1835), 653.

91 João Carlos de Oliveira Duan, Marquis of Saldanha (1790-1876), Portuguese politician and general; considered radical.

92 Buxton moved for a select committee to inquire whether the conditions for the grant of £20,000,000 to the West Indian planters, as stipulated by the Emancipation Act of

1833, had been complied with. The government and the sentiment of the House was opposed, and Buxton withdrew his motion. *3 Hansard,* XXVIII (19 June 1835), 918-60.

93 Admiral Sir William Hall Gage (1777-1864), became commander in chief at Lisbon, Apr.-Dec. 1837; admiral of the fleet, 1862.

94 The breach between Dona Maria and her step-mother, Amélie of Leuchtenberg, developed after the death of Maria's husband of two months, the second Duke of Leuchtenberg. England opposed Maria's preference for the Duc de Nemours as her next husband, as did Maria's step-mother, a Bonapartist, who pressed the claims of her brother, Maximilien (1817-52) third Duke of Leuchtenberg. In 1839 he married the eldest daughter of Czar Nicholas.

95 Francisco D'Almeida Portugal, Count of Lavradio (1797-1870), Portuguese diplomat.

96 Lord Dudley Coutts Stuart (1803-54), eighth son of the first Marquess of Bute. MP Arundel, 1830-7, Marylebone, 1847-54. He obtained a vote for £10,000 for the relief of Polish rebels who had come to England, and became an advocate of Polish independence; solicited public subscriptions and obtained further parliamentary grants; m. (1824) the daughter of Lucien Bonaparte, Prince Canino.

97 Robert Cutlar Fergusson (1768-1838), associated with Lord Dudley Stuart in advocating Polish independence. MP Kirkcudbrightshire, 1826-38; Judge Advocate General, 1834, 1835-8.

98 Sir Edward Hall Alderson (1787-1857), Baron of the Exchequer, 1834-57.

99 It passed its second reading in Commons on 15 June. Among the several amendments anticipated in committee were those for the preservation of freeman's rights and property qualifications for members of parliament. Neither passed in the Commons' committee, but were later added by the Lords.

100 Sir George Grey (1799-1882), nephew of the prime minister. MP Devonport, 1832-47, North Northumberland, 1847-52, Morpeth, 1853-74; Under Secretary for Colonies, 1834, 1835-9; Judge Advocate General, 1839-41; Home Secretary, 1846-52, 1855-8, 1861-6; Colonial Secretary, 1854-5.

101 Its report later initiated the bill that created the Great Western Railway from London to Bristol. 5 & 6 Will IV, c. cvii.

102 The Reform Act had retained the freeman franchise in perpetuity by birth or servitude. The Municipal Corporations Bill, as it reached this stage, preserved the rights of existing freemen only. The franchise would then expire with the death of existing freemen and the parliamentary franchise could not therefore be perpetuated. The clause passed 278-232. *3 Hansard,* XXVIII, 1112-16. In similar votes on 16 July, amendments to preserve the freeman franchise in perpetuity were again defeated. *Ibid.,* XXIX, 669-73, 678. But the Lords' amendments restored the freeman franchise. See below, p. 479 n. 144.

103 Sir Harford Jones Brydges (1764-1847), diplomat; originally in the service of the East India Company; a Whig in politics.

104 Richmond's brothers: Lord John George Lennox (1793-1873), MP West Sussex, 1832-41; Lord William Pitt Lennox (1799-1881), MP Lynn, 1832-5; Lord Arthur Lennox (1806-64), MP Chichester, 1832-46.

105 As Spanish Finance Minister. He became the effective head of the ministry in September 1835.

106 Henry Malthus (1806-82), rector of Poughill, Devonshire, 1832; vicar, Effingham, Surrey, 1837, translated to Donnington, Sussex, September 1837. See the correspondence in his behalf in HHP, BM Add. MSS 51839, ff. 157-8; 51539, ff. 236-9.

107 Edmund Goodenough Bayly (1804-86) became rector of St Andrews, Hertford, 1835, translated to Ackworth, Yorks, 1840, both livings in the gift of the Chancellor of the Duchy of Lancaster.

108 Holland had inherited Ampthill Park, near Woburn, from his uncle, Lord Ossory, in 1818.

109 Thomas Lloyd (1772-1851), rector of Sacombe, Hertford, since 1807; appointed rector of Swafield, Norfolk, 1837, a living in the gift of the Chancellor of the Duchy; he had been a friend of Lord Holland since his days at Eton, 1784-92; an intimate of Lord and Lady Cowper.

110 John Lumley Savile (1788-1856), styled Viscount Lumley, 1832-5, eighth Earl of Scarborough (I); MP Notts 1826-32, North Notts, 1832-5.

111 William Courtenay (1777-1859), succeeded his cousin as twentieth Earl of Devon in 1835. He had been Clerk-Assistant of the House of Lords, 1826-35.

112 William Brougham (1795-1886), MP Southwark, 1831-4; Master in Chancery, 1835-40; he succeeded his brother as Lord Brougham.

113 Montagu Bertie (1784-1854), fifth Lord Abingdon.

114 George William Frederick Howard (1802-64), styled Viscount Morpeth, afterwards (1848) seventh Earl of Carlisle, MP Morpeth, 1825-30, Yorkshire, 1830-2, West Riding, 1832-41, 1846-8; Irish Secretary, 1835-41, in cabinet from 1839; Lord Lieutenant of Ireland, 1855-8, 1859-64.

115 Printed in part: Melbourne to the king, 29 June 1835, in Sanders, *Melbourne,* pp. 333-4.

116 Sir Charles Edward Grey (1785-1865), judge of Supreme Court of Madras, 1820-5; Chief Justice in Bengal, 1825-35; one of the three commissioners dispatched to Canada in 1835 to determine the causes of discontent. MP Tynemouth, 1838-41; Governor of Barbados, 1841-6; Governor of Jamaica, 1847-53.

117 Bateman's abstract of 1883 lists the Holland family estates in Wiltshire comprising 5,514 acres valued at £6695; 227 acres in Surrey valued at £762. Large holdings in the metropolis were not listed. John Bateman, *The Great Landowners of Great Britain and Ireland* (London, 1883), p. 223. Lord Holland had also acquired interests in estates in the West Indies after his marriage.

118 The draft of the minute is printed in Sanders, *Melbourne,* pp. 334-5. Holland had submitted a corrected minute to Melbourne on this occasion, emphasizing that the first draft be toned down, 'that our object should on the face of the paper be less that of censure on what has been done, than assertion of the necessity of avoiding its recurrence.' 7 July [1835], BP, CAB/A/22/1.

119 Tomas de Zumalacárregui (1788-1835), Spanish Carlist general and a master strategist; he died in the siege of Bilbao, 1835.

120 Henry Seymour, who was not Black Rod but Serjeant at Arms of the House of Commons, and retired in 1835. Gossett did succeed him.

121 Cf. Hobhouse's account in *Recollections of a Long Life* (London, 1910), V, pp. 41-2.

122 Canada Act of 1791, not 1792.

123 The Duchess of Northumberland (1787-1866) was governess to Princess Victoria.

124 John Kaye (1783-1853), Bishop of Bristol, 1820-7, of Lincoln, 1827-53.

125 Charles Goddard (1770-1845), archdeacon of Lincoln, 1817-44. The Bishop and Archdeacon of Lincoln and the Chancellor of the Duchy were listed as commissioners in 58 Geo. III, c. 145 to supervise the building of additional churches.

126 Aberdeen's Instructions to Amherst, 2 Apr. 1835, are printed in H.C. 1838, *PP,* XXXIX (231), 863-94; Glenelg's Instructions to Gosford and the Canada Commissioners, 17 July 1835, printed in H.C. 1836, *PP,* XXXIX (113), 1-54.

127 Archbishop Whately had been Senior's tutor at Oxford, and then became Professor of Political Economy. Senior recommended Whately as Chairman of the Commission of Inquiry on the Irish Poor, established in 1833. Senior to Spring Rice, 5 May 1833, Monteagle Papers, N.L.I.; Macintyre, *The Liberator,* pp. 211-12.

128 Phillpotts attacked Dr Murray, the Catholic Bishop of Dublin and one of the Commissioners of Public Instruction, for promoting Dens' *Theology*. Peter Dens was a professor of theology at the University of Louvain in the mid-eighteenth century, his work of a Catholic orientation. *3 Hansard,* XXIX, 603-16.

129 Reform of Irish municipal corporations had been recognized as a necessary 'remedial measure' by the Whigs as early as 1831. Melbourne to Stanley (priv.), 2 Jan. 1831,

P.R.O., HO 122/15, f. 118; *3 Hansard*, I (3 Feb. 1831), 119-21. Like the reform bills, the Irish Municipal Corporations Bill was a corollary to its counterpart for England and Wales. It was not passed until 1840, but reportedly remained one of O'Connell's conditions for supporting Melbourne's government. Littleton's Diary, 11 Apr. 1835, HP, S.R.O., D/260/M/F/26/9, ff. 80-1; *3 Hansard*, XXVI (26 Feb. 1835), 398; for the legislative struggle to reform Irish corporations, see Macintyre, *The Liberator*, pp. 227-61.

130 The four reports of the select committee are in H.C. 1835, *PP*, XV (377); *ibid.*, XVI (475), *ibid.*, (476); *ibid.* XVII (605).

131 The Sinecure Church Preferment Bill, 5 & 6 Will. IV, c. 30, prevented the lapse of benefices where there was no cure of souls. It was designed as a prerequisite to a bill to be proposed the next session to enforce residence and restrict pluralities.

132 Kenneth Alexander Howard (1767-1845), eleventh Baron Howard of Effingham; earldom, 1837; general.

133 Berkeley Thomas Paget (1780-1842), Anglesey's youngest brother. MP Anglesey, 1807-20, Melborne Port, 1820-6; a commissioner of excise.

134 Probably George Frederick Young, MP Tynemouth and North Shields, 1831-8, when he was unseated on petition by Sir Charles Edward Grey; MP Scarborough, 1851-2.

135 Philip Pusey (1799-1855), Conservative MP Berks, 1835-52.

136 John Nicholas Fazakerley (?1788-1852), MP 1812-20, 1826-41, sitting for Peterborough, 1830-41.

137 Jerome Bonaparte (1784-1860), Napoleon's youngest brother, was King of Westphalia, 1807-13; Louis Bonaparte (1778-1846), brother of Napoleon, was King of Holland, 1805 to 1810, when he abdicated.

138 The division of the bill would have made the appropriations question a separate bill, a procedure which the Whigs had themselves contemplated in 1833.

139 The yield of the newspaper stamp tax had been considered by both Althorp and his successor, Spring Rice, too important to be surrendered, though the latter pledged himself to the principle of reduction. *3 Hansard*, XXIII (22 May 1834), 1210-13; *ibid.*, XXX (18 and 21 Aug. 1835), 623, 845-9, 862.

140 39 Geo. III, c. 79.

141 Sir Frederick Adair Roe (1786-1866), chief magistrate of police at Bow Street, 1832-7; baronetcy, 1836.

142 A contrivance devised to assassinate Louis Philippe and used in the celebrations to commemorate the July Revolution on 28 July 1835, when it killed fourteen people. See the description of it in the *Annual Register 1835* (History), p. 411.

143 Holland refers here to the action of the Lords during the committee stage of the bill in August 1835. Lyndhurst assumed the leadership of opposition Tory peers who sought to destroy the bill by amendments. The most damaging provided for the appointment of aldermen for life, chosen from those who already held such title in the unreformed corporations and who were to constitute one-quarter of any town council. The amendment passed, 126-39. *3 Hansard*, XXX (17 Aug. 1835), 601-2. The final version of the bill contained a compromise on this matter; one-third of a council would be comprised of aldermen elected by the councillors for a term of six years.

144 The amendments which Russell and the government accepted included division of larger towns into wards, appointment of magistrates vested in the crown, preservation of the special privileges of freemen, and a property qualification for town councillors, varying according to the size of the town. This last amendment was modified by the Commons. For the intricate parliamentary manoeuvring which led to the passage of the act, see George Kitson Clark, *Peel and the Conservative Party* (London, 1929), pp. 261-93; G.B.A.M. Finlayson, 'The Politics of Municipal Reform, 1835,' *Eng. Hist. Rev.*, LXXXI (Oct. 1966), 673-92.

145 The act was restricted to 178 existing boroughs, provisions made for the future application by towns which were not royal burghs. Manchester and Birmingham were incorporated under the act in 1838.
146 Sir George Elliot (1784-1863), admiral; MP Roxburghshire, 1832-5; secretary of the Admiralty, 1830-4; a lord commissioner of the Admiralty, 1834-7.
147 The act reducing the militia – 5 & 6 Will. IV, c. 37 – specified that reductions were to be implemented by orders in council.
148 Probably a reference to the Marriage and Registration bills for Dissenters (see text, p. 340), but possibly to the Irish Registration Bill which was defeated on second reading in Lords. *3 Hansard,* XXX (2 Sept. 1835), 1263.
149 The Lords had defeated the appropriations clause on 27 August, and government then abandoned the bill for the session.
150 Alexander Hamilton (1767-1852), tenth Duke of Hamilton.
151 After the prorogation, O'Connell undertook a speaking tour in northern England and Scotland, where he was severely critical of the House of Lords.
152 The Liddell family competed with the Greys and Lambtons in north Durham and southern Northumberland. Sir Thomas Henry Liddell (1775-1855), cr. (1821) first Baron Ravensworth, was Tory MP co. Durham, 1806-7; his son, Henry Thomas Liddell (1797-1878), later second Lord Ravensworth, earldom, 1874, was Tory MP Northumberland, 1826-30, North Durham, 1837-47, Liverpool, 1853-5.
153 The Sunday collections, referred to at various stages of O'Connell's career as the Catholic rent, National rent or Repeal rent.
154 Brooks's.
155 A commission to inquire into charities in England and Wales until 1837 was established by 5 & 6 Will. IV, c. 71.
156 Henry Charles Somerset (1766-1835), sixth Duke of Beaufort.
157 On 1 September 1835 Czar Nicholas and King Frederick William met on the Polish frontier at Kalisch and then proceeded on 19 September to Toeplitz in Bohemia, where they were joined by Emperor Ferdinand of Austria.
158 Nicholas condemned the past ingratitude of the Poles, their aspirations for an independent Poland, and threatened to destroy Warsaw should an independence movement be resumed. Printed in the *Annual Register 1835* (History), pp. 487-9.
159 The controversy stemmed from claims for spoliations under the Berlin and Milan Decrees. Louis Philippe's government agreed to pay the United States $5,000,000 in return for a reduction of duties on French wine. Congress passed the necessary legislation, but French delay in payment led President Jackson to order the navy to prepare for service, and recommend to Congress reprisals on French property. Britain successfully mediated the dispute.
160 Sir Thomas Maitland (?1759-1824), lieutenant general; Governor of Malta, 1813-24; Lord High Commissioner of the Ionian islands and commander in chief in the Mediterranean, 1815-24.
161 Napier's Portuguese honorific.
162 Bartolomeo Alberto Capellari (1765-1846), Pope Gregory XVI, 1831-46.
163 Francesco IV, Duke of Modena (d. 1846), inherited the Duchy in 1814, though he had ruled it since 1806. Expelled in the revolution of 1831, he was restored to his dukedom by Austrian troops.
164 Howard Peter Browne (1788-1845), second Marquess of Sligo (I), Governor General of Jamaica, 1833-6.
165 *Parliamentary Talk; or the Objections to the Late Irish Church Bill considered in a letter to a friend abroad.* By a disciple of Selden (London, James Ridgeway & Sons, 1836, 2nd ed.), 52 pp.
166 Nuno José Severo de Mendoça Rolim de Moura Barreto, Marquis and later (1862) Duke of Loulé (1804-1875), m. (1827) Dona Ana de Jesus Maria, youngest daughter of John VI, sister of Pedro and Miguel. She had renounced any claim to the crown for

herself and her descendants. Loulé was Minister of Foreign Affairs, 1835-6, and supported the revolution of September 1836.

167 Francisco Antonio de Campos, later first Baron and Viscount Vila Nova de Fozcoa (1780-1873), Minister of Finance, 1835-6.

168 Ferdinand of Coburgh (1816-1885) became Dona Maria's second husband in 1836. His name had first been put forward in July 1835.

169 Cracow was occupied by forces of Russia, Austria, and Prussia, the three powers having agreed at Kalisch in 1835 that the free state of Cracow be abolished.

170 David Urquhart (1805-77), diplomat; attached to Sir Stratford Canning's mission in Constantinople, 1831-2; secretary to the embassy at Constantinople, 1836; recalled, 1837, for hostility to Russia. MP Stafford, 1847-52. He agitated for Turkish autonomy and vehemently opposed Palmerston's foreign policy.

171 See text, p. 387.

172 Joseph Ewart (1759-92), Ambassador to Prussia, 1788-91. In 1791 he had been openly hostile to Russia.

173 Francis Osborne (1751-99), Marquess of Carmarthen, fifth Duke of Leeds; Foreign Secretary, 1783-91.

174 Lord Grenville (1759-1834) succeeded Carmarthen as Foreign Secretary, 1791-1801; First Lord of the Treasury, 1806-7.

175 Akif Pasha, Reis Effendi or Ottoman Foreign Minister, had been under the influence of the Russian party at Constantinople.

1836

1 The Constitution of 1813 was imposed upon Maria Cristina in August 1836 at La Granja.

2 Adolphe Thiers (1797-1877), one of the conspirators of the July Revolution; politician and historian; Prime Minister, 1836. His projected intervention against the Carlists led to his removal by Louis Philippe; President of the Republic, 1871-3.

3 Arthur Aston, secretary of the embassy at Paris, 1833-9; minister at Madrid, 1840-3; knighted, 1843.

4 These were bills to revise the Court of Chancery by separating the lord chancellor's political and judicial functions, the latter to be vested in a new lord chief justice of Chancery, and a bill to enable the House of Lords to sit in its appellate capacity even if parliament had been prorogued or dissolved. The government also lost another bill to abolish imprisonment for debt.

5 6 & 7 Will. IV, c. 71 provided for the compulsory commutation of tithes, which were converted to a rent charge. It hardly differed from Peel's bill of 1835.

6 Russell had introduced three bills based upon the recommendations of the Commission. One sought to equalize the revenues of bishoprics by redrawing boundaries of episcopal sees and permanently establishing the Ecclesiastical Commission. This Established Church Act – 6 & 7 Will. IV, c. 77 – was the only one to pass in the 1836 session. The other two, providing for the reduction of pluralities and the application of surplus revenues of deans and chapters to general church purposes, passed in 1838 and 1840 respectively.

7 Henry Hobhouse (1776-1854), permanent Under Secretary of State for the Home Department, 1817-27.

8 6 & 7 Will. IV, c. 85, c. 86.

9 William Vesey-Fitzgerald (1783-1843), second Baron Fitzgerald (I), cr. (1835) Baron Fitzgerald (UK); MP 1808-32; he was defeated by O'Connell in the famous Clare by-election of 1828; President of the Board of Control, 1841-3.

10 For the exchange with Lyndhurst, see *3 Hansard*, XXXV (15 Aug. 1836), 1224-5; for that with the Bishop of Exeter, *ibid.* (25 July 1836), 507-13.

11 Robert Ferguson of Raith (?1768-1840), then MP for Haddingtonshire. The subscription was to defray O'Connell's expenses in the election proceedings brought against him. Ferguson contributed £25, the Duke of Bedford, £100. BP, MIS A/6/1-2.
12 William George Grey (1819-65), then embarking upon a diplomatic career, was soon to become secretary of the legation at Paris.
13 John Grey (1812-95), fifth son of Earl Grey, m. (1836) Elizabeth, second daughter of the Marquis of Bristol; curate of Chenies, Bucks, 1835-6; vicar of Wooler, Northumberland, 1836-43, rector of Houghton-le-Spring, Durham, 1836-95. The patron of the first living was the Duke of Bedford, the Bishop of Durham having the gift of the other two.
14 Lady Howick (1803-79) was the younger daughter of Sir Joseph Copley, third baronet.
15 *3 Hansard,* XXXV (25 July 1836), 478-83.
16 Par excellence.
17 Renn Dickson Hampden (1793-1868) was appointed by Melbourne as Regius Professor of Divinity in 1836, and encountered considerable opposition; Bishop of Hereford, 1848-68.
18 Edward Hawkins (1789-1882), Provost of Oriel College, Oxford, 1828-74.
19 Henry Reynolds (1806-69), proctor, 1835; fellow of Jesus College, 1831-49; rector of Rotherfield, Peppard, Oxon, 1848-69.
20 Henry Pickthall, vicar of Millom, Cumberland, 1836, the living in the gift of the Chancellor of the Duchy.
21 William Blamire (1790-1862), Whig MP Cumberland, 1831-2, East Cumberland, 1832-6; Chief Tithe Commissioner, 1836-51.
22 William Van Mildert (1765-1836), Bishop of Durham, 1826-36, was succeeded by Maltby who was translated from Chichester. Van Mildert was one of the founders of Durham University.
23 Philip Nicholas Shuttleworth (1782-1842), Warden of New College, Oxford, 1822-40. He did become Bishop of Chichester, 1840-2. An opponent of the Tractarians.
24 Charles Thomas Longley (1794-1868), headmaster of Harrow, 1829-36; Bishop of Ripon, 1836-56, of Durham, 1856-60; Archbishop of York, 1860-2, of Canterbury, 1862-8, Melbourne appointed him to the newly founded see of Ripon in 1836.
25 Samuel Butler (1774-1839), headmaster at Shrewsbury, 1798-1836; Bishop of Lichfield and Coventry, 1836-9.
26 William Otter (1768-1840), first principal of King's College London, 1830-6; Bishop of Chichester, 1836-40.
27 Thomas Arnold (1795-1842), headmaster of Rugby, 1828-42.
28 Richard Whately (1787-1863), Archbishop of Dublin, 1831-63.
29 George Chapple Norton (1800-75), MP Guildford, 1826-30.
30 Germaine de Staël (1766-1817), Necker's daughter, m. (1786) Baron de Staël.
31 Catherine Worlée, known as Madame Grand after her marriage to an employee of the East India company; divorced in 1802; Talleyrand's mistress and then his wife.
32 In August 1836, on the House of Lords' amendments to the Municipal Corporations Act, rejected by the Commons. It was the only free conference between representatives of the two Houses to have occurred since 1740. Joseph Redlich, *The Procedure of the House of Commons* (London, 1908, reprinted New York, 1969), II, p. 83; *Annual Register 1836* (History), pp. 158-62.
33 Thomas Creevey (1768-1838), Whig MP 1802-18, 1820-6, 1831-2; Treasurer of the Ordnance, 1830-4; Treasurer of Greenwich Hospital, 1834-8.
34 'Through their own folly.' See *Odyssey,* Book I, line 7 (Loeb Classical Library edition).
35 Ferdinand of Coburgh and Dona Maria had eleven children.
36 The Revolution reinstated the Constitution of 1822 in place of the Charter of 1826.
37 George Nugent-Grenville (1789-1850), second Baron Nugent (I), Whig MP 1812-32, 1847-50; a lord of the treasury, 1830-2.

38 James Stuart (1775-1849), editor of the *Courier*, 1833-6; appointed a factory inspector by Melbourne in 1836.

39 Sir Thomas Dick Lauder (1784-1848), author and naturalist; appointed secretary to the board of Scottish manufactures, 1839.

40 Probably William Henry Lytton Bulwer (1801-72), cr. (1871) Baron Dalling and Bulwer, the diplomat. MP Wilton, 1830-1, Coventry, 1831-4, Marylebone, 1835-7, Tamworth, 1868-71; secretary of legation and Chargé d'Affaires at Brussels, 1832-6; secretary of embassy at Constantinople, 1837; Chargé d'Affaires at Paris, 1839; Ambassador to Spain, 1843-8; to USA 1849. But it might refer to his brother, Edward Lytton Bulwer (1803-73), cr. (1866) Baron Lytton; novelist and dramatist; MP St Ives, 1831-2, Lincoln city, 1832-41; Herts, 1852-66; Secretary for Colonies, 1858-9. Both were members of Brooks's, as was their eldest brother, Earl L. Bulwer (1799-1877).

41 'So, too, may any other also be destroyed who does such deeds.' See *Odyssey*, Book I, line 47 (Loeb Classical Library edition).

42 Thomas Burgess (1756-1837), Bishop of Salisbury, 1825-37.

43 Alexis Guignard, Comte de Saint-Priest (1805-51), historian and diplomat; French minister at Brazil, 1833-5, Portugal, 1835-7.

44 Jean Isidore Harispe (1768-1855), French marshall; commanded the French army at the Pyrenees during the Spanish civil war.

45 Holland's son, Charles Richard Fox, became Receiver-General of the Duchy of Lancaster in October 1836 and retained the post until his death in 1873.

46 William Frederick Chambers (1786-1855), physician to St George's Hospital, 1816-39; gazetted physician in ordinary to Queen Adelaide, 1836; to William IV, 1837; to Queen Victoria.

1837

1 Miguel Gómez, Spanish Carlist general.

2 Baldomero Espartero (1793-1879), Spanish general and politician.

3 Lord John Hay (1793-1851), MP Haddingtonshire, 1826-31, Windsor, 1847-50; commander of a squadron on the north coast of Spain during the civil war; rear-admiral, 1851.

4 Probably James Nisbet Colquhoun (1791-1853), raised and commanded a corps of artillery attached to Colonel De Lacy Evans' legion to serve the constitutionalist forces during the Carlist wars.

5 William Frederick Lapidge commanded a vessel on the north coast of Spain in the service of the constitutionalists; captain, 1837; rear-admiral, 1857.

6 England opposed French activity in Algeria, which it still recognized as part of the Ottoman Empire.

7 *3 Hansard*, XXXVI (31 Jan. 1837), 1-4.

8 John Arthur Roebuck (1801-79), MP Bath, 1832-7, 1841-7, Sheffield, 1849-68, 1874-9; radical politician; original member of the Reform Club, and associate of Hume, Grote, Warburton, and Place.

9 Sir George Crewe (1795-1844), Conservative MP South Derbyshire, 1835-41.

10 Charles Buller (1806-48), MP West Looe, 1830-1, Liskeard, 1832-48; radical politician; Durham's secretary when Governor General of Canada; credited, along with Wakefield, with writing the Durham Report.

11 Appointed in 1833, the commission of inquiry on the Irish poor submitted its final report in 1836. It opposed the application to Ireland of the principles of the Poor Law Amendment Act of 1834. The government's bill was based on the subsequent report of George Nicholls, an English commissioner, who toured Ireland for six weeks in the autumn of 1836, and favored the English system. The bill passed in 1838 – 1 & 2 Vict. c. 56.

12 Different from Althorp's bill of 1834, Spring Rice's unsuccessful Church Rate Bill of 1837 sought to abolish the rates, by having the ecclesiastical commissioners provide for the repair of churches on behalf of government from the anticipated surplus to be derived from government's management of church leases. Government abandoned the bill in committee.

13 *3 Hansard,* XXXVII (9 Mar. 1837), 147-9.

14 On the resolution in the Commons to cease the collection of church rates, 273-250. *Ibid.* (15 Mar. 1837), 549-54.

15 John Mitchell Kemble (1807-57), philologist and historian; editor of the *British and Foreign Review,* 1835-44.

16 Probably Sir Henry Rich (1803-69), baronetcy, 1863. MP Knaresborough, 1837-41, Richmond, 1846-61; a lord of the treasury, 1846-52; contributor to the *Edinburgh Review.*

17 Albany Fonblanque (1793-1872), radical journalist; editor of the *Examiner,* 1830-47, and its proprietor until 1865; frequent contributor to the *Westminster Review.*

18 Edward Denison (1801-54), Bishop of Salisbury, 1837-54; opposed admission of dissenters to the colleges at Oxford, 1835.

19 William Herbert (1778-1847), third son of the Earl of Carnarvon. MP Hants, 1806-7, Cricklade, 1811-12; rector of Spofforth, West Riding, 1814-40; dean of Manchester, 1840-7.

20 George Abercromby (1770-1843), second Baron Abercromby, eldest brother of the Speaker; Lord Lieutenant of co. Stirling, 1837-43.

21 James Graham (1755-1836), third Duke of Montrose (S) and Earl Graham (GB); Lord Lieutenant of co. Stirling, 1794-1836.

22 Whately had been chairman of the commission whose report, in 1836, opposed the application of the English system to Ireland.

23 Probably a reference to the investigation of joint stock banks which was renewed this session. *3 Hansard,* XXXVI (6 Feb. 1837), 155-203.

24 Possibly the registration of voters bill, lost in committee, but probably the bill suspending for four months legislation of the previous session for the registration of births, marriages, and deaths. The Poor Law commissioners had complained that, by July, 1300 parishes not previously in union would be, and the legislation could then be more effectively implemented. 1 Vict. c. 22.

25 William Collins (1793-1859), MP Warwick, 1837-52.

26 Thomas Thynne (1765-1837), second Marquess of Bath, KG, had been Lord Lieutenant of Somersetshire since 1819. His son and successor to the title died four months later.

27 Edmund Boyle (1767-1856), ninth Earl of Cork. He did not receive the lieutenancy of Somerset, which was given to the third Earl of Ilchester.

28 Edward Adolphus Seymour (1775-1855), eleventh Duke of Somerset, did receive the garter, 19 April 1837.

29 Edward Stanley (1779-1849), succeeded Bathurst as Bishop of Norwich, 1837-49.

30 Sir John Thomas Stanley (1766-1850), cr. (1839) Baron Stanley of Alderley.

31 See J. H. Adeane and M. Grenfell (eds), *Before and After Waterloo: Letters from Edward Stanley* (1907).

32 I.e. the marriage of Louis Philippe's son, Duc d'Orléans, to Helène Louise of Mecklenburg-Schwerin on 30 May 1837.

33 The government's majority was 36, 278-242. *3 Hansard,* XXXVIII (18 April 1837), 120-4.

34 Stephen Lushington (1782-1873), MP 1806-8, 1820-41, sitting for Tower Hamlets, 1832-41; reformer and abolitionist; Judge of the High Court of Admiralty, 1838-67; Dean of Arches, 1858-67.

35 Sir William Webb Follett (1798-1845), Conservative MP Exeter, 1835-44; Solicitor General, 1834-5, 1841-4; Attorney General 1844-5.

36 Leslie Grove Jones (1779-1839), soldier during peninsular war; author of letters to *The Times* in favor of parliamentary reform, which he had signed under the name, RADICAL.

37 Frederick Byng (1784-1871), clerk in the Foreign Office, 1801-39; gentleman usher of the privy chamber, 1831-71; earned the sobriquet 'Poodles' because of his curly hair.

38 John Temple Leader, Radical MP Bridgewater, 1835-7, Westminster, 1837-47.

39 *3 Hansard,* XXXVII (10 Apr. 1837), 981-93.

40 Louis de Beaupoil, Comte de Sainte Aulaire (1778-1849), French diplomat.

41 Prince Karl of Leiningen (d. 1856), Victoria's half-brother.

42 Maria, Countess of Klebelsberg, m. (1829) the Duke of Leiningen.

43 In a similar account, Allen refers to Sir B. Stevenson. HHP, BM Add. MS 52204F, f. 22. See above, p. 424 n. 17.

44 William Thomas Horner Fox-Strangways (1795-1865), afterwards (1858), fourth Earl of Ilchester; secretary of the embassy at Vienna, 1832-5; parliamentary under secretary for foreign affairs, 1835-40; minister at Frankfurt, 1840-9.

45 George Bell, a British merchant in Constantinople, was persuaded by Urquhart to send his vessel, the *Vixen,* to assist the rebels in Circassia. The Russians intercepted it in Nov. 1836, and arrested the crew and confiscated the cargo. See Webster, II, pp. 570-5.

46 Sir Charles Richard Vaughan (1774-1849), Ambassador to USA, 1825-35; proceeded by way of Malta as special envoy to Constantinople, 1837.

47 Hugh Percy (1785-1847), third Duke of Northumberland, Lord Lieutenant of Ireland, 1829-30.

48 Caroline Fox (1767-1845).

49 Sir Henry Wheatley (1777-1852), Keeper of the Privy Purse and Receiver General of the Duchy of Cornwall, 1830-47.

50 Maria Anne FitzHerbert (1756-1837), m. (1785), the Prince of Wales, later George IV, and received £6000 per year when they separated, 1803.

51 Arthur Chichester (1797-1837), cr. (1831) Baron Templemore, Whig MP Melborne Port, 1826-30, co. Wexford, 1830-1; a lord of the bedchamber, 1835-7, and a lord in waiting, 1837.

52 Francis Charles Seymour-Conway (1777-1842), third Marquess of Hertford.

53 Lady Forbes (d. 1861), née Elizabeth Cotgrave, m. (1791) William Ashburner (d. 1798), and m. (1800) Charles Forbes (d. 1849), baronetcy, 1823, an ardent Tory.

54 Lady Durham (1797-1841) was the eldest daughter of Lord Grey; lady of the bedchamber, 1837-8.

55 Lady Clanricarde (1804-76), daughter of George Canning, married Lord Clanricarde in 1825.

56 Duchess of Sutherland (1806-68), third daughter of the sixth Earl of Carlisle, m. (1823) Earl Gower, later Duke of Sutherland; Mistress of the Robes to Queen Victoria, 1837-41, 1846-52, 1853-8; 1859-61.

57 Buckingham House had been built for John Sheffield, first Duke of Buckingham (1648-1721), in 1703 and sold by his descendants to George II in 1761. Buckingham Palace was built on its site in 1825.

58 Henry Fox, first Lord Holland, 'Memoir on the Events Attending the Death of George II and the Accession of George III' in Countess of Ilchester and Lord Stavordale (eds), *Life and Letters of Lady Sarah Lennox 1745-1826* (London, 1901), 2 vols. (See I, pp. 30-4).

59 Thomas Musgrave (1788-1860), Bishop of Hereford, 1837-47; Archbishop of York, 1847-60.

60 Whig estimates generally put the results in English counties as 46 for ministers, 109 for opposition, and 4 doubtful (Wm Cowper to Holland, 14 Aug. [1837], HHP, BM Add. MS 51559; Russell to Melbourne, 13 Aug. 1837, P.R.O. Russell Papers, P.R.O. 10/22/2F, ff. 9-10; Russell to the queen, 15 Aug. 1837, *ibid.,* ff. 12-14). Goulburn wrote to Peel that the English counties would return 111 opponents and 48 supporters of

government. (15 Aug. 1837, P.P., BM Add. MS 40333, ff. 372-4.) Total returns in each of the above documents were listed as follows: Cowper estimated 342 government supporters, 311 opponents, 5 doubtful; Russell to Melbourne – 338 ministerial supporters, 316 opponents, 4 doubtful; Russell to the queen – 340 ministerial supporters, 313 opponents, 5 doubtful; Goulburn gave government a probable majority of 34; Bonham's estimate to Peel was that government would have a majority of not more than 9. (Peel to Graham, 11 Aug. 1837, Graham Papers.) Henry Hardinge calculated a government majority of 26 votes. (To Graham, 13 Aug. [1837], *ibid.*).

61 'Draft Memorandum for Communication to the Duke of Wellington, Earl Grey, Viscount Melbourne and Sir Robert Peel,' Royal Archives, 50594-50601; endorsed in Sir Herbert Taylor's hand as 'Draft prepared in consequence of Rumour of Resignation 1836-37 Intended by His Majesty to apply to any such contingency.'

62 See text, p. 391.

63 HHP, BM Add. MS 52204F, ff. 23-4.

64 In July 1837, the ex-ministers Saldanha and Terceira led an abortive counter-revolution to abolish the more liberal constitution of 1822 in Portugal. In Spain the Carlists enjoyed continued military success.

65 Louise, Baroness Lehzen (d. 1870), Victoria's governess.

66 Selected from HHP, BM Add. MS 52204F, ff. 25-6.

67 Sir William Molesworth (1810-55), MP East Cornwall, 1832-7, Leeds, 1837-41, Southwark, 1845-55; began the *London Review,* 1835, and joined it with the *Westminster Review* in 1837; associated with the Philosophical Radicals; opponent of government's colonial policy; First Commissioner of Public Works in Aberdeen's cabinet, 1853-5; Colonial Secretary, 1855.

68 Thomas Wakley (1795-1862), medical reformer; founded the *Lancet* in 1823; radical MP Finsbury, 1835-52.

69 The Countess of Tankerville (1783-1865).

70 See above, p. 377.

71 Andrew Spottiswood, one of the Queen's printers, organized a subscription to contest the Irish elections of 1837, charging intimidation of voters by O'Connell's supporters. Resolutions in the Commons against the institution of the Spottiswood fund were discouraged by Russell and no vote was taken.

72 Russell is recorded in Hansard as having said, not that the act was final, but that some had thought it would be so considered. The people could reconsider and amend it, 'but I am not myself going to do so.' *3 Hansard* (vol. 39), XXIX (20 Nov. 1837), 70.

73 'fleeting remarks.'

74 John Hely-Hutchinson (1787-1851), third Earl of Donoughmore (I) and Viscount Hutchinson (UK). Whig MP co. Tipperary, 1826-30, 1831-2. He turned Tory in the late 1830s.

75 For the debate see *3 Hansard,* XXXIX (27 Nov. 1837), 212-82.

1838

1 As High Commissioner of British North America and Governor General of Canada.

2 1 Vict. c. 9 suspended the constitution of Lower Canada until November 1840, and provided for a special council which, with the governor, would administer and legislate for the colony.

3 *3 Hansard,* XL (25 and 26 Jan. 1838), 504, 543-5 (Peel and Russell).

4 From Ovid's *Metamorphoses,* Book V, line 678.

5 Margaret, Lady Keith (1788-1867), daughter of the first Baron Keith and Jane Mercer, was in Princess Charlotte's household. She succeeded to the title in 1823; she had married (1817) Comte de Flahaut.

6 On the Scottish Church question, see *3 Hansard,* XLI (8 Mar. 1838), 701-2; (9 Mar.), 707-12; XLII (30 Mar.) 110-52. On the reduction of the Yeomanry: *ibid.,* XLI (13 Mar. 1838), 797-802; (15 Mar.) 901; XLII (7 May), 944-51.

7 Sir Thomas Dyke Acland (1787-1871), MP co. Devon 1812-18, 1820-30, North Devon, 1837-57. He had voted for Catholic Emancipation but turned conservative during the Reform Bill struggle. His motion was that the Commons' resolutions of 7 April 1835 for appropriation be rescinded. *3 Hansard,* XLII (14 May 1838), 1213.

8 Cornelia Knight, one of Victoria's ladies in waiting, had succeeded Lady de Clifford in 1812 upon the latter's resignation as governess.

9 Probably Henry Hallam (1777-1859), the historian; a frequent guest at Holland House. The death of his son, Arthur Hallam (1811-33) inspired Tennyson's *In Memoriam.*

10 Prince Friedrich Wilhelm Augustus of Prussia (1779-1843).

11 HHP, BM Add. MS 52204F, ff. 28-32.

12 Sir Richard Hussey Vivian (1775-1842), cr. (1841) Baron Vivian. Commander of the Forces in Ireland, 1831-5; MP Truro, 1820-5, Windsor, 1826-31, East Cornwall, 1837-41.

13 O'Connell's allegation at the Crown and Anchor on 21 February that Tory politicians had committed perjury in committees of the Commons induced Lord Maidstone to move for a breach of privilege against him. The motion that the question be put carried, 263-254. *3 Hansard,* XLI (26 Feb. 1838), 162-6. After a series of subsequent votes, O'Connell was reprimanded by the House, the government opposing the censure. *Ibid.* (27 Feb. 1838), 233-6.

14 *Ibid.,* 261-2. The vote was 100-87.

15 Frances Mary Gascoyne (d. 1839) m. (1821) the second Marquess of Salisbury.

16 Sandon's motion to censure the government for its conduct in Canada was defeated. 316-287. *3 Hansard,* XLI (7 Mar. 1838), 684-9.

17 I.e., Sandon's motion, which was an amendment to Molesworth's original motion to censure the Colonial Secretary, Lord Glenelg. Molesworth withdrew his motion.

18 Brougham's Poor Law Amendment Bill, refuting criticism about the operation of the Act of 1834.

19 The Neutrality Act of 1838 amended the neutrality laws of 1794 and 1818, and was designed to prevent involvement by US nationals in foreign or colonial territories contiguous to the USA. The debates were particularly concerned with the Canadian rebellion.

20 For an address to the queen not to renew the suspension of the Foreign Enlistment Act, thereby removing British subjects from involvement in the Spanish civil war.

21 The Speaker put the question, no one having risen to address the House. The unexpected division was narrowly won by government, the motion rejected, 70-62. See the ensuing debate on procedure, *3 Hansard,* XLI (28 Mar. 1838), 1384-1400.

22 Chandos's motion was to prohibit the expenses of Durham's administration of Canada from exceeding those of his predecessor, Lord Gosford. On the division that the question be put, it was rejected, 160-158, *3 Hansard,* XLII (3 Apr. 1838), 422-5.

23 William Ewart Gladstone (1809-98) began his parliamentary career as Tory MP for Newark, 1832-5.

24 A bill protecting the status of apprenticed labourers under the provisions of the 1833 abolition. 1 & 2 Vict. c. 19.

25 1 & 2 Vict. c. 107.

26 Durham's Ordinances banished eight of the Lower Canada political prisoners to Bermuda and pardoned the others. Printed in *Annual Register, 1838* (Chronicle), pp. 304-7.

27 Follett's clause, incorporated in the Canada Act, had prohibited the Governor General from altering or suspending any existing act of the imperial parliament or of the colonial legislature. *3 Hansard,* XL (26 Jan. 1838), 590-2, 595.

28 Brougham's Indemnity Bill in effect pardoned Durham for having issued and acted under the subsequently controverted Ordinances. Enacted as 1 & 2 Vict. c. 112. See Brougham, *Life and Times,* III, p. 511.
29 Sir Robert Grant (1779-1838), MP 1818-34; Governor of Bombay; 1835-8.

1839

1 Sir Herbert Taylor to the queen, 8 July 1837, Royal Archives, 50490-6. Taylor indicated that from the beginning of Melbourne's second administration until his death, King William differed with his ministers cnly on the appointment of Dr Hampden to the Regius Professorship, the proposed abolition of church rates, the attempted consolidation of military affairs under the Secretary at War, and the proposed rearrangement of the Canadian legislative council – the latter characterized by the King as 'a *Radical* step towards an alteration of the Constitution of the House of Lords.'
2 William Downe Gillon (1801-46), MP Lanark burghs, 1831-2, Falkirk burghs, 1832-41.
3 Russell opposed the motion on grounds that it ought properly to have come from the ministers. *3 Hansard,* XLIII (6 July 1838), 1291-1303.
4 The King of Holland accepted the Twenty-four Articles on 14 March 1838, whereupon the Belgians balked on giving up Luxemburg and Limburg which they had retained since the convention of 1833. Britain and France refused to alter the Articles and, except for some modification in reducing the interest payable by Belgium on the public debt of the Netherlands, a final treaty was signed on 19 April 1839.
5 The commercial and navigation treaties with Austria (3 July 1838) and with Turkey (16 Aug. 1838) are in *BFSP,* XXVI, 677-91.
6 Holland's error. Fitzwilliam sought a revision of the corn laws. His motion was rejected, 224-24. *3 Hansard,* XLVI (14 Mar. 1839), 624.
7 Technically, Roden's motion was to establish a select committee to inquire into the state of Ireland since 1835, particularly concerning crime. *Ibid.* (21 Mar. 1839), 974.
8 The vote was 63-58. *Ibid.,* 1047-8.
9 See text, pp. 343, 361.
10 After five nights of debate, Russell's motion for a vote of confidence in the Irish government was carried, 318-296. *3 Hansard,* XLVII (19 Apr. 1839), 447-51.
11 Lady Flora Hastings (1806-39) eldest daughter of the first Marquess Hastings; lady of the bedchamber to the Duchess of Kent.
12 Lady Portman (1809-65), a lady of the bedchamber, 1837-51.
13 Sir James Clark (1788-1870), naval surgeon and physician to Prince Leopold; physician to the Duchess of Kent since 1834; physician in ordinary to the queen; baronetcy, 1837.
14 See the exchange between Brougham and Normanby in *3 Hansard,* XLVI (21 and 22 Mar. 1839), 1045-6, 1108-17.
15 On the motion that the Commons go into committee on the Jamaica government bill. *Ibid.,* XLVII (6 May 1839), 967-72.
16 Melbourne rejected the proposal that he advise the queen to call Spencer, on grounds that Lord Spencer could not be lured from retirement and that a government led by him would be no stronger than the existing government. Melbourne to Holland, 6 May 1839, HHP, BM Add. MS 51559 (unfoliated).
17 Not quite. The queen kept Melbourne informed of the state of negotiations. See her letter to Melbourne and replies of 8 and 9 May 1839 in Arthur Christopher Benson and Viscount Esher (eds), *The Letters of Queen Victoria* (London, 1908), I, pp. 157-62.
18 John Elphinstone (1807-60), thirteenth Lord Elphinstone (S), cr. (1859) Baron Elphinstone (UK). Scottish representative peer, 1832-5, 1847-59; a lord of the bedchamber, 1832-4, 1835-6; Governor of Madras, 1837-42; of Bombay, 1853-60. Melbourne sent him off to India when it was rumored that the queen had fallen in love with him.

19 For the debate, primarily between Russell and Peel, see *3 Hansard,* XLVII (13 May 1839), 979-1003.
20 Lady Normanby (1798-1882), daughter of Thomas Henry Liddell, first Baron Ravensworth, was a lady of the bedchamber.
21 The Jamaica bill passed the third reading in Commons, 267-257, on 10 June 1839. *3 Hansard,* XLVIII, 524-9.
22 Stanley's motion, not Peel's. The order of 10 April 1839 appointed a committee of council to superintend any funds voted by parliament for promoting public education. Stanley's motion was defeated, 280-275. *Ibid.* (20 June 1839), 681-6. The division of 24 June in committee of supply for funding the order was carried by only two votes 275-273, *ibid.,* 793-8.
23 The Lords expunged the first clause of the Jamaica bill, which would have empowered the Governor in Council to issue ordinances on contracts for labor and occupation of waste lands. *Ibid.* (2 July 1839), 1151-4. The Archbishop of Canterbury's resolutions against the Education measure were carried on 5 July 1839. *Ibid.,* 1332-6.
24 Sir Charles Mansfield Clarke (1782-1857), an authority on midwifery.
25 Hamilton FitzGerald, Lady Flora Hastings' uncle. His letter was printed in the *Examiner,* 24 Mar. 1839, reprinted in *Annual Register, 1839* (Chronicle), pp. 351-2.
26 The Dowager Marchioness of Hastings (1780-1840). She published her correspondence with Melbourne in the *Morning Post.*
27 *3 Hansard,* XLIX (11 July 1839), 128.
28 'All is laughter, all is dust, all is nothingness.'
29 The vote was 86-52. *3 Hansard,* XLIX (6 Aug. 1839), 1381-3.
30 Holland's protest is in *ibid.,* 1383-4.
31 *Ibid.* (1 Aug. 1839), 1073-4.
32 See Wellington's protests on the passage of the second and third readings. *Ibid.,* L (15 and 19 Aug. 1839), 336-9, 386-7.
33 2 & 3 Vict., c. 73.
34 2 & 3 Vict., c. 97.
35 Francis Thornhill Baring (1796-1866), baronetcy, 1838, cr. (1866) Baron Northbrook. MP Portsmouth, 1826-65; Joint Secretary to the Treasury, 1834, 1835-9; Chancellor of the Exchequer, 1839-41; First Lord of the Admiralty, 1849-52.
36 For Howick's defense of his resignation, see Howick to Ellice, 6 Sept. 1839, EP, N.L.S., E/22, ff. 43-8.
37 From the Chinese attempt to suppress the opium trade and the question whether Chinese courts had jurisdiction over British subjects. The 'Opium War' commenced in 1840.
38 Hugh Elliot (1752-1830), diplomat; Governor of Madras, 1814-20; brother of the Earl of Minto; his son, Charles Elliot (1801-75), was chief superintendent of the commission on trade in China; Chargé d'Affaires in Texas, 1842-6; Governor of Bermuda, 1846-54; of Trinidad, 1854-6; of St Helena, 1863-9; knighted, 1856.
39 Philip Ivanovitch, Baron Brunnow (1797-1875), Russian minister and subsequently Ambassador to England, 1840-54, 1858-70; Ambassador to France, 1871-4; cr. count, 1871; he came to London in September 1839 on a special mission to solve the Eastern question.
40 *BFSP,* XXVIII, 408-9.
41 George Hay (1787-1876), eighth Marquess of Tweedale (S), a Scottish representative peer, 1818-76; aide-de-camp to George IV and William IV; Governor and Commander in Chief of Madras, 1842-8.
42 Prince Albert (1819-61) and Prince Ernest (1818-93); the latter succeeded as Duke of Saxe-Coburg, 1844.
43 Lord Wriothesley Russell (1804-86), fourth son of the sixth Duke of Bedford; rector of Cheneys, Bucks (1829) and canon of Windsor (1840); chaplain to Prince Albert.

1840

1 Cf. the printed version in Sir Herbert Maxwell, *Life and Letters of George William Frederick fourth Earl of Clarendon* (London, 1913), I, pp. 196-7.

2 The Treaty of London, whereby Britain, Austria, Prussia, and Russia agreed to the closure of the straits while Turkey was at peace, and offered the possession of Egypt and South Syria to Mehemet Ali for the remainder of his life, the other territories occupied by the Pasha to be returned to the Sultan along with the Turkish fleet, which had defected to Mehemet Ali. If the Pasha refused to accept the terms, the concessions could be withdrawn. *BFSP*, XXVIII, 342.

3 Philipp, Baron von Neumann (1781-1851), Austrian Ambassador at London, 1839-41; m. (1844) Lady Augusta Somerset, daughter of the Duke of Beaufort.

4 John Arthur Douglas Bloomfield (1802-79), afterwards (1846) second Baron Bloomfield (I), cr. (1871) Baron Bloomfield (UK); secretary of the embassy at St Petersburg, 1839-44; envoy to St Petersburg, 1844-51; to Berlin, 1851-60; Ambassador to Austria, 1860-71.

5 Friedrich Wilhelm IV (1795-1861).

6 The Emir Bechir (1763-1850), Prince of the Lebanon and Emir of the Druses in Syria; he had supported Mehemet Ali during the latter's invasion of Syria; surrendered to the English, Oct. 1840, and died in exile.

7 HHP, BM Add. MS 52204 H, f. 3.

8 Lord Holland died on 22 October 1840.

APPENDIX: THE WHIG CABINETS 1830–40

LORD GREY'S CABINET

	Nov. 1830	*April 1833*	*June–July 1834*
First Lord of the Treasury	Lord Grey	Grey	Grey
Chancellor of the Exchequer	Viscount Althorp	Althorp	Althorp
Lord Privy Seal	Lord Durham	Earl of Ripon	Carlisle
Lord President of the Council	Marquess of Lansdowne	Lansdowne	Lansdowne
Lord Chancellor	Lord Brougham	Brougham	Brougham
Home Secretary	Lord Melbourne	Melbourne	Melbourne
Foreign Secretary	Lord Palmerston	Palmerston	Palmerston
Chancellor of the Duchy of Lancaster	Lord Holland	Holland	Holland
Secretary for War and Colonies	Viscount Goderich (cr. Earl of Ripon, Apr. 1833)	Stanley	*Thomas Spring Rice*
First Lord of the Admiralty	Sir James Graham	Graham	*Lord Auckland*
President of the Board of Control	Charles Grant	Grant	Grant
President of the Board of Trade			
Master of the Mint			*James Abercromby*
Secretary at War			*Edward Ellice*
First Commissioner of Woods and Forests			
Paymaster General	*Lord John Russell* (from June 1831)	Russell	Russell
Irish Secretary	*E. G. Stanley* (June 1831–Mar. 1833)		
Postmaster General	Duke of Richmond	Richmond	
Minister without Portfolio	Earl of Carlisle (to June 1834)	Carlisle	

* Italics indicate new members of the cabinet.

LORD MELBOURNE'S CABINET

July–Nov. 1834	*April 1835*	*Feb. 1839*	*Aug.–Sept. 1839*
Melbourne	Melbourne	Melbourne	Melbourne
Althorp	Spring Rice	Spring Rice	*Sir Francis Baring*
Earl of Mulgrave	Duncannon	Duncannon	[Duncannon]: *Earl of Clarendon* (from Jan. 1840)
Lansdowne	Lansdowne	Lansdowne	Lansdowne
Brougham	*Lord Cottenham* (from Jan. 1836)	Cottenham	Cottenham
Viscount Duncannon	Russell	Russell	Normanby
Palmerston	Palmerston	Palmerston	Palmerston
Holland	Holland	Holland	Holland
Spring Rice	Grant cr. (May 1835) Lord Glenelg	*Marquess of Normanby*	Russell
Auckland	Auckland (Gov. Gen. of India, 1835) *Earl of Minto* (from Sept. 1835)	Minto	Minto
Grant	Hobhouse	Hobhouse	Hobhouse
	Charles Poulett Thomson	Thomson	*Henry Labouchere*
Abercromby			
Ellice	*Viscount Howick*	Howick	*Thomas Babington Macaulay*
Sir John Cam Hobhouse	[Duncannon] – also Privy Seal	[Duncannon]	Duncannon
Russell			
		Viscount Morpeth	Morpeth

INDEX

Abdul Mejid I (1823-61), Sultan (1839-61), 416-17, 420
Abercromby, George, 2nd Baron, 359
Abercromby, James (1st Baron Dunfermline), xxviii, 6, 27, 79, 190, 192, 207, 223, 254, 271, 279-80, 284, 349, 364-5, 377, 380, 395, 410; chosen Speaker, 1835, 279; reelected, 1837, 377
Abercromby, Ralph (2nd Baron Dunfermline), 25
Aberdeen, George Hamilton Gordon, 4th Earl of, xxxix, 24, 48, 55, 57, 59, 63, 90-1, 93, 96, 117-19, 122, 125, 153, 156, 178, 199, 204, 214, 219, 222, 291, 294, 306, 311, 317, 319, 321, 340, 386-7, 393
Abingdon, Montagu Bertie, 5th Lord, 312
Abinger, 1st Baron, *see* Scarlett, James
Acland, Sir Thomas Dyke, 382, 385
Adair, Sir Robert, xli, 12, 14, 16, 18-20, 29, 32, 67, 111, 125, 174, 316
Adam, Sir Frederick, 157
Adam, William George, 5, 297
Adam family, 157
Addington, Henry, Viscount Sidmouth (1757-1844), xiv, xviii, 258
Addington, Henry Unwin, 173, 237
Adelaide, Princess of Orléans, 133, 362
Adelaide, Queen (1792-1849), xx, 15-18, 20, 22, 35, 37, 50, 53, 65-7, 69, 71-4, 122, 169-70, 180, 187, 189, 191-3, 198, 202, 219, 259, 274, 277, 349-50, 354-5, 365-8
Affleck, Lady (Lady Holland's mother), 184, 193
Agnew, Sir Andrew, 280
Ailesbury, Charles Brudenell-Bruce, 1st Marquess of, 137, 155
Ailsa, Archibald Kennedy, 1st Marquess of, 239
Akif Pasha, Reis Effendi, 337, 416-17
Alava, Don Miguel Ricardo de, 19, 291, 294, 297, 301-2, 304-7, 310-11, 313, 316-17, 325
Albemarle, William Charles Keppel, 4th Earl of, 22, 35, 387
Albert of Saxe-Coburg, Prince Consort, 414-15
Alderson, Sir Edward Hall, 310
Alexander I, Czar (1777-1825), 387
Allen, John, xiv, xxiii, 78, 250, 260, 265, 276, 309, 354, 399; diary entries of, 279-84, 373, 375-6, 383-7, 422
Allen, Joseph, Bishop of Bristol, of Ely, 265
Althorp, John Charles Spencer, styled Viscount, 3rd Earl Spencer (1782-1845), xxvi, xxxiii-v, xxxvii-viii, xlv-vi, l-iv, 5-7, 10, 29-30, 33-5, 46-7, 58-9, 66-7, 69, 79, 81-2, 86-8, 90-5, 99, 109, 119, 120-2, 126-7, 129, 134, 138, 144, 147-9, 151, 158, 160, 163-4, 183, 189, 192, 194, 196, 210, 212-15, 218, 220, 222-3, 225-6, 228, 230, 233, 235, 238, 241, 243, 248, 252, 254-62, 264-5, 269-71, 274, 299, 389, 400-1; offers compromise on borough franchise, 30; suggested as possible prime minister (1839), 397
Alvanley, William Arden, 2nd Baron, 53, 262, 291, 294, 360
Amélie of Leuchtenberg (Don Pedro's wife), 240, 246, 267-8, 307-8
Amherst, William Pitt, 1st Earl, 104, 292, 296, 306
Ancillon, Johann Peter Friedrich, 106, 114, 173, 338
Ancona: French invasion of, 145-6, 150; discussed in House of Lords, 153; Austria and, 160
Anglesey, Henry William Paget, 1st Marquess of, xxxiv, xxxvi-viii, liii, 12, 29-31, 33, 41, 61-2, 66-8, 70, 78, 121, 128-9, 197-8, 202, 204-6, 231-2, 238, 243, 245, 251, 299-301, 328, 331, 346; reform plans for Ireland, 30, 202, 204-5, 435 n.190, 451 n.62
Anne, Queen (1665-1714), 275, 362
Anson, Thomas William, Viscount (1st Earl of Lichfield), 192
Appointments, *see* patronage
Apponyi, Count Anton Rudolph, 150, 164
Arbuthnot, Charles, 294
Argüelles, Agustin, 19, 103, 251
Argyll, Duchess of, 16
Argyll, George William Campbell, 6th Duke of, 244-5, 297, 387, 414

Aristocracy: necessary for preservation of liberty, xviii; quality of honor among, xix-xx; and constitution, xx-i
Armagh, Archbishop of, *see* Beresford, Lord John George
Armistead, Mrs, xiv
Arnold, Thomas, 344
Ashbrook, Henry Jeffrey Flower, 4th Viscount, 187
Ashburton, 1st Baron, *see* Baring, Alexander
Ashley, Anthony Ashley Cooper, styled Lord, 7th Earl of Shaftesbury (1801-85), xxiii-iv
Astell, William, 157
Aston, Arthur, 339
Attorney General: *see* Denman, Sir Thomas (to Nov. 1832), Horne, Sir William (to Feb. 1834), Campbell, Sir John (from Feb. 1834)
Attwood, Thomas, 209
Auckland, George Eden, 2nd Baron, 61, 126, 150, 191, 254-5, 292, 310, 313, 411
Augusta Sophia, Princess, 35, 74, 363
Augustus of Prussia, Prince, 383
Aylmer, Frederick Whitworth William, 6th Baron, 296

Backhouse, John, 59, 387
Bagot, Sir Charles, 23, 29, 47, 65, 67, 71, 84, 191
Bagot, Henrietta Maria, 239
Bank of England, 88, 192-3
Bankruptcy bill, 38, 67, 69, 436 n. 209, 437 n. 227
Barbacena, Marquis of, 8
Baring, Alexander, 1st Baron Ashburton, 119, 178-9, 219, 322
Baring, Sir Francis Thornhill, 409-10, 411
Barnes, Thomas, 262
Barrett, Richard, 222, 230
Barrow, John 292
Barthe, Felix, 24
Bath, Thomas Thynne, 2nd Marquess of, 359
Bath and Wells, Bishop of, *see* Law, George Henry
Bathurst, Henry, Bishop of Norwich, 43, 359
Bathurst, Henry, 3rd Earl, 58, 186, 265
Baudrand, Comte Marie Etienne Francois, 43-5, 49, 211
Bauza, Don Felipe, 19
Bayard, Ildefonso Leopoldo, 269, 276
Bayly, Edmund Goodenough, 312, 343
Beaufort, Henry Charles Somerset, 6th Duke of, 332
Bedchamber controversy, 397-402
Bedford, John Russell, 6th Duke of, 131, 313, 342, 414
Beer houses, licensing of, xxxiii, 23, 433 n. 63
Beira, Maria Theresa, Princess of, 294
Belgium, 9, 28, 31-2, 112, 212; Dutch advances in, 23-4; French march into, 25-6; French designs on, 30-1; discussed in House of Lords, 31-2, 41; armistice in, 37-8, 42; Austria, Prussia and Russia press for French withdrawal from, 45
Belgium, fortresses in: xli, 19-21, 25, 32-4, 36, 39-40, 42, 44, 99-102, 104, 110, 112-4, 118, 123-4, 146, 431 n.134; France and, 21, 25, 36, 99-102, 104, 110; Prussia and, 44, 114
Belgium, London Conference on: xl, 12-14, 24-6, 32-3, 37-8, 42, 44, 49, 52, 58, 69, 71-2, 74, 79, 114, 120, 122, 172, 239, 392, 443 n. 334, 444 n. 355, 488 n. 4
Belgium, National Congress of, 14, 427 n. 67
Belgium, Revolution of 1830 in, xli, 2-3
Belhaven, Robert Montgomery Hamilton, 8th Lord (and 1st Baron Hamilton), 47
Bell, George, 364
Belliard, Comte Augustin Daniel, 22, 29
Belmore, Somerset Lowry-Corry, 2nd Earl, 140, 142, 150
Bentham, Jeremy, xvii, xxxiii, 190
Bentinck, Lord William Cavendish, 116, 295, 331
Beresford, Lord John George, Archbishop of Armagh, 31, 141, 164, 223, 263, 405
Beresford, William Carr, 1st Viscount, 19, 225, 229, 294
Bernal, Ralph, 219
Bernstorff, Count Christian Günther von, 14, 19, 114, 125
Berri, Duchesse de, 189, 211
Bessborough, Frederick Ponsonby, 3rd Earl of, 54
Bethune, John Elliot Drinkwater, 296
Bexley, Nicholas Vansittart, 1st Baron, 177
Bickersteth, Henry, 1st Baron Langdale, 265, 331, 345-6, 354, 387
Binning, Lord, *see* Haddington
Blackburne, Francis, 41, 51
Blackburne, John, 296
Blake, Anthony Richard, 112, 206, 316
Blamire, William, 344
Blayney, Andrew Thomas, 11th Lord, 116
Blomfield, Charles James, Bishop of London (1828-56), 7, 19, 20, 31, 58, 82, 84, 129, 137, 141, 149, 157, 161, 169-70, 177, 184, 231-3, 236, 262, 358
Bloomfield, John Arthur Douglas, later Baron, 421
Bonaparte, François Charles Joseph (Duc de Reichstadt and King of Rome), 245
Bonaparte, Jerome (King of Westphalia), 323
Bonaparte, Joseph, 212, 245
Bonaparte, Louis (King of Holland), 323
Bonaparte, Louis-Napoleon, later Napoleon III, 245
Bonaparte, Lucien, Prince Canino, xl, 212, 245-6
Bonaparte, Napoleon, *see* Napoleon I
Bosanquet, Sir John Bernard, 293
Bourbon, Louis Henri, Duc de, 105
Bourmont, Comte Louis Auguste Victor de Ghaisne de, 225, 229, 231
Bradford, George Augustus Frederick Bridgeman, 2nd Earl of, 137
Breadalbane, John Campbell, 4th Earl and 1st Marquess of, 44, 55

Breadalbane, Mary, Lady, 5, 55
Bresson, Comte Charles, 22, 114-15
Broglie, Duc de, 251, 272, 310, 313, 333, 338-9
Brougham, James, 39, 264
Brougham, William, 312
Brougham and Vaux, Henry Peter Brougham, 1st Baron (1778-1868), xxiv, xxvi, xxx, xxxiii, xxxvii-viii, xlv xlix, li, 6-9, 12, 15, 18, 26-7, 32, 39, 40-1, 46, 49-52, 54-6, 58-65, 71-2, 74-6, 78-9, 81, 83-4, 87-9, 92, 94-5, 106-7, 112, 116-17, 123-4, 126-7, 131, 133, 135-6, 140-2, 147-9, 151-2, 157-8, 162-3, 165-9, 172, 176-8, 182, 186, 189, 193, 195-6, 198, 200, 203, 207-8, 212, 214-5, 219-24, 227-9, 231-5, 238, 241, 243, 248, 253-7, 259, 260, 262-6, 269-70, 273-8, 280-1, 291, 293-4, 302-3, 306, 309-10, 313, 324, 327-8, 331-2, 346-7, 352, 371, 375-6, 379, 381-2, 384-8, 396, 401-3, 406-8, 413-14; account of dissolution of Parliament in 1831, 43; on creation of peers to carry Reform Bill, 41, 46, 135; defends death penalty, 50; attacks West Indian slaveowners, 55-6; defends unions, 75-6; objects to wording of Stanley's Irish tithe bill, 90; opposes parliamentary inquiry on West Indies, 142; suspected of wanting to break up ministry (1832), 166; equivocal attitude toward emancipation of slaves, 208; on coronation oath and Irish Church Reform bill, 232; ambition to become prime minister, 256-7; angry exchange with Melbourne, 376; curries favor with Tories, 384; his isolation, 401-2; rumored to have died, 414
Brownlow, Lady, 15
Brunnow, Baron Philip Ivanovitch, 416, 421
Brunswick, Karl Friedrich, Duke of, 213
Brydges, Sir Harford Jones, 311
Buccleugh, Walter Francis Montagu-Douglas-Scott, 5th Duke of, 190, 192-3, 198
Buckingham and Chandos, Richard Temple Chandos Grenville, 1st Duke of, 118, 133, 177, 227, 233
Buckingham and Normanby, John Sheffield, 1st Duke of (1648-1721), 370
Buller, Charles, 357, 376
Bülow, Baron Heinrich von, 14, 33-4, 37, 44, 58, 123, 125, 139, 173, 175, 421
Bulwer, William Henry Lytton, 351
Burdett, Sir Francis, xix-xx, 49, 76, 95, 195, 210, 233, 309, 330-1, 357, 361
Burge, William, 137, 212, 222, 225
Burgess, Thomas, Bishop of Salisbury (1825-37), 352, 358
Burke, Edmund (1729-1797), xix-xx
Butler, Samuel, Bishop of Lichfield and Coventry (1836-9), 344, 415
Buxton, Sir Thomas Fowell, 55-6, 140, 234, 307, 310
Byng, Frederick, 361
Byng, George, 136
Byng, Sir John, 1st Baron Strafford and Earl Strafford, 49-50, 322-3
Byron, George Gordon, Lord (1788-1824), xv

Cabinet (Introductory essay): composition of Grey's, xxvii; corporate assumptions of, xxxii; Irish policy of, xxxiv-ix; collective responsibility in, xliii-liv; size of, xlv, 48; monarch and, xlix, 318; House of Lords and, xlix-l; House of Commons and, l, 86, 230; tactic of concession for stability, l; factional alignments in Grey's, xlv-vi; subcommittees of, xlvi-vii, 163, 192-3; lack of decision in, xlvii-viii; role of prime minister in, xlvii, lii-iv; formal votes in, xlviii-ix
Cabinet changes: resignation of Grey's in 1832, 177-8; of personnel in 1833, 207; resignation of four ministers from in 1834, 251-3; their replacements in spring 1834, 253-5; resignation of Grey's in 1834, 256-8; formation of Melbourne's first, 258-60; dismissal of Melbourne's, 269-76; resignation of Peel's, 285; formation of Melbourne's second, 286-90; their resignation on Jamaica bill, 1839, 397; changes in composition of, 1839, 409-11
Cabinet deliberations: response to French offer of mediation in Poland, 13; draft of protocol on Eighteen Articles, 13; on £10 qualification in Reform Bill, 20; on Portugal, 59, 80, 87, 89-90, 237; on creation of peers for Reform Bill, 46-7, 97-9, 107-10, 113-16, 124-5, 130-1, 134-5, 138, 141, 143-5, 148-9, 151-3, 158, 160, 162-3, 165, 167-8, 177, 180-1; on Belgium, 64, 120, 154, 210; on defeat of second reading of Reform Bill in House of Lords (Oct. 1831), 64-6; on attaching O'Connell to government, 68; convening Parliament (Nov. 1831), 79, 82; on Russia in Poland, 80; on franchise in Reform Bill, 81-2, 85; on borough freeholders, 81, 445 n. 362; on freeman franchise, 81, 445 n. 363; division of counties in Reform Bill, 81, 444 n. 361; constituency boundaries, 81, 99; size of reformed House of Commons, 86; preparation of King's Speech in convening Parliament (Dec. 1831), 87, 89; Irish Reform Bill, 94-5, 194; relief granted to victims of hurricane in West Indies, 96-7; treaty on fortresses in Belgium, 101-2; grant to Roman Catholic clergy in Ireland, 112-13; Russian Dutch loan, 122-3; Irish tithes, 125-6, 129, 130, 194-5; coercion proposals for Ireland, 125-6, 129; West Indian sugar duties, 127, 158; magistrates at Bristol, 128-9; Lord Dundonald's pardon, 133, 154; French in Ancona, 154; Greece, 158; resignation as an alternative to creation of peers, 160, 167, 177; municipal corporations, 163, 292, 298, 300, 303; refusal to postpone House of Lords consideration of Schedule A, 176; insist on guarantee of creating peers if necessary, 181, 183-4; foreign affairs (July 1832), 200; defense of liberal principles in foreign affairs, 201-2;

reform of Irish Church, 205 ff; emancipation of slaves, 213, 218, 225; arrears of tithe in Ireland, 213-14; East India Company, 214; House of Lords resolution on Portugal (1833), 215-16; grant to West Indians, 216, 218, 225; appropriation of surplus Irish Church revenues, 205, 251-2, 467 n.14; appropriations clause in Irish Church Reform Bill, 222, 226, 251-2, 298; Brougham's Local Judicature bill, 227; alternatives in July 1833, 227-8; decide not to resign after Lords' amendments to Irish Church Reform Bill, 235; urge Grey not to retire (Aug. 1833), 241 (Jan, 1834), 248-9; assistance to Pedro's forces in Portugal (1834), 248; division on renewal of Irish Coercion Bill (1834), 255-6; Heytesbury's appointment to India, 291-2; Irish Tithe bill (1835), 299, 304, 313; Spain (1835), 302; on using troops to collect tithe in Ireland, 302; decide to send a steamer to West Africa, 318; consider creation of peers after censure of Normanby's government (1839), 393-4; appeal to House of Commons after censure of Irish government by House of Lords, 394; Near East crisis (1839-40), 412-13, 417-21

Cabinet, meetings of: xlvi-vii, 5-6, 8-9, 11, 13, 20-1, 23-4, 26, 29-30, 32, 34, 36, 42, 45, 46-8, 51, 54, 55, 58, 64, 66-9, 79-84, 87, 89-93, 97, 99, 101, 106-7, 112, 114-15, 118, 120, 122, 124-6, 128, 130, 133, 138, 141, 143, 148, 150, 154, 158, 160, 162-3, 165, 167, 170, 175-7, 180, 183, 186, 190, 194, 199, 201, 210, 212-14, 218-20, 223, 225-6, 233, 235, 237, 248, 291-2, 295, 297, 299, 301-2, 304-6, 308, 312-13, 316, 318, 321-2, 324, 329, 411

Calcraft, John, 53

Cambridge, Augusta, Duchess of, 17

Cambridge, George, 7th Duke of, 22

Campbell, Sir John, 49

Campbell, Sir John, later 1st Baron (Attorney General), 292-3, 302, 331-2, 345

Camperdown, Robert Dundas Duncan Haldane, 2nd Viscount Duncan, 1st Earl of, 6, 44, 90

Campomanes, Count of, 20

Campos, Francisco Antonio de, 336

Canada, 297, 306, 315, 317, 318-20, 335, 347, 359, 370, 380, 388-90, 392, 413; bill suspending constitution of Lower Canada, 381; motion in House of Commons to censure government's conduct on (1838), 384; insurrection in and Durham's ordinances on, 386-7

Canino, Prince, *see* Bonaparte, Lucien

Canning, George (1770-1827), xxiv-v, 156

Canning, Sir Stratford, 244, 250

Canterbury, Archbishop of, *see* Howley, William

Capital punishment, 49-50, 148, 195, 203, 453 n.99, 458 n.211; Holland on, xxxiii

Carew, Robert Shapland, later 1st Baron, 130

Carlisle, George Howard, 6th Earl of, xxvii, lii, 5, 9-10, 16-18, 39, 46, 48-9, 51, 68, 79, 82, 94, 109, 126, 130, 133, 140, 144, 197, 213, 223-4, 226, 248, 254, 260, 359

Carlisle, Lady, 5

Carlists, 211, 242, 304-5, 311, 351; and France, 333, 353

Carlos, Don, 20, 220, 247, 250-1, 292, 294, 297, 310, 336, 354

Carmarthen, Francis Osborne, Marquess of, 5th Duke of Leeds (1751-99), 337

Carnarvon, Henry George Herbert, 2nd Earl of, 7, 27-8, 40, 64, 96, 133, 161-2, 178-9, 183

Caroline, Queen (1768-1821), xxvi

Carr, Robert James, Bishop of Chichester (to 1831), Bishop of Worcester (1831-41), 52

Cartwright, Major John (1740-1824), xix

Cartwright, Thomas, 201

Carvalho, *see* Silva Carvalho

Caulfield, Henry, 50

Cave, Robert Otway, 280

Cawdor, John Frederick Campbell, 1st Earl, 20, 227

Cea Bermudez, Francisco, 220, 225, 250

Celles, Comte Antoine Philippe de, 49

Chad, George William, 106, 114-15, 125

Chambers, Dr William Frederick, 354

Chandos, Richard Temple-Nugent-Grenville, styled Marquess of (2nd Duke of Buckingham and Chandos), xxxii, 55-6, 92, 97, 219, 282, 385

Charity commission, 332

Charlemont, Francis William Caulfield, 2nd Earl and 1st Baron, 50, 52

Charles I (1600-49), 351

Charles II (1630-85), 53

Charlotte, Princess (1796-1817), 5, 363, 382-3

Charlotte, Queen (1744-1818), 370

Chateaubriand, Vicomte François René de, 211

Chatham, John Pitt, 2nd Earl of, 244, 328-9, 332

Chaves, Marquis of, 267

Chester, Bishop of, *see* Sumner, John Bird

Chichester, Bishop of, *see* Carr, Robert James (to 1831), Maltby, Edward (1831-6), Otter, William (to 1840)

Choiseul, Duc de, 137

Cholera, 74, 76, 78, 87, 129, 179; in Russia, 5, 19; in Scotland, 13; at Sunderland, 73-4; in the metropolis, 129-30; Prevention bill, 131

Cholmondely, George Horatio, 2nd Marquess of, 4

Church of England: in colonies, 5; Buildings bill, 19, 431 n.129; Pluralities bill, 42, 54, 58, 159; Peel ministry's plans for reform of, 280; church rates, 300, 340, 358, 361, 483 n.12; building of churches, 320; Sinecure Church Preferment bill, 323, 479 n.131; legislation of 1836 on, 340, 481 n.6, *see also* Church of Ireland, Dissenters, Tithes (England), Patronage, ecclesiastical

Church of Ireland: vestry cess, 27, 434 n.176; plans for reform of, xxxvii-viii, 204-5, 459 n. 2; Temporalities Act (1833), xxxvii-viii; amendments to Temporalities Bill in Lords'

committee, 234; dissension on appropriation of surplus revenues of, 205, 222-3, 251-2, 282-3, 285, 287-8, 291, 296, 304, 321, 323, 357, 382-3, 386, 451 n.62, 464 n.64, 476 n.85; divides Stanley and Whigs, 286; plans for reform affect King's decision to dismiss Melbourne, 273-4; *see also* Ireland, Tithes (Ireland)
Clanricarde, Lady, 369, 371
Clanricarde, Ulick John de Burgh, 2nd Marquess of, 63, 96, 133, 150, 153, 192, 222, 236, 254, 341, 369-70, 371, 387, 410, 414
Clare, John Fitzgibbon, 2nd Earl of, 222
Clarendon, John Charles Villiers, 3rd Earl of, li, 244-5, 410, 414, 416, 419-21
Clark, Sir James, 395, 403-4
Clarke, Sir Charles Mansfield, 403-4
Clements, Robert Bemingham, styled Lord, 300
Clerk, Sir George, 196
Clerk, John (Lord Eldin), 190
Cleveland, William Harry Vane, 1st Duke of, 47, 65, 333
Clive, Edward Herbert, styled Viscount, later 2nd Earl of Powis, 93
Cloncurry, Valentine Browne Lawless, Baron, 41, 124, 206, 341
Clubs: Brooks, 330-1, 351; Fox (Whig), 29, 194; Johnson, 167; Reform, 375
Cobbett, William, 209, 309
Cochrane, Lord and Lady, *see* Dundonald
Codrington, Sir Edward, 23, 100
Coke of Holkham, Thomas William, 1st Earl of Leicester, 44, 107, 226, 301, 370
Coleridge, Samuel Taylor (1772-1834), xx
Collins, assaults King at Ascot, 193, 195
Collins, William, 359
Colquhoun, John Nisbet, 354
Compton, Sir Spencer, 1st Earl of Wilmington, 245, 258
Conroy, Sir John, 53, 56, 225, 349-50, 363, 365, 368-9, 371, 374, 379-80, 391, 394, 402-4
Constantine, Grand Duke of Russia, 104, 387
Conyngham, Francis Nathaniel, 2nd Marquess of, 254, 299, 317, 370, 387
Conyngham, Lady, 16
Copleston, Edward, Bishop of Llandaff, 86, 343
Córdoba, Antonio López de (Spanish Chargé d'Affaires in London), 225
Córdoba, Luis Fernández de, 220, 242, 249, 302
Cork, Edmund Boyle, 9th Earl of, 359
Cornwall, Duchy of, 52, 128, 354; estate of, in Scilly Islands, 132-3, 139
Coronation: of George IV, 3; of William IV, 17, 20, 38, 40, 45, 48, 50-1, 53; of Victoria, 388; creation of peers at, 39, 44-5, 46-7
Cottenham, Lord, *see* Pepys, Sir Charles
Cotton, Sir Willoughby, 150
Courier, 40, 114, 350, 352
Courtenay, Thomas Peregrine, 42, 127
Courtenay, William, 20th Earl of Devon, 214, 312
Court of Chancery, 15, 24, 40, 212, 275, 340, 434 n.170, 481 n.4
Coventry, Lady, 220
Cowley, Henry Wellesley, 1st Baron, 276, 298
Cowper, Emily Mary Lamb, Lady (later Lady Palmerston), 102, 384
Cowper, Peter Leopold Clavering-, 5th Earl, 312
Cowper, William, 1st Earl (d. 1723), 275
Crabbe, George, 220
Crampton, Philip Cecil, Irish Solicitor General, 51
Creevey, Thomas, 348
Crewe, Sir George, 356
Croker, John Wilson, 51, 97, 331
Croley, Dr George, 41
Cumberland, Duchess of, 185, 187, 191, 202
Cumberland, Ernest Augustus, Duke of (King of Hanover), 22, 48, 50, 67, 171, 185-8, 190-1, 198-9, 224, 227, 231-3, 239, 301, 311, 322, 325, 344, 348, 356, 366-7, 370
Cumberland, William Augustus, Duke of (1721-65), 35, 370
Currey, Mr, 5
Czartoriski, Prince Adam Jerzy, 40, 104, 128, 387

Dacre, Thomas Brand, 20th Lord, 5-7, 254
Daine, Nicholas Joseph, 28
Dalrymple, Sir John Hamilton Macgill (later 10th Earl of Stair), 189, 191-2
Dalrymple, William Tombes, 74
Danvers, Frederick Dawes, 3, 58, 114, 126, 173, 193
Da Ponza, *see* Napier, Sir Charles
Davies, Thomas Henry Hastings, 217
Dawson, George Robert, 96, 153
Dedel, Salomon, 210-12, 217, 316
De Grey, Thomas Philip Weddell, Baron Grantham, 1st Earl, 232
De Lisle, Sophia FitzClarence, Lady Sidney, Lady, 15, 362
De Mauley, 1st Baron, *see* Ponsonby, William Francis Spencer
Denison, Edward, Bishop of Salisbury (1837-54), 358
Denison, John Evelyn, 30, 358
Denman, Sir Thomas, 1st Baron, 39, 52, 82, 92, 128, 185, 303, 306, 317, 320
De Rigny, Comte Henri Gauthier, 251
Derry, Bishop of, *see* Ponsonby, Richard
D'Este, Augusta Emma, 15, 53, 311
D'Este, Sir Augustus, 52
Devon, 20th Earl of, *see* Courtenay, William
Devonshire, William George Spencer, 6th Duke of, 22-3
Dino, Duchesse de, 13, 72, 173, 333
Dissenters, 280, 282, 284, 302, 358, 373, 379; Marriage and Registration Bills, 302, 329, 340, 476 n. 82

Donoughmore, John Hely-Hutchinson, 3rd Earl of, 378
Dover, George James Welborne Agar-Ellis, 1st Baron, 5, 12, 14, 143, 167
Downshire, Athur Hill, 3rd Marquess of, 266, 270
Doyle, James Warren, Bishop of Kildare and Leighlin, 96
Drinkwater, John Elliot, *see* Bethune, John
Drummond, Henry, 87
Dublin, Archbishop of, *see* Whately, Richard
Dudley, John William Ward, 1st Earl of, 165
Duff, Mrs 16
Duncan, Lord, *see* Camperdown, Robert
Duncannon, John William Ponsonby, Viscount, later 4th Earl of Bessborough, xxvii, xxxvii, xlviii, 27-9, 86, 99, 124, 128, 133, 149, 191-2, 197, 220, 230, 254, 260, 263, 266-7, 270, 273, 278, 287-8, 293, 295, 299, 302, 304, 322, 329, 357, 370, 380, 387, 389, 395, 401
Duncombe, Thomas Slingsby, 125-6, 292
Dundas, Robert Adam, 191
Dundas 'of Berkshire', Charles, 1st Baron Amesbury, 47, 98, 110
Dundonald, Lady, 56, 133, 192
Dundonald, Thomas Cochrane, 10th Earl of, 11, 51-2, 54, 56, 95, 154, 192, 334
Dunning, John, 89
Durant de Mareuil, Joseph Alexandre Jacques, styled, 193
Durham, John George Lambton, 1st Earl, xxiv, xxvii, xxxvii, xlv-viii, liii, 5-6, 8-11, 14, 16-18, 28, 44-5, 47, 56, 72, 80, 87-9, 93, 98, 100-2, 104, 109, 112, 124-9, 135, 145-9, 158, 164, 169, 186, 256, 260, 320, 347, 364-5, 369-71, 388, 391-2, 394; his character and ill-humor, 8, 11; asks for earldom, 44; illness and death of his son, 60, 88; anger toward Grey, 88-9, 138, 146, 148-9; offers to go to China, 104; calculates Whig strength in Lords, 124; threatens to resign, 131; on creation of peers, 152, 154; rumors of his resignation, 166; special mission to Russia (1832), 195-6, 200; resignation from cabinet and elevation to earldom, 207; declines Paris embassy, 253; objections to possibility of his joining cabinet (1834), 254; controversy with Brougham and Russell about credit for Reform Bill, 264, 269, 294; ministers' fear of, as an opposition leader, 272; and appointment to Canada, 298, 370, 381; appointed ambassador to Russia (1835), 313-15; his role as ambassador, 334, 337, 351; alleged to be an advisor to Duchess of Kent, 349, 362, 372; issues illegal ordinances, 386
Durham, Lady, 369, 371

East India Company, 157, 174-5, 214; renewal of charter, 88, 92, 455 n.145, 462 n.34; and factory at Canton, 93, 116-17
Eaubrink drainage bill, 3, 5
Ebrington, Hugh Fortescue, styled Viscount, later 2nd Earl Fortescue, 65, 93, 125-6, 130, 179, 197, 206, 215, 350, 392, 407
Eden, Robert John, 3rd Baron Auckland, 275
Edinburgh Review, xv, 264, 294; origin of, 115
Egremont, Sir George O'Brien Wyndham, 3rd Earl of, 13, 15-17
Eldon, John Scott, 1st Earl of, 7, 11, 24, 38, 48, 58, 61, 123, 140, 149, 153, 195, 224
Elections: of 1830, 3, 424 n.11; of 1835, 279; of 1837, 371-3, 383-4, 485 n.60; by-elections (1835), 295, 301
Eliot, Edward Granville, Lord, later 3rd Earl of St Germans, 291, 298, 304, 385
Ellenborough, Edward Law, 2nd Baron, 93, 96, 123, 150, 169, 177, 184, 224, 226, 233, 236, 239, 261, 361, 386, 387
Ellice, Edward, xlvi, 207-8, 230, 248, 253-5, 270, 283, 286-8, 293-4, 299-300, 399, 413, 417
Elliott, Charles, 411
Elliott, Sir George, 327
Elliott, Hugh, 411
Ellis, Henry, 3
Elphinstone, John, 13th Lord, 399
Elphinstone, John Fullerton, 103
Emancipation of slaves, xxix, 55-6, 60, 91, 136-7, 207, 379-80, 385; and sugar duties, 60, 62, 213; Lords' committee to inquire into, 137, 141-2; Stanley's bill of 1833 for, 208, 213, 216-18, 223-4, 460 n.10; Buxton's resolutions on (1835), 307, 310; *see also* 'Saints', Slave trade, Slavery
Emir Bechir, The, 422
Ernest of Saxe-Coburg, 414
Errol, Elizabeth FitzClarence, Lady, 53
Errol, William George Hay, 18th Earl of, 183
Erskine, David Montagu Erskine, 2nd Baron, 199, 201-2
Espartero, Baldomero, 354
Essex, George Capel-Coningsby, 5th Earl of, 50, 244, 309
Esterhazy, Prince Paul Anton, 55, 105
Eton, xiii, 17-18; cabinet ministers and, 8, 16, 427 n.58
Euston, Henry Fitzroy, styled Earl of, later 5th Duke of Grafton, 279
Evans, George De Lacy, 207, 307, 309, 310-11, 317, 319, 325, 328, 354, 360
Ewart, Joseph, 337
Examiner, 399
Exeter, Bishop of, *see* Phillpotts, Henry

Fagel, Barton Hendrik, 200
Falck, Baron Anton Reinhard, 22, 34-5, 120, 128, 192-3
Falmouth, Edward Boscawen, 1st Earl of, 19
Faraday, Michael, 294
Farnham, John Maxwell-Barry, 5th Baron, 99, 302
Fazakerly, John Nicholas, 323

Ferdinand I, Austrian Emperor (1835-48), 298
Ferdinand VII, King of Spain, 23, 93, 103, 220, 250
Ferdinand of Saxe-Coburgh, Prince, 336, 353
Ferguson of Raith, Robert, 342
Fergusson, Robert Cutlar, 309
Fife, James Duff, 4th Earl and 1st Baron, 37
FitzClarence, Lord Adolphus, 53, 138, 203
FitzClarence, Lord Augustus, 323
FitzClarence, Lord Frederick, 370-1
Fitzgerald, Hamilton, 403-4
Fitzgerald, William Vesey-, 1st and 2nd Baron, 341, 361
Fitzherbert, Maria Anne, 369
Fitzwilliam, Charles William Wentworth-, styled Lord Milton, 3rd and 5th Earl, 11, 29, 296, 392
Flahault, Comte Auguste Charles Joseph de, 19, 193, 244
Flahault, Margaret, Lady Keith, Comtesse de, 382-3
Floridablanca, Count of, 20
Foley, Lady, 192
Foley, Thomas, 5th Baron, 49-50, 192
Follet, Sir William Webb, 360, 386
Fonblanque, Albany, 358, 403
Forbes, George John, styled Viscount, 41
Forbes, Lady, 369
Foreign Enlistment Act, xxii, 40, 61, 97, 103, 106, 302, 307, 310, 385, 437 n.226, 443 n.345
Fortescue, Hugh, 1st Earl, 219, 227
Fox, Caroline (diarist's sister), xiii, 366
Fox, Charles James (1749-1806), xiii, xv-xxi,xli, xliv, xlvi, 16, 119, 156, 418
Fox, Charles Richard (diarist's eldest son), xiv, 72, 76, 184-7, 191, 203, 295-7, 300, 354, 366
Fox, Henry Edward, later 4th Lord Holland (diarist's son), xxv, 18, 20, 32, 42, 49, 71, 76, 185, 190, 192, 212, 323, 362
Fox, Henry Stephen, 117, 328
Fox, Lady Mary, 16-17, 35, 53, 178-9, 185, 329, 366, 380
Fox-Strangways, William Thomas Horner (4th Earl of Ilchester), 364, 387
Francesco IV, Duke of Modena, 335
Frederick William IV (1795-1861), King of Prussia (1840-61), 422
Freire, Augustinho José, 249, 268, 307-8
Frias, Bernardino Fernández de Velasco, Duke of, 291, 313
Friends of the People, xviii-xix
Funchal, Count of, 12, 55, 237

Gage, Henry Hall, 4th Viscount, 186
Gage, Sir William Hall, 307, 333, 353
Galloway, Lady, 16
Gascoyne amendment, xxvii, xxxi
Genlis, Comtesse de, 49, 333
George I (1660-1727), 15
George II (1683-1760), 328
George III (1738-1820), xv, 44, 66, 153, 179, 188, 200, 226, 289, 382, 415
George IV (1762-1830), xxiv-v, 1, 3, 16, 354, 382, 384
Gérard, Etienne Maurice, 39, 41, 49, 52, 71
German Confederation, 9, 93, 201, 427 n.67
Giddy (Gilbert), Davies, 179
Gillon, William Downe, 391
Gisborne, Thomas, 223, 281
Gladstone, William Ewart, 385
Glasgow, George Boyle, 4th Earl of, 139
Glenelg, Charles Grant, 1st Baron, xx, 296, 299-300, 306, 323, 335, 351, 380-1, 384, 410, 414; censured by king, 315-17; instructs Canada Commissioners, 318-21; king's dislike of, 348, 350; distressed by agitation for immediate emancipation, 385; removed from Colonial Office and resigns, 389-90, 392; *see also* Grant, Charles
Glenorchy, John, Lord, 5th Earl of Breadalbane, 13
Globe, 40, 277, 352
Gloucester, Bishop of, *see* Monk, James Henry
Gloucester, Duchess of (Princess Mary), 21, 82, 355, 415
Gloucester, William Frederick, Duke of, 189, 383
Glove trade, 150
Goddard, Charles, 320
Goderich, Frederick John Robinson, Viscount, 1st Earl of Ripon, xx, xxiv, xxvi, xxxviii, xli, 8-9, 27, 30, 46, 56, 62-4, 69, 79, 82, 86-7, 91, 94, 107, 116, 123, 127, 137, 142-4, 148, 150-2, 169, 196, 199, 202, 206; suspicious of France, 25, 33, 100, 120, 158; questions association with Dom Pedro, 59, 61; inability to devise colonial policy, 143; mortified at his removal from Colonial Office to Lord Privy Seal, 207; *see also* Ripon, Frederick, 1st Earl of
Godwin, William (1756-1836), xx
Gómez, Miguel, 354
Goodwin, John Thomas, 111, 117, 274
Gordon, Captain, 160
Gore, Sir John, 116
Gormanston, Jenico Preston, Viscount, 124
Gosford, Archibald Acheson, 2nd Earl of, 140, 159, 303, 306, 317-18, 335
Gossett, Sir William, 300, 317
Goulburn, Henry, 95, 276
Gower, George Granville Sutherland Leveson-, Baron (later 2nd Duke of Sutherland), 32, 191, 369
Grafton, Augustus Henry Fitzroy, 3rd Duke of (1735-1811), 179
Grafton, George Henry Fitzroy, 4th Duke of, 244-5, 265-6, 274
Graham, Sir James, xxvii, xxxvii-viii, xlv-viii, li, 14, 34, 51, 54, 56, 59-60, 80-1, 100, 103, 106-7, 117, 125, 127, 215, 219, 225, 251, 279, 292, 311, 323, 347, 357; favors support of Dom Pedro in Portugal, 52, 248; and creation of

peers for Reform Bill, 144, 152; wants to resign after Lords' resolution on Portugal but defers to majority of cabinet, 215; resignation, 252-3; reported anxious for junction with Peel, 281; considers opposition to appropriation a matter of religious principle, 283
Grand, Mme, 346
Grant, Charles, 1st Baron Glenelg, xxv-vi, xlii, xlvi, 10, 14, 30, 61, 91-2, 94, 103, 109, 116, 141, 145, 212-14, 248, 271, 291-2; *see also* Glenelg
Grant, Marcia Maria, 300
Grant, Sir Robert, 389
Grant, Sir William, 190
Grant of Rothiemurchus, John Peter, 222
Granville, Lord Granville Leveson-Gower, 1st Earl, xli, 9, 18, 20-1, 24-5, 31-2, 34-6, 42, 65-7, 84, 102, 106, 111, 145-6, 150, 154, 173, 190, 231, 235, 286, 298, 301, 305, 310, 335, 339, 351
Great Western Railway, 310, 315-16
Greece, London Conference on, xl, 21-2, 433 n.151
Green, Richard Wilson, 125, 129
Gregory XVI, Pope (1831-46), 145-6, 335
Gregson, William, 79
Grenville, William Wyndham, Baron (1759-1834), xv-xvi, xliv, xlvi, 337
Greville, Charles Cavendish Fulke, 4, 149
Grey, Charles, 285
Grey, Charles, 2nd Earl (1764-1845), xvi-xxix *passim,* xxxiii-liv *passim,* 3-299 *passim,* 316, 322, 330-1, 342, 347, 349, 354, 368, 372, 383, 399-401, 405, 410; consults Holland on foreign affairs, 13, 44; and creation of peers for Reform Bill, 42, 64, 102-3, 109-10, 113, 121, 146-7, 149, 151; overruled by cabinet on summoning Parliament (1831), 82; skill in debate compared to Pitt and Fox, 156; constantly agonizes about retirement, 158, 209, 239-50; prefers Althorp as his successor, 226; suggests Althorp or Melbourne for prime minister, 260; *see also* Cabinet, 'Waverers'
Grey, Sir Charles Edward, 315
Grey, Edward, Bishop of Hereford (1832-7), 174, 219, 232, 234, 263, 306, 344, 370
Grey, Sir George, 310, 385, 387, 410
Grey, John, 342
Grey, Lady, 39, 72, 103, 128, 130, 260-1, 294
Grey, William George, 342
Grote, George, 223, 284, 375-6, 383
Guardian, 283
Guizot, François, 251, 417
Gurwood, John, 304

Haddington, Thomas Hamilton, 9th Earl of, 69, 118, 130, 183, 190, 192, 233
Halford, Sir Henry, 118, 165, 395
Halkett, Sir Colin, 222
Hallam, Henry, 383
Hamilton, Alexander, 10th Duke of, 329, 332, 359
Hampden, Dr Renn Dickson, 343
Harcourt, Edward Vernon, Archbishop of York, 132, 155, 184, 219
Hardinge, Sir Henry, 151, 360
Hardwicke, Philip Yorke, 1st Earl of (1690-1764), 123, 332
Hardwicke, Philip Yorke, 3rd Earl of, 125
Hardy, Sir Thomas Masterman, 51-2, 56
Harewood, Henry Lascelles, 2nd Earl of, 224, 386
Harispe, Jean Isidore, 353
Harley, Alfred, styled Lord, 6th Earl of Oxford, 6
Harley, Robert, 1st Earl of Oxford (1661-1724), 118
Harper, Robert John, 192
Harrowby, Dudley Ryder, 1st Earl of, 54, 64, 69, 91-2, 97, 118, 125-39, 144, 147-9, 151, 161-3, 165, 172, 176, 188-9, 194, 219, 227, 233, 306, 340; negotiations with Grey on Reform Bill, 125-39; *see also* 'Waverers'
Harvey, Daniel Whittle, 209, 332, 375-6
Hastings, Dowager Marchioness of, 403
Hastings, Lady Flora, 394-5, 401-5
Hastings, George Augustus Francis Rawdon, 2nd Marquess of, 20, 395, 403
Hatherton, Lord, *see* Littleton, Edward John
Hawkins, Edward (Provost of Oriel, Oxford), 343
Hay, Lord John, 354, 360
Hay, Robert William, 292
Head, Sir Francis Bond, 18, 335
Heathcote, Lady, 16
Hélène of Württemburg, Grand Duchess, 71-2
Herbert, William, 359, 371
Hereford, Bishop of, *see* Huntingford, George Isaac (1815 to Apr. 1832), Grey, Edward (1832 to June 1837), Musgrave, Thomas (1837-47)
Hereford, Henry Fleming Lee Devereux, 14th Viscount, 19-20, 24, 310
Herries, John Charles, 120
Hertford, Francis Charles Seymour-Conway, 3rd Marquess of, 369
Hertford, Lady, 214
Heytesbury, William A'Court, 1st Baron, 80, 171, 291-2, 295
Hill, Rowland, 1st Baron, 116, 150, 184-5, 187-8, 228, 300, 319
Hillsborough, Arthur Hill, styled Earl of, later 4th Marquess of Downshire, 267
Hobhouse, Henry, 340
Hobhouse, Sir John Cam, xxxiii, 70, 121-2, 126, 207, 260, 281, 290-2, 316, 324, 357, 419
Hodgson, Christopher, 280
Holland, Henry Fox, 1st Baron (1705-74) (diarist's grandfather), xiii, l, 348, 370
Holland, Henry Richard Vassall Fox, 3rd Baron (1773-1840), the diarist (introductory essay and Allen's entries only): his devotion to

Charles James Fox, xiii; education of, xiii; continental travels, xiii-xiv; marriage, xiv; inherits Fox's principles, xv-xvi, xli; conception of liberty, xvi-xxii; revives protests in House of Lords, xvii; sense of party, xviii; and the Friends of the People, xviii-xix; sense of honor, xix-xx; on property, xx-i; and French Revolution, xx; conception of constitution, xx-i, xxx; opposition to slavery, xxi; hierarchical and corporate conception of society, xxi-ii, xxix-xxx; indifference to factory bills and social reform legislation, xxi-ii, xxxiii; associates national aspirations with liberty and constitutionalism, xxii, xxxix, xli; ambivalence toward Napoleon, xxii-iii; an heir of the Enlightenment, xxiii; Lord Ashley on, xxiii-iv; declines joining Canning's government, xxiv-v; laments absence of constitutional issues in 1820s, xxv; declines foreign office, xxvi; becomes Chancellor of Duchy of Lancaster, xxvii; ideas on representation, xxx, xxxii; and legal reform, xxxiii; on Irish demands, xxxv-vi; and Irish Church reform, xxxvii; distaste for coercive legislation, xxi, xxxviii; distinguishes Whigs from Tories on foreign as well as domestic affairs, xxxix; intimacy with foreign diplomats, xl-i; and Palmerston, xl, xlii-iii; Francophilia of, xli; desire to maintain alliance of constitutional powers, xli-iii; attitude toward Polish provisional government, xlii; isolation within cabinet on foreign affairs in 1840, xliii-iv; role in Whig cabinets, xlv-viii, liii; and Melbourne, lii; and Grey, lii-iii; 280, 284, 376, 387, 411

Holland, Lady (1770-1845), xiv-xv, xxii-iii, 8, 35, 165, 296-7, 399

Holland, Stephen Fox, 2nd Baron (diarist's father), xiii

Holland House, xiii-xv; xxiv, xxxix-xl, text *passim*; parodied by Caroline Lamb, xv

Holmes, William, 123, 180, 281

Holt, Francis Ludlow, 122

Home, William Archibald, 275

Hoppner, Richard Belgrave, 4, 42, 49, 53, 240-2, 250

Horne, Sir William (Solicitor General 1830-2, Attorney General 1832-4), 62, 82, 128, 265

Horner, Francis, xv, 115

House and window tax, 207

House of Commons: express confidence in government after defeat of Reform Bill in Lords (Oct. 1831), 65-6; address to king to retain Grey ministry, 179; reformed, of 1833, 208-9, 461 n.12; address supporting ministry on Portugal (1833), 217; pledge support to Grey's government (1834), 253; election of Speaker (1835), 279-80 (1837), 377; alleged failure of government to command, 348; division on ballot (1838), 383

House of Lords: *passim*; appellate jurisdiction of, 38, 437 n.210; defeat Reform Bill on second reading, 64; third Reform Bill introduced, 162; and Belgium, 27, 31-2, 39, 41, 63, 91-2, 118; and foreign affairs, 48-9, 118-19, 215-16; and Portugal, 57, 63, 214; and Irish tithes, 126, 149; Irish peers in, 155; and ministry's Irish education plan, 141, 158-9, 164; postpone consideration of Schedule A, 176-7; pass third reading of Reform Bill, 189; address on Portuguese neutrality, 214; amendments to Irish Church Temporalities bill in committee, 234; and diplomatic peerages, 244; defeat bill to eliminate subscription to thirty-nine articles for university entrance, 320; and constitution, 332; consideration of reform of (1836), 348; and Church Rates bill (1837), 358; and British Legion in Spain (1837), 360; and Irish Corporations bill, 361; weakness of government in (1838), 387; censure of Lord Normanby's administration of Ireland (1839), 393; resolution against government's education measure (1839), 405; committee on crime in Ireland (1839), 406; attempt to establish ascendancy over Commons and Crown, 408

Howard, Henry Thomas, 293

Howard de Walden, Charles Augustus Ellis, 6th Baron, 247, 249, 268, 307, 333, 336, 350-1, 353

Howard of Effingham, Kenneth Alexander, 11th Baron, 323

Howe, Richard William Penn Curzon, 1st Earl, 15, 45, 48, 65-7, 69, 222, 354, 414

Howick, Henry George Grey, styled Viscount, later 3rd Earl Grey, xlv-vi, liv, 39, 150, 217, 234, 238, 260, 269, 271, 281-2, 285, 288, 290, 293, 304, 319, 323, 325, 336, 342, 347, 356, 381, 400, 409; favors immediate emancipation of slaves, 207-8; forces change in Colonial Office, 389-90; resigns from cabinet, 409-10

Howley, William, Archbishop of Canterbury, 5-7, 11, 19-20, 31, 42, 50, 95, 98, 127, 129, 149, 216-19, 221, 231, 234, 236, 320, 323, 343-4, 358, 405

Hudson, Sir James, 275, 277

Hume, Joseph, 58, 93, 95, 186, 199, 209, 281-2, 322, 361

Hunt, Henry 'Orator', xxiv, 38, 97, 179

Huntingford, George Isaac, Bishop of Hereford (1815-32), 139, 173

Huskisson, William (1770-1830), xxv

Ilchester, Henry Stephen Fox-Strangways, 3rd Earl of, 54, 323

Ingestre, Henry John Chetwynd-Talbot, styled Viscount, 179

Ireland: education in, 26-7, 141, 158-9, 164, 316, 321-2, 434 n.176, 453 n.92, 476 n.85; agitation for dissolution of Union in, 27-8; Subletting Act in, 27, 434 n.176; Orange strength in, 28, 107; O'Connell's associations in, 99; illegal associations in, 107; coercive laws for, xxxviii, xlv,

107, 128, 197, 255, 448 n.1; emigration from, 117; crime in, 200, 406; dissension within government of (1832), 202, 205-6; juries in, 206, 460 n.5
Ireland, legislation for: bill on growth of tobacco in, 24; Arms Bill (1831), xliv-v; Reform Bill, xxxv, liii, 54, 58, 94-5, 186-7, 194, 446 n.387-8; Coercion bill (1833-4), xxxviii, xlv, 206, 255, 460 n.4 (1835), 322, 324, 328; Church Millions bill (1833), 249; Municipal Corporations bill, 322, 324, 340-2, 356-7, 361, 386, 478 n.129; Poor Law, 358-9, 386, 483 n.11; *see also:* Church of Ireland, Kildare Street Society, Tithes (Ireland), Yeomanry
Irish MPs, 26, 28; those friendly to government, 33; disappointed at only five additional representatives in Irish Reform Bill, 93; press for extension of county franchise, 194; threaten to oppose Russian-Dutch loan, 197

Jamaica, 140, 143, 150-1, 335, 389; insurrection in, 136-7; bill to suspend legislature of (1839), 396-7, 402
Jeffrey, Francis, xv, xix, 115
Jersey, George Child Villiers, 5th Earl of, 3, 276
Jersey, Lady, 178, 231, 384
Jewish Civil Disabilities bill, xviii, 236-7
John Bull, 283
Johnson, Samuel, 37
Johnston, Edward, 243
Jones, Leslie Grove, 361
Junius, identity of, 179

Kaye, John, Bishop of Lincoln (1827-53), 320, 344
Keith, Lady, *see* Flahault, Comtesse de
Kemble, John Mitchell, 358
Kempt, Sir James, 185, 188, 191, 203, 224
Kenmare, Valentine Browne, 2nd Earl of, 124
Kennedy, Thomas Francis, 120-1, 243
Kent, Edward, Duke of, 244
Kent, Victoria Mary Louisa, Duchess of, 17, 38, 45, 51-3, 56, 143, 224-6, 239, 311, 320, 349-50, 362-5, 368, 369, 371-5, 378-81, 394-5, 401-4
Kenyon, George, 2nd Baron, 19, 38, 153, 157, 234
Kerry, Maurice Fitzgerald, Knight of, 28
Kildare Street Society, 26, 138, 141, 434, n.176; *See also* Ireland, education in
King of Ockham, Peter, 7th Baron, 54, 95, 217
Kinnaird, George William Fox, 9th Lord (1st Baron Rossie), 192
Knight, Cornelia, 383
Knighton, Sir William, 128, 353
Knox, Edmund (Bishop of Killaloe, 1831; tr. Limerick, 1834), 51, 158
Kosciusko, Tadeusz, 104

Laborde, Etienne de, 246
Labouchere, Henry (1st Baron Taunton), 20, 93, 119, 295, 387, 410-11
Lafayette, Marquis de (1757-1834), xiv, 2
Lafitte, Jacques, 19, 21
Lamb, Frederick (later 2nd Viscount Melbourne), 19, 47, 85, 146, 196, 286
Lamb, Lady Caroline (1785-1828), xv
Lambert, Henry, 213
Lambton, *see* Durham, John, 1st Earl
Lancaster, Duchy of, 52, 62-3, 128, 303, 354, 370; and treasure belonging to, 3, 23, 58; county palatine court of, 122, 310; patronage of chancellor of, lvi n.75, 126; rents due to, 380
Landon, Whittington, Dean of Exeter, 173
Langdale, 1st Baron, *see* Bickersteth, Henry
Lansdowne, Sir Henry Petty-Fitzmaurice, 3rd Marquess of, xxiv-vii, xxxi, xxxvii, xl, xlvii-viii, 9, 12-14, 18, 25, 29-30, 35, 38-40, 43, 51, 60, 64-6, 68, 73-4, 81-2, 84, 87, 96, 99, 106-9, 113, 120, 125-6, 128-9, 135, 144-6, 148-50, 152, 158, 160-1, 167, 169, 183, 190, 200, 202-4, 215, 226, 228, 230-1, 233, 235, 238, 241, 245, 252-4, 266, 272-3, 286-7, 290-1, 299, 304, 324, 328-9, 332-3, 340, 366, 387, 389, 390, 392, 400, 402, 419
Lansdowne, William Petty, Lord Shelburne, 1st Marquess of, 267
Lapidge, William Frederick, 354
Larkin, 185
La Rochefoucault, 23
Latour-Maubourg, Marquis de, 36, 38, 49
Lauder, Sir Thomas Dick, 350
Lauderdale, James Maitland, 8th Earl of, 7, 13, 414
Lavradio, Francisco D'Almeida Portugal, Count of, 308, 336
Law, George Henry, Bishop of Bath and Wells (1828-45), 59, 232
Leach, Sir John, 99, 265
Leader, John Temple, 361, 375-6
Leeds, George William Frederick Osborne, 6th Duke of, 133
Lees, Harcourt, 12
Lefanu, Thomas Philip, 51
Lehon, Charles Aimé Joseph, 12, 25, 36, 49
Lehzen, Louise Baroness, 374-5, 394, 401
Leicester, 1st Earl of, *see* Coke of Holkham
Leiningen, Maria Duchess of, 362
Leiningen, Prince Karl of, 362
Leinster, Augustus Frederick FitzGerald, 3rd Duke and Viscount, 41, 203, 308
Leitrim, Nathaniel Clements, 2nd Earl of, 301
Le Marchant, Denis, 247
Leopold, Prince, of Saxe-Coburg, King of the Belgians, 4-5, 7, 9, 12, 14-15, 21-6, 28, 34-7, 39, 41-2, 44, 48-9, 54, 63, 71, 74, 79, 101-2, 111, 118, 123, 125, 154, 164, 175, 200, 212, 333, 350, 352, 364, 368, 372, 374-5, 378, 383, 391-2; *see also* Belgium
Le Tellier, 110

Leuchtenberg, Auguste, 2nd Duke of, 240, 246, 268-9, 276, 303, 333
Leuchtenberg, Maximilien, 3rd Duke of, 308
Lichfield, Thomas William Anson, 1st Earl of, 299, 387
Liddell family, 330
Lieven, Dorothea, Princess, 34-5, 67, 102, 200, 204, 213, 243-4, 333, 338, 369
Lieven, Prince, 128, 173-6, 337
Lilford, Lady (Mary Elizabeth Fox, diarist's daughter), 32
Lilford, Thomas Atherton Powys, 3rd Baron, 32
Lima, Luis Antonio D'Abreu e, Count of Carreira, 59
Lincoln, Bishop of, *see* Kaye, John
Lisbon: cabals at, 4; French at, 18; ship of line dispatched to, 51; *see also* Portugal
Lismore, Cornelius O'Callaghan, 1st Viscount and Baron, 124
Littleton, Edward John, 1st Baron Hatherton, xxxviii, li, 255-7, 260, 266, 270, 299, 387, 406
Liverpool, Robert Banks Jenkinson, 2nd Earl of (1770-1828), xxiv-v, xxix, 312, 390
Llandaff, Bishop of, *see* Copleston, Edward
Llandaff, Francis James Mathew, 2nd Earl of, 124
Lloyd, Thomas, 312
Local Judicature bill, xxxiii, 220-1, 224, 226-7; defeated in House of Lords, 227-8
London, Bishop of, *see* Blomfield, Charles James
London, Treaty of (1840), 421, 489 n.2
Londonderry, Charles William Stewart-Vane, 3rd Marquess of, 4, 19, 22, 24, 27, 29, 31-2, 36, 39, 41, 48, 55, 61-3, 67, 122, 126, 141, 143, 145-6, 153-5, 183, 185, 222, 282, 290, 294, 301, 305, 340
Londonderry, Lady, 122
London University, 283, 301, 303, 306, 475 n.76
Longley, Charles Thomas, 344
Lorton, Robert Edward King, 1st Viscount, 99, 140-1
Louis, Baron Joseph Dominique, 24
Louis XIV, King of France (1643-1715), 53
Louis XVI, King of France (1774-93), 351
Louis Philippe (1773-1850), King of the French (1830-48), xli-ii, 1-2, 8, 18-22, 42-3, 58, 61, 93, 101-2, 110, 155-6, 170, 172, 193, 204, 240, 244, 245-6, 251, 268, 272, 297, 305, 308, 332-3, 338-9, 351-2, 355, 360-2, 421
Loulé, Duke of, 336
Lovat, Simon Fraser, 11th Lord, 74
Lushington, Stephen, 360, 407
Luttrell, Henry (?1765-1851), xv
Luxemburg, Duchy of, 9, 24, 93, 427 n.67
Lyndhurst, John Singleton Copley, 1st Baron, 29, 38, 43, 56, 58, 64, 67, 92, 123, 176, 178, 180, 182, 189, 221, 223-4, 226-7, 276, 278, 280-1, 288-90, 292-3, 326-7, 331, 341-3, 345-8, 356, 382, 386-8, 392, 401, 406; as possible leader of Tory party, 235
Lyndhurst, Lady, 29, 38, 58, 67, 169, 235
Lyttleton, William Henry, 3rd Baron, 90, 210

Macartney, George, 1st Earl, 104
Macaulay, Thomas Babington, xiv, xxxiv, xlvi, 15, 97, 106, 120, 410-12
Macdonald, Sir James, 108
McDonald, Lt Col. John, 192
Mackintosh, Sir James, 61, 72, 190
Macmahon, Sir William, Master of the Rolls, 62, 117, 212
McTaggert, John, 280
Magee, William, Archbishop of Dublin, 35
Mahmoud II, Sultan (1808-39), 213, 281, 418
Maitland, Sir Thomas, 334
Maltby, Edward, Bishop of Chichester (1831-6), Bishop of Durham (1836-56), 52, 140, 158, 164, 236, 277, 306, 344
Malthus, Henry, 312
Malthus, Thomas Robert, 275
Manners-Sutton, Charles (later 1st Viscount Canterbury), 19, 178, 229, 245, 258, 266, 276, 279-80, 377
Mansfield, David William Murray, 3rd Earl of, 64, 169, 181, 183, 192, 231, 386
Mansfield, Lady, 191
Mansfield, William Murray, 1st Earl of (1705-93), 123
Maria Cristina, Queen Regent of Spain, 220, 291, 297, 300, 302, 305, 307, 310-12, 320, 338, 351, 372, 374
Maria II da Gloria, Dona, Queen of Portugal, xl, xlii, 8, 12, 20, 24, 31, 34, 72-3, 78-80, 86, 90, 99, 133, 160, 211, 230, 237-8, 240, 246-7, 251, 267-9, 276, 297, 312, 333, 336, 350-2, 372, 374; proclaimed Queen, 237; her arbitrary behavior, 307-8
Marie Amélie, Queen of France, 170
Markham, Frederick, 191
Marriage and Registration bills, *see* Dissenters
Marshal, Sir John, 139
Marshall, Dr, 13
Martin, Sir Thomas Byam, 70, 117
Martínez de la Rosa, Francisco De Paula, 250, 304
Maryborough, William Wellesley-Pole, Baron, 276
Matuszewic, Count André Joseph, 26, 35, 122, 171, 174, 204, 337
Mauguin, François, 100
Maule, Fox, later 2nd Baron Panmure and 11th Earl of Dalhousie, 281
Maule, William, 1st Baron Panmure, 6, 44
Mayo, John Bourke, 4th Earl of, 139
Meath, John Chambré Brabazon, 10th Earl of, Baron Chaworth, 54
Mee, Anne, 16
Mehemet Ali, Pasha of Egypt, xxxiv, xlii-iii, 211, 218, 337, 386, 411-13, 415-22
Melbourne, William Lamb, 2nd Viscount (1779-1848), xx, xxv, xxvii, xxix-xxxviii, xliii-liv, 9, 14, 17-19, 25, 39-40, 42, 51, 55, 70, 73-4, 76,

82-3, 96, 108, 115-16, 118, 140, 157, 163, 168, 187, 192-4, 200, 202, 206, 213, 215-16, 222, 225, 231-3, 235-6, 239, 243, 254, 263, 265-6, 269-78, 280, 284-95, 298-301, 306-8, 310-18, 320-1, 325-8, 330-3, 340-6, 348-9, 351, 353-5, 359, 361-74, 376, 379-82, 384-97, 399-403, 406, 408-11, 417-20; his indolence, 47-8; alarmed by state of country, 79; reports to cabinet on public mood, 82; and creation of peers for Reform Bill, 131, 145; defends Anglesey, 231-2; succeeds Grey, 258-61; dismissed, 269-74; forms new government (1835), 290; takes responsibility for Palmerston's letter to Nesselrode, 314; defies opposition in Lords, 343; and Mrs Norton, 344-5; as a public speaker, 345-6; consulted by the new queen, 366-8; fears dissolution of his government (1837), 376; angry outburst at Brougham, 376; his confidence in the queen's good sense, 379; his resignation (1839), 397; recalled by the queen, 399; Holland's assessment of, 410; his cabinet divided by Palmerston's policies, 420.

Mendizábal, Juan Alvarez, 241, 269, 301-3, 307, 311-12, 316-17, 329, 333, 338-9, 352

Mercer, Miss, *see* Flahault, Comtesse de

Metcalfe, Charles Theophilus, later Baron, 295

Metternich, Prince Klemens Lothar (1773-1859), 104, 146, 173, 238, 338, 412, 422

Middleton, Henry Willoughby, 6th Baron, 195, 312

Miguel, Dom, xl, xlii, 4, 24, 38, 42, 57, 59, 72, 74, 79-80, 87, 90, 103, 105, 160, 199, 220, 229-30, 232, 242, 249-51, 267, 294; Wellington's predilection for, 48

Militia, reduction of (1835), 308, 313, 325, 328

Milltown, Joseph Leeson, 4th Earl of, 124

Milton, Lord, *see* Fitzwilliam, Charles, Earl

Mina, Francisco Espoz y, 251

Minchin, William, 126

Minto, Gilbert Elliot, 2nd Earl of, 164, 191, 198, 298, 327-8, 351, 370, 392, 410, 419

Miraflores, Marquis of, 251, 333

Modena, Duke of, *see* Francesco IV

Molé, Comte Louis Matthieu, 2, 351, 353

Molesworth, Sir William, 375-6, 384

Monk, James Henry, Bishop of Gloucester (1830-56), 137

Monteagle, Lord, *see* Spring Rice, Thomas

Montrond, Comte Casimir de, 84, 172

Montrose, James Graham, 3rd Duke of, 359

Moore, Stephen, 126, 137

Moore, Thomas, 294

Morier, David Richard, 291

Morning Chronicle, 280, 394; reports dismissal of Melbourne's government, 274, 277

Morning Post, 403

Morpeth, George William Frederick Howard, styled Viscount, later 7th Earl of Carlisle, xxxiii, 312-13, 324, 330, 347, 357, 359, 387, 389-90, 419, 420

Mulgrave, Sir Constantine Henry Phipps, 2nd Earl of, 1st Marquess of Normanby, 38, 140, 143, 150, 183, 212, 218, 253, 260, 301-2, 232, 325, 330, 371, 378; *see also* Normanby, Marquess of

Münchengrätz, Convention of, xlii

Municipal corporations, 86, 115, 163, 210, 243, 280, 282, 292-3, 296, 446 n.375; bill of 1835, xxxii, 297-300, 303, 306, 310, 325-7, 473 n.42

Munster, George Augustus FitzClarence, 1st Earl of, 6, 15-17, 138, 188, 366, 370-1

Murray, John, 192

Musgrave, Thomas, Bishop of Hereford (1837-47), 371

Napier, Sir Charles, 34, 230, 237, 241, 305, 310, 334, 422

Napier, Sir William Francis Patrick, 66

Napoleon I (1769-1821), xiv, xxii-iii, 49, 153, 245-6

Nemours, Duc de, 22, 35, 308, 328, 333, 336

Nesselrode, Count Karl Robert, 173, 313-14

Nesselrode, Mme, 102

Netherlands, *see* William I, King of the

Neumann, Baron Philipp von, 421

Newburgh, Thomas Eyre, assumed title Earl of, 50

Newcastle, Henry Pelham Clinton, 4th Duke of, 177, 181, 184, 188, 231

Newport, Sir John, 28-9, 94, 130, 195, 389

Newspapers, 78, 324-5, 330; ministerial, 437 n.222; and dismissal of Melbourne's government, 274, 277-9; stamp duties on, 324, 409; Tory, 283; *see also* individual newspaper listings

Nicholas I (1796-1855), Czar, 2, 4, 19, 92, 102, 104-5, 175, 196, 200, 213, 244, 298, 313-14, 333-4, 336, 338, 421

Niemcewicz, Julian Ursin, xl, 104

Norfolk, Bernard Edward Howard, 12th Duke of, 265, 311

Normanby, Sir Constantine Henry Phipps, 2nd Earl of Mulgrave, 1st Marquess of, xlix, 392, 396, 402, 413-14, 419; joins cabinet, 389-90; his administration of Ireland censured by House of Lords, 393, 405-7; alleged inefficiency of, as Colonial Secretary, 410; *see also* Mulgrave, 2nd Earl of

Normanby, Lady, 402

North, Frederick, Lord (1732-92), xv

Northampton, Spencer Joshua Alwyne Compton, 2nd Marquess of, 84

Northumberland, Duchess of, 320, 365

Northumberland, Duke of, 365

Northwick, John Rushout, 2nd Baron, 123

Norton, Caroline Elizabeth Sarah, 300, 345

Norton, George Chapple, 344

Norwich, Bishop of, *see* Bathurst, Henry

Nottingham, Daniel Finch, 2nd Earl of (1647-1730), 118
Nugent, George Nugent-Grenville, 2nd Baron, 350, 352

O'Connell, Daniel, xxiv, xxxiv-v, xxxviii-xlv, li, 27-8, 40, 54, 58, 66, 68-9, 72, 78, 86, 94, 96, 99, 107, 194, 197, 199, 203, 206, 208-9, 217, 223, 229-30, 252-3, 256, 261-3, 267, 279-82, 285, 287, 289, 291, 294, 297, 299-301, 329-31, 341-3, 355-6, 358, 373, 375, 384-5, 415
O'Hanlon, Henry M., 295
Orange, William Frederick, Prince of, 21, 28-9, 32, 239, 383
Orangemen and Orange societies, 107, 117, 122, 126, 141, 266-7, 322, 408; Orange corporations, 341
Orford, Horatio Walpole, 3rd Earl of, 31
Orléans, Duc de, 21, 85, 211, 213, 237, 362
Orloff, Count Alexis Feodorovich, 150, 163-4, 174-5
Osborne, Lord Francis (later 1st Baron Godolphin), 98, 110
Otter, William, Bishop of Chichester (1836-40), 344
Otto of Bavaria (1815-67), King of Greece (1833-62), 158, 336
Ouvrard, Gabriel Julien, 84, 91
Owen, Sir Edward, 116
Oxford, Edward Harley, 5th Earl of, 6
Oxford University, and Regius professorship, 344-5

Paget, Sir Arthur, 146, 299
Paget, Berkeley Thomas, 323
Palgrave, Sir Francis, 115, 139, 282
Palmella, Marquis of, xl, 12, 57-9, 61-2, 72-3, 78-81, 86, 99, 202, 210-12, 229, 240-4, 249-50, 267-8, 307-8, 333, 336
Palmer, John Horsley, 81
Palmerston, Henry John Temple, 3rd Viscount (1784-1865), xxv-vii, xxxiii, xl-xlvi, xlviii, li, 4, 8, 9-14, 21, 23-4, 29-30, 38, 40, 43, 45-6, 48, 51, 55, 57-9, 62, 65-6, 71, 79, 82, 87, 89, 91, 99, 104-5, 114, 117, 119-20, 122, 128, 130, 134-5, 145-6, 151-2, 154, 164, 171-5, 183, 189-90, 192-3, 196-7, 199-204, 210-11, 213, 215, 217, 225, 228, 237-8, 240-1, 245-50, 253, 270-2, 278, 286-7, 291-3, 297-8, 301-5, 307, 309-10, 313-14, 318, 323, 334-8, 342, 350-1, 353, 360, 364, 373, 387, 415-21; rejects French proposal for mediation in Poland, 9-10; consults cabinet on Belgian policy, 13, 26, 37, 44; suspicious of French designs in Belgium, 30; supposed hostile to Dutch, 34; on Belgian fortresses and France, 36-7, 101-2, 112; hesitant to recognize Polish delegation, 40; recognizes impolicy of neglecting Dom Pedro, 52; leans towards intervention in Portugal, 59; objects to extending borough franchise to non-householders, 29-30; reluctant to agree on creation of peers for Reform Bill, 65, 108-10, 113, 144, 152, 167; writes to Grey deprecating creation and urging modification of Bill, 66; opposes pledging government to Reform Bill, 69; recommends concessions in bill, 98, 165, 167-8; king tries to retain him in government after cabinet's resignation (1832), 178; concludes Miguel must abdicate or be deposed, 74; Holland's criticisms of, for lukewarmness to causes of party and ministry, 100; accuses Spanish chargé d'affaires of meddling, 225; favors intervention in Portugal, 246-8; consults cabinet on Russian appointment, 293; Holland's doubts about his Turkish policy, 411; offers his resignation (1840), 417-18; his policy provokes Holland's resignation, 419
Paris; insurrection in, 190; 'infernal machine' at (1835), 325
Parke, Sir James, 122
Parker, Sir William, 237, 240-1, 248
Parliament: *passim*; dissolution of (1831), 3, 43; jurisdiction over slavery in colonies, 137, 142; fire destroys houses of, 266; *see also* House of Commons, House of Lords, Reform Bill
Parnell, Sir Henry Brooke (1st Baron Congleton), 41, 120-1
Patronage, xiii, xxiv, 139, 153, 174, 187, 244, 370; diplomatic, 117-18, 328; ecclesiastical, 12, 21, 43, 51-2, 174, 265, 312, 344, 358-60, 371, 415; garter, 266, 274, 332-3, 359; dispute on Irish, 62; and Lord Chancellor, 55, 92, 212, 275; of Duchy of Lancaster. lvi n.75, 126
Paul of Württemberg, Prince, 21-2, 383
Pedro, Dom, xl, xlii, 4, 7-8, 12, 20, 23, 31, 34, 38, 40, 57-61, 63, 72, 74, 79-80, 86, 90, 99-100, 103, 127, 133, 157, 160, 199, 211, 232, 240-2, 247, 249-51, 269, 307, 352; his character, 237; death of, 267-8
Peel, Lady Jane, 74
Peel, Sir Robert (1788-1850), xxxiv, xlix, l, 15, 21, 67, 84, 93, 96, 127, 135, 168, 178, 193, 197, 199, 229, 231, 238, 253, 258, 275, 277-9, 281-7, 290, 306, 311, 323, 326-7, 344, 348, 357, 360-1, 368, 371-2, 377, 381, 383-4, 386, 397-8, 400-2; resigned to Reform Bill 97; declines to help form Tory ministry in 1832, 178; rejects coalition with Melbourne (1834), 258; forms ministry (Dec. 1834), 277-8; fall of his government, 281-5; and literary pensions, 294; and public opinion, 327; his moderation, 340-1, 355-6; reports of his illness, 371; called to form new ministry (1839), 398; *see also* Bedchamber controversy
Pelham, Thomas, 2nd Earl of Chichester, 197
Pembroke, George Augustus Herbert, 11th Earl of, 16
Penny postage, xxxiii, 409
Pensions, literary, 294
Pepys, Sir Charles Christopher, 1st Baron Cot-

tenham, 265, 293, 332, 346, 354, 387-8, 392, 402, 419
Périer, Casimir, 9-10, 18, 21, 24, 31, 33, 58, 105-6, 112, 126, 145-6, 150, 153, 155-6, 170-2, 178; assessed by Talleyrand, 110-11
Périer, Casimir (the younger), 104
Pewsey, *see* Pusey, Philip
Philip V, King of Spain (1700-46), 20
Phillpotts, Henry, Bishop of Exeter (1830-69), 158, 169, 217, 231-2, 262, 302, 321, 342, 359
Pickthall, Henry, 344
Pitt, William (1759-1806), xiv, xviii, 16, 119, 156, 337
Plunket, Thomas Span (Dean of Down), 45, 153
Plunket, William Conyngham, 1st Baron, 7, 12, 21, 25, 29, 37-8, 41-2, 45, 51, 53-4, 62, 64, 67-8, 107, 117, 126, 129, 133, 138, 140-1, 143, 153, 159, 192, 227, 229, 231-3, 243, 266, 270, 281, 350, 359, 406
Poinsett, Joel Roberts, 29
Poland: revolution of 1830 in, 19, 104; French offer for mediation of revolution in, 8-12; British response, xliii, 13; deputies from provisional government of, 40; Russian capture of Warsaw, 57; Russian authority in, according to Treaty of Vienna, 57, 80, 170; Czar Nicholas and, 92
Polignac, Prince de, 246
Poltimore, George Warwick Bampfylde, 1st Baron, 222
Ponsonby, Lady Fanny, 329
Ponsonby, John, 2nd Baron, 25, 106, 145-6, 219, 334, 337, 364, 411, 416, 422
Ponsonby, Richard, Bishop of Derry (1831-53), 12, 21, 43, 223, 263
Ponsonby, William Francis Spencer, 1st Baron de Mauley, 54
Poor Law Amendment bill, xxxiii, 261-2; and elections of 1837, 373; Brougham's bill of 1838, 385
Pope, The, *see* Gregory XVI
Portman, Edward Berkeley, 12, 403
Portman, Lady, 395, 404-5
Portugal: French capture corvettes of, 12, 23; ex-ambassadors in London, 12; and constitutional government, 72; French urge recognition of Dona Maria in, 73; associated with Spain, 78-9; Pedro's capture of Oporto, 199; British indecision about, 210-11, 230; Dom Pedro's conduct in, 240; Don Miguel's troops in, 251; and death of Dom Pedro, 267-9; in 1835, 307-8, 333, 336; in 1836, 350-3
Powys, Thomas Lyttleton (diarist's grandson), 224
Pozzo di Borgo, Count Carlo Andrea, 2, 106, 292, 298, 313-14, 337, 423 n.6
Prisons bill (1835), 301
Privy Council, 3-4, 43, 120, 366, 370; Orders in Council, 140, 142-3, 151, 176, 328, 402, 446, n.383
Pusey, Philip, 323

Quadruple Alliance, xlii, 251, 267, 294, 304, 333, 336, 351, 353, 360, 467 n.9
Queen Anne's Bounty, 31, 33, 280

Radnor, William Pleydell-Bouverie, 3rd Earl, 64, 159, 185-6, 254, 301, 312, 320, 387
Rayneval, François Gerard, Comte de, 302, 304, 333
Reform Bill (England and Wales): provisions of when first introduced, xxvii-viii; traditional interpretation of, xxviii-ix, xxxii; revisionist interpretation of, xxviii-xxxii; principles of, xxxi; relationship to other reform legislation, xxxii; commissioners in 5, 42, 425 n.38; land and town representation in, xxx-i, 11, 29-30, 85, 99; Milton's plan for double representation to twenty-six boroughs, 12; tenants-at-will in, 12, 428 n.75; fear of, by royal females, 16; £10 qualification in boroughs, 20, 432 n.146; county franchise in, 29-30, 435 n.187; leaseholder franchise in, 29; borough freeholder franchise in, xxxi-ii, 29-30, 81, 445 n.362; copyholder franchise in, 29-30; division of counties in, 81, 444 n.361; freeman franchise in, 81, 445 n.363; criterion for disfranchisement and enfranchisement in, 81, 445 n.364; proposal for representation of colonies, 86; second reading of in Commons (Dec. 1831), 97; constituency boundaries, 81, 99; principles of, xxxi, 130, 132, 147; third bill brought into House of Lords (1832), 162; Lord John Russell of 'finality' of, xxxi, 377-8; *see also* Cabinet
Reis Effendi; *see* Akif Pasha
Revolution, fear of, should Reform Bill not pass, xxviii, 164
Revolutions of 1830, xxvi-vii, xli, 1-3, 104
Reynolds, Henry, 344
Rich, Sir Henry, 358
Richmond, Charles Gordon Lennox, 5th Duke of (1791-1860), xxvii, xxx, xxxiii, xxxviii, xli, xlvi, li-iv, 8, 10, 12, 14, 25-6, 34, 36, 42-3, 46, 48, 51, 55, 59, 62, 65, 82-3, 86-8, 90, 94-5, 98, 108, 113, 116, 124, 127, 130-1, 133, 135, 144, 148-9, 152, 154, 158, 160, 167-8, 177-8, 182, 193-4, 199, 205, 215, 220, 238, 248, 254, 256, 281, 311, 403, 413; interest in Beer bill, xxxiii, 23; fears extension of borough franchise to non-householders, 29-30; opposes post for O'Connell, 68; proposes representation for colonies, 86; refuses to remain in cabinet if peers are created, 177; resigns from cabinet, 251-2
Richmond, Dowager Duchess of, 74
Ripon, Frederick John Robinson, Viscount Goderich, 1st Earl of, xxxviii, li, 212, 215, 224, 226, 233, 251, 254, 292, 390; *see also* Goderich, Viscount
Rockingham, Charles Watson-Wentworth, 2nd Marquess of (1730-82), xv, xvii
Roden, Robert Jocelyn, 3rd Earl of, 138, 140-1, 164, 189, 192-3, 231, 306, 378, 393

Roe, Sir Frederick Adair, 324
Roebuck, John Arthur, 356, 375
Rogers, Samuel, xv, 3, 32, 128, 220, 294
Rolfe, Henry Monsey, 265
Romilly, Sir Samuel, 43
Rosebery, Archibald John Primrose, 4th Earl of, 159, 222
Ross, Charles, 283
Rosse, Lawrence Parsons, 2nd Earl of, 233
Rosslyn, Alexander Wedderburn, 1st Earl of, 179
Rosslyn, Sir James St Clair Erskine, 2nd Earl of, 3, 149, 227, 276
Rothschild, Nathan Meyer, 180, 280
Roussin, Admiral Albin Reine, 18, 54, 57
Russell, Lord George William, 20, 29, 32, 37, 42, 49, 220, 237, 241-2, 249
Russell, Lord John, xiv, xx, xxii, xxvi-vii, xxxi, xxxvii-viii, xlv, xlviii, li, liii, 5, 7, 10, 25, 30, 34-5, 58-9, 66, 79, 81, 97, 119, 121-2, 126, 138, 144, 148-9, 157, 161, 167, 220, 249, 255, 266, 278, 286-8, 290, 302, 306, 308, 311, 313, 324-6, 335, 342, 350, 352, 355, 358, 364, 371, 382, 387, 391, 393-4, 397, 400-1, 406, 413, 419; favors creation of peers, 39, 80, 109; writes letter to people of Birmingham, 70, 443 n. 336; wants assurances from 'waverers', 151; would resign if Durham did, 154; suspects Brougham wishes to break up government (Apr. 1832), 166; favors dividing Irish Church Temporalities bill (1833), 222; on Lord Hill's absence from House of Lords on Local Judicature Bill, 228; threatens to resign (1833), 230; on appropriation of surplus Irish Church revenues (1834), 251-2; controversy with Brougham and Durham on credit for Reform Bill, 264; considered for leadership of House of Commons before dismissal of 1834, 269-72; and opposition to Peel's government in 1835, 279, 281, 283, 285; as leader of House of Commons, 292, 347, 356-7; defeated in by-election for Devonshire (1835), 295; returned for Stroud, 296-7, 300; disliked by king, 309; king reconciled to, 327, 329-30, 332; and church legislation of 1836, 340, 481 n. 6; announces government's insistence on Irish Corporations bill (1837), 357, 361; and 'finality' of Reform Bill, xxxi, 376-7; and change in Colonial Office (Feb. 1839), 388-90; becomes Secretary for War and Colonies, 410
Russell, Lady William, 50, 242, 249
Russell, Lord William, 121
Russell, Lord Wriothesley, 415
Russian-Dutch loan, 119, 120, 122-3, 125, 197, 199, 450 n. 30
Rutland, John Henry Manners, 5th Duke of, 138

Sacheverell, Dr Henry (?1674-1724), 219
St Albans, Duchess of, 16
Saint-Priest, Comte Alexis Guignard de, 353
St Vincent, Edward Jervis, 2nd Viscount, 55, 222, 225
Sainte-Aulaire, Comte de, 362, 422
'Saints', 55-6, 122, 136, 139-41, 158, 176, 213, 306
Saldanha, Marquis of, 307, 336
Salisbury, Bishop of, *See* Burgess, Thomas
Salisbury, James William Gascoyne-Cecil, 2nd Marquess of, 22, 183
Salisbury, Lady, 384
Sampaio, Francisco Teixeira, 61
Sandon, Dudley Ryder, styled Lord, later 2nd Earl of Harrowby, 131
Santarem, 2nd Viscount of, 242
Sarmento, Cristovao Pedro de Morais, Viscount of Torre de Moncorvo, 276, 308, 336, 352, 407
Sartorius, George Rose, 40, 103, 106, 133, 305, 334
Saumarez, Sir James, 44, 52, 59
Saxe-Meinüngen, Bernhard Erich, Duke of, 35
Saxe-Weimar, Bernhard, Duke of, 16-17, 29, 32, 37
Saxe-Weimar, Duchess of, 17
Saxe-Weimar, Princess Louise of, 198
Scarborough, John Lumley Savile, styled Viscount Lumley, 8th Earl of, 312
Scarlett, James, 1st Baron Abinger, 3, 16, 281, 293, 345
Scotland: Reform Bill, 54, 58, 196; election of peers, 159; reform of Court of Exchequer, 190, 192-3, 457 n.190; elections (1832), 191; church in, 382; municipal corporations, 296, 474 n.58
Seaford, Charles Rose Ellis, 1st Baron, 55, 60, 137, 140, 218, 298
Sébastiani, Comte François Horace, 8-9, 20-1, 24-6, 31-2, 34, 42, 54, 57, 59, 99, 102, 105-6, 110, 116, 298, 302, 310, 328, 333, 421
Sedgwick, Adam, 275, 344
Sefton, William Philip Molyneux, 2nd Earl of and 1st Baron, 7, 42, 49, 123, 124, 170
Segrave, William Fitzhardinge Berkeley, 1st Baron, 147, 236-7
Selwyn, George, 16
Semonville, Charles Louise Huget, Marquis de, 21
Senior, Nassau William, 247, 283
Seymour, Sir George Francis, 52
Seymour, Sir George Hamilton, 173, 196, 328
Seymour, Henry, 317
Seymour, Jane Georgina Sheridan, Lady, 300
Seymour, Lord Webb, 115
Shadwell, Sir Lancelot, 293
Sharpe, Henry Edward, 213, 230
Shee, Sir George, 40, 59
Sheil, Richard Lalor, 15, 41, 324, 356, 413
Sheridan, Richard Brinsley (1751-1816), 16, 51
Shuttleworth, Dr Philip Nicholas, 344
Sidney, Lady Sophia, *see* De Lisle, Lady
Silva Carvalho, Jos´e da, 268, 312, 336, 350
Sinclair, Sir George, 139, 280, 331, 376

Skrzynecki, Jan Zygmunt, 104
Slavery, xxi, 55-6, 83, 91, 142, 208; *see also* Emancipation of slaves, Slave trade
Slave trade, 328, 407-8; project of convention with France, 83-4; *see also* Emancipation of slaves, Slavery
Sligo, Henry Peter Browne, 2nd Marquess of, 335, 409
Smith, Sydney, xiv-xv, 52, 115, 226, 344
Solicitor General (England and Wales), *see* Horne, Sir William (to Nov. 1832), Campbell, Sir John (to Feb. 1834), Pepys, Sir Charles
Somerset, Edward Adolphus Seymour, 11th Duke of, 359
Somerset, Lord Fitzroy, later 1st Baron Raglan, 151
Sophia, Princess (1777-1848), 57
Sorrell, Thomas, 241
Soult, Nicholas Jean de Dieu, 21, 35, 85, 126, 190, 204
Southey, Robert, 294
Spain: Salic law of, 20, 220, 432 n.145; associated with Portugal, 59, 79-80, 243; misleading report of revolution in, 93; troops of, reported in Portugal (1834), 247, 250-1; after death of King Ferdinand, 250; Eliot (Logrono) Convention (1835), 291; in 1835, 302, 304-5, 311-12; in 1836, 339, 351, 353; in 1837, 354-5, 360-1
Spain, Queen of, *see* Maria Cristina
Special Constables bill, 52, 440 n.279
Spencer, George John, 2nd Earl, 6-7, 144, 269-71, 276
Spencer, 3rd Earl, *see* Althorp, John, Viscount
Spottiswood subscription, 376
Spring Guns bill, 52, 440 n.279
Spring Rice, Thomas, 1st Baron Monteagle, xxxiii, 95, 153, 207, 242, 254, 271-3, 287-8, 292, 296-7, 299, 301-2, 304, 306, 324, 340, 351, 358, 409-10
Staël, Mme de, 346
Stafford, George Granville Leveson-Gower, 2nd Marquess of, 1st Duke of Sutherland, 47, 65, 71
Standard, 277
Stanley, Edward, Bishop of Norwich (1837-49), 359-60
Stanley, Edward Geoffrey, later 14th Earl of Derby, xxiv, xxvii, xxxvi-viii, xliv-vii, li, liii-iv, 6-7, 10, 12, 30, 44, 46, 56, 59, 81-2, 90-1, 93-5, 97, 99, 108, 112-13, 117, 122, 126, 129-30, 181, 183, 200, 204-8, 212-14, 216, 218, 223, 228, 238, 245, 247-8, 256, 259, 272-3, 279-83, 285-7, 290, 292, 306, 311, 347, 357, 383; plans for reorganizing Yeomanry, 14; wants to disband Kildare Street Society, 26; fails to consult leading Irishmen, 29; meets Irish MPs, 33; opposes place for O'Connell, 68; criticized by O'Connell, 78; on Irish tithes, xxxvi, 88, 90, 95, 127, 194-5, 197-8, 453 n.93 (*see also* Tithes, Ireland); Irish dislike of, 124, 200; differences with Anglesey, 202; Irish Church Temporalities bill and appropriations question, 204-6, 251-3, 272-3, 279, 282, 285-6 (*see also* Church of Ireland; Tithes, Ireland); becomes Colonial Secretary, 207; plans for Negro emancipation, 208, 213 (*see also* Emancipation of slaves); enmity toward O'Connell, 230; resigns from Grey's cabinet, 251-3; his coterie, 280-1, 283, 286
Stanley, Edward John, later 2nd Baron Stanley of Alderley, 260, 384
Stanley, Sir John Thomas, 1st Baron Stanley of Alderley, 359
Stephen, James, 207, 218, 319, 381
Stephenson, Sir Benjamin Charles, 3, 363
Stockmar, Baron Christian Friedrich von, 42, 364, 368-9
Stormont, William David Murray, styled Viscount, later 4th Earl of Mansfield, 91
Strafford, Lord, *see* Byng, Sir John
Strangford, Percy Clinton Sydney Smythe, 6th Viscount, 117, 126, 150, 154, 294, 306
Strangways, *see* Fox-Strangways, William
Stuart, Lord Dudley Coutts, 309
Stuart, James, 350, 352
Stuart de Rothesay, Charles Stuart, 1st Baron, 199
Stuart-Wortley-Mackenzie, John, later 2nd Baron Wharncliffe, 97
Suffield, Edward Harbord, 3rd Baron, 166
Suffolk, Thomas Howard, 16th Earl of, 147
Sugar duties, 60, 127, 158; *see also* Emancipation of slaves, West Indian interest
Sultan, *see* Mahmoud II, Abdul Mejid I
Summer, Charles Richard, Bishop of Winchester, 82
Sumner, John Bird, Bishop of Chester, 177
Sussex, Augustus Frederick, Duke of, 6, 49-50, 52, 123, 184-5, 187, 190, 198, 220, 225, 226, 232, 239, 366, 370-1, 377, 383, 391, 414
Sutherland, Duchess of, 369-70, 375
Sutherland, 2nd Duke of, *see* Gower, Baron

Talbot, Charles Chetwynd-, 2nd Earl, 139, 148
Talleyrand, Prince, xiv, xl-i, 7-9, 12-14, 22, 25-6, 28, 30, 32-4, 36-8, 40, 44-5, 53, 55, 58-9, 61-3, 65, 69-71, 79, 85, 93, 95, 97, 99, 101, 104-6, 110-11, 114-15, 119, 122-5, 139, 145-6, 150, 157, 164, 170-3, 175-6, 189-90, 192-3, 200, 211-13, 219, 226, 244, 272, 304, 322, 346; proposes joint mediation in Poland, 8; opinions of Casimir Périer and Louis Philippe, 18-19; shows letters from Paris to Holland, 34, 42; confers with Palmerston on Belgium, 36; explains British policy to Paris, 104; attacked by *The Times,* 114; reads his memoirs to Holland, 117; anticipates Tory ministry in 1832, 178; resentment of Palmerston, 338
Tankerville, Countess of, 376
Tavistock, Francis Russell, styled Marquess of, later 7th Duke of Bedford, 29, 403-4

Taylor, Henry, 294
Taylor, Sir Herbert, 48, 50-1, 55, 59, 66, 70, 74-9, 86, 92, 109-10, 112, 118, 127-8, 130, 137-9, 154-5, 168, 174, 179, 181, 183-5, 189, 192, 212, 216, 218-19, 226, 253, 259-60, 264, 274, 276-7, 290, 292, 315-16, 336-7, 366, 368, 382, 387, 391
Templemore, Arthur Chichester, 1st Baron, 369
Tennyson, Charles, 120
Tenterden, Charles Abbot, 1st Baron, 50, 58, 189, 195
Terceira, Antonio José de Sousa, Count of Villa Flor, Duke of, 57, 229, 237, 267-8, 276
Theirs, Adolphe, 338-9, 417
Thirlwall, Connop, 275, 344
Thirty-nine articles, bill to abolish requirement for subscribing to, 301, 320
Thompson, Charles Poulett, later 1st Baron Sydenham, 39, 193, 281, 290, 297, 304, 387, 410, 413
Tierney, George (1761-1830), xxiv
Times, The, 29, 40, 109, 114, 149, 274, 277, 301, 435 n.185; opposes Poor Law Amendment bill, 262; attacks Lord Brougham, 264
Tithes (England), 33; Dacre's bill for commutation of, 5-7, 425 n. 33; Archbishop's bill for composition of, 5-7, 425 n. 33; bill of 1835, 329; bill of 1836, 340
Tithes (Ireland): Composition Act of 1823, 11; composition of parliamentary committees on, 91, 95, 129; Stanley's plan for commutation of, xxxvi, 88, 90, 194-5, 197, 453 n.93; commutation bill in House of Lords (1831-2), 96, 126, 203; reform of, associated with coercion, 128-9, 142; suspension of collections for arrears of, 213; Millions Bill (1833), 243; bill of 1834, xlix, 262-3, 469 n.37; bill of 1835, 295-6, 299, 304, 309, 321, 323, 329, 476 n. 85; bill of 1836, 340; bill of 1838 passes with abandonment of appropriations clause, 386, *see also* Church of Ireland, Cabinet
Torre de Moncorvo, Viscount of, *see* Sarmento
Torrens, Robert, 60, 62
Torrijos, José Mariá de, 103
Truck bills, 19, 431, n.130
Tweedale, George Hay, 8th Marquess of, 413

Unions, 73, 75-8, 82-3, 85, 87, 89, 112, 118, 157, 178, 194
Unkiar Skelessi, Treaty of, 238, 465 n.91
Upper Ossory. John Fitzpatrick, 2nd Earl of (1745-1818), xiii
Urquhart, David, 337, 364, 387
Uxbridge, Henry Paget, styled Lord, later 2nd Marquess of Anglesey, 239

Valence, Comte Cyrus de, 49
Van de Weyer, Jean Sylvain, 74, 123, 125, 163, 174-5, 387
Vassall, Richard (d. 1795), xiv
Vaughan, Sir Charles Richard, 365
Vaughan, Sir John, 122
Vial (Spanish minister in London), 225, 251
Victoria, Queen (1819-1901), xlix, lii, 53, 143, 349, 362-75, 378-9, 382, 384, 391-2, 394-401, 406-8, 410-11, 419, 421-2; succeeds William IV, 366; eager for continuation of Melbourne's government, 385; coronation of, 388; distressed at Melbourne's resignation, 397; refuses to place her household at Peel's disposal, 398; and affair of Lady Flora Hastings, 402-5; proposes to Prince Albert, 414-15; *see also* Bedchamber controversy
Vila Real, Count of, 12, 267-8
Villa Flor, *see* Terceira
Villiers, George William Frederick, later 4th Earl of Clarendon, 250, 304, 339, 351
Vivian, Sir Richard Hussey, 129, 383
Vyvyan, Sir Richard Rawlinson, 126

Wakeley, Thomas, 375
Waldegrave, John James, 6th Earl, 60
Walewsky, Comte Alexandre Florian Joseph Colonna, 9
Walter, John 262
Warburton, Henry, 282, 284, 376
Ward, Henry George, 252-3
'Waverers', 84, 92, 127-8, 130, 132, 134-40, 147-8, 169, 172, 176, 219, 227-8, 284; ministers' dependence upon, 228, 233
Webster, Sir Godfrey, xiv
Webster, Henry Vassall, 12, 23, 29, 40, 55, 57, 179
Weimar, Duke and Duchess of, *see* Saxe-Weimar
Wellesley, Richard Colley, 1st Marquess of, 17-18, 25, 85, 157, 189, 219, 232, 243, 245, 255-7, 261, 266, 271, 290, 293, 297, 301, 331, 347, 371, 396
Wellesley-Pole, William Pole Tylney Long-, 4th Earl of Mornington, 6
Wellington, Arthur Wellesley, 1st Duke of (1769-1852), xx, xxv-vii, xxxix, xl, 2-3, 6-7, 15, 17-18, 20-1, 25, 27, 32-3, 40-1, 48, 50, 55, 57-8, 63, 74-8, 87, 91, 96, 100, 116, 122-3, 127, 130, 135, 140-1, 149-51, 153-4, 159, 162, 168-9, 189-90, 192-3, 196, 199, 203-4, 214, 217, 221-2, 224, 226, 228-9, 231-6, 238-9, 243, 256, 258-9, 261, 275-8, 280, 282, 284, 289, 291-2, 294, 300, 305-6, 309, 311-12, 320-2, 326, 337, 339, 340-2, 345, 348, 355-6, 360-1, 366, 368, 372, 376-8, 381-2, 384, 386-8, 393, 395, 397-9, 401-4, 407, 415; resignation of, 1; and revolutions of 1830, 1; opposes demolition of Belgian fortresses, 39; letter to king on unions, 75-7; hints at compromise with Grey on Reform Bill, 84-5; encourages Dutch king, 93; on Belgian revolution, 155-6; attempts to form ministry (1832), 178-80; protest on passage of Reform Bill, 182; on coronation oath and Irish Church Temporalities bill, 228-31; as an 'enemy of

political liberty', 236; rejects coalition government (1834), 258; tactless speech on Grey's retirement, 259; holds all the seals after Melbourne's dismissal, 277; approves Palmerston's foreign policy, 291-2, 305
Werther, Baron Heinrich August Alexander Wilhelm von, 1-2, 44
Wessenberg, Baron Johann Philipp von, 13-14, 33-4, 37, 42, 123, 173, 190, 192
West Indian interest, 55-6, 62, 92, 136-7, 141-2, 150, 208, 212-13, 222, 225, *see also* Emancipation of slaves, Slavery, Sugar duties
Westmeath, Emily, Lady, 17
Westmeath, George Thomas John Nugent, Marquess of, 203
Wetherall, Frederick Augustus, 56
Wetherell, Sir Charles, 87, 89, 283
Wharncliffe, James Archibald Stuart-Wortley-Mackenzie, 1st Baron, 19, 64, 67, 81, 84, 92, 117-18, 127-8, 131-9, 147-8, 151, 161, 169, 172, 176-7, 189, 233, 261, 290, 306, 347
Whately, Richard, Archbishop of Dublin, 159, 226, 232, 236, 304, 316, 321-2, 324, 344, 359
Wheatley, Sir Henry, 368
Whigs: descent of, xv; and liberty, xvi-xxi; and radicals, xviii-xix, 309; and ascendancy of aristocracy, xviii-xx; and property, xx; and hierarchical conception of society, xxi-ii, xxx; in the 1820s, xxiv; formation of government in 1830, xxv-vii; fear of revolution should Reform Bill not pass, xxviii; tactic of concession for sake of stability, xxix, xxxiii-v; and social reform legislation, xxxiii; and legal reform, xxxiii; and Irish policy, xxxiv-ix; and limited government, xxxv-vi; dismissal of, 276; in opposition (1834-5), 279-85
Whishaw, John, 300
Whitbread, Samuel (1758-1815), xix
Wicklow, William Howard, 4th Earl of, 36, 42, 61, 96, 133, 158, 164, 222, 233
Wilde, Sir Thomas, later 1st Baron Truro, 15, 265
Wilkes, John (1727-97), 330
William I (1772-1844), King of the Netherlands (1815-40), 2, 4, 12-17, 23-5, 34, 37, 42, 44, 54, 62, 71-2, 74, 84, 87, 91-3, 107, 111, 119, 123, 125, 128, 139, 154, 163, 199, 200, 210, 212, 308, 392
William IV (1765-1837), xx, xxviii, xliv, xlviii-liv, 3-375 *passim,* 380, 384, 408; on expense of coronation, 3-4; and coronation oath, 3, 50-1, 288; after-dinner speeches of, 35, 53; wants Duke of Weimar reprimanded, 37; and creation of peers for Reform Bill, 48, 59-60, 102-3, 110-12, 115, 127, 131-2, 155, 164-5, 168-9, 180, 183; quarrels with Duchess of Kent, 51-2, 239, 311, 320, 349-50, 362-3; finds fault with King Leopold, 53; on aristocracy, 59; fears unions, 76-8, 112, 194; has confidence in Grey, 78, 111, 132; promises to support Grey on Reform Bill (Feb. 1832), 131-2; fears too close a connection with France, 170-1; insists on making Grey's brother a bishop, 174; and resignation of Grey's ministry (1832), 177-9; negotiates with Grey for return of Whig ministry, 180-4; makes Charles Richard Fox his aide-de-camp, 184-5, 187-8; excludes Duke of Sussex from court, 185, 187; urges final modifications of reform bills, 186-7; struck by a stone at Ascot, 193; praises Talleyrand upon his departure from England, 193; differs with cabinet on German affairs and foreign policy generally (1832), 201; evaluates Near Eastern situation (1833), 211, 217-18; and House of Lords resolutions on Portuguese neutrality (1833), 216; writes to Archbishop of Canterbury to rebuke bench (1833), 216-17, 219; laments government's insistence on Irish Church Temporalities bill, 235; insists Mr Johnston not to accompany Lord Wellesley to Ireland, 243; entreats Grey to remain in office (Jan. 1834), 248; urges Grey to remain in office after resignation of four cabinet ministers (May 1834), 253; seeks coalition government after resignation of Grey's cabinet, 256-7; alarmed by ministry's plan to reform Irish church (1834), 273-4, 470 n.60, 471 n.61; dismisses Melbourne's government, 269-78, 470 n.59, 471 n.62; seeks a coalition government (Apr. 1835), 285-7; tries to elecit pledge from Melbourne against appropriation of surplus Irish church revenues, 287; negotiates with Melbourne to form a government, 287-91; his incivility to Pozzo di Borgo and Count Sebastiani (1835), 298; consents to establishment of British legion to serve in Spain (1835), 303; fears increase of Russian military capability, 308, 313, 328, 336; objects to reduction of militia, 308, 313, 325, 328; acquiesces in but disapproves of Irish tithe bill (1835), 309; censures Palmerston for negotiating with Nesselrode without his consent, 313-14; upholds royal prerogative in colonial affairs, 315; disagrees with cabinet on Canada, 315, 317-20; says cabinet is not his and he will have them impeached (1835), 318; criticizes Mulgrave's administration of Ireland, 325; seems reconciled to his ministers, 327, 329-30, 332; and appointment of Dr Hampden to Regius professorship, 343; and Lord Melbourne's affair with Mrs Norton, 345; his alleged expectation of a change of government (1836), 348-9; and gift to Princess Victoria upon her majority, 362-4; death of, 365-6; eulogized, 367; his political advice to Victoria, 368, 391; his memorandum justifying his conduct as king, 372-3
Williams, 306
Wilson, Robert, Lord Berners, 174
Winchelsea, George William Finch-Hatton, 10th Earl of, 164, 188, 231, 395, 402
Winchester, Bishop of, *see* Sumner, Charles Richard

Windham, William, 40
Wood, Charles, later Viscount Halifax, 131, 160, 410
Worcester, Bishop of, *see* Carr, Robert James
Wordsworth, William, xx, 294
Wortly, John, *see* Stuart-Wortley-Mackenzie, John
Wrottesley, Sir John, 229-30
Wyatville, Sir Jeffry, 35
Wylde, Serjeant, *see* Wilde, Sir Thomas
Wylde, William, 304, 354, 360
Wynford, William Draper Best, 1st Baron, 11, 29, 37-8, 54, 59, 91, 120, 123, 126, 185, 195, 224, 226, 239, 344
Wynn, Charles Watkin Williams, 179
Wyse, Thomas, 41

Yeomanry, xlvii, 27, 117, 323, 382, 429 n.97; plan for re-modelling of, 14, 30, 33; and Irish MPs, 28; and friends of ministry, 30; and Irish members friendly to government, 33; Wicklow's speech on, in House of Lords, 36; *see also* Ireland
York, Archbishop of, *see* Harcourt, Edward Vernon
Young, George Frederick, 323

Zea Bermudez, *see* Cea Bermudez
Zumalacárregui, Tomas de, 316
Zuylen van Nyevelt, Hugo van, 23-4, 120, 125, 200